World Economic Forum
Geneva, Switzerland 2003

Professor Klaus Schwab
World Economic Forum

Professor Michael E. Porter
Harvard University

Co-Directors, The Global Competitiveness Report

The Global Competitiveness Report 2002–2003

D1352520

Peter K. Cornelius
World Economic Forum
Editor

New York • Oxford
Oxford University Press
2003

The Global Competitiveness Report 2002–2003 is published by the World Economic Forum within the framework of the Global Competitiveness Programme.

Professor Klaus Schwab
President

Dr Peter K. Cornelius
Director

Jennifer Blanke
Economist

Fiona Paua
Economist

Emma Loades
Manager

We thank Hope Steele for her superb editing work and Ha Nguyen for her great interior graphic design and layout.

We are very grateful to Gabrielle Antille Gaillard and Frederic Davier from the Laboratory of Applied Economics, Department of Economic and Social Sciences, University of Geneva, for their invaluable collaboration in the data analysis.

Thank you to Yonas Biru, from The World Bank's International Comparison Program (ICP), for kindly providing the most recent World Bank GDP per capita (PPP) data.

Thanks also to Ibrahima Djeinabou Barry, Gonçalo Domingos Felicio, Henri de La Grandville, Catherine Vindret, and Ken Watanabe for invaluable research assistance.

The terms *country* and *nation* as used in this report do not in all cases refer to a territorial entity that is a state as understood by international law and practice. The term covers well-defined, geographically self-contained economic areas that may not be states but for which statistical data are maintained on a separate and independent basis.

Oxford University Press

Oxford   New York
Auckland   Bangkok   Buenos Aires
Cape Town   Chennai   Dar es Salaam
Delhi   Hong Kong   Istanbul   Karachi
Kolkata   Kuala Lumpur   Madrid
Melbourne   Mexico City   Mumbai
Nairobi   São Paulo   Shanghai
Singapore   Taipei   Tokyo   Toronto

Copyright © 2003
by the World Economic Forum

Published by
Oxford University Press, Inc.
198 Madison Avenue
New York, New York 10016
http://www.oup.com

Oxford is a registered trademark of Oxford University Press

ISBN 0-19-515981-0

9 8 7 6 5 4 3 2 1

Printed in the United States of America on acid-free paper.

Contents

Partner Institutes

Argentina
IAE—Universidad Austral
Marcelo Paladino, Research Director
José del Tronco, Research Assistant

Australia
Business Council of Australia
Katie Lahey, Chief Executive

Austria
Vienna University of Economics and Business Administration
Dr Christian Bellak

Bangladesh
Centre for Policy Dialogue
Professor Rehman Sobhan, Chairman
Dr Debapriya Bhattacharya, Executive Director

Belgium
Vlerick Leuven Gent Management School
Professor Dr Lutgart Van Den Berghe, Executive Director, Chairman Competence Centre—Entrepreneurship, Governance & Strategy

Bolivia
Universidad Catolica Boliviana
Lic. Marcela A. De Guzman, Directora, Depto. Economia

Botswana
Botswana Institute for Development Policy Analysis (BIPDA)
Dr N.H. Fidzani, Executive Director

Brazil
Fundação Dom Cabral
Professor Carlos Arruda, Associate Dean for Development
Fabiana Santos

Bulgaria
Center for Economic Development
Anelia Damianova, PhD, Senior Expert

Canada
Institute for Competitiveness and Prosperity
Roger Martin, Dean of the Rotman School and Head of the Institute for Competitiveness and Prosperity
James Milway, Executive Director of the Institute for Competitiveness and Prosperity

Chile
Universidad Adolfo Ibañez
Andres Allamand Zavala, Dean of the School of Government
Victoria Hurtado Larrain, Academic Coordinator of the School of Government

China
Institute of Economics Systems and Management
State Council Office for Restructuring Economic
Chen Li, Executive Deputy Director
Dr Gao Shi-Ji, Deputy Director For Research
Zhou Mei, Assistant Fellow

Colombia
National Planning Department
Juan Carlos Echeverry, General Director

Croatia
Institute of Economics, Zagreb
Dr Ivan Teodorovic, Director
Dr Sonja Radas, Research Fellow

Czech Republic
CMC—Graduate School of Business
Peter Loewenguth, President
Professor Jaroslav A. Jirasek, Honorary Dean

Denmark
Copenhagen Business School
Heather Alison Hazard, Associate Professor, Program Director, Vice President for International Affairs
Jens Soegaard Jacobsen, Program Administrator

Ecuador
ESPAE—Escuela Politecnica del Litoral (ESPOL), Guayaquil
Juan Alvarado, Director

Egypt
Egyptian Center for Economic Studies
Dr Ahmed Galal, Executive Director

Estonia
Estonian Chamber of Commerce and Industry
Mart Relve, Director General
Siim Raie, Acting Director General

Finland
ETLA The Research Institute of the Finnish Economy
Pentti Vartia, President
Pekka Ylä-Anttila, Managing Director
Petri Rouvinen, Research Director

France
HEC School of Management—Paris
Bernard Ramanantsoa, Professor, Dean of HEC School of Management
Bertrand Moingeon, Professor, Associate Dean for Executive Education

Germany
Wissenschaftliche Hochschule für Unternehmensführung Koblenz
WHU—Otto Beisheim Graduate School of Management
Professor Michael Frenkel

Greece
Federation of Greek Industries
Antonis Tortopidis, Co-ordinator, Research and Analysis
Theodora Aivazoglou, Economist, Research and Analysis

Haiti
SOGEBANK—Société Général Haïtienne de Banque S.A.
Claude Pierre-Louis, Director-General
Pierre-Marie Boisson, Chief Economist
Reginald Saint-Fleur, Economist

Hong Kong
The Hong Kong General Chamber of Commerce
Ian K. Perkin, Chief Economist

Hungary
Kopint-Datorg, Economic Research
Dr Éva Palócz, Deputy General Director
Ágnes Nagy, Project Manager

Preface

KLAUS SCHWAB

President, World Economic Forum

Last year's *Global Competitiveness Report* was published in the aftermath of the terrorist attacks of September 11, 2001, an event that created an unprecedented degree of uncertainty. How would we recover from such a shocking event? To be sure, the terrorist attacks were not the only shocks during the past year, and perhaps they were not even the most shocking. The world is presently faced with a full-fledged crisis of confidence, and it is about much more than just September 11.

Revelations of dishonesty in some of what were once the world's most venerated firms abound: failed CEOs departing with severance packages worth millions, top managers cooking the books, shareholder and employee welfare subjugated to the greed of the few. To put it bluntly, the public has (with reason) lost confidence in its business leaders. Even if these cases turn out to be spectacular exceptions, the image of global business has already been tarnished, and along with it, that of the globalized economy. In this context, it not surprising that stock prices around the world have fallen to such lows, barely fighting to come back.

The loss of trust has been coupled with discouraging news on the economic front. World GDP growth over the past year has been extremely disappointing. We now know that the United States, the largest economy in the world, was already in recession when the terrorist attacks occurred, with output contracting for the first nine months of 2001. At present most analysts agree that US GDP growth will have remained below potential for 2002, and will only slowly recover in 2003. In the meantime, growth within Europe has remained sluggish at best, and Japan has yet to pull itself out of its economic malaise. A number of emerging markets have also seen a slowdown over the period, in great part linked to contractionary forces within the industrialized countries. All this anxiety is now exacerbated by the prospect of war in Iraq.

In other words, the crisis of confidence comes at a time when the world needs to trust its economic and political leaders more than ever. But how can we hope to steer ourselves out of the present situation when we no longer trust those at the helm of our economies? A first step toward restoring the world economy to healthy growth must therefore be for policymakers and business leaders to gain back the public's trust. This will take time, and will be no easy task. Trust cannot be bought. Trust must be earned.

A key goal of the World Economic Forum is to help the public to regain this trust through our various activities, by providing a platform for dialogue and by increasing transparency. *The Global Competitiveness Report 2002–2003* aims to contribute to this effort by providing a thorough assessment of the world economy.

The present gloom and uncertainty make it all the more crucial to identify the factors that drive growth in the medium and the long run. This is because the ability of countries to weather the storm will also depend on the robustness of their economies. This, in turn, is determined by the factors driving international competitiveness: the set of institutions, policies, and regulations that support high levels of productivity and sustained increases in output. More competitive countries can be expected to return to a sustained growth path faster and earlier than those that are less competitive. This is precisely what the *Report* is concerned with—the five-to-eight-year economic prospects within individual economies.

This year's *Report* differs from those of past years in the diversity of its analytical chapters. An entire section of the *Report* is devoted to a series of regional studies, covering the latest economic developments in Asia, Africa, Latin America, and eastern Europe. Another section includes a number of topical studies, with a particular emphasis on innovation and productivity. Important subjects such as governance and environmental sustainability are also covered. All of these issues are essential for economic growth in the long term.

We have also continued to expand our coverage this year, adding six countries to our analysis, all from developing and transition countries, in our effort to reflect the rising integration of these countries into the global economy. These new countries are Botswana, Croatia, Haiti, Morocco, Namibia, and Tunisia. With the exception of Croatia and Haiti, all of the new entrants are from Africa, reflecting an important increase in our coverage of the region and our continuing commitment to it. We will continue to expand the list of countries covered in future *Reports*.

This *Report* remains our flagship publication within our Global Competitiveness Programme, a family of research studies that truly mirror the increased integration of the world economy. Concurrent complementary publications include *The Arab World Competitiveness Report 2002–2003, The Global Information Technology Report*

2002–2003, and *Corporate Governance and Capital Flows in a Global Economy*.

We would like to thank Professor Michael E. Porter, Director of the Institute for Strategy and Competitiveness at the Harvard Business School, for his partnership and dedication to this project. Our appreciation goes to Peter K. Cornelius, who has been charged with heading the Global Competitiveness Programme under which this *Report* is published, and to his team, Jennifer Blanke and Fiona Paua. We also extend our gratitude to all the committed business leaders who responded to our Executive Opinion Survey. Finally, we extend a very special thanks to KPMG, our partner in this *Report*, for their support in this important venture.

Executive Summary

PETER K. CORNELIUS, World Economic Forum

Last year's *Global Competitiveness Report* was published in an environment of exceptional uncertainty. In the two weeks following the terrorist attacks of September 11, 2001, the world equity markets lost approximately two trillion US dollars, with 20 of the world's major stock exchanges dropping more than 10 percent. There was widespread agreement that in the near term the horrific event would accelerate and deepen the slowdown in the global economy that had already been underway by causing substantial disruptions of the global transport networks and production chains and a fall in consumer and business confidence. There was less agreement, however, about how fast the global economy would recover and return to a sustained growth path in the medium term. Even greater uncertainty existed with regard to the long-term impact of the terrorist attacks. In the introduction to last year's *Report* we wrote:

> In the longer term, the terrorist attacks will have a lasting negative impact if the policy responses trigger a reversal of the global economic integration that has characterized the past 20 years. The possibility of large-scale global conflict, terrorism, political backlash, and market uncertainty have the potential to raise the costs of cross-border business to levels not seen in decades, and thereby to limit the gains in economic well-being that global economic integration can yield.
>
> Cornelius et al. (2002, p 8).

Over the last 12 months, the world economy seems to have proved quite robust. Although global output growth has fallen, arguably the situation could have been considerably worse. However, this should not give rise to complacency. The risks we highlighted last year have hardly become smaller. Even if new terrorist attacks do not occur and large-scale conflicts can be avoided, the global economic outlook remains clouded with tremendous uncertainty.

Short-term uncertainties and longer-term growth dynamics

The prospects of a war in Iraq, corporate scandals, the bursting of the IT asset bubble, and the uncertain outlook in some emerging markets continue to weigh heavily on investors' confidence. Asset prices have remained subject to substantial volatility. In the two-and-a-half-year period between March 2000 when equity prices peaked and end-

September 2002, some of the major stock indices lost up to two thirds of their value, with the Nikkei having hit a 19-year low. The NASDAQ and other tech-laden stock exchanges have suffered even greater losses, with some markets—including Germany's Neuer Markt and Switzerland's New Market—being dissolved. Moreover, the latest GDP revisions in the United States confirm that the situation a year ago was actually worse than thought. Rather than merely slowing, we now know that the largest economy in the world was already in recession when the terrorist attacks occurred, with output having shrunk for the first nine months of 2001.

Nevertheless, in each of the three subsequent quarters GDP growth has been positive, and judging by the fears many had a year ago, one might argue that the US economy has weathered the economic impact of the tragic events of September 11 reasonably well. The terrorist attacks were not the only shock to the world economy, however. The failure of Enron and WorldCom and other high-profile collapses, the disappearance of Argentina's currency board, and the severe tensions in the Middle East might each have been expected to have a considerable impact on the global economic outlook, too. Taken together, their impact could have been far more serious, possibly pushing the world economy into a prolonged recession. Considering the potential damage these shocks could have caused, the world economy and the global financial system seem to have proved surprisingly resilient thus far.

Economic developments in the emerging markets are largely explicable in terms of the same contractionary forces affecting the industrialized countries. Asia's substantial reliance on exports of IT-related products made the region particularly vulnerable to the slowdown in the US economy, which was driven by a major decline in activity in the high-tech sector. Latin America, with the notable exception of Mexico, was generally less affected, while several emerging market economies in central and eastern Europe seemed almost immune. The economic crises in Argentina and Turkey have proved very costly, but the contagion effects have remained relatively limited.

Much credit for the global economy's resilience is due to the sharp monetary easing in most countries, especially the United States. This monetary easing has been accompanied by a more expansionary fiscal stance. In the United States, sizeable tax cuts were implemented and public expenditure has been rising strongly, especially in the aftermath of the terrorist attacks, and in 2002, the easing of the budgetary stance is estimated to amount to around 1.5 percent of GDP. Fiscal policy has become significantly more expansionary in several other countries, including Canada, Norway, Sweden, and especially the United Kingdom.

In the United States, the economy has also benefited from the fact that banks entered the recession with strong balance sheets. Moreover, capital markets provided a ready alternative supply of credit, shielding the economy from the financial implications of the recession. Unlike many previous recessions, there was no oversupply of housing, a factor that—combined with low interest rates—helped shore up consumer spending. Finally, it has been argued that trend growth in the United States is now in the range of 3 to 3.5 percent thanks to increased productivity, around half a percentage point higher than it was in 1980–1995. This means that if output growth falls by 3 percent, the economy simply stalls, whereas in previous cycles it would have contracted.

Although the mildness of America's recent recession may seem surprising—from peak to trough, GDP fell by only 0.6 percent, compared with an average decline of over 2 percent during recessions in the postwar era—it is important to note that nominal GDP growth in the G-7 countries fell to one of its slowest rates for decades. It is too early to tell whether the worst is already over. To begin with, the recovery in the United States seems rather slow, and there remains considerable concern about a possible "double dip." Although massive adjustments in inventories boosted growth to an annual rate of 5 percent in the first quarter of 2002, the rate of expansion fell back to just 1.1 percent in the months from April to June. With consumption having increased by less than 2 percent, economic growth has fallen considerably short of what could be expected in a normal recovery. In other major industrialized countries, economic growth has also remained sluggish, and world trade actually shrank by around 1 percent in 2001—one of the worst performances in the last few decades.

To be sure, the relative resilience of the global economy should not lead to complacency. The short-term economic risks are considerable, and they exist regardless of the enormous uncertainties associated with the possibility of a protracted war in Iraq or new terrorist threats. For one thing, corporate and private debts still appear rather large in the United States. Lower interest rates have encouraged a house-price boom that has partially offset losses in the stock market, helping insulate private wealth and maintain consumer spending. Once households reduce their borrowing propped up by higher mortgages, they will spend less and save more, which could lead to a prolonged period of sluggish growth. The United States

will not have much monetary policy ammunition left if, under such a scenario, the economy stumbles. With the US current account deficit becoming harder to be financed, there is concern that a sharp fall in the US dollar could help export deflationary pressures to other countries. At the same time, to the extent that the economy has become more open, fiscal policy might have become less effective to cushion downturns than it was in previous cycles.

How well the United States and the rest of the world can weather the potential turbulence will depend, first and foremost, on the robustness of their economies. Primarily, this ability is a function of the factors determining their competitiveness—that is, the set of institutions, policies, and regulations that support high levels of productivity and drive productivity growth and sustained increases in output. Competitive countries can be expected to return to a sustained growth path faster and earlier than those that are less competitive. This is what *The Global Competitiveness Report* is concerned with—the five-to-eight-year prospects in a large number of individual economies.

As in the two previous years, *The Global Competitiveness Report* employs two distinct but complementary approaches to the analysis of competitiveness. The first one focuses on growth competitiveness. Introduced originally by Jeffrey D. Sachs and Andrew Warner and developed with the assistance of John McArthur, it has been further refined in this edition. This year covering 80 countries, the Growth Competitiveness Index (GCI) represents a best estimate of the underlying prospects for growth. Six new countries are covered by the Index this year: Botswana, Croatia, Haiti, Morocco, Namibia, and Tunisia. On the other hand, Egypt had to be dropped this year due to the lack of Survey data.

The *Report*'s second approach to competitiveness has been developed by Michael E. Porter of the Institute for Strategy and Competitiveness at the Harvard Business School. In contrast to the GCI, the Microeconomic Competitiveness Index (MICI) uses microeconomic indicators to measure the "set of institutions, market structures, and economic policies supportive of high current levels of prosperity," referring mainly to an economy's effective utilization of its current stock of resources. Covering the same countries, the Index thus assesses the current productive potential. Together, the GCI and the MICI present distinct yet highly complementary insights into sources of national competitiveness.

The two indexes reflect that there exist circumstances that contribute to the level of income per capita and those that contribute to the change in income per capita, or growth.[1] In its simplest form, the theory of growth supposes that the level of income per capita depends on the amount of capital per person—the capital intensity of the economy—and the level of technology determining the average productivity of a unit of capital. With a fixed proportion of income assumed to be saved, which is equal to the change in the capital stock, economic growth, then, has two major components: technological change and capital deepening.

Of course, in reality things are more complex. Although in theory a clear distinction can be made between the factors explaining the *level* of economic prosperity as opposed to those that drive economic *growth*, in practice this proves substantially more difficult. One important problem stems from the fact that some of the same institutions, regulations, attributes, and practices affect both level and growth. The intensity of rivalry, for instance, drives current productivity, but it also fosters innovation and technological progress and hence productivity growth.

In actual economies, technological change and capital deepening are highly complex processes. The capital stock of an economy includes not just the accumulated physical capital of machinery, structures, and physical infrastructure (roads, ports, telecommunications), but also the level of education, workforce skills and attitudes, managerial talent, and social capital. Moreover, the stock of capital encompasses a country's set of legal institutions and regulatory practices governing businesses. In the same way, the conditions that lead to rapid economic growth include not just the aggregate investment or saving rates in an economy, but also the mix of public and private institutions that support innovation, the diffusion of ideas across sectors, and the inflows of ideas from foreign companies into the domestic economy. Similarly, technology and technological progress include multiple dimensions, going beyond the technological know-how embedded in a nation's scientific and technological institutions to also include the technology rooted in firms, which is embodied in every activity they perform and in the strategy they employ to compete.

Understanding the factors that explain current levels of economic prosperity and growth requires employing a dataset that reflects the complexity of the development process in a large cross-section of countries. Using publicly available information and statistics is not enough. Therefore, our competitiveness assessments also include Survey evidence. This evidence appears particularly important in areas where no reliable hard data sources exist for many of the most important aspects of an economy, such as the efficiency of government institutions, the sophistication of local supplier networks, or the nature of competitive practices. But even where hard data exist, the data often do not cover all the countries in our sample. The Executive Opinion Survey, conducted annually by the World Economic Forum with the assistance of a large number of partner institutes, reflects the perspectives of business leaders around the world by asking them to compare aspects of their local business environment with global standards.

This year, more than 4,700 respondents participated in the Survey. Given that these business leaders actually make many of the investment decisions that drive economic growth, their responses provide an invaluable source concerning the current state of economic affairs in 80 countries.

The Growth Competitiveness Index

The Growth Competitiveness Index is based on three broad categories of variables that are found to drive economic growth in the medium and long term: technology, public institutions, and the macroeconomic environment. Without technological progress, countries may achieve a higher standard of living, for example, through a higher rate of capital accumulation, but they will not be able to enjoy continuously high economic growth. Institutions are crucial for their role in ensuring the protection of property rights, the objective resolution of contract and other legal disputes, efficiency of government spending, and transparency in all levels of government. In the absence of good governance, the division of labor is likely to be impeded and the allocation of resources inefficient. Monetary and fiscal policies, and the stability of financial institutions, have important effects on short-term economic dynamics as well as on the long-term capacity to grow.

These drivers play a critical role at all stages of economic development. As far as technology is concerned, however, the way this driver affects economic growth varies according to the level of economic prosperity a country has already achieved. At early stages of economic development, a country's ability to launch its economy on a steeper growth path depends primarily on the transfer of technology from abroad. Countries that have experienced rapid economic growth are typically those that are successful in adopting and adapting a technology that has been developed abroad, a process known as *technological diffusion*. At more advanced stages of economic development, however, it becomes increasingly important that a country itself *innovate* new technologies in order to sustain rapid economic growth. In the high-income countries, each new technological innovation triggers yet further innovation, in a kind of chain reaction that fuels long-term economic growth.

Taking into account the different channels through which technology affects economic growth at different stages of development, in this *Report* we continue to distinguish between two groups of countries. The group of *core innovators* (a term introduced last year, and in no way to be construed as a value judgment) includes those countries whose companies have registered at least 15 US utility patents per million population in 2001. This criterion is met in 24 economies. All other countries are said to be *non-core innovators*. Empirical tests find that technology plays a particularly critical role in the core innovating countries, which is reflected in the weights we attach to the different growth drivers. For these countries, technology has a weight of 50 percent in the overall GCI, compared with 25 percent each for public institutions and the macroeconomic environment. By contrast, equal weights of one third are attached to the three drivers in the case of the non-core innovators.

For the core innovators, the technology index is a simple average of the innovation subindex and the information and communication technology subindex, both of which are comprised of hard and soft data (note that the innovation subindex is different from the "innovative capacity index" constructed by Michael E. Porter and Scott Stern in Chapter 3.1. While the innovation subindex seeks to explain the elements of innovation that are linked to economic growth, the innovative capacity index seeks to explain the underlying factors that contribute to innovation). In the case of non-core innovators, by contrast, technology transfer plays a considerably more important role than innovation, which is reflected in relative weights of three eighths versus one eighth in the innovation index. Information and communication technology represents the other subindex of the technology index, with a weight of one half.

This year's *Report* includes one important adjustment: the technology transfer subindex includes new Survey evidence on the licensing of foreign technology as an important source of new technology. This evidence replaces a variable that was created to measure the extent of manufacturing technology in the export structure of non-core countries. The reasoning behind that variable was that countries with a technology-based export sector may be expected to be more adept at absorbing technologies from abroad than economies with a primarily commodity-based export structure. Empirical tests suggest that the new variable has significant explanatory power.

The composition of the public institutions index and the macroeconomic environment index has remained unchanged. The public institutions index consists of two subindexes, one that reflects the perceived degree of corruption and one that focuses on the role of contracts and law. Both subindexes have equal weights and are based solely on Survey evidence. The macroeconomic environment index includes a subindex on macroeconomic stability (mirroring, among other things, inflation, national savings, and real exchange rate developments) as well as country credit ratings and general government expenditure.

This year's rankings are presented in Table 1. The United States leads the Growth Competitiveness Index, swapping positions with Finland, last year's number 1 and now ranked number 2. Taiwan, Singapore, and Sweden follow. While Singapore has retained its fourth rank,

Taiwan and Sweden enjoy a significant improvement of three and four positions, respectively. An even greater improvement in its relative position concerns Switzerland, however, a country that is being ranked sixth this year (see Chapter 2.3 in this *Report*, which contains a case study on Switzerland).

The United States owes its position mainly to its stellar performance on technology-related factors (see Table 2). Research and development, collaboration between universities and businesses, the level of tertiary education, and a sophisticated and innovative business and academic community all contribute to the high ranking of the United States. The United States also receives high scores for its venture capital markets, receptivity to innovation, and leadership in information and communication technology. In addition, during the 1990s, fiscal consolidation helped the United States, contributing to a second place on the macroeconomic environment index. By contrast, the respondents to the Executive Opinion Survey perceive public institutions to be in need of reform, an area where the United States is ranked only 16. However, this relatively poor reading does not jeopardize the country's top position on the overall Index, given its strong performance in technology and the macroeconomic environment.

Finland also enjoys a very high level of technological sophistication, being ranked third in this dimension of competitiveness. In addition, Finland's public institutions are perceived to be the best in the world. On the other hand, Finland has slipped slightly in terms of its macroeconomic environment. Taiwan's high overall score also results primarily from its very high position on the technology index, whereas Singapore's strengths are found especially in the macroeconomic area.

As far as emerging-market economies are concerned, China and India register substantial improvements in their relative positions, to 33 and 48, respectively. The world's two most populous countries—but especially China—have outperformed most other countries in terms of economic growth in recent years. Much of the countries' overall rankings is owed to their stable macroeconomic environment, although in the case of China potential risks have been flagged more recently with regard to contingent liabilities for the budget stemming from problems in the banking sector.

Conversely, the overall rankings of Argentina and Turkey decline substantially, to 63 and 69, respectively. Both countries have suffered from severe financial crises that have caused real output to shrink dramatically. Relative to their overall position, both countries do moderately well on the technology dimension. Major problems are identified in the areas of public institutions and the macroeconomic environment, however.

Tunisia is the highest new entrant at number 34. Further down the list are Botswana at number 41,

Table 1: Overall competitiveness rankings

GROWTH COMPETITIVENESS INDEX RANKINGS

Country	Growth Competitiveness ranking 2002	Growth Competitiveness ranking 2002 among GCR 2001 countries*	Growth Competitiveness ranking 2001
United States	1	1	2
Finland	2	2	1
Taiwan	3	3	7
Singapore	4	4	4
Sweden	5	5	9
Switzerland	6	6	15
Australia	7	7	5
Canada	8	8	3
Norway	9	9	6
Denmark	10	10	14
United Kingdom	11	11	12
Iceland	12	12	16
Japan	13	13	21
Germany	14	14	17
Netherlands	15	15	8
New Zealand	16	16	10
Hong Kong SAR	17	17	13
Austria	18	18	18
Israel	19	19	24
Chile	20	20	27
Korea	21	21	23
Spain	22	22	22
Portugal	23	23	25
Ireland	24	24	11
Belgium	25	25	19
Estonia	26	26	29
Malaysia	27	27	30
Slovenia	28	28	31
Hungary	29	29	28
France	30	30	20
Thailand	31	31	33
South Africa	32	32	34
China	33	33	39
Tunisia	34	—	—
Mauritius	35	34	32
Lithuania	36	35	43
Trinidad and Tobago	37	36	38
Greece	38	37	36
Italy	39	38	26
Czech Republic	40	39	37
Botswana	41	—	—
Uruguay	42	40	46
Costa Rica	43	41	35
Latvia	44	42	47
Mexico	45	43	42
Brazil	46	44	44
Jordan	47	45	45
India	48	46	57
Slovak Republic	49	47	40
Panama	50	48	53
Poland	51	49	41
Dominican Republic	52	50	50
Namibia	53	—	—
Peru	54	51	55
Morocco	55	—	—
Colombia	56	52	65
El Salvador	57	53	58
Croatia	58	—	—
Sri Lanka	59	54	61
Jamaica	60	55	52
Philippines	61	56	48
Bulgaria	62	57	59
Argentina	63	58	49
Russian Federation	64	59	63
Vietnam	65	60	60
Romania	66	61	56
Indonesia	67	62	64
Venezuela	68	63	62
Turkey	69	64	54
Guatemala	70	65	66
Nigeria	71	66	74
Paraguay	72	67	72
Ecuador	73	68	68
Bangladesh	74	69	71
Nicaragua	75	70	73
Honduras	76	71	70
Ukraine	77	72	69
Bolivia	78	73	67
Zimbabwe	79	74	75
Haiti	80	—	—

MICROECONOMIC COMPETITIVENESS INDEX RANKINGS

Country	Microeconomic Competitiveness ranking 2002	Microeconomic Competitiveness ranking 2002 among GCR 2001 countries*	Microeconomic Competitiveness ranking 2001**
United States	1	1	2
Finland	2	2	1
United Kingdom	3	3	7
Germany	4	4	4
Switzerland	5	5	5
Sweden	6	6	6
Netherlands	7	7	3
Denmark	8	8	8
Singapore	9	9	9
Canada	10	10	12
Japan	11	11	10
Austria	12	12	11
Belgium	13	13	15
Australia	14	14	14
France	15	15	13
Taiwan	16	16	21
Iceland	17	17	16
Israel	18	18	17
Hong Kong SAR	19	19	18
Ireland	20	20	22
Norway	21	21	19
New Zealand	22	22	20
Korea	23	23	26
Italy	24	24	23
Spain	25	25	24
Malaysia	26	26	37
Slovenia	27	27	32
Hungary	28	28	27
South Africa	29	29	25
Estonia	30	30	28
Chile	31	31	29
Tunisia	32	—	—
Brazil	33	32	30
Czech Republic	34	33	34
Thailand	35	34	38
Portugal	36	35	33
India	37	36	36
China	38	37	43
Costa Rica	39	38	48
Lithuania	40	39	50
Dominican Republic	41	40	60
Slovak Republic	42	41	40
Greece	43	42	46
Trinidad and Tobago	44	43	31
Latvia	45	44	41
Poland	46	45	42
Sri Lanka	47	46	58
Morocco	48	—	—
Mauritius	49	47	51
Panama	50	48	49
Namibia	51	—	—
Croatia	52	—	—
Jordan	53	49	47
Turkey	54	50	35
Mexico	55	51	52
Colombia	56	52	57
Botswana	57	—	—
Russian Federation	58	53	56
Jamaica	59	54	39
Vietnam	60	55	62
Philippines	61	56	53
Uruguay	62	57	45
El Salvador	63	58	64
Indonesia	64	59	55
Argentina	65	60	54
Peru	66	61	63
Romania	67	62	61
Bulgaria	68	63	68
Ukraine	69	64	59
Zimbabwe	70	65	65
Nigeria	71	66	66
Venezuela	72	67	67
Guatemala	73	68	69
Bangladesh	74	69	73
Nicaragua	75	70	71
Paraguay	76	71	70
Ecuador	77	72	72
Honduras	78	73	74
Bolivia	79	74	75
Haiti	80	—	—

* Only 74 countries out of the 75 covered last year are shown, as Egypt is not included in this year's *Report*. ** Using 2002 formula

Table 2: Rankings on growth competitiveness component indexes

Country	GCI ranking	Technology index ranking	Public institutions index ranking	Macroeconomic environment index ranking
United States	1	1	16	2
Finland	2	3	1	14
Taiwan	3	2	27	6
Singapore	4	17	7	1
Sweden	5	4	15	34
Switzerland	6	6	8	5
Australia	7	9	5	4
Canada	8	8	9	12
Norway	9	10	12	7
Denmark	10	11	2	31
United Kingdom	11	15	6	16
Iceland	12	16	3	24
Japan	13	5	25	29
Germany	14	12	14	22
Netherlands	15	19	10	19
New Zealand	16	27	4	17
Hong Kong SAR	17	32	13	3
Austria	18	23	11	23
Israel	19	7	17	62
Chile	20	33	19	13
Korea	21	18	32	10
Spain	22	24	26	15
Portugal	23	13	21	40
Ireland	24	31	18	9
Belgium	25	22	22	26
Estonia	26	14	28	46
Malaysia	27	26	33	20
Slovenia	28	25	23	50
Hungary	29	21	30	49
France	30	28	29	28
Thailand	31	41	39	11
South Africa	32	38	34	30
China	33	63	38	8
Tunisia	34	60	24	37
Mauritius	35	45	35	36
Lithuania	36	40	36	45
Trinidad and Tobago	37	42	43	25
Greece	38	30	44	47
Italy	39	39	37	27
Czech Republic	40	20	50	59
Botswana	41	61	31	48
Uruguay	42	50	20	73
Costa Rica	43	37	46	43
Latvia	44	29	52	55
Mexico	45	47	58	21
Brazil	46	35	45	67
Jordan	47	51	40	57
India	48	57	59	18
Slovak Republic	49	34	53	64
Panama	50	49	55	42
Poland	51	36	61	54
Dominican Republic	52	48	60	41
Namibia	53	59	41	66
Peru	54	64	49	52
Morocco	55	62	56	44
Colombia	56	58	54	51
El Salvador	57	69	48	33
Croatia	58	43	57	70
Sri Lanka	59	67	42	60
Jamaica	60	46	51	74
Philippines	61	52	70	32
Bulgaria	62	56	47	75
Argentina	63	44	66	65
Russian Federation	64	66	65	35
Vietnam	65	68	62	38
Romania	66	55	67	58
Indonesia	67	65	77	53
Venezuela	68	53	73	72
Turkey	69	54	63	78
Guatemala	70	74	74	56
Nigeria	71	71	78	61
Paraguay	72	76	71	63
Ecuador	73	70	75	69
Bangladesh	74	79	79	39
Nicaragua	75	73	64	79
Honduras	76	78	76	71
Ukraine	77	72	72	77
Bolivia	78	77	69	76
Zimbabwe	79	75	68	80
Haiti	80	80	80	68

Namibia at number 53, Morocco at number 55, Croatia at number 58, and Haiti at number 80. Tunisia owes its ranking to moderately good performance on macroeconomic environment variables and especially to good public institutions. Botswana is also perceived to perform well with regard to its public institutions relative to its overall position on the GCI, whereas its position on the technology index is sub-par, given its overall competitiveness score. Haiti, at the bottom, is known to be going through one of the most difficult periods in its history. Its competitiveness suffers from rock-bottom scores on technology and public institutions and only a slighter better position regarding the country's macroeconomic environment.

The Microeconomic Competitiveness Index

Whereas the GCI strives to estimate the underlying conditions for growth over the medium term, the Microeconomic Competitiveness Index (MICI) examines the underlying conditions defining the sustainable level of productivity in each of the 80 countries covered in the *Report*.[2] Productivity and the creation of wealth are rooted in the sophistication of companies and operating practices as well as in the quality of the microeconomic business environment in which a nation's firms compete. As important as the macroeconomic, political, and legal contexts are, unless there is appropriate improvement at the microeconomic level, other reforms will not bear full fruit. Accordingly, the MICI is composed of two subindexes: one that reflects the degree of company sophistication and another that mirrors the quality of the national business environment. Both subindexes draw on a complex array of variables with demonstrated statistical relationships to GDP per capita (PPP) using common factor analysis. The weights for the two subindexes are determined from the coefficients of a multiple regression of the subindexes on GDP per capita and are 0.37 and 0.63, respectively.

This year's MICI rankings are shown in Table 1, while subrankings on the sophistication of company operating practices in each country and the quality of the business environment are presented in Table 3. The United States retakes the leading position over Finland after two years of being ranked second. Consistent with its top position on the GCI, the United States appears to be in an excellent position to return to a sustained growth path. Other advanced nations improving their MICI rankings include the United Kingdom, Canada, Belgium, Taiwan, and Ireland. Of these, the improvement of the United Kingdom's position is particularly remarkable, with its jump from 7 in 2001 to 3 this year, reflecting, inter alia, notable improvements in venture capital availability, intellectual property rights protection, the effectiveness of antitrust policy, and buyer sophistication. By contrast, the Netherlands, France, and New Zealand are found to have become relatively less competitive in terms of their foundations of productivity and economic prosperity. The drop of the Netherlands from 3 to 7 is particularly significant, where deteriorations relative to other nations were found in both the business environment and company sophistication, including financial market sophistication, the context for firm strategy and rivalry, public administrative effectiveness, R&D spending, and marketing.

Of the countries newly added to the sample, Tunisia is the top-ranked performer, coming in 32nd. Morocco, Namibia, and Croatia all enter at around 50. Although the increase in the number of countries make intertemporal comparisons difficult, these three new entrants appear significantly less competitive than, say, Lithuania, which jumped from 49 in 2001 to 40 this year. Other developing nations whose competitiveness improved significantly include Slovenia, the Dominican Republic, and Sri Lanka. The largest increase, however, has been achieved by Malaysia, reflecting improvements in a number of dimensions including cluster vitality, the rules governing competition, value chain presence, branding, and the nature of competitive advantage.

Conversely, several developing countries have suffered from a decline in their competitiveness as mirrored in a lower position in the MICI. Apart from the Philippines and Indonesia, this group includes Argentina and Turkey, two countries that have experienced major financial crises. Turkey's drop by 19 ranks is particularly sharp; Argentina's fall is slightly less, but ranked 65th now, it is clear that the country faces enormous challenges in most dimensions of competitiveness.

In general, there exists a fairly close correlation between company sophistication and the quality of the business environment in which the firms operate. But there are some interesting outliers. Countries whose company development is ahead of the business environment include four G-7 countries: Japan, Germany, France, and Italy. In these countries, significant changes in public policy are necessary to improve the environment for competition. Unless such improvements are implemented, companies will be prone to move operations or make new investments outside the countries. However, significant deficits relative to the degree of firm-level sophistication are also found in several emerging-market economies, including Argentina, the Dominican Republic, and Indonesia.

Advanced countries whose business environment ranks ahead of current company sophistication include Portugal, New Zealand, Australia, Hong Kong, and Singapore. This constellation is also found in several developing nations and transition economies, such as Tunisia, Botswana, and Estonia. Many leading companies in these countries still rely on natural resource extraction or are local subsidiaries of foreign multinationals that are not

Table 3: Rankings on microeconomic competitiveness component subindexes

Country	MICI ranking	Company operations and strategy ranking	Quality of the national business environment ranking
United States	1	1	1
Finland	2	4	2
United Kingdom	3	3	3
Germany	4	2	4
Switzerland	5	5	6
Sweden	6	6	8
Netherlands	7	8	10
Denmark	8	9	9
Singapore	9	14	5
Canada	10	13	7
Japan	11	7	17
Austria	12	12	12
Belgium	13	11	15
Australia	14	19	11
France	15	10	21
Taiwan	16	16	13
Iceland	17	17	14
Israel	18	20	18
Hong Kong SAR	19	24	16
Ireland	20	15	22
Norway	21	23	19
New Zealand	22	25	20
Korea	23	21	23
Italy	24	18	24
Spain	25	22	25
Malaysia	26	27	26
Slovenia	27	26	27
Hungary	28	29	29
South Africa	29	31	33
Estonia	30	36	28
Chile	31	35	31
Tunisia	32	37	30
Brazil	33	28	36
Czech Republic	34	34	34
Thailand	35	33	35
Portugal	36	41	32
India	37	40	37
China	38	38	38
Costa Rica	39	32	47
Lithuania	40	39	39
Dominican Republic	41	30	53
Slovak Republic	42	43	40
Greece	43	47	41
Trinidad and Tobago	44	44	44
Latvia	45	48	42
Poland	46	46	45
Sri Lanka	47	52	43
Morocco	48	50	46
Mauritius	49	42	50
Panama	50	54	52
Namibia	51	58	49
Croatia	52	53	54
Jordan	53	59	48
Turkey	54	56	55
Mexico	55	45	60
Colombia	56	51	57
Botswana	57	64	51
Russian Federation	58	62	56
Jamaica	59	60	59
Vietnam	60	67	58
Philippines	61	49	67
Uruguay	62	63	61
El Salvador	63	61	62
Indonesia	64	55	65
Argentina	65	57	68
Peru	66	65	66
Romania	67	69	64
Bulgaria	68	72	63
Ukraine	69	66	69
Zimbabwe	70	68	70
Nigeria	71	71	71
Venezuela	72	73	72
Guatemala	73	70	73
Bangladesh	74	76	74
Nicaragua	75	75	76
Paraguay	76	77	75
Ecuador	77	74	77
Honduras	78	78	79
Bolivia	79	79	78
Haiti	80	80	80

competing with sophisticated enough strategies. In some cases, it appears that the rapid improvements in the business environment have not yet been taken advantage of by companies that remain focused on traditional ways of competing. In these, improvements in entrepreneurship, strategic thinking, managerial practice, and business education seem particularly crucial.

A time-series analysis confirms that there has been a clear upgrading in national business environments since 1998, when the MICI was introduced. The bar is rising, and countries need to make considerable progress just to maintain position vis-à-vis other countries. Areas where particular improvements have been registered over the last five years include, for instance, infrastructure, financial markets, import tariffs, and the reduction of red tape. This year's data, however, reveal an interesting development. Developing countries were less successful in improving their business environments than advanced countries. In company operations and strategy, there are also clear areas where companies in many countries are progressing but also signs that the growing intensity of competition is making it hard to keep up. For example, companies in many countries report difficulties in mastering the full value chain. While companies in developing countries seem to be struggling with developing brands, those in advanced countries report greater difficulties in innovating on the global knowledge frontier.

Finally, in constructing the MICI, it is recognized that in the short and medium term, nations can overperform their microeconomic fundamentals, for example, because of surges of inbound foreign direct investment or natural resource windfalls. However, unless the microeconomic fundamentals are improved, countries will find it difficult to sustain their levels of prosperity when these special factors disappear. Conversely, a country may underperform in the sense that it has not fully achieved the level of GDP per capita that would appear reachable given the country's microeconomic foundations. A positive gap between the MICI and GDP per capita signals upside potential; a negative gap indicates vulnerability. Countries with upside potential include the United Kingdom, Malaysia, Brazil, Chile, Estonia, Lithuania, and India. Norway, Iceland, Ireland, Canada, Greece, Portugal, Bolivia, and Haiti are countries, in contrast, whose current GDP per capita exceeds that predicted by their microeconomic competitiveness.

Structure of the *Report*

The second part of this *Report* discusses competitiveness issues from a global and regional perspective. In his chapter "The Year in Review," Martin Baily (Institute for International Economics) provides the background for analyzing the challenges the world economy is facing today. Specifically, Baily examines the global slowdown among the main industrial economies of Europe, the United States, and Japan, which have been remarkably synchronized. Discussing the role of equity markets in perpetuating this slowdown, the chapter also focuses on the importance of corporate governance issues that have profoundly affected investors' confidence. As Baily argues, Enron, WorldCom, and other corporate scandals, further fueled by financial crises in several emerging markets, have led to a backlash against market liberalization and American-style capitalism. At the same time, as Baily notes, companies have begun to reassess the potential benefits of a business strategy of full-tilt globalization. Today it appears that an increasing number of executives view the imperative of global expansion as less compelling, and the terrorist attacks have left companies even more aware than before of the political risks of cross-border activities. Although it is imperative to restore investor confidence in the information they have available, Baily argues that over-regulation must be avoided since this could discourage risk taking and new ventures.

Another threat hanging over the United States and the world economy is the impending war with Iraq. Although a short war could help lift some of the clouds currently hanging over the markets, a protracted war would clearly have negative effects on economic growth. Although in the short term it cannot be ruled out that, even under these optimistic assumptions, economic growth in the United States will remain sluggish, in the longer term, according to Baily the US economy looks set to recover, given an expansionary financial policy stance and the overall resilience of the economy. The "new economy" is alive and well, and although productivity growth is less than initially thought, its trend does appear to be continuing at a faster rate than it did in the 1970s and 1980s. As Baily emphasizes, however, microeconomic evidence suggests that faster productivity growth has not come simply from the contribution of IT capital, but rather from successful business innovations.

By comparison, the longer-term outlook for Europe and especially Japan appear, in Baily's view, less sanguine. Short term, a relatively tighter monetary policy stance appears less supportive of a recovery, and the stability pact severely limits the room for maneuvering. In the longer term, the key challenge in the core European countries remains making their economies more flexible. In Japan, these challenges are even greater, especially with regard to

financial restructuring, and macroeconomic policies have become largely impotent. Finally, Baily discusses recent financial crises in emerging-market economies, especially in South Korea, Argentina, and Brazil, taking into account both macroeconomic and microeconomic factors. For the microeconomic factors, Baily finds that institutional failures and policy interventions have seriously distorted incentives and created barriers to growth in several sectors.

One of Baily's main conclusions is that the market economy remains the best system available. Although the market economy works well with good stabilization policies and with legal and regulatory systems that provide accurate information to market participants, problems almost inevitably arise if screwball restrictions are put in place with an incoherent rationale behind them. The market-based system works worse, however, if fiscal and monetary policies follow paths that are unsustainable over the long run and if policies are implemented that prevent industries from evolving and old firms from dying.

Focusing on Baily's latter point, John Llewellyn and the Global Economics Team of Lehman Brothers discuss "Reinvigorating Structural Reform." Whereas there exists a nontrivial degree of risk that recent economic developments reduce policymakers' appetite for market-oriented reforms, Lewellyn and his team argue that a reinvigoration of supply-side policies is vital and overdue, mainly for two reasons: first, because they are the major determinant of economic performance over the medium to long term. To illustrate the importance of their argument, the authors reckon that adding just half a percent to a potential output growth rate of 2.5 percent per annum would mean that material living standards would double in 20 years rather than 40. Second, structural rigidities make it harder for economies to absorb shocks—resulting, for example, in high and more persistent unemployment than would otherwise be the case.

Llewellyn and his coauthors focus in their assessment of current structural impediments primarily on the major OECD countries. To this group belongs Switzerland, one of the richest countries in the world, whose economy, however, has not been growing much over the past decade. Given an average annual growth rate of just around 1.5 percent, Franz Jaeger (Research Institute for Empirical Economics and Economic Policy at the University of St. Gallen) asks what has held Switzerland back in a case study on the country. His analysis is broadly consistent with Llewellyn's. Although Switzerland enjoys an exceptional macroeconomic environment and many Swiss companies operate at the global frontier of innovation and technological progress, substantial parts of the domestic economy have remained highly protected. One immediate consequence, according to Jaeger, is Switzerland's comparatively low labor productivity. Against this background,

Jaeger concludes that "a policy change toward more competition and structural changes in the domestic sector would help Switzerland grow faster."

The remaining chapters in this part of the *Report* focus primarily on emerging-market economies in different regions of the world. Depending on the stage of development, each region—and indeed, each country—face different challenges. A very poor country with rudimentary levels of education and health will generally not be competing on the basis of technological innovation. Rather, its goal should be to attract capital investment and use the proceeds of economic growth to invest in improved health, education, and infrastructure. As a country progresses further, it becomes increasingly important to speed up the process of technological diffusion into the country, in part by attracting high-tech foreign direct investment. Probably the most challenging transition, however, is the one from technological diffusion to technological innovation. Indeed, the group of countries identified in the *Report* as "core innovators" has remained small.[3] As our analysis in this and previous editions of the *Global Competitiveness Report* suggests, the transition through the different stages of economic development is not necessarily linear or gradual, nor does it happen automatically. Countries may get stuck if they are not able to achieve a wholesale transformation of many interdependent dimensions of competition.

This is, of course, not to say that non-core innovators cannot achieve rapid economic growth. On the contrary, it is often the countries in the earlier stages that achieve the world's highest growth rates, by rapidly absorbing the advanced technologies and capital of the advanced innovators. This process of "catch-up" growth has been very important for many developing countries. However, this process has its inherent limits. As the income gap between the technological leaders and followers narrows, the ability of the latter to narrow the gap still further tends to diminish; in order to close the gap fully, a country needs to become a core innovator itself. In other words, a country's competitive advantage must become the development of unique products at the global technology frontier.

Against this background, Chapter 2.4, "Africa: A Union Open for Growth, Trade, and Business?" written by Lisa D. Cook (Harvard University and Stanford University), discusses recent economic developments in Africa and policy challenges for the future that remain to be addressed if higher economic growth and better living standards are to be achieved. As a framework for discussion, Cook focuses on the New Partnership for Africa's Development (NEPAD), a much-discussed new initiative centering on a wide range of issues including economic growth, integration, peace, security, democracy, and human development. To be sure, the NEPAD goals are ambitious: importantly, poverty is to be reduced by 50 percent by

2015, a target whose achievement requires economic growth of 7 percent annually, as Cook emphasizes. Given the experience of a large sample of countries, Africa's further global integration through trade and investment will need to play a key role in the continent's development strategy. For this, an economic and business environment is needed that is conducive to private entrepreneurship. In her analysis, Cook focuses especially on two areas: physical infrastructure and financial sector development. As she stresses, however, these are just two examples that stand for the multidimensional challenges Africa is facing in upgrading the continent's long-term competitiveness.

Asia's emerging markets face different challenges. Many of them have already achieved a relatively high level of economic prosperity. However, that does not automatically guarantee that the Asian economies will continue to grow at rates many had enjoyed in the 1980s and the first half of the 1990s. Given that economic development represents a sequential process of building interdependent microeconomic capabilities, evolving the modes of competing, improving incentives, and increasing rivalry, lack of improvement in one area can lead to a plateau in productivity growth and stalled development. In her chapter entitled "Asia: The Productivity Imperative," Diana Farrell (McKinsey Global Institute) examines four economies whose stages of development and economic structures are highly diverse: India and Thailand, with per capita incomes (PPP basis) of around 2,500 and 6,500 US dollars; and South Korea and Japan, two of the richest OECD member countries in the world. But as different as they are, in each of these countries there are industries and services that are highly efficient, whereas others are found to be woefully inefficient. A key message that emerges from Farrell's assessment is that "the efficiencies engendered by international markets need to be emulated in the domestic, non-tradable sectors," which frequently continue to be burdened by overregulation and structural ossification.

Although in some countries in central and eastern Europe economic growth has slowed noticeably in the wake of lower output growth in the world economy, others have proved remarkably resilient. As Barry W. Ickes (Pennsylvania State University), Jürgen von Hagen (Zentrum für Europäische Integration, University of Bonn; Indiana University; and CEPR), and Iulia Traistaru (Zentrum für Europäische Integration, University of Bonn) find, several countries that are now close to accession into the European Union have managed to reach a sustainable path of economic growth and macroeconomic stability. In their chapter on "Central and Eastern Europe: Economic Developments, Reforms, and Geography," the authors first examine the basic economic structures of the transition economies and the extent to which these have changed since the transformation process began in earnest. Achieving sustained economic growth requires, as the authors argue, first and foremost a stable macroeconomic environment. Noting that the real engines of growth are embedded in a business environment that is conducive to private risk taking and entrepreneurship, the chapter then discusses the state of economic reforms in the region. Against the background of the EU enlargement process, the chapter specifically examines the quality of institutions and governance, the business environment, and the location of industrial activity and the pattern of regional specialization in the accession candidates. Finally, the authors discuss macroeconomic and structural developments in Russia, whose economic performance has been quite remarkable since the financial crisis in 1998.

Arguably, the most vulnerable region right now is Latin America, where most countries are trying to cope with an environment of high economic fragility, partly resulting from the current global slowdown but also reflecting internal political trouble and policy mismanagement. As Felipe Larrain B. (Ponticifia Universidad Católica de Chile and Harvard University) argues in his chapter on "Lights and Shadows of Latin American Competitiveness," the latter set of factors suggests that the region's problems are of a more long-term nature than merely cyclical and therefore need to be tackled accordingly, taking into account country-specific circumstances. Although Latin America's large distance from world markets, the region's complicated topography, and the tropical climate pose particularly important challenges, one important policy conclusion Larrain B. draws from his analysis concerns the quality of domestic institutions. Cross-country variances notwithstanding, he argues, important deficits persist, holding back economic growth. On the macroeconomic front, Larrain B. notes that the fiscal policy stance has deteriorated significantly in several countries, sending them into a dangerous spiral of increasing debts and deficits despite important efforts to generate primary surpluses in the public budget. On a positive note, Larrain B. observes, however, that encouraging reforms have been implemented in some areas, notably regarding foreign trade and financial liberalization. As a result, exports have deepened and become more diversified, which bodes well when the external environment becomes more favorable again.

The third part of the *Report* deals with specific topics of economic development and competitiveness. This part opens with an assessment of "The Impact of Location on Global Innovation: Findings from the National Innovative Capacity Index" by Michael E. Porter (Harvard University) and Scott Stern (Northwestern University and National Bureau of Economic Research). Given that innovation measures provide the most important explanation of cross-country differences in economic prosperity among high-income countries, their analysis addresses the following two key questions: why does the intensity of innovation vary across countries and how does innovation depend on location? Extending their research from prior years' *Reports*, Porter and Stern stress that innovation output depends on the interaction between private-sector and public-sector policies and investments and rank 73 countries according to their "national innovative capacity." Their analysis finds striking evidence for the hypothesis that the national environment for innovation plays a very important role for innovative output. Consistent with Porter's analysis of the microeconomic foundations of competitiveness published in the present *Report*, the authors argue that countries that have aggressively invested in innovative capacity look set to become more competitive and achieve higher levels of prosperity. Conversely, Porter and Stern express concern that those countries in which innovative capacity lags behind overall productivity are likely to find it difficult to sustain their current levels of competitiveness.

According to Porter and Stern's analysis, the United States continues to enjoy the highest innovative capacity. Whether the US productivity miracle of the 1990s can be sustained is a different issue, however, and one that remains at the core of the policy debate. Employing a novel approach, Robert J. Gordon (Northwestern University, National Bureau of Economic Research, and Center for Economic and Policy Research) tackles this issue within a supply-demand framework. Specifically, Gordon asks: "High-Tech Innovation and Future Productivity Growth: Does Supply Create Its Own Demand?" This question is particularly relevant with regard to the computing power of a microprocessor chip that, according to Moore's Law, doubles in each cycle. But will the growth in demand be adequate to continue to keep up with the explosion in supply? Gordon provides a rich set of references to the real world that casts considerable doubt on the absorptive capacity of demand. His analysis is not confined to computing power, however. The huge overcapacity created in particular by telecom investment, but also in other areas, argues Gordon, suggests that the 1990s boom was unique, implying that the productivity miracle does not appear sustainable.

Gordon's conclusions do not mean, of course, that innovation and new information and communication technology (ICT) do not matter for economic growth and development. They do matter substantially. Indeed, ICT has long been recognized as a catalyst for organizational transformation and change. At the firm level, ICT plays a key role in creating new products, exploiting new distribution channels, and delivering differentiated value-added services to customers. At the national level, ICT is found to serve as a catalyst for economic development, helping bridge existing divides in different areas and integrate a country into the global economy. But how ready are individual countries for the networked world? Building upon

xxi

the work that the World Economic Forum, in collaboration with the Center for International Development at Harvard University, has previously undertaken, Soumitra Dutta and Amit Jain (INSEAD) explicitly consider the roles played by the major stakeholders—individuals, businesses, and governments (see World Economic Forum 2002). In their chapter entitled "The Networked Readiness of Nations," which represents a synopsis of a new edition of the *Global Information Technology Report*, Dutta and Jain examine the networked readiness of 80 economies according to three dimensions: first, the environment for ICT—that is, the market conditions, the political and regulatory framework, and the infrastructure for ICT. The second dimension is the readiness of individuals, the business community, and government. The third is the actual usage of ICT by the three stakeholders. Based on this framework, the authors develop a networked readiness index.[4]

Foreign direct investment (FDI) represents an important channel through which countries may gain access to technology developed abroad. An increasing number of developing countries, once hostile to the entry of FDI or inclined to restrict it severely, now compete to attract firms. "Something must have been observed in the last couple of decades to change attitudes in so many countries," Robert E. Lipsey writes in his chapter on "Foreign Direct Investment, Growth, and Competitiveness in Developing Countries." This "something" is, first, that larger inflows of FDI have, in general, been associated with higher growth, especially in countries and industries not too far behind the most advanced economies. Second, as Lipsey finds, there is clear evidence that some countries have succeeded in using inward direct investment, especially investment oriented toward exports, effectively to promote their growth and the transition of their economies. As Lipsey cautions, however, openness to inward FDI is no magic potion that can eliminate the effects of poor policies or poor endowments. Rather, FDI needs to be embedded in a comprehensive development strategy.

Openness to trade can also play an important role in helping nations to achieve greater prosperity. However, one of the main difficulties in measuring the benefits of opening to trade is that, for the most part, trade performance has not been measured systematically. The chapter on "Export Performance and Stages of Development" by Jennifer Blanke of the World Economic Forum, along with International Trade Centre economists Friedrich von Kirchbach, Mondher Mimouni, and Jean-Michel Pasteels, aims to provide such an analysis, employing a framework for assessing national trade performance at the sectoral level. The authors find that while for the most part the rich industrialized countries presently outperform developing countries in practically all export sectors, developing and transition countries are seeing important

improvements in their exports performance over time. Curiously, these improvements are not taking place in the sectors in which one might expect them based on trade theory, such as labor-based or low-technology goods. In fact, the authors find that improvements in performance are taking place at the higher end of the investment and technology ladder—in sectors with higher value added goods, such as IT and consumer electronics. These improvements seem to be driven in large part by increasing FDI flows. Since FDI can play a crucial role in inserting these countries into the production chain of higher value added export sectors, the authors conclude that lower-income countries should implement policies that foster economic environments attractive to such investment.

For countries to be an attractive location for FDI, certain governance standards need to be met. Countries that are well governed tend to attract more foreign capital. Conversely, where good public institutions are lacking and corruption is widespread, foreign investors will be discouraged. But FDI is just one channel through which governance affects economic growth. That institutional reforms need to be an integral part of any policy strategy is therefore becoming increasingly accepted. And yet, as Daniel Kaufmann (World Bank Institute) argues, there exist several misperceptions regarding governance and the way it affects economic development. Employing the results of the Executive Opinion Survey, Kaufmann challenges some popular views in his chapter on "Governance Crossroads." Unbundling corruption, he looks at intra-regional differences and examines corruption perceptions over time. A key finding of his analysis is that voice, oversight, and transparency matter—and not only in the public sector. Good governance in the public and private sectors are closely intertwined, and as Kaufmann argues, improvements require collective action through a systematic participatory and consensus-building approach involving all key stakeholders in society. The international community needs to play a critical role as well. Unless improved governance is made a paramount objective, grounded on political commitment from both national and international quarters, Kaufmann cautions that the Millennium Development Goals are unlikely to be met.

Finally, the *Report* recognizes that standards of living are inextricably tied to the quality of the environment. Previous editions of the *Global Competitiveness Report* included analyses that found that, both at the macro- and microeconomic levels, better environmental performance does not need to come at the expense of economic performance. Indeed, considerable empirical evidence was found that cross-country differences in environmental performance are associated with the quality of the environmental regulatory regime in place. Although these findings are good news, much work remains to be done in order to draw the right policy conclusions. One particularly pressing question concerns what *sustainability* really means—the focus of a chapter by Forest Reinhardt (Harvard Business School) entitled "Tests for Sustainability." His analysis begins with the various approaches that have been applied in the long tradition of economics at the national level. Reinhardt then discusses different ways in which conceptually similar sustainability tests may be conducted at the firm level, drawing on principles of financial accounting. He emphasizes that environmental sustainability at the firm level cannot be viewed in isolation from the business fundamentals of the firm. This applies also to the national level, where environmental sustainability must be considered in the context of a country's overall economic activity. In order for private and social costs to converge, argues Reinhardt, an appropriate regulatory regime is needed. Comprehensive compilations of potential externalities are equally important at the national level, in the absence of which tests for sustainability will remain elusive.

Part four of the *Report*, finally, contains country profiles for each individual economy covered. This part includes data tables for the individual variables used to assess national competitiveness. How the country profiles and the data tables work is explained in a separate section. Moreover, technical notes explain individual variables and the results of the World Economic Forum's Executive Opinion Survey.

Notes

1 This section follows Porter, Sachs, and Warner (2000).

2 Conceptually, the Microeconomic Competitiveness Index is identical with last year's Current Competitiveness Index. Although the latter has been renamed to emphasize its focus on micro- as opposed to macroeconomic issues, this year's results are comparable with those estimated last year and in previous years.

3 The concept of *core innovators* was introduced in last year's *Global Competitiveness Report* by John W. McArthur and Jeffrey D. Sachs in their chapter "The Growth Competitiveness Index: Measuring Technological Advancement and the Stages of Development" in *The Global Competitiveness Report 2001–2002* (McArthur and Sachs 2002). According to this concept, a country is defined as a *core innovator* if it has achieved at least 15 patents registered in the United States per million population.

4 Note that the index in this *Report* deviates slightly from the one in the forthcoming *Global Information Technology Report* in that it does not include Egypt and Luxembourg.

References

Cornelius, P. K. et al. 2002. "Introduction." In *The Global Competitiveness Report 2001–2002*. New York: Oxford University Press for the World Economic Forum.

McArthur, J. W. and J. D. Sachs. 2002. "The Growth Competitiveness Index: Measuring Technological Advancement and the Stages of Development." In *The Global Competitiveness Report 2001–2002*. New York: Oxford University Press for the World Economic Forum.

Porter, M. E., J. D. Sachs, and A. M. Warner. 2000. "Executive Summary: Current Competitiveness and Growth Competitiveness." In *The Global Competitiveness Report 2000*. New York: Oxford University Press for the World Economic Forum.

World Economic Forum. 2002. *The Global Information Technology Report 2001–2002: Readiness for the Networked World*, ed. by G. Kirkman et al. New York: Oxford University Press for the World Economic Forum.

———. 2003. *The Global Information Technology Report 2002–2003*, ed. by S. Dutta, B. Lanvin, and F. Paua. New York: Oxford University Press for the World Economic Forum.

xxiii

Part 1

The Competitiveness Indexes

CHAPTER 1.1

The Growth Competitiveness Index: Recent Economic Developments and the Prospects for a Sustained Recovery[1]

PETER K. CORNELIUS, World Economic Forum

JENNIFER BLANKE, World Economic Forum

FIONA PAUA, World Economic Forum

World output growth has slowed to one of its lowest rates in decades. According to the September 2002 issue of the International Monetary Fund's *World Economic Outlook,* global output expanded by only 2.2 percent in 2001. In 2002, a moderate recovery to 2.8 percent is expected, which would still be the second-lowest reading since the global slowdown in the early 1990s. These estimates mask important regional differences: although the slowdown in the advanced countries has been remarkably synchronized, it has been particularly pronounced in the United States where economic growth fell from 3.8 percent in 2000 to just 0.3 percent in 2001. In Japan, output actually shrank in 2001, and in the European Union economic growth more than halved to just 1.6 percent in that year.

The developing countries have not remained unaffected by the economic slowdown in the industrialized world. The adverse external environment has had a particularly pronounced impact on Latin America, exacerbating the domestic economic problems in several countries, notably in the Southern Cone—Argentina's output fell by almost 4.5 percent in 2001—but also in Mexico, where economic activity shrank after an expansion of more than 6.5 percent the year before. In developing Asia, by contrast, output growth remained relatively robust, registering an increase of around 5.5 percent in 2001. Similarly, in the transition countries in central and eastern Europe, the decline in economic growth from 3.8 percent in 2000 to 3 percent in 2001 was relatively modest. The only region where economic growth accelerated in 2001 was Africa.

The short-term economic outlook remains clouded with exceptional uncertainty. Although the United States seems to have weathered the economic impact of the terrorist attacks of September 11, 2001, reasonably well, global asset prices continue to show a high degree of volatility. Taking into account that the terrorist attacks were not the only shock—Enron and other corporate scandals, the severe tensions in the Middle East, and the financial crises in some emerging markets could each have caused serious effects—the recent recession in the United States and the global slowdown appear relatively mild. At the same time, however, the recovery seems rather slow, and important risks exist that could derail the expected return to a steeper growth trajectory. Private institutions, governments, and international organizations have continued to lower their economic forecasts for 2002 and 2003. According to the consensus forecasts, a considerable output gap is expected to persist in the short term in the advanced economies. In the developing world, output growth is expected to accelerate markedly in 2003. However, important interregional differences are forecast to remain.

Although the short-term outlook for a sustained recovery is currently subject to a huge amount of uncertainty, the longer-term growth itself is determined by the set of institutions, market structures, and economic policies supportive of higher productivity growth and increases in output. This set of factors is precisely what the Growth Competitiveness Index (GCI) is concerned with. Rather than attempt to make short-term economic forecasts, we are interested primarily in the potential of a large cross-section of countries to achieve sustained economic growth over the next five to eight years.

To put our analysis in an appropriate context, we begin by reviewing global economic developments over the last five years and discuss the extent to which these developments were broadly consistent with our assessment of national competitiveness five years ago. We then review the recent growth performance in the industrialized countries and the main emerging-market economies and discuss the short-term risks countries are currently facing in struggling to return to a sustained growth path. In the second part of the chapter, we outline the construction of the Index and then discuss the empirical results.

Recent economic developments and short-term outlook

Global economic growth since 1997

In the last few years of the past decade, the world economy enjoyed a period of rapid economic growth. Between 1997 and 2000, global output expanded by almost 4 percent per year (IMF 2002). As far as the industrialized countries are concerned, the United States outperformed most other advanced economies, with real activity expanding by more than 1 percentage point per annum faster than in the European Union. In Japan, by contrast, economic growth averaged less than 1 percent during that period. In 2001, however, economic growth in virtually all industrialized countries fell in a remarkably synchronized fashion.

Most Asian economies recovered reasonably well from the financial crises in 1997–98. Korea, for example, achieved a turnaround in output from a decline of almost 7 percent (year-over-year) in 1998 to gains of almost 11 and 10 percent in 1999 and 2000, respectively. In Malaysia, the Philippines, and Thailand, the recovery was somewhat less pronounced, but still considerable. China proved largely unaffected by the crisis and has continued to grow at a rapid rate of around 7 to 8 percent per year.

The Asian financial crisis radiated more widely, however, affecting especially Brazil where market forces led the authorities to introduce a flexible exchange rate regime in January 1999. Greater exchange rate flexibility helped Brazil recover after output growth was essentially flat in 1998 and 1999. In Argentina, whose economy had enjoyed rapid economic growth in the mid 1990s, serious doubts emerged as to whether the currency board arrangement could be sustained. In contrast to Brazil, the crisis in Argentina deepened beginning in the late 1990s. With output shrinking at an increasing rate—real activity in 2001 is estimated to have fallen by around 4.5 percent—the currency board of Argentina was abandoned and the exchange rate has depreciated by around 70 percent since then. In Chile, economic growth also slowed markedly in 1998–99, but recovered strongly thereafter. Mexico, finally, has largely followed the US economy, recording strong economic growth in the second half of the 1990s and a significant slowdown in 2001.

In Africa, average economic growth in 1997–2001 hovered around 3 to 3.5 percent per year. However, with population growth remaining relatively strong, standards of living have not much improved. In many African countries, economic growth continues to be driven primarily by commodity prices and domestic factors. By contrast, few countries are integrated enough to have felt the global business cycle. One exception is, of course, South Africa, whose economy suffered in 1998–99 from the flight to quality in the wake of the Asian financial crisis. Since then, South Africa has enjoyed a moderate recovery. One of the worst performers remains Zimbabwe, where the economic downturn accelerated substantially in 2001 and 2002.

Finally, regarding the transition economies in central and eastern Europe, Russia has shown a sharp turnaround, after having defaulted on its foreign debt and moving to a flexible exchange rate regime in 1998. Although real output shrank by almost 5 percent in 1998, economic growth was already positive in 1999, and in 2000 activity expanded by 9 percent. In the Ukraine, the turnaround was achieved somewhat later, but in 2000 and 2001 the country outperformed most other economies in the region. Among the EU accession candidates, the Baltic countries have shown solid economic performance, although they all suffered in 1999 from a temporary slowdown in growth. Among the more advanced transition economies, Hungary and Poland have enjoyed the relatively fastest growth rates.

How do the competitiveness rankings we published in 1997 appear in light of the actual performance over the past five years? Recall that the competitiveness index "... is intended to identify factors determining economic growth. More specifically, it is designed to measure the capacity of national economies to achieve high rates of per capita GDP growth in the medium term. . . ." (Hu and Sachs 1997, p 23).

Table 1 shows the growth performance in 1997–2001 of the 53 countries included in the 1997 competitiveness rankings, with the first column showing average annual economic growth in percent and the second column showing the countries' relative position ranging from 1(best) to 53 (worst). In general, countries that were found to be relatively competitive tended to outperform those that were found to be less competitive. Note that the table shows average absolute economic growth rates rather than growth rates per capita, which represents the endogenous (or left-hand side variable) in the competitiveness analysis. In some cases where population growth has remained particularly rapid (eg, Egypt) or slow or even negative (eg, Germany and Japan), this will obviously affect the results. Overall, however, the picture remains materially unchanged.

Although the 1997 Competitiveness Index was adjusted for income levels, in a period as short as 1997–2001 it is difficult to detect a catch-up effect. Of the ten best growth performers, five belonged to the group of high-income countries (Ireland, Luxembourg, Singapore, Finland, and Iceland). Among the low-income countries, China, India, and Vietnam enjoyed the highest average growth rates in absolute terms.

There are four broad groups of countries where the 1997 rankings clearly missed something: a group of Asian economies (Thailand, Indonesia, Hong Kong SAR, and Korea); post-socialist countries (China, Vietnam, Hungary, Poland, Czech Republic, Ukraine, and Russia); countries in the European periphery (Ireland Spain, Portugal, and Greece); and "banking centers" (Luxembourg and Switzerland).

The experience in Asia is particularly interesting. Clearly, the 1997 rankings missed the negative impact of the financial crisis. To the extent that this crisis was precipitated by international financial panic, this is precisely the kind of surprise that the rankings were not designed to predict and in fact never were expected to predict. With the important exception of Indonesia, five of the countries hit by this crisis in 1997 or 1998 have bounced back with positive and fairly high economic growth, suggesting that despite the crisis, there remains a strong underlying growth potential. Korea had two years with growth above 7 percent, Hong Kong grew just under 6 percent in 2000, Malaysia had back-to-back growth of 3.5 and 4 percent in 1999 and 2000, Singapore achieved growth of 3.9 and 6.4 percent in the same two years, and even Thailand achieved a more modest 3.2 and 4.0 percent in 1999 and 2000. Most Asian countries subsequently suffered from the global demand slowdown in 2001–02.

The 1997 rankings also underpredicted the performance of European post-socialist economies such as Hungary and Poland. Since these economies were in the midst of restructuring toward private enterprises, it is probably not surprising that a framework designed to explain global growth of countries not in this circumstance did poorly in accounting for growth in these countries. For these countries, the transition entailed a major structural change characterized by a massive movement of resources from state industries and the elimination of subsidies for ineffi-

Table 1: Average annual growth 1997–2001 and 1997 competitiveness index rankings

Country	Average annual real GDP growth 1997–2001 (in %)	Growth rate rankings	Competitiveness index rankings
Argentina	0.66	50	37
Australia	3.88	16	17
Austria	2.38	36	27
Belgium	2.76	31	31
Brazil	2.04	40	42
Canada	3.94	15	4
Chile	3.20	24	13
China	7.80	2	29
Colombia	0.78	48	41
Czech Republic	1.06	47	32
Denmark	2.36	37	20
Egypt	5.08	6	28
Finland	4.40	9	19
France	2.92	30	23
Germany	1.78	44	25
Greece	3.42	19	48
Hong Kong SAR	2.66	34	2
Hungary	4.54	8	46
Iceland	4.36	10	38
India	5.40	4	45
Indonesia	0.06	51	15
Ireland	9.54	1	16
Israel	3.08	26	24
Italy	2.02	41	39
Japan	0.70	49	14
Jordan	3.52	18	43
Korea	4.30	12	21
Luxembourg	6.36	3	11
Malaysia	2.96	29	9
Mexico	4.34	11	33
Netherlands	3.36	21	12
New Zealand	2.44	35	5
Norway	2.74	32	10
Peru	2.10	39	40
Philippines	3.12	25	34
Poland	4.14	13	50
Portugal	3.36	22	30
Russian Federation	3.08	27	53
Singapore	4.72	7	1
Slovak Republic	3.28	23	35
South Africa	2.22	38	44
Spain	3.88	17	26
Sweden	3.00	28	22
Switzerland	1.92	43	6
Taiwan	4.14	14	8
Thailand	−0.22	52	18
Turkey	1.20	46	36
Ukraine	1.98	42	52
United Kingdom	2.74	33	7
United States	3.38	20	3
Venezuela	1.30	45	47
Vietnam	5.28	5	49
Zimbabwe	−1.72	53	51

Sources: IMF (2002); WEF (1997)

cient enterprises. In this context, the post-socialist countries remain a difficult case for our competitiveness rankings, since there is so little empirical history on which to base the rankings.

On the whole, however, if we take into account the fact that we do not pretend to predict the unpredictable, such as the Asian financial crisis, the rankings appear moderately satisfactory. Nevertheless, there remains considerable room for improvement. Since 1997, we have changed the ranking procedure in a number of ways. We are now placing more emphasis on fundamental drivers of growth such as technology and innovation. Moreover, since the 2000 *Report*, we are no longer sticking to a one-size-fits-all approach. Introduced in last year's *Report*, we distinguish between two groups of countries, the "core innovators" and the "non-core innovators" (a terminology not to be construed as a value judgment, as explained below). This year's approach remains basically unchanged, with one slight refinement. We review the rankings in more detail after considering the current economic situation.

The current situation and short-term prospects

Seldom has there been a period with greater uncertainty than the year after the publication of last year's *Global Competitiveness Report* in October 2001. In the two weeks following the terrorist attacks of September 11, 2001, the world equity markets lost approximately two trillion US dollars, with 20 of the world's major stock exchanges dropping more than 10 percent. There was widespread agreement that in the near term the horrific event would accelerate and deepen the slowdown in the global economy that had already been underway, by causing substantial disruptions of the global transport networks and production chains and also by causing a steep drop in consumer and business confidence. There was less agreement, however, as to how fast the global economy would recover and return to a sustained growth path in the medium term. Even greater uncertainty existed with regard to the long-term impact of the terrorist attacks.

A year later, the global economic outlook still remains clouded by tremendous uncertainty. Asset prices have remained subject to substantial volatility. In the two-and-a-half-year period between March 2000, when equity prices peaked, and end-September 2002, some of the major stock indices lost up to two-thirds of their value, with the Nikkei having hit a 19-year low. The NASDAQ and other tech-laden stock exchanges have suffered even greater losses, with some markets—including Germany's Neuer Markt and Switzerland's New Market—being dissolved. Moreover, the latest GDP revisions in the United States confirm that the situation a year ago was actually worse than thought. Rather than merely slowing, we now know that the largest economy in the world was already in recession when the terrorist attacks occurred, with output having shrunk for the first nine months of 2001.

Nevertheless, in each of the three subsequent quarters GDP growth has been positive, and judged by the fears many had a year ago, one might argue that the US economy has weathered the economic impact of the tragic events of September 11 reasonably well. In fact, from the peak to trough, GDP fell by only 0.6 percent, compared with an average decline of over 2 percent during recessions in the post-war era. Although it is true that nominal GDP growth in the G-7 countries fell to its slowest rates for decades, it is important to bear in mind that the terrorist attacks were not the only shock. The failure of Enron, WorldCom, and other high-profile corporate scan-

dals; the collapse of Argentina's currency board; and the severe tensions in the Middle East might each have been expected to have a considerable impact on the global economic outlook, too. Taken together, their impact could have been far more serious, possibly pushing the world economy into a prolonged recession. Considering the potential damage these shocks could have caused, the world economy and the global financial system seems to have proved surprisingly resilient thus far.

One important reason for the robustness that the global economy has shown so far is the resilience of the global financial system. The infrastructure of the system proved strong, and even in the immediate aftermath of massive disruptions in New York City, the world's leading financial center, the system continued to function effectively. The same can be said with regard to the energy market after the collapse of Enron, one of the world's biggest energy traders. Although the US commercial paper market was most affected, corporate bond issuance rose to record levels and many firms were able to fall back on prenegotiated arrangements with their banks. Moreover, consumers in many industrialized countries as well as in some emerging-market economies gained greater access to consumer and mortgage credit, helping private consumption and residential construction to hold up well.

Another remarkable aspect of the robustness of the global economy is that, unlike the cases of the Long-Term Capital Management (LTCM) and Russian crises in 1998, in 2001 there was no panic flight to liquidity (Bank for International Settlements 2002, pp 3 ff); nor was there a sudden drying up of financing for countries with current account deficits due to increased risk aversion. The external funding requirements of the United States continued to be met, and emerging markets of good credit standing seeking funds in the international bond markets still had ready access, with sovereign spreads actually narrowing for several countries.

Much credit for the global economy's resilience is due to the sharp monetary easing in most countries, especially in the United States where at the time of this writing the federal funds target rate stood at just 1.25 percent. This monetary easing has been accompanied by a more expansionary fiscal stance. In the United States, sizeable tax cuts were implemented and public expenditure has been rising strongly, especially in the aftermath of the terrorist attacks, and in 2002, the easing of the budgetary stance is estimated to amount to around 1.5 percent of GDP. Fiscal policy has become significantly more expansionary in several other countries, including Canada, Norway, Sweden, and especially the United Kingdom.

That the global economy has been relatively resilient should not lead to complacency, however. The short- and medium-term economic risks are considerable, and they exist regardless of the enormous uncertainties associated

Figure 1: Recession expectations

(1 = your country's economy will likely be in a recession next year; 7 = your country's economy will have strong growth next year)

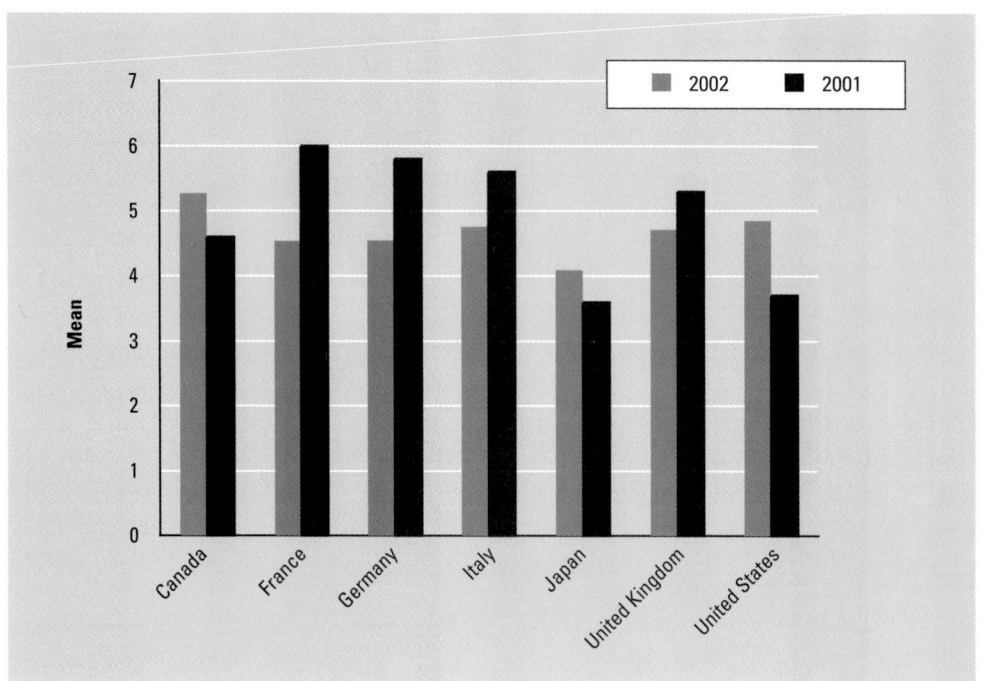

with the possibility of a protracted war in Iraq or new terrorist threats. For one thing, corporate and private debts still appear rather large in the United States. Lower interest rates have encouraged a boom in the housing market that has partially offset losses in the stock market, helping insulate private wealth and maintain consumer spending. Once households reduce their borrowing propped up by higher mortgages, they will spend less and save more, which could lead to a prolonged period of sluggish growth. US monetary policy has not much ammunition left if, under such a scenario, the economy stumbles. The rest of the world would not remain unaffected, and with the US current account deficit becoming harder to finance, there is concern that a sharp fall in the US dollar could help export deflationary pressures to other countries. At the same time, to the extent that the economy has become more open, fiscal policy might have become less effective to cushion downturns than in previous cycles.

Given the enormous uncertainties that continue to exist, forecasters have continually lowered their 2003 forecasts for the United States and most other OECD countries. Although economic activity in the "Triad" of the United States, Europe, and Japan is expected to increase, the recovery is forecast to be rather gradual, with output remaining below production potential for the foreseeable future. Under this scenario, inflation is expected to remain tame, but unemployment in many countries will remain high or even rising. A slower-than-expected recovery in the OECD countries has obvious implications for the

developing world, where in many countries economic growth has also slowed considerably.

This scenario is more or less in line with the responses to our Executive Opinion Survey, which was conducted in the spring of 2002. Asked about their recession expectations (1 = very high probability of a recession next year; 7 = very low probability of a recession next year), respondents from Canada were most optimistic among G-7 participants, with a mean score of 5.3 (see Figure 1). By contrast, Japanese executives showed the highest degree of pessimism, with a mean score of 4.1. Overall, however, the Survey results show relatively little variation. Although a rapid recovery does not appear to be in the cards, responses of the senior executives who participated in the Survey do not suggest a particular fear of a recession in any of the G-7 countries.

Interestingly, US executives were actually considerably more optimistic in early 2002, with a mean score of 4.8, than they had been 12 months earlier, when the mean response to our question was a 3.7. Although in retrospect US executives showed a considerable degree of foresight—the unforeseeable terrorist attacks and other shocks notwithstanding—the global slowdown took their European counterparts by surprise, with their mean responses ranging from 5.3 (United Kingdom) to 6.0 (France) in early 2001. Japanese executives have also become slightly more optimistic, with the mean response increasing from 3.6 in early 2001 (for 2002) to 4.1 in early 2002 (for 2003).

Figure 2: Terrorism and the cost of doing business

(1 = the threat of terrorism imposes significant costs on business; 7 = the threat of terrorism does not impose significant costs on business)

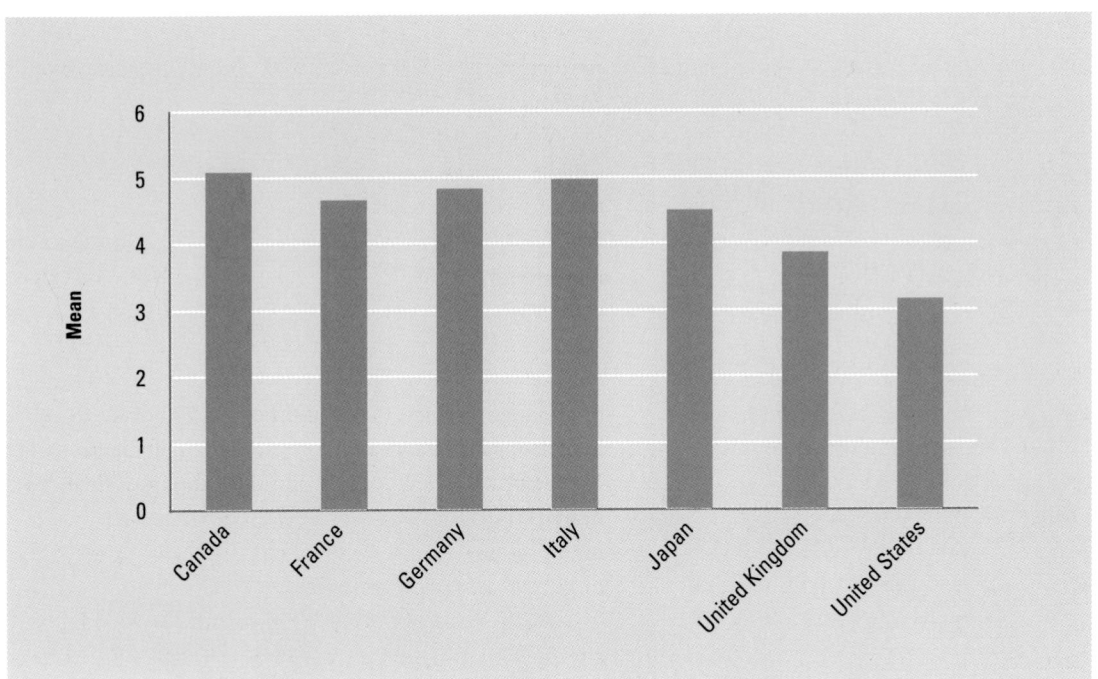

Asked about the cost impact of the threat of terrorism on their business, US executives show by far the highest degree of skepticism, followed by their fellow executives in the United Kingdom. Although executives in continental European countries and in Japan were less pessimistic, the results suggest a high degree of caution in the sense that none of the respondents ruled out the possibility that terrorism could seriously affect their businesses (see Figure 2).

Notwithstanding the tremendous short-term uncertainties currently facing the world economy, those countries that have in place the set of institutions, policies, and regulations that support high levels of productivity and drive productivity growth should be expected to return to a sustained growth path faster than less competitive countries. Which are these countries? How much growth can they reasonably expect once the clouds of uncertainty disappear? This is precisely what the growth competitiveness rankings are concerned with: estimating the underlying prospects for growth over the next five to eight years in a large number of individual economies. Our analysis includes 80 economies, with six new countries being covered by the Growth Competitiveness Index this year: Botswana, Croatia, Haiti, Morocco, Namibia, and Tunisia. Egypt, however, had to be dropped this year due to the lack of Survey data.

The Growth Competitiveness Index

The overall Growth Competitiveness Index (GCI) aims to measure the capacity of the national economy to achieve sustained economic growth over the medium term, controlling for the current level of development.

There are several issues in this definition that are worth noting. First of all, we say *sustainable* to emphasize that we are thinking beyond the shorter-term business cycle. Moreover, our calculations aim to track growth potential after taking into account the temporary catch-up phenomena, whereby poorer countries can grow quickly for a time as they catch up to richer countries. The catch-up phenomenon is temporary because it disappears after countries have caught up to richer countries; however, it can take many years for this to happen. Roughly speaking, our rankings rate growth potential after taking out the part of growth that is related to catching up. For a poorer country such as China, this adjustment can make a large difference. China's growth rate during the period 1991–2001 was over 8 percent per year, the highest of the 80 countries in the *Report*. If our rankings were keyed to unadjusted growth rates, China would look highly competitive.

The rankings are fact driven in the sense that we aspire to include in the rankings only those factors that have some demonstrated correlation with rates of economic growth over the medium term. We construct the rankings on the basis of recent theoretical literature on the determinants of economic growth, as well the past 10 years' empirical evidence on economic growth. The Index is tested each year to confirm that it does indeed correlate with rates of economic growth from the recent past.

The rankings provide a "rough guide" to the potential for growth. There are two reasons that the rankings are rough. The first is that the rankings inevitably leave out any special circumstances in each country. This means essentially that a significant fraction of growth is left unexplained. Sometimes the rankings are criticized for encouraging the view that there is a single recipe that all countries should follow to achieve competitiveness and fast growth. There is nothing in the *Global Competitiveness Report* that denies the importance of each country's special circumstances. At the same time, the international evidence shows that there are indeed important common factors that influence growth in all countries.

The second reason the rankings are rough is that there is little meaningful distinction between countries ranked close to each other. Very fine differences in the data can shift countries up or down in the rankings if the countries happen to be similar in terms of the underlying indicators. Therefore small changes in the rankings are best attributed to statistical error. A reasonable rule of thumb is that any given country could easily have been ranked five positions in either direction due to random differences in the data. However, if two countries differ by more than ten positions, it is very likely that the difference reflects something real rather than a random error.

Therefore the rankings provide a rough summary of the environment for rapid growth in each country, as best as can be judged by recent evidence. We identify critical determinants of growth and use them to construct the index. As in previous years, the rankings are built from a base that starts with an extensive data set. This data set includes information from official sources such as national statistical agencies and international organizations such as the United Nations (UN), the World Bank, the World Trade Organization (WTO), the International Monetary Fund (IMF), and the World Intellectual Property Organization (WIPO). It also includes data collected through the annual Executive Opinion Survey of the *Global Competitiveness Report*. The Executive Opinion Survey is relied on to provide qualitative data or data on issues that are not measured by alternative sources. A discussion of the characteristics and methodology behind this year's Executive Opinion Survey can be found in Part 4 of this *Report*.

The construction of the GCI essentially follows last year's approach. Developed by Jeffrey D. Sachs and John W. McArthur (McArthur and Sachs 2002), this approach represents the result of continuous research efforts published in previous *Global Competitiveness Reports*. As outlined in

detail in last year's *Report* and summarized in the Appendix of this chapter, the GCI is based on three broad categories of variables that are found to drive economic growth in the medium- and long-term. These categories are technology, public institutions, and the macroeconomic environment.

Without technological progress, countries may achieve a higher standard of living, for example, through a higher rate of capital accumulation, but they will not be able to enjoy continuously high economic growth. Institutions are crucial for their role in ensuring the protection of property rights, the objective resolution of contract and other legal disputes, efficiency of government spending, and transparency in all levels of government. In the absence of good governance, the division of labor is likely to be impeded and the allocation of resources inefficient. Monetary and fiscal policies, and the stability of financial institutions, have important effects on short-term economic dynamics as well as on the long-term capacity to grow.

The role of technology in the growth process has attracted a particularly great deal of attention in the literature. Since the onset of the first industrial revolution, economists have struggled to understand why growth proceeds slowly at some times and in some nations, but rapidly in others. During the past two decades, a new growth theory has taken the economics profession by storm, identifying technological change as a key factor in economic development.

Given the central role technology plays in the growth process, the key question for the future, of course, is whether a brisk pace of technological advance can be sustained. As Scherer (1999, p 119) emphasizes, "(t)here is a centuries-old tradition of gazing with wonder at recent technological achievements, surveying the difficulties that seem to thwart further improvements, and concluding that the most important inventions have been made and that it will be much more difficult in the future to achieve comparable rates of advance. Such views have always proved to be wrong in the past, and there is no reason to believe that they will be any more valid in the foreseeable future."

Whether the recent pace of technological progress can be sustained is also a key issue in the present *Report*. Perhaps the most hotly debated question in this regard is currently whether the acceleration in US productivity growth in the second half of the 1990s can be expected to continue, an issue that represents the focus of Chapter 3.2 by Robert Gordon. But even if this acceleration in productivity growth proved to be a temporary phenomenon, the most fundamental observation in the growth literature remains intact—namely that each new technological innovation triggers yet further innovation, in a kind of chain reaction that fuels long-term economic growth. Examining national competitiveness thus requires, first and foremost, analyzing the extent to which individual countries are able to achieve technological progress.

Technology plays a critical role at all stages of economic development, but the way this driver affects economic growth varies according to the level of economic prosperity a country has already achieved. At early stages of economic development, a country's ability to launch its economy on a steeper growth path depends primarily on the transfer of technology from abroad. Countries that have experienced rapid economic growth are typically those that are successful in adopting and adapting a technology that has been developed abroad, a process known as *technological diffusion*. At more advanced stages of economic development, technological diffusion becomes increasingly important for countries to sustain rapid economic growth.

Taking into account the different channels through which technology affects economic growth at different stages of development, in this *Report* we continue to distinguish between two groups of countries. The group of *core innovators* comprises those countries whose companies have registered at least 15 US utility patents granted per million population in 2001. This criterion is met in 24 economies (see Table 2). All other countries are said to be *non-core innovators*. Empirical tests find that technology plays a particularly critical role in the core innovating countries, a finding that is reflected in the weights we attach to the different growth drivers. In these countries, technology has a weight of 50 percent in the overall GCI, compared with 25 percent each for public institutions and the macroeconomic environment. By contrast, equal weights of one third are attached to each of the three drivers in the case of the non-core innovators.

For the core innovators, the technology index is a simple average of the innovation subindex and the information and communication technology subindex, both of which are comprised of hard and soft data (note that the innovation subindex is different from the "innovative capacity index" constructed by Michael E. Porter and Scott Stern in Chapter 3.1. While the innovation subindex seeks to explain the elements of innovation that are linked to economic growth, the innovative capacity index seeks to explain the underlying factors that contribute to innovation). In the case of non-core innovators, by contrast, technology transfer plays a considerably more important role than innovation, which is reflected in relative weights of three eighths for the technology transfer index versus one eighth in the innovation subindex. Information and communication technology represents the other subindex of the technology index, with a weight of one half.

This year's *Report* includes one important adjustment: the technology transfer subindex includes new Survey evidence on the licensing of foreign technology as an impor-

Table 2: Core technology-innovating economies in the 1980s and in 2001

Country	Average annual US utility patents granted per million population, 1980 to 1989	1980s rank	US utility patents granted per million population, 2001	2001 rank
1980s Core technology innovators				
Switzerland	189.70	1	195.65	4
United States	165.90	2	314.43	1
Japan	101.30	3	260.99	2
Sweden	94.40	4	195.62	5
Germany	85.10	5	135.73	8
Netherlands	52.00	6	83.27	11
Canada	50.40	7	115.80	9
United Kingdom	43.30	8	66.44	17
France	43.00	9	68.15	16
Israel	42.20	10	163.32	6
Austria	40.40	11	72.43	13
Finland	37.10	12	140.21	7
Denmark	31.80	13	89.55	10
Belgium	26.50	14	70.25	15
Norway	22.70	15	58.82	19
Australia	21.50	16	44.99	20
Italy	16.50	17	29.64	24
New Zealand	15.20	18	32.28	23
1980s Non-core economies that became core innovators by 2000				
Taiwan	12.80	19	239.78	3
Iceland	9.00	21	63.33	18
Ireland	8.80	22	37.24	21
Hong Kong SAR	5.40	23	34.34	22
Singapore	2.40	25	72.12	14
Korea	1.30	28	73.99	12

Source: US Patent and Trademark Office, April 2002

tant source of new technology. This evidence replaces a variable that was created to measure the extent of manufacturing technology in the export structure of non-core innovators. The reasoning behind including this variable was that countries with a technology-based export sector may be expected to be more adept at absorbing technologies from abroad than economies with a primary commodity-based export structure. Empirical tests suggest that the new variable has significant explanatory power.

Technology can not be examined in isolation. As discussed in Chapter 3.1, Porter and Stern find a substantial degree of variation among a large sample of countries in terms of their innovative capacity. Although this study focuses primarily on innovation rather than technology transfer, a country's ability to adopt and adapt new technologies developed abroad also depends on a complex set of factors determining the quality of the business environment. Reviewing the growth and technology literature, Scherer (1999, p 124) emphasizes three main barriers in developing countries. The most important one is the lack of, or critical shortcomings in, a legal and institutional framework that encourages vigorously independent risk-taking and dynamic competition. The second barrier lies in the scarcity of business entrepreneurs willing and able to take advantage of the opportunities for development offered by modern technology. And third, because devel-

Table 8: Public institutions index components

Country	Public institutions index		Contracts and law subindex		Corruption subindex	
	Rank	Score	Rank	Score	Rank	Score
Argentina	66	3.38	76	2.35	58	4.42
Australia	5	6.23	4	6.03	8	6.44
Austria	11	5.90	8	5.79	19	6.02
Bangladesh	79	2.56	66	2.93	80	2.20
Belgium	22	5.36	22	5.14	30	5.58
Bolivia	69	3.13	70	2.69	71	3.56
Botswana	31	5.14	23	5.01	36	5.27
Brazil	45	4.45	45	4.08	46	4.82
Bulgaria	47	4.30	67	2.87	27	5.73
Canada	9	6.00	14	5.52	7	6.49
Chile	19	5.62	24	4.90	10	6.34
China	38	4.68	44	4.18	39	5.19
Colombia	54	4.10	64	3.05	41	5.14
Costa Rica	46	4.33	43	4.25	59	4.41
Croatia	57	4.04	60	3.26	45	4.83
Czech Republic	50	4.20	49	3.75	51	4.65
Denmark	2	6.50	2	6.28	3	6.72
Dominican Republic	60	3.93	56	3.42	57	4.43
Ecuador	75	2.98	78	2.29	69	3.67
El Salvador	48	4.24	58	3.33	40	5.16
Estonia	28	5.22	36	4.58	25	5.86
Finland	1	6.60	1	6.32	1	6.89
France	29	5.15	32	4.62	28	5.69
Germany	14	5.85	10	5.64	17	6.06
Greece	44	4.53	40	4.46	52	4.61
Guatemala	74	2.98	79	2.15	66	3.81
Haiti	80	2.11	80	1.80	79	2.41
Honduras	76	2.93	75	2.45	74	3.41
Hong Kong SAR	13	5.88	13	5.53	15	6.24
Hungary	30	5.15	30	4.66	29	5.65
Iceland	3	6.39	3	6.05	2	6.73
India	59	3.96	39	4.48	73	3.43
Indonesia	77	2.90	68	2.80	77	2.99
Ireland	18	5.76	20	5.25	14	6.26
Israel	17	5.76	12	5.55	22	5.97
Italy	37	4.71	47	4.03	32	5.39
Jamaica	51	4.18	52	3.61	49	4.75
Japan	25	5.27	37	4.56	21	5.97
Jordan	40	4.67	27	4.78	54	4.56
Korea	32	4.96	28	4.72	38	5.20
Latvia	52	4.12	50	3.66	53	4.59
Lithuania	36	4.89	51	3.64	16	6.13
Malaysia	33	4.94	34	4.59	34	5.29
Mauritius	35	4.91	25	4.88	42	4.94
Mexico	58	3.99	62	3.17	47	4.82
Morocco	56	4.05	46	4.07	64	4.03
Namibia	41	4.65	31	4.62	50	4.68
Netherlands	10	5.95	11	5.59	13	6.30
New Zealand	4	6.32	5	5.95	4	6.69
Nicaragua	64	3.50	69	2.69	60	4.31
Nigeria	78	2.89	61	3.18	78	2.60
Norway	12	5.89	16	5.46	12	6.32
Panama	55	4.06	53	3.60	55	4.52
Paraguay	71	3.09	72	2.63	72	3.55
Peru	49	4.24	59	3.27	37	5.21
Philippines	70	3.11	63	3.14	76	3.07
Poland	61	3.83	54	3.55	62	4.11
Portugal	21	5.50	17	5.43	31	5.57
Romania	67	3.38	65	2.96	67	3.80
Russian Federation	65	3.45	71	2.69	61	4.22
Singapore	7	6.17	9	5.78	5	6.55
Slovak Republic	53	4.11	57	3.39	44	4.84
Slovenia	23	5.33	26	4.83	26	5.82
South Africa	34	4.93	35	4.59	35	5.28
Spain	26	5.25	41	4.46	18	6.05
Sri Lanka	42	4.57	29	4.67	56	4.48
Sweden	15	5.81	18	5.28	11	6.33
Switzerland	8	6.07	7	5.79	9	6.36
Taiwan	27	5.25	33	4.61	23	5.89
Thailand	39	4.68	38	4.49	43	4.86
Trinidad and Tobago	43	4.56	42	4.35	48	4.78
Tunisia	24	5.31	19	5.28	33	5.34
Turkey	63	3.52	48	3.78	75	3.27
Ukraine	72	3.07	73	2.57	70	3.58
United Kingdom	6	6.19	6	5.85	6	6.54
United States	16	5.76	15	5.50	20	6.01
Uruguay	20	5.54	21	5.20	24	5.88
Venezuela	73	3.07	77	2.29	65	3.85
Vietnam	62	3.65	55	3.50	68	3.80
Zimbabwe	68	3.31	74	2.54	63	4.07

Finland, swapping positions with the United States this year, continues to perform extremely well with regard to its public institutions. Moreover, it is one of the most technologically advanced economies in the world, ranked number 3 on both the innovation subindex and the information and communication technology subindex. However, Finland falls to the 14th rank in terms of its macroeconomic environment, a decline that is primarily due to Finland's deteriorating position with regard to government expenditure.

Taiwan, ranked 7th last year, overtakes Singapore, whose overall position remains unchanged. Taiwan owes the improvement to the 3rd rank to very high scores on the technology index. Although Taiwan enjoys a macroeconomic environment that is quite favorable relative to most other countries, considerable competitive disadvantages are perceived to exist with regard to Taiwan's public institutions.

Switzerland and Japan have also been able to improve their overall positions. In both cases, technology represents the key driver behind these improvements. In the case of Switzerland, the country's dramatic rise in the technology index by 18 positions mirrors a 7-percent increase in the number of utility patents Swiss firms have registered in the United States in 2001. Swiss public institutions are also perceived to have improved relative to other countries, whereas the country slips slightly in the macroeconomic dimension of national competitiveness (a more detailed discussion of Switzerland's competitiveness can be found in Chapter 2.3). Japan's companies are even more competitive in terms of innovation, putting the country in the 5th position on that subindex as well as the technology index. Not surprisingly, however, Japan's position on the macroeconomic environment index and, to a somewhat lesser extent, the public institutions index drops markedly, reflecting the massive problems the country continues to face in these areas. These problems pose a formidable challenge to policymakers. The good news is, however, that the country's innovative power has remained very strong, and once the macroeconomic situation improves and the governance problems are addressed efficiently, Japan should be able to recover and resume economic growth.

It is more difficult to trace France's decline in the overall GCI back to an individual subset of factors. France slips on all counts: in the area of technology by 11 positions to number 28, with regard to the quality of its public institutions to 29, and concerning the macroeconomic environment to 28. Tables 6, 7, and 8 allow a more detailed assessment of France's relative ranking in all these dimensions.

As far as emerging-market countries are concerned, India represents a particularly interesting case. As noted earlier, India's overall position on the GCI improves this year by 8 positions to 48. In terms of technology, India ranks 2nd among the non-core innovators for the technology transfer index, a position that mirrors the country's overall strong performance in terms of the prevalence of foreign technology licensing and a relatively high score in terms of foreign direct investment and technology. However, India's overall improvement also mirrors a relatively stronger macroeconomic environment, driven for example by its jump from the 33rd to the 9th position on government expenditure.

Countries that have been experiencing financial turmoil show considerably lower readings on the overall GCI, primarily reflecting a much more difficult macroeconomic environment. Argentina's relative credit rating falls from the 43rd to the 72nd position. Access to credit is reported to have become much more difficult, putting Argentina at the 76th rank of the entire sample of 80 countries. A substantial deterioration also concerns the country's public institutions, with a rock-bottom score for property rights protection. Relative to its previous year's position, Turkey slips even more, by 16 positions to 69 on the overall GCI. Turkey faces a similarly complex mix of serious challenges, especially pertaining to its macroeconomic environment and its public institutions.

Conclusions

In closing, we stress again that the GCI rankings are empirically based rankings, whose quality is as good as the available evidence from recent worldwide experience with growth. Because we cannot observe future growth, we must look backward in testing and developing the rankings. Of course, if the future is not like the recent past, the rankings will not be good indicators of future growth. We are not suggesting that a country can *necessarily* grow rapidly if it reorients its policy to score high on the criteria listed in the *Global Competitiveness Report*. Still less are we suggesting that countries can guarantee rapid growth by concentrating exclusively on the small subset of variables that make up the GCI. Nevertheless, in the public discussion about economic policy, it is helpful to know which variables have been most strongly correlated with recent growth rates. The various subindexes aggregate these variables and, put together in the overall GCI, can help identify specific impediments to growth. Together with other chapters of this *Report*, it is hoped that our analysis help design policies to remove such impediments.

Notes

1 We would like to thank Frederic Davier of the Laboratory of Applied Economics, Department of Economic and Social Sciences, University of Geneva, for assisting us in analyzing the hard and Survey data used to calculate the Growth Competitiveness Index. We also wish to thank Andrew M. Warner, J. E. Austin Associates, Arlington, VA, and the Center for International Development at Harvard University, Cambridge, MA, for his assistance in examining the performance of the Growth Competitiveness Index over time. Some parts of this paper follow an earlier draft provided by Andrew M. Warner.

2 Note that the inflation rankings are based on a normalization of the data that is based on the ranks rather than the actual inflation rates.

3 Employing the European Union's own criteria to measure the region's progress toward becoming "the most competitive and dynamic knowledge-based economy in the world by 2010, capable of sustainable economic growth, with more and better jobs and greater social cohesion," one comes to slightly different results. However, even using the European Union's own benchmarks puts France into the bottom half of the competitiveness rankings among the individual member states (World Economic Forum 2002).

References

Bank for International Settlements. 2001. *72nd Annual Report.* Basle: Bank for International Settlements.

Barro, R. J. 1997. *Determinants of Economic Growth: A Cross-Country Empirical Study* Cambridge, MA: MIT Press.

Ghosh, A. R. and S. Phillips. 1998. "Warning:Inflation May be Harmful to Your Growth." *IMF Staff Papers* 45(4): 672–710.

Hu, F. and J. D. Sachs. 1997. "Executive Summary." In: *The Global Competitiveness Report 1997.* Geneva: World Economic Forum.

International Monetary Fund (IMF). *World Economic Outlook: September 2002.* Washington, DC: International Monetary Fund.

McArthur, J. W. and J. D. Sachs. 2002. "The Growth Competitiveness Index: Measuring Technological Advancement and the Stages of Development." In: *The Global Competitiveness Report 2001–2002* New York: Oxford University Press for the World Economic Forum.

Scherer, F. M. 1999. *New Perspectives on Economic Growth and Technological Innovation.* Washington, DC: Brookings Institution Press.

US Patent and Trademark Office. 2001. Historical data come from *Patent Counts by Country/State and Year—Utility Patents.* February. Online. http://www.uspto.gov/web/offices/ac/ido/oeip/taf/cst_utl.pdf.

———. 2002. 2001 data come from *Patent Counts, States and Countries of Origin Calendar Year 2001.* April 2002. Online. http://www.uspto.gov/web/offices/ac/ido/oeip/taf/st_co_01.htm.

World Economic Forum. 1997. *The Global Competitiveness Report 1997.* Geneva: World Economic Forum.

———. 2002. *The Lisbon Review 2002–2003: An Assessment of Policies and Reforms in Europe.* World Economic Forum and Center for European Integration Studies at the University of Bonn.

19

Appendix: Composition of the Growth Competitiveness Index

The Growth Competitiveness Index is composed of three component indexes: the technology index, the public institutions index, and the macroeconomic environment index. These indexes are calculated on the basis of both "hard data" and "Survey data."

The responses to the Executive Opinion Survey are what we refer to as *Survey data*, with responses ranging from 1 to 7 (see the chapter at the end of the *Report* for further information on the Executive Opinion Survey); the hard data were collected from various sources, described in the Technical Notes and Sources at the end of the *Report*. Virtually all of the data used in the calculation of the Growth Competitiveness Index can be found in the data tables section of the *Report*.

The standard formula for converting each hard data variable to the 1-to-7 scale is:

$$6 \times \frac{(\text{country value} - \text{sample minimum})}{(\text{sample maximum} - \text{sample minimum})} + 1$$

The sample minimum and sample maximum are the lowest and highest values of the overall sample, respectively. In some instances, adjustments were made to account for extreme outliers in the data.

Calculating the Growth Competitiveness Index

As explained in the chapter, the sample of countries is divided into two groups: the core innovators and the non-core innovators. Core innovators are countries with more than 15 US utility patents registered per million population in 2001; non-core innovators are all other countries.

For the core innovators, we place extra emphasis on the role of innovation and technology. The weightings for the core innovators are as follows:

Growth Competitiveness
Index for core innovators = (1/2 technology index)
+ (1/4 public institutions index)
+ (1/4 macroeconomic environment index)

For the non-core innovators, we calculate the Growth Competitiveness Index values as a simple average of the three component indexes:

Growth Competitiveness
Index for non-core
innovators = (1/3 technology index)
+ (1/3 public institutions index)
+ (1/3 macroeconomic environment index)

Technology index components

The technology index is calculated for the core and non-core innovators as follows:

technology index for
core innovators = (1/2 innovation subindex)
+ (1/2 information and communication technology subindex)

technology index for
non-core innovators = (1/8 innovation subindex)
+ (3/8 technology transfer subindex)
+ (1/2 information and communication technology subindex)

Innovation subindex

innovation subindex = (1/4 Survey data)
+ (3/4 hard data)

Innovation Survey questions

3.01 What is your country's position in technology relative to world leaders'?
3.02 Does continuous innovation play a major role in generating revenue for your business?
3.07 How much do companies in your country spend on R&D relative to other countries?
3.09 What is the extent of business collaboration in R&D with local universities?

Innovation hard data

3.15 US utility patents granted per million population in 2001
3.18 Gross tertiary enrollment rate in 1998 or most recent available year

Technology transfer subindex

technology transfer
subindex = unweighted average of two technology transfer Survey questions

3.04 Is foreign direct investment in your country an important source of new technology?
3.05 Is foreign technology licensing in your country a common means of acquiring new technology?

Appendix: Composition of the Growth Competitiveness Index *(cont'd.)*

Information and communication technology (ICT) subindex

information and
communication
technology subindex = (1/3 information and communication
technology Survey data)
+ (2/3 information and communication
technology hard data)

Information and communication technology Survey questions

4.02 How extensive is Internet access in schools?

4.03 Is there sufficient competition among ISPs in your country to ensure high quality, infrequent interruptions and low prices?

4.04 Is ICT an overall priority for the government?

4.05 Are government programs successful in promoting the use of ICT?

4.06 Are laws relating to ICT (electronic commerce, digital signatures, consumer protection) well developed and enforced?

Information and communication technology hard data

4.07 Cellular mobile subscribers per 100 inhabitants, 2001

4.08 Internet users per 10,000 inhabitants, 2001

4.09 Internet hosts per 10,000 inhabitants, 2001

4.10 Main telephone lines per 100 inhabitants, 2001

4.11 Personal computers per 100 inhabitants, 2001

Public institutions index components

public institutions index = (1/2 contracts and law subindex)
+ (1/2 corruption subindex)

Contracts and law subindex (Survey questions)

6.01 Is the judiciary in your country independent from political influences of members of government, citizens or firms?

6.03 Are financial assets and wealth clearly delineated and well protected by law?

6.09 Is your government neutral among bidders when deciding among public contracts?

6.15 Does organized crime impose significant costs on business?

Corruption subindex (Survey questions)

7.01 How commonly are bribes paid in connection with import and export permits?

7.02 How commonly are bribes paid when getting connected with public utilities?

7.03 How commonly are bribes paid in connection with annual tax payments?

Macroeconomic environment index components

macroeconomic
environment index = 1/2 macroeconomic stability subindex
+ 1/4 country credit rating[1] in March 2002
+ 1/4 government expenditure[2] in 2001

Macroeconomic stability subindex

macroeconomic
stability subindex = (2/7 macroeconomic stability Survey data)
+ (5/7 macroeconomic stability hard data)

Macroeconomic stability Survey questions

2.01 Is your country's economy likely to be in a recession next year?

2.05 Has obtaining credit for your company become easier or more difficult over the past year?

Macroeconomic stability hard data

2.15 Government surplus/deficit in 2001

2.17 National savings rate in 2001

2.19 Inflation in 2001

2.21 Real exchange rate relative to the United States in 2001

2.28 Lending– borrowing interest rate spread in 2001

Institutional Investor **country credit rating,**[1] **March 2002**

Government expenditure[2] **as a percentage of GDP, 2001**

Notes

1 The *Institutional Investor* country credit ratings are taken from http://www.iiplatinum.com/rr/countrycredit/ccr/2002.htm

2 This refers to variable 2.16 in the Data Tables in Part 4 of the *Report*.

Building the Microeconomic Foundations of Prosperity: Findings from the Microeconomic Competitiveness Index[1]

MICHAEL E. PORTER, Harvard University

Introduction

Competitiveness has become a central preoccupation of both advanced and developing countries in an increasingly open and integrated world economy. Despite its acknowledged importance, the concept of competitiveness is often misunderstood. Here, we define *competitiveness* concretely and outline its direct relationship to a nation's standard of living. The Microeconomic Competitiveness Index provides a conceptual framework and a data-rich approach to measuring and analyzing the fundamental competitiveness of a large number of countries in a comparative context.

Much discussion of competitiveness and economic development has focused on the macroeconomic, political, legal, and social circumstances that underpin a successful economy. It is well understood that sound fiscal and monetary policies, a trusted and efficient legal context, a stable set of democratic institutions, and progress on social conditions contribute greatly to a healthy economy. However, these broader conditions are necessary but not sufficient, providing the opportunity to create wealth but not by themselves creating wealth. Wealth is actually created in the microeconomic level of the economy, rooted in the sophistication of company strategies and operating practices as well as in the quality of the microeconomic business environment in which a nation's firms compete. Unless there is appropriate improvement at the microeconomic level, macroeconomic, political, legal, and social reforms will not bear full fruit.

Beginning in 1998, we began an effort to examine statistically the microeconomic foundations of competitiveness and prosperity across a wide array of countries, a daunting task given the myriad of attributes involved. The microeconomic approach focuses on measuring and comparing the complex array of national circumstances that support a high and sustainable level of productivity, measured by GDP per capita. The effort aims to move beyond the examination of broad, aggregate variables typical of most economic growth analyses and provide a framework for countries and companies to understand their detailed competitive strengths and weaknesses. The microeconomic approach also highlights the fact that improvement in competitive potential is not a simple linear process in which all nations must progress on a constant set of dimensions. Instead, successful economic development requires nations to develop the ability to compete in increasingly sophisticated ways to support higher levels of wages and national income.

The Microeconomic Competitiveness Index examines the microeconomic bases of a nation's prosperity measured by its level of GDP per capita. The focus is on whether current prosperity is sustainable, and on the specific areas that must be addressed if GDP per capita is to achieve higher levels in the future. A separate Growth Competitiveness Index, discussed in the previous chapter of this *Report*, examines the sources of GDP per capita growth, which is more dependent than microeconomic prosperity on investment rates and other macroeconomic policies. The sustainable level of current GDP per capita and its rate of growth are related in the long term, and each area requires its own distinctive policy agenda.

This year's Microeconomic Competitiveness Index includes 80 countries, up from 75 last year. One country, Egypt, had to be dropped because its government chose not to make all the Survey responses available. In this chapter, we present findings on the competitiveness of individual countries, on the different challenges of countries on different stages of economic development, and on the patterns of change in microeconomic conditions across all countries.

The analysis here proceeds pragmatically, making use of available data and statistical methods that remain far from perfect. It would be desirable to supplement our Survey with more "hard" data but there are simply no such data available. However, our Survey data prove to be powerful in revealing differences across countries and in capturing national conditions. We provide new tests to document the statistical validity of the Survey data. Establishing causality also remains a challenge because of still limited time-series data. However, even if definitive tests of causality are not yet possible, understanding the microeconomic correlates of prosperity remains crucial. There may be a natural tendency for some microeconomic conditions to improve as GDP per capita grows but the differences across countries reveal that this improvement is far from automatic. Microeconomic conditions can be influenced markedly by purposeful action in both government and the private sector, so that the findings here carry strong implications for policy.

Despite more countries and enhancements in the model, the statistical findings are remarkably stable and robust compared with the 2001 and earlier *Reports*. The results again provide strong support for the importance of microeconomic competitiveness for economic development and prosperity. Our findings also verify the striking and regular pattern of microeconomic changes that accompany economic development.

The measured microeconomic differences among nations prove to account for 81 percent of the variation across countries in the level of GDP per capita.[2] These findings highlight the pressing need to better incorporate microeconomic competitiveness into efforts to stimulate economic growth. In advanced countries, which have largely gotten their macro policies right, it is micro reform that holds the key to reversing unemployment problems, to growing exports, and to translating economic growth into a rising standard of living. The United Kingdom, which improved its ranking markedly this year, is an example of a country that has begun to address microeconomic reforms after a phase of macroeconomic consolidation.

Developing countries, again and again, are tripped up by microeconomic failures. By accessing global capital markets, countries can engineer spurts of growth through macroeconomic and financial reforms that bring floods of capital and create the illusion of progress as construction cranes dot the skyline. Without microeconomic reforms, however, growth will be snuffed out as exports and jobs fail to materialize, wages stagnate, and the return on investments proves disappointing. This disappointment, and the austerity that results from such cycles, is at the heart of the backlash against globalization.

Argentina is a vivid example of this problem. Argentina's progress on macroeconomic conditions and investments in physical infrastructure masked severe weaknesses at the microeconomic level. These weaknesses meant that exports did not grow, few jobs were created, and productivity growth was slow. Pegging the Argentine peso to the US dollar, while valuable in establishing macroeconomic stability, meant that Argentine productivity growth had to match or exceed US productivity growth rates to avoid growing overvaluation. Microeconomic weaknesses held back productivity growth, and collapse was inevitable.

Successful economic development requires progress on multiple fronts simultaneously. Reform efforts need to be tightly connected to the country's current stage of development. As an economy progresses, the constraints to its continued advancement shift. At strategic points in the development process, the whole basis of national competitiveness must be transformed. This requires changing many aspects of company strategy as well as new requirements for the national business environment. Our analysis provides the conceptual framework and comparative data to define such national agendas and measure progress.

What is competitiveness?

Competitiveness remains a concept that is not well understood, despite widespread acceptance of its importance. The most intuitive definition of *competitiveness* is a country's share of world markets for its products. This makes competitiveness a zero-sum game, because one country's gain comes at the expense of others. This view of competitiveness is used to justify intervention to skew market outcomes in a nation's favor (so-called industrial policy). It also underpins policies to hold down local wages and devalue the nation's currency, both aimed at expanding exports. In fact, it is still often said that lower wages or devaluation "make a nation more competitive." Business leaders are drawn to the market-share view because these policies seem to address their immediate competitive concerns.

The misleading metaphor of direct market competition, however, is a deeply flawed view of competitiveness, and acting on it works against national economic progress. The need for low wages reveals a lack of competitiveness and holds down prosperity. Devaluation causes a nation to take a collective pay cut by discounting its products and services in world markets while paying more for the goods and services it purchases abroad. Exports based on low wages or a cheap currency, then, do not support an attractive standard of living.

To understand competitiveness, the starting point must be the sources of a nation's prosperity. A nation's standard of living is determined by the productivity of its economy, which is measured by the value of goods and services produced per unit of the nation's human, capital, and natural resources. Productivity depends both on the value of a nation's products and services, measured by the prices they can command in open markets, and the efficiency with which they can be produced.

True competitiveness, then, is measured by productivity. Productivity allows a nation to support high wages, a strong currency, and attractive returns to capital—and with them a high standard of living. Productivity is the goal, not exports *per se*. Only if a nation expands exports of products or services it can produce productively will national productivity rise. Domestic or foreign firms are neither good nor bad for competitiveness *per se*; what matters is the productivity of their activities in a country. The productivity of local industries has a major influence on the cost of living and the cost of doing business, not to mention their level of wages. The productivity of the entire economy matters for the standard of living, then, not just the traded sector.

The world economy is not a zero-sum game. Many nations can improve their prosperity if they can improve productivity. The central challenge in economic development, then, is how to create the conditions for rapid and sustained productivity growth.

Microeconomic foundations of productivity

Stable political, legal, and social institutions and sound macroeconomic policies create the potential for improving national prosperity. But wealth is actually created at the microeconomic level—in the ability of firms to create valuable goods and services using efficient methods. Only in this way can a nation support high wages and the attractive returns to capital necessary to support sustained investment (see Figure 1).

Figure 1: Determinants of productivity and productivity growth

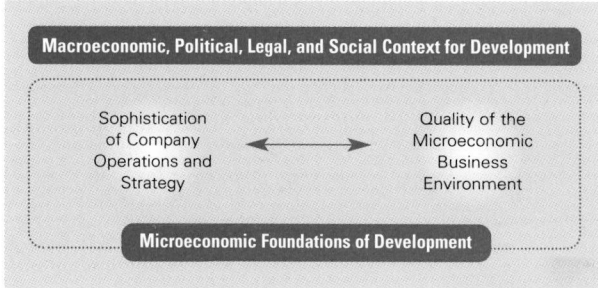

The microeconomic foundations of productivity rest on two interrelated areas: (1) the sophistication with which domestic companies or foreign subsidiaries operating in the country compete, and (2) the quality of the microeconomic business environment.

The productivity of countries is ultimately set by the productivity of their companies. An economy cannot be competitive unless companies operating there are competitive, whether they are domestic firms or subsidiaries of foreign companies. However, the sophistication of companies is inextricably intertwined with the quality of the national business environment. More sophisticated company strategies require more highly skilled people, better information, improved infrastructure, better suppliers, more advanced research institutions, and stronger competitive pressure, among other things.

Companies in a nation must upgrade their ways of competing if successful economic development is to occur. A nation's companies must shift from competing on comparative advantages (low-cost labor or natural resources) to competing on competitive advantages arising from unique products and processes. Companies must move from tapping foreign distribution channels to building their own channels. Some of the transitions in corporate strategies and operating practices required for successful development are shown in Figure 2.

Figure 2: Company sophistication and economic development

Low-Income Countries	Middle-Income Countries	High-Income Countries
• Competitive advantages beyond cheap inputs • Production process sophistication • Degree of customer orientation • Extent of marketing • Extent of regional sales • Reliance on professional management	• Broad value chain presence • Control of international distribution • Extent of branding • Company spending on R&D • Prevalence of foreign technology licensing • Extent of staff training	• Capacity for innovation • Breadth of international markets • Extent of incentive compensation • Willingness to delegate authority

What were strengths in competing at earlier stages of development become weaknesses at more advanced levels of development. Rapid copying of foreign technology, for example, must give way to internal development of innovative technology if a country is to compete on the advanced-economy level. Necessary changes are often resisted by the corporate sector because past approaches were profitable and because old habits are deeply ingrained.

Moving to more sophisticated ways of competing depends on parallel changes in the microeconomic business environment. The business environment can be understood in terms of four interrelated areas: the quality of factor (input) conditions, the context for firm strategy and rivalry, the quality of local demand conditions, and the presence of the related and supporting industries. Because of their graphical representation (see Figure 3), the four areas have collectively become referred to as the *diamond*.

Government plays an inevitable role in economic development because it affects many aspects of the business environment. Government shapes factor conditions, for example, through its training and infrastructure policies. The sophistication of home demand derives in part from regulatory standards, consumer protection laws, government purchasing practices, and openness to imports. Similar policy influences are present in all four parts of the diamond. There are distinct roles for government in improving the business environment at the national, state, and local levels.[3] National productivity can also be enhanced through coordinating policies among neighboring countries. A concerted effort to improve the business environment is needed at all these governmental levels.

In addition to government, however, many other national and local institutions in an economy have a role in economic development. Universities, schools, infrastructure providers, standard-setting agencies, and a myriad of other organizations contribute in some way to the microeconomic business environment. Such institutions must not just develop and improve their capabilities, but must also become more connected to the economy and better linked with the private sector.

The private sector itself is not only a consumer of the business environment, but it also can and must play a role in shaping it. Individual firms can take steps such as establishing schools, attracting suppliers, or defining standards that not only benefit themselves but also improve the overall national environment for competing. Collective industry bodies, such as trade associations and chambers of commerce, also have important roles to play in improving infrastructure, providing training, and export marketing that are often overlooked. The private sector can also take collective steps to enhance the ability of individual companies to improve operating practices and strategies, such as quality certification programs and manufacturing assistance centers.

Clusters and economic development

An improving business environment gives rise to the formation of clusters. *Clusters* are geographically proximate groups of interconnected companies, suppliers, service providers, and associated institutions in a particular field, linked by commonalities and complementarities. Clusters such as software in India or high-performance cars in Germany are often concentrated in a particular region within a larger nation, and sometimes in a single town.

Clusters affect competitiveness in three broad ways: first, by increasing the productivity of constituent firms or industries. In the California Wine Cluster, for example, the local presence of specialized suppliers of machinery and inputs enables wineries to lower transaction costs and reduce capital costs by keeping stocks of material inputs low. The intense local rivalry between competing wineries then provides incentives to mobilize these assets and drives the productivity to allow wineries to support the high costs of real estate and labor in northern California.

Second, clusters increase the capacity for innovation and thus for productivity growth. Opportunities for innovation can often be perceived more easily within clusters, and the assets, skills, and capital are more available to pursue them. For example, new prototypes can be tested with sophisticated local customers.

Third, clusters stimulate and enable new business formation that supports innovation and expands the cluster. The local presence of experienced workers and access to all the needed inputs and services, for example, reduces the barriers to entry. In California, introducing a new line of wine or starting a new winery are much easier than at other locations.

Figure 3: The microeconomic business environment

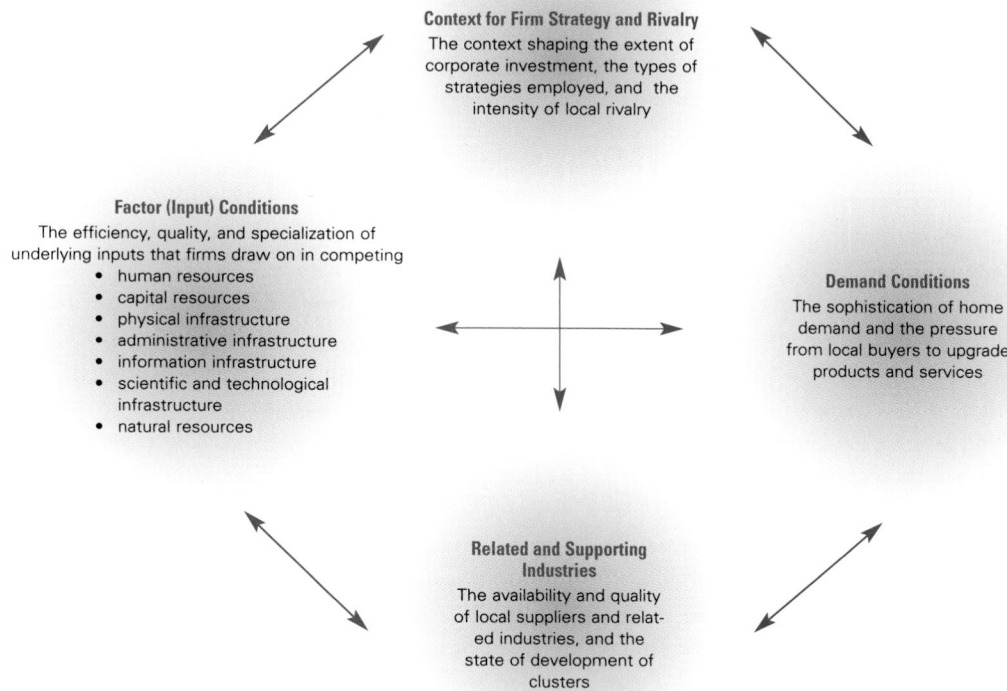

Figure 4: The California Wine Cluster

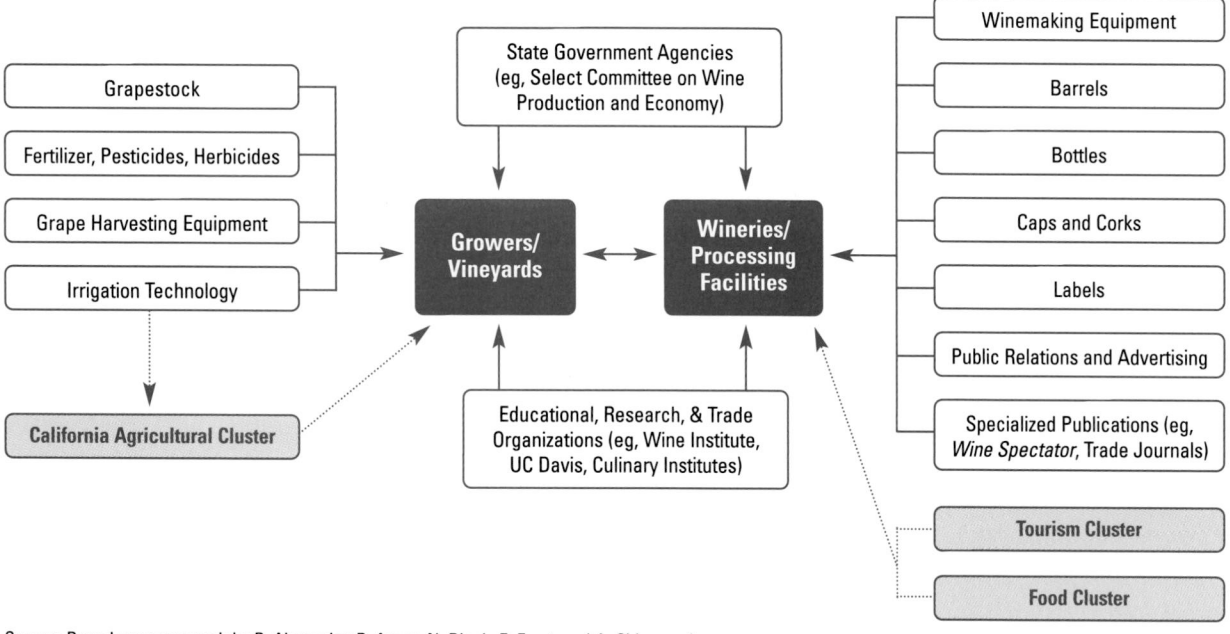

Source: Based upon research by R. Alexander, R. Arney, N. Black, E. Frost, and A. Shivananda

National economies tend to specialize in particular clusters, which account for a disproportionate share of their output and exports. The shape of clusters varies with the state of development of the economy. In developing countries, clusters are normally shallow or underdeveloped. Firms compete based on cheap labor or local natural resources, and they depend heavily on imported components, machinery, and technology. Specialized local infrastructure and institutions are absent. As economies advance, clusters develop and deepen to include suppliers of specialized inputs, components, machinery, and services; specialized infrastructure; and institutions providing specialized training, education, information, research, and technical support. More-developed clusters also include trade associations and other collective private-sector bodies that support cluster members.

It is rare that there is only a single cluster in the world in a given field. In most cases, there is an array of clusters in different locations with different levels of sophistication and specialization. Only a small number of clusters tend to be true innovation centers, such as Silicon Valley and Japan in semiconductors. These may tend to specialize in particular market segments. Other locations may be manufacturing centers. Still other clusters can be regional assembly and service centers. Firms based in the most-advanced clusters often seed or enhance clusters in other locations as they disperse some activities to reduce risk, access inputs, or seek to better serve particular regional markets. The challenge for an economy is to move from isolated firms to an array of clusters, and upgrade the sophistication of clusters to more advanced activities.

Stages of competitive development

Successful economic development is a process of successive upgrading, in which a nation's business environment evolves to support and encourage increasingly sophisticated and productive ways of competing by firms and subsidiaries based there. Nations at different levels of development face distinctly different challenges (see Figure 5).

Figure 5: Stages of economic development

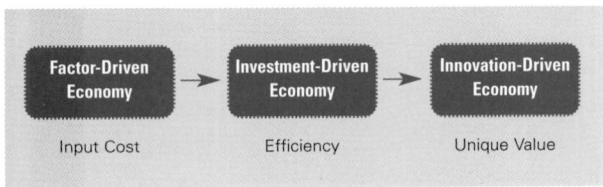

Source: Porter (1990)

As nations develop, they progress in terms of their characteristic competitive advantages and modes of competing.[4] In the Factor-Driven stage, basic factor conditions such as low-cost labor and access to natural resources are the dominant sources of competitive advantage and exports. Firms produce commodities or relatively simple products designed in other, more-advanced countries. Technology is assimilated through imports, foreign direct investment, and imitation. In this stage, companies compete on price and lack direct access to consumers. They have limited roles in the value chain, focusing on assembly, labor-intensive manufacturing, and resource extraction. A Factor-Driven economy is highly sensitive to world economic cycles, commodity price trends, and exchange rate fluctuations.

In the Investment-Driven stage, efficiency in producing standard products and services becomes the dominant source of competitive advantage. Heavy investment in efficient infrastructure, business-friendly government administration, and strong investment incentives and access to capital allow major improvements in productivity. The products and services produced become more sophisticated, but technology and designs still largely come from abroad. Technology is accessed through licensing, joint ventures, foreign direct investment, and imitation. However, nations at this stage not only assimilate foreign technology but also develop the capacity to improve on it. Companies serve a mix of original equipment manufacturer (OEM) customers and their own customers. They extend capabilities more widely in the value chain. An Investment-Driven economy is concentrated on manufacturing and on outsourced service exports. It is susceptible to financial crisis and external, sector-specific demand shocks.

In the Innovation-Driven stage, the ability to produce innovative products and services at the global technology frontier using the most advanced methods becomes the dominant source of competitive advantage. The national business environment is characterized by strengths in all areas together with the presence of deep clusters. Institutions and incentives supporting innovation are well developed. Companies compete with unique strategies that are often global in scope. An Innovation-Driven economy has a high share of services in the economy and is resilient to external shocks.

Seeing economic development as a sequential process of building interdependent microeconomic capabilities, shifting company strategies, improving incentives, and increasing rivalry exposes important pitfalls in economic policy. The influence of one part of the microeconomic business environment depends on the state of others. Lack of improvement in any important area can lead to a plateau in productivity growth and stalled development. Worse yet, it can undermine the whole economic reform process. When well-trained college graduates cannot find appropriate jobs because companies are still competing based on cheap labor, for example, a backlash against business is created.

This analysis also begins to make it clear why countries find the transition to a new stage of development so difficult. Such inflection points require wholesale transformation of many interdependent dimensions of competition. In Asia, for example, successful economies at the Investment-Driven stage such as Taiwan and Singapore have found that their reliance on OEM manufacturing for multinationals, heavy infrastructure investments, and government guidance of the economy to boost efficiency were insufficient to support higher levels of prosperity. Yet relatively high levels of wages and domestic costs made them vulnerable to competition from lower-wage countries such as China. The challenge for both Taiwan and Singapore is to move to an Innovation-Driven economy and develop deep clusters. This is a slow process, however, as companies need to move to new types of strategies, investment priorities must change, and new institutions must be developed. Although government policy can have comparatively rapid (5 to 10 years) effects at the Investment-Driven stage, the move to the Innovation-Driven stage is a slow process in which government must rely more on the private sector.

The relationship between macroeconomic and microeconomic policy

Our analysis makes it clear why the traditional focus on macroeconomic policy alone is insufficient. Macroeconomic policies fostering high rates of capital investment, for example, will not translate into rising productivity unless the forms of investment are appropriate, the company skills and supporting industries are present to make the investments efficient, and strong competitive pressures and adequate corporate governance provide the needed market discipline. The prudence of foreign debt levels depends on exactly what the foreign capital is invested in, together with the microeconomic fundamentals surrounding its deployment and governance. Regulating overall debt levels is less important, in many ways, than improving the microeconomic foundations. High rates of public investment in human capital will not pay off unless a nation's microeconomic circumstances create the demand for skills in companies. Privatization will not boost prosperity unless companies can improve efficiency and are pressured by local competition.

Sound monetary and fiscal policies and the removal of distortions in exchange rates and other prices will eliminate impediments to productivity, but microeconomic foundations must be in place if productivity is actually to increase. For sound policies at the macroeconomic level to translate into an increasingly productive economy, then, parallel microeconomic improvements must take place.

The effects of trade agreements and other market opening measures, a major focus in today's international economic policymaking, also depend on microeconomic policies. Market opening is good, but its benefits in terms of prosperity depend on microeconomic progress. If the local business environment does not become more efficient and local companies do not improve their productivity and sophistication, market opening will boost imports but there will be slow growth in exports. Improvement in the microeconomic business environment is also necessary if the country is to win its fair share of foreign investment even if investment is opened.

In Asia, for example, it was weaknesses in these sorts of areas that brought down economies that looked solid in terms of macroeconomic indicators. Although macroeconomic reforms and the selective opening of foreign exchange markets created a huge inflow of foreign capital, the absence of microeconomic reforms in areas such as competition policy, financial market regulations, and corporate governance encouraged a misallocation of this capital into nonproductive investments such as real estate, trophy infrastructure projects, and excess productive capacity. Imports boomed but the lack of improvements in fundamental competitiveness led to unsustainable trade deficits and the inability to service loans. Without microeconomic reforms, this pattern of boom and bust repeats itself over and over again.

A greater focus on microeconomic reforms will pay another essential dividend. Although macro reforms almost inevitability inflict hardship in the short and medium run through raising interest rates and prices while cutting public expenditures, micro reforms can produce tangible and visible benefits for citizens. Breaking up local cartels and monopolies, for example, lowers the cost of food, housing, electricity, telephone service, and other costs of living. Regulatory reform can rapidly begin to ease inefficiencies, reduce pollution, raise product and service quality, and improve unsafe practices. Bold steps to improve the quality of education and training are particularly important, because they offer the hope of a better life for children. If citizens see businesses reforming themselves and having to confront tough competitive challenges, they themselves will be more willing to live with personal sacrifices and less likely to side with antireform interest groups. The political will and public support to make real economic change will be elevated.

Measuring competitiveness

The Microeconomic Competitiveness Index (MICI) is constructed from measures drawn primarily on a survey of more than 4,700 senior business leaders in 80 countries. The 80 countries included in this year's index are shown in Table 1. Compared to 2001 we have added six countries: Botswana, Croatia, Haiti, Morocco, Namibia, and Tunisia. One country, Egypt, had to be dropped, as mentioned earlier, because its government declined to make the Survey responses available.

Only through a detailed survey can textured measures of the competitive environment and company practices be assembled across many countries. The Survey questions aim to capture the state of circumstances in a nation, but do so in way that is meaningful for Survey respondents. For example, we get at the stock of basic human capital with a question on the quality of public schools because this is something that respondents can compare more readily across countries. The quality of schools, a flow measure, will be highly correlated with the stock of basic skills. We use quantitative measures for patenting rates, Internet penetration, and cellular phone penetration. For all of the other dimensions we measure, however, quantitative data are simply unavailable, especially for so many countries. The Survey not only offers many unique measures, but it also captures the informed judgments of thousands of actual participants in the economies examined. The Survey responses are important in their own right, because they reflect the attitudes of the decision makers who ultimately determine economic activity.

We use the *average* response of Survey respondents within each country as independent variables. To assess the validity of responses within countries, we conducted an ANOVA analysis for each GCR Survey measure. Regressing individual Survey responses on a complete set of country dummy variables allows us to calculate the share of the variation (across individual responses) that results from systematic differences in the average response across countries. The results are reported in Appendix A.

Considering that there is an average of more than 60 respondents per country, the degree of within-country consensus is striking. For all measures, the proportion of variation due to country differences is statistically significant. For most measures, between one third and one half of the overall variation in the responses is driven by country-specific differences for that measure. As would be expected, the within-country consensuses are higher for cross-cutting business environment indicators, such as overall infrastructure quality, and lower for measures where there would be variation within the country across companies and clusters, such as stage of cluster development. The country averages, then, capture meaningful differences across countries in competitive circumstances while

limiting idiosyncratic biases that would result if there were only a handful of responses per country.

The dependent variable used to develop the MICI is the level of GDP per capita in 2001, adjusted for purchasing power parity (PPP). GDP per capita is the broadest measure of national productivity and is strongly tied over time to a nation's standard of living.[5] It is the best single, summary measure of microeconomic competitiveness available across all countries.[6] GDP per employee is also a desirable measure of overall productivity, but it relies on comparative employment levels that are considerably less reliable than population data; consistent data are not available for all countries. Using the best available numbers, we find a very high correlation between GDP per capita and GDP per employee ($R^2 = 0.94$). We utilize GDP per capita because of its broader coverage and lower susceptibility to biases.

To explore differences in the sources of competitiveness across countries at different levels of development, we divided countries into three groups based on income. There were 31 low-income countries with a purchasing power–adjusted US-dollar GDP per capita in 2001 below $6,800; 26 middle-income countries with GDP per capita between $6,800 and $20,000; and 23 high-income countries with a GDP per capita above $20,000. As will be reported, these groups exhibited different patterns of statistical relationships among variables.

Although GDP per capita will reflect structural fundamentals over the medium and long term, it is also influenced by a wide array of short-term and idiosyncratic factors such as natural disasters, macroeconomic shocks, and windfalls in particular export industries. The proportion of the variation in GDP per capita across all countries that can be explained by microeconomic fundamentals is interesting in its own right.

Measuring sources of competitiveness

To construct an overall index of competitiveness, we validated the statistical relationship of a wide array of measures of microeconomic competitiveness with GDP per capita. Table 2 gives bivariate regressions of the Survey responses and available quantitative measures on GDP per capita reporting variables that are statistically significant. Variables are grouped into those measuring the sophistication of company operations and strategy and those measuring the quality of the national business environment. Included in the table is the slope of the regression relationship, a measure of statistical significance, and the adjusted R^2 (or proportion of variation in GDP per capita adjusted for statistical degrees of freedom).[7] Microeconomic indicators individually and collectively explain a meaningful proportion of the variation in the level of GDP per capita across countries. This compares favorably with macroeconomic variables, such as the national savings rate,

Table 1: The Microeconomic Competitiveness Index

Country	MICI ranking					Company operations and strategy ranking					Quality of the national business environment ranking					2001 GDP per capita (PPP-adjusted)
	2002	2001*	2000	1999	1998	2002	2001	2000	1999	1998	2002	2001	2000	1999	1998	
United States	1	2	2	1	1	1	1	2	1	2	1	2	2	1	1	34,888
Finland	2	1	1	2	2	4	2	3	7	8	2	1	1	2	2	25,611
United Kingdom	3	7	8	10	5	3	7	11	13	9	3	8	9	8	5	24,421
Germany	4	4	3	6	4	2	4	1	5	1	4	4	6	5	8	25,715
Switzerland	5	5	5	5	9	5	5	5	2	3	6	5	10	9	10	29,587
Sweden	6	6	7	4	7	6	6	6	3	4	8	6	11	7	9	24,978
Netherlands	7	3	4	3	3	8	3	7	8	5	10	3	3	3	4	26,242
Denmark	8	8	6	7	8	9	9	8	9	10	9	10	4	6	7	28,342
Singapore	9	9	9	12	10	14	15	15	14	12	5	9	5	12	6	23,250
Canada	10	12	11	8	6	13	14	16	12	15	7	11	8	4	3	28,611
Japan	11	10	14	14	18	7	8	4	4	7	17	16	19	19	19	27,101
Austria	12	11	13	11	16	12	11	12	10	11	12	12	12	13	17	27,518
Belgium	13	15	12	15	19	11	12	10	11	13	15	14	13	15	18	27,912
Australia	14	14	10	13	15	19	24	20	19	22	11	7	7	10	12	26,552
France	15	13	15	9	11	10	10	9	6	6	21	13	15	11	13	25,074
Taiwan	16	21	21	19	20	16	20	18	17	16	13	21	21	22	21	22,559
Iceland	17	16	17	22	24	17	16	14	21	28	14	15	16	21	23	30,725
Israel	18	17	18	20	21	20	18	13	18	21	18	18	20	20	20	19,867
Hong Kong SAR	19	18	16	21	12	24	21	23	24	17	16	17	14	18	11	25,581
Ireland	20	22	22	17	13	15	17	19	20	18	22	22	22	17	14	27,457
Norway	21	19	20	18	14	23	23	21	23	14	19	19	18	16	15	30,727
New Zealand	22	20	19	16	17	25	19	22	16	19	20	20	17	14	16	20,725
Korea	23	26	27	28	28	21	26	25	27	24	23	29	28	30	28	18,149
Italy	24	23	24	25	26	18	13	17	15	20	24	24	26	27	27	24,510
Spain	25	24	23	23	22	22	22	24	22	23	25	23	23	23	22	20,374
Malaysia	26	37	30	27	27	27	37	30	25	34	26	37	30	31	26	8,424
Slovenia	27	32	—	—	—	26	28	—	—	—	27	35	—	—	—	18,233
Hungary	28	27	32	33	31	29	33	34	36	39	29	25	31	33	31	12,941
South Africa	29	25	25	26	25	31	25	26	28	33	33	27	25	25	25	9,565
Estonia	30	28	—	—	—	36	32	—	—	—	28	26	—	—	—	10,380
Chile	31	29	26	24	23	35	30	27	26	25	31	30	24	24	24	9,753
Tunisia	32	—	—	—	—	37	—	—	—	—	30	—	—	—	—	6,769
Brazil	33	30	31	35	35	28	29	29	32	27	36	32	32	37	39	7,759
Czech Republic	34	34	34	41	30	34	41	41	55	31	34	31	34	36	33	14,885
Thailand	35	38	40	39	37	33	42	47	43	37	35	39	40	39	36	6,630
Portugal	36	33	28	29	33	41	38	35	37	48	32	28	27	26	30	17,571
India	37	36	37	42	44	40	40	40	48	50	37	34	37	43	42	2,464
China	38	43	44	49	42	38	39	38	31	35	38	46	45	50	44	4,329
Costa Rica	39	48	43	38	—	32	34	39	35	—	47	51	42	41	—	8,490
Lithuania	40	50	—	—	—	39	47	—	—	—	39	47	—	—	—	7,764
Dominican Republic	41	60	—	—	—	30	59	—	—	—	53	61	—	—	—	6,198
Slovak Republic	42	40	36	48	36	43	57	31	51	40	40	36	36	47	37	11,739
Greece	43	46	33	36	38	47	51	32	45	32	41	43	33	34	38	17,482
Trinidad and Tobago	44	31	—	—	—	44	27	—	—	—	44	38	—	—	—	10,018
Latvia	45	41	—	—	—	48	35	—	—	—	42	42	—	—	—	7,750
Poland	46	42	41	37	41	46	55	36	38	38	45	40	41	38	40	9,327
Sri Lanka	47	58	—	—	—	52	58	—	—	—	43	56	—	—	—	3,634
Morocco	48	—	—	—	—	50	—	—	—	—	46	—	—	—	—	3,787
Mauritius	49	51	38	30	—	42	49	37	29	—	50	50	38	29	—	10,400
Panama	50	49	—	—	—	54	40	—	—	—	52	49	—	—	—	5,986
Namibia	51	—	—	—	—	58	—	—	—	—	49	—	—	—	—	6,650
Croatia	52	—	—	—	—	53	—	—	—	—	54	—	—	—	—	8,414
Jordan	53	47	35	32	32	59	56	46	44	42	48	41	35	28	32	4,080
Turkey	54	35	29	31	29	56	44	28	33	26	55	33	29	32	29	6,716
Mexico	55	52	42	34	39	45	46	42	30	29	60	52	43	35	41	8,969
Colombia	56	57	48	52	49	51	52	48	40	43	57	59	48	53	49	6,202
Botswana	57	—	—	—	—	64	—	—	—	—	51	—	—	—	—	8,196
Russian Federation	58	56	52	55	46	62	54	33	42	45	56	55	53	55	47	8,948
Jamaica	59	39	—	—	—	60	31	—	—	—	59	44	—	—	—	3,890
Vietnam	60	62	53	50	43	67	64	50	41	36	58	62	52	49	43	2,130
Philippines	61	53	46	44	45	49	45	43	34	41	67	54	46	46	45	4,113
Uruguay	62	45	—	—	—	63	48	—	—	—	61	45	—	—	—	8,781
El Salvador	63	64	51	47	—	61	66	57	46	—	62	64	50	48	—	4,603
Indonesia	64	55	47	53	51	55	50	51	47	52	65	58	47	52	51	3,059
Argentina	65	54	45	40	34	57	53	45	39	30	68	53	44	40	34	12,098
Peru	66	63	49	46	47	65	65	53	56	49	66	63	51	44	46	4,797
Romania	67	61	—	—	—	69	63	—	—	—	64	60	—	—	—	7,036
Bulgaria	68	68	55	54	—	72	70	54	52	—	63	65	54	54	—	6,182
Ukraine	69	59	56	56	52	66	62	52	50	51	69	57	56	56	52	4,224
Zimbabwe	70	65	50	45	48	68	60	56	54	46	70	67	49	45	48	2,406
Nigeria	71	66	—	—	—	71	61	—	—	—	71	68	—	—	—	898
Venezuela	72	67	54	51	50	73	67	49	53	44	72	66	55	51	50	5,966
Guatemala	73	69	—	—	—	70	69	—	—	—	73	69	—	—	—	3,879
Bangladesh	74	73	—	—	—	76	72	—	—	—	74	73	—	—	—	1,644
Nicaragua	75	71	—	—	—	75	73	—	—	—	76	70	—	—	—	2,514
Paraguay	76	70	—	—	—	77	68	—	—	—	75	71	—	—	—	4,379
Ecuador	77	72	57	57	—	74	71	55	57	—	77	72	58	57	—	3,295
Honduras	78	74	—	—	—	78	74	—	—	—	79	75	—	—	—	2,505
Bolivia	79	75	58	58	—	79	75	58	58	—	78	74	57	58	—	2,439
Haiti	80	—	—	—	—	80	—	—	—	—	80	—	—	—	—	1,444

* Using 2002 formula

investment as a percentage of GDP, and the level of taxation, that are either not significantly related to the level of GDP per capita or are associated with a minor share of its variation across countries.[8]

In addition to last year's variables, one new variable measuring the quality of the nation's electricity supply has been included; the question measuring the presence of corruption has also been modified. Hard data have been substituted for two Survey variables: Internet penetration and mobile phone penetration. All the reported variables are highly statistically significant in the full sample of countries. A wide range of company practices and multiple dimensions of the business environment prove strongly related to competitiveness. These findings are highly consistent with results from earlier *Global Competitiveness Reports*.

Among the company variables, production process sophistication, the nature of the competitive advantage of a nation's companies (reliance on low cost inputs versus unique products and processes), the extent of training, and the extent of marketing have the strongest bilateral association with per capita GDP. By itself, the measure of overall competitive approach—the nature of competitive advantage—explains a remarkable 65 percent of the variance in GDP per capita.

All four parts of the business environment prove important. Among factor conditions, overall infrastructure quality, the quality of electricity supply, venture capital availability, the quality of public schools, and university-industry research collaboration have the strongest bilateral association with GDP per capita. Many of the most important influences on GDP per capita relate to policies and institutions rather than factor stocks.

Measures of local demand conditions perform particularly strongly. Demanding regulatory standards, stringent environmental regulations, and buyer sophistication, among others, are strongly associated with the variation in GDP per capita. These results run counter to the perceived wisdom that local demand and local market conditions are not important in a global economy. Cluster linkages, especially the quality of local suppliers and the presence of specialized local research and training providers, also prove significant and suggest a powerful role of clusters in competitiveness. Finally, the rules and context governing competition are strongly related to measured productivity. Intellectual property protection, the influence of illegal payments (corruption), and the effectiveness of antitrust policy are particularly potent variables.

It is important to acknowledge that causality can be argued in both directions for some of the variables, though the Survey questions were worded to avoid spurious reverse causality. The quality of scientists and engineers or the sophistication of buyers, for example, could be partly the result of high per capita GDP and not the cause. Note that the same causality issue applies in macroeconomic and economic growth analyses. We provide some evidence of causality from microeconomic conditions to GDP per capita later in this chapter, but more years of surveying will be required to establish definitive cause and effect relationships.

Competitiveness and economic development

As has been discussed, the appropriate company strategies and operating practices and the influence of particular elements of the business environment will differ for countries at different levels of development. The transition is likely to be particularly challenging, as economies must shift from, for example, Factor-Driven to Investment-Driven to Innovation-Driven. Each stage involves very different bases of competitive advantage, very different forms of integration with the global economy, and different priorities in the diamond.

To examine these issues, we explored the impact of measures of microeconomic competitiveness in the three country groups based on per capita GDP. All the reported variables are statistically significant across the entire sample, and strongly distinguish countries across groups. However, as expected, individual variables differ in their influence within groups.

The right-hand side of Table 2 presents income subgroup regressions. We explore the pattern of statistical significance of each variable as well as the differences in slope. Limitations on subgroup sample size and the variation of the dependent variable within subgroups reduce statistical power, so that only robust variables will register high levels of statistical significance.

Low-income countries

For low-income countries at the Factor-Driven stage of development, the ability to move beyond competing solely on cheap labor/natural resources *per se* is the essential challenge revealed in the regressions. At the company level, improving the sophistication of production processes, becoming more customer-oriented, and beginning to practice marketing are revealed as most significant. At this stage, progress on other dimensions of corporate strategy and operations, especially those related to technology, is premature.

Low-income countries score low on many measures of the business environment, especially on cluster development and measures related to technology and innovation. Priorities for improving the business environment in low-income countries revealed in the regressions start with upgrading the quality of infrastructure, including electricity, communications, and transportation networks. Also revealed as important are establishing a sound regulatory environment (eg, environmental standards, laws governing IT), reducing barriers to competition (eg, hidden trade barriers and distortive government subsidies), and strengthening antitrust policy. All these steps create a foundation of efficiency, transparency, and competitive pressure that support Factor-Driven competition. Other aspects of the business environment, such as financing, venture capital, and expanding the availability of scientists and engineers, are not yet priorities at this stage of development.

Middle-income countries

Moving into middle income, the challenge is to move beyond Factor-Driven competition to the Investment-Driven stage. The regressions suggest the following patterns: corporate priorities must expand to include building brands (versus relying on commodities or products designed by foreign OEMs), licensing foreign technology, company spending on R&D, and widening the presence in the value chain.

To reach middle income, countries must have achieved improvements in basic factor conditions such as physical infrastructure and human resources. Middle-income countries score higher on such measures in absolute terms than do low-income countries. The regressions reveal that to progress as a middle-income country requires new challenges in the business environment. University-industry research collaboration and the quality of research institutions start to become important. The quality of financial markets becomes much more important, as better financial markets are needed to mobilize debt and equity capital. Improving local demand conditions are needed to pressure improvements in producer quality. Cluster development begins to become essential to support higher levels of efficiency, though middle-income countries still score relatively low in absolute terms on measures of cluster development and of company innovation. As nations reach upper middle income, companies must have also developed the capacity to absorb the best available foreign technology, and to produce products at quality levels reaching world standards.

High-income countries

To reach high-income status, improvement in quality and efficiency are no longer enough. The hurdle is to move to the Innovation-Driven stage. The patterns of regressions suggest the following priorities: companies must develop the ability to innovate at the world technology frontier, create unique product designs, and sell their products and services globally. Reliance on foreign technology becomes a negative. In order to accomplish this transformation, a series of organizational changes such as greater incentive compensation and the ability to delegate authority becomes necessary.

High-income countries have all achieved strengths in many aspects of the business environment. The differences in success among high-income countries are concentrated in areas connected to innovation: the supply of scientists and engineers, the quality of research institutions, the extent of research collaboration with universities, venture capital availability, the sophistication of demand conditions (eg, demanding regulatory standards), and intense local competition.

Trends in competitiveness in the global economy

Now that there are several years of consistent Survey data, we can examine the overall patterns of change in dimensions of competitiveness between the 1998 Survey and the 2002 Survey.[9] Table 3 identifies those areas where substantial absolute changes in company practices and the quality of the business environment (either positive or negative) were registered in eight more countries, or 10 percent of our sample. Overall, there is clear upgrading in national business environments. The bar is rising, and improvement here is needed just to maintain position vis-à-vis other countries. In company operations and strategy, there are clear areas where companies in many countries are progressing but also signs that the growing intensity of competition is making it hard to keep up.

Table 3 shows that governments around the world are continuing to improve infrastructure, upgrade financial markets, lower tariffs, and reduce bureaucratic red tape. Progress in these areas is increasingly becoming a *given* if countries are to participate fully in the world economy.

This year's data revealed a new trend: *developing economies were less successful in improving their business environments than advanced economies.* Hence, the competitive gap between economies at different stages of development is rising again; this is a trend especially pronounced in overall infrastructure quality. The recent economic conditions, coupled with debates about globalization, appear to have made it more difficult for less-developed countries to sustain the investments and policies needed to improve their competitiveness, an ominous development.

Global trends among companies are also shown in Table 3. Companies are working to professionalize management in increasingly competitive markets, the single most widespread global development among companies. However, companies from less-developed countries are finding it hard to keep up with the pace of improvement by competitors from more-advanced countries. Improvements in marketing and customer orientation are more prevalent in middle- and high-income countries compared with previous years, while there is only a slight improvement on this dimension in low-income countries. Companies in high-income countries are also gaining in staff training, an indicator of the increasing competitive pressure to attract and retain talent.

Table 2: Bivariate regression results, dependent variable: 2001 GDP per capita (PPP-adjusted)

	All countries (N = 80)		Low-income countries GDP per capita < $6,800 (N = 31)		Middle-income countries GDP per capita > $6,800 and < $20,000 (N = 26)		High-income countries GDP per capita > $20,000 (N = 23)	
	Slope	Adj. R^2	Slope	Adj. R^2	Slope	Adj. R^2	Slope	Adj. R^2
I. COMPANY OPERATIONS & STRATEGY								
Production Process Sophistication	7387.66**	0.835	1690.02**	0.318	3761.03**	0.307	3271.62**	0.167
Nature of Competitive Advantage	6886.32**	0.647	1636.95**	0.228	2362.42**	0.180	1020.99	0.024
Extent of Staff Training	8394.08**	0.737	1485.58**	0.246	2914.42**	0.163	3074.21**	0.142
Extent of Marketing	8563.98**	0.692	1458.79**	0.226	2198.63	0.070	2184.68	0.048
Willingness to Delegate Authority	8023.01**	0.702	1547.73**	0.241	2003.44	0.029	2387.62**	0.226
Capacity for Innovation	7203.04**	0.714	1191.34**	0.111	3150.27**	0.295	936.61	0.001
Company Spending on R&D	7838.43**	0.659	1447.16**	0.119	2586.00**	0.196	1566.64*	0.092
Value Chain Presence	6023.44**	0.621	1052.80**	0.173	2569.28**	0.259	197.56	−0.044
Breadth of International Markets	6202.84**	0.680	994.64**	0.147	1948.74**	0.138	40.77	−0.048
Degree of Customer Orientation	9950.43**	0.674	1595.67**	0.296	3115.55**	0.117	5150.22**	0.156
Control of International Distribution	10760.47**	0.617	1665.21**	0.148	1084.26	−0.028	1964.16	0.037
Extent of Branding	6760.75**	0.703	1450.90**	0.218	4248.05**	0.407	395.69	−0.036
Reliance on Professional Management	7087.02**	0.564	140.43	−0.030	1478.89	0.018	1743.11	0.033
Extent of Incentive Compensation	9052.86**	0.645	1524.38**	0.204	1984.30	0.043	1770.95	0.026
Extent of Regional Sales	6259.20**	0.505	886.06**	0.163	76.56	−0.041	1879.54	−0.006
Prevalence of Foreign Technology Licensing	6331.88**	0.180	666.42*	0.062	3462.10**	0.149	−4581.96**	0.153
II. NATIONAL BUSINESS ENVIRONMENT								
A. FACTOR (INPUT) CONDITIONS								
1. Physical Infrastructure								
Overall Infrastructure Quality	5507.30**	0.684	1039.40**	0.335	2138.11**	0.177	1233.79	0.057
Railroad Infrastructure Quality	4141.32**	0.471	279.78	0.002	894.40	0.036	−62.68	−0.047
Port Infrastructure Quality	5199.12**	0.569	756.18**	0.199	1380.57*	0.073	575.51	−0.026
Air Transport Infrastructure Quality	6336.32**	0.512	970.85**	0.246	1671.12*	0.088	565.51	−0.037
Electricity Supply Quality	5526.18**	0.682	972.76**	0.393	3013.30**	0.331	3260.02**	0.240
Telephone/Fax Infrastructure Quality	5029.39**	0.479	789.54**	0.390	2105.74**	0.208	4396.72*	0.094
Cellular Telephones per 100 people (2001)	289.26**	0.782	120.65**	0.323	151.46**	0.806	−61.63	0.025
Internet users per 100 people (2001)	484.21**	0.816	420.69**	0.323	231.12**	0.458	127.56**	0.199
2. Administrative Infrastructure								
Police Protection of Businesses	5665.35**	0.586	674.34**	0.162	2223.03**	0.232	2194.59*	0.090
Judicial Independence	4749.43**	0.533	447.76*	0.062	1326.24*	0.113	1358.16	0.075
Adequacy of Public Sector Legal Recourse	5397.78**	0.563	537.54*	0.065	1283.09	0.068	1284.61	0.048
Administrative Burden for Startups	5267.95**	0.280	524.45	0.033	1387.46	0.048	582.56	−0.019
Extent of Bureaucratic Red Tape	9298.68**	0.167	824.68	0.015	−893.63	−0.033	244.28	−0.047
3. Human Resources								
Quality of Management Schools	7171.45**	0.537	566.41	0.035	1556.86	0.020	1340.93	0.020
Quality of Public Schools	5224.64**	0.649	830.12**	0.198	1545.93*	0.104	793.42	−0.029
Quality of Math and Science Education	5530.09**	0.377	621.68*	0.074	1089.93	0.029	−355.21	−0.044
4. Technology Infrastructure								
Patents per Capita (2001)	107.76**	0.530	2828.98**	0.122	73.34**	0.335	15.80*	0.113
Availability of Scientists and Engineers	6704.53**	0.366	421.69	0.006	1487.41	0.046	3101.19*	0.102
Quality of Scientific Research Institutions	7750.44**	0.599	618.74	0.020	2724.06**	0.198	2052.59*	0.110
University/Industry Research Collaboration	7808.58**	0.630	986.15*	0.090	3092.10**	0.285	1224.49	0.016
Intellectual Property Protection	6495.56**	0.753	1249.89**	0.318	3039.71**	0.324	1978.78*	0.093
5. Capital Markets								
Financial Market Sophistication	6178.36**	0.570	1008.21**	0.181	936.95	0.003	985.93	0.007
Venture Capital Availability	8249.44**	0.655	633.01	0.012	2989.94**	0.222	1660.77	0.036
Ease of Access to Loans	8260.16**	0.560	1263.15**	0.200	2355.93*	0.107	1518.44	0.025
Local Equity Market Access	4858.16**	0.317	70.82	−0.032	690.23	−0.010	435.04	−0.043
B. DEMAND CONDITIONS								
Buyer Sophistication	7495.61**	0.730	754.91*	0.081	4065.31**	0.343	1854.61	0.000
Consumer Adoption of Latest Products	8663.17**	0.635	1011.76**	0.141	3779.82**	0.254	1794.19	0.000
Government Procurement of Advanced Technology Products	7816.57**	0.368	564.45	0.030	3371.51**	0.208	−40.36	−0.048
Presence of Demanding Regulatory Standards	7793.06**	0.786	1600.79**	0.362	3782.11**	0.271	3632.80**	0.173
Laws Relating to Information Technology	7960.61**	0.575	1476.24**	0.367	2533.06**	0.198	1453.70	−0.012
Stringency of Environmental Regulations	6431.95**	0.731	1539.68**	0.435	2244.56*	0.107	1011.46	0.001

(cont'd.)

Figure 6: The relationship between microeconomic competitiveness and GDP per capita

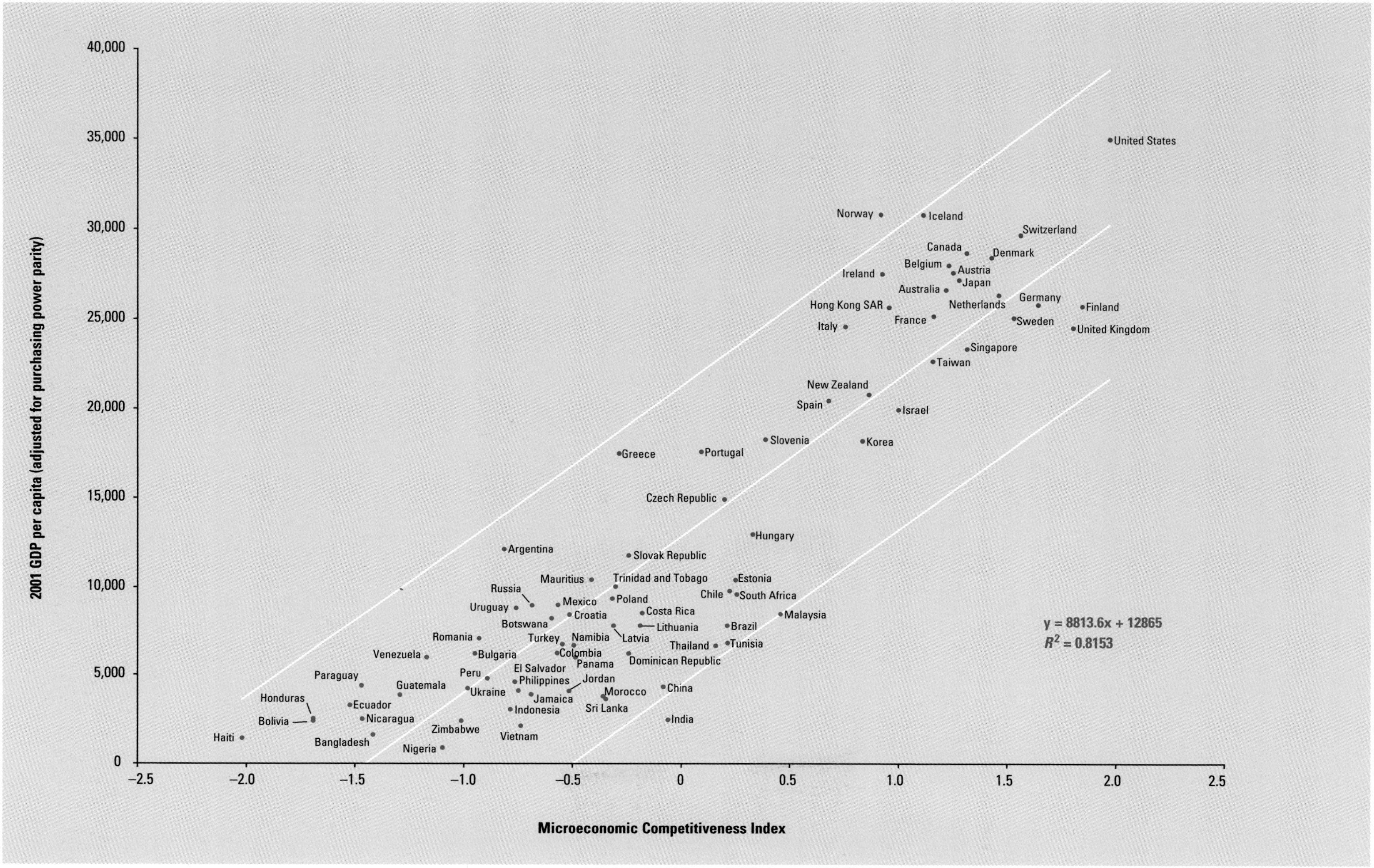

$y = 8813.6x + 12865$
$R^2 = 0.8153$

Microeconomic Competitiveness Index

2001 GDP per capita (adjusted for purchasing power parity)

Developing countries falling in microeconomic competitiveness include Turkey, Argentina, the Philippines, and Indonesia. Turkey's drop by 19 ranks (15 for a constant sample of countries) is driven by a relative decline in factor quality (eg, university-industry research collaboration, quality of management schools, administrative burden for startups, and others) and context for strategy and rivalry (eg, effectiveness of antitrust policy). Company sophistication is holding up better, but technology licensing and staff training have suffered. Turkey's political and macroeconomic problems seem to have taken their toll on the ability to make progress in competitiveness.

Argentina's economic crisis of 2002 was a vivid illustration of the importance of microeconomic policy. The country made significant progress on macroeconomic stabilization, market opening, and investments in the physical infrastructure, but not enough attention was focused on serious weaknesses on the microeconomic level. Without microeconomic reforms, few jobs were being created and unemployment remained stubbornly high, putting pressure on the government budget. Internationally, pegging the Argentine peso to the US dollar added to the problems: in the short run, the currency peg helped the country to overcome a legacy of high inflation and achieve macroeconomic stability. In the medium run, however, the fixed exchange rate to the US dollar had to be matched by productivity growth equal or above the US productivity growth rate in order to avoid a real appreciation of the peso. In the absence of sufficient microeconomic upgrading in Argentina, such high levels of productivity growth did not materialize. The subsequent real appreciation of the peso further increased the pressure on the trade balance, reducing the country's foreign reserves. Deteriorating public finances and unsustainable external balances culminated in the Argentine crisis of 2002.

Country overperformance and underperformance

We can gain insights into the sustainability of a country's prosperity by looking at its level of microeconomic competitiveness versus its current income. Table 4 lists countries in order of the absolute divergence between actual GDP per capita and the expected GDP given their microeconomic competitiveness. Countries lying above the regression line in Figure 6 are those whose current GDP per capita *exceeds* that predicted by their microeconomic competitiveness, as measured by the MICI factor. This is a danger sign, because it means that a country's per capita income may be unsustainable. Among high-income countries, Norway, Iceland, Ireland, and Canada all continue to enjoy a level of prosperity that exceeds their microeconomic fundamentals. Greece, Argentina, and, to a lesser extent, Portugal are among a group of middle-income countries whose levels of income will be unsustainable without substantial microeconomic reform. Bolivia and Haiti are among other low-income countries in this category.

Reasons for country overperformance seem to vary and can be either stable over time or transitory. Overperformance can persist for many years if it is based on natural resource endowments, as in Norway, Bolivia, and Canada, as long as the natural resources are not exhausted and commodity price levels are maintained at high enough levels. Persistent foreign aid inflows can also support otherwise unsustainable prosperity levels, which may explain the overperformance of countries such as Bangladesh. Overperformance can be more transitory if it is based on a boom in foreign investment inflows, as in Ireland. Overperformance can also reflect a lag in income behind deteriorating microeconomic conditions, as in Argentina.

Countries lying below the regression line in Figure 6 are those whose microeconomic competitiveness is *stronger* than current GDP per capita. We term them *underperformers*. Underperformance bodes well for the future, because the platform is in place to support higher GDP per capita if macro, political, or other constraints can be eased.

The United Kingdom leads the advanced countries with upside potential. Malaysia, Brazil, Chile, Estonia, and Lithuania are among the middle-income countries that should be able to support a higher GDP per capita given microeconomic fundamentals. India continues to head the list of low-income countries with upside potential.

Table 4: GDP per capita relative to microeconomic competitiveness

	High-income countries	Middle-income countries	Low-income countries
UPSIDE POTENTIAL			
Microeconomic competitiveness would support higher per capita income	Finland United Kingdom	Korea Hungary Estonia Chile South Africa Costa Rica Malaysia Lithuania Brazil Latvia Romania	Tunisia Turkey Namibia Thailand Colombia Dominican Republic Panama El Salvador China Philippines Jordan Jamaica Morocco Sri Lanka Indonesia India Zimbabwe Vietnam Nigeria
NEUTRAL			
Competitiveness and income are balanced	Netherlands Germany France Sweden Singapore Taiwan New Zealand Spain	Israel Czech Republic Slovak Republic Trinidad and Tobago Poland Croatia Botswana	Peru Ukraine
CURRENT OVERACHIEVERS			
Per capita income is high relative to microeconomic competitiveness	United States Norway Iceland Switzerland Canada Denmark Belgium Austria Ireland Hong Kong SAR Italy Japan Australia	Slovenia Portugal Greece Argentina Mauritius Mexico Russian Federation Uruguay	Bulgaria Venezuela Paraguay Guatemala Ecuador Nicaragua Honduras Bolivia Bangladesh Haiti

Reasons for country underperformance also seem to vary. Stable underperformance results from persistent structural, political, or social challenges. For India and China, for example, measured underperformance on a per capita basis may well result from the sheer number of people living at the subsistence level outside the mainstream economy. The average prosperity of these countries will remain below measured microeconomic potential until reforms are spread throughout the country. Transitory underperformance can occur in the aftermath of a macroeconomic crisis that has not led to a deterioration of the microeconomic fundamentals, as in Thailand. Underperformance may also reflect a lag prosperity adjusting upward to improving microeconomic conditions. This seems to be the case in Estonia, Finland, and the United Kingdom.

Company competitiveness versus the quality of the business environment

Normalized subindexes of company sophistication and the quality of the microeconomic business environment are plotted against each other in Figure 7. Countries near the line enjoy the positive interaction of the two subindexes. Countries lying above the 45-degree line are those whose companies are more advanced than the state of their business environment. Those below the line are countries whose business environment is more advanced than their companies.

Countries whose company development is ahead of the business environment include Japan, Germany, France, Sweden, Italy, Argentina, the Dominican Republic, and Indonesia. Significant changes in public policy are necessary in these countries to improve the environment for competition. Unless the business environment improves, companies will be prone to *move operations or make new investments outside the country.* Japan remains the advanced economy with the most glaring weaknesses in the business environment, despite strong companies. The consequences for Japan's economic growth have been severe, and Japanese companies have fled the country.[11]

Figure 7: The relative development of companies and the microeconomic business environment

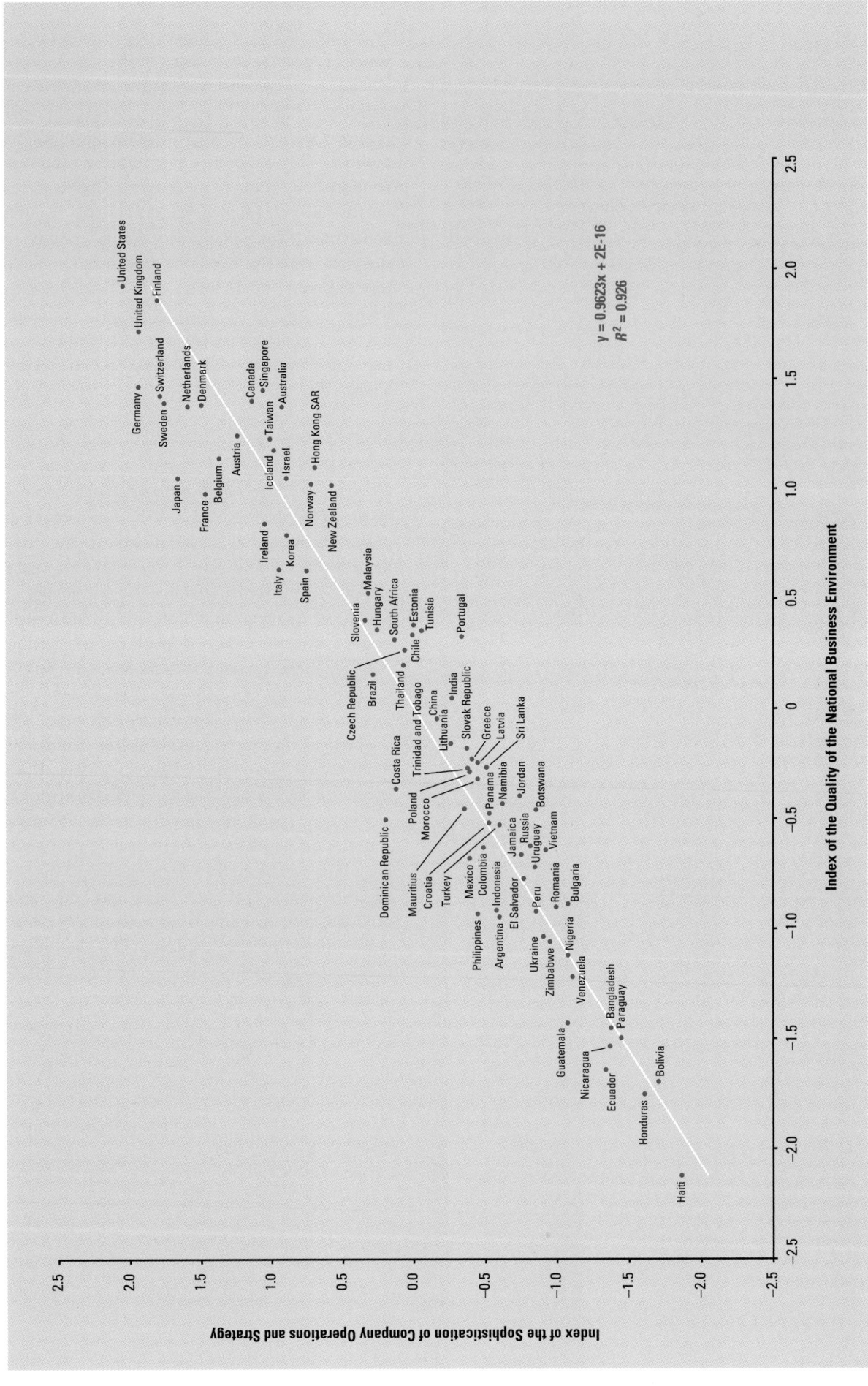

$y = 0.9623x + 2E\text{-}16$
$R^2 = 0.926$

Index of the Sophistication of Company Operations and Strategy

Index of the Quality of the National Business Environment

Countries whose business environment ranks ahead of current company sophistication include Portugal, New Zealand, Australia, Tunisia, Botswana, Hong Kong, Estonia, and Singapore. Many leading companies in these countries still rely on natural resource extraction (eg, Australia), depend heavily on OEM production, or depend on local subsidiaries of foreign multinationals that are not competing with sophisticated enough strategies (eg, Portugal, Singapore, and Tunisia). In some countries, such as Australia, part of the problem stems from rapid improvements in the business environment that have not yet been taken advantage of by companies who remain focused on traditional ways of competing. Efforts to improve entrepreneurship, strategic thinking, managerial practice, and business education are high priorities in these countries.

Change in microeconomic competitiveness and the growth of prosperity

A final area of analysis is addressed by examining whether changes that are improving or worsening their ranking register corresponding results in terms of GDP per capita growth. MICI rank changes should affect per capita GDP growth as prosperity responds to a new sustainable level. Microeconomic adjustments and other shocks may also affect growth, but the relationship between shifts in MICI ranking and prosperity growth provides a tentative indication of causality.

Regressing GDP per capita growth between 1998 and 2001 on countries' MICI rank changes between 1999 and 2002, we find a statistically significant relationship that explains about 25 percent of the total variation in GDP per capita growth across countries. Two outliers, Ireland and Zimbabwe, reduce the fit. Ireland's foreign direct investment inflows have been extraordinary and probably unsustainable; the severe political crisis for Zimbabwe has been devastating. Dropping the outliers and introducing a dummy variable for the low-rank and high-ranked countries to control for the boundedness of the ranking from above and below, the R^2 moves up to 35 percent. The coefficient is highly significant and implies that a 1.9 percent higher GDP per capita growth rate is associated with an increase of 10 ranks over the four-year time period.

Conclusions

National prosperity is strongly affected by competitiveness, which is the productivity with which a nation uses its human, capital, and natural resources. Competitiveness is rooted in a nation's microeconomic fundamentals, manifested in the sophistication of its companies and the quality of its microeconomic business environment. Political stability, sound macroeconomic policies, market opening, and privatization have long been considered the cornerstones for economic development. The results here suggest that these are necessary but not sufficient. More than 80 percent of the variation of GDP per capita across countries is accounted for by microeconomic fundamentals. We find strong evidence that microeconomic upgrading is a sequential process in which countries at different levels of development face distinctly different challenges.

Although institutions such as the International Monetary Fund (IMF) have strongly encouraged macro reforms, our findings suggest that micro reforms are equally if not more important. Without micro reforms, growth in GDP induced by sound macro policies, market opening, and privatization will be unsustainable or will not translate into improvements in GDP per capita. Appropriate micro reforms, which boost productivity and productivity growth, can greatly ease the challenge of meeting government's fiscal obligations and reducing macroeconomic distortions. Microeconomic reforms can also ease the political pressure on governments trying to defend macroeconomic stabilization and market opening against vested interests. Citizens who see monopolies loosing their grip, businesses reforming themselves, and opportunities for employment and entrepreneurship increasing are much less likely to be seduced by populism and government intervention.

Our results again challenge the notion that microeconomic improvement is automatic if proper macroeconomic policies are instituted. Although there may be a tendency for microeconomic conditions to improve because GDP per capita rises, such improvement appears to be far from automatic. Moreover, the rate of improvement in microeconomic competitiveness can be affected markedly by purposeful action in both government and the private sector. As our results reveal, microeconomic conditions can move ahead of or fall behind current GDP per capita, and shifts in rankings have a significant influence on future economic growth.

41

Our findings indicate that it is unwise to view micro reforms narrowly as reducing the role of government and abolishing market distortions. Such steps remain a critical challenge for many countries to master. Yet government has a range of positive roles that are fundamental to prosperity, such as investing in human resources, stimulating advanced demand via regulatory standards, and building innovative capacity. Many nations need to move beyond first-stage reforms and address these agendas. The private sector too has an important role in improving a nation's competitive platform through collective activities and cluster development initiatives. Second-stage micro reforms require a new perspective on the role of the private sector.

Our analysis also makes it clear that microeconomic reform is much more than cluster development. The proliferating efforts to develop and enhance clusters around the world are highly encouraging. Yet countries also need to pursue the full range of areas in the microeconomic business environments, or cluster initiatives will ultimately be stymied.

Finally, our results highlight the need to align a nation's economic priorities with its level of development. We describe the differing challenges for low-, middle-, and high-income countries, and the difficult transitions between broad development stages. Countries that have been very successful in one mode of competing need to recognize the multifaceted adjustments necessary for managing the transition to the next one.

If there is to be continued momentum for economic reform in nations around the world, there is a pressing need to move to the next level of thinking and practice about economic development. Approaches centered largely on responding to international financial markets and ceding choices to impersonal global forces are producing a backlash that erodes the consensus for global economic progress and encourages populist national policies that are fundamentally self-defeating. Economic reform must move beyond now-standard approaches and embrace domestic competition, stringent environmental standards, and policies that meaningfully boost the skills and opportunities of citizens.

Countries are converging on macroeconomic stabilization, trade opening, privatization, and financial markets that penalize laggards. The central challenge to the world economy is now microeconomic reform. Progress in improving the sophistication of companies and the quality of the business environment is the only way to produce real improvements in efficiency, product quality, and new business opportunities that support a rising standard of living for citizens.

Notes

1 I would like to thank Christian Ketels and Weifeng Weng for their major role in the analyses reported here. Lyn Pohl provided able supervision of the final production of the paper, and Janice Long provided production assistance.

2 The proportion has grown modestly over the last several years as the model has been improved.

3 See the *Clusters of Innovation* reports (Porter, Council on Competitiveness, and Monitor Group, 2001a; 2001b; 2001c; 2001d; 2002a; and 2002b).

4 Stages of economic development were first introduced in Porter (1990).

5 GDP per worker is employed as a productivity measure in some studies. We used the broader measure here because GDP per worker can be increased by high unemployment or low workforce participation, which do not increase wealth. Also, holders of capital, not only workers, contribute to national productivity. In comparing the United States and France, for example, the United States has absorbed a huge influx of new workers (higher workforce participation) over the last decade, while France has maintained high GDP per worker but with high unemployment and a large student population not counted as part of the potential workforce.

6 In the case of Ireland, we used GNP instead of GDP because of the size of dividend outflows to foreign investors. Ireland's GDP is about 20 percent higher than its GNP.

7 Statistical significance at ** = 5 percent and * = 10 percent (all two-tailed tests) is noted in the table.

8 We conducted additional bivariate regressions (not reported here) using macroeconomic indicators collected for the *Global Competitiveness Report*. These regressions show no statistical relationship between GDP per capita and individual macroeconomic indicators. See also Easterly (2001), who shows similar results.

9 This analysis covers the questions that have been common over the years, which comprise the great majority of questions.

10 The forecast region has wider bands than a 95 percent mean confidence region. The latter provides a confidence interval for a given level of competitiveness over repeated observations. The forecast region method, in contrast, reflects a higher degree of inherent uncertainty in predicting a single observation. As a result, interpretation of the proximity of data points to the regression line should be undertaken with appropriate caveats. Note that the forecast region widens slightly as it moves away from the "center" of the graph. The center is the point located at the intersection of the mean GDP per capita level and mean factor score.

11 For a more detailed examination of Japan's competitive situation, see Porter, Takeuchi, and Sakakibara (2000).

Selected References

Baumol, W. J. 2002. *The Free-Market Innovation Machine: Analyzing the Growth Miracle of Capitalism*. Princeton, NJ: Princeton University Press.

Barro, R. J. 1991. "Economic Growth in a Cross Section of Countries," *Quarterly Journal of Economics* 106 (2): 407–443.

Competitiveness Policy Council. 1995. "Lifting All Boats: Increasing the Payoff from Private Investment in the US Economy," Report of the Capital Allocation Subcouncil, Washington, DC: Competitiveness Policy Council.

Department of Trade and Industry. 2001. *UK Competitiveness Indicators*, 2nd Edition London: Department of Trade and Industry.

Easterly, W. 2001. *The Elusive Quest for Growth: Economists' Adventures and Misadventures in the Tropics*. Cambridge, MA: MIT Press.

Easterly, W. and R. Levine. 2002. "Tropics, Germs, and Crops: How Endowments Influence Economic Development," NBER Working Paper No. 9106. Cambridge, MA: National Bureau of Economic Research.

Enright, M. J., A. Francés, and E. S. Saavadra. 1994. *Venezuela: El Reto de la Competitividad.* Caracas, Venezuela: Ediciones IESA.

European Commission. 2002. *European Competitiveness Report 2002.* Brussels: European Commission.

Fagerberg, J. 1988. "International Competitiveness," *The Economic Journal* 98(2): 355–374.

Fairbanks, M. and S. Lindsay. 1997. *Plowing the Sea: The Challenge of Competitiveness in the Developing World* Boston: Harvard Business School Press.

Ghemawat, P., M. E. Porter, and U. S. Rangan. 1995. "A New Vision for Indian Economic Development: The Corporate Agenda," Working Paper, October 17.

Hall, R. E. and C. I. Jones. 1999. "Why Do Some Countries Produce So Much More Output per Worker than Others?" *Quarterly Journal of Economics* 114 (1): 83 –116.

Hirschman, A. O. 1958. *The Strategy of Economic Development* New Haven, CT: Yale University Press.

Ingham, V. H. 1995. "The Competitiveness of Argentina: From Sheltered Markets to Global Rivalry." PhD dissertation, Fletcher School of Law and Diplomacy, Tufts University.

Ketels, C. H. M. 2001/2002. "Why the European Context Matters." *European Business Forum* 8 (Winter 2001/2002): 13–16.

Lucas, R. E., Jr. 1988. "On the Mechanics of Economic Development," *Journal of Monetary Economics* 22 (July 1988): 3–42.

Mankiw, N. G. 1995. "The Growth of Nations," *Brookings Papers on Economic Activity* 1 (1): 275–310.

Mankiw, N. G., D. Romer, and D. N. Weil. 1992. "A Contribution to the Empirics of Economic Growth," *Quarterly Journal of Economics* 107(2): 407–437.

Nickell, S. 1996. "Competition and Corporate Performance," *Journal of Political Economy* 104 (1996): 724-746.

Nordhaus, W. D. 1994. "Climate and Economic Development." In *Proceedings of the World Bank Annual Conference on Development Economics 1993.* Washington, DC: The International Bank for Reconstruction and Development/The World Bank.

North, D. C. 1990. *Institutions, Institional Change and Economic Performance: Political Economy of Institutions and Decisions.* Cambridge: Cambridge University Press.

Oughton, C. 1997., "Competitiveness Policy in the 1990s," *The Economic Journal* 107: 1486–1503.

Panayotou, T. and J. R. Vincent. 1997. "Environmental Regulation and Competitiveness." In *The Global Competitiveness Report 1997.* Geneva, Switzerland: World Economic Forum.

Porter, M. E. 1990. *The Competitive Advantage of Nations.* New York: The Free Press.

———. 1995. "Comment on 'Interaction Between Regional and Industrial Policies: Evidence From Four Countries,' by J. Markusen. "In *Proceedings of The World Bank Annual Conference on Development Economics 1994.* Washington, DC: The International Bank for Reconstruction and Development/The World Bank.

———. 1996. "What Is Strategy?" *Harvard Business Review* 74 (6): 61–78.

———. 1998a. "Introduction." In M. Porter, ed., *The Competitive Advantage of Nations: With a New Introduction.* New York: The Free Press.

———. 1998b. "Clusters and Competition: New Agendas for Companies, Governments, and Institutions." In M. Porter, ed., *On Competition.* Boston: Harvard Business School Press.

———. 2000. "Attitudes, Values, Beliefs, and the Microeconomics of Prosperity," in L. E. Harrison and S. P. Huntington, eds., *Culture Matters,* New York: Basic Books, 2000: 14–28.

Porter, M. E., with G. T. Crocombe and M. J. Enright. 1991. *Upgrading New Zealand's Competitive Advantage.* Auckland, New Zealand: Oxford University Press.

Porter, M. E., Council on Competitiveness, and Monitor Group. 2001a.*Clusters of Innovation Initiative: San Diego Report.* Washington, DC: Council on Competitiveness.

———. 2001b.*Clusters of Innovation Initiative: Regional Foundations of U.S. Competitiveness.* Washington, DC: Council on Competitiveness.

———. 2001c. *Clusters of Innovation Initiative: Atlanta-Columbus.* Washington, DC: Council on Competitiveness.

———. 2001d. *Clusters of Innovation Initiative: Wichita.* Washington, DC: Council on Competitiveness.

———. 2002a. *Clusters of Innovation Initiative: Research Triangle.* Washington, DC: Council on Competitiveness.

———. 2002b.*Clusters of Innovation Initiative: Pittsburgh.* Washington, DC: Council on Competitiveness.

Porter, M. E., P. Ghemawat, and U. S. Rangan. 1995. "A New Vision for Indian Economic Development," Harvard Business School Working Paper, March 17.

Porter, M. E., S. Stern, and Council on Competitiveness.1999. *The New Challenge to America's Prosperity: Findings from the Innovation Index.* Washington, DC: Council on Competitiveness.

Porter, M. E. and H. Takeuchi with M. Sakakibara. 2000. *Can Japan Compete?* Basingstoke, England, and New York: Macmillan and Basic Books.

Porter, M. E. and C. van der Linde. 1995. "Toward a New Conception of the Environment-Competitiveness Relationship," *Journal of Economic Perspectives* 9(4): 97–118.

Romer, P. M. 1990. "Endogenous Technological Change," *Journal of Political Economy* 98(5): S71–S102.

Sachs, J. D. and A. Warner. 1995. "Economic Reform and the Process of Global Integration," *Brookings Papers on Economic Activity* 1(1): 1–118.

Sakakibara, M. and M. E. Porter. 1998. "Competing at Home to Win Abroad: Evidence from Japanese Industry," Harvard Business School Working Paper No. 99-036. Cambridge, MA: Harvard Business School Press.

Solow, R. M. 1956. "A Contribution to the Theory of Economic Growth," *Quarterly Journal of Economics* 70(1): 65–94.

43

Appendix A: ANOVA Analysis for Survey Responses

I. COMPANY OPERATIONS & STRATEGY	R^2
Production Process Sophistication	0.471
Nature of Competitive Advantage	0.376
Extent of Staff Training	0.387
Extent of Marketing	0.391
Willingness to Delegate Authority	0.330
Capacity for Innovation	0.427
Company Spending on R&D	0.362
Value Chain Presence	0.436
Breadth of International Markets	0.441
Degree of Customer Orientation	0.265
Control of International Distribution	0.188
Extent of Branding	0.426
Reliance on Professional Management	0.362
Extent of Incentive Compensation	0.252
Extent of Regional Sales	0.362
Prevalence of Foreign Technology Licensing	0.162

II. NATIONAL BUSINESS ENVIRONMENT	R^2

A. FACTOR (INPUT) CONDITIONS

1. Physical Infrastructure

Overall Infrastructure Quality	0.612
Railroad Infrastructure Quality	0.633
Port Infrastructure Quality	0.514
Air Transport Infrastructure Quality	0.447
Electricity Supply Quality	0.555
Telephone/Fax Infrastructure Quality	0.533

2. Administrative Infrastructure

Police Protection of Businesses	0.459
Judicial Independence	0.477
Adequacy of Public-Sector Legal Recourse	0.471
Administrative Burden for Startups	0.310
Extent of Bureaucratic Red Tape	0.121

3. Human Resources

Quality of Management Schools	0.399
Quality of Public Schools	0.527
Quality of Math and Science Education	0.389

4. Technology Infrastructure

Availability of Scientists and Engineers	0.303
Quality of Scientific Research Institutions	0.329
University/Industry Research Collaboration	0.292
Intellectual Property Protection	0.464

5. Science & Technology

Financial Market Sophistication	0.509
Venture Capital Availability	0.268
Ease of Access to Loans	0.260
Local Equity Market Access	0.329

II. NATIONAL BUSINESS ENVIRONMENT (Cont'd.)	R^2

B. DEMAND CONDITIONS

Buyer Sophistication	0.377
Consumer Adoption of Latest Products	0.304
Government Procurement of Advanced Technology Products	0.249
Presence of Demanding Regulatory Standards	0.443
Laws Relating to Information Technology	0.298
Stringency of Environmental Regulations	0.466

C. RELATED AND SUPPORTING INDUSTRIES

Local Supplier Quality	0.354
State of Cluster Development	0.252
Local Availability of Process Machinery	0.292
Local Availability of Specialized Research and Training Services	0.270
Extent of Product and Process Collaboration	0.220
Local Supplier Quantity	0.248
Local Availability of Components and Parts	0.216

D. CONTEXT FOR FIRM STRATEGY AND RIVALRY

1. Incentives

Extent of Distortive Government Subsidies	0.257
Favoritism in Decisions of Government Officials	0.324
Cooperation in Labor-Employer Relations	0.260
Efficacy of Corporate Boards	0.206

2. Competition

Hidden Trade Barrier Liberalization	0.293
Intensity of Local Competition	0.181
Extent of Locally Based Competitors	0.155
Effectiveness of Antitrust Policy	0.345
Decentralization of Corporate Activity	0.342
Costs of Other Firms' Illegal/Unfair Activities	0.240
Tariff Liberalization	0.286

Appendix B: The Microeconomic Competitiveness Index (Constant Country Sample)

Country	MICI ranking					Company operations and strategy ranking					Quality of the national business environment ranking					2001 GDP per capita (PPP-adjusted)
	2002	2001*	2000	1999	1998	2002	2001	2000	1999	1998	2002	2001	2000	1999	1998	
United States	1	2	2	1	1	1	1	2	1	2	1	2	2	1	1	34,888
Finland	2	1	1	2	2	4	2	3	7	8	2	1	1	2	2	25,611
United Kingdom	3	7	8	10	5	3	7	11	13	9	3	8	9	8	5	24,421
Germany	4	4	3	6	4	2	4	1	5	1	4	4	6	5	8	25,715
Switzerland	5	5	5	5	9	5	5	5	2	3	6	5	10	9	10	29,587
Sweden	6	6	7	4	7	6	6	6	3	4	8	6	11	7	9	24,978
Netherlands	7	3	4	3	3	8	3	7	8	5	10	3	3	3	4	26,242
Denmark	8	8	6	7	8	9	9	8	9	10	9	10	4	6	7	28,342
Singapore	9	9	9	12	10	14	15	15	14	12	5	9	5	12	6	23,250
Canada	10	12	11	8	6	13	14	16	12	15	7	11	8	4	3	28,611
Japan	11	10	14	14	18	7	8	4	4	7	17	16	19	19	19	27,101
Austria	12	11	13	11	16	12	11	12	10	11	12	12	12	13	17	27,518
Belgium	13	15	12	15	19	11	12	10	11	13	15	14	13	15	18	27,912
Australia	14	14	10	13	15	19	24	20	19	22	11	7	7	10	12	26,552
France	15	13	15	9	11	10	10	9	6	6	21	13	15	11	13	25,074
Taiwan	16	21	21	19	20	16	20	18	17	16	13	21	21	22	21	22,559
Iceland	17	16	17	22	24	17	16	14	21	28	14	15	16	21	23	30,725
Israel	18	17	18	20	21	20	18	13	18	21	18	18	20	20	20	19,867
Hong Kong SAR	19	18	16	21	12	24	21	23	24	17	16	17	14	18	11	25,581
Ireland	20	22	22	17	13	15	17	19	20	18	22	22	22	17	14	27,457
Norway	21	19	20	18	14	23	23	21	23	14	19	19	18	16	15	30,727
New Zealand	22	20	19	16	17	25	19	22	16	19	20	20	17	14	16	20,725
Korea	23	26	27	28	28	21	26	25	27	24	23	29	28	30	28	18,149
Italy	24	23	24	25	26	18	13	17	15	20	24	24	26	27	27	24,510
Spain	25	24	23	23	22	22	22	24	22	23	25	23	23	23	22	20,374
Malaysia	26	37	30	27	27	27	37	30	25	34	26	37	30	31	26	8,424
Slovenia	27	32	—	—	—	26	28	—	—	—	27	35	—	—	—	18,233
Hungary	28	27	32	33	31	29	33	34	36	39	29	25	31	33	31	12,941
South Africa	29	25	25	26	25	31	25	26	28	33	33	27	25	25	25	9,565
Estonia	30	28	—	—	—	36	32	—	—	—	28	26	—	—	—	10,380
Chile	31	29	26	24	23	35	30	27	26	25	31	30	24	24	24	9,753
Brazil	33	30	31	35	35	28	29	29	32	27	36	32	32	37	39	7,759
Czech Republic	34	34	34	41	30	34	41	41	55	31	34	31	34	36	33	14,885
Thailand	35	38	40	39	37	33	42	47	43	37	35	39	40	39	36	6,630
Portugal	36	33	28	29	33	41	38	35	37	48	32	28	27	26	30	17,571
India	37	36	37	42	44	40	43	40	48	50	37	34	37	43	42	2,464
China	38	43	44	49	42	38	39	38	31	35	38	46	45	50	44	4,329
Costa Rica	39	48	43	38	—	32	34	39	35	—	47	51	42	41	—	8,490
Lithuania	40	50	—	—	—	39	47	—	—	—	39	47	—	—	—	7,764
Dominican Republic	41	60	—	—	—	30	59	—	—	—	53	61	—	—	—	6,198
Slovak Republic	42	40	36	48	36	43	57	31	51	40	40	36	36	47	37	11,739
Greece	43	46	33	36	38	47	51	32	45	32	41	43	33	34	38	17,482
Trinidad and Tobago	44	31	—	—	—	44	27	—	—	—	44	38	—	—	—	10,018
Latvia	45	41	—	—	—	48	35	—	—	—	42	42	—	—	—	7,750
Poland	46	42	41	37	41	46	55	36	38	38	45	40	41	38	40	9,327
Sri Lanka	47	58	—	—	—	52	58	—	—	—	43	56	—	—	—	3,634
Mauritius	49	51	38	30	—	42	49	37	29	—	50	50	38	29	—	10,400
Panama	50	49	—	—	—	54	40	—	—	—	52	49	—	—	—	5,986
Jordan	53	47	35	32	32	59	56	46	44	42	48	41	35	28	32	4,080
Turkey	54	35	29	31	29	56	44	28	33	26	55	33	29	32	29	6,716
Mexico	55	52	42	34	39	45	46	42	30	29	60	52	43	35	41	8,969
Colombia	56	57	48	52	49	51	52	48	40	43	57	59	48	53	49	6,202
Russian Federation	58	56	52	55	46	62	54	33	42	45	56	55	53	55	47	8,948
Jamaica	59	39	—	—	—	60	31	—	—	—	59	44	—	—	—	3,890
Vietnam	60	62	53	50	43	67	64	50	41	36	58	62	52	49	43	2,130
Philippines	61	53	46	44	45	49	45	43	34	41	67	54	46	46	45	4,113
Uruguay	62	45	—	—	—	63	48	—	—	—	61	45	—	—	—	8,781
El Salvador	63	64	51	47	—	61	66	57	46	—	62	64	50	48	—	4,603
Indonesia	64	55	47	53	51	55	50	51	47	52	65	58	47	52	51	3,059
Argentina	65	54	45	40	34	57	53	45	39	30	68	53	44	40	34	12,098
Peru	66	63	49	46	47	65	65	53	56	49	66	63	51	44	46	4,797
Romania	67	61	—	—	—	69	63	—	—	—	64	60	—	—	—	7,036
Bulgaria	68	68	55	54	—	72	70	54	52	—	63	65	54	54	—	6,182
Ukraine	69	59	56	56	52	66	62	52	50	51	69	57	56	56	52	4,224
Zimbabwe	70	65	50	45	48	68	60	56	54	46	70	67	49	45	48	2,406
Nigeria	71	66	—	—	—	71	61	—	—	—	71	68	—	—	—	898
Venezuela	72	67	54	51	50	73	67	49	53	44	72	66	55	51	50	5,966
Guatemala	73	69	—	—	—	70	69	—	—	—	73	69	—	—	—	3,879
Bangladesh	74	73	—	—	—	76	72	—	—	—	74	73	—	—	—	1,644
Nicaragua	75	71	—	—	—	75	73	—	—	—	76	70	—	—	—	2,514
Paraguay	76	70	—	—	—	77	68	—	—	—	75	71	—	—	—	4,379
Ecuador	77	72	57	57	—	74	71	55	57	—	77	72	58	57	—	3,295
Honduras	78	74	—	—	—	78	74	—	—	—	79	75	—	—	—	2,505
Bolivia	79	75	58	58	—	79	75	58	58	—	78	74	57	58	—	2,439

*Using 2002 formula

Part 2

Global and Regional Analyses

CHAPTER 2.1

The Year in Review: A Turning Point?

MARTIN NEIL BAILY, Institute for International Economics

Introduction

There was a golden age of globalization in the last part of the 19th century. The push for globalization weakened over time, however, and tariffs and restrictions were enacted that created barriers to international trade and investment. During the last decades of the 20th century, there was another golden age of globalization and market liberalization. But there has been a new backlash against this trend, stimulated by a set of economic problems that have become evident in the past couple of years. The responses to these problems threaten once again to send globalization into reverse. Are we seeing in the current economic situation a parallel to the end of the first golden age of globalization?

This review begins by describing the cycle of enthusiasm and then disillusionment associated with globalization and market liberalization. It then evaluates four of the economic problems that have contributed to the backlash. These are: the global slowdown; the decline of the "new economy"; the continuing financial crises, particularly those in Latin America; and, finally, the barriers to economic development that have prevented many poor countries from growing. Of necessity, this review will leave out much that is important, and it draws freely on the work of others.[1]

The review concludes that some of the problems have been the result of market failures, exacerbated by institutional failures and inadequate policy responses. Other problems, however, were the direct result of bad policies, at either the macroeconomic or the microeconomic level, or both. Forceful use by government policymakers of stabilization policies is vital to economic success, while failure to control government budgets is a recipe for eventual disaster in developing economies. The appropriate extent and nature of regulation is a key issue. For corporate governance, for banks, and in many individual product markets, smart regulation is better than no regulation. In practice, however, there is no guarantee that actual regulation will be so smart; regulation can, and often does, cause more problems than it solves. Because many markets have unique properties, it may be better to think about policies to promote competition and flexibility in markets, rather than pushing for deregulation or even market liberalization as goals in their own right. Finally, some "problems" are the result of changes in technology and productivity and cannot be "solved" without hurting economic growth. They are part of the process of economic evolution and the playing out of competition at the national and global level.

It is possible that some countries will pull back from the path of globalization and competition. This review concludes that if this were to happen, it would be a setback for global growth.

49

Enthusiasm for globalization and competitive markets

There have been large steps made toward a world economy based on competitive and flexible markets, in which goods, services, and capital are traded freely. Most dramatic have been the shifts in China, Russia, and eastern Europe away from central planning and toward market-based economic systems. But the change did not come just among the former communist countries. In Asia, Latin America, and through much of the rest of the world as well, a prevailing view developed in the last decade of the 20th century that market liberalization was the key to economic growth. The World Economic Forum has played its own part in this, by stressing the desirability of competitiveness and measuring each country's performance in achieving favorable economic conditions.

Many Europeans have reservations about freer and more flexible markets, stressing that they should not come at the expense of social welfare concerns. Education and worker training has long been the favored tool for generating equal opportunity, while income-support programs for the disadvantaged and the elderly were preserved as part of the European "third way" between pure laissez-faire capitalism and socialism. Support for free-market capitalism has always been stronger and less ambivalent in the United States, and maybe in Britain—but even in the United States, the Administration in the 1990s stressed government support for worker training and the importance of social welfare programs such as the Earned Income Tax Credit that supplements the incomes of low-wage workers.

The last two decades of the 20th century provided perhaps a high point in enthusiasm for a liberal, competitive, global world economy. Europe moved further toward its goal of creating a single market, including the adoption of a common currency. In the United States, innovation and competition were perceived as fostering much faster rates of productivity growth and an unparalleled stock market boom (although of course the perceptions got ahead of the reality). World trade and investment flows expanded rapidly. China and India, the world's two most populous countries, grew rapidly and liberalized their markets. They gave promise that the scourge of endless poverty and underdevelopment around the developing world could be lifted by the adoption of a market system.

Of course there were reasons to question the optimistic view of globalization even during the boom of the 1990s. In developing and transition countries there were recurrent economic crises. In a majority of countries, the gap between rich and poor widened as the majority of low-income countries failed to achieve sustained growth, most notably the countries of Africa. In Russia and other countries of the former Soviet Union, the road to a market economy was very rocky and chaotic. The Russian economy experienced a sharp decline in its GDP after the fall of communism, a rise in unemployment and underemployment, and created a system where a few lucky or unscrupulous individuals prospered while the bulk of the population suffered sustained economic hardship.

There were problems in the United States, Europe, and Japan, too. In the United States, the distribution of wages and family incomes started to widen in the 1980s, with more-educated and higher-wage individuals faring far better than lower-skilled, lower-wage workers. There has been a huge increase in the number of people incarcerated in the United States, disproportionately young African-American males. In Europe there has been a chronic employment shortage since 1973. Measured unemployment has been high. In addition, a variety of programs that address issues such as youth training, early retirement, work sharing, and disability and general income support have disguised an even greater employment problem than is revealed by the unemployment statistics. The Japanese economy was the envy of the world for many years, but it has now become the sickest of the major economies. By 1989, per capita GDP in Japan had reached around 85 percent of the US level of the same year. Since then, the US economy has continued to grow strongly, but the Japanese economy has all but stagnated, falling to around 74 percent of the US level of GDP per capita in 2000. Reported unemployment is low, but underemployment is reportedly widespread and problems in the financial sector are extreme.

These difficulties, however, did not weaken the support for globalization and market liberalization among the majority of policymakers and economists in the 1990s. On the contrary, the problems were seen as confirmation of the basic value of open markets. It was argued that financial crises occurred, for example in Asia, because of incomplete liberalization. The poorest countries in Africa had too *little* globalization, not too much, as they had largely insulated themselves from the global trading system. Europe needed a more flexible market system, and Japan's economy was seen as rigid and sclerotic, its financial institutions having failed to use rational lending criteria.

Disillusionment

The mood is very different today. A slowdown in global economic growth started in 2000 and became more severe in 2001. Then came the terrorist attacks on New York and Washington. Last year's issue of *The Global Competitiveness Report* warned that these "attacks will have a lasting negative impact if the policy responses trigger a reversal of the global economic integration that has characterized the past twenty years." It went on to note the dangers of political backlash and market uncertainty that could follow and their potential for "derailing the benefits of global business" (Cornelius et al. 2002, p 8).

The benefits of globalization are now being questioned by business, by policymakers, and by the public. The economic difficulties present in Asia and Latin America have resulted in a reassessment by multinational companies of the benefits of the strategy of full-tilt globalization. Many companies' efforts at direct investment in Asia or in Latin America have failed to pay off, and the imperative of global expansion now seems less compelling to many CEOs. The terrorist attacks reinforced in the minds of business executives the importance of a review of the successes and failures of their global strategies and left companies even more aware than before of the political risks of cross-border activities.

In Latin America, there is a severe public backlash against globalization and the liberalization of markets. Brazil and Argentina privatized their state-owned companies and liberalized their markets to a significant extent. In the early or mid 1990s, they linked their exchange rates to the dollar in order to give credibility to their anti-inflation policies. Yet today Argentina is in a terrible crisis in which the exchange rate of the peso has now collapsed and the banks are insolvent. Brazil faces the threat of partial default on its debt, having already faced crisis and devaluation in 1999. Globalization has been under attack from Genoa to Seattle.

Nobel prize–winning economist Joseph Stiglitz (2002) has provided an intellectual framework for opponents of globalization. He argues that, although globalization does provide potential benefits, the way it has taken place in practice has imposed substantial costs on developing countries and on the poor. The existence of market failures, notably the lack of perfect information, and the fragility of industries in developing economies undermine the case for rapid market opening and liberalization, in his view. Stiglitz argues the International Monetary Fund (IMF), a major proponent and architect of globalization, has failed to recognize the implications of market failures and has abandoned the use of Keynesian policies to preserve full employment.

There are, of course, political and military dimensions to globalization, and these too may have experienced a turning point. With the fall of the Iron Curtain it seemed possible that there would be an end to global political and military tensions. No one expected an end to local and regional conflicts, which often suffer with terrible bloodshed. But with cooperation among Russia, Europe, and the United States, the framework for a more peaceful world seemed to be in place.

Although the threat of nuclear annihilation remains much lower than it was during the Cold War, the attacks of September 11th, the endless Middle East war, and the prospect of a US war with Iraq that is opposed by many other countries remind us of the difficulty of achieving real global consensus and cooperation. There is neither the space nor the ability to assess this dimension adequately here, but it does affect the economic situation and cannot be ignored. Political and military uncertainties weaken stock markets and increase risk premiums, and sharp increases in oil prices have been triggers to global recession or barriers to recovery.

A major reassessment of economic returns has also taken place within the advanced economies. This started with the bursting of the bubble in equity prices for technology stocks. Then the broader equity market declined in the United States, in Europe, and in Japan. Many small investors had been caught up in the idea of easy gains from stock price increases. They bought into the market near the peak and have lost money, sometimes a large portion of their savings.

The reassessment of US economic performance has taken place, in part because official economic data have been substantially revised. At the end of 2000 it looked as if productivity in the United States (output per hour in the non-farm business sector) was actually accelerating, with growth getting faster and faster each year. Based on data available a year ago, it looked as if GDP growth from mid 1999 to mid 2000 would be at a 6 percent annual rate, driven by the rapid increase in productivity combined with a buoyant labor market. Even the recession of 2001 seemed to be barely recognizable, with only one quarter of the year showing a decline in GDP based on preliminary data.

Revised data are very different, with productivity estimates scaled back (2.9 percent in 2000 and 1.1 percent in 2001) and overall growth noticeably slower. Revised GDP growth in 2000 was 3.8 percent—still strong but no longer a blockbuster—and the latest data show three consecutive quarters of GDP declines in 2001. An important reason for these revisions is that new surveys suggested there had been less investment in both information technology hardware and software than originally thought. The "new economy" lost a lot of its shine after the data were revised.

Figure 1: A synchronized decline in GDP growth

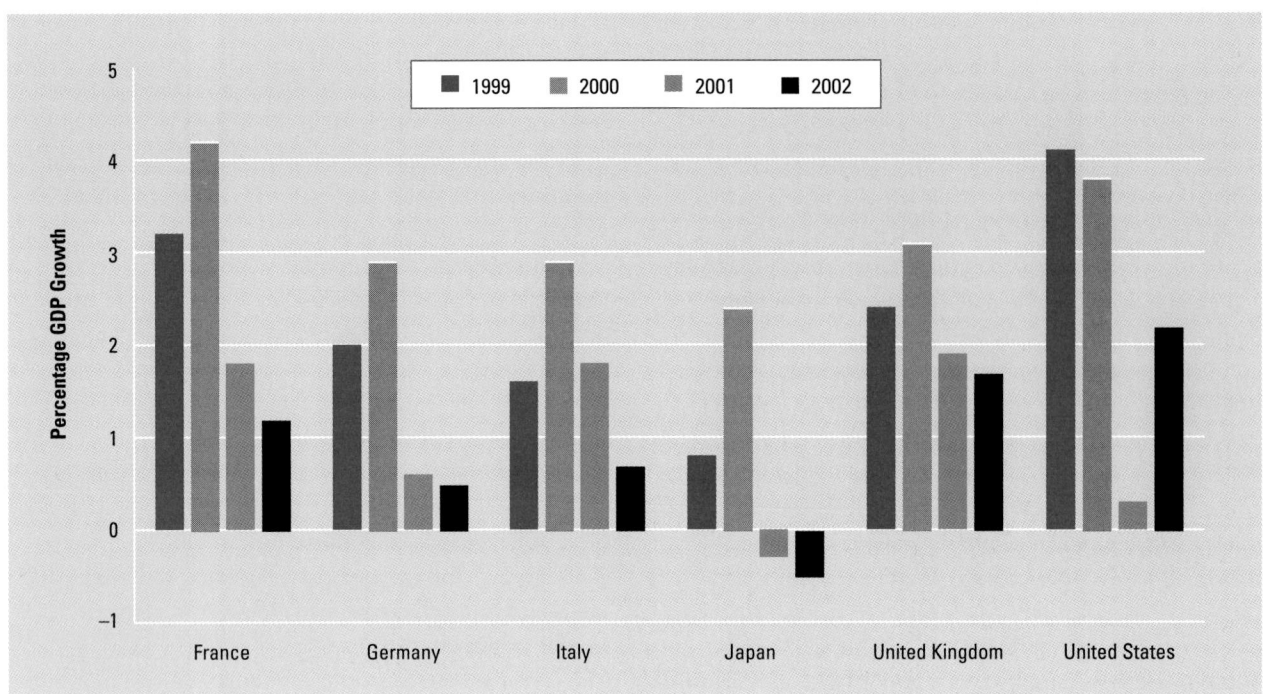

Note: IMF forecast for 2002 data.
Source: IMF *World Economic Outlook*, September 2002

52

For the government data, the restatement of economic performance reflected the availability of new data. For corporations, the restatement of performance reflected, in many cases, the fact that the books were being cooked. Profits had been overstated through a variety of accounting tricks and outright falsification. There were signs that this was happening even in the late 1990s, as reported corporate profits weakened even while the economy continued to grow strongly. Creative accounting can often move profits forward to exaggerate growth for a while, but then there are no new tricks and reality sets in. The collapse of Enron revealed wholesale distortions of the company's financial position, sanctioned by auditors from Arthur Andersen, which had been one of the most respected accounting firms. These revelations were followed by earnings restatements at Worldcom, Tyco, Adelphia, Global Crossing, and others. One hundred and fifty-seven US public companies restated profits following the collapse of Enron.

Although the United States led the way in this bout of corporate excess, Europe and Japan have faced similar problems. The telecom industry around the world has gone through a massive boom and bust cycle. Corporate scandals have affected Europe, while in Japan hiding bad news is almost a way of life, both in business and government.

A synchronous global slowdown

Europe, Japan, and the United States (often called the *Triad*) have all experienced a slowing in economic growth, or outright recession, at about the same time. Figure 1 shows the growth of real GDP in France, Germany, Italy, Japan, the United Kingdom, and the United States for 1999 to 2002. The figures for 2002 are IMF forecasts released September 2002. All of the countries show a growth slowdown in 2001. The United States had the sharpest decline in growth, but also seems to be the economy that is recovering most quickly. The slowdown in the United Kingdom appears to be very mild, while Germany and Japan are the hardest hit.

These synchronous movements of GDP are matched in equity markets. Figure 2 shows the similarity of movements in equity prices among the same group of countries. Indexed to 100 in January 1999, they all rose strongly through that year and into early 2000 and then slumped through mid 2002. The stock indices did not move exactly together, but the correlation is very strong. According to Consensus Economics (2002), the 52-week correlation between the US stock market and stocks in Europe has increased from 40 to 60 percent in the early 1990s, to around 80 percent more recently. The Japanese stock market has certainly moved on its own separate path since the Japanese bubble burst in the late 1980s. Even in Japan,

Figure 2: Synchronized movements of equity markets

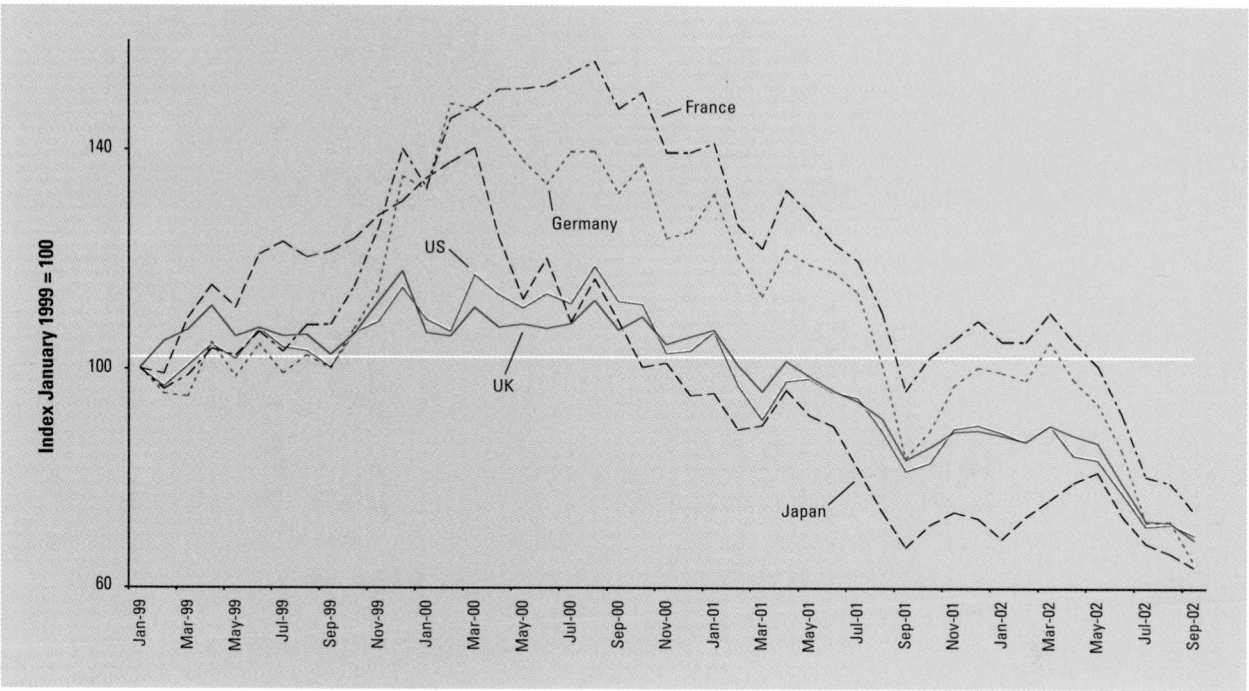

Source: Yahoo Finance: France (CAC 40), UK (FTSE 100), Germany (DAX), Japan (NIKKEI 225), US (S&P 500)

however, stock prices have tracked a similar pattern of rise and fall over the past two and a half years.

The weakness in equity markets has been an important trigger for overall economic weakness. An early sign of trouble in equities came in the United States with the collapse in the prices of technology stocks. The NASDAQ stock index peaked in March of 2000, having doubled over the previous year and risen by a factor of around 10 over the previous decade. It lost more than half its value by the spring of 2001, recovered modestly, and then fell again. As of the fall of 2002, the NASDAQ index is down to its level of the mid 1990s. The Dow Jones, the S&P, and other broader stock indices did not go through the same massive bubble as the NASDAQ, which is so heavily dominated by technology stocks. But the overall market clearly had reached unsustainable levels at the end of the boom. Overall stock market valuation in the United States had declined by $7 trillion from its peak by the spring of 2002, and it has fallen more since then.

The weakness in equities adversely affected US consumer and business confidence, which dropped sharply in the fall of 2000. The US manufacturing sector had been under pressure from a strong dollar even in the late 1990s, and when the strong dollar was combined with a slowdown in the growth of domestic demand, layoffs in manufacturing increased rapidly. Over two million jobs were lost in the United States in this sector from its peak

through August of 2002. For the US economy as a whole, the sharp growth slowdown of 2000 turned into a mild recession by the spring of 2001.

The US Federal Reserve started to raise short-term interest rates in early 1999 and continued to increase them through mid 2000. Inflation had not yet increased significantly, but there were signs that it might. Wages were rising faster, oil prices were up substantially, and the Fed wanted to cool off the economy before it overheated. In particular, the rise in equity prices had encouraged a buying spree among American consumers and businesses.

In some respects, the US slowdown and the recession that followed the interest rate increases was unexceptional. The growth slowdown of 2000 was at first largely an inventory correction. Production was greater than sales, and inventories needed to be reduced. This was followed by a drop in investment, with a large drop-off in purchases of high-tech equipment. This pattern of inventory and investment adjustment is pretty normal for recessions. After all, the US economy had been expanding for nearly 10 years, so a slowdown or recession was hardly surprising.

Europe's growth had not been quite as rapid as that of the United States, and the expectation was that it could avoid a recession. Historically, there has been some correlation of the business cycle among the major economies, but it is far from exact. The direct link between the United States and Europe, in terms of bilateral trade, does not seem large enough to drive synchronous downturns. The United States is the destination of only 9.5 percent of EU exports. There seemed no clear reason why a cyclical decline in the United States should trigger a similar decline in Europe, yet that is what seems to have happened. There is some diversity of outcomes within Europe, but the euro zone as a whole has slipped into a downturn, especially its largest economy, Germany.

Japan's economy lacked the resilience to absorb the growth decline in the United States and it too fell into recession, prolonging the long agony of slow GDP growth and deterioration in the financial sector. Japan's GDP declined by 0.7 percent for the four quarters ending mid 2002.

One possible explanation of the synchronous cycle is that it is the result of the attacks of September 11, 2001, but that is not a perfect or even a very good explanation. US real GDP grew in the fourth quarter of 2001, so the US recession may have ended in the fourth quarter of 2001, rather than beginning then! Real GDP rose at a 2.8 percent annual rate over the three quarters, starting with the fourth quarter of 2001, so it is pretty hard to say that the US economy was knocked down by the attacks. In Japan, when consumers are nervous they save more. In the United States, when consumers are nervous they go out and buy houses and sport utility vehicles (SUVs)—ready for all emergencies. In the United States, equity markets were weak prior to the attack and there was a very sharp drop in prices after the attack, when Wall Street re-opened. But prices bounced back fairly quickly over subsequent weeks.

In Europe, the growth slowdown occurred a bit later than it did in the United States, so arguably the attacks were a contributory factor. Europe is more vulnerable to a disruption of oil supplies than is the United States. But overall, it is hard to see why Europe should have been more affected than the United States by attacks on New York and Washington by terrorists whose enmity is focused on the United States.

Perhaps it is just coincidence that the business cycles and equity markets in the Triad have moved so closely together. A more likely explanation, however, is that globalization has created stronger links among the economies than are visible in the bilateral trade flows among them. Globalization has created a network of multilateral trade flows, so that, for example, when the United States went into a downturn, this negatively affected East Asia, which supplies it with high-tech and low-tech products. This

reduced the demand for capital goods and hurt Germany as a major supplier of capital goods to the world. Many industries, especially in the high-tech sector, are global industries with global sourcing. Weakness in the United States, which has been the great consuming engine of the world economy, has a contagion effect that ripples round the global economy.

Allowing for multilateral trade linkages is still not enough, though. Beyond trade flows, there is a confidence factor that also spreads through the global economy. In this case, weakness that starts in the United States flows overseas and then comes back to affect the United States again. As this is written, in October of 2002, it seems likely that the United States is on the path of economic recovery, but the strength of that recovery remains quite uncertain and the recovery in Europe is yet to show itself. The US stock market, having weathered the terrorist attacks, has been overwhelmed by the blizzard of corporate scandals and profit warnings. And as Figure 2 shows, other markets have fallen as much or even more. The collapse of the high-tech sector, the fall of Enron and a raft of telecom companies—quintessential new-economy companies—have done what the fall of the World Trade Center did not do—shake the faith of investors around the world. As equity markets weakened, the recovery of business and consumer spending has been threatened.

Although some aspects of the recession in the United States were very typical of past recessions, others were not. This business cycle was driven in large part by an excessive rise and then sharp drop in asset prices. In contrast, most previous recessions were the result of an excessive rise in overall goods and services price inflation. The stock market boom of the 1990s created a "wealth effect," encouraging consumers and businesses to increase their spending which then led to an overheated economy. In the downturn, the negative effect of the loss of stock market wealth is holding back the recovery.

The volatility of asset markets, therefore, can be an important source of economic instability. Why does it occur? Purists argue that markets are always rational and absorb efficiently any available information. If you do not believe that, they say, there is clearly an opportunity for you to make money by outguessing the market. Market critics reply that Wall Street is a gambling hall that is subject to herd behavior. Investors get caught up in optimism or pessimism and drive the market above or below the level that is consistent with the underlying profit fundamentals.

The experience of the past two years makes the market purist view hard to accept. In principle, the volatility of markets does imply a profit opportunity, but in practice it would take a lot of patience, a lot of wealth, and a strong appetite for risk to take advantage of that opportunity. Alan Greenspan warned in 1996 that the US stock market was experiencing irrational exuberance, and he was certainly correct—but someone betting on his view would have lost money for four years before being proven correct. Investors who are right about the market fundamentals can still lose money if everyone else believes something else. That said, the message of the market should not be dismissed completely. As will be explored later, there were new opportunities that opened in the United States and the world economy in the 1990s, and these raised potential economic growth and profits. Some exuberance was called for; it is just that the market went way too far.

Restoring growth in the Triad

It appears that asset markets can over-react to economic news and be subject to speculative swings. The question is how serious a problem this is for overall economic stability and how quickly growth will be restored in the Triad. Some previous examples of recessions linked to asset price bubbles are not encouraging. The Great Depression of the 1930s followed the end of the stock market boom of 1929, and full economic recovery did not occur until 1941. Japan has gone through economic ups and downs since its stock market and real estate bubbles ended in 1989, but has failed to generate sustained economic growth for over 10 years. Many in Japan have warned that the United States is destined to suffer a long period of weak or negative growth following the end of the 1990s boom.

Recovery and uncertainty in the United States

The chances that the United States will slip into a prolonged Japan-style period of very slow or negative growth are very low indeed; it is almost impossible. The Great Depression is the only time the US economy has ever experienced a long period of very high unemployment, and there have been tremendous institutional and policy regime changes since then. In contrast to the 1930s, the US financial system today is in generally good shape, better than in the early 1990s recession, and with adequate reserves. It has lost money on bad loans, but not enough to imperil the system. Deposit insurance adds great stability to the system. Moreover, the growth of securitized markets means banks no longer carry as much risk as they used to.

In a world with well-developed securities markets, the consequences of economic shocks or changes fall heavily on asset holders. Assets are re-priced, and the impact is spread widely to people and institutions that (should) hold widely diversified sets of assets. Asset re-pricing in response to changes in the fundamentals reduces the incidence of bank failures or other more costly alternatives. Of course, for this to work well, the risks associated with

asset price variations have to be borne by those who can understand and accept them, and recently this has not always been the case.

Another precondition for a securitized market system to work well is that there has to be honest reporting of financial information; this condition has not been met either. There can be a market failure caused by asymmetric information. Company managers may have an incentive to mislead investors about how well their company is doing in an attempt to raise the share price of their companies. Because of this lack of information, or lack of trust in the market, even good companies will trade at discounted prices because investors do not know whether or not to believe the managers. The current weakness in equity markets reflects a necessary correction to an overvalued market earlier. But it also reflects investors' concerns that some companies that look good on the surface are overstating their profits.

This problem in financial markets is mitigated by the presence of independent auditing companies that certify a company's economic performance using generally accepted accounting principles (GAAP). This process broke down because the auditors were receiving large accounting and consulting fees, and allegedly turned a blind eye to false or misleading reporting. The research departments of investment banks were another way in which investors could be informed about companies, but in some cases this source of guidance seems to have been biased because the researchers were told to give favorable reports on companies generating large underwriting fees to the investment banks. Finally there is the problem of stock options granted to managers as a large part of their company remuneration. These options were reported in the footnotes of company statements, but were not accounted for in the profit-and-loss statements. In the 1990s, the amounts of employee stock options were very large and affected reported profits substantially. Some shareholders may not have realized how large these options were; hence the likely impact on future reported profits. The existence of these options often provided a major incentive for CEOs to inflate their stock prices with false or misleading information, and then cash out the options before the profit inflation was revealed to the public.

Clearly the problem of incomplete information was not being solved by the regulatory system that was in place. There was a need for US and world markets to restore investor confidence in the information they have available as they decide what securities to buy. At the same time, not too much should be done. Over-regulation would discourage risk taking and new ventures.

It looks as if the right steps are currently being taken to restore confidence in corporate accounts. The US Congress passed a bill (Sarbanes-Oxley) whose provisions should improve accounting practices. There are negotiations taking place on rules that would separate investment banking and research. Changes are also being made at the Securities and Exchange Commission to improve enforcement. The market itself is responding as investors, notably large institutional investors, are demanding that companies meet higher standards—in reporting stock options, for example. It will take some time before investors regain their confidence.

Another threat hanging over the United States and the world economy as this chapter is being written is the impending war with Iraq. Thus far, the conflict with Iraq and the uncertainty about the outcome have been a negative for growth. Financial markets do not like uncertainty, oil prices have risen, and consumer confidence has fallen again. There is the possibility that US consumers will finally lose their appetite for houses and SUVs.

A short successful war with Iraq in which Hussein was replaced by a new government that was less hostile to the West would certainly be a positive for the United States and the world economy. It would lift some of the clouds currently hanging over markets. Of course, opinions differ as to the appropriateness of US Iraq policy: this comment is not concerned with its appropriateness, but merely with the likely economic outcome. The uncertainty would be reduced, oil prices would probably fall, and the expenses of the war would actually provide a boost to total demand in the United States. A more protracted or a wider war, in which the United States was faced with street-to-street fighting in Baghdad and heavy casualties, would have negative effects on the economy. Oil supplies could be disrupted by terrorist attacks on tankers or other facilities. A new wave of terrorist attacks against the United States or others could be initiated.

Barring an adverse outcome in Iraq, the weight of the evidence suggests the US economy will make a normal recovery from the mild recession of 2001. GDP growth will probably be uneven, but it should average over 3 percent a year going forward. A big reason why solid recovery is likely is that the correct macroeconomic policies were followed. Monetary policy moved quickly and aggressively to counteract the downturn. Fiscal policy became expansionary also, as the tax cuts kicked in, followed by increased federal government spending in the aftermath of the terrorist attacks. Down the road, the United States will have to confront the possibility of a return to chronic budget deficits, but that is another story and is not an issue that will derail the current recovery.

As well as the right policies in the United States, there is also the overall resilience of the US economy. Microeconomic and labor market policies in the United States also favor growth. Many Europeans dislike the harshness of the US economic system, which is understandable. But the current US economic system does have distinct advantages by creating very strong incentives for people to work and by making it very easy for new businesses to start and existing businesses to grow. The fact that US businesses have easy access to land is one important growth incentive.

It is certainly possible that the prediction of a continuing US economic recovery will not pan out in the short run. The fragility of business and consumer confidence and the economic weakness in the rest of the world could pull the United States into a second downturn. This would be costly for the United States and for other countries that rely on US growth. However, it would not derail longer-run US growth prospects. Within a year or so there would be a return to solid economic growth in the United States. Forceful and appropriate use of macro policies, a sound financial system, and growth-friendly micro policies are the three-part foundation for this prediction.

The need for faster growth in Europe

Europe does not have all three of these parts in place (Japan has none of them). Europe has a sound, if somewhat fragile, financial system, but it has used macroeconomic policies less forcefully than it should have. The European Central Bank (ECB) does have a mandate to consider both inflation and growth, but in practice the inflation target has dominated its decision-making. This imparts an unfortunate degree of caution to its actions in response to a weak European and global economy. Although it has been argued that the ECB has acted sufficiently to the downturn,[2] many economists (this author included) judge that this is not the case. Current short-term interest rates are higher in Europe than they are in the United States even though the euro has appreciated against the dollar. The ECB should have lowered interest rates more than it did in 2001. It did not do so then, and it is reluctant to cut interest rates now because core inflation in the euro zone is holding around 2.5 percent. In addition, there is a fairly widespread impression in Europe that the introduction of the euro provided an excuse for companies to raise prices. The ECB argues that the data do not support this view, but this impression still makes the ECB anxious to be perceived as tough on inflation. If the economic weakness in Europe continues or worsens, as seems quite likely, the ECB should reconsider and provide further monetary easing. In the current world economic environment, the threat of inflation is much less than the threat of recession.

Figure 3: US labor productivity accelerated in 1995

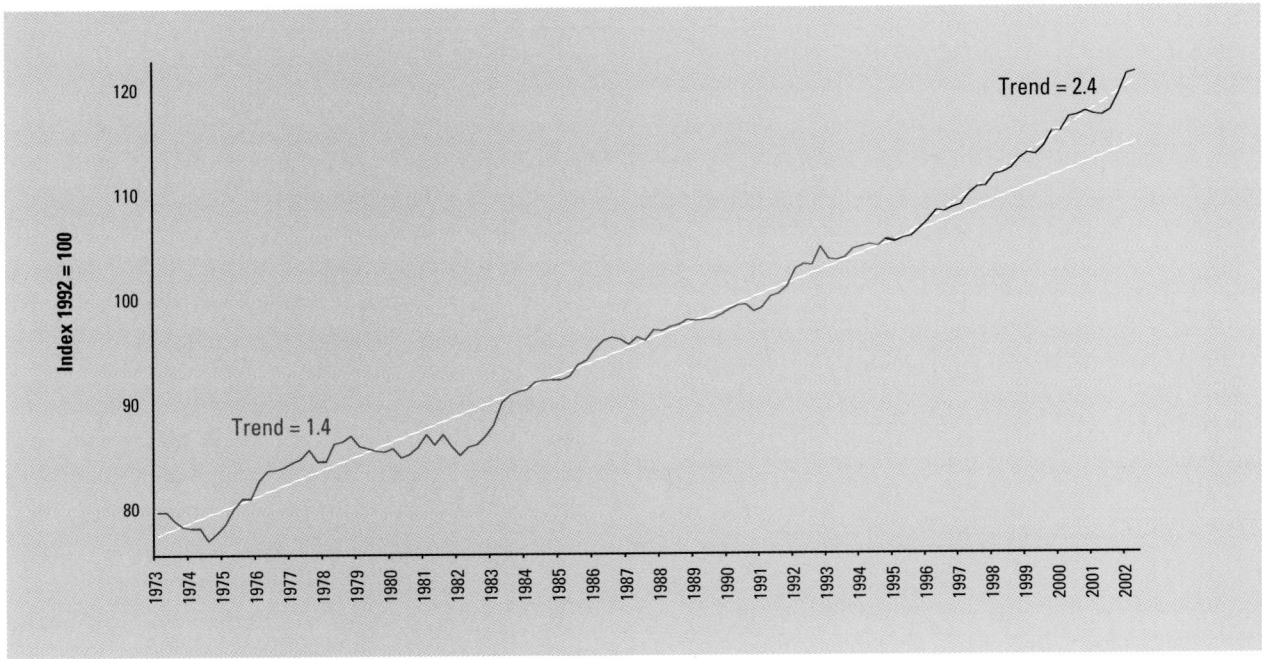

Source: US Bureau of Labor Statistics; index on logarithmic scale

Despite the data revisions, the trend of productivity growth in the United States does appear to be continuing at a higher rate than it did in the 1970s and 1980s. Output per hour in the non-farm business sector of the United States is rising at about 2.4 percent a year. This is not as fast as it rose in the post–World War II period, but a sharp improvement over the record of the prior 20 years (see Figure 3). In addition, the improvement in productivity growth has occurred not just within high-tech manufacturing, but also within service industries (Baily 2002; Triplett and Bosworth 2002). Faster productivity growth, the most important element of the new economy, remains in place, if a little attenuated.

The slowing of overall productivity growth in the United States in the early 1970s had been associated with a collapse of productivity growth in the service sector. Economists' explanations of this phenomenon ranged from skepticism about the data for service industries to a belief that the service sector was intrinsically unable to raise productivity. The resurgence of productivity growth in services after 1995, therefore, was an important sign that there might be a new economy. If there is a new economy it cannot be based just on the ability of the high-tech sector to make faster and faster computers. There also has to be evidence that the rest of the economy is able to make productive use of the new technologies. Since the service industries are heavy IT users, the productivity improve-

ment in services seemed to suggest that IT had allowed the sector to overcome whatever intrinsic problems it had with improving productivity.

These same ideas seemed to carry strong implications for Europe and Japan. Real GDP per hour worked is not an ideal measure of productivity in the market economy, but it is available on a timely basis across countries. According to the Conference Board (2002), real GDP per hour worked grew at 2.0 percent a year in the United States from 1995 to 2000, compared with 1.4 percent a year in the European Union and 1.8 percent a year in Japan. This meant that the United States has had the most rapid productivity growth among the three regions after 1995. In earlier periods, Europe and Japan had experienced much faster rates of productivity growth than did the United States.[4] On the basis of this turnaround in relative productivity performance, international organizations and many academics said the key to raising productivity growth in Europe and other countries was to increase or improve the use of IT.

Australia was seen as a pure test case of the benefits of using IT. Productivity growth has increased in Australia, and yet it produces almost no IT hardware. It has billed itself as a country that is a successful user of IT.

The view that IT is the key to improving productivity growth was a plausible one that seemed to fit the facts of relative growth performance across countries. However, it now seems incomplete and even misleading, both as a description of the US productivity resurgence and as a prescription for faster European growth. Using the standard tool of growth accounting, Jack Triplett and Barry Bosworth (2002) look at the US service industries where productivity growth increased, and they find that most of the resurgence in these industries came not from the contribution of IT capital, but instead from *multifactor productivity growth* (also called *total factor productivity growth*). Multifactor productivity growth is computed as a residual. It is the fraction of growth that cannot be explained by the standard quantifiable inputs, so this exercise does not reveal an alternative reason for the speedup in growth. It could be the result of innovations enabled by IT, or it could be from changes in business practices that were largely unrelated to IT.

Another approach to understanding the role of IT in growth was provided by the McKinsey Global Institute (2001). This research goes behind the mystery of multifactor productivity growth to determine what companies were actually doing. It looked at case studies of specific industries, concentrating on those that had contributed heavily to the overall productivity increase. Among the service-sector case studies, retail and wholesale trade and securities were important in this regard. In turned out that a variety of changes and innovations were at work, including the increased use of "big box" stores in retailing and the shift to higher value added products and services. IT did play a direct role in improving productivity, in the securities industry, for example. In other situations, IT was an enabling technology—for example, large retailers would find it impossible to operate their current business systems without a strong IT backbone. In these cases it was often the technology that was installed prior to 1995 that was most important in boosting productivity after 1995.

The most important conclusion of the study is that productivity had increased only when companies made successful business innovations. Those companies that simply invested in IT systems with the vague promise that this would help their performance were generally disappointed. High-powered PCs do not do much if the users cannot take advantage of them. Advanced data management systems do not help performance if the data comes from different and incompatible sources, or if the company has not figured out how to take advantage of the new information it gains. The case studies of the banking and hotel industries revealed clear examples of IT investments that had failed.

These findings about the productivity impact of IT investment, combined with the fact that IT capital spending slumped so badly in the downturn, suggest that companies in the United States overinvested in IT capital during the boom years. This is surely true of investment in communications equipment and fiber optic cables, an area where overinvestment also occurred in other countries. Once again, therefore, with the benefit of hindsight, one can point to a "market failure." Irrational enthusiasm for the hoped-for benefits of IT contributed to the boom-and-bust cycle and wasted resources. This is not a situation that calls for policy intervention, however. The new technologies held out considerable promise, and sometimes delivered on that promise. Policymakers were often cheerleaders for the new economy and would not have directed the economy in a better direction with more interventionist policies. Businesses have now learned and become more discriminating in their choices. Grand successes and failures are to be expected with a new technology.

If IT was only a part of the explanation of faster productivity growth in the United States in the 1990s, what else was at work, and will the faster growth continue? Definitive evidence is not available to answer that question, but the most likely explanation is that strong competitive intensity, driven in part by the increase in globalization, started to pay off in the 1990s. In autos, for example, strong competition from Japanese transplants as well as from imports put pressure on the US domestic automotive industry. The deregulation movement has been accompanied by mistakes (California power, for example) but on balance it encouraged competition and fostered innovation. Even in domestic US industries, competitive intensity increased as the strongest competitors in retailing expanded nationwide and forced adjustments from the rest of the industry (a sign of the potential for Europe from the single market).

Going forward, competitive intensity in the US economy remains high, and the potential for productive use of IT is still strong. This warrants cautious optimism for a continuation of strong productivity growth in the United States. From the second quarter of 2000 through the second quarter of 2002, labor productivity in the United States rose at an annual rate of 2.5 percent a year, a pretty solid performance during a period of economic weakness, one that is consistent with the trend growth of 2.4 percent from 1995 on. So far so good, in terms of the new productivity trend surviving the recession. One reason for caution is because of uncertainty about the data—further revisions are possible. Another reason is that business cycle fluctuations have a short-term effect on productivity and make it hard to estimate the underlying trend.[5] Despite these reservations, Figure 3 makes a pretty convincing case that there was a shift to faster trend growth after 1995 that has continued through the downturn.

What are the implications of the new economy for Europe? Many Europeans are comfortable with the way things are and see no cause for change. After all, productivity growth in Europe was much faster than in the United States for many years, and the level of productivity is pretty high in France and West Germany. Companies in Europe are making use of IT and may have avoided the overinvestment of the US boom years.

Not all Europeans agree, however. They recognize the need for better productivity growth performance now, particularly since the number of retirees will be rising so rapidly in the future. The Centre for European Studies (2002) points out that not only has productivity growth in Europe been slower than in the United States since 1995, lately it has been slowing down even more. Growth in GDP per employee has come in well below its predicted growth rate 1999–2001, even after adjusting for the impact of the business cycle. They see a threat of stagnation and even stagflation. Moreover, concerns about productivity growth come on top of existing concerns about employment that were mentioned earlier. In 2001, average GDP per capita in the member countries of the EU was 67 percent of the US level, with 69 percent in France and Germany (Conference Board 2002). Given that they choose to work so few hours, Europeans need to make sure each hour counts. They need create an economic environment in which productivity grows.

With hindsight, perhaps talking about a "new economy" in the United States was an overstatement. But it would be a mistake to see the pendulum of opinion swing too far in the other direction. Economic performance did improve sharply in the United States in the 1990s, and IT did play an important enabling role for business innovation. The surge in US productivity growth suggests that the pace of business innovation is enhanced by competitive, flexible markets; by land-use policies that encourage business expansion; by a sophisticated financial market that can fund risky investments, encourage entrepreneurship, and weather storms; and by a labor market that encourages people to try new jobs. The single market in Europe provides an important way in which competitive intensity can increase as best practice companies spread regionwide. But this is only a potential that could be thwarted by restrictive regulation. With an economic environment that fosters business innovation, Europe could ensure it leverages the full benefits of IT use. A policy that tries to force-feed technology to the economy would probably result in wasted investments.

The lessons for the rest of the world from the new economy experience in the United States are similar. Create a good economy and let companies use IT in ways they find best. A certain amount of infrastructure development or standard setting may be needed, but this should not be an excuse to direct or control an industry. One useful lesson of the past couple of years is that being a producer of IT hardware is not as valuable as it looked. The number of jobs in the IT hardware sector was never all that large. At one time, the wealth creation in that sector was stupendous, but much of that wealth has collapsed as the technology bubble burst. Industrial policies that fostered high-tech manufacturing in developing countries are not good investments.

Financial crises: market failures or policy failures

Repeated and costly economic crises are a terrible failure of the global economic system. The dynamics of each crisis varies by country, so there is no single cause or cure. Since the focus of this chapter is on the past year or so, I will look mostly at the lessons from Brazil and Argentina, but a preamble on the crisis in South Korea is helpful to illustrate that not all crises are alike.

The South Korean crisis

The South Korean economy has been one of the great success stories of economic development. It quintupled its GDP between 1970 and 1995, transforming itself into a major economic power. South Korea did a lot of things right, but its rapid industrialization also contained some pitfalls. It never developed a modern banking system or financial markets that were able to assess risk and deal with company failures. It funneled a huge amount of capital into industries that were the chosen favorites of industrial policy, even though they could not use it productively. The close relationship between government and industry gave rise to favoritism and corruption. Corporate governance problems are not confined to South Korea, but theirs were extreme, with unwieldy and opaque *chaebol* relationships. Investment decisions were not based on reasonable expectations of future profits.

The consequence of these difficulties was that very highly leveraged companies started to have trouble servicing their debts in the 1990s. The rate of return to capital had been driven down, not because South Korea had too much capital overall, but because the capital was concentrated in industries that had overexpanded and overinvested. Rather than face up to the bad assets and bad loans, the banks borrowed from overseas, often with loans denominated in US dollars, to make up the shortfall. This made them highly vulnerable to crisis when contagion spread from Thailand and other Asian countries in 1997.

Other economists have described the South Korean crisis, and the crises elsewhere in Asia, in somewhat different terms, focusing on the problems of fixed exchange rates, contagion, and short-run liquidity. Indeed those things were important, especially for the timing and short-run dynamics of the crisis. When the value of the Korean won fell, this left banks with a mismatch between their assets, in the form of won-denominated loans, and their liabilities, in the form of dollar-borrowing from the global capital market. But the underlying structural problems that created the vulnerability to crisis in the first place are also important.[6]

The Argentinean crisis

Argentina did not achieve the stunning sustained growth that occurred in South Korea. It did, however, grow strongly in the 1990s, with real GDP growth averaging 4.4 percent in the years 1993–1998 and inflation at only about 3 percent a year (Mussa 2002). The relative price stability was in marked contrast to earlier periods of very high inflation. Argentina had taken the powerful but dangerous medicine of fixing its exchange rate to the US dollar in order to establish credibility for its monetary policy and reduce inflation. It had also taken major steps to establish a sound financial system, encouraging international banks to take over Argentine banks and ensuring that these banks had adequate reserves and were well regulated. Given that growth was strong over this period, it should have been possible for government deficits to remain low and for the debt-to-GDP ratio to grow modestly or even decline. That was not the case. The debt-to-GDP ratio rose from 29 percent in 1993 to 41 percent in 1998, despite the fact that reported government deficits were rather small (Mussa 2002).

A serious problem in Argentina, paralleled until recently in Brazil and Russia, is that spending decisions are made at the regional or local level, but the central or federal government is responsible for the resulting debts. This undermines fiscal discipline. It also undermines the confidence of investors, who see the instability in the budget process. As the debt-to-GDP ratio rises, they begin to doubt the government's ability to pay back its obligations. This problem is intensified if a significant fraction of the debt is held internationally and denominated in US dollars, as was the case in Argentina. As confidence erodes, interest rates rise and the problem of debt service increases, even if the level of the debt-to-GDP ratio is not high by the standards of developed countries. Argentina became vulnerable to crisis because of its fixed exchange rate and its fiscal problems.

In early 1999, the Brazilian real was allowed to float and the exchange rate dropped sharply. Brazil is a major trading partner of Argentina, so the crisis in Brazil put heavy pressure on Argentina, increasing the likelihood of a devaluation of its currency, a breakdown of the one-to-one relation with the US dollar. With the US dollar itself being very strong against other world currencies and the Brazilian currency depreciated, the Argentine peso had become unsustainably overvalued. Interest rates increased, and the economy went into a recession as GDP contracted by 4 percent between 1998 and 2000. The debt-to-GDP ratio rose to 50 percent in 2000, and the debt service rose even faster. With a currency that was way out of line and worsening fiscal problems, it was only a matter of time before the crisis took place. In the course of responding to the crisis, the government has managed to bankrupt its previously sound banking system. It will take some time for Argentina to recover.

The Brazilian crisis

After the devaluation of the real in 1999, Brazil managed to avoid the serious threat of runaway inflation. The fact that Brazil was able to end its fixed exchange rate and yet maintain reasonable stability was an achievement, and credit goes to the policies of the central bank under Arminio Fraga. The Brazilian government was not able to deal adequately with its fiscal problem, however, and it is now in danger of another crisis, involving restructuring (partial default) on its government debt. Some of the same ingredients that were at play in Argentina have also been at work in Brazil, notably the failure (until recently) of the national government to control the fiscal situation in the regions. One issue that is worth stressing in the Brazil context is the instability of the debt dynamics in a country threatened by crisis.

Take a hypothetical example to illustrate. Suppose a country has a government debt-to-GDP ratio of 50 percent, and the interest rate paid on that debt is 10 percent. This means that total interest payments on the debt are equal to 5 percent of GDP. Suppose government revenues, less government spending on everything except interest (the "primary surplus"), amounts to 3 percent of GDP. This means the overall budget deficit is 2 percent of GDP. Provided nominal GDP grows at even a moderate rate (anything over 4 percent a year), the government debt-to-GDP ratio will be falling. The country is a model of fiscal rectitude and investor confidence remains high.

Consider now a situation that differs from the above example only with respect to the interest rate the government must pay on its obligations. The debt-to-GDP ratio is the same, at 50 percent, the primary budget surplus is the same at 3 percent of GDP, and real growth and inflation are the same. What is different, however, is that investors no longer have confidence in the government's ability to service its debt. There is a large risk premium imposed, and in order to roll over its debt, the government must offer an interest rate of 25 percent. The debt service is now a massive 12.5 percent of GDP and the overall budget deficit is 9.5 percent of GDP. Nominal GDP would have to rise 19 percent a year to keep the debt-to-GDP ratio constant. Lower rates of growth will result in an upward spiral of rising debt to GDP, leading to even lower investor confidence and a rising interest rate, until a crisis occurs.

A high rate of nominal GDP increase is certainly possible with a large enough rate of inflation. There are many historical examples of countries using an increase in inflation as a way to get out of debt problems. But faster inflation creates its own difficulties and, in the case of countries such as Brazil, will not even solve the problem. The government debt often carries floating interest rates (tied to the overnight rate for some bonds) and may be indexed to the exchange rate. This means that the debt service costs will increase about as fast as any increase in the rate of inflation. Investors are well aware of the inflation risk and will not hold long-term bonds at fixed interest rates.

The particulars of Brazil's situation obviously differ in detail and are more complex than the example. Its net public debt-to-GDP ratio in June 2002 was 59 percent, having risen from 30 percent in 1994 (using more conservative numbers on government assets, the net debt in 2002 is as high as 66 percent; see Williamson 2002). It has recently been paying an interest premium of 20 percentage points over the rate on US Treasuries in order to borrow. Some of the debt is international, denominated in US dollars. This means that devaluation immediately raises the ratio of public (and private) debt to GDP. It also adds additional concerns about the availability of foreign exchange to service the foreign debt. Despite these additional elements, however, Brazil's overall situation does reflect in a central way the problem shown in the above example. It has made major fiscal reforms, including bringing discipline to the regions, and is running a primary budget surplus of 3.75 percent of GDP. But Brazil is paying very high interest rates and is in imminent danger of default and a debt restructuring.

The numerical example given earlier illustrates a phenomenon in economics of broader application—the existence of multiple equilibria. If everyone believes a country will be able to contain inflation and repay its debts, then interest rates will be low and the expectation is fulfilled. If expectations turn sour and interest rates rise, then the chances of default rise also and the expectations may be fulfilled. Economists often insist that expectations are rational and based on the underlying economic fundamentals. The above example, however, argues that there are actually two (or more) possible outcomes for which expectations turn out to be correct.

Interpreting this model is tricky, however. Investor expectations are not formed out of nothing. Whether a country ends up with a high-interest-rate equilibrium or a low-interest-rate equilibrium depends on the policies it followed along the way. Brazil has a long history of borrowing to cover an excess of government outlays over revenues. The government chose to borrow in US dollars (or with bonds indexed to the exchange rate) as a way of reducing the cost of borrowing. But this strategy made the risks of borrowing much greater, and when the exchange rate slumped, the debt obligations jumped in value. Even in the past few years, when there has been greater budget discipline, new government obligations have been uncovered that have pushed up the debt-to-GDP ratio.[7] A different policy path in the past would have prevented Brazil from moving to the bad equilibrium.

Lessons from the crises

The crises in South Korea, Argentina, and Brazil were not the result of the liberalization of domestic markets in these countries, or of trade liberalization. In fact, if South Korea had moved sooner to liberalize its domestic economy and reform its corporate governance structure and its banks, it might well have avoided a crisis. Argentina and Brazil did derive some benefit from the deregulation and market reforms they followed, and Argentina developed a strong banking system by bringing in multinational banks. None of the three countries fully liberalized or opened their economies.

Further liberalization in Brazil and Argentina would not have been enough because the problems at the macro level limited the benefits of microeconomic liberalization. In Brazil, for example, it was hard for companies to invest and expand when real interest rates of 30 to 100 percent prevailed on loans for working capital or for purchases of consumer durables. South Korea regained macroeconomic stability more quickly after its crisis and resumed solid growth. It has made substantial strides toward liberalization after its crisis, although it does still have further to go.

All three countries had problems resulting from fixed exchange rates. Possibly there are occasions when fixing the exchange rate will help overcome a history of exchange rate instability or of hyperinflation. It is very hard, however, to preserve a fixed exchange rate in the long run without subordinating domestic monetary policy completely to this goal, which can create its own problems. In particular, if the currency does not adjust, then wages and prices in the domestic economy have to adjust, and that may come only with a severe recession or with chronically high unemployment. Exchange rate intervention may be helpful if currencies are prone to instability, but some flexibility is needed to avoid crises (Goldstein 2002a). Inflation targeting is not a policy that is useful for most developed economies, but it may well be a good option for countries with a history of hyperinflation—a better alternative than trying to fix the exchange rate.

It is hard to distinguish clearly between the extent to which the crisis countries suffered purely from self-inflicted wounds and the extent to which they were hurt by the workings of the global capital market. The promise for developing countries of integration into the global capital market is that it can provide easier and cheaper access to funds and access to financial skills to provide better allocation of capital. These are important benefits—but the global capital market is a harsh taskmaster. A country that has sinned in the past (by running unsustainable budget deficits, for example) may find it very hard to recover. Investors, both domestic and foreign, are suspicious of promises to maintain fiscal discipline and avoid excessive inflation in the future. This is particularly the case when such policies will worsen a domestic recession. Therefore interest rates remain high and the country is stuck in a high-interest-rate equilibrium. If a country's economic institutions are not ready to operate in the global environment, or if governments use the global market to finance unwise policies, then the costs of integration into the global capital market may outweigh the benefits.

The IMF can and has played a valuable role in helping countries get back on track. It has also made mistakes. There is a contentious debate at present about the role of the IMF, but that cannot be addressed here. What is important to note, however, is only that the IMF is in a tough situation as it responds to crises. It may not have enough funds to shift an economy from a high-interest-rate equilibrium to a low-interest-rate equilibrium. Even if it did, like private investors, it may be suspicious of the promises that governments make about the future. Frequent large-support packages by the IMF would tempt countries to avoid dealing with the problems in their fundamentals.

The clearest lesson from the experience of crisis countries is that it is vital to avoid trouble in the first place. As the famous Watergate saying notes, "once the toothpaste is out of the tube, it is very hard to get it back in again." Once a country has lost credibility for its monetary or fiscal policy, it is very hard to regain it.[8] The credibility with its own citizens is just as important as the credibility of the global market. Lacking that credibility, policymakers may be faced with either making drastic cuts in government spending or going into default.[9] Argentina has chosen to default and has bankrupted its banks in the process. Brazil faces very tough choices.

Development failures and the market development path

Views about the desirability of alternative paths to economic development have shifted in the last couple of years. As noted earlier, there is a profound backlash in

Latin America against the market approach to economic development. Even in the transition economies, some policymakers are looking to the Asian model of growth instead of the market model.[10] This section argues that the failures of economic development do not represent a failure of the market model.

William Easterly, a long-time World Bank economist, argues that past development efforts have been based on the belief that increases in capital and education, combined with control over population, would lead to economic growth (Easterly 2001). The World Bank has had an input-driven view of growth, he says. Standard economics assumes that output in an industry or at the economy-wide level depends upon the inputs of capital, labor, skills, and technology. Increases in output depend upon increasing the inputs, and so if output grows faster than population, the country is developing. Of course there is a simple legitimacy to this view, since after all no one can operate a factory or office or retail establishment without these inputs. But as a development strategy, Easterly argues, this input-based approach is flawed. Education, in particular, has been a development favorite, but there are many examples of countries that have invested heavily in education but failed badly in their efforts to develop. Easterly says that development policy failed to account for people's response to incentives. If the economic incentives are wrong, educated workers take jobs in large government bureaucracies or move to the United States. Capital investment projects create gleaming new highways, but there is no economic activity to take advantage of them.

One can question the assumption here that economic development really has failed. India and China contain a large proportion of the world's population; based on the number of people in poverty in these two countries, the economic situation has been improving for two decades, according to a study by Surjit Bhalla.[11] Neither India nor China is a model of market forces, but both have been moving toward rather than away from the market model. Easterly's focus on economic incentives is the correct one, however. Many developing economies fail to get the economic incentives right for development.

The series of developing country studies by the McKinsey Global Institute have documented, industry by industry, the institutional failures and policy interventions that have distorted incentives and created barriers to growth in a wide range of countries. The body of information in these studies is very large, but a few examples can illustrate the conclusions drawn. India placed restrictions on apparel producers, limiting the amount of capital (machinery) that could be used by any single company. The idea of this restriction was to protect employment. The result was that apparel companies could not achieve optimal scale and their productivity was low. The levels of productivity *and employment* in the industry in India is far lower than they are in China, where there were no such restrictions. India placed restrictions on foreign direct investment, and its auto industry remained very small and with low productivity. Licensing requirements were abolished and foreign investment permitted in the early 1990s. From 1992–1993 to 1999–2000, labor productivity in this industry increased 256 percent, output rose 280 percent, and employment increased 11 percent. In South Korea, industrial policy favored investment to expand capacity at the expense of profitability. The semiconductor, confectionary, and auto industries in 1995 all had capital per worker that was about the same as it was in the United States, but productivity was at only half the US level. There was widespread excess capacity even before the crisis in 1998. In the confectionary industry, there were brand new production lines standing idle, lines that had been built without adequate market research on whether people would buy the products.

In Brazil and Russia, high-productivity supermarkets must pay taxes. Their expansion has been slowed because they have trouble competing against low-productivity retailers that evade taxes and do not abide by safety and sanitary rules. A playing field that is tilted against high-productivity companies or small companies with the potential to grow often showed up in these studies as a barrier to growth.

There is a crazy quilt of restrictions, distortions, and regulations in Brazil, Argentina, India, Russia, Turkey, and probably most developing countries. They do not solve any market failures, and they create an environment that often breeds corruption as well. A large and even growing share of employment is in the informal sector—held there by restrictive policies, the difficulty of getting clear title to land, and problems of contract enforcement. It is not surprising that many economists and policymakers have suggested sweeping market reforms. There is something to be said for this approach to development, and it could work in any country that could maintain a reasonable level of inflation and avoid an unstable fiscal situation. Market reforms, accompanied by a sound legal system, would likely get incentives a lot straighter than they are now, even if there were some market failures along the way.

In other countries, however, such shock therapy might cause more dislocation in the short run than the political process can stand. Perhaps it is a dangerous approach in countries that lack adequate institutions, a sound legal system, or a sound financial sector. The right sequencing of market liberalization is a tough issue that goes beyond the scope of this chapter. The important point for our purposes is that it is possible to look directly at the workings of a developing country economy and see why its industries are not growing and why productivity is low. It is information that is not available from official statistics and does not come from short visits to a country. It

is essential information for developing an understanding of the barriers to development and how to create the right microeconomic environment for growth.

Finally, there is the question of whether the Asian development model refutes the argument made here. Japan, South Korea, Taiwan, and Singapore all grew very rapidly in periods when they had a lot of government intervention in the economy.

Developing countries would do well to copy many of the features of the successful Asian economies. They achieved moderate inflation and fiscal discipline. They educated their workforces and, although education is no magic bullet for development, the availability of an educated workforce was helpful to growth. They exposed many of their industries to competition with the world's best practice companies with export incentives. They provided incentives for saving and directed the flow of funds into industrialization, which was appropriate at their level of development. Corruption existed but was kept under control.

The specific industrial policies that favored some industries over others were not the basis for success in Asia. A careful review of industrial policy by Marcus Noland and Howard Pack (2002) concludes that it accounts for very little of the strong growth in Japan, South Korea, and Taiwan. In fact, the industrial policies followed by these Asian countries have costs that have grown larger over time. The period of rapid economic growth in each country was achieved with extraordinary rates of savings and investment, levels that squeezed consumption among households at a time when they had very low standards of living. If these economies had been more open and their domestic industries competitive, they could have relied more on productivity growth and less on input growth. Singapore, a very rich country, encouraged the inflow of foreign direct investment, bringing capital, skills, and technology with it.

South Korea's industrial policy made it vulnerable to crisis, in the manner described earlier, while the example of Japan suggests that the Asian growth model can run into a brick wall at some point. Making the transition to a more open flexible market economy at that point is hard. There are many virtues to the Asian development model, but industrial policy is not one of them.

65

Conclusion

Some of the economic dislocations of the past year or so can be linked to market problems. Examples include the equity market boom and bust cycle in the United States and elsewhere, and the corporate greed and corruption. Policymakers in Brazil and Argentina who were trying to solve their economic crises can be forgiven for thinking that the global capital market is a tough master.

At the end of the day, getting the incentives right is the answer to economic growth and, generally, getting the incentives right means using competitive markets. For all its problems it is the best system available. It is made much better with good stabilization policies and with legal and regulatory systems that provide accurate information to market participants. It works better when it encourages competition and regulates monopolies (sensibly), if these are the only workable structure for an industry. It can be combined with redistribution policies without eroding the incentives unduly. The market system works worse when screwball restrictions are put in place with an incoherent rationale behind them. It works worse when regulation becomes an excuse to protect one set of jobs in the economy at the expense of potential new jobs elsewhere. It works worse when policies prevent industries from evolving and old firms from dying. It works much worse if fiscal and monetary policies follow paths that are unsustainable over the long run.

Notes

1 I am particularly indebted to my colleagues at the Institute for International Economics and at the McKinsey Global Institute. Pavel Trcala provided helpful research assistance.

2 See for example, the Bank for International Settlements (2002).

3 Adam Posen (2002) and R. Glen Hubbard (2002), Chair of the Council of Economic Advisers, have suggested such an approach.

4 After World War II, the US economy achieved sustained and rapid economic growth, but the European economies and Japan achieved even faster growth, allowing their economies to close the productivity gap with the United States. There was strong "convergence" among this group of countries. In the early 1970s, there was a sharp slowdown in the rate of productivity growth among almost all the advanced economies, although the rates of productivity growth remained faster in Europe and Japan than in the United States until the mid 1990s.

5 Robert J. Gordon, who writes "High-Tech Innovation and Future Productivity Growth: Does Supply Create Its Own Demand?" in this year's *Report*, has argued that the business cycle explains some of the strong productivity growth of the 1990s.

6 Structural problems are often dismissed, on the basis that "how can they be important when Korea grew so fast for 25 years?" That is a false argument considered later in this chapter.

7 Morris Goldstein (2002b) provides a critical assessment of Brazil's budget situation and how it developed.

8 This is another example of asymmetric information in markets and the problems it creates. A government may have a genuine commitment to sound policies, but investors may not know this.

9 Cuts in government spending have been deplored on the grounds that such spending provides support for the poor. Some does, but the spending often goes to pay the salaries or pensions of bloated government bureaucracies or overstaffed government enterprises. That does not make the cuts any easier politically, however.

10 Economic development also appears to have failed in Africa, where per capita incomes have actually been falling for 20 years. This situation is beyond the scope of this chapter.

11 Surjit S. Bhalla (2002) explains the difference between his findings and earlier, more pessimistic reports from the World Bank. Africa is a notable exception to the general rule of poverty reduction.

References

Baily, M. N. 2002. "The New Economy: Post Mortem or Second Wind?" *Journal of Economic Perspectives* 16(2): 3–22.

Bank for International Settlements (BIS). 2002. *72nd Annual Report*. Basel, Switzerland: Bank for International Settlements.

Bhalla, S. S. 2002. *Imagine There's No Country: Poverty, Inequality, and Growth in the Era of Globalization*. Washington, DC: Institute for International Economics.

Centre for European Studies. 2002. *Fiscal and Monetary Policy for a Low-Speed Europe*. Brussels: Centre for European Studies.

Conference Board. 2002. *Performance 2001: Productivity, Employment, and Income in the World's Economies*. New York: Conference Board.

Consensus Economics, Inc. 2002. *Current Economics*. London: Consensus Economics, Inc.

Cornelius et al. 2002. "Introduction." In *The Global Competitiveness Report 2001–2002*. New York: Oxford University Press for the World Economic Forum.

Council of Economic Advisers. Online at http://www.whitehouse.gov/cea/

Easterly, W. 2001. *The Elusive Quest for Growth*. Cambridge, MA: MIT Press.

Goldstein, M. 2002a. *Managed Floating Plus*. Washington, DC: Institute for International Economics.

———. 2002b. "Is a Debt Crisis Looming in Brazil?" Lecture at the Institute for International Economics, Washington, DC, June 27.

Hubbard, R. G. 2002. *Economic Growth and Reform: Lessons from the United States and Japan*, Speech delivered at Airlie Center, Warrenton VA, September 21, 2002.

McKinsey Global Institute (MGI). 1997. *Removing Barriers to Growth and Employment in France and Germany*. Washington, DC: McKinsey Global Institute.

———. 2000. *Why the Japanese Economy Is not Growing: Micro Barriers to Productivity Growth*. Washington, DC: McKinsey Global Institute.

———. 2001. *US Productivity Growth 1995–2000*. Washington, DC: McKinsey Global Institute.

———. 2002 *Reaching Higher Productivity Growth in France and Germany*. Washington, DC: McKinsey Global Institute.

Mussa, M. 2002. *Argentina and the Fund: From Triumph to Tragedy*. Washington, DC: Institute for International Economics.

Noland, M. and H. Pack. 2002. *Reconsidering the Washington Consensus: The Lessons from Asian Industrial Policy*. Washington, DC and Philadelphia, PA: Institute for International Economics and University of Pennsylvania. Mimeograph (June 3).

Posen, A. S. 2002. "The Looming Japanese Crisis," Institute for International Economics Policy Brief No. 02-5, May. Washington, DC: Institute for International Economics. Online at http://www.iie.com/policybriefs/news02-5.pdf

Stiglitz, J. E. 2002. *Globalization and Its Discontent.* New York and London: W.W. Norton & Company.

Triplett, J. and B. Bosworth. 2002. "Baumol's Disease Has Been Cured." Washington, DC: The Brookings Institution. Mimeograph (September 18).

Williamson, J. 2002. "Is Brazil Next?" Institute for International Economics Policy Brief 02-7, August. Washington, DC: Institute for International Economics. Online at http://www.iie.com/policybriefs/news02-7.pdf

Yahoo Finance (2002). Index data for each country downloaded from http://finance.yahoo.com/?u, under International Indices, September.

CHAPTER 2.2

Reinvigorating Structural Reform

JOHN LLEWELLYN and the **GLOBAL ECONOMICS TEAM,**
Lehman Brothers[1]

For much of the postwar period, macroeconomic policy focused on managing the fluctuations of aggregate demand. This Keynesian concentration on demand management helped to prevent a repeat of the 1930s slump and enjoyed considerable success in taming the business cycle. Progressively, however, it became clear that greater demand-side stability was coming at a growing supply-side cost. Some important programs put in place to help to stabilize the economy and facilitate full employment or other ostensibly worthy social or equity-related objectives were reducing the efficiency and flexibility of many economies. Minimizing cyclical variations in output was of limited value if trend growth in the economy was reduced and inefficiencies left economies poorly equipped to absorb shocks.

Over the last 25 years, policymakers have begun to address important structural issues. Progress has been hesitant and uneven, however, and latterly some countries have taken retrograde steps in certain areas. Political opposition to structural change is often strong, because the benefits tend to accrue widely but thinly to society as a whole, whereas the costs tend to be concentrated on smaller but vocal groups.

In this chapter, we review the state of structural policies in the major economies and the progress being made in reforming these policies, and argue that a reinvigoration of supply-side policy is vital and overdue. Our main findings and recommendations are as follows.

Why are structural policies important?
Structural policies are important for two principal reasons:

- First, through operating on the supply side of the economy, they are the major determinant of economic performance over the medium to long term. As we discuss later, adding just half a percent to a potential growth rate of 2.5 percent per annum would mean that material living standards would double in 20 years rather than 40.

- Second, structural rigidities make it harder for economies to absorb shocks, resulting, for example, in higher and more persistent unemployment than would otherwise be the case.

Economies with the best structural underpinnings tend to perform best. This is also reflected in financial market performance, with, for example, the economies that have the best structural policies also having the best-performing stock markets, and vice versa.

Who is winning and who is losing the structural policy marathon?

Based on a ranking of the 400-odd structural variables in the Lehman Brothers Structural Database at the end of the last millennium:

- The United States had the best structural policies, while both Europe (especially the euro zone) and Japan had significant structural policy weaknesses. This judgment extends to each of three key areas reviewed: policies to improve potential growth, the functioning of labor markets, and the functioning of product markets.

- The number one ranking of the US economy clearly sits well with its impressive performance of the 1990s, and with the fact that economists generally underpredicted US growth and overestimated inflation over this period.

- European performance was diverse, but generally unsatisfactory, and this was mirrored in the unspectacular economic growth and high unemployment that characterized the 1990s.

- A GDP-weighted average of the individual euro area country rankings occupies a low 15th place out of the 21 countries assessed. A broader European average that includes the non-EMU countries would score more highly than Japan, but still lag behind the United States, Canada, New Zealand, and Australia. The larger continental countries generally scored poorly, with France the best.

- However, the United Kingdom was a consistently high scorer and some European economies scored well in particular areas. Sweden came top in policies to promote potential growth; the other Nordic countries too did well in this area, and some of the smaller economies, including the Netherlands, Ireland, and Switzerland, were among the leaders in areas such as education and training, and workplace flexibility.

- Furthermore, there is some good news for Europe: the euro area labor market is becoming more flexible, and the output/inflation tradeoff is improving, probably by more than the ECB recognizes.

- Even after successive episodes of structural reform over the last two decades, Japan's supply-side shortcomings remain many and various. Japan finished a mediocre 12th in our country-by-country structural league table, and was last if all the European scores are combined into a weighted average. One problem is predominant: Japan's dysfunctional financial sector. Beyond that, Japan is let down by poor policies to promote product market competition.

- These considerations help to explain why, in terms of real GDP growth, Japan was one of the worst-performing economies in the 1990s and why this period also saw a dramatic escalation of government debt and the consistent erosion of the full employment that had characterized its postwar development.

What are the major challenges for structural policy going forward?

Structural performance is not a constant. The situation is in a perpetual state of flux, with countries improving in some areas and falling back in others. The reality is that, despite their continued shortcomings, structural policies in Europe and Japan have been generally moving in the right direction, although the pace of change has often been disappointing. In the United States, some aspects of structural policy have latterly been moving in the wrong direction, although the US response to its corporate governance crisis would appear to have been both rapid and appropriately framed.

Much structural work still needs to be done in all the major economies. But this process is complicated by the fact that structural theory and policy are, by the standards of the familiar and well-trodden road of aggregate-demand analysis, very much in their infancy. Furthermore, the dynamics of structural performance are, to a significant extent, determined by the interrelated and often rather opaque considerations of institutional history and the broader contemporary political context. The ability to instigate and adapt to change is itself a function of a country's pace of long-term development and the institutional forces that have grown up as a result. The broader political context exerts a strong influence, as the adjustment costs of structural change tend to be immediately concentrated on homogeneous and well-organized groups, while the benefits are spread more thinly across society as a whole and take time to become clear.

We judge the priorities to be as follows:

- In the United States, corporate governance remains the burning issue. Otherwise, the priority should be to unwind the recent imposition of tariffs on imports of steel and lumber and the increased subsidies to agriculture.

- European policymakers, particularly in the euro zone, face serious challenges in all the three areas of structural policy: potential growth and labor and product market flexibility. Despite the evidence of employment flexibility, the priority must remain the labor market; but a lower tax burden, less administrative interference, and the promotion of stronger competition are also of high importance.

- In the case of Japan, it is impossible to see how the economy can ever grow vigorously again unless the banking sector functions properly. That will not happen unless the government addresses the central issue of nonperforming loans decisively and effectively. Thereafter, the government will need to tackle the many other inefficiencies that constrain growth and reduce the economy's ability to absorb shocks.

Changing priorities

Supply/demand imbalance

Just as generals often stand accused of fighting the last war, so too can macroeconomic policymakers be accused of focusing too much on what is increasingly the wrong issue—in this case, aggregate demand rather than aggregate supply.

It was natural, following the misery of the Great Depression, that policymakers should seek to ensure that such an economic (and human) catastrophe would never happen again. Thus, the principal cause of that depression having been identified by Keynes and his disciples as a chronic shortage of final demand, economic policy was, for three decades after 1945, overwhelmingly directed at maintaining aggregate spending power at a high level.

This preoccupation with aggregate demand by and large produced the desired result. Not only has there been no repeat of the 1930s experience, but also the downturns in activity in the principal OECD countries have become shallower and shorter. To some extent, this almost certainly came about as a result of basic changes in the structure of economies. Government expenditure, more stable than that of the private sector, has risen substantially as a share of countries' GDP, from well under 20 percent before the war to some 38 percent today (and more like 48 percent in Europe). Also, in contrast to the prewar era, governments generally have allowed the counter-cyclical automatic stabilizers of falling tax revenues and higher entitlement spending to function more or less unfettered during slowdowns. Furthermore, the underlying commitment to maintain aggregate demand has served to provide a floor for private-sector confidence, expectations, and spending and, in contrast to the interwar period, there has been a high degree of international economic cooperation.

However, economies were becoming increasingly inflation-prone, and in the 1960s the Keynesian consensus began seriously to be questioned. That criticism, which has a number of strands, was somewhat confused, and remains so to this day: it is useful to separate these various strands.

One strand is the allegation that the rising inflation-proneness was the direct result of the discretionary fiscal fine-tuning, and some critics have even gone so far as to allege that that fine-tuning was unsuccessful even in its own terms. But there is a wide body of evidence that fine-tuning generally did succeed in reducing cyclical fluctuations in the 1950s and 1960s.[2]

The second strand of criticism is that the general trend toward a higher share of government expenditure in economies crowded out private-sector expenditure, importantly including business fixed investment, and that this damaged the growth of productive potential and made economies more inflation prone. This criticism may well have some validity.

The third strand of criticism is that macroeconomic policymaking all too frequently relegated monetary tools to the secondary, subservient, role of accommodating the "needs" of fiscal policy. The role of monetary policy, it was often considered at the time, was simply to produce low interest rates, regardless of what fiscal policy was doing; accordingly, monetary policy played no effective role in inflation control. This criticism has considerable validity. Fortunately, however, this problem has now been addressed in many countries, by the conferring of a high degree of independence upon central banks.

Most recently a fourth criticism has come to the fore, which is that scant attention has been paid, not only in the 1950s and 1960s but also in the more recent period, to supply-side considerations. Our judgment is that this charge has considerable validity, and it is with policies that address that charge that this chapter is concerned.

Shock therapy

The relegation of the supply side of the economy to a secondary consideration has resulted in a range of inefficiencies and significant damage to longer-term economic performance. For example, policy decisions taken in the name of full employment or other, ostensibly worthy, objectives, rendered labor markets progressively more rigid. This in turn hindered the basic functional requirement of an economy that it offer employment and rising material living standards to all who wish to work.

It was the two great oil shocks, of 1973–1974 and 1978–1979, that finally brought supply-side performance into the policy limelight. These shocks, which wrought deep and fundamental structural change on economies, cruelly exposed the inappropriateness of demand-side policies for dealing with supply-side shocks. Pressure for structural change was augmented by other powerful forces, including rapid technological change, the intensification of global competition, and the emergence of new and dynamic competitor economies.

Today, there is an acceptance among economists that structural change is both necessary and unavoidable: technological advancement, the heightened contestability of markets, and the emergence of new, low-cost producers contribute importantly to satisfying the desire of consumers for growing material living standards. But the adjustments required are not easy to make, and they can be very painful.

To understand this, it is worth remembering that the evidence across a range of different OECD countries, from the United States to Sweden, is that at least one job in every ten is destroyed each year. Aggregate unemployment does not typically change a great deal from one year to the next, so it follows that something like the same number of new jobs is also created each year. Hence, the image of comparative stability presented by the aggregate employment and unemployment statistics is misleading. Beneath the placid surface of the headline figures lies a turbulent process of continual job creation and job destruction.

This is in relatively tranquil periods. When an economy is hit by a shock, such as a jump in the oil price or a sudden change in the pattern of expenditure, as occurred last year following the attacks of September 11, the pressures for structural adjustment are multiplied. Unless the required change can be effected rapidly and smoothly, the result will be rising and more persistent unemployment and slower economic growth. That is as unacceptable to those who are unable to find employment as slow growth in living standards is to those in employment.

The capacity for adjustment

A country's ability to undertake structural change is dictated by a range of complex considerations, not least of which are history and the broader contemporary political context.

History is important because all societies are to some extent prisoners of their own past. Even in today's increasingly globalized world, each economy retains its own social, cultural, and institutional idiosyncrasies. The ability to instigate and adapt to change is itself a function of a country's pace and pattern of long-term development, the crises it has faced, and the institutional forces that have grown up as a result. Hence the impact of common structural policy changes will differ in both a micro- and a macroeconomic sense from country to country.

The broader contemporary political context is important because the adjustment costs of structural change tend to be immediately concentrated on homogeneous and well-organized groups, while the benefits are spread more thinly across society as a whole and take time to become clear. This leaves politicians at a disadvantage. They often have to endure the political costs during their own electoral lifetime, while the benefits may accrue to subsequent administrations, which could, of course, be of an altogether different political hue.

Equally important, there are times when structural change is easier to instigate than others. Indeed, there are occasions when a particular shock (discrete or progressive) to the psyche of a nation means that there is a headlong rush toward structural change that politicians can barely keep up with or control. It could be argued that the record of industrial unrest and chronic economic underperformance inherited by the Thatcher government in the United Kingdom in 1979 offered one such opportunity for accelerated change. On a smaller scale, the recent crisis in US corporate governance could be characterized as a similar cathartic moment. But there are also times, such as in major wars, when formal structural policy must be relegated to a very low level of priority (although this is not to deny that wars can have positive externalities in the form of technological advance, social inclusion and high levels of resource utilization).

Change or else

Ignoring structural change and structural policy is no longer an option open to governments. Ensuring good supply-side performance is now an imperative in all OECD countries, as well as many beyond, and is increasingly being seen as such. As former UK Prime Minister John Major observed, adding just half a percent to a potential growth rate of 2.5 percent per annum would mean that material living standards would double in 20 years rather than 40.

Indeed, the importance of a good supply-side performance can even extend beyond purely domestic considerations: it can assume geopolitical importance. Despite occasional crises, the US economy's underlying dynamism and flexibility, and in particular its ability to absorb a rapidly expanding population into the workforce while consistently delivering a large defense program, led to the Cold War coming to an end without a shot being fired. By the late 1980s, the sclerotic and rapidly disintegrating former USSR simply could not afford to match the US military buildup.

Although the Soviet analogy is perhaps an extreme one, most of Europe is now also starting seriously to be confronted by a similar issue: the unfortunate consequences of its supply-side failures. The European economy is not delivering the growth of post-tax real incomes that many desire; it is persistently unable to employ all of its present citizens; and it is far from clear that, on present policies, it will be able to employ the substantial influx of labor that will result if, as is currently envisaged, the single market and monetary union is swelled by some 75 million-odd over the next decade.

Virtually no economist would seriously suggest that these problems could be more than partially addressed by demand-side policies. They are rooted in the growth of supply, not in the proportion of it that is taken up. In short, the time has come when, if it is to remain a global economic and political force, Europe's policymakers have to turn their increasingly encouraging supply-side rhetoric into more meaningful action.

Japan, too, has deep-seated and fundamental problems with the supply side of its economy. Once the world's growth-miracle economy, it has now languished for more than a decade. The net result is that not only is the Japanese economy unable to employ all of its labor force—including hidden unemployment, its jobless rate is now similar to, if not higher than, that of the European Union—it is also threatened by a burgeoning government debt crisis and could soon abdicate its leadership of the Asian region to China. The Chinese economy is growing at something like 7 percent per year. If both economies continue on their present diverse trajectories, the Chinese GDP will exceed Japanese GDP by 2020. This would have profound global geopolitical implications.

Again, scarcely any economist would suggest that Japan's travails can be put right purely by demand-side policies. Indeed, these have already been pushed close to their limits over recent years, and have manifestly failed. The time has come when Japan, too, has to take structural, supply-side policies seriously or risk becoming a second-class power.

Assessing the opposition

The growing focus on structural, supply-side issues may seem natural and obvious to the economist; but as hinted earlier, the costs it imposes on vested interests mean that it evokes considerable resistance from them. This is especially the case as, to many, the espousal of better supply-side policies is akin to saying, "make your economy more like that of the United States." And the United States, to a significant proportion of public opinion in Europe and beyond, is regarded as a relatively harsh society that exhibits little social solidarity and even less compassion.

Whatever the validity of these judgments, it does not follow that policies designed to promote flexibility and dynamism and to ensure that adjustment to shocks takes place more smoothly are necessarily harsh or socially divisive. To give some examples:

- First, consider the employment protection legislation (EPL) seen in a number of European countries, including France. The motive behind such legislation is to protect the individual against capricious dismissal by the employer. But the effect at the aggregate level, particularly if the provisions are strong, is to inhibit employers from hiring, producing the paradoxical result that the person in work is protected not from the employer but rather from someone unemployed and seeking a job. Refining this legislation would ease the problem of "insiders" and "outsiders" in the labor force.

- Second, what of the European trait of discouraging part-time working supposedly to encourage more "real, full-time jobs," either through explicit legislative prevention of part-time jobs or by levying the same employer-paid rates of tax on part-time workers as full-time workers? The recent softening of such measures has resulted in a surge in part-time employment, while surveys conducted by the European Commission reveal that the majority of these part-time workers prefer not to work full time. Many, for example, are women who, with a partner at work and children at school, prefer to work, but for limited hours.

- Third, there are the Active Labor Market Policies (ALMPs), which equip, retrain, or upgrade the skills of displaced workers for a new job. These have been developed and applied most fully in the Nordic and Scandinavian countries and they work well, to the benefit of workers, employers, and society alike.

It is also worth reflecting on the experiences of the Netherlands. Dutch society is generally perceived as having a deeply ingrained social conscience, yet over the last two decades Dutch structural policy has been extremely innovative. Although macroeconomic policy has been severely constrained by a combination of a fixed exchange rate (even pre-EMU) and the European Union's budgetary rules, a cocktail of tax reform, liberalization, and a strong social safety net has generated rapid private-sector employment growth and one of the lowest jobless rates in the OECD. Dutch structural policy is now held up as the model for the rest of Europe.

Some definitions

Before progressing further, it is appropriate to define exactly what we mean by supply-side policies. In essence, we take *structural policies* to be **all those policies beyond fiscal and monetary stabilization policy that materially affect macroeconomic performance—the so-called supply side of the economy—over the medium term.**

This definition encompasses everything from bank restructuring and the strengthening of the regulatory framework to capital market development, corporate governance, enterprise reform and corporate debt restructuring, competition policies, labor market reform and social safety nets, transparency, monitoring and information disclosure, privatization and public enterprise reform, and the environment.

That said, some structural policies are likely to be more important than others in improving economic performance, and it is important to identify which these are. Policy effort should be focused where it is likely to have the greatest effect. Most economists today are convinced that the main thrust of a program of structural reform or improvement should be both to encourage allocative efficiency, so that more resources are channeled into the most productive uses, and to speed up the process of adjustment.

That, as we have already suggested, is easier said than done. But one thing is clear. Policies designed to facilitate structural change would be easier to accept if their precise benefits could be explained with confidence. But the theory of structural analysis is both complex and underdeveloped. On the empirical side, merely measuring the narrow sectoral effects of a single policy change entails the collection of detailed data on output, employment, costs, prices, and profits in an industry group over several years and covering differing levels of regulatory intensity. Measuring the effects of such changes on the entire economy is more tortuous still, requiring an understanding of the intricate processes of how a change in the institutional environment in one sector interacts with all other sectors, both upstream and down. Compared with the, by now familiar, well-trodden road of aggregate-demand analysis, supply-side policy analysis is convoluted and still very much in its infancy.

Many of these difficulties lie beyond the scope of this chapter. In what follows, we summarize the use that we have been making of Lehman Brothers' unique structural database (LSD), in order to shine some light on the importance of supply-side issues in economic performance in the major economies (the United States, Europe, and Japan); to identify some of the key areas where change would seem to be a priority; and to offer some insights into the potential positive effects of such changes.

Database and method

Making sense of the numbers

To investigate the scale of contemporary structural problems, and to compare these problems across countries, we assembled a wide range of different structural data on a cross-country comparative basis. We made this decision partly because we knew that there were only a limited number of such data, and also because, the state of the theory of structural adjustment being largely undeveloped, we did not wish to prejudge the importance of one variable vis-à-vis another. However, we stress that our coverage of financial sector indicators was relatively sparse and that this area should be looked at separately, as indeed we do when we evaluate Japan's structural situation.

We also elected to collect information relating both to structural policies themselves, and to the macro- and microeconomic variables that we judge to be most likely to be directly influenced by such policies. This distinction between "policy" variables and "performance" variables is, in our judgment, a crucial one. The European Commission, in its otherwise very useful work on structural policy change, fuses these two categories in its monitoring reports on Europe's structural progress. This does seem to mix up apples and oranges.[3]

On this basis, the complete LSD—policy and performance variables taken together—currently extends to some 400 variables, covering 21 OECD countries.[4]

For the purposes of analysis, we have divided our structural policy variables according to how we judge they may influence economic performance over the medium and long term: potential GDP growth; the non-accelerating wage rate of unemployment, or NAWRU; and pricing behavior. Each of these three areas contains four subsets, giving twelve in all, as shown in Figure 1. Of course, these three areas of influence are in reality interrelated, as indeed are many of the subsets, but this analytical framework seemed to us to be helpful. Naturally, the data can be divided in other ways, depending upon the purpose.

Figure 1: Organization of Lehman Structural Database

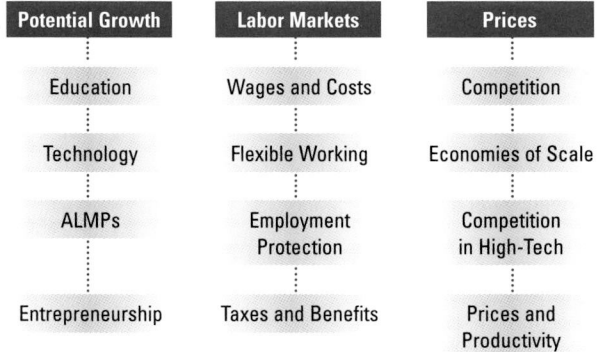

Potential Growth	Labor Markets	Prices
Education	Wages and Costs	Competition
Technology	Flexible Working	Economies of Scale
ALMPs	Employment Protection	Competition in High-Tech
Entrepreneurship	Taxes and Benefits	Prices and Productivity

Policies affecting potential output

A good education system, which provides ready access to life-long training, is essential to provide a high-quality labor force. Accordingly, the first of our subsets in the area of potential growth is Education and Training. This subset contains variables that measure, among other things, the resources devoted to education (from nursery through to tertiary level) as well as vocational training and in-work training. Other variables assess educational achievements and the effectiveness of these policies (as measured, for example, by youth unemployment rates). In recognition of the importance of new technologies in boosting both the quality of the capital stock and technical progress, our second subset is Technology. Variables in this group include those measuring resources devoted to research and development (R&D) and the production of information and communication technologies (ICT) as well as the utilization of such technologies.

Variables in the third Active Labor Market Policy (ALMP) subset measure the amount of government spending devoted to retraining the unemployed and the provision of job placements and subsidies. Other variables measure the effectiveness of these policies (as measured, for example, by the number of people who start to work in the unsubsidized labor market after their training). In the same way that a good education system can, ALMPs can also boost the quality of the labor force and total factor productivity (TFP).[5] The fourth subset, Entrepreneurship, includes variables that measure whether the environment is constructive for companies, in particular small companies, to do business. It includes such variables as corporate tax rates, the administrative burden for small and medium-sized enterprises (SMEs), help for start-ups, and the cost of corporate failure. A vibrant corporate sector is needed to exploit technological advances commercially, thereby increasing the capital stock and TFP.

Policies affecting the NAWRU and labor markets

The first subset in labor markets is Wage Flexibility. This subset contains variables that measure the power of trade unions and the type of wage bargaining system. Powerful unions and centralized wage bargaining inhibit wage differentiation (reflecting differences in labor productivity). They also limit the adjustment of overall wages to changes in productivity. This can result in lower demand for labor and a higher NAWRU than otherwise would be the case. Flexible Working (our second subset) and low Employment Protection (our third subset) facilitate the adjustment of a company's workforce to variations in demand. Low employment protection also allows those people who are unemployed to compete for jobs with current employees, so helping to curtail wage increases in excess of productivity. Flexible working arrangements can also raise labor supply, for example by encouraging housewives and the elderly to join the labor force rather than remaining outside it.

Finally, high Taxes and Benefits (subset four) reduce employment in two ways: first, high income taxes and social security contributions create a wedge between the take-home wage and labor costs, reducing labor supply and demand for a given wage level. Second, high benefits combined with high taxes for low incomes can create a poverty trap, whereby an unemployed person gains little in net income if he or she starts to work. Our subset includes a multitude of tax and benefit variables, which captures the interaction between the two systems.

Policies affecting competition and prices in product markets

The relative price level of goods and services depends to some extent on the level of competition in the corporate sector. Our first subgroup in the area of prices, Competition, contains variables that measure the degree of competition in a number of sectors in the economy, including the utility sector. Other variables measure the power of the competition authorities. Because of the importance of the ICT sector for other industries, these variables are put a separate subgroup: Competition in High-Tech. Separately, in the retail industry, we judge competition already to be sufficient. Hence in the subset, Economies of Scale, we favor larger retail outlets and longer opening hours that allow retailers to exploit economies of scale.

To gain an overall impression of policy strengths and weaknesses in each country, we have scored each variable. This allows us to "add up" the results across each area and subset. Accordingly, we have scored each variable on a scale of 0 to 10, with 10 being the maximum "best" score attained and 0 the "worst." Scores of between 1 and 4 represent below-average performers, and scores of 6 to 9 above-average performers. The scores are then ranked, with 1 the highest rank and 21 the lowest.

Health warning

Under this system, the scoring ranges generally reflect the variability of the data rather than a definitive judgment about a particular country's performance in one or more areas. Furthermore, in some areas our analysis contains value judgments about what constitute "good" and "bad" structural policies. We are implicitly assuming that we are right in these judgments, but acknowledge that we do not yet have all the requisite evidence. Different value judgments would, in places, result in different conclusions. Research projects currently being undertaken by Lehman Brothers' economists will help determine whether we are right or not. However, we are encouraged by our initial findings. We are also investigating whether some of our indicators are more important than others; this would, of course, lead us to weight some scores more highly than others when we come recompile our composite scores.

The structural league table

What is immediately clear from our turn-of-the-millennium snapshot is that the cross-country differences in the scale of these problems are considerable.

The United States tends to come out on top in any comparative study, and (as Figure 2 demonstrates) it certainly does in ours, finishing first in two of the three broad policy areas that we have surveyed (labor markets and prices). It also comes top but one in the third area (potential output), being beaten only narrowly to the post by Sweden.

Figure 2: Rankings from Lehman Structural Database

Rankings from LSD (1 = best, 21 = worst)

US 1	Ireland 8	Norway.................14
Canada................2	Finland 9	Germany...............15
New Zealand 3	Netherlands...........10	Belgium 16
UK 4	Denmark...............11	Spain....................17
Australia..............5	Europe* 11	Austria 18
Sweden................6	Japan...................12	Portugal................19
Switzerland..........7	France.................13	Italy 20
		Greece..................21

*GDP-weighted average of country scores

Rankings from LSD (1 = best, 6 = worst)

US 1
Canada.................2
New Zealand 3
Australia...............4
Europe*................5
Japan...................6

*GDP-weighted average of country scores

This overall result fits well with the extremely impressive US economic performance of the second half of 1990s. It is supported also by the fact that economists generally underpredicted US growth and overpredicted inflation over this period, implying that an improvement took place in the growth-inflation tradeoff. This in turn, of course, has important positive feedback effects for the mechanics of stabilization policy.

A GDP-weighted average of the individual euro area country rankings occupies a low 15th place out of the 21 countries assessed. A broader European average that includes the United Kingdom, Sweden, and Norway scores more highly than Japan, but still lags behind the United States, Canada, New Zealand, and Australia. Overall, European policies to increase potential growth are somewhat further behind best practice than those to promote product market competition or to reduce structural unemployment. Again, this fits with the fact that, although economists did a good job in forecasting growth on average during the second half of the 1990s, they tended to overpredict inflation.

Japan ranks a mediocre 12th in the individual country scores. Even after successive episodes of structural reform, its supply-side shortcomings remain many and various, but one problem predominates. The financial sector remains in need of radical surgery. What is more, Japan is let down by poor policies to promote product market competition, where it ranks a very low 17th. It is no great surprise, therefore, that when the asset price bubble burst in 1990, relative prices did not adjust quickly, causing resources to be misallocated and the economic pain to extend over the subsequent decade. In terms of real GDP growth, Japan was one of the worst-performing economies in the 1990s.

Financial market implications

It is also interesting to note that these indicators correlate reasonably well with stock market performance (Figure 3). The better the structural policy scores, the better the stock market performance. The next section looks at the evidence in more detail, region by region.[6]

Figure 3: Stock market performance and structural policies*

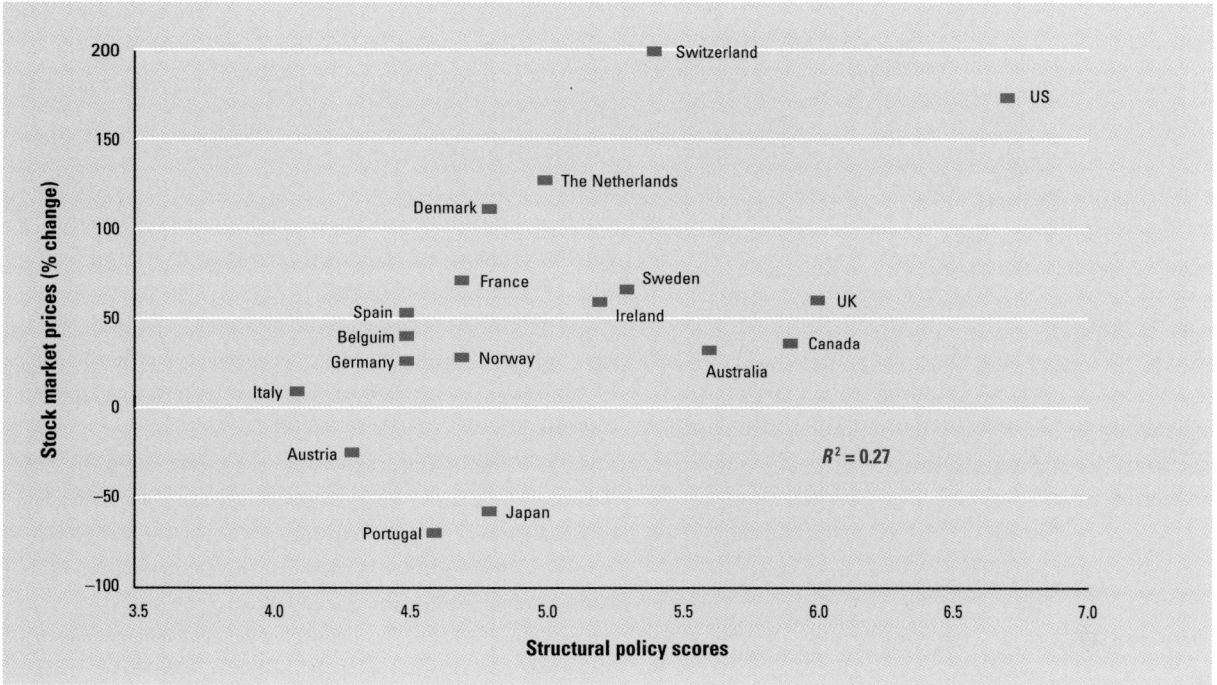

* Percent change in stock market prices between January 1990 and September 2002 in US dollars are shown on the vertical axis, against the scores across all variables in our dataset, with 10 the maximum score and 0 the minimum on the horizontal axis.

United States: simply the best

Summary

On the basis of our definitions of what constitute good structural policies, the United States had the fewest short-comings at the end of the 1990s: it came top in our aggregate scores based on all the variables in LSD (see Figure 4). Notwithstanding a burgeoning current account imbalance, this favorable structural backdrop contributed to a remarkable macroeconomic performance during the 1990s, especially during the second half of the decade. Annual real GDP growth averaged 3.2 percent, taking the unemployment rate down to just 4.2 percent in 1999—a rate not seen for 30 years. And although the labor market tightened throughout this period, core consumer price inflation fell to less than 3 percent in the mid 1990s, then to around 2.5 percent in the late 1990s—and has remained subdued ever since.

A flexible supply-side should stand the US economy in good stead to weather the prevailing downturn in demand. Productivity-enhancing technical advances, strong competition in its product markets, and a supple labor market should keep prices stable, and thereby allow the Federal Reserve to continue to cut interest rates further if necessary. Moreover, the Bush Administration has taken action in some key structural areas where US policies fall short: education spending and reform, tax cuts to reduce work disincentives for the low paid, personal bankruptcy, and, of course, corporate governance.

Nevertheless, there are numerous areas where there is room for improvement and, over the last 12 months, there have been some disturbing retrograde steps in the important areas of trade policy and agricultural subsidy. What is more, the war on terrorism and its attendant defense-related costs threaten to crowd out private-sector activity.

Potential output policies: nearly the best

In terms of our potential output variables, the United States was let down by its score for education and training and narrowly beaten to first place by Sweden (Figure 5). Indeed, education appears to be one of the very few areas where US policy and performance falls a long way behind best practice. To increase the productivity of low-income, low-skilled workers, the quality of education needs to be improved: youth unemployment rates are high relative to prime unemployment rates. In addition, surveys suggest that relatively few people train once they are employed. Part of the problem is that education has traditionally been the province of local governments. There is, for example, considerable variation in state government per-child spending—from $1,500 to $15,000. In response to these shortcomings, the federal government in the No Child Left Behind Act has boosted education spending and reformed the curriculum, teaching, and assessment

Figure 4: Impressive overall scores in all three categories: United States

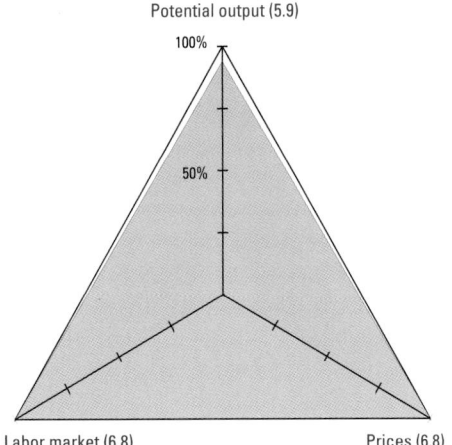

Note: We illustrate structural policy strengths and weaknesses by four "radar" diagrams. The first diagram (above) shows the aforementioned scores for each country in the three areas: potential growth, the labor market, and prices. The subsequent three diagrams show similar calculations for the 12 subsets, which make up the three separate areas. In each case, the shaded region shows the scores as a percentage of the best performing country in our sample (100% = best performer, 0% = worst performer, implying that the larger the shaded area, the better the structural policies).

Figure 5: Potential output scores: United States

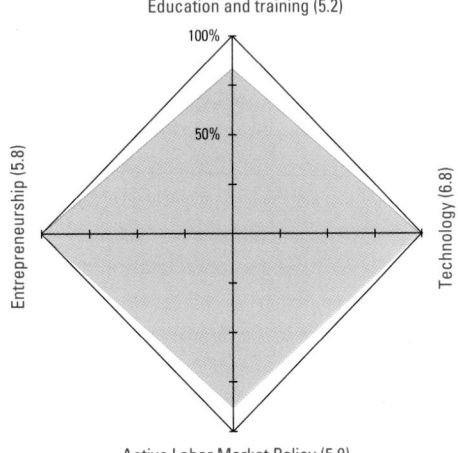

methods. However, greater efforts should be made to offer improved English-language training to immigrants.

Although booming economic conditions in the 1990s reduced the need for active labor market policies to retrain the unemployed, the United States scored very well in this subgroup, coming fourth overall. In 1998, the Workforce Investment Act overhauled and consolidated federal job training programs into state-administered block grants, giving adults individual training accounts. Some states have increased the finance available to move people off welfare and into training.

The United States scored well in terms of both the use made of technology and the production of high-tech goods, being beaten, by only the narrowest of margins, by Sweden.

The United States also came top in the subgroup that measured policies to encourage entrepreneurship, scoring particularly well where help for small businesses is concerned. Our indicators singled out the United States as a low-tax country, but the balance of income and corporate tax remains an issue. For example, the double taxation of dividends (at a combined rate as high as 62 percent in some states) introduces a large bias in favor of corporate bond financing, and this may have helped fuel the recent equity market bubble. The US tax system's shortcomings are sufficiently broad-based for the OECD to have called for a complete overhaul, centering on the lowering of capital gains and capital income taxes relative to consumer taxes and the reform of state and local sales taxes (the United States has no value added tax).

Finally, there are concerns that the positive incentive effects of low overall taxation could be undermined if this leaves the budget in persistent deficit. Large fiscal shortfalls run the risk of exerting sustained upward pressure on real interest rates and the cost of capital for the private sector.

Labor market policies: the best
Despite a sub-par score for policies affecting flexible working arrangements, the United States comes top in labor market policies as a whole, gaining the highest scores in the other three subgroups, and the government has already taken action in a number of areas to improve the tax and benefit systems (Figure 6). "Workfare"—a scheme requiring people to work in order to receive welfare payments—has been introduced in some states, and in-work benefits are paid to people with low family income.

Remaining poverty traps and work disincentives, caused by high personal income tax rates for the low-paid, should be alleviated in the United States by tax cuts this year (the bottom rate of tax will be cut to 10 percent, from 15 percent) and further adjustments will be made through 2006.

Figure 6: Labor market scores: United States

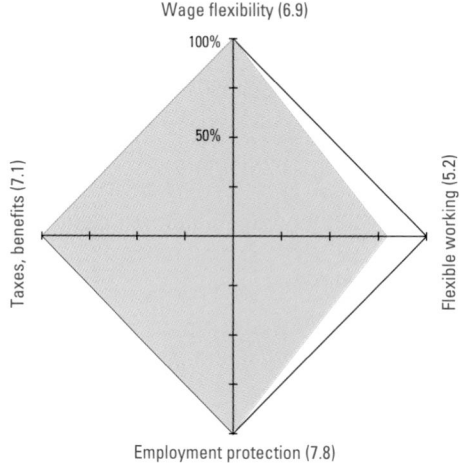

Wage flexibility (6.9)

Taxes, benefits (7.1)

Flexible working (5.2)

Employment protection (7.8)

Figure 7: Product market scores: United States

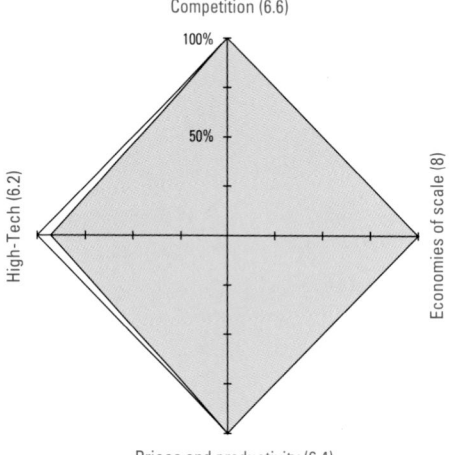

Competition (6.6)

High-Tech (6.2)

Economies of scale (8)

Prices and productivity (6.4)

Wage flexibility is high, and despite an increase in the minimum wage in 1997, it remains at a relatively low level, while employment protection is strictly limited. On the other hand, part-time working has been falling and the evidence on increased flexibility full-timers appears mixed. Until recently, the only observable flexibility in hours worked for full-timers was a persistent increase. What is more, there is limited access to health and child care, especially for low-income workers. In response to these problems, however, in 1998 Congress approved the Head Start Program to improve the availability of child-care services, especially for one-parent families.

Product market policies: the best
The United States also scores best in the area covering prices, which includes the subset of variables measuring competition (Figure 7). Many sectors of the economy—including transport, energy, telecoms, financial services, and increasingly IT—have been subject to federal pro-competition legislation by the antitrust authorities. However, more competition in the local telephone market is required, and there are infrastructure shortfalls in the electricity transmission and generation industries. Electricity markets in some states are not deregulated and, in California in particular, a move to real-time retail pricing is needed. Airport infrastructure, including the system of air traffic control, also needs to be upgraded. And as recent events have shown, the regulatory framework in the financial sector has not kept up with the rapid pace of change (see the section below on corporate governance).

In addition, in the last year or so, there has been some backpedaling in the areas of agricultural subsidy and trade protection. Recent financial support of the farmers had a strong political bias and needs to be wound back. But the most notable new protectionist measures have been the imposition of import tariffs to protect the steel and lumber industries. All of these measures are retrograde in terms of their effects on the economy, but the greater risk is that they lead other countries to take retaliatory measures, which would ultimately damage global growth. Recently, the European Union won its case in the WTO against US subsidies to export industries. Although this ruling strengthens the hand of the European Union in its dispute with the United States, it has chosen not to impose permitted sanctions yet—clear evidence that both sides, the United States and the European Union, want to avoid an escalation into a trade war.

Nailing down corporate governance
Our structural database does not systematically extend to indicators of financial market efficiency. However, clearly the depth and transparency of US capital markets has been an important determinant of US economic performance. Until recently, the US system of corporate governance was generally viewed as one of the best in the world. The scandals of the last year have tarnished that reputation and present a major structural challenge to the United States. Although it is early in the process, policymakers appear to have responded appropriately to the crisis, averting major structural damage to the economy.

Figure 8: S&P 500 and corporate scandals

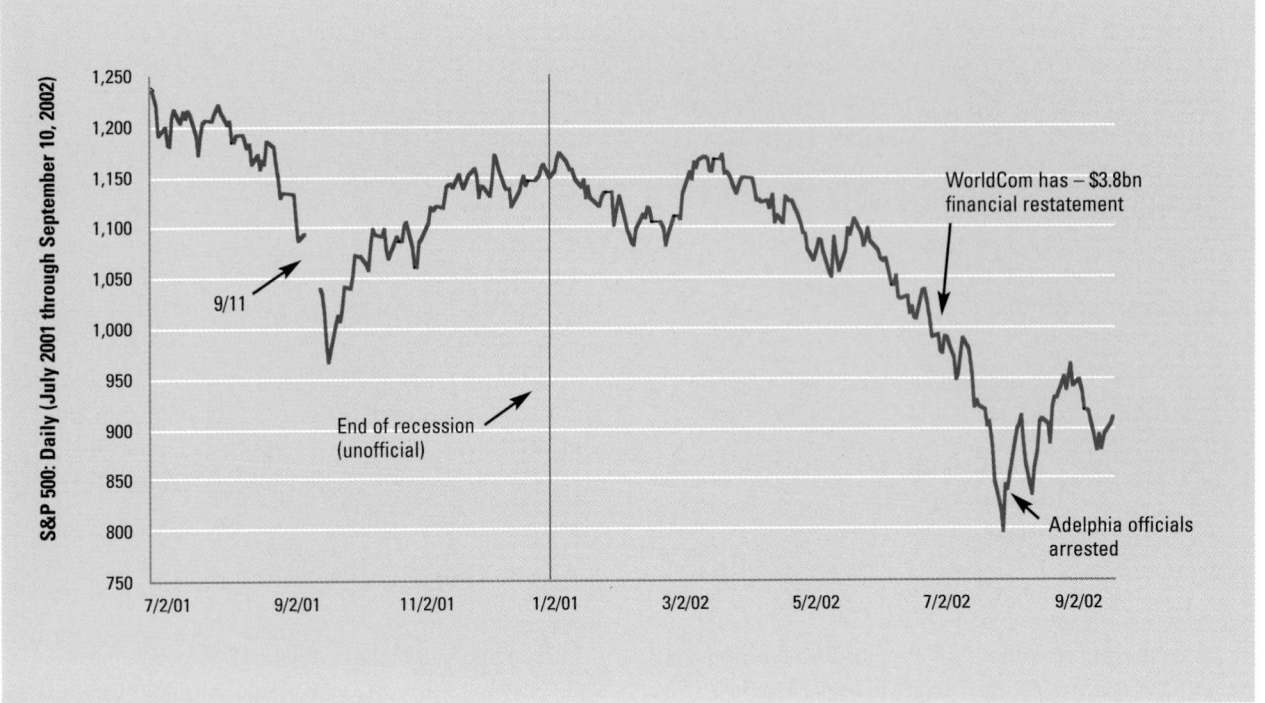

Corporate governance has become a catchall phrase in the press, but ultimately it comes down to one question: "How can outside investors be protected from insider expropriation?" A good system of corporate governance helps to overcome the inherent conflicts of interest that arise with the modern corporation, in which management and finance are separated. Managers have many opportunities to enrich themselves at the expense of shareholders. Effective governance requires a system of checks and balances, including independent auditors, independent boards of directors, and effective government regulators. The current crisis reflects a potent combination of two trends: (1) the tremendous incentive to cheat created by a record bull market, and (2) a successive weakening in the checks and balances in the system.

The stakes in resolving corporate governance issues are considerable. In the near term, the primary concern is the damage to aggregate demand. The Brookings Institution has tentatively estimated that the simple wealth effects of the recent corporate accounting scandals could take US$35 billion (0.34 percent) off US GDP over 12 months. Yet even bigger estimates are possible. It is not unreasonable to ascribe the entire 15 percent or so drop in the stock market this summer (Figure 8) to the corporate scandals, and this would have a negative wealth effect of over a percentage point. In the long term, the primary concern is the damage to the growth potential of the

economy: if investors distrust the corporations they give money to, the whole system of financial intermediation risks becoming inefficient.

Governance around the world

Ironically, before the recent crisis, a number of academic studies argued that the United States had one of the better systems of corporate governance. These studies asserted that the widely held firms in the United States tend to protect shareholders better than firms with concentrated ownership in families or governments, which are common outside the United States. Common-law countries such as the United States and the United Kingdom tend to have stronger securities laws—such as those relating to shareholder rights, the protection of minority shareholders, creditor rights, and legal and accounting quality—than do civil-law regimes, such as most of continental Europe. Fundamentally, this is because judges in common-law countries tend to interpret the law as circumstances change, whereas judges in civil-law countries are expected to stick more rigidly to the letter of the law. Crudely put, the issue is the difficulty for legislation alone to keep up with the new ways to circumvent corporate control.

Conflicted accountants

The decline in auditing quality has been the necessary condition for most other governance problems to fester and grow. Accounting always involves large gray areas of judgment, but three forces combined to weaken accounting standards in the 1990s. First, with executive pay tied to stock market performance, executives put considerable pressure on their accountants to cook the books. Second, accounting has long been a self-regulated industry, and regulatory oversight by the Securities and Exchange Commission (SEC) had become increasingly lax over the years. Third, the conflict of interest within accounting firms has grown as they have become increasingly involved in providing consulting services as well as audits. None of these problems is new, but all were accentuated in the 1990s.

In the boardroom

Along with quality auditing, corporate boards are a pivotal feature of the structure of quality governance. Securities law gives boards and directors a duty to the stockholder, with the responsibility of hiring and firing the most senior management and overseeing the most important decisions. The CEO therefore has a strong incentive to attempt to "capture" the board—to pack it full of friends who will be happy essentially to rubber-stamp management's choices. Hence, states and stock exchanges have various requirements on the sizes of boards, their various committees, degrees of independence, and so forth. It appears that in the late 1990s a number of boards did not provide effective, independent oversight.

Academic research shows that both the size and composition of boards are important. An effective board should have relatively few insiders and should be sufficiently small that each member takes "ownership" of the decisions of the overall board. More independent boards, without firm insiders, provide a more objective and less conflicted monitoring of management. Smaller boards also force each member to provide a more rigorous monitoring, rather than simply free riding on other board members to do the job. Research also shows that companies with smaller boards tend to have higher stock valuations; the evidence is more mixed on the importance of independent members.

At the top

Generating many of the news stories across both the business and front pages have been the tales of executive compensation in the United States. Executives appear to be enriching themselves at the expense of the firm's outside investors. Executive pay in the United States has changed quite dramatically over the past generation. In 1980, only 30 percent of CEOs of large firms received stock options. By 1994, that proportion rose to 70 percent, just in time

to take advantage of the extraordinary bull market of the late 1990s. The bulk of the increase in compensation came not from cash salaries and bonuses, but from the distribution of stock and stock options.[7] Moreover, with executives often receiving new and repriced options after a fall in the firm's stock price, the perception is that they have been rewarded for poor performance. Also, because CEO compensation is often decided through peer comparisons, the surge in pay for some more aggressive CEOs has pulled up the general level of pay.

From a macroeconomic perspective, the issue is not whether CEOs truly "deserve" the enormous sums of money that they receive, but rather whether the high pay is symptomatic of a more general erosion of oversight. The academic literature has generally found that firms with weaker corporate governance mechanisms tend to pay their CEOs more.[8] In particular, the United States appears to pay their CEOs a "wage premium" that does not exist in other countries, but only the very top executives in US companies enjoy that premium, not other employees.

Reform

Reforms that are forged hurriedly in the heat of political outrage do not always lead to the desired outcome. For example, it has been argued that anti-takeover sentiment after the 1980s led to legislation in some states that effectively killed off one of the more austere variants of corporate governance. Similarly, previous efforts to rein in executive pay have failed. The Omnibus Budget and Reconciliation Act (OBRA) of 1993 sought to reduce it by limiting the corporate tax deduction for compensation paid to the CEO and the next four highest-paid officers to $1 million each. However, OBRA contained exceptions for "performance-based" pay, and there is little evidence that the cap restrained executive compensation.

Fortunately, the most recent reforms appear to be more or less on target. The major legislative reform, the Sarbanes-Oxley Act of July 30, 2002, focused on accounting issues. The Act established an oversight board for accountants, which will have the authority to set accounting standards, investigate possible infractions with subpoena power, and impose civil sanctions. The board will be responsible for the direct monitoring of the behavior and results of accounting firms—moves are already afoot for firms to deduct the value of stock options from their bottom lines every three months. Moreover, the conflicts of interest prevalent among accounting firms will be mitigated, as they will no longer be permitted to provide the consulting services. A mandatory rotation of lead and coordinating auditors every five years (as has long been the case in Germany, for example) is designed to reduce the incentive to provide continually soft, non-rigorous audits in the hope of continuing to win business, although there are concerns that it takes time (perhaps a number of years) for an auditor to learn enough about some larger companies to do a thorough audit. This measure still leaves open the possibility of auditors colluding to continue past practices, however.

Internally, companies will now have to have an auditing committee that is responsible for hiring, compensating, and overseeing their selected accountants. Attorneys, who have often been accused of being complicit both with auditors and with corporations to provide legal cover for shoddy financial statements, will now be obligated to report lawbreaking within a company to either the firm's chief counsel or its CEO, and follow up with further reports if there is no "appropriate" response. The upshot is that accountants will no longer be essentially self-regulating, but rather will have to answer to the oversight board.

Sarbanes-Oxley also established a number of provisions more directly related to corporate governance, including faster filing of financial reports and of disclosure of trading by insiders, and an end to special personal loans to insiders. The Act further mandated stronger criminal penalties for fraud, obstruction of justice, destruction of evidence, and the requirement of forfeiture of unwarranted profits by CEOs and CFOs.

Finally, funding for the SEC has been greatly increased to enable it to play a more active role in monitoring the overall system. The SEC has already called for the CEOs and CFOs of the largest publicly held US companies to verify their 2001 annual statements, and under the Act this is now required for every future quarterly and annual report filed with the SEC. The SEC will also frame new rules regarding the independence of securities analysts.

It is far too early to make any definitive judgment about the seriousness, from an economic performance standpoint, of the recent bout of corporate malfeasance. It is similarly too soon to judge the likely efficacy of the Sarbanes-Oxley Act. That said, our tentative conclusions are that:

- Important though the recent corporate governance episodes have been in a number of respects, they are unlikely materially to harm US macroeconomic performance over the longer term.

- We see the provisions of Sarbanes-Oxley as founded on an essentially correct analysis both of the causes of the problem and the likely consequences of the Act itself being in force. As hurried legislation goes, this is probably one of the better examples.

Europe: well behind best practice but closing the gap

Summary

Structural policies in Europe lagged behind those in the United States at the end of the 1990s (see Figure 9). But European performance was diverse. If Germany and Italy generally scored poorly, France did not do much better, and the lower positions in our structural league tables were typically occupied by European economies. The United Kingdom was a consistent high scorer, however, and other economies scored well in particular areas. For example, in addition to Sweden's coming in on top in policies to promote potential growth, the other Nordic countries, too, do well in this area. Some of the smaller European economies, including the Netherlands, Ireland, and Switzerland, were among the leaders in areas such as education and training, and workplace flexibility.

There is evidence that unemployment in European countries with relatively good structural policies rises less and persists less long when the economy is hit by a shock than is the case in countries with poor structural policies.

Figure 9: Mediocre at best; poor at worst: Europe

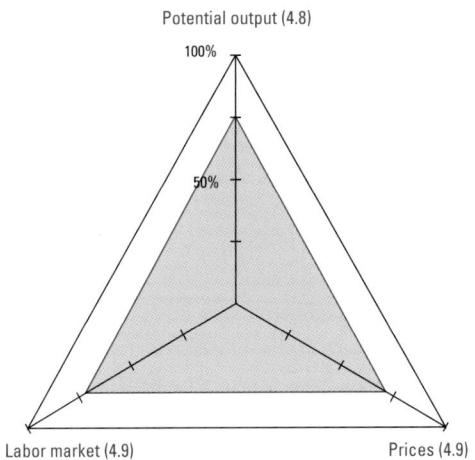

Note: We illustrate structural policy strengths and weaknesses by four "radar" diagrams. The first diagram (above) shows the aforementioned scores for each country in the three areas: potential growth, the labor market, and prices. The subsequent three diagrams show similar calculations for the 12 subsets, which make up the three separate areas. In each case, the shaded region shows the scores as a percentage of the best-performing country in our sample (100% = best performer, 0% = worst performer, implying that the larger the shaded area, the better the structural policies).

Figure 10: Cumulated private-sector employment growth since 1970

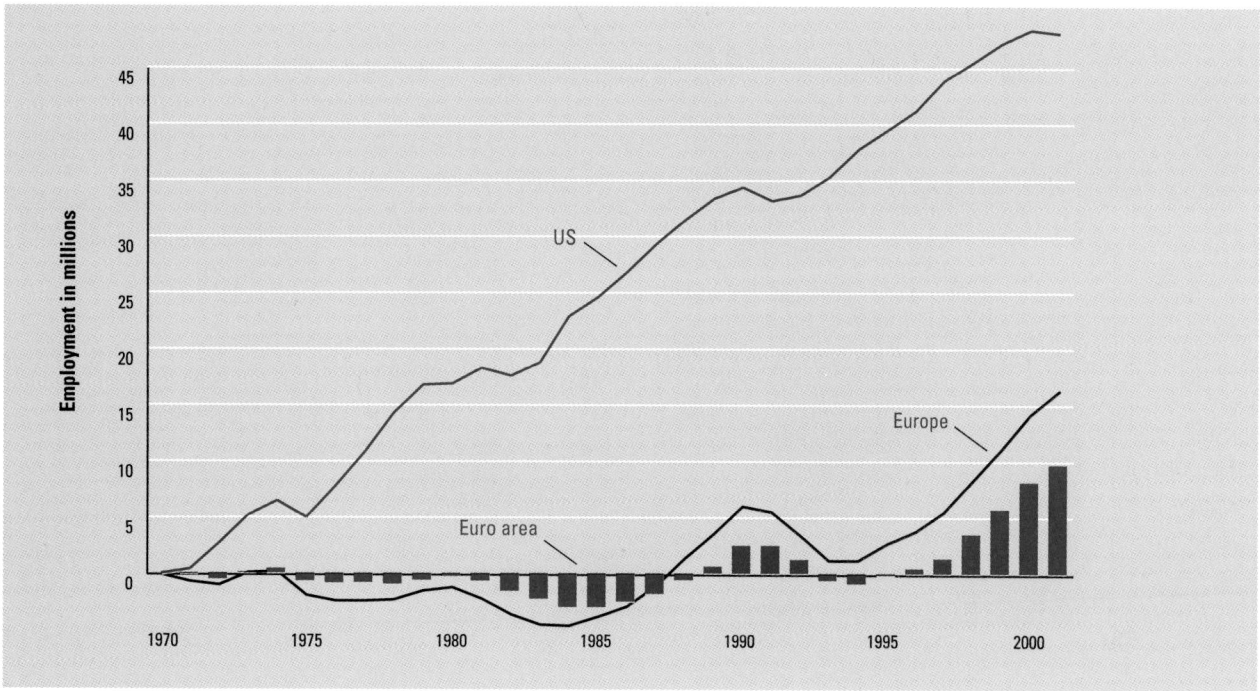

Note: European data adjusted for German reunification.
Source: OECD and Lehman Brothers

A GDP-weighted average of the individual euro area country rankings occupies a low 15th place out of the 21 countries. But a broader European average that includes the United Kingdom, Sweden, and Norway would score more highly than Japan, even if it still lagged the United States, Canada, New Zealand, and Australia. However presented, Europe's structural performance is less than satisfactory, and this was mirrored in the unspectacular economic growth, poor growth of private sector employment (Figure 10), and consistently high unemployment of the 1990s.

Europe has been making progress, however. The gap between Europe and the United States has been narrowing, albeit more slowly than hoped over the last year or so. After a long period of stagnation, private-sector employment has begun to pick up (Figures 11 and 12). There is general agreement that the number of areas where structural policy needs improvement has declined significantly since the early 1990s, and there is a widespread acceptance among European policymakers that the positive momentum of reform needs to be maintained if the European Union (and Europe generally) is to compete satisfactorily with its major trading partners. Indeed, European struc-

tural policy initiatives have become progressively more ambitious over the years. The Lisbon Special European Council on Employment, Economic Reform and Social Cohesion of March 2000 set the strategic goal of making the EU "the most competitive and dynamic knowledge-based economy in the world, capable of sustainable economic growth, with more and better social cohesion." Heads of government ostensibly took personal responsibility for an associated timetabled plan covering a broad range of areas, although thus far their rhetoric has been more impressive than their ability to deliver policy change.

One particular concern is that structural reforms in the largest countries in the euro zone are lagging behind those in some of the smaller countries, as well as the United Kingdom and Sweden. In Italy, poor policies to promote potential growth and competition in product markets cause Italy to have nearly the lowest score in our sample of 21 countries. Only Greece ranks below it. Germany is on a par with the euro area as a whole, pulled down by shortcomings in the same areas as in Italy. France, which scores quite well in policies to support potential output, scores better than Germany, Italy, and the euro area as a whole.

Figure 11: Structural policy scores in Europe

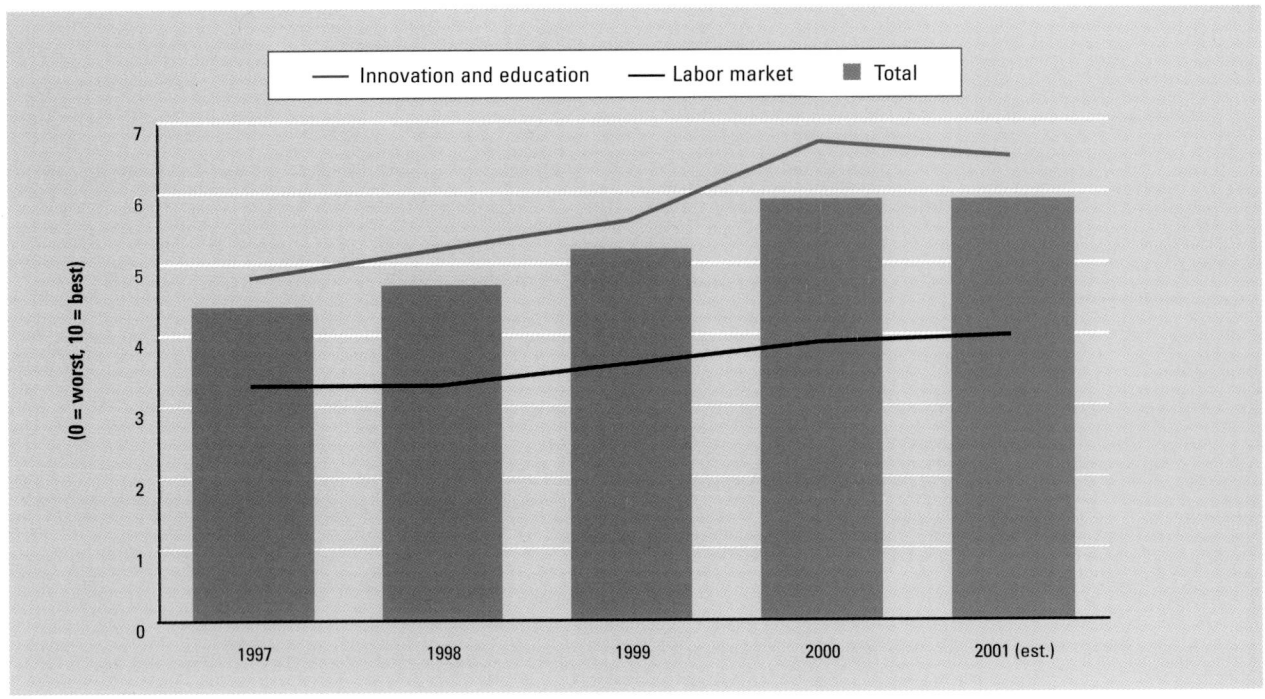

Note: Scores are based on a number of structural indicators selected by Lehman Brothers from those published by the European Commission. Changes are relative to the position in 1997.

Figure 12: Structural policy scores in Germany, France, Italy, and the United Kingdom

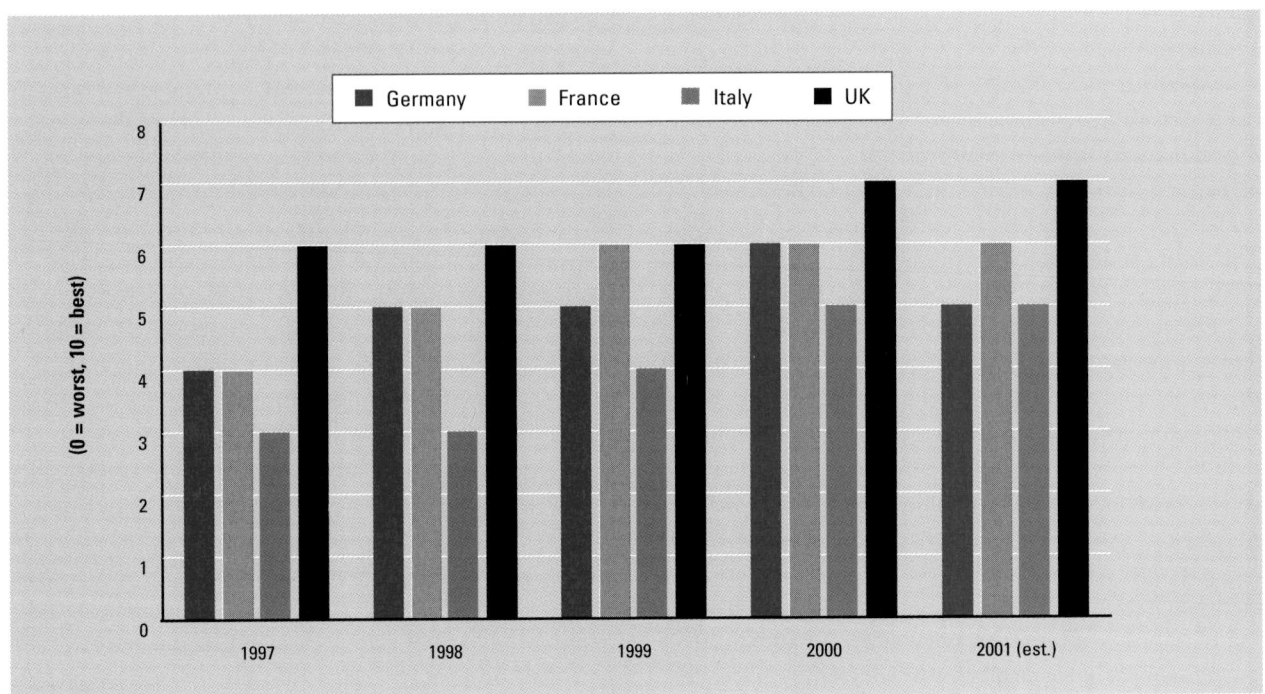

Note: Scores are based on a number of structural indicators selected by Lehman Brothers from those published by the European Commission. Changes are relative to the position in 1997.

Potential output policies: unsatisfactory

Across the three broad policy areas covered, euro area policies to increase potential output are somewhat further behind best practice than policies to reduce the natural rate of unemployment or to promote competition in product markets (Figure 13), although the scores in all three categories are very disappointing. By contrast, the United Kingdom scores quite highly (ranked sixth) and Sweden is first.

Policies to promote entrepreneurship and the application of new technologies are the main areas where the euro area falls short in terms of policies to raise potential output, although active labor market policies (ALMPs) also leave much to be desired. High tax rates and administrative burdens, especially for small companies, stifle entrepreneurship and, with the exception of Finland and Ireland, European countries generally fall short in the production of new technologies. But more importantly, there is a much bigger gap in terms of utilization of new technologies. In contrast, in education and training, the gap with best practice is much less pronounced, although shortages of ICT, science, and engineering specialists endure. In this area, the Nordic economies (rather than the that of the United States) lead the field.

Labor market policies: hints of flexibility to come?

Labor markets in Europe (Figure 14) are still characterized by restrictive employment protection legislation, high taxes on labor, relatively generous benefit systems (particularly regarding the duration of unemployment benefits) and limited wage flexibility. However, the United Kingdom is a positive exception to the general rule: the introduction of more flexible working contracts and practices over the 1990s has caused the gap with the best-performing systems to close and even reverse, and recent and programmed tax cuts aimed at indirect wage costs and on the incomes of the lower paid, even if modest, should pay further dividends.

The euro area's labor participation ratio is around eight percentage points lower than in the United States, while long-term unemployment is around six times higher, indicating that particularly strong efforts need to be made to develop the necessary employment skills and incentives to work. Some countries have seen a significant rise in female participation in the labor force, but progress vis-à-vis the elderly has been negligible. Although there has been some progress in some countries, many benefit systems, including eligibility criteria, enforcement of availability requirements, and the duration of payments, still require a major overhaul.

Figure 13: Potential output scores: Europe

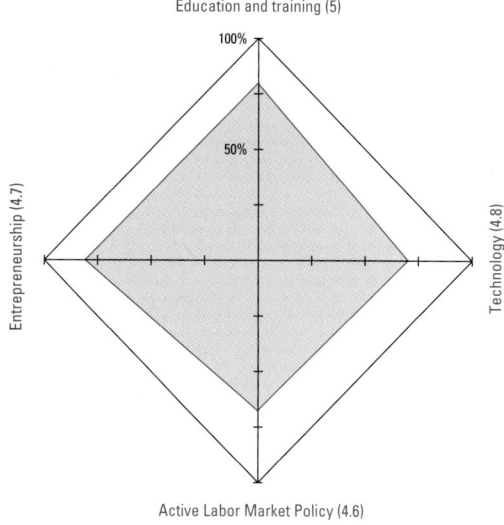

Figure 14: Labor market scores: Europe

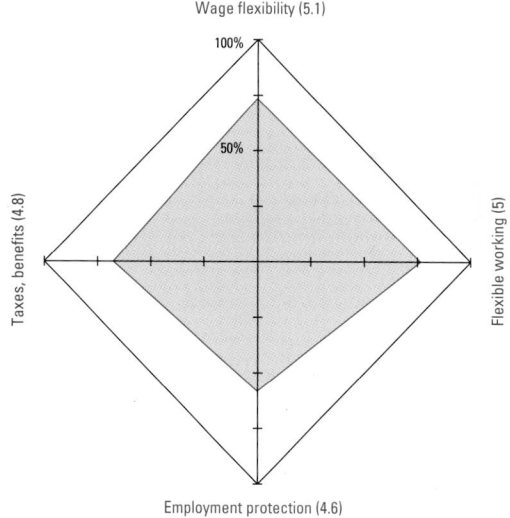

Product market policies: plenty of room for improvement
European product markets still have more regulation and are less open to competition than is the case elsewhere (Figure 15), particularly in the industries that were former state monopolies, such as utilities, transport (rail and air), and postal services. Overall single market effects have thus far been disappointing, but progress has been made in privatizing and introducing competition into the telecommunications industry, and prices have fallen as a result. In this area too, the United Kingdom stands out as the star performer within Europe.

Reforms in product markets need to be speeded up, especially with respect to liberalization and promotion of stronger competition in network industries (telecommunications, energy, and transportation) as well as in a significant number of service sectors. Other required reforms include increasing the transparency and efficiency of public procurement and services and reducing the backlog of implementation of legislation. Several countries also still have much to do in terms of strengthening their competition authorities.

Growing European labor market flexibility
Of all the areas of structural policy in which the euro area lags behind best practice, that which stands out most is labor market flexibility. Certainly our Lehman Structural Database (LSD) confirms this, according much of continental Europe a poor structural score in respect of these policies.

That finding probably surprises few people. After all, many studies have suggested that the inflexibility of the labor market is the fundamental reason why much of the continent has suffered from such high unemployment for so long. What people find more surprising is that our recent research suggests that, notwithstanding its starting out way behind best practice—the United States and the United Kingdom being the two principal exemplars of this—the euro area now appears to be catching up, and quite quickly.

In addition to measuring what has been happening with policy, we have also been undertaking more fundamental research in order to see which of the many structural policies stand the best chance of improving labor market performance.

Figure 15: Product market scores: Europe

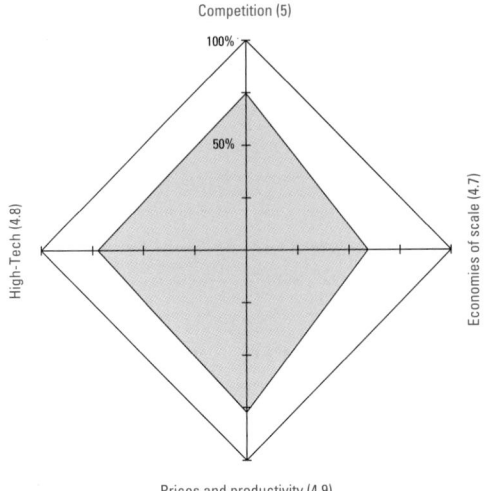

Of shocks and structural factors
The basic idea that shapes our research in this area of crucial importance to Europe is that what drives unemployment—beyond the short-term cyclical influences—is a combination of shocks and structural (or, as some people prefer to call them, "institutional") factors. By a *shock* we mean something such as a big change in oil prices, as occurred in 1973–74 and 1978–79; by a *structural factor* we mean things such as tax rates or unemployment benefit levels.

The theory behind this empirical work has a medical analogy. Shocks might be thought of as akin to viruses, which people occasionally catch regardless of their health. (In that sense, they can be characterized as exogenous processes that arrive, from a victim's perspective, randomly, and against which people can do little or nothing to protect themselves). However, the consequences of catching a virus differ from person to person, depending in part on how fit each person is. That level of fitness can be influenced by, say, diet and/or exercise. So, a given virus may have different impacts on different people.

In much the same way, a "fit" economy is one with good structural policies, whereas an "unfit" one has poor policies. So, a negative shock—such as the big jump in oil prices in the early 1970s (and the resultant drop in total factor productivity)—may have had a much longer-lasting impact in "unfit" Europe than it did in the "fit" United States. Recent empirical research by Blanchard and Wolfers[9] has used this sort of model to explain shifts in structural (ie, non-cyclical) unemployment—examining the record from the early 1960s through to the mid 1990s across 20-odd OECD countries.

The shocks that apparently matter particularly, in the sense that they appear to play a significant role (in statistical terms) in driving unemployment, are:

Total factor productivity (TFP), that is, that component of growth that cannot be accounted for in terms of increased inputs to the production process, and that must therefore be due to increased efficiency of these inputs (or increased productivity of the factors of production). The United States enjoyed a better TFP performance during the 1990s than in the previous two decades (Figure 16). The euro area, by contrast, experienced a marked deterioration (Figure 17).

The cost of capital, that is, real long-term interest rates. These rates rose smartly during the early 1980s, worldwide, as policymakers began to bear down on inflation by hiking short-term rates.

Shifts in labor demand—proxied by looking at shifts in the labor (or nonprofit) share of GDP. In effect, this comprises wages and salaries, so it represents that proportion of income that ends up in households' pockets. The labor share has been fairly stable in the United States and the United Kingdom—fluctuating a little with the cycle. But, in the euro area, it rose during the 1970s, before dropping back during the second half of the 1980s and right through the 1990s.

Theory suggests that fast TFP growth, low interest rates, and a falling labor share are all good for employment. Our empirical work, like that carried out by Blanchard and Wolfers, accords with theory.

As regards structural policies, the sorts of factors that research has found to be particularly important are:

Taxes and benefits. Three measures in particular help to account for unemployment: the tax wedge (ie, the total tax rate—comprising income taxes, payroll taxes, and consumption tax); the replacement ratio (ie, the rate of unemployment benefit measured against the average wage for someone in work), and benefit duration (ie, the length of period over which unemployment benefits are paid).

Active Labor Market Policies, that is, spending on programs to help the unemployed get back to work.

Union "power". This is usually measured either in the form of union density (the proportion of the workforce that are union members) or union coverage (the proportion of the workforce that are affected by pay deals struck by unions).

Union-employer coordination. The institutional framework used to set wages and terms of working conditions certainly affects unemployment. At one extreme, the United States and the United Kingdom systems are highly "atomistic." At the other, countries such as Sweden and Denmark have highly centralized systems for wage bargaining and settlement.

Theory suggests that high tax rates, generous benefit systems, and strong unions all raise the structural level of unemployment, while high spending on ALMPs can ameliorate the effects of these factors somewhat. The empirical evidence supports such a contention. As regards the bargaining system, however, theory is less clear. In practice, it appears that countries with highly centralized systems for bargaining have generally enjoyed lower unemployment than those without, ceteris paribus.

Our own work adds a role for part-time working and the use of temporary contracts in affecting labor market flexibility, finding that the effects of changing these variables can be quite strong. Differentiating between the roles of part-time work and temporary contracts, and for that matter between their impact and the impact of Employment Protection Legislation, turns out to be quite hard. All three variables are strongly correlated with one another. However, in an econometric horse race, part-time working and temporary contracts come out just ahead.

Europe is catching up
Part-time work and temporary contracts matter rather a lot when it comes to assessing how Europe's structural policies in this area have changed over time—the "time variation" issue. For it turns out that having been, 20 years ago, a long way behind the United States in terms of the proportion of workers who are part-timers, the euro area has since the mid-1990s actually overtaken the United States (Figure 18). Moreover, the pattern appears to be common to all of the euro area's big four economies (Figure 19).

Our econometric work also suggests that the combination of a falling labor share and improved structural policies means that the euro area is, at last, starting to catch up with best practice, as regards the "natural rate of unemployment." One mechanism by which this is taking place is a decline in union density.

This decline, it seems, helps to explain why, in a statistical sense, the labor share is falling (Figure 20). Of course, it may be that there is another ultimate driver of both processes. For example, the rise in the service sector share of total output may be the driving factor. A second mechanism is the trend in part-time working and temporary contracts.

Our present best guess is that the euro area NAWRU might now be as low as 8 percent, and still falling. (Note that it was above 10 percent as recently as five years ago.) If this is so, it compares favorably with what others have been suggesting. (The OECD, for example, in its recent Economic Survey of the euro area, showed estimates from the European Commission, the IMF, and the OECD averaging 8.25 percent.)

Figure 16: Total factor productivity in the United States

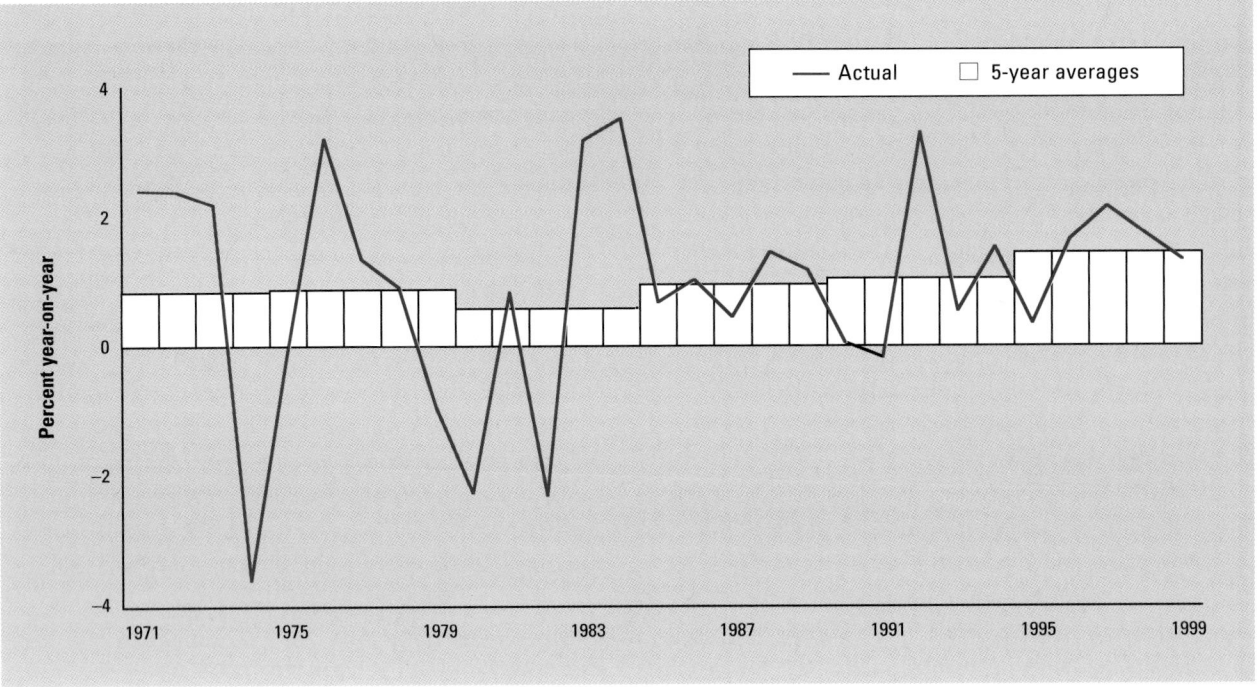

Figure 17: Total factor productivity in the euro area

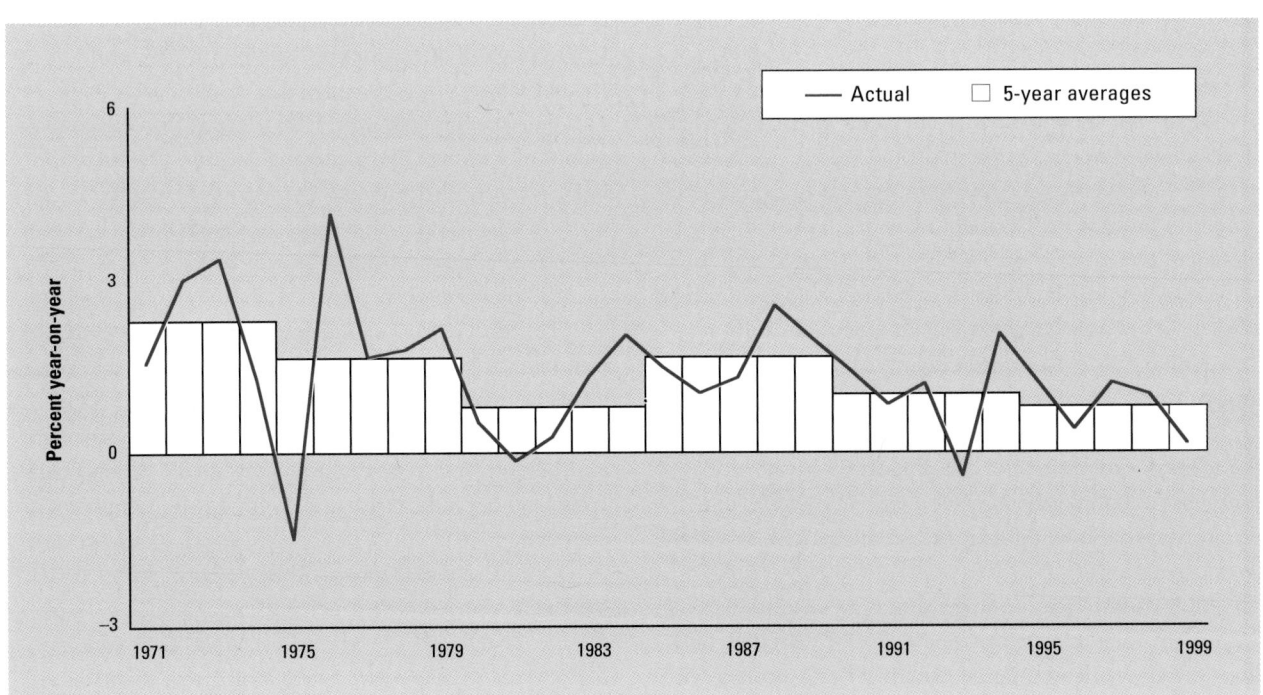

Figure 18: Part-time work: United States and euro area compared

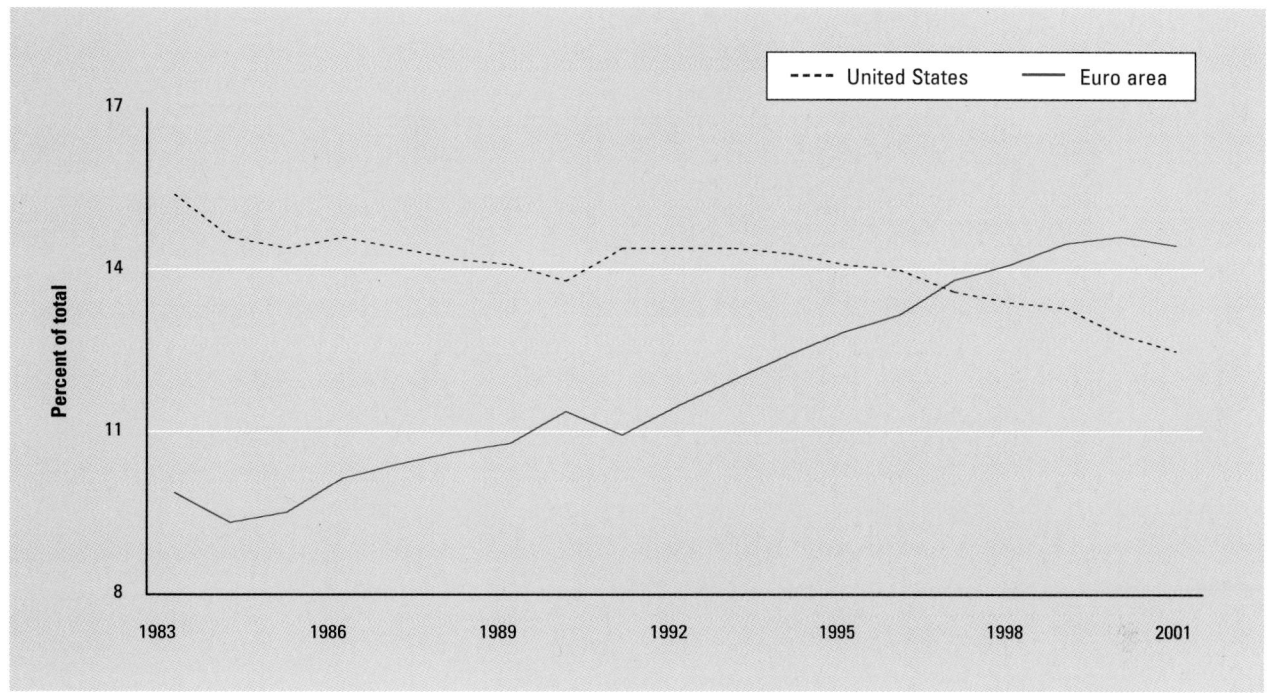

Figure 19: Part-time work: Germany, France, Italy, and Spain

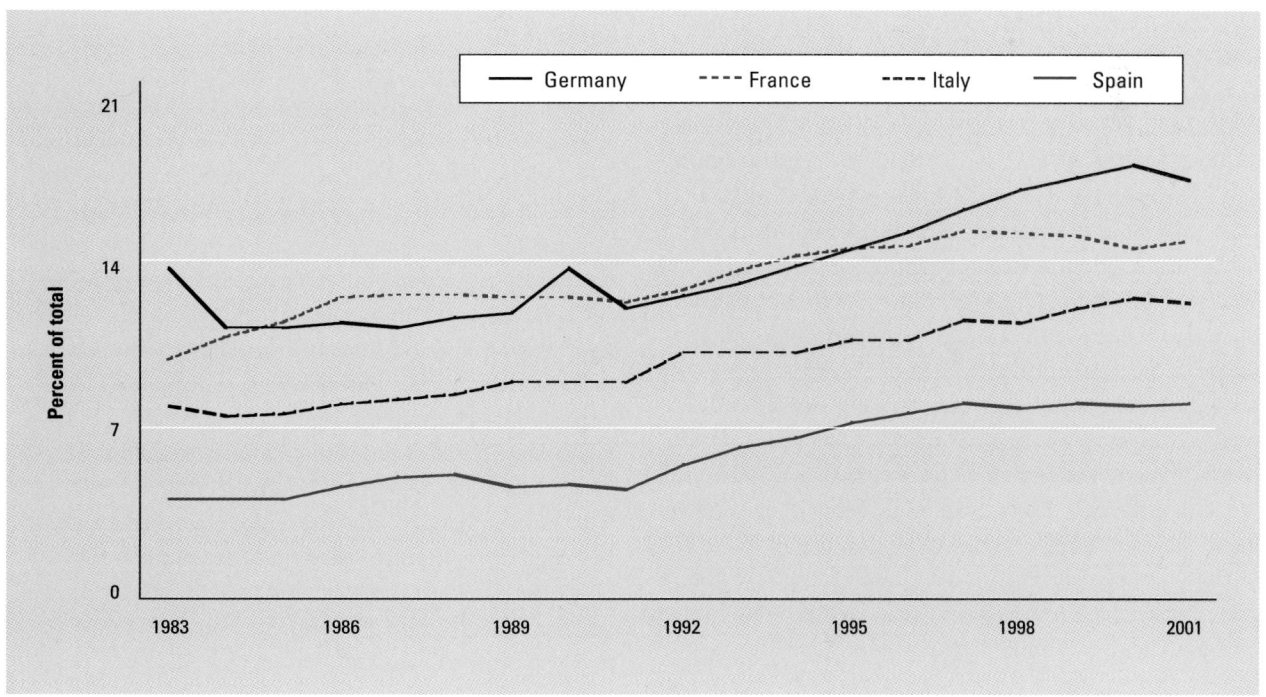

Figure 20: Labor share and union density

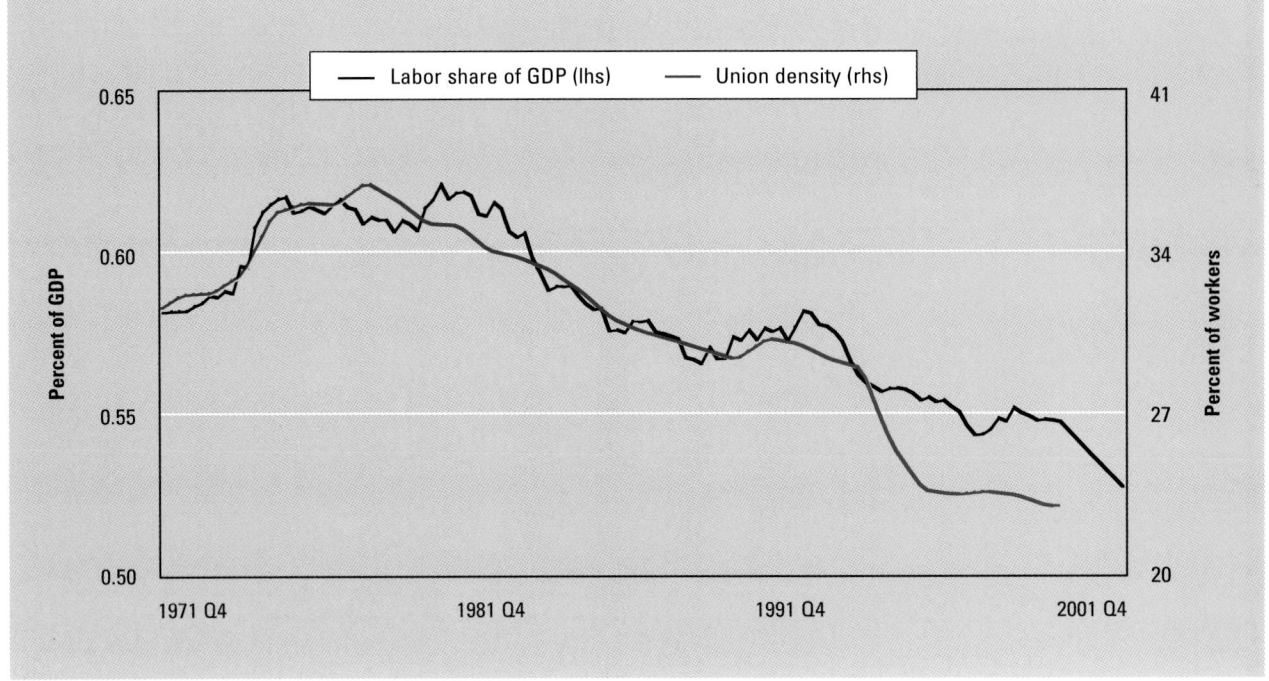

But the ECB remains cautious

All this matters because the ECB stands out as having a very hawkish view on this matter. Their own model suggests that the rate of unemployment required to stop wage growth from accelerating—the non–accelerating wage rate of unemployment (NAWRU)—is more like 8.75 percent. So, the ECB may well judge that, with the actual unemployment rate now down to 8.3 percent—that is, below what they think the "natural" rate is—a marked and protracted acceleration in wage growth is on the cards. If, however—as we consider is the case—the true NAWRU is close to 8 percent and falling, then, apart from a bit of payback—because inflation turned out higher than when wage deals were struck two years ago and workers now want recompense—wages are unlikely to show any significant acceleration over the next year or two.

Using the ECB's own Area-Wide Model, and adjusting it allow for what we judge to be the "true" NAWRU of close to 8 percent, we find that the ECB is likely to be overestimating the required level of interest rates (to hit its inflation target) by about 50 basis points (Figure 21).

Japan: the slow pace of reform has hindered restructuring

Summary

In terms of output, Japan was one of the worst-performing OECD economies in the 1990s—average annual GDP growth was just 1.3 percent over the decade 1990–99 (see Figure 22). The bursting of the asset-price bubble in 1990 and the subsequent collateral damage inflicted on the banking sector and credit creation process was largely responsible, but poor macroeconomic policy and a reluctance to implement structural and labor market reforms were also to blame. Policymakers have pursued financial deregulation, but successive governments have been slow to clean up the banking system, taking the important decision to use public money to help solve banks' balance sheet problems only in 1998, and then with little enthusiasm. More recently, policymakers have launched new efforts to speed up the resolution of the nonperforming loan problem, but there is little evidence yet that this represents a fundamental break with the failed policy approach of the past.

Figure 21: The NAWRU

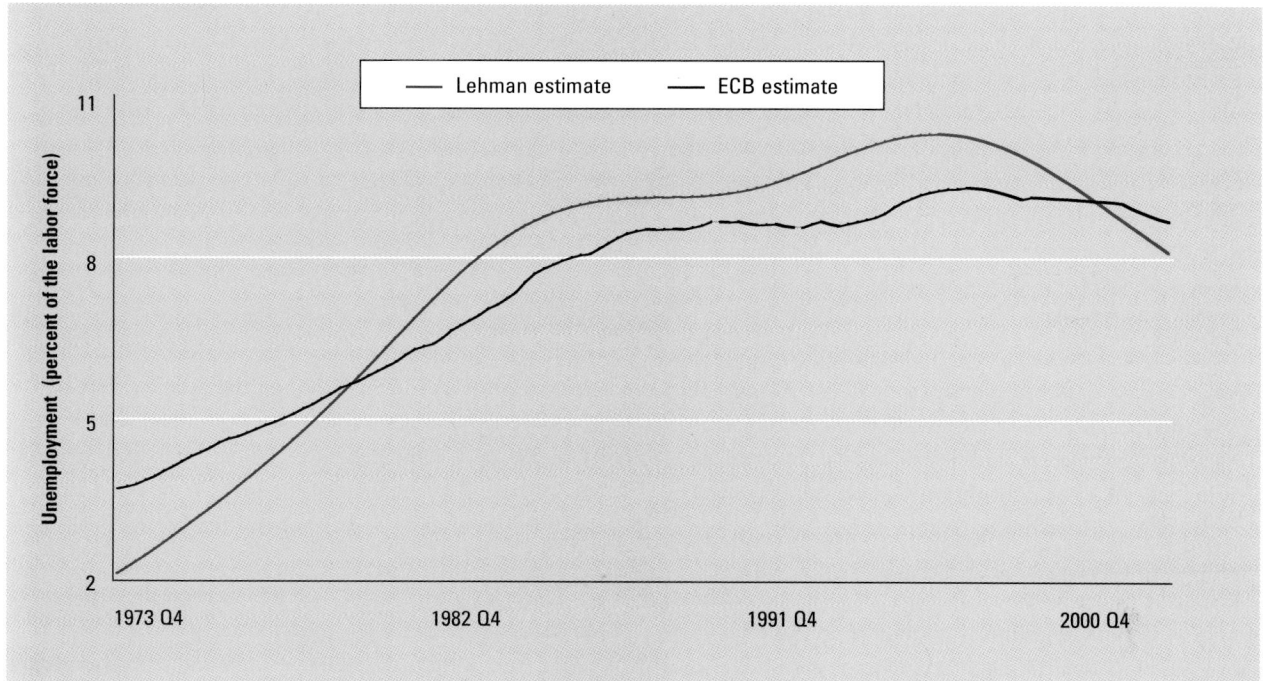

Our analysis suggests that, apart from the failure of financial sector policies, a major problem was the lack of competition in the markets for goods and services, which prevented relative prices from adjusting. This in turn caused a misallocation of resources. In addition, the practice of offering lifetime employment resulted in an inflexible labor market and led to high levels of "hidden" unemployment. Government decision-making also needs reform—something that has only just begun.

Instead of biting the bullet with thoroughgoing structural policy reform, in the past the government responded with multiple (and increasingly ineffective) fiscal support packages, which have caused government debt to rise to the highest level (as a proportion of GDP) in the OECD, supported by successive monetary easing culminating in an extended period of 0 interest rates. On the positive side, the workforce is well educated and excels in the production of high-tech goods. Belatedly, in response to the protracted downturn, the government is enacting a plethora of structural reforms, including measures in the area of pensions, information technology, and the public sector.

Figure 22: Japan: structural shortcomings all too obvious

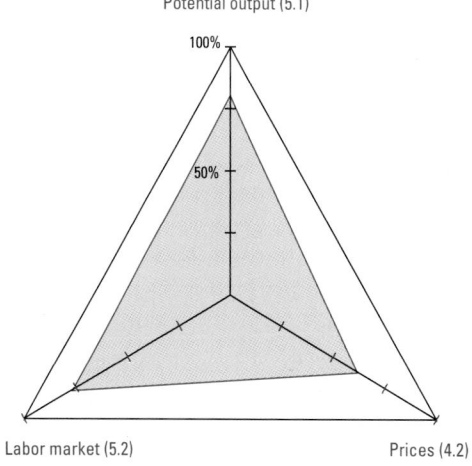

Potential output policies: above average, behind the leaders
Japan scores quite well (Figure 23) in terms of education and training (although this assessment is based on fewer variables than for other countries) as well as in active labor market policies. Pupil-teacher ratios are low, and this results in a good achievement record. An efficient system places graduates with companies which, together with the "lifetime" employment system and in-work training, has resulted in low unemployment. However, slow growth in the 1990s and corporate restructuring put the lifetime employment system under pressure for change.

Continued business sector reforms, which aim to increase competition and raise profitability, will probably result in a further rise in unemployment. Accordingly, the government has started to emphasize the importance of improving labor market mobility rather than subsidizing existing jobs. Recent reforms in the financial sector, to increase competition and to dispose of bad loans, have resulted in a decline in relationship-based lending and a greater role for open capital markets. In turn, the *keiretsu* system of corporate groups is starting to break down. However, there are still major problems in the life insurance industry, which remains underfunded.

Japan's entrepreneurship score is poor. Restructuring has been hindered by regulation and hopes that fiscal stimulus would lead to a recovery. However, more demanding capital markets and an expanded set of corporate restructuring tools should lead to increased restructuring and M&A activity. In the past several years, legislation has been introduced to allow holding companies, share buybacks, stock options, stock swaps, and corporate dissolutions. Accounting rules, bankruptcy laws, and tax incentives have also been improved. Although corporate tax rates have been cut and are now just above average, the taxation of corporate debt, land, property, and inheritance remains distortionary.

Separately, Japan's score for technology combines a high score for production of high-tech goods with a low score for usage, although usage is increasing rapidly, encouraged by policy.

Labor market policies: lifetime employment under pressure
Japan does not score well in the area of labor market policies (Figure 24). The pressure to reform Japan's lifetime employment system increased when growth slowed. Firms were forced to emphasize profitability rather than market share, but tough employment protection laws and the desire to provide lifelong employment have inhibited restructuring. A reduction in bonuses, which make up around a third of salary, helped, but did not solve the problem of insufficient labor flexibility. The government has responded by introducing employment subsidies and reducing restrictions on temporary work agencies and job placement firms.

Japan scores well on taxes and benefits: marginal tax rates are low—encouraging people to work—while the VAT rate is the lowest among OECD countries. However, the personal tax base is narrow and the unemployment benefit system needs revising in order to encourage greater labor market mobility. Given future demographic trends (a particularly rapidly aging population structure), the tax burden would appear to be unsustainably low and a major rebalancing in favor of taxes on consumption is required.

Product market policies: a lack of competition
Japan also scores poorly in the area of product market competition (Figure 25). Although the public sector has been slimmed down and the system of public works tendering has been reformed, government intervention remains pervasive. Reform of the giant Trust Fund Bureau and Fiscal Investment Loan Program has begun, but it is proceeding at a snail's pace.

Little privatization has taken place, and there is a reluctance to liberalize the agricultural and construction sectors. Agricultural subsidies are high and many goods are effectively protected from foreign competition. Cartels remain widespread, partly because the Fair Trade Commission lacks teeth. The retail sector is still dominated by a few manufacturers. The result is higher prices than in Japan's major competitors.

The keystone: financial sector reform
Probably all of the above areas of structural policy will need to be reformed if Japan is again to become one of the best-performing countries in today's world. But the single, most critical, structural issue for policymakers in Japan to get right, and the one that they have finally started to focus on, is fixing the banks.

In our judgment, an economy of Japan's size, in which the banking system is so dominant, cannot possibly attain its medium- and longer-term growth potential while the banking system remains overloaded with non-performing loans, and while financial stability is maintained because of implicit or explicit government guarantees on bank liabilities rather than by virtue of the strength of balance sheets and the discipline of markets.

Figure 23: Potential output scores: Japan

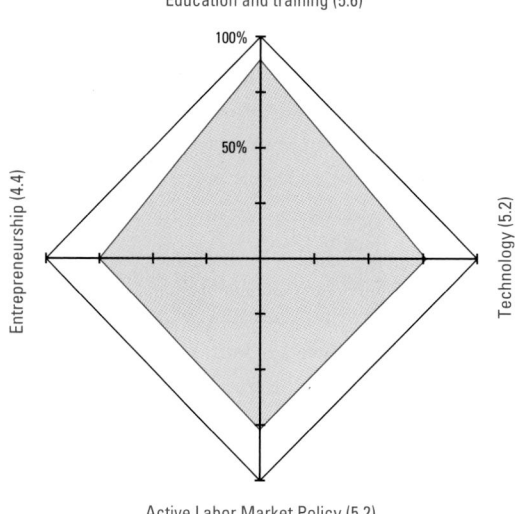

Figure 24: Labor market scores: Japan

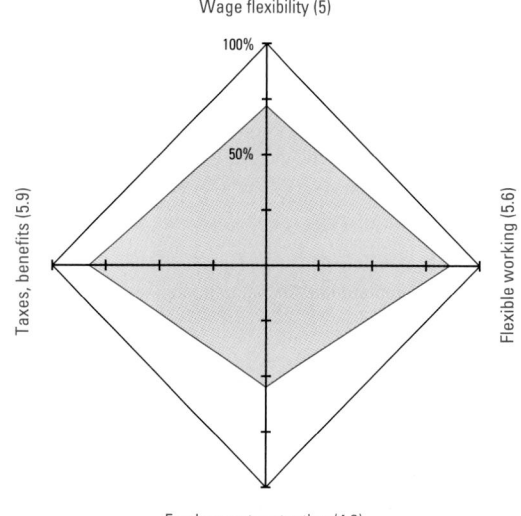

Figure 25: Product market scores: Japan

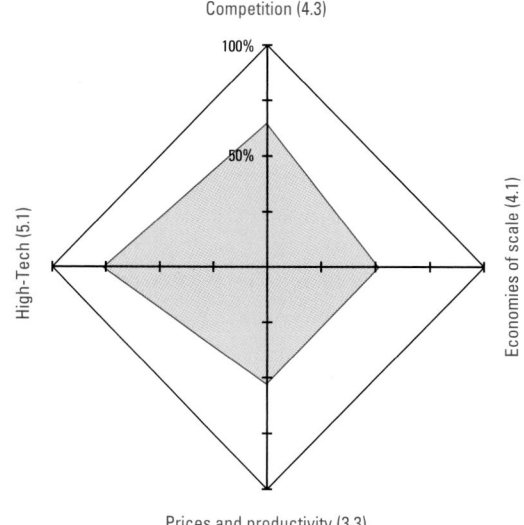

The banking system sits between the household sector and the corporate sector, and its state of health impacts both. On the household sector side, there is a need for households to diversify their portfolios of financial assets away from a strong bias towards bank deposits and cash, and this has been an aim of policy in recent years. By so doing, the household sector can start to play a greater role in supplying risk money and in supporting, as a supplier of funds, the development of a more sophisticated and diversified financial system. However, as long as the banking system remains sick, the government has to continue to intervene to maintain stability and this distorts household portfolio choices.

The counterparts to the banking system's nonperforming assets are, of course, the corporate sector's liabilities. It follows that delay in resolving the banks' assets means that corporate balance sheet restructuring is delayed too, and along with it much needed organizational and operational restructuring. This makes for a less efficient and dynamic economy all round. And the banking system in Japan plays a critical role not just in supplying funds to the corporate sector to finance asset ownership and new investment, but also as the main locus of corporate governance. As long as the banks remain sick, corporate governance remains seriously impaired.

93

A mountain of a problem

The latest official figures (for the end of FY2001) show that, 13 years after the 1980s asset bubble began to diminish, the level of nonperforming loans (NPLs) in Japan has never been higher (Figure 26). Some 8.8 percent of all bank loans are classified as nonperforming, and the figure rises to 14.2 percent if doubtful (category II special mention) loans are included.

True, banks have written off (or accumulated reserves against) large amounts of NPLs: a cumulative ¥81.5 trillion in the past 10 years. This is equivalent to 16 percent of total bank lending outstanding at the start of the period, and accounts for a similar proportion of GDP. But new NPLs have been accumulated at an even faster rate—a total of ¥89.8 trillion over the past nine years—as previously unrecognized NPLs have been disclosed and ongoing asset deflation and three recessions have caused good loans to turn sour. Asset deflation is the key culprit: urban commercial land prices—the collateral behind much lending—have fallen continually since September 1990, to a level now just 15 percent of that inflated peak (Figure 27).

It is easy to get lost in the detail of the Japanese bank workout, a saga that has dragged on for years and that has generated endless debate. We consider, however, that the issues involved, and their potential solutions, are relatively straightforward, even if their handling by policymakers has been anything but. The seriousness of Japan's current banking system problem reflects two things. First, the original cause—a huge asset bubble of the 1980s, the bursting of which in the 1990s severely damaged bank balance sheets; and second, despite its largesse elsewhere, an extreme reluctance of the government in the past to use fiscal resources to deal with the problem. The first explains where the problem came from, the second why it is still present.

Policy failure

The current banking system problems in Japan, and the related deflationary stagnation of the economy, stem largely from a failure of policy, which itself may reflect a lack of political will. In the past decade, policymakers in Japan appeared to have three goals: to implement reforms, to maintain financial stability, and to minimize the use of fiscal resources to clean up the banking system. Given the damage done to bank balance sheets by the bursting of the asset bubble, these three goals are mutually incompatible. The government has been able to secure financial stability by maintaining a guarantee on bank deposits, but this "socialization" of financial risk has delayed the banking system workout and slowed reform.

The aversion of the government either to allow financial disruption to play a role in the workout process or to dedicate fiscal resources to the cleanup of balance sheets leaves forbearance as the default policy option. The continued use of government guarantees to shore up the system becomes the principal instrument for implementing that policy.

However, forbearance has not worked. When the government, in mid 1995, realized that it had a systemic problem on its hands, it averted a collapse of the banking system by announcing a blanket guarantee on all deposits. About half the deposits in the system by total amount were below ¥10 million per depositor, and these "small-lot deposits" carried a deposit insurance guarantee. The significance of the June 1995 policy decision was to extend the deposit insurance guarantee to "large-lot depositors," those having ¥10 million or more on deposit at an institution. Given the latent losses generated on the asset side of bank balance sheets by the collapse of the bubble, and the rational expectation that losses would continue to mount, had the government treated large-lot depositors according to their legal status at the time—as unsecured creditors of banks—there can be little doubt that runs on banks would have ensued—they did in some cases even with the guarantee—which likely would have turned into
a run on the system as a whole.

By guaranteeing all deposits, the government was able to buy time to deal with the underlying problems. But that did nothing to solve those problems. The guarantee merely converted risky paper claims on rapidly depreciating underlying real estate assets into (contingent) government bonds, in effect nationalizing the deposit base. Having won a reprieve on the liability side of their balance sheets, banks could slowly turn their attention to dealing with the problems on the asset side—so the thinking went.

Figure 26: Bank nonperforming loans in Japan

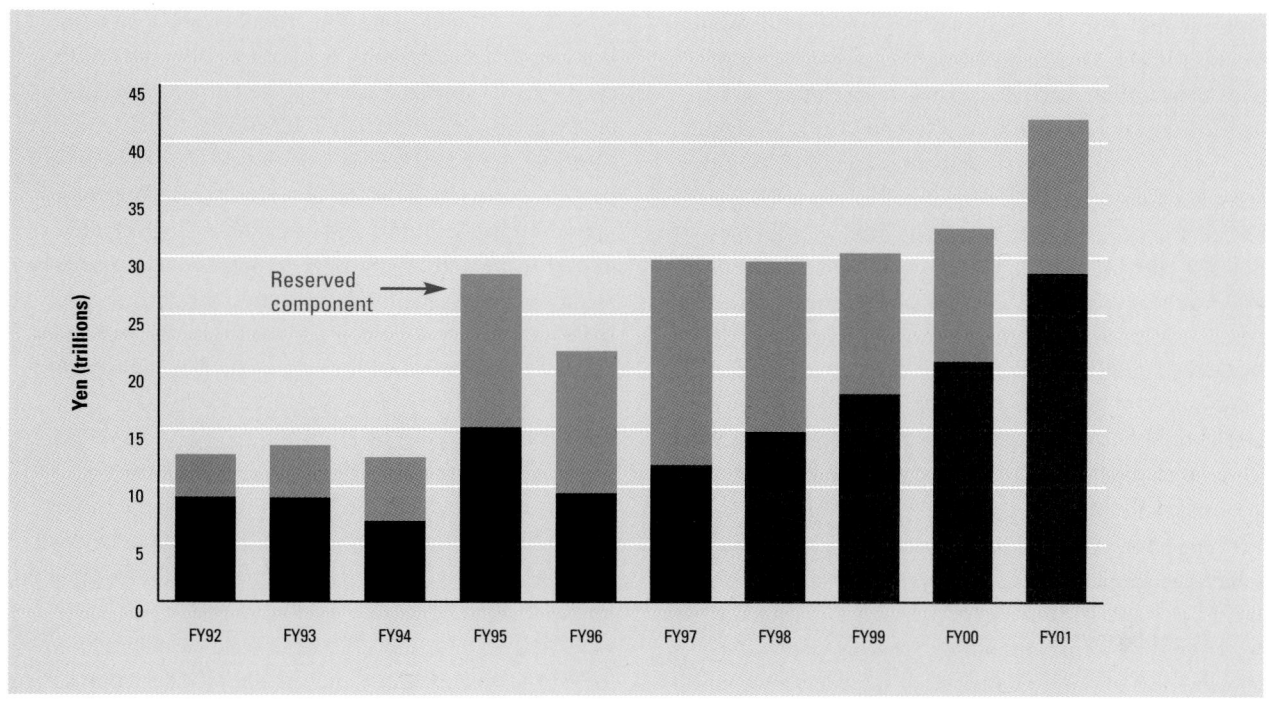

Figure 27: Japan's commercial real estate bubble

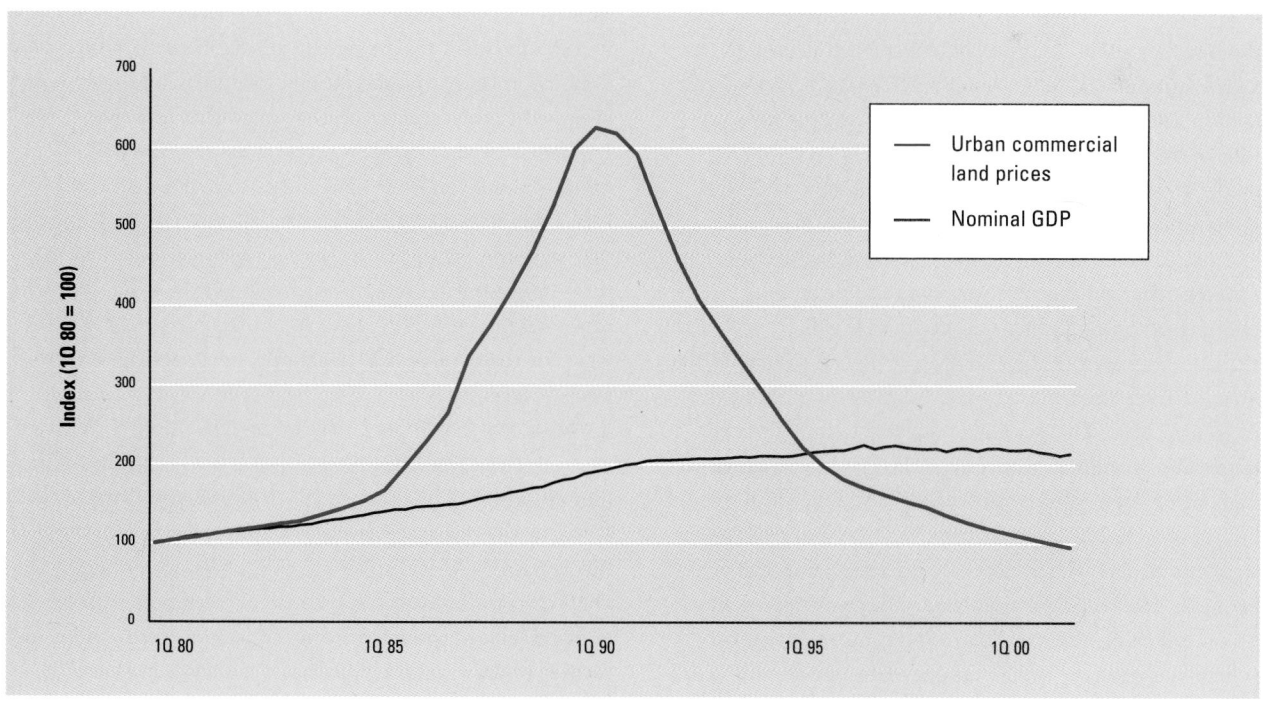

Too little, too late

At the time, policymakers underestimated the scale of the problem and were oblivious to the opportunity costs in terms of lost dynamism and foregone growth associated with their forbearance policy. They believed that, by raising deposit insurance premiums sevenfold and by giving the banks five years to deal with their asset problems, the bank workout could be accomplished without the government itself needing to spend any money. From day one, the Japanese banking system workout has been predicated on two principles: taking as much time as necessary and being self-financing, unless sticking to that policy threatened a full-fledged crisis. Only in 1998, after the November 1997 surprise failures of a "big-four" broker and a city bank shook confidence, did the government put in place a proper workout infrastructure and back it with a promise of up to ¥60 trillion of public funds.

Even here the government exhibited its extreme reluctance to spend public money. Despite the government's characterizing the 1998 policy as involving the injection of ¥60 trillion into the banking system, and allowing this notion to obtain wide currency, it was nothing of the sort. ¥60 trillion was the total amount of guarantees that the government authorized the Deposit Insurance Corporation (DIC) to tap in order to raise funds for its various workout accounts to disburse. Given that all deposits were already guaranteed, the ¥60 trillion merely attached numbers to the problem. Up to ¥60 trillion was to be available in a worst-case scenario, but this did not mean that the government spent this money: the actual amount ended up being much smaller, around ¥25 trillion. Much of that was injected into the banking system on the premise that the funds would later be recovered, the assumption being that the guarantee from the government would never need to be called in.

Meanwhile, at the end of December 1999, the government decided that five years would not be long enough, notwithstanding that up to ¥60 trillion was now available to expedite the workout. It moved to extend the guarantee on large-lot deposits, due to expire at the end of March 2001. The extension was to be done in two stages: the guarantee on large-lot time deposits (about 40 percent of large-lot deposits) would continue until the end of March 2002, and that on large-lot demand deposits until the end of March 2003. At the same time, the government enacted legislation to introduce a permanent "financial crisis response" framework, one element of which was to grant it the authority, through the DIC, to fully guarantee deposits in a failed or threatened institution, should that be deemed necessary in order to maintain financial stability. In effect, this legislation converted what had been a limited-term explicit guarantee into a permanent optional one.

In the event, the first stage of the reimposition of a cap on deposit insurance, predictably, triggered a huge shift in deposits from large-lot time to other deposits, mainly large-lot demand deposits, the latter swelling by 53 percent year-on-year to reach ¥150 trillion (30 percent of GDP) by the end of March 2002. Ahead of the scheduled expiry of the guarantee on large-lot demand deposits at the end of March 2003, the government, facing strong pressure from within its ranks to extend the guarantee, moved at the end of July 2002 to open up a loophole by retaining a permanent guarantee on some categories of large-lot demand deposits—accounts used for settlement purposes and individual 0-interest-rate demand deposits.

Moving the goal posts

A significant part of the 1998 workout infrastructure expired at the end of March 2001, most notably the capital injections framework for banks. The collapse in stock prices leading up to this point, particularly the collapse in the bank stock index to a level substantially below the peak attained after the 1999 large-scale recapitalization, forced the government to unveil a new policy approach to the bank workout in April 2001.

The centerpiece was a pledge by the prime minister "to aim for a final resolution in the NPL problem within two to three years." However, it soon transpired that this announcement represented only a shift in rhetoric rather than a substantive break with the favored forbearance approach of the past.

Rather than follow up the announcement with a new initiative to inject public money into the banking system to expedite the cleanup on the suggested time frame, the government was forced to reveal what it really had in mind—to take another seven years to bring the ratio of NPLs down to a reasonable level. Specifically, in August of that year, the Financial Services Agency presented to the prime minister its "image" for resolving the NPL problem: this envisaged the NPL ratio for major banks going sideways for three years (FY01–03), dropping to the 3.5 to 4 percent level by March 2005, and then steadily coming down to the 2 to 3 percent level by March 2008. Without any retraction, the commitment to a "two- to three-year final resolution" had turned into a seven-year workout scenario, the policy preference for forbearance winning out yet again. As if this backtracking was not enough, the first year of the seven has seen the NPL ratio, far from going sideways, shoot up from 5.7 percent to 8.7 percent, further undermining credibility in policymakers and in the policy framework. At this rate, the resolution of a banking problem that has its origins in the 1980s seemed likely to drag on until the end of this decade.

The costs to Japan of not getting structural policy in this area right are potentially very high. We do not consider that Japan can attain a sustainable economic recovery without having a healthy and well-functioning banking system as the cornerstone of an increasingly market-oriented financial system. The government's own prognosis appears to concede this point. It has billed the current two years (FY02–03) as a "period of concentrated adjustment" in which banking, corporate, and other reforms are expedited. Recognizing the short-term dislocation involved, the government expects growth in these two years to be "in the vicinity of zero," but argues that, as long as the reforms are implemented, from FY2004 it will be possible to overcome deflation and attain stable real GDP growth of around 1.5 percent.

On the other hand, the government warns that, should reforms not be implemented, the economy will grow at an average of only 0.5 percent over the remainder of the decade. And more: should this prolonged economic stagnation shake confidence in the bond market and lead to a spike in government bond yields, growth could average close to 0. The failure by the government to take policy actions consistent with its own rhetoric risks pushing the economy down this path of long-term stagnation.

Anatomy of a slow workout

The government's plan (introduced in April 2001) to resolve the problem contained a number of elements: a step-by-step removal of the guarantee, tougher inspections, time limits on keeping NPLs on balance sheet, more active use of the government asset management company (the Resolution and Collection Corporation), and a well-articulated deposit insurance framework with abundant government guarantees on which to draw. However, each of these has its flaws, and all are part of an approach predicated on a slow, rather than a rapid, workout.

Removing the government guarantee on large-lot deposits increases market pressure on all parties, and needs to happen as part of a resolution of the banking system problems. However, the sequencing is key: rolling back the guarantee is something that follows from having solved the problems rather than being the solution itself. Given that the government is committed to avoiding a financial crisis, the only way credibly to remove the guarantee is to first restore confidence in the banking system by having solved the underlying problems. This the government has singularly failed to do.

Tougher inspections are welcome, but the "toughness" of the inspections and disclosure requirements in Japan to date has always seemed to be carefully calibrated not to allow too much bad news out too quickly. The "special inspections," incorporating market signals about creditworthiness of borrowers, the results of which were announced in April 2002, are the most recent case in point. The inspections led to 58 percent of the bank lending to the targeted borrowers being downgraded, but the inspections covered only 2.8 percent of total bank lending, or about 6 percent if the flow-on effect to other lenders to the same borrowers is included. The market is left to wonder: if the 6 percent turned out to be so bad, what about the other 94 percent, even granted that the average quality of those loans is likely to be much better?

A key element of the April 2001 initiative was the introduction of the "three-year rule": banks would have to dispose of existing loans in the at-risk-of-bankruptcy category or worse within two years (by the end of March 2003), and would have three years to dispose of any new NPLs that entered this category. The three-year rule was tightened up in April 2002, to require banks in principle to dispose of half of any new at-risk loans within a year, and 80 percent within two years, the balance by the end of the third year. The problem with this approach is that three years is too long, and it is on a rolling basis, the three years starting each time that a new wave of NPLs is recognized. Indeed, it is precisely this rule that lies behind the current scenario envisioning the resolution stretching out to March 2008.

A related key element of the approach so far has been the upgrading of the role of the Resolution and Collection Corporation (RCC). The role of the RCC has evolved, but until recently its principal role was as the vehicle for liquidating the distressed assets of failed institutions. When the 1998 framework was put in place, the RCC was given the ability to purchase NPLs from viable institutions, but it had to do so at a discount to market rates. Effectively this meant that the RCC could buy NPLs only when it was the sole bidder. Consequently, the RCC purchased only a few loans during the two-and-a-half-year life of this scheme (¥1.1 trillion in book value), and this at a very heavy discount to book (96.4 percent). In late 2001, legislation was enacted to allow the RCC to purchase NPLs from viable institutions at market value. This improved matters. In the first half of 2002, the RCC purchased NPLs at an 80 percent higher (annualized) rate than under the earlier rules, and at a smaller average discount (90.0 percent).

A number of problems remain, however. The scale of planned purchases (in the low trillions of yen) is still far too limited relative to the size of the total problem (in the several tens of trillions). Because of the aversion to incurring secondary losses, the RCC's incentives are skewed toward warehousing loans rather than disposing of them rapidly; the RCC cannot purchase NPLs above market value and certainly not at book value (adjusted for reserves) and therefore, as currently constituted, lacks the wherewithal to "bail out" the banking system in a truly effective way.

The RCC is a wholly owned corporate subsidiary of the Deposit Insurance Corporation (DIC). As a result of the 1998 and subsequent initiatives, the DIC has a number of accounts that are earmarked and funded to fulfill various functions relating to the protection of depositors and cleanup of the banking system, financing the RCC being just one. In FY02, the DIC is authorized to borrow up to ¥70 trillion for these purposes, of which some ¥21 trillion is already accounted for. Thus the infrastructure and funding would appear to exist now to deal with the banking system problems in a resolute and rapid manner.

The problems are twofold. First, as a workout framework, the DIC is reactive (the emphasis being on measures to protect depositors in failed or threatened institutions) rather than proactive (in the sense of seeking to remove the underlying source of erosion of asset values and confidence). Second, although adequately funded, the political allergy to using public funds to "bail out the banks" creates an inherent bias toward minimizing the use of public funds, rather than maximizing the effective use of them. The two features complement: if the intent is to avoid injecting public money, better to design a reactive system in the hope that the existence of the system itself is enough to prevent a crisis.

Light at the end of the tunnel
Recently, however, there have been some new positive developments. First, the Bank of Japan put pressure on the government by announcing that it would take the unprecedented step of buying equities held by banks as a measure to help stabilize the financial system and would conduct a "comprehensive review of the nonperforming loan problem." Then, Prime Minister Junichiro Koizumi sent a strong signal that he has finally decided to move the reality of the NPL workout closer to the rhetoric by appointing Economic and Fiscal Policy Minister Heizo Takenaka as the Financial Service Agency (FSA) Minister, replacing Hakuo Yanagisawa. In contrast to Mr Yanagisawa, Mr Takenaka has long argued for the use of public funds to restore the health of the banking system. In a further positive move, Mr Takenaka appointed high profile critics of the FSA's past policy position as members of a task force created to tackle the NPL issue. The government

also announced its intention to keep the guarantee on large-lot demand deposits in place for another two years (until April 2005), after which time the government intends to fully guarantee zero-interest accounts for corporations and individuals. While this is a disappointing back-down, it does serve to bring the timetable for the withdrawal of the guarantee in line with the new policy goal of "bringing an end to the NPL problem by FY2004."

It is to be hoped that these developments signal that policymakers have learnt the lessons from their past mistakes and the workout is entering a new phase of accelerated and coordinated action by the government and the central bank.

Notes

This paper was very much a team effort. Jane Edwards was responsible for much of the cross-country analysis; John Shin provided the detail on corporate governance; and major contributions were made by Lehman Brothers' regional chief economists: Ethan Harris (US), Michael Dicks (Europe), and Paul Sheard (Asia). The final draft was assembled and edited by John Llewellyn (Global Chief Economist, Lehman Brothers) and Russell Jones (Chief International Economist, Lehman Brothers).

1 The paper draws on research carried out by the Lehman Brothers Global Economics team, under the general direction of John Llewellyn, over the past eight years. In particular, Michael Dicks wrote a seminal paper on the ways in which structural policy change can be expected to change macroeconomic performance. A bibliography containing Lehman Brothers' principal writings on structural policies and performance, together with other key related works, is provided in the selected bibliography at the end of this chapter.

2 For a summary of the (generally positive) effects of fine-tuning, see Llewellyn, Samuelson, and Potter (1985), Part II, pp 121–187, and the references cited therein.

3 See, for example, European Commission (2002).

4 Full details can be found in Edwards and Schanz (2001b).

5 It could be argued that ALMPs belong in the NAWRU category rather than the potential growth category. The bottom line is that the categorization system that we have employed is very much an imprecise science.

6 Further details, especially of the relative structural performance of individual European countries can be found in Edwards and Schanz (2001b).

7 See Hall and Liebman (1998).

8 Murphy (1999) and Bebchuk, Fried, and Walker (2001).

9 See particularly Blanchard and Wolfers (2000).

References

In addition to the specific references in the text, the following publications, and the references contained therein, provide a wealth of information on structural policies and their effects on macroeconomic performance.

Ashenfelter, O. and D. Card, eds. 1999. *Handbook of Labor Economics*, Volume 3. North Holland.

Bebchuk, L., J. Fried, and D. Walker. 2001 "Executive Compensation in America: Optimal Contracting or Extraction in Rents?" NBER Working Paper No. 8661. Cambridge, MA: National Bureau of Economic Research.

Blanchard, O. and J. Wolfers. 2000. "The Role of Shocks and Institutions in the Rise of European Unemployment: The Aggregate Evidence," *Economic Journal* 110 (March):

Dicks, M. 2000. *The Search For A Perfect Model . . . Or the Importance of Being Structural.* Lehman Brothers Structural Research Papers No. 2 (July).

———. 2001. *The Causes of Unemployment.* Lehman Brothers Structural Research Papers, No. 5 (April).

Edwards, J. 2000. *Euro 2000: They Think It's All Over . . . .* Lehman Brothers Structural Economics Papers No. 1 (June).

Edwards, J. and J. Schanz. 2001a. (*Faster, Higher, Stronger: An International Comparison of Structural Policies.* Lehman Brothers Structural Research Papers No. 3 (March).

———. 2001b. *Lehman's Structural Database: Sources and Methods.* Lehman Brothers Structural Research Papers No. 4 (March).

European Commission. 2001.*Report on the Implementation of the 2000 Broad Economic Policy Guidelines.* (March) 2001.

———. 2002. *Annual Report on Structural Reforms 2002*, No. 167. March.

Hall, B. and J. Liebman. 1998. "Are CEOs Really Paid Like Bureaucrats?" *Quarterly Journal of Economics* 113(3): 653–691.

Jones, R. 1999. *Phoenix from the Ashes: The East Asian Economy Two Years on.* Lehman Brothers Research Papers (September).

Jones, R. and J. Llewellyn. 1999. *Japan: A Radical Proposal.* Lehman Brothers Research Papers (January).

Layard, R., S. Nickell, and R. Jackman. 1991.*Unemployment: Macroeconomic Performance and the Labor Market.* Oxford University Press.

Lisbon Special European Council on Employment, Economic Reform and Social Cohesion. March 2000.

Llewellyn, J., S. Potter, and L. Samuelson. 1985. *Economic Forecasting and Policy: The International Dimension.* Routledge & Keegan Paul.

Llewellyn, Samuelson, and Potter (1985), Part II, pp 121–187,

Murphy, K. J. 1999. "Executive Compensation." In O. Ashenfelter and D. Card, eds. *Handbook of Labor Economics*, Volume 3. North Holland.

Organisation for Economic Co-operation and Development (OECD). 1994. *The OECD Jobs Study: Facts, Analysis, and Strategies.* Paris: Organisation for Economic Co-operation and Development.

———. *OECD Economic Surveys.* Paris: Organisation for Economic Co-operation and Development.

Case Study: Switzerland

FRANZ JAEGER, Research Institute for Empirical Economics and
Economic Policy at the University of St. Gallen

Introduction

The Swiss economy may be characterized as "stagnating at a very high level." Other economies are catching up while a number of established Swiss advantages are being eroded. However, even though Switzerland is the sole Organisation for Economic Co-operation and Development (OECD) country that was unable to increase its GDP per capita over the last decade, it still features one of the highest levels of prosperity worldwide.

Figure 1a illustrates that only Luxembourg and the United States have a higher per capita GDP than Switzerland. Austria, France, Germany, and other European countries, in turn, rank behind Switzerland. Until 1974, Switzerland experienced growth rates similar to those of the European and the G7 countries. After the 1975–76 recession, Switzerland's GDP recovered at roughly the same speed as that of other European countries. But after 1990, Swiss growth fell behind (SECO 2002a, p 3). With respect to the per capita growth rates of income during the 1990s, Switzerland ranks last. Even Japan, heavily burdened with a structural crisis, was able to increase per capita income by 1 percent on average. One potential explanation for this shortcoming is the observation that at high levels of prosperity, it tends to become more difficult to sustain high expansion rates of GDP per capita. Figures 1a and 1b indicate, however, that Luxembourg and the United States actually do well in terms of both prosperity *and* growth.

The next section of this case study aims to illustrate Switzerland's position relative to a selection of countries with respect to the macroeconomic environment. Labor productivity, one of the main growth drivers, is analyzed in the following section, where we also discuss the role of technological progress and human capital as well as the market setup in some detail. The final section summarizes the results of the study.

Throughout the study, our selection of countries for making comparisons comprises Austria, Denmark, Finland, Germany, the Netherlands, Sweden, and the United States.[1] These European countries are comparable with Switzerland because of a similarly high standard of living, geographical closeness, a highly developed economy, and intense business contacts. Nevertheless, there are remarkable differences in growth rates that demand an explanation. The US economy—being the world's leading economy—serves as a further benchmark.

In accordance with the methodology of the *Global Competitiveness Report*, the focus of this case study is on the supply-side factors that explain the slow growth in Switzerland. Although a lack of aggregate demand, especially in the 1990s, may also have contributed to the exceedingly slow growth process, the analysis of demand-side effects is beyond the scope of the present study.

Figure 1a: GDP per capita in 2000, based on PPP

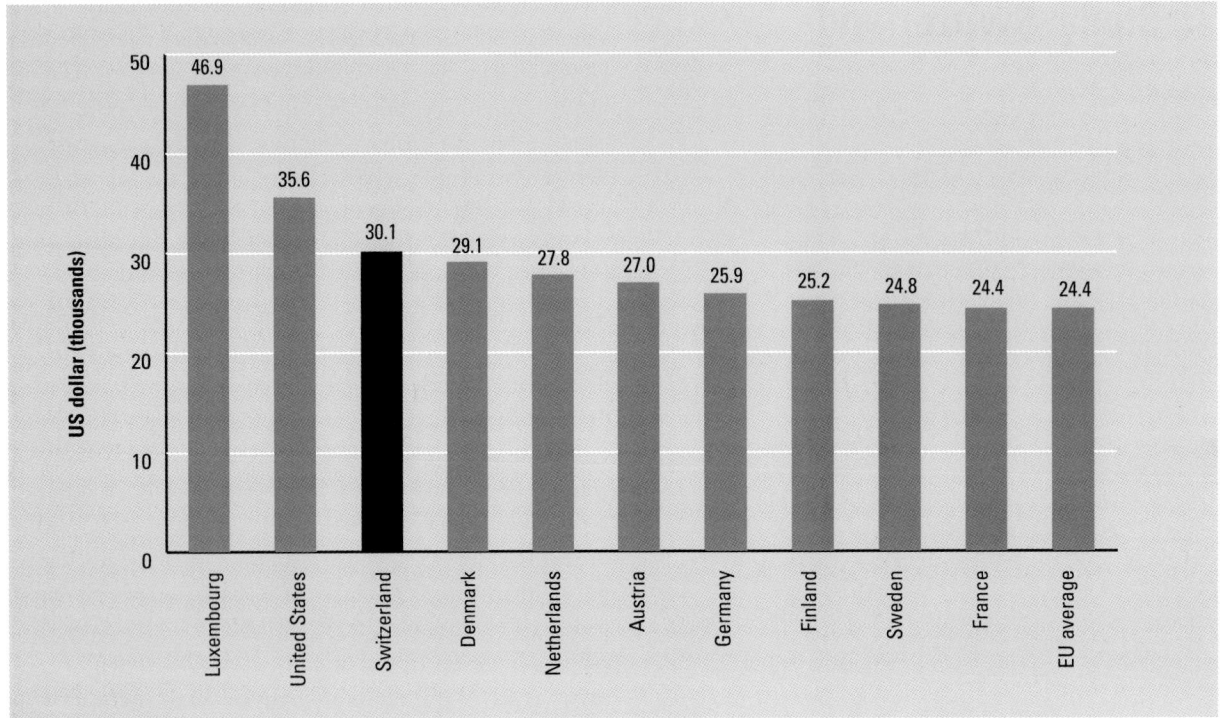

Source: OECD (2002b)

Figure 1b: Growth rate of income per capita, average of the 1990s

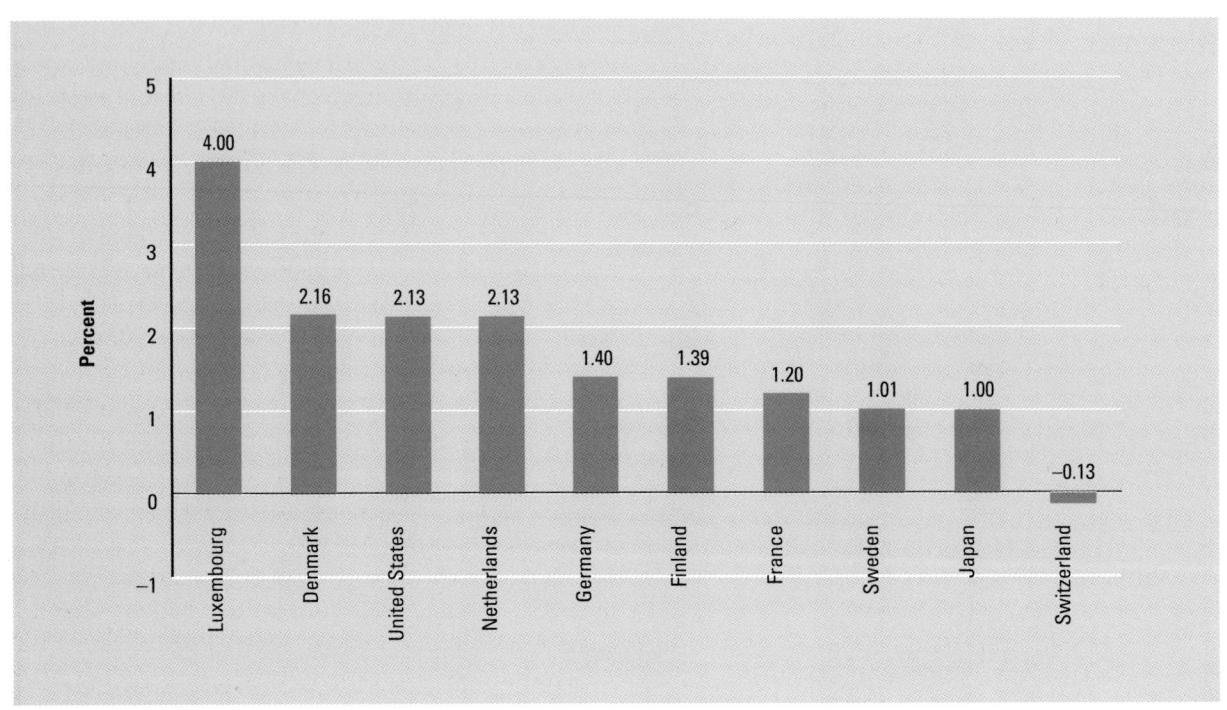

Source: SECO (2002a, p 4)

Figure 18: Total patents granted per 1,000 researchers

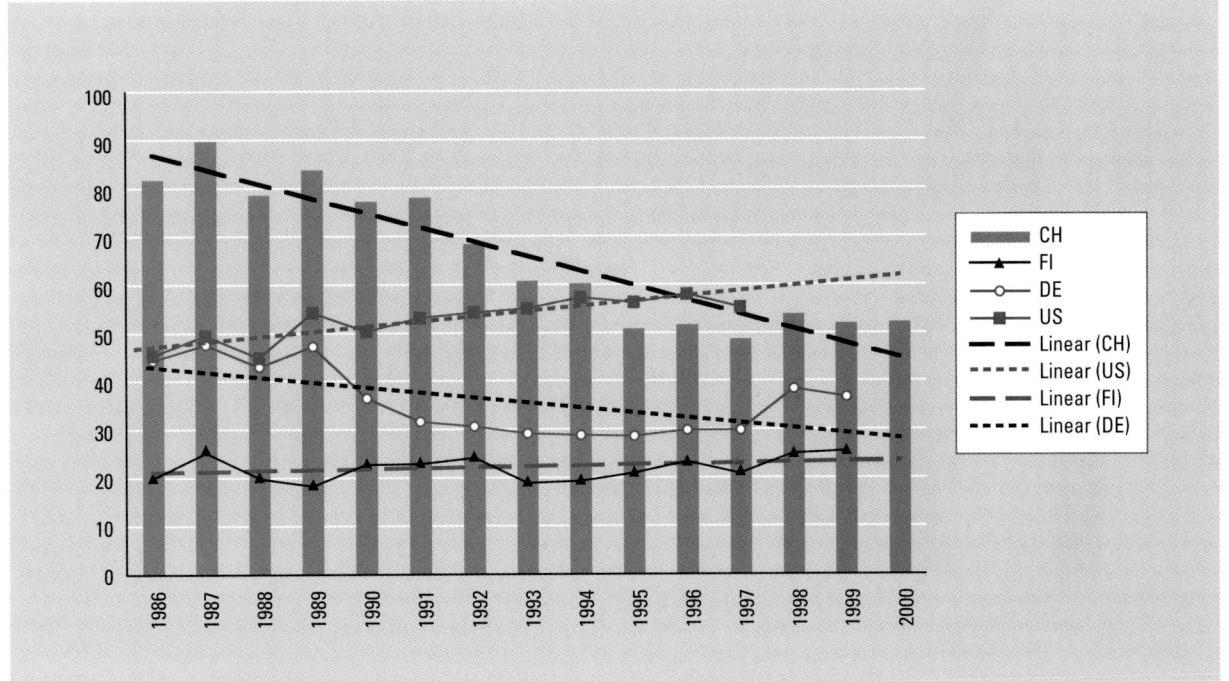

Note: CH = Switzerland, FI = Finland, DE = Germany
Source: OECD (2002d), author's calculations

Nonetheless, there are further drivers that have an influence on the level of technological sophistication. In all these countries, *research institutions*[23] are perceived to be very good, with Survey answers ranging in the same area. Quality of research institutions being a driver for scientific prowess, the finding is in line with the above results.

In order to translate science into technology, the *collaboration*[24] between research institutions, universities, and business enterprises is an important element. In all countries analyzed, collaboration has reached a relatively high level. Finland is leading in this collaboration, followed by Sweden, Germany, and the United States. Switzerland seems to be lagging behind to some extent.

As commercialization is a defining element of innovation,[25] it is an important aspect for its success. To a significant extent, technological innovation is commercialized through startup companies. For these companies, having developed the basis of scientific knowledge and personnel, financing becomes the critical factor for success. This is also true for established national and international technology firms, as their research operations prove to be extremely cost-intensive. Therefore, *availability of financing* becomes an important driver for macroeconomic technological sophistication.

Because of this, we look at the availability of venture capital,[26] as well as access to local equity markets[27] and the degree to which banks offer loans in a particular country.[28]

Although all our chosen countries rank relatively high in a worldwide comparison, answers indicate that venture capital is no longer perceived to be widely available. However, entrepreneurs seem to obtain venture capital financing more easily in Scandinavian countries and in the United States than in German-speaking countries. This corresponds to the finding that financing a company on the local stock market is perceived to be likely possible for a good company. This is true for all countries we compare. On the other hand, obtaining a bank loan is not so easy *per se*. Again, we see a more optimistic perception in Scandinavia and the United States. In comparison, German-speaking countries perceive this as more difficult.

It is important to note that these findings result from questions concerning the availability of financing in all sectors of the economy and as such reflect a general climate. With venture capital being primarily focused on technology, it shows that technology firms currently face problems obtaining financing. Even though these results have important implications for current funding possibilities, they are influenced and therefore changing according to the general development in financial and capital markets.

Protection of intellectual property[29] is another important driver of innovation. Because innovation usually is an expensive and time-consuming process, as, for example, in the biotechnology industry, patent protection gives the innovator the possibility of realizing an economic gain by

Figure 19: Comparison of relative price levels (GDP based)

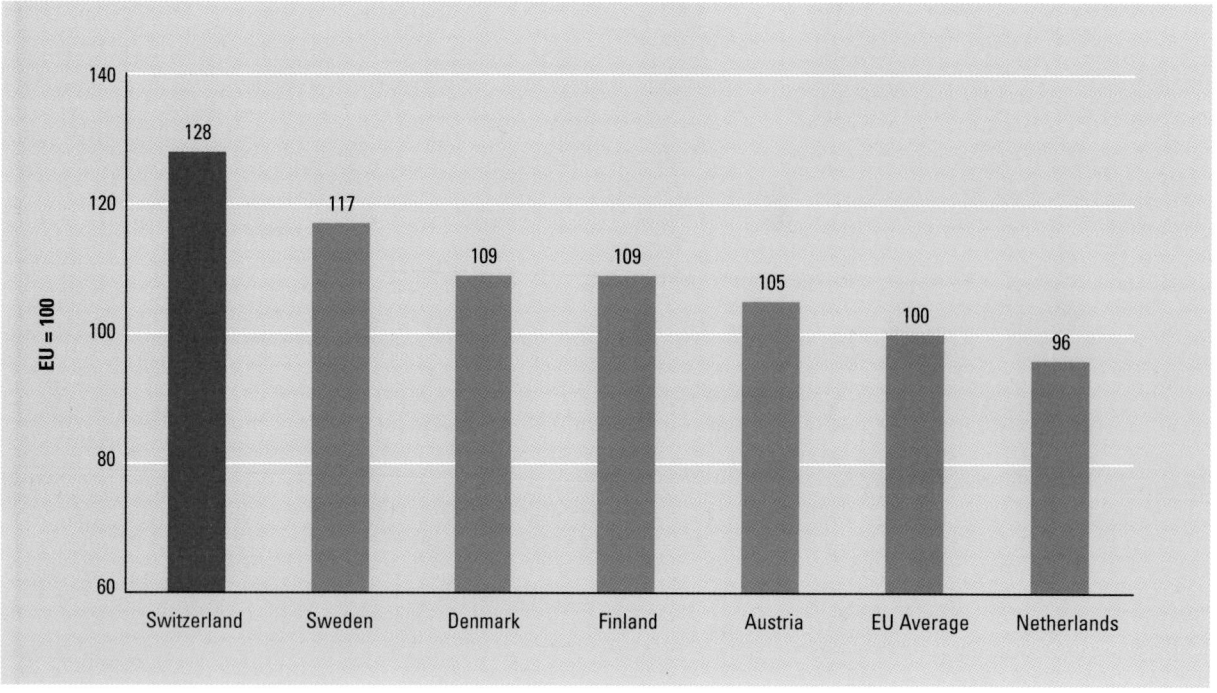

Source: BfS (2002)

offering a temporary monopoly on the innovation. According to the Survey, all relevant countries rank on a similar, relatively high level. This indicates that intellectual property protection in Switzerland is close to the world's most stringent.

Swiss market setup

A dual economy

As already discussed, the growth rate of the Swiss GDP continually appears among the lowest within Europe in spite of a macroeconomic environment that looks exceptional. This section tries to examine some specific Swiss issues that could partially explain this situation. In addition to the low overall productivity rate (of labor), the relative price level is remarkably high (see Figure 19). Switzerland's relative price level continually tops all other price levels of the OECD countries.

Is the discouraging situation described above characteristic for the overall economy? Looking a bit closer at the figures, a striking discrepancy appears. On one side there is a highly competitive export sector (dominated by pharmaceuticals, financial services, machinery, and engineering industries) and on the other side a still rather well protected and administrated domestic sector (in particular public transport, agriculture, postal services, property rent, health services, and electricity) (see Figure 20).

Export-orientated, competitive sectors are those that show the highest labor productivity in Switzerland. Even compared with economies such as those of the United States, France, and Germany, labor productivity in competitive sectors (like the pharmaceutical industry, financial services, watches) is high (see Figure 21). It is therefore the protected and strongly administrated domestic market that pushes down the overall productivity to its remarkably low level.

Overall labor productivity is the weighted average of the labor productivity of each sector of the economy. By protecting unproductive sectors from competition, their relative weight is increasing within the overall economy and thus additionally reduces average aggregate productivity (see Figure 22). It thus becomes evident that the low overall productivity is also due to structural factors.

Examining price levels, the same gap exists: the high aggregate price level in Switzerland is caused to a large extent by the remarkably high relative prices of domestically produced goods and services. These are exactly the sectors that show a low productivity.

Looking at the dynamics of the overall price level, it again becomes evident that the goods and services that are produced in the administered domestic market pushed up the overall price level (see Figure 23). Between 1992 and 2002, administered prices have been increased by 11.9

Figure 20: Labor productivity in selected sectors

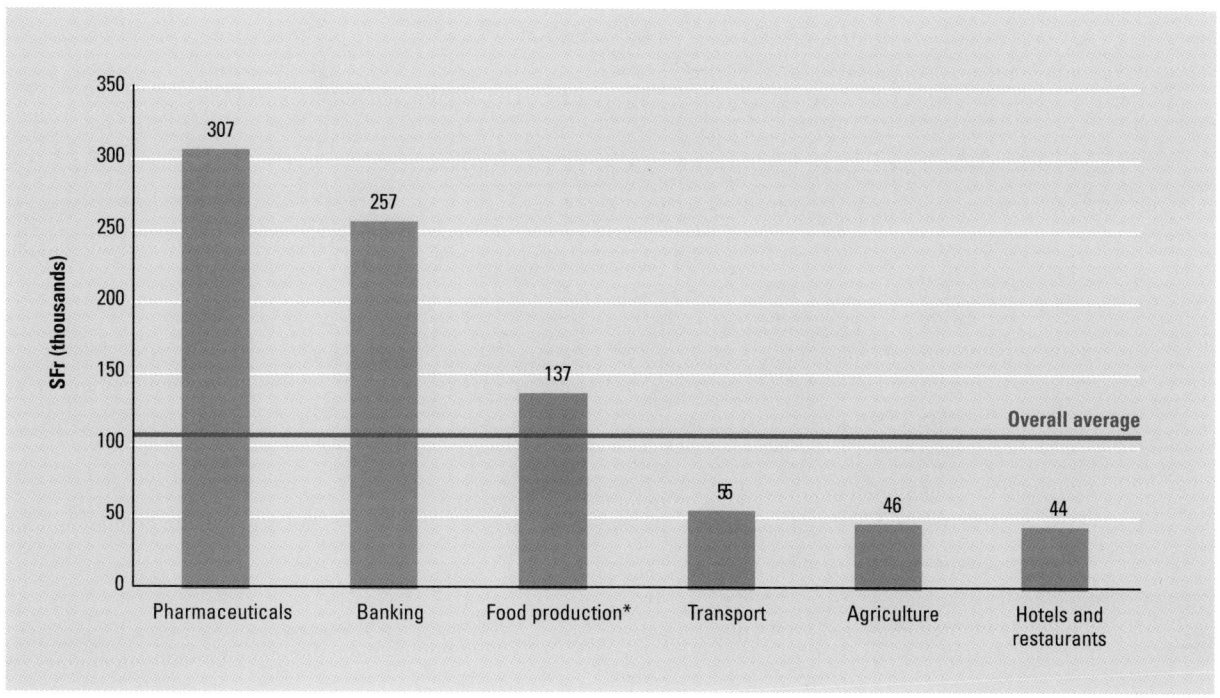

* Without agriculture
Note: 1998 data; 1990 prices; full-time equivalents on a yearly basis
Source: BfS (2001)

Figure 21: International labor productivity measured relative to the Swiss level (lower level implies a higher Swiss productivity; 1998 data, productivity by working hour, PPP adjusted)

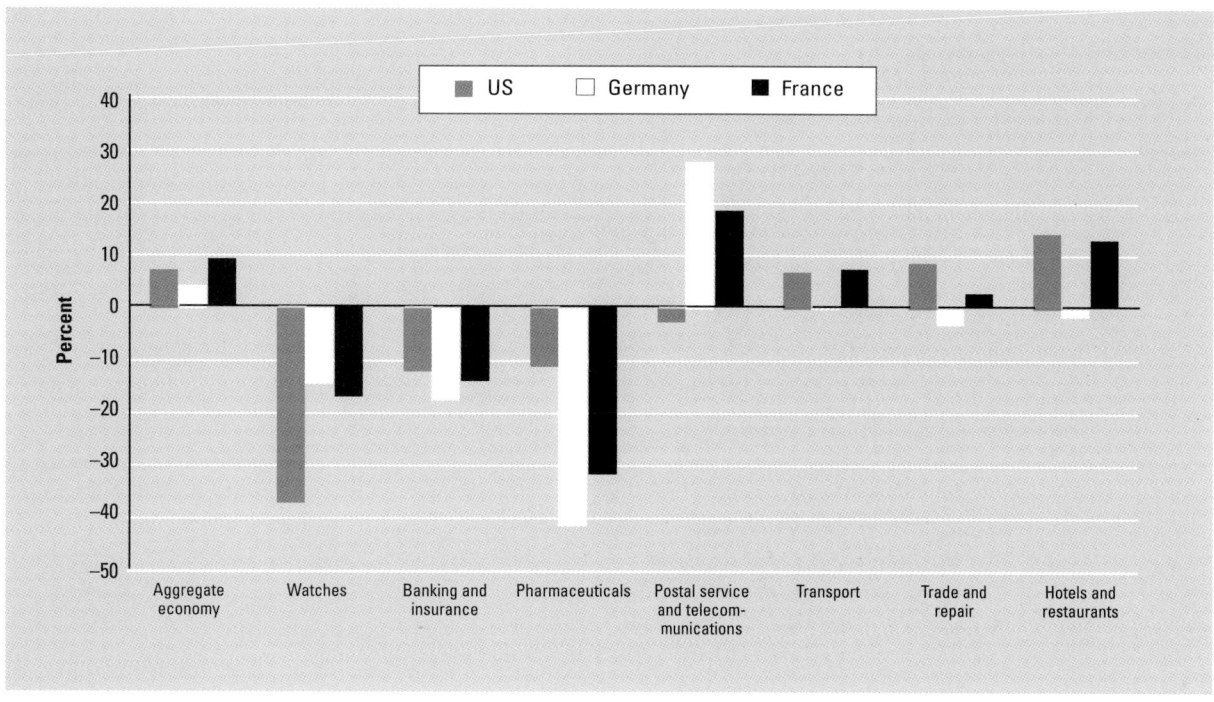

Source: SECO (2002b, p 12)

Figure 22: Relative price levels of selected sectors

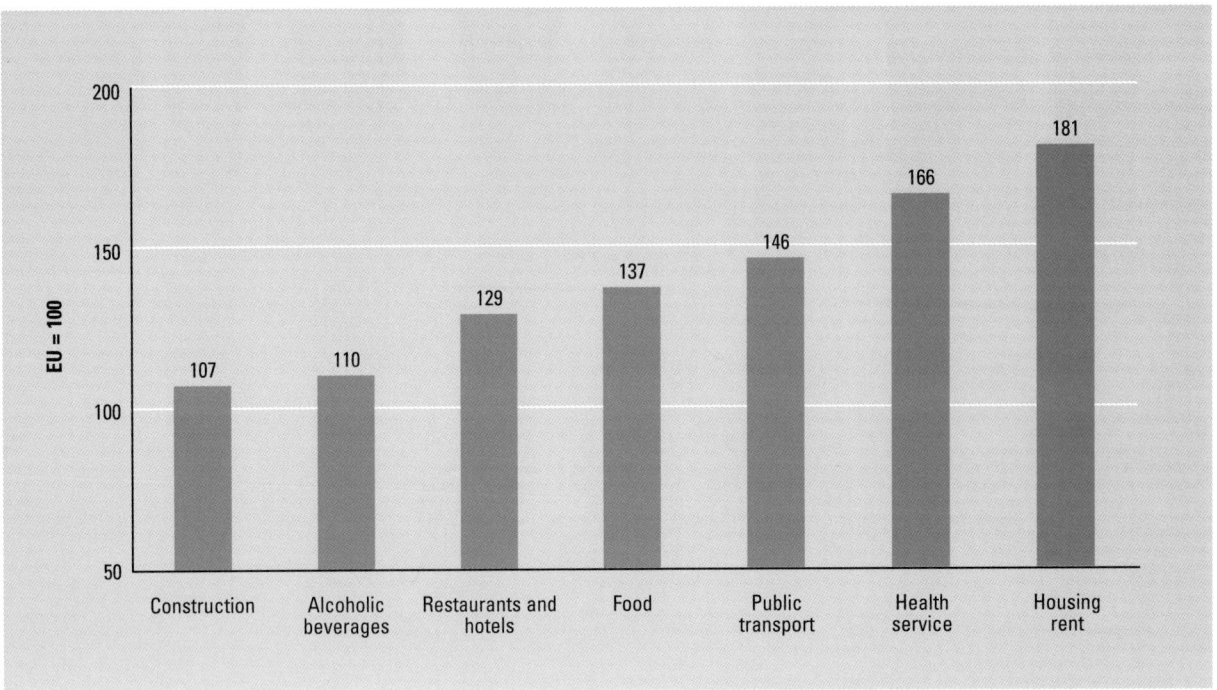

Source: SECO (2002c, pp 22, 23)

percent.[30] As a result, the overall economy's price level increased by 7.6 percent.

As the administered prices' share of the overall price level is 31.2 percent, it can be claimed that it is also because of government regulations that the high price level could not have been significantly reduced. These regulations—at least to this extent—can be imposed only in a protected market like Switzerland's domestic sector.

Obviously, productivity and relative price levels are determined (among other things) by competition. A high competitive pressure, as imposed on Switzerland's successful export-oriented sector, goes along with high labor productivity and a moderate price level. Therefore, it is the domestic market—still set up to avoid efficient competition—that causes low productivity (and high price levels) and strongly contributes to the low growth of the overall economy. The telecom sector is an example that reveals the effects on prices and productivity that result from transforming a once-protected domestic industry into a competitive, open-market business.

Between 1993 and 2002, overall consumer prices in Switzerland increased by 7.6 percent, but telecommunication prices have decreased by 39 percent (see Figure 24). Such a price decrease indicates—besides the vanished monopoly rent—a respectable increase in labor productivity.

Unlike the telecom example, many markets within the domestic sector of the Swiss economy forestall effective competition:

Housing rent: Housing rents are highly regulated in Switzerland. Increases in housing rents are limited to the increase in mortgage interest rates. These regulations discourage investment in housing and keep the supply inflexible. Consequently, prices stay high. In 1998, housing rents were almost twice as high as the EU average (see SECO 2002c). In addition, the effectiveness of monetary policy becomes an issue under such a regulation. If the Swiss National Bank raises interest rates in order to combat inflationary pressure, higher interest rates result in higher rents, which in return push up the overall price level (Edel and Hartwig 2001).

Agriculture: In spite of some recent deregulations, the Swiss agricultural market is still (at least compared with other European countries) strongly regulated and subsidized.[31] International competition is almost totally blocked; the gap between (European) market prices and Swiss producer prices is still tremendous. Food prices in Switzerland are almost 1.4 times higher than the EU average (see SECO 2002c).

Health services: Due to the federal system in Switzerland, the health system is mainly supervised and managed by the cantons (states). National competition has not been implemented. In 1998, the Swiss health services system was over 1.6 times more expensive than the EU average (see SECO 2002c).

Figure 23: Drivers of the increasing consumer prices* (May 1992 to February 2002)

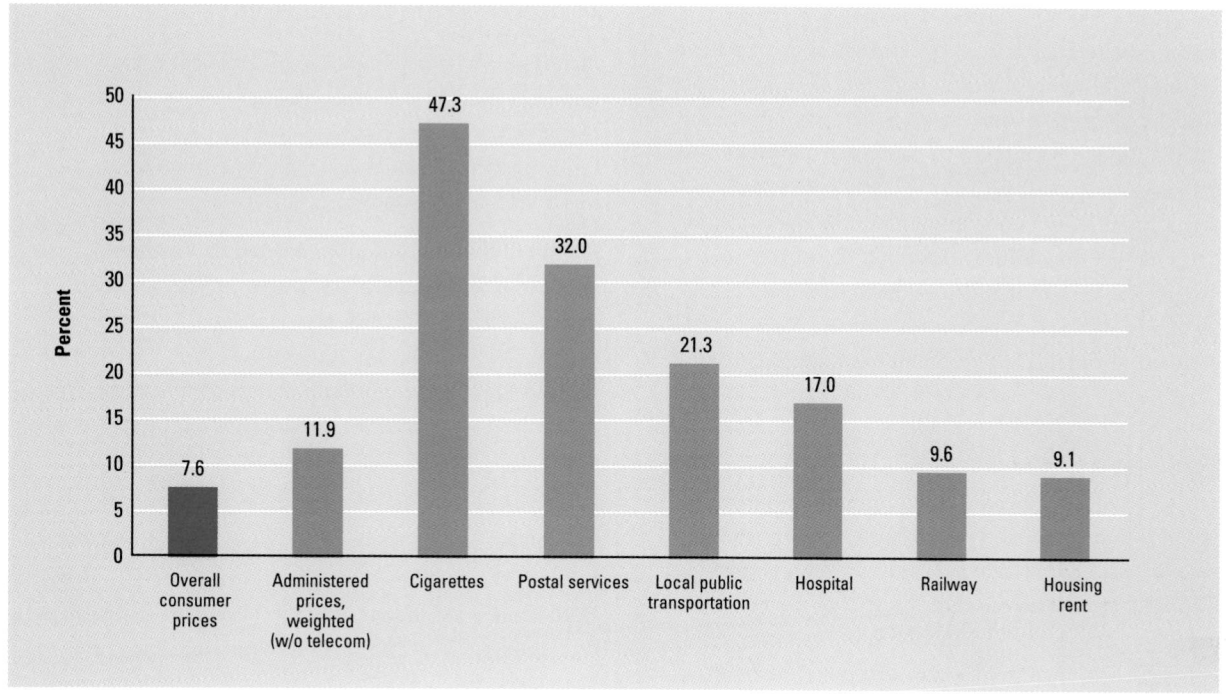

* Based on national consumer price index
Source: BfS (2002)

Figure 24: Liberalization of the telecommunication sector

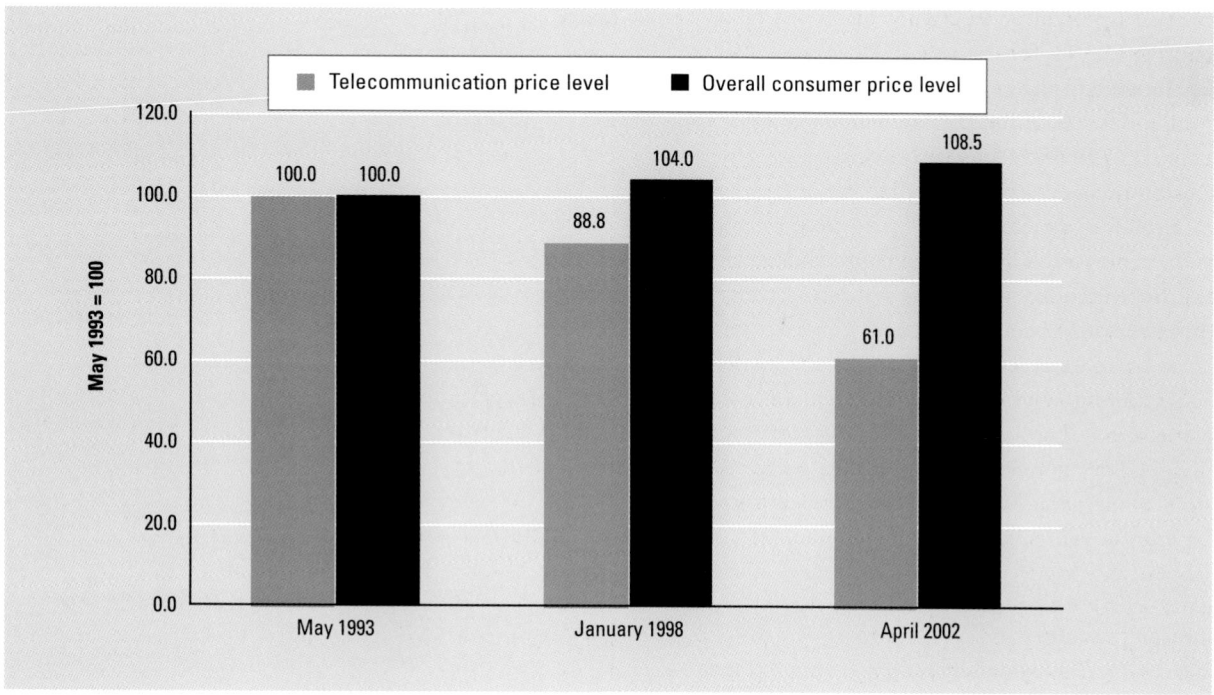

Source: BfS (2002)

Policy outlook

1. Electricity market liberalization

The liberalization of the electricity market was up on a referendum in late September 2002. It basically involved the free choice of the electricity supplier and required the owner of the electricity cable network (that would still be controlled by the government) to allow any competitor to use it. Switzerland voted against the liberalization and is one of the last OECD countries not to have liberalized its electricity market. In addition, this outcome of the referendum makes it very difficult to implement other potential liberalizations (such as postal services or railway) as the vote will be interpreted as a reluctance toward liberalization in general.

2. Cartel policy legislation

The Swiss Cartel Act, introduced in 1996, has been widely criticized for one clause: in order to punish companies that have illegally cartelized, an already-existing condemnation for the very same cartel is required. It is obvious that this "one shot for free" principle does not really hold companies back from cartelizing. In addition, Swiss cartel legislation is not applicable to (domestic) markets where prices are regulated. This legislation excludes prices in many markets (eg, housing rent, cheese and milk) from being determined by competition (Jaeger and Kaiser forthcoming). A revision of this law is in progress.

3. Domestic market competition legislation

The political system of Switzerland is highly federalist. This setup can be an obstacle on the way toward a competitive domestic market. Cantons tend to try to protect their local businesses against the competition of other cantons' companies. In 1996, a law was passed whose objective was to guarantee open competition within Switzerland and to tear down barriers built up by the 26 cantons. An evaluation performed by the federal parliament in 2000[32] revealed that within many domestic sectors (eg, sanitary, taxis, and hotel and restaurant industry), domestic competition has not yet been really in effect. This is basically due to different cantonal authorizations that are still required to run a business, as well as the possibility of maintaining trade barriers for "common welfare." A revision of this legislation, which should further increase domestic competition, has not yet started.

Summary and conclusions

- Switzerland has an exceptional macroeconomic environment with a strong currency, but with less growth of the real GDP than the EU average and the United States. A matter of concern is the development of the public finances.

- Switzerland still has a very high number of patents per capita, which indicates superior technological prowess and thus a high level of innovation.

- Although Switzerland allocates significant capital resources for R&D, it has only a low density of scientists compared with other countries. Even though this indicates substantial capital availability per researcher, research efficiency shows significant depreciation.

- Although Switzerland ranks among the leading countries according to the reached level of the analyzed drivers, it has not managed to realize any growth at those drivers. Countries such as the United States and Finland have improved these drivers significantly over the same time period. This resulted in equivalent economic growth, although it remains to be statistically proven.

- Dual economy: The protected domestic sector slows down GDP growth and pushes down labor productivity. Both figures are driven only by the export sector. A policy change toward more competition and structural changes in the domestic sector would help Switzerland grow faster.

- Prices in Switzerland could be considerably lower in many (domestic) sectors if they were not excluded from competition.

Notes

1 In all figures, the countries are abbreviated as follows: Austria = AT, Switzerland = CH, Germany = DE, Denmark = DK, Finland = FI, Netherlands = NL, Sweden = SE, United States = US, and EU = European Union.

2 The figure provides a broad overview of Switzerland's benefits and drawbacks in comparison with those of the European Union and the United States. Measurement problems make a comparison between the countries difficult; basic tendencies can be gathered from the figure.

3 OECD (2002a, Annex Table 1).

4 OECD (2002a, Annex Table 15); this is the Standardised Unemployment Rate.

5 OECD (2002a, Annex Table 19).

6 OECD (2002a, Annex Table 33); the data for Switzerland are taken from BSV (2002, p 250).

7 To calculate the real interest rates, the OECD long-term interest rates are corrected for the inflation rate measured by the consumer price index.

8 The Economist (2002, http://www.economist.com/markets/bigmac/index.cfm)

9 There is empirical evidence that, for example, expenditures for infrastructure or R&D correlate with long-term sustainable economic growth. See the section on technological innovation and human capital.

10 Data source: Executive Opinion Survey 2002, question 6.12 "Your country's tax system is" with possible answers from "1 = highly complex and distortive on business decisions" to "7 = simple and transparent."

11 The characteristics of an inflexible labor market are, for example: general wage agreements for whole industries negotiated between employers associations and national labor unions, a long period of notice for individual dismissal, strong dismissal protection, regulation of working hours by law, and no flexible arrangement regarding immigration.

12 Data source: Executive Opinion Survey 2002, question 10.19 "Wages in your country are" with possible answers from "1 = set by a centralized bargaining process" to "7 = up to each individual company."

13 Note that measurement of labor productivity and—to some extent—of the relative price level is often based on different methods and prerequisites. In spite of that, the key results should not be affected by this unavoidable issue.

14 Of course, the high growth rate of the GDP is also due to its low initial level.

15 Regression based on growth rates between 1993 and 2002; business-sector labor productivity only; sample based on 25 selected OECD countries. Dependent Variable: Prod. Growth; Coefficient: 1.333; T-Value: 4.18; R^2: 44.2 percent.

16 McArthur and Sachs (2002, p 40); for futher argument, see Porter and Stern (2002, p 107).

17 Labelling of driver consistent with OECD (source).

18 Labelling of driver consistent with OECD (source).

19 Data source: Executive Opinion Survey 2002, question 3.07 "Companies in your country" with possible answers from "1 = do not spend money on research and development" to "7 = spend heavily on research and development relative to international peers."

20 Data source: Executive Opinion Survey 2002, question 3.11 "Math and science education in your country's schools" with possible answers from "1 = lag far behind most other countries" to "7 = are among the best in the world."

21 Data source: Executive Opinion Survey 2002, question 3.12 "Scientists and engineers in your country are" with possible answers from "1 = nonexistent or rare" to "7 = widely available."

22 Because there are many further strong influences, these results only show tendencies.

23 Data source: Executive Opinion Survey 2002, question 3.06 "Scientific research institutions in your country (eg university laboratories, government laboratories) are" with possible answers from "1 = nonexistent" to "7 = the best in their field."

24 Data source: Executive Opinion Survey 2002, question 3.09 "In its R&D activity, business collaboration with local universities" with possible answers from "1 = minimal or nonexistent" to "7 = intensive and ongoing."

25 We define *innovation* as the generation of something new or a significant improvement of an existing technology that is viable for commercialization.

26 Data source: Executive Opinion Survey 2002, question 2.06 "Entrepreneurs with innovative but risky projects can generally find venture capital in your country" with possible answers from "1 = not true" to "7 = true."

27 Data source: Executive Opinion Survey 2002, question 2.07 "Raising money by issuing shares on the local stock market is" with possible answers from "1 = nearly impossible" to "7 = quite possible for a good company."

28 Data source: Executive Opinion Survey 2002, question 2.04 "How easy is it to obtain a bank loan in your country with only a good business plan and no collateral" with possible answers from "1 = impossible" to "7 = easy."

29 Data source: Executive Opinion Survey 2002, question 6.04 "Intellectual property protection in your country" with possible answers from "1 = is weak or nonexistent" to "7 = is equal to the world's most stringent."

30 Not including telecommunication prices.

31 OECD (2002c). Switzerland has one of the highest ratios of agricultural subsidies per GDP.

32 Parlamentarische Verwaltungskontrollstelle (2000).

References

Bassanini, A. et al. 2000. "Economic Growth in the OECD Area: Recent Trends at the Aggregate and Sectoral Level," OECD Economics Department Working Paper No. 248. Paris: Organisation for Economic Co-operation and Development.

Bernegger, U. et al. 2002. "Analyse der Einnahmen der öffentlichen Hand in der Schweiz mit besonderer Berücksichtigung der nicht steuerlichen Einnahmen und der Sozialversicherung," FEW-HSG Working Paper St.Gallen: Forschungsinstitut für Empirische Ökonomie und Wirtschaftspolitik.

Bundesamt für Sozialversicherung, (BSV). 2002. *Schweizerische Sozialversicherungsstatistik 2002*. Bern: Bundesamt für Sozialversicherung.

Bundesamt für Statistik (BfS). 2000. *Ausländerinnen und Ausländer in der Schweiz, Bericht 2000*. Neuchâtel: Bundesamt für Statistik.

———. 2001. *Volkswirtschaftliche Gesamtrechnung. Arbeitsproduktivität in der Schweiz 1998*. Neuchâtel: Bundesamt für Statistik.

———. 2002. *Statistisches Jahrbuch 2002*. Neuchâtel: Bundesamt für Statistik.

Christoffel, J. 1995. "Unproduktive Schweizer Wirtschaft?" *Die Volkswirtschaft* 8: 36–41.

Economiesuisse. 2002. *Ausgabenkonzept—Diskussionsplattform der Wirtschaft zu den öffentlichen Finanzen*. Zürich: Economiesuisse.

The Economist. *Big Mac Index, Apr. 25th 2002*. Rev. September 18, 2002. Online. http://www.economist.com/markets/bigmac/index.cfm.

Edel, K. and J. Hartwig. 2001. "Das Reich der Möglichkeiten," In J. Furrer and B. Gehrig, eds., *Aspekte der schweizerischen Wirtschaftspolitik*. Chur: Rüegger.

Eidgenössische Finanzverwaltung (EFV). 2000. *Internationale Vergleiche*. Rev. September 18, 2002. Online. http://www.efv.admin.ch/d/finanzen/intvergl/index.htm.

Jaeger, F. and Ch. Kaiser. Forthcoming. "Das Konzept einer wirksamen Wettbewerbsordnung aus ökonomischer Prespektive, illustriert am Fallbeispiel Schweiz." In Carl Baudenbacher ed., *Internationales und europäisches Wirtschaftsrecht* (forthcoming).

McArthur, J. W. and J. D. Sachs. 2002. "The Growth Competitive Index: Measuring Technological Advancement and the Stages of Development." In *The Global Competitiveness Report 2001–2002*. New York: Oxford University Press.

Organisation for Economic Co-operation and Development (OECD). 2002a. *OECD Economic Outlook No. 71: June 2002*. Paris: Organisation for Economic Co-operation and Development.

———. 2002b. *National Accounts of OECD Countries, Main Aggregates, Volume 1, Update July 2002*. Rev. September 18, 2002. Online. http://www.oecd.org/pdf/M00018000/M00018518.pdf.

———. 2002c. *Highlights of Agricultural Policies in OECD Countries—Monitoring and Evaluation 2002*. Paris: Organisation for Economic Co-operation and Development.

———. 2002d. *OECD Statistical Compendium 01/2002* (CD-ROM). Paris: Organisation for Economic Co-operation and Development.

Parlamentarische Verwaltungskontrollstelle. 2000. *Evaluation: Wie offen ist der Schweizer Binnenmarkt? Schlussbericht zuhanden der Geschäftsprüfungskommission des Nationalrates*. Bern: Parlamentsdienste.

Porter, M. E. and S. Stern. 2002. "National Innovative Capacity." In *The Global Competitiveness Report 2001–2002*. New York: Oxford University Press.

125

Schweizerische Nationalbank (SNB). 2002. *Monatsbericht: August 2002.* Bern: Schweizerische Nationalbank.

Staatssekretariat für Wirtschaft (SECO). 2002a. *Der Wachstumsbericht.* Bern: Staatssekretariat für Wirtschaft.

———. 2002b. "Produktivitätsrückstand der Schweiz," WP Discussion Paper No. 4. Bern: Staatssekretariat für Wirtschaft.

———. 2002c. "Wettbewersbbedingungen im Schweizer Binnenmarkt," WP Discussion Paper No. 6. Bern: Staatssekretariat für Wirtschaft.

Weber, B. and B. Zürcher. 2001. "Fleissige Schweiz: Über den Zusammenhang zwischen Arbeitsproduktivität und Reichtum," *Die Volkswirtschaft* 3: 28–33.

CHAPTER 2.4

Africa: A Union Open for Growth, Trade, and Business?

LISA D. COOK, Harvard University and Stanford University

African economies are vulnerable because of their dependence on primary production and resource-based sectors, and their narrow export bases. There is an urgent need to diversify production. . . . Private enterprise must be supported, both micro-enterprises in the informal sector and small and medium enterprises in the manufacturing sector, which are principal engines of growth and development. Governments should remove constraints to business activity and encourage the creative talents of African entrepreneurs.

—*The New Partnership for Africa's Development*
Section V.C.156, p 23, October 2001, www.nepad.org.

Although a significant portion of the much-discussed New Partnership for Africa's Development (NEPAD) statement centers on issues of peace, security, democracy, political governance, and human development, a nontrivial portion of it is related to economic growth and integration for the new 53-member African Union. Focusing on economic outcomes is warranted, since one-third of sub-Saharan African countries have not yet returned to 1960 living standards (see Rodrik 1998 and Sachs and Warner 1997). Half of Africa's population—300 million people—live in poverty, on less than $1 a day. Just over half of Africa's population have access to clean water. On average, at birth Africans are expected to live to be 54 years old.

Certainly, there are observable differences among the 53 countries listed in Table 1. Along with the other 135 heads of state who attended the Millennium General Assembly at the United Nations, leaders of these countries agreed to pursue the Millennium Development Goals (MDGs). These objectives are ambitious but consistent with the immense and persistent challenges faced.

The MDG objectives include:

1. Eradicate extreme poverty and hunger:
    Between 1990 and 2015, halve the proportion of people whose income is less than $1 a day and halve the proportion of people who suffer from extreme hunger
2. Achieve universal primary education:
    By 2015, ensure that children everywhere, boys and girls, will be able to complete a full course of primary schooling
3. Promote gender equality and empower women:
    By 2005, eliminate gender disparity in primary and secondary education and, by 2015, in all levels of education
4. Reduce child mortality:
    Between 1990 and 2015, reduce by 67 percent the under-five mortality ratio

Table 1: Growth and progress toward the Millennium Development Goals in Africa

Country	Real GDP growth, average, per capita 1975–2000 (%)	GDP per capita, PPP, 2000 (US$)	Undernourished people (% of total population)	Female gross primary enrollment, ratio as % male ratio	Under-five mortality (per 1,000 live births)	Population using improved water sources (%)
Algeria	−0.3	5,308	OT	OT	SB	OT
Angola	−1.9	2,187	OT	—	SB	—
Benin	0.5	990	OT	FB	FB	—
Botswana	**5.1**	**7,184**	**SB**	**A**	**SB**	**—**
Burkina Faso	1.4	976	OT	FB	FB	—
Burundi	−0.7	591	SB	FB	FB	—
Cameroon	−0.6	1,703	OT	—	SB	OT
Cape Verde	3.0	4,863	—	OT	OT	—
CAR	−1.6	1172	FB	—	FB	FB
Chad	−0.8	871	OT	FB	FB	—
Comoros	−1.4	1,588	—	—	OT	A
Congo	−3.4	825	FB	OT	FB	—
Congo, DR	−4.7	765	SB	—	FB	—
Côte d'Ivoire	−2.1	1,630	OT	FB	SB	OT
Djibouti	−5.0	—	—	FB	FB	OT
Egypt	**2.9**	**3,635**	**OT**	**OT**	**OT**	**OT**
Equatorial Guinea	10.4	15,073	—	—	OT	—
Eritrea	1.1	837	—	—	OT	—
Ethiopia	−0.1	668	—	SB	FB	FB
Gabon	−1.5	6,237	OT	—	FB	—
Gambia	−0.3	1,649	OT	OT	FB	—
Ghana	0.1	1,964	A	—	L	OT
Guinea	1.4	1,982	OT	FB	OT	FB
Guinea-Bissau	0.4	755	—	—	FB	—
Kenya	0.4	1,022	FB	OT	SB	L
Lesotho	2.6	2,031	L	A	FB	OT
Liberia	—	—	SB	—	FB	—
Libya	−6.7	—	—	—	OT	FB
Madagascar	−1.7	840	SB	OT	FB	FB
Malawi	0.2	615	OT	OT	L	L
Mali	−0.5	797	FB	OT	FB	OT
Mauritania	−0.1	1,677	OT	OT	FB	FB
Mauritius	**4.1**	**10,017**	**OT**	**A**	**OT**	**OT**
Morocco	**1.3**	**3,546**	**OT**	**OT**	**OT**	**OT**
Mozambique	1.5	854	OT	FB	FB	
Namibia	**−0.1**	**6,431**	**FB**	**A**	**FB**	**L**
Niger	−2.1	746	FB	FB	FB	FB
Nigeria	**−0.7**	**896**	**A**	**—**	**FB**	**L**
Rwanda	−1.3	943	SB	—	SB	—
Sao Tome and Principe	−0.9	—	—	—	FB	—
Senegal	−0.2	1,510	FB	OT	FB	OT
Seychelles	2.8	—	—	—	OT	—
Sierra Leone	−2.6	490	L	—	FB	—
Somalia	—	—	SB	—	FB	—
South Africa	**−0.7**	**9,401**	**—**	**OT**	**SB**	**—**
Sudan	0.6	1,797	OT	OT	FB	OT
Swaziland	1.9	4,492	FB	OT	SB	—
Tanzania	0.1	523	SB	OT	FB	FB
Togo	−1.2	1,442	OT	FB	FB	FB
Tunisia	**2.0**	**6,363**	**—**	**OT**	**OT**	**—**
Uganda	2.5	1,208	FB	OT	L	FB
Zambia	−2.3	780	FB	OT	SB	OT
Zimbabwe	**0.3**	**2,635**	**FB**	**OT**	**SB**	**OT**
AVERAGE	0.02	2,649.13	—	—	—	—

Notes: GDP growth data for Chad, Congo, Eritrea, and Tanzania are for 1990–2000. The countries that appear in bold are the ones included in the GCR and Egypt.
A = Achieved, FB = Far behind, L = Lagging, OT = On track, SB = Slipping back
Source: UNDP (2002)

5. Improve maternal health:

Between 1990 and 2015, reduce by 75 percent the maternal mortality ratio

6. Combat infectious diseases:

By 2015, halt and reverse the spread or incidence of HIV/AIDS, malaria, and other diseases

7. Ensure environmental sustainability:

By 2015, halve the proportion of people without sustainable access to safe drinking water

By 2020, improve significantly the lives of no less than 100 million slum dwellers

8. Develop a global partnership for development that includes an open, rule-based, predictable, and non-discriminatory trading and financial system through which issues of official development assistance, market access, and indebtedness might be addressed.[1]

Given their divergent initial conditions, which include institutions, geography and human-capital endowments, and policy choices, African countries have made predictably uneven progress on the Millennium Development Goals (MDGs). A subset of the indicators used to measure change in the variables relevant for achieving the above objectives is extracted from the 2002 Human Development Report and included in Table 1. Each of the last four columns represents an MDG target, and the scores indicate whether countries are moving in the direction of halving hunger, attaining gender equity in schooling, reducing child mortality rates by two thirds, and increasing access to clean water by 50 percent. It is encouraging that 20 of the 41 countries for which we have data have been assessed by UNDP researchers as either "on track" or having achieved the goal of halving the proportion of the population living with hunger. Predictably, the slowest-growing (negative-growth) economies are less likely to have registered progress along the relevant dimensions. Only three among the slowest growing—Algeria, Comoros, and Gambia—have been able to stay more "on track" than not. Similarly, higher income (levels and rates) is associated with positive change in these indicators.[2] Nonetheless, Egypt, Mauritius, and Morocco are the only countries that have either achieved or are "on track" for all measures presented. It is interesting that a number of countries that are either higher-income or had traditionally invested in health and development, such as Botswana, Gabon, Lesotho, Namibia, Nigeria, South Africa, Swaziland, and Zimbabwe, are far behind or losing ground with respect to infant mortality. This deterioration is likely due, among other things, to the disproportionate effect that the HIV/AIDS pandemic has had on these countries.

On the whole, the scorecard for Africa is not good. It, for example, has a growing number of the world's poor:[3] in 1999, it had 300 million, and without further interven-

tion, it is anticipated to have 340 million by 2015. To reduce poverty by the recommended 50 percent and to simultaneously meet other Millennium and NEPAD goals, it has been determined that African economies will need to grow at 7 percent annually. To put this in perspective, between 1975 and 2000, the median African economy grew more slowly than its rate of population growth, that is, by −0.1 percent. Seven percent growth is a pace faster than that of the five fastest growing economies—Botswana (5.1 percent), Mauritius (4.1 percent), Cape Verde (3 percent), Egypt (2.9 percent), and Seychelles (2.8 percent)—over the same period.[4] On balance, only a few of the fastest-growing Newly Industrialized Countries (NICs) have been able to sustain growth rates above 5 percent in the same 25-year interval: Singapore (5.2 percent), Korea (6.2 percent), Thailand (5.5 percent), and China (8.1 percent). Over the same period, the least developed countries and the Arab States grew at a rate of 0.3 percent; Latin America and the Caribbean, 0.7 percent; and South Asia, 2.4 percent (UNDP 2002).

These statistics are no surprise to even the most casual observers of economic growth and development, and Africa remains the biggest challenge in this regard. Will 7 percent growth be simply a one-time Herculean task? Or will it be a Sisyphean exercise of incessantly pushing the boulder up to an elusive summit? Is this a feasible goal for Africa?

Before attempting to answer these questions, one might first consult data on Africa's growth path over a longer time period than 25 years. Angus Maddison identifies and examines five major subperiods in African economic history: 1820–1870 (pre-colonial period); 1870–1913 (colonial period); 1914–1949 (World War I, the Great Depression, World War II); 1950–1972 (pre- and early independence period); and 1973–1992 (current period). He finds that the last 30 years of slow growth, relative to the rest of the world, are an isomorph of the entire period and each subperiod of much of the last two centuries. He estimates that the world (56 countries in the sample) grew at an average yearly rate of 1.2 percent between 1820 and 1992, while Africa grew at a rate of 0.6 percent. Even when growing relatively rapidly (2.1 percent) during the period 1950–1972, the region lagged behind the other regions of the world: western Europe, 3.9 percent; Western "offshoots," 2.4 percent; southern Europe, 4.9 percent; eastern Europe, 3.5 percent; Latin America, 2.5 percent; and Asia, 3.8 percent. An African's income in 1992, $1,284, was equivalent to a European's in 1820 (Maddison 1995).

A number of hypotheses related to Maddison's results have traditionally found empirical support in the economics literature. Among them are specialization in a narrow range of primary-commodity exports, which are characterized by declining and volatile price movements; political instability and other factors affecting internal and regional politics, including Cold War–related international competition; suboptimal economic policies, including protectionism; and the legacy of natural- and human-resource extraction during the colonial period. In the mid to late 1990s, other factors were emphasized or added to the list of explanatory variables.

Bloom and Sachs (1998) show that Africa's geographic position, 93 percent of it located in the tropics, is associated with low income levels in three important ways: clustering of endogenous technical change in temperate-zone countries, impediments to technological diffusion across ecological zones, and health and agricultural disadvantages related to the tropics. Geography and demography account for 60 to 90 percent of slow growth in Africa, according to their estimates. Sachs and Warner (1995) also introduce openness as a source of Africa's slow growth.[5] Easterly and Levine (1997) emphasize ethnic heterogenity and divisions as an impediment to economic growth. Acemoglu, Johnson, and Robinson (2001a, 2001b) invoke institutions to explain variation in per capita income levels. The establishment of institutions, property-rights protection for example, allowed investment to flow to poorer regions where it might not have otherwise.

Recent economic research has also focused on the relation between globalization and economic growth. Africa is markedly less integrated in the global economy than it was in the 1950s or even 12 years ago. The continent accounted for 3.4 percent of all merchandise exports and 2.8 percent of all merchandise imports in 1990. In 2001, the region was responsible for 2.4 percent of merchandise exports and 2.2 percent of merchandise imports (WTO 2002).

The NEPAD architects assign partial responsibility for Africa's sustained experience of sluggish economic growth to globalization, which has "increased the cost of Africa's ability to compete" and has marginalized Africa and Africans (NEPAD 2001, p 6).

Researchers at the World Bank take a different view (see Collier and Dollar 2001). They have recently examined three periods of globalization and found significant variation across periods, among countries, and within Africa. They show that the first period of globalization, 1870 to 1914, saw the doubling of international trade, which was based largely on the provision of primary commodities from developing countries to rich countries in exchange for manufactures; increases in migration from poorer to richer countries; and increases in international flows of capital.[6] The second period, the post-war era, was characterized by a return to pre-WWI levels of trade flows but not to pre-war levels of migration and capital flows. In the most recent period, the last 35 years, trade as a proportion of world GDP has reached levels higher than in the two previous periods, and the composition of trade has shifted such that developing countries are producing and exporting manufactures. The authors identify two chief features critical to large increases in manufactured exports from developing countries: the reduction of trade barriers by the rich countries and enhancement of the investment environment in the developing countries.

NEPAD and World Bank authors acknowledge that globalization affects regions and countries unevenly. The latter authors divide those affected into three groups. Since 1980, rates of economic growth, on average, fell by 1 percent in the "less globalized" economies, the rich countries grew at 2 percent, and the "more globalized" economies grew at 5 percent per annum. African countries were not excluded from any of the three groups. Côte d'Ivoire and Zimbabwe were among those in the group of "globalizers," along with Bangladesh, Brazil, China, India, and Uruguay. Consistent with the aforementioned UN data, the economies that were more integrated into the world economy fared well with respect to reducing the incidence of poverty in their countries. At the same time that Uganda began to participate more fully in the global economy, between 1992 and 1998, its average growth rate was just below 6 percent per year and poverty there fell by 40 percent.

These empirical results have shed light on the puzzle of economic growth in developing countries such that the growth targets set by NEPAD do not appear as untenable as they might have seemed prior to the 1980s.

In largely accepting these and other findings, NEPAD's architects announced both the objectives and measures deemed necessary to achieve the desired 7 percent rate of growth per year and poverty alleviation. Among the targets are ones related to corporate governance, domestic-savings mobilization, and private investment flows. The shortcomings of economic incentives and outcomes articulated by the document are corroborated not only by the foregoing empirical evidence but also by business leaders in Africa. According to the 2002 World Economic Forum Executive Opinion Survey (simply termed *Survey* hereafter), for example, it is reported that African economies are too dependent on natural resources and that infrastructure is not as good as the world standard. This finding, among others, will be discussed more fully below.

Nonetheless, the problem of addressing the inextricably intertwined problems of economic growth, international trade, and poverty reduction is not a finite Herculean effort that is required of economic policymakers in Africa. It is a sustained, infinite-horizon Sisyphean

Table 2: The economic and business environment, selected African countries

Country	Real GDP growth, average, %, 1998–2001	Quality of nat'l. business environment, rank	Index of economic freedom, 2002, rank	Anti-monopoly enforcement	Start-up procedures, survey score	Start-up procedures, number	Legal dispute settlement	Intellectual property rights protection	Crime and violence	Environmental regulation	Extra payments, public contracts	Extra payments, influencing law, policy	Corruption perceptions index 2002, rank
Botswana	6.5	51	60	3.4	4.5	8	5.1	3.9	4.3	3.6	4.7	5.0	24
Egypt	4.8	na	121	na	na	13	na	na	na	na	na	na	62
Mauritius	5.0	50	72	3.2	4.5	na	4.6	3.5	4.9	3.8	3.6	4.5	40
Morocco	2.1	46	76	4.0	3.6	13	3.9	3.4	5.0	2.8	3.3	3.8	52
Namibia	3.3	49	60	3.6	4.8	na	5.1	4.4	3.3	4.1	3.5	4.3	28
Nigeria	2.2	71	125	3.1	3.5	9	3.0	2.4	2.4	2.0	2.0	2.7	101
South Africa	2.1	33	60	4.9	4.5	9	5.4	5.0	2.9	4.3	4.2	4.7	36
Tunisia	5.2	30	58	4.4	5.3	9	5.0	4.9	5.9	5.2	4.9	5.1	36
Zimbabwe	−1.0	70	147	3.4	3.6	10	2.4	3.0	3.0	3.2	2.5	3.4	71
Mean, Africa	3.4	50	87	3.8	4.3	10.1	4.3	3.8	4.0	3.6	3.6	4.2	50
Mean, All	na	na	na	4.0	4.1	9.8	4.0	4.0	4.4	4.2	4.2	4.4	na
N	9	80	161	80	80	72	80	80	80	80	80	80	102

Notes and sources: GDP growth data are either for fiscal years 1998/1999, 1999/2000, and 2000/2001 or for 1998, 1999, and 2000 and are taken from country pages of www.imf.org. The Index of Economic Freedom data come from http://www.heritage.org/. The start-up procedure data are taken from the World Bank, http://rru.world-bank.org/DoingBusiness/SnapshotReports/Default.aspx. The Corruptions Perceptions Index data come from http://www.transparency.org/. Survey responses are on a scale of 1 to 7, where "1" is the worst outcome and "7" is the best. See Part 4 of the *Report* for further explanation of Survey responses and of the quality of national business environment index. Data on the number of start-up procedures are not available for El Salvador, Estonia, Iceland, Mauritius, Namibia, Nicaragua, Paraguay, the Slovak Republic, and Trinidad and Tobago.

effort that must be undertaken such that globalization's current opportunities are maximized and that the last 180 years are not replicated in the next 180 years. Growth and trade will be central to the analysis that follows.

The African countries included in the rankings of this *Report*—Botswana, Mauritius, Morocco, Namibia, Nigeria, South Africa, Tunisia, and Zimbabwe—plus Egypt account for 97 percent of manufactured exports from Africa and are among the fastest growing in the region.[7] An implicit objective of an African analog of the European Union (EU) or the North American Free Trade Agreement (NAFTA) appears to be to improve these African economies and, simultaneously, to replicate the success of most of these economies across the continent. In order to effect and measure the meaningful economic change envisaged by NEPAD, explicit and more refined economic benchmarks may be useful. What are the elements of economic policy and practice and of an underdeveloped private sector that inhibit innovation, entrepreneurship, trade, and integration in Africa? Using a few but important measures articulated in the NEPAD document, this chapter will attempt to answer this question by focusing on (1) the overall economic or business environment, (2) infrastructure, (3) international and regional trade, and (4) finance. Both published statistical data and data from the Executive Opinion Survey will be used in assessing the current situation in the African countries reviewed.

Economic and business environment

The 49 least developed countries (LDCs), 27 of which are in Africa, accounted for US$5 billion of the US$1 trillion in foreign direct investment (FDI) flows in 1999 (see UNCTAD 2002). NEPAD relates the low level of domestic savings to the scarcity of attractive investment opportunities in African countries. Traditionally, in Africa this scarcity has been reflected in underinvestment by both domestic and foreign savers. To what extent are African economies attractive destinations for savings? Are the conditions in Africa conducive to promoting meaningful economic activity—that is, starting, operating, and growing viable firms? To what extent are African economies able to capture and support innovation in the private sector? The data in Table 2 respond at least partially to these questions, and the results are mixed.

On the one hand, firms reported that starting a business in Africa was somewhat easier (score of 4.3) than in the rest of the world (4.1) and that the legal mechanism for resolving disputes was more useful (4.3) than in the rest of the world (4.0).[8] This finding suggests that the laws on the books are clear. On the other hand, it is clear that some constraints in the business and economic environment are binding in African economies relative to others.

When asked about enforcement and the actual conduct of business in the economy, firms analyze conditions differently. As reported in Table 2, with respect to enforcement of competition (anti-monopoly) policy, intellectual property rights agreements, and environmental regulation, Africa falls below the sample means. With respect to enforcement of environmental regulation, for instance, the means for the Asia region (4.1) and for the central and eastern European and CIS countries (4.0) are closer to the sample mean of 4.2 rather than the Africa mean of 3.6. These findings are consistent with other measures of a country's economic flexibility and depth of economic activity, such as the quality of the national business environment index and the Index of Economic Freedom.[9] With the globalization of capital markets, economies face stiffer competition in mobilizing the resources of domestic and foreign savers. Much improvement is needed to enhance the quality and level of economic interactions in these and other African countries.

International and regional trade

As aforementioned, the opportunity cost of exporting primary products relative to manufactures has grown immensely in the last four decades. In 2001, manufactures accounted for 75 percent of the value of global merchandise trade. The rich countries of western Europe and North America were responsible for 61 percent of manufactured exports (Figure 1), while Africa accounted for less than 1 percent of all trade in manufactures between 1990 and 2001.

The passage from the NEPAD document at the beginning of the chapter rightfully points out a correlation between manufacturing and economic development and growth. A positive relationship has been established in the economics literature between exports of manufactures and rates of economic growth. In addition to the World Bank research mentioned above, Radelet and Sachs (1998), for example, find a positive correlation between rates of economic growth among rapidly growing Asian economies and the expansion of exports in manufactures. This linkage is not surprising, as industrial production typically requires a complex of resources—human, physical, and financial—of an economy and that they function at least somewhat well together.

African countries in the sample have increased manufacturing value-added per capita by 86 percent, on average, between 1985 and 1998. However, these countries are more successful at industrial production than most of their immediate neighbors, and there is tremendous variation within this group. Table 3 shows that Mauritius and Tunisia have had triple-digit increases in manufacturing value added, while it has declined in Nigeria and Zimbabwe by more than one quarter over the same period. Further, the gains in value added in manufacturing have not been captured uniquely by domestic economies. Change in manufacturing value added is positively correlated with the value of manufactured exports as a propor-

tion of total merchandise exports. From the data, three areas emerge in which significant change is needed in order to create an African common market: breadth and depth of the export base, the set of destinations for exports, and trade policy and practices.

Africa's share of the trade in natural resource exports has declined. Prices for the commodity exports are lower than they were in the 1960s, for example, and African countries face stiffer competition from countries with comparable natural resource bases. During the period 1962–1964, sub-Saharan Africa supplied OECD countries with $448 million in green groundnuts, which represented 80.1 percent of OECD imports. By the period 1991–1993, sub-Saharan Africa's share had fallen to 1.7 percent of total OECD green groundnut imports. Ng and Yeats (1996) suggest that, if Africa had maintained its 1962–1964 OECD import market share, its exports would be 75 percent higher.

Export markets, in general, are limited and shrinking for most African economies. Low-income Asian countries began to account for 29.6 (share points) more of green groundnuts imports to OECD countries and Latin America began to account for 11.7 (share points) more by 1991–1993. Ng and Yeats (1996) also find that, between 1962 and 1993, Africa's market share of primary-commodity imports to OECD countries declined in 21 of 30 product groups, while for Latin America, the share increased in 20 of 30 primary-commodity product groups. This feature of African export markets is consistent across the continent and among those firms in the GCR sample, even though these countries export most of the continent's manufactured goods. More African firms say that their economy's export opportunities are constrained (3.1) relative to the entire sample (3.9). Among these, South African firms report being less constrained, with a score of 4.3.

Firms also report that there is too little intraregional trade (4.1) relative to the entire sample (4.8). This perception is borne out by the data (see Figure 2). With respect to overall trade, only the southern region appears to be somewhat integrated. In 2000, the Southern African Custom Union's (SACU) exports to the Southern African Development Community (SADC) alone totaled $3.3 billion and represented one third of overall trade within Africa.[10] With respect to trade in manufactures, African exports to Africa constituted 12 percent of exports to the region in 1990 and 14 percent in 2001. Although the increase in share over time is admirable, it still lags behind most other regions: western Europe, 65 percent; Asia, 44 percent; North America, 37 percent; central and eastern Europe, 23 percent; the Middle East, 16 percent; and Latin America, 15 percent (WTO 2002).

Table 5: Financial indicators, selected African countries

Country	Market capitalization, level, end-2001, US$ mil.	Number of listed companies	Average value of listed company, end-2001, US$ mil.	Value traded/ GDP, 2001	Overall sophistication of financial markets	Protection of assets and wealth	Difficulty of obtaining bank loan	Extra payments for loan application	Difficulty of securing venture capital	Raising funds by issuing shares
Botswana	1,269	16	79.3	1.3	3.5	5.5	3.5	5.1	3.2	5.2
Egypt	24,335	1,110	21.9	7.1	na	na	na	na	na	na
Mauritius	1,063	40	26.6	2.3	3.3	5.4	3.4	5.1	3.0	5.2
Morocco	9,087	55	165.2	3.5	3.0	4.3	2.9	3.5	3.5	4.9
Namibia	151	13	11.6	0.2	3.9	5.3	3.1	4.5	2.9	4.9
Nigeria	5,404	194	27.9	1.1	3.5	3.9	1.9	3.7	2.9	6.2
South Africa	139,750	542	257.8	31.0	5.4	5.5	3.5	5.4	3.7	5.8
Tunisia	2,303	46	50.1	1.6	3.5	5.4	3.3	5.0	3.7	5.5
Zimbabwe	7,972	72	110.7	16.6	4.0	2.6	2.8	4.5	2.9	6.2
Mean, Africa	21,259	232	83	7.2	3.8	4.7	3.1	4.6	3.2	5.5
Mean, All	449,338	576	401	37.52	4.1	4.7	3.3	5.0	3.3	4.8
N	74	74	74	74	80	80	80	80	80	80

Note: Published financial data are not available for Costa Rica, the Dominican Republic, Haiti, Honduras, Nicaragua, Paraguay, and Vietnam.
Sources: *World Development Indicators 2002* (financial data); author's calculations

Figure 4: Value of traded companies, selected African countries

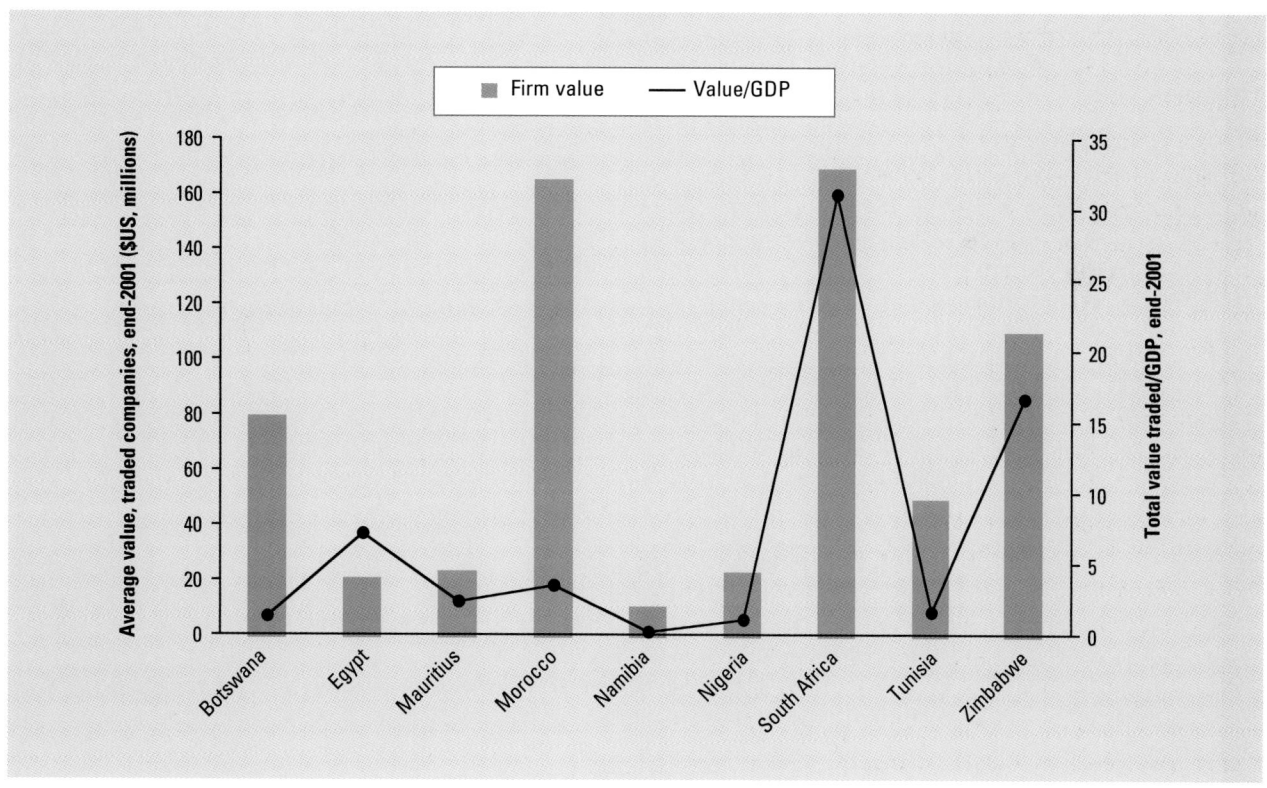

Source: Data are from the World Bank, *World Development Indicators 2002*, http://www.worldbank.org/data/wdi2002

10 Economist Intelligence Unit (2002) and WTO (2002). Members of SACU are Botswana, Lesotho, Namibia, South Africa, and Swaziland. SACU members also belong to SADC, which has 14 members total, including Mauritius and Zimbabwe. Data for SACU/SADC trade are for 2000; data for intraregional trade are for 2001.

11 Variation in AGOA exports may be partially explained by the timing of confirmation of eligibility for privileges under the program. Eligibility is declared on a rolling basis.

12 The European Union web site http://www.eurunion.org/news/press/2000/w000055.htm contains more information on the program.

13 World Economic Forum in *Latin American Competitiveness Report 2001–2002*, p 55, and *Africa Competitiveness Report 2000–2001*, p 271.

14 Further, firms in Africa found the AfDB to be less helpful relative to the entire sample of 2002 GCR countries on issues of private-sector development and poverty alleviation.

15 Caprio, Atiyas, and Hanson (1994), Gelb (1989), King and Levine (1993), Levine (1997), Levine and Zevros (1998), Neusser and Kugler (1998), Stiglitz (2000), and the World Bank (2001) have generated insightful research on this topic.

16 See World Bank (1998) for an exemplary case related to the Senegalese financial system and the *Union Monetaire Ouest Africaine*.

17 The ratio of value traded to GDP for Namibia will be artificially low, because the Namibia Stock Exchange has largely been integrated into the Johannesburg Stock Exchange since 1998. For the same reason, the South African ratio might be slightly overstated.

References

Acemoglu, D., S. Johnson, and J. Robinson. 2001a. "The Colonial Origins of Comparative Development: An Empirical Investigation," *American Economic Review* 91(5): 1339–1401.

———. 2001b. "Reversal of Fortune: Geography and Institutions in the Making of the Modern World Income Distribution," NBER Working Paper No. 8460. Cambridge, MA: National Bureau of Economic Research.

African Growth and Opportunity Act (AGOA). Online. www.AGOA.gov

Agence de Promotion de l'industrie. 1997. "Coûts des factuers de Production en Tunisie et Comparaisons Internationales," Tunis.

Bloom, D. and J. Sachs. 1998. "Geography, Demography, and Economic Growth in Africa," *Brookings Papers on Economic Activity* 1998(2): 207–273.

Caprio, G., I. Atiyas, and J. Hanson, eds. 1994. *Financial Reform: Theory and Evidence.* Cambridge, England: Cambridge University Press.

Clark, X., D. Dollar, and A. Micco. 2002. "Maritime Transport Costs and Port Efficiency," WB Policy Research Working Paper No. 2781. Washington, DC: World Bank.

Collier, P. and D. Dollar. 2001. *Globalization, Growth, and Poverty: Building an Inclusive World Economy.* New York: Oxford University Press for the World Bank.

Collier, P. and C. Udry. 1998. "Geography, Demography, and Economic Growth in Africa: Comments and Discussion," *Brookings Papers on Economic Activity* 1998(2): 274–295.

Cook, L.D. 1999. "Free Zones and Export Growth in Ghana." Harvard University, Mimeo.

———. 2000. "Background Paper on Tunisia." Prepared for CAER Export Platforms Project, Center for International Development at Harvard University.

———. 2001. "Madagascar Needs Assessment Report." Prepared for UNCTAD, Center for International Development at Harvard University.

Cook, L. D. and J. D. Sachs 1999. "Regional Public Goods in International Assistance." In I. Kaul, I. Grunberg, and M. A. Stern, eds., *Global Public Goods: International Cooperation in the 21st Century.* New York: Oxford University Press, 1999.

Dollar, D. 2001. "Globalization, Inequality, and Poverty since 1980." Washington: World Bank, http://www.worldbank.org/research/global

Dollar, D. and A. Kraay 2001. "Growth is Good for the Poor," WB Policy Research Working Paper No. 2587. Washington, DC: World Bank.

Easterly, W. and R. Levine. 1997. "Africa's Growth Tragedy," *Quarterly Journal of Economics* 112(4):1203–1250.

Economist Intelligence Unit. 2002. "Southern Africa: Moving towards an 'African EU,' " July 1, 2002, http://www.eiu.com

European Union. 2001. "Everything but Arms." Online. http://europa.eu.int/comm/trade/miti/devel/eba4_sum.htm

Gelb, A. H. 1989. "Financial Policies, Growth, and Efficiency." World Bank Policy Research Working Paper No. 202. Washington, DC: World Bank.

Heritage Foundation. 2002. *Index of Economic Freedom 2002.* http://www.heritage.org/research/features/index/.

International Monetary Fund (IMF). Country Information. Online. http://www.imf.org/external/country/index.htm

International Monetary Fund (IMF) and World Bank. 2002. "Market Access for Developing Country Exports—Selected Issues." Online. http://econ.worldbank.org/view.php?type=5&id=18875

International Road Federation. 2002. *World Road Statistics.* Online. http://www.irfnet.org/wrs.asp

International Telecommunications Union. Online. http://www.itu.int/home/

King, R. G. and R. Levine. 1993. "Finance and Growth: Schumpeter Might Be Right," *Quarterly Journal of Economics* 108(3): 717–737.

Levine, R. 1997. "Financial Development and Economic Growth: Views and Agenda," *Journal of Economic Literature* 35: 688–726.

Levine, R. and S. Zervos. 1998. "Stock Markets, Banks, and Economic Growth." *American Economic Review* 88(3): 537–558.

Limao N. and A. Venables. 1999. "Infrastructure, Geographical Disadvantage, and Transport Costs." World Bank Policy Research Working Paper No. 2257. Washington, DC: World Bank.

MTC Consulting. 1998. "Etude sur l'offre de biens tunisiens." Mimeo. Tunis.

Maddison, A. 1995. *Monitoring the World Economy 1820–1992.* Paris, France: Development Centre, Organization for Economic Co-opera-tion and Development.

Ministry of Economic Development, Financial Services, and Corporate Affairs of Mauritius, Central Statistics Office. 2002. *The Export Processing Zone and Pioneer Status Enterprises, Second Quarter 2002.* Online. http://ncb.intnet.mu/cso/ei391/epz/intro.htm

The New Partnership for Africa's Development (NEPAD). October 2001. Online. www.nepad.org.

Neusser, K. and M. Kugler. 1998. "Manufacturing Growth and Financial Development: Evidence from OECD Countries," *Review of Economics and Statistics* 80: 636–646.

Ng, F. and A. Yeats. 1996. "Open Economies Work Better! Did Africa's Protectionist Policies Cause Its Marginalization in World Trade?" Policy Research Working Paper No. 1686. Washington, DC: World Bank.

O'Rourke, K. and J. Williamson. 1999. *Globalization and History.* Cambridge, MA: MIT Press.

Price Waterhouse. 1998. *Tunisia Information Guide.* Tunis.

Radelet, S. and J. D. Sachs. 1998. "Shipping Costs, Manufactured Exports, and Economic Growth." Harvard Institute for International Development. Online. http://www2.cid.harvard.edu/hiidpapers/ship-cost.pdf

Rodriguez, F. and D. Rodrik. 1999. "Trade Policy and Economic Growth: A Skeptic's Guide to the Cross-National Evidence," NBER Working Paper No. w7081. Cambridge, MA: National Bureau of Economic Research.

Rodrik, D. 1998. "Trade Policy and Economic Performance in Africa," NBER Working Paper No. w6562. Cambridge, MA: National Bureau of Economic Research.

Sachs, J. D. and A. Warner. 1995. "Economic Reform and the Process of Global Integration." *Brookings Papers on Economic Activity*. 1995(1): 1–118.

———. 1997. "Sources of Slow Growth in Africa," *Journal of African Economies* 6: 335–376.

Stiglitz, J. E. 2000. "Capital Market Liberalization, Economic Growth, and Instability," *World Development* 28(6): 1075–1086.

Transparency International. 2002. "The Corruptions Perceptions Index." Online. http://www.transparency.org/

United Nations Development Programme (UNDP). 2002. *Human Development Report 2000*. Online. http://www.undp.org

UNCTAD. 2002. "Foreign Direct Investment Database." Online. http://www.unctad.org/

UNIDO, *Industrial Development Report 2002/2003* http://www.unido.org/doc/511836.htmls

US International Trade Center. 2002. "U.S. Exports, Imports, GSP Imports, and AGOA Imports." Online. http://reportweb.usitc.gov/africa/by_country.jsp

World Bank. 1998. *Financial Sector Reform*. Washington, DC: World Bank.

———. 2001. *Finance for Growth*. New York: Oxford University Press.

———. 2002. *World Development Indicators 2002*. Online. http://www.worldbank.org/data/wdi2002/.

World Economic Forum. 2000.*Africa Competitiveness Report 2000–2001* Cape Town and New York: Oxford University Press.

———. 2002. *Latin American Competitiveness Report 2001–2002* . New York: Oxford University Press.

World Trade Organization (WTO). 2002. "International Trade Statistics 2002." Online. http://www.wto.org/english/res_e/statis_e/statis_e.htm

CHAPTER 2.5

Asia: The Productivity Imperative

DIANA FARRELL, The McKinsey Global Institute[1]

Post–World War II, the phrase *the Asian Economic Miracle* was commonly used to describe the phenomenon of Asia's strong economic growth. Unsurprisingly, this epithet is no longer in common usage. The stalling of Japan's economy, combined with the "Asian Flu," the regional economic crisis of 1997–1998, have raised serious questions about whether Asia is able to build on its past economic success. It is now commonly understood that these problems have roots in a fundamental economic malaise that goes to the heart of Asia's economies. Such failures have severely shaken business confidence throughout the region and, although a number of the economies now show an apparent return to form in exhibiting higher growth rates, doubts remain. Japan's economy, the most important in Asia, continues to be stagnant after 10 years of reforms and pump-priming investment. There, as elsewhere in the region, there is a clear sense that what has worked well in the past no longer does so. Something more is needed if sustainable growth is to be achieved.

In examining the region's potential, we have studied a wide range of industries across Asia. In doing so, we have been cognizant that it is difficult to make meaningful generalizations about a region as diverse as Asia. Not only does the region account for a good portion of the world's population, but it also encompasses the most disparate range of economic models anywhere on earth. Having said this, our examination of four essentially divergent economies—those of India, Japan, Korea, and Thailand—show that these economies exhibit underlying similarities in a number of important aspects. Despite their obvious differences, useful generalizations can be made about the path that Asian economies need to take if they are to achieve greater prosperity.

The most striking observation is that in each of these countries many sectors are woefully inefficient. Each of the economies studied can be clearly divided in two. On the one side are industries and services that are relatively efficient and productive; on the other, in clear contrast, those that are inefficient and underproductive. McKinsey Global Institute (MGI) studies have shown that the dividing line is no mere accident.

Asia's export-led growth has ensured that many industries have been subject to the shaping forces of rigorous market competition. In these industries, labor productivity is relatively high. In contrast, those industries and services that are domestically oriented—the non-tradable sectors—have had to face less rigorous competition and have lagged in their productivity growth. In the domestically oriented industries that we studied, we found levels of Asian labor productivity to be a fraction of US levels. It is here that the opportunity lies.

This opportunity is underlined by changes in the relative competitive position of the Asian economies considered here. Whereas many countries in Asia have in the past

145

competed largely on factor input–based competitive advantages, particularly in terms of labor costs and natural resources, new competition is now emerging that will make this strategy harder to sustain. China's factor-input costs in manufactured goods have enabled it to make inroads into the world's major export markets, taking an increasing share of total exports. These factor advantages are attracting substantial foreign direct investment (FDI) including investment from elsewhere in the region. Japan, in particular, has relocated substantial manufacturing capacity to China. Similarly, though it has yet to attract substantial FDI, India is emerging with similar advantages in services.

This new competition, combined with rising wages, suggests that Asia's other economies need increasingly to emphasize labor productivity advantages if they are to grow rapidly. This is not to say that the root causes of the current malaise, nor the required responses, are similar in each country's case. Indeed, a clear distinction can be made between Japan and Korea on the one hand and India and Thailand on the other. Whereas the former are relatively high-wage economies that have a successful export-led track record now facing low-cost competition, India and Thailand are emerging as global players without many clear factor-input advantages.

Underlying these distinctions, however, the challenges of these four countries show surprising commonality. India's remote services sectors, though currently highly competitive, are seeing rapid increases in wage costs as they integrate with the global economy. Japan's economy, in many ways highly advanced, is hamstrung because of the inefficiency of its domestic sector (Figure 1). India and Thailand, as much as Japan and Korea, need to see improvements in their labor productivity if they are to see sustainable growth at the higher levels they have come to expect.

The common difficulty faced by Asia's economies is therefore clear. The efficiencies engendered by international markets need to be emulated in the domestic, non-tradable sectors. Whereas international markets define the nature of the competition—the type of goods and services required and the attributes of those services—domestically oriented industries and services are largely shaped by domestic conditions. Such considerations have all too frequently led to substantial regulation that has inadvertently promoted structural ossification rather than increased productivity.

A corollary of the forces that have shaped the competitive environment in domestic-oriented industries is that each country's requirements are likely to be fairly unique or, at the very least, will exhibit unique characteristics. Food, housing, and retailing are all subject to national tastes, culture, and demands. Yet the case can be overstated. Though these differences are undeniable, such differences are usually somewhat exaggerated by those with vested interests in protecting the status quo. Although, almost by definition, domestic goods and services cannot be physically traded for practical reasons, less direct forms of international competition can be encouraged, better methods and technologies can be introduced, and markets can be reshaped.

History has shown that in other parts of the world productivity gains can be achieved in domestic areas of the economy without sacrificing national tastes, culture, and demands. There is nothing inevitable about the low productivity of Japanese retailing or Korean housing. The productivity of Japanese retailing can be improved without making it un-Japanese; Korean housing can meet the needs of Korea and yet be more productive.

Yet it is undeniable that Asia's policymakers will have to make some difficult choices if they are to realize the potential productivity gains. Tradeoffs will need to be made. It is likely that some of the people and businesses that currently benefit from the inefficiencies will lose out. Yet, if the status quo is maintained at the cost of greater productivity, then a substantial opportunity for growth will be lost and the malaise will continue unchecked. This chapter sets out to highlight some of these tradeoffs. It sketches what has led to the current situation and highlights the challenges that need to be faced and the decisions that policymakers need to make. It highlights the significant cost to the economy of specific product, market, and land regulations and, in some cases, the cost of lack of enforcement. In what follows we raise the major challenges facing each economy, examine the opportunities within specific sectors, and look briefly at how these opportunities have been realized in specific cases.

Asia's dilemma: improving productivity

Today's challenges in Asia do not exist in isolation. They are the result of historical patterns of growth that have been shaped by national economic policy. This section focuses primarily on a brief description of these economic challenges, placing the issues in the context of the role that needs to be played by productivity improvements.

Japan

Japan's economy was the great success story of the post-War years. From the 1940s through to the 1980s it achieved unparalleled and rapid economic growth. Much of this growth was driven by ever-increasing exports, a strategy that focused the industries concerned on continuous improvement in their efficiency, quality, and the productivity of their manufacturing. Many Japanese products, in such areas as electronic consumer goods and automobiles, have come to be seen as best in class. Japanese production processes and innovation techniques have been widely imitated.

Figure 1: Productivity performance in Japan

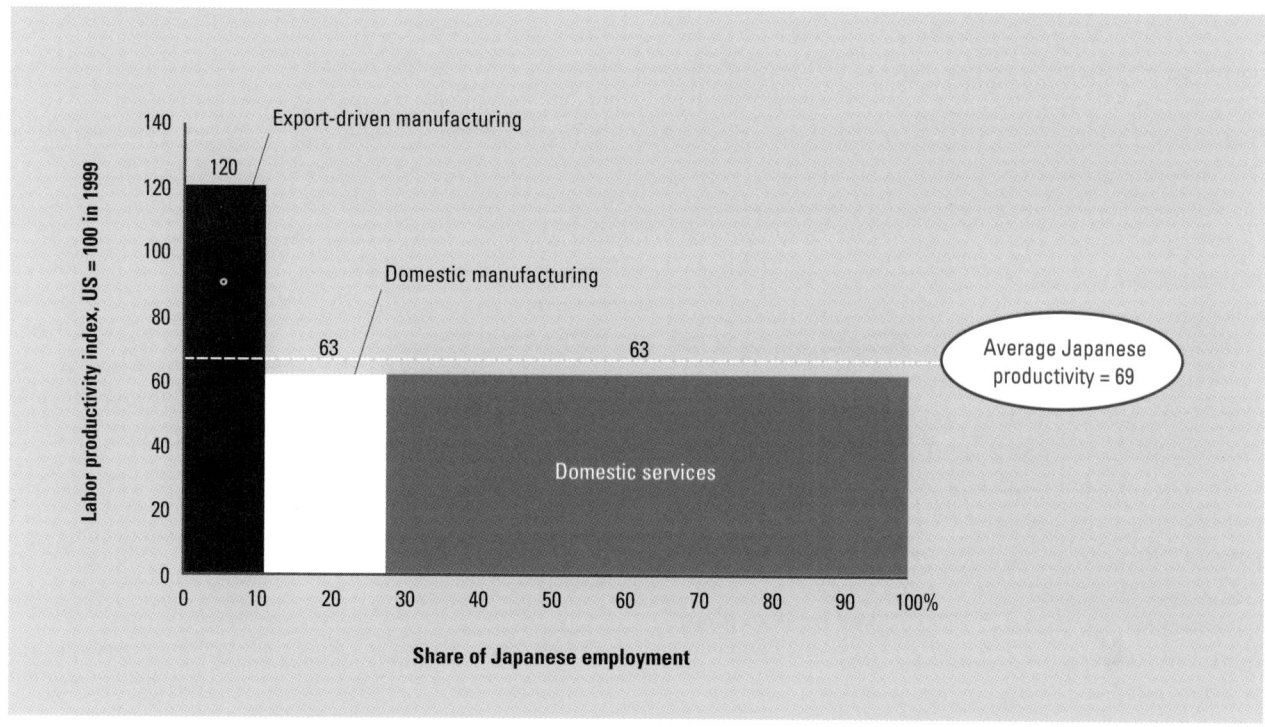

Sources: OECD; O'Mahoney, *Britain's Productivity Performance 1950–96: An international perspective*; McKinsey analysis

In the 1990s this success and the continuous expansion came to a grinding halt. GDP growth for the decade slowed to an average of just 0.6 percent per year. Unemployment rose from 2.3 percent in 1990 to 5.4 percent in 2002, shocking the Japanese workforce, who were used to guaranteed lifetime employment. Despite the government's best efforts, nothing appears to be able to pick up the economy. Extensive fiscal spending and loose monetary policy failed to have any positive impact. Between 1991 and 1998, the government approved stimulus packages worth nearly $800 billion. This helped push up the government debt to GDP ratio from 60 percent in 1990 to nearly 120 percent in 2000, twice the level of the government debt of the United States and Germany. Yet despite all the spending, the economy stubbornly refused to grow, leaving many bewildered by the powerful deflationary forces at work.

What stands out about Japan's current economic performance is that, despite its earlier successes, Japan lags well behind the United States in certain fundamental, crucial respects. At the aggregate level, the Japanese use 11 percent more effort and 20 percent more capital per worker than America. Despite the efficiency of the export-led sectors, much of Japan's economy is, in other words, woefully underproductive.

Korea

Korea is considered a prime example of what has been referred to by commentators as *the Asian economic miracle*. In many ways Korea emulated Japan's earlier development path in building up infrastructure and focusing on export-led growth of manufactured goods. As a result of this policy, Korea's economy grew rapidly from the 1970s onward and is currently a major manufacturing power in such areas as electronics and automobiles. This development led to a fivefold increase in real income per capita between 1970 and 1995, making Korea the world's 12th largest economy today.

This spectacular growth has not been without its costs. It has been possible only because of the combination of a high level of savings and long working hours. Productivity is, as a result, relatively low. Today's youth in Korea, as in Japan, are questioning the degree of personal sacrifice needed to sustain this level of growth, suggesting that the past pattern of development might well need to be modified if growth is to continue. As elsewhere in the region, these challenges have been compounded by the economic shock of 1997 combined with the current downturn in the world economy. This has led many Koreans to question the wisdom of continuing a growth path so dependent on exports. If Korea's aspirations are to be met, then improvements in productivity are essential.

Thailand

When Thailand emerged on a path of rapid economic development in the 1980s, it epitomized the notion of the Asian "tiger economy." Over a period of three decades it sustained a GDP growth rate averaging more than 6 percent a year, reaching close to 9 percent for the whole of the 1980s and early 1990s. This growth, as in the case of other Association of South-East Asian Nations (ASEAN) countries, was to a large extent based in the competitive advantages derived from low-cost inputs—in particular, labor costs and natural resources (eg, rubber).

As with other economies in the region, the Asian Flu came as a severe jolt, temporarily reversing the gains that had been made in previous years. The past two administrations in Thailand have explored a variety of strategies for reviving economic growth. These efforts started with fiscal measures and trade liberalization guided by the International Monetary Fund (IMF) and have since included economic pump-priming and technical support to small manufacturing enterprises. However, now growing strongly, the economy has yet to recover its previous "tiger" growth levels, and the experience of the 1997 crisis has left many ordinary Thai people uneasy and distrustful of the role of the international financial community. Some doubt that it can reach the former levels of growth. The MGI examination of the economy suggests that a core part of the solution lies in improving productivity.

India

Unlike the other countries considered here, India long relied on import-substitution in its economic policy. As a result, India's economy grew slowly for many years, with GDP growth averaging just 1.6 percent a year per capita from Independence through till the mid 1980s. From then until 1990 GDP growth averaged 2.6 percent. In 1991-3 India went through substantial policy liberalization. This resulted in the rate of GDP growth picking up to 4.2 percent per capita a year. India is still no tiger, but it is certainly exhibiting a healthier growth than in earlier years.

The many years of slow growth saw India fall behind its traditional competitors. Whereas India's per capita GDP was historically within shooting distance of China's, today it is a little over half that of its neighbor's. Part of the problem is the result of demographic growth. Total GDP growth has always been several points higher than per capita growth because of the country's rapidly expanding population. Its population is currently growing at 1.8 percent per year, having dropped from above 2 percent for most of this period. India has done well in these circumstances to see the proportion of population below the poverty line decline from around 45 percent in 1980 to 26 percent in 2000. Life expectancy has similarly been raised by over 25 percent between 1980 and 1998, from 50 to 63 years.

These successes, combined with the high rate of population growth, will place a great deal of strain on future labor productivity. The labor force is currently expanding at 2.4 percent a year. In the recent past, India has derived much of its improved growth rate from improvements in labor productivity, illustrating the vital role productivity improvements play in its economy.

The vital role of competition

We earlier suggested that the domestic, non-tradable sector of the economy can be characterized as being shaped by domestic and cultural considerations and that, with all good intentions, these considerations are often translated into regulation that inadvertently limits the opportunity for productivity improvement. How does this happen? Our work in Asia suggests that the prime cause is that regulation inadvertently restricts the competitive intensity in the non-tradable sector. Such inadvertent curbing of competitive intensity can have numerous outcomes, ranging from preventing consolidation—including preventing the industry from reaching the scale where automation becomes possible—to substantially limiting the desire to adopt best practices because of the comfortable relationships that are enabled to continue within the industry.

The problems of the non-tradable sector are often interlocking. This in part helps explain why reform has proved so difficult and productivity improvements so elusive. In Japan, for instance, the regulations that restrict large-scale retailers interact with those that inadvertently provide incentives to small-scale retailers not to exit. As a result, land ownership changes very slowly. The resulting retail fragmentation then has a knock-on effect that prevents consolidation of the food processing industry. The dairy industry, for example, exists in two parallel systems: one in which inefficient small-scale processors typically supply small, inefficient local stores, and the other in which large processors supply large, efficient retailers. Improvements seen elsewhere suggest that small retailers need not necessarily be inefficient, so there is nothing inevitable about this situation. Land regulation also prevents any change in the housing construction industry. The same tax incentives that discourage small-scale retailers from exiting also prevent large-scale housing construction. As a result, the housing construction industry remains sub-scale and there is little to drive Design for Manufacturing (DFM) processes or standardization of materials. It is clear that for reform to be successful, it needs to tackle the interlocking nature of the problems.

In order to better understand the effects of government regulation on productivity we have chosen to look at four industries in the non-tradable sector: housing construction, retail, food processing, and telecom.

Figure 2: Size of housing construction industry*

Share of GDP (%)

Japan — 5
Korea — 5
India — 1
US — 4

Share of employment (%)

Japan — 4
Korea — 3
India — 1
US — 3

* Japanese and Korean data are for 1995, Indian and US data are for 1997.
Source: McKinsey Global Institute country reports

Housing construction

At the outset, let us be clear that housing is an emotive subject. Families are very important in Asia and the home is central to the family. Hence, when we talk of housing, emotion is likely to be generated. Housing is also the very articulation of tradition. Regions and even countries are identified with traditional forms of housing.

It can be argued that local regulation has sought to protect these things. But if it has, it has succeeded only in part. Indeed, modern housing construction in India, Japan, Korea, and Thailand have much more in common with each other than they do with the traditional forms of housing in any of these countries. Modernity has already won in terms of construction form. Modernity, however, is not the same thing as efficiency. A very wide range of productivity levels was observed across the countries studied, from 8 percent of US levels in India to 69 percent in Korea. With the exception of India, where productivity potential is constrained by the very low levels of income of large sections of the population, productivity could potentially reach around 90 percent of US levels. By way of comparison, the Netherlands show labor productivity levels comparable with those seen in the United States. Many would also say that the Netherlands have been more successful than most in integrating modern construction with its traditional urban landscape.

We have studied housing construction in detail in Japan, Korea, and India. This sector is important economically: in each case housing construction accounts for between 1 and 5 percent of each nation's economy and between 1 and 4 percent of employment (Figure 2). It is important socially: housing is a basic social need. Changes in housing construction have a very direct impact in improving a society's and an individual's standard of living. Few would dare argue against lower housing prices and the wider availability of affordable housing.

Housing construction is non-tradable; it places many obstacles in the way of successfully transferring technology, systems, skills, and knowledge between markets. Safety and planning regulation, climate, the community's expectations of housing densities and housing forms, and the house buyer's product expectations all play their part in creating these obstacles. The resulting equations of regulation and expectation are complex, and the potential for limiting efficiency great. As a result, housing construction is one of the few markets where, even with a fully open market, few foreign firms would be prepared to enter. To be successful, the industry requires access to a vast amount of hard and soft information and deep knowledge of local operating conditions. As a result of these difficulties there are few global construction companies. Skanska, a Swedish company, is one of the few in the industry that appears to be set to become global. These two problems need to be resolved before progress can be made.

If policymakers cannot look to FDI to rescue housing construction productivity, where will help come from? In answering that question, our analysis of the industry suggests that low productivity in housing construction is in large part due to two key factors: first, to the product mix of different types of housing available; second, to the degree of price competition. The product mix can directly affect productivity as well as distort competition within the industry as a whole. Price competition is very easily disrupted, both in the market for developers and in that for contractors.

Product mix

Product mix is very important. Though individual house buyers are presented with a limited set of options within their price range, the potential set of options is much wider than the currently limited set on offer. In examining this problem we have framed the product mix as exhibiting four dimensions: single family versus multi-family housing, primary versus secondary housing, large-scale construction versus small-scale, and higher quality versus lower. We will discuss each of these four dimensions in turn.

1. The first of these dimensions is *single family versus multi-family housing*. Multi-family housing (apartments, condominiums, or flats) is higher density, providing for greater efficiency in land utilization, but typically creating lower value added per unit, which translates into lower productivity. In Korea the high percentage of multi-family housing is the result of limited land availability due to zoning and price cap regulations. Multi-family housing accounts for 81 percent of all new construction in Korea, compared with only 20 percent in the United States. However, Korean single-family housing is 56 percent more productive than its multi-family housing counterpart. This is a common pattern. For a number of reasons (discussed below), including its greater reliance on traditional building forms, its high population density, and its high land costs, Japan is the exception to this rule. It has a fairly high percentage of multi-family housing, which comprises a little over half of all new construction. In Japan, such housing is slightly more productive than single-family housing. However, it is still only 60 percent as productive as US levels (Figure 3).

If land prices are high, surely more multi-family housing is the answer? Our view is that this should not be assumed to be the right answer in every case. It is often thought to be so because the right question is not being asked, which, in richer markets, is not how cheap can housing be built, but how can its construction create the greatest value? Looking at the problem in this light makes it clear that there are alternative approaches to building

the current multi-family constructions because house buyers are looking for "good value." Good value might well derive, for example, from a higher price or from a single-family dwelling. Alternatively, it might derive from better (or shared) amenities in a multi-family dwelling (such as shops, a gymnasium, or a swimming pool). Nor should the inputs be assumed to be static. Though land prices might be high, regulation is helping keep them artificially so, as in the zoning regulation found in Korea.

Experience elsewhere in the world, such as in the Netherlands, also shows that single-family units can be relatively high density when planned effectively, and that improved transport infrastructure can quickly revalue otherwise unpopular locations. The garden suburb is not a one-size-fits-all solution, but neither is the multi-family skyscraper. Greater productivity can be achieved by imaginative use of the land available and by making a variety of options available to home buyers.

2. The second of the four dimensions that determine the product mix in the housing market is the level of importance of the *secondary housing market*, the market for buying and selling "used homes." In both Japan and India, the secondary housing market is very weak. Some would no doubt argue that the lack of a secondary housing market is in many ways a good thing. It is no doubt true that if people own only one house in a lifetime, this speaks of the likelihood of high social stability and strong community bonds. The clear tradeoff, however, is that the reverse side of social stability is a consequent lack of social mobility. In the United States, 66 percent of all moves are within the same area and only 10 percent are caused by job relocation, suggesting that fulfilling personal aspirations plays a large part in shaping the secondary housing market there. One outcome of this is that each house in the United States has 17 times as many transactions as does the average Japanese house. Each transaction creates value.

Why is it that India and Japan have failed to develop a secondary housing market? There are two main reasons: information transparency and tax disincentives. In both countries, there is insufficient information transparency on transactions, particularly in terms of the market price and quality. This leads to buyers and sellers finding it difficult to agree on a price acceptable to both, as there is no objective way of measuring what premium, if any, is being paid. Similarly, in both countries potential sellers see transaction taxes as disincentives to selling. In Japan the tax structure actively discourages short-term ownership: a tax of 40 percent is imposed on properties owned for less than five years, compared with 14 percent for those owned for more than ten years.

3. The third dimension that determines the product mix in housing construction is *scale*. The economies of scale in housing construction come from the efficient use of prefabricated materials, better equipment utilization,

Figure 3: Comparison of housing mix, 1999

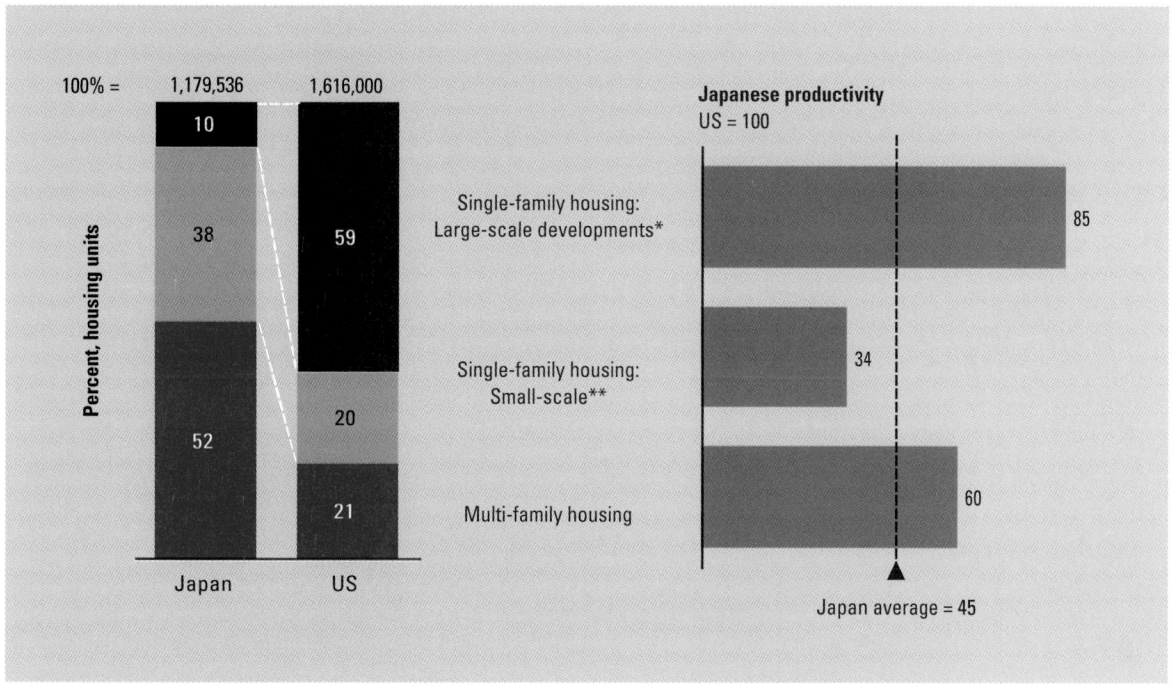

* 10 percent of total output is built by developers, therefore this is an upper boundary. ** Mostly post and beam
Source: McKinsey Global Institute Japan report

bulk purchasing of materials, and the spreading of architecture fees. Together such economies can reduce construction costs by 25 percent (as, for example, in constructing 50 single-family row homes at a time as compared with constructing a single unit). Achieving such economies of scale has two dimensions to it: large housing volumes and standardization. Large volumes are the result of large-scale investment. Smaller builders are not typically in a position to realize these economies. Standardization is the result of policy regulation, the outcome of large-scale construction, or the two acting in combination. Unfortunately, scale is lacking in each of the housing markets we studied. As a result there are no consequent economies of scale and little standardization. In turn, this limits the opportunity for skills and systems transfer. In Japan, for example, there are some 150 regional systems for the construction of traditional post-and-beam housing, and 10 systems even for pre-fabricated housing. In more advanced markets, Design for Manufacturing (DFM) has a shaping influence on construction as it improves planning and changes the way the contractor views the project from one of craftsmanship to that of assembly. The use of standardized materials in such areas as doors and windows, plumbing and wiring, flooring and roofing, and wall and roof components leads to task specialization and reductions in installation time.

What causes this lack of standardization? In India, large-scale construction is difficult for two reasons. First, the underlying infrastructure is poorly developed, so "green-field" sites are relatively unattractive to developers. Second, high population densities and fragmented land ownership patterns mean that there is, in any case, a shortage of suitable land for development. Japan faces similar constraints in that the supply of suitable land plots for large-scale construction is limited. There are two causes of this: the tax disincentives to sell property mentioned earlier (the property and inheritance tax), and land fragmentation caused by urban development laws. In the case of both India and Japan it is difficult to see the benefits of scale being realized without policy intervention.

4. The fourth and final element in the housing mix is *quality*. "You get what you pay for" is a maxim that does not apply to much of the Asian housing market. In Japan, for example, the high levels of design customization combined with a shortage of the requisite skills (in such areas as carpentry and joinery) has led to inefficient design and a relatively low quality of execution. The 1998 Survey on the Demand for Housing conducted by the Japanese Ministry of Construction found that 48 percent of all households were dissatisfied with their housing conditions. The primary causes of this dissatisfaction was cited to be the lack of provision for the elderly, soundproofing and

insulation, inadequate space, high levels of wear and tear, and inadequate air-conditioning and water supply.

Market constraints mean that there is insufficient higher-quality property available in both Japan and Korea, the market mix favoring the lower end. Again, this reduces the potential for the value added per worker in construction. This situation is the result of well-intended regulation. In Korea, price cap regulation, intended to protect lower-income groups, results in builders lowering quality to come within the price constraints. Under these constraints, Korean construction firms supply just the bare walls, whereas in the United States builders will add a large number of fixtures and fittings, such as refrigerators, ovens, fireplaces, carpets, and the like. Approximately one-third of the productivity gap between Korea and the United States is accounted for by the differences in quality and content mix.

Price competition

Apart from these four dimensions determining the product mix, the other major factor determining the productivity of the sector is the level of price competition. In all the markets we studied, price competition for contractors and developers proved to be easily disrupted, thereby directly reducing incentives to improve productivity in the industry.

The lack of enforced standards for materials and construction methods in India and Japan is a major contributing factor to the reduced levels of competition found there. The lack of information transparency prevents house buyers from making like for like comparisons, giving contractors considerable power in shaping the production outcome. In India, for example, inadequately enforced materials standards lead contractors to focus on procuring materials at the lowest cost. These cost savings in inputs are, however, not passed on to the home buyer. As a result, materials are often of poor or of substandard quality, leading to profit levels substantially higher than the international average. Developers and contractors collude in materials procurement and neglect any focus on improving site design or project management. Similarly, in Japan, the multiplicity of construction techniques and lack of standardization in design leads to high levels of customization and very little focus on project management or design for manufacturing.

In both India and Japan, competition between developers primarily takes the form of securing access to land, as opposed to price-based competition. Large-scale land plots are seldom available, so when they are, such competition is intense. Whoever controls the land controls the market. Although this is true to a large extent elsewhere in the world, it is important to recognize that a poorly functioning land market exacerbates the lack of pricing transparency.

What needs to be done?

Housing construction represents a set of interlocking problems that are unlikely to be unraveled independently. The product mix and level of price competition have been shaped by a number of historical factors that hold down productivity. Policymakers need to consider what they can do to unlock this logjam. As was mentioned earlier, changes cannot be made without tradeoffs. The two most important things to consider to help shape the outcome in this context are housing mix and competition. This decision needs to be taken in the context of the economy as a whole.

There are two key interventions that can raise Asia's housing construction labor productivity: creating the scale to optimize DFM techniques and achieving greater pricing transparency. The current lack of scale prevents the introduction and use of DFM techniques. The resulting lack of standardization and inefficiency of design leads to significantly lowered productivity levels. The lack of standardization also contributes to the difficulty in maintaining price transparency, as individual houses vary enormously in their methods of construction, in their design, and in the quality of materials that have been used in their construction.

It is clear that a crucial determinant of the success of the outcome will be the balance of the housing mix. Policymakers need to examine this in the light of this requirement for scale. The right strategy could enable well-funded developers to drive through simultaneously large-scale housing projects, DFM, better project management, and materials standardization.

Retail

The challenges to retail productivity in Asia in many ways follow a pattern similar to those facing housing construction. Firstly, retail is a very large and important sector of Asia's economies, representing between 5 and 10 percent of each nation's economy and from 6 to 16 percent of its employment (Figure 4). Secondly, there is a large productivity gap as compared to the US. Although a wide range of productivity levels were observed across the countries studied, none reached a level more than half that of the US. Thirdly, the retail industry is subject to many of the same cultural and regulatory pressures as housing construction.

Because retail is essentially linked to personal, regional, and national consumption preferences, it is harder for policymakers to commit to restructuring this sector than it is for those less in the public eye. Retail reform has a definite impact on the lifestyle and behaviors of individuals. As with housing construction, because retail growth is driven by consumption, this impact is likely to be seen as positive rather than negative.

Figure 4: Size of retail industry*

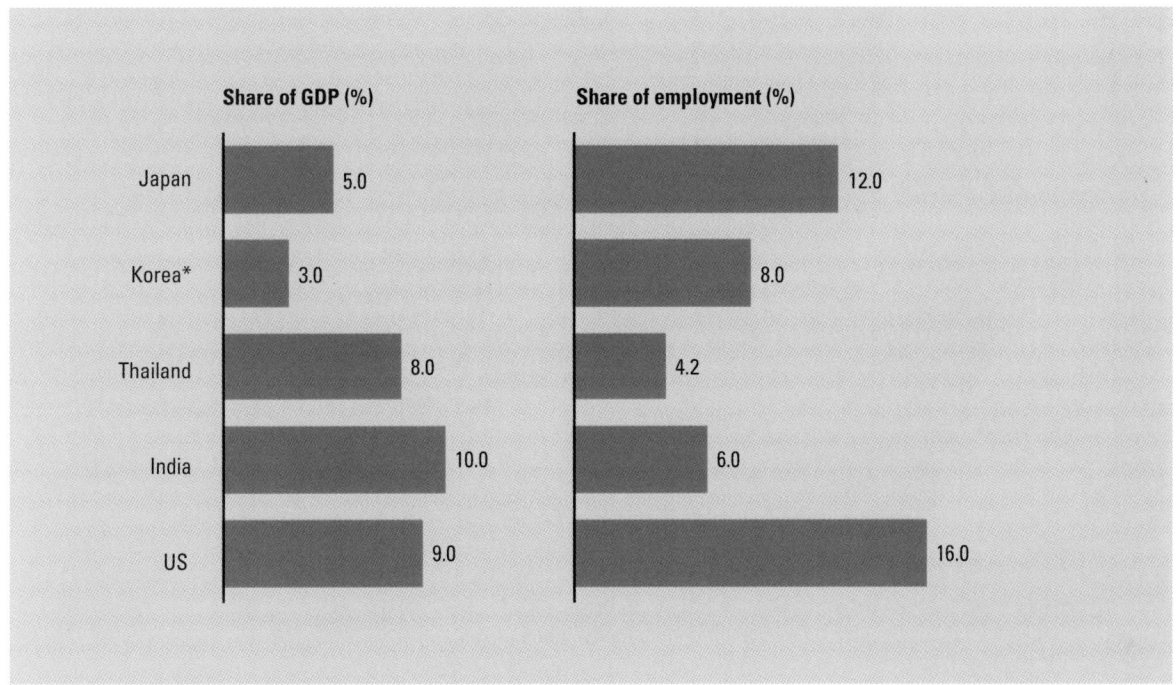

* Only general merchandise retail; Korea and Japan data are for 1995; India and US data are for 1997.
Sources: McKinsey Global Institute country reports

From a wider perspective, the imperative for improving productivity is great, as demand for improvements in retailing productivity put similar pressures on a wide range of upstream industries supplying the retailers. Productivity improvements are also highly visible, as they tend to be quickly translated into lower retail prices. This in turn stimulates demand and raises the standard of living across the economy.

Modern retail format

The low productivity of the retail sector in Asia stems primarily from the limited share of modern retail formats in the sector and the ensuing reliance on traditional store formats (Figure 5). In Japan, for example, the productivity gap between Japanese discounters and general merchandise stores and those in the United States is negligible. However, such stores account for only 12 percent of retail employment in Japan, compared with 35 percent in the United States. In contrast, the share of employment derived from traditional stores in Japan is 55 percent compared with 19 percent in the United States, while productivity is only 33 percent of the US levels of "mom & pop" stores. Of course, what is considered to be traditional varies widely between countries, from wet markets in Thailand to street vendors in India to small local stores in Korea and Japan.

There are two sets of causes that determine why traditional stores continue to be dominant throughout Asia: factors that reduce the competitive position of modern formats as compared with traditional formats, and factors that explicitly bar the entry of modern formats.

1. *The factors that reduce the competitive position of modern formats* are typically those that provide an artificial cost advantage to traditional retailers. In Thailand and India, these advantages take the form of a combination of regulatory differentiation and weak regulatory enforcement that allows traditional retailers to reduce their tax burden and skirt minimum wage requirements. In India, underdeveloped upstream industries also add costs and complicate sourcing for modern formats, preventing them from reaching the necessary levels of scale and standardization. In Japan, low property taxes, high capital gains taxes, and inheritance tax reductions discourage traditional retailers from exiting and selling off land. Government loan guarantees and subsidies also help support the position of traditional retailers in Japan.

2. *Policy plays a large role in preventing the entry of modern retail formats.* Land availability is one of the biggest issues in all the countries examined. In India, the unavailability of appropriate real estate for modern formats is due to generous tenancy laws and unclear land titles. In Japan, the large-scale retail location law essentially allows local traditional retailers to limit the entry of large-scale

Figure 5: Size and productivity of traditional and modern retail industry*

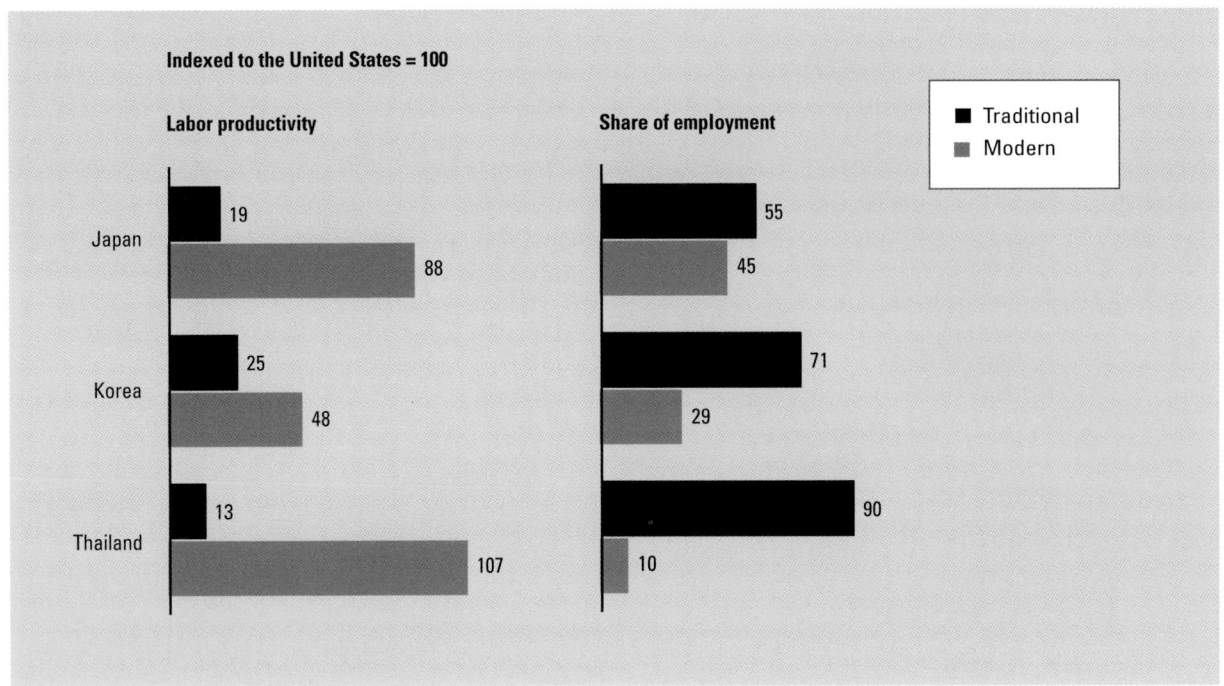

Indexed to the United States = 100

* Korean data are for 1992, Japan and Thailand data are for 1999.
Sources: McKinsey Global Institute country reports

retailers. In Korea, restrictive zoning and land development laws restrict the use of land and reduce its availability, especially as regards large buildings such as shopping malls. Additionally, explicit or implicit restrictions on FDI are another way in which the entry of modern formats (and the introduction of best practices) is prevented. In Korea, for example, FDI is expressly forbidden in department stores and shopping malls. Complicated and time-consuming application processes for entering the Korean market act as an additional deterrent. As a result of this restricted competition, even where modern formats do exist, they frequently exhibit fairly low levels of productivity due to the lack of exposure to best practice skills and methods. This is certainly the case in India, where there are explicit bans on FDI in the retail sector.

What needs to be done?
Quite simply, policy needs to encourage greater competitive intensity. This will in turn lead to a greater focus on merchandizing. For example, traditional stores have faced intense competition from large chains in France, but they continue to survive next door to supermarkets with highly focused merchandizing in the form of gourmet cheese stores, fresh-from-the-farm vegetable stores, ethnic grocery stores, patisseries, and the like. In Japan, the lack of merchandizing in traditional stores accounts for more than two thirds of the productivity gap as compared with US

traditional stores (the remainder mainly derives from the absence of point-of-sale information technology). In conclusion, it is evident that greater competitive intensity would encourage the migration to more productive retail formats. For example, in Japan, though large and regional supermarkets exhibit respectable levels of productivity, some 70 percent of supermarket employment is still in small, local stores. Here the productivity is just 65 percent that of the larger Japanese supermarkets (and barely half US levels).

To return to the issues about consumer preferences, it should be clear that increased competitive intensity can lead to a solution that, rather than completely eliminating local stores, gives them a more productive role better focused on consumer needs. High productivity is not synonymous with complete uniformity—far from it—but it is synonymous with greater competition.

Food processing
Food consumption, even more than housing or retail, is defined to a very large extent by cultural and national preferences, resulting in many of the challenges to productivity that have already been discussed in the sections on housing construction and retail. Processed foods, unlike housing and retail, are sometimes tradable. Though perishable processed foods, such as dairy products, are restricted in their tradability, commodities such as flour, frozen

Figure 6: Productivity impact of import restrictions on commodity food products, Japan

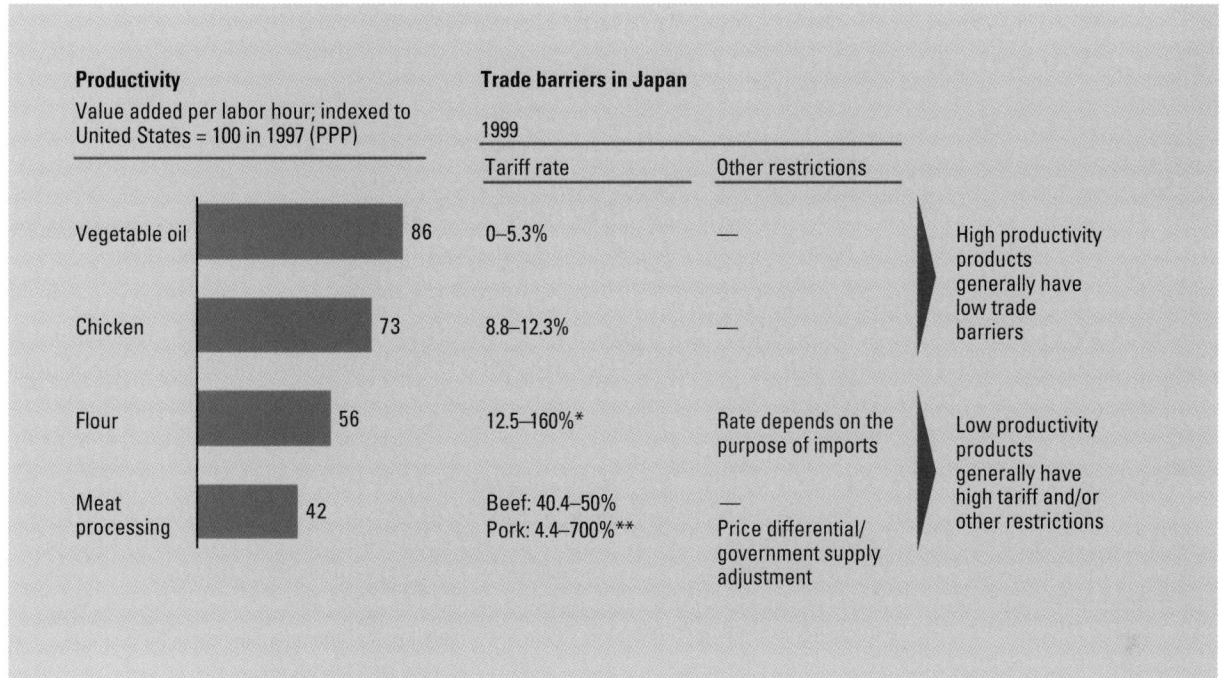

* 12.5 to 25 percent applied to imports for specific purposes only; most are subject to ad valorem rates and other duties; estimated to be 160 percent of market price
** Actual tariff is ad valorem rate of ¥ 371.67/kg.; rate calculated based on pork prices in the market
Sources: Census of Manufacture; Economic Census; *Agro-Trade Handbook*, JETRO (1999); *Trade Policy Review Japan*, WTO (1998); interviews

produce, and sugar are fully tradable. It is significant that, though there are exceptions, generally there are large differences in the productivity of tradable categories as compared with that of perishable ones. In Japan, for example, the productivity of perishables is just 32 percent of US levels, while that of commodities is 60 percent of that of the United States. This limited tradability gives the processed foods industry many of the characteristics of the non-tradable sector. In Japan, traditional processed foods—which include soy sauce, miso, fish products, and pickles—exhibit labor productivity just 18 percent of US levels (Figure 6). In Korea, of the categories studied, traditional foodstuffs such as seasoning and noodles also exhibited low levels of productivity.

Although the trade of certain types of processed food is increasingly global, much processed food production remains remarkably local. Korea, for example, produces more than 70 percent of its processed food consumption locally. Traditional foodstuffs are the least productive category.

We have examined the food processing industry in Korea and Japan, as well as specific food processing sectors in India and Thailand. In all these economies, food processing is an important sector, not the least because the impact of changes in the quality, range, or prices of processed foods have an immediate impact on the well-being of the populations concerned. Food processing is also a large employer. In Korea, it accounts for 2.2 percent of total employment and 11 percent of manufacturing employment. Its contribution to Korea's GDP is even greater, at 3.3 percent. Similarly, in Japan, 11.2 percent of those employed in manufacturing are engaged in the food processing industry.

Unfortunately, food processing is a woefully unproductive sector of these economies at present. The total factor productivity of the industry in Japan is just 39 percent of US levels; in Korea it is 46 percent. In contrast, France reaches 96 percent of the US level. The French figure is significant, however, as it indicates, as has already been seen in the retail industry, that far from sacrificing local culture, high levels of productivity can be synonymous with meeting local needs and tastes.

The unforeseen consequences of legislation

After several decades of market reform, it might come as a surprise just how large a role government regulation plays in Asia in restricting the food processing market. As part of the non-tradable sector, food processing has been subject to fairly limited impact from the forces that are shaping the tradable part of the economy. As a result, government regulation still plays a crucial role in restricting food processing productivity throughout the region. Such regulation has a shaping influence on many of the factors upstream and downstream of the industry, as well as directly on the industry itself. The most important impact is that regulation severely hampers the potential shaping influence of the retail industry by restricting land ownership patterns in both Japan and Korea and by making taxation an exit disincentive for inefficient retailers in Japan. Regulation also restricts the productivity of the Thai poultry industry by raising feedstuff prices and preventing the import of poultry meat, thereby restricting price competition. In India, milk marketing regulation severely constrains the entry of new players and has prevented the necessary consolidation and increase of scale. In Japan, pork processing, which is owned and controlled by the government, has low productivity because of insufficient investment in automation. The Japanese government also provides subsidies to a range of perishable processed foods segments, such as dairy products. In Korea, a raft of practices protects the Korean food processing industry from full free market competition. For example, foreign multinationals find it difficult to gain access to broadcaster's advertising time, as all advertising is regulated by a state-owned organization that has allocated the airtime on long-term contracts. Burdensome and complex administrative processes that rely on strong relationships for their completion also play a role in restricting entry. Regulation restricts entry in Korea by protecting small companies in a range of product categories, as is the case in India.

In looking across the range of food processing product categories in the countries concerned, MGI's study suggests that such government regulation has had a direct and negative impact in determining the generally low competitive intensity and the lack of scale in a number of product categories. To give some sense of this, we examine the impact of regulation in the retail, dairy, and poultry categories.

Retail

The degree of competitive intensity is particularly important in helping raise productivity. In Korea, the level of consolidation in the food processing industry is similar to that in the United States in categories such as confectionery, wet-corn milling, and cookies. However, the overall competitive intensity of the industry remains substantially lower because the retail industry, downstream of processing, is insufficiently consolidated to play the shaping role it has done in other countries. As has already been mentioned in the section on the retail industry, restrictive land regulation has played a significant role in determining the situation in Korea, where around 80 percent of retail outlets are local, small-scale stores. As a result, there is little pressure on food processors to improve productivity levels. The low competitive intensity also correlates with weak product development and marketing. Industries that are fully exposed to international competition, in contrast, quickly shape up to the demands of the international

marketplace. Thus the productivity improvements that can come from better product management are largely absent. In the United States, in contrast, it is the retail chains that help drive through productivity improvements, as they ruthlessly focus on value.

Dairy

The crucial role downstream retailers can play in producing scale in the retail industry is mirrored in both supply and processing in the milk-processing industry in India and Japan. In Japan, the lack of consolidation downstream in retail means there is insufficient pressure to produce increase of scale. This in turn results in limited automation and inadequate marketing. As a result, in Japan, there are 718 milk-processing plants, four times the number per capita seen in the United States, half of which produce less than 2 tons per day. It is therefore not surprising that milk-processing productivity is just 48 percent of US levels. However, though the small plants account for the vast majority of the processing units, a few large processors have a good market share. The top three largest processors supply 51 percent of the total milk supply and 68 percent of the needs of the national and regional supermarkets. The bulk of the produce of the other 715 goes to supply the small local stores. In other words, the small processors rely primarily on local relationships with local stores, where they can command higher prices because of the lack of bargaining power of the small stores. This situation, where the two types of processors exist side by side supplying different markets, results in an overall low level of competitive intensity and low productivity. This lack of scale accounts for 69 percent of the productivity gap as compared with the United States. Again, as has already been mentioned, the lack of consolidation in the retail industry that causes this is the outcome of Japanese land and taxation regulation.

In India, the situation is even more extreme. A combination of low levels of investment, government regulation, and the lack of industry concentration conspire to reduce the competitive intensity to very low levels overall. The average Indian farmer has three or fewer cows, making milk collection a multi-stage process and reducing supply chain productivity. As a result, most dairy processing plants are small-scale. Larger processing plants that employ more than 20 people are legally part of the "registered sector" in India. Such plants account for over 85 percent of the processed milk output but only 35 percent of the employment. The Milk & Milk Products Order (MMPO) regulation, rather than trying to resolve this situation, actively reinforces it by restricting the licensing of new, large-scale processing plants. As a result of the absence of scale, chilling infrastructure is underdeveloped and milk processing is highly decentralized and very

tive reform. Competition and investment need to be encouraged. Typically, legislative intervention has removed restrictions that have in the past actively prevented competition, allowing a sudden influx of capital that is able to reshape the industry. The other common theme, true in two out of the three examples, is that FDI has played this role. Though, because of the nature of the non-tradable sector, it is unlikely that FDI can play this role in every case, when it can, the requisite change needed to drive through the productivity enhancements happen all the more quickly.

Korean dairy processing industry

We have talked extensively about the problems facing the dairy processing industry in India and Japan, but what about that industry in Korea? Korea's dairy processing industry shows factor productivity of 97 percent of the US level. Labor productivity is 101 percent of US levels overall and 98 percent of US levels in liquid milk. Liquid milk accounts for 81 percent of dairy sales. Capital productivity is 92 percent of US levels, which is one thing that clearly distinguishes this product category from many others in Korea.

How has Korea achieved this admirable state of affairs? The simple answer is scale. Korea, though it has a relatively small market compared to that of the United States, has made wise investments in up-to-date technology and automation. The result is that it faces no disadvantages in terms of scale. Korean plants also exhibit output levels similar to those of US counterparts and show similar rates of value added. This contrasts greatly with the situation in India and Japan, where large processors have a smaller share of the total market and the economies of scale have not been achieved.

Indian automotive industry

Though India's dairy processing industry generally paints a particularly depressing picture, not all is so gloomy in India. Our study of the automotive industry there reveals how quickly a sector can grow and evolve once regulatory barriers are removed. The continuous liberalization of the sector since 1983 has led to an increasing growth not only in output but also in productivity and employment. Although output growth before 1983 was around 3 percent per year, the growth rate in the passenger car segment rose to 17 percent thereafter due largely to the entry of Maruti-Suzuki, an Indian subsidiary of Suzuki of Japan. After de-licensing in 1993, the growth rate further increased, to 21 percent a year. Productivity improvements of existing plants and the entry of other productive companies also resulted in an increase in labor productivity of the passenger car segment by 20 percent a year. In turn, since output growth outpaced productivity growth, employment in the sector also grew.

Maruti-Suzuki's entry into the market in 1983 was the first step in liberalizing a sector that had been heavily regulated for three decades prior to that. Until Maruti-Suzuki's entry, the sector had been notorious for producing grossly outdated models, of which the best-selling one dated back to the mid 1950s! Maruti-Suzuki's entry was followed by the entry of several other companies, mostly Japanese and Korean, that focused on the commercial vehicle and components segments through joint ventures with Indian partners. The next major step toward liberalization was the de-licensing of the sector in 1993, which allowed foreign companies to set up wholly owned subsidiaries in India. The large size and growth potential of the Indian market, coupled with the inability to serve it through exports, caused many transnational companies to set up production facilities in India. In April 2001, the sector made a further transition toward an open market, as WTO commitments compelled the Indian government to abolish quantitative restrictions on the import of vehicles.

Maruti-Suzuki's entry into the Indian automotive sector shows the transforming effects that increased productivity can have in shaping an industry. Prior to its entry, automobile ownership was restricted to a tiny segment of the population. With the introduction of more efficient designs, technology, and manufacturing practices, Maruti-Suzuki was able to substantially reduce the price to the consumer and greatly expand the market, growing it at 21 percent a year whilst productivity grew at 20 percent a year. Within a few years, car ownership became the aspiration of the increasingly large middle class, and a whole upstream industry was able to be built from it. This, in turn, led the government to realize the benefits of increasing competition, further liberalization making the market more attractive to new entrants. As the competitive intensity quickly increased, it served to drive productivity to higher levels, further lowering prices to the consumer in real terms.

Thai retail industry

Finally, let us look at the Thai retail industry. Evidently, retail plays a crucial role in driving up productivity in upstream industries in any economy and has a particularly significant impact in shaping the non-tradable sector. Thailand's progress in retail therefore offers particular encouragement.

Overall, the level of Thailand's retail sector productivity, at 20 percent that of the United States, does not appear particularly encouraging, but this figure hides a far more interesting story. Modern formats are in the process of transforming the industry. They show a productivity level 91 percent of that of similar formats in the United States. Within specific segments of the modern formats, the story is even more encouraging. Thailand's supermarkets show labor productivity to be 122 percent of US levels, and

161

space efficiency, in terms of value added per square meter, to be 210 percent of US levels. Though such formats currently account for only 10 percent of retail employment in Thailand, this is changing rapidly, as Thailand's retail industry evolves along a path witnessed elsewhere. Modern formats now account for 44 percent of retail sales, and their penetration has been growing at an annual rate of 3.3 percent over the past 12 years.

All this has been achieved in very few years. How? The Thai retail revolution was one beneficial effect of the Asian Flu of 1997. The economic crisis led the government to liberalize FDI regulation in the retail industry and to allow enterprises with 100 percent foreign control from then on. This led to a dramatic increase in the intensity of competition, as seven multinational retailers entered the market: Carrefour, Casino Group, Delhaize Group, Food Lion, Royal Ahoid, SHV Group, and Tesco. As a result, the proportion of sales of modern formats rose from 5 percent to 44 percent in just 12 years.

The productivity imperative

How Asia's economies will ensure that productivity continues to rise is one of the biggest challenges facing Asia today. On the one hand, countries at an early stage in the demographic shift, such as India and Thailand, face burgeoning populations where demographics will ensure a rapid expansion of those available for work. By 2010, as much as 62 percent of India's population will be aged between 15 and 59. The danger here is that labor productivity will drop. In contrast, Japan and Korea's populations are aging rapidly. The number of 15- to 64-year-olds in Japan will decline by 0.5 percent per year between 2000 and 2010. This will make Japan highly reliant on productivity improvements for it to sustain its standard of living, as labor will be less easily available.

The issues discussed here are therefore of vital importance if the quality of life in Asia's economies is to rise. The productivity improvements seen in recent years in tradable goods and services need to be realized in the domestic non-tradable sector. Achieving this is no mean task. FDI can be a critical component of the answer, but alone it will not be the solution. Besides, many of the non-tradable sectors are of only limited attractiveness to foreign players. What is clear, however, is that in each of the industries visited here, international best practices can greatly help improve productivity. These practices range from Design for Manufacturing in the housing construction industry and improved supply chain management and marketing in retail to the use of further automation in food processing.

We believe the greatest boost to productivity will derive from legislative reform. This reform needs to be shaped so as to enhance and reinforce competition. This will require legislators to make difficult tradeoffs between conflicting objectives. Restrictions on land ownership in Japan and Korea, FDI limits in India, tariff and other domestic protections in Thailand are all cases in point.

There is nothing to suggest that India, Korea, Japan, and Thailand cannot dramatically improve their productivity performance. On the contrary, our work suggests that the right kind of product-level regulatory reforms will go a long way to close the gaps with global best practice. However, if things stay the way they are, then productivity is unlikely to rise very quickly. With the demographic changes already afoot, this could create an unprecedented threat to Asia's economic well-being.

Note

1 This chapter is based on the following four country studies the McKinsey Global Institute has prepared over the last few years: *India: The Growth Imperative* (September 2001); *Why the Japanese Economy Is not Growing* (July 2000); *Productivity-Led Growth for Korea* (March 1998); and *Thai Productivity Report: Prosperity through Productivity* (February 2002). The latter represents a joint project undertaken by McKinsey's Thailand office, supported by the MGI in collaboration with two leading Thai economic research think tanks: the National Economic and Social Development Board (NESDB) and the Thai Development Research Institute Foundation (TDRI).

References

Japan External Trade Organization (JETRO). 1999. *Agro-Trade Handbook*. Tokyo: Japan External Trade Organization.

McKinsey Global Institute (MGI). 1998. *Productivity-led Growth for Korea*. Seoul and Washington, DC: McKinsey & Company.

———. 2000. *Why the Japanese Economy Is Not Growing: Micro Barriers to Productivity Growth*. Washington, DC: McKinsey & Company.

———. 2001. *India: The Growth Imperative: Understanding the Barriers to Rapid Growth and Employment Creation*. Mumbai: McKinsey & Company.

———. 2002. *Thai Productivity Report: Prosperity through Productivity*. Bangkok: McKinsey & Company.

O'Mahoney, M. 1999. *Britain's Productivity Performance 1950–96: An International Perspective*. London: National Institute of Economic and Social Research.

Organisation for Economic Co-operation and Development (OECD). 1999. *Japan: 1999–2000*. Paris: Organisation for Economic Co-operation and Development.

Statistics Bureau and Statistics Center. 1999. *1999 Establishment and Enterprise Census*. Tokyo: Statistics Bureau and Statistics Center.

———. 2000. *Japan Statistical Yearbook, 2000*. Tokyo: Statistics Bureau and Statistics Center.

World Trade Organization (WTO). 1998. *Trade Policy Review—Japan*. Geneva: World Trade Organization.

Central and Eastern Europe: Economic Developments, Reforms, and Geography

BARRY W. ICKES, Pennsylvania State University

JÜRGEN VON HAGEN, ZEI, University of Bonn, Indiana University, CEPR

IULIA TRAISTARU, ZEI, University of Bonn

Introduction

The weakening of economic growth in the United States and western Europe led to a slowdown of economic growth in the transition economies of central and eastern Europe, including Russia. The fall in real growth rates has been significant in Russia, Poland, and Hungary. Other countries, however, have remained on a more robust growth path in 2001. In contrast to its response in the mid 1990s, the region has shown no signs of contagion from the financial turmoil in Argentina and Brazil, either. This indicates that the advanced transition countries, in particular those that are now close to accession into the European Union, have managed to reach a sustainable path of economic growth and macroeconomic stability.

This chapter reviews the recent economic, reform, and regional developments in central and eastern Europe, focusing on Russia and the countries seeking accession to the European Union. The size and specific circumstances and developments in Russia justify the analysis of this country separately from the other EU accession candidate countries. The second section reviews the economic trends among the EU accession candidates, beginning with a review of basic economic data and recent macroeconomic developments. A discussion of recent reform policies and conditions for foreign direct investment (FDI) follows. The section ends with a discussion of regional economic developments in these countries. The following section is dedicated to the economic performance of Russia.

Economic performance of central and eastern European countries

Basic economic data

Ten countries in central and eastern Europe are currently considered for EU membership: Bulgaria, the Czech Republic, Estonia, Hungary, Latvia, Lithuania, Poland, Romania, the Slovak Republic, and Slovenia. These 10 central and eastern European countries (CEEC) together have a population of 104.3 million people, about 28 percent of the combined population of the current European Union. Birth rates have fallen dramatically in the past 10 years; even in Poland, which traditionally had a high and stable population growth rate before 1990, population growth has slowed significantly. If this trend persists, the CEEC will, before too long, be confronted with the same challenges of aging populations that western European countries are facing today. Life expectancy in the CEEC reaches 68.9 years for men and 76.8 years for women. The countries have well-educated workforces, with literacy rates of virtually 100 percent for men and women above the age of 15 years. Primary school enrollment rates are around 100 percent; the average secondary school enrollment rate is 90 percent, with Bulgaria (76.8 percent) and Romania (78.4 percent) having the lowest and the Baltic countries and the Czech Republic (above 97 percent) having the highest rates.

The combined GDP of this group reached US$401.8 billion in 2001 (up from US$364.8 billion in 2000), or 5.1 percent of EU GDP. In purchasing power parity (PPP), per capita GDP is highest in Slovenia, where it reached 52 percent of US per capita GDP (70 percent of EU average per capita GDP) in 2001, followed by the Czech Republic (43 percent of US and 60 percent of EU per capita GDP) and Hungary (37 percent and 51 percent, respectively). With 18 percent of US per capita GDP and 24 percent of EU per capita GDP, Bulgaria has the lowest level of per capita income in the group. On average, CEEC per capita GDP has moved from 44 to 46 percent of EU per capita GDP between 1997 and 2001. This convergence process was faster in Estonia, which caught up from 38 to 42 percent; Latvia (28 percent to 32 percent); and Slovenia (66 percent to 70 percent), while Romania fell back from 26 percent to 24 percent of EU per capita GDP. Compared with pre-transition levels, Poland's GDP today is larger by almost one third, reflecting a relatively mild decline of GDP in the early 1990s and a string of years of strong growth in the late years of the same decade. Slovenia and Hungary have surpassed their pre-transition levels of GDP significantly, while Bulgaria, Romania, and the Baltic states are still far below the pre-transition level. This reflects the much more severe initial output crunches in these countries.

As shown in Table 1, agricultural sectors in CEE countries remain relatively large. In Romania and Bulgaria, agriculture still exceeds 12 percent of GDP. Manufacturing sectors are large compared with these sectors in western countries; they still account for one quarter to one third of GDP. This suggests considerable growth potential in the services industries, but also a continued restructuring of the manufacturing sector, which will be accompanied by relatively high unemployment rates.

Within the manufacturing sectors, large-scale restructuring processes have occurred in the past 10 years (see Landesmann and Stehrer 2002), which have reduced the pre-transition dominance of low-tech, labor-intensive industries in favor of industries that are more high tech. Only Bulgaria and Romania have experienced increases in the share of employment in the former sector between 1993 and 2000 (Landesmann and Stehrer 2002). In the other CEE countries, the rise in relative employment in medium- and high-tech industries has been accompanied by a rise in relative wages in these industries, suggesting that the changing employment patterns reflect changes in production technologies and expanding capital stocks. In contrast, relative wages have declined in the low-tech industries in most CEE countries. The picture is more diverse regarding resource-intensive industries, where relative wages have increased in most CEE countries, but

employment shares have increased in some and fallen in other countries.

Employment in most CEE countries has continued to fall from pre-transition levels in recent years, with Poland, Latvia, and Slovenia being the exceptions (see Table 2). Correspondingly, unemployment rates remain high. Both processes reflect structural shifts in the labor markets. Meanwhile, macroeconomic productivity is rising. Apart from Romania, countries in the region have reached inflation rates of less than 10 percent, and inflation rates are coming down further in most countries. Still, inflation remains a concern in Hungary, Bulgaria, and Slovenia, where consumer price inflation (CPI) still stands at 9.2 percent, 7.5 percent, and 8.4 percent, respectively. The same countries had producer price inflation rates of 5.7 percent, 6.7 percent, and 9 percent in 2001. In contrast, Latvia and Lithuania recorded virtual price stability in 2001. Overall, the region has achieved a remarkable degree of macroeconomic stability compared with other regions in transition.

As shown in Table 1, macroeconomic investment rates are generally high in the region, reaching 30 percent and above in the Czech Republic and Slovenia. With the exception of Bulgaria, in all countries these rates are considerably larger than the investment rate in the United States (which was 16.6 percent in 2001), and they are not much different from the German rate (22 percent in 2001). Gross national savings rates are similarly large and exceed the US rate (11.9 percent in 2001).

All countries in the region are relatively open economies, as witnessed by the high share of trade (exports plus imports of goods and services) in GDP shown in Table 3. Only in Poland and Romania does trade account for less than 30 percent of GDP. In all other countries in the region, it involves more than half of GDP, and its share has been growing rapidly in the past 10 years. This growth reflects the effects of trade liberalization under the EU Association Agreements, which opened trade for most industrial products. The main export markets for all countries are in the European Union today (see Table 4). The largest economies in the region, Poland, Hungary, and the Czech Republic, send more than 70 percent of their exports to the European Union. The European Union's share in exports is below 60 percent only for Lithuania, Bulgaria, and the Slovak Republic. Similarly, the European Union is the main source of imports for all countries in the region. In contrast, trade within the region is relatively small. It is important in terms of the shares in total export only for the Czech and the Slovak Republics, where it reflects mainly bilateral trade between the two countries that split up in the 1990s, and for the Baltic economies. Trade with Russia has lost importance on the export side, where its share is well below 5 percent except for the Baltic countries (where it is 6 to 9 percent). In contrast,

Table 1: Basic economic data

	Population, 2001 (in millions)	GDP per capita (PPP), (2001 in US$)	GDP per capita (PPP, % of US), 2001	GDP (2001 as % of 1989)	Manufacturing industry (% of GDP)	Agriculture (% of GDP)	Investment (% of GDP), 2001	Gross national savings (% of GDP, 2001)
Bulgaria	7.93	6,182.1	0.18	78.3	25.1	14.5	13.7	13.8
Czech Republic	10.29	14,884.8	0.43	102.2	36.0	3.9	29.6	26.0
Estonia	1.43	10,380.4	0.30	89.8	14.6	6.3	26.5	20.1
Hungary	10.11	12,941.3	0.37	108.3	26.9	4.8	23.2	25.1
Latvia	2.37	7,749.6	0.22	69.1	16.3	4.5	22.8	18.9
Lithuania	3.69	7,764.2	0.22	69.9	22.8	7.6	22.5	16.8
Poland	38.63	9,326.9	0.27	128.1	29.0	3.3	24.0	17.6
Romania	22.41	7,036.2	0.20	83.5	27.6	12.6	19.8	16.0
Slovak Republic	5.41	11,738.7	0.34	106.2	25.8	4.5	24.9	26.6
Slovenia	1.99	18,233.0	0.52	113.7	27.7	3.2	33.8	25.1

Sources: Economic Commission for Europe (2002); Foders, Piazolo, and Schweickert (2002); Data tables, Part 4.3 of this *Report*

Table 2: Real growth, inflation, and unemployment

	Real growth rate (%)		Employment growth (%) (average)	CPI inflation (%)		Unemployment (%)	
	1996–2000	2001	1996–2000	1996–2000	2001	2000	2001
Bulgaria	1.1	4.8	−2.7	10.3	7.5	16.4	17.5
Czech Republic	4.7	3.6	−2.0	3.9	4.7	8.8	8.5
Estonia	5.4	5.3	−1.5	3.9	5.8	13.7	12.7
Hungary	4.9	3.8	1.3	9.8	9.2	6.4	5.7
Latvia	5.1	7.5	0.5	2.6	2.5	14.6	7.7
Lithuania	3.0	5.8	−1.1	0.9	1.3	15.4	12.5
Poland	5.2	1.1	0.0	10.1	5.4	16.1	16.2
Romania	−2.4	5.3	−2.1	45.7	34.5	7.1	8.6
Slovak Republic	3.6	3.3	−1.4	8.9	7.3	7.0	n.a.
Slovenia	4.6	3.0	0.8	12.0	8.4	18.6	n.a.

Note: *n.a.* = not available.
Sources: Authors' calculations from EBRD transition reports (various issues) and the Economic Commission for Europe (2002); Data tables, Part 4.3 of this *Report*

Russia still accounts for sizable shares of total imports for Bulgaria (18.5 percent), the Baltic countries (between 10 and 20 percent), and the Slovak Republic (12 percent).

At the end of the 1980s, the trade patterns of CEE countries largely corresponded to the patterns typically observed of less-developed countries—that is, a relative specialization in labor-intensive and energy-intensive industries and a low representation of capital-intensive, R&D–intensive, and skill-intensive industries (see, eg, Landesmann 2000). These patterns have changed dramatically for most countries in the region, and there is a tendency of differentiation among them. As shown in Landesmann and Stehrer (2002), one group of countries, led by Hungary and Estonia and including the Czech and the Slovak Republics and Poland, has shown an increasing relative export specialization in technology-driven industries at the cost of declining relative specializations in labor- and capital-intensive industries.[1] In contrast, Bulgaria, Romania, Latvia, and Lithuania have become more specialized in exporting labor-intensive products. Looking at skill intensities, these authors find an increase in the relative export specialization in products intensive in the use of medium-skilled or blue-collar workers and a decline in the relative specialization in low-skill intensive products for the first group of countries. However, a sig-

nificant increase in the relative export specialization in high-skill intensive products can be observed only in the cases of Hungary and the Slovak Republic; Estonia even records a decline in that product segment. Bulgaria and Lithuania are the only countries with increasing relative specialization in low-skill intensive industries. Thus, trade developments in recent years suggest that the countries in the region are quite heterogeneous as regards comparative advantages.

As part of the EU accession process, countries in the region have largely, if not completely, abolished capital and foreign exchange controls (Begg et al. 2001). As a result, and reflecting the favorable growth perceptions, capital inflows have been significant in recent years. Table 3 shows that most countries in the region ran sizable current account deficits in 2000 and 2001, but were able to finance these deficits with inflows of FDI. Meanwhile, international reserves, also shown in Table 4, stand at about one third or more of international debt.

General government spending accounts for 30 to 40 percent of GDP in most countries (see Table 5), much lower than in the early phase of transition in most countries. The exception is Romania, where general government spending amounts to only 16 percent of GDP. In general, there has been a remarkable process of

Table 3: External performance

	Trade (% of GDP)	Current account balance (% of GDP)	FDI inflow (% of GDP)	International reserves (% of foreign debt)	Exchange rate (national currency units per US dollar)	
		2000	2000	2000	2000	2001
Bulgaria	51.0	−5.9	8.4	31.2	2.12	2.19
Czech Republic	62.0	−4.4	9.0	56.7	38.6	38.0
Estonia	82.9	−6.3	7.8	29.6	16.97	17.48
Hungary	50.3	−3.2	3.5	37.7	282.2	286.5
Latvia	54.1	−6.9	5.7	31.6	0.61	0.63
Lithuania	52.6	−6.0	3.4	33.3	4.00	4.00
Poland	29.2	−6.3	5.9	45.2	4.35	4.09
Romania	30.5	−3.7	2.8	28.7	21,709	29,061
Slovak Republic	64.6	−3.6	10.7	36.8	46.2	48.4
Slovenia	56.5	−3.4	1.0	59.0	222.68	242.75

Source: Authors' calculations from EBRD transition reports (various issues) and the Economic Commission for Europe (2002)

Table 4: Export and import shares

	Export shares (%), 1999			Import shares (%), 1999		
	EU	CEEC	USA	EU	CEEC	USA
Bulgaria	54.1	4.2	4.0	50.9	4.8	2.9
Czech Republic	69.2	17.6	2.4	64.7	12.1	3.9
Estonia	62.7	13.8	2.5	57.8	7.4	4.4
Hungary	76.2	6.4	5.2	64.5	6.4	3.5
Latvia	62.6	14.9	5.7	53.7	21.3	2.0
Lithuania	50.1	21.1	4.4	46.5	13.2	3.8
Poland	70.6	10.8	2.8	65.0	7.2	3.6
Romania	65.7	6.8	3.8	60.6	9.0	3.5
Slovak Republic	59.5	30.0	1.4	51.7	22.7	2.6
Slovenia	66.2	6.9	3.1	68.8	7.6	3.0

Source: Foders, Piazolo, and Schweickert (2002)

convergence of the size of governments among these countries (Gleich and von Hagen 2000). Compared with EU standards, this means that the governments are economically relatively small. Consolidated government deficits are still a concern in the Czech Republic, Poland, and the Slovak Republic, where they exceeded 4.5 percent of GDP in 2001. In contrast, the Baltic states, Bulgaria, and Slovenia comfortably meet the Maastricht deficit criterion of 3 percent of GDP. Public-sector debts seem relatively stable. Compared with the Maastricht debt criterion of 60 percent, the debt-GDP ratios are clearly too high in the Czech Republic, Hungary, and the Slovak Republic, and the ratio must be watched carefully in Poland and Slovenia to avoid overshooting the Maastricht limit. The other countries have much more comfortable debt ratios. On average for all CEEC, direct taxes contribute merely 22.3 percent of all revenues to the general government budget, while taxes on goods and services contribute 48 percent and social security taxes almost 30 percent (Gleich and von Hagen 2000). Since indirect taxes are regressive, this suggests that tax reforms have not paid sufficient attention to the distributional concerns of tax policy. In addition, the high burden of social charges on labor may eventually lead to similarly severe labor market

distortions in CEE countries as they do today in many EU countries.

One remaining weakness of the economies in the region is the state of their financial systems. The low degrees of monetization, measured by the ratio of broad money to GDP, reflect the lack of a well-developed banking system (see Table 6). For comparison, note that this ratio is around 140 percent in the euro area. Even the more advanced countries in the region are still far from

Table 5: Government finance

	Government spending (% of GDP)		Government budget balance (% of GDP)		Government debt (% of GDP)
	2000	2001	2000	2001	2000
Bulgaria	38.4	n.a.	−0.20	−0.86	26.2
Czech Republic	32.1	32.1	−4.20	−4.75	85.7
Estonia		n.a.	−0.50	0.52	42.2
Hungary	43.2	42.1	−3.40	−2.85	78.5
Latvia	32.6	30.4	−3.00	−1.85	23.2
Lithuania	27.5	n.a.	−2.70	−1.50	23.1
Poland	34.5	n.a.	−2.50	−4.50	49.4
Romania	n.a.	15.9	−3.70	−3.10	26.6
Slovak Republic	39.5	n.a.	−3.40	−4.60	72.2
Slovenia	40.0	40.4	−1.70	−1.40	52.7

Note: n.a. = not available.
Sources: Authors' calculations from EBRD transition reports (various issues) and the Economic Commission for Europe (2002); Data tables, Part 4.3 of this *Report*

Table 6: Financial sector

	Real loan rates on short-term credit (%, 2001)	Interest rate spread (%, 2001)	Equity and debt market capitalization (% of GDP, 2000)	M3/GDP (%, 2000)	Total credit to private sector/ GDP (%, 2000)	State-owned banks (% of total bank assets, 2000)	Bad loans (% of total loans, 2000)
Bulgaria	4.4	8.6	5.0	31.9	16.6	19.8	10.9
Czech Republic	4.0	4.0	38.0	72.4	52.2	28.2	19.3
Estonia	3.2	3.7	37.0	35.6	35.4	0.0	1.5
Hungary	5.5	2.8	52.0	42.7	26.1	8.6	3.1
Latvia	9.2	5.9	25.0	26.3	18.0	2.9	19.6
Lithuania	10.2	5.3	31.0	20.9	13.5	10.8	10.1
Poland	16.4	8.6	43.0	48.7	28.5	15.9	18.8
Romania	2.2	18.8	3.0	19.0	11.8	3.8	7.2
Slovak Republic	4.4	6.1	28.0	63.6	46.3	49.1	26.2
Slovenia	5.7	5.3	24.0	50.9	35.9	42.2	8.5

Note: *Interest rate spread* is the difference between bank lending and deposit rates on short-term credit and deposits, respectively.
Sources: UNECE (2002), Bonin and Wachtel (2002)

that level. The low degree of monetization is a key indicator of the low level of financial intermediation that characterizes CEE countries. The volume of bank assets varies between 30 percent and 120 percent of GDP in the CEE countries, compared with a euro area average of about 265 percent (Caviglio, Krause, and Thimann. 2002). The supply of credit to the private sector remains relatively low, too. The largest ratios of credit to GDP in the region are found in the Czech and the Slovak Republics; there, they correspond to about two fifths of the corresponding values in the euro area. At the same time, real loan rates are high. Poland stands out for its extremely high real interest rate of 16.6 percent in 2001, reflecting a tight monetary policy in the face of falling inflation rates. But in the other states, except Romania, real lending rates are also high compared with rates in the euro area, especially given the absence of controls on international capital mobility. The weakness of financial intermediation is also reflected in relatively large spreads between loan and deposit rates, pointing to a lack of competition in the deposit markets.

Securities and stock markets remain relatively weak. Equity and debt markets are extremely small relative to GDP in Bulgaria and Romania, but even in the other CEE countries they remain underdeveloped compared with those of more advanced industrial countries (see Table 6). Despite the weaknesses of the banking industry, financial intermediation is bank-dominated. A significant feature of the new banking industries in CEE countries is the strong presence of foreign banks. Foreign investors own more than two thirds of the banking system in CEE countries. Foreign ownership is biased toward large institutions and controls about half of the existing banks; often, foreign owners control three or more of the five largest banks in a country (Caviglia, Krause, and Thimann 2002). Foreign investors have contributed positively to intensifying competition and improving efficiency in the financial sector.

Recent macroeconomic performance

Macroeconomic performance in the region has been relatively favorable in recent years. Table 2 reports the average growth rates for 1996 to 2000. Romania is the only country where real output continued to fall during that period, and Bulgaria saw an average growth rate of merely 1.1 percent annually. All other countries in the region witnessed real growth rates of 3 percent and above annually, with the leading growth performances in Estonia, Poland, and Latvia, where average growth exceeded 5 percent annually. The most surprising observation arising from Table 2 is the continued strong growth in most countries during 2001—in the face of a weakening world economy. Although growth slowed down somewhat relative to the 1996–2000 average in the Czech Republic, Slovenia, and Hungary, it actually accelerated in Bulgaria, Latvia, Lithuania, and Romania. The data thus suggest that the reform processes and the expectation of entry to the European Union have generated a sustained growth process that is able to weather a slowdown in the economies of the main trading partners. Poland is the significant exception from the group in 2001, as growth fell drastically to 1.1 percent on average in 2001. An attitude of complacency about the reform progress in the mid 1990s that led to a postponement of further reforms still necessary, together with a relatively tight monetary policy in 2000–2001, explain this deviation from the more general pattern.

US dollar exchange rates have tended to devalue in recent years, but real exchange rates have appreciated. This is most likely a result of the "Samuelson Balassa effect," which holds that small open economies experiencing faster productivity growth than their trade partners will have real exchange rate appreciations reflecting the rising price of nontradable goods relative to tradable ones. The management of capital inflows of significant scale poses a challenge to macroeconomic policies in upcoming years. The experience of the 1990s teaches that capital inflows can dry up or even revert quickly when market perceptions change, whether because of inconsistent domestic economic policies or because of a general change in investor attitudes in international markets (also called *contagion effects*). This makes old-style regimes of fixed exchange rates, such as the European Monetary System, vulnerable to speculative attacks; these regimes are more vulnerable the less they are protected by capital controls. This experience notwithstanding, the predominant view among EU policymakers is that countries joining the European Union will have to join the new Exchange Rate Mechanism (ERM-2) before they can become full members of the European Monetary Union. The policy implication of this requirement is that countries in the region should either avoid pegging their exchange rates to the euro too narrowly and use the full exchange rate band of +/− 15 percent in the ERM-2, or move all the way to adopting currency boards with the euro to eliminate any expectation of future devaluations. The more desirable and rational alternative, to let countries adopt the euro unilaterally as national currency if they wish to do so, is currently being ruled out as an option by the European Commission and the European Council (Begg et al. 2001).

EU accession, economic reforms, and liberalization

Quality of institutions and governance
The EU Summit in Copenhagen in 1993 declared that EU membership was an option for countries in the region provided they fulfill two types of criteria: political stability, as manifested by the existence of a functioning democratic and legal order, protection of human rights, and protection of minorities; and economic maturity, witnessed by the existence of a viable market economy and the ability to withstand the competitive pressures and market forces within the European Union. In addition, EU membership requires the ability to adopt and implement the *Acquis Communautaire*—the body of EU law and regulations. The European Commission has further specified the economic criteria. A viable market economy is thought to exist, if

- prices and trade are sufficiently liberalized,
- there are no significant barriers to market entry and exit,
- a legal order compatible with a market economy exists and protects property rights and the enforcement of contracts,
- macroeconomic stability has been achieved,
- the financial system is able to channel savings into productive investments, and
- there is a broad consensus about the main elements of economic policy.

The ability to withstand competitive market pressures is assessed on the basis of

- the existence of a stable planning and decision environment,
- a satisfactory endowment with human and real capital,
- the effectiveness of regulatory policies and legislation,
- a high degree of trade integration with the European Union, and
- improved market access for small and medium enterprises.

Since 1997, the European Commission has published annual progress reports on the countries in the region. Accession negotiations were opened with all 10 CEE countries in the late 1990s. They are structured into 31 chapters, each negotiated separately. Currently, 30 of these chapters have been opened for all candidate countries. Most countries have closed negotiations on at least 24 (Poland) and a maximum of 27 (Czech Republic, Lithuania, Slovenia) chapters; only Romania and Bulgaria lag behind with 11 and 17 chapters closed, respectively. Regional policy, agricultural policy, and budgetary issues remain the most contentious issues. Initially, the general perception was that accession would occur in two waves, with Poland, Hungary, the Czech Republic, Estonia, and Slovenia being in the first wave together with Malta and Cyprus. The European Summit of Nice in 2001 officially stated the expectation that the first new members would be able to participate in the European Parliament elections of 2004.

Meanwhile, a "big-bang" accession is expected in 2003–2004, which would make all CEE countries except Bulgaria and Romania members of the European Union. This would leave Bulgaria and Romania alone with Turkey in a group of officially acknowledged candidates for EU membership. Economically, such an outcome might be less problematic for these two countries than it seems at first glance, since free trade and capital mobility with the European Union are available to the accession countries. Politically, however, such an outcome could be problematic since Turkey would probably try hard to be a member of the next round of accessions, and this very prospect could make the European Union reluctant to proceed with the accession of Bulgaria and Romania.

Assessment and comparison of economic reform across countries is inherently difficult, as the information is qualitative in nature, and the implementation and enforcement of new rules is much more difficult to evaluate than the existence of legal or administrative provisions. A number of international organizations provide such measurements. One is the index of economic liberty, published by the Fraser Institute (see Table 7). The index ranges from 0 to 10, with 10 indicating complete economic liberty. It includes assessments of the size and market-friendliness of the public sector, the regulation of the market environment, and legal order and security. Table 7 shows that the CEE countries had values ranging between 3.8 (Slovak Republic) and 4.7 (Hungary) at the beginning of the 1990s, much lower than the EU average of 7.5. By the end of the 1990s, however, most countries had made strong progress, the only exception being Romania. Scores are now close to 6 or above, much closer to the EU average of 8.0 in 1999. Interestingly, the CEEC average is above the EU average in the assessment of the public sector, but it remains below the EU average in the other two dimensions (market environment and legal environment). In both dimensions, however, the CEEC average is close to or above the lowest scores in the European Union. Overall, the CEE economies have attained a much greater degree of liberty than they had at the beginning of the transition experiment.

The European Bank for Reconstruction and Development (EBRD) reform index, also reported in Table 7, gives another picture of the reform progress. The initial conditions index measures the state of the economic systems at the start of the transition phase, taking into account economic dependence on trade with the COMECON, macroeconomic stability, trading potentials with the European Union, and resource endowments. Accordingly, the worst conditions prevailed in the Baltic countries and Romania. The reform index measures progress attained since then. It ranges from 1 (central planning) to 4+ (market conditions of advanced industrial countries). The index confirms the low levels of reform achieved in Bulgaria and Romania, and puts Poland, Estonia, and the Czech Republic into leading positions in the region. Interestingly, the EBRD's subindexes for commercial and financial services law are consistently close to 4 for all countries,

attesting to strong progress in the legal systems. The difference between the strong performance on this legal index and the overall index suggests continuing weaknesses in the practical implementation of reform policies, and may reflect the emphasis on legal rapprochement in the EU accession process.

Economists and policymakers have recently recognized the importance of good government institutions (*governance* for short) for strong and sustainable economic development. Governance determines the conditions under which economic transactions evolve, business contracts are made, and commitments to invest capital are entered into. Kaufmann, Kraay, and Zoida-Lobatón (2002) present an extensive database that allows international comparisons in this regard. They look at governance in six dimensions: voice and accountability, political stability, government effectiveness, regulatory quality, rule of law, and control of corruption.[2] The data are based on surveys and polls. Table 8 reports these data for the CEE countries. Each index varies between −2.5 and 2.5, with higher numbers indicating better governance. We also report the values for Russia and Indonesia, which we will discuss below.

A first point to note from this table is that democracy is the strongest element in governance in all CEE countries: only Bulgaria and Romania remain weak with regard to voice and accountability. In contrast, rule of law and control of corruption are generally weak in all CEE countries. Hungary, Estonia, Slovenia, and the Czech Republic have achieved a quality of governance comparable with Greece or better, but Poland still performs considerably worse in terms of government effectiveness, regulatory quality, and control of corruption. Significantly, Kaufmann, Kraay, and Zoido-Lobatón (2002) find some slippage in the quality of individual elements of governance comparing 1997–1999 with 2000–2001 data.

Table 7: Economic liberty, reform, and the cost of entry

	Fraser Institute Index of Economic Liberty		EBRD Index of Economic Reform		Cost of market entry	
	1990	1999	1989	2000	USD 1999	% of start-up capital
Bulgaria	3.9	5.9	2.1	2.4	348	3.42
Czech Republic	3.8*	6.6	3.5	3.2	1,732	2.52
Estonia	5.9*	7.4	−0.4	3.1	n.a.	n.a.
Hungary	4.7	7.1	n.a.	n.a.	4,718	10.15
Latvia	5.5*	7.0	−0.2	2.6	1,273	5.15
Lithuania	5.5*	6.5	0.0	2.8	625	2.39
Poland	4.6	5.7	1.9	3.3	1,927	4.87
Romania	4.2	3.8	1.7	2.3	822	5.41
Slovak Republic	3.8	6.3	2.9	2.8	1,799	5.01
Slovenia	5.9*	6.2	3.2	2.8	3,939	3.98

Note: *a* indicates data from 1995.

Business environment and competitiveness

Costs of entering a market and starting up a new business are an important determinant of FDI, and they depend heavily on the business-friendliness or unfriendliness of entry regulations. A recent study by Djankov et al. (2001) estimates the cost of setting up a *standardized firm* in a large number of countries, including most CEE countries. These costs include actual monetary costs and the time spent with bureaucratic procedures.[3] Table 8 shows that Hungary has the most costly entry regulations; setting up a new firm can cost up to 10 percent of the startup capital. In most other CEE countries, these costs are about 5 percent; the Czech Republic and Lithuania have even lower setup costs in terms of initial capital. Djankov et al. estimate that setup costs amount to 1.1 percent of the initial capital in Finland, 3.3 percent in Germany, 3.6 percent in France, 4.5 percent in Italy, and 7.3 percent in Greece. In absolute dollar amounts, entry costs are highest in Hungary (US$4,718) and Slovenia (US$3,939) and lowest in Bulgaria (US$348). This compares with US$2,559 in Finland, US$8,362 in Germany, US$8,335 in France, US$8,834 in Italy, and US$8,592 in Greece. Thus, CEE countries offer relatively friendly entry conditions for FDI compared with current EU countries.

At the Lisbon Summit in March 2000, Europe's heads of state declared their ambition to make the European Union "the most competitive and dynamic knowledge-based economy in the world by 2010, capable of sustainable economic growth, with more and better jobs and greater social cohesion."[4] This declaration forms the basis of the *Lisbon strategy*, a program of economic reforms and improvements in the legal, information, and physical infrastructure of the EU economy. The Lisbon strategy aims at making progress in eight dimensions of economic policy that the European governments perceived to be of key importance for gaining better competitiveness and growth: (1) the establishment of an information society; (2) the creation of a European area for innovation, research, and development; (3) further liberalization of the European markets for goods and services, including the completion of the Single Market Program especially in the areas of services and the reorientation of state aids to more targeted sectoral assistance; (4) liberalization of network industries; (5) the improvement of the efficiency and integration of financial markets in the European Union; (6) the strengthening of entrepreneurship through reduced regulatory burdens for business and improved conditions for business startups; (7) social inclusion through bringing people back to work, upgrading skills, and modernizing social protection; and (8) sustainable development, including policies for improving the environment and addressing climate change. A recent study conducted by the World Economic Forum and the Center for European Integration Studies at the University of Bonn presents an assessment of where the European Union stands in terms of these dimensions and in comparison with the United States and several other Organisation for Economic Co-operation and Development (OECD) economies (Cornelius et al. 2002).

The study also provides evidence for the CEE countries by computing *Lisbon scores* for each country. For this purpose, the study uses data from the World Economic Forum's *Executive Opinion Survey*. The Survey questions are answerable on a scale ranging from 1 to 7. The study uses responses to questions that relate specifically to the eight dimensions of the Lisbon strategy. These responses reflect a timely view of a country's economic environment from the perspective of its business leaders. Each Lisbon score is an average of the responses to all questions related to a particular aspect of the Lisbon strategy. The Lisbon scores can be used to compare the business environment and the competitiveness of the CEE countries and the countries of European Union.

Table 9 reports the Lisbon scores for the EU mean, and the differences between the individual (average) scores and the EU average for the following groups of countries:

Table 8: Governance indicators

	Voice, accountability		Political stability		Government effectiveness		Regulatory quality		Rule of law		Control of corruption	
	2000–01	1997–98	2000–01	1997–98	2000–01	1997–98	2000–01	1997–98	2000–01	1997–98	2000–01	1997–98
Russian Federation	−0.35	−0.19	−0.41	−0.69	−0.57	−0.59	−1.40	−0.30	−0.87	−0.72	−1.01	−0.62
Indonesia	−0.40	−1.13	−1.56	−1.29	−0.50	−0.53	−0.43	0.12	−0.87	−0.92	−1.01	−0.80
Bulgaria	0.59	0.47	0.37	0.43	−0.26	−0.81	0.16	0.52	0.02	−0.15	−0.16	−0.56
Czech Republic	1.04	1.20	0.74	0.81	0.58	0.59	0.54	0.57	0.64	0.54	0.31	0.38
Estonia	0.94	0.86	0.73	0.79	0.86	0.26	1.09	0.74	0.78	0.51	0.73	0.59
Hungary	1.19	1.22	0.75	1.25	0.60	0.61	0.88	0.85	0.76	0.71	0.65	0.61
Latvia	0.81	0.75	0.50	0.46	0.22	0.07	0.30	0.51	0.36	0.15	−0.03	−0.26
Lithuania	1.00	0.88	0.29	0.35	0.26	0.13	0.30	0.09	0.29	0.18	0.20	0.03
Poland	1.21	1.12	0.69	0.84	0.27	0.67	0.41	0.56	0.55	0.54	0.43	0.49
Romania	0.50	0.29	−0.08	0.02	−0.54	−0.57	−0.28	0.20	−0.02	−0.09	−0.51	−0.46
Slovak Republic	0.99	0.52	0.62	0.65	0.23	−0.03	0.27	0.17	0.36	0.13	0.23	0.03
Slovenia	1.07	1.03	0.87	1.09	0.70	0.57	0.52	0.53	0.89	0.83	1.09	1.02

Source: Kaufman, Kraay, and Zoido-Lobatón (2002)

Table 9: Lisbon scores

	EU mean	Four worst EU countries mean less EU mean	CEEC mean less EU mean	Bulgaria	Czech Republic	Estonia	Hungary	Latvia	Lithuania	Poland	Romania	Slovak Republic	Slovenia
Information society (average)	**5.42**	**-1.04**	**-0.91**	**-1.56**	**-0.04**	**0.32**	**-0.01**	**-0.70**	**-0.84**	**-1.10**	**-1.36**	**-0.80**	**-0.21**
Innovation, R&D (average)	**5.15**	**-1.57**	**-1.35**	**-1.96**	**-0.65**	**-0.87**	**-0.79**	**-1.26**	**-1.33**	**-1.29**	**-1.95**	**-1.14**	**-0.71**
Liberalization (average)	**4.78**	**-0.77**	**-1.27**	**-1.59**	**-0.77**	**-0.66**	**-0.55**	**-1.17**	**-1.03**	**-1.27**	**-1.92**	**-1.16**	**-0.46**
Completing the single market	5.17	-0.93	-1.35	-1.71	-1.04	-0.94	-0.80	-1.33	-1.08	-1.27	-1.92	-1.23	-0.66
State aids	4.39	-0.60	-1.19	-1.46	-0.50	-0.34	-0.30	-0.81	-0.99	-1.26	-1.92	-1.08	-0.27
Network Industries (average)	**5.31**	**-1.37**	**-0.95**	**-1.49**	**0.01**	**0.01**	**-0.33**	**-0.73**	**-0.82**	**-1.07**	**-1.52**	**-0.70**	**-0.12**
Telecommunications	5.31	-0.97	-0.53	-1.13	0.35	0.52	0.21	-0.47	-0.50	-0.62	-1.06	-0.43	0.04
Utilities, Transportation	5.30	-1.76	-1.39	-1.87	-0.34	-0.51	-0.88	-1.00	-1.14	-1.53	-2.00	-0.98	-0.29
Financial services (average)	**5.13**	**-1.05**	**-1.25**	**-1.84**	**-1.78**	**-0.24**	**-0.55**	**-0.94**	**-0.90**	**-1.08**	**-1.61**	**-1.27**	**-0.53**
Enterprise environment (average)	**3.48**	**-1.37**	**-0.44**	**-1.14**	**-0.62**	**0.60**	**0.02**	**-0.21**	**-0.32**	**-0.45**	**-1.12**	**-0.69**	**0.04**
Conditions for startups	4.20	-1.87	-1.00	-1.90	-1.12	0.22	-0.37	-0.61	-0.50	-0.72	-1.62	-1.03	-0.18
Regulatory burden	2.76	-0.87	0.12	-0.39	-0.13	0.98	0.42	0.19	-0.14	-0.18	-0.62	-0.36	0.26
Social inclusion (average)	**4.85**	**-0.91**	**-1.04**	**-1.73**	**0.36**	**-0.36**	**-0.53**	**-1.49**	**-1.27**	**-1.27**	**-1.47**	**-0.32**	**-0.05**
Life-long learning	5.16	-1.21	-0.75	-1.43	0.02	-0.30	-0.20	-0.97	-0.96	-0.85	-1.03	-0.35	-0.41
Modernizing social protection	4.53	-0.61	-1.33	-2.03	0.71	-0.43	-0.86	-2.01	-1.57	-1.70	-1.91	-0.28	0.32
Sustainable development (average)	**5.46**	**-1.20**	**-1.38**	**-1.98**	**-0.41**	**-0.76**	**-0.80**	**-1.08**	**-1.16**	**-1.45**	**-1.95**	**-1.25**	**-0.47**
Environment	4.82	-0.65	-1.05	-1.40	-0.45	-0.46	-0.49	-0.83	-0.92	-1.20	-1.48	-0.55	-0.16
Climate change	6.09	-1.75	-1.70	-2.55	-0.38	-1.06	-1.11	-1.33	-1.39	-1.70	-2.41	-1.95	-0.78

Note: Numbers in italics indicate scores better than the average of the four worst EU performers. The four worst EU performers vary according to the different categories. They always include Greece and in most cases Italy.

Figure 1: The trade of CEE countries with the world and the EU, 1990–2000 (millions of US dollars)

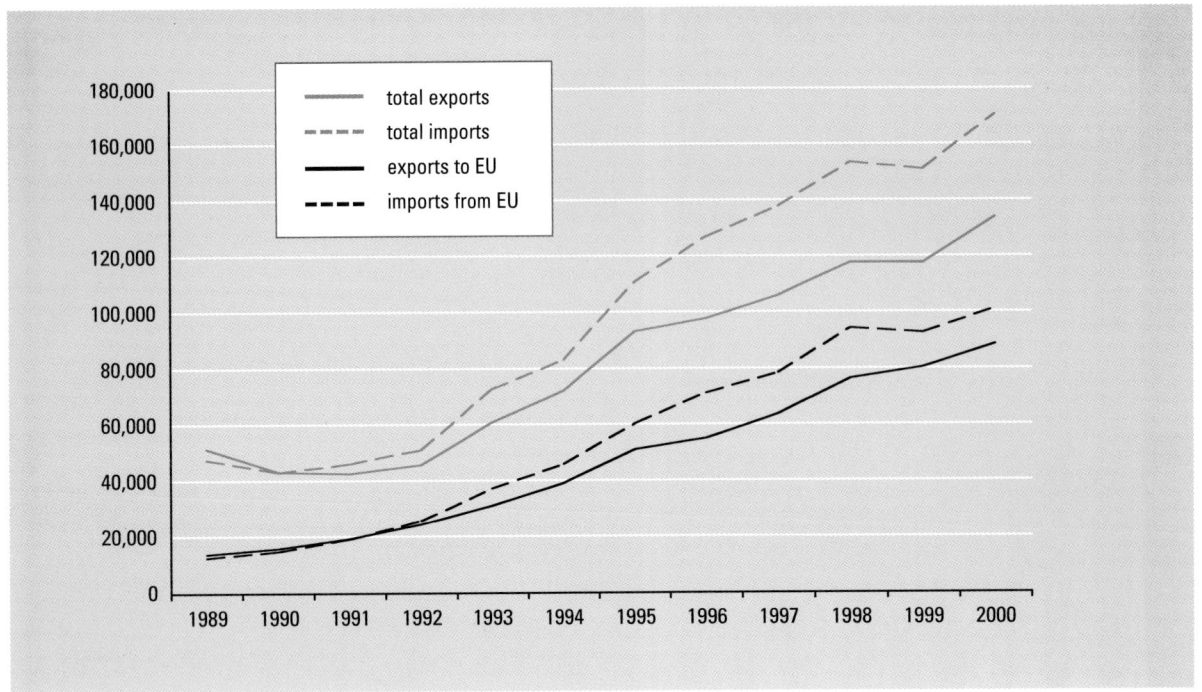

Source: Based on authors' calculations from IMF (2002)

the four worst-performing EU members, the CEE countries, and each CEE country individually. The table gives the average scores for eight main targets of the Lisbon strategy and the scores for several sub-items. A number of observations are noteworthy. First, the CEEC average is below the EU average in all dimensions except one, namely regulatory burden, where it is very close to the EU average score. Second, the four best-performing CEE countries—Estonia, Hungary, Slovenia, and the Czech Republic—are above the four worst-performing current EU members in almost all dimensions. These countries score nearly as high as the EU average in a few items listed in Table 9. If the dimensions of the Lisbon strategy capture the determinants of competitiveness in the European Union well, these countries will enter the European Union with relatively strong competitive conditions.

Third, there is an intermediate group of CEE countries including Latvia, Lithuania, and the Slovak Republic that outperform the four worst-performing EU members in terms of the information society, innovation and R&D, network industries, and enterprise environment. This may reflect the adoption of modern, competition-friendly market regulation in the accession process and the effects of technological leapfrogging in network and communication technologies.

Finally, Bulgaria, Romania, and Poland lag significantly behind even the four worst-performing countries in the current European Union, with scores below the EU average in almost all dimensions. The case of Poland is especially worrying, since Poland is the largest country of the group and, in contrast to Bulgaria and Romania, it is expected to be in the first round of enlargement.

Overall, these results suggest that the CEE countries have made good progress toward joining the competitive environment of the European Union in a couple of years.

The changing economic geography in central and eastern Europe

Over the last decade, the integration of central and eastern European countries into the world economy, in particular with the European Union, has progressed via trade and FDI. Exports of CEE countries to the world were 3 times larger and imports were 4 times larger in 2000 than in 1990. CEE countries' exports to the European Union were 5.5 times larger and the imports from the EU 6.7 times larger in 2000 than in 1990 (IMF 2002) (see Figure 1).

The relative share of CEE countries in extra-EU trade grew, over the same period, from 3 percent to 9 percent in the case of extra-EU imports and from 3 percent to 12 percent in the case of extra-EU exports. As indicated above, the European Union has become the main trading partner for CEE countries. The FDI flows from the

European Union to the CEE countries increased from 2 billion ecu in 1992 to 11.2 billion euros in 1999 amounting to 45.7 billion euros over the period 1992–1999 (Eurostat 2001). Trade reorientation and increasing economic integration caused a reallocation of resources across sectors and space, creating both opportunities and challenges for the CEE countries. At the aggregate level, welfare and efficiency gains may hide the uneven distribution of costs and benefits associated with this structural change, creating winners and losers. Sectoral shifts at the national level in the CEE countries have been analyzed frequently (see, for instance, Landesmann and Stehrer 2002), but the reallocation of resources across space requires investigation in more depth. What types of regions are winners and what types of regions are losers in the CEE countries? Where is industrial activity located? Have patterns of regional specialization and industrial concentration changed from 1990 to 1999? How does regional specialization relate to economic performance? What are the determinants of industrial location patterns? How has increased trade liberalization affected regional relative wages? The remainder of this section provides some answers to these questions based on recent research findings.

Winning and losing regions in central and eastern Europe

The analysis of regional economic performance in the CEE countries over the last decade[5] reveals two types of winning regions: metropolitan areas and border regions close to the European Union. There are also two types of losing regions: declining industrial regions and rural areas. A brief description of the common economic features of these regions is given below.

Metropolitan areas (in particular, capital city regions) have benefited from the increased concentration of skilled labor, high investment, good infrastructure, and a favorable geographical location. These regions have lower unemployment rates and higher wages than the rest of regions. Employment is shifting from manufacturing to services, with privately owned small enterprises and foreign investment as the main sources of employment growth.

Border regions close to EU markets (western border regions and coastal areas), which were disadvantaged areas during the communist regime,[6] have experienced increased trade and investment and falling unemployment rates due to their proximity to the European Union, well-developed infrastructure, low labor costs, and labor force skills. These regions have good prospects for employment growth and economic development in the long term.

Declining (old) industrial regions, which were advantaged areas during the communist regime,[7] have suffered from the opening of economies and trade reorientation, which has led to restructuring and enterprise closures. They have failed to attract new business and foreign investment. These regions have high unemployment rates and the

laid-off workers experience difficulties finding jobs due to their low and outdated qualifications. These regions are likely to have serious social and economic problems unless they can create new jobs.

Rural areas are the most disadvantaged regions in the CEE countries due to their poor infrastructure; low investment; weak economic structure, which is dominated by agriculture; and low educational attainment of the labor force. Subsistence farming and outward migration have kept unemployment from rising. Employment is, however, falling and large job losses are expected to follow the needed structural reforms in agriculture.

Patterns of regional specialization and industrial concentration

Recent international trade theories[8] and existing empirical evidence from current EU member states and the United States[9] suggest that falling trade barriers and trade costs are likely to lead to relocation of industrial activity and, thereby to an increased specialization of regions and geographic concentration of industries. The increased specialization and concentration are likely to increase productivity via increasing returns to scale. Nevertheless, they create a reason for concern because industry-demand shocks may become region-specific shocks, and the short-run adjustment costs may be high in the case of relocation of firms.

Specialization of regions and geographic concentration of industries can be measured in relation to production structures (Aiginger et al. 1999), as shown in Box 1. A region is specialized if a few industries have a large share in the production at regional level. An industry is geographically concentrated if a large percentage of its production is in just a few regions.

The effects of economic integration on patterns of regional specialization and location of industrial activity were investigated in a recent research project[10] that considered five EU accession countries: Bulgaria, Estonia, Hungary, Romania, and Slovenia. This analysis is interesting, in particular, because these countries differ with respect to size, progress with accession, and geographical position. Romania is relatively large, Hungary and Bulgaria are small, and Estonia and Slovenia are very small. Estonia, Hungary, and Slovenia are closer to EU accession than Bulgaria or Romania. Hungary and Slovenia are closer to the European core, Estonia is part of northern Europe, and Bulgaria and Romania have a peripheral position in the southeastern part of Europe. Romania has no border with any current EU Member State. Finally, Hungary is land-locked, while the other four countries have coastal areas.

For the purpose of identifying manufacturing relocation patterns across regions in the above-mentioned accession countries, we use here the following taxonomy of regions proposed by Resmini (2002): regions bordering

Box 1: Indicators of regional specialization and geographic concentration of industries*

E = employment

s = shares

i = industry (sector, branch)

j = region

S_{ij}^S = the share of employment in industry i in region j in total employment of region j

S_{ij}^C = the share of employment in industry i in region j in country employment of industry i

S_i = the share of country employment in industry i in total country employment

S_j = the share of total employment in region j in country employment

$$S_{ij}^S = \frac{E_{ij}}{E_j} = \frac{E_{ij}}{\Sigma_i E_{ij}} \qquad S_{ij}^C = \frac{E_{ij}}{E_i} = \frac{E_{ij}}{\Sigma_i E_{ij}}$$

$$S_i = \frac{E_i}{E} = \frac{\Sigma_j E_{ij}}{\Sigma_i \Sigma_j E_{ij}} \qquad S_j = \frac{E_j}{E} = \frac{\Sigma_i E_{ij}}{\Sigma_i \Sigma_j E_{ij}}$$

The dissimilarity index

Specialization measure

$$SPEC_j = \Sigma_i \left| S_{ij}^S - S_i \right|$$

Concentration measure

$$CONC_i = \Sigma_j \left| S_{ij}^C - S_j \right|$$

* Indicators are defined following Aiginger et al. (1999).

Table 10: Structural changes in regional employment, 1992–1999

	BEU	BAC	BEX	INT
BULGARIA				
Food, beverages, tobacco	0.00	−0.04	−0.01	0.04
Textiles, clothing and leather	0.05	−0.01	0.00	−0.04
Wood and paper products	−0.02	−0.03	−0.02	0.07
Fuel, chemicals, rubber, plastics	0.00	−0.02	−0.01	0.02
Non-metallic mineral products	−0.01	−0.01	−0.01	0.03
Metallurgy, machinery, equipment, motor vehicles	−0.01	−0.02	0.00	0.03
Furniture and other manufacturing	0.02	−0.04	−0.01	0.05
HUNGARY				
Food, beverages, tobacco	0.01	0.01	−0.01	−0.01
Textiles, clothing and leather	0.03	0.04	0.02	−0.08
Wood and paper products	0.00	0.00	0.01	0.00
Fuel, chemicals, rubber, plastics	0.04	0.00	0.01	−0.06
Non-metallic mineral products	0.05	0.08	−0.01	−0.11
Metallurgy, machinery, equipment, motor vehicles	0.04	−0.02	0.03	−0.05
Furniture and other manufacturing	0.05	−0.08	−0.02	0.05
ROMANIA				
Food, beverages, tobacco	—	−0.03	−0.01	0.05
Textiles, clothing and leather	—	0.02	−0.01	−0.01
Wood and paper products	—	−0.03	0.08	−0.05
Fuel, chemicals, rubber, plastics	—	0.02	0.00	−0.01
Non-metallic mineral products	—	−0.03	0.00	0.03
Metallurgy, machinery, equipment, motor vehicles	—	0.01	0.02	−0.04
Furniture and other manufacturing	—	0.01	0.00	−0.01
ESTONIA				
Food, beverages, tobacco	0.02	−0.02	—	
Textiles, clothing and leather	−0.01	0.01	—	
Wood and paper products	−0.21	0.21	—	
Fuel, chemicals, rubber, plastics	−0.17	0.17	—	
Non-metallic mineral products	−0.12	0.12	—	
Metallurgy, machinery, equipment, motor vehicles	0.08	−0.08		
Furniture and other manufacturing	−0.05	0.05	—	
SLOVENIA				
Food, beverages, tobacco	0.01	—	−0.01	0.00
Textiles, clothing and leather	0.00	—	0.00	0.00
Wood and paper products	0.00	—	0.00	0.00
Fuel, chemicals, rubber, plastics	0.03	—	−0.02	0.00
Non-metallic mineral products	0.02	—	−0.02	0.00
Metallurgy, machinery, equipment, motor vehicles	0.00	—	0.00	0.00
Furniture and other manufacturing	−0.01	—	0.01	0.00

BEU = regions bordering the EU; BAC = regions bordering accession countries BEX = regions bordering countries outside the EU enlargement; INT= regions other than border regions
Source: Authors' calculations, based on Resmini (2002)

the EU are abbreviated *BEU*, regions bordering accession countries are abbreviated *BAC*, regions bordering countries outside the EU enlargement are abbreviated *BEX*, and regions other than border regions are abbreviated *INT*.

As shown in Table 10, during the 1990s there was a relocation of manufacturing activities in these countries. The structural changes in regional manufacturing employment are country-specific.

In Bulgaria, most industries seem to move away from border regions, in particular from regions bordering accession countries and regions bordering countries that are outside the EU enlargement. Regions bordering the European Union have gained employment in textiles, clothing, and leather goods as well as furniture and other manufacturing, while nonborder regions have increased their employment shares in food, beverages, tobacco, wood, and paper products as well as furniture and other manufacturing mainly at the expense of regions bordering accession countries.

Figure 2: Average* regional specialization in EU accession countries, 1990–1999

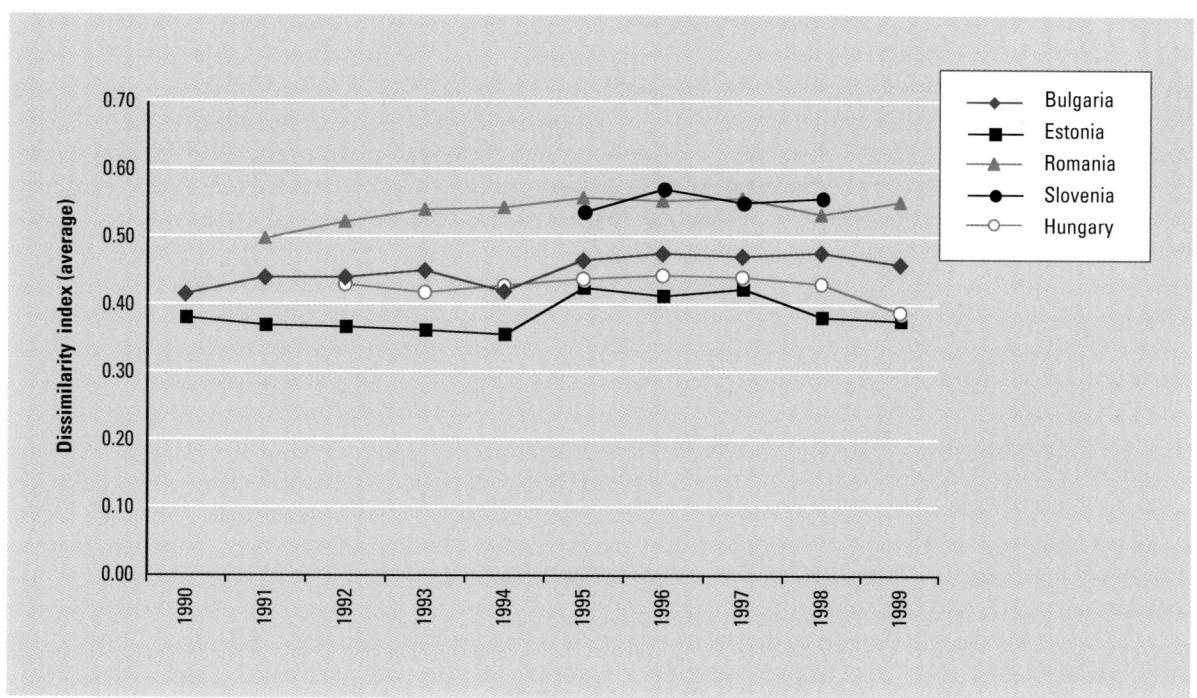

*weighted averages using regional employment shares
Source: Based on calculations by Traistaru, Nijkamp, and Longhi (2002)

In Hungary, there is a clear pattern of the relocation of manufacturing to regions bordering the European Union and those bordering other accession countries at the expense of nonborder regions and regions bordering countries outside the EU enlargement area. Regions bordering the European Union have increased their employment shares, in particular in resource-intensive industries (non-metallic mineral products, fuel, chemicals, rubber and plastics, and furniture) and high-technology industries (machinery, equipment, and motor vehicles); regions bordering accession countries have gained employment in resource-intensive industries (non-metallic mineral products) and labor-intensive industries (textiles, clothing, and leather).

In Romania, the pattern of manufacturing relocation is less clear. Nonborder regions have gained employment in labor-intensive (food, beverages, and tobacco) and resource-intensive (non-metallic mineral products) at the expense of regions bordering accession countries. Regions bordering countries outside the EU enlargement have attracted, in particular, the manufacturing of wood and paper products (resource intensive) as well as machinery, equipment, and motor vehicles. Regions bordering accession countries have gained employment in particular in the manufacturing of textiles, clothing, and leather.

In Estonia, manufacturing has moved away from regions bordering the European Union to regions bordering accession countries, with the exception of machinery, equipment, and motor vehicles as well as food, beverages, and tobacco. The biggest shifts in regional employment shares have taken place in the cases of resource-intensive industries.

In Slovenia,[11] there have been very few changes in the regional employment shares. The tendency seems to be to relocate manufacturing activities to regions bordering the European Union at the expense of bordering countries outside the EU enlargement area. In particular, regional employment shares in regions bordering the European Union have increased in the cases of resource-intensive industries (fuel, chemicals, rubber, and plastics, as well as non-metallic mineral products).

Patterns of regional specialization and geographic concentration of manufacturing and their determinants in the above-mentioned five accession countries are identified and explained by Traistaru, Nijkamp, and Longhi (2002). They use regional manufacturing employment data and other regional variables[12] for the period 1990–1999. Their main findings are discussed below.

Average regional specialization has increased in Bulgaria and Romania, decreased in Estonia and Hungary, and has not changed much in Slovenia (see Figure 2). This result indicates that countries closer to the EU markets have become less specialized while peripheral countries have become more specialized. A possible explanation is

Figure 3: Average* manufacturing concentration in EU accession countries, 1990–1999

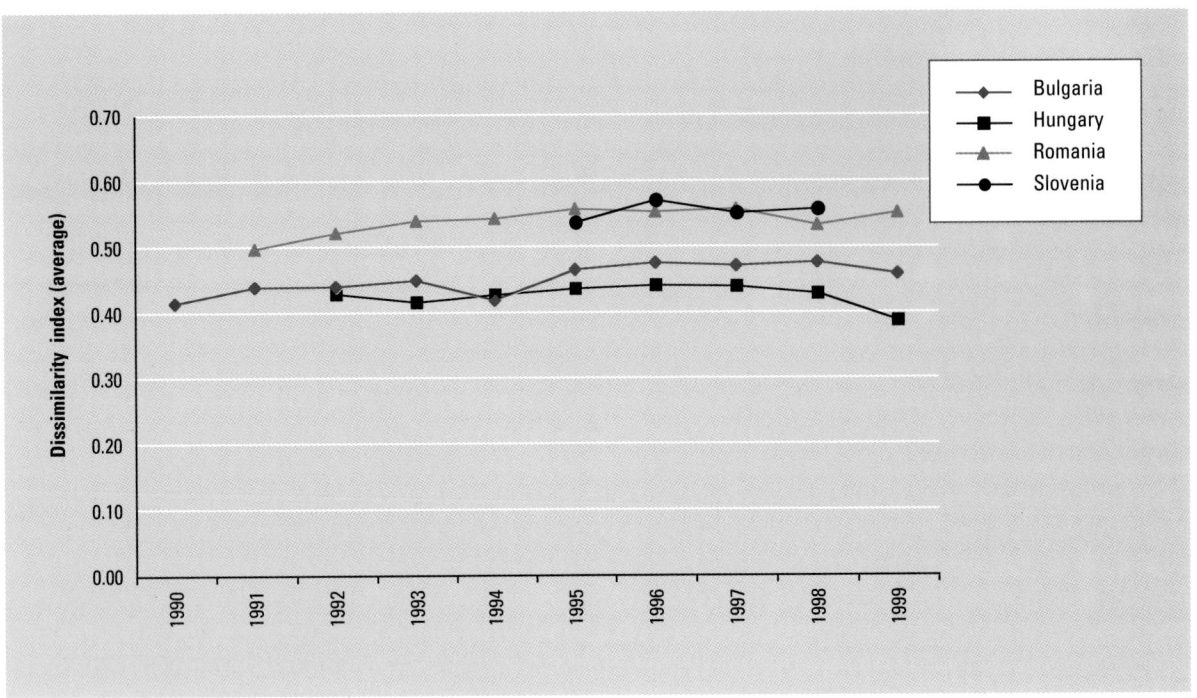

*weighted averages using manufacturing employment shares
Source: Based on calculations by Traistaru, Nijkamp, and Longhi (2002)

the inherited regional economic structures. For example, Romania started the transition to a market economy with a fairly even distribution of manufacturing while in Hungary and Estonia manufacturing was geographically more concentrated.

Patterns of regional manufacturing specialization differ depending on the geographical position of regions and their proximity to the EU markets. For the countries closer to accession (Estonia, Hungary, and Slovenia), regions bordering the European Union are less specialized than the countries' other regions. In Bulgaria, which lags behind with the accession, regions bordering the European Union are more specialized than the other regions. Moreover, regions bordering other accession countries are more specialized than the national averages in Hungary, while in Bulgaria, Estonia, and Romania they are less specialized. Regions bordering countries outside the European Union enlargement (non-EU, non-accession countries) have become more specialized with the exception of Romania. Nonborder regions are less specialized in Bulgaria and Hungary and more specialized in Romania and Slovenia.

Higher specialization is in most cases associated with below-average economic performance,[13] while diversified regions are above average. This result suggests that highly specialized regions in accession countries are specialized in declining industries and/or in industries with low added value.

Average manufacturing concentration has increased in Bulgaria, Romania, and Slovenia and decreased in Hungary, as shown in Figure 3.

Manufacturing concentration patterns depend on industry characteristics such as economies of scale, technology intensity, and wages.[14] Industries with greater economies of scale, higher levels of technology, and higher wages are more concentrated than the national average concentration, while industries with low technology levels and low wages are more dispersed.

Determinants of industrial location patterns
Patterns of location of industrial activity are likely to be determined by an interaction of regional and industry characteristics (Midelfart-Kvarnik et al. 2000). Thus, regions differ in size, factor endowments, and their geographical position relative to industry centers. Industries differ depending on economies of scale, technology, and wages as well as factor intensities.

A model of location of manufacturing activity has been estimated for five EU accession countries by Traistaru, Nijkamp, and Longhi (2002).[15] The empirical results suggest that both factor endowments and geographical proximity to industry centers (capital cities and the European core) explain industrial location. On average, and other things being equal, industries are attracted by large markets. Industries with large economies of scale tend to locate in regions closer to industry centers (the capital city regions in Bulgaria, Romania, and Hungary; European markets in the cases of Estonia, Hungary, and Romania). Research-intensive industries are attracted by regions endowed with researchers. Labor-intensive industries locate in regions endowed with a large labor force.

Economic integration and regional relative wages

Previous theoretical and empirical studies indicate that regional nominal and relative wages are decreasing with transport cost to industry centers (Krugman and Livas 1996; Hanson 1996; Hanson 1997a, 1997b). In a closed economy, the industrial center is, in most cases, the capital region, which concentrates human and capital resources in the process of industrialization. After trade liberalization, access to foreign markets becomes important and some industrial activity is likely to relocate to border regions. As a consequence of a larger labor demand, wages in border regions will rise, reducing the importance of the distance to the capital region in determining regional wage differentials.

Using data on regional manufacturing wages in Mexico before and after trade liberalization, Hanson (1996; 1997a, 1997b) found support for the hypothesis that regional nominal and relative wages decrease with transport cost (proxied with distance) to industry centers (Mexico City and the regions bordering the United States). He found an increased importance of distance from the border regions after trade liberalization.

In the case of EU accession countries, a number of recent papers have tested the above-mentioned hypothesis and found empirical support for the increasing importance of geographical proximity to EU markets as a determinant of regional relative wages.[16] Regional relative wages decrease with the distance to the capital cities, which remain the main industrial centers. The effect of the distance to the capital city on regional relative wages is, however, smaller for border regions,[17] and it becomes less important after the European Association Agreements entered into force.

The adjustment of regional relative wages in response to falling trade barriers in EU accession countries is examined by Damijan and Kostevc (2002a). In particular, these authors investigate whether the response of regional relative wages to increasing economic integration via trade liberalization and FDI has resulted in regional convergence or regional polarization.[18] Their results suggest that the integration forces lead to regional divergence in Estonia and Romania, and a catching-up process is at work in Hungary and Slovenia. No clear pattern is found for Bulgaria.

Economic developments in the Russian Federation

The Russian economy in 2002 once again displays a dual character. On one hand, there are developments in some sectors—oil and gas and retail sales, especially in Moscow—that are very impressive. On the other hand, necessary structural changes that are crucial for economic growth still fail to take place. Unlike 1998, when a fiscal crisis led to devaluation and default, the budget situation is not out of kilter.[19] Russia's strong international position—a current account surplus of US$35 billion in 2001, for example—implies that servicing of external debt is not a problem. The main economic policy issue right now is the failure to take advantage of a significant opportunity to establish growth on a sustainable basis. Although President Vladimir Putin has called for 8 percent annual growth rates in real GDP to make Russian per capita income catch up with Portugal's within a decade, this challenge will almost surely remain unmet.[20]

In 2001, Russian GDP was approximately US$309 billion at official exchange rates. Valued in terms of purchasing power parity, GDP was approximately US$1,235 billion, and per capita GDP in 2001 was approximately $8,900. The absolute size of Russia's GDP at purchasing power parity is thus about equal to that of the CEEC's,[21] and about double the size of the rest of the Commonwealth of Independent States (CIS) economies.

Macroeconomic changes

The pace of the Russian recovery has slowed in 2002 compared with 2001, though it still remains strong compared with the early period of transition. Figure 4 shows that, although GDP has been growing since the August 1998 crisis, output is expected to reach its 1993 level no earlier than 2003.[22] This recovery is primarily attributable to the devaluation of the ruble and the increase in fuel prices, Russia's major export. The impact of these two factors is difficult to overstate. Figure 5 indicates the importance of oil prices for the Russian economy. Higher oil prices increased the revenues of major exporters, increasing cash payments that filtered throughout the economy and led to a higher share of taxes paid in cash as well.[23]

Devaluation, which was a key result of the August 1998 crisis, has been sustained in real terms. This has given a boost to Russian competitiveness.[24] Figure 6 illustrates the relationship between the real exchange rate and GDP. This figure also suggests that the erosion of the gains in competitiveness has led to slower growth more recently. Russia suffers from a classic Dutch Disease syndrome: the value of the ruble that would make its manufacturing sector competitive is inconsistent with its position as a large exporter of oil and gas. Real appreciation threatens to erode the competitiveness advantage that Russia has enjoyed since the August 1998 crash.

Figure 4: Real GDP and GDP growth

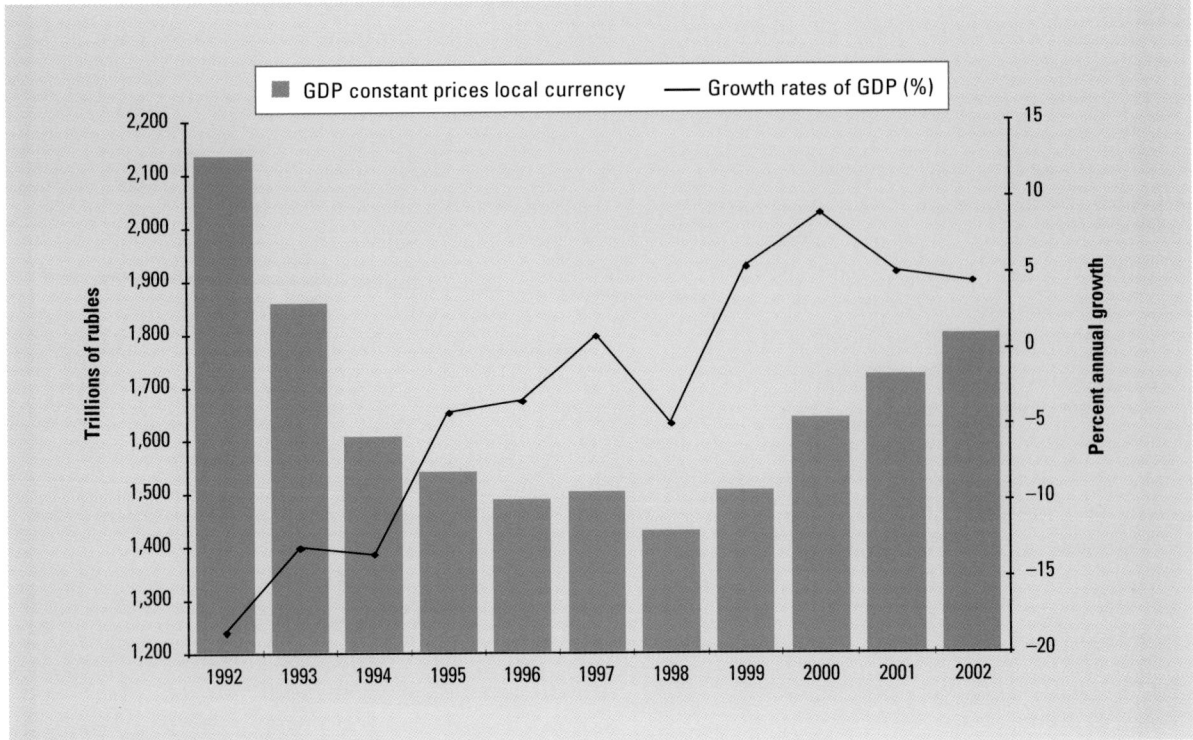

Source: Authors' calculations

Figure 5: Oil prices and GDP

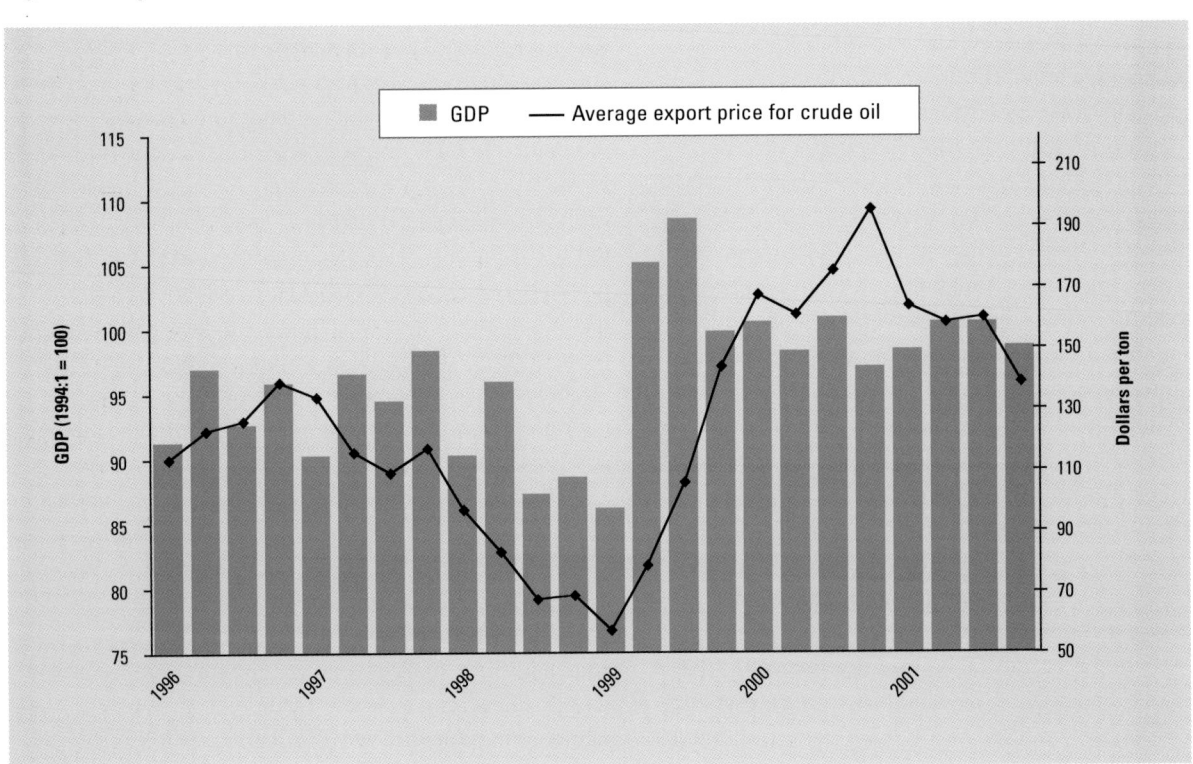

Source: Authors' calculations

Figure 6: GDP and the real exchange rate

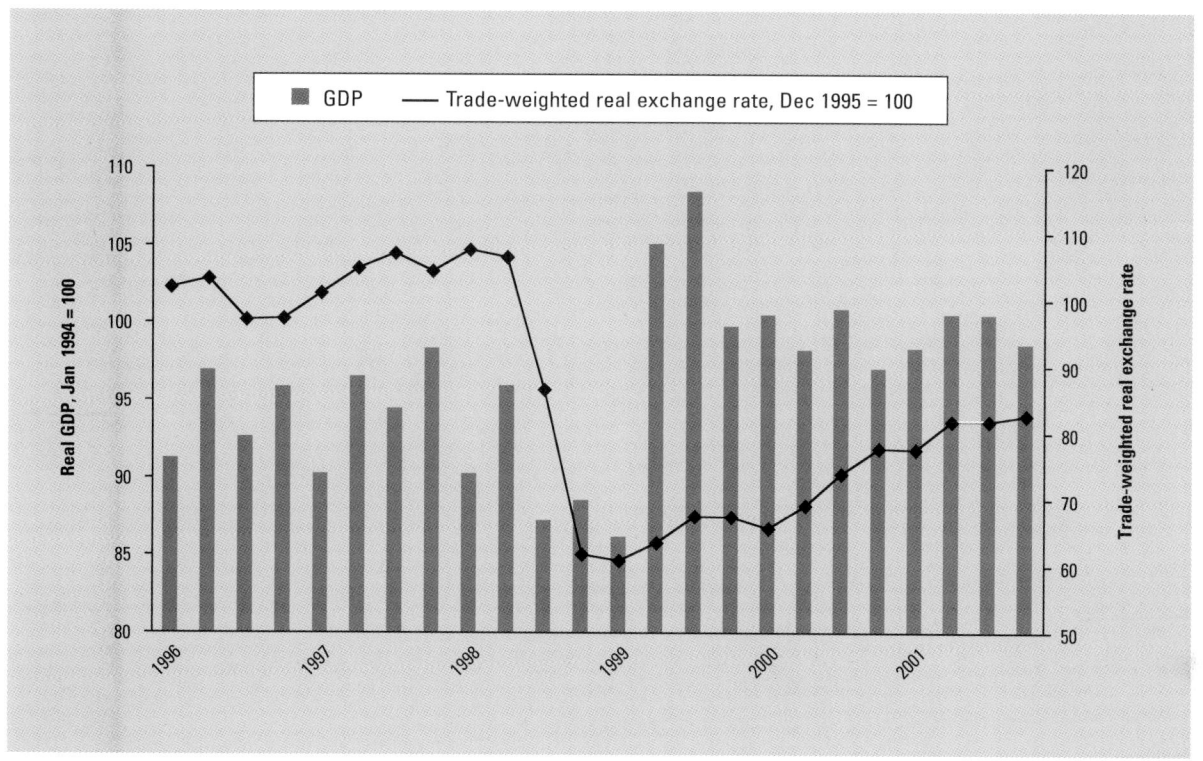

Source: Authors' calculations

These figures illustrate the sensitivity of Russian growth to future paths of oil prices and of the real exchange rate, which is unlikely to decrease in the near future despite the evident desire of the government to diversify the economy. This sensitivity greatly complicates economic policy in Russia. High oil revenues and large capital inflows lead to ruble appreciation that weakens competitiveness. If this is offset through monetary expansion, it leads to excessive inflationary pressures.

The improvements in competitiveness have also led to large current account surpluses—nearly $40 billion in 2001. These surpluses are inconsistent with some elements of Russia's need of foreign capital to finance investment and restructure the economy, but they have allowed Russia to build up its international reserves and to pay down its international debt ahead of schedule. As a result, there is no longer much fear of the "2003 problem," a bulge in repayments of debt that will be due that year. The large current account balance, however, also threatens competitiveness. Although the Russian central bank maintains a tight corridor for the ruble's exchange rate, the large current account surpluses have forced foreign exchange interventions to absorb pressures for appreciation. This has led to an increase in official reserves and an expansion of the monetary base because the central bank's ability to sterilize reserve inflows is limited by the underdeveloped financial markets. Without the early repayment of debt, and

without the large capital flight that Russia has not been able to shake, the expansion in the money base would create further inflationary pressure and erode the competitive advantage that Russia obtained from the real depreciation of the ruble in the wake of the August 1998 crisis.

Income and expenditure

Real disposable income and real expenditure by households have increased significantly since 1999, though the latter has expanded more rapidly (see Figure 7). This suggests that real incomes may be statistically understated. It may also indicate that Russian households expect that incomes will continue to increase. This expenditure growth is an important source of demand and a reflection of increasing consumer credit opportunities. One of the most encouraging signs at the macro level is precisely this development on the consumer side. It is especially important because investment has been less robust than consumer demand.

Investment

Investment is the key to restoring Russia's competitiveness. The core manufacturing sector remains largely unrestructured. Assets are old and getting older. The capital stock in manufacturing has aged during the transition period—in 1990, the average age of the capital stock was 10.8 years; by 1996 it was 14.9 years.[25] Some recent

Figure 7: Real household income and expenditure (January 1994 = 100)

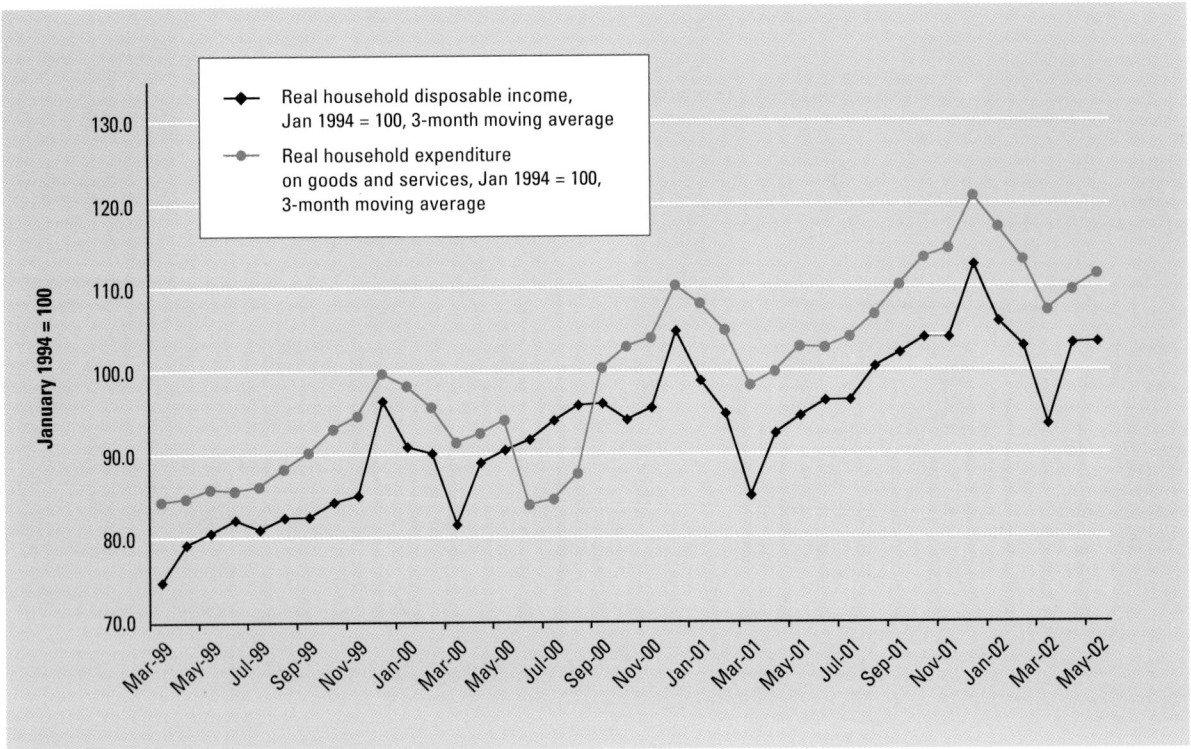

Source: Authors' calculations

estimates put it as high as 17 years (see Bush 2002). To modernize manufacturing requires an acceleration of investment spending. Yet during this period, investment in Russia has been tepid at best, and most investment spending has been concentrated in the energy sector. In fact, although the total volume of real gross fixed investment was 21 percent higher in the first half of 2001 than in the first half of 1998, the entire increase was concentrated in fuels and transportation. For all other sectors of the economy, investment was actually 10 percent lower than in the first half of 1998.[26]

In addition to industry, massive investment is also required for infrastructure[27] and for the exploitation of new oil fields, such as in the Caspian basin. The required amounts of investment for these various purposes are staggering. Figure 8 shows that investment has been increasing since the crisis, but the levels are still low, both compared with what is needed and with pre-transition levels.[28] In 2001, for example, private investment in Russia was just over 12 percent of GDP and public investment was around 7 percent. In advanced transition economies, these rates are closer to 20 to 25 percent of GDP for private investment; there is also another 3 to 6 percent in public investment in advanced transition economies. Figure 8 indicates that the recovery in investment still does not bring it back to the levels experienced early in transition, which were already significantly lower than they were

during the Soviet period. One could argue, of course, that investment is better deployed now. This does not, however, alter the fact that the capital stock seems to be aging quite dramatically in Russia, and hence, the need for investment is increasing.

FDI is especially low in Russia. In 2000, it was $4.4 billion, compared with some $46 billion in China. In 2001, FDI fell to just under $4 billion. Most of it is concentrated in the energy sector. The conventional explanations for the low levels of FDI in Russia are twofold. First are the restrictions imposed by the Russian government on foreign investors and the lack of a level playing field for those without good connections. Second are the corporate governance problems that seem endemic in Russia. Problems of minority shareholders imply that rates of return may be very low if the foreign investor does not hold a majority stake. Yet an enterprise that has majority foreign ownership may suffer from the problem of poor government connections (the first problem). These are both essentially problems of the business environment. Related to these is a third problem, which is a legacy of the Soviet economy: expected rates of return, outside the energy and commodity sectors, are simply too low.

There are two theories that attempt to explain the low level of investment in Russia. The conventional view is that investment is constrained by an inefficient financial system and weak corporate governance. The idea is that

Figure 8: Quarterly fixed investment since 1992

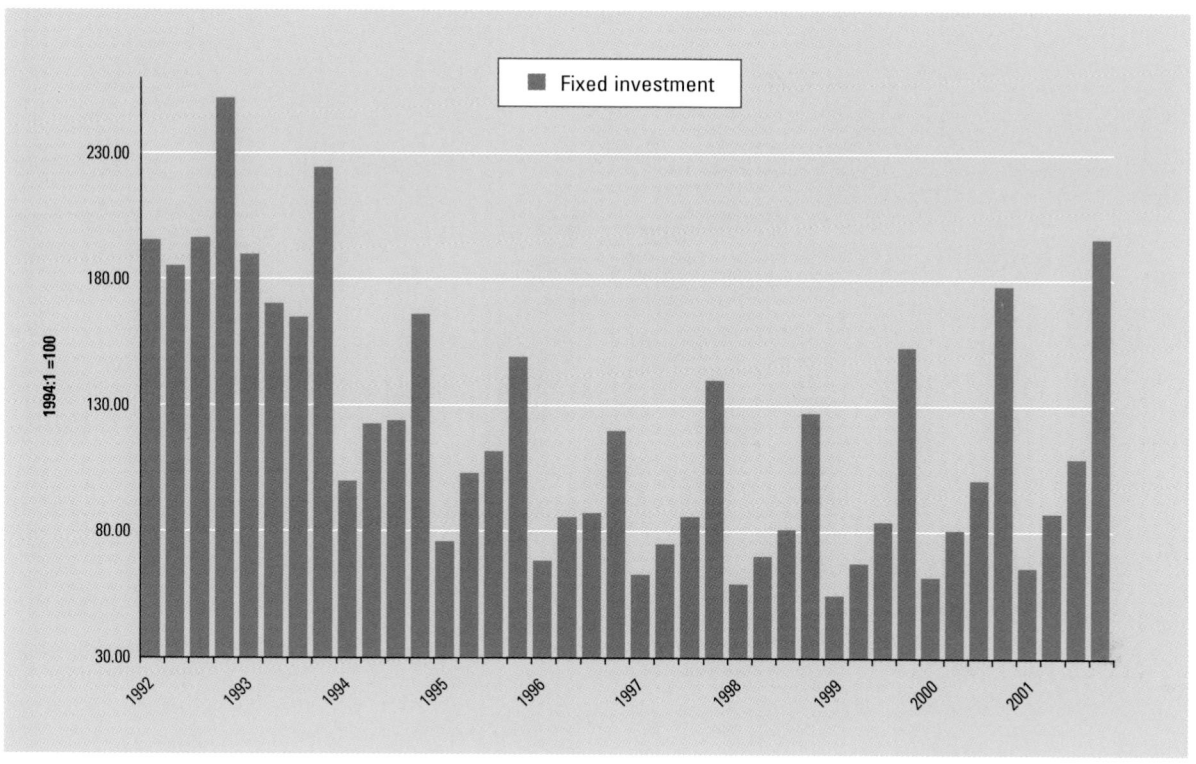

Source: Authors' calculations

institutional failures cause the risk premium to be too high to stimulate investment in non-energy sectors. If the financial system were fixed and corporate governance straightened out, this view predicts that investment into the non-energy sectors of the economy would pick up.

The alternative view is that investment in non-energy sectors is constrained by low profit potential. The problem is that the existing capital-labor bundles are too inefficient. On this theory, which has a lot to do with the notion of potentially viable enterprises, it is the internal aspects that are critical, not the external, institutional, aspects. As Gaddy and Ickes (2002, p 7) note: "Of course, a sufficient infusion of outside resources can guarantee successful restructuring for any enterprise, because this makes it possible to reconstruct the entire enterprise from scratch. Therefore, any meaningful notion of restructuring has to consider the opportunity cost of making a given enterprise viable." Part of the problem is the location of manufacturing assets in Russia. Even with zero cost of capital, it may not be rational to reinvest in Perm (where the average January temperature is lower than −14 centigrade).[29] Instead, you would build a new factory in Rostov.

One important indicator of the extent to which restructuring is incomplete is the large share of manufacturing enterprises that are unprofitable, yet continue to operate. This share remains above 40 percent 10 years into transition.[30] As is evident in Figure 9, the number of loss-making industrial enterprises is higher today than it was in 1995. Although there has been some decline since the August 1998 crisis, the share of loss-makers appears to be on the rise again. This is especially problematic given the underdeveloped state of the financial system. Most investment in Russia comes from retained earnings. Hence, the enterprises with the greatest need to restructure are often the least able to do so.

Although the aggregate figures on the share of loss-making enterprises are sufficiently alarming, they mask regional variations. In Moscow (at 21 percent) and St. Petersburg (at 28 percent), the shares are much lower than the national average. Regions that are farther to the east show much higher ratios. Thus, the shares are 51.5 percent in the Siberian and 54.5 percent in the Far Eastern Federal Districts, and in some constituent regions they top 60 percent (for example, Yakutia at 61.7 percent, Magadan at 62.9 percent, and Kamchatka at 63.5 percent). Thirty districts in Russia have more than 50 percent of their enterprises losing money, and 9 have a share over 60 percent.[31] To a great extent this is due to the legacy of investments in the Soviet era that were made without regard to transportation and other location-specific costs. Enterprises in these regions are simply not viable.

The fact that such a large share of enterprises continues to operate despite being unprofitable indicates that much remains to be done on the reform agenda. To some

Figure 9: Percentage of loss-making industrial enterprises

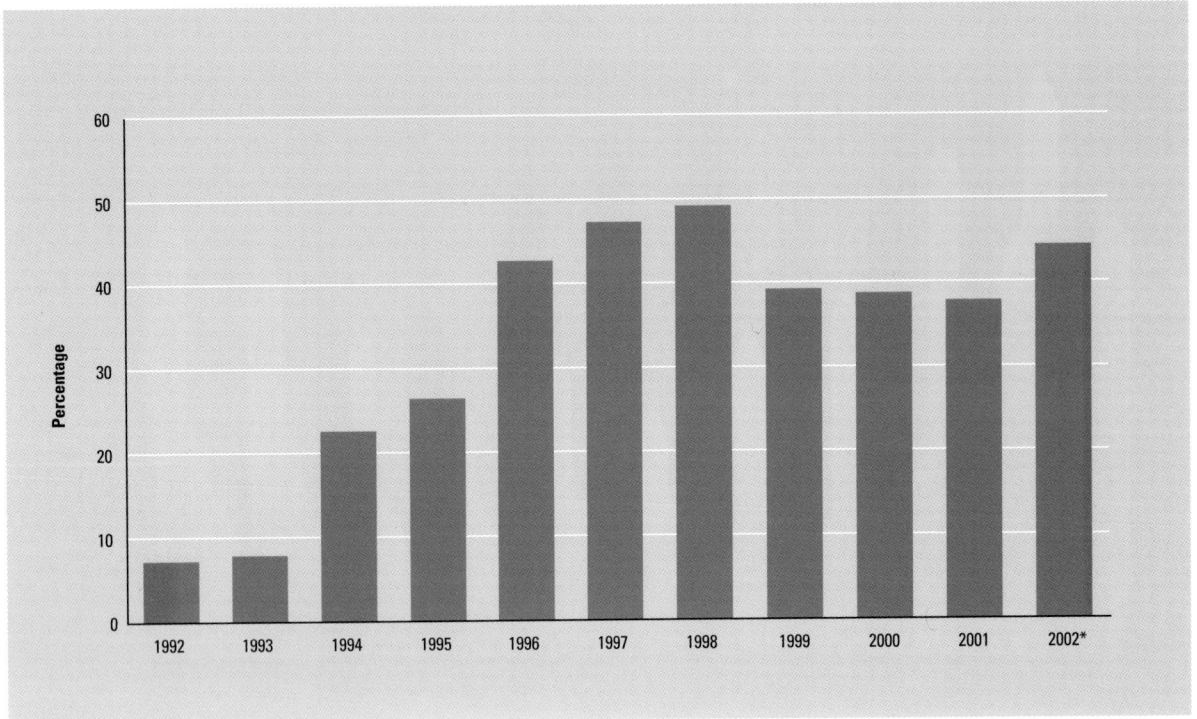

* 2002 refers to data for the first half of the year
Source: Authors' calculations

extent, this continued need for reform reflects weaknesses in the bankruptcy process and lack of creditor rights. In addition, it represents the fact that the Russian government is still unwilling, or unable, to tolerate the closure of so many enterprises; these enterprises can remain open because of subsidized energy.

World Trade Organization accession

World Trade Organization (WTO) accession is a key policy issue for Russia. President Putin has called for a rapid accession. This is partly for political reasons—Russia wants to be accepted as part of the international community. But it also is an important element in reform. Accession is viewed as an incentive to implement key structural reforms. Russia is in a somewhat anomalous situation with regard to accession compared with other countries. Markets are fairly liberalized in Russia. Russian tariffs are relatively low; in September 2000 the average tariff on merchandise trade was approximately 15 percent.[32] The major problems are with services and with changes in institutions and rules. The service sector was restricted in the Soviet era and it is still underdeveloped. Partly due to the influence of powerful interests from this sector, the Russian proposal utilizes an infant industry approach to defend the continued protection of the service sector against international competition.

The key problem for Russia is harmonizing laws to comply with WTO regulations. A rather sticky problem is the domestic price of natural gas. The current level of domestic prices is less than 20 percent of international prices. Russia claims that this is appropriate because it is a major gas producer. Moreover, low gas prices are critical to maintaining a large part of the manufacturing economy. But, for just this reason, the WTO insists that gas prices be brought toward international levels. President Putin has recently argued that this cannot be accepted.

Russia and the WTO face difficult negotiations to reach the goal of Russia joining by 2004. Yet achieving this target—in time for the next presidential election—may be an important consideration for President Putin. It is unclear whether Russia and the WTO will be able to conclude such an agreement, but if this can be accomplished it will be of great importance for the future development of the Russian economy.

Human capital

In addition to investment in physical capital, human capital plays a key role in Russia's attempt to catch up with Europe. Russia's 90 percent primary school enrollment rate is in line with the average for comparable, fast-growing economies and almost twice that of slow-growing ones. In secondary education, Russia is far ahead—at three times the average for fast growers and nine times the average for slow growers. This is a primary advantage for Russia. However, investment in human capital has been low during the transition process, and if we take a broader view there are other important considerations.

In important ways, human capital is on decline in Russia due to health and demographic trends. Russia's population, for example, is expected to decline from its current 144 million to 135 million by 2015. The concomitant decline in the size of the workforce will put even more pressure on growth in total factor productivity (TFP) as a source of growth. Moreover, the population is aging. By 2015, the dependency ratio is expected to be four workers for every three nonworkers. In addition, health conditions are deteriorating. Alcohol abuse is growing and HIV exploding (Russia and Ukraine are believed to have the highest growth rates of HIV cases in the world). In 2002, Russia allocated only $5.4 million for AIDS treatment.

It is difficult to assess the economic consequences of the decline in health conditions. In most countries, the elderly and the very young are the first to experience rises in morbidity and mortality. Unique to the Russian case is that much of the increased mortality is concentrated in working-age males. Many of these prime working-age males are employed in the decaying, noncompetitive manufacturing enterprises, and these individuals would probably be very costly to re-train for work in more modern industries. Hence, although increased mortality in this cohort represents a loss of human capital inherited from the past, this loss may have limited effects on the economy. This is not true, however, for the increase in HIV infections, which tend to be concentrated in younger-age groups. A study by the World Bank suggests that, in the worst-case scenario, Russian GDP could be reduced by more than 10 percent by 2020 due to the consequences of HIV (see Rühl, Pokrovsky, and Vinogradov 2002).

Competitiveness

A general finding is that the impact of privatization on productivity growth is much harder to detect in Russia (and the CIS in general) than it is for CEE countries (see, for example, Djankov and Murrell 2002). One possible reason for this is that institutions that are necessary for privatization to be effective are missing in Russia. This could also be related to the nature of privatization and how it was implemented in various regions. Competition also seems very important, and the fact that CEE countries are more open than Russia may play a role. Alternatively, these differences could be the result of differing initial conditions, which include the share of defense industry, structure of industry, age of plant, and also location. Most likely it is a confluence of these factors that explains this finding, though assessing the relative weight of each factor is important.

It is instructive to compare Russia with the CEE countries in terms of the governance indicators collected by Kaufmann, Kraay, and Zoido-Lobatón (2002); see also Table 8. Russia scores significantly lower than Romania on all indicators, and Romania is the clear laggard in the region. Indeed, as shown in Table 8, Russian scores are much closer to those of Indonesia (added for comparison) than to other CEE economies. This low ranking on governance categories stands in stark contrast to Russia's rather high levels of education. Its weak performance is especially noteworthy with respect to such indicators as rule of law and control of corruption. These are elements that are clearly seen to be inimical to foreign investment.

An argument can be made that significant changes are currently at work with regard to governance in Russia. The argument is that the consolidation of ownership into a small number of significant groups has transformed the incentives for predation. Prior to this consolidation, rent-seeking and asset stripping was the predominant strategy of key decision makers. As insiders have consolidated ownership, the incentive to increase value has risen relative to predation. The Yukos oil company, for example, has witnessed a significant rise in its value relative to other Russian oil companies, including the leading firm, Lukoil. An important question is whether this change in behavior can extend to sectors outside of energy and resources.

Some observers, however, worry that the consolidation of ownership in Russia's industrial sector leads to a problem of *chaeobolization*, and that this will be an impediment to the growth of small- and medium-sized firms in the longer run. Thus, Gavrilenkov argues that the Russian economy is becoming too Asian-like in that *chaebols* are forming (see Gavrilenkov 2002). The fear is that this will lead to an increasing lack of transparency of the financial system, and subsequently to even poorer investment. The lack of competition and transparency would also reduce savings by offering worse assets. Yet, if Russia could achieve a Korean-type economic performance, it would make the economic costs of *chaebolization* seem rather tolerable! In fact, it may well be that, under current conditions in Russia, where most apparent investment opportunities are not really worth investing in, *chaebols* would attract at least as much, and perhaps more, investment than arms-length investors operating with more conventional, weak institutions of financial mediation. *Chaebols* can cherry-pick pretty well when there are few cherries to pick, and they can add substantial relational capital to an enterprise in a way that a normal investor cannot, thus making the enterprise even more valuable in some cases.[33] Where the *chaebol* approach would pose problems would be in an economy in which there were really a lot of alternative profitable investment opportunities.

An important factor that affects Russia's competitiveness is its location and climate. Fifty-four percent of its territory is covered by permafrost. Russia began its economic transition with a locational legacy from the past that was especially severe. Soviet location policies moved population to colder climates to such an extent that Russia's temperature per capita actually decreased during the 20th century.[34] About 45 million people live and work east of the Urals, where average January temperatures range between −15 and −40 degrees centigrade.[35] Canada has a climate that is very similar to Russia's—both have the same share of their territories north of the Arctic Circle—but the share of Canada's population that lives in territory north of the Arctic Circle is about 1 percent that of Russia's.

The location of Russian industrial activity thus provides an extra burden. In addition to competitive inefficiency due to poor investments, Russia suffers from the fact that plants are in the wrong places—both from the perspective of the cost of production and the distance to markets. The difficulties of climate make it harder to attract investment to the regions where manufacturing needs to be restructured.

Structural reforms

Russia's improved economic performance since the August 1998 crisis has been due to high energy prices and a cheap ruble. These are not forces that can be relied upon to achieve sustained economic growth and to catch up with Portugal. Rather, Russia must accelerate the process of structural reforms.[36] To a great extent these reforms were ignored until the August 1998 crisis. Since the election of President Putin, emphasis on structural reforms has intensified and progress has been seen in the field of tax reform. How far and deep such reforms will go is crucial to the future performance of the economy.[37]

Some reforms, primarily tax reform, have been implemented during the window of opportunity created by the confluence of Putin's election, high oil prices, and real depreciation. Crucial elements of structural reform remain, however. One area of intense interest is the reform of natural monopolies, primarily the "three fat boys"—the electricity company RAO UES, Gazprom, and the Ministry of Railways. Rationalization of tariff structures for these bodies is sensitive, given the magnitude of the implicit subsidy.[38] Raising tariffs to world levels could push a large portion of manufacturing into bankruptcy.[39]

As Tompson (2002, p 941) notes, reform of the electricity monopoly RAO UES is at the heart of the matter. The current system cross-subsidizes inefficient firms and prevents needed investment in the electricity sector. Reform threatens vested interests, but it would have long-run benefits to the economy. One has to recall that important elements in Russian manufacturing were built on a foundation of cheap electricity—reform threatens not only their competitive advantage but also their survival.[40]

It is important to recognize the interaction between these reforms and the burdens of the Soviet legacy. Cross-subsidization is one means by which enterprises can survive (barely) in such extreme climates. The costs of locating manufacturing enterprises in cold climates far from markets would be much larger if energy and transportation costs approached world prices. Structural reforms may thus make the regional and locational imbalances in the economy more transparent. At the same time, they will have large differential effects on the economy. This may explain the hesitation of the government to implement such reforms.[41]

One can also see that WTO accession may be one of the strongest forces pushing for structural reforms. This may prove to be a sufficient prize to enable the government to withstand the special interests that are opposed to structural reform. In isolation, each structural reform may be successfully opposed by special interest. As a package deal, however, it may be possible to overcome such opposition. EU accession has certainly posed such a "prize" for CEE economies. Whether WTO accession is a sufficient prize remains to be seen.

Conclusions

The Russian Federation and the central and eastern European countries have maintained high real economic growth rates despite the economic slowdown in the West. This indicates that economic performance in the general region has become more resilient to shocks from elsewhere and is now more sustainable than in the first years of transition. Macroeconomic trends have improved significantly, as growth has been accompanied by falling rates of inflation in recent years. In contrast to the region's precarious position of the late 1990s, the region's external balance does not now seem to be endangered by risks of currency crises or problems of lingering default on external liabilities.

The CEE countries have made significant progress in improving market institutions and the competitiveness of their economies. The candidates for EU accession in 2004, in particular, have used the pre-accession phase to implement reforms and achieve better investment and market conditions. Several of the countries attain the EU average in terms of the Lisbon strategy, the European Union's own ambitious program, to strengthen the competitiveness of its member economies. These countries can be expected to perform quite well in the market environment provided by the European Union. A disappointment in this regard, however, is the relatively poor performance of Poland, the largest CEEC economy, in terms of the Lisbon strategy.

Aggregate economic gains in the CEE countries may, however, hide an uneven distribution across space of costs and benefits associated with the transition reforms and increasing integration with the world economy, in particular with the European Union. Metropolitan areas and border regions close to the European Union are the winners, while declining old industrial regions and rural areas are the losers of the economic transformation processes taking place in the CEE countries. Proximity to EU markets seems to be associated with a diversified industrial activity and better-than-average economic performance, while proximity to other accession countries and countries outside the EU enlargement seems to be associated with high specialization and below-average economic performance.

In Russia, rapid growth and an improvement in the external debt position have been carried mainly by the rise in oil prices in recent years and the real devaluation of the ruble. Outside the oil and natural resources sector, investment remains too weak and the economy has not yet reached a sustainable growth path. Investment is held back by continued weaknesses in the financial system and corporate governance. But the low level of investment is also a result of a lack of profitable opportunities, a lack that is due to the uneconomical capital-labor-location combinations inherited from the past. These problems are becoming more important as the competitiveness boost from the weak ruble is rapidly being eroded through real appreciation. There is still a broad agenda of economic reforms that must be implemented before Russia can hope to attain the goal formulated by President Putin to attain Portugal's level of per capita income.

Notes

1 Landesmann and Stehrer measure relative export specialization by comparing the export shares of individual industries with the export shares of the same industries for the northern EU countries.

2 *Voice and accountability* refers to the ability of citizens to participate in the selection of their governments. *Political stability* indicates perceptions of the likelihood that a government will be overthrown by unconstitutional means. *Government effectiveness* refers to the perceptions of the quality of the bureaucracy and public service provision, and *regulatory quality* measures the quality of regulatory policies in terms of market friendliness and regulatory burden. *Rule of law* indicates the extent to which agents have confidence in the rules of society, and *control of corruption* measures the perception of how prevalent corruption is in society. See Kaufmann, Kraay, and Zoido-Lobatón (2002).

3 These authors account for all required administrative costs of setting up a firm. A *standardized firm* is defined as one that performs general industrial or commercial activities, operates in the largest city, and does not engage in foreign trade. It is not subject to special industry or environmental regulations and does not trade in goods subject to excise taxes. Its capital, which amounts to 10 times per capita GDP in 1999, is domestically owned and subscribed in cash. Data for Estonia are not provided.

4 The full text (Presidency Conclusions, Lisbon European Council, 23 and 24 March 2000) can be downloaded from http://www.europa.eu.int/comm/off/index/_en.htm.

5 See, for instance, European Commission (2001), Petrakos (2000), Resmini (2002), and Traistaru, Nijkamp, Longhi (2002).

6 Trade barriers and the threat of military invasion are, for instance, two reasons explaining the unfavorable position of these regions during the communist regime (Anderson and O'Dowd 1999).

7 Heavy industries were the main engine of industrialization during the communist regime, and they enjoyed large subsidies due to their strategic importance for the defense sector.

8 The new trade theory models (Krugman 1979; 1980; 1981; Helpman and Krugman 1985; and Krugman and Venables 1990) predict that the lowering of trade barriers, and implicitly of trade costs, will result in the concentration of production in large regions, primarily in the "core" regions with good market access, and relocating from remote regions, "the periphery." However, the relationship between trade costs and location of activity is not monotonic. When trade barriers and trade costs are low enough, the geographical advantage of the regions with good market access become less important. At this stage, factor production costs will motivate firms to move back to peripheral regions. More recently, new economic geography models (Krugman 1991a; 1991b; Krugman and Venables 1995; Venables 1996; Fujita, Krugman, and Venables 1999) suggest that the regional specialization may be the result of the spatial pattern of agglomeration of economic activities. Regions with an initial scale advantage in particular sectors are predicted to attract more activity via a mechanism of "cumulative causation."

9 See, for instance, Krugman (1991a), Amiti (1999), Aiginger et al. (1999), Brülhart (1998a, 1998b; 2001), Hanson (1996; 1997a, 1997b), and Midelfart-Knarvik et al. (2000).

10 The project, "European Integration, Regional Specialization and Location of Industrial Activity in Accession Countries," was undertaken with financial support from the European Community PHARE ACE Programme and coordinated by the Center for European Integration Studies, University of Bonn.

11 Data for Slovenia were limited to three years only, 1997–1999.

12 Geographic and demographic variables, average earnings, GDP, infrastructure, and R&D indicators at NUTS 3 level.

13 Regional economic performance indicators included are GDP per capita, productivity, unemployment, and average wages.

14 Manufacturing branches have been grouped in industries with high, medium, and low economies of scale following the classification given in Pratten (1988). Technology-based industry groups include high-, medium-, and low-technology industries classified by OECD (1994) on the basis of R&D intensities. The classification of industries into high, medium, low wages follows the OECD (1994) classification, which is based on the average labor compensation (wages and salaries plus supplementary benefits paid by the employer). Industries in the high-wage group have wages more than 15 percent higher than the median wage; industries in the medium-wage group have wages within 15 percent of the median wage; industries in the low-wage group have wages at least 15 percent below the median wage.

15 The model is similar to the one estimated by Midelfart-Knarvik et al. (2000) for EU Member States. The dependent variable is the share of employment of manufacturing branches in regional employment. The tested determinants of location included the size of regions and regional manufacturing, regional characteristics such as labor and research abundance (factor endowments), market potential (measuring proximity to industrial centers), industry characteristics (economies of scale, labor, technology, and research intensities) and interacted regional and industry characteristics such as market potential and scale economies, research endowment and research intensity, research endowment and technology intensity, labor abundance, and labor intensity. The model has been tested for Bulgaria, Estonia, Hungary, Romania, and Slovenia.

16 See Spiridonova (2002) for Bulgaria; Fainshtein and Lubenets (2002) for Estonia; Maffioli (2002) for Hungary; Traistaru and Pauna (2002) for Romania; and Damijan and Kostevc (2002b) for Slovenia.

17 Southern and eastern border regions in the case of Bulgaria; western border regions in the cases of Estonia and Romania; western and northern border regions in the cases of Hungary and Slovenia.

18 The model tested by Damijan and Kostevc (2002a) has as dependent variable regional wages relative to the wages in the capital city and their determinants include FDI, interregional trade costs, and border effects.

19 On a consolidated basis, Russia ran a budget surplus of 3.8 percent of GDP in the first half of 2002. To some extent this was due to unspent funds; a figure closer to 2.3 percent might be a more accurate portrayal of the situation. Still, this represents a significant change from the pre-August 1998 period, when budget deficits on the order of 8.8 percent (1997) were typical.

20 Given that Portugal is in the bottom tier of EU economies, this may seem like a modest goal. Yet the difficulty of achieving parity with Portuguese per capita income in a decade attests to the challenge that lies ahead for Russia. See Aris (2002).

21 For our purposes in this chapter, and for this calculation in particular, the CEE countries include the Baltic States.

22 The decline in GDP in Russia in the early phase of transition certainly reflects some rationalization of production and looks smaller if post-transition relative prices are used. See OECD (1995) and Gavrilenkov and Koen (1994).

23 See Gaddy and Ickes (2002, chapter 9) for a discussion of the effects of devaluation on the remonetization of the economy after 1998.

24 In January 1999, the average monthly dollar wage was $50.8, only 29 percent of its July 1998 level of $178. By July 2000, the dollar wage had climbed back to about $82.7, but this was still less than 46 percent of the July 1998 level. By May 2002, the dollar wage had reached $134, still only 75 percent of the July 1998 level.

25 *Rossiyskiy statisticheskiy yezhegodnik* (1997, p 340).

26 *Russian Economic Trends*, volume 10, number 2, 2001: 37.

27 For example, roads, railways, power lines, water supply, and sewers need to be replaced and maintained. In addition, there is great need for investment in pipelines, which lose an estimated 17 to 20 million tons of oil each year (see Bush 2002).

28 Some indication of the problem is evident if we extend the period to the beginning of transition, as in Figure 4.

29 Note that Perm is a city with a population of over 1 million.

30 The share of unprofitable enterprises for the first half of 2002 approaches 46 percent; see Interfax (2002). It could be argued that these data overstate the true level of loss-making, due to inadequate amortization of capital expenses, or simple cheating. However, the important point is the trend of the loss-making share, and that is clearly moving in the wrong direction.

31 Data are from Interfax (2002), Table 3.

32 Although this is higher than those in WTO Member economies, it probably overstates the true levels since most firms do not pay tariffs anyway. For example, the nominal official weighted average tariff rates were 14 percent, 14 percent, 12 percent, and 8 percent in 1996, 1997, 1998, and 1999, respectively. But the actual duty collected as a percent of the value of imports in the same years were only 4 percent, 7 percent, 7 percent, and 5 percent (Gorban, Guriev, and Yudaeva 2001, p 6).

33 *Relational capital* refers to the stock of goodwill that an enterprise can use to avoid the strictures of the budget constraint. An enterprise that has high relational capital can undertake transactions (barter, using tax offsets, and delaying payment) that other enterprises cannot get away with. Relational capital is support for informal activity that can aid the operation of an enterprise. See Gaddy and Ickes (2002, chapter 3).

34 Temperature per capita (TPC) is a population-weighted mean temperature. In most countries, TPC increased as population moved to warmer climates. In the United States, for example, TPC rose more than 3 degrees centigrade during the century. In Russia, on the other hand, it fell by more than 1 degree centigrade, as industry moved to the Urals region. See Clifford Gaddy and Barry W. Ickes, "The Cost of the Cold" unpublished working paper, Brookings Institution.

35 For example, in 1997 four of the top ten largest cities in Russia (each with a population over 1 million) had average January temperatures of −14 degrees centigrade or below. In 1897, on the other hand, none of the ten largest cities had such low temperatures.

36 Structural reforms can be thought of as microeconomic reforms that deal with incentives to pay taxes and obey budget constraints. The most important example, perhaps, is the elimination of soft-budget constraints through the ending of implicit subsidies for energy use.

37 See Tompson (2002) for an analysis of the politics of structural reform in Russia.

38 In his work "The Politics of Structural Reform in Russia," Tomspon points out that "At the beginning of 2002—a decade after Gaidar's 'big bang' price liberalization—the domestic price of oil was under 30 percent of the world market price of Urals crude, and the average domestic wholesale price of natural gas was about 12.5 percent of the export price" (Tompson 2002, p 945).

39 Of course, this would be the case only if a viable bankruptcy plan—another significant structural reform—were in place.

40 One might see a similar force at work in the financial sector, where domestic interests have limited the penetration of foreign banks. Hence, the financial sector remains underdeveloped.

41 It would be more efficient, of course, to reform tariffs and compensate regions with transfers out of general revenues to cope with the burdens posed by the Soviet legacy. Such policies are rarely implemented even in developed economies, however.

References

Aris, B. 2002. "In Pursuit of Portugal," *The Moscow Times*, September 30.

Aiginger, K. et al. 1999. "Specialisation and (Geographic) Concentration of European Manufacturing," *Enterprise DG Working Paper No. 1*, Background Paper for *The Competitiveness of European Industry: 1999 Report*. Brussels: European Commission

Amiti, M. 1999. "Specialisation Patterns in Europe," *Weltwirtschaftliches Archiv*, 134(4): 573–593.

Anderson, J. and L. O'Dowd. 1999. "Borders, Border Regions and Territoriality: Contradictory Meanings, Changing Significance," *Regional Studies* 33(7): 593–604.

Begg, D. et al. 2001. *Sustainable Capital Account Regimes for Accession Countries*. Mimeo: University of Bonn.

Bonin, J. and P. Wachtel. 2002. "Financial Sector Development in Transition Countries – Lessons From the First Decade." Mimeo: Stern School, New York University.

Brülhart, M. 1998a. "Economic Geography, Industry Location and Trade: The Evidence," *The World Economy* 21(6): 775–801.

———. 1998b. "Trading Places: Industrial Specialization in the European Union," *Journal of Common Market Studies* 36(3): 319–346.

———. 2001. "Growing Alike or Growing Apart? Industrial Specialization of EU Countries." In C. Wyplosz, ed. *The Impact of EMU on Europe and the Developing Countries*. Oxford: Oxford University Press.

Bush, K. 2002. "Russian Economy, June 2002." Mimeo. Washington DC: Center for Strategic and International Studies.

Caviglia, G., G. Krause, and C. Thimann. 2002. "Key Features of the Financial Sectors in EU Accession countries." In: C. Thimann, ed., *Financial Sectors in EU Accession Countries*. Frankfurt: European Central Bank.

Cornelius, P. et al. 2002. *The Lisbon Review 2002–2003. An Assessment of Policies and Reforms in Europe*. Geneva: World Economic Forum.

Damijan, J. and C. Kostevc. 2002a. "The Impact of Economic Integration on the Patterns of Adjustment of Regional Wages in Accession Countries." In I. Traistaru, P. Nijkamp, and L. Resmini, eds., *The Emerging Economic Geography in EU Accession Countries*. Aldershot: Ashgate Ltd. Publishing.

———. 2002b. "The Emerging Economic Geography in Slovenia." In I. Traistaru, P. Nijkamp, and L. Resmini, eds., *The Emerging Economic Geography in EU Accession Countries*. Aldershot: Ashgate Ltd. Publishing.

Djankov, S. et al. 2001. "The Regulation of Entry." Working Paper, Washington, DC: World Bank.

Djankov, S. and P. Murrell. 2002. "Enterprise Restructuring in Transition: A Quantitative Survey," *Journal of Economic Literature* XL(3): 739–792.

Economic Commission for Europe. 2002. *Economic Survey of Europe*. New York: United Nations.

European Commission. 2001. *Unity, Solidarity, Diversity for Europe, Its People and Its Territory. Second Report on Economic and Social Cohesion*. Luxembourg: Office for Official Publications of the European Communities.

European Council. 2000. Presidency Conclusions, Lisbon European Council, 23 and 24 March 2000. Online. http://www.europa.eu.int/comm/off/index/_en.htm.

"European Integration, Regional Specialization and Location of Industrial Activity in Accession Countries." 2002. Project undertaken with financial support from the European Community PHARE ACE Programme and coordinated by the Center for European Integration Studies, University of Bonn.

Eurostat. 2001. European Union direct investment data. Luxembourg: Office for Official Publications of the European Communities.

Fainshtein, G. and N. Lubenets. 2002. "The Emerging Economic Geography in Estonia." In I. Traistaru, P. Nijkamp, and L. Resmini, eds., *The Emerging Economic Geography in EU Accession Countries*. Aldershot: Ashgate Ltd. Publishing.

Foders, F., D. Piazolo, and R. Schweickert. 2002. "Fit für die EU? Indikatoren zum Stand der Wirtschaftsreformen in den Kandidatenländern." *Kieler Diskussionsbeitrage* 389/390 Juni.

Fujita, M., P. Krugman, and A. Venables. 1999. *The Spatial Economy*. Cambridge, MA: MIT Press.

Gavrilenkov, E. 2002. "Russia's Chaebols: Why Conglomerates Are Dangerous for Russia," *Troika Dialog Research*, July 25, 2002.

Gaddy, C. and B. W. Ickes. 2002. *Russia's Virtual Economy*. Washington, DC: Brookings.

———. "The Cost of the Cold" unpublished working paper, Brookings Institution.

Gavrilenkov, E., and V. Koen. 1994. "How Large Was the Output Collapse in Russia? Alternative Estimates and Welfare Implications," IMF Research Department Working Paper No. WP/94/154, Washington, DC: International Monetary Fund. December 1994.

Gleich, H. and J. von Hagen. 2000. "Fiscal Policy in Transition: Convergence, Hysteresis, and the Role of Institutions." In S. Eijffinger, K. Koedijk, and S. Yeo, eds., *Vivent les Differences. Heterogeneous Europe*. London: Centre for Economic Policy Research.

Gorban, M., S. Guriev, and K. Yudaeva. 2001. "Russia in the WTO: Myths and Reality," CEFIR and Club 2015, Moscow: Center for Economic and Financial Research. Online. http://www.cefir.org/wto_pub.html

Haaland, J. I. et al. 1999. "What Determines the Economic Geography of Europe?" CEPR Discussion Paper No. 2072. London: Centre for Economic Policy Research.

Hanson, G. H. 1996. "Economic Integration, Intra-Industry Trade, and Frontier Regions," *European Economic Review* 40 (3-5): 941–949.

———. 1997a. "Localization Economies, Vertical Organization, and Trade," *American Economic Review* 86 (5): 1266–1278.

———. 1997b. "Increasing Returns, Trade, and the Regional Structure of Wages," *Economic Journal* 107(January): 113–133.

Helpman, E. and P. Krugman. 1985. *Market Structure and Foreign trade: Increasing Returns, Imperfect Competition and the International Economy*. Brighton: Harvester Wheatsheaf.

Interfax. 2002. *Statistical Report* XI(40): September 28.

International Monetary Fund (IMF). 2002. *Direction of Trade Statistics Yearbook*. Washington, DC: International Monetary Fund.

Kaufmann, D., A. Kraay, and P. Zoido-Lobatón. 2002. "Governance Matters II: Updated Indicators for 2000–01," World Bank Working Paper, Washington, DC: World Bank.

Krugman, P. 1979. "Increasing Returns, Monopolistic Competition and International Trade," *Journal of International Economics* 9(4): 469–479.

———. 1980. "Scale Economics, Product Differentiation, and the Pattern of Trade," *American Economic Review* 70(5): 950–959.

———. 1981. "Intra-Industry Specialization and the Gains from Trade," *Journal of Political Economy* 89: 959–973.

———. 1991a. *Geography and Trade*. Cambridge, MA: MIT Press.

———. 1991b. "Increasing Returns and Economic Geography," *Journal of Political Economy* 99(3): 484–499.

Krugman, P. and R. Livas. 1996. "Trade Policy and the Third World Metropolis," *Journal of Development Economics* 49(1): 137–150.

Krugman, P. and A. Venables. 1990. "Integration and the Competitiveness of Peripheral Industry." In C. Bliss and J. Braga de Macedo, eds., *Unity with Diversity in the European Community*. Cambridge: Cambridge University Press.

———. 1995. "Globalisation and the Inequality of Nations," *Quarterly Journal of Economics* 110(4): 857–880.

Landesmann, M. 2000. "Structural Change in the Transition Economies, 1989–1999." In UN Economic Commission for Europe, ed., *Economic Survey of Europe*. Vienna: The Vienna Institute for International Economic Studies.

Landesmann, M. and R. Stehrer. 2002. "The CEECs in the Enlarged Europe: Convergence Patterns, Specialization, and Labor Market Implications." The Vienna Institute for Comparative Economic Studies (WIIW) Research Report No. 286, July.

Maffioli, A. 2002. "The Emerging Economic Geography in Hungary." In I. Traistaru, P. Nijkamp, and L. Resmini, eds., *The Emerging Economic Geography in EU Accession Countries*. Aldershot: Ashgate Ltd. Publishing.

Midelfart-Knarvik, K. H. et al. 2000. "The Location of European Industry," *Economic Papers* No. 142, Report prepared for the Directorate General for Economic and Financial Affairs, European Commission.

Organisation for Economic Co-operation and Development (OECD). 1994. *Manufacturing Performance: A Scoreborard of Indicators*. Paris: Organisation for Economic Co-operation and Development and OCDE.

———. 1995. *Russia Survey*. Paris: Organisation for Economic Co-operation and Development.

———. 2002. *OECD Economic Outlook* 71 (June). Paris: Organisation for Economic Co-operation and Development.

Petrakos, G. 1996. "The Regional Dimension of Transition in Eastern and Central European Countries: An Assessment," *Eastern European Economics* 34(5): 5–38.

———. 2000. "The Spatial Impact of East-West Integration." In G. Petrakos, G. Maier, and G. Gorzelak, eds. *Integration and Transition in Europe: The Economic Geography of Interaction*. London: Routledge.

Pratten, C. 1988. "A Survey of the Economies of Scale." In European Commission, 2: Studies on the Economics of Integration, vol. 2, Luxembourg: Office for Official Publications of the European Communities.

Resmini, L. 2002. "Specialization and Growth Prospects in Border Regions of Accession Countries," ZEI Working Paper No. B02-17. In I. Traistaru, P. Nijkamp, and L. Resmini, eds., *The Emerging Economic Geography in EU Accession Countries*. Aldershot: Ashgate Ltd. Publishing.

Rossiyskiy statisticheskiy yezhegodnik (Russian Statistical Yearbook). 1997. Moscow: State Committee of Statistics of Russia, p 340.

Rühl, C., V. Pokrovsky, and V. Vinogradov. 2002. *The Economic Consequences of HIV in Russia*. World Bank. Online at http://www.worldbank.org.ru/eng/statistics/hiv/default.htm#4f

Russian Economic Trends. 2001. London: Basil Blackwell, vol. 10.

Spiridonova, J. 2002. "The Emerging Economic Geography in Bulgaria." In I. Traistaru, P. Nijkamp, and L. Resmini, eds., *The Emerging Economic Geography in EU Accession Countries*. Aldershot: Ashgate Ltd. Publishing.

Tompson, W. 2002. "Putin's Challenge: The Politics of Structural Reform in Russia," *Europe-Asia Studies* 54(6): 933–957.

Traistaru, I., P. Nijkamp, and S. Longhi. 2002, forthcoming. "Regional Specialization and Concentration of Industrial Activity in Accession Countries," ZEI Working Paper No. B02-16.

Traistaru, I. and C. Pauna. 2002. "The Emerging Economic Geography in Romania." In I. Traistaru, P. Nijkamp, and L. Resmini, eds., *The Emerging Economic Geography in EU Accession Countries*. Aldershot: Ashgate Ltd. Publishing.

Traistaru, I., P. Nijkamp, and L. Resmini, eds. 2002. *The Emerging Economic Geography in EU Accession Countries*. Aldershot: Ashgate Ltd. Publishing.

United Nations Economic Commission for Europe (UNECE). 2002. *Economic Survey of Europe 2002, No. 1*. New York and Geneva: United Nations.

Venables, A. 1996, "Equilibrium locations of vertically linked industries", International Economic Review, 37, 341–359.

CHAPTER 2.7

Lights and Shadows of Latin American Competitiveness

FELIPE LARRAIN B., Pontificia Universidad Católica de Chile,
and Harvard University

Introduction

Latin America is going through very difficult times indeed. Most countries are trying to cope with an environment of high economic fragility, which is partly a result of the world recession in 2001, but which is also exacerbated by internal political trouble and policy mismanagement. The region as a whole grew by less than half of 1 percent in 2001, following growth of over 4 percent in 2000. Economic prospects for 2002 are significantly worse, and in some cases—such as Argentina—they are abysmal. Political fragility is also being felt strongly in several countries, most notably in Argentina and Venezuela, but also in Peru, Colombia, and Brazil.

The short-term outlook

As Figure 1 shows, growth expectations for the region in 2002 have been consistently revised downward. To a significant extent, this dire situation is due to external factors: the US recession in 2001 and half-hearted recovery in 2002, extremely slow activity in Europe, and recession in Japan have all conspired against the recovery of external demand for Latin America's exports. As a result, most commodity prices—with the exception of oil—have taken a downward trend. Net private capital inflows have also suffered a dramatic decline (see Figure 2): from over US$70 billion in 1998–99, they have scaled back to US$40 billion in 2000 and slightly over US$20 billion in 2001. The forecast for 2002 is even worse: according to the IMF (2002), total net private inflows to Latin America will be on the order of US$10 billion, the lowest level in more than a decade.

The deep economic and political crisis in Argentina is perhaps the most visible problem nowadays in Latin America. As we discuss later in this chapter, the roots of this crisis go well beyond economic factors, into the weakness of institutions and the divisiveness of politics. Argentina suffered a GDP decline of 4.5 percent in 2001, which has been followed by a much worse performance in 2002—a contraction of GDP approaching 15 percent. The country not only is excluded from international private financial markets, but also has important difficulties in conducting regular foreign trade operations. The problems are compounded by a deposit freeze that, after devaluation and conversion rates for dollar deposits that were well below market, resulted in a significant expropriation for depositors. Banks and other foreign investors have also suffered substantial losses. Beyond the immediate concerns, a key question is how Argentina will restore confidence to domestic and foreign investors so that it can start a sustained recovery. This task seems beyond the country's capabilities in the short to medium term.

Figure 1: The fall in 2002 growth expectations (%)

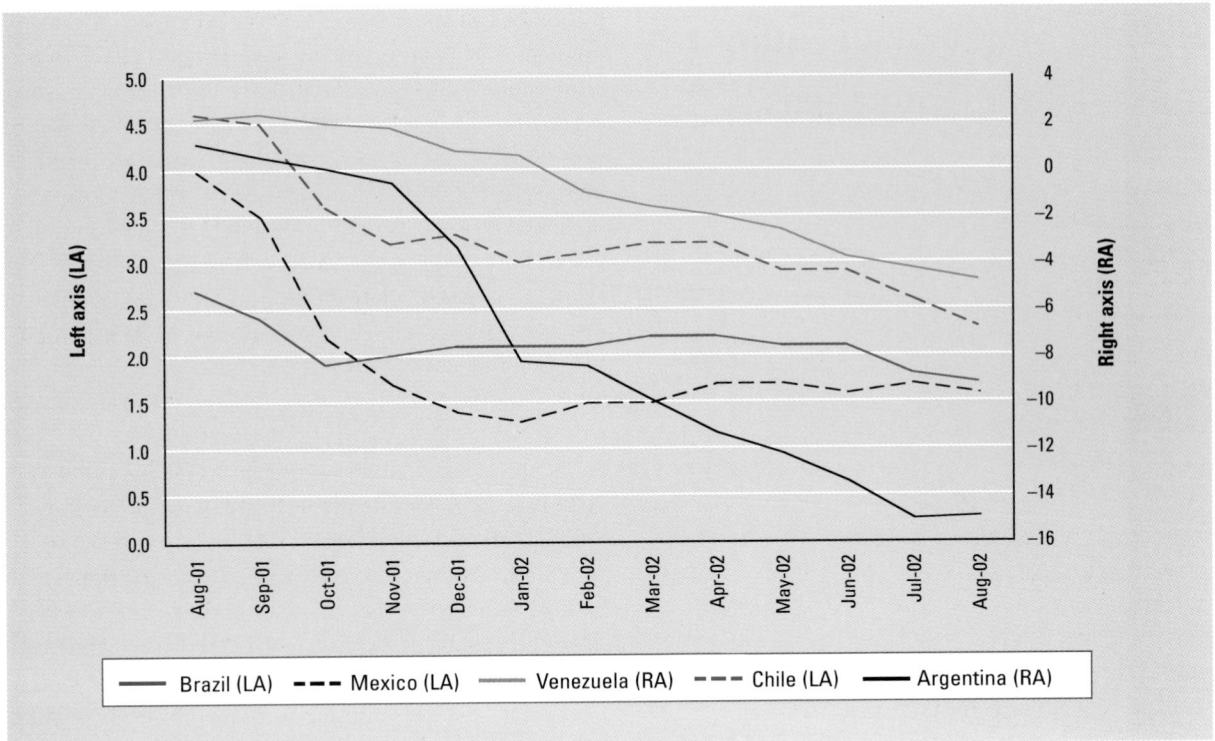

Source: Consensus Economics, various years

Figure 2: Capital inflow drought

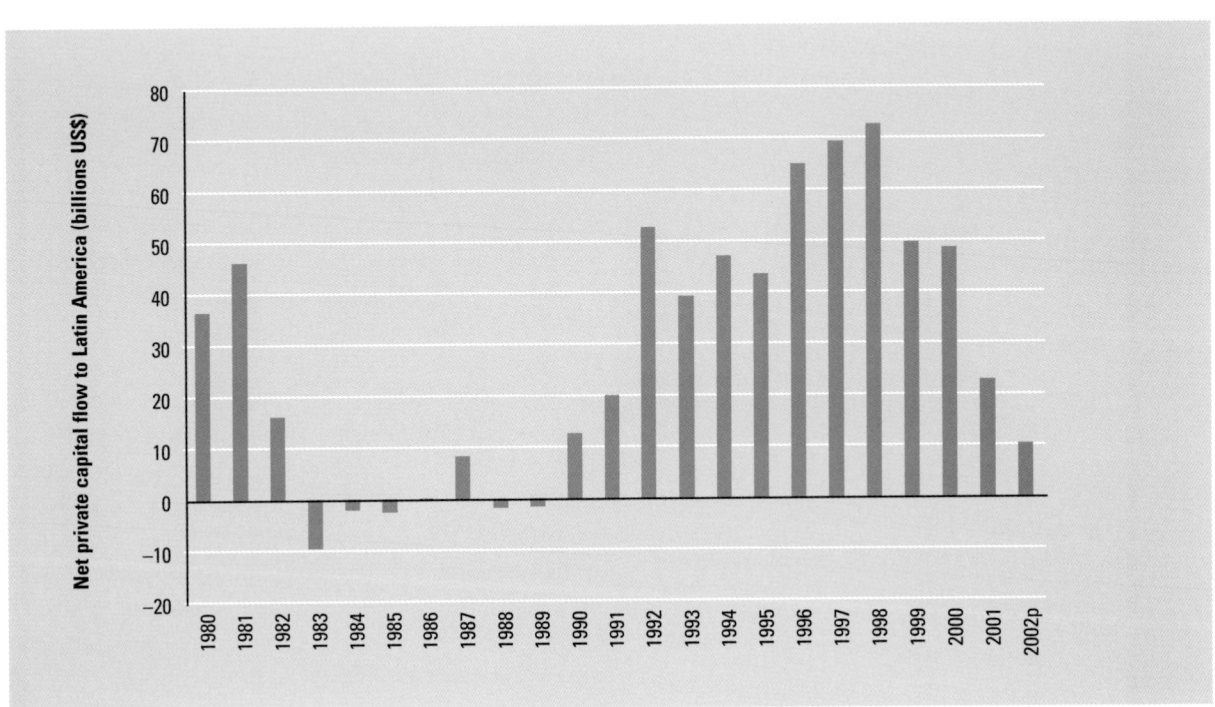

Note: *p* = projected
Source: IMF (2002)

After the collapse in Argentina, market focus turned to Brazil, which—amid political uncertainty—has been on the brink of economic collapse during the last few months. The IMF's US$30 billion rescue package in August 2002 allowed the country to avoid debt default and crisis for the short term. There are, indeed, significant differences between Brazil and Argentina. Unlike Argentina, Brazil has been able to improve its public finances significantly. Its primary fiscal surplus has increased consistently since 1996, and currently runs around 3.5 percent of GDP, which covers almost half the fiscal interest bill. Additionally, a large part of the public debt is in reales (the local currency). Also, Brazil's floating exchange rate regime helps cushion the shocks, in sharp contrast to Argentina's defunct currency board. Nonetheless, the country needs more than outside financial assistance to avoid economic collapse and improve its growth prospects over the medium to long term. It needs serious internal policy commitments and actions. In particular, the new government would need to increase the primary surplus beyond the 3.75 percent of GDP target set in the IMF agreement to allow a reduction of interest rates and the sovereign spread. This fiscal effort could more than pay off in lower debt-service costs. The new government should also continue with structural reforms, especially in the state sector and labor markets. This combination of policies would improve Brazil's prospects and those of Latin America.

Beyond the desperate plight of millions of Argentineans and the problems in Brazil, attention has been placed, too, on the "contagion effect" of these troubles on the rest of the region. Most of the contagion effect from Argentina has already occurred. Countries that trade with Argentina have been hurt, capital inflows to the region have declined, and exchange rates have depreciated. The trade link has hurt many Brazilian exporters, but its overall macroeconomic effect is relatively small for Brazil—partly because Brazilian exports are less than 10 percent of GDP, and partly because export dependence on Argentina is low. For the rest of the region—with the exception of Uruguay and Paraguay—trade contagion from Argentina is not significant. Neighboring Chile, for example, sends only 3 percent of its exports to Argentina.

Contagion has a more important effect on financial flows to the region. This is evidenced by the steep decline in net private capital inflows during 2001–2002, shown in Figure 2. Even foreign direct investment (FDI), which has proved the most resilient type of capital inflow in times of crisis, has dropped significantly. Perhaps the clearest case of financial contagion from Argentina has been Uruguay. Only last January this country had an investment grade status; a few months later, the spread over US Treasury bonds topped 2,000 percent (see Figure 3), the government declared a bank holiday in the face of a stampede of depositors, and recession hit hard (GDP declined 10 percent in the first quarter of this year).

Figure 3a: Sovereign spreads in Latin America (1997–2002)

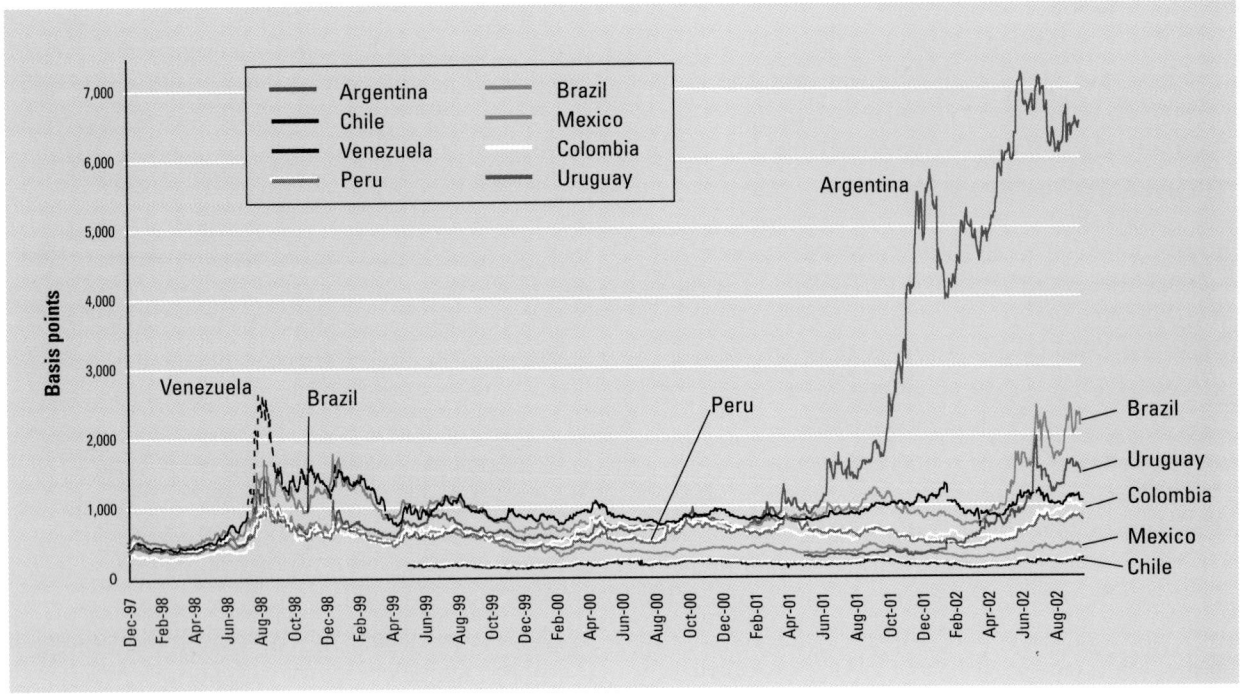

Source: JPMorgan Chase Online

Figure 3b: Sovereign spreads in Latin America (2001–2002)

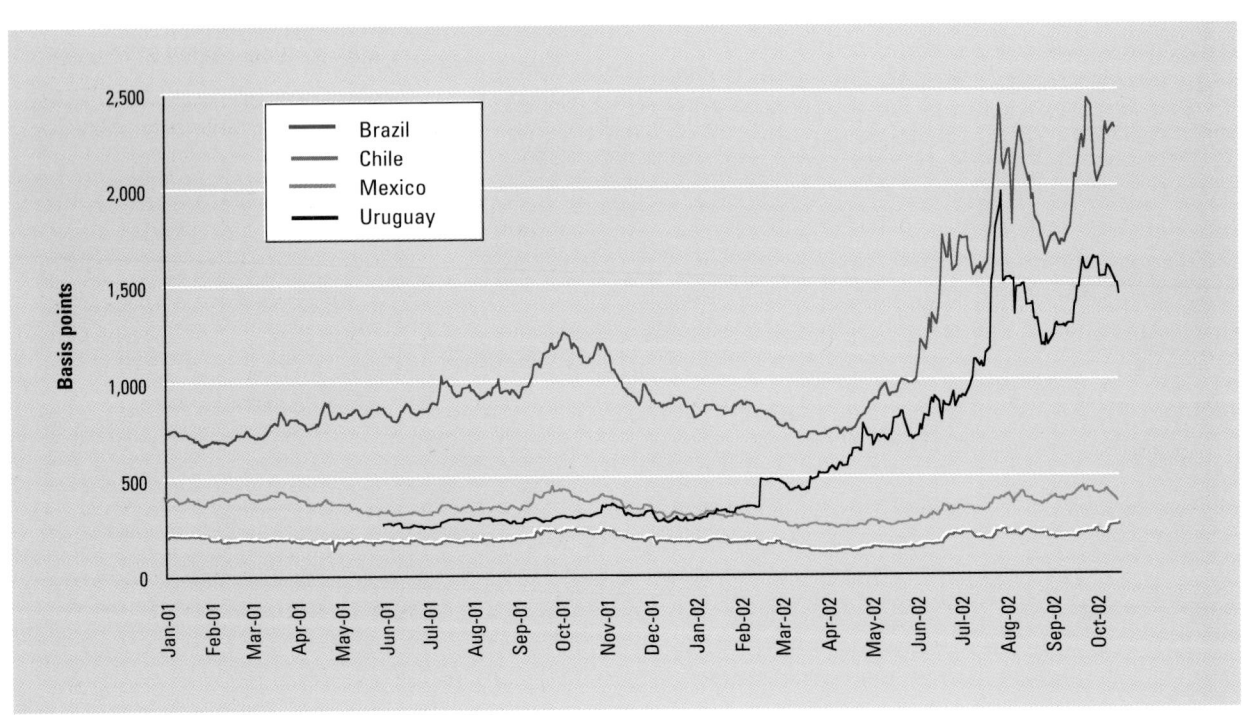

Source: JPMorgan Chase Online

Figure 4: Latin American countries in the Growth Competitiveness rankings since 1994

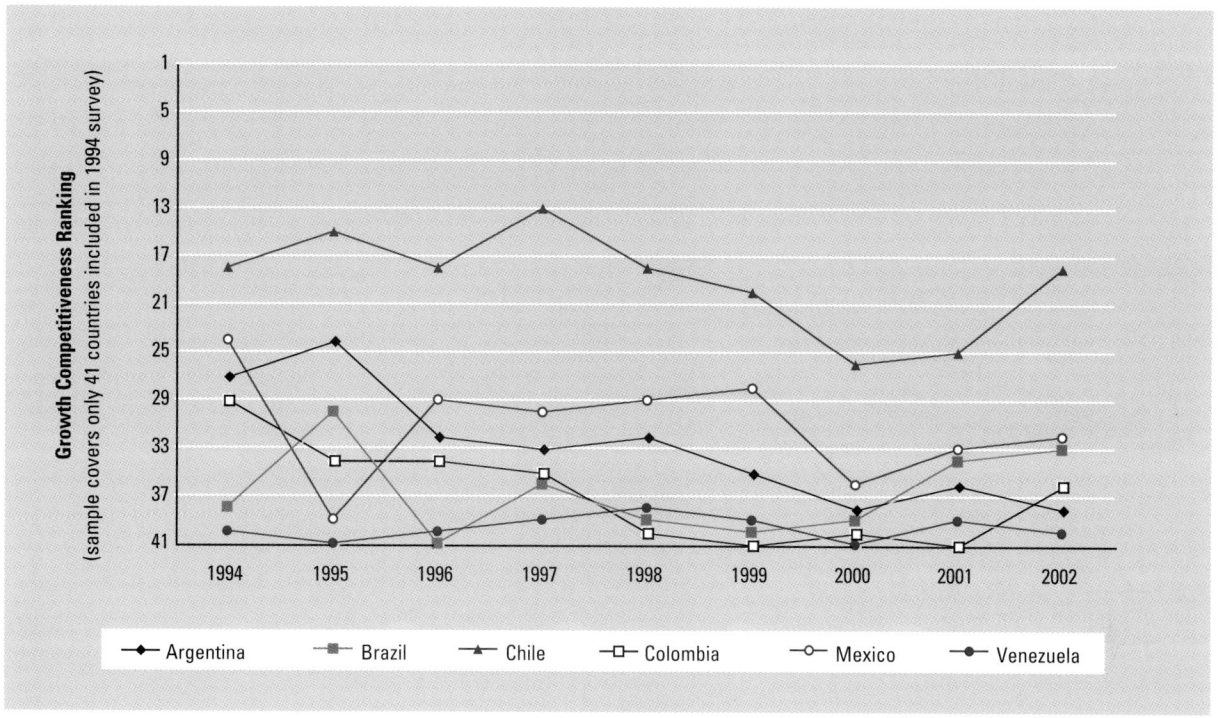

Note: Beginning in 2000, *The Global Competitiveness Report* has contained two distinct rankings: the "Growth Competitiveness Index" (GCI) and the "Microeconomic Competitiveness Index" (MICI). The numbers in this figure correspond to the GCI rankings. Note that there have been methodological changes during the nine-year period under consideration.
Source: Executive Opinion Survey, various years

A longer-term view

Economic recovery in the outside world would certainly help, but it would not solve all of Latin America's problems. In fact, as the Global Competitiveness rankings show over time, the region's problems have a more long-term nature than merely a cyclical one. Latin America as a whole has been slowly losing ground relative to other countries since the mid 1990s (see Figure 4). Chile still appears as the best-ranked country in the region, at a distance from the others. Even this country, however, lost ground from 1997 to 2000, although in 2001and 2002 Chile has slowly started to recover.

If we compare GDP per capita growth between selected Latin American and Asian economies over the last four decades, it is clear that a reversal of fortunes has occurred (see Table 1). In 1960, (nonweighted) Latin American GDP per capita was more than 40 percent higher than emerging Asia's. The situation now is totally different: Asian GDP per capita is three and a half times that of Latin America. This is a result of very slow growth in Latin America, where GDP per capita has expanded at annual average rates between 1 and 2 percent over the last five decades; exceptions were Brazil in the 1970s and Chile in the 1990s. Meanwhile, emerging Asia has grown at around 5 percent annually. Thus, while Latin America doubled its average income over the last forty years, Asia's income rose ninefold.

A longer perspective is even more suggestive. For example, in 1820, Mexico's GDP per capita was higher than Japan's and close to Canada's. Nearly two centuries later, these two countries have about four times Mexico's income (see Table 2). Also note that at the beginning of the 20th century, Argentina's per capita income was similar to Canada's and France's and was nearly three times Japan's. One century later, in 2001, Argentina's average income was about one third of the per capita income of those countries. Behind these shocking facts lie factors such as economic policies, structural conditions, and institutions, which have made the difference for economic competitiveness and growth. These are the focus of the present chapter.

This quick overview strongly suggests that there is a lot the region has to do to improve its competitiveness and, thus, its growth and development prospects. This chapter examines five main issues. The next section analyzes Latin America's structural characteristics, especially its geographical conditions and the effects of natural resource abundance. The section concerned with policy effects discusses the role of economic policies, with special emphasis on two aspects: labor markets and institutions, and fiscal reforms and the current fiscal crisis. The following section studies the important role of domestic institutions, and the next discusses the important impact of trade issues and the

Table 1: Latin America and Asia

	Period	GDP per capita growth (%)						GDP per capita (1995 US$)		
		1950–59	1960–69	1970–79	1980–89	1990–2001	Whole period	1960	2001	2001/1960 ratio
Latin America										
Argentina	1950–2001	0.4	2.4	1.2	-2.9	2.5	0.9	5,419	7,550	1.39
Brazil	1950–2001	3.6	2.9	5.8	0.2	1.2	2.6	1,742	4,636	2.66
Chile	1950–2001	1.1	2.0	0.6	2.1	4.7	2.4	1,968	5,443	2.77
Mexico	1950–2001	2.4	3.5	3.3	-0.7	1.5	2.1	1,639	3,739	2.28
Peru	1950–2001	2.1	2.3	0.9	-2.5	1.9	1.0	1,875	2,334	1.24
Venezuela	1950–2001	3.9	1.2	0.0	-2.3	-0.1	0.3	3,721	3,326	0.89
Median		**2.3**	**2.4**	**1.0**	**-1.5**	**1.7**	**1.6**	**1,921**	**4,187**	**2.18**
Asia										
Hong Kong SAR	1960–2001	ND	6.8	6.4	5.5	2.3	5.2	3,008	24,187	8.04
Korea	1953–2001	2.4	5.5	6.6	7.3	4.9	5.2	1,325	13,420	10.13
Malaysia	1955–2001	0.9	3.5	5.3	2.8	3.9	3.7	975	4,709	4.83
Singapore	1960–2001	ND	6.9	7.3	4.8	4.0	5.8	2,676	27,180	10.16
Taiwan	1951–2001	4.2	5.4	7.8	6.8	4.7	5.7	1,405	15,800	11.25
Thailand	1950–2001	-0.1	4.6	4.2	5.6	3.3	3.8	465	2,853	6.14
Median		**1.7**	**5.5**	**6.5**	**5.6**	**3.9**	**5.2**	**1,365**	**14,610**	**10.71**

Source: Author's calculations based on World Bank (2002) and Heston and Summers (1991)

Table 2: GDP per capita (1995 PPP constant dollars)

	1820	1900	1925	1950	1980	2001
Argentina		2,957	4,205	5,351	8,846	8,619
Brazil		756	1,051	1,795	5,628	5,589
Chile	649	2,341	3,285	3,943	6,066	11,474
Colombia			1,346	2,241	4,586	5,687
Mexico	816	1,242	1,734	2,237	5,638	5,949
Peru			1,242	2,429	4,512	3,718
Mean (A)	**733**	**1,824**	**2,144**	**2,999**	**5,879**	**6,839**
Average growth (%)		1.1	0.6	1.4	2.3	0.7
Australia	1,726	4,613	6,129	7,745	14,813	20,588
Canada	958	2,960	4,413	7,561	17,468	22,485
France	1,307	3,056	4,428	5,602	16,073	22,097
Japan	756	1,218	1,946	2,010	14,070	22,318
United Kingdom	1,880	4,929	5,270	7,347	13,710	20,548
United States	1,503	4,395	6,749	10,271	19,603	28,301
Mean (B)	**1,355**	**3,529**	**4,823**	**6,756**	**15,956**	**22,723**
Average growth (%)		1.2	1.3	1.4	2.9	1.7
(B) / (A) Ratio	1.8	1.9	2.2	2.3	2.7	3.3

Source: Author's calculations based on Madison (1995) and Braun et al. (2000)

Free Trade Area of the Americas (FTAA), followed by an analysis of the potential that the ICT revolution poses for the region.

Structural determinants of Latin America's economic growth

To understand Latin American competitiveness and growth prospects, it is not enough to analyze the economic policies or the external shocks to which the region has been exposed. It is necessary also to start by considering some important structural factors that have affected regional economic performance, such as the impact of geography, natural resource abundance, and the role of institutions. As we will see, economic policy frequently reflects a reaction to these structural factors.

The main question that arises when we compare economic performance across countries is what types of conditions are associated with productivity and growth. Earlier economic studies gave primary emphasis to economic policies, mainly to those that encouraged capital accumulation. In recent years, however, analysts have become more eclectic and are looking into other types of variables as well, especially into the structural and institutional conditions of countries. One goal of this chapter is to analyze all these elements and to be able to understand the interaction that exists among them, because growth experiences are quite varied. Good policies have often been undermined by structural problems and/or weak institutions. In other cases, bad policies have undermined institutional bases.

Figure 5: Malaria in the world (1994)

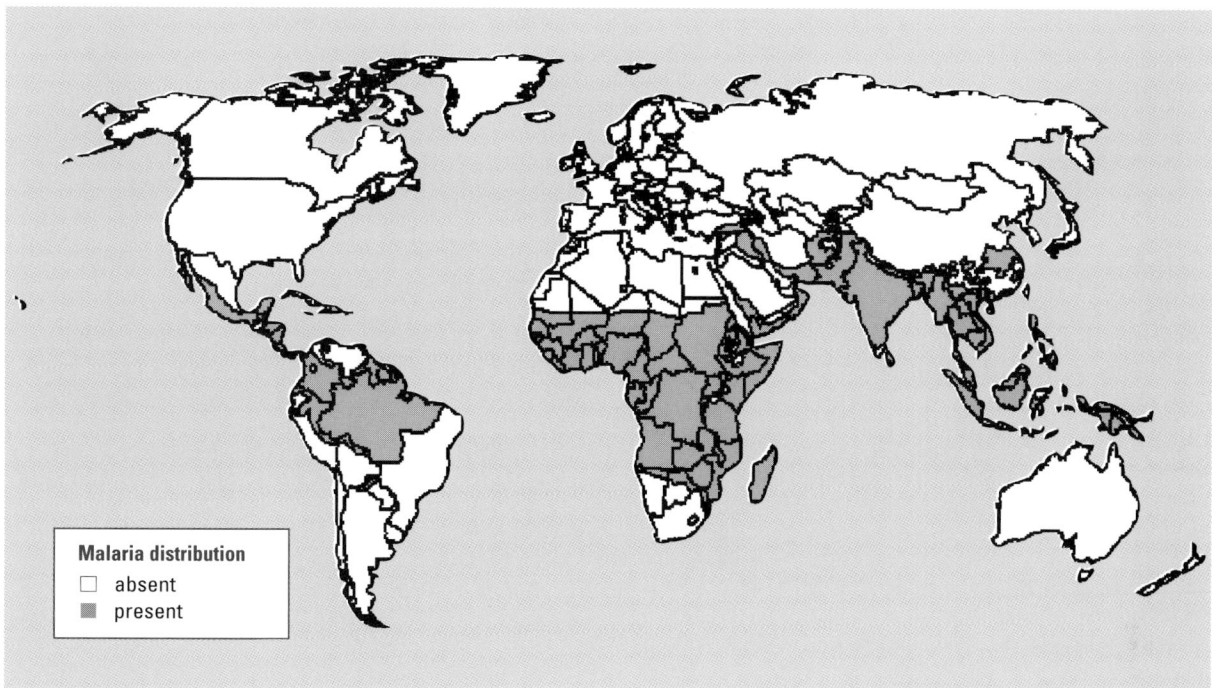

Source: Center for International Development at Harvard University, Online

This section analyzes the structural factors that have determined Latin America's competitiveness and economic performance, such as geographical conditions and natural resource abundance, and their effect on economic fluctuations and long-term performance. It starts with the effects of geographic location on competitiveness. Then it analyzes the implications of Latin America's natural resource abundance.

Geography and competitiveness

Latin America is a clear example of the importance of geography as a determinant of competitiveness and long-term growth prospects. The abundance of natural resources, for example, has been a key determinant of the economic behavior of the region throughout its history, and economic policies have been greatly influenced by this. In fact, the hypothesis that the prices of Latin America's exports (mainly minerals and agricultural goods) suffered a secular downward trend (Prebisch 1950; Singer 1950) was the single largest influence in the adoption of the import substitution model from the 1950s to the late 1970s.

Geography is probably the only truly exogenous determinant of economic competitiveness and growth. It affects countries through elements such as the distance and ease of access to world markets, through the consequences of climate, and through the endowment of natural resources. Consider, for example, that the vast majority of

tropical countries, with the notable exceptions of Hong Kong and Singapore, are classified as low- or middle-income economies. Going beyond per capita income, of the 40 highest-ranked countries in the latest Human Development Index, 35 are in temperate zones (UNDP 2001).

The main reasons behind this are not difficult to discover. Tropical zones, for example, have lower agricultural productivity in comparison with that of other climatic zones (Gallup 1998), and suffer from a variety of plagues and sicknesses that have not yet come under control. Growing recent evidence shows that malaria, a sickness of the tropics, has important costs in terms of the level and growth rate of per capita income, though this impact could be mitigated through greater access to health centers. Significant parts of most countries in Latin America are in a tropical climate, with the exception of Argentina, Chile, and Uruguay; and malaria has still not been eradicated from Brazil, Colombia, Ecuador, Haiti, Nicaragua, and Venezuela (see Figure 5).

The link between geography and competitiveness can be more subtle, through historic roots and institutions. Acemoglu, Johnson, and Robinson (2001), for example, argue that the first European colonizers of America built strong institutions where they could more easily settle, whereas in more difficult territories with significant natural resource potential, institutions were weaker from the start. The important role of institutions in Latin America's competitiveness is explored in further detail in its own section below.

Geographic location has another important effect on competitiveness in relation to natural disasters. Carvériat (2000) analyzes the natural risks that Latin America has had to confront, and concludes that these phenomena have an annual cost of between US$700 and US$3,300 million for the region. A country affected by a natural disaster typically loses 3 percent of its GDP the year of the impact, though an important part of the cost is recovered in subsequent years. Within the region, Central America and the Caribbean have been the hardest hit.

Although the occurrence of disasters cannot be avoided, it is, indeed, possible to reduce their associated damage through both prevention and the use of financial mechanisms. This is all the more important, considering that Latin America is the region with the second heaviest occurrence of natural disasters in the world—23 percent of total disasters over the period 1900–1995 (IADB 2000). Unfortunately, there is very little progress in risk prevention. Latin America stands in last place in insurance coverage in the world: only 4 percent of events that occurred in the last 20 years have been covered by insurance. There is, indeed, a lot of progress to be made in this area.

The outward orientation of countries is clearly related to its geography. As far back as the seminal work of Adam Smith (1776, reprinted in Cannan 1965), it was noted that the division of labor is limited principally by the size of the market. Also the enlargement of the market for a country's products is limited both by trade policy and geography. The main geographic variables that determine a market's size are:

- the physical conditions of local transportation, which are favored by access to navigable routes and a regular topography;
- the closeness to markets in the neighboring countries and their size; and
- the proximity to the main world markets.

From a geographical standpoint, Latin America can be considered as divided into two subregions: Southern Hemisphere countries (Argentina, Bolivia, Brazil, Chile, Ecuador, Peru, Paraguay, and Uruguay) and Northern Hemisphere ones (the rest). This division is relevant when we consider trade opportunities inside and outside the region.

Table 3 summarizes some important geographic conditions of Latin America. The main points to be highlighted are:

Latin American countries in the Northern Hemisphere
- Main advantages are uniform topography, proximity to rivers and sea, and geographic location (closeness to some of the main world markets).
- Climate, in contrast, is a disadvantage, as 92 percent of these countries—on average—are in tropical areas.

Latin American countries in the Southern Hemisphere
- Advantages include climatic zones and wide land extensions that favor the extensive cultivation of several agricultural products and the breeding of livestock. Oil and mineral resources are abundant.
- The complicated topography is a clear barrier to competitiveness; it implies high transport costs to reach navigable routes, which are the main export routes.
- There is considerable distance between this subregion and the main world markets. Given the modest size of the domestic market and the complicated geography, this fact is clearly an obstacle for regional competitiveness.

To a large extent, these characteristics have determined the economic performance of Latin America. In the case of Southern Hemisphere countries, exports have been centered in mineral and agricultural products that exploit the advantage of natural resource abundance. This is a way to mitigate the effects of long-distance costs and complicated regional geography. On the other hand, Latin

Table 3: Physical characteristics of Latin America

	Latitude of centroid (degree)	Mean elevation (masl)*	Distance from centroid to nearest coast or sea-navigable river (km)	Percent land area in geographical tropics (%)	Minimum distance to one of three capital-goods supplying regions (km) **
World countries	21.5	627	452	49	4,034
Latin America	1.5	613	280	82	4,651
Northern Hemisphere	14.2	468	132	92	3,237
Southern Hemisphere	−20.7	867	539	59	7,215

* *masl* = meters above mean sea level   ** New York, Rotterdam, and Tokyo
Sources: Based on Gallup, Sachs, and Melligner (1999); Sachs and Warner (1995)

Figure 14: Perceptions on quality and composition of public spending, 2002
(1 = strongly disagree, 7 = strongly agree)

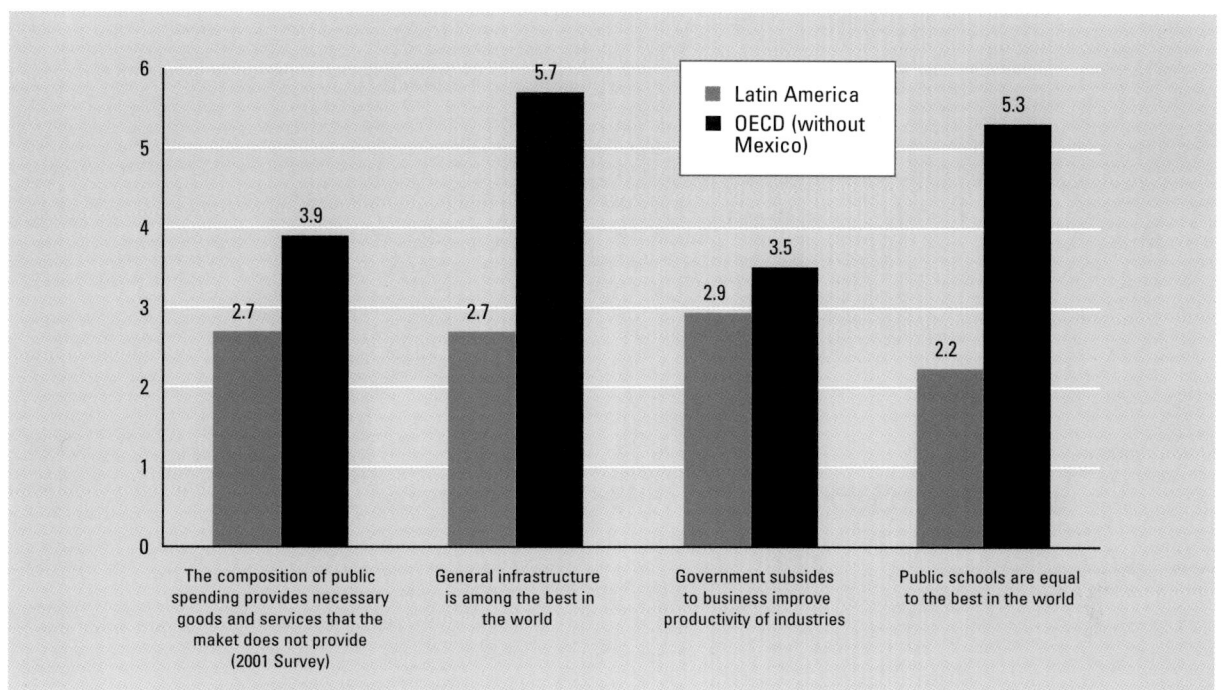

Sources: Executive Opinion Surveys 2001, 2002

One of the first items to be cut during structural reforms has been public investment, including investment aimed at social infrastructure. In fact, five of the nine major Latin American countries covered in a recent study (Calderón, Easterly, and Serven 2002) show cuts on infrastructure investment that contributed over half of total fiscal adjustment. This type of public spending, however, is positively related to economic growth (Easterly and Rebelo 1993). A current challenge is to increase public capital formation, especially in infrastructure, but with a solid financial base. Concessions of public infrastructure have opened an interesting opportunity for private contribution in this area, which should be deepened.

Educational expenses were also cut in several cases, mainly at the basic level. In recent years, educational reforms are attempting to reverse this situation and trying to improve the use of resources.

In several countries, public social security expenses have grown as a result of pension reforms. The transitional costs of social security privatization, due to a reduction in contributions to the public system, have increased public deficits.

The burden of government debt
Previously, excessive fiscal spending was financed partly through significant increases in public debt. This has generated a long-term impact through higher interest rates on public debt. This effect currently remains: interest expenses

are twofold larger (as a percentage of GDP) than the average of the 1970s, and more than offset the efforts made to increase the primary fiscal surplus. A prime example of this is Brazil, where the primary surplus is around 3.5 percent of GDP, but interest payments on public debt reach almost 9 percent of GDP.

Figure 15 shows the burden of consolidated public debt (as a percent of GDP and net of international reserves) for some of the main countries in Latin America as of the end of 2001. Some important observations emerge. First, Argentina and Brazil have the highest levels of debt—around 55 percent of GDP—while Chile has the lowest—around 15 percent of GDP. Second, Argentina's public debt is overwhelmingly in dollars; thus, the huge devaluation of around 270 percent in 2002 and the slump in economic activity has raised the rate to well over 100 percent of GDP. Third, the majority of Brazil's public debt is in reales, which provides some cushion against the devaluation of 2002 (in spite of this, the current level of this debt is close to 70 percent of GDP). One important aspect not shown in Figure 15, however, is debt maturity. A government facing the distrust of financial markets typically faces a recomposition of its debt toward foreign currency, an increase in interest rates, and a shortening of maturities. In some notable cases (Mexico in 1994 and Argentina in 2000), this process ends in a fiscal and external payments crisis.

Figure 15: Foreign and domestic government debt, 2001

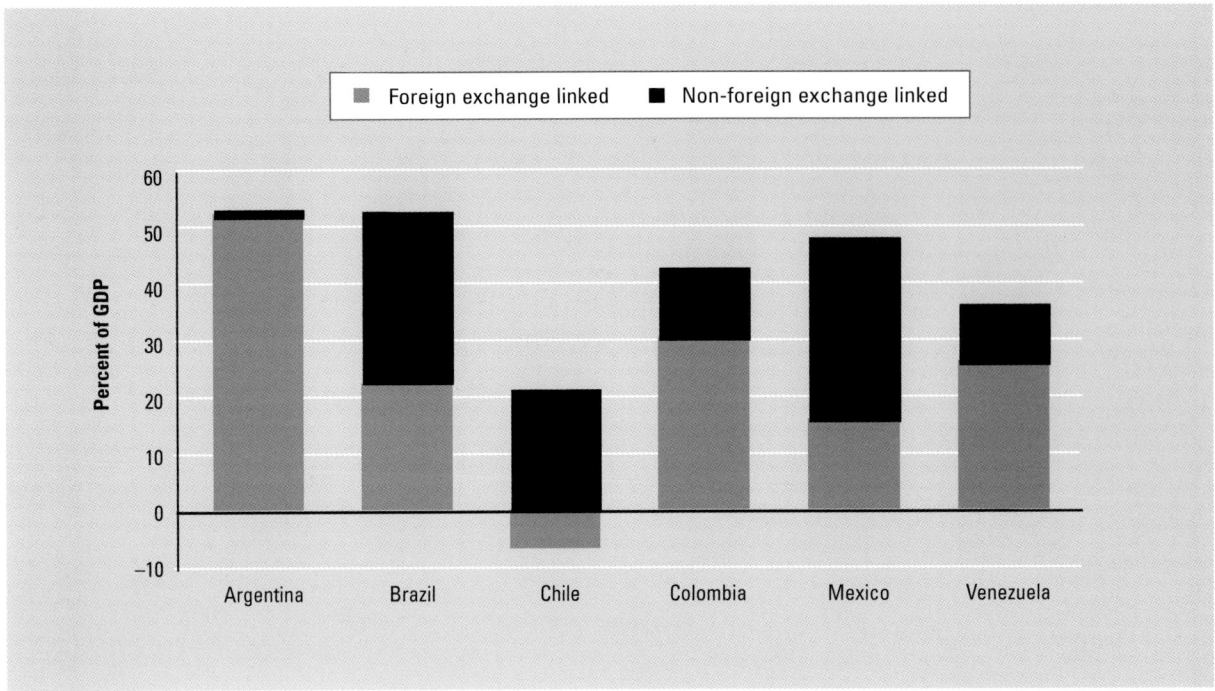

Source: IMF (2002)

The importance of institutions

There is a growing perception that applying the "right" economic policies is a necessary but not a sufficient condition for competitiveness and growth. The right policies applied in economies with weak institutions fail to deliver their potential. Throughout the years, the World Economic Forum's *Global Competitiveness Reports* and other interesting work at the World Bank and the Inter-American Development Bank (IADB) have helped to explain that the relatively low rankings of Latin America's competitiveness are closely associated with the weakness of its institutions.

Institutions can be defined as the set of rules, their application mechanisms, and the organizations that are related to economic transactions (World Bank 2001). Thus, institutions include the respect for the rule of law and property rights, access conditions and the working of the judiciary system as a way of resolving commercial disputes, and the mechanisms of law creation and application. Figure 16 shows the very close relationship between the rule of law index produced by the World Bank (Kaufmann et al. 2001) and *The Global Competitiveness Report*'s public institutions index.

Recent research concludes that the quality of a country's institutions is crucial to explaining differences in competitiveness and economic performance. Figure 17 shows an index with respect to the rule of law (a measure of institutional quality), which is closely associated with

the level of GDP per capita. The IADB (2000) estimates that 60 percent of the income gap between developed countries and Latin American nations is explained by institutional quality. The importance of this factor in explaining the gap between Latin America and Southeast Asia is even higher, as it explains 80 percent of the income gap.

More detailed analysis shows that institutions are also essential to understanding differences in the productivity and efficiency with which factors of production are used (Hall and Jones 1999), gaps in investment rates (Brunetti, Kisunko, and Weder 1998), and the development of the financial system (Levine 1999).

Empirical evidence is robust in showing that better governance and higher quality of institutions promote higher rates of economic growth. Dollar and Kraay (2000) studied the importance of political rights and the rule of law on economic growth in a vast number of countries; their results suggest that the rule of law has a more significant effect on per capita income than political participation. This latter result is limited, however, because a good democratic system allows voters to control administrative responsibility, which helps reduce corruption and improve efficiency in public administration, thus strengthening competitiveness and growth prospects (Adserà, Boix, and Payne 2000).

Figure 16: Measures of institutional quality

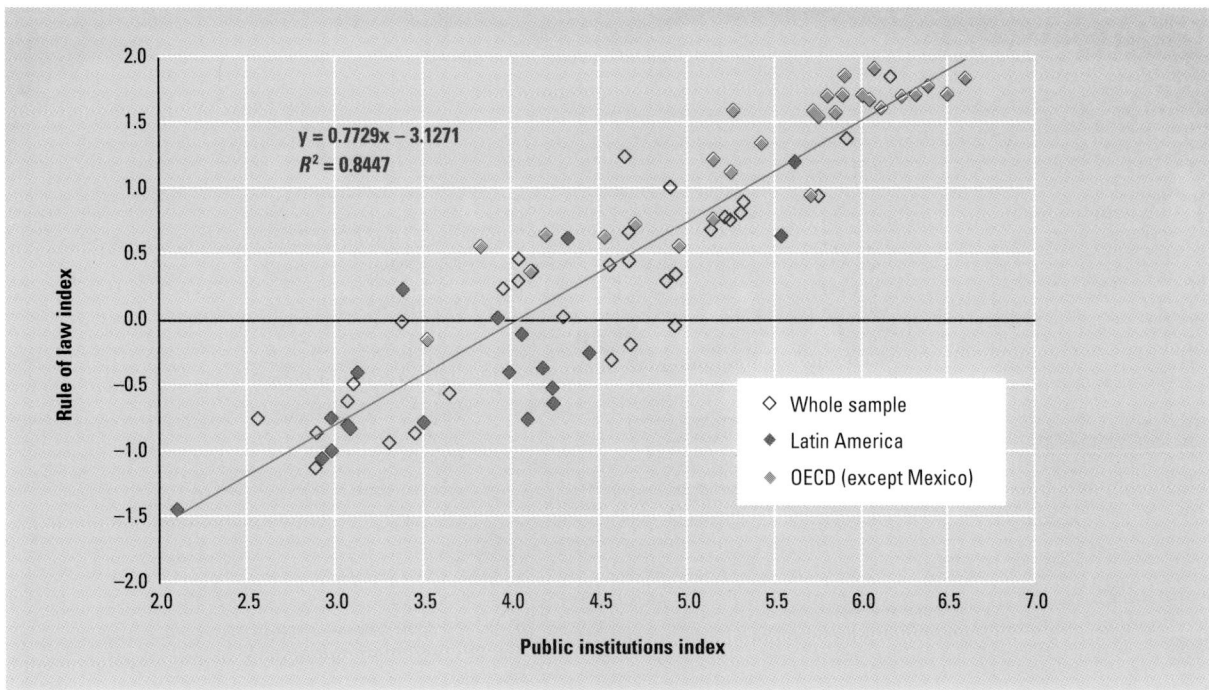

Sources: The rule of law index is from Kaufmann et al. 2001; the public institutions index is from Chapter 1.1 of this *Report*

Most empirical analyses about the effects of institutions are carried out using statistical methods applied to panel data. One limitation of this line of research is that sometimes it is hard to identify causality and the specific quantitative effect of one variable over another. This is particularly the case with variables that show little fluctuation through time. One such case is present when we try to distinguish the separate effects of geography and institutions on competitiveness and growth. We stated that the effects of geography may be perceived through various elements such as distance to world markets, climate, natural resource abundance, and natural disasters. Both geographic and institutional factors generally remain constant time and suffer only small fluctuations year to year, so that sometimes it is difficult to decompose the separate effects of each factor. Using the example of the early American colonies, Acemoglu, Johnson, and Robinson (2002) have recently suggested that institutional factors may be the channels through which geographic characteristics affect economic performance.

The quality of institutions also appears to have a close relationship with social conflict. Rodrik (1999), for example, has suggested that social problems with ethnic, political, or economic origin are likely to result in lower economic growth. The argument goes as follows. A country facing a negative external shock will generally have winners and losers; a weak institutional structure cannot manage the conflict arising from the distribution of losses and benefits. Therefore, authorities postpone as much as possible the policy measures necessary to face the shocks—such as fiscal adjustment or exchange rate depreciation—thus resulting in lower economic growth. The empirical evidence provided by Rodrick (1999) and by Gaviria et al. (2000) supports this hypothesis.

The informal sector

One other link between the quality of institutions and economic competitiveness and growth comes through the effects of bureaucracy, discretionary power, and corruption on the size of the informal sector. Countries where the informal economy is more significant, in turn, tend to grow less than those that have a better institutional environment and, thus, less informality.

Note that perceptions about the size of the informal economy (inferred from the Executive Opinion Survey) are smaller than actual estimates (for example, see Friedman et al. 2000), as shown in Figure 19. This may be due to the characteristics of interviewed companies: formal companies with high interaction with the outside world may underestimate the true extent of informality.

Figure 17a: Measures of institutional quality and GDP per capita, rule of law index

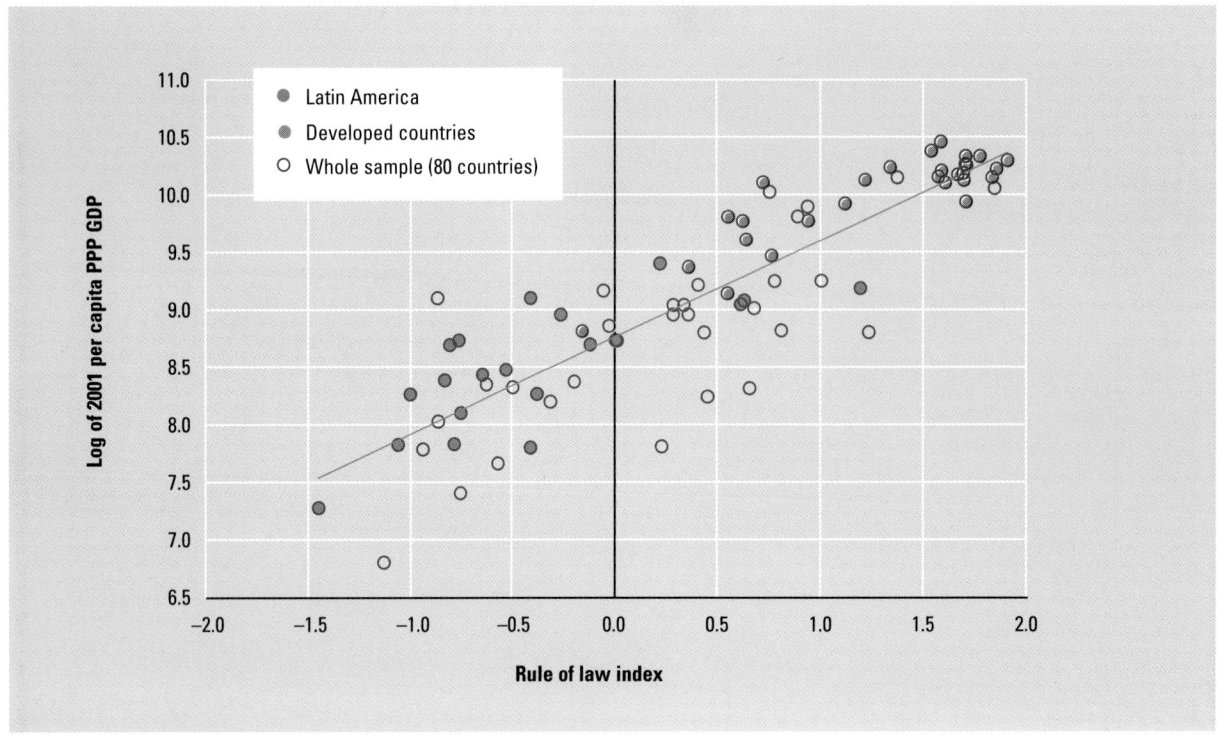

Sources: The rule of law index is from Kaufmann et al. (2001); 2001 per capita PPP GDP are from the data tables, Part 4.3 of this *Report*

Figure 17b: Measures of institutional quality and GDP per capita, public institutions index

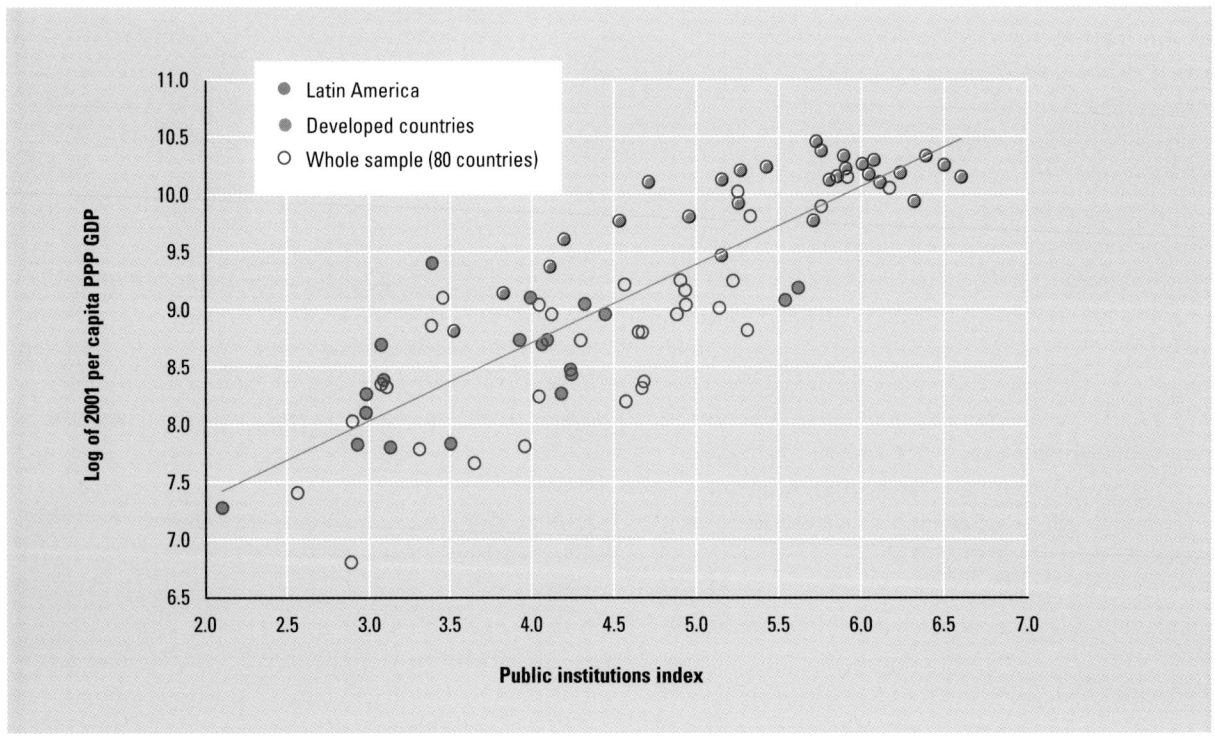

Sources: The public institutions index data are from Chapter 1.1 of this *Report*; 2001 per capita PPP GDP are from the data tables, Part 4.3 of this *Report*

Figure 18: The informal economy in Latin America (percent of GDP)

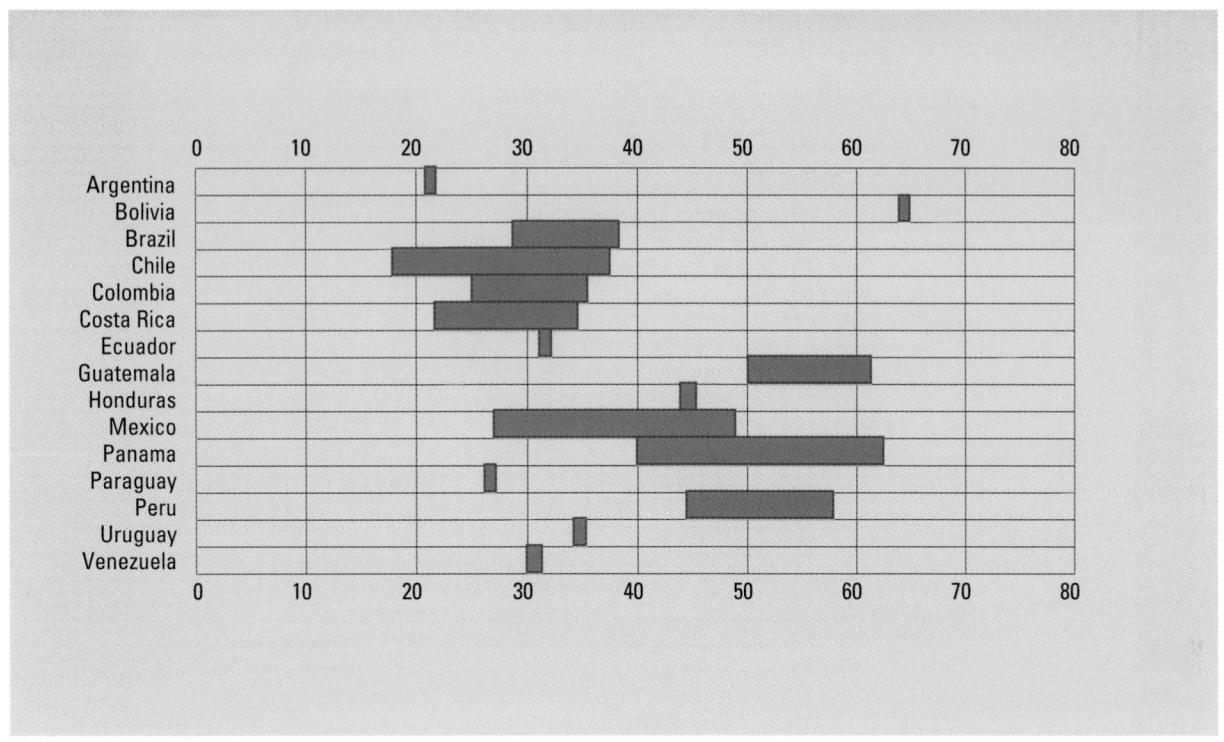

Source: Friedman et al. (2000)

Figure 19: Informal economy perceptions and estimates (percent of GDP)

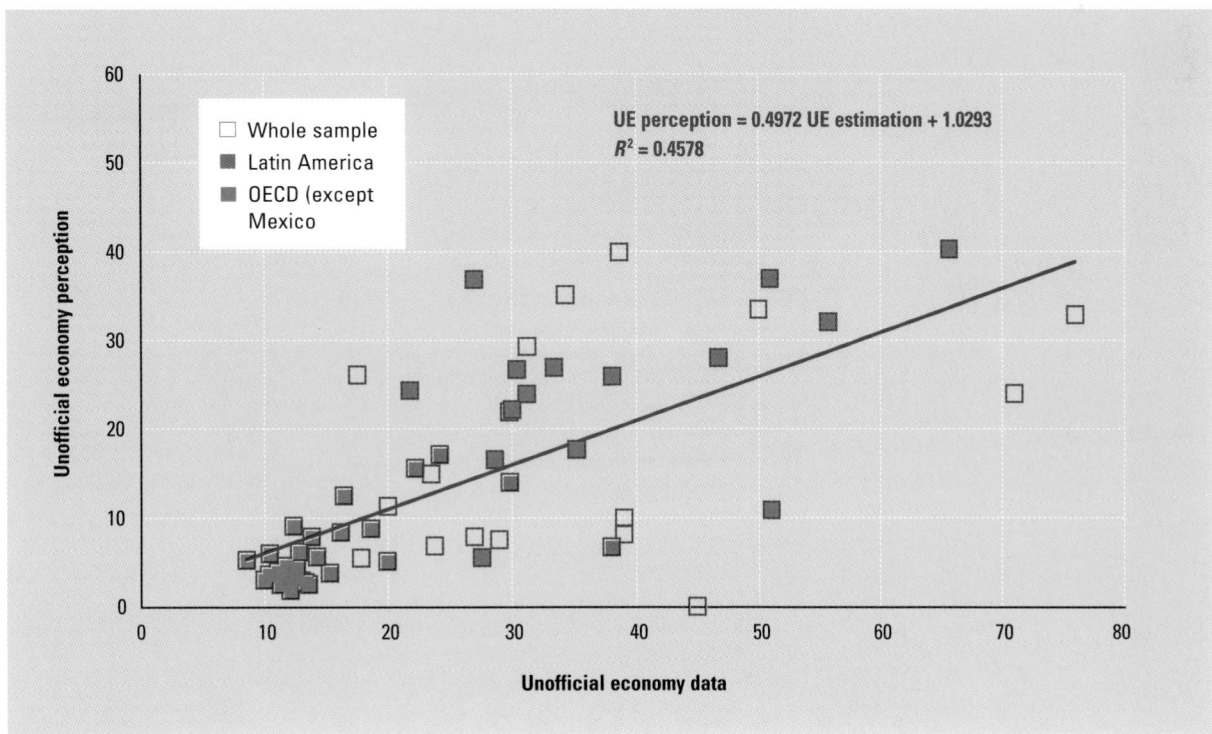

Note: *UE* = unofficial economy.
Sources: Author's calculations based on the Executive Opinion Survey 2002; Friedman et al. (2000)

According to several studies, the main determinants of the size of the informal sector are:

- a high tax burden,
- rigid labor market regulations, and
- public-sector inefficiency.

Larrain (2002) has argued that public-sector bureaucracy and inefficiency and rigid labor market regulations are probably more important in determining informality; high tax burdens exist only in a few Latin American countries, where they may represent an obstacle to formal economic activity.

Public-sector efficiency

The efficiency of the public sector and the extent of bureaucratic hurdles are, on their own, important determinants of competitiveness and of the extent of informality. This is precisely one of the weakest points of Latin America. A recent study by Djankov et al. (2002) reports that starting a new company in Latin America requires on average five additional bureaucratic procedures, double the number of days, and over three times the cost (as a percent of GNP) as in the OECD. This study finds evidence that the state has used bureaucracy as a source of money and power (*the grabbing hand*) instead of helping in the promotion of efficiency (*the helping hand*). Evidence presented in this *Report* corroborates these findings, as shown in Table 8.

Consider the additional evidence on institutional quality provided by the governance and public efficiency indicators prepared by Kauffman et al. (2001). Once again, OECD has a large advantage over Latin America in political stability, government effectiveness, quality of the regulatory framework, rule of law, control of corruption, and accountability (see Figure 20).

Until this point, we have considered three main factors to explain the economic performance of Latin America: structure, policies, and institutions. These give us the

Table 8: Entry and contract enforcement regulations in Latin America and OECD countries

(a) Djankov et al. (2002)

	Latin America	OECD
Number of procedures to start new business	13.5	8.0
Days to complete procedures (days)	94	53
Cost (as % of 1997 GDP per capita)	44.7	13.3

(b) Doing Business Database 2002 (World Bank)

	Latin America	OECD
Contract enforcement:		
Number of procedures	32.5	16.5
Duration (days)	292.0	186.0
Entry regulations:		
Number of procedures	13.0	9.0
Duration (days)	81.0	41.0
Cost (US$)	802.2	1,188.9
Cost (% of GNP per capita)	22.4	13.2

Sources: Djankov et al. (2002); data tables, Part 4.3 of this *Report*

Figure 20: Governance indicators in Latin America and OECD countries (indices from 0 to 100)

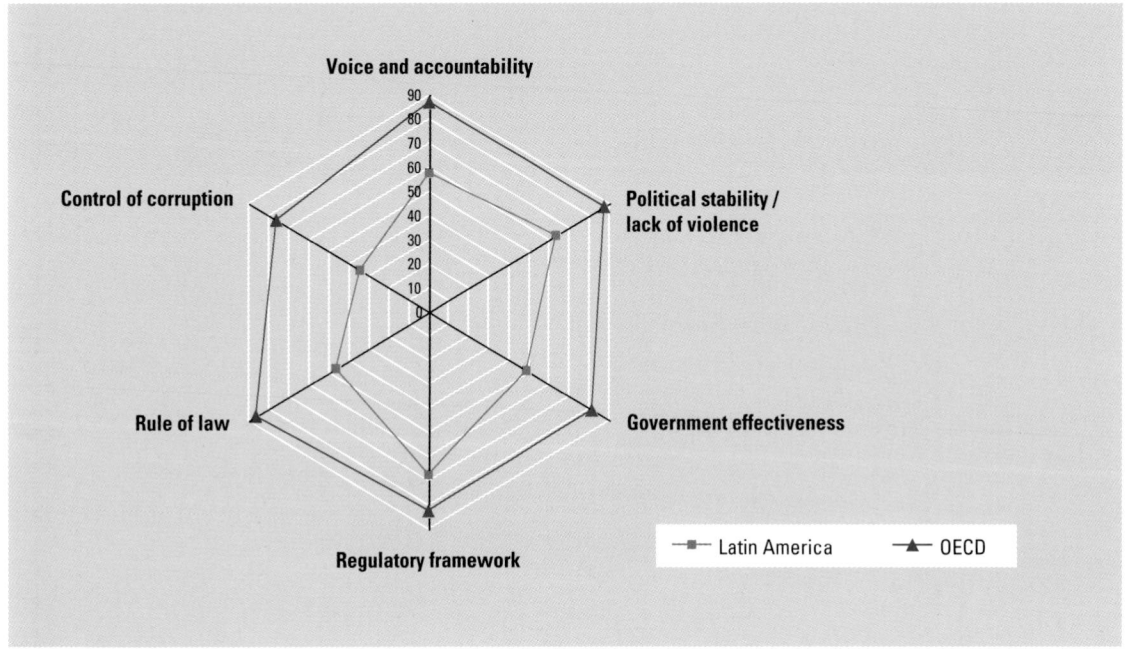

Source: Kauffman et al. (2001)

general framework to understand regional competitiveness and growth. Nonetheless, the increasing interaction that exists among different economies in the process of globalization, and the important technological advances reached mainly in the last decades, indicate that Latin America is confronted with two well-known challenges: how to accelerate integration with the rest of the world, and how to take advantage of the revolution of information and communication technologies. We consider these aspects next.

The trade challenge

So far, Latin America has made important progress in deepening its trade integration with the outside world.

Exports are now a much larger share of GDP than 30, 20, or even 10 years ago. In countries such as Chile and Mexico, exports represent over 30 percent of GDP; in Costa Rica, Ecuador, and Honduras, this ratio exceeds 40 percent (see Table 9). There is, too, a notable diversification away from natural resources, although primary goods still represent over half of total regional exports (Table 10). The most interesting experiences of this process are those of Costa Rica and Mexico, helped by Intel and NAFTA, respectively.

The next few years will bring an important opportunity for Latin America to gain greater access to external markets through trade integration in bilateral, regional, and multilateral agreements. Start with the latter. The new

215

Table 9: Export deepening (exports of goods and services as percentage of GDP)

	1960	1970	1980	1990	2000
Argentina	7.6	5.6	5.1	10.4	10.8
Bolivia	19.7	29.4	24.5	22.8	17.6
Brazil	7.1	7.0	9.1	8.2	10.8
Chile	13.5	14.6	22.8	34.6	31.8
Colombia	15.7	14.3	16.2	20.6	21.3
Costa Rica	21.4	28.2	26.5	34.6	48.1
Dominican Republic	25.6	17.2	19.2	33.8	29.9
Ecuador	16.3	14.0	25.2	32.7	42.4
El Salvador	20.3	24.8	34.2	18.6	27.6
Guatemala	12.6	18.6	22.2	21.0	19.9
Haiti	20.0	13.8	21.6	16.0	12.5
Honduras	21.4	27.9	36.2	36.4	42.4
Mexico	8.5	7.7	10.7	18.6	31.1
Nicaragua	23.7	26.7	24.2	24.9	36.8
Panama	—	—	50.7	38.4	32.7
Paraguay	17.7	14.9	15.3	33.2	20.3
Peru	20.8	17.9	22.4	15.8	16.0
Uruguay	13.9	13.9	15.0	23.5	19.3
Venezuela	27.1	20.9	28.8	39.4	28.4
Latin America & Caribbean	10.3	9.5	12.4	14.1	17.3

Source: World Bank (2002)

Table 10: Export composition (percentage of merchandise exports)

	Primary exports		Manufactures		High-technology	
	1965	2000	1965	2000	1994	2000
Argentina	94.4	66.5	5.6	32.2	1.4	2.9
Bolivia	95.7	71.0	4.3	28.9	1.1	2.3
Brazil	91.6	39.5	7.7	58.5	2.6	10.9
Chile	95.9	81.4	3.9	16.2	0.4	0.6
Colombia	93.5	65.9	6.3	34.1	1.9	2.5
Costa Rica	84.2	34.4	14.6	65.6	1.5	8.6
Ecuador	97.6	90.1	2.4	9.9	0.3	0.6
El Salvador	83.7	50.3	16.3	48.4	3.1	2.9
Guatemala	86.0	68.0	14.0	32.0	2.3	2.5
Honduras	95.6	67.1	4.4	32.7	0.3	0.8
Mexico	83.6	16.5	16.3	83.5	10.7	18.7
Nicaragua	94.5	92.1	5.3	7.8	0.6	0.4
Panama	98.1	84.1	1.9	15.9	0.1	0.0
Paraguay	91.6	80.7	8.4	19.3	0.2	0.6
Peru	99.3	79.7	0.5	20.3	0.4	0.7
Uruguay	95.0	58.1	5.0	41.9	0.9	0.8
Venezuela	98.3	90.9	1.7	9.1	0.3	0.3
Latin America & Caribbean	91.5	50.7	8.6	48.5	3.2	7.6

Source: World Bank (2002)

round of talks of the World Trade Organization launched at Doha offers the prospects of freer trade and enhanced market access for developing countries. Nonetheless, it is clear that the Doha round will not reach a successful conclusion if Europe and the United States do not reduce significantly the protection of their agricultural sectors. This amounts to no less than the elimination of export subsidies and a major reduction of production subsidies and other forms of protection to farmers.

Free trade agreements will also share in the action. A few countries in the region are currently in negotiations for free trade pacts with the European Union. Mexico already has a free trade agreement (FTA) with the European Union. Chile, on the other hand, has recently concluded negotiations for a similar FTA, which is likely to obtain legislative ratification soon. Yet the most ambitious initiative on this front for Latin America is the Free Trade Area of the Americas (FTAA), whose target date has been set for 2005. According to the current plan, negotiations must be concluded in January 2005; agreements must be ratified by national legislative branches during the rest of the year. The role of the United States in this process is essential. To make significant progress toward the FTAA, US leadership has no substitute. In the short term, the clearest test of US commitment to the FTAA is the conclusion of a free

trade agreement with Chile. Eleven rounds of negotiations have already been completed, and the terms of the agreement are relatively close to completion at the technical level. Negotiations resumed in September 2002, under the welcome background of the Trade Promotion Authority (TPA). The effects of an FTA with Chile would go much beyond this particular country. It would be a powerful signal for the other economies of Latin America that now—with the exception of Mexico—have grounds to be skeptical about the prospects of free trade with the United States.

The economic effects of the FTAA will be significant for the region. Latin America, the United States, and Canada will form together the largest free trade area of the world, significantly larger than the European Union, even considering all possible expansions of the European Union (see Figure 21). A recent study by Monteagudo and Watanuki (2001), for example, shows that the FTAA would be more beneficial for the Southern Cone Common Market (MERCOSUR) than an FTA with Europe, even if MERCOSUR has very strong trade ties with Europe. Part of the benefits from the FTAA would come from making more viable regional infrastructure projects on energy, roads and ports.

Figure 21a: FTAA 2001 GDP
US$12,678 billion

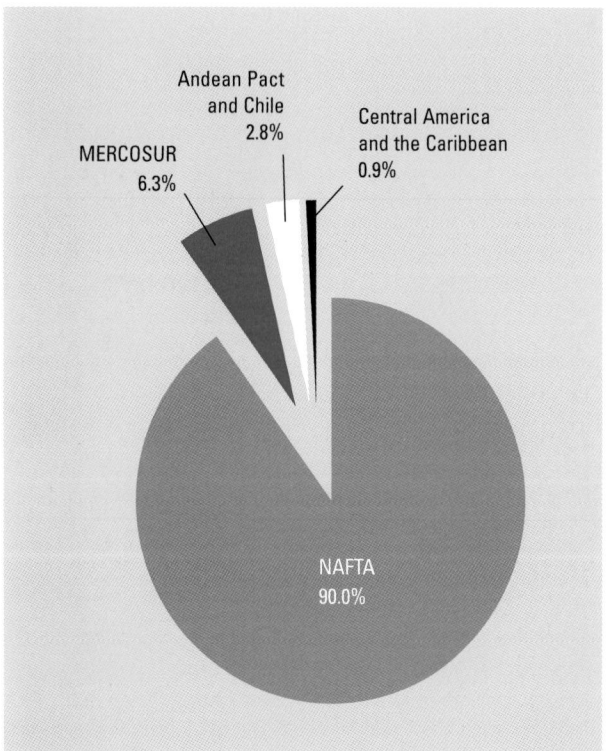

Source: based on IMF (2002)

Figure 21b: European Union and candidate countries 2001 GDP
US$8,443 billion

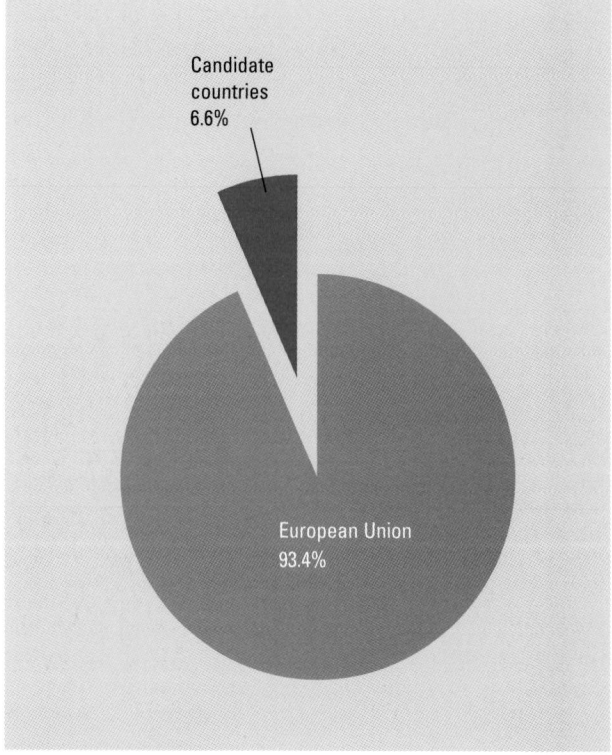

Source: based on IMF (2002)

On the trade front, tariff and non-tariff barriers will come down, and will eventually be eliminated. A salient feature of trade policy in the United States—and elsewhere in the industrialized world—is the fact that higher value added goods are protected with higher tariffs. Because of this fact—known as *tariff escalation*—the trade effects will be stronger on exports of higher value added from Latin America, precisely what the region needs to deepen the process of export diversification. In addition, many of today's exports from Latin America enter the United States with zero import tariffs under the generalized system of preferences (GSP). This is, however, a unilateral concession of the United States, which can be taken away at any time. The FTAA will, thus, act as a guarantee of free long-term access to the US and regional markets. In this way, it will act as an insurance against any outburst of protectionism in the region.

The most important effects of the FTAA would probably occur, however, in the attraction of capital inflows to the region. If it is loosely modeled after NAFTA, such an agreement will go far beyond trade issues into areas such as guarantees on foreign investment, protection of competition, and market-friendly rules; these provisions would reduce the risk premium of investing in the region and will therefore help attract capital back to Latin America. Coeymans and Larrain (1994) have estimated, for example, that an FTA with the United States would increase foreign direct investment flows to Chile up to 2 percent of GDP per year. Schott (2001) has made a similar general argument for Latin America as a whole.

Clear progress toward the FTAA would also have an expectational advantage for the region. At times of great difficulty in Latin America, the focus on the FTAA would shift attention from the Argentinean crisis and Brazilian problems to the vision of a more prosperous and shared future in the Americas.

The ICT revolution and Latin America

This section analyzes whether the revolution of information and communication technologies has the potential to contribute significantly to Latin American competitiveness and growth. This is a very recent phenomenon, indeed, and its macroeconomic effects have only recently begun to be understood. Therefore, research on ICT is recent and conclusions are tentative.

The information communication technologies (ICT) revolution

Internet and "dot-com" companies are perhaps the most visible face of the ICT revolution, but these are manifestations of a more general revolution. In fact, the largest part of its effect takes place precisely in the companies of the "old" economy, especially in those sectors whose capital is intensive in the use of new technology (Van Ark 2001).

The United States is the world leader in information technologies, but there are several other countries that are at the forefront of this revolution. The world is increasingly connected through ICT. But this revolution is also dividing the world into three fundamental groups (see Table 11).

217

Table 11: ICT indicators in selected countries

	IT use as % of GDP		IT use per capita (dollars)		Personal computers (per 100 people)		Telephone lines (per 100 people)		Cellular telephones (per 100 people)	Internet users (per 10,000 people)	Internet hosts (per 10,000 people)
	Change 1992–99	1999	Growth 1992–99	1999	Change 1992–2001	2001	Growth 1992–2001	2001	2001	2001	2001
Latin America											
Argentina	1.0	3.4	78.0	294.3	4.6	5.3	10.8	21.6	18.61	800.28	124.14
Brazil	2.3	5.8	199.4	267.4	6.0	6.3	12.1	21.8	16.73	465.58	95.71
Chile	1.1	5.7	121.8	321.0	7.3	8.4	14.7	23.9	34.02	2001.99	79.20
Mexico	ND	4.2	30.6	231.8	6.1	6.9	6.4	13.7	21.68	362.23	91.49
Asia											
China	3.0	4.9	465.7	37.9	1.9	1.9	12.9	13.8	11.17	260.00	0.69
India	1.8	3.5	220.8	15.4	0.6	0.6	2.9	3.4	0.63	68.16	0.81
Indonesia	-0.3	1.4	7.0	13.7	1.0	1.1	4.2	3.7	2.47	186.19	2.13
Korea	-0.5	4.4	53.8	521.5	21.4	25.1	13.9	47.6	60.84	5,106.83	92.14
Malaysia	2.1	5.5	61.8	168.4	11.8	12.6	10.1	19.9	29.95	2,394.96	31.10
Philippines	0.9	2.7	82.6	33.6	1.9	2.2	2.9	4.0	13.70	259.30	4.00
South Africa	1.8	7.2	49.5	240.6	6.1	6.8	1.7	11.4	21.00	700.58	54.45
Developed Countries											
Canada	1.6	5.3	31.6	1,808.7	28.3	39.0	9.4	65.5	32.00	4,352.73	931.90
Denmark	1.0	4.5	45.3	2,540.3	31.6	43.1	12.5	72.3	73.67	4,471.77	1,045.38
France	0.8	3.8	27.5	1,706.6	26.2	33.7	7.4	57.4	60.53	2,637.72	132.94
Germany	0.9	4.1	29.4	1,699.9	23.4	33.6	14.8	63.5	68.29	3,642.54	294.58
United Kingdom	0.7	4.7	52.0	1,979.5	25.8	36.6	11.6	58.8	78.28	3,995.01	371.37
United States	0.9	5.2	57.9	2,792.1	40.5	62.2	11.1	66.5	44.42	4,995.10	3,714.01

Sources: based on IMF (2001) and data tables, Part 4.3 of this *Report*

Innovative countries provide the latest advances in information technology. The United States leads this group, followed by a few countries in Europe, Japan, and—something interesting from the point of view of small countries—Sweden and Finland. These countries are not only strong users of IT, but rather they are in the vanguard of innovation with leading companies such as Nokia in Finland and Ericsson in Sweden. Nokia currently has around 25 percent of the world market of cellular phones, one of the industries with the most explosive growth in the world.

A second group of countries successfully adopt and adapt innovations. Whole regions of Asia and the south of China belong in this group. These countries do not create new technologies—rather they use the technologies created by the leaders. Still a third group of countries is excluded from this revolution: these include large parts of Africa, especially sub-Saharan Africa, and the poorest regions in Asia. The case of China is very asymmetrical, because innovation is much more pronounced in the south of the country.

Where is Latin America in this world division? With luck, it is in the periphery of the second group. Realistically, the region cannot aim to become a leader of ICT, but should aim to become an active member of the second group. As Barro and Sala-i-Martin (1997) state, it is not required to be among the leaders to grow quickly; in fact, successful "followers" can grow even more than the leaders at certain stages of the development.

The concentration of innovation is very strong in the world. This is perceived, for example, in patents and scientific publications. Latin America has around 8.5 percent of world GDP (at PPP), but contributes only 1.6 percent of published scientific papers, 0.6 percent of research and development (R&D) expenditure, and less than 0.2 percent of total patents.

Patent production is closely related to R&D expenditure. In small countries that are in the vanguard of investigation and creation of new technologies—such as Sweden and Finland—R&D absorbs around 3 percent of GDP. Similar statistics apply to South Korea and a few other East Asian countries. The United States, for example, spends about US$90 billion annually only on research in basic sciences. Part of this is channeled through the National Science Foundation (NSF), an entity of great prestige. Latin American countries, on average, spend significantly less than 1 percent of GDP on R&D.

What produces such different innovation rates among countries? There are no simple answers in this area. Innovation systems are complex. Market forces and incentives are central to the innovation process, but there is much more. Successful countries have been able to create a close and efficient relationship between private companies, universities, and the government. The Internet started as a project of the US Department of Defense, which was looking for protection mechanisms in the event of a large-scale armed conflict. Universities took over from there and developed the World Wide Web. Private companies followed closely in their footsteps and developed numerous innovations and applications.

The contribution of ICT revolution to US economic growth

The effect of ICT on economic growth is of big magnitude: it is estimated that around 30 percent of GDP growth in the United States from 1995 to 2002 came from ICT sectors (CEA 2001). Other authors estimate that the contribution has been even bigger in the United States: around 45 percent of recorded growth over the period 1990–1998 (Van Ark 2001). This recent research indicates that ICT has induced faster growth of the US economy on the order of one percentage point per year in the second half of 1990s (see Table 12). This means an additional creation of wealth on the order of US$100 billion per year, or roughly 5 percent of annual Latin American GDP.

Of course, the ICT revolution has not finished with the economic cycle, as some of the wildest optimists expected. The United States continues living with expansions and contractions, although it appears that better inventory management through the use of ICT has reduced the volatility of GDP growth (IMF 2001).

Faster growth of the US economy since the second half of the 1990s has come fundamentally from improvements in productivity. Average increases in productivity in the 1990s were around 1.5 percent annually for the economy as a whole. In the ICT industry, however, average productivity growth was 11 percent annually over the same period (Larrain 2001). Productivity growth comes from three different sources: technical progress of ICT producer companies, applications of ICT in traditional companies, and, less significantly, from the creation of "dot.com" companies.

ICT revolution and previous technological revolutions

Comparing the ICT revolution with previous important technological changes such as steam machines, electric power, or railroads, we can find important similarities and differences (IMF 2001). Among the similarities, we have:

- Gains in these revolutions come initially from capital deepening caused by fall in relative prices.

- Initial gains are generally concentrated on industrial countries.

- Benefits of these revolutions are felt more by users than by producers.

- Technological revolutions induce wide fluctuations in financial markets, such as important rises in the stock prices of new technology companies.

Table 12: ICT revolution and economic growth in developed countries

| | GDP growth (%) 1990–98 | of which ICT contribution is: | Contribution of | | Non–ICT-related sectors |
| | | | ICT-related industries | | |
			ICT-using	ICT-producing	
Canada	2.1	0.8	28.6	9.5	61.9
Denmark	1.8	0.5	11.1	16.7	72.2
Finland	1.6	0.7	0.0	43.8	56.3
France	1.3	0.5	15.4	23.1	61.5
Germany	1.1	0.5	36.4	9.1	54.5
Italy	1.4	0.7	35.7	14.3	50.0
Japan	1.4	0.8	35.7	21.4	42.9
Netherlands	2.5	1.0	28.0	12.0	60.0
United Kingdom	2.1	1.0	28.6	19.0	52.4
United States	3.2	1.4	28.1	15.6	56.3
Mean	**1.9**	**0.8**	**24.8**	**18.4**	**56.8**

Source: Author's calculations based on Van Ark (2001) and IMF (2001)

The main differences between the ICT revolution and the previous technological revolutions are:

- The fall in the relative prices of ICT goods has been much stronger, thus reflecting a faster pace of technological innovation.

- The production of goods with ICT involves more globalized processes than occurred in previous episodes.

- The rate of diffusion of new technology from developed countries to emerging economies is quicker than in previous revolutions.

This latter characteristic is important for Latin America, because the region can benefit from ICT at a faster speed than it could during other technological revolutions. ICT use indicators point out that the adoption of new technologies in developing economies has been remarkable.

Can the ICT revolution accelerate convergence?

The convergence hypothesis for economic growth states that poor countries will grow faster than rich economies, thus producing a convergence in per capita income through time. The ICT revolution has the potential of being a convergence (catch-up) factor for developing countries, because it allows cheap access to information, quick diffusion of knowledge advances, and participation in world production nets.

Convergence will only happen, however, if developing nations can take advantage of ICT—that is, if they participate in the ICT revolution. In contrast, if developing countries cannot accede to improvements of knowledge because those improvements are not a public good, the possibility of convergence is limited. In this case, the most likely result is that faster growth would concentrate on innovative countries, thereby pushing toward divergence.

How can Latin America take advantage of the ICT revolution?

Productivity increases allowed by the ICT revolution open up an opportunity to raise Latin American competitiveness and growth. How can public policies promote the participation of countries in the ICT revolution? The role of government in this process is mainly that of a facilitator, not the main actor. Through its policies, however, government can affect decisively the way in which the private sector faces this challenge. Several areas for action are outlined below.

Stimulate research and development. A first step is to allocate more resources to R&D, through public grants and (tax) incentives for private companies. To be successful, though, it is necessary to use resources well. Part of this process should involve stimulating the cooperation between universities and private companies.

Foment risk capital. Another important step is to stimulate capital risk. This is a very poorly developed industry in Latin America. Part of the reason may be an unattractive tax treatment, especially in terms of the capital gains tax. An alternative that deserves attention is to set a lower tax rate on capital gains than on other forms of income. Some countries have even opted to abolish the capital gains tax. Another important area to address is the protection of minority shareholder rights.

Reduce regulatory barriers. Another obstacle for ICT adoption is the presence of important regulatory barriers, especially in telecommunications. There has been a fall in Internet connection costs in Latin America, but they are still relatively high, generally involving a fixed charge plus a payment for the time of use of the Internet.

Labor market flexibility and human capital development. Deepening labor market flexibility is key, in general, for a country's competitiveness, but it seems to be even more essential for taking good advantage of the ICT revolution. A related and central need is to improve human capital through formal education and on-the-job training. Several

Latin American countries have started programs to connect all primary schools, public and private, to the Internet.

The government as a user. Internet use by government should also be deepened. There are two important examples of this: first, government procurement above a minimum value should be carried out entirely through the Internet; second, revenue services should increasingly rely on the Internet both for information and for the filing of tax reports.

Attracting foreign investment. It is desirable to attract world-leading companies in sectors of high technology to invest in Latin America. This does not necessarily require tax incentives, which have many potential problems. Within a framework of neutral incentives, however, countries can do much more to market themselves. An active policy of IT foreign investment attraction may bear fruit. It is necessary to understand that the world-leading companies have hundreds of countries from which to choose as hosts. Consider the positive externalities that world-leading companies can have on the host country: in education, in training, in the "signaling" effect that helps attract other companies to the region, and in improving the productivity of other companies that belong to more traditional sectors.

The successful diffusion of ICT needs better infrastructure and qualified human resources. It also requires, however, a healthy institutional atmosphere that involves minimum levels of rule of law and respect for property rights, solid financial markets, and a degree of openness that allows the country to absorb new knowledge (Chong and Micco 2002).

The ICT revolution provides an extraordinary challenge for Latin America. Although it has great potential for the region, there are still a series of barriers that preclude massive access to new technologies and interconnection to the Internet. Full use of new ICT expertise and tools would improve strongly the prospects for national and regional competitiveness and growth.

Concluding remarks

This chapter has analyzed Latin American economic competitiveness and growth prospects as the result of three main forces: structural characteristics such as geography and natural resource abundance, the quality of domestic institutions, and the soundness of economic policies.

We have argued that structural factors have been more of a hurdle than a boost for the region, particularly Latin America's large distance from world markets, the complicated topography, and the tropical climate. Of course, these factors are not all present in all countries at the same time: distance is more of a factor in the Southern Hemisphere, while tropical climate is a feature

mainly of Northern Hemisphere countries. Natural resource abundance, however, is a generally shared feature of the region. Recent research casts an important doubt on the apparent benefits of natural resource abundance. Reliance on abundant natural resources appears detrimental to growth in several studies.

Domestic institutions are also essential for competitiveness, and Latin America shows significant weaknesses in this area. In fact, several studies have estimated that this is the most important factor explaining the difference in competitiveness and growth between Latin America and East Asia. Countries in the region generally rank low with respect to the rule of law and high with respect to corruption. A notable exception is Chile, which presents significantly better institutions than the rest of the region, many times at the level of the OECD average.

Economic policy reforms, however, appear to have a large potential to improve competitiveness in the region. A lot has happened in this area since the mid 1980s. Progress has been especially remarkable on trade and financial liberalization, less so on the increasing flexibility of labor markets. Unfortunately, the region has not been able to reap the full benefits of its economic reforms due to a very unfavorable external scenario in recent years, and to the weakness of its institutions.

Over the last few years, however, the fiscal policy stance has deteriorated significantly in several important countries. Fiscal deficits have increased and the public debt has risen, quite dramatically in some cases, thus increasing the interest rates governments have to pay on their debt. This has provoked a dangerous spiral of increasing debts and deficits, in spite of important efforts to generate primary surpluses in the public budget.

Not all is somber for the region, however. In spite of important difficulties, exports have deepened and diversified, most notably in Mexico and Costa Rica since the second half of the 1990s. This process should continue in the future. In addition, the prospects of the Free Trade Area for the Americas, whose target date has been set for 2005, loom large on the region's horizon. Although progress has so far been slow, prospects have improved with the approval of the Trade Promotion Authority by the US Congress and the imminent conclusion of a free trade agreement between the United States and Chile, the first for the United States in the region since the approval of NAFTA in 1993.

Overall, the prospect of being part of the largest free trade area in the world and the opportunities that the revolution of information and communication technologies provide are two of the most welcome recent developments in the region. Working hard on increasing labor market flexibility, on strengthening public finances, and on improving the quality of local and regional institutions will help Latin America enhance its competitiveness. With these improvements, it can respond more adequately to the challenges and opportunities of globalization.

Notes

1 Professor of Economics, Pontificia Universidad Católica de Chile, and Faculty Fellow, Harvard University. I am grateful to Peter Cornelius for very helpful comments and to Pablo Mendieta for highly efficient research assistance.

2 The five exceptions are Barbados, Hong Kong, Singapore, Bahrain, and Brunei.

3 See, for instance Gallup, Sachs, and Mellinger (1999) and McCarthy, Wolf, and Wu (2000).

4 Barahona et al. (2001) study the effects of natural disasters in Central America and explore ways to prevent their negative consequences.

5 This subsection is partially based on Larrain, Sachs, and Warner (1999).

6 Additional evidence may be found in Knack and Keefer (1995) and Chong and Zanforlin (2001).

7 See, for example, Loayza (1997) and Johnson, Kaufmann, and Zoido-Lobatón (1999).

8 Calculations are based on USPTO (2001) and World Bank (2002).

References

Acemoglu, D., S. Johnson, and J. Robinson. 2001. "The Colonial Origins of Comparative Development," *American Economic Review* 91(December): 1369–1401.

———. 2002. "Reversal of Fortune: Geography and Institutions in the Making of the Modern World Income Distribution," *Quarterly Journal of Economics* (forthcoming).

Adserà, A., C. Boix, and M. Payne. 2000. "Are You Being Served? Political Accountability and Quality of Government," IADB Working Paper No. 438. Washington, DC: Inter-American Development Bank.

Baldwin, R. and P. Martin. 1999. "Two Waves of Globalisation: Superficial Similarity and Fundamental Diffrerences." In H. Siebert, ed., *Globalisation and Labour.* Tubingen: Institute of World Economics.

Barahona, J. et al. 2001 "Reducing the Vulnerability to Natural Disasters: Hurricane Mitch and Central America." In F. Larrain, ed. *Economic Development in Central America, Vol. II: Structural Reforms.* Cambridge, MA: Harvard University Press.

Barro, R. and J. Lee. 2000. "International Data on Educational Attainment: Updates and Implications," CID Working Paper No. 42. Cambridge, MA: Center for International Development.

Barro, R. and X. Sala-i-Martin. 1997. "Technological Diffusion, Convergence, and Growth," *Journal of Economic Growth* 2(1): 1–26.

Bidarkota, P. and M. Crucini. 2000. "Commodity Prices and the Terms of Trade," *Review of International Economics* 8(4): 647–666.

Braun, J. et al. 2000. "Economía Chilena 1810–1995. Estadísticas Históricas," Universidad Católica de Chile Working Paper No. 187. Santiago de Chile, Universidad Católica de Chile.

Brunetti, A., G. Kisunko, and B. Weder. 1998. "Credibility of Rules and Economic Growth: Evidence from a Worldwide Survey of the Private Sector," *The World Bank Economic Review* 12(3): 353–384.

Caballero, R. 2002. "Enfrentando la Vulnerabilidad Externa de Chile: Un Problema Financiero," *Economía Chilena* 5(1): 11–36.

Calderón, C., W. Easterly, and L. Serven. 2002. "Infrastructure Compression and Public Sector Solvency in Latin America," Central Bank of Chile Working Paper No. 187. Santiago de Chile: Central Bank of Chile, October.

Cannan, E., ed. 1965. *Adam Smith's Wealth of Nations.* New York: Modern Library.

Carvériat, C. 2000. "Natural Disasters in Latin America and the Caribbean: An Overview of Risk," IADB Working Paper BID No. 434. Washington, DC: Inter-American Development Bank.

Center for International Development at Harvard University. Online. http://www.cid.harvard.edu

Council of Economic Advisers (CEA). 2001. *Economic Report of the President 2001.* Washington, DC: United States Government Printing Office.

Coeymans, J. E. and F. Larrain. 1994. "Efectos de un Acuerdo de Libre Comercio entre Chile y Estados Unidos: Un Enfoque de Equilibrio General," *Cuadernos de Economía* 31(94): 357–399.

Consensus Economics. Various years. *Latin American Consensus Forecast.* London: Consensus Economics.

Chong, A. and A. Micco. 2002. "The Internet and the Ability to Innovate in Latin America," IADB Working Paper No. 464. Washington, DC: Inter-American Development Bank, January.

Chong, A. and L. Zanforlin. 2001. "Inward-Looking Policies, Institutions, Autocrats, and Economic Growth in Latin America: An Empirical Exploration," IADB Working Paper No. 446. Washington, DC: Inter-American Development Bank, April.

Djankov, S. et al. 2002. "The Regulation of Entry," *Quarterly Journal of Economics* 117 (1): 1–37.

Dollar, D. and A. Kraay. 2000. "Property Rights, Political Rights, and the Development of Poor Countries in the Post-Colonial Period." Rev. October 2002. Online. http://www.worldbank.org/research/growth/pdfiles/dollarkraay2.pdf

———. 2001. "Trade, Growth and Poverty," World Bank Policy Research Working Paper No. 2199. Washington, DC: World Bank.

Easterly, W., N. Loayza, and P. Montiel. 1997. "Has Latin America's Post-Reform Growth Been Disappointing?" *Journal of International Economics* 43(3-4): 287–311.

Easterly, W. and S. Rebelo. 1993. "Fiscal Policy and Economic Growth: An Empirical Investigation," *Journal of Monetary Economics* 32(3): 417–458.

Ernst & Young. 2002. *Worldwide Corporate Tax Guide 2002.* Ernst & Young Global Ltd. Online. http://newsweaver.ie/ernst/e_article000073333.cfm.

Fajnzylber, P. and D. Lederman. 1999. "Economic Reform and Total Factor Productivity Growth in Latin America and the Caribbean, 1950–95: An Empirical Note," World Bank Policy Research Working Paper No. 2114. Washington, DC: World Bank.

Fatás, A. 2002. "The Effects of Business Cycles on Growth," Central Bank of Chile Working Paper No. 156. Santiago de Chile: Central Bank of Chile.

Fernández-Arias, E. and P. Montiel. 1997. "Reform and Growth in Latin America: All Pain, No Gain?" IADB Working Paper No. 351. Washington, DC: Inter-American Development Bank.

Friedman, E. et al. 2000. "Dodging the Grabbing Hand: The Determinants of Unofficial Activity in 69 Countries," *Journal of Public Finance* 76(3): 459–493.

Gallup, J. L. 1998. "Agricultural Productivity and the Tropics," CID Mimeo. Cambridge, MA: Center for International Development.

Gallup, J., J. Sachs, and A. Mellinger. 1999. "Geography and Economic Development," CID Working Paper No. 1. Cambridge, MA: Center for International Development at Harvard.

Gavin, M. 1997. "A Decade of Reform in Latin America: Has It Delivered Lower Volatility?" IADB Working Paper No. 349. Washington, DC: Inter-American Development Bank.

Gavin, M. and R. Hausmann. 1998. "Nature, Development and Distribution in Latin America: Evidence on the Role of Geography, Climate and Natural Resources," IADB Working Paper No. 378. Washington, DC: Inter-American Development Bank.

221

Gaviria, A. et al. 2000. "Political Institutions and Growth Collapses," IADB Working Paper No. 419. Washington, DC: Inter-American Development Bank.

Gylfason, T. and G. Zoega. 2002. "Natural Resources and Economic Growth: The Role of Investment." Prepared for the International Conference *Natural Resources and Growth*, Santiago de Chile: Central Bank of Chile, January 18th.

Hall, R. and C. Jones. 1999. "Why Do Some Countries Produce So Much More Output per Worker Than Others?" *Quarterly Journal of Economics* 114(1): 83–116.

Herrera, S., G. Perry, and N. Quintero. 2000. "Output Fluctuations in Latin America: What Explains the Recent Slowdown?" World Bank Policy Research Working Paper No. 2333. Washington, DC: World Bank.

Heckman, J. and C. Pagés. 2000. "The Cost of Job Security Regulation: Evidence from Latin American Labor Markets," *Economía* 1(1): 109–154.

Heston, A. and R. Summers. 1991. "The Penn World Table (Mark 5): An Expanded Set of International Comparisons, 1950–1988," *Quarterly Journal of Economics*, 106(2): 327–368.

Inter-American Development Bank (IADB). 1996. *Progreso Económico y Social en América Latina 1996*. Washington, DC: Inter-American Development Bank.

———. 2000. *Desarrollo: Mas Allá de la Economía. Progreso Económico y Social en América Latina 2000*. Washington, DC: Inter-American Development Bank.

International Monetary Fund (IMF). 2001. *World Economic Outlook: The Information Technology Revolution*. Washington, DC: IMF World Economic and Financial Surveys.

———. 2002. *World Economic Outlook: Trade and Finance*. Washington, DC: IMF World Economic and Financial Surveys.

Johnson, S., D. Kaufmann, and P. Zoido-Lobatón. 1999. "Corruption, Public Finances and the Unofficial Economy," World Bank Policy Research Working Paper No. 2169. Washington, DC: World Bank.

JPMorgan Chase. Online. http://mm.jpmorgan.com

Kaufmann, D., A. Kraay, and P. Zoido-Lobatón. 2001. "Governance Matters II: Updated Indicators for 2000–01," World Bank Policy Research Working Paper No. 2772. Washington, DC: World Bank.

Knack, S. and P. Keefer. 1995. "Institutions and Economic Performance: Cross-Country Test Using Alternative Institutions Measurers," *Economics and Politics* 7(3): 207–227.

Lane, P. and A. Tornell. 1995. "Power Concentration and Growth," Harvard Institute of Economics Research, Discussion Paper No. 1720. Cambridge, MA: Harvard Institute of Economics Research.

Larrain, F. 2001. "Cuán Real es la Nueva Economía?" *Revista de Derecho Universidad Finis Terrae*, Santiago de Chile.

Larrain, F. 2002. "Política Fiscal y Rol del Estado en Latinoamérica." In M. Braun, ed., *Hacia un Nuevo Estado en Latinoamérica*. Buenos Aires: CIPPEC and Grupo Columbus.

Larrain, F. and M. Selowsky. 1991. *The Public Sector and the Latin American Crisis*. San Francisco: ICS Press.

Larrain, F, J. Sachs, and A. Warner. 1999. "A Structural Analysis of Chile's Long-Term Growth: History, Prospects and Policy Implications." Document prepared for Chile Government. Online. http://www.minh-da.cl/castellano/contenido/prensa/publica/Chiles%20Long-Term%20Growth.pdf

Lederman, D. and W. Maloney. 2002. "Open Questions about the Link Between Natural Resources and Economic Growth: Sachs and Warner Revisited." Prepared for the International Conference *Natural Resources and Growth*. Santiago de Chile Central Bank of Chile, January 18th.

Leite, C. and J. Weidmann. 1999. "Does Mother Nature Corrupt? Natural Resources, Corruption and Economic Growth," IMF Working Paper No. 99/85. Washington, DC: International Monetary Fund.

Levine, R. 1999. "Law, Finance and Economic Growth," *Journal of Financial Intermediation* 8(1–2): 8–35.

Loayza, N. 1997. "The Economics of the Informal Sector: A Simple Model and Some Empirical Evidence from Latin America," World Bank Policy Research Working Paper No. 1727. Washington, DC: World Bank.

Lora, E. 2001. "Structural Reforms in Latin America: What Has Been Reformed and How to Measure It," IADB Working Paper No. 466. Washington, DC: Inter-American Development Bank.

Madison, A. 1995. *Monitoring the World Economy: 1820–1995*. Paris: Organisation for Economic Co-operation and Development.

Martin, W. 2002. "Outgrowing Resource Dependence: Theory and Evidence." Prepared for the International Conference *Natural Resources and Growth* Central Bank of Chile, Santiago de Chile, January 18th.

McCarthy, F, H. Wolf, and Y. Wu. 2000. "The Growth Costs of Malaria," NBER Working Paper No. 7541. Cambridge, MA: National Bureau of Economic Research.

Monteagudo, J. and M. Watanuki. 2001. "Regional Trade Agreements for MERCOSUR: the FTAA and the FTA with the European Union." Prepared for the Conference *Impacts of Trade Liberalization Agreements on Latin America and the Caribbean* organized by the Inter-American Development Bank, Washington, DC, November 5–6.

O'Driscoll Jr, G. P., K. Holmes, and M. A. O'Grady. 2002. *2002 Index of Economic Freedom*. The Heritage Foundation and *The Wall Street Journal*, co-publishers.

Prebisch, R. 1950. "The Economic Development of Latin America and Its Principal Problems" New York: United Nations Reprinted in Prebisch, R. 1962. *Economic Bulletin for Latin America* 7(1): 1–22.

Rodrik, D. 1999. "Where did All the Growth Go? External Shocks, Social Conflict, and Growth Collapses," *Journal of Economic Growth* 4: 358–412.

———. 2000. "Institutions for High-Quality Growth: What They Are and How to Acquire Them," *Studies in Comparative International Development* 35(3): 3–31.

Sachs, J. 1998. "International Economics: Unlocking the Mysteries of Globalization," *Foreign Policy* 110: 97–111.

Sachs, J. and A. Warner. 1995. "Natural Resources Abundance and Economic Growth," NBER Working Paper No. 5398. Cambridge, MA: National Bureau of Economic Research.

Schott, J. 2001. *Prospects for Free Trade in the Americas*. Washington, DC: Institute for International Economics.

Singer, H. 1950. "The Distribution of Gains between Investing and Borrowing Countries," *American Economic Review* 40(2): 473–485.

Straub, S. 2000. "Empirical Determinants of Good Institutions: Do We Know Anything?" IADB Working Paper No. 423. Washington, DC: Inter-American Development Bank.

Tanzi, V. and H. Davoodi. 2000. "Corruption, Growth and Public Finances," IMF Working Paper No. 00/182. Washington, DC: International Monetary Fund.

United Nations Development Programme (UNDP). 2001. *Human Development Report 2001*. New York: Oxford University Press.

United States Patent and Trademark Office (USPTO). 2001. "Patents Counts by Country/State and Year: Utility Patents." Washington, DC: United States Patent and Trademark Office.

Van Ark, B. 2001. "The Renewal of the Old Economy: An International Comparative Perspective," OECD – STI Working Paper No. 2001/5. Paris: Organisation for Economic Co-operation and Development.

Venables, A. 2001. "Geography and International Inequalities: The Impact of New Technologies." Prepared for the World Bank *Conference on Economic Development*, Washington, DC, May 1–2.

World Economic Forum (WEF). 2000. *The Global Competitiveness Report 2000*. New York: Oxford University Press.

———. 2002. *The Global Competitiveness Report 2001–2002*. New York: Oxford University Press.

World Bank, 2001. *World Development Report 2001/2002*. Washington, DC: World Bank.

———. 2002. *The Global Development Network Database*. Online. http://sima-ext.worldbank.org/wbq

Part 3

Special Topics

CHAPTER 3.1

The Impact of Location on Global Innovation: Findings from the National Innovative Capacity Index

MICHAEL E. PORTER, Harvard University

SCOTT STERN, Northwestern University and National Bureau of Economic Research

Introduction

International competitiveness increasingly depends on innovation, especially in more developed economies. After a decade of structural reforms, with continued operational improvement in education and infrastructure now a given and with local companies able to rapidly acquire and deploy technologies from around the world, producing standard products using standard methods no longer sustains competitiveness. Prosperity, particularly in advanced economies, flows from the ability of companies in a nation to create and then globally commercialize new products and processes, shifting the innovation frontier as fast as rivals catch up. In Chapter 1.2, we found that innovation measures are the most important explanation of differences in prosperity among high-income countries. As global markets and sourcing reduce the value of low-cost inputs, the ability to access and develop technology also becomes a more fundamental driver of competitiveness for developing nations.

A higher level of innovation in one nation need not come at the expense of other nations. Raising the rates of innovation improves the productivity and prosperity of all nations and collectively speeds the rate of world economic growth. Innovation is also crucial for addressing pressing social challenges, by relaxing the tradeoffs between economic growth and health, safety, and environmental impact.

Although R&D investments are undertaken widely, the process of international innovation tends to be concentrated in a relatively small though growing number of countries. The United States and Switzerland had per capita patenting rates well in excess of other economies during the 1970s and 1980s, but the number of innovator nations has grown over the past 15 years (see Figure 1). Within nations, innovation tends to be dominated by geographically concentrated clusters of firms supported by local institutions. For example, more than three-fourths of all bio-pharmaceutical patents have their origin in a handful of regional clusters in the United States.

There remain large and persistent differences among leading countries in innovation performance. Whereas the Scandinavian countries and Japan have registered sharp increases, western European nations such as France and Italy have lagged, with innovation output at roughly the same level as a generation ago. Some emerging economies such as Singapore and Taiwan have become innovators, while many other economies, notably those of Latin America, still depend on low labor costs and imitation of foreign technologies.

Why does the intensity of innovation vary across countries? How does innovation depend on location? Innovation arises from private sector initiative, but the R&D productivity of firms at a given location is importantly shaped by local policies, local institutions, and other

227

Figure 1: International patents per capita, leading countries (1975–2001)

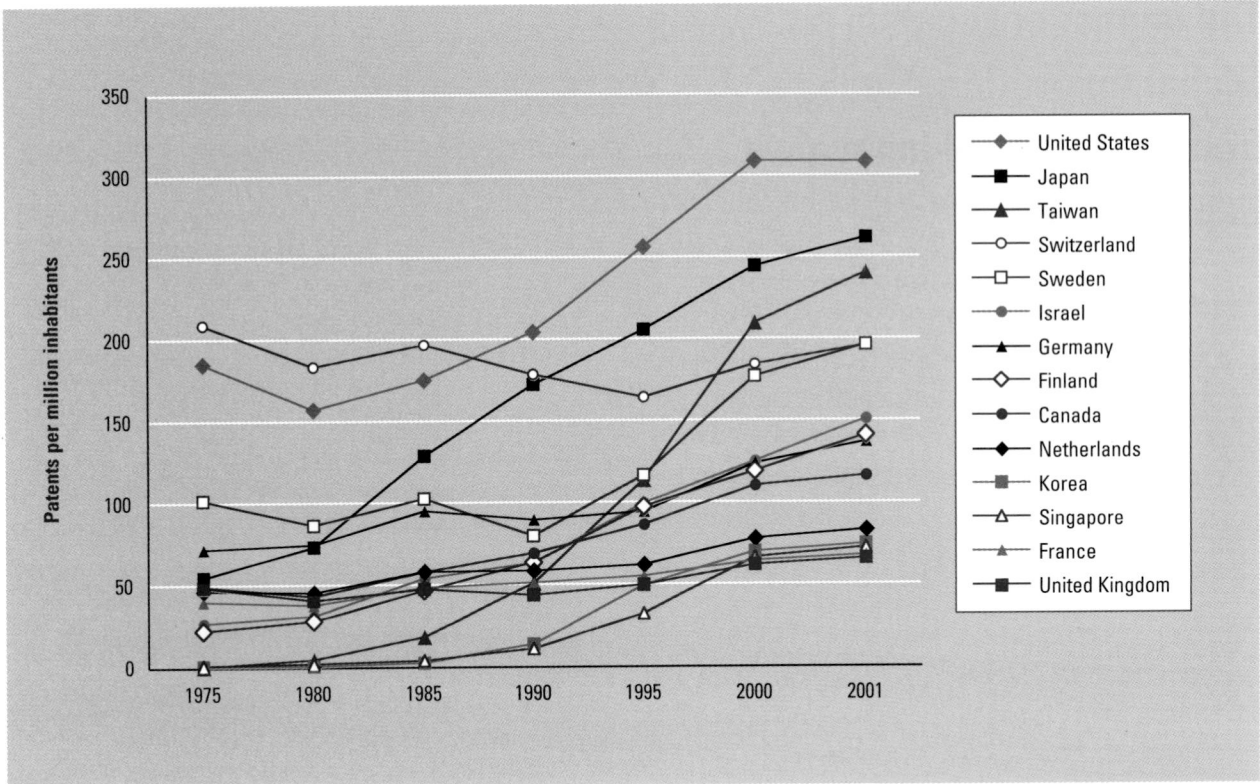

local circumstances. Innovation output, then, depends on the interaction between private-sector and public-sector policies and investments. We term this constellation of factors *national innovative capacity*, or the degree to which a nation offers a favorable environment for global innovation.

This chapter extends our prior research on the role of location in innovation, using new data from the Executive Opinion Survey 2002 to assess the innovative capacity of 73 countries.[1] We examine a wide range of nuanced measures suggested by the national innovative capacity framework and available from the Survey data to construct a national innovative capacity index (NICI). We rank countries on the NICI as well as five subindexes measuring important components of innovative vitality (see Table 1).

Our statistical findings reveal the striking degree to which measures of the national environment for innovation affect innovative output. We also find that the bar for innovation is rising; even countries with an *absolute* increase in innovative capacity over their 2001 capacity

can register a *relative* decline because of their inability to improve local conditions as fast as other nations. Some countries have aggressively invested in innovative capacity, going ahead of their expected investment given current income, in order to lead competitiveness and prosperity; conversely, innovative capacity in other nations lags overall productivity and income rankings, raising concerns about the sustainability of their competitiveness. Finally, the extent that firms choose innovation-oriented strategies is closely connected to the national environment of the countries in which they operate; improvements in the measured national innovation environment raise the propensity of firms to choose strategies and investments consistent with innovation. Though these findings are subject to caveats common to any quantitative study of the causes and consequences of innovation, our results provide consistent support for the role of policy choices in enhancing the national environment for innovation, and, with it, international competitiveness.

Table 1: National innovative capacity rankings

Country	National Innovative Capacity Index 2002 RANK	INDEX	Scientific and Engineering Manpower Subindex RANK	INDEX	Innovation Policy Subindex RANK	INDEX	Cluster Innovation Environment Subindex RANK	INDEX	Innovation Linkages Subindex RANK	INDEX	Company Innovation Orientation Subindex RANK	INDEX	Innovative Capacity Index 2001	Microeconomic Competitiveness Index 2002	GDP per capita 2001
United States	1	30.98	4	8.33	7	3.95	1	6.31	1	5.62	1	6.77	1	1	1
United Kingdom	2	29.66	15	7.89	10	3.84	2	6.06	2	5.50	2	6.37	4	3	19
Finland	3	29.05	8	8.12	4	4.06	5	5.83	3	5.26	9	5.79	2	2	14
Germany	4	28.52	10	8.04	6	3.98	7	5.77	7	4.79	4	5.95	3	4	13
Japan	5	28.28	2	8.56	13	3.79	6	5.77	17	4.31	7	5.85	12	11	10
Switzerland	6	27.89	11	8.03	18	3.67	14	5.39	12	4.49	3	6.32	5	5	4
Sweden	7	27.86	3	8.41	24	3.52	11	5.46	6	4.81	13	5.66	8	6	17
Taiwan	8	27.76	16	7.87	5	4.00	4	5.98	15	4.43	14	5.49	14	16	21
Canada	9	27.64	12	8.00	3	4.08	13	5.43	8	4.78	18	5.35	10	10	5
Singapore	10	27.59	17	7.86	1	4.33	12	5.44	22	4.22	10	5.75	13	9	20
Netherlands	11	27.31	18	7.85	12	3.81	9	5.52	9	4.77	17	5.35	6	7	12
Denmark	12	27.14	6	8.15	21	3.58	23	4.99	11	4.52	6	5.90	19	8	6
France	13	27.12	14	7.91	15	3.73	18	5.22	10	4.58	11	5.69	9	15	16
Austria	14	27.03	19	7.75	11	3.82	17	5.22	14	4.43	8	5.81	17	12	8
Israel	15	26.82	29	7.36	2	4.20	31	4.55	4	5.05	12	5.67	11	18	24
Belgium	16	26.75	13	7.99	19	3.66	28	4.77	5	4.88	15	5.44	15	13	7
Australia	17	26.58	9	8.12	9	3.85	15	5.34	18	4.31	22	4.96	7	14	11
Iceland	18	26.49	1	8.65	23	3.53	25	4.93	24	4.11	19	5.27	20	17	3
Norway	19	26.35	5	8.32	22	3.58	16	5.26	16	4.39	25	4.81	18	21	2
Ireland	20	26.22	24	7.67	14	3.76	19	5.18	13	4.48	20	5.14	16	20	9
Italy	21	26.00	37	7.19	38	3.15	3	6.05	20	4.26	16	5.36	22	24	18
Korea	22	25.92	23	7.67	20	3.65	10	5.49	25	4.10	21	5.00	23	23	26
Spain	23	24.95	30	7.35	25	3.47	22	5.04	23	4.21	23	4.88	21	25	23
New Zealand	24	24.32	20	7.69	47	2.94	29	4.70	21	4.25	27	4.73	24	22	22
Slovenia	25	24.11	22	7.68	27	3.44	34	4.34	26	3.99	29	4.66	31	27	25
Hong Kong SAR	26	23.82	63	4.54	30	3.33	8	5.75	19	4.27	5	5.93	NA	19	15
Portugal	27	23.62	28	7.37	16	3.72	20	5.09	44	3.34	45	4.11	25	36	27
Hungary	28	23.28	33	7.27	28	3.43	39	4.17	31	3.73	28	4.68	28	28	30
Estonia	29	22.97	21	7.68	44	3.01	44	4.07	28	3.88	35	4.34	27	30	34
South Africa	30	22.34	39	7.05	39	3.14	32	4.49	34	3.68	50	3.98	29	29	37
Lithuania	31	22.33	26	7.62	53	2.76	43	4.11	37	3.66	41	4.19	37	40	46
Czech Republic	32	22.25	36	7.21	33	3.22	53	3.96	35	3.67	42	4.19	26	34	29
Brazil	33	22.21	48	5.68	36	3.17	21	5.09	29	3.88	33	4.39	33	33	47
Russian Federation	34	21.89	7	8.13	61	2.59	37	4.19	46	3.32	64	3.66	30	58	40
Poland	35	21.87	34	7.26	57	2.70	41	4.11	32	3.70	46	4.10	36	46	38
China	36	21.87	43	6.13	26	3.45	30	4.69	42	3.38	38	4.22	43	38	62
Greece	37	21.75	35	7.25	42	3.03	49	4.01	45	3.33	44	4.14	42	43	28
Costa Rica	38	21.74	42	6.28	32	3.24	36	4.19	50	3.20	24	4.82	39	39	42
Malaysia	39	21.67	57	5.04	17	3.69	27	4.79	36	3.66	31	4.49	52	26	43
Slovak Republic	40	21.63	27	7.52	41	3.06	64	3.58	43	3.37	47	4.09	34	42	32
Chile	41	21.33	45	5.91	49	2.92	35	4.34	38	3.54	30	4.62	35	31	36
Croatia	42	21.32	32	7.31	37	3.16	69	3.46	49	3.24	43	4.14	NA	52	44
India	43	21.00	56	5.06	29	3.36	24	4.94	27	3.95	61	3.70	38	37	74
Latvia	44	20.91	40	6.99	51	2.80	65	3.58	40	3.46	48	4.07	41	45	48
Tunisia	45	20.72	60	4.82	8	3.91	45	4.05	30	3.73	40	4.21	NA	32	50
Thailand	46	20.59	61	4.63	35	3.19	26	4.83	39	3.49	32	4.45	46	35	53
Ukraine	47	20.56	25	7.66	70	2.40	60	3.75	52	3.18	69	3.56	32	69	63
Romania	48	20.10	31	7.34	59	2.66	63	3.65	60	2.95	71	3.51	55	67	49
Dominican Republic	49	19.79	71	3.91	34	3.20	38	4.18	33	3.70	26	4.80	62	41	55
Bulgaria	50	19.58	38	7.16	66	2.50	72	3.29	55	3.05	68	3.58	50	68	56
Mexico	51	19.50	51	5.37	40	3.09	42	4.11	57	2.98	54	3.94	53	55	39
Argentina	52	19.30	41	6.37	78	2.22	59	3.81	59	2.96	53	3.95	49	65	31
Vietnam	53	19.14	49	5.61	52	2.77	40	4.14	56	2.99	67	3.63	61	60	77
Turkey	54	19.13	47	5.72	67	2.47	33	4.43	64	2.85	63	3.67	44	54	51
Mauritius	55	18.98	44	6.00	58	2.68	62	3.66	58	2.97	62	3.68	47	49	33
Sri Lanka	56	18.98	53	5.24	54	2.75	48	4.02	48	3.25	60	3.72	57	47	69
Panama	57	18.95	59	4.82	55	2.75	56	3.89	53	3.18	36	4.31	45	50	57
Trinidad and Tobago	58	18.95	58	4.98	50	2.83	52	3.97	47	3.28	57	3.89	40	44	35

Note: For Ireland, GNP per capita is shown instead of GDP per capita because of the size of the dividend outflows to foreign investors. Ireland's GDP is about 20 percent higher than its GNP.

(cont'd.)

Table 1: National innovative capacity rankings *(cont'd.)*

Country	National Innovative Capacity Index 2002 RANK	INDEX	Scientific and Engineering Manpower Subindex RANK	INDEX	Innovation Policy Subindex RANK	INDEX	Cluster Innovation Environment Subindex RANK	INDEX	Innovation Linkages Subindex RANK	INDEX	Company Innovation Orientation Subindex RANK	INDEX	Innovative Capacity Index 2001	Microeconomic Competitiveness Index 2002	GDP per capita 2001
Indonesia	59	18.48	46	5.86	77	2.24	54	3.93	65	2.83	66	3.63	54	64	71
Philippines	60	18.08	55	5.16	74	2.39	50	4.00	74	2.50	49	4.02	56	61	64
Colombia	61	18.05	65	4.38	43	3.01	46	4.03	61	2.88	59	3.75	59	56	54
Peru	62	17.66	50	5.43	68	2.47	74	3.20	68	2.66	56	3.89	60	66	59
Uruguay	63	17.46	54	5.17	60	2.63	75	3.19	73	2.58	55	3.90	51	62	41
Venezuela	64	17.41	52	5.27	76	2.29	67	3.52	62	2.87	72	3.47	58	72	58
El Salvador	65	16.64	73	3.85	75	2.38	71	3.34	63	2.86	39	4.21	67	63	60
Nicaragua	66	16.08	68	4.30	72	2.40	68	3.49	78	2.26	65	3.63	63	75	72
Guatemala	67	16.07	66	4.32	65	2.52	73	3.21	71	2.61	76	3.11	69	77	70
Ecuador	68	15.75	64	4.42	62	2.59	77	3.03	69	2.65	80	2.81	65	70	76
Zimbabwe	69	15.68	72	3.91	69	2.47	58	3.83	77	2.32	75	3.22	64	76	61
Paraguay	70	15.47	62	4.61	71	2.40	78	2.92	77	2.32	78	2.98	70	74	78
Bangladesh	71	15.23	70	3.93	73	2.39	66	3.57	75	2.36	79	2.97	68	78	73
Honduras	72	15.17	67	4.32	63	2.57	76	3.09	79	2.22	79	2.97	71	79	75
Bolivia	73	14.60	69	4.23	79	2.12	79	2.83	76	2.35	77	3.08	71	79	75
Botswana	NA	NA	NA	NA	45	2.99	51	3.99	66	2.74	37	4.25	NA	57	45
Haiti	NA	NA	NA	NA	80	1.99	80	2.36	80	2.02	74	3.34	NA	80	79
Jamaica	NA	NA	NA	NA	56	2.74	70	3.42	67	2.67	34	4.35	NA	59	66
Jordan	NA	NA	NA	NA	48	2.93	61	3.74	51	3.20	58	3.87	NA	53	65
Morocco	NA	NA	NA	NA	46	2.97	47	4.02	41	3.42	51	3.97	NA	48	68
Namibia	NA	NA	NA	NA	31	3.24	57	3.87	70	2.62	52	3.96	NA	51	52
Nigeria	NA	NA	NA	NA	64	2.52	55	3.91	54	3.12	70	3.54	NA	71	80

230

The determinants of national innovative capacity

The vitality of innovation in a location is shaped by *national innovative capacity*. National innovative capacity is a country's potential—as both a political and economic entity—to produce a stream of commercially relevant innovations. National innovative capacity is distinct from purely scientific or technical achievements; it focuses on the economic application of new technology. Innovative capacity is not simply the realized level of innovation but aims to measure the fundamental conditions that create the environment for innovation in a particular location. Innovative capacity depends in part on past technological sophistication and the size of the scientific and technical workforce, and it also reflects a series of investment and policy choices by government and the private sector that affect the incentives for research, development, and commercialization activities in a country and their productivity.

Sharp differences in innovative output across locations make clear the importance of local circumstances in R&D productivity. However, taking advantage of the local environment for innovation is far from automatic. Companies based in the same location can and do differ markedly in their success at innovation. Harnessing the local environment for innovation requires that companies pursue appropriate strategies and make appropriate investment choices.

National innovative capacity is composed of four broad elements that define how location shapes the ability of a company to innovate at the global frontier (see Figure 2). Although the framework was created for application at the national level, it can also be employed to evaluate innovative capacity at the regional or local level.

Common innovation infrastructure

A nation's common innovation infrastructure is the set of cross-cutting factors supporting innovation throughout an entire economy, including the pool of human and financial resources devoted to scientific and technological advances, the economywide public policies bearing on innovative activity, and the economy's inherited level of technological sophistication. The foundation of a nation's common innovation infrastructure is its cadre of scientists and engineers involved in innovation. Common innovation infrastructure also includes investments and institutions engaged in basic research, which advances fundamental understanding and underpins much commercial technology. Government funding remains the mainstay of virtually every nation's investment in truly frontier research. Areas of cross-cutting policy affecting innovation include the protection of intellectual property; the extent of tax-based incentives for innovation; the degree to which antitrust enforcement motivates and encourages innovation; the extent to which innovation is spurred versus impeded by the structure of safety, quality, and environmental regulations; and the openness of the economy to trade and investment. Overall, a strong common innovation infrastructure requires national investments and policy choices stretching over decades.

The cluster-specific innovation environment

Although the common innovation infrastructure sets the basic conditions for innovation, the development and commercialization of new technologies take place disproportionately in clusters—geographic concentrations of interconnected companies and institutions in a particular field. The cluster-specific innovation environment is captured in the "diamond" framework (see Figure 3).[2] Four attributes of the microeconomic environment surrounding a cluster bear on its overall competitiveness and innovative vitality—the presence of high-quality and specialized inputs; a local context that encourages investment together with intense rivalry; pressure and insight gleaned from sophisticated local demand; and the local presence of high-quality related and supporting industries.

The importance of clusters reflects important externalities in innovation that are contained in particular geographic areas. Presence within a cluster offers advantages to firms in perceiving both the need and the opportunity for innovation. Equally important, however, are the flexibility and capacity present in clusters to turn new ideas into reality. Within a cluster, a company can rapidly assemble the components, machinery, and services necessary for commercialization. Suppliers of essential inputs and "lead" buyers become crucial partners in the innovation process; the relationships necessary for effective innovation are more easily achieved among participants that are nearby. Reinforcing these advantages for innovation within clusters is sheer pressure—competitive pressure, peer pressure, customer pressure, and constant comparison. We focus on clusters (eg, information technology) rather than individual industries (eg, printers), then, because of powerful spillovers and externalities across discrete industries that are vital to the rate of innovation.

The innovation environment of a cluster is fundamental to its competitiveness. For example, the Finnish pulp-and-paper cluster benefits from the advantages of pressures from demanding domestic consumers, intense rivalry among local competitors, and local Finnish process-equipment manufacturers who are world leaders, with companies such as Kamyr and Sunds leading the world in the commercialization of innovative bleaching equipment. Similar examples of cluster vitality in innovation occur in many fields, from pharmaceuticals in the United States to semiconductor fabrication in Taiwan.

Figure 2: National innovative capacity framework

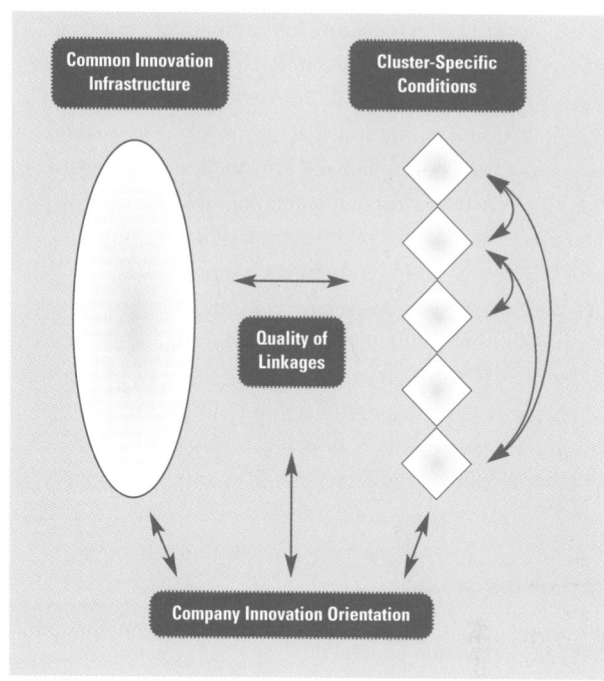

Figure 3: The microeconomic business environment

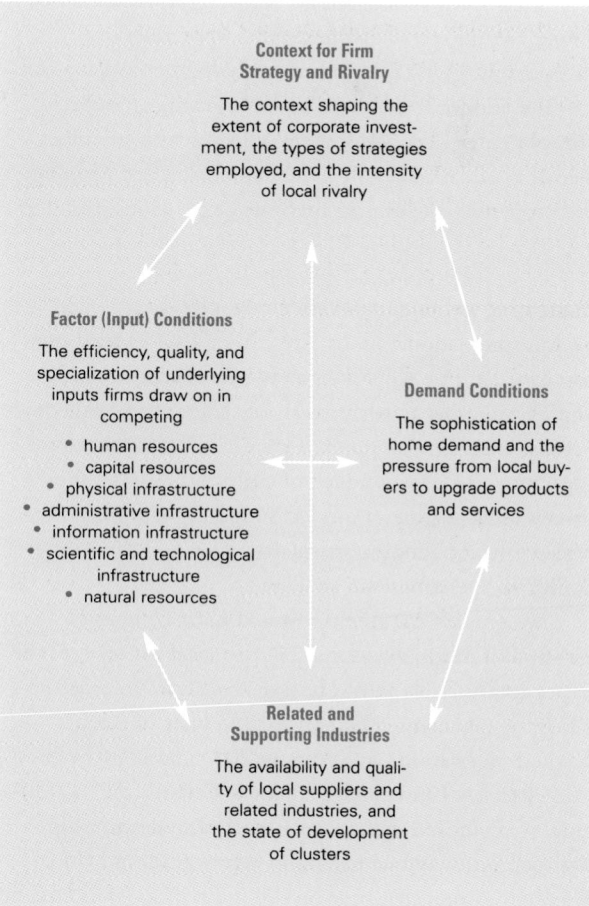

The quality of linkages

The quality of the connections between a nation's common innovation infrastructure and individual industrial clusters is crucial to innovation. It is also reciprocal: strong clusters feed the common infrastructure and also benefit from it. Without strong linkages, upstream scientific and technical advances can actually diffuse to other countries more quickly than they can be exploited at home. For example, although early elements of VCR technology were developed in the United States, it was three companies in the Japanese consumer electronics cluster that successfully commercialized this innovation on a global scale in the late 1970s.

A particularly important linking institution is a nation's university system, which can play the role of bridging researchers and companies. A variety of formal and informal organizations and networks—which we term *institutions for collaboration*—are present in many nations and link the two areas.

Company innovation orientation

Finally, taking advantage of these elements of the innovation environment depends on appropriate choices by companies. Companies must embrace strategies based on innovation and choose supportive operating policies in areas such as R&D spending, customer orientation, and recruiting and training. Simply investing in R&D is not enough; companies need to draw purposefully on strengths in the local innovation environment such as universities and local suppliers. In other words, appropriate corporate practices and strategy interact with the other elements of national innovative capacity in determining the propensity of firms to innovate at the global frontier.

Measuring national innovative capacity

To measure national innovative capacity, we extend our prior research by employing new data drawn from the Survey. Standard governmental data sources are inadequate because they fail to capture many drivers of innovative capacity across a wide range of countries. Among these drivers are the array of innovation policy variables, the cluster-specific innovation environment, and the nature of company operations and strategy.

We employ the single best and most comparable measure of innovative output, *international patenting*, as the dependent variable in our statistical analysis. International patenting is measured by the total number of patents granted to a nation's inventors in 2000 and 2001 by the United States Patent and Trademark Office (USPTO).[3] We employ regression analysis to evaluate the relationship between international patenting and over 30 individual Survey measures that bear on the innovation environment and corporate practices. The regression analysis allows us to assign *relative* weights to individual variables. We use these weights to calculate subindexes of the four dimensions of each nation's innovative capacity, and then combine them into an overall ranking. This procedure ensures that country-level assessments of innovative capacity are closely tied to measures that have a demonstrated relationship to long-term international innovative performance.

We employ USPTO patents in constructing the dependent variable for several reasons.[4] First, when a foreign inventor files for a US patent, it is a sign of the innovation's potential economic value because of the costs involved. Patents with significant economic consequences are highly likely to be filed in the United States because it is the world's largest market. Second, the US patent system tests applications against the global technology frontier and offers a common standard comparable across innovations.

Since no single measure of innovation output is ideal, we have explored several alternatives, including the pattern of exports in international high-technology markets and the flow of technology licensing revenues across countries. Overall, international patenting offers by far the best and most consistent measure across time and location.

The use of Survey data to measure the innovation environment also raises some methodological questions. There are no quantitative data at all available for most of the areas measured, much less for a meaningful number of countries, so that Survey data are the only alternative. However, there is a legitimate question of whether the Survey responses truly capture cross-country differences. Each country-level Survey measure is computed as the *average* response by respondents within each country. To assess the reliability of aggregating across respondents, we conducted an analysis of variance (ANOVA) analysis for each measure. We regressed individual Survey responses on a complete set of country-level dummy variables, allowing us to calculate the share of the variation (across individual responses) that results from systematic differences in the average response across countries. The results are reported in Appendix B.

Considering that there is an average of more than 60 respondents per country, the degree of within-country consensus is striking. For most measures, between one third and one half of the overall variation in the responses is driven by country-specific differences for that measure. For example, more than 45 percent of the dispersion across respondents from all countries on "Effectiveness of intellectual property protection in promoting innovation" reflects country-specific consensus. As a result of this substantial within-country consensus, country averages are meaningfully different from each other; for each of the 34 Survey measures employed in this chapter, the ANOVA analysis statistically rejects equality of the country-level means. By aggregating across the large number of individual respondents within each country, then, country-level averages isolate the meaningful differences across countries in the competitiveness environment, while limiting idiosyncratic biases.

Since variation in the number of Survey responses per country and the degree of consensus within countries are important concerns when conducting multivariate regression analysis, we also checked the robustness of our country rankings by weighting the key regressions by the number of respondents and the degree of consensus within each country. The results remain virtually unchanged.[5]

Determinants of innovative capacity across countries

We first regress the national level of international patenting in 2000 and 2001 in a sample of 73 countries, on three base variables: (1) total population, (2) the number of scientists and engineers employed within the nation, and (3) the "stock" of international patents generated by the country between 1981 and 1995.[6] The control for population focuses the analysis on per capita rates of international patenting; it is a nation's intensity of innovation, controlling for country size, that should matter for its international competitiveness.[7] Both the number of technological personnel and the patent stock vary substantially across countries and over time. For example, the percentage of the workforce that is comprised of scientists and engineers is three times higher in Japan than in Italy or Spain, though the national living standards of all these countries are similar. The number of scientists and engineers is a baseline measure of the effort devoted to innovative activity. Historical patenting is a control variable for historical technological sophistication, as well as differences across countries in the propensity to patent inventions in the United States.[8] Over 80 percent of the total variance in international patenting across the world can be explained by the baseline variables.

We use the share of scientists and engineers in a country's workforce to create a scientific and engineering manpower subindex.

Despite the predictable explanatory power of the baseline variables, some countries—such as Singapore, Israel, and the United States—have patenting levels well above that predicted by the baseline model. Others such as Spain and Russia are substantially below the baseline. Controlling for the baseline variables, we explore measures of the innovation environment suggested by our framework to explain the "gap" between predicted and realized international innovation performance.

There are 34 Survey measures related to innovative capacity that can be divided into four groupings: those bearing on innovation-related public policies (eg, the effectiveness of intellectual property protection and the effectiveness of competition policy), those assessing the cluster innovation environment (eg, the sophistication of local buyers and the quality of local suppliers), those meas-

uring the strength of linkages; and those bearing on the degree of innovation orientation in company operations and strategies. The complete list of national innovative capacity measures and baseline regressions including each individual measure are reported in Appendix A.

We introduce each variable, one at a time, into the baseline specification. Of the 34 measures, 33 are statistically significant, and no measure is associated with a negative relationship with innovation performance.[9] In other words, even after controlling for the size of a country, the aggregate level of resources devoted to innovation and the stock of past ideas to build on, a series of measures of the national innovation environment is strongly associated with the level of innovative output actually realized by countries.

To calculate an innovative capacity index, it was not feasible to include all 34 variables in a multivariate regression analysis. The reason is straightforward: nearly all of the measures are correlated with each other, and our analysis relies on a single cross-section of 73 countries. For measures addressing similar parts of the business environment (eg, domestic competition), the correlation sometimes reaches over 0.9. Rather than attempt to disentangle the distinct effects associated with each measure, we create a parsimonious specification for four additional subindexes using a few key variables drawn from the range of variables relevant to that area. Our choice of variables for each of the subindexes relied on an extensive analysis that identified the particular variables from the set of relevant variables with the most statistically robust relationship to our measure of innovative output. The regression results, along with all other subindex regressions, are reported in Appendix C.

The innovation policy subindex

Three measures were selected to capture the innovation policy environment, each with a strong and robust relationship to international patenting:

- the effectiveness of intellectual property protection,
- the size and availability of R&D tax credits and R&D subsidies for the private sector, and
- the effectiveness of environmental regulation in promoting long-term competitiveness.

These three variables were added to the baseline regression. The innovation policy subindex for a country is calculated as the weighted sum of the three measures, where the weights are based on the regression coefficients for each measure in the specification presented in Appendix C.

Together, these measures are highly statistically significant, and each is predicted to have a substantial impact on the level of international patenting. For example, increasing the Survey response on the availability of R&D tax credits from 4 to 5 (one standard deviation) is associated with a 30 percent increase in a country's level of international patenting.

The third column of Table 1 presents country rankings on the innovation policy subindex. Singapore registers the highest ranking, followed by Israel, Canada, and Finland. Surprisingly, three non-OECD economies (Singapore, Israel, and Taiwan) are among the top five. The OECD economies of the United States, Germany, Australia, and the United Kingdom all rank within the top ten. Despite weakness in other areas, Tunisia is ranked eighth in innovation policy, driven by its favorable scores for R&D tax credits and environmental policies.

A number of OECD economies, including Italy and New Zealand, lag substantially behind on this subindex. There is an increasing gap between countries in their willingness and ability to implement innovation-oriented policy reforms.

The innovation policy subindex rankings also reveal substantial variation across broad geographic regions. For example, Latin American nations exhibit a weak innovation policy record relative to their ranking in overall competitiveness. All Latin American innovation policy rankings are below the top 30, including countries such as Costa Rica and Mexico that have improved international competitiveness over the past decade. Eastern European economies such as Russia and Estonia also lag substantially behind in terms of implementing an effective innovation policy agenda, despite their large pools of science and engineering personnel. India and China, often cited as emerging innovator economies, register innovation policy rankings far below those of the main OECD economies (both are outside of the top 25). These countries have yet to put in place the type of innovation policy environment found in emerging innovator economies such as Singapore and Israel.

The cluster innovation environment subindex

A similar methodology underlies the cluster innovation environment subindex. We selected three measures relating to the quality of the cluster environment for creating and commercializing innovation:

- the state (prevalence and depth) of cluster development,
- the extent of locally based competition, and
- the sophistication of domestic customers.

Each of the measures has a statistically significant and quantitatively significant impact on the rate of international patenting, even after controlling for population, the historical propensity to innovate, and the size of the R&D workforce. The cluster innovation environment subindex

is calculated by adding together these three factors, using the weights calculated in the regression (reported in Appendix C).

The United Kingdom, Italy, and the United States form a "top tier" in terms of the cluster environment for innovation. Relative to their policy rankings, Japan and Sweden register relatively high rankings on the cluster subindex, while Canada has a significantly lower ranking.

These patterns reflect important differences across countries that are often misunderstood by more conventional analyses that focus solely on policy indicators. Innovative capacity results not just from overall policies but also from strong clusters. Over the past five years, for example, the United Kingdom has made a commitment to cluster development in its most innovative sectors, from the life sciences to financial services. Although this has yet to show up in outcome measures such as international patenting, the focus on clusters lays an important foundation for future innovation performance.

Three emerging East Asian economies—Taiwan, Singapore, and Hong Kong—each have cluster innovation environments comparable with those of mainstream OECD economies, outdistancing countries such as Denmark, France, and Spain in this regard. Rather than reflecting erosion on the part of the OECD countries, however, our findings reveal substantial and sustained advancement in cluster development across an increasing number of East Asian economies.

The record for other emerging economies is more mixed. Israel's growth over the past decade has been led by strong cluster development. However, this subindex registered a decline in this area in 2002, perhaps because of instability and security concerns. China and India register modest cluster development, though they are well positioned when compared with most eastern European and Latin American economies, where cluster development continues to be at a relatively low level.

The linkages subindex

The strength of linkages between the common innovation infrastructure and a country's clusters and firms is perhaps the most difficult area to measure of the drivers of national innovative capacity, because it reflects the subtle but crucial collaboration between public-sector institutions and private-sector initiatives. Given the limited number of measures available, this subindex is based on just two Survey measures closely associated with the process by which a country's innovation resources are directed toward the needs of individual clusters and firms:

- the local availability of specialized research and training institutions, and
- the availability of venture capital for innovative but risky projects.

The availability of specialized research and training institutions highlights the importance of leading universities and other independent research institutions in fostering linkages. The availability of venture capital reflects the importance of venture capital providers in seeking out commercializable research and moving it to the marketplace. Each measure is statistically and quantitatively significant in its predicted impact on the rate of international patenting. The linkages subindex is the weighted sum of the two linkages measures, with the weights determined by the regression coefficients reported in Appendix C.

Countries vary widely in their ability to foster connections between the public, university, and private sectors. As reported in the fifth column of Table 1, the United States stands out at the top of this ranking, followed by the United Kingdom, Finland, and Israel. Even during a period in which Israeli cluster development is threatened, linkages have so far remained strong. Relative to the other two subindexes, Japan records its poorest performance, falling out of the top 15, while Sweden and Belgium improve in relative performance. Sustained weakness by Japan in fostering linkages contributes to explaining the ineffectiveness of multiple economic policy initiatives over the past decade in reversing macroeconomic stagnation.

No emerging economy except Israel registers in the top 10 on linkages. Relative weakness in this area is endemic in East Asia, Latin America, and eastern Europe. This is not surprising. Most developing countries have a history of sharp divisions across government, business, and universities. The development of linkages requires policy attention, resource investments, institution building, and attitude shifts that require patience and perseverance. In contrast to instituting policy choices such as the presence of R&D tax credits, developing effective linkages is a slow process.

The company innovation orientation subindex

The final subindex measures the extent to which company strategies and operating practices are oriented toward innovation versus other modes of competing. The national environment shapes the opportunities and constraints that firms face when setting strategy, but managers must act on these through their choices. By choosing strategies that depend on innovation, companies link their competitive advantage to the innovative capacity of their local environment.[10]

We take advantage of three Survey measures to capture the impact of corporate practices on innovative capacity:

- the degree to which companies' competitive advantage depends on introducing unique goods and services,
- the extent and sophistication of marketing, and
- the degree to which pay is linked to productivity.

At its heart, innovation-oriented strategies result from a choice by managers to seek competitive advantage from sustained introduction of unique products and processes rather than rely on low cost inputs. Premising strategy on innovation affects all aspects of a company's business, from product positioning to internal organization. The second and third measures capture practices that support innovation-based strategies. As in the other subindexes, each measure is statistically and quantitatively linked to the rate of international patenting. As in the prior subindexes, the company innovation orientation subindex is the weighted sum of these three measures, with the weights determined by the regression coefficients reported in Appendix C.

As reported in Table 1, the United States leads this ranking, followed closely by the United Kingdom and Switzerland. A number of countries are closely bunched together in a second tier, including several European countries such as Germany and Austria. Relative to the other subindexes, Finland, Sweden, and Australia register poor performance in this area, while Hong Kong achieves its strongest subindex ranking. Four emerging economies—Hong Kong, Singapore, Taiwan, and Israel—are within the top 15, suggesting that innovation-oriented firm strategies and operating practices are not limited to historically advanced economies.

There should be a positive relationship between the quality of the innovation environment and the innovation orientation of firm strategies. The relationship is far from automatic, however, as firms may fail to recognize or have the skills to take advantage of national assets. To gain insight into this complex relationship, Figure 4 shows the relationship between the company innovation orientation subindex and the other subindexes. While the company innovation orientation subindex is correlated with each subindex, the relationship is closer for the cluster subindex and the linkage subindex than for the innovation policy subindex.[11] Merely setting broad policies supporting innovation appears not to be sufficient to assure innovation. The other dimensions of the innovation environment must progress to raise the odds that companies embrace innovation as a way of competing.

Looking across the graphs in Figures 4a, 4b, and 4c, company innovation orientation leads to innovation environment indicators in some countries while, in other countries, companies do not seem to be taking full advantage of the innovative capacity of their local environment. For example, Swiss companies remain focused on innovation despite weaknesses in national conditions. In contrast, Australia's companies lag behind the quality of the nation's innovation environment. The benefits of innovative capacity for long-term competitiveness depend on the willingness and ability of companies to exploit the potential in the local environment. Hence, an important policy priority is to champion innovation to the private sector and ensure that enhancements in national innovative capacity are both recognized by and accessible to local firms.

Ranking overall innovative capacity

The national innovative capacity index, reported as the first column of Table 1, is calculated as the unweighted sum of the five subindexes. Each of the subindexes registers a high individual proportion of explained variance in innovative output, but there are not enough data points to derive statistically robust weights. The five subindexes are:

- science and engineering manpower subindex,
- the innovation policy subindex,
- the cluster innovation environment subindex,
- the innovation linkages subindex, and
- the company innovation orientation subindex.

The United States ranks first, reflecting its leadership in three of the five subindexes, closely followed by the United Kingdom and Finland. Germany and Japan round out the first tier. The remainder of the top 10 countries are closely bunched in terms of their absolute scores; only small differences distinguish the second tier of international innovators. Two non-OECD economies, Taiwan and Singapore, are included among the top 10. A third tier, composed of another dozen countries (from the Netherlands [11th] to Korea [22nd]), are also closely bunched, with small differences in the absolute scores for this group of countries determining the relative positioning within the group.

These findings strongly confirm our earlier research and research by others on patterns of international innovation. Over the past quarter century, the set of leading innovator economies has expanded to include as many as 15 European economies (including nearly all the nations of northern Europe) as well as several emerging economies, highlighted by the presence of three Asian nations that rank within the top 10. Although OECD nations continue to be responsible for the great majority of global innovation, a growing number of emerging economies have achieved the conditions to support innovation. Overall, since the end of the Cold War, steady "convergence" in innovation output has resulted from a substantial upgrading in the innovation environment in a group of about 25 nations.

The remainder of the world lags in innovative capacity. As was revealed in our analysis of each of the subindexes, the large Asian economies, most notably China and India, are still at an early but promising stage of development in terms of innovation at the global frontier. Despite improvements in macroeconomic stability over the past two decades in Latin America and positive political and economic changes in eastern Europe, these areas of the world do not yet offer environments conducive to innovation at the global frontier. In eastern Europe, a large pool of scientists and engineers at the end of the Cold War did not lead to comprehensive strategies to develop innovative capacity; as a result, these nations continue to register unfulfilled promise. Similarly, African nations have so far developed only the ability to absorb new technologies: none is ranked within the top 30. Even South Africa underperforms on innovation relative to its overall level of economic development.

The subindexes differ in the extent of variation across countries and so in their relative impact on the overall innovative capacity ranking. The innovation policy subindex exhibits the least amount of variation: many countries around the world have adopted the essential elements of effective innovation policy, so that the ability to achieve global innovation leadership purely through policy differentiation has eroded. The gap in innovative capacity among top-tier countries is driven by large differences in the linkages and company innovation orientation subindexes. Differences among middle-tier countries (ranking from 20th to 40th overall in innovative capacity) are more closely linked to differences in cluster innovation environment and the science and engineering manpower subindexes.

Figure 4a: The relationship between company innovation orientation and innovation policy

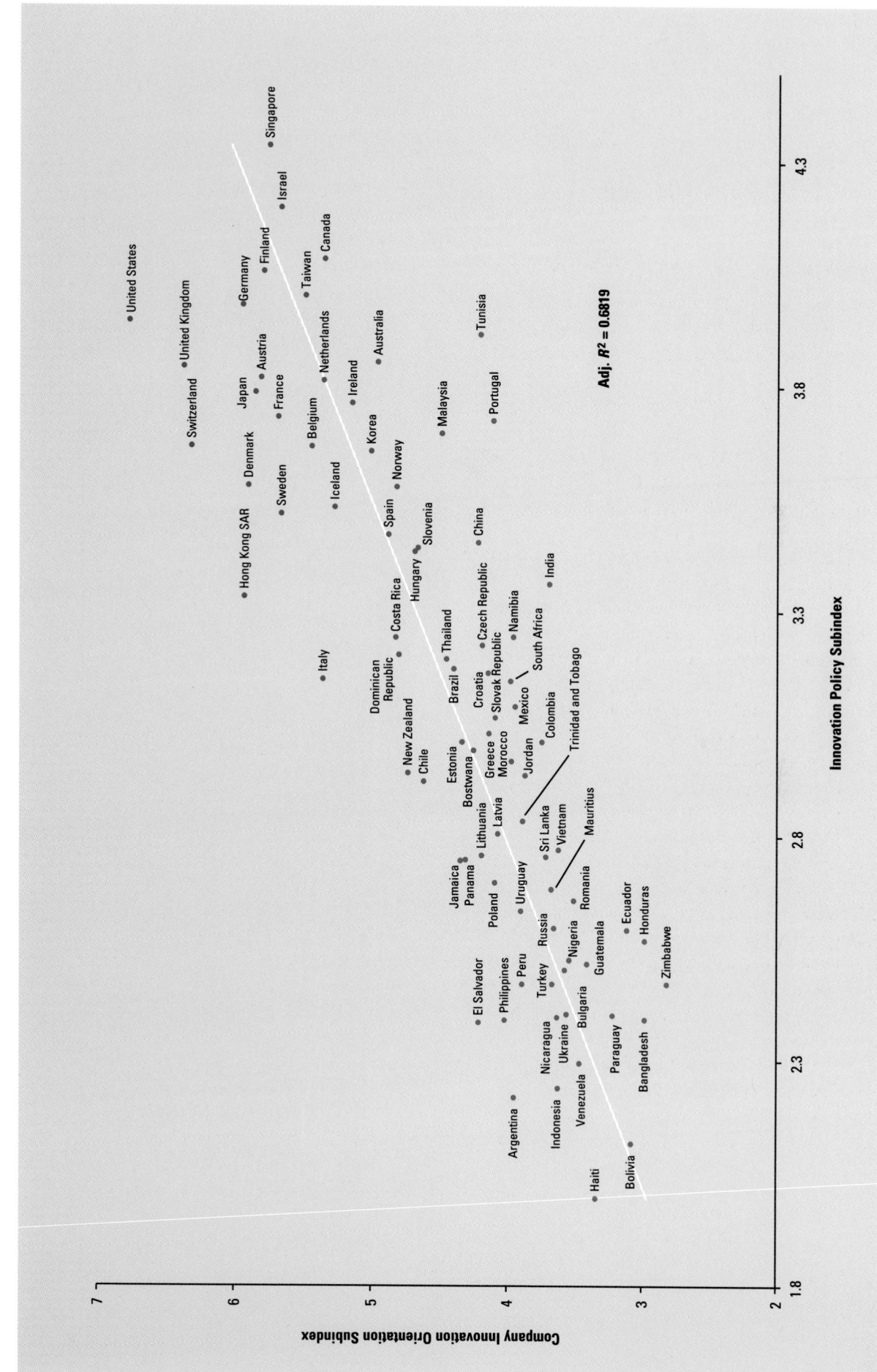

Figure 4b: The relationship between company innovation orientation and cluster environment

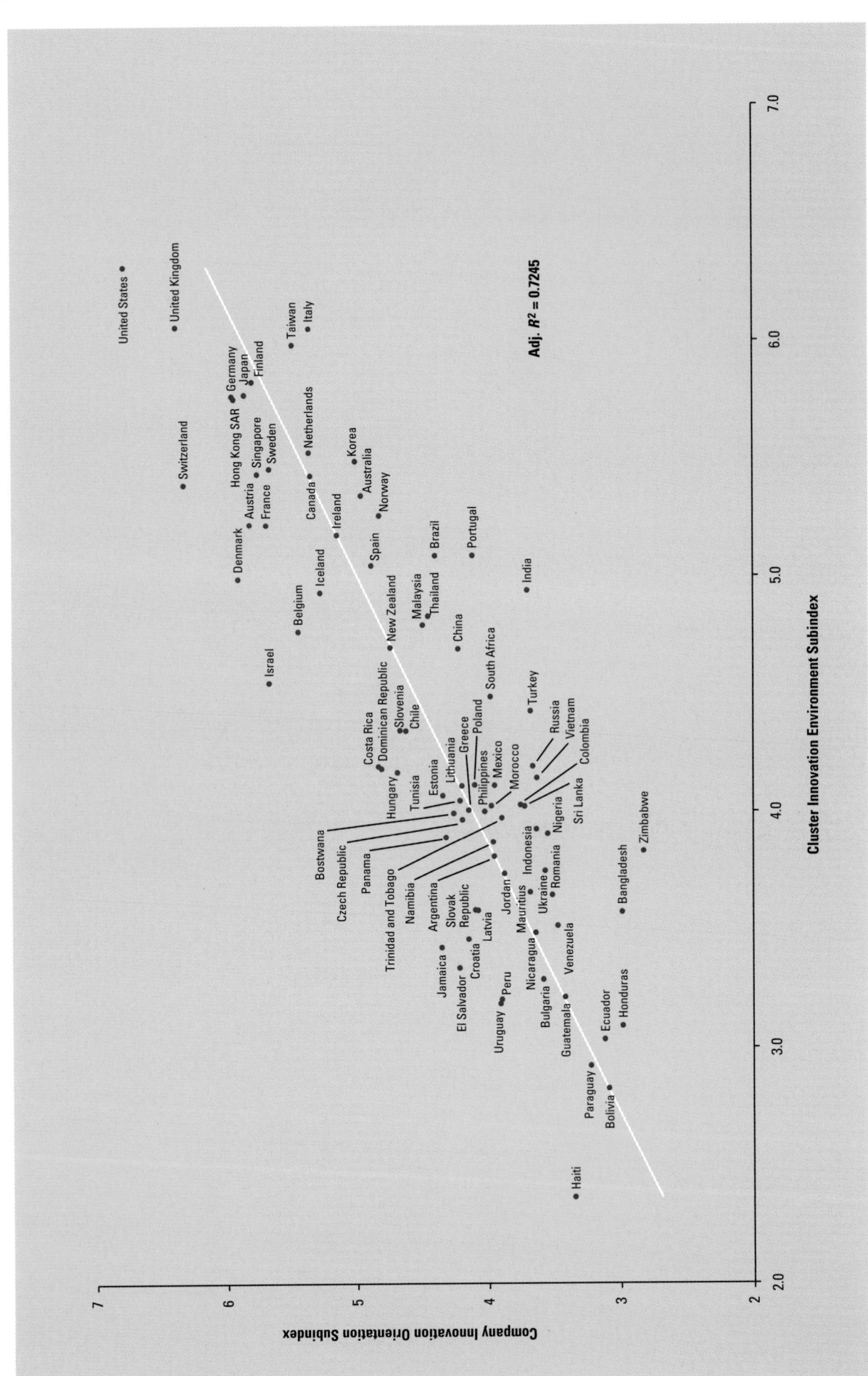

Figure 4c: The relationship between company innovation orientation and innovation linkages

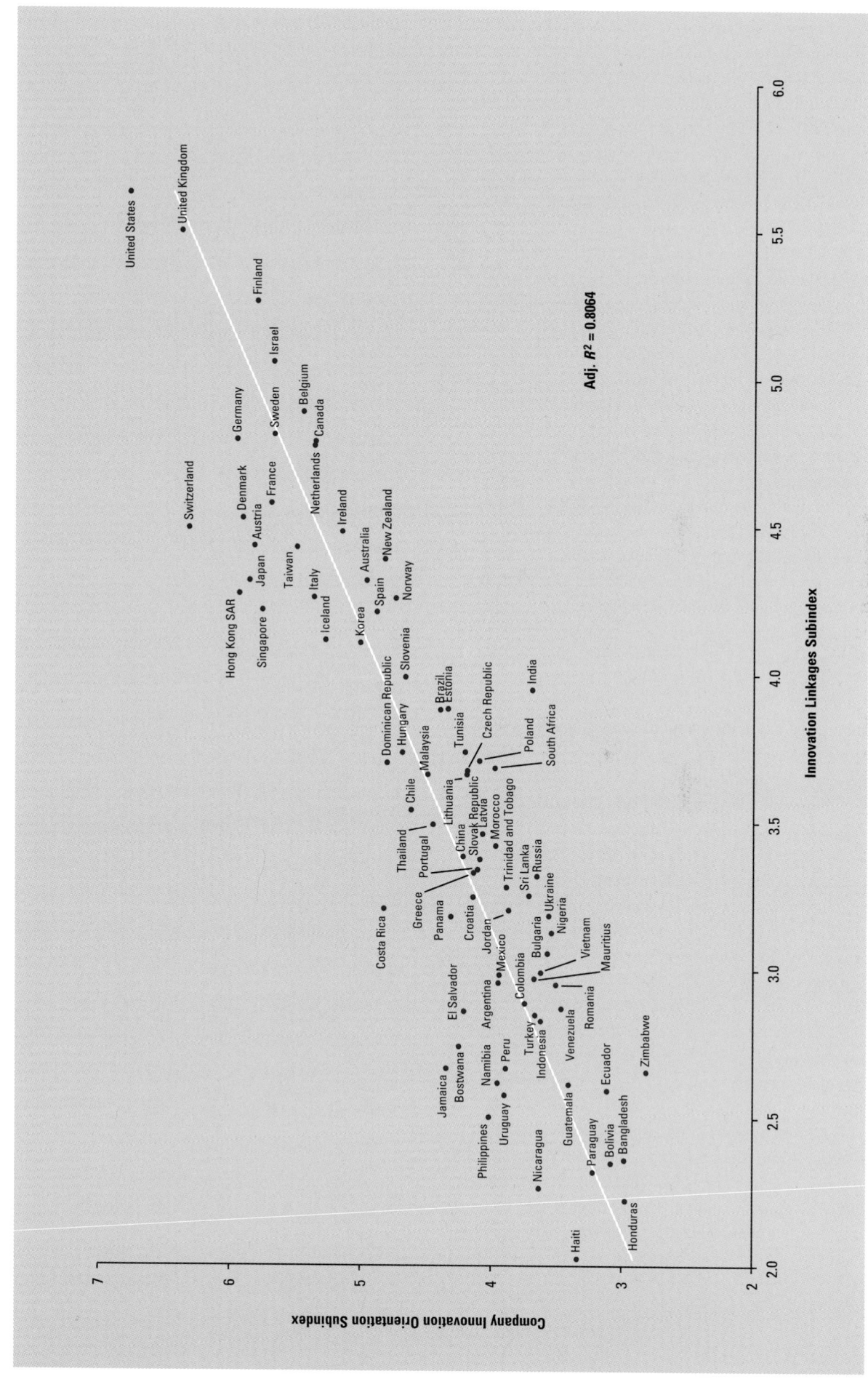

239

To gain insight into how innovative capacity has shifted around the globe, Table 2 provides a comparison of our national innovative capacity index (NICI) for 2001 and 2002. To make the results comparable, we use the data from the Survey for each year but impose the same model for both years. In other words, we recalculated innovative capacity rankings for 2001 using last year's data and using the model developed for this year's ranking.

Across the world, absolute innovative capacity seems to be improving, with nearly all countries experiencing improvements in innovative capacity over the last year. Not surprising, per capita patenting is also rising. Countries experiencing a decline in their NICI ranking between 2001 and 2002 often have improved on an *absolute* basis but have failed to advance as rapidly as other nations within the same tier. For example, Australia's decline from 7th to 17th over the last year is due to the fact that its improvements in the company innovation orientation subindex as well as the linkages subindex are far behind that of the other top 20 innovators. However, despite some substantial shifts in rankings (such as for Australia and Japan),[12] the relative rankings of most countries have remained relatively stable: the United States, United Kingdom, Germany, and Finland still comprise the top 4 nations, and lagging OECD countries such as Italy and Spain remain outside the top 20.

Innovative capacity, competitiveness, and prosperity

We are now in a position to explore the complex interplay between innovative capacity, competitiveness, and economywide prosperity. We begin, in Figures 5 and 6, by comparing the innovative capacity ranking with the overall Microeconomic Competitiveness Index and with GDP per capita, a summary measure of prosperity.

The innovative capacity index is highly correlated with the overall Microeconomic Competitiveness Index (the correlation is just over 0.9). A high level of innovative capacity is integral to achieving the high levels of productivity necessary to achieve and sustain overall competitiveness. Innovative capacity and competitiveness are linked even for lower-income countries. The ability and incentive to embrace new technology is now a *sine qua non* of international competition.

Although most countries are positioned quite close to the regression line, interesting groups of outliers stand out. Among leading nations, the United States' razor-thin leadership in overall competitiveness contrasts with its significant (and stable) advantage in innovative capacity.

Table 2: 2001 versus 2002 innovative capacity rankings (common sample and methodology)

Country	2002 NICI	2001 NICI (Using 2002 Formula)	Change in Innovative Capacity
United States	30.98	27.38	3.60
United Kingdom	29.66	24.90	4.76
Finland	29.075	26.14	2.91
Germany	28.52	24.62	3.90
Japan	28.28	24.12	4.16
Switzerland	27.89	24.97	2.92
Sweden	27.86	24.47	3.38
Taiwan	27.76	24.22	3.54
Canada	27.64	23.93	3.70
Singapore	27.59	24.23	3.36
Netherlands	27.31	23.91	3.40
Denmark	27.14	23.48	3.66
France	27.12	24.72	2.41
Austria	27.03	23.25	3.78
Israel	26.82	23.77	3.05
Belgium	26.75	23.09	3.66
Australia	26.58	24.81	1.78
Iceland	26.49	22.79	3.69
Norway	26.35	22.74	3.61
Ireland	26.22	22.90	3.32
Italy	26.00	21.79	4.22
Korea	25.92	21.55	4.37
Spain	24.95	21.54	3.41
New Zealand	24.32	20.41	3.91
Slovenia	24.11	19.07	5.04
Portugal	23.62	19.35	4.27
Hungary	23.28	19.32	3.96
Estonia	22.97	19.34	3.63
South Africa	22.34	19.28	3.05
Lithuania	22.33	17.75	4.58
Czech Republic	22.25	18.64	3.62
Brazil	22.21	18.67	3.54
Russian Federation	21.89	18.59	3.30
Poland	21.87	18.61	3.26
China	21.87	17.48	4.39
Greece	21.75	17.21	4.54
Costa Rica	21.74	17.89	3.85
Malaysia	21.67	15.93	5.74
Slovak Republic	21.63	18.37	3.25
Chile	21.33	18.26	3.07
India	21.00	17.15	3.85
Latvia	20.91	17.51	3.40
Thailand	20.59	15.99	4.60
Ukraine	20.56	18.15	2.41
Romania	20.10	15.35	4.76
Dominican Republic	19.79	13.71	6.08
Bulgaria	19.58	15.96	3.63
Mexico	19.50	15.94	3.56
Argentina	19.30	16.90	2.40
Vietnam	19.14	13.82	5.32
Turkey	19.13	17.17	1.96
Mauritius	18.98	15.53	3.45
Sri Lanka	18.98	14.43	4.55
Panama	18.95	16.95	2.00
Trinidad and Tobago	18.95	17.87	1.08
Indonesia	18.48	15.21	3.27
Philippines	18.08	15.29	2.78
Colombia	18.05	15.05	2.99
Peru	17.66	14.13	3.53
Uruguay	17.46	16.18	1.29
Venezuela	17.41	13.43	3.98
El Salvador	16.64	12.49	4.15
Nicaragua	16.08	12.87	3.20
Guatemala	16.07	12.67	3.40
Ecuador	15.75	11.94	3.81
Zimbabwe	15.68	12.42	3.26
Paraguay	15.47	12.95	2.51
Bangladesh	15.23	11.19	4.04
Honduras	15.17	11.54	3.63
Bolivia	14.60	11.48	3.12
Average	**22.21**	**18.64**	**3.57**

Figure 5: The relationship between the innovative capacity index and the Microeconomic Competitiveness Index

$y = 5.2415x - 154.98$
$R^2 = 0.6819$

2002 Innovative Capacity Index

2002 Microeconomic Competitiveness Index

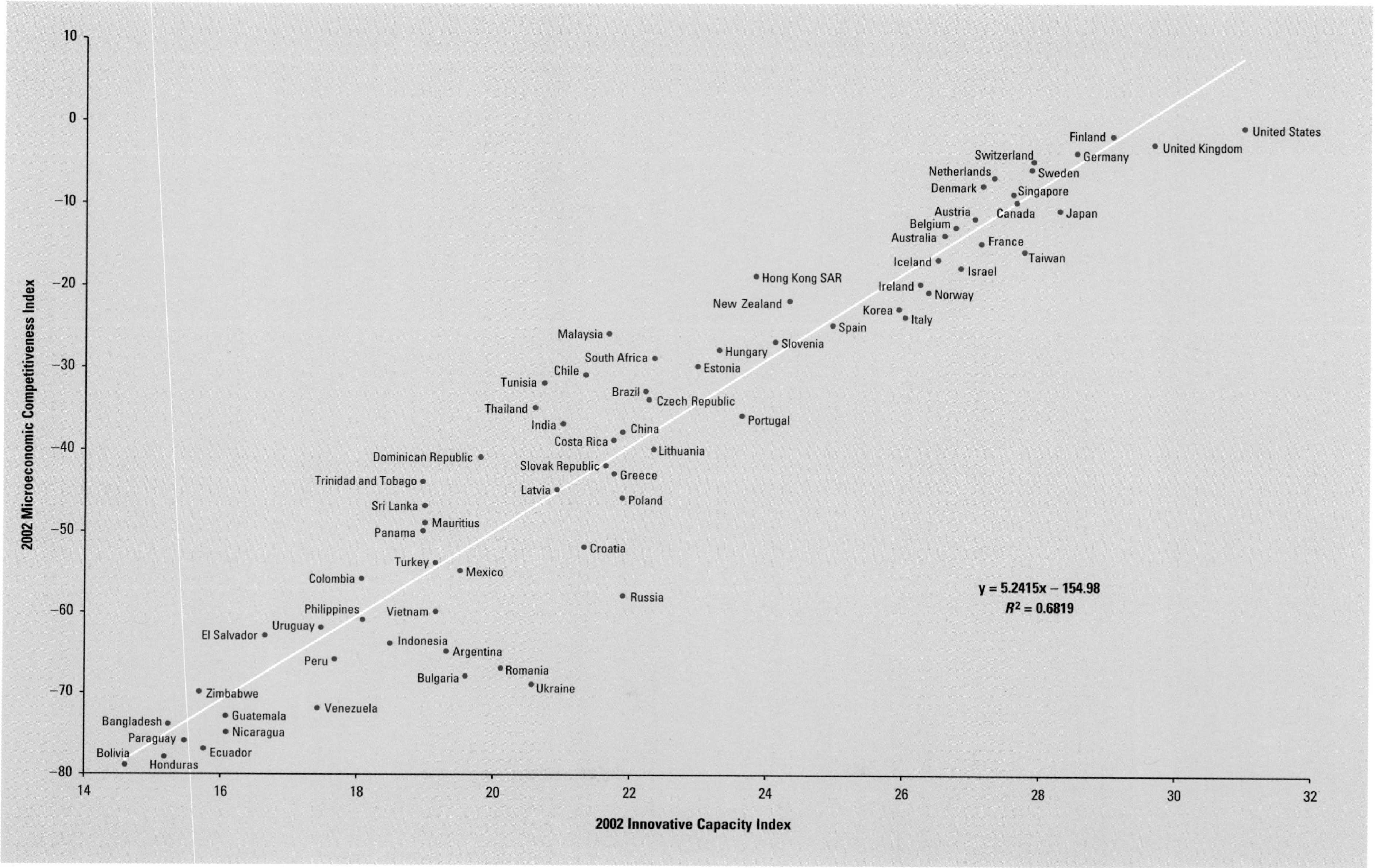

Figure 6: The relationship between innovative capacity and GDP per capita

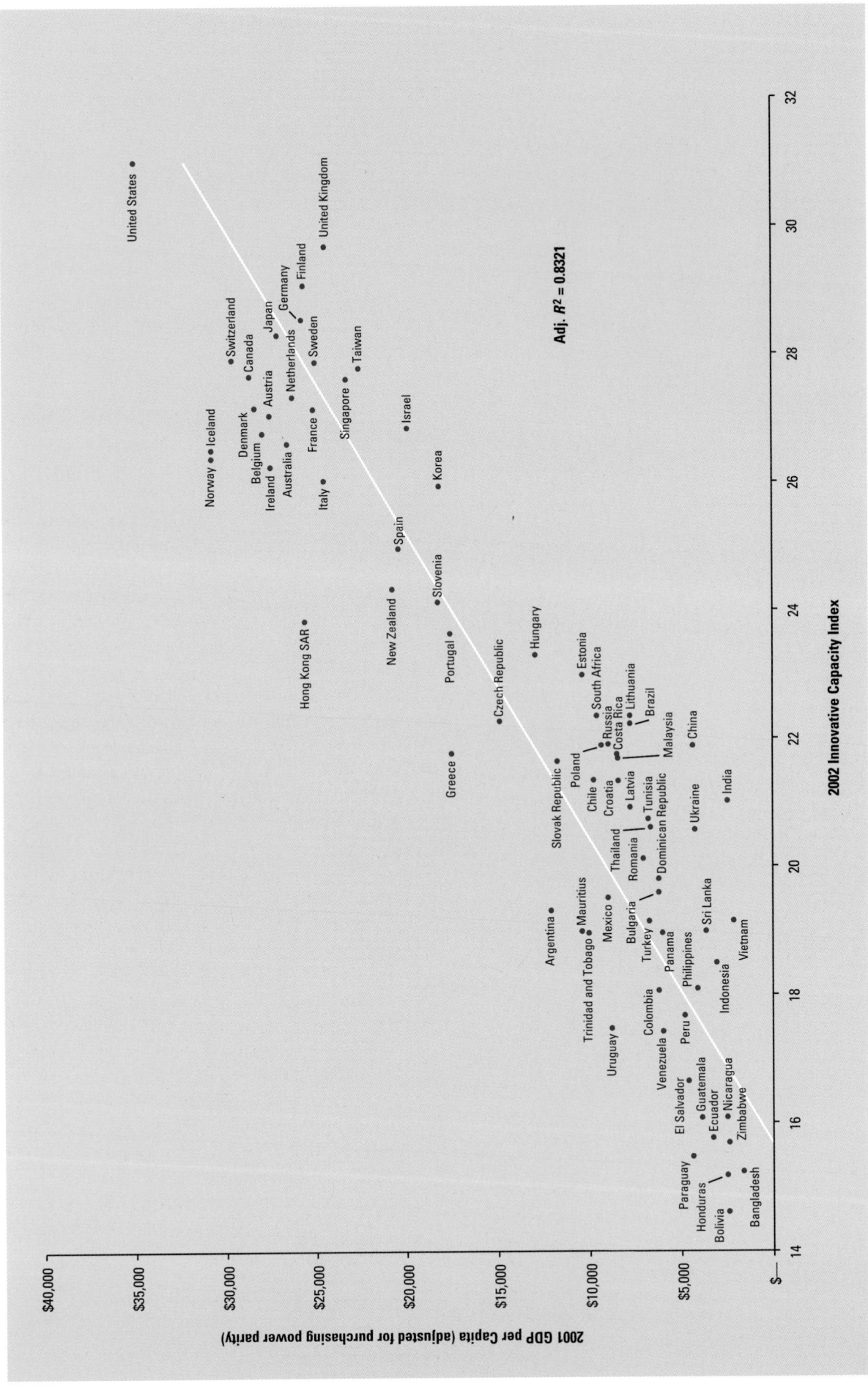

The largest discrepancies between the level of innovative capacity and the level of competitiveness arise in a group of eastern European countries (Ukraine, Romania, Bulgaria, and Russia), which score much lower on competitiveness than on innovative capacity, which is elevated because of their substantial science and engineering workforces. A chief disappointment of the post–Cold War era has been the inability of the former Soviet bloc nations to leverage their legacy and upgrade innovative capacity. An even bigger disappointment has been their slow progress on overall competitiveness. Another outlier country is Malaysia, with a level of competitiveness substantially above its measured level of innovative capacity. Malaysia still competes largely as a low-cost assembler. Its relative weakness in innovative capacity, despite some highly visible national projects focused on advanced technology, highlights the challenges that Malaysia will face in sustaining long-term prosperity.

Turning to the comparison between innovative capacity and GDP per capita, the relationship is still strong but not as close as the relationship with competitiveness.[13] A number of distinct development models seem to be present, even among leading nations. Some advanced economies, such as the United Kingdom, Finland, and Israel, developed a level of innovative capacity *ahead of the overall competitiveness of the economy*. In these countries, increases in innovative capacity reflected public- and private-sector consensus about the priority of innovation in driving long-term competitiveness. For example, Finland's current prosperity can be tied closely to investments from the early 1980s onward that have nurtured the development of the telecommunications cluster, stepped-up investment in basic research, and improved advanced education, among other things.

In contrast, countries such as Norway and Greece have continued to rely on favorable natural resources or proximity to major markets. Despite increasing evidence of the role of innovation in long-term prosperity, these countries have as yet made little change in their economic development strategies, raising the possibility of long-term stagnation. Finally, several leading nations, such as France, are located close to the regression line, suggesting a "balanced" path in which innovative capacity and the overall environment for productivity progress at roughly the same rate.

The United States continues to lead the world in innovative capacity, competitiveness, and current GDP per capita. The leadership of the United States in innovative capacity is more pronounced than its leadership in competitiveness because of weakness in areas such as education and environmental standards. Policymakers in the United States remain highly focused on innovative capacity at both the federal and regional levels, which bodes well for sustaining US prosperity. The greater US challenge today seems to be in addressing its weaknesses in other areas.

Creating versus absorbing new technology

Although innovative capacity and competitiveness are related even among countries with low incomes, the initial challenge for developing countries is to access and exploit technology from elsewhere. Effective technology absorption is a precursor to the development of the capacity to innovate at the international frontier. Many of the same attributes affect the ability to absorb technology as affect the ability to create technology. However, it is revealing to separate the two, especially for lower-income nations.

For all countries below median income in our sample (less than US$ 8,900 per year), we computed a "technology absorptive capacity" score by adding together Survey responses to two questions seeking to establish:

- the prevalence of foreign technology licensing, and
- the ability to absorb foreign technology.

Although imperfect, these measures provide a summary of the extent to which foreign technology is accessed in a country. We then plot this score against the 2002 GCR innovative capacity score in Figure 7. Perhaps not surprisingly, there is a close relationship between absorptive and innovative capacity. Also, countries appear to differ in the balance among activities. Notably, among lower-income countries, India registers the highest absorptive capacity score but a modest level of innovative capacity, trailing countries such as Malaysia. In contrast, the pattern for China is the opposite: China scores high on innovative relative to absorptive capacity. Though most analyses of China and India assume that their aggressive approach to technology reflect similar strategies, these findings suggest a more subtle relationship: India's positioning has been based more on *exploiting* global technology, while China is making systematic investments (relative to its level of development) in *developing* global technology.

Figure 8 plots technology absorptive capacity against GDP per capita. The results are revealing. India, Malaysia, Thailand, and Brazil register an ability to exploit global technology far higher than would be predicted by their current level of economic development. Conversely, many other Latin American and eastern European nations register a low level of technology absorptive capacity relative to income. Interestingly, while China is a bit above the regression line linking absorptive capacity and GDP per capita, its rapid improvement in per capita income over the last decade has resulted in a position where its ability to absorb foreign technology is now roughly consistent with the level of prosperity it has achieved.

Figure 7: The relationship between technology absorptive capacity and innovative capacity, lower-income countries

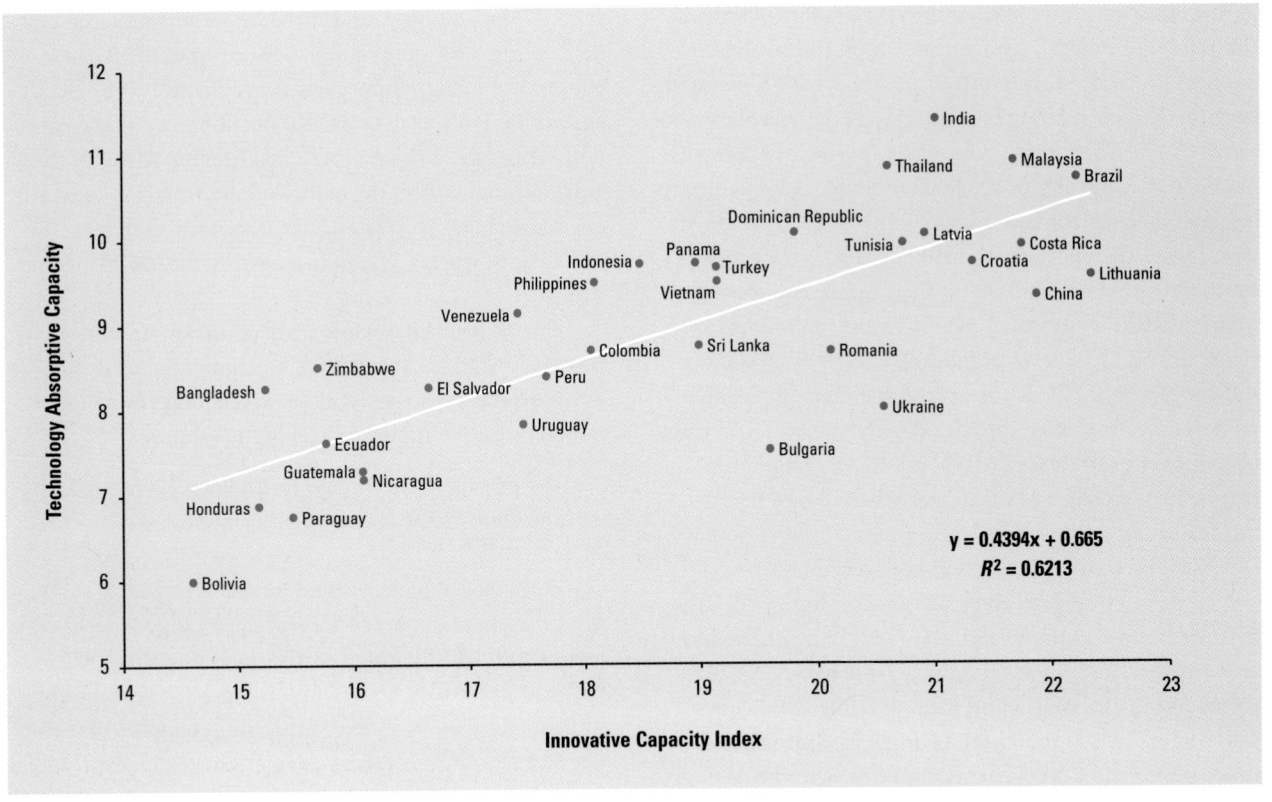

Figure 8: The relationship between technology absorptive capacity and 2001 GDP per capita, lower-income countries

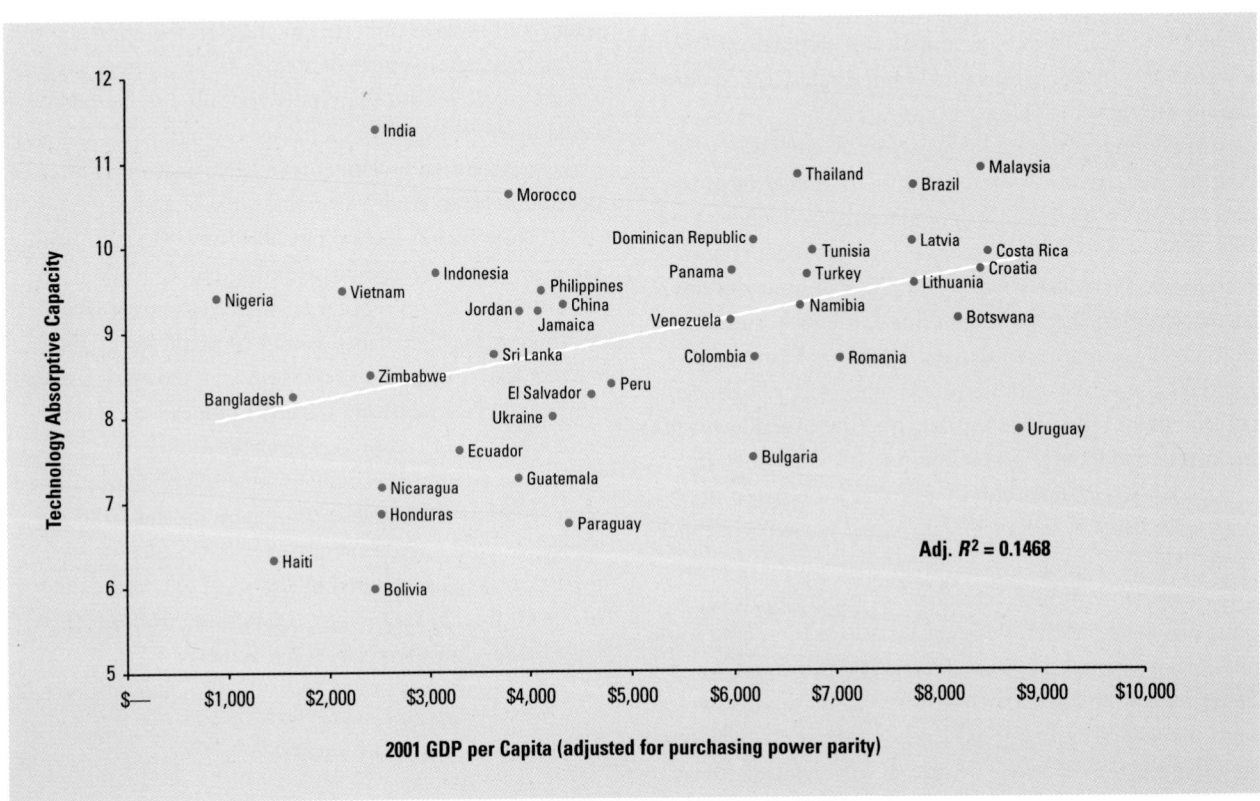

Conclusions

Innovation has become perhaps the single most important source of competitiveness in advanced economies, and building innovative capacity has a strong relationship to a country's overall competitiveness and level of prosperity. The national innovative capacity framework allows a detailed examination of sources of the large and persistent differences across countries in innovation performance. This chapter provides an assessment of the comparative performance in national innovative capacity around the world in 2002, providing a scorecard for national policy-makers about their relative standing and policy priorities. Although the data available and feasible statistical procedures are limited by the inherent difficulties in measuring innovation and its causes, the rankings are consistent with our knowledge about individual countries and provide insight into the strengths and challenges facing both advanced and emerging economies.

Those economies, such as Finland and Singapore, that have proactively built innovative capacity have prospered. In contrast, limited investment in innovative capacity has retarded the competitive potential of countries such as Spain and New Zealand. The continuing economic uncertainty in Latin America, contrasted with the rapid rebound experienced by leading East Asian economies after the 1998 Asian flu, highlights the crucial importance of innovative capacity to long-term economic prosperity.

Notes

1 For a complete exposition of the national innovative capacity framework, see Furman, Porter, and Stern (2001) and Porter, Stern, and Council on Competitiveness (1999). While innovative capacity has long been a subject of interest (Pavitt 1980; Suarez-Villa 1993), we offer a new framework that synthesizes and extends three areas of prior theory: ideas-driven endogenous growth (Romer 1990), cluster-based national industrial competitive advantage (Porter 1990), and national innovation systems (Nelson 1993).

2 For a more complete exposition of the diamond framework and its role in understanding the origins of national competitive advantage, see Porter (1990; 1998).

3 We sum patents from the two most recent years in order to smooth short-term fluctuations.

4 For a thorough discussion of the use of patenting and international patenting data (and alternatives) in studying the causes and consequences of innovation, see Furman, Porter, and Stern (2001). Also, Trajtenberg (1990) provides a thorough discussion of the role of patents in understanding innovative activity, stretching back to their use by Schmookler (1966) and noting the ever-increasing use of patent data by scholars in recent years (eg, Griliches 1984; 1990; 1994). The use of international patents also has precedent in prior work comparing international inventive activity (see Dosi, Pavitt, and Soete 1990; Eaton and Kortum, 1996).

5 See Appendix D for the coefficients from these "weighted" regression specifications.

6 This specification is simply the "ideas" production function, as developed in endogenous growth theory (Romer 1990). See Porter and Stern (2000) for a full derivation of our empirical formulation.

7 Although controlling for differences in GDP per capita is feasible in this regression (and we have used this formulation in our related work), the focus here is on explaining the drivers of prosperity. We focus our analysis on measures more closely related to the microeconomic foundations of competitiveness.

8 More precisely, we first take the natural logarithm of all of these variables, to smooth out the variation in country size and also to provide for easily interpretable coefficient estimates. Science and engineering resources are drawn from several data sources, as summarized in *World Development Indicators*. Specifically, data for OECD countries are drawn from the OECD Main Science and Technology Indicators, Latin American data are drawn from the RICYT, and the Asian data are drawn primarily from the science and technology statistics from individual countries.

9 Although there is a close relationship between patenting and the Survey measures closely related to the innovative capacity framework, there is no statistical relationship between patenting and Survey variables distant from the framework. For example, after controlling for the baseline variables, overall measures of governance such as the "availability of an independent judiciary" and the "rarity of insider trading" have no statistical relationship to international patenting. Although not dispositive, the absence of correlation between patenting and measures distant from the national innovative capacity framework increases our confidence in our specification and statistical approach.

10 While our prior work emphasizes the conceptual link between the national innovation environment and company strategy (Porter and Stern 2001), this chapter, exploiting nuanced measures available from the Survey, represents the first quantitative study of the contribution of corporate practices and orientation to national innovative capacity.

11 If the company innovation orientation score for each nation is plotted against the sum of the innovation policy, clusters, and linkages scores, a similar graph emerges; we break out the individual relationships to highlight the closeness of the relationship between company Innovation orientation and the cluster environment and the strength of linkages scores (relative to the innovation policy score).

12 The shift observed for Japan between 2001 and 2002 is informative about the stability (and informativeness) of the innovative capacity rankings. When Japan ranked 12th in the 2001 rankings, we remarked that this result was both anomalous (as our earlier research that Japanese innovative capacity in the mid 1990s was at or near the global frontier) but explicable (since Japan's continued economic stagnation has diverted resources away from innovation and investment in linking institutions, etc.). The 2002 Microeconomic Competitiveness Index rankings bear out both concerns; although the 2001 result was somewhat anomalous, Japan has lost position competing with the United States for global leadership in innovative capacity.

13 Overall, the relationship between international patenting and the measures included in each of the subindexes holds across the country income distribution. Each subindex regression specification was repeated on two subsamples, composed of countries above or below median GDP per capita. Although specific estimates became more noisy (sometimes becoming marginally insignificant), no clear anomalies emerged (such as a reversal of the sign of a significant coefficient).

References

Dosi, G., K. Pavitt, and L. Soete. 1990. *The Economics of Technical Change and International Trade*. New York: New York University Press; distributed by Columbia University Press.

Eaton, J. and S. Kortum. 1996. "Trade in Ideas: Patenting & Productivity in the OECD," *Journal of International Economics* 40(3–4): 251–278.

Furman, J. L., M. E. Porter, and S. Stern. 2001. "The Determinants of National Innovative Capacity," *Research Policy* 31(6): 899–993.

Griliches, Z. 1984. *R&D, Patents, and Productivity*. Chicago: University of Chicago Press.

————. 1990. "Patent Statistics as Economic Indicators: A Survey," *Journal of Economic Literature* 92: 630–653.

————. 1994. "Productivity, R&D, and the Data Constraint," *American Economic Review* 84(1): 1–23.

Nelson, R., ed. 1993. *National Innovation Systems: A Comparative Analysis*. New York: Oxford University Press.

Pavitt, K. 1980. "Industrial R&D and the British Economic Problem," *R&D Management* 10: 149–158.

Porter, M. E. 1990. *The Competitive Advantage of Nations*. New York: Free Press.

————. 1998. "Clusters and Competition: New Agendas for Companies, Governments, and Institutions." In *On Competition*. Boston: Harvard Business School Press.

Porter, M. E. and S. Stern. 2000. "Measuring the 'Ideas' Production Function," NBER Working Paper No. 7891. Cambridge, MA: National Bureau of Economic Research.

————. 2001. "Innovation: Location Matters," *MIT Sloan Management Review*, 42(4): 28–36.

Porter, M. E., S. Stern, and Council on Competitiveness. 1999. *The New Challenge to America's Prosperity: Findings from the Innovation Index*, Washington, DC: Council on Competitiveness.

Romer, P. 1990. "Endogenous Technological Change," *Journal of Political Economy* 98: S71–S102.

Schmookler, J. 1996. *Innovation and Economic Growth*. Cambridge, MA: Harvard University Press.

Suarez-Villa, L. 1993. "The Dynamics of Regional Invention and Innovation: Innovative Capacity and Regional Change in the Twentieth Century," *Geographical Analysis* 25(2): 147–164.

Trajtenberg, M. 1990. "Patents as Indicators of Innovation," *Economic Analysis of Product Innovation*. Cambridge, MA: Harvard University Press.

World Bank. 2002. *World Development Indicators 2002*. Washington, DC: International Bank for Reconstruction and Development/The World Bank.

World Economic Forum. 2002. *Global Competitiveness Report 2001–2002*. New York: Oxford University Press.

Appendix A: Bilateral regressions for each of the four subindex areas

Dependent Variable — Log of U.S. Patents, 2000-2001

Independent Variables	Baseline			Innovation Policy Variables			Cluster Variables			Linkages Variables			Company Innovation Orientation Variables		
	Coeff	t-stat	adj. R^2	Coeff	t-stat	adj. R^2	Coeff	t-stat	adj. R^2	Coeff	t-stat	adj. R^2	Coeff	t-stat	adj. R^2
Log of Patent Stock Metric (patents issued between 1981 and 1995)	0.786	14.670	0.924												
Log of Population in 2001	0.143	1.730													
Log of Proportion of Full-time Employed Scientists and Engineers	0.374	3.590													
Intellectual Property Protection				0.389	2.940	0.932									
Quality of Math and Science Education				0.223	1.720	0.926									
Attractiveness of National Environment for Retaining Talented People				0.370	3.050	0.932									
Government R&D Tax Credits and Subsidies				0.450	3.740	0.936									
Government Procurement of Advanced Technology Products				0.475	2.890	0.931									
Presence of Demanding Regulatory Standards				0.611	3.460	0.935									
Effectiveness of Anti-Trust Policy				0.470	3.080	0.932									
Environmental Compliance Helps Long-Run Competitiveness				0.687	3.290	0.934									
Buyer Sophistication							0.636	4.610	0.942						
Local Supplier Quality							0.719	3.890	0.937						
Consumer Adoption of Latest Products							0.706	4.660	0.942						
State of Cluster Development							0.717	4.700	0.942						
Extent of Product and Process Collaboration							0.845	3.880	0.937						
Production Process Sophistication							0.862	5.780	0.945						
Extent of Locally Based Competitors							0.818	4.180	0.939						
Absorption of New Technology										0.788	4.720	0.942			
Quality of Scientific Research Institutions										0.581	3.260	0.933			
Local Availability of Specialized Research and Training Institutions										0.815	3.720	0.936			
University/Industry Research Collaboration										0.587	0.159	0.936			
Venture Capital Availability										0.595	4.200	0.939			
Nature of Competitive Advantage													0.577	4.210	0.940
Value Chain Presence of Exporting Firms													0.404	3.600	0.935
Extent of Branding for Exporting Companies													0.497	3.480	0.935
Capacity of Innovation													0.684	4.000	0.938
Extent of Marketing													0.633	3.450	0.935
Degree of Customer Orientation													0.704	3.970	0.938
Control of International Distribution													0.710	3.190	0.933
Breadth of International Markets													0.543	4.380	0.940
Company Spending on R&D													0.686	4.000	0.938
Extent of Staff Training													0.596	3.550	0.935
Pay Linked to Productivity													0.424	3.340	0.934
Willingness to Delegate Authority													0.472	3.010	0.932
Reliance on Professional Management													0.285	1.780	0.926
Quality of Management Schools													0.297	2.000	0.927

Appendix B: ANOVA analysis for each subindex area

	IP Subindex	Cluster Subindex	Linkages Subindex	CIO Subindex
	Adj. R^2	Adj. R^2	Adj. R^2	Adj. R^2
Intellectual Property Protection	0.4549			
Quality of Math and Science Education	0.3786			
Attractiveness of National Environment for Retaining Talented People	0.4191			
Government R&D Tax Credits and Subsidies	0.3209			
Government Procurement of Advanced Technology Products	0.235			
Presence of Demanding Regulatory Standards	0.4329			
Effectiveness of Anti-Trust Policy	0.3336			
Environmental Compliance Helps Long-Run Competitiveness	0.1222			
Buyer Sophistication		0.3661		
Local Supplier Quality		0.3424		
Consumer Adoption of Latest Products		0.2915		
State of Cluster Development		0.2377		
Extent of Product and Process Collaboration		0.2036		
Production Process Sophistication		0.4615		
Extent of Locally Based Competitors		0.1405		
Absorption of New Technology			0.2483	
Quality of Scientific Research Institutions			0.3171	
Local Availability of Specialized Research and Training Institutions			0.2561	
University/Industry Research Collaboration			0.2792	
Venture Capital Availability			0.2556	
Nature of Competitive Advantage				0.3649
Value Chain Presence of Exporting Firms				0.4255
Extent of Branding for Exporting Companies				0.4158
Capacity of Innovation				0.4164
Extent of Marketing				0.3799
Degree of Customer Orientation				0.2521
Control of International Distribution				0.1878
Breadth of International Markets				0.4315
Company Spending on R&D				0.3513
Extent of Staff Training				0.3764
Pay Linked to Productivity				0.2453
Willingness to Delegate Authority				0.3179
Reliance on Professional Management				0.3503
Quality of Management Schools				0.3884

Appendix C: Regressions for each of the four subindexes

Innovation Policy Subindex

Regression Statistics

Adj. R^2	0.9382
Observations	69

	Coef.	Std. Error	t-stat	P-value
Intercept	−5.1150	1.0335	−4.9500	0.0000
Log (Patent Stock Metric)	0.6608	0.0648	10.1900	0.0000
Log (S&E Proportion)*	0.3170	0.9523	3.3300	0.0010
Log (Population)	0.2418	0.9402	2.5700	0.0130
Intellectual Property Protection	0.0982	0.1591	0.6200	0.5400
Government R&D Tax Credits and Subsidies	0.2964	0.1478	2.0000	0.0490
Environmental Compliance Helps Long-Run Competitiveness	0.3894	0.2354	1.6500	0.1030

Cluster Innovation Environment SubIndex

Regression Statistics

Adj. R^2	0.9500
Observations	69

	Coef.	Std. Error	t-stat	P-value
Intercept	−5.6361	0.7458	−7.5600	0.0000
Log (Patent Stock Metric)	0.5794	0.0574	10.0900	0.0000
Log (S&E Proportion)*	0.2941	0.0853	3.4500	0.0010
Log (Population)	0.1729	0.0818	2.1100	0.0380
Buyer Sophistication	0.3103	0.1607	1.9300	0.0580
State of Cluster Development	0.4515	0.1609	2.8100	0.0070
Extent of Locally Based Competitors	0.3617	0.2161	1.6700	0.0990

Linkages SubIndex

Regression Statistics

Adj. R^2	0.9420
Observations	69

	Coef.	Std. Error	t-stat	P-value
Intercept	−4.8123	0.7049	−6.8300	0.0000
Log (Patent Stock Metric)	0.5964	0.0623	9.5800	0.0000
Log (S&E Proportion)*	0.2348	0.0998	2.3500	0.0220
Log (Population)	0.2690	0.0800	3.3600	0.0010
Local Availability of Specialized Research & Training Institutions	0.5015	0.2369	2.1200	0.0380
Venture Capital Availability	0.4376	0.1568	2.7900	0.0070

Company Innovation Orientation SubIndex

Regression Statistics

Adj. R^2	0.9487
Observations	69

	Coef.	Std. Error	t-stat	P-value
Intercept	−6.2520	0.8664	−7.2200	0.0000
Log (Patent Stock Metric)	0.5252	0.0707	7.4300	0.0000
Log (S&E Proportion)*	0.3431	0.0919	3.7300	0.0000
Log (Population)	0.3693	0.0817	4.5200	0.0000
Nature of Competitive Advantage	0.4452	0.1338	3.3300	0.0010
Extent of Marketing	0.3296	0.1763	1.8700	0.0660
Pay Linked to Productivity	0.3176	0.1154	2.7500	0.0080

• Log of Proportion of Full-Time Employed Scientists and Engineers

Appendix D-1: Alternative regressions weighted by number of respondents

Country	Baseline NICI rank	Baseline NICI index	Country	Weighted NICI rank	Weighted NICI index	Scientific and engineering manpower subindex	Innovation policy subindex	Cluster innovation environment subindex	Innovation linkages subindex	Company innovation orientation subindex
United States	1	30.98	United States	1	36.80	8.33	5.15	8.56	6.80	7.96
United Kingdom	2	29.66	United Kingdom	2	35.24	7.89	5.03	8.09	6.63	7.61
Finland	3	29.05	Finland	3	34.51	8.12	5.25	7.90	6.34	6.90
Germany	4	28.52	Germany	4	33.92	8.04	5.13	7.75	5.74	7.25
Japan	5	28.28	Japan	5	33.21	8.56	4.76	7.68	5.12	7.10
Switzerland	6	27.89	Sweden	6	33.04	8.41	4.63	7.31	5.81	6.88
Sweden	7	27.86	Switzerland	7	32.70	8.03	4.80	7.09	5.39	7.39
Taiwan	8	27.76	Taiwan	8	32.69	7.87	5.02	8.21	5.33	6.25
Canada	9	27.64	Netherlands	9	32.55	7.85	4.97	7.41	5.74	6.58
Singapore	10	27.59	Canada	10	32.54	8.00	5.23	7.26	5.75	6.30
Netherlands	11	27.31	Singapore	11	32.45	7.86	5.51	7.35	5.10	6.64
Denmark	12	27.14	France	12	32.03	7.91	4.81	6.90	5.51	6.90
France	13	27.12	Denmark	13	31.91	8.15	4.69	6.61	5.46	7.00
Austria	14	27.03	Austria	14	31.79	7.75	4.97	6.95	5.32	6.81
Israel	15	26.82	Belgium	15	31.53	7.99	4.75	6.25	5.88	6.66
Belgium	16	26.75	Israel	16	31.43	7.36	5.28	5.97	6.10	6.71
Australia	17	26.58	Italy	17	31.19	7.19	4.07	8.31	5.10	6.51
Iceland	18	26.49	Australia	18	31.15	8.12	5.00	7.01	5.18	5.83
Norway	19	26.35	Norway	19	31.03	8.32	4.58	7.06	5.31	5.75
Ireland	20	26.22	Iceland	20	30.96	8.65	4.60	6.59	4.99	6.14
Italy	21	26.00	Ireland	21	30.90	7.67	4.77	6.98	5.44	6.05
Korea	22	25.92	Korea	22	30.52	7.67	4.61	7.44	4.95	5.85
Spain	23	24.95	Spain	23	29.43	7.35	4.42	6.71	5.07	5.88
New Zealand	24	24.32	Hong Kong SAR	24	28.56	4.54	4.35	7.67	5.19	6.81
Slovenia	25	24.11	New Zealand	25	28.41	7.69	3.90	6.18	5.13	5.51
Hong Kong SAR	26	23.82	Slovenia	26	27.90	7.68	4.41	5.66	4.78	5.38
Portugal	27	23.62	Portugal	27	27.79	7.37	4.75	6.89	4.04	4.74
Hungary	28	23.28	Hungary	28	27.13	7.27	4.38	5.61	4.47	5.40
Estonia	29	22.97	South Africa	29	26.46	7.05	4.10	6.01	4.45	4.86
South Africa	30	22.34	Estonia	30	26.43	7.68	3.89	5.31	4.68	4.87
Lithuania	31	22.33	Brazil	31	26.40	5.68	4.01	6.87	4.62	5.22
Czech Republic	32	22.25	Lithuania	32	25.83	7.62	3.47	5.60	4.42	4.72
Brazil	33	22.21	Czech Republic	33	25.67	7.21	4.12	5.21	4.35	4.78
Russian Federation	34	21.89	Malaysia	34	25.63	5.04	4.65	6.38	4.40	5.16
Poland	35	21.87	Poland	35	25.46	7.26	3.42	5.54	4.45	4.79
China	36	21.87	China	36	25.43	6.13	4.30	6.32	4.05	4.63
Greece	37	21.75	Costa Rica	37	25.41	6.28	4.08	5.57	3.80	5.68
Costa Rica	38	21.74	Greece	38	25.34	7.25	3.83	5.28	4.02	4.96
Malaysia	39	21.67	India	39	25.09	5.06	4.17	6.65	4.74	4.46
Slovak Republic	40	21.63	Chile	40	25.03	5.91	3.74	5.77	4.24	5.36
Chile	41	21.33	Russian Federation	41	24.93	8.13	3.20	5.65	3.95	3.99
Croatia	42	21.32	Slovak Republic	42	24.84	7.52	3.86	4.81	4.02	4.63
India	43	21.00	Croatia	43	24.58	7.31	3.92	4.63	3.87	4.86
Latvia	44	20.91	Thailand	44	24.50	4.63	4.04	6.51	4.19	5.13
Tunisia	45	20.72	Tunisia	45	24.48	4.82	4.95	5.30	4.51	4.90
Thailand	46	20.59	Latvia	46	24.12	6.99	3.52	4.79	4.16	4.64
Ukraine	47	20.56	Dominican Republic	47	23.60	3.91	3.99	5.62	4.47	5.63
Romania	48	20.10	Ukraine	48	23.43	7.66	2.95	5.07	3.80	3.94
Dominican Republic	49	19.79	Romania	49	23.07	7.34	3.30	5.00	3.52	3.90
Bulgaria	50	19.58	Mexico	50	23.00	5.37	3.83	5.60	3.54	4.65
Mexico	51	19.50	Panama	51	22.64	4.82	3.50	5.18	3.86	5.27
Argentina	52	19.30	Turkey	52	22.50	5.72	3.09	6.03	3.35	4.31
Vietnam	53	19.14	Sri Lanka	53	22.42	5.24	3.54	5.36	3.92	4.37
Turkey	54	19.13	Trinidad and Tobago	54	22.41	4.98	3.61	5.27	3.98	4.58
Mauritius	55	18.98	Argentina	55	22.40	6.37	2.79	5.04	3.51	4.69
Sri Lanka	56	18.98	Bulgaria	56	22.37	7.16	3.15	4.45	3.64	3.97
Panama	57	18.95	Mauritius	57	22.31	6.00	3.42	4.89	3.58	4.43
Trinidad and Tobago	58	18.95	Vietnam	58	21.94	5.61	3.39	5.47	3.58	3.89
Indonesia	59	18.48	Indonesia	59	21.70	5.86	2.79	5.38	3.38	4.28
Philippines	60	18.08	Colombia	60	21.55	4.38	3.80	5.40	3.44	4.52
Colombia	61	18.05	Philippines	61	21.32	5.16	3.00	5.36	3.01	4.79
Peru	62	17.66	Peru	62	20.62	5.43	3.09	4.37	3.17	4.56
Uruguay	63	17.46	Venezuela	63	20.45	5.27	2.86	4.70	3.41	4.22
Venezuela	64	17.41	Uruguay	64	20.34	5.17	3.36	4.19	3.08	4.54
El Salvador	65	16.64	El Salvador	65	19.62	3.85	3.11	4.50	3.46	4.70
Nicaragua	66	16.08	Nicaragua	66	19.12	4.30	2.98	4.81	2.73	4.30
Guatemala	67	16.07	Guatemala	67	19.06	4.32	3.16	4.37	3.14	4.07
Ecuador	68	15.75	Zimbabwe	68	18.81	3.91	3.13	5.11	3.22	3.43
Zimbabwe	69	15.68	Ecuador	69	18.71	4.42	3.18	4.23	3.06	3.82
Paraguay	70	15.47	Paraguay	70	18.11	4.61	2.99	3.92	2.77	3.83
Bangladesh	71	15.23	Bangladesh	71	18.00	3.93	2.95	4.85	2.85	3.43
Honduras	72	15.17	Honduras	72	17.86	4.32	3.19	4.21	2.65	3.49
Bolivia	73	14.60	Bolivia	73	17.22	4.23	2.59	3.92	2.81	3.67
Botswana	NA	NA	Botswana	NA	NA	NA	3.81	5.31	3.35	4.87
Haiti	NA	NA	Haiti	NA	NA	NA	2.43	3.22	2.45	3.70
Jamaica	NA	NA	Jamaica	NA	NA	NA	3.48	4.53	3.19	5.23
Jordan	NA	NA	Jordan	NA	NA	NA	3.77	5.04	3.84	4.44
Morocco	NA	NA	Morocco	NA	NA	NA	3.73	5.47	4.13	4.52
Namibia	NA	NA	Namibia	NA	NA	NA	4.15	5.15	3.18	4.56
Nigeria	NA	NA	Nigeria	NA	NA	NA	3.12	5.28	3.76	4.10

Appendix D-2: Alternative regressions weighted by consensus (within-country standard deviation)

Country	Baseline NICI rank	Baseline NICI index
United States	1	30.98
United Kingdom	2	29.66
Finland	3	29.05
Germany	4	28.52
Japan	5	28.28
Switzerland	6	27.89
Sweden	7	27.86
Taiwan	8	27.76
Canada	9	27.64
Singapore	10	27.59
Netherlands	11	27.31
Denmark	12	27.14
France	13	27.12
Austria	14	27.03
Israel	15	26.82
Belgium	16	26.75
Australia	17	26.58
Iceland	18	26.49
Norway	19	26.35
Ireland	20	26.22
Italy	21	26.00
Korea	22	25.92
Spain	23	24.95
New Zealand	24	24.32
Slovenia	25	24.11
Hong Kong SAR	26	23.82
Portugal	27	23.62
Hungary	28	23.28
Estonia	29	22.97
South Africa	30	22.34
Lithuania	31	22.33
Czech Republic	32	22.25
Brazil	33	22.21
Russian Federation	34	21.89
Poland	35	21.87
China	36	21.87
Greece	37	21.75
Costa Rica	38	21.74
Malaysia	39	21.67
Slovak Republic	40	21.63
Chile	41	21.33
Croatia	42	21.32
India	43	21.00
Latvia	44	20.91
Tunisia	45	20.72
Thailand	46	20.59
Ukraine	47	20.56
Romania	48	20.10
Dominican Republic	49	19.79
Bulgaria	50	19.58
Mexico	51	19.50
Argentina	52	19.30
Vietnam	53	19.14
Turkey	54	19.13
Mauritius	55	18.98
Sri Lanka	56	18.98
Panama	57	18.95
Trinidad and Tobago	58	18.95
Indonesia	59	18.48
Philippines	60	18.08
Colombia	61	18.05
Peru	62	17.66
Uruguay	63	17.46
Venezuela	64	17.41
El Salvador	65	16.64
Nicaragua	66	16.08
Guatemala	67	16.07
Ecuador	68	15.75
Zimbabwe	69	15.68
Paraguay	70	15.47
Bangladesh	71	15.23
Honduras	72	15.17
Bolivia	73	14.60
Botswana	NA	NA
Haiti	NA	NA
Jamaica	NA	NA
Jordan	NA	NA
Morocco	NA	NA
Namibia	NA	NA
Nigeria	NA	NA

Country	Weighted NICI rank	Weighted NICI index	Scientific and engineering manpower subindex	Innovation policy subindex	Cluster innovation environment subindex	Innovation linkages subindex	Company innovation orientation subindex
United States	1	30.75	8.33	3.96	6.40	5.35	6.70
United Kingdom	2	29.42	7.89	3.85	6.15	5.23	6.29
Finland	3	28.83	8.12	4.08	5.91	5.01	5.71
Germany	4	28.31	8.04	4.01	5.85	4.57	5.84
Japan	5	28.14	8.56	3.85	5.86	4.13	5.75
Switzerland	6	27.70	8.03	3.67	5.48	4.28	6.25
Taiwan	7	27.68	7.87	4.08	6.06	4.22	5.46
Sweden	8	27.60	8.41	3.51	5.54	4.57	5.56
Canada	9	27.50	8.00	4.13	5.51	4.56	5.30
Singapore	10	27.49	7.86	4.39	5.51	4.01	5.71
Netherlands	11	27.08	7.85	3.83	5.61	4.55	5.25
France	12	26.94	7.91	3.76	5.30	4.36	5.60
Denmark	13	26.93	8.15	3.58	5.07	4.31	5.82
Austria	14	26.86	7.75	3.84	5.30	4.23	5.75
Israel	15	26.66	7.36	4.28	4.63	4.81	5.59
Belgium	16	26.52	7.99	3.69	4.85	4.65	5.34
Australia	17	26.46	8.12	3.88	5.43	4.11	4.92
Iceland	18	26.32	8.65	3.54	5.01	3.91	5.22
Norway	19	26.19	8.32	3.61	5.34	4.17	4.75
Ireland	20	26.09	7.67	3.82	5.25	4.26	5.09
Italy	21	25.82	7.19	3.17	6.13	4.06	5.26
Korea	22	25.81	7.67	3.72	5.57	3.91	4.95
Spain	23	24.80	7.35	3.51	5.13	4.01	4.80
New Zealand	24	24.15	7.69	2.92	4.77	4.05	4.71
Slovenia	25	24.01	7.68	3.47	4.42	3.81	4.63
Hong Kong SAR	26	23.67	4.54	3.34	5.84	4.06	5.90
Portugal	27	23.55	7.37	3.77	5.16	3.17	4.08
Hungary	28	23.19	7.27	3.47	4.23	3.56	4.66
Estonia	29	22.88	7.68	3.02	4.14	3.70	4.34
Lithuania	30	22.25	7.62	2.80	4.17	3.48	4.18
Czech Republic	31	22.19	7.21	3.26	4.03	3.51	4.18
South Africa	32	22.19	7.05	3.15	4.56	3.50	3.93
Brazil	33	22.12	5.68	3.21	5.16	3.71	4.36
Russian Federation	34	21.88	8.13	2.65	4.25	3.17	3.67
China	35	21.86	6.13	3.52	4.76	3.23	4.23
Poland	36	21.77	7.26	2.73	4.17	3.53	4.07
Costa Rica	37	21.66	6.28	3.28	4.26	3.07	4.77
Greece	38	21.66	7.25	3.07	4.08	3.17	4.09
Malaysia	39	21.62	5.04	3.76	4.87	3.49	4.47
Slovak Republic	40	21.57	7.52	3.11	3.64	3.22	4.09
Chile	41	21.24	5.91	2.95	4.41	3.38	4.59
Croatia	42	21.24	7.31	3.22	3.51	3.10	4.10
India	43	20.93	5.06	3.44	5.01	3.76	3.65
Latvia	44	20.83	6.99	2.85	3.64	3.29	4.06
Tunisia	45	20.65	4.82	3.97	4.12	3.56	4.18
Ukraine	46	20.53	7.66	2.46	3.80	3.04	3.57
Thailand	47	20.53	4.63	3.24	4.90	3.33	4.43
Romania	48	20.08	7.34	2.71	3.70	2.82	3.52
Dominican Republic	49	19.71	3.91	3.26	4.25	3.52	4.76
Bulgaria	50	19.53	7.16	2.54	3.34	2.92	3.58
Mexico	51	19.45	5.37	3.15	4.17	2.85	3.91
Argentina	52	19.23	6.37	2.25	3.87	2.83	3.92
Vietnam	53	19.17	5.61	2.84	4.21	2.85	3.65
Turkey	54	19.10	5.72	2.51	4.49	2.73	3.64
Mauritius	55	18.88	6.00	2.71	3.71	2.83	3.63
Sri Lanka	56	18.88	5.24	2.78	4.09	3.09	3.68
Trinidad and Tobago	57	18.85	4.98	2.86	4.04	3.12	3.86
Panama	58	18.81	4.82	2.77	3.95	3.02	4.24
Indonesia	59	18.41	5.86	2.28	3.98	2.70	3.60
Philippines	60	18.01	5.16	2.43	4.06	2.38	3.97
Colombia	61	17.97	4.38	3.05	4.09	2.76	3.70
Peru	62	17.59	5.43	2.51	3.25	2.55	3.86
Uruguay	63	17.39	5.17	2.65	3.24	2.46	3.87
Venezuela	64	17.34	5.27	2.34	3.57	2.74	3.42
El Salvador	65	16.54	3.85	2.39	3.39	2.72	4.20
Nicaragua	66	16.02	4.30	2.44	3.53	2.15	3.59
Guatemala	67	15.99	4.32	2.55	3.26	2.49	3.38
Ecuador	68	15.68	4.42	2.65	3.07	2.48	3.06
Zimbabwe	69	15.60	3.91	2.49	3.89	2.52	2.78
Paraguay	70	15.41	4.61	2.44	2.97	2.21	3.19
Bangladesh	71	15.20	3.93	2.44	3.63	2.24	2.97
Honduras	72	15.13	4.32	2.61	3.13	2.12	2.95
Bolivia	73	14.53	4.23	2.17	2.86	2.24	3.04
Botswana	NA	NA	NA	3.02	4.06	2.60	4.21
Haiti	NA	NA	NA	2.04	2.40	1.92	3.34
Jamaica	NA	NA	NA	2.77	3.48	2.54	4.27
Jordan	NA	NA	NA	2.96	3.79	3.05	3.85
Morocco	NA	NA	NA	3.02	4.08	3.25	3.96
Namibia	NA	NA	NA	3.27	3.93	2.49	3.93
Nigeria	NA	NA	NA	2.58	3.96	2.98	3.53

CHAPTER 3.2

High-Tech Innovation and Future Productivity Growth: Does Supply Create Its Own Demand?

ROBERT J. GORDON, Northwestern University, National Bureau of Economic Research, and Centre for Economic Policy Research[1]

Introduction

No macroeconomic magnitude is more important for the future evolution of the economy than productivity growth, and none is harder to predict. Productivity growth forecasts are needed by monetary policymakers attempting to gauge the growth rate of potential output, the economy's "speed limit." So too is a predicted path of future productivity growth needed for forecasts of future government budgets, deficits, debt, and dates of potential Social Security crises, not to mention the future revenue and employment requirements that guide capital spending plans in every sector of private industry.

Yet, without exception, economists failed to forecast the marked acceleration of US productivity growth after 1995, just as they had failed to anticipate in advance the two-decade slowdown in productivity growth after 1972. With both of these major failures as precedents, it is surprising that there is such a widespread consensus that the post-1995 productivity revival will continue into the indefinite future—that is, that the productivity growth recorded from 1995 to 2002 is more relevant to the long-term future over the next decade or two than the more dismal precedent of 1972 to 1995. The very phrase "New Economy" connotes such a permanent change in regime, in contrast to a hypothetical alternative label, such as "bubble economy," that would treat the change in regime as temporary and short-lived. Is such an assumption of permanence in the productivity growth revival warranted? Did the revival contain onetime elements that are unlikely to be repeated?

Productivity growth and ICT investment

Important studies of the post-1995 productivity growth revival have concluded that its primary source, and perhaps its only source, was the post-1995 acceleration of growth in real investment in information and communication technology (ICT). This chapter begins with the record of US productivity growth, distinguishes between cyclical and structural elements of the post-1995 revival, and then reviews evidence on the role of ICT investment in achieving the revival. The major conclusion is that the magnitude of ICT investment's contribution to the productivity growth revival has been exaggerated; ICT deserves substantial credit, but not all the credit that it has previously received. In reaching this conclusion, we focus primarily on the example of the retail trade sector, which emerges both as a primary location of the revival in the United States and as by far the most important industry explaining why the United States enjoyed a revival while Europe did not.

Whether ICT investment explained half, most, or all of the US productivity growth revival, clearly a critical ingredient in predicting future productivity growth is a determination of whether ICT investment will soon return to the heady growth rates of the late 1990s, or instead that growth rested on unsustainable elements that are unlikely to be repeated. The core of the chapter is suggested by its subtitle, "Does Supply Create its Own Demand?" In an environment in which steady advances in chip-making technology create geometric increases in the *supply* of computer power, does the marketplace automatically generate a *demand* for all that new computer power? This chapter argues that supply does not *automatically* create its own demand, and that a continuing explosion of computer power over the next decade may lead to a steady decline in the share of nominal GDP devoted to current-dollar spending on ICT investment, rather than a return to the high growth rates of real ICT investment experienced in the 1990s. "The real problem is demand. It seems that the supercharged spending on technology between 1998 and 2000 owed much to the coincidence of business, product, and liquidity cycles" (*Financial Times* 2001).

Macro: The positive feedback loop

The treatment of supply and demand for ICT investment is divided into two parts, which, in shorthand, can be considered the "macro" component and the "micro" component. The macroeconomic environment of the late 1990s reflected a remarkable "positive feedback loop" in which four major factors each achieved historically unprecedented performance and, in doing so, fed back and reinforced the behavior of the others. The boom in ICT investment, created by a confluence of microeconomic supply and demand elements described separately, fueled the stock market boom and contributed to low inflation. The stock market provided cheap finance to spur the ICT investment boom and added to output growth through its wealth effect on consumer behavior. Low inflation made it possible for the Federal Reserve (the Fed) to avoid tight monetary policy, while monetary policy, by keeping interest rates relatively low, boosted the demand for ICT investment and supported the stock market boom. Each of these elements made the demand for ICT investment higher than it would have been otherwise, and created a larger response of real ICT investment to rapid declines in ICT prices than would have occurred without the macro positive feedback loop.

Micro: The unsustainable demand for ICT equipment in the late 1990s

An acceleration in the rate of decline of computer prices, made possible by a faster "Moore's Law" cycle in the development of new computer chips, kicked off the New Economy ICT boom of the late 1990s. Prices that fell more rapidly encouraged firms and consumers to replace old computers more quickly. Yet the demand for these ever-cheaper computers depended in part on the development of new reasons to buy them, and several factors, most notably the invention of the World Wide Web (WWW), spurred an explosion in demand that matched the expansion of supply. A continuing pace of technological development in the supply of computer power may not, however, generate a repeat occurrence of the demand for ICT equipment experienced in the late 1990s. Our analysis begins with the overhang of underutilized fiber-optic cable and telecom equipment, perhaps the greatest technological bubble in the history of the modern world. We continue with the surfeit of equipment no longer needed by failed e-commerce firms, the "dot.coms," the dimming prospect that the Internet will live up to its initial promise for either consumer e-commerce or business-to-business commerce, and our most important and controversial proposition that software innovation has failed to take advantage of explosive growth in hardware capacity, leaving both business firms and consumers lacking reasons to replace their old computers at anything like the pace that was common in the 1990s. The section on the micro demand for computer power can be summarized as saying "there can be many slips between the cup of semiconductor technology and the lip of economic performance."

The chapter begins with the bare facts about the productivity revival, the distinction between cyclical and structural components of the post-1995 revival, and the contribution of ICT investment to the revival. We then argue that previous studies may have overstated the importance of ICT investment in the revival and link this overstatement to the puzzling failure of Europe to achieve a productivity growth revival of its own. Whether the ICT investment boom was the sole cause of the productivity growth revival or only a large cause, its role in the revival was central, raising the question of whether it can recur in the future or was fundamentally a temporary phenomenon. The middle section of the chapter is devoted to the macro elements, the "positive feedback loop" that fed the economy's strength and created a greater response of demand for ICT equipment than would have occurred otherwise. The final section of the chapter is devoted to the micro elements of unsustainability in the late 1990s ICT investment boom.

Dimensions of the post-1995 productivity growth revival

This section describes the basic dimensions of US productivity behavior over the postwar period and in greater detail for the 1990s. We then turn to an analysis of the cyclical component of the late 1990s' productivity growth revival and to an interpretation of the more recent upsurge of productivity growth experienced in late 2001 and early 2002.

The record of productivity growth since 1950

Table 1 presents the basic dimensions of the post-1995 US productivity growth revival in contrast to the previous postwar period. The analysis is based on quarterly data for four sectors published by the US Bureau of Labor Statistics (BLS): nonfarm private business, manufacturing, and two subdivisions within manufacturing: durables and nondurables. In addition, data for nonfarm nonmanufacturing, although unpublished, can be calculated as a residual.[2] The left three columns of Table 1 exhibit annual growth rates of output per hour in each sector for the longer intervals divided in 1972:Q2 and 1995:Q4. The right three columns divide the most recent 1995–2002 interval into three subintervals divided in 2000:Q2 and 2001:Q3, quarters chosen to encompass the period of slow growth in real GDP.

Table 1: Annual growth rates of output per hour, 1950–2002, selected sectors and intervals, in percent

Sector	1950:Q2–1972:Q2	1972:Q2–1995:Q4	1995:Q4–2002:Q2	1995:Q4–2000:Q2	2000:Q2–2001:Q3	2001:Q3–2002:Q2
Nonfarm Private Business	2.66	1.42	2.53	2.59	0.68	5.46
Manufacturing	2.56	2.60	3.95	4.47	1.11	5.93
Durables	2.34	3.05	4.94	5.94	0.07	7.09
Nondurables	2.97	1.95	2.85	2.94	2.11	4.22
Nonfarm Nonmanufacturing	2.64	1.00	2.05	2.04	0.98	5.31

Source: Bureau of Labor Statistics. Calculation of nonfarm nonmanufacturing is explained in endnote 2.

Looking first at the broadest aggregate, the nonfarm private business sector in the top line, we see that the annual rate of productivity growth accelerated by 1.11 percentage points after 1995, and the rate achieved after 1995 of 2.53 percent almost matched the 2.66 rate of the earlier postwar era, 1950–1972. The post-1995 revival for nondurable manufacturing was similar, with a pickup of 0.90 percent and a post-1995 growth rate almost as fast as in 1950–1972. The pattern for durable manufacturing is different, with no slowdown at all but rather an initial acceleration after 1972 and an even greater second-stage acceleration after 1995. The residual nonfarm nonmanufacturing sector (most of the economy) did worse in 1995–2002 relative to pre-1972 than did the entire economy, simply because durable manufacturing did so much better. The post-1995 acceleration was 1.05 percent, but the post-1995 growth rate of 2.05 percent fell well short of the pre-1972 growth rate of 2.64 percent. A puzzle that has perplexed many observers, including Griliches (1994), is that, in the earlier postwar era, productivity growth proceeded at roughly equal rates in manufacturing and the rest of the economy (ie, the residual sector). This is validated in Table 1, but the 1972–1995 slowdown period was entirely concentrated in nonmanufacturing with no slow-

down at all in manufacturing. The post-1995 period witnessed a substantial recovery in nonmanufacturing, but not enough to close the gap with the manufacturing sector.

The right half of Table 1 decomposes the post-1995 period into the boom period of the late 1990s ending in 2000:Q2, the period of slow output growth over the following five quarters, followed by the recovery period after 2001:Q3. Productivity growth responded to the output growth slowdown by decelerating sharply during the five quarters of slow output growth, and in the durable manufacturing sector productivity growth was essentially zero during this interval. Then, when the economy recovered after 2001:Q3, productivity growth exploded to rates even faster than in 1995–2000 in each sector.

Cyclical dimensions of productivity growth

Ever since the early work of Hultgren (1960) and Okun (1962), economists have recognized and attempted to quantify the procyclical component of productivity growth. But the nature of this behavior is not widely understood, and it does not correspond to the official dates at which expansions end and recessions begin. As examined by Gordon (1993), productivity growth is cyclical because the change in hours of labor input lags behind changes in output, so that an acceleration or deceleration of output growth causes a short-run acceleration or deceleration of productivity growth. In addition, the elasticity of hours growth to output growth (relative to the trends in both hours and output) is less than unity, implying that productivity grows faster than its trend whenever output grows faster than its trend.

Several methods are available to separate the cyclical component of productivity from its underlying trend. The most straightforward method to estimate the trend in any time-series variable is the Hodrick-Prescott (1981) filter.[3] Figure 1 displays two different growth rates of output per hour for the aggregate US economy (the nonfarm private business sector). The colored line is simply a four-quarter moving average of aggregate productivity growth, while the black line is the Hodrick-Prescott trend.[4] The trend displays a more subtle version of postwar productivity growth history than the simple "fast-slow-fast" version of Table 1. Trend growth peaked in the early 1960s, slowed down steadily until about 1980, and then revived in stages through the late 1990s. Also visible in Figure 1 is an excess of actual over-trend productivity growth in the late 1990s, a shortfall below trend growth in 2001, and then a resurgence to above-trend growth in early 2002.

Table 2 summarizes the information in Figure 1 for decades prior to 1995 and three intervals since 1995. Prior to 1995 each decade exhibits small cyclical effects, alternating across decades. It is interesting that a period as long as a decade is not enough to extinguish the cyclical effect; this depends on economic conditions in the initial and

Figure 1: Output per hour in the nonfarm private business sector, actual change from four quarters prior and Hodrick-Prescott trend, 1960–2002, percentage changes at annual rate

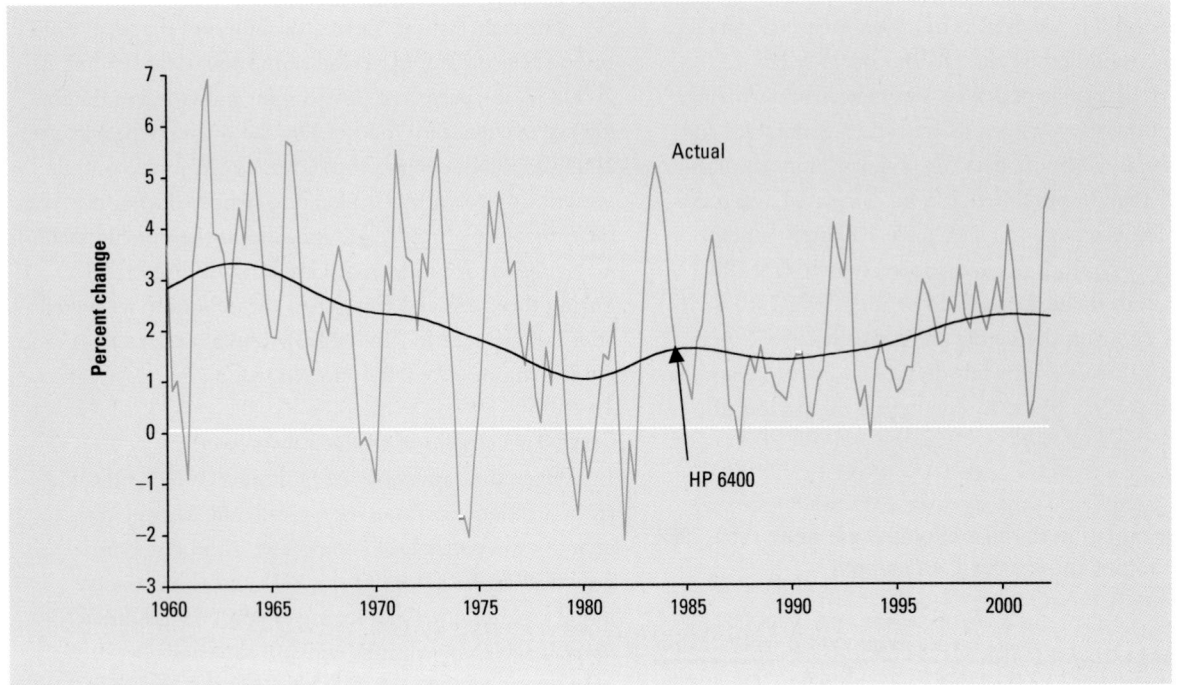

Sources: Bureau of Labor Statistics; author's research

terminal years chosen for each decade. Since 1995 there has been a positive cyclical effect during 1995–2000, then a negative cyclical effect for the five quarters of slow real GDP growth between mid 2000 and 2001:Q3, followed by a very strong cyclical growth resurgence in the final three quarters. The cyclical effect of 0.44 points for the 1995–2000 period is consistent with my previous writing, which argued that a significant fraction, perhaps one third, of the post-1995 productivity growth revival through mid 2000 could be interpreted as cyclical rather than structural.[5]

This leaves the final upsurge of productivity growth in late 2001 and early 2002 open to interpretation. Most commentators have interpreted this episode as indicating that trend growth may have accelerated again to 2.50 or even 2.75 percent at an annual rate. However, their optimism is countered by three historical precedents, as shown in Table 3. Very strong productivity growth was registered in the first four quarters of the economic recoveries that began in early 1975, late 1982, and early 1991, yet in each case the following two years registered dismal productivity growth at or below the trend rate for that period. These precedents make it likely that productivity growth will settle back at or below its trend value of 2.25 percent per year, displayed in Table 2. Stated another way, the initial quarters of a business recovery typically combine a jump in output growth with the lagged effect of firms to cut costs and reduce employment. Only after the recovery is well underway does hiring begin in earnest.

Table 2: Growth rates of output per hour, nonfarm private business sector, selected intervals, 1955–2002

Interval	Actual Growth	Trend Growth	Cyclical Effect
1955:Q4–1965:Q4	2.99	2.90	0.09
1965:Q4–1975:Q4	2.02	2.25	−0.23
1975:Q4–1985:Q4	1.44	1.33	0.11
1985:Q4–1995:Q4	1.39	1.54	−0.15
1995:Q4–2000:Q2	2.59	2.15	0.44
2000:Q2–2001:Q3	0.68	2.25	−1.57
2001:Q3–2002:Q2	5.46	2.22	3.24

Source: Author's research. The trend in the middle column refers to the same series as is plotted in Figure 1.

Table 3: Growth rates of output per hour, nonfarm private business sector, four quarters at start of recovery and next eight quarters

Interval	Initial Four Quarters	Next Eight Quarters
1975:Q1–1976:Q1	4.63	0.99
1982:Q3–1983:Q3	5.19	1.58
1991:Q1–1992:Q1	4.01	1.15
2001:Q3–2002:Q2	5.46	—

Source: Bureau of Labor Statistics

The contribution of high-tech investment to the productivity growth revival

The post-1995 productivity growth revival has generated a growth industry of its own, in the form of academic analyses of the sources of the revival. In this section we examine the latest decomposition of the sources of the revival by one of the leading research teams on this topic and then raise questions about their results.

The sources of growth

The leading studies of the interplay between ICT investment and the productivity growth revival are by Jorgenson and Stiroh (2000), Jorgenson (2001, 2002), and Oliner and Sichel (2000, 2001, 2002). The most recent results of Oliner and Sichel are presented in Table 4. Fortunately, this analysis over the post-1995 productivity growth revival, which extends through 2001, can be examined in a straightforward way without any need to separate changes in trend from cyclical effects, since the Oliner-Sichel 1995–2001 growth rate of 2.25 percent (Table 4, top line, middle column) is almost identical to the trend estimate for the same period in Table 2 above.[6] Stated another way, when the analysis includes both the positive cyclical effect for 1995–2000 and the negative cyclical effect for 2001, these effects exactly cancel out.

The Oliner-Sichel method is to start with labor productivity growth and then subtract the contribution of capital deepening and changes in labor quality, arriving at the growth rate of multifactor productivity (MFP) as a residual. Then the location of multifactor productivity growth by industry is examined, and the total of MFP growth is disaggregated into the portion occurring in the ICT sector and a residual for other sectors. The findings reported in Table 4 are very striking. The total post-1995 acceleration in labor productivity is *more than entirely*

explained by information technology investment, with nothing left over for the contribution of other types of capital or for any independent sources of the revival of growth in labor productivity and MFP growth. As shown in the right column, the total revival of labor productivity growth is 0.85 points, divided into contributions of 0.55 points of ICT capital deepening, 0.43 points of acceleration in MFP growth in the ICT industries, −0.10 contribution of capital deepening for non-ICT capital, and a −0.02 contribution of the acceleration of MFP growth in the non-ICT part of the economy. In short, Oliner and Sichel *overexplain* the post-1995 productivity growth revival without any reference to innovation or organizational improvements outside of the production and use of ICT capital. Their conclusion coincides to an uncanny degree of precision with that reached more than two years earlier by Gordon (2000).[7]

Has the contribution of high-tech investment been exaggerated? The Oliner-Sichel results do not imply that the only "action" in the economy has been located in sectors making computers, servers, peripherals, routers, software, and fiber-optic cable. Their contribution from the *use* of ICT equipment (0.55 points in Table 4) is higher than their contribution from the *production* of ICT equipment (0.43 points). There has clearly been great dynamism in some industrial sectors that make heavy use of computers. Numerous studies, especially those of Triplett and Bosworth (2002) and Nordhaus (2002b), pinpoint wholesale and retail trade and securities trading as the industries outside of ICT manufacturing where the productivity growth revival is most evident.

Two questions may be raised about the implication of Table 4, that the post-1995 productivity revival was a song with one note: namely the production and use of ICT equipment. First, the Oliner-Sichel technique requires that the full productivity payoff from the use of computers occurs at the exact moment that the computer is produced.[8] Leaving aside any delay between production and installation, they assume that the computer produces its ultimate productivity benefit on the first day of use. Numerous observers, led by David (1990), argue instead that there is a substantial time delay necessary for firms to make the organizational changes needed to take advantage of new hardware and software. If there is a substantial delay in the real world that is not taken into account by the Oliner-Sichel method, then they exaggerate the contribution of ICT capital-deepening to the post-1995 revival. A corollary is that, in years such as 2001 and 2002 when ICT investment has declined, there are substantial leftover benefits from the previous ICT boom of the late 1990s that may support productivity growth even if ICT investment remains in a slump.

Table 4: Contributions to growth in labor productivity by source, 1973–1995 versus 1995–2001 and post-1995 growth acceleration

	1973– 1995	1995– 2001	Post-1995 change
Labor Productivity	**1.40**	**2.25**	**0.85**
Contributions from:			
Capital Deepening	0.71	1.17	0.46
Information Technology Capital	0.42	0.97	0.55
Other Capital	0.30	0.20	-0.10
Labor Quality	**0.27**	**0.25**	**-0.02**
Multifactor Productivity	0.42	0.83	0.41
Information Technology Capital	0.30	0.73	0.43
Other Sectors	0.12	0.10	-0.02

Source: Unpublished update to Oliner and Sichel (2002), provided by Daniel Sichel to the author on October 6, 2002

A second qualification relates to the robust productivity revival recorded in the retail sector. This was concentrated in "large stores offering a wide array of goods accompanied by low prices and relatively high use of self-service systems" (Sieling, Friedman, and Dumas 2001, p 10). A complementary finding by Foster, Haltiwanger, and Krizan (2002) based on a study of a large set of individual retail establishments shows that *all* of the retail productivity growth (not just the revival but the entire measured amount of productivity growth in the 1990s) can be attributed to more productive entering establishments that displaced much less productive existing establishments. The average establishment that continued in business exhibited zero productivity growth, and this despite the massive investment of the retail industry in ICT equipment that presumably went to both old and new establishments. In the Foster results, productivity growth reflects the greater efficiency of newly opened stores, and the Sieling comment implies that most of these highly efficient new stores are large discount operations, the proverbial "big boxes" such as Wal-Mart, Home Depot, Best Buy, Circuit City, and new large supermarkets.

But the Sieling and Foster findings seem to conflict with the Oliner-Sichel implication that all of the productivity revival in retailing was achieved by purchasing new computers, software, and communications equipment. All retailers, whether new establishments of the 1990s or older establishments of the 1980s or prior decades, have adopted ICT technology. Bar-code readers have become universal in new *and* old stores. The check-out process at Home Depot involves laser bar-code readers that operate identically to the bar-code readers in the ancient hardware store in the town of Evanston, Illinois, for example.[9] It is likely that the productivity revival in retailing associated with newly built "big box" stores involves far more than the use of computers, including large size, economies of scale, efficient design to allow large-volume unloading from delivery trucks, stacking of merchandise on tall racks with fork-lift trucks, and large-scale purchases taken by customers to vehicles in large adjacent parking lots.

In the taxonomy of Table 4, these sources of efficiency gains should count as a contribution of non-ICT capital (ie, big-box structures and fork-lift trucks) and organizational improvements that raise MFP in the non-ICT sector. The possibility that Oliner-Sichel exaggerate the role of ICT capital deepening, or indeed of ICT gains in MFP, would imply that the residual role of non-ICT MFP growth is greater than it appears from Table 4. One may speculate that computers in reality earned less than the competitive rate of return assumed by Oliner-Sichel, and that non-ICT capital earned more than a competitive rate of return. This or some other related discrepancy between reality and the Oliner-Sichel framework would be necessary to reconcile their results with those of Foster, and this

possibility may extend beyond retailing to the wholesale trade and securities trading sectors, where impressive productivity gains have also been recorded. It may also help in confronting another puzzle of the 1990s: the divergent productivity growth experiences of the United States and Europe.

The puzzling contrast between the United States and Europe

If the decomposition of growth sources is a booming academic industry on the west side of the Atlantic, laments about Europe's performance are the corresponding concern of academics on the east side of the Atlantic. Although the United States enjoyed a productivity growth revival after 1995, a growth *deceleration* occurred in numerous European countries as well as in the European Union as a whole. How could ICT be the main source of the US growth revival, as described in the work of Oliner-Sichel summarized in Table 4 above, while Europe fell behind? Business firms, not to mention university professors, use the same PCs and Microsoft software everywhere in Europe, and Europe is widely acknowledged to be ahead in the use of mobile telephones.

Part of the European puzzle is resolved when we recognize that heterogeneity among European countries is more pronounced than the difference between the European Union and the United States. Numerous studies have shown a relatively strong positive correlation between MFP growth and measures of ICT intensity, for example, the ratio of ICT expenditure to GDP or the change in PC intensity per 100 inhabitants over the 1990s. In such comparisons, numerous countries achieve higher MFP growth rates than the United States over the 1990s—these countries include Ireland, Finland, Sweden, Denmark, Norway, Canada, and Australia. Some, but not all, of these countries surpass the United States in PC intensity and/or in the share of ICT expenditure. What differs most between Europe and the United States is the low level of PC adoption and ICT expenditure in the "olive belt" ranging from Portugal and Spain in the west to Italy and Greece in the east.[10] The contrast between the Nordic and olive-belt countries suggests irreverent comments about how Scandinavians in their dark winters find PCs more appealing than do olive-belt residents cavorting on their sunny beaches.

Contrasts within Europe also suggest that perhaps we could try to disaggregate the United States to provide a more appropriate comparison with Europe. Silicon Valley could be compared with Ireland and Finland; New England could be compared with Denmark and Sweden; Texas with Australia, and the midwestern heartland with France and Germany. What stands out in this suggestion is the absence of any US equivalent for the European olive-belt countries. Political borders are a product of history, and perhaps the United States would look more like Europe, which includes the olive belt, if we were to aggregate US data with those for the "tequila belt" (Mexico).

A comprehensive recent study by van Ark, Inklaar, and McGuckin (2002) provides a few answers at a more formal level. As shown in Table 5, van Ark and colleagues support the widespread impression that the United States accelerated while Europe fell behind. The top line in Table 5 shows that US productivity growth accelerated by 1.1 percent in the late 1990s while European growth decelerated by 0.9 percent, a mirror-image performance. An initial caveat is that Europe looks much better when the two halves of the 1990s are aggregated into a single 1990–2000 period; European productivity growth for 1990–2000 averages out to 1.95 percent per year, considerably higher than US growth of 1.65 percent per year.

The van Ark study allows us to trace the location of productivity growth accelerations and decelerations to particular industrial sectors, divided into ICT-producing, ICT-using, and non-ICT industries. As we have already seen in Table 4, there has been no productivity revival in US industries that are classified as neither ICT-producing nor ICT-using, and this is confirmed on the bottom line of Table 5 for the United States. These industries are also the core of the European problem, exhibiting a deceleration in the late 1990s greater than the deceleration of the European economy as a whole. Surprisingly, ICT-producing industries exhibited both higher productivity growth and a greater acceleration in the late 1990s in Europe than in the United States. The core of the US success story appears to have been in *ICT-using* industries—that is, the same retail, wholesale, and securities trading industries already discussed. A separate analysis by van Ark, Inklaar, and McGuckin (2002, Figure 2a) shows that literally *all* of the productivity growth differential of the United States over Europe in the late 1990s came from these three industries, with retail contributing about 55 percent of the differential, wholesale 24 percent, and securities trading 20

percent. The remaining industries had small positive or negative differentials, netting out to zero. As might have been expected, the United States–Europe differential was negative in telecom services, reflecting US backwardness in mobile phones.

These results for Europe bring together our discussion of retailing in the previous section and here as a major factor explaining Europe's poor performance in the late 1990s. Just as we argued earlier that the US retailing sector has achieved efficiency gains for reasons not directly related to computers, including physical investments in a new type of "big box" organization, so we can suggest in parallel that Europe has fallen back because European firms are much less free to develop the "big box" retail formats.[11] Impediments include land use regulations that prevent the carving out of new "greenfield" sites for "big box" stores in suburban and exurban locations, shop-closing regulations that restrict the revenue potential of new investments, congestion in central-city locations that are near the nodes of Europe's extensive urban public transit systems, and restrictive labor rules that limit flexibility in organizing the workplace and make it expensive to hire and fire workers with the near-total freedom to which US firms are accustomed.

Overall, we conclude that ICT investment has been exaggerated as the sole source of the US productivity revival of the late 1990s, and it is even clearer that lack of ICT investment has been wrongly cited as the main source of the contrasting productivity performance in Europe. The main US advantage was in retail and wholesale trade, where the expansion of new establishments raised productivity growth for many reasons that go well beyond ICT investment, and the ability of Europe to expand in tandem was hampered by regulations and institutions that have long been cited as a drag on European economic growth.

Positive feedback loops among the ICT investment boom, the stock market, low inflation, and monetary policy

We have now examined the extent to which the post-1995 productivity growth revival may have contained a cyclical component, how much of it can be attributed to the boom in ICT investment, whether standard estimates of ICT's contribution may have been exaggerated, and why Europe did not experience a productivity growth revival. Whether the ICT investment boom was the sole cause of the US productivity growth revival or only a very large cause, there is no doubt that the ICT investment boom deserves substantial credit for the productivity growth revival. Accordingly, the future growth of productivity will depend at least in part on whether ICT investment soon returns to growth rates typical of the late 1990s

259

Table 5: Labor productivity by industry group, United States versus Europe, 1990–1995 versus 1995–2000, annual growth rates in percent

	United States		European Union	
	1990–1995	1995–2000	1990–1995	1995–2000
Total Economy	1.1	2.2	2.4	1.5
ICT-Producing Industries	6.1	6.5	6.0	8.5
ICT-Using Industries	1.4	4.2	1.9	1.3
Non-ICT Industries	0.4	0.4	2.4	1.0

Source: van Ark, Inklaar, and McGuckin (2002, Table 5).

or settles down to much slower growth rates, perhaps even slower than in the 1987–1995 period.

We now turn to the core of this chapter, which is to identify unsustainable sources of the ICT investment boom of the late 1990s. All of these sources fall under the general heading suggested by the chapter's subtitle, "Does Supply Create Its Own Demand?" We treat the geometric increase in computer power as a given, and attempt to identify the sources of the robust demand for computer power in the late 1990s that might not recur in the future. These fall into two general categories: macroeconomic and microeconomic. The macro sources of demand are described as a multidimensional feedback loop in which the ICT investment boom interacted positively with the stock market, inflation behavior, and monetary policy. The micro sources of demand are traced to particular events in the evolution of telephone equipment, computer hardware, and software technology.

The high-tech investment boom

The late 1990s were notable both for an amazing acceleration in the growth of real computer investment and for a simultaneous acceleration in the rate of price decline of computer power. In fact, one hypothesis is that the investment boom simply reflected the faster rate of price decline. With a price elasticity of demand of 1.0, one would expect a faster rate of price decline to be reflected one-for-one in an equivalent acceleration in the growth rate of real investment.

The dimensions of this phenomenon are illustrated in Figure 2. Plotted on the same scale are four-quarter growth rates of real investment in computers and peripherals and the change in the deflator for the same category of equipment. The upper line is the real investment series, with growth rates accelerating from 19 percent per year during 1987–1995 to 33 percent per year between mid 1995 and mid 2000. During the two years following mid 2000, the growth rate decelerated sharply to 4.6 percent per annum, well below the average of 1987–1995.

The lower line is the growth rate of the computer deflator, with a rate of change accelerating from around −15 percent per year before 1995 to between −30 and −35 percent per year during 1995–1999, followed by a return closer to the pre-1995 growth rates. Was the investment boom simply the counterpart of the accelerated rate of price decline? If the boom reflected only substitution with a price elasticity of unity, then nominal spending on computers would not have increased. As shown in Figure 3, the investment boom went beyond that. Computer investment as a share of nominal GDP was not constant in the late 1990s, but rather jumped after 1995 from about 0.75 percent to close to 1.0 percent before falling back to 0.7 percent in 2001–2002. The drop in the nominal computer share in 2001–2002 reminds us that a rapid rate of price

decline for high-tech equipment is not enough to guarantee a continuous investment boom; if the demand is not there, then the nominal share can decline as prices continue to fall relative to prices in the rest of the economy.

The phrase *New Economy* became widely adopted to describe the US macroeconomic miracle of the late 1990s, and definitions of the New Economy centered not just on the productivity growth revival but also on the burst of growth in high-tech investment visible in Figure 2. In fact it became common in the late 1990s for some commentators (see Gordon 2000) to treat the accelerated rate of price decline of computers as the defining characteristic of the New Economy. However, this emphasis on the rate of price decline implicitly treats the acceleration of technological change in high-tech equipment as both necessary and sufficient to generate an investment boom and a productivity revival. As we shall see, a technological acceleration in supply does not guarantee that the demand for all that equipment will emerge, and in this sense any definition of the New Economy has to include innovation *both* in computer technology *and* in new uses for computers.

Thus far we have emphasized the computer part of ICT investment to the exclusion of software and telecom investment, mainly because the price deflators for computers are much better than those for software and telecom (where the rate of price decline is generally assumed to be understated).[12] However, deflators do not matter for nominal shares, and we see in Figure 4 that the nominal share of all ICT investment (computers, peripherals, software, and telecom) experienced more robust growth than for computers alone in the 1990s. While the computer share in Figure 3 fell back in 2001–2002 to its level of 1984, the share of all ICT investment in 2001–2002 was a full percentage point higher than in the mid 1980s, although more than half a point below its peak of 1999–2000. Why did the prior upsurge in the ICT investment share in the 1980s *not* create a productivity revival like that of the late 1990s? This is one of several circumstantial pieces of evidence implying that the role of ICT investment in the late 1990s productivity revival, as argued above, may have been exaggerated in analyses like that of Table 4.

Pillar of the positive-feedback loop: the stock market

Whatever the rate of price decline in computer equipment, as displayed in the bottom frame of Figure 2, the growth rate of real investment depended crucially on the sources of demand for computers and other types of ICT investment. This growth rate was increased by the stock market boom, both directly through the role of stock market finance in helping old and new firms alike buy massive amounts of ICT equipment, and also through the role of the stock market in propelling overall economic growth that was more rapid than otherwise.

Figure 2: Real investment in computers and peripherals and its deflator, change from four quarters prior, 1987–2002, percentage changes at an annual rate

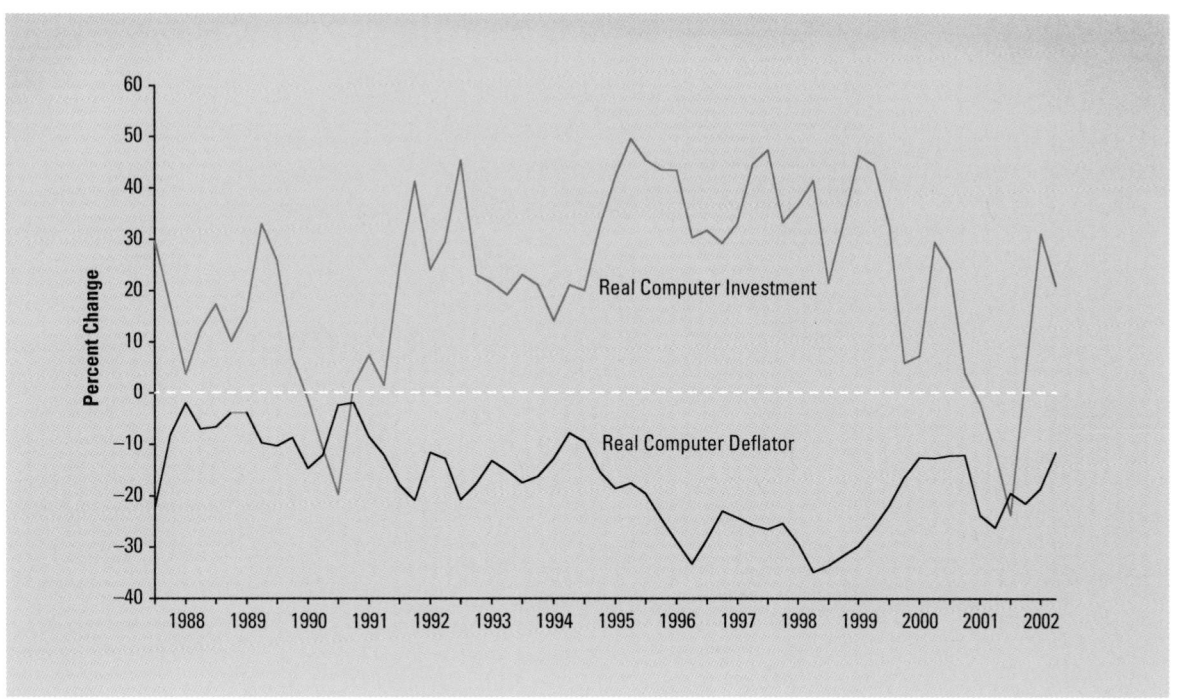

Source: Bureau of Economic Analysis

Figure 3: Ratio to nominal GDP of nominal investment in computers and peripherals, quarterly data, 1960–2002

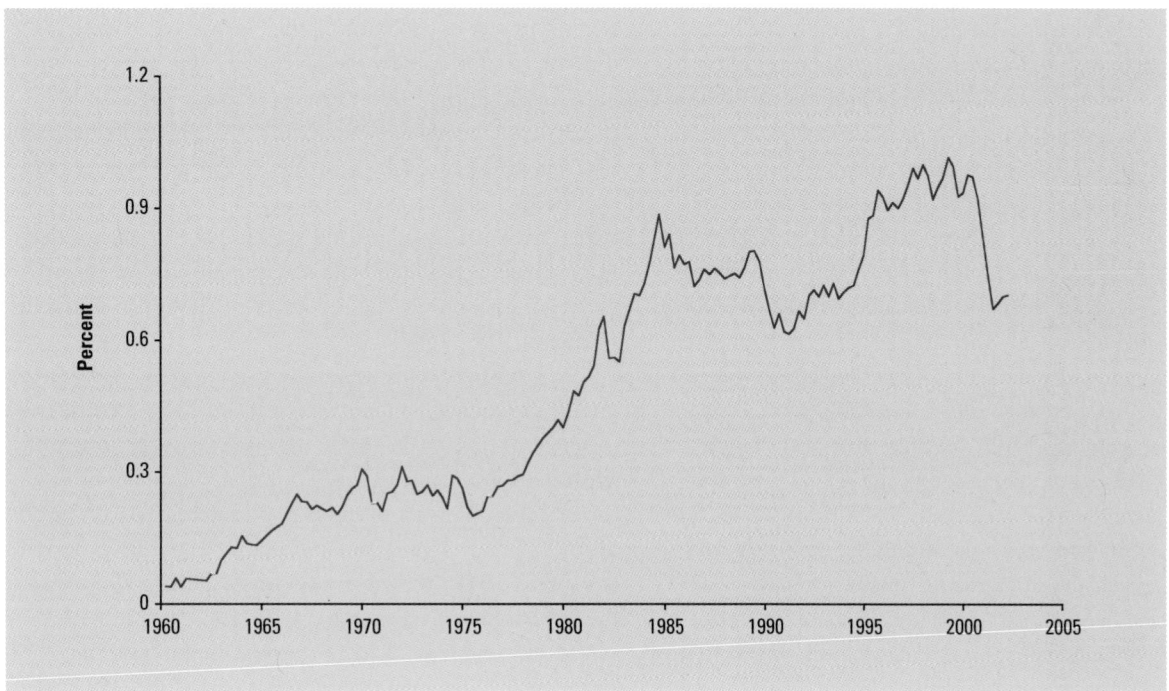

Source: Bureau of Economic Analysis

Figure 4: Ratio to nominal GDP of nominal investment in information technology, quarterly data, 1960–2002

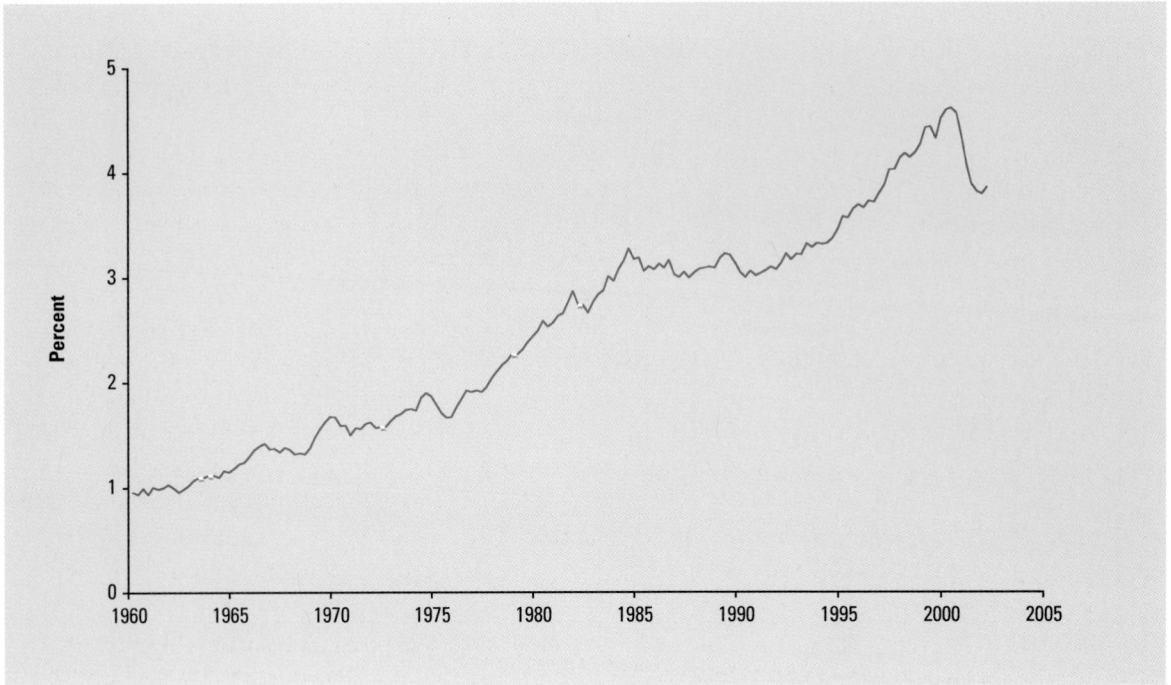

Source: Bureau of Economic Analysis

The S&P 500 stock market average exactly tripled from May 1995 to March 2000 and then fell by almost half by October 2002.[13] This reflected in large part the marked increase in corporate profits at roughly the same time. The most widely watched measure of profits refers to the reported profits of the S&P 500 companies, an amount that roughly quadrupled from about $125 billion in 1991 to about $500 billion in mid 2000 before collapsing to around $200 billion in late 2001. If the S&P measure of reported profits were the only available measure, there would be no mystery surrounding either the stock market boom or its collapse, since the S&P index increased and then decreased by roughly the same percentage as profits. However, as pointed out by Nordhaus (2002a), several other profit measures show different timing, particularly the national accounts (NIPA) measure that peaks much earlier, in 1997 rather than in 2000, and which decreases much less than the S&P series from 2000 to late 2001.[14] If market investors had been watching NIPA profits rather than S&P profits, the stock market might not have increased as much in 1997–2000 nor declined nearly as much after 2000. Nordhaus speculates that the much later peak in S&P profits may have reflected creative accounting schemes of the type that have created the recent crisis in US corporate governance involving Enron, WorldCom, Global Crossing, Tyco, and others.

If the S&P 500 stock market index simply echoed reported S&P earnings, however misleading or inaccurate these may have been, then the stock market boom of the late 1990s was not a "bubble" since it was based on a fundamental factor, namely the perceived value of S&P earnings. Although the price-earnings ratio for the S&P 500 did increase substantially between 1995 and 2000, most of this can be explained by a decline in the real interest rate on bonds. Nordhaus (2002a, Figure 8) shows that the spread between the return on equities (the inverse of the price-earnings ratio) and the real interest rate on government bonds was only slightly lower in 2000 than it was in 1992 and 1985–1987.

In assessing the future of the stock market, and hence one of the critical components of the positive-feedback mechanism of the late 1990s, we must assess the future of all three components of the Nordhaus spread: the profits, the price-earnings ratio, and the real interest rate on government bonds. During the prosperous 1960–1973 period, the spread was in the range of 3 to 4 percent, followed by the depressed and inflationary 1973–1983 period with spreads ranging from 5 to 14 percent. In contrast, the spread after 1984, except for a short period in 1989, was in the narrow and lower range of −1 to 2 percent. In fact, the collapse in stock prices through October 2002, together with the decline in bond yields, brought the spread back up to at least 4, as high as at any time since 1984. At that point the market had itself corrected the widespread perception of irrational exuberance.

Could the spread go back to the range of 0 to 2 percent that has characterized most of the post-1984 period? Another way to pose this question is to ask whether the 1963–1973, 1973–1983, or post-1984 periods are more relevant to post-2002 stock market spreads and hence prices. An important change that can be dated to 1983–1984 is a decline in macroeconomic volatility, as measured by various volatility measures of real GDP growth (Blanchard and Simon 2001); this would be expected to decrease the spread between stock and bond yields. Another factor working in the same direction has been the shift from defined benefit to defined contribution pension plans, leading many workers to make regular monthly investments in equities independent of the current state of the stock market.

The previous discussion suggests that the spread could well decline from its value of mid October 2002 of about 4 percent back toward the 0-to-2 percent range that has been the norm since 1984. Interest rates on bonds in late 2002 are abnormally low and could plausibly increase by more than any hypothetical future increase in inflation (discussed below). As Nordhaus shows, S&P reported profits have been abnormally low in 2001–2002 as the dirty linen of creative accounting has been cleansed. Future S&P profits may bounce back substantially as this one-time element disappears, even if economic profits do not change appreciably as a share of GDP.[15] This discussion on causes of the stock market boom of the late 1990s concludes that the bubble element of prices has been squeezed out and that substantial stock market returns for the period after October 2002 are quite likely.

The effects of the late 1990s stock market boom are easier to describe than its causes. Easy stock market finance fueled start-up companies and the expansion of existing high-tech companies. New companies with only vague business plans and remote prospects for profit were flooded with funds from aggressive venture capital firms and then proceeded to initial public offerings (IPOs) that have since become notorious for providing privileged insiders and friends of brokerage houses with opportunities for guaranteed first-day gains at the expense of ordinary investors. The heady optimism as market participants anticipated unending gains ("Dow 36,000") doubtless led to more finance being shoveled into ICT investment than would otherwise have occurred; the abuses since discovered, as well as the collapse in high-tech stocks, make it unlikely that this supporting component of the ICT investment boom will recur in the foreseeable future, if ever in our lifetimes.[16]

The ICT investment boom was propelled not just by the stock market but also by the prosperity of the overall economy, feeding back to investment as part of the stan-dard "accelerator" effect. One impetus to economywide growth was a two-step feedback from the stock market to ICT investment, working through the wealth effect of the stock market on consumption expenditures. This connection is most vividly illustrated by Figure 5, which compares the household savings rate with the ratio of the S&P 500 stock market index to nominal GDP. This S&P ratio more than doubled in the four short years between 1995 and 1999, after declining by two thirds between 1965 and 1982. The negative correlation between the stock market ratio and the household savings rate is evident in the data and is just what would be expected as a result of the wealth effect embedded in Modigliani's original life-cycle hypothesis of consumption behavior. Rapid economic growth in the late 1990s was fueled not just by the ICT investment boom, but also by a consumption binge financed by capital gains that allowed consumption expenditures to grow more rapidly than personal disposable income for four straight years. Another source of positive feedback came from the rest of the world outside of the United States. The stock market boom attracted foreign investment that financed the US current account deficit, and this allowed US consumers to expand their purchases of imports far faster than the rest of the world was willing to buy US exports. The resulting appreciation of the US dollar played its own role in the positive-feedback mechanism, as it was the most important single source of the surprisingly low rate of inflation experienced by the United States in the late 1990s.

Low inflation enabled easy monetary policy

Low inflation in the late 1990s allowed monetary policy to avoid a move toward the restrictive spike in short-term interest rates that had ended previous expansions in 1969, 1981, and 1989. The nature of the inflationary surprise is evident in Figure 6, which plots the unemployment rate on the same scale as the inflation rate for the personal consumption expenditures (PCE) deflator.[17] The unemployment rate in 1999–2000 fell to 4 percent, the lowest rate since 1966–1970, yet in 1998 and early 1999, inflation not only failed to accelerate but actually decelerated.

Taking a general view of the unemployment-inflation relationship, it appears superficially that the only support for a negative Phillips-curve unemployment-inflation tradeoff is based on the 1960s Vietnam-era experience, with a bit of further support from the economic expansion of 1987–1990. In other periods, especially during 1972–1985 and 1995–1999, the unemployment and inflation rates appear to be positively correlated, with the unemployment rate behaving as a lagging indicator, moving a year or two later than inflation. Although this appearance of a positive tradeoff led some economists—notably Robert E. Lucas, Jr. and Thomas Sargent—in the 1970s to declare the Phillips curve to be "lying in

263

Figure 5: Household savings rate and ratio of S&P 500 stock market index to nominal GDP, 1972 = 100, annual data, 1970–2002

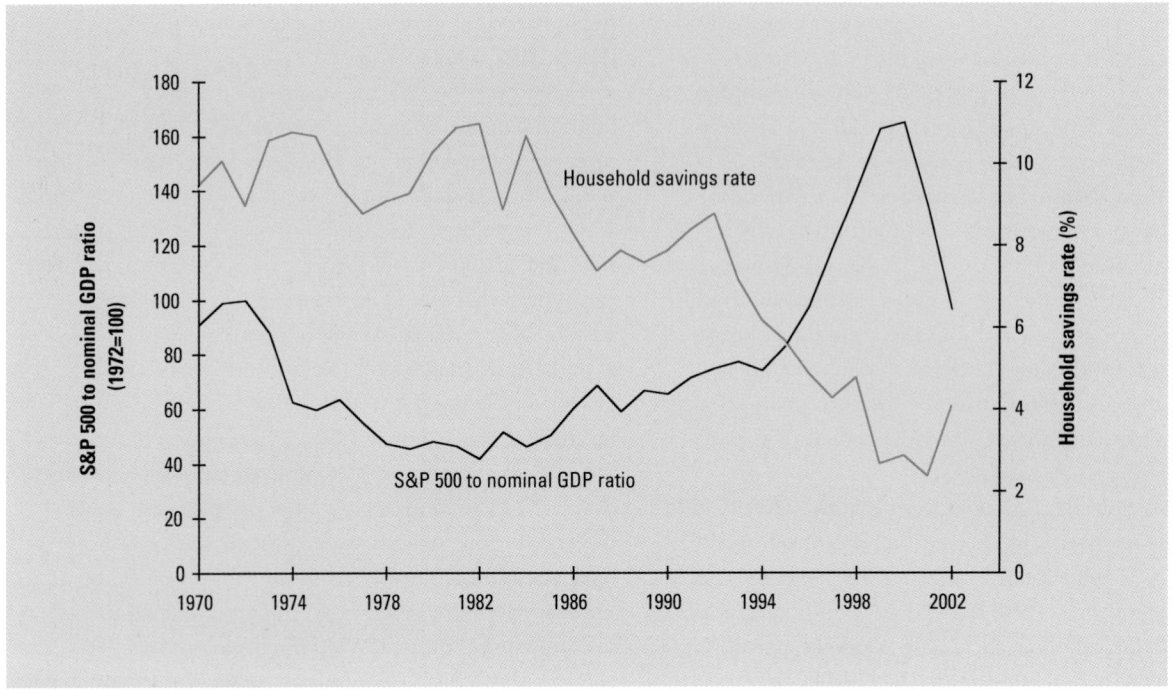

Sources: Standard & Poor's Corporation; Bureau of Economic Analysis

Figure 6: The unemployment rate and the change, from four quarters prior, of the deflator for personal consumption expenditures, quarterly data, 1960–2002

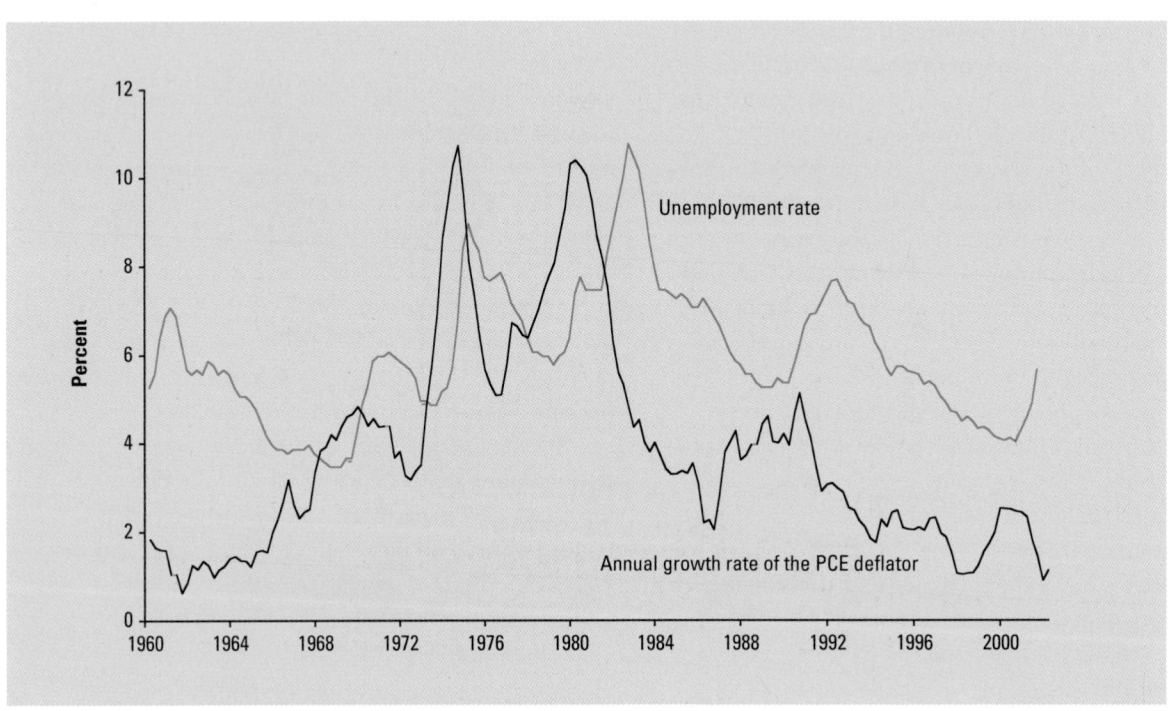

Sources: Bureau of Labor Statistics; Bureau of Economic Analysis

wreckage," at the same time a more general model of inflation determination was developed that combined an influence of demand (ie, a negative short-run relation between inflation and unemployment), supply (in the form of "supply shocks" such as changing real oil prices that created a positive inflation-unemployment relation), slow inertial adjustment, and long-run independence of inflation and the unemployment rate.[18] During the 1980s and the first half of the 1990s, this more general model was adopted as the mainstream approach to inflation determination by textbook authors and policymakers alike, but in the late 1990s it was challenged again by the simultaneous decline in unemployment and deceleration of inflation evident in Figure 6.

At the end of the decade, no consensus had yet emerged to explain the positive correlation of inflation and unemployment in the late 1990s. I have attempted (1998) to use a common framework to explain why the performance of the 1970s was so bad and the performance of the 1990s was so good, pointing to the role of adverse supply shocks in the earlier episode and beneficial supply shocks more recently. The first beneficial shock was the basic topic of this chapter: the post-1995 productivity growth revival, which directly reduced the growth in unit labor costs, and hence inflation, for any given growth rate of nominal wages. If there was a substantial lag in the response of nominal wage changes to faster productivity growth, then the productivity revival contributed directly to lower inflation.

The second and third beneficial shocks were the familiar "old" supply shocks, the falling real prices of imports and energy. Of these by far the most important was the declining real price of imports that was a counterpart to the flood of capital inflows and appreciation of the dollar over the entire period between 1995 and early 2002. I have estimated (1998) that in early 1998 inflation was being held down by more than 1 percent at an annual rate by the behavior of real import prices. The role of real energy prices was short-lived, having its maximum impact in holding down inflation in early 1998. Productivity, import prices, and energy prices were joined by two "new" supply shocks: the accelerating decline in computer prices (see Figure 2 above) and a sharp decline in the prices of medical care services made possible by the managed health care revolution.

The confluence of this set of five beneficial supply shocks was central to the longevity of the boom of the 1990s. Low inflation, as we shall see below, allowed the Fed to pursue a very different monetary policy than in the late 1980s. Yet none of the beneficial shocks was guaranteed to last forever. Indeed, the first to disappear was the energy price effect, which turned around and accounted for most of the doubling of inflation in the price deflator for personal consumption expenditures (plotted in Figure 6) from 1.1 percent in 1998 to 2.6 percent in 2000.[19]

If low inflation in the late 1990s was mainly caused by the beneficial supply shocks, and low inflation in 2001–2002 was caused by a weakening of demand in product and labor markets, what are the prospects for inflation when the economy recovers? This is relevant to the overall themes of this chapter, because if there is a substantial risk that inflation will reignite, the response of monetary policy may look more like the late 1980s than the late 1990s, and any bounce back of interest rates on bonds will throw cold water on housing and car sales, on housing refinance, and on any incipient stock market recovery.

A case can be made that, in addition to energy prices, all four of the remaining supply shocks that shifted in a beneficial direction in the late 1990s may turn in the adverse direction and indeed may already have done so. Even if productivity growth remains strong, eventually real wage growth will recognize and absorb the productivity growth revival. Indeed, this had already happened in the late 1990s, as annual growth in real compensation per hour accelerated from a mere 0.7 percent during 1992–1998 to 2.8 percent during 1998–2000.[20] The beneficial role of falling real import prices has already greatly lessened in impact, from an annual rate of decline of −3.3 percent per year in 1992–1998 to −1.2 percent per year in 1998–2002. A continuing decline in real import prices is unlikely, as the dollar has begun to decline from its peak reached early in the year 2002.

Perhaps the greatest single concern for the future of inflation involves medical care prices. Between 1993 and 1996 medical care inflation exhibited a sharp deceleration from roughly double the economywide inflation rate to a number almost equal to the overall inflation rate. Yet recently the inflation rate of the personal consumption deflator for medical care has begun to creep up, from 2.1 percent in 1999, to 2.9 percent in 2000, to 3.6 percent in 2001, relative to an overall inflation rate in 2001 of only 2.0 percent. This may be the tip of the iceberg, however, because health care prices are once again becoming a leading edge of inflation. The growth rate of one index of health insurance premiums decelerated from 18 percent in 1989 to 0.8 percent in 1996, only to reaccelerate again to 13 percent in 2002.[21] The final beneficial shock of the late 1990s was the more rapid rate of decline in computer prices, and we have already seen (in Figure 2) that the rate of price decline retreated from −30 percent per year in 1995–1999 to an average rate of about −20 percent in 1999–2002.

The response of the Fed's monetary policy is summarized in Figure 7, which compares quarterly values of the Federal funds rate with the output ratio or "gap"—that is, the ratio of actual to potential real GDP. The gap is

Figure 7: The Federal funds rate and the log ratio of actual to natural real GDP, quarterly data, 1984–2002

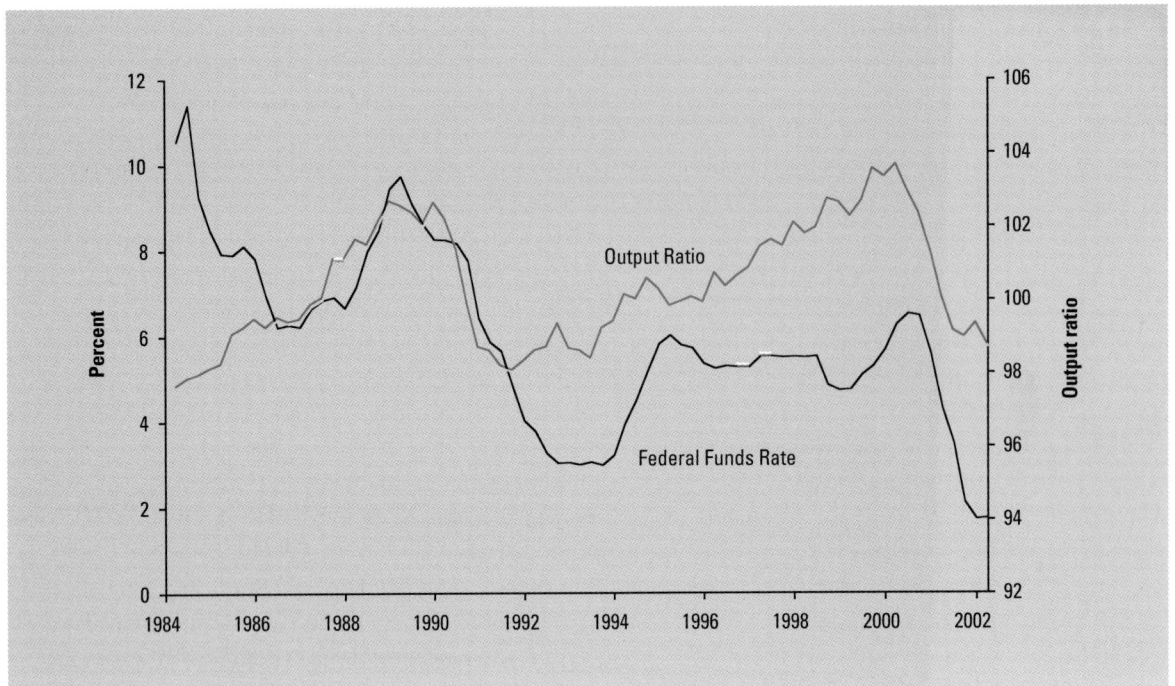

Sources: Federal Reserve Board; author's research

commonly used to measure how much actual output differs from potential output—that is, the amount the economy is capable of producing without generating extra inflation. As shown by the right scale, the output ratio rose above 100 percent both in 1988–1990 and in 1997–2000, but the response of the Fed was quite different. In the episode of the late 1980s, the Fed responded to excess output by quickly tightening policy and creating a spike in the Federal funds rate to 9.25 percent in early 1989. In the late 1990s, the output ratio rose above 100 percent for a longer period and to a higher level, but the Fed barely touched the Federal funds rate, which varied only in the range of 4.5 to 6.5 percent during the entire period between early 1995 and late 2000. The distance between the two lines in Figure 7 during the period 1997–2000 can be interpreted as showing the influence of low inflation on monetary policy, and hence low inflation as an enabler of the continued output boom. Once again, there was a positive feedback system, with relatively low interest rates fostering ICT investment and the productivity revival, and the productivity revival feeding back to make its own contribution toward keeping inflation low.

The interplay of supply and demand in the ICT investment boom

We have now seen that the ICT investment boom of the late 1990s, although initially stimulated by technological advances that pushed the price of computer power downward more rapidly than before, did not occur in isolation. In addition to the pure technological stimulus, ICT investment was funded by ample finance made possible by the stock market boom and relatively easy monetary policy, and ICT investment responded to the boom in the overall economy, which in turn reflected positive feedback among the productivity revival, beneficial shocks that held down inflation, and low interest rates. Stated another way, if the initial technological stimulus had not been supported by the positive macro feedback loop, a given rate of decline in computer prices would have been accompanied by less real ICT investment and a lower share of nominal ICT investment in nominal GDP than the actual ratio displayed in Figure 3.

But there is another requirement necessary for a technological advance to result in an investment boom and an increased share of computer spending in nominal GDP. There must be a *use*—that is, a *demand*—for all that extra computer power. A unique element of the late 1990s is that technological advances in the manufacture of computers coincided with new stimuli to the demand for computers, including but not limited to the invention of the WWW. This interdependence of supply and demand is missed by commentators, such as Jorgenson, who see a simple chain of causation between information technology as an input and economic performance as an output: "... the foundation for the American growth resurgence is the development and deployment of semiconductors" (Jorgenson 2001, p 1).

Moore's Law and the explosion of supply

The specific technological event that made the growth resurgence possible was an acceleration in technical change in the manufacture of microprocessors, the computer chips that provide a computer's computation capacity. The idea of a product cycle in computer chips is summarized by "Moore's Law," a name later given to a 1969 observation by Gordon E. Moore, one of the two founders of the Intel Corporation, that each new microprocessor chip contained twice as many transistors as the previous generation and was released within 18 to 24 months of its predecessor. This implied a logarithmic growth rate of computing capacity at between 35 and 47 percent per year. Rarely if ever has any scientist been so accurate in forecasting the future development of an innovative process. The actual price of computer memory chips declined by 40.9 percent per year during 1974–1996. The price of logic chips, a narrower category more directly comparable to computer microprocessors, declined during 1985–1996 at 54.1 percent per year, followed by an acceleration to a rate of price decline of more than 90 percent per year. As characterized by Jorgenson (2001), "the semiconductor industry shifted from a three-year-product cycle to a greatly accelerated two-year cycle."

The calendar of product cycles and Moore's Law may seem confusing at first, because the pre-1995 schedule in which the number of transistors doubled every 18 months seems to conflict with the idea of a three-year product cycle. This apparent conflict is reconciled by the fact that each new generation of chips produced an increase in computation power by more than a factor of two—it is rather more like a factor of four.[22] If the shortening of the product cycle from three years to two was an ephemeral phenomenon of the late 1990s, then this is one more reason to expect that an ICT investment boom on the same scale will not recur. In the rest of this chapter, we will assume that the faster two-year cycle continues for at least another decade. The issue, then, is whether there is sufficient demand for computation power to absorb an increase in computer power *by a factor of 1,000* from a starting date of 2002?[23]

Why the demand for ICT power matters

Whether Moore's Law proceeds with a cycle time of two years or three years, there is no doubt that future progress will provide an unbelievable further explosion of computer power beyond what already existed at the peak of the ICT investment boom in mid 2000. But, as we have seen, a rapid decline in the price of computer power does not guarantee a robust expansion in ICT investment. An annual rate of decline in computer prices of, say, 30 percent per year could be accompanied by an annual rate of growth of real computer investment of +60 percent, +30 percent, 0, or −30 percent. Growth of real investment in this example of +30 percent would imply no change in nominal computer investment. Any lower growth rate in real investment, whether 0, −30, or any number between, would imply a sharp decline in the share of ICT investment in nominal GDP, as has already occurred between 2000 and 2002. It is this possibility of a continuing decline in the share of ICT investment in nominal GDP that creates the sharpest divide between the economic environment of the late 1990s and the next few years.

Shifting supply and demand: theory and facts

The evolution of the price and quantity of computer power can be displayed in a simple theoretical diagram, as in Figure 8. Throughout its history, the economics of the computer has featured a steady downward shift in the supply curve of computer attributes at a rate much faster than the upward shift in the demand for computer services. In fact, the story is often told with a theoretical diagram like the top panel of Figure 8, in which the supply curve slides steadily downwards from S_1 to S_2 with no shift in the demand curve at all.[24] Ignoring the possibility of a rightward shift in the demand curve from D_1 to D_2 (we return to this possibility below), the second distinguishing feature of the development of the computer industry is the unprecedented speed with which diminishing returns set in; while computer users steadily enjoy an increasing amount of consumer surplus as the price falls, the declining point of intersection of the supply curve with the fixed demand curve implies a rapid decline in the marginal utility or benefit of computer power.

The accelerated rate of price decline in computer attributes has been accompanied since 1995 by the invention of the Internet.[25] In perhaps the most rapid diffusion of any invention since television in the late 1940s and early 1950s, by the end of the year 2000 the percentage of US households hooked up to the Internet reached 50 percent. Surely the invention of web browsers and the explosive growth of e-commerce should be interpreted as a rightward shift in the demand curve in the top panel of Figure 8 from D_1 to D_2. Such a rightward shift in the demand curve would imply an increase in the benefits provided by all computers, both old and new.[26]

Figure 8: Theoretical relation (top) and actual data (bottom) on the relation of the price to the quantity of computer characteristics (annual data)

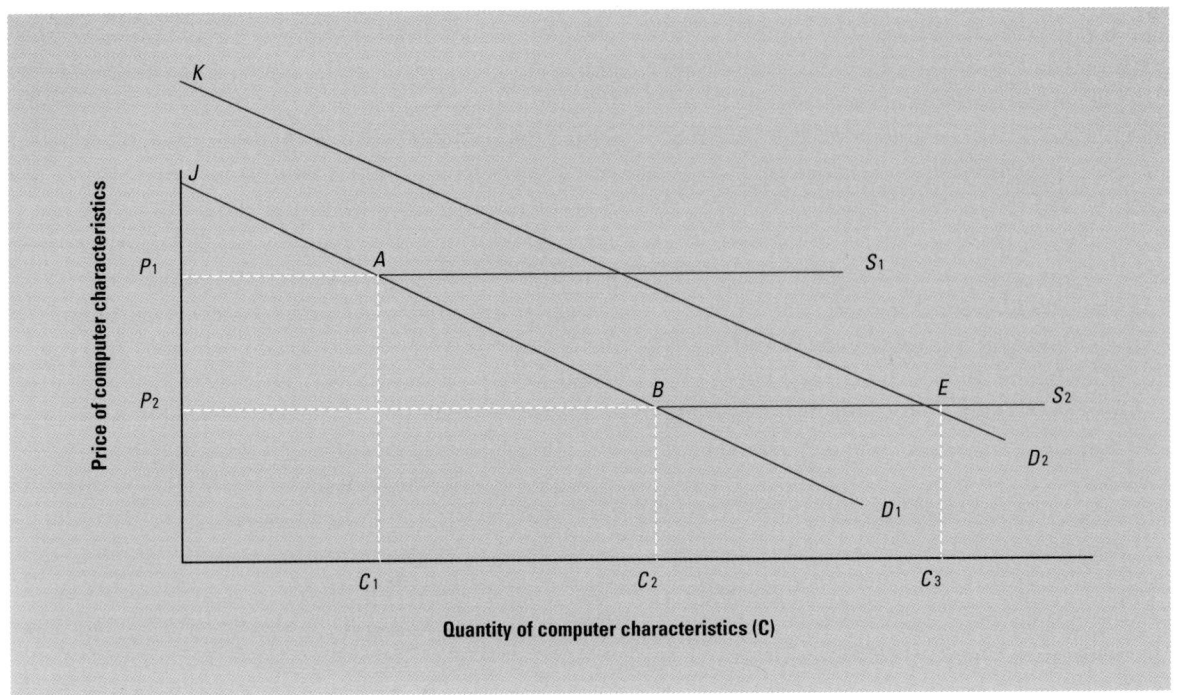

Source: Bureau of Economic Analysis

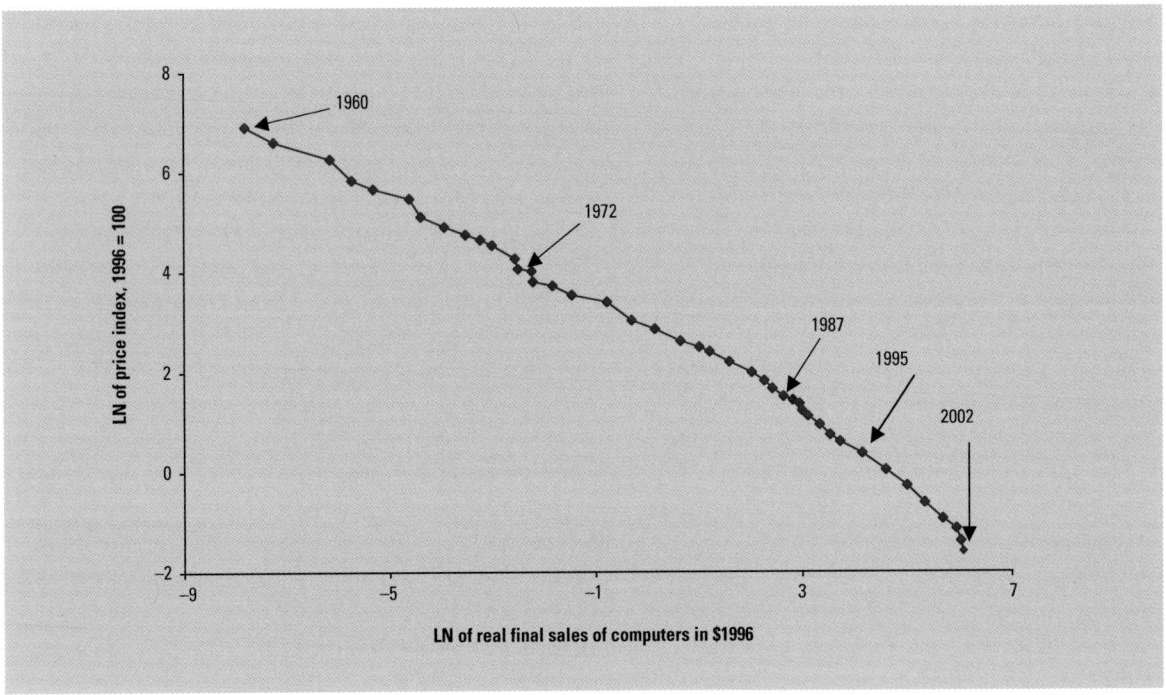

Source: Bureau of Economic Analysis

Although the invention of the Internet is usually treated as revolutionary, a simple analysis of the supply and demand for computer hardware may suggest a more limited role. We have already seen that the rate of decline of prices for computer hardware, including peripherals, accelerated sharply after 1995. This fact is shown in the bottom panel of Figure 8, which plots the price and quantity of computer characteristics since 1960. The implicit price deflator for computer hardware, including peripherals, declined from 70,969 in 1961 to 20 in 2002 (with a base 1996 = 100), for a rate decline of 20.0 percent per annum. There has been a corresponding increase in the quantity of computer attributes, and both the rate of price decline and quantity increase accelerated after 1995.

Although the rate of price change has varied over time, a rapid price decline in 1995–2000 does not distinguish the New Economy from the 1960–1980 interval dominated by the mainframe computer or the 1980–1985 interval dominated by the transition from mainframe to PC applications prior to the invention of the Internet.[27] If there had been a discontinuous rightward shift in the demand curve for computer hardware due to the spread of the Internet, we should have observed a noticeable flattening of the slope of the price-quantity relationship in the bottom panel of Figure 8, as the rate of increase of quantity accelerated relative to the rate of decline in price, but we do not. The rate of change of price and quantity both accelerate after 1995 (as indicated by the greater spacing between annual observations) but the slope does not change appreciably, suggesting that the spread of the Internet is a byproduct of rapid technological change that is faster than in previous decades but not qualitatively different in the relationship between supply and demand than earlier advances in the computer industry.

The data on the price and quantity of computer characteristics have previously been used to "map out" the demand curve (Brynjolfsson 1996, p 290). In fact, the slope of the price-quantity relationship was appreciably flatter during 1972–1987 than during 1987–1995 or 1995–2000. If the demand curve has not shifted, the inverse of these slopes is the price elasticity of demand, namely −2.03, −1.33, and −1.19 in these three intervals, which can be compared with Brynjolfsson's (1996, p 292) estimated price elasticity of −1.33 over the period 1970–1989 (the implied elasticity in the slump period 2000–2002 was only −0.28). The apparent decline in the price elasticity is consistent with the view that the most important uses of computers were developed prior to 1987, not currently.

Unsustainable sources of demand for ICT investment in the late 1990s

Our discussion of unsustainable demand for ICT investment begins with the least controversial component of the argument that supply does not create its own demand. It is uncontroversial because it—the bubble and subsequent meltdown in telecom equipment investment, especially in fiber-optic cable and in the communication infrastructure of the Internet—has already happened. We then turn to computer equipment, peripherals, and software, where optimists like Jorgenson point to the inexorable future explosion of computer power made possible by Moore's Law, and we assemble a growing body of evidence showing that much of the extra computer power is not needed and will not be purchased.

The telecom equipment bubble and meltdown

Of all the different components of ICT investment, the most staggering mismatch between supply and demand occurred in fiber-optic telephone lines. During the late 1990s, new technology made possible an explosion in the carrying capacity of a given fiber-optic line at a pace that made progress in computer microprocessors look anemic by comparison. Until 1995 it was possible to transmit only one color of data-carrying light through fiber-optic lines, but the development of "dense-wave division multiplexing" split the single beam into a spectrum of colors and multiplied capacity by as much as a factor of 300. Over a seven-year period, the capacity of telephone lines increased by more than in the previous 100 years; the number of one-page e-mails that could be sent over one fiber-optic strand increased from 25,000 in 1995 to 25 million in 2002. Yet the cost of providing 1,000 times more capacity increased minimally and in some cases declined.

Oversupply was so great that the cost of renting an intercity data line dropped at a rate of 67 percent per year between 2000 and 2002, but despite the stimulus to demand from these lower prices, the growth of demand fell so far behind the growth in supply that, in 2002, fully 97 percent of fiber-optic capacity remained unutilized. The implied 3 percent utilization rate was without precedent in industrial history and led to an unparalleled series of corporate bankruptcies and the evaporation of $2 trillion in shareholder wealth and 500,000 industry jobs.[28]

Given the advance in technology, another outcome was possible. If each fiber-optic line had such an increase in its capacity, then supply could have remained matched to demand if fewer lines were built. The underlying assumption that led to overinvestment was heady optimism, the same factor that propelled the NASDAQ stock market bubble. One frequently quoted number, which has been traced to a corporate memo written in 1997, was that Internet traffic was doubling every 100 days, implying an annual growth rate of around 1,100 percent (Dreazen

2002). It never occurred to telecom executives, or the Wall Street analysts promoting their stocks, that such growth rates would imply that within a few years every member of the US population would be spending 24 hours per day connected to the Internet, and that Internet revenues would exceed 100 percent of GDP. In actual fact, the annual growth rate of Internet traffic for 2003 has been estimated to be closer to 50 percent per year than 1,000 percent.[29] Telecom equipment, even more than the stock market, appears to have been history's classic example of "irrational exuberance" in several meanings of that term, including irrational demand forecasts, stock price increases, and debt incurred, resulting in an unprecedented value of equity wiped out in one after another debt-heavy bankruptcy.

Differences between the unsustainable nature of computer and telecom investment

At first glance, the telecom equipment investment bubble may seem quite irrelevant for computers, peripherals, and software, the heart of the New Economy that made possible the WWW and the dot.com e-commerce revolution. Nothing like the overbuilding of telecom equipment capacity occurred with computer hardware, and the utilization of the equipment devoted to making computer chips, personal computers, laptops, and peripherals such as monitors and printers was closer to 100 percent than the 3 percent recorded for fiber-optic cable.

Yet a central topic of this chapter is not utilization rates, but the extent to which the growth rate of ICT investment in the late 1990s was unsustainable. For computers, the annual rate of decline of prices provided an ever-growing supply of computer characteristics—that is, speed and memory—and the demand for these characteristics was sufficient to boost temporarily the share of nominal computer investment in nominal GDP, as was displayed in Figure 3. However, the core factors that created the demand for computers in the late 1990s were in part unsustainable, and this implies that similar increases in the supply of computer power over the next decade (2002–2012) may be accompanied by a less than proportionate increase in the quantity of computer power demanded by the marketplace.

The Web could be invented only once

The period between 1995 and 1999 witnessed the instant deployment and diffusion of the World Wide Web (WWW). Whereas no business firm knew anything about web sites in 1995, by 1998–1999 every business, government agency, university, and other nonprofit organization was compelled to develop its own web site. Constructing a web site required buying one or more servers and hiring numerous software engineers to design the pages, their interaction within the site, and the hyperlinks to external

sites. The period 1998–2000 represented the peak of this investment activity, with its required purchases of hardware and software, but this level of frenetic activity did not have to be sustained forever.[30] Once each component of the web site "went live," subsequently it would need only to be maintained and incrementally improved. The hardware requirements of such incremental improvements may have been minor, even negligible, while the software investment was far less than had been needed to create the initial site.

The wave of investment in Internet infrastructure went beyond web sites available to external customers. During the same period in the late 1990s, many business firms reorganized their internal communications systems as "intranets," web-based internal communication systems. Once the bugs were sorted out and these systems became operational, the investments had been made. Although computer manufacturers had become accustomed to a three-year replacement cycle in which old computers were routinely replaced by new computers, many firms currently view their late 1990s intranet investments as long-lasting and do not need to repeat the hardware or software purchases of the boom years. In the words of the Chief Information Officer of Mohawk Carpets, "We're not spending as much because we already spent it" (Thurm 2001).

Legacy of the failed dot.coms

Another pillar of the ICT investment boom of the late 1990s was the demand for computer hardware and software by the thousands of newly established e-commerce business firms collectively known as the *dot.coms*. Spurred by easily available finance from venture capitalists and IPOs, a booming economy, and overblown expectations, the dot.coms were touted as a new industrial revolution:

> The Internet has become a powerful symbol of society's expectations about the future—a future of fast-moving, disruptive technology that is shifting the terrain not only in business, but also in politics and culture. . . . Because it is such a low-cost communications technology, the Internet holds the promise of drastically reducing transactions costs. . . . Organizational bureaucracies of every kind—corporate, government, and union—suddenly look vulnerable to the Internet's decentralizing powers. (Lohr 1999, p C1)

But the heralded dot.coms soon came crashing to the ground, leaving a legacy of failed business models, not to mention a surfeit of unneeded computer hardware that soon flooded the market for used equipment, in turn bringing to a halt the previously rapid growth in the demand for new equipment. Some of the used equipment eventually found new users, but much of the software dedicated to the specific requirements of individual e-commerce web sites became instantly worthless.

An early virtue of e-commerce was the intense competition fostered by low costs of entry, pushing the economy toward the classroom model of perfect competition. But e-commerce firms soon learned that competition brings benefits to the consumer but leaves little if any residual in the form of operating profits. Thus much of the investment in computer hardware and software infrastructure for the dot.com boom ultimately had a zero or negative rate of return. Further, the extent of reduction in transactions costs was exaggerated. For many products, e-commerce was just a new type of mail-order catalogue, providing an electronic interface for placing orders that eliminated the need for telephone operators, but no change in the technology of warehouses or delivery. As failed companies such as the e-grocer Webvan were soon to discover, the costs of the warehouses and delivery swamped the savings provided by the electronic order interface.[31]

If consumer e-commerce provided benefits to consumers without profits for dot.coms, then surely business e-commerce ("B2B") delivered benefits to businesses that flowed directly to the bottom line. Unfortunately B2B did not live up to its original promise; "many exchanges have shut down, and virtually all the rest are badly behind schedule in implementing their business plans" (Gomes 2001). What business firms need from their suppliers are "relationships, consistency, quality, and reliability" (Tedeschi 2001). For instance, a produce wholesaler had no use for produce Internet sites, because they lacked the element of trust that reassured customers that produce was fresh and top quality rather than rotting on the vine. Firms found that public e-commerce sites for buying supplies offered the same price to everyone, whereas firms had become used to developing individual relationships with suppliers and having price arrangements that were confidential. The produce wholesaler was quoted as rejecting the Internet for making public information that was previously confidential: "The Internet is very good at taking one message and sending it out to the whole world. . . . That's not the way our world works" (Gomes 2001, p A1). Firms also were concerned about reliability and the chance that some B2B web sites would not remain in business, a fear that soon came to be realized.[32]

Software innovation is falling behind hardware innovation

Throughout the history of the computer industry, purchase and replacement decisions have been driven by the need to purchase new hardware in order to be able to operate increasingly complex software. Computer chip makers continually increased the speed and memory capability of computers, and hard drive manufacturers more than kept pace.[33] But the minimum performance required to run the latest software also continued to increase, and users were continually under pressure to replace obsolescent machines with new ones capable of keeping up with software improvements. As the saying went, "What Intel giveth, Microsoft taketh away."

Perhaps the most controversial assertion of this chapter is that this race is over, Intel has won, and Microsoft is lagging badly behind. Evidence keeps accumulating that computer users do not feel the same impetus to buy replacement computers as before, because improvements in software have ground nearly to a halt. Consider this comment by the dean of computer columnists, Walter Mossberg of the *Wall Street Journal*, in reflecting on the tenth anniversary of his column:

> The upgrade cycle in PCs has all but petered out. Back in 1991, we still lived in an era when people needed to buy the latest and greatest processors and other hardware, just to run all the new software. But it has been at least four years since software challenged hardware in that way. Today, the killer app is the Internet, and it doesn't require the fastest, biggest PCs. It only thirsts for faster connection speeds, greater bandwidth (Mossberg 2001).

Mossberg is not alone in his assessment. Everyday, forecasts of slumping computer sales now routinely refer to the absence of compelling software: "Though PCs have grown more powerful, a lack of new software has dulled their shine for holiday sales . . . Consumers no longer are excited by faster processors running the same old programs" (McWilliams and Tam 2002). "Consumers and businesses have shown little inclination to shell out for new computers that do not offer significant improvements. . . . After Windows 95 was released PCs have not changed so much." (Reuters 2002, p C3). Other computer columnists concur: "There are many reasons for the current slump in personal computer sales, but one of the most important is the lack of software that gives us a compelling reason to replace our machines" (Wildstrom 2001).

Simple increases in computer speed and memory are not enough: "Even personal computer industry veterans acknowledge the paucity of new ideas that currently troubles the computer industry. . . . computers have reached a point where for the most common home purposes—Web surfing, e-mail, and word processing—they are already more than fast enough to suit a typical home user's needs. As long as new PC's are just faster, cheaper, better than old PC's, you're going to get slow growth" (Markoff 2002).

To be sure, some computer users always value more speed and memory, especially those whose main uses are games and the downloading of photos, video, and audio. But we are primarily interested in business rather than consumer uses of computers, since business uses are presumably those that contribute to productivity growth in the private business economy. Consumer use of computers for games, video, and audio may raise consumer welfare, but not in a way that increases measured output per hour.

The lack of compelling new types of software has translated into a stalling out of the advance of computer penetration in the US home. After growing from 30 to 60 percent between 1995 and 2001, the share of households with PCs remained unchanged at 60 percent in 2002. Worse yet, the reason most holdouts gave for not owning a computer at home was not price or technological ignorance, but that they "just had no compelling reasons to own PCs" (Gaither 2002). Part of the problem may be that the initial novelty of the web has worn off for early users, while current non-users are not persuaded to access the web. Another issue is the very source of the demise of many early dot.com firms: they could not figure out how to make a profit. The web now teems with advertising and user fees, repelling some early users: "Everywhere you go someone is jumping on you to buy something . . . It's like walking down the streets of Tijuana." For some users the novelty value of the web has started to wear off: "I'm a frontiersperson, and the Web is not a frontier anymore . . . It is simply a place" (both quotes from Guernsey 2002).

Y2K compressed the replacement cycle

The final, and probably least important, of the factors that temporarily boosted the demand for computers in the late 1990s was the much-publicized potential crisis regarding the inability of existing software, primarily older versions of programs written before the mid 1990s, to handle the transition from years beginning in "19XX" to "20XX." An enormous investment in software reprogramming occurred throughout 1998 and 1999 at almost every corporation, large and small, with frequent reports that each particular corporation had reached a certain percentage of the required reprogramming by a particular date. Some unknown part of the rapid growth of real computer investment displayed above in Figure 2 was related to the Y2K phenomenon, and particularly the compression of the normal replacement cycle as computers scheduled for normal replacement in 2000 and 2001 were instead replaced in 1998 and 1999.

Is broadband the answer?

If anything can stimulate purchases of ICT equipment in the next few years, it is the adoption of broadband in every US household that currently accesses the Internet via slow dial-up connections. An immediate qualification is that US corporate business already has fast connections, and even college freshmen have lightning-fast access to the Internet from their dorm rooms. Whatever impact on business productivity made possible by universal adoption of broadband in the US corporate and institutional world

has already occurred. A rush to install broadband connections in the US household would not have a direct impact on business productivity, since its major effect would be to allow faster downloading of video, music, and games.

But US households are not rushing to convert to broadband. In early 2002, adoption rates for all types of broadband were below 10 percent and were not rising at the rate that had been expected. Noam (2002) provides three reasons. First, broadband is not free, and it costs substantially more to provide than ordinary dial-up on an existing residential telephone line. Second, the network effects that multiply the benefits of an invention such as e-mail when it is universally adopted does not apply to broadband, since if Uncle Harry switches from dial-up to broadband, it has no effect on the benefits to Cousin Sarah of dialing up to send an e-mail to Uncle Harry. Third is "the absence of a strong reason to have it. . . . There is only so much free time and attention to go around in a day, and there is no indication that broadband users use the Internet much differently than narrowband users . . . we must push the demand side of broadband to catch up with the supply" (Noam, 2002, pp 4, 9).

Conclusion

Many studies have linked the post-1995 productivity growth revival in the United States to the acceleration in the growth of ICT investment that occurred at the same time. At first glance, their link between productivity and ICT would seem to imply that the revival had a single source—ICT investment—achieved both in its production and use. An acceleration in the growth of real investment in computers made possible more rapid MFP growth in the production of computers, as well as a greater contribution to productivity growth through capital deepening as the rest of the economy purchased more computers.

This chapter brings both bad news and good news to the debate over the role of ICT capital and the future outlook for productivity growth. The bad news, and the main contribution of the chapter, is that the ICT investment boom of the late 1990s was inherently transitory and unsustainable for both macroeconomic and microeconomic reasons. The growth rate of ICT investment did not occur in isolation but was supported by a positive feedback loop among an unusual confluence of positive *macroeconomic* shocks, including the stock market boom, a set of beneficial supply shocks that reduced inflation, and the role of low inflation in creating the benign tolerance by the Federal Reserve of unusually rapid output growth and a decline in the unemployment rate without precedent in the preceding three decades. At the same time, the growth rate of ICT investment was supported by a set of transitory *microeconomic* sources of demand for ICT equipment, including the telecom investment bubble, the fact that the World Wide Web could be invented only once, the equipment and software purchases by the dot.coms that promptly failed, and the last gasp of Microsoft and other software makers as they struggled to find ways for firms and consumers to use the explosion in the growth of computer power made possible by the inexorable advance of Moore's Law.

The good news is that a failure of ICT investment growth to return to the heady days of the late 1990s does not doom productivity growth to return to the dismal decades prior to 1995. The best recent work on the sources of the productivity revival between 1995 and 2001 attributes all of this revival, to the growth acceleration in ICT investment. Taken literally, this work implies that if the growth rate of ICT investment falls back to its pre-1995 pace, productivity growth will likewise return to its pre-1995 rate. But this recent research can be criticized, and it is possible that it overstates, perhaps substantially, the contribution of ICT investment to the productivity revival. Recent writing on productivity growth points to retail trade as a key locus of the role of computers in creating productivity growth, reasoning that for the aggregate economy ICT investment is the entire story and retailing is an industry that both uses ICT equipment heavily and displays a robust productivity growth revival at the level of industry data.

But much more has been going on in the retail sector, and presumably in other industrial sectors that are heavy users of ICT equipment, than just buying lots of computers and software. Micro evidence at the level of individual establishments shows that *all* of the productivity growth in the retail sector in the 1990s was achieved by new establishments, and that none of it was achieved by establishments already existing in 1990, no matter how many computers they bought. This suggests that a central role in the productivity growth revival of the 1990s was a set of non-ICT investments and organizational innovations that we associate with "big box" retailers such as Wal-Mart, Home Depot, Best Buy, and others. Old establishments checked out their customers with bar coder scanners, just as did new establishments, but ICT investments were apparently "necessary but not sufficient" for retail productivity to increase. New establishments were big, computers enabled them to be big, but computers by themselves were not enough to achieve a revival in retail productivity.

The confluence of the bad news and good news leaves the future of productivity growth highly uncertain. The macro and micro foundations of the late 1990s ICT investment boom may not reappear in our lifetimes, and it may be decades before we see five straight years of annual growth rates of ICT investment of greater than 30 percent

per year. But the role of ICT investment as a foundation of the productivity growth revival has been exaggerated, leaving other kinds of investment and organizational improvements playing a role that has not been sufficiently appreciated. This conclusion, albeit not susceptible to quantification, has one important byproduct: it helps us understand why Europe failed to duplicate the US productivity revival despite using the same computer hardware and software as Americans did. Europe's troubles lie elsewhere and cannot be solved by purchasing more computers. The environment of product and labor market regulation in Europe still, despite recent improvements, inhibits the bold new types of retailing formats that formed the vanguard of the US productivity revival. Whether Europe can loosen its straightjacket of regulations, and whether the United States can sustain these organizational improvements in the absence of a new ICT investment boom, remain unanswered questions.

Notes

1 This research has been supported by the National Science Foundation. I am grateful to Henry Chen for creating the figures, to John Haltiwanger and Jack Triplett for helpful discussions, to Daniel Sichel for providing his latest data as summarized in Table 4, and to William Nordhaus for an updated version of his stock market spread data.

2 This calculation is performed using 1996 weights of nominal (current-dollar) spending in each sector. The nonfarm private business sector is about 78 percent of GDP, the manufacturing sector is 16 percent, and the nonfarm nonmanufacturing "residual" sector is about 62 percent of GDP.

3 Gordon's (1993) technique was to conduct a grid search for the productivity trend that provides the best fit in an econometric equation relating changes in hours to lagged changes in hours and current and lagged changes in output. Results using this technique on recent data yield conclusions similar to the Hodrick-Prescott results discussed in the text and displayed in Figure 3 and Table 2.

4 Users of the Hodrick-Prescott method must specify a "smoothing parameter." Most users choose the same parameter (1600) used in the original Hodrick-Prescott research, but this yields too variable a trend that, for instance, exhibits a substantial decline in output during the Great Depression of the 1930s. The trend displayed in Figure 1 uses a parameter of 6400 that imposes slightly more smoothness.

5 Based on data through 1999:Q4, Gordon (2000, Table 2, p 55) estimated a cyclical effect of 0.50 points, almost identical to that displayed in Table 2.

6 The combined annual growth rates in Table 2 of actual and trend for the period 1995:Q4–2001:Q3 are both 2.17 percent, implying a cyclical effect of 0.00 percent.

7 Gordon (2000, Table 2) calculated a residual acceleration in MFP outside the ICT sector of 0.02 percent per year for the period ending in 1999:Q4, compared with Oliner and Sichel's –0.02 percent per year for the period ending with the full year 2001.

8 Recall that the GDP statistics on which they rely measure output by production and treat any unsold goods as inventory accumulation, a part of GDP.

9 Virtually the only remaining traditional hardware store in Evanston, Lemoi Hardware advertises that it is "Evanston's oldest store, established in 1896."

10 Scatter plots supporting these correlations between MFP growth and computer intensity are presented in Bartelsman et al. (2002, Figures 8 and 9).

11 Any generalizations here about "Europe" must be qualified by differences across countries. The Germans until recently were notorious for restrictive shop-closing hours, while the French firm Carrefour and the Swedish firm Ikea are innovators in "big box" retailing formats.

12 On the issue of software and telecom deflators, see Jorgenson and Stiroh (2000, pp 153–160).

13 The monthly average of the S&P 500 index for May 1995 was 508, and the peak reached on March 24, 2000, was 1527. The value reached on October 7, 2002, was 785, fully 49 percent below the peak.

14 Nordhaus (2002a, Figure 5) displays four different measures of profits. There are two S&P indexes, both including and excluding accounting changes, discontinued operations, extraordinary items, and special items. The measure discussed in the text is reported S&P profits, which includes all these items. There are also two NIPA indexes, including and excluding an inventory valuation adjustment and capital consumption allowances, and the measure discussed in the text includes such adjustments. Major differences in the NIPA indexes compared with the S&P include their greater comprehensiveness in applying to the entire economy, exclusion of capital gains, basis on economic rather than accounting profits, and treating of stock options as an expense.

15 Nordhaus (2002a, Figure 6) shows that reported S&P profits were not unusually high as a percent of GDP at the 2000 peak and indeed were lower at that peak than in virtually every year between 1960 and 1980. This suggests that a substantial rebound in S&P profits relative to GDP from the 2001–2002 lows is quite likely.

16 One is reminded of the famous and chilling remark of the British Foreign Minister Sir Edward Grey on August 3, 1914, after the British cabinet had made its fateful decision to go to war: "The lamps are going out all over Europe; we shall not see them lit again in our lifetime."

17 The deflator for Personal Consumption Expenditures, part of the National Income and Product Accounts, is preferable to the Consumer Price Index because it has been revised retrospectively to use a consistent set of measurement methods, whereas the CPI is never revised.

18 The more general approach was developed in Gordon (1977, 1982), and its evolution is described in Gordon (1997).

19 Measures of "core inflation" that exclude food and energy prices exhibited only a negligible acceleration from 1998 to 2000, but these core measures are influenced by the other beneficial shocks discussed in this section—namely the productivity revival, the decline of real import prices, the temporary cessation of medical care inflation, and the accelerated rate of decline of computer prices.

20 The growth rate of real compensation per hour subsequently slowed back to 0.7 percent per year between 2000:Q2 and 2002:Q2.

21 "Small Employers Severely Cut Health Care," *The New York Times*, September 6, 2002, p. C4.

22 The arithmetic of Moore's Law can be better understood as related to the fact that the natural logarithm of 1.0 is 0 and of 2.0 is 0.7. Thus a doubling of computation power raises the logarithm by 0.7, which represents a logarithmic growth rate of 46.7 percent over 18 months or 1.5 years. At that rate, the logarithm of computation power over 3 years increases by 1.4, or by a factor of 4.0 (the antilogarithm or exponent of 1.4).

23 With a product cycle of two years, computation power quadruples every two years and doubles every 12 months. Any variable that doubles in one year must increase by a factor of 1,024 over one decade.

24 Three examples of this graph applied to computers exhibiting no shift in the demand curve are Brynjolfsson (1996, p 290), Gordon (1990, p 46) and Sichel (1997, p 17). The supply curves in this graph have been drawn as horizontal lines, both to simplify the subsequent discussion and because there is no evidence of a rising marginal cost of producing additional computer speed, memory, and other characteristics at a given level of technology.

25 Here to simplify the presentation we will take the Internet as being synonomous with the World Wide Web and the invention of web browsers, although the use of the Internet for e-mail, at least in the academic and scientific community, dates back at least to the early 1980s.

26 In terms of elementary economics, there is an increase in the consumer surplus associated with the lower supply curve S_2 from the triangle JP_2B to the larger triangle KP_2E.

27 Existing computer price deflators fail to take account of the radical decline in the price per calculation that occurred in the transition from mainframes to PCs (which have been studied only separately, not together). Gordon (1990, p 239) calculates that the annual rate of price decline between 1972 and 1987 would have been 35 percent per annum rather than 20 percent per annum if this transitional benefit had been taken into account. This consideration further reduces the unique quality of technological advance created by the New Economy.

28 Facts in this section come from Berman (2002). The loss in stock market value and in jobs comes from Yang (2002).

29 If supply quadruples every year while demand grows by 50 percent per year, and if demand and supply are equal in year 1, then by year 5 the ratio of demand to supply is only 2 percent.

30 My own web site http://faculty-web.at.northwestern.edu/economics/gordon was developed by two undergraduate economics majors in the fall of 1998.

31 On the demise of Webvan, see Spurgeon (2001). Among the problems cited, besides the costs of huge warehouses and truck fleets, were the reluctance of "busy people who have little time to sit home waiting for a delivery. . . the challenge remains being able to develop a large enough customer base to offset the costs of picking and delivering those groceries on a profitable basis." Further, time-pressed consumers chose not to turn to web delivery services but to buying prepared food in traditional supermarkets: "It turns out, however, that shopping isn't the step that busy consumers are eliminating. Cooking is."

32 Ironically, the much heralded e-business technological revolution that was supposed to increase dramatically the efficiency of inventory management did not prevent one of the largest pile-ups of excess inventory in economic history, not only in ICT equipment but also in the economy as a whole, where inventory accumulation was negative for five straight quarters, 2001:Q1 to 2002:Q1.

33 My first PC in 1983 had a hard drive capacity of a mere 10MB. Today's standard 40GB hard drives represent an increase in capacity by a factor of 4,000. Over the same period speed and memory have increased somewhat less, by a factor of about 1,000. This represents an annual rate of performance change of about 36 percent for speed and memory, and about 44 percent for hard drive capacity.

References

Bartelsman, E. et al. 2002. "The Spread of ICT and Productivity Growth: Is Europe Really Lagging Behind in the New Economy," OECD draft report presented at *The Information Economy: Productivity Gains and the Digital Divide* Conference, Catania, Sicily, June 15.

Berman, D. K. 2002. "Innovation Outpaced the Marketplace," *Wall Street Journal*, September 26, p B1.

Blanchard, O., and J. Simon. 2001. "The Long and Large Decline in U.S. Output Volatility," *Brookings Papers on Economic Activity* 32(1): 135–164.

Brynjolfsson, E. 1996. "The Contribution of Information Technology to Consumer Welfare," *Information Systems Research* 7(3): 281–300.

David, Paul A. (1990). "The Dynamo and the Computer: An Historical Perspective on the Modern Productivity Paradox," *American Economic Review* (Papers and Proceedings) 80(2): 355–361.

Dreazen, Y. J. 2002. "Behind the Fiber Glut," *Wall Street Journal*, September 26, p B1.

Financial Times. 2001. Lex Column "Technical Difficulties," April 18, p 14.

Foster, L., J. Haltiwanger, and C. J. Krizan. 2002. "The Link Between Aggregate and Micro Productivity Growth: Evidence from Retail Trade," NBER Working Paper No. 9120. Cambridge, MA: National Bureau of Economic Research.

Gaither, C. 2002. "The Many, the Skeptical, the Folks Without PC's," *The New York Times*, March 18, p C3.

Gomes, L. 2001. "How Lower-Tech Gear Beat Web Exchanges at Their Own Game," *Wall Street Journal*, March 16, p A1.

Gordon, R. J. 1977. "Can the Inflation of the 1970s Be Explained?" *Brookings Papers on Economic Activity* 1:1977, 253–277.

———. 1982. "Inflation, Flexible Exchange Rates, and the Natural Rate of Unemployment." In M. N. Baily, ed., *Workers, Jobs, and Inflation*. Washington, DC: Brookings.

——— 1990. *The Measurement of Durable Goods Prices*. Chicago: University of Chicago Press.

———. 1993. "The Jobless Recovery: Does It Signal a New Era of Productivity-Led Growth?" *Brookings Papers on Economic Activity* 24(1): 271–316.

———. 1997. "The Time-Varying NAIRU and its Implications for Economic Policy." *Journal of Economic Perspectives* 11(1): 11–32.

———. 1998. "Foundations of the Goldilocks Economy: Supply Shocks and the Time-Varying NAIRU," *Brookings Papers on Economic Activity* 29(2): 297–333.

———. 2000. "Does the New Economy Measure Up to the Great Inventions of the Past?" *Journal of Economic Perspectives* 14(4): 49–74.

Guernsey, L. 2002. "As the Web Matures, Fun Is Hard to Find," *The New York Times*, March 28, p D1.

Griliches, Z. 1994. "Productivity, R&D, and the Data Constraint," *American Economic Review* 84(March): 1–23.

Hodrick, R., and E. C. Prescott. 1981. "Postwar U.S. Business Cycles: An Empirical Investigation." Discussion Paper No. 451. Minneapolis, MN: University of Minnesota (May).

Hultgren, T. 1960. "Changes in Labor Cost during Cycles in Production and Business." NBER Occasional Paper 74. New York: National Bureau of Economic Research.

Jorgenson, D. W. 2001. "Information Technology and the U.S. Economy," *American Economic Review* 91(1): 1–32.

———. 2002. *Economic Growth in the Information Age: Econometrics*. Vol. 3. Cambridge MA: MIT Press.

Jorgenson, D. W. and K. J. Stiroh. 2000. "Raising the Speed Limit: U.S. Economic Growth in the Information Age," *Brookings Papers on Economic Activity* 31(1): 125–211.

Lohr, S. 1999. "The Economy Transformed, Bit by Bit," *The New York Times*, December 20, p C1.

Markoff, J. 2002. "PC Makers Hit Speed Bumps; Being Faster May Not Matter," *The New York Times*, September 30, p C1.

McWilliams, G., and P.-W. Tam. 2002. "Season Looks Gloomy for PCs," *Wall Street Journal*, October 17, p B4.

Miller, R. 2001. "Too Much of Everything," *Business Week*, April 9: 28–30.

Mossberg, W. 2001. "Decade Yields Dramatic Progress in Personal Technology," *Wall Street Journal*, October 25, p B1.

The New York Times. "Small Employers Severely Cut Health Care," *The New York Times*, September 6, 2002, p C4.

Noam, E. 2002. Panel presentation in "Broadband: Opportunities and Challenges for the Telecommunications Industry," transcript of a Forum presented by the Economic Strategy Institute. Washington, DC: Economic Strategy Institute, pp 1–9.

Nordhaus, W. D. 2002a. "The Recent Recession, the Current Recovery, and Stock Prices," *Brookings Papers on Economic Activity* 33(1): 199–220.

———. 2002b. "Productivity Growth and the New Economy," *Brookings Papers on Economic Activity* 33(2): forthcoming.

Okun, A. M. 1962. "The Gap between Actual and Potential Output," *Proceedings of the American Statistical Association*, reprinted in Edmund S. Phelps, ed., *Problems of the Modern Economy*. New York: Norton, 1965.

Oliner, S. D. and D. E. Sichel. 2000. "The Resurgence of Growth in the Late 1990s: Is Information Technology the Story?" *Journal of Economic Perspectives* 14(Fall): 3–22.

———. 2001. "The Resurgence of Growth in the Late 1990s: Is Information Technology the Story?" Updated presentation presented at the meetings of the American Economic Association, January 7.

———. 2002. "Information Technology and Productivity: Where Are We Now and Where Are We Going?" *Atlanta Federal Reserve Bank Review* (forthcoming).

Reuters. 2002. "PC Sales Fail to Rev Up as School Starts," *Chicago Tribune*, September 9, p. C3.

Sichel, D. E. 1997. *The Computer Revolution: An Economic Perspective*. Washington, DC: Brookings.

———. 2002. Personal communication, update to Oliner and Sichel (2002), October 6.

Sieling, M., B. Friedman, and M. Dumas. 2001. "Labor Productivity in the Retail Trade Industry, 1987–99," *Monthly Labor Review* (December): 3–14.

Spurgeon, D. 2001. "Traditional Grocers Feel Vindicated by Webvan's Failure," *Wall Street Journal*, July 12, p B3.

Tedeschi, B. 2001. "E-commerce Report," *The New York Times*, March 5, p C11.

Thurm, S. 2001. "The Broader Slowdown Isn't the Only Cause of Tech Industry's Ills," *Wall Street Journal*, March 21, p A1.

Triplett, J. E. and B. P. Bosworth. 2002. "Baumol's Disease Has Been Cured: IT and Multifactor Productivity in U.S. Services Industries," Presentation at Brookings Workshop on Services Industry Productivity. Washington, DC, May 17.

van Ark, B. , R. Inklaar, and R. H. McGuckin. 2002. "Changing Gear: Productivity, ICT and Service Industries: Europe and the United States," Paper presented to Brookings Workshop on Services Industry Productivity. Washington, DC, May 17.

Wildstrom, S. H. 2001. "Buying a New PC? Not So Fast," *Business Week*, April 2, p 26.

Yang, C. 2002. "The Decision that Could Reshape Telecom," *Business Week*, September 30, p 86.

CHAPTER 3.3

The Networked Readiness of Nations

SOUMITRA DUTTA, INSEAD

AMIT JAIN, INSEAD

Overview

The fundamental role of Information and Communication Technology (ICT) has long been recognized as a catalyst for organizational transformation and change. As a consequence, gaining a better understanding of the economic and business impact of ICT has been identified as a key research priority, giving rise to a multitude of research streams. The Networked Readiness Index 2002–2003 discussed in this chapter is the product of one such research effort.[1]

ICT forms the backbone of several industries such as banking, airlines, and publishing, and is an important value-adding component of consumer products such as television sets, cameras, cars, and mobile phone sets. ICT is today a dominant force in enabling companies to exploit new distribution channels, create new products, and deliver differentiated value-added services to customers.[2] ICT is also an important catalyst for social transformation and national progress. Disparities in the levels of ICT readiness and usage could translate into a disparity in levels of productivity—and hence could influence a country's rate of economic growth. Understanding and leveraging ICT is critical to a nation striving for continued economic progress.[3]

Over the past few years, numerous attempts have been made to measure the comparative levels of ICT development of nations.[4] The multitude of these efforts, and the diversity of the organizations conducting them, only helps underline the importance of ICT as a key factor contributing to a nation's development and as a cohesive force for integrating a nation in the global economy. The speed with which technological forces affect us and the rapidity of the ensuing changes require a mechanism for measurement that takes into account not only the factors enabling the spread and usage of ICT, but also explicitly considers the roles played by the major stakeholders—individuals, businesses, and governments.

This chapter presents the Networked Readiness Index (NRI) that has been used to assess the comparative progress of 80 countries along different dimensions of ICT progress. The discussion in this chapter is divided into four main sections. First, there is a discussion on the "Networked Readiness Framework" and the procedure used to arrive at the NRI results. Second, the results of the research and analysis are presented—the relative ranking of nations based on their degrees of networked readiness. Third, we take a closer look at the three component indexes (and their constituent subindexes) composing the NRI, and how various countries have fared on each of these dimensions. Finally, the fourth section investigates the relationship of networked readiness with key variables such as GDP per capita, ICT expenditure, and Internet usage, in addition to presenting some of the key challenges faced while conducting the study.

The Networked Readiness Index framework 2002–2003

The Networked Readiness Index (NRI) framework 2002–2003 represents an effort to untangle the underlying complexity behind the role of ICT in a nation's development. The framework and its components not only provide a model for computing the relative development and use of ICT in countries, but also allow for a better understanding of a nation's strengths and weaknesses with respect to ICT.

Figure 1 depicts the structure of the NRI framework. The NRI framework is based upon the following premises:

- There are three important stakeholders to consider in the development and use of ICT: individuals, businesses, and governments.
- There is a general macroeconomic and regulatory environment for ICT in which the above stakeholders play out their respective roles.
- The degree of usage of ICT (and hence the impact of ICT) on the three stakeholders is linked to their degree of readiness (or capability) to use and benefit from ICT.

The *NRI* is defined as "the degree of preparation of a nation or community to participate in and benefit from ICT developments." As shown in Figure 1, the index is a composite of three components: the environment for ICT offered by a given country or community; the readiness of the community's key stakeholders (individuals, businesses, and governments) to use ICT; and finally the usage of ICT amongst these stakeholders. A discussion in greater detail on the structure of the framework is presented in a following section titled "Disaggregating the Networked Readiness Index."

NRI results for 2002–2003

The overall results for the Networked Readiness Index 2002–2003 are presented in Table 1.[5] Finland comes out with the top rank, followed by the United States. Finland, as shall be seen later, has performed well across all the component indexes of the NRI framework. Singapore, Sweden, and Iceland occupy the third, fourth, and fifth places, respectively. Canada gets the sixth place, followed by the United Kingdom, Denmark, and Taiwan with almost equal NRI scores. Germany comes in tenth place. Of note also are:

- Israel, with its rapidly developing e-business sector and large technically skilled workforce, has a current rank of 12.
- Korea, with its very high Internet penetration and one of the highest usages of broadband in the world, is ranked 14.
- Estonia is the leader amongst the eastern European countries with a rank of 24.

One sees in the top 25 rankings the following regional groupings:

- The Americas: two countries—the United States and Canada.
- Western Europe: fourteen countries led by Finland.
- Asia and Oceania: seven countries led by Singapore.
- Middle East and North Africa: one country—Israel.
- Central and eastern Europe: one country—Estonia.

Furthermore, one can observe that

- The top-ranked South American countries are Brazil (28), Chile (34), and Argentina (44). As a block, Latin America fares poorly in the NRI rankings. Secondary analysis leads us to believe that this is partially explained by the relatively low levels of e-readiness of the governments of these countries.
- In Asia, India with its immense pool of trained IT staff is ranked 36 and Thailand follows at rank 40. China is ranked 42.
- Russia comes in with an overall ranking of 67.
- There are few countries from Africa and Central Asia that are included in the rankings. This is due to limitations in obtaining reliable data from these nations (see last section for more details on limitations of the research).

Interpreting the results

The NRI permits business leaders and public policymakers to investigate the reasons leading to a nation's ranking and relative performance. It captures key factors relating to the environment, and the readiness and usage of the three stakeholders in ICT (individuals, businesses, and governments), and can be used to understand the performance of a nation or even a region with regards to ICT development. The component index and subindex rankings serve to identify key areas where a nation is under- or overperforming. One would, for instance, be able to identify relative imbalances in development across the three component indexes of environment, readiness, and usage, or even go one level deeper.[6]

We would like to emphasize that although rankings are useful as relative indicators of a nation's ICT excellence, there are several limitations to the analytic process. For one, caution should be exercised in comparing countries that are closely ranked. Countries ranked close together can show very small variation in the index scores. Costa Rica (Index = 3.57, rank 48) and Turkey (Index = 3.57, rank = 49) even have the same overall score. In this case, Costa Rica had an overall index score marginally higher than that of Turkey, but it was at the third decimal place. Additionally, small differences in the index may be outside the limits of statistical significance due to the fact

Table 1: The Networked Readiness Index (NRI)

Country	NRI score	NRI rank	Country	NRI score	NRI rank	Country	NRI score	NRI rank
Finland	5.92	1	Czech Republic	4.43	27	Sri Lanka	3.45	53
United States	5.79	2	Brazil	4.40	28	Uruguay	3.45	54
Singapore	5.74	3	Hungary	4.30	29	Mauritius	3.44	55
Sweden	5.58	4	Portugal	4.28	30	Dominican Republic	3.40	56
Iceland	5.51	5	Malaysia	4.28	31	Trinidad and Tobago	3.36	57
Canada	5.44	6	Slovenia	4.23	32	Colombia	3.33	58
United Kingdom	5.35	7	Tunisia	4.16	33	Jamaica	3.31	59
Denmark	5.33	8	Chile	4.14	34	Panama	3.30	60
Taiwan	5.31	9	South Africa	3.94	35	Philippines	3.25	61
Germany	5.29	10	India	3.89	36	El Salvador	3.17	62
Netherlands	5.26	11	Latvia	3.87	37	Indonesia	3.16	63
Israel	5.22	12	Poland	3.85	38	Venezuela	3.11	64
Switzerland	5.18	13	Slovak Republic	3.85	39	Peru	3.10	65
Korea	5.10	14	Thailand	3.80	40	Bulgaria	3.03	66
Australia	5.04	15	Greece	3.77	41	Russian Federation	2.99	67
Austria	5.01	16	China	3.70	42	Ukraine	2.98	68
Norway	5.00	17	Botswana	3.68	43	Vietnam	2.96	69
Hong Kong SAR	4.99	18	Argentina	3.67	44	Romania	2.66	70
France	4.97	19	Lithuania	3.65	45	Guatemala	2.63	71
Japan	4.95	20	Mexico	3.63	46	Nigeria	2.62	72
Ireland	4.89	21	Croatia	3.62	47	Ecuador	2.60	73
Belgium	4.83	22	Costa Rica	3.57	48	Paraguay	2.54	74
New Zealand	4.70	23	Turkey	3.57	49	Bangladesh	2.53	75
Estonia	4.69	24	Jordan	3.51	50	Bolivia	2.47	76
Spain	4.67	25	Morocco	3.50	51	Nicaragua	2.44	77
Italy	4.60	26	Namibia	3.47	52	Zimbabwe	2.42	78
		(cont'd.)			*(cont'd.)*	Honduras	2.37	79
						Haiti	2.07	80

Figure 1: The Networked Readiness Index framework 2002–2003

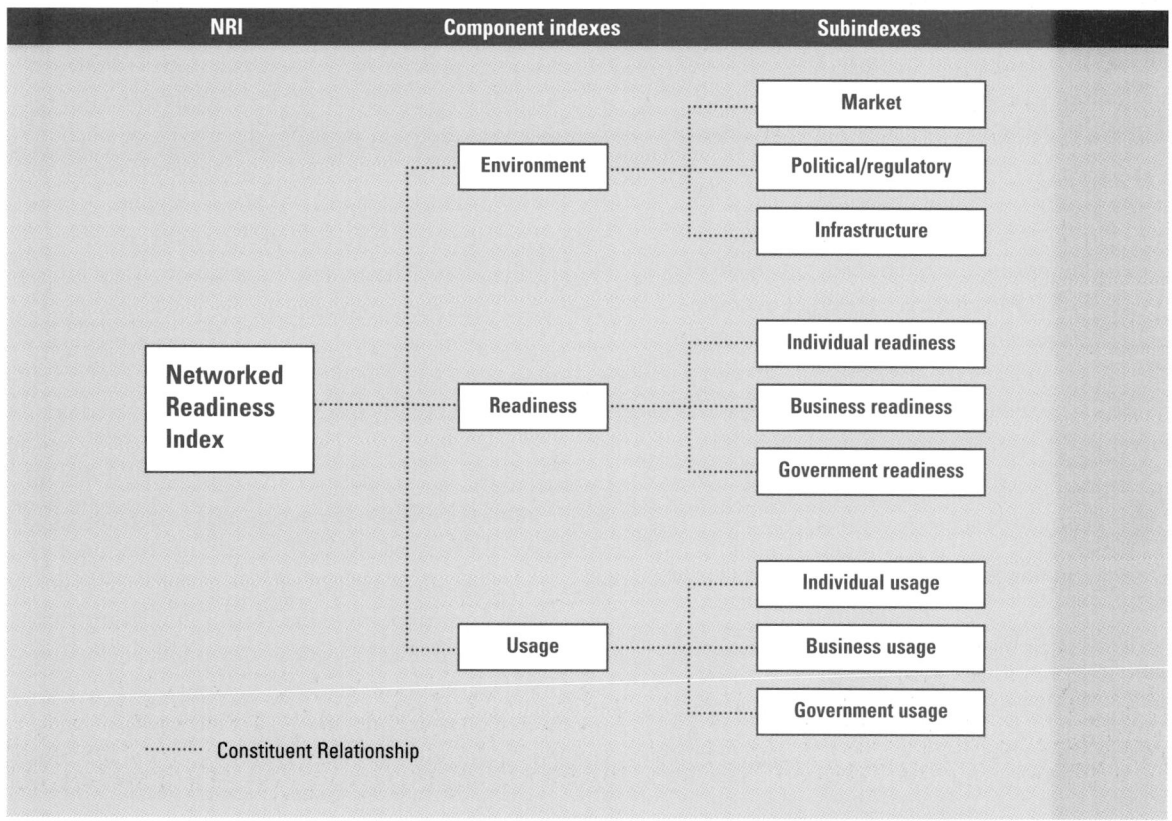

Source: INSEAD

that a number of missing observations were estimated using analytic techniques such as regression and clustering.

Also, only 80 countries were considered in our analysis due to limitations in the availability of data from reliable sources. Ranking other countries remains a challenge for the future. Any overall ranking on a global basis needs to account for these countries where data are unavailable, and any inferences drawn on the current rankings should be done with this taken into consideration.

Finally, the complexity of ICT issues in a nation can get obscured behind the numerical figure of the NRI. A country such as India, for instance, shows enormous geographic and demographic divides in ICT usage. It has one of the largest workforces in the world in ICT. One can find intense ICT usage in technology clusters such as Bangalore and Gurgaon (near New Delhi), or amongst the upper-middle bracket of incomes. The other side of the story is that there is not even telephone connectivity in large parts of the country. Singapore, on the other hand is a country where there is high ICT usage across all stakeholders—individuals, businesses, and governments.

Disaggregating the Networked Readiness Index

The NRI provides a quick and relative benchmark of the overall success of a country in participating in and benefiting from ICT. Although this is useful, one may need to gain further insights into areas of over- and underperformance of a nation, and to understand the key drivers determining the results. One can do so by looking at the component indexes: environment, readiness, and usage. See Table 2 for the overall results of each component index. Further insight may be obtained by looking at the subindexes composing each component index. The final level of detail can be obtained by having a close look at the 64 variables comprising the subindexes, which are presented in the Technical Appendix at the end of the chapter. Figure 2 gives a schematic diagram of the relationships between the various indexes and how they add up to form the NRI. The Technical Appendix to the chapter provides more details on the computation of the NRI.

Figure 2: Disaggregating the Networked Readiness Index

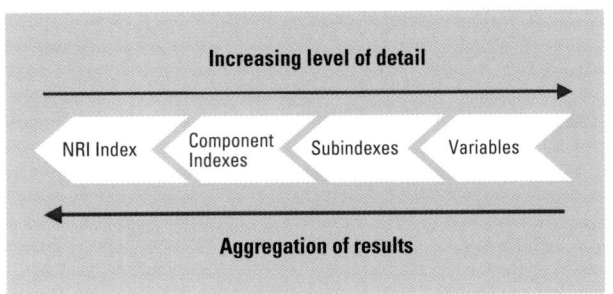

Environment

The environment component index is designed to measure the conduciveness of an environment that a country can provide for the development and usage of ICT. As can be seen from Table 2, the top countries with regard to the environment are the United States, Finland, and Iceland, and the results are consistent with the overall index. An exception is Israel, which has a rank of 12 on the overall index, and that of 5 for environment. The primary driver for Israel's excellent rank is the political/regulatory environment provided to ICT in the country, and this reflects the high priority given to ICT by the government.

Table 3 presents the detailed ranking and scores for each of the three subindexes comprising the environment dimension:

Market: This entails the assessment of the presence of the appropriate human resources and ancillary businesses to support a knowledge-based society. The forces that play an important role in determining the market environment for ICT are varied and include fundamental macroeconomic variables, commercial measures such as availability of funding and skilled labor, and the level of development of the corporate environment. The leader for this subindex is the United States followed by Finland, the United Kingdom and Sweden. It is noteworthy that Israel ranks highly at 5th place.

Political/Regulatory: The priorities of a nation are reflected in its policies and laws, which in turn influence its rate of growth and direction of development. This component of the NRI measures the impact of a nation's polity, laws, and regulations and their implementation on the development and use of ICT. The leaders from the political/regulatory perspective are Singapore, Israel, Finland, the United States, and Canada, not a surprising result given that these governments are known for their strong support of and emphasis on ICT. Box 1 presents a case study of Canada highlighting how government policy can be used aggressively to promote networked readiness.

Infrastructure: *Infrastructure* is defined as the level of availability and quality of the key access infrastructure for ICT within a country. A quality ICT access infrastructure facilitates the adoption, usage, and impact of these technologies, which in turn promote investment in infrastructure. Infrastructure thus plays a critical role in influencing the networked readiness of a nation. The top ranks for this component go to Iceland, the United States, Japan, and Sweden. One notes that India at 68th place for infrastructure—a very low rank compared with its overall 33rd position in environment—is perhaps an indication of the heterogeneous proliferation of ICT across different socioeconomic and geographic segments in the country. Box 2

Table 2: Networked Readiness Index (NRI) component indexes

Country	Environment score	Rank	Country	Readiness score	Rank	Country	Usage score	Rank
United States	5.83	1	Singapore	6.41	1	Finland	5.85	1
Finland	5.58	2	Finland	6.34	2	Singapore	5.58	2
Iceland	5.32	3	United States	6.06	3	Sweden	5.53	3
Canada	5.30	4	Sweden	5.95	4	United States	5.49	4
Israel	5.27	5	Canada	5.87	5	Iceland	5.36	5
Sweden	5.26	6	Iceland	5.86	6	Denmark	5.32	6
United Kingdom	5.24	7	Taiwan	5.82	7	Taiwan	5.22	7
Singapore	5.22	8	Israel	5.81	8	Korea	5.22	8
Germany	5.18	9	Switzerland	5.73	9	Netherlands	5.17	9
Netherlands	5.12	10	United Kingdom	5.72	10	Canada	5.17	10
Denmark	5.05	11	Denmark	5.62	11	Germany	5.14	11
Austria	4.95	12	Korea	5.60	12	United Kingdom	5.08	12
Switzerland	4.94	13	Japan	5.56	13	Norway	4.94	13
Australia	4.89	14	Germany	5.56	14	Australia	4.88	14
Taiwan	4.88	15	Netherlands	5.51	15	Switzerland	4.87	15
Ireland	4.86	16	France	5.51	16	Hong Kong SAR	4.80	16
France	4.85	17	Hong Kong SAR	5.46	17	Belgium	4.66	17
Japan	4.79	18	Austria	5.44	18	Austria	4.64	18
Norway	4.78	19	Australia	5.35	19	Israel	4.60	19
Hong Kong SAR	4.71	20	Ireland	5.31	20	France	4.55	20
New Zealand	4.66	21	Estonia	5.29	21	Estonia	4.51	21
Belgium	4.64	22	Norway	5.29	22	Japan	4.51	22
Italy	4.61	23	Belgium	5.20	23	Ireland	4.50	23
Spain	4.58	24	New Zealand	5.12	24	Italy	4.40	24
Korea	4.50	25	Czech Republic	5.04	25	Spain	4.38	25
Portugal	4.28	26	Spain	5.03	26	Brazil	4.32	26
Estonia	4.28	27	Tunisia	5.01	27	New Zealand	4.32	27
Malaysia	4.24	28	Hungary	5.00	28	Portugal	4.15	28
Hungary	4.24	29	Malaysia	4.95	29	Czech Republic	4.08	29
Czech Republic	4.18	30	Italy	4.78	30	Slovenia	4.04	30
Brazil	4.17	31	Slovenia	4.75	31	Chile	3.88	31
Chile	4.04	32	Brazil	4.72	32	Argentina	3.84	32
India	3.98	33	Chile	4.50	33	Poland	3.79	33
Tunisia	3.98	34	China	4.50	34	South Africa	3.73	34
Slovenia	3.89	35	Thailand	4.49	35	Hungary	3.67	35
Slovak Republic	3.86	36	Portugal	4.41	36	Mexico	3.67	36
South Africa	3.86	37	Latvia	4.41	37	Malaysia	3.64	37
Greece	3.79	38	Slovak Republic	4.38	38	Latvia	3.54	38
Thailand	3.68	39	India	4.35	39	Turkey	3.53	39
Latvia	3.66	40	Lithuania	4.33	40	Tunisia	3.50	40
Botswana	3.66	41	Sri Lanka	4.29	41	Greece	3.39	41
Jordan	3.64	42	Costa Rica	4.23	42	India	3.33	42
Namibia	3.61	43	South Africa	4.23	43	Croatia	3.33	43
Lithuania	3.57	44	Poland	4.20	44	Slovak Republic	3.30	44
Dominican Republic	3.56	45	Botswana	4.16	45	Uruguay	3.25	45
Poland	3.56	46	Greece	4.13	46	Thailand	3.24	46
Croatia	3.52	47	Croatia	4.02	47	Botswana	3.22	47
Morocco	3.50	48	Morocco	4.01	48	Costa Rica	3.18	48
Trinidad and Tobago	3.49	49	Jamaica	3.99	49	Venezuela	3.13	49
China	3.49	50	Namibia	3.98	50	China	3.12	50
Uruguay	3.48	51	Mexico	3.97	51	Lithuania	3.05	51
Argentina	3.47	52	Jordan	3.95	52	El Salvador	3.01	52
Mauritius	3.43	53	Mauritius	3.91	53	Philippines	2.99	53
Sri Lanka	3.39	54	Vietnam	3.90	54	Mauritius	2.99	54
Turkey	3.38	55	Dominican Republic	3.88	55	Panama	2.98	55
Philippines	3.33	56	Bulgaria	3.84	56	Morocco	2.98	56
Costa Rica	3.30	57	Trinidad and Tobago	3.80	57	Colombia	2.94	57
Colombia	3.30	58	Turkey	3.79	58	Jordan	2.93	58
Mexico	3.24	59	Russian Federation	3.78	59	Peru	2.85	59
Panama	3.22	60	Colombia	3.76	60	Namibia	2.83	60
Jamaica	3.20	61	Indonesia	3.72	61	Trinidad and Tobago	2.79	61
Venezuela	3.10	62	Panama	3.71	62	Dominican Republic	2.76	62
Indonesia	3.01	63	Argentina	3.70	63	Indonesia	2.76	63
El Salvador	3.01	64	Uruguay	3.61	64	Jamaica	2.75	64
Peru	2.95	65	Ukraine	3.58	65	Sri Lanka	2.68	65
Russian Federation	2.88	66	Peru	3.50	66	Ecuador	2.62	66
Bulgaria	2.87	67	El Salvador	3.48	67	Ukraine	2.58	67
Ukraine	2.77	68	Philippines	3.43	68	Nigeria	2.56	68
Romania	2.75	69	Romania	3.35	69	Nicaragua	2.50	69
Nigeria	2.69	70	Venezuela	3.11	70	Paraguay	2.50	70
Vietnam	2.61	71	Guatemala	2.89	71	Guatemala	2.45	71
Guatemala	2.55	72	Zimbabwe	2.87	72	Bangladesh	2.40	72
Bolivia	2.41	73	Ecuador	2.85	73	Bulgaria	2.38	73
Zimbabwe	2.41	74	Paraguay	2.85	74	Bolivia	2.38	74
Bangladesh	2.37	75	Bangladesh	2.81	75	Vietnam	2.37	75
Ecuador	2.32	76	Honduras	2.66	76	Russian Federation	2.30	76
Paraguay	2.28	77	Bolivia	2.62	77	Honduras	2.25	77
Honduras	2.20	78	Nicaragua	2.62	78	Haiti	2.19	78
Nicaragua	2.19	79	Nigeria	2.61	79	Zimbabwe	1.97	79
Haiti	1.83	80	Haiti	2.19	80	Romania	1.88	80

Table 3: Environment subindexes

Environment subindex = 1/3 market + 1/3 political/regulatory + 1/3 infrastructure

Country	Market score	Rank	Country	Political/regulatory score	Rank	Country	Infrastructure score	Rank
United States	6.08	1	Singapore	5.86	1	Iceland	5.94	1
Finland	5.92	2	Israel	5.84	2	United States	5.75	2
United Kingdom	5.56	3	Finland	5.76	3	Japan	5.46	3
Sweden	5.56	4	United States	5.67	4	Sweden	5.23	4
Israel	5.36	5	Canada	5.62	5	Germany	5.22	5
Germany	5.16	6	Netherlands	5.44	6	Canada	5.20	6
Taiwan	5.12	7	Malaysia	5.41	7	Australia	5.15	7
Netherlands	5.11	8	Ireland	5.37	8	Denmark	5.13	8
Canada	5.08	9	Iceland	5.31	9	Switzerland	5.09	9
Singapore	4.93	10	United Kingdom	5.28	10	Finland	5.05	10
France	4.93	11	Austria	5.28	11	France	4.89	11
Ireland	4.91	12	Denmark	5.19	12	Singapore	4.89	12
Switzerland	4.88	13	Australia	5.18	13	United Kingdom	4.87	13
Norway	4.86	14	Germany	5.15	14	New Zealand	4.86	14
Denmark	4.84	15	India	5.00	15	Netherlands	4.80	15
Austria	4.78	16	Sweden	4.99	16	Austria	4.78	16
Iceland	4.70	17	Hong Kong SAR	4.98	17	Hong Kong SAR	4.77	17
Japan	4.63	18	Spain	4.95	18	Taiwan	4.71	18
Korea	4.59	19	Belgium	4.91	19	Norway	4.70	19
Italy	4.53	20	Italy	4.85	20	Spain	4.62	20
Belgium	4.43	21	Switzerland	4.85	21	Israel	4.61	21
New Zealand	4.42	22	Taiwan	4.82	22	Belgium	4.57	22
Hong Kong SAR	4.38	23	Tunisia	4.81	23	Italy	4.43	23
Australia	4.35	24	Portugal	4.81	24	Korea	4.39	24
Brazil	4.21	25	Norway	4.78	25	Ireland	4.31	25
Spain	4.17	26	France	4.73	26	Czech Republic	4.15	26
Estonia	4.12	27	New Zealand	4.70	27	Estonia	4.12	27
India	4.12	28	South Africa	4.61	28	Slovenia	4.11	28
Hungary	4.10	29	Estonia	4.58	29	Portugal	4.10	29
Chile	4.00	30	Hungary	4.54	30	Hungary	4.07	30
Czech Republic	3.97	31	Brazil	4.52	31	Greece	4.04	31
Portugal	3.95	32	Korea	4.50	32	Argentina	3.97	32
Tunisia	3.76	33	Czech Republic	4.42	33	Chile	3.93	33
Malaysia	3.65	34	Slovenia	4.31	34	Uruguay	3.86	34
Costa Rica	3.63	35	Botswana	4.30	35	Slovak Republic	3.79	35
Slovak Republic	3.61	36	Japan	4.28	36	Brazil	3.78	36
Poland	3.58	37	Namibia	4.27	37	Croatia	3.76	37
Lithuania	3.45	38	Thailand	4.25	38	Lithuania	3.72	38
South Africa	3.45	39	Chile	4.21	39	Malaysia	3.67	39
Latvia	3.38	40	Slovak Republic	4.20	40	Latvia	3.58	40
Thailand	3.36	41	Mauritius	4.16	41	Namibia	3.58	41
Botswana	3.33	42	Jordan	4.14	42	Jordan	3.56	42
Greece	3.30	43	Trinidad and Tobago	4.13	43	Mauritius	3.54	43
Colombia	3.29	44	Morocco	4.05	44	Turkey	3.52	44
Slovenia	3.25	45	Philippines	4.05	45	South Africa	3.52	45
Dominican Republic	3.25	46	Greece	4.04	46	Poland	3.48	46
Jordan	3.23	47	Latvia	4.03	47	Dominican Republic	3.42	47
Morocco	3.23	48	Dominican Republic	4.00	48	Thailand	3.42	48
China	3.20	49	Turkey	3.97	49	Trinidad and Tobago	3.42	49
Sri Lanka	3.11	50	Jamaica	3.96	50	Peru	3.40	50
Uruguay	3.09	51	China	3.91	51	Tunisia	3.38	51
Panama	3.08	52	Sri Lanka	3.85	52	China	3.36	52
Argentina	3.04	53	Croatia	3.77	53	Botswana	3.36	53
Croatia	3.03	54	Indonesia	3.70	54	Mexico	3.32	54
Namibia	2.98	55	Nigeria	3.70	55	Panama	3.32	55
Trinidad and Tobago	2.93	56	Mexico	3.64	56	Morocco	3.22	56
Russian Federation	2.91	57	Poland	3.61	57	Sri Lanka	3.21	57
Vietnam	2.90	58	Lithuania	3.56	58	Bulgaria	3.20	58
Philippines	2.90	59	Venezuela	3.54	59	Costa Rica	3.17	59
Indonesia	2.85	60	Colombia	3.48	60	El Salvador	3.16	60
Mexico	2.75	61	Uruguay	3.48	61	Colombia	3.13	61
Ukraine	2.74	62	Argentina	3.40	62	Venezuela	3.08	62
Zimbabwe	2.72	63	Bangladesh	3.36	63	Philippines	3.05	63
El Salvador	2.71	64	Panama	3.26	64	Guatemala	3.01	64
Jamaica	2.70	65	El Salvador	3.16	65	Jamaica	2.93	65
Venezuela	2.69	66	Costa Rica	3.11	66	Bolivia	2.87	66
Turkey	2.65	67	Ukraine	3.06	67	Russian Federation	2.85	67
Bulgaria	2.63	68	Romania	3.06	68	India	2.84	68
Mauritius	2.58	69	Peru	2.97	69	Ecuador	2.83	69
Romania	2.58	70	Vietnam	2.94	70	Romania	2.61	70
Peru	2.47	71	Zimbabwe	2.89	71	Paraguay	2.57	71
Paraguay	2.24	72	Russian Federation	2.88	72	Ukraine	2.49	72
Bangladesh	2.16	73	Bulgaria	2.77	73	Indonesia	2.48	73
Nigeria	2.16	74	Honduras	2.65	74	Nigeria	2.21	74
Guatemala	2.12	75	Nicaragua	2.59	75	Honduras	2.10	75
Nicaragua	2.12	76	Guatemala	2.50	76	Vietnam	1.99	76
Bolivia	2.01	77	Bolivia	2.36	77	Nicaragua	1.86	77
Haiti	1.97	78	Ecuador	2.22	78	Zimbabwe	1.63	78
Ecuador	1.90	79	Paraguay	2.03	79	Bangladesh	1.60	79
Honduras	1.84	80	Haiti	1.97	80	Haiti	1.55	80

presents a case study of how active steps were taken to develop infrastructure and service offerings in Japan by promoting competition within the telecommunications industry. As a consequence, Japanese consumers can today access one of the most competitive broadband services in the world.

Readiness

The readiness of a nation measures the capability of the principal agents of an economy (citizens, businesses, and governments) to leverage the potential of ICT. This capability is lent to the nation's community by a combination of factors such as the presence of relevant skills for using ICT among individuals, access and affordability of ICT for corporations, and the local government using ICT for its own services and processes. As shown in Table 2, Singapore ranks highest on overall readiness, in spite of its 11th place score on business readiness. Singapore is supported by a very strong performance in government readiness, reflect-

ing the fact that ICT is a top priority item on the government's agenda. Third-ranked United States, on the other hand, benefits from high scores in business readiness. Second-placed Finland shows a consistent performance across all three readiness subindexes, and illustrates the basic concept behind the NRI: that a nation's readiness is determined by the degree to which technology permeates across all three stakeholders of the community—individuals, businesses, and government.

Detailed results for each of the subindexes used for measuring readiness (listed below) can be found in Table 4.

Individual Readiness: Individual readiness measures the readiness of a nation's citizens to utilize and leverage ICT. Factors that are used to measure this include literacy rates, mode and locus of access to the Internet, and the degree of connectivity of individuals. The top three positions on individual readiness go to Finland, Singapore, and Iceland. Korea (6) has an exceptional score on individual readiness,

---

Box 1: Case Study: e-business roundtable in Canada

An e-business roundtable was set up in 1999 as a voluntary cooperation in the private sector with the objective of growing the e-economy in Canada. It had 35 members: mainly leaders from the ICT industry and industry associations, and one representative from the government—the deputy minister of industry. The roundtable advised Industry Canada, which lobbied the federal government to enforce selected recommendations.

Action: The roundtable consisted of five groups, each working with the objective of improving Canada's performance in a particular area. The five areas in which the members worked were (1) government online service, (2) ICT talent pool, (3) capital markets, (4) SME access to ICT, and (5) Canada as a place for e-commerce. Members from one group interfaced with corresponding members from industry. The roundtable was dissolved in 2002 since it was originally set with a one-year mandate. But the public and private initiatives continue.

Result: The roundtable became an effective adviser to the government on e-commerce strategy, enabling the government to make meaningful changes in a short period of time. The capital gains tax has been reduced to 50 percent in response to the 30 percent recommended by the roundtable. Provisions have been made for 600 million Canadian dollars to implement government online strategy by 2005. Corporate tax rates are to be reduced from 28 percent to 21 percent over the five-year period starting 2002.

Box 2: Case Study: Broadband rollout in Japan

Japan's incumbent telecom service provider NTT had invested heavily in Integrated Services Digital Network (ISDN) with the result that Japan had the world's highest ISDN penetration in 1999. NTT planned to upgrade ISDN to Fiber To The Home (FTTH) as the next generation high-speed network. However, Tokyo Metallic convinced the Ministry of Post & Telecom (MPT) to open up the NTT infrastructure for DSL service.

Action: MPT swiftly enacted policies to unbundle local loops of NTT and in this way to allow other operators. NTT upgraded all exchanges for ADSL. However, it continued to provide ISDN to its users. Other operators joined Tokyo Metallic in providing DSL service, which began to take away share from NTT's ISDN subscribers. NTT was thus forced to offer DSL service itself. Yahoo! marked its entry in September 2001 with a DSL offering at half the price of NTT, driving the prices further down.

Result: Japan today has one of the world's most competitive and cheapest broadband services. The uptake has grown exponentially since DSL was introduced.

Table 4: Readiness subindexes

Readiness component index = 1/3 individual readiness + 1/3 business readiness + 1/3 government readiness

Country	Individual readiness score	Rank	Country	Business readiness score	Rank	Country	Government readiness score	Rank
Finland	6.71	1	United States	6.65	1	Singapore	7.00	1
Singapore	6.38	2	Finland	6.45	2	Taiwan	5.86	2
Iceland	6.38	3	Israel	6.34	3	Finland	5.86	3
Canada	6.30	4	Sweden	6.30	4	Tunisia	5.56	4
Sweden	6.29	5	Germany	6.30	5	Israel	5.54	5
Korea	6.27	6	Switzerland	6.28	6	Canada	5.47	6
United States	6.13	7	Japan	6.03	7	United States	5.41	7
Australia	6.07	8	Iceland	5.94	8	United Kingdom	5.36	8
United Kingdom	6.06	9	Taiwan	5.91	9	Iceland	5.27	9
Denmark	6.06	10	France	5.88	10	Sweden	5.27	10
Netherlands	6.05	11	Singapore	5.85	11	Hong Kong SAR	5.26	11
Hong Kong SAR	6.03	12	Canada	5.83	12	Ireland	5.24	12
Austria	6.01	13	Denmark	5.77	13	Estonia	5.15	13
Belgium	6.00	14	United Kingdom	5.72	14	China	5.14	14
Norway	5.99	15	Netherlands	5.66	15	Korea	5.12	15
New Zealand	5.92	16	Austria	5.63	16	Switzerland	5.08	16
Switzerland	5.84	17	Belgium	5.54	17	Denmark	5.04	17
Estonia	5.78	18	Korea	5.41	18	Malaysia	4.94	18
France	5.77	19	Ireland	5.29	19	Japan	4.91	19
Germany	5.76	20	Norway	5.29	20	France	4.87	20
Japan	5.75	21	Australia	5.24	21	Netherlands	4.81	21
Taiwan	5.68	22	Hong Kong SAR	5.08	22	Hungary	4.74	22
Czech Republic	5.67	23	Brazil	5.03	23	Australia	4.74	23
Israel	5.54	24	Czech Republic	5.01	24	Austria	4.66	24
Slovenia	5.52	25	Spain	5.00	25	Sri Lanka	4.66	25
Hungary	5.47	26	India	5.00	26	Spain	4.65	26
Spain	5.45	27	Estonia	4.95	27	Germany	4.61	27
Italy	5.41	28	New Zealand	4.93	28	Norway	4.58	28
Ireland	5.39	29	Italy	4.93	29	New Zealand	4.50	29
Slovak Republic	5.17	30	Costa Rica	4.79	30	Czech Republic	4.45	30
Malaysia	5.12	31	Hungary	4.78	31	Brazil	4.37	31
Croatia	5.03	32	Malaysia	4.78	32	India	4.18	32
Latvia	5.02	33	Slovenia	4.75	33	Chile	4.18	33
Portugal	5.01	34	South Africa	4.66	34	Lithuania	4.16	34
Poland	4.93	35	Tunisia	4.64	35	Portugal	4.14	35
Argentina	4.92	36	Chile	4.59	36	Jamaica	4.06	36
Panama	4.91	37	Thailand	4.56	37	Belgium	4.06	37
Thailand	4.88	38	Slovak Republic	4.54	38	Thailand	4.04	38
Greece	4.87	39	Latvia	4.39	39	Morocco	4.01	39
Lithuania	4.81	40	China	4.38	40	Italy	4.00	40
Tunisia	4.81	41	Greece	4.36	41	Slovenia	3.99	41
Bulgaria	4.79	42	Poland	4.31	42	Vietnam	3.99	42
Chile	4.75	43	Botswana	4.27	43	Botswana	3.86	43
Brazil	4.75	44	Namibia	4.25	44	Latvia	3.82	44
Costa Rica	4.72	45	Turkey	4.20	45	South Africa	3.69	45
Turkey	4.68	46	Morocco	4.18	46	Mexico	3.68	46
Russian Federation	4.68	47	Mexico	4.13	47	Namibia	3.63	47
Romania	4.49	48	Mauritius	4.09	48	Jordan	3.48	48
Trinidad and Tobago	4.45	49	Portugal	4.09	49	Croatia	3.47	49
Jordan	4.43	50	Indonesia	4.07	50	Slovak Republic	3.44	50
Colombia	4.37	51	Lithuania	4.03	51	Mauritius	3.40	51
Botswana	4.34	52	Dominican Republic	4.02	52	Poland	3.37	52
South Africa	4.33	53	Argentina	3.97	53	Dominican Republic	3.34	53
Sri Lanka	4.32	54	Jordan	3.94	54	Bulgaria	3.25	54
Uruguay	4.30	55	Sri Lanka	3.91	55	Colombia	3.25	55
Dominican Republic	4.29	56	Jamaica	3.90	56	Costa Rica	3.18	56
Ukraine	4.25	57	Panama	3.80	57	Greece	3.17	57
Mauritius	4.23	58	Trinidad and Tobago	3.78	58	Trinidad and Tobago	3.15	58
Indonesia	4.20	59	Peru	3.73	59	Uruguay	3.07	59
Mexico	4.10	60	Ukraine	3.72	60	Russian Federation	2.95	60
Philippines	4.08	61	Vietnam	3.72	61	Indonesia	2.88	61
Namibia	4.07	62	Russian Federation	3.71	62	El Salvador	2.88	62
Peru	4.01	63	Colombia	3.66	63	Philippines	2.87	63
Jamaica	4.00	64	El Salvador	3.58	64	Ukraine	2.77	64
El Salvador	3.99	65	Croatia	3.56	65	Peru	2.76	65
Vietnam	3.98	66	Venezuela	3.51	66	Nigeria	2.71	66
China	3.96	67	Bulgaria	3.48	67	Nicaragua	2.55	67
India	3.87	68	Uruguay	3.47	68	Bangladesh	2.53	68
Venezuela	3.84	69	Guatemala	3.42	69	Turkey	2.48	69
Morocco	3.84	70	Zimbabwe	3.41	70	Romania	2.42	70
Guatemala	3.69	71	Philippines	3.35	71	Panama	2.41	71
Bolivia	3.63	72	Paraguay	3.34	72	Ecuador	2.30	72
Paraguay	3.61	73	Bangladesh	3.25	73	Argentina	2.20	73
Zimbabwe	3.60	74	Romania	3.15	74	Honduras	2.01	74
Ecuador	3.23	75	Ecuador	3.02	75	Venezuela	1.96	75
Honduras	3.06	76	Nigeria	2.95	76	Bolivia	1.84	76
Nicaragua	2.84	77	Honduras	2.91	77	Zimbabwe	1.61	77
Haiti	2.75	78	Nicaragua	2.47	78	Paraguay	1.60	78
Bangladesh	2.66	79	Bolivia	2.40	79	Guatemala	1.58	79
Nigeria	2.18	80	Haiti	2.29	80	Haiti	1.52	80

having both a high penetration of the Internet in general, and one of the highest penetrations of broadband in the world. Box 3 presents a case study of how Sweden succeeded in using innovative policy and tax measures to increase its PC penetration, and hence achieved increases in both individual and business readiness.

Business Readiness: Business readiness measures the readiness of a cross-section of businesses to participate in and benefit from ICT. The aim is to not just focus on the largest corporations, but also to include small and medium-sized businesses and their willingness to exploit ICT and invest in the ICT skills of their employees. The United States has a no-surprise first place on business readiness, followed by Finland, Israel, and Sweden. Also noteworthy is India's rank on business readiness of 26 compared with individual readiness of 68, reflecting a growing digital divide among the different ICT stakeholders in the country.

Government Readiness: Government readiness measures the readiness of a government to employ ICT. It is reflected in the policymaking machinery and internal processes of the government, and the availability of government services online. If the polity of a nation decides to make ICT a priority, this becomes visible in the short- and long-term policy measures and laws that help encourage ICT deployment and use. It is also reflected in the government itself using ICT and equipping its people to do the same. Singapore leads on government readiness, followed by Taiwan and Finland. Of note is Estonia at 13th place, reflecting the government's push in ICT, and one of the factors contributing to its overall rank of 24. Box 4 presents a case study of BundOnline in Germany, illustrating how the government was proactive in putting its services online and thus promoting the use of ICT.

Usage

The usage component aims to measure the level of impact of ICT on the principal stakeholders of the NRI framework: individuals, businesses, and governments. This includes changes in behaviors, lifestyles, and other economic and noneconomic factors brought about by the adoption of ICT. Finland, Singapore, and Sweden are the top three performers with regard to overall usage, as shown in Table 2. One can observe variances in country performance across the three subindexes, reflecting uneven impact across the three principal stakeholders. For example, Germany ranks high for business usage (1) but relatively low for individual (16) and government (20) usage. Another notable example is Estonia, with high government readiness (13) and usage (8) but relatively low positions for individual (27) and business (31) usage.

Box 3: Case Study: PC penetration in Sweden

The Swedish government set its goals to increase Internet connectivity, PC penetration, and ICT literacy.

Action: The PC Tax Reform Act was passed in 1998, by which tax relief was provided on purchases of computers. Companies would buy the PCs and offer them to their staff at tax-free monthly installments deducted from their salary. Every worker in a permanent position was eligible, irrespective of job titles.

Results: PC penetration in households increased from 48 percent to 67 percent in one year. Spread of PCs has led to awareness of information and services on the Internet. The government has been able to close the digital divide, since PCs were available cheaply to all permanent workers. All parties involved in the process benefited: employees got PCs at cheap prices, employers gained from the greater ICT literacy of their staff, banks that financed the loan perceived it as low-risk investment, and the government attained its goals.

Box 4: Case Study: BundOnline2005 in Germany

The federal government launched the BundOnline2005 program to provide online all government services that can be placed on the Internet. Over 350 services have been identified for this purpose and 1.65 billion euros committed over the period till 2005. Infrastructure will be coordinated centrally and implemented locally. Several model projects have been implemented, for example, BAföG online (online repayment of student loans), Arbeitsamt online (online job search and placement service), DEPATISnet (online search for patents and trademarks), and Öffentlicher Einkauf online (online procurement platform of federal administration).

Table 5 gives the detailed results and scores for each of the three subindexes (described below) used for measuring usage.

Individual Usage: Individual usage gives an indication of the level of adoption and usage of ICT technologies by a nation's citizens. This is done by assessing the deployment of connectivity-enhancing technologies such as telephones and Internet connections, levels of Internet usage, and money spent online. The individual usage rankings differ significantly from those of individual readiness. The top performers here are Korea, Finland, Denmark, the Netherlands, and Sweden. Korea and the Netherlands stand out in particular, as they are significantly lower on both the overall NRI and on overall usage.

Business Usage: Business usage measures the level of deployment and use of ICT across all businesses in a nation. Business usage is measured by factors such as the level of business-to-business and business-to-consumer e-commerce, the use of ICT for activities such as marketing, and levels of online transactions. The top five performers are Germany, Sweden, the United States, Finland, and Iceland.

Government Usage: Government usage is the level of use of ICT by the government of a given country. The government, besides making ICT a priority, can also benefit from the usage of ICT itself. This usage can help the government streamline the services to its citizens and improve its overall functioning. Factors used to measure this include the volume of transactions that businesses have with governments and the presence of government services online. The top ranking countries on this measure are Finland, Singapore, Iceland, Taiwan, and Sweden. Of note is Estonia at 8th place, reflecting the fact that the country's government is "walking the talk"—both promoting ICT in the country and also using ICT for its own functioning. Box 5 presents the case of Carte Vitale and how the French government has been benefiting from the use of ICT in the health care sector.

Understanding networked readiness

More than a single measure

The degree of networked readiness of a nation is the result of a multitude of effects. Our research started with a set of over 130 different variables or indicators for evaluating networked readiness, which were narrowed down by statistical analysis to a set of 64 variables. These 64 vari-

Box 5: Case Study: Health industry in France

In 1996, the French government launched the Sesam-Vitale program to control health expenditures (10 percent of GDP). The objective of the program was to fully replace the paper-based system of reporting doctor visits with an electronic system. The program was expected to help better understand expenditure, to improve efficiency, and to enhance quality of healthcare.

Action: A card (Carte Vitale) with an embedded microchip has been handed out to individuals covered by healthcare insurance. Healthcare Professionals (HCP) and pharmacists received similar identification cards. When visiting a doctor, the visitor's card is inserted into a dedicated terminal, which automatically records the visit. Information at the end of the day is transmitted via Internet to the appropriate organization.

Results: About 41 percent of HCPs currently transmit forms online. About 80 percent of doctors possess a PC (compared to 10–15 percent in 1995). Individuals get automatically reimbursed within five days versus several weeks before. Net annual savings to government: 150–200 million euros.

ables were grouped among the 9 subindexes of the NRI framework. This provides us with an opportunity to study some of the interrelationships across the variables and the components/subindexes of the NRI framework.

GDP and Networked Readiness

Any attempt to use a single measure to approximate the Networked Readiness Index would remain a simplification. One of the most intuitive and appealing measures that one may be tempted to use as a proxy is the Gross Domestic Product per capita of a country. If one has a closer look at the NRI results, one would find that Estonia with a GDP per capita PPP of US$10,066 has an NRI score of 4.69 and is ranked 24 overall. Mauritius, with a very close GDP per capita of US$10,017, on the other hand, has a score of 3.44 and overall ranking of 55. One thus sees a wide spread in the NRI score for a given GDP PPP per capita. This is only one of many examples that could be cited.

Nevertheless, one could look at the relation between the NRI and GDP in order to obtain a better understanding of trends, and also to identify over- and underperformers with respect to the trend. Figure 3 gives a plot between GDP PPP per capita and the Networked

Table 5: Usage subindexes

Usage component index = 1/3 individual usage + 1/3 business usage + 1/3 government usage

Country	Individual usage score	Rank	Country	Business usage score	Rank	Country	Government usage score	Rank
Korea	5.19	1	Germany	6.19	1	Finland	6.73	1
Finland	4.90	2	Sweden	5.96	2	Singapore	6.72	2
Denmark	4.87	3	United States	5.95	3	Iceland	6.46	3
Netherlands	4.81	4	Finland	5.93	4	Taiwan	6.23	4
Sweden	4.64	5	Iceland	5.58	5	Sweden	5.98	5
Japan	4.62	6	Netherlands	5.51	6	United States	5.94	6
United States	4.57	7	Singapore	5.49	7	Canada	5.91	7
Singapore	4.53	8	United Kingdom	5.42	8	Estonia	5.75	8
United Kingdom	4.51	9	Denmark	5.40	9	Denmark	5.69	9
Canada	4.46	10	Switzerland	5.39	10	Brazil	5.49	10
Norway	4.46	11	Norway	5.23	11	Hong Kong SAR	5.39	11
Belgium	4.39	12	Korea	5.20	12	Australia	5.35	12
Taiwan	4.38	13	France	5.14	13	United Kingdom	5.32	13
Switzerland	4.28	14	Canada	5.14	14	Korea	5.26	14
Australia	4.24	15	Hong Kong SAR	5.08	15	Netherlands	5.18	15
Germany	4.17	16	Australia	5.06	16	Norway	5.14	16
Slovenia	4.13	17	Argentina	5.05	17	Austria	5.11	17
Iceland	4.05	18	Taiwan	5.05	18	Ireland	5.09	18
Israel	3.99	19	Brazil	5.03	19	Israel	5.09	19
Ireland	3.97	20	Spain	5.03	20	Germany	5.08	20
Austria	3.96	21	Italy	5.01	21	Chile	4.96	21
Hong Kong SAR	3.91	22	Belgium	4.96	22	Switzerland	4.95	22
New Zealand	3.79	23	Japan	4.90	23	Tunisia	4.89	23
France	3.68	24	Austria	4.85	24	France	4.83	24
Portugal	3.66	25	Poland	4.72	25	India	4.80	25
Italy	3.62	26	Israel	4.72	26	Portugal	4.79	26
Estonia	3.44	27	Czech Republic	4.71	27	Spain	4.72	27
Greece	3.43	28	South Africa	4.69	28	Hungary	4.68	28
Spain	3.39	29	New Zealand	4.54	29	Belgium	4.63	29
Czech Republic	3.14	30	Ireland	4.45	30	New Zealand	4.62	30
Latvia	3.11	31	Estonia	4.35	31	Italy	4.58	31
Uruguay	3.02	32	Mexico	4.31	32	Malaysia	4.48	32
Hungary	2.91	33	Venezuela	4.01	33	China	4.44	33
Slovak Republic	2.84	34	Portugal	3.99	34	Czech Republic	4.38	34
Argentina	2.78	35	Chile	3.98	35	Mexico	4.26	35
Turkey	2.74	36	Malaysia	3.95	36	Thailand	4.20	36
Chile	2.71	37	Slovenia	3.94	37	South Africa	4.19	37
Lithuania	2.63	38	Turkey	3.89	38	Poland	4.07	38
Trinidad and Tobago	2.62	39	Botswana	3.80	39	Slovenia	4.05	39
Poland	2.58	40	Costa Rica	3.76	40	Latvia	4.03	40
Croatia	2.54	41	Croatia	3.74	41	Japan	4.01	41
Malaysia	2.50	42	India	3.71	42	Turkey	3.97	42
Brazil	2.44	43	Tunisia	3.65	43	Lithuania	3.96	43
Mexico	2.43	44	Slovak Republic	3.63	44	Botswana	3.93	44
Venezuela	2.40	45	Thailand	3.60	45	Croatia	3.71	45
Bulgaria	2.37	46	El Salvador	3.60	46	Argentina	3.69	46
Jamaica	2.35	47	Indonesia	3.59	47	Mauritius	3.67	47
South Africa	2.31	48	Philippines	3.58	48	Jordan	3.65	48
Panama	2.29	49	Latvia	3.48	49	Greece	3.57	49
Mauritius	2.28	50	Jordan	3.44	50	Costa Rica	3.57	50
Costa Rica	2.21	51	Morocco	3.44	51	Colombia	3.56	51
Ukraine	2.18	52	Panama	3.43	52	Morocco	3.55	52
El Salvador	2.14	53	Hungary	3.43	53	Namibia	3.50	53
Colombia	2.08	54	Ecuador	3.40	54	Slovak Republic	3.43	54
Peru	2.06	55	Uruguay	3.36	55	Philippines	3.42	55
Philippines	1.98	56	Peru	3.31	56	Dominican Republic	3.40	56
Russian Federation	1.97	57	Namibia	3.24	57	Uruguay	3.37	57
Paraguay	1.96	58	Nicaragua	3.23	58	El Salvador	3.29	58
Tunisia	1.96	59	Nigeria	3.18	59	Sri Lanka	3.26	59
China	1.95	60	Colombia	3.17	60	Panama	3.24	60
Romania	1.95	61	Greece	3.17	61	Jamaica	3.23	61
Morocco	1.93	62	Honduras	3.13	62	Peru	3.19	62
Thailand	1.92	63	Bolivia	3.10	63	Indonesia	3.16	63
Botswana	1.91	64	Dominican Republic	3.06	64	Vietnam	3.09	64
Nicaragua	1.91	65	Bangladesh	3.05	65	Nigeria	2.99	65
Bolivia	1.86	66	Haiti	3.04	66	Venezuela	2.96	66
Dominican Republic	1.84	67	Guatemala	3.02	67	Trinidad and Tobago	2.84	67
Guatemala	1.79	68	Mauritius	3.01	68	Ukraine	2.84	68
Sri Lanka	1.78	69	Sri Lanka	3.00	69	Russian Federation	2.80	69
Ecuador	1.76	70	China	2.98	70	Paraguay	2.73	70
Namibia	1.74	71	Trinidad and Tobago	2.89	71	Ecuador	2.70	71
Jordan	1.71	72	Paraguay	2.80	72	Bangladesh	2.70	72
Honduras	1.68	73	Ukraine	2.72	73	Bulgaria	2.61	73
Zimbabwe	1.65	74	Jamaica	2.65	74	Guatemala	2.53	74
Indonesia	1.53	75	Vietnam	2.56	75	Nicaragua	2.37	75
Nigeria	1.51	76	Lithuania	2.55	76	Haiti	2.20	76
India	1.47	77	Zimbabwe	2.40	77	Bolivia	2.18	77
Bangladesh	1.47	78	Bulgaria	2.16	78	Honduras	1.94	78
Vietnam	1.44	79	Russian Federation	2.12	79	Romania	1.89	79
Haiti	1.32	80	Romania	1.82	80	Zimbabwe	1.87	80

Figure 3: GDP PPP per capita versus Networked Readiness Index, partial log regression

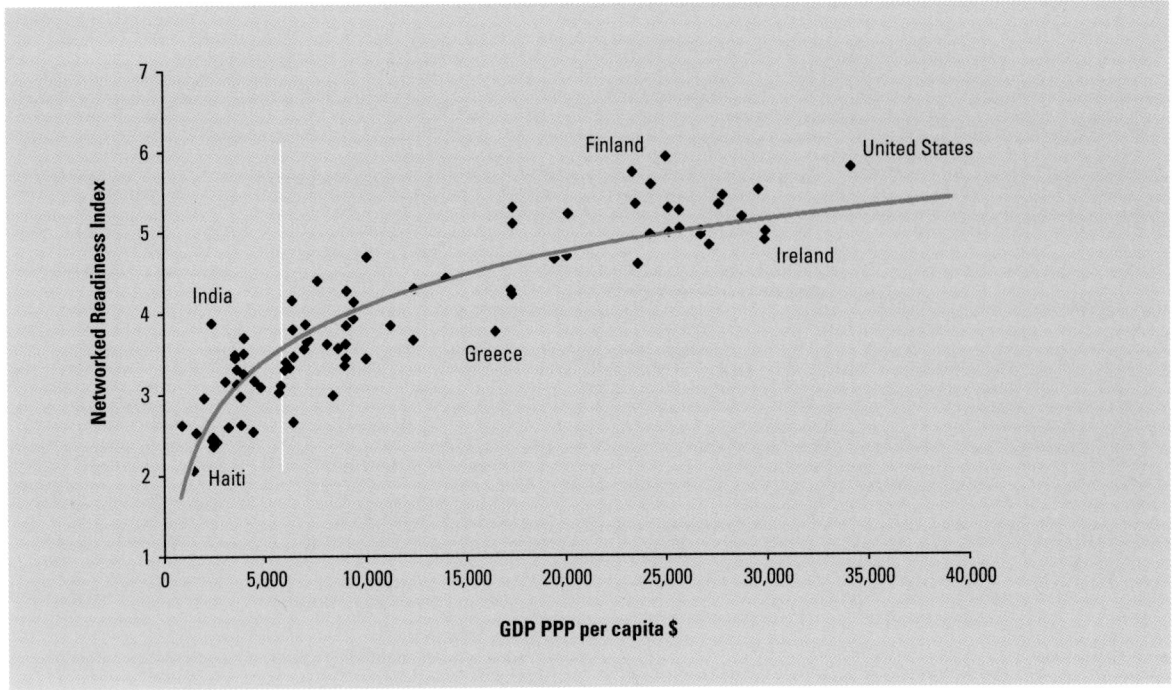

Source: Technology Management Department, INSEAD

Readiness Index. The partial log regression plot presents a possible trend. One would note immediately the following points:

- For a given GDP PPP per capita, there is a spread in the NRI scores around the regression plot as presented in Figure 3.
- The impact of GDP seems to be very high at low GDP values, and the NRI score increases rapidly with small increases in GDP.
- Around a GDP per capita of US$9,000 the curve tapers off and the effect of increasing GDP is much less pronounced.

Countries widely distanced from the regression plot could be examples of underperforming or overperforming countries. Thus one sees that Finland leads the NRI ranking, whereas Ireland—with a significantly higher GDP per capita—relatively underperforms on the overall NRI score. Similarly, India would be overperforming on its NRI score with respect to its GDP per capita.

ICT spending and networked readiness
Plotting ICT spending versus NRI gives a similar trend to that of GDP PPP per capita versus NRI. Notable, however, is that there is a very large spread in the NRI score (see Figure 4) at a given ICT expense (as a percentage of GDP), making one reflect on the effectiveness of the ICT

dollar toward promoting networked readiness. For example, Spain has a lower spending on ICT (as a percent of GDP) than Vietnam, but has a significantly higher score on the NRI. This emphasizes the importance of other variables (such as market and regulatory factors), which play an important role in determining the degree of networked readiness of a nation. Some notable points from Figure 4 are:

- The United States, Finland, and Spain are among the leading overperformers.
- Romania, Vietnam, Colombia, and New Zealand are among the leading underperformers.
- New Zealand, with the highest ICT expenditure (percent GDP), has a modest NRI score of 4.70.

Internet users per 100 and readiness component index
One could be tempted to use the number of Internet users in a country as a proxy estimate of the networked readiness of a country. Figure 5 shows a plot between the number of Internet users/100 persons (number of Internet accounts) and the readiness component index. One would thus see the existence of a possible relationship between these, represented by the partial logarithmic regression plot. One sees that the readiness score increases sharply from 0 to 20 Internet users per 100 people, and much more gradually thereafter. The relatively flat curve above

Figure 4: ICT spending (percent GDP) versus Networked Readiness Index, partial log regression

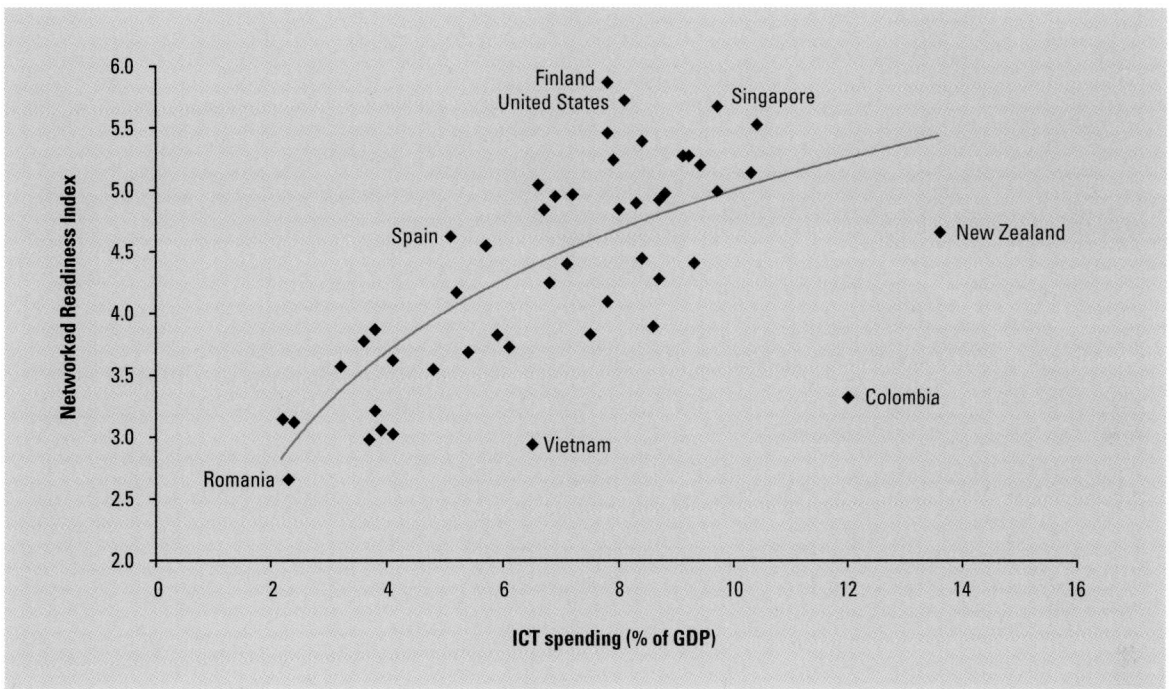

Source: Technology Management Department, INSEAD

20 to 30 Internet users per 100 implies the importance of other factors beyond this point in influencing the degree of readiness of a nation: for example, the quality of connectivity, speed, and availability of online services among others. Some of the interesting observations one could make from this plot are:

- Singapore, with one of the highest numbers of Internet users per 100, outperforms the trend line with the highest readiness component index scores. Singapore benefits from a strong government push in ICT, apart from a high concentration of businesses, and the presence of a skilled workforce.

- Korea, with the second highest number of Internet users, performs relatively moderately on the readiness component index in 12th place—despite having one of the best broadband connectivities in the world. Korea shows a higher readiness on the individual dimension as compared with the business and government readiness.

- India and China, with relatively low numbers of Internet users, have relatively higher readiness scores, probably due to regional and demographic digital divides existing within these countries.

- A number of South American countries, such as Nicaragua and Uruguay, are just starting to witness the propagation of the Internet, and this is being reflected in lower readiness scores.

Is there a threshold for usage to take off?

One would expect the readiness and usage scores of a nation to move together hand in hand. A country having a high degree of readiness would be able to transform this ICT capability into usage statistics, and hence show a consequent high score on the usage component index. For instance, Singapore and Finland have among the highest readiness component index scores, and one sees this readiness translating into real ICT usage, as represented by high usage scores (see Figure 6).

If one has a closer look at the trend of readiness versus usage at lower values of readiness, one sees that usage remains rather flat, with initial increases in readiness. This leads us to believe that there is a threshold to readiness: a country needs to have a certain level of readiness with regard to ICT before there can be an effective usage of ICT, and a consequent impact. A certain critical mass in terms of number of users, or the availability of narrowband and broadband services, or of services online is essential before this is reflected in real usage metrics. Thus one sees that:

- Haiti with a readiness score of 2.19 has a low usage score of 2.19 and has to still develop its readiness before usage starts increasing significantly.

Figure 5: Number of Internet users per 100 versus readiness component index, partial log regression

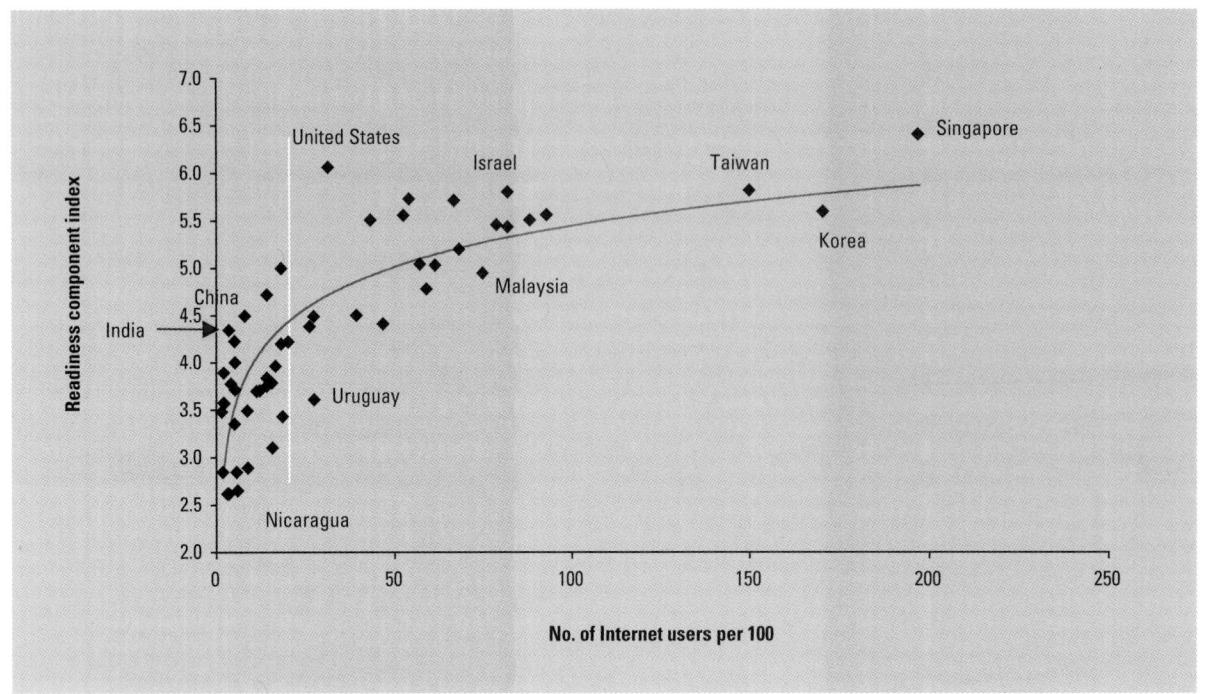

Source: Technology Management Department, INSEAD

Figure 6: Readiness component index versus usage component index, partial log regression

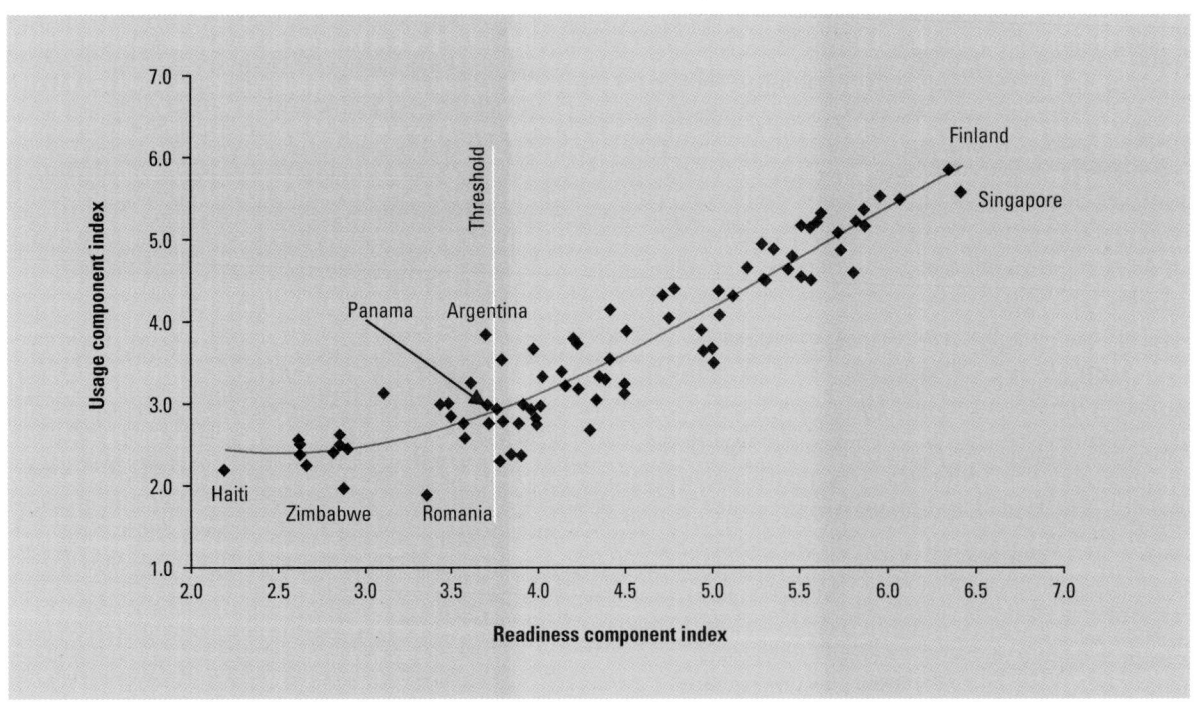

Source: Technology Management Department, INSEAD

- Romania is a significant underperformer, below the threshold level. Although it has a readiness score of 3.35, this does not result in a corresponding usage level.
- Panama and Argentina find themselves at the threshold level. Argentina, however, is a significant overperformer with its usage level of 3.84.

Research challenges

Finding the Facts: The best laid out frameworks can face seemingly insurmountable roadblocks in their implementation due to the lack of accurate and reliable data. The overriding aim in our research and analysis has been to provide a scientific and credible interpretation of reality. Thus, the first step in our research has been to collect the most complete and highest quality set of data relating to ICT. We used two types of data in our research: soft data, which is subjective data gathered as a result of questionnaires (such as the Executive Opinion Survey), and hard data, which is driven by statistics collected by reputed independent agencies (such as the World Bank and International Telecommunications Union [ITU]). Both these sets of data play a crucial role in the overall analysis. The soft data are critical in determining the opinion of the decision makers and influencers who are intimately familiar with a nation's economy. On the other hand, the hard data capture fundamental elements related to the development of infrastructure, human capital, and ICT.

Absence of Key Usage Metrics: Key ICT such as mobile telephony and the Internet are still undergoing rapid development. Owing to this, accurate usage metrics are difficult if not impossible to obtain and/or are not up to date. In the absence of such usage metrics, one has to devise ways to best estimate the development of a country's ICT. For example, metrics on cost savings realized, on high-speed Internet access costs and usage, on key measures of policy and regulation, and on the use of ICT by governments remain elusive.

Selection of Countries: Availability of objective and reliable data is critical while preparing a study of this type. To ensure quality of information we have restricted the study to 80 countries. Availability of data has in fact been a key factor in selecting the countries in this study. As a consequence, regions suffering from a chronic lack of reliable statistics, such as Africa and Central Asia, find themselves underrepresented in the NRI.

Ensuring Statistical Significance: Once solid and reliable facts had been accumulated, a comprehensive statistical analysis was conducted. Following the classic steps of any such analysis, correlation and factor analyses were conducted to drop closely correlated or interrelated variables. Following this, missing data in the dataset were estimated using regression and clustering techniques. The variables were then classified along the lines of the NRI framework.

Data Estimation: Despite our best efforts to collect data from all major international sources, it has been necessary at times to cope with incomplete sets of data for the countries under consideration. In order to compensate for this, statistical procedures have been used to estimate missing data: mainly regression and clustering techniques. Control procedures and checks have been devised to ensure that estimations were reasonable and not overly favorable or disadvantageous in their representation of the country concerned.

Calculating the Index: In order to calculate the index, the data were first transformed on a scale of 1 to 7, in order that each piece of information has an equal weight. Next, each of the subindexes was computed as a mathematical average of the variables composing it. The same approach was used to calculate the component indexes, averaging the subindexes. Finally, the NRI was computed as an average of the three component indexes. Details are provided in the Technical Appendix.

Summary

Measuring a country's networked readiness remains a significant challenge, and any framework or model representing networked readiness remains, at best, a simplified representation of reality. The NRI framework attempts to interpret the underlying complexity of the development and use of ICT in an intuitive and easy-to-comprehend model. The overall NRI is a summary measure of a nation's ability to participate in and benefit from ICT. The NRI provides guidance to business leaders and public policy makers to enhance the impact of ICT on all key stakeholders—individuals, businesses, and governments.

The essence of networked readiness extends beyond any single metric, and that all said, there are under- and overperforming countries: countries that have put ICT on the national agenda and have strived to make it an area of excellence, and others that have not done so. The former countries have succeeded in going beyond individual measures of national income, or national ICT spending, in an effort to provide an optimal environment for ICT development, thus promoting high levels of readiness and usage within all three key stakeholders. Finland, Singapore, and Korea are some such leaders, and could serve as role models for other nations in their quest for ICT excellence. The NRI allows a nation to benchmark its ICT performance and determine the effectiveness of policy. It also permits a country to learn from the policy and performance of other countries with similar profiles, and to identify best practice.

ICT hold the keys to evolution of our practices in many domains—education, work, personal relations, work effectiveness, and national productivity. An interesting characteristic of ICT such as the Internet and mobile communications is that overall value increases nonlinearly with the number of connected individuals and organizations. Increasing the levels of participation of developing countries in ICT creates benefits not only for these countries; it enlarges the overall potential of all connected stakeholders to realize value.

Notes

1 A more detailed description of this research can be obtained from the forthcoming publication: *The Global Information Technology Report 2002–2003*, S. Dutta, B. Lanvin, and F. Paua, World Economic Forum, Oxford University Press, New York, (January 2003).

2 *The Global Information Technology Report 2001–2002: Readiness for the Networked World*, G. Kirkman, P. Cornelius, J. Sachs, and K. Schwab. New York: Oxford University Press for the World Economic Forum, 2002.

3 *Human Development Report: Making New Technologies Work for Human Development*, United Nations Development Programme, New York: Oxford University Press, 2001. *The Global Competitiveness Report 2001–2002*, K. Schwab, M. Porter, J. Sachs, P. Cornelius, and J. McArthur. New York: Oxford University Press for the World Economic Forum, 2002.

4 Comparison of e-Readiness Assessment Models, Bridges.org, October 2001. http://www.bridges.org/ereadiness/tools.html

5 An NRI ranking of nations was presented for 2001–2002 in the following publication: *The Global Information Technology Report 2001–2002: Readiness for the Networked World*, G. Kirkman, P. Cornelius, J. Sachs, and K. Schwab. New York: Oxford University Press for the World Economic Forum, 2002. The NRI 2002–2003 ranking cannot be directly compared with this earlier ranking as the underlying framework and variables used in our research differ from those used in the earlier research by Kirkman et al. A full explanation of these differences is beyond the scope of the current chapter.

6 For example, Israel at an overall ranking of 12 does well on the environment (6) and readiness (8) dimensions, as compared to the usage dimension where it is ranked 21. See Table 2.

References

Comparison of e-Readiness Assessment Models, Bridges.org, October 2001. Online. http://www.bridges.org/ereadiness/tools.html

International Telecommunications Union. 2001. *World Telecommunications Indicators*. Online. http://www.itu.int/ITU-D/ict/publications/world/world.html

Organization for Economic Co-operation and Development (OECD). 2001. *Science, Technology and Industry Outlook: Drivers of Growth: Information Technology, Innovation, and Entrepreneurship*. Online. http://www.fedpubs.com/subject/techno/scitec.htm

United Nations Development Programme (UNDP). 2001. *Human Development Report: Making New Technologies Work for Human Development*. New York: Oxford University Press.

World Economic Forum. 2002a. *The Global Competitiveness Report 2001–2002*. New York: Oxford University Press.

———. 2002b. *The Global Information Technology Report 2001–2002: Readiness for the Networked World*. New York: Oxford University Press.

World Bank. 2002. *World Development Indicators 2001*. The World Bank Group: 2002. Online. http://www.worldbank.org/data/wdi/index.htm

Technical Appendix: Constructing the Networked Readiness Index

The Networked Readiness Index 2002–2003 separates environmental factors from ICT readiness and usage, and hence there are three component indexes for each of environment, readiness, and usage. Starting from a set of over 130 ICT-related variables, we have divided these variables amongst the nine subindexes. We then eliminated variables on the basis of number of countries for which data were available and used analytical procedures such as correlation analysis. Our final index computation is based on a set of 64 variables.[1]

Definitions of the Networked Readiness Index, component indexes, and subindexes

A. The *Networked Readiness Index* is defined as follows:

$$\text{Networked Readiness Index} = 1/3 \text{ environment} + 1/3 \text{ readiness} + 1/3 \text{ usage}$$

B. The environment component index is defined as follows:

$$\text{Environment} = 1/3 \text{ market} + 1/3 \text{ political/regulatory factors} + 1/3 \text{ infrastructure}$$

1. The *market subindex* is defined by the following data variables:
- Venture capital availability
- State of cluster development
- Competition in the telecommunication sector
- Availability of scientists and engineers
- Brain drain
- Public spending on education (% of GDP)
- Domestic software companies in international markets
- Domestic manufacturing of IT hardware
- ICT expenditure (% of GDP)

2. The *political/regulatory subindex* is defined by the following data variables:
- Effectiveness of law-making bodies
- Legal framework for ICT development
- Subsidies for firm-level research and development
- Government restrictions on Internet content
- Prevalence of foreign technology licensing

3. *Infrastructure* is defined by the following variables:
- Overall infrastructure quality
- Local availability of specialized IT services
- Number of telephone mainlines (per 1,000 people)
- Number of telephone faults (per 100 main lines)
- Number of telephone mainlines per employee
- Number of fax machines (per 1,000 people)
- Local switch capacity (per 100,000 people)
- Ease of obtaining new telephone lines
- Waiting time for telephone mainlines (in years)
- Number of secure Internet servers

C. The *readiness component index* is defined as follows:

$$\text{Readiness} = 1/3 \text{ individual readiness} + 1/3 \text{ business readiness} + 1/3 \text{ government readiness}$$

1. *Individual readiness* is defined by the following variables:
- Sophistication of local buyers' products and processes
- Availability of mobile Internet access
- Availability of broadband access
- Public access to the Internet
- Secondary school enrollment (% net)
- Total adult illiteracy rate (%)
- Quality of math and science education
- Cost of local call (US$ per 3 min)
- Cost of off-peak local cellular call (US$ per 3 min)
- Cost of residential telephone subscription (US$ per month)

2. *Business readiness* is defined by the following variables:
- Firm-level technology absorption
- Firm-level innovation
- Capacity for innovation
- Business Intranet sophistication
- Quality of local IT training programs
- Cost of business telephone subscription (US$ per month)

3. *Government readiness* is defined by the following variables:[2]
- Government prioritization of ICT
- Government procurement of advanced technology products
- Competence of public officials
- Government online services

293

Technical Appendix: Constructing the Networked Readiness Index *(cont'd.)*

D. The *usage component index* is defined as follows:

$$\text{Usage} = \text{1/3 individual usage} \\ + \text{1/3 business usage} \\ + \text{1/3 government usage}$$

1. *Individual usage* is defined by the following variables:

- Use of online payment systems
- Number of radios (per 1,000 people)
- Number of television sets (per 1,000 people)
- Number of cable television subscribers (per 1,000 people)
- Number of mobile telephones (per 1,000 people)
- Number of Internet users (per 100 people)
- Number of narrowband subscriber lines (per 100 people)
- Number of broadband subscriber lines (per 100 people)
- Household spending on ICT (US$ per month)

2. *Business usage* is defined by the following variables:

- Use of Internet for coordination with customers and suppliers
- Businesses using e-commerce (%)
- Use of Internet for general research
- Sophistication of online marketing
- Presence of wireless e-business applications
- Use of email for internal correspondence (%)
- Use of email for external correspondence (%)
- Pervasiveness of company web pages

3. *Government usage* is defined by the following variables:[3]

- Use of Internet-based transactions with Government
- Government online services
- Government success in ICT promotion

Notes

1 Our research used the most recent data available from the concerned sources (such as the Executive Opinion Survey 2002 from the World Economic Forum and data from World Bank and ITU). A more detailed description of the variables and data tables used for computing the NRI 2002–2003 can be obtained from the forthcoming publication: *The Global Information Technology Report 2002–2003*, S. Dutta, B. Lanvin, and F. Paua, New York: Oxford University Press for the World Economic Forum, (January 2003).

2 We could not find more variables with both statistical significance and reliable coverage for a sufficiently large number of countries for evaluating the readiness of governments for using ICT. This should be an area of focus for international data collection agencies in the future.

3 We could not find more variables with both statistical significance and reliable coverage for a sufficiently large number of countries for evaluating the usage of ICT by governments. Clearly this is an area where international data collection agencies need to focus in the future.

Foreign Direct Investment, Growth, and Competitiveness in Developing Countries

ROBERT E. LIPSEY, National Bureau of Economic Research

Introduction

Many developing countries, once hostile to the entry of foreign direct investment (FDI) or inclined to restrict it severely, now compete to attract foreign firms. Something must have been observed in the last couple of decades to change attitudes in so many countries.

There have always been reasons to suspect that an inflow of foreign direct investment would be favorable for economic growth in the recipient country. One is the evident superiority of multinational firms over local firms and their command over the most productive segments of the world economy. Over the world as a whole, workers in affiliates of multinational firms—apart from those in the parent companies—each produce about seven times as much as the average worker (Lipsey 1998). The margin in developing countries is even greater, perhaps as much as 15 times the average output per worker. There are many reasons for this superiority other than the talents of the multinationals. Most affiliates are located in developed countries, or in higher-income developing countries, where output per worker is high in general. Also, most affiliates are in manufacturing, mining, and financial services, where output per worker is higher than it is in other industries. Still, whatever the reason, multinationals are highly productive firms, and their operations in host countries reflect the productivity of the parent firms.

The superiority of foreign-owned firms does not necessarily imply an effect on the economic growth of the host countries, but many writers have suggested that there are such effects. One of the most favorable appraisals was made by Romer (1993), who suggested that for a developing country trying to keep up with or gain on more advanced countries, the main obstacle was the gap in knowledge, or ideas, rather than in physical capital. Much of that intellectual gap was the human or organizational capital of multinational firms, which is what enabled them to be multinational. For more rapid growth in a developing country, "... one of the most important and easily implemented policies is to give foreign firms an incentive to close the idea gap, to let them make a profit from doing so. ... The government of a poor country can therefore help its residents by creating an economic environment that offers an adequate reward to multinational corporations when they bring ideas from the rest of the world and put them to use with domestic resources" (p 548).

This emphasis on the intellectual capital of the investing firm fits with what Markusen and Maskus (2001) have described as the "knowledge-capital model" of the multinational firm. It reflects also the earlier observation by Dunning and Steuer (1970), describing the views of Hymer and Kindleberger, that the multinational firm "... is primarily a vehicle for the transfer of entrepreneurial talent rather than financial resources" (p 321). One problem with accepting this view is that it throws a cloud over most empirical attempts to examine the consequences of direct investment. The reason is that the statistical measures of FDI most widely available are of financial flows and stocks. It is quite a leap to assume that these are a good reflection of the transfer of intellectual capital. Even the measures of production or employment used in the studies based on firm microdata described below, while preferable, are questionable proxies for the flow of intellectual capital.

A further obstacle to identifying the impact of FDI on growth is that economic growth is a complex phenomenon, related to many factors. These include the world economic environment, which is outside the control of individual countries; natural catastrophes or favorable changes; wars and preparation for military action; a country's legal system; governmental economic policies; and many others. Changes in flows of FDI are related to all of these, and changes in policies toward FDI are often linked to changes in other economic policies. In particular, liberalization of rules on FDI is often accompanied by trade liberalization and other moves toward freer markets, and it is a difficult task to extract the effects of FDI from these combinations of events. These other policies may not only affect growth but also may affect any impact of FDI on growth.

Attempts to measure the effect of inward FDI flows on growth across all developing countries have been rare. The comprehensive review by Levine and Renelt (1992) of the variables used in growth studies did not even include FDI inflows as one of the variables. The few studies that did include FDI inflows produced mixed results; these studies are reviewed below. Some studies found that countries that were closer in income levels to countries in the developed world were better able to benefit from the presence of foreign firms. Others found that the favorable effects of FDI inflows depended on the presence of other country characteristics, such as high education levels or developed financial markets.

More common than cross-country studies have been analyses of individual countries, particularly their manufacturing sectors. These analyses have compared levels of productivity in foreign-owned and locally owned firms and attempted to learn whether productivity in individual establishments was higher because they were foreign, or productivity in a sector was higher because of the presence of foreign-owned firms. The analyses have also searched for evidence of spillovers of technology from foreign to domestic firms, in the sense that locally owned firms' productivity was raised by learning from foreign firms. Local firms might learn by imitating foreign firms, by competing with them, by dealing with them as buyers or sellers, or by hiring workers or executives from them.

Another way of studying the effects of foreign entry is to examine the experience of countries with different policies or countries that changed their policies toward inward foreign investment, mostly from very restrictive to more liberal policies. Malaysia and Singapore are examples of countries that particularly encouraged inward FDI; Ireland, China, and former Communist countries in Europe are examples of sharp policy change. The latter cases are attractive as experiments, but they still suffer from the fact that changes in policy toward FDI were usually part of programs of liberalization that included other policy changes that may have been favorable to growth.

Comprehensive cross-country statistical studies

Blomström, Lipsey, and Zejan (1994) reported that, across all developing countries in 1960–1985, ratios of FDI inflow to GDP in a five-year period were positively and significantly related to growth in per capita GDP across all developing countries in subsequent five-year periods. When the developing countries were subdivided between higher- and lower-income countries, it was found that higher FDI inflow ratios raised growth rates only in the higher-income group. The reason, the authors suggested, was that ". . . the least developed countries may learn little from the multinationals, because local firms are too far behind in their technological levels to be either imitators or suppliers to the multinationals . . ." (pp 250–251). If that is the correct interpretation of these results, it is important also for understanding the results of many other studies.

Other comprehensive cross-country studies found that FDI inflows had little or no effect on growth by themselves, but did have an effect in combination with other factors. Borensztein, De Gregorio, and Lee (1995) found, in a set of 69 developing countries from 1970 to 1989, that FDI inflows, by themselves, were only a marginally significant positive influence on growth, but FDI that interacted with a measure of educational attainment was a stronger influence. The higher the level of education of the labor force in a country, the greater the gain in growth from a given FDI inflow. Aside from that direct effect, FDI inflows also promoted growth by raising the level of aggregate capital formation. The induced capital formation was larger than the FDI inflow, possibly because local firms were induced or forced to increase their capital formation.

Lipsey (2000a), examining the effects of FDI inflows in five-year periods on the growth of real per capita GDP in subsequent five-year periods among developing countries, found that the combination of FDI inflows with schooling levels was the most consistent positive influence on growth rates. That was the case for both the time-series cross-section combination and over time for individual countries.

One possible reason for the mixture of results on the growth effects of inward FDI is that the effect can be either favorable or unfavorable, depending on the incentives offered to the foreign investors. Bhagwati (1978) suggested that the direction of the effect may depend on whether the host country followed an export promotion (EP) trade strategy or an import substitution (IS) strategy. "Under the EP strategy, both the magnitude of the private (direct) investment inflow and its efficacy in promoting economic growth will be greater over the long haul than under the IS strategy. . . . an EP strategy, with its lack of discrimination against foreign markets, is likely to attract foreign firms essentially on the nineteenth-century pattern of 'factor endowment' advantages. . . . On the other hand, by creating 'artificial' inducement to invest via tariffs and/or QRs [quantitive restrictions], so that one gets 'tariff-jumping' investments oriented to the domestic market alone, the IS strategy provides an artificially limited incentive to invest in the country" (p 212). The effect of the trade regime is not only on the amount of foreign investment received but also its efficiency. As Bhagwati points out, "tariff-jumping investments, induced by the IS strategy, are more likely to imply social losses or (at minimum) reduced gains than investments attracted by Heckscher-Ohlinesque factors" (p 214).

Balasubramanyam, Salisu, and Sapsford (1996) attempted to test Bhagwati's hypothesis by relating annual growth rates of real GDP to changes in labor input and exports, ratios of fixed investment, and FDI inflows to GDP in 46 countries, divided between EP and IS trade regimes. A variety of statistical methods and of definitions of trade policy were applied to the data. Significant positive effects of FDI inflows were found only in EP countries; the effects in IS countries were never significant and often negative. Furthermore, the equations explained much more of the variations in growth in the EP countries. Most of the equations for the IS countries explained little of the variation in growth rates among them.

Balasubramanyam et al. took these results as confirming Bhagwati's hypothesis. Higher inward FDI flows apparently were associated with higher rates of growth in GDP in the EP countries, which include, in different data sets, 10 to 18 developing countries. No such effect was found for the 24 to 28 remaining developing countries, a fact that suggests that the positive relationship is far from universal.

Campos and Kinoshita (2002) use panel data for 25 central and eastern European and former Soviet transition countries to test for the effects of FDI inflows on growth from 1990 to 1998. They argue that FDI flows to these countries represent more of a pure transfer of technology than is typical of investment in developing countries, because the transition countries were technologically backward, but were substantially industrialized, and had

relatively well educated labor forces. Their results indicate that ". . . FDI is a crucially important explanatory variable for growth in transition economies . . . ," a finding that survives ". . . correcting for reverse causality, endogeneity, and omitted variable bias" (p 22).

A recent paper by Carkovic and Levine (2002) on this issue uses new data sets and different statistical techniques. Their dependent variable is per capita GDP growth in a sample of 72 developed and developing countries over the whole period from 1960 to 1995 and in a panel of five-year periods. They find no "robust, positive influence on economic growth" from "the exogenous component of FDI" (p 3).

In equations that do not subdivide the sample, FDI inflows are not significant in the rate of growth over 1960 to 1995, and only irregularly significant in equations for five-year periods. Once variables for trade openness, the black market currency premium, or financial development are included, the coefficients for FDI are insignificant. Carkovic and Levine then test the results of other studies indicating that education levels, trade openness, or per capita income determine which countries gain in their rates of growth from higher levels of FDI. They find that none of these country characteristics consistently determine the effect of FDI on growth, although some are significant in some combinations of conditioning variables.

It is difficult to draw strong conclusions from these cross-country studies. Where they differ, it is not always clear whether differences in definitions of growth, in equation forms, in country coverage, or in the underlying data used account for the large differences in results. Carkovic and Levine do say, but do not show, that limiting their country sample to developing countries does not affect their conclusions.

It does seem safe to conclude that there is no universal relationship between the ratio of inward FDI flows to GDP and the rate of growth of a country. Sometimes a relationship seems to be there and sometimes not. High rates of growth seem to be accompanied often by a collection of country characteristics that usually occur together, making it difficult to discern separate effects. The combinations of presumably growth-enhancing or growth-discouraging characteristics that have been assembled by various investigators still leave most differences in growth rates unexplained.

All of these analyses are based on the idea that FDI is important mainly as a financial flow, an addition to the sources of financing, presumably for physical capital formation. However, physical capital formation is more a consequence of previous growth than a determinant of future growth (Blomström, Lipsey, and Zejan 1996). Furthermore, if the importance of FDI is seen mainly from the transfer of technology to affiliates and imitation by local firms, or from learning by suppliers or customers of the affiliates, the nominal flow of FDI would be a very poor measure of it. The extent of production, employment, local purchases, and sales are more suitable proxies for the sources of technology transfer, and these measures are the main ingredients of industry and microdata studies.

Affiliate productivity and spillovers

Most theoretical discussions of the possible role of inward FDI refer to the transmission of superior technology. Productivity measurement is an attempt to measure productivity gaps between foreign and domestic firms and changes in technology. That is an aspect of technology, but it is a narrow view of it. The technology advantages of foreign firms may involve more their knowledge of world markets or of ways of coordinating production and distribution in many countries than their efficiency in manufacturing processes themselves, although manufacturing efficiency is presumably part of these technology advantages. The productivity studies are confined to manufacturing activity, which is a large part of multinational activity but far from all of it, and ignore the other aspects of a firm's competitiveness.

One of the main ways in which foreign investment might raise the growth rate of a host country is by introducing methods of production more efficient than those of local firms. They might not improve their own efficiency faster than local firms once they are established, but the addition of the more efficient foreign firms would raise the aggregate growth rate as long as their share increased. The possibility of such gains depends on whether foreign affiliates are, in fact, more efficient and, if they are, whether this higher efficiency stems simply from their acquisition of local firms that are more efficient than average. If the higher efficiency results from improvements in the efficiency of acquired local firms or from the establishment of new operations of above-average efficiency, it should result in more efficient production on average and higher rates of productivity growth as long as the foreign share is increasing.

Another source of productivity gains for the host country, which has almost monopolized the attention of investigators, is the possibility of spillovers of productivity advantages from the foreign affiliates to locally owned firms. Locally owned firms might increase their efficiency by copying the procedure of foreign firms to raise profits, to reach export markets, or to survive in competition with the foreign firms. There could be negative spillovers also, if foreigners, by taking markets from local firms, force them to less efficient scales of production.

Whether spillovers to local firms are positive, negative, or nonexistent, the effect of the entrance of foreign firms or their expansion on the country's growth will depend on the combination of two components. One is the efficiency of the foreign firms themselves and the other is spillovers to local firms in the same industry and in other industries. The focus should be on the aggregate efficiency of industries, but only a few studies deal with this issue.

There could be increases in aggregate efficiency even if there were no visible differences in productivity between foreign and domestic firms. If the industry is sufficiently competitive, the entry of foreign firms could force domestically owned competitors to match them quickly to survive.

The choices among productivity measures in these studies range from value added per worker, the simplest and most universally available measure, to value added per unit of labor and capital input and value of output per unit of labor, capital, and intermediate product input. Some studies fit production functions that also incorporate scale economies. The result of including capital input is to ignore any host country benefits from the accumulation of fixed capital or from any advance in technology that is inseparable from the adoption of new capital goods. The result of including scale economies is to ignore any benefits from increases in the scale of production introduced by foreign firms.

Productivity comparisons between foreign and domestic operations have been made in many ways. Some are very aggregated for industry or manufacturing as a whole. Others are within individual industries, but without accounting for differences in the characteristics of establishments. Others take account of size of establishments, capital intensity, or use of intermediates. Partly depending on the availability of data, some use value added as the measure of output and use labor input, or labor and capital input, as measures of input. Others use the total value of output as the output measure and include intermediate purchases in inputs. Some comparisons include the scale of operations as a determinant of productivity, moving further toward fitting production functions. Most investigators add as many establishment characteristics as the underlying data permit, on the theory that differences in production functions are the best measure of differences in technology.

It is rare not to find that productivity is higher, on average, in foreign-owned firms and establishments. Large margins were reported, for example, in Mexico (Blomström and Wolff 1994), Uruguay (Kokko, Zejan, and Tansini 2001), and Venezuela (Harrison 1996), and five east Asian countries (Ramstetter 1999).

These aggregate differences reflect the fact that FDI tends to be in industries of higher than average productivity, because they are more capital intensive than average or employ workers of higher than average skills and wages. However, within individual industries also, foreign-owned firms and establishments typically have higher productivity, as was reported for Mexico (Blomström and Wolff 1994), Taiwan (Chuang and Lin 1999), Côte d'Ivoire, Morocco, and Venezuela (Harrison 1996).

Within industries, the higher productivity of foreign operations is usually associated with higher capital intensity, if the productivity measure is labor productivity, larger scale of operations, or greater use of intermediate inputs. With the effects of all or some of these removed, foreign operations were found to have higher productivity in the great majority of industries in Indonesia (Sjöholm 1999), Morocco (Haddad and Harrison 1993), and Venezuela (Harrison 1996).

By and large, productivity comparisons between foreign-owned and locally owned firms have found that the former had higher productivity. That finding of the superiority of foreign-owned firms persisted, although not in all cases, when various firm or establishment characteristics were included as explanatory variables. The logic of taking account of all these factors is the assumption that, for example, higher capital intensity, larger scale of production, and greater input of intermediates are all available to domestic firms and should not be attributed to any technological superiority of the foreign firms. That is a questionable assumption for developing countries. There may be no domestic firms capable of operating some types of equipment, of managing large-scale production, or of finding the same quality of intermediate products. Intermediate products, in particular, may be purchased by an affiliate from other units of the same multinational firm, an option that may not be available to a local firm.

Reviews of the literature on productivity spillovers to local firms have come to mixed conclusions. One view is that there is some evidence for spillovers, but that they are more likely to occur when the local firms or their countries are not too far behind the foreign firms or their home countries (Blomström and Kokko 1998; Blomström, Kokko, and Globerman 2001). Another view is that spillovers depend on the degree of competition in the host country and the extent of technological investment by local firms (Wang and Blomström 1992; Kinoshita 2000). A more agnostic view is that there is little evidence for spillovers, particularly in studies using panel data. It is argued that most of the evidence for positive spillovers is from cross-section studies that fail to remove the effects of selection of highly productive establishments for takeover by foreign firms (Görg and Greenaway 2001; Görg and Strobl 2001).

Another possibility is that the effects of FDI on local firms depend on broad aspects of government policy, particularly the trade regime, as suggested in the earlier quotation from Bhagwati about effects on growth. A highly protective regime may encourage inward investment, particularly "tariff-jumping" investment, in sectors that are economically unsuitable for the host country and not viable for unsubsidized local firms. They may be capital intensive in a capital-poor country, or require large-scale production to be efficient, in a country with a small market and little likelihood of finding export markets. When host-country subsidies are involved, there is often the additional drawback that the subsidies direct the investment to backward areas of the host country that would not be selected in a free choice. An example of inward investment under a restrictive trade regime that included all these defects was that of auto production in Chile in the 1960s, described in Johnson (1966). Chile ended up with about 20 auto assembly plants, together assembling only about 8,000 units, in a city a thousand miles from Santiago, the main market. Foreign investors can create white elephants, given the incentives to do so. It would be surprising if much in the way of spillovers to domestically owned plants could be found in Chilean microdata. This is probably an extreme example, but it provides one reason why spillovers might be elusive.

If there is any validity to the finding that the extent of spillovers to domestic firms depends on country factors such as trade policy, education levels, and the technological sophistication of its industries, the selection of countries studied may affect the conclusions drawn. For example, of the four developing countries for which Görg and Greenaway (2001) and Görg and Strobl (2001) report panel data results—Colombia, India, Morocco, and Venezuela—three were described (World Bank 1987) as "inward-oriented" during the period studied. Similar rankings were given to these countries by Wheeler and Mody (1992).

Although some commentators give a heavy weight to the evidence from panel data studies, the findings from these studies may reflect the weakness of the manufacturing sectors in the few countries examined. There may not be enough local firms capable of learning new technologies. The number of countries for which panel data studies have been performed is, so far, insufficient to form definitive judgments from them, especially since the small number may also be a biased sample of developing countries.

New exports and new industries

One way in which FDI inflows have been said to promote growth has been to introduce new industries into a host country and into its portfolio of export products. The role of FDI would be important when a host country possesses the factor proportions suitable for economical production, but lacks either the technological knowledge, in the conventional sense, or the requisite knowledge of consumer tastes or fashions. Another case is an intermediate product that is suitable for a country's factor proportions and skills, but is part of a chain of production requiring such close coordination with the rest of the chain that it can be produced efficiently only in a plant managed by the same owner. This type of fragmentation is often found in the parts of the electronics industry. Lipsey (2000b) described the large role of US affiliates in that industry in East Asia, especially in the early development of the industry. Data from the early stages of the industry in that region, not necessarily the earliest beginnings, show US affiliates accounting for three quarters of exports, a share that eventually declined as the industry matured. He summarized the country studies in Dobson and Chia (1997) as showing how foreign firms ". . . saw a way to integrate these countries into worldwide networks of production . . . Foreign firms supplied the technology and the links to other parts of the production networks that completed the set of resources necessary for the growth of these industries" (p 163).

In a study of "Export Catalysts in Low-Income Countries," Rhee and Belot (1990) refer in their summary to ". . . the critical role of transnational corporations (TNCs) in the transfer of technical, marketing, managerial know-how to developing countries—a role more important than the transfer of financial resources associated with FDI by TNCs" (p viii).

Policies toward FDI

Large differences among host countries and, especially, sharp changes in host-country policy toward FDI provide a set of experiments in which basic country characteristics are held constant, although there are changes in other policies, particularly toward trade, that usually accompany shifts in direct investment policy.

A conspicuous case, although it is not a developing country, is that of Ireland. Ireland had a severely restrictive, almost prohibitive, policy toward inward direct investment until 1959. In the late 1950s, its export comparative advantage, the share of a product in Ireland's exports relative to its share in world exports, was that of a developing country. Ireland reported comparative advantages in only two one-digit SITC (Standard International Trade Classification) sections: Food and Live Animals, and Beverages and Tobacco. Along with other nonmanufactured products, they made up more than 80 percent of Irish exports, as can be seen in Figure 1. In every other SITC section, including all types of manufacturing, Ireland had a comparative disadvantage in exporting.

Once the barriers to inward investment in Ireland were removed, direct investment began to flow in. US direct investment in manufacturing, which had been reported as 0 in 1958, rose to $242 million in 1972, with most of the output destined for export. Even before Ireland joined the European Union (EU), this inflow had

started to transform the economy and Ireland's export structure, to the point where Ireland had a comparative advantage in Chemicals and, slightly, in one other manufactured goods sector. Joining the European Union gave a large boost to both inward investment and the growth of manufactured exports. By 1997, Ireland's export comparative advantage was much greater in Chemicals than in Foods and Beverages, and more than half of Ireland's exports were in Chemicals and in Machinery and Transport Equipment, as can be seen in the figure. Foreign firms, exporting over 70 percent of their output (more in relatively high-tech sectors), accounted for two-thirds of manufacturing employment (Ruane and Görg 1999, pp 51–53).

The results of this transformation of the economy in terms of the standard of living can be seen in Figure 2. Before 1960, Ireland was losing ground in per capita income relative to the EU average. After the liberalization of 1959 and the beginnings of FDI inflow, Ireland kept up with the other EU countries. Ireland joined the EU in 1973, and after that, the inward flow of FDI accelerated and Ireland's growth began to outpace that of the other EU countries. Inward investment exploded in the 1990s, as did Ireland's relative income. Ireland went from being a poor relation in the EU, with per capita income 40 percent below the EU average at the time of its accession, to parity with the other countries and then above-average income in 20 years.

The rapid growth of the inward FDI stock in Ireland in the 1990s was accompanied by an acceleration in per capita income growth to a rate much higher than in previous decades. Although income growth in general seems to have some effect in promoting inward FDI flows, according to most studies, that direction of causation is less likely for Ireland because most of the output of foreign-owned firms is exported. Increases in per capita income could be expected, if anything, to discourage inward investment for export production because such increases represent rising labor costs. It seems most likely, then, that it was the growth of inward FDI that propelled the rise in per capita income.

China is another example of a country that was virtually closed to inward FDI until the late 1980s. Its export structure in 1985 (Figure 3) was still that of a country in the early stages of development, with well over half in Foods, Beverages, Crude Materials, and Mineral Fuels. Once it opened up to inward FDI, even though it restricted investment geographically at first, the inflow started slowly and then became large. By 1993, foreign establishments accounted for a third of industrial production in Guangdong Province, one of the favored ones (Lipsey, Blomström, and Ramstetter 1998, p 106). By the late

Figure 1: Ireland: Composition of exports, 1950 and 1997

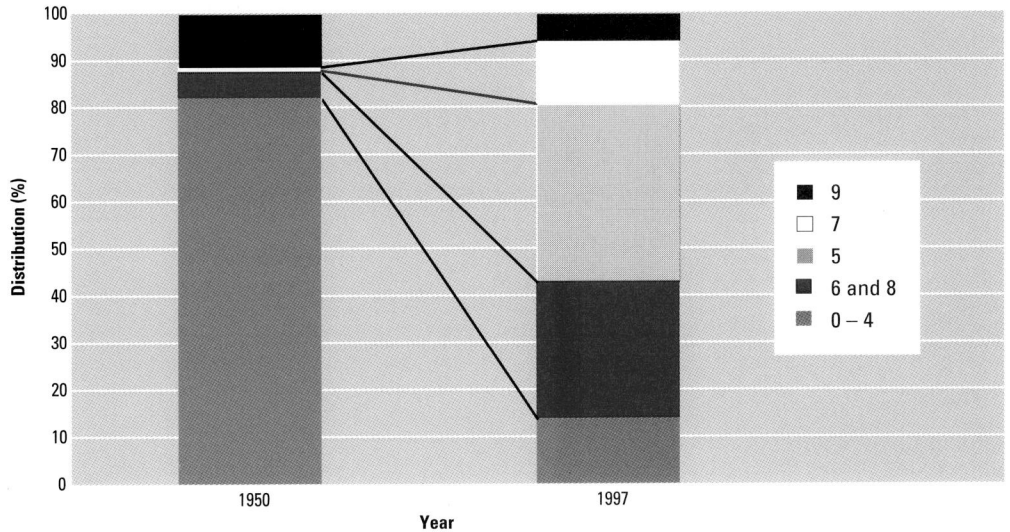

Note: SITC Revision 2, 0–4: Food and Live Animals; Beverages and Tobacco; Mineral Fuels, Lubricants, Related Materials; Crude Materials, Inedible, except Fuels; Animal and Vegetable Oils and Fats. 6 & 8: Manufactured Goods classified by material; Miscellaneous Manufactured Articles. 5: Chemicals. 7: Machinery and Transport Equipment. 9: Commodities and Transactions, n.e.s.
Sources: United Nations (1953); Statistics Canada (1999).

Figure 2: Ireland real per capita GDP and inward FDI stock, 1950–2000

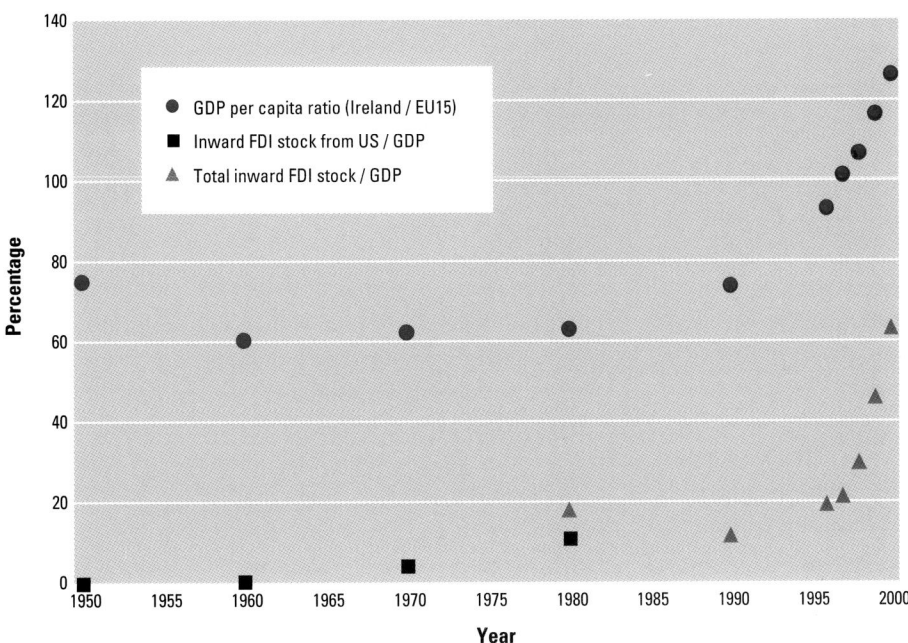

Sources: PennWorldTables; UNCTAD (2001) and earlier issues in the same series; World Bank (2002); US Dept. of Commerce (1982) and (1986).

1990s, manufactures accounted for more than 85 percent of Chinese exports. Foreign affiliates were the source of more than 40 percent of total exports (UNCTAD 1997, p 93), and must have accounted for a higher proportion of manufactured exports.

Malaysia and Singapore were two countries that welcomed inward FDI at an early date. They relied heavily on foreign firms to enlarge their manufacturing industries and manufactured exports. In 1970, both countries' export comparative advantages were outside the manufacturing sector. Manufactured exports comprised about a quarter of total exports in Malaysia and a third in Singapore (Figure 4). By the late 1990s, more than half of each country's exports were in Machinery and Transport Equipment—in Singapore, this was almost two thirds. Foreign-owned firms accounted for more than half of manufacturing production in both countries in the 1970s. The share declined in Malaysia to a little over 40 percent by the mid 1990s, but remained around 70 percent in Singapore (Ramstetter 1999, Table 1). In both countries, foreign firms accounted for larger shares of exports of manufactures than of manufacturing production: 70 percent in Malaysia and 85 percent in Singapore. As in Ireland, it was the foreign firms that turned both countries into major producers and exporters of manufactured products. That is not to say that a shift to manufacturing requires dependence on foreign firms: Korea and Taiwan became major manufactures exporters with much lower foreign participation, although foreign firms played some role in each case.

Conclusions

There is enough ambiguity in the results of many studies of the effects of inflows of FDI to show that no straightforward, universal impact exists. Studies across the universe of developing countries, or most of it, do not find that increased inflows of FDI guarantee faster growth. Some countries do gain, but some do not, although there is little evidence to suggest losses. Whether a country gains or not apparently depends on its initial economic level, its trade and other government policies, and the quality of its labor force. The closer a developing country is to the economic level of the developed countries in per capita income, the greater the benefit from inflows of FDI. That is true even though initially low income levels, by themselves, are usually found in growth equations to be associated with faster subsequent growth. The less restrictive the trade regime and the more open the economy in general, the greater the gain from any given level of FDI inflow. The higher the degree of education of the labor force, the greater the growth benefits from FDI.

These relationships are blurred in practice by the fact that the factors that are supposed to enhance the positive effects of FDI on growth are usually positively correlated with flows and stocks of inward FDI. FDI tends to flow more to higher-income developing countries, and to those with more open trade regimes, more educated labor, and more efficient and honest governments. If these factors by themselves promote growth, it is difficult to disentangle their influence from that of the FDI itself.

All of the cross-country studies depend on the use of data on flows or stocks of inward FDI. These are only rough approximations to the provision of additional funds for plant and equipment investment. They are even rougher approximations to transfers of technology through FDI. With all their weaknesses, the conclusions drawn from the cross-country studies range from no effect of inward FDI to a positive impact in combination with other variables.

Studies of FDI in individual recipient countries can make use of data on employment, sales, production, and fixed investment closer to activities through which the presumably superior technology of the investing multinationals might be transferred to the host country economy. *Superior technology* is usually identified in empirical studies as higher output per unit of labor input or per unit of labor, capital, and intermediate product inputs. Sometimes allowances can be made for the scale of production.

Foreign-owned firms in developing countries almost always have higher labor productivity, on average, than domestically owned firms. They are in higher productivity industries, they are larger, they are more capital-intensive, and they use more purchased intermediate inputs in production. It is usually assumed that any superior technology of the foreign firms will not be represented by their factor inputs or their scale of production, but only by higher output from any given combination of inputs. However, some country data sets are limited in the number of inputs that can be accounted for, and all have problems in capital estimation.

As more determinants of output are added to the production functions for individual countries and industries, the margin of superiority of the foreign firms declines. In general, however, some foreign firm advantage remains. Cross-section studies across industries and regions for individual years, the most common type of analysis, generally find that there are spillovers of productivity to domestically owned firms. Domestic firms in the industries or regions, or the industries within regions, where foreign firms are more important have higher productivity. There are a few studies based on panel data for individual firms or plants, which remove the risk that the cross-section results reflect only the acquisition of superior local firms by foreigners. However, these studies cover only a few countries, and not very successful ones, and they give ambiguous results on spillovers. There are even some cases of apparent negative spillovers, perhaps from competition too strong for local firms. Thus, the evidence for positive

Figure 3: China: Composition of exports, 1985 and 1997

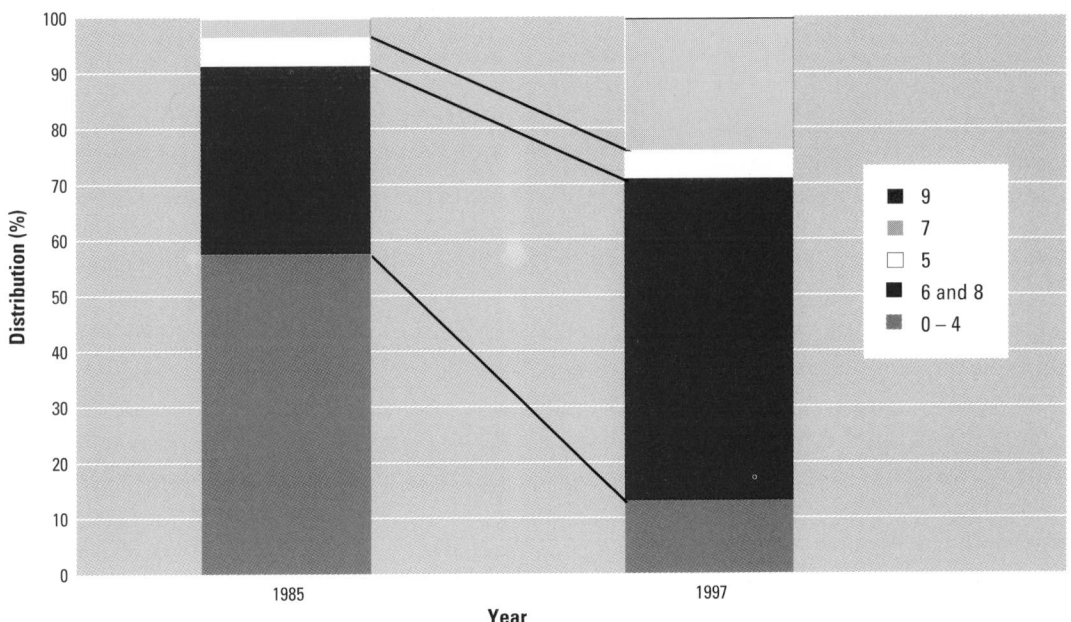

Note: SITC Revision 2, 0–4: Food and Live Animals; Beverages and Tobacco; Mineral Fuels, Lubricants, Related Materials; Crude Materials, Inedible, except Fuels; Animal and Vegetable Oils and Fats. 6 & 8: Manufactured Goods classified by material; Miscellaneous Manufactured Articles. 5: Chemicals. 7: Machinery and Transport Equipment. 9: Commodities and Transactions, n.e.s.
Sources: NBER (1997); Statistics Canada (1999).

Figure 4: Malaysia and Singapore: Composition of exports, 1970 and 1997

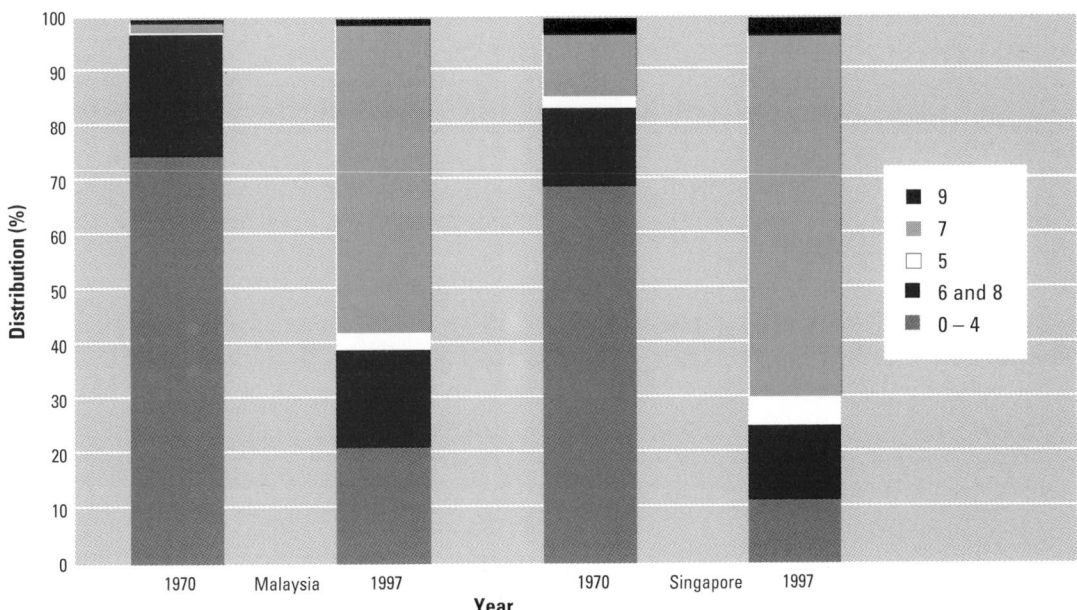

Note: SITC Revision 2, 0–4: Food and Live Animals; Beverages and Tobacco; Mineral Fuels, Lubricants, Related Materials; Crude Materials, Inedible, except Fuels; Animal and Vegetable Oils and Fats. 6 & 8: Manufactured Goods classified by material; Miscellaneous Manufactured Articles. 5: Chemicals. 7: Machinery and Transport Equipment. 9: Commodities and Transactions, n.e.s.
Sources: NBER (1997); Statistics Canada (1999).

spillovers is not strong. Spillovers may depend not only on the country characteristics discussed earlier, but also on the characteristics of particular host-country industries and firms.

The impact of multinationals on host countries is clearer with respect to exports. Multinational corporations' affiliates are almost always more export-oriented than domestic firms. Their entrance into a country, or their expansion, often leads to new products among exports and new markets. That phenomenon has been a particular feature of electronics industries in East Asia.

Differences in policy toward FDI, and especially sharp changes in policy, provide another type of evidence of the effects of inward FDI. Malaysia and Singapore, by encouraging production by foreign firms, have become major producers and exporters of various types of machinery. It is difficult to imagine that these industries would have grown in countries with such small local markets if foreign firms had been barred or discouraged. Even stronger evidence is provided by countries that sharply changed their policies toward inward FDI. Both Ireland and China moved from virtual prohibition of inward FDI to active encouragement. Ireland's export trade was transformed from that of a developing agricultural country to that of an industrial economy. Its per capita income, falling relative to other European countries in the 1950s and far below the average by 1960, reached a level above the EU average in the late 1990s.

China also exhibited the export structure of a developing country as late as the mid 1980s. Once it opened up to inflows of FDI, it moved to the export structure of an industrialized country. Foreign affiliates were the producers of more than 40 percent of China's total exports by 1996. Their share of manufactured exports must have been much larger.

Openness to inward FDI is no magic potion that can eliminate the effects of poor policies, poor endowments, and bad luck. However, larger inflows of FDI have, in general, been associated with higher growth, especially in countries and industries not too far behind the leaders. And there is clear evidence that some countries have succeeded in using inward direct investment, especially investment oriented toward exports, effectively to promote the growth and the transformation of their economies.

References

Balasubramanyam, V. N., M. Salisu, and D. Sapsford. 1996. "Foreign Direct Investment and Growth in EP and IS Countries," *The Economic Journal* 106 (January): 92–105.

Bhagwati, J. N. 1978. *Anatomy and Consequences of Exchange Control Regimes*, Special Conference Series on Foreign Trade Regimes and Economic Development, Vol. XI. Cambridge, MA: Ballinger.

Blomström, M. and A. Kokko. 1998. "Multinational Corporations and Spillovers," *Journal of Economic Surveys* 12: 247–277.

Blomström, M., A. Kokko, and S. Globerman. 2001. "The Determinants of Host Country Spillovers from Foreign Direct Investment: a Review and Synthesis of the Literature." In N. Pain, ed., *Inward Investment, Technological Change, and Growth*. Basingstoke, Hampshire, and New York: Palgrave in Association with the NIESR.

Blomström, M., R. E. Lipsey, and M. Zejan. 1994. "What Explains the Growth of Developing Countries?" In W. J. Baumol, R. R. Nelson, and E. N. Wolff, eds., *Convergence of Productivity: Cross-national Studies and Historical Evidence*. New York: Oxford University Press.

———. 1996. "Is Fixed Investment the Key to Economic Growth?" *Quarterly Journal of Economics* 111(1): 269–276.

Blomström, M. and E. N. Wolff. 1994. "Multinational Corporations and Productivity Convergence in Mexico." In W. Baumol, R. Nelson, and E. N. Wolff, eds., *Convergence of Productivity: Cross-national Studies and Historical Evidence*. New York: Oxford University Press.

Borensztein, E., J. De Gregorio, and J.-W. Lee. 1998. "How Does Foreign Direct Investment Affect Economic Growth?" *Journal of International Economics* 45(1): 115–135.

Carkovic, M. and R. Levine. 2002. "Does Foreign Direct Investment Accelerate Economic Growth?" University of Minnesota Department of Finance Working Paper, June.

Campos, N. F. and Y. Kinoshita. 2002. "Foreign Direct Investment as Technology Transferred: Some Panel Evidence from the Transition Economies," *The Manchester School* 70(3): 398–419.

Chuang, Y.-C. and C.-M. Lin. 1999. "Foreign Direct Investment, R&D, and Spillover Efficiency: Evidence from Taiwan's Manufacturing Firms," *Journal of Development Studies* 35(4): 117–134.

Dobson, W. and C. S. Yue, eds. 1997. *Multinationals and East Asian Integration*. Ottawa: International Development Centre; Singapore: Institute of Southeast Asian Studies.

Dunning, J. H. and M. Steuer. 1970. "The Effects of United States Direct Investment on British Technology." In J. H. Dunning, ed., *Studies in International Investment*. London: George Allen & Unwin.

Görg, H. and D. Greenaway. 2001. "Foreign Direct Investment and Intra-Industry Spillovers: A Review of the Literature." Research Paper 2001/37, Globalisation and Labour Markets Programme, Leverhulme Centre for Research on Globalisation and Economic Policy, Nottingham.

Görg, H. and E. Strobl. 2001. "Multinational Companies and Productivity Spillovers: A Meta-Analysis," *The Economic Journal* 111(November): 723–739.

Haddad, M. and A. Harrison. 1993 "Are There Positive Spillovers from Direct Foreign Investment?" *Journal of Development Economics* 42: 51–74.

Harrison, A. 1996. "Determinants and Effects of Direct Foreign Investment in Côte d'Ivoire, Morocco, and Venezuela." In M. J. Roberts and J. R. Tybout, eds., *Industrial Evolution in Developing Countries*. New York: Oxford University Press for the World Bank.

Johnson, L. J. 1966. "Problems of Import Substitution: The Chilean Automobile Industry," *Economic Development and Cultural Change* 15: 202–216.

Kinoshita, Y. 2000. "R&D and Technology Spillovers via FDI: Innovation and Absorptive Capacity," CEPR Discussion Paper No. 2775.

Kokko, A., M. Zejan, and R. Tansini. 2001. "Trade Regimes and Spillover Effects of FDI: Evidence from Uruguay," *Weltwirtschaftliches Archiv* 137(1): 124–149.

Levine, R. and D. Renelt. 1992. "A Sensitivity Analysis of Cross-Country Growth Regressions," *American Economic Review* 82(4): 942–963.

Lipsey, R. E. 1998. "Galloping, Creeping, or Receding Internationalization," *International Trade Journal* XII(2): Summer.

———. 2000a. "Inward FDI and Economic Growth in Developing Countries," *Transnational Corporations* 9(1): 67–95.

———. 2000b. "Affiliates of U.S. and Japanese Multinationals in East Asian Production and Trade." In T. Ito and A. O. Krueger, eds., *The Role of Foreign Direct Investment in East Asian Development and Trade*, NBER East Asian Seminar on Economics, Vol. 9. Chicago: University of Chicago Press.

Lipsey, R. E., M. Blomström, and E. D. Ramstetter. 1998. "Internationalized Production in World Output." In R. E. Baldwin, R. E. Lipsey, and J. D. Richardson, eds., *Geography and Ownership as Bases for Economic Accounting*. Chicago: University of Chicago Press.

Markusen, J. and K. E. Maskus. 2001. "General Equilibrium Approaches to the Multinational Firm: A Review of Theory and Evidence," NBER Working Paper No. 8334. Cambridge, MA: National Bureau of Economic Research.

National Bureau of Economic Research (NBER). 1997. "NBER Trade Database, Disk 2, World Trade Flows, 1970–1992," Robert C. Feenstra, Robert E. Lipsey, and Harry P. Bowen, Cambridge, MA: National Bureau of Economic Research.

Penn World Tables, Version 5.6. On National Bureau of Economic Research Web Site.

Ramstetter, E. D. 1999. "Comparisons of Foreign Multinationals and Local Firms in Asian Manufacturing Over Time," *Asian Economic Journal* 13(2): 163–203.

Rhee, Y.- W. and T. Belot. 1990. "Export Catalysts in Low-Income Countries," World Bank Discussion Paper No. 72. Washington, DC: World Bank.

Romer, P. 1993. "Idea Gaps and Object Gaps in Economic Development," *Journal of Monetary Economics* 32(3): 543–573.

Ruane, F. and H. Görg. 1999. "Irish FDI Policy and Investment from the EU." In R. Barrell and N. Pain, eds., *Innovation, Investment, and the Diffusion of Technology in Europe*. Cambridge: Cambridge University Press.

Sjöholm, F. 1999. "Technology Gap, Competition, and Spillovers from Foreign Direct Investment: Evidence from Establishment Data," *Journal of Development Studies* 36(1): 53–73.

Statistics Canada. 1999. *World Trade Database, 1980–1997* (CD-ROM). Ottawa: Statistics Canada.

United Nations (UN). 1953. *Yearbook of International Trade Statistics, 1953*. New York: United Nations.

United Nations Conference on Trade and Development (UNCTAD). 1997. *World Investment Report, 1997*. New York and Geneva: United Nations.

———. 2001. *World Investment Report, 2001*. New York and Geneva: United Nations.

US Department of Commerce. 1982. *Selected Data on U.S. Investment Abroad, 1950–1976*. Bureau of Economic Analysis, February.

———. 1986. *U.S. Direct Investment Abroad: Balance of Payments and Direct Investment Position Estimates, 1977–81*. Bureau of Economic Analysis, November.

Wang, J. Y. and M. Blomström. 1992. "Foreign Investment and Technology Transfer: A Simple Model," *European Economic Review* 36: 137–155.

Wheeler, D. and A. Mody. 1992. "International Investment Location Decisions: The Case of U.S. Firms," *Journal of International Economics* 33(1/2): 57–76.

World Bank. 1987. *World Development Report, 1987, Trade Policy and Industrialization*. Washington, DC: World Bank.

———. 2002. *World Development Indicators* (CD-ROM). Washington, DC: World Bank.

World Economic Forum. 2002. *Global Competitiveness Report 2001–2002*. New York: Oxford University Press for the World Economic Forum.

305

CHAPTER 3.5

Export Performance and Stages of Development

JENNIFER BLANKE, World Economic Forum

FRIEDRICH VON KIRCHBACH, International Trade Centre

MONDHER MIMOUNI, International Trade Centre

JEAN-MICHEL PASTEELS, International Trade Centre

A number of chapters of this *Report* explore the drivers of national competitiveness, focusing on such aspects as the macroeconomic environment and the quality of public institutions. It is also generally recognized that openness to trade can play an important role in helping nations to achieve greater prosperity. In this regard, a number of studies have explored the relationship between freer trade and economic growth (ie, Sachs and Warner 1995; Dollar and Kraay 2000). These studies have shown that by opening to trade countries can raise their economic growth rates.

It is important to note, however, that openness to trade is not, in itself, a panacea. In recent years, some authors have questioned the link between openness and stronger growth. These studies have looked most particularly at the mixed experiences of developing countries that have opened their markets to trade.[1] Although it is indeed true that opening to trade does not always lead to higher growth, it also seems clear that the variation in national experiences stems in large part from differences in the internal conditions of the countries in question. Among these differing conditions are critical factors such as governance, the quality of institutions, levels of education and health, and law and order. In other words, trade can act as an important catalyst for growth, but countries must have the right institutions in place and an overall business environment that allows countries to benefit most from the expanded opportunities it provides, and to confront the foreign competition it ushers in. These issues are precisely those related to national competitiveness that are explored in depth throughout the other chapters of this *Report*, so they will not be explored further here.

The argument traditionally used to explain the benefits of free trade has been based on the classical theory of *comparative advantage*. According to this theory, gains from trade are due to the relative efficiency of different countries in producing a variety of goods. A key determinant of comparative advantage is the international distribution of factor endowments. Specifically, the theory predicts that a country that is well endowed with labor would be expected to export goods that use labor intensively in production, such as agricultural goods and simple manufactures. Wealthier, more capital abundant countries, on the other hand, would be expected to export goods that use capital more intensively, such as more complex manufactured goods. A technological advantage in the production of a good would also give a country a comparative advantage.

Although comparative advantage demonstrates that gains can be made from opening to trade, it has also been recognized that in today's international economic landscape, competing successfully, particularly when moving into higher technology exports, requires a concept that goes beyond simple factor endowments and "given" technological advantages. In this context, an approach has been

307

developed that aims to explain how countries move from a factor-based competition stage to one based on innovative capacity. This concept, *competitive advantage*, was first proposed by Michael Porter in his book *The Competitive Advantage of Nations* (1990). This is a more microeconomic approach, based on the analysis of the competitiveness of nations in specific industrial sectors.

As Porter outlines in Chapter 1.2 of this *Report*, countries can be seen as moving through three stages of development, during which they produce increasingly sophisticated products: the Factor-Driven stage, the Investment-Driven stage, and the Innovation-Driven stage. During each of these phases, national competitive advantage is based on different determinants, which would also be expected to drive national trade performance. The first stage, the Factor-Driven stage, is based on relative factor endowments such as abundant, low-cost labor. In other words, in this stage, trade performance would be expected to follow a logic similar to comparative advantage. For later stages of development, other factors become critical. In the Investment-Driven stage, competitive advantage is driven by higher levels of efficiency in the production of standard products, with increased levels of investment driving productivity growth. In the final, Innovation-Driven stage, competitive advantage is driven by a country's innovative capacity, particularly in the production of the most high-technology products.

Central to the concept of competitive advantage is where firms decide to set up shop internationally. As Martin Wolf explained in a recent article in *The Financial Times*, what matters for economic success today is "location, location, location."[2] In fact, we see that decisions on location—and relocation—can have an enormous impact on a country's sectoral trade performance.

One of the main difficulties in measuring the benefits of opening to trade is that, for the most part, trade performance has not been measured systematically. This is precisely what this chapter aims to do. We assess the trade performance of individual countries at different stages of development, within specific industrial sectors. To accomplish this, we employ an approach developed by the International Trade Centre,[3] based on United Nations COMTRADE data. This approach, referred to as the *trade performance index* (TPI), allows us to examine a country's trade performance both as a snapshot of a particular year and in terms of its evolution over a five-year period. In both cases, the approach is based on a number of different dimensions, taking into account not only world market share in exports or export growth, but also a number of other aspects, such as the extent to which trade is diversified across markets and across individual products.

It is important to point out that the TPI data cover only trade in goods, and not trade in services. Although

this means that this methodology does not give an entirely complete picture of a country's trade profile, it does provide valuable insights into the competitive advantages of countries in specific goods sectors, particularly considering that goods exports account for approximately 80 percent of overall world exports.[4]

The trade performance index

In this chapter we use the same approach applied in the "Sectoral Trade Perfomance" chapter of last year's *Global Competitiveness Report* (Cornelius et al. 2002). Again we look at two measures of trade competitiveness of specific countries: the *trade performance current index* (which measures the current level of competitiveness of a country in a given sector), and the *trade performance change index* (which measures how the competitive position has changed over a period of five years).

The *current index* summarizes a country's present competitiveness standing in a given sector, and is composed of the following five variables:

1. the share of the country's export sector in world trade,
2. the sectoral trade balance (net exports),
3. per capita exports (to control for the size of the economy),
4. the level of differentiation of export products within a given sector, and
5. the level of diversification of export markets.

The *change index* reflects the improvement or weakening of a country's competitiveness position in the sector (the "dynamics" of competitiveness in the given sector), and is composed of:

1. the change in the country's sector-specific share in world trade,
2. the increase or decrease in the trade balance within the given sector,
3. the degree of specialization in particularly dynamic products within a given sector,
4. the change in product differentiation, and, finally
5. the change in market diversification.

Box 1 provides further details on the methodology used to construct these two indexes. The trade performance index positions 14 broad export sectors in 184 countries in terms of sector-specific trade competitiveness. The overall findings are shown in Table 1, which presents the rankings of both the current and the change index for 14 sectors of each of the 80 countries covered in this *Report*. Box 2 explains how this table is constructed and interpreted.

Box 1. Measuring trade performance

This chapter employs two composite trade performance indexes (TPIs) to measure trade performance: the *current TPI* and the *change TPI*.

The *current TPI* provides an assessment of the *current position* of the country and sector under review. It is like a snapshot of country- and sector-specific trade performance at a given point in time.

The *change TPI* provides an assessment of the *change in trade performance* of the country and sector under review over the most recent *five-year period*. In other words, it examines trade performance from a dynamic perspective.

The current TPI is calculated as an average ranking of the following five criteria:

1. Share in world exports

The *share in world exports* is probably the single most important indicator for the overall competitive position of the export sector in the country under review. By taking an aggregated national approach, it complements per capita exports.

2. Value of net exports

Net exports are defined as exports less imports. A country's net exports are an interesting indicator of its position in the world market for three reasons: first, they show whether local production can meet local demand and generate, in addition, an exportable surplus or not. Second, the indicator takes into account the fact that a growing share of inputs for exports is imported and often belongs to the same product category. Third, the concept of net exports helps to eliminate re-exports from the analysis.

3. Per capita exports

Per capita exports is one of the most significant indicators of the degree of outward orientation of an economy and the per capita income derived from international trade. It is independent of the size of the economy.

4. Product diversification

Export *product diversification* within a given sector provides a measure of the complexity of the sector under review. It sheds light on the sector's capacity for product differentiation. Diversification also reduces the vulnerability to product-specific shocks in external markets. Product diversification is measured in terms of the equivalent number of products of equal value and by the spread of export markets.

5. Market diversification

Export *market diversification* measures the success in pursuing a truly global marketing approach. Export market diversification also diminishes the dependence on shocks in any target market. Market diversification is measured in terms of the equivalent number of target markets and the spread of export markets.

The change TPI is calculated as an average ranking of the following five criteria:

1. Change in world market share

The *change in world market share* is the most obvious indicator for assessing the dynamics of sectoral export performance. It demonstrates the extent to which countries are gaining or losing out in global markets. It is expressed as the percentage change in market share (not percentage points).

2. Trend in the coverage of imports by exports

This indicator assesses the ability of exporters in the sector under review to increase the sectoral trade surplus, or reduce the deficit, of exports over imports. It is calculated as the least square trend of the sector-specific export coverage of imports over the five years under review.

3. Specialization in the most dynamic products within a sector

This indicator measures the specialization in products for which world demand is rapidly growing. It indicates whether countries are focusing on sunrise or sunset sectors. It is calculated as the rank correlation between the share of specific products within the exporting country's sector under review, on the one hand, and the global growth trend of world imports in the sector, on the other.

4. Change in product diversification

Changes in product diversification provide an idea of the evolution of the extent of integration into the international division of labor. They are measured as average annual variations in the number of equivalent export products and the spread of export products.

5. Change in market diversification

Changes in market diversification are measured as average annual variations in the number of equivalent export markets and the spread of target markets.

Table 1: Trade performance index

No. of exp countries	Basic manufactures 127		Chemicals 123		Clothing 114		Electronic components 90		Fresh food 163		IT & Consumer electronics 66		Leather products 85		Minerals 137		Miscellaneous manufacturing 122		Nonelectronic machinery 95		Processed food 139		Textiles 107		Transport equipment 83		Wood products 110	
	Cu.l.	Ch.l.	Cu.l.	Ch.l.	Cu.l.	Ch.l.	Cu.l.	Ch.l.	Cu.l.	Ch.l.	Cu.l.	Ch.l.	Cu.l.	Ch.l.	Cu.l.	Ch.l.	Cu.l.	Ch.l.	Cu.l.	Ch.l.	Cu.l.	Ch.l.	Cu.l.	Ch.l.	Cu.l.	Ch.l.	Cu.l.	Ch.l.
ARGENTINA	39	81	49	38			63	69	9	145	31	60	24	61	24	7	62	61	50	15	11	107	72	69	43	8	58	92
AUSTRALIA	14	106	39	42			32	79	2	58	3		43	48	62	60	28	25	22	86	5	63	30	53	37	37	44	14
AUSTRIA	9	56	24	33	38	106	13	38	46	28	18	11	28	23	62	123	25	68	11	55	21	73	18	90	16	23	4	33
BANGLADESH		76	120	63	23	5			91	105			21	28	12	16	95	37					68	18				
BELGIUM	104	108	3	13	21	22	10	45	18	45	6	20	4	25	65	117	12	55	13	32	4	52	4	56	5	51	16	10
BOLIVIA	20	77	113	97	95	102			87	144			72	82	48	63	99	39	82	64	73	114	96	4	67	24	79	96
BRAZIL	30	122	42	73	65	52	39	84	15	21	53		16	5	55	34	43	31	38	76	20	19	43	84	21	44	22	67
BULGARIA	38	59	30	117	12	13	48	88	33	52	33	37	39	67	9	72	38	64	35	95	32	30	49	103	44	36	38	79
CANADA	22	83	34	49	56	10	49	39	10	84	30	13			34	67	34	29	32	52	31	36	38	54	13	22	10	45
CHILE	16	34	51	17					16	26					51	47	60	100	55	5	18	102	59	41	53	60	11	22
CHINA	58	4	28	60	2	14	23	23	37	92	10	51	6	3	39	100	56	73	29	26	24	16	12	5	11	13	43	42
COLOMBIA	63	16	60	67	54	65	59	41	37	91			22	32	58	23	56	28	57	58	48	11	53	80	60	6	60	24
COSTA RICA	48	38	61	65	68	16	54	30	29	86	35	21	54	66	47	118	63	45	72	62	25	72	75	26	77	2	56	56
CROATIA	15	65	48	70	43	85	37	47	75	82	54		41	9	15	84	41	43	36	37	47	83	55	73	49	7	37	26
CZECH REPUBLIC	29	23	27	81	28	95	28	22	55	103	32	9	27	65	66	89	18	106	15	72	35	79	13	36	8	33	13	28
DENMARK	86	104	11	25	16	19	15	72	3	129	20	7	29	21	128	31	5	30	6	78	3	81	20	11	15	26	31	23
DOMINICAN REPUBLIC	89	33	100	109	40	57	50	13	92	72		34			32	55	61	70			91	128	98	9				
ECUADOR	75	10	90	24	87	21			31	117			67	49	66	89	77	13			40	14	84	79	78	18	66	95
EL SALVADOR	47	26	76	53	76	32	74	61	90	156			26	14	32	31	69	15	37	36	70	5	58	33		20	70	64
ESTONIA	6	86	40	45	37	37	51	11	53	89	34	29			19	55	27	22			42	60	26	13	40		20	59
FINLAND	19	71	21	55	47	92	20	34	72	155	8	14	10	31	53	95	7	56	7	68	37	123	37	59	30	78	2	82
FRANCE	1	57	5	66	13	88	11	77	5	123	12	42	11	53	20	14	14	99	12	77	1	84	5	76	1	57	14	55
GERMANY	36	116	1	102	18	98	1	87	21	110	14	56	37	78	19	82	1	93	1	94	14	92	2	100	2	48	3	25
GREECE	74	21	35	105	26	84	44	83	32	111	47	49	66	30	40	115	39	108	40	90	38	111	31	96	51	79	47	100
GUATEMALA	123	31	68	83	81	67	82	50	39	8			82	84	118	6	71	59	81	21	46	26	65	57			74	61
HAITI	103	44			82	29	87	55	159	158					116	50	116	115			126	56	104	24				
HONDURAS	66	80	103	22	98	24	86	27	68	126					14		89	94			87	2	95	51			76	36
HONG KONG	42	67	81	120	25	51	40	81			40	65			43		36	119	64	80	60	99	40	89			65	80
HUNGARY	57	78	25	29	6	49	26	32	13	128	17	1	33	19	42	44	40	98	44	48	13	121	36	29	31	59	32	12
ICELAND	56	101	83	1					36	99			58	71	33	48	49	84			28	113	56	55	62	54		
INDIA	41	6	43	95	24	38	42	80	22	121	45	55	12	40	68	88	48	118	41	88	69	131	11	85	25	69	6	19
INDONESIA	46	54	32	12	5	73	17	3	25	48	19	22	13	15	80	25	22	21	58	25	23	46	11	12	41	28	48	7
IRELAND	54	39	15	18	59	35	9	24	11	104	4	25			49	54	11	47	20	54	10	20	34	38	39	19	19	7
ISRAEL	3	95	13	36	36	79	29	42	38	22	23	19	1	68	75	57	29	9	30	39	43	59	42	83	58	32		
ITALY		50	18	58	1	103	4	89	30	93	24	53			69	54	4	120	2	93	7	85	1		10	73	43	
JAMAICA	4		108	106	92	105			107	137					8	126					80	48						
JAPAN			7	56	80	34	2	36			1	54	73	45	126		6	90	10	83			14	62	7	76	35	62
JORDAN	76	36	56	20	4	42	71	17	111	43			5	64	44	44	78	8	76	2	86	22	79	14			75	9
KOREA	12	11	10	40	7	80	7	46	70	41	5	17	52	74	49	12	24	54	18	50	50	50	3	15	6	45	42	21
LATVIA	61	68	75	80	48	53	43	71	104	100	43	40	30	43	75	24	48	40	42	31	56	110	32	45	50		34	30
LITHUANIA	49	9	53	98	20		43		52	77	42	33			69	52	33	35	23	33	34	68	15	25	38	16	33	46
MALAYSIA	33	5	23	9	30	61	24	5	41	124	7	30			8	27	9	19	31	20	12	66	15	8	28	17	5	48

Table 1: Trade performance index (cont'd.)

No. of exp countries	Basic manufactures 127		Chemicals 123		Clothing 114		Electronic components 90		Fresh food 163		IT & Consumer electronics 66		Leather products 85		Minerals 137		Miscellaneous manufacturing 122		Nonelectronic machinery 95		Processed food 139		Textiles 107		Transport equipment 83		Wood products 110	
	Cu.I.	Ch.I.	Cu.I.	Ch.I.	Cu.I.	Ch.I.	Cu.I.	Ch.I.	Cu.I.	Ch.I.	Cu.I.	Ch.I.	Cu.I.	Ch.I.	Cu.I.	Ch.I.	Cu.I.	Ch.I.	Cu.I.	Ch.I.	Cu.I.	Ch.I.	Cu.I.	Ch.I.	Cu.I.	Ch.I.	Cu.I.	Ch.I.
MAURITIUS	110	2	94	19	29	87			135	113	15		40	34	121	78	57	88	68	40	63	108	71	35	24	40	53	57
MEXICO	55	51	45	96	35	3	34	10	64	17	15	4	36	55	35	91	44	42	48	9	62	34	52	48	73	55	69	13
MOROCCO	73	35	66	91	15	1	53	1	35	61	13	36	15	29	73	35	90	34	5	59	57	53	69	74	14	30	21	65
NETHERLANDS	23	46	2	94	31	94	14	74	1	63	38	31	20	51	18	65	51	36	27		2	88	9	75	54	34	17	49
NEW ZEALAND	53	98	55	85	79	83	47	52	6	157			76	41	87	62	115	49		43	82	44	73	58			85	91
NICARAGUA									49	50					29	37		76	14	46	26	21	102	93	22	47		
NIGERIA	13	92	33	27					14	42	21	35	81	63	5	45	26	77			88	96					30	76
NORWAY	109	87	87	41	85	70	21	65	48	12			48		127	33	118	85	14		92	13		81		9	73	11
PANAMA	120	117	112	92	102	46			69	141				12	21	113	88	24	60	30	39	91	93	88	45		63	93
PARAGUAY	52	93	64	59	69	58			47	24			38	39	85	40	30	72	47	71	72	82	39	40	27	29	89	17
PERU	67	3	65	5	27	62	19	2	80	73	27	12	34	69	52	110	23	63	33	23	17	28	60	22	36	64	77	73
PHILIPPINES	35	66	31	93	19	100	35	31	45	37	48	32	9	76	56	94	37	95	25	57	41	95	41	47	34	39	18	16
POLAND	45	49	37	23	3	99	25	35	67	107	39	26	19	10	54	8	53	58	34	29	67	120	22	68	18	41	9	70
PORTUGAL	21	89	50	111	8	66	57	9	73	125	46	8			2	49	31	26	24	73	58	49	48	16	20	50	2	2
ROMANIA	11	22	14	39	34	33	36	68	71	90	28	23	44	42	16	29	42	16	34	38	9	61	29	63	18	41	12	83
RUSSIAN FEDERATION			4	4	61	64	5	48	19	32	2	61			16	15	20	105	19	66	29	87	25	16	17	50	7	44
SACU*	27	41	17	4	33	56	27	48	26	64	21	2	14	22	2	61	35	102	28	60	54	127	46	63	29	72	26	34
SINGAPORE	2	47	12	32	32	76	41	44	83	39	41	18	25	59	86	61	19	78	21	41	36	45	24	105	33	53	15	41
SLOVAK REPUBLIC	24	53	44	101	32	76	5	44	83	39	36		25	59	88	74	8	113	16	89	19	37	8	91	26	67	8	60
SLOVENIA	26	70	22	30	41	107	12	40	94	95	36	41	3	58	54	42	19	107	21	91	51	15	10	28	9	27	27	40
SPAIN	8	105	19	43	34	45	16	76	7	62	25	39	2	73	22	2	21	92	17	73	6	64	19	66	4	43	83	63
SRI LANKA	92	112	77	50	10	26	56	25	26	36	59	62	46	27	91	99	55	17	71	1	83	18	64	19	3	31	1	68
SWEDEN	2	75	9	32	44	89	8	51	40	115	3	10			30	102	52	83	3	70	30	40	23	21	26	67	28	50
SWITZERLAND	25	20	9	57	50	93	3	56	57	59	26	59			25	64	8	113	4	89	19	37	8	91	9	27	36	103
TAIWAN	10	28	20	100	17	75	6	15	12	98	9	41	3	58	60	41	8	107	16	91	51	57	10	28	23	10	23	1
THAILAND	37	12	26	10	9	91	30	7	57	16	22	16	8	54	37	3	13	27	26	17	15	47	10	61			52	51
TRINIDAD AND TOBAGO	51	88	54	87			38	8	112	109	56	63	31	13	17	90	50	66	67	35	33	38	74	44	56	5	61	15
TUNISIA	65	91	47	82	11	54	33	58	100	29	51	24	32	26	61	66	59	87	63	45	53	69	7	34	32	3	45	53
TURKEY	31	64	36	35	51	17	55	73	34	161	50	52	50	56	31	21	52	52	39	79	16	9	78	64	42	66	41	29
UKRAINE	17	40	29	72	22	111	18	43	62	149	11	47	17	80	4	43	79	111	43	81	22	89	21	82	12	58	24	87
UNITED KINGDOM	18	99	8	86	67	109	55	73	27	131	50		23		60		16	23	8	44	44	76	61	94	55	14	67	58
URUGUAY	88	84	71	11	46	101	22	59	17	114	16	57	23	38	23	83	75	71	74	65	27	74	27	60	19	56	25	94
UNITED STATES	32	82	6	69					114	87	44	5	7		26	119	17	86	9	8	81	55	67	1	68	83	78	81
VENEZUELA	34	102	58	61			64	28	114	76	44		7	4	57	39	32	14	80	8	76	12	67				94	97
VIET NAM	71	17	92	15	39	11			28	38			61	8	67	51	91	69	85	47	85	106	80	50			78	81
ZIMBABWE	60	111	101	54	93	112																					94	97

Note: Color codes indicate 5 quintiles in rankings: most competitive > > > least competitive

* The Southern African Customs Union (SACU) includes Botswana, Lesotho, Namibia, South Africa, and Swaziland
For full explanatory notes see: http://www.intracen.org/mas
Source: International Trade Centre UNCTAD/WTO

Box 2. Interpreting the trade performance index table

The trade performance index (TPI) table, shown in Table 1, ranks the performance of the 80 countries covered in the *Report* within 14 broad export sectors. Each country receives two performance rankings in each sector: one for its performance according to the current TPI (Cu. I), and one for its performance on the change TPI (Ch.I). Each ranking is constructed based upon the country's performance across five TPI indicators (see Box 1 for details).

Within each sector and each index, the level of performance is indicated by two elements: the *rank number* and the *color* attributed to the box itself:

Rank numbers range from 1 to 184, covering all countries covered by the TPIs (or several more countries than the 80 that are covered by the *Report* and this chapter). A rank of "1" corresponds to the highest performing country within the sector and index, while a rank of "184" corresponds to the lowest performer. This indicates the specific position of the country within the rankings. It is important to note that—since for several of the 14 sectors, a number of countries do not export at all—the worst possible score on the two indexes can be much lower than 184 (eg, if a sector includes only 120 exporting countries, the worst possible score is 120) .

Five color codes range from darkish blue (indicating the highest trade performing quintile of countries in the sector) to white (indicating the lowest performing quintile of countries). The color coding is critical since, as mentioned above, the total number of countries actually exporting in each of the 14 sectors varies considerably. This means that the rank number is not enough to give a full sense of the positioning of the country's trade performance in some sectors. Another useful aspect of the color coding is that by looking across an entire line for a particular country, the reader gets a sense of where the country stands across all of the 14 sectors covered, based on which colors predominate.

In cases where countries carry out no trade in a particular sector, the boxes contain a period and are not counted in the numbering.

We take the case of Singapore to illustrate how to read the table. The TPI table is reproduced below for four export sectors: basic manufactures, chemicals, IT and consumer electronics, and leather products.

	Basic manufactures		Chemicals		IT & consumer electronics		Leather products	
	127		123		66		85	
	Cu.I.	Ch.I.	Cu.I.	Ch.I.	Cu.I.	Ch.I.	Cu.I.	Ch.I.
SINGAPORE	27	47	4	4	2	61	.	.

Reading from left to right provides the following information:

In the basic manufactures sector, Singapore ranks 27 on the current TPI, indicating that it is performing relatively well in this sector at present. It ranks 47 on the change TPI, indicating that its evolution in this sector over the five-year period 1996–2000 has been a bit less strong. The color indicates that in both indexes Singapore falls into the second highest quintile of countries in this particular sector.

In the chemicals sector, Singapore performs extremely well, as indicated both by the dark blue shading of the boxes, and the high score of 4 in each index.

In the IT and consumer electronics sector, Singapore performs extremely well at present, as measured by the current TPI rank of 2, and the blue shading of the box. Its evolution over the five-year period, on the other hand, has been much less favorable, with a low score of 61 on the change TPI and a color coding that indicates that it falls into the worst-performing quintile. Singapore exports a negligible amount of leather products, or none at all.

A reading of the table by country (by row) provides an overview of the sectors in which the country exports and its present trade performance in the relevant sectors, as well as the evolution of its performance in these sectors over a five-year period. The table is thus useful for an analysis of specific country performances.

Similarly, an analysis of the table by sector (by column) allows for cross-country comparisons within the different sectors.

Of course, since the trade data are presented in aggregated format, a number of details on the strengths and evolutions in specific product groups within each of the sectoral categories escape our analysis. However, the goal of this chapter is not to provide every detail of what is happening within each broad sector, but rather to give an overview of the general trends taking place in international trade across a large sample of counties. To this end, the level of aggregation allows us to capture these broad trends in a tractable manner.

The rest of this chapter is organized as follows. We begin by analyzing the trade performance of individual countries covered by the *Report* in a number of key industrial sectors. We place particular emphasis on how countries perform as they progress through the different stages of development. A primary goal of this analysis is to assess where developing country trade performance is evolving most positively in the sectors covered, and why this is occurring.

Assessing national export trade performance: a sectoral analysis

This section will provide an overview of the present international trading situation as well as the evolution of the trade performance of individual countries in a number of key trade sectors. Since, as mentioned above, trade performance among developing countries has been highly variable, a primary aim of this analysis is to identify specific sectors in which we see encouraging progress.

Our goal is to give an overview of trade performance among the countries covered by the *Report*, as well as to provide some insight into areas where the lower-income countries are faring best and what this means for trade policy for developing countries.

Before beginning the analysis, we should point out that since most trade presently takes place among wealthy industrialized countries, we would a priori expect these countries to outperform developing countries in all export sectors in their *present trade performance*. We also note that the patterns of international trade in goods are constantly changing. There is a steady shifting away from the production of primary, labor-intensive goods to more advanced manufacturing and higher-technology goods. Moving into the production of these more advanced products requires much higher levels of capital and technological sophistication. We might therefore also expect the *evolution of trade performance* in these sectors to be stronger in the wealthier industrialized countries that are at the most advanced stages of development.

Throughout the analysis, we will note specific industrialized country success stories, and the reasons behind their strong performances, in an effort to better understand the factors that make countries strong players in the different sectors. We will also note the progress over the recent five-year period to see how these countries are improving or diminishing their export performance over time.

For developing and transition countries we will highlight specific cases of currently strong performance, as these can serve as useful benchmarks for other developing countries. Perhaps most interesting in the case of these particular countries, however, is to evaluate how they are improving their performance over time—that is, who are the emerging winners, and where are they succeeding? We will do this by carrying out a systematic analysis of the evolution of developing-country performance in different sectors as measured by the change TPI. This will allow us to discern the sectors in which we might expect them to perform well in the future.

Before proceeding, a number of caveats related to trade performance should be mentioned. There are three important macroeconomic factors affecting country specific trade performance hovering in the background of the analysis that are not directly captured by the TPIs. The first factor is the presence of *regional trade agreements*. Trade agreements will tend to increase the level of trade among countries, allowing for increased market and product diversification within a region. This, in turn, will almost automatically improve each member country's individual trade performance. We note, for example, that with regard to the current TPI, many countries within the European Union (EU) perform well in almost every sector. This is linked to their complete trade integration.

A second factor is *trade protectionism*. In a number of sectors, particularly labor-intensive sectors such as textiles and agriculture, wealthy countries lavish large subsidies on national producers. This has a negative impact on developing-country producers by reducing both demand for their products and the prices at which they can sell their products on the world market. Developing countries also maintain trade barriers in a number of industries. Barriers such as tariffs increase prices within their own countries, protecting local producers to the detriment of consumers.

The third important factor is *exchange rate competitiveness*. A country's trade performance will be automatically affected by its real exchange rate. For example, Argentina is underperforming in a number of export sectors. This is due in part to the fact that during the period under review, the peso was pegged to the dollar through the country's currency board system, creating a situation in which the Argentinean currency was too highly appreciated vis-à-vis its trading partners and regional competitors. This resulted in much less competitive exports.

Furthermore, it is important to remember that trade data are not perfect. The TPI data do not capture things such as unreported trade and re-exports. *Re-exports* are

313

goods that are temporarily imported into a country and then exported again with no or little further processing, and are therefore less representative of production patterns of a country. In countries such as Panama and Hong Kong, re-exports can account for at least 50 percent of exports in some sectors.

We begin our analysis with a hypothesis based on the stages of development, and competitive advantage. Based on this concept we would expect to find developing country export strengths in labor-intensive and low-technology industries. (We note that under the theory of comparative advantage we would make a similar prediction for these relatively labor abundant countries). We therefore begin by exploring country-specific trade performance in three such industries—the fresh food, textiles, and basic manufactures industries—to see how well performance is explained by these concepts. We then move up the investment and technology ladder to assess country-specific trade performance in more capital intensive and innovation-driven sectors.

Labor-intensive and low-technology industries

Based on the framework of competitive advantage and stages of development outlined above (as well as on the theory of comparative advantage), we would expect developing countries to perform particularly well in labor-intensive, and low-technology industries, such as agriculture and clothing. What do the data tell us?

Fresh food and agrobased products

This sector comprises all types of foods and other agro-based goods that have not been processed. This includes products such as live animals, rice, unmilled grains, vegetables, and unprocessed tobacco. International trade in these products, estimated at approximately US$238 billion, accounts for about 14 percent of world trade. Table 2 presents the countries covered by the *Report* ranking in the top 10 of the current TPI of the fresh food sector, followed by those in the top 20 of the change TPI. All of the tables in the following sectoral analysis also include the following two key indicators: "share in world exports" and "change in world export share" over the five-year period from 1996 through 2000, as these are perhaps the most illustrative indicators of trade performance within each index.

Looking at the table, we see that the industrialized nations strongly dominate this sector. At present, the United States is a key leader as indicated by the high score on the current TPI and almost 16 percent of world market share in fresh food exports in 2000. A number of EU countries also have strong positions in this area, indicated by both the current TPI and the share in world exports.

Table 2: Top performers in the fresh food and agrobased products sector

Country	Current TPI	Share in world exports 2000	Change TPI	Change in world export share
Netherlands	1	6.50%	63	−0.09%
Australia	2	4.83%	58	0.06%
Denmark	3	2.29%	129	−0.01%
United States	4	15.69%	114	−0.42%
France	5	5.89%	123	−0.15%
New Zealand	6	1.58%	157	−0.04%
Spain	7	3.92%	62	0.07%
SACU*	8	0.57%	32	−0.02%
Argentina	9	2.49%	145	−0.03%
Canada	10	5.12%	84	0.18%
Guatemala	39	0.50%	8	0.04%
Panama	48	0.19%	12	0.02%
Trinidad and Tobago	112	0.01%	16	0.00%
Mexico	64	2.28%	17	0.15%

*Member countries of the Southern African Customs Union (SACU) are Botswana, Lesotho, Namibia, South Africa, and Swaziland.

The European Union, as a whole, accounts for more than 31 percent of world market share in fresh food, approximately double that of the United States. In the case of the European Union, most of these volumes are intra-EU trade. In both the cases of the European Union and the United States, this position is also clearly reinforced by a strong support of agriculture (including producer and consumer support), which, combined, accounted for approximately US$195 billion in 2000 (OECD 2001, pp 197).

It is important to note that the value of world trade in agriculture has been shrinking steadily in past years, primarily due to the fall in world commodity prices. This means that in order for countries to increase their share of the market, leading to improved performance, this must necessarily be at the expense of other exporting countries. This is one reason that the rich-world subsidies are so painful for developing countries trying to improve their performance in this sector.

Despite heavy rich-world subsidies, some developing countries are performing well. The Southern African Customs Union (SACU) stands out as a particularly successful case. The strong performance is related to strong product and market diversification in the fresh food sector, as well as relatively high per capita exports (a variable that controls for population size). The strong performance has been facilitated by the fact that the five countries within the SACU (South Africa, Botswana, Lesotho, Namibia, and Swaziland) opened their borders to trade among themselves in 1970, making it one of the oldest customs unions in the world. This has allowed them to expand their markets and diversify their products. The success of southern Africa is also largely explained by its geography, as it can produce fruits and vegetables for export to Europe during the winter, for example.

Figure 1: Change TPI in fresh food, by income level

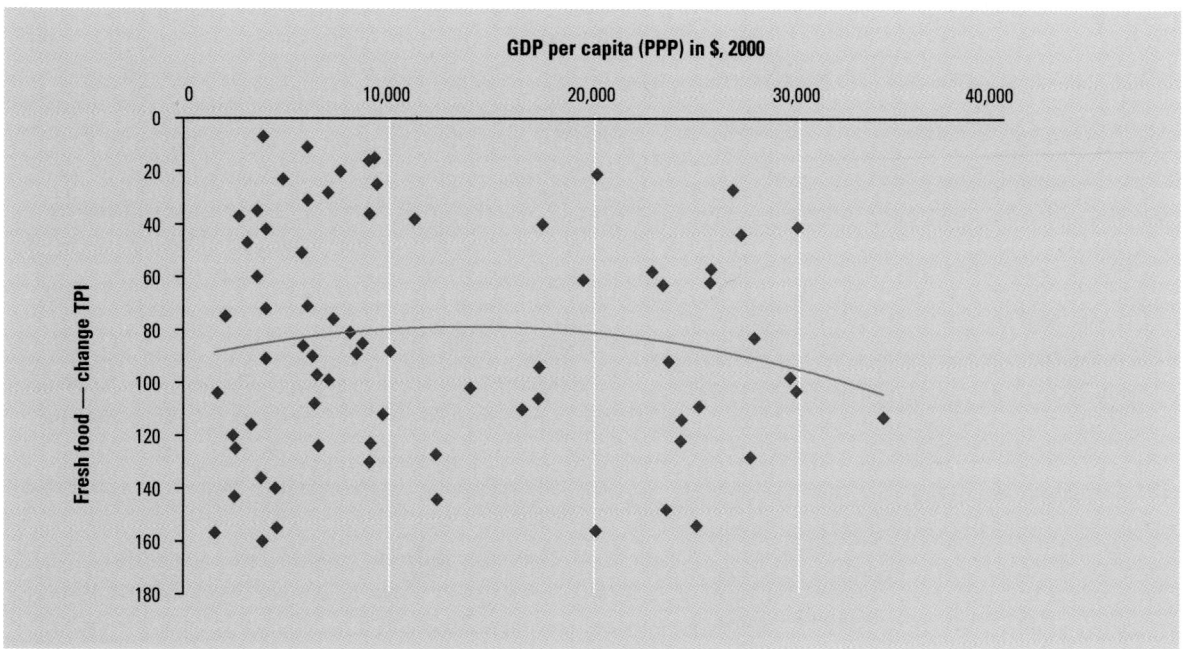

Source: GDP data were obtained from the International Comparison Programme (ICP) of the World Bank.

Turning to changes in performance over time, as indicated by the scores on the change TPI, however, we see that all of the EU countries and the United States fare rather poorly. For most countries in Europe, this can be traced mainly to a decline in market share over the five-year period, and issues such as the failure to diversify products within the sector (eg, Denmark), or the specialization within sectors where world demand is not very dynamic (eg, France). The United States has also faced a decline in world market share. In this case, the negative evolution in trade performance is largely linked to a negative trend in the import coverage by exports, in particular with US bilateral trade with Mexico. During the five-year period in question, the United States experienced a 10 percent decrease in its sectoral surplus (going in the same direction as the country's notorious current account deficit). The deterioration in performance of both the European Union and the United States might be linked to the reduction of subsidies and customs duties over the period in question, in the context of the Uruguay Round agreement on agriculture, which would have decreased market share.

Given the rather poor rankings of the developed countries on the change TPI, and also given the fact that this is a labor-intensive sector, we might expect to find developing countries (generally in the Factor-Driven Stage of development) catching up in this sector. To see whether this is the case, it is informative to compare country performances on the change TPI directly to income levels. Although national income levels are not directly correlated with levels of development, they do provide a useful proxy (see Figure 1).

Figure 1 shows that there seems to be no trend in favor of developing-country performance in the fresh food sector (the trend line is basically flat). So, contrary to what we might have expected based on theory, this is not an area in which developing countries are improving their performance. This example infers that the evolution of developing-country performance does not seem to be explained by factor endowments and price competition alone.

We also note that there is a large variation in the performances of the low-income countries as a group. The data for these countries are shown in Table 3.

We note that of the countries on the top half of the list, many enjoy preferential trade agreements with rich-world markets. For example, just regarding EU preferential trade agreements, we note that Turkey has a customs union agreement with the European Union. Other countries on the list, including Morocco, Bulgaria, Poland, Jordan, Lithuania, Romania, and Tunisia have free trade agreements with the European Union. Further, all of the African, Caribbean, and Pacific (ACP) countries enjoy one-way trade preferences with the European Union. This includes Trinidad and Tobago, Zimbabwe, Haiti, Mauritius, and the countries of the SACU. Mexico has benefited greatly from US market access through NAFTA. Although not all of these countries fall into the top half of the list, the great majority do. It is clear that access to these mar-

Table 3: Fresh food: performance of low-income countries

Country	Fresh food — change TPI	GDP per capita (PPP), 2000
Guatemala	8	3,841
Panama	12	5,999
Trinidad and Tobago	16	9,274
Mexico	17	8,985
Brazil	21	7,604
Peru	24	4,799
Chile	26	9,417
Turkey	29	7,014
SACU	32	6,017
Sri Lanka	36	3,530
Poland	37	9,051
Zimbabwe	38	2,635
Jordan	43	3,972
Indonesia	48	3,054
Bulgaria	52	5,710
Morocco	61	3,546
Dominican Republic	72	6,017
Philippines	73	3,987
Vietnam	76	1,996
Lithuania	77	7,278
Croatia	82	8,091
Costa Rica	86	8,696
Venezuela	87	5,797
Russian Federation	90	8,406
Colombia	91	6,257
China	92	3,976
Thailand	98	6,467
Latvia	100	7,062
Bangladesh	105	1,602
Tunisia	109	6,363
Mauritius	113	9,698
Ecuador	117	3,251
India	121	2,358
Malaysia	124	9,095
Romania	125	6,540
Honduras	126	2,462
Uruguay	131	9,035
Jamaica	137	3,722
Paraguay	141	4,426
Bolivia	144	2,424
El Salvador	156	4,497
Haiti	158	1,467
Ukraine	161	3,818

Source: GDP per capita (PPP) was obtained from the International Comparison Programme (ICP) of the World Bank.

It would therefore seem that differences in improvements across developing and transition countries in the fresh food sector is driven to a large extent by trade policy and preferential access to markets rather than by factor endowments alone. Adaptation to consumer preferences in developed-market economies is also an important factor.

To see whether this finding is corroborated in other, similar sectors we now turn to another labor-intensive sector, and one that is also characterized by high levels of protectionism.

Clothing

This sector includes all types of clothing products, including apparel, accessories, and headgear for adults and children. International trade in this sector is estimated at US$187 billion, or approximately 3 percent of world trade (see Table 4).

Two quite different countries lead the sector, as reflected by the current TPI as well as by international market share: Italy and China. There is a notable difference in the trade performance of these two leaders. Italy, traditionally perceived as the ultimate producer of elegant clothing, does indeed come in number 1 in the current TPI. This placement is based on its large share in the world clothing market and its well-diversified products and markets. Further, it is producing at the high end of the market, leading to a very high world market value for its products. However, in terms of the change TPI, Italy performs much less well. This can be linked to three factors: a reduction in Italy's world export share of clothing, a negative trend in import coverage by exports, and, most particularly, the specialization in sectors that have not been matched by increases in overall world demand over the period.

kets has facilitated the positive evolution in their trade performance in this sector.

It can also be seen from the table that countries such as Chile, Guatemala, and the SACU countries have been able to profit from the rising import demand in developed markets for off-season products.

Another key factor explaining the disappointing performance of the poorest countries is their difficulty in complying with environment-related trade barriers, which can be seen as a rising form of protectionism. According to Fontagné, Kirchbach, and Mimouni (2001), technical barriers are a major obstacle to trade in developing countries, since approximately half of their exports in 2000 consisted of environment-sensitive products, compared with 15 percent on average for the rest of the world.

Table 4: Top performers in the clothing sector

Country	Current TPI	Share in world exports 2000	Change TPI	Change in world export share
Italy	1	7.07%	103	−0.77%
China	2	19.31%	14	0.87%
Portugal	3	1.51%	99	−0.19%
Korea	4	2.69%	42	0.01%
Indonesia	5	2.53%	73	0.07%
Hungary	6	0.66%	49	−0.01%
Turkey	7	3.50%	89	−0.08%
Romania	8	1.25%	66	0.06%
Thailand	9	2.01%	91	−0.08%
Sri Lanka	10	1.39%	45	0.05%
Morocco	15	1.29%	1	0.20%
Mexico	35	4.62%	3	0.56%
Bangladesh	23	2.68%	5	0.22%
Canada	56	1.11%	10	0.08%
Vietnam	39	0.87%	11	0.04%
Costa Rica	68	0.21%	16	0.05%
Ukraine	51	0.26%	17	0.02%
Denmark	16	0.93%	19	0.03%
India	24	2.60%	38	−0.01%

dynamics of world demand over the period. Additional strengths leading to high scores on the change index are improvements in market diversification (for the Philippines, Singapore, Taiwan and Thailand) or improvements in product diversification (in the case of Indonesia). This progress has been driven by the ability of these countries to attract higher levels of FDI in recent years.

Morocco is also an interesting case of a developing country that has been strongly improving its trade performance in this sector in recent years. It ranks first on the change TPI, linked to an improvement in import coverage by exports, matching the dynamics of world demand, and most importantly, increased product diversification. This has clearly been at least partially driven by Morocco's special trade relationship with the European Union, culminating with the Euro-Mediterranean Association Agreement in March 2000, which has given it improved access to one of the world's largest economies.

To summarize, it seems that in these higher-investment sectors, country performance is explained in large part by access to markets and the ability to attract FDI. In this sense, performance improvements can be described to a certain extent by competitive advantage, insofar as we would expect countries to attract FDI when they have the right business environment in place to attract firms.

Innovation-driven industries

We complete this analysis by turning to the most innovation- and technology-driven industries. Countries at the Innovation-Driven stage of development should have a competitive advantage in these sectors, with high levels of investment complemented by business environments fostering high levels of innovation. We would generally expect the wealthiest, most industrialized countries to perform best in this sector.

IT, Consumer Electronics, and Telecommunications

The IT, consumer electronics, and telecommunications sector is one of the most important sectors in terms of value added. This sector includes such products as office machines, data processing equipment, televisions, stereo equipment, radios, and telecommunications equipment. International trade in this sector is estimated at around US$632 billion in 2000, or approximately 11 percent of world trade (see Table 8).

Industrialized countries presently account for approximately 62 percent of world trade in the IT and consumer electronics sector. Japan demonstrates the strongest export performance based on its top score on the current TPI. The United States, with a slightly higher market share than Japan, is several ranks lower, at 16 on the index. This is due to weak performance in terms of per capita exports and negative net exports (as a very high consumer of these

Table 8: Top performers in the IT, consumer electronics, and telecommunications sector

Country	Current TPI	Share in world exports 2000	Change TPI	Change in world export share
Japan	1	10.40%	54	−0.75%
Singapore	2	6.23%	61	−1.01%
Sweden	3	2.02%	10	−0.06%
Ireland	4	3.37%	25	0.19%
Korea	5	5.38%	17	0.50%
Belgium	6	1.54%	20	0.03%
Malaysia	7	5.32%	30	0.12%
Finland	8	1.61%	14	0.11%
Taiwan	9	6.68%	41	0.07%
China*	10	6.03%	51	0.60%
United Kingdom	11	6.33%	47	−0.19%
France	12	3.80%	42	−0.01%
Netherlands	13	4.80%	36	0.11%
Germany	14	5.11%	56	−0.13%
Mexico	15	4.90%	4	0.49%
United States	16	11.79%	57	−0.48%
Hungary	17	1.09%	1	0.25%
Austria	18	0.39%	11	0.02%
Indonesia	19	1.03%	22	0.09%
Denmark	20	0.50%	34	−0.01%
Slovak Republic	41	0.03%	2	0.00%
Brazil	53	0.34%	3	0.04%
Vietnam	44	0.02%	5	0.00%
Czech Republic	32	0.17%	7	0.02%
Romania	46	0.07%	8	0.02%
Croatia	54	0.01%	9	−0.00%

* China's relatively poor ranking in change TPI despite strong growth in market share is explained by a faster increase of imports than exports in this sector and a reduction in target markets and the number of export products.

goods, the United States imports substantially more IT and consumer electronics products than it exports).

The Nordic countries such as Finland, Denmark, and Sweden do relatively well on both indexes (driven by the activities of companies such as Nokia and Ericsson). This is due in great part to the rise in their exports of telecommunications equipment during the period in question. In terms of present strength, Finland and Sweden perform well due to a high world market share, accompanied by high net exports, high per capita exports, and strong market diversification. Denmark's present strength is linked to high per capita exports and relatively diversified markets. Finland's strong evolution has been supported by an increase in world market share, an improvement in import coverage by exports, and improvements in market diversification. Denmark's and Sweden's evolutions are reinforced by an improvement of import coverage by exports. Of course, the reader must keep in mind that since these data cover the late 1990s and 2000, they do not capture the deceleration in world trade in the telecommunications sector. This deceleration will likely have had a negative impact on the performance of these countries.

We once again look to see how the performance of countries at different income levels has been evolving over the five-year period in this high value added sector (see Figure 6).

Figure 6: Change TPI in IT, consumer electronics, and telecommunications, by income level

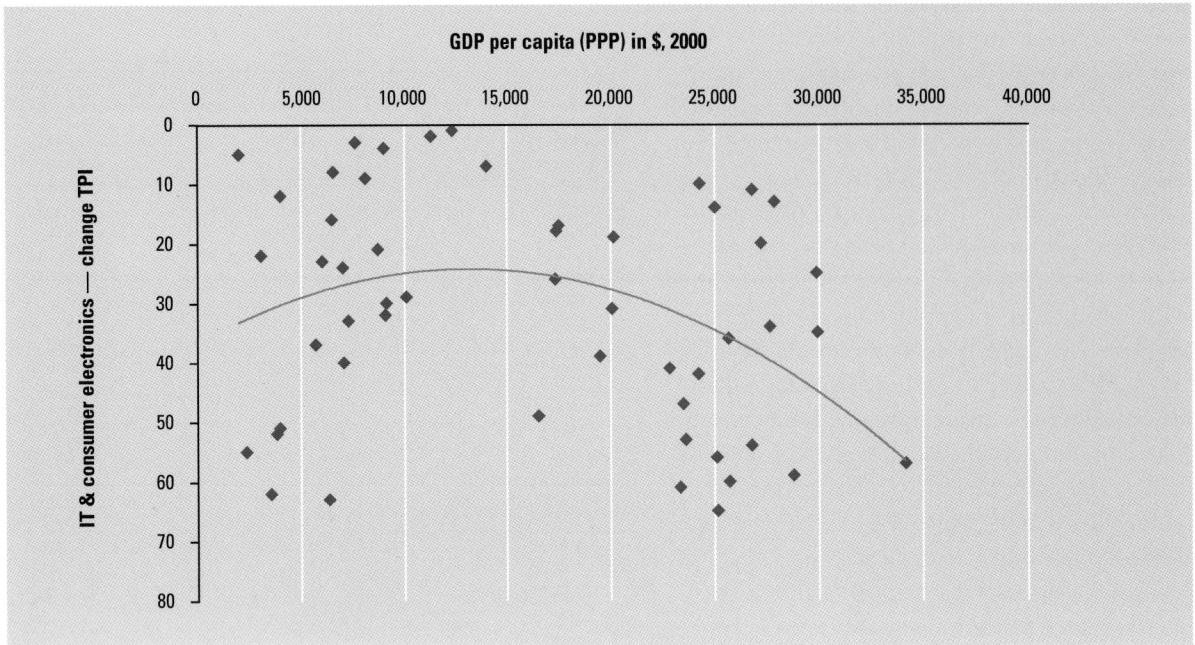

Source: GDP data were obtained from the International Comparison Programme (ICP) of the World Bank.

326

A number of the lower-income countries are not included since they do not export any IT or consumer goods. This indicates the concentration of high-tech exports in a limited number of developing and transition countries. Looking at the graph, we do notice that— unlike what we might have expected—on average, performance improvements do not favor the highest-income countries. In fact, improvements over time seem to favor lower- and middle-income countries.

A number of the developing Asian countries are presently performing well on the current TPI. Of particular interest are Korea and Malaysia, which in fact demonstrate strong performance based on the criteria of both indexes. Both countries' present strong performances are linked to a high share in the world market, a high value of net exports, and high per capita exports. Further, their strong evolution over the five-year period is supported by an increase in market share, improvements in their import coverage by exports, and the fact that the products they have been exporting have matched dynamics of world demand. Korea's particularly strong improvement over the period can be linked in part to important FDI inflows following the liberalization of its FDI policy in the late 1990s.

Mexico is another particularly strong performer in this sector, as measured by both indexes. Recent performance improvements, as measured by the change TPI, can be attributed to an increase in market share, products that correspond with dynamics of world demand and improvements in product diversification. As mentioned in the

section above, improvements in Mexico's trade performance have been driven by access to the US market, accompanied by a large increase in FDI in this sector.

A number of transition economies are also improving their trade performance in this sector, as well as performing quite well according to the current index. Hungary tops the change TPI, due to a healthy increase in market share as well as very strong improvements in the four other areas measured by the index. Hungary is joined in the top 10 of the change TPI by the Slovak Republic, the Czech Republic, and Romania. All of these countries experienced important FDI inflows over the period, which helped them to increase their export performance within this sector.

FDI has been an important driver of improvements in export performance in this very high innovation sector for a number of developing and transition countries. We note that of the low- to middle-income countries covered by our *Report*, of the top 16 recipients of FDI in the period 1996–2000, 11 of them are in the top 20 performers in the change TPI. These 11 top performers include countries such as Brazil, Hungary, Mexico, and Thailand.

There are two possible conclusions to draw from this phenomenon. The first and more optimistic one for developing countries is that changes in performance in this sector are out of line with competitive advantage, in the sense that countries are able to leapfrog over stages of development to higher levels of performance by attracting FDI. Specifically, it is possible that the progress from one stage of development to another is not as smooth a progression as we might expect based on competitive advantage. Perhaps countries with low per capita incomes are nonetheless in the position, through FDI, to perform quite well in sophisticated markets.

The second, more pessimistic, conclusion is based on the fact that much of what these countries are exporting in this sector are in fact based on low value added manual tasks: local production in many of the low-income countries mainly consists of assembling imported components (with a few exceptions). According to this line of reasoning, improvements in export performance can in many cases be explained by both comparative and competitive advantage, as multinational corporations are investing in countries based on labor costs. In other words, these developing countries have integrated themselves into the international value chain only through their comparative/competitive advantage based on their relative endowment of low-cost labor.

Either way, FDI and increased trade in these high-tech products offers developing countries the possibility of reaping the positive effects of technological diffusion. This is a classic argument in favor of trade, and increasingly of FDI. Of course, the extent to which countries are actually benefiting from technological diffusion is the subject of much debate. If it is true that these countries are being used only for low-cost labor and re-exports, it would make technology diffusion to the rest of the economy more problematic. In other words, it could be that at present many of these countries are doing well in terms of trade performance, but this does not necessarily mean that there has been an improvement in the overall economic development of the country. However, given their declining export performance in the more basic industries, it would seem that the attraction of FDI and the movement into these higher-technology sectors should remain a goal of developing country governments.

Conclusion

This chapter has assessed the trade performance of individual countries across a number of broad industrial sectors. The aim of this assessment has been to provide readers with a sense of the general international trade landscape across a variety of sectors. A particular focus has been on the areas in which developing and transition countries are performing best.

The current TPI has shown that richer countries tend to demonstrate better current trade performance throughout all sectors; this is not surprising, since most world trade still takes place among wealthy industrialized nations. The wealthy nations are joined by a few emerging developing countries such as Mexico and China, which are also performing very well.

For developing and transition countries as a whole, we have observed some progress as measured by the change TPI. However, improvements are not necessarily taking place in the sectors in which we would expect them. These countries are not systematically improving their export performance in the labor-based and low-technology exports such as fresh food. In fact, what we see is that, as we move up the investment and technology ladder and into higher value added goods, the average performance of lower-income countries actually increases. In other words, for the most part, our analysis contradicts what we would expect based upon the theories of comparative and competitive advantage.

We have seen that progress in the highest-technology sectors has been based in large part on the ability of certain countries to attract important inflows of FDI. According to UNCTAD's *World Investment Report 2002*, Transnational Corporations (TNCs), through FDI, can play a key role in improving the export performance of developing countries. In particular, they can help countries move into more value-added export sectors. The report notes that:

> The role of TNCs in expanding exports of host developing countries derives from the additional capital, technology and managerial know-how they can bring with them, along with access to global, regional, and especially, home-country markets. The resources and market access TNCs can bring can complement a country's own resources and capabilities and can provide some of the missing elements for greater competitiveness. Host countries can build upon these to enter new export activities and improve their activities in existing ones. . . . TNCs can provide host countries with competitive assets for export-oriented production in technology-intensive and dynamic products in world trade. Such assets are often firm-specific, costly and difficult for firms in developing countries and economies in transition to acquire independently (UNCTAD 2002, pp 151–152).

Despite the current debate on the benefits of technology diffusion, given their decreasing performance in the lower-tech sectors, increasing FDI in the nonprimary goods and resources sectors should be a goal of policymakers in the developing world. FDI can play a crucial role in inserting these countries into the production chain of higher value added export sectors. However, it is also clear that for countries to be attractive targets for FDI, they must implement policies that foster economic environments attractive to investment. Foreign firms will go only to places where they find good frameworks in place. The key to high performance remains location, location, location.

Notes

1 Dani Rodrik of Harvard University has been highly vocal on this issue in recent years. A number of critiques, including "Trade Policy and Economic Growth: A Skeptic's Guide to the Cross-National Evidence" are available online at http://ksghome.harvard.edu/~.dro-drik.academic.ksg/papers.html

2 Wolf was referring to the importance of location for economic success in general, but this can be extended to apply to trade performance as well.

3 The International Trade Centre is a joint subsidiary organ of the United Nations Conference on Trade and Development (UNCTAD) and the World Trade Organization (WTO).

4 This percentage is calculated from export data in the World Bank's *World Development Indicators 2002*.

5 We note that only 90 of the 184 countries export electronic components. This eliminates 16 of the countries covered by this *Report*, 15 of which have per capita annual incomes less than US$10,000 at purchasing power parity. A relatively large number of low- and high-income countries do export in this sector, and are included in the graph, however, providing useful information on relative levels of progress in trade performance.

References

Avisse R. and M. Fouquin. 2001. "Textile and Clothing Trade: Comparing Multilateral Agreement to Regional Free Trade Agreements," CEPII Working Paper. Paris: Centre d'Etudes Prospectives et d'Informations Internationales. Revised as Fouquin, M. et al. 2002. "Mondialisation et régionalisation: le cas des industries du textile et de l'habillement," CEPII Working Paper No. 2002-08. Paris: Centre d'Etudes Prospectives et d'Informations Internationales. Online. www.cepii.fr, click on "Documents de travail."

Cornelius, P. et al. 2002. "Sectoral Trade Performance." In *The Global Competitiveness Report 2001–2002*. New York: Oxford University Press for World Economic Forum.

Dollar, D. and A. Kraay. 2000. *Trade, Growth and Poverty*. Washington, DC: Development Research Group, World Bank.

Fontagné, L., F. von Kirchbach, and M. Mimouni, 2001. "A First Assessment of Environment-Related Trade Barriers." Centre d'Etudes Prospectives et d'Informations Internationales (CEPII), Document de travail No. 2001-10.

Fouquin, M. et al. 2002. "Mondialisation et régionalisation: le cas des industries du textile et de l'habillement, " CEPII Working Paper No. 2002-08. Paris: Centre d'Etudes Prospectives et d'Informations Internationales.

International Trade Centre (ITC). Online. http://www.intracen.org

Li S. and F. Zhai. "China's WTO Accession and Implications for Its Regional Economies." Presented at the workshop on *China's Economy*, organized by the CEPII in Paris on December 12, 2001.

Organisation for Economic Co-operation and Development (OECD). 2001. *Agricultural Policies in OECD Countries, Monitoring and Evaluation, Agriculture and Food*. Paris: Organisation for Economic Co-operation and Development.

Porter, M. E. 1990. *The Competitive Advantage of Nations* New York: The Free Press.

———. 1998. *On Competition*. Cambridge, MA: Harvard Business School Press.

Rodrik, D. and F. Rodríguez. 2001. "Trade Policy and Economic Growth: A Skeptic's Guide to the Cross-National Evidence." Newly revised. In B. Bernanke and K. S. Rogoff, eds. *Macroeconomics Annual 2000*. Cambridge, MA: MIT Press for NBER.

Sachs, J. D. and A. M Warner. 1995. "Economic Reform and the Process of Global Integration," *Brookings Papers on Economic Activity* 1: 1–118.

Wolf, M. 2002. "Location, Location, Location Equals the Wealth of Nations," *Financial Times (London)*, September 25, p 23.

World Bank. International Comparison Programme (ICP) of the World Bank.

———. *World Development Indicators 2002*. Washington, DC: World Bank.

UNCTAD. 2002. *World Investment Report 2002: Transnational Corporations and Export Competitiveness*. UNCTAD 2002, Division on Investment, Technology and Enterprise Development. Online. www.unctad.org/wir/index.htm

CHAPTER 3.6

Governance Crossroads

DANIEL KAUFMANN,[1] World Bank Institute

Introduction: challenging orthodoxy

Less than a decade ago, governance issues were not even at a crossroads in the agenda of development institutions. Then there was no road: the absence of institutional and governance reforms was arguably the most glaring omission of the "Washington consensus" of the past decade on the 10 tenets of sound economic policies and management. In fact, the challenges of governance and corruption were often ignored altogether. It was frequently argued that even though there were ethical concerns, governance and corruption were not central to economic development, and thus outside the mandate of the international financial institutions (IFIs). Some analysts even argued that corruption could at times be beneficial to development—the "grease-of-the-wheels-of-commerce" argument. Yet in terms of starting to face up to the corruption challenge in the international fora, a turning point took place at the time of the International Monetary Fund (IMF)/World Bank Annual Meetings in late 1996, when the President of the World Bank placed the corruption issue center stage as a worldwide challenge for development (Wolfensohn 1996). This was followed by support from the IMF and other such institutions, all of which complemented the work of the premier nongovernmental organization (NGO) in the anticorruption arena, Transparency International (TI).

Since those meetings, supporting local initiatives in a number of countries, many IFIs and bilateral donor agencies have significantly scaled up their support of anticorruption and public-sector reform programs. These efforts have taken place against the backdrop of a relatively undeveloped state of the art in the complex and multidisciplinary field of governance and anticorruption—especially compared with well-established areas such as public finance, international trade, and financial sector reforms. It is thus timely to try to distill some lessons from experience and recent research, and also—where warranted—to challenge received wisdom. The increasing availability of data on governance issues in general, and in particular the opportunity to distill the insights emerging from this year's Executive Opinion Survey (referred to hereafter as the *Survey*), permit us to address thorny governance issues from an empirical perspective and question some orthodoxies.

In this chapter we present an analysis of the evidence on governance from the Survey—complementing it with the worldwide aggregate governance research indicators dataset that we have built in a multiyear project. In taking this empirical route, we question received conventions, namely that: (1) corruption and misgovernance are virtually synonymous; (2) addressing them requires a similar approach across countries; (3) it is virtually impossible to define and measure key concepts in this field, and thus a "softer" qualitative approach is needed; (4) to attain concrete progress, the focus has to be on traditional public sector management and judicial/legal measures; (5) steady progress, however gradual, has been recently attained in governance worldwide; (6) reduction of administrative bribery within the public sector bureaucracy in all developing countries ought to continue being the key for corruption control; and (7) the shaping of the investment climate is essentially in the hands of the public sector, and the policies that matter most for the investment climate are outside the governance realm.

We challenge these views, contending that they may contain myths—implying little support from recent evidence—or that they miss elements within a broader multidisciplinary and cross-sectoral framework. In this context, we present data on cross-thematic links between capture, corruption, finance, money laundering, political funding, transparency, and citizen voice, thus moving beyond the confines of narrow notions of governance. This analysis has practical implications, since the emerging evidence in fact does suggest that currently we may be at a crossroads in the governance field. Which path the international community and emerging countries embark on in the coming years on governance may prove critical for success or failure in providing for an appropriate climate for renewed investment and private-sector growth in emerging markets, for poverty alleviation and, related, the attainment of the Millennium Development Goals (MDGs).

Indeed, the analysis of the evidence will enable us to move beyond challenging the above orthodoxies and put forth a set of concrete forward-looking propositions. Our aim is to provide a framework for analysis and to inform, based on fresh evidence, in order to generate debate to help us move ahead to the next phase in addressing governance and anticorruption challenges around the globe.

Governance and corruption: basic analytics and empirics

Good governance: beyond corruption control—a broader framework

Although there are crucial links between both, which necessitate further in-depth analysis, corruption and governance are distinct notions.

Corruption is commonly defined as the abuse of public office for private gain. *Governance* is defined as the exercise of authority through formal and informal traditions and institutions for the common good, thus encompassing: (1) the process of selecting, monitoring, and replacing governments; (2) the capacity to formulate and implement sound policies and deliver public services; and (3) the respect of citizens and the state for the institutions that govern economic and social interactions among them.

For measurement and analysis, the three dimensions in this definition of governance can be further unbundled

to comprise two measurable concepts per each of the dimensions above, for a total of six components: (1) *voice and external accountability* (ie, the government's preparedness to be externally accountable through citizen feedback and democratic institutions, and a competitive press); and also (2) *political stability and lack of violence, crime, and terrorism;* then (3) *government effectiveness* (including quality of policymaking, bureaucracy, and public service delivery); and (4) *lack of regulatory burden;* and, finally, (5) *rule of law* (protection of property rights, judiciary independence, and so on); and (6) *control of corruption. Governance* is thus a much broader notion than *corruption,* the latter being *one* (albeit admittedly very important) among a number of closely intertwined governance components.

The power of data: governance can be measured, monitored, and rigorously analyzed.

> Not everything that can be counted counts, and not everything that counts can be counted.
> —Einstein

Less than a decade ago, in fact, most dimensions of governance were regarded as not measurable, and often writings were subject to long prose—and even rhetoric. At times, misplaced efforts to count concepts that in essence "do not count" do in fact take place. Consider, for instance, an attempt to measure the quality of rule of law by focusing on official statistics on the number of jailed citizens as a percentage of the population. At the top of the high end of this indicator stand together Russia and the United States, while on the very low end one finds Japan and Indonesia. Interpretation of this numerical indicator as contrasting excellent versus poor quality of rule of law is futile. Indeed, these types of ill-advised attempts to over-interpret official statistics—which in fact can be subject to an even larger margin of error than data from surveys and expert polls—are potent illustrations of the first part of Einstein's assertion (counting what does not count): the result of a search for measures when a conceptual framework is lacking.

Thus, the real challenge has been to count what used to be considered uncountable, yet that does count—focusing on conceptually rigorous notions of governance. Significant advances in the analysis and measurement of governance allow in-depth and rigorous analysis and monitoring. Applying the definition of governance advanced in the previous subsection, and gathering data from many different sources (including Survey data of various years in the past), we have analyzed hundreds of cross-country indicators as proxies for various aspects of governance.[2] Imposing structure on these many available variables from diverse sources, the data are mapped to the six subcomponents of governance listed above, are expressed in com-

Figure 1: Rule of law, voice and accountability, and control of corruption—regional averages

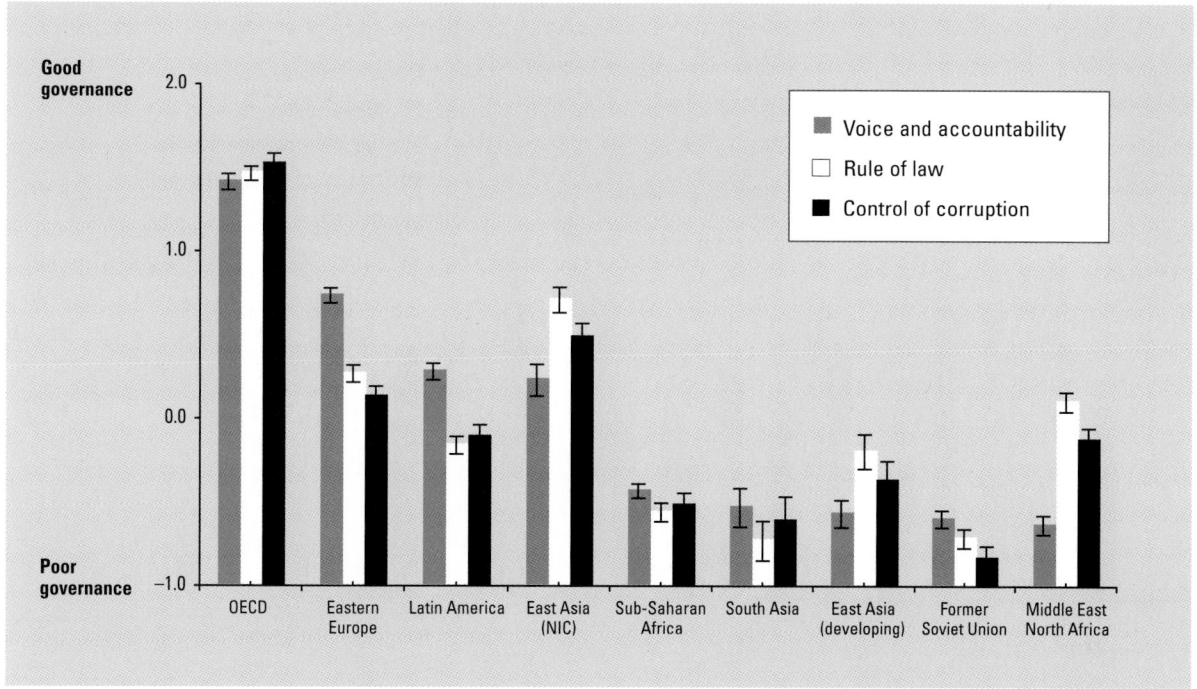

Source: Worldwide Governance Research Indicators based on data in Kaufmann and Kraay (2002) for 175 countries. Details online at http://www.world-bank.org/wbi/governance/pubs/growth.gov.htm. Units in vertical axis are expressed in terms of standard deviations around zero. Country and regional average estimates are subject to margins of error (illustrated by thin line atop each column), implying caution in interpretation of the estimates and that no precise country rating is warranted. See also regional clarifications in note 4.

mon units, its margins of errors (which are not small) are measured, and, thanks to a statistical aggregation methodology, aggregated into the six governance indicators—hereby improving the reliability of the resulting composite indicator and the analysis.

Based on the results from the updated worldwide composite measures from 2000–2001, in Figure 1 we illustrate three of the six composite governance components: control of corruption, rule of law, and voice and external accountability. The height of each column presents the average governance estimate for a given region, while the thin line atop the column depicts the margin of error—or statistical confidence interval—for the each component's estimated governance level. Since, at the country level, the margins of error generally are not small, it is misleading to have countries "run" in seemingly precise worldwide "horse race" rankings in governance. Instead, grouping countries into a limited number of broad categories (ranging from "green light"/examplary to "yellow/orange" vulnerable to "red light" governance crisis) for each governance dimension is more appropriate and statistically consistent. Thus, this broad grouping of governance indicators (and transparently presenting the margin of error for each data point) is the way we have organized the overall governance indicators dataset for 175 countries, available

interactively on the web at www.worldbank.org/wbi/governance/govdata2001.htm.

Even after fully accounting for its margins of error, the data turn out to be highly informative and yield many insights. As shown in Figure 1, there is a substantial cross-regional variation in the quality rating of governance. Further, although there is a correlation within each region across the various governance components, these variables do not move fully together. Some regions do not rate very poorly in the voice/civil liberties dimension, although they face a very large challenge in rule of law and control of corruption; this is the case of Latin America for instance, and to an extent eastern Europe (although the latter has made strides over the past decade).[3] Yet there is evidence for a contrasting situation in the case of Middle East and developing East Asia (and, in relative terms, for industrialized East Asia), where the voice and external accountability dimension remains as a significant challenge.[4] In the former Soviet Union, South Asia, and Africa, the challenges in all three governance components are rather substantial.

Yet these are generalizations based on regional averages, which hide significant variation in the quality of governance across countries in the same region. Indeed, a more in-depth review of the country data reveals that there are countries in Latin America, Africa, Asia, eastern

Figure 2: Unbundling corruption—Executive Opinion Survey regional averages, 2002

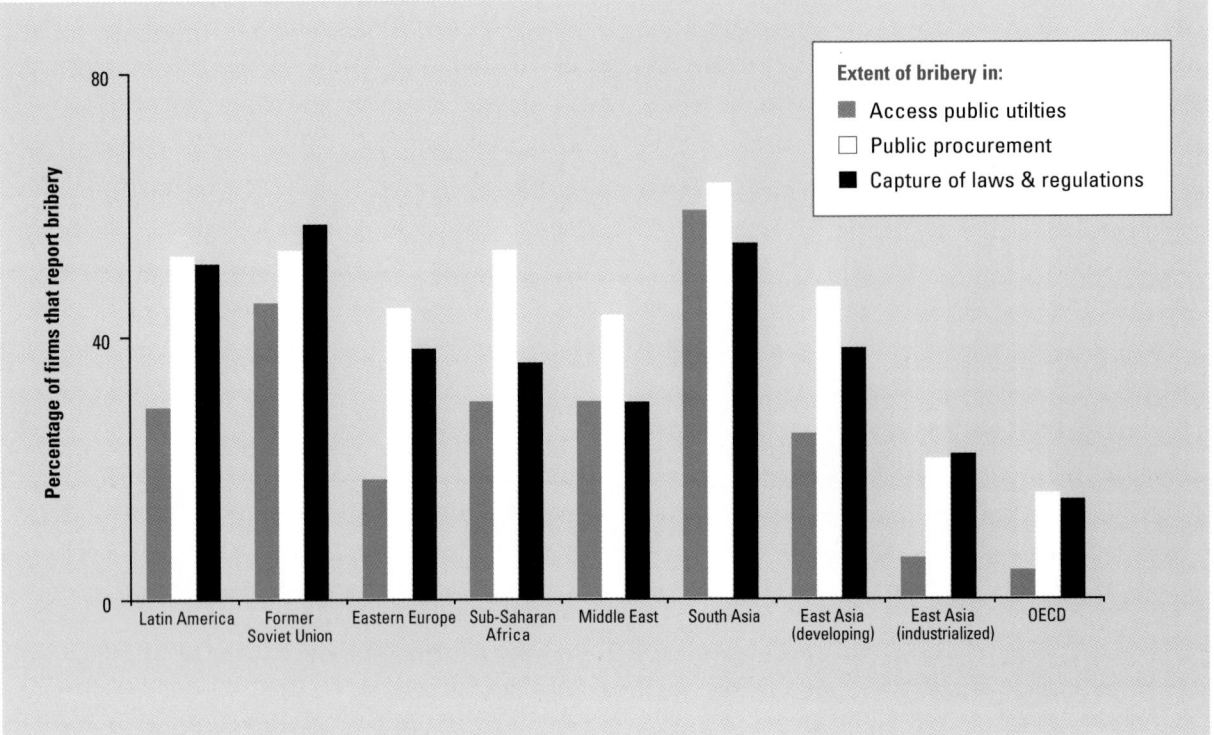

Europe, and Asia that rate above some OECD countries on a number of governance dimensions, challenging the notion that being fully industrialized or wealthy is a prerequisite for good governance. Furthermore, these worldwide composite governance indicators, although covering a much larger set of countries than is available under any individual survey or poll, do not permit a detailed unbundling of particular manifestations of misgovernance.

Stagnating governance and corruption control performance: unbundling and assessing trends based on the Survey

The Survey permits unbundling

Complementing the analysis with surveys such as the Executive Opinion Survey of the World Economic Forum, which this year utilized a comprehensive and specially designed module on governance, is warranted. Figure 2, based on the firm responses, presents an unbundling of selected types of corruption and depicts the regional averages of the extent of bribery in connection to public utilities (as a proxy of administrative corruption), in public procurement, and in the illicit "purchase" of laws and regulations (this illicit purchase is termed *capture*).[5] It is again clear that although types of corruption are correlated with each other within a country or region, there is not neces-

sarily one-to-one mapping: in some regions public procurement corruption is rated as the most prevalent form, while in others it is the extent of illicit purchase (or capture) of laws, policies, and regulations.

The data provided by the enterprises surveyed in this year's Survey suggest, for instance, that in Latin America the challenges of capture and corruption in public procurement and the judiciary (not shown) are particularly acute, in contrast to administrative corruption associated with connections to public utilities, export/imports or taxes. By contrast, in Africa public procurement corruption stands out relative to all other forms, while in South Asia the extent of corruption in all types, except for judiciary bribery, is reported to be very high. Even in OECD countries there are relative differences: the virtual absence of administrative types of bribery compared with the reported existence of procurement corruption and capture.

Equally telling, however, is the extent of variance *across* countries within each region. For instance, on the question measuring the extent of provision of transparent and clear information to the enterprise sector by the government, the evidence suggests that some countries in Africa—such as South Africa, Namibia, Mauritius, and Botswana—perform rather well: Botswana, in fact, is well within the top quartile in the sample, and rating above 11 OECD countries. Then, more specifically on corruption, these four countries in Africa rate in the top half in most every dimension measured in corruption, and often in the top third and above some OECD countries. For instance, in terms of control of misuse of public funds, Botswana is in the top quartile, above many OECD countries in fact, while in terms of independence of the judiciary, and in control of bribery in the judiciary and for tax evasion, Botswana, Mauritius, and South Africa perform relatively well, above some countries in Europe according to the reports by the firms.

Trends in governance over time: time-series analysis of the *Global Competitiveness Report* (GCR) Executive Opinion Surveys

Reviewing trends in recent times can be done thanks to the common questions that have been asked in Surveys for a number of years. A troubling finding from the comparison over the past five to six years is that overall there has been stagnation—or, in some cases, even deterioration—in key dimensions of governance, in apparent contrast with other important areas, where overall an improvement over time is detected. Based on the various Surveys over the period 1997–2002, we see this stagnation in governance in Figures 3a–3f, which depict the trends in six different dimensions—four in governance, and two in other areas. The first four panels (Figures 3a, 3b, 3c, and 3d) depict respectively the firms' reports on corruption trends over the previous three years, the extent of independence in the judiciary, the effectiveness of antimonopoly policy, and the reported costs to business from organized crime. In none of these governance dimensions has there been an improvement over time on average. This is also the case regarding the extent of corruption in the judiciary (not shown). In fact, there even appears to be deterioration in some governance dimensions, such as judiciary independence, as seen in Figure 3b. Some important differences in regional trends from region to region are also evident: for the Survey country sample in South Asia, Latin America, Africa, and the former Soviet Union, enterprises report a deteriorating trend in corruption on average, in contrast with the other regions.

These disappointing trends in governance contrast with the improvements in other dimensions outside core governance, such as in the overall quality of infrastructure and in the effective absorption of new technologies (shown in the last panels, 3e and 3f, respectively), as well as in the quality of math and science education, and in the soundness of the banking—where overall there is also an improvement; not shown in Figure 3).

In terms of the corruption trend performance *within* regions, there are salient differences again. For instance, in

Africa, Mauritius and Botswana exhibit a clearly improving trend in reported control of corruption, in sharp contrast to countries such as Zimbabwe and Nigeria, and also with countries such as Venezuela, Guatemala, Paraguay, Ukraine, Romania, Indonesia, Bangladesh, and Germany in other regions. In each region there are cases of improving as well as clearly deteriorating governance dimensions, pointing to the limits of inferences that can be made based on regional averages alone.

Probing further on the within-regional variance by focusing on a region currently facing enormous socioeconomic and financial challenges, Latin America, provides insights. On average, the firms in the region report a deterioration in corruption control, as seen in Figure 3a. This reported deterioration set in a couple of years ago, following a few years where, on balance, there appeared to be some incipient improvement in the trend. Yet again, these regional averages mask important variation. For instance, Chile in many governance dimensions rates in the top quartile of the Survey country sample, even rating above some OECD countries. Until the year 2000, Chilean entrepreneurs had been reporting an improvement in control of corruption for some years. Yet over the past two years this trend appears to have been reversed, with the majority of respondents reporting a deterioration, even though the *level* of probity in general is still rather high (see Box 1 on Chile).[6] Brazil, on the other hand, from a lower initial starting point in control of corruption, over the past two years has continued to exhibit an improved trend. Countries such as Venezuela and Paraguay exhibit both significantly deteriorating trends in corruption as well as very low current levels of probity, as reported by the firms, while Costa Rica shows relatively high levels of probity, as well as relatively neutral trends over the past few years.

Latin America is not unique in exhibiting significant cross-country variation within a region—that is the case in virtually every region. Furthermore, as we have seen, each country has relative strengths and weaknesses. The variation within a region is also illustrated in the case of the Middle East. This year's Executive Opinion Survey included relatively few countries from that region (and, in the case of Egypt, which was part of the covered country sample for this year's Survey implementation, the data were not available to the World Economic Forum). Yet a few months earlier an enterprise survey dedicated to 10 countries in the Middle East had been carried out by the World Economic Forum, permitting an analysis with a larger country coverage (where *inter alia* data from Egypt was made available). Selected results on governance-related variables are summarized in Box 2.

Trends in selected governance and other variables
Figure 3a: Trends in corruption as reported by firms, regional averages

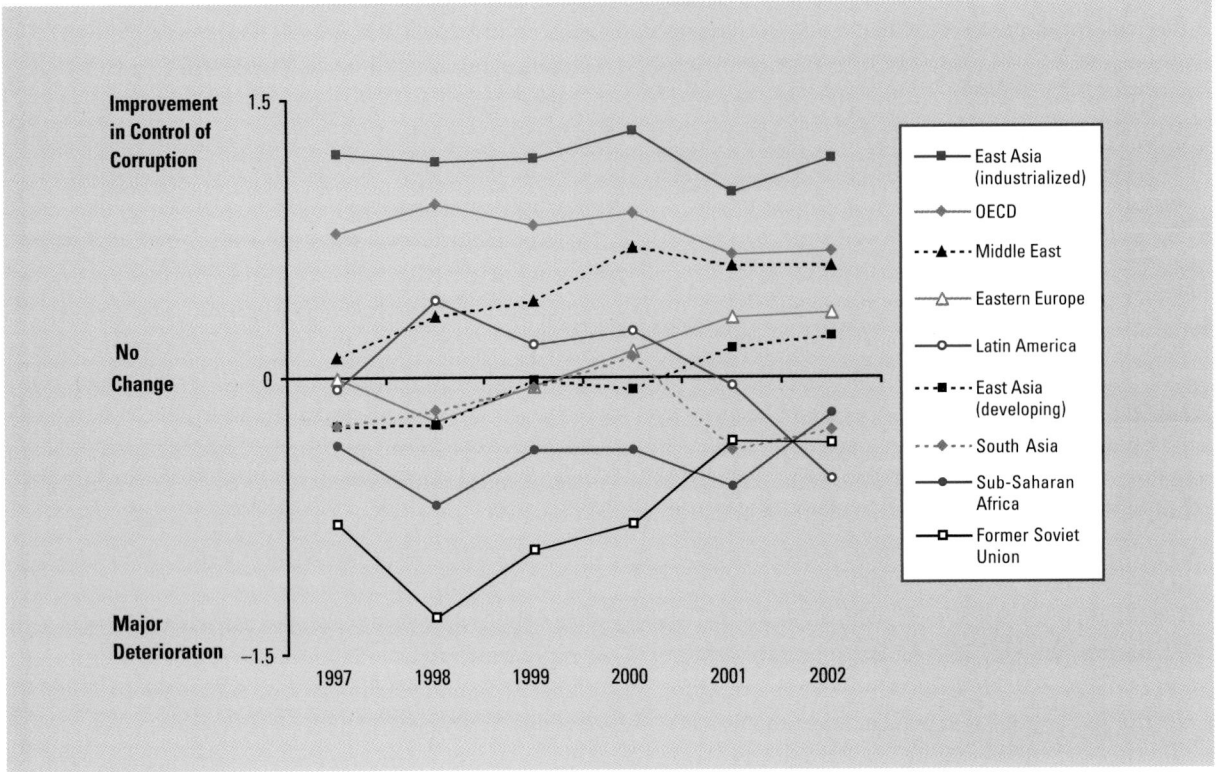

Note: Since this variable was based on the question about deteriorating or improving trend in corruption, the scale was modified to have the maximum range between −4 and +4, where the value 0 means no change in control of corruption, while positive values signify improvement in controlling corruption.
Source: Executive Opinion Survey, 1997–2002

Figure 3b: Extent of independence of the judiciary, regional averages

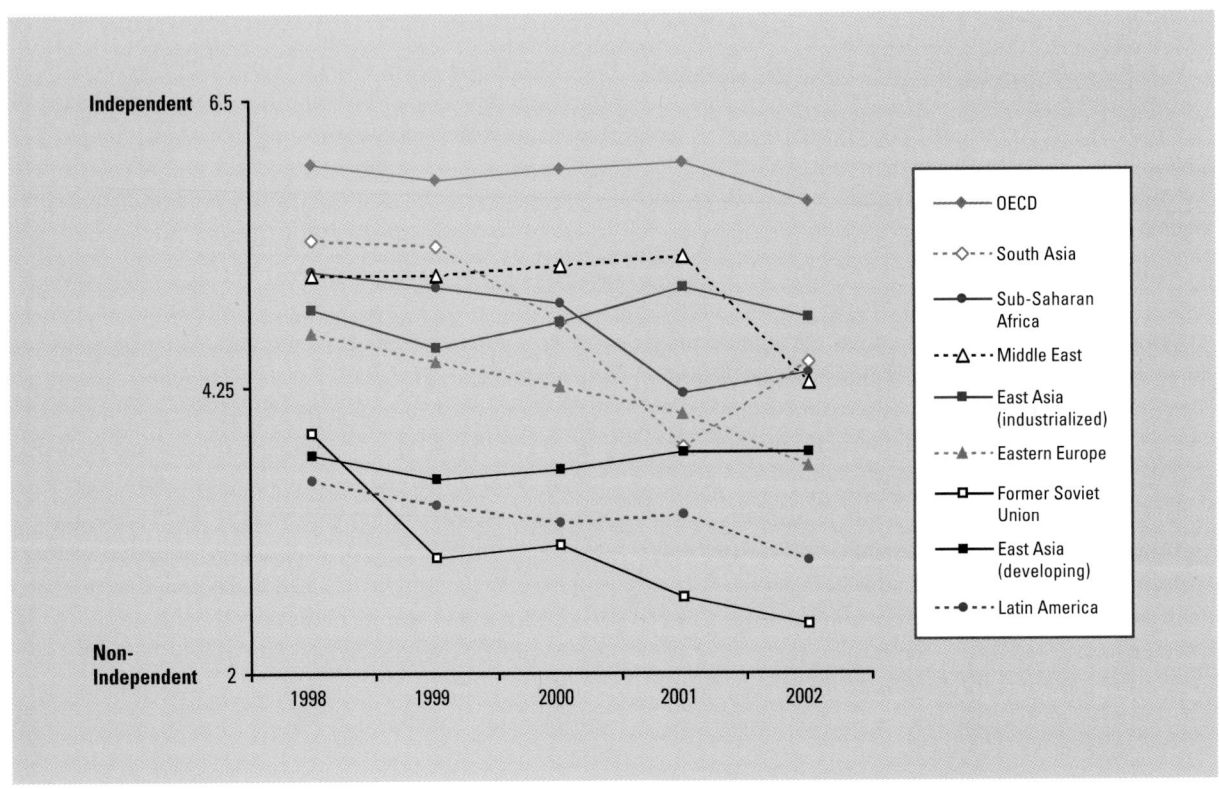

Note: Scale in this trend variable is 1 to 7; where 4 is neutral/no change, lower than 4 signifies a deterioration and higher than 4 an improvement in the control of corruption.
Source: Executive Opinion Survey, 1998–2002

Figure 3c: Effectiveness of antimonopoly policy, regional averages

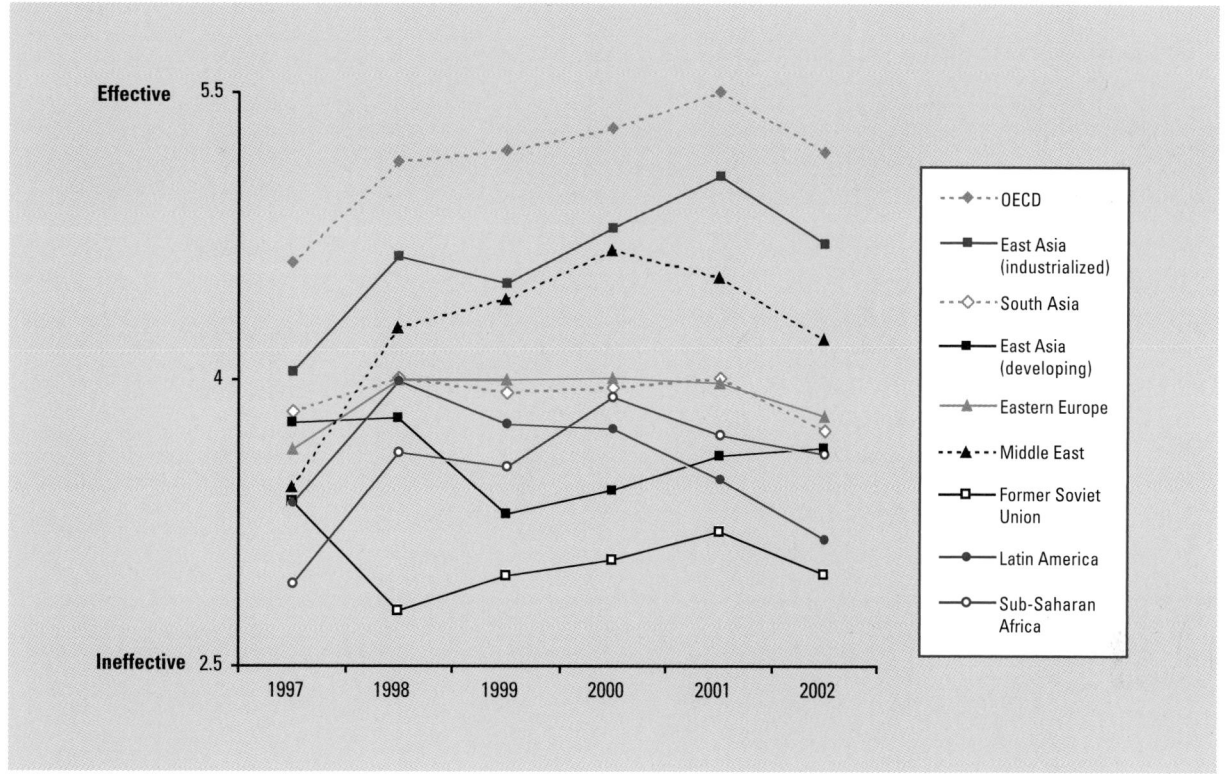

Source: Executive Opinion Survey, 1997–2002

Figure 3d: Extent of cost to business of organized crime, regional averages

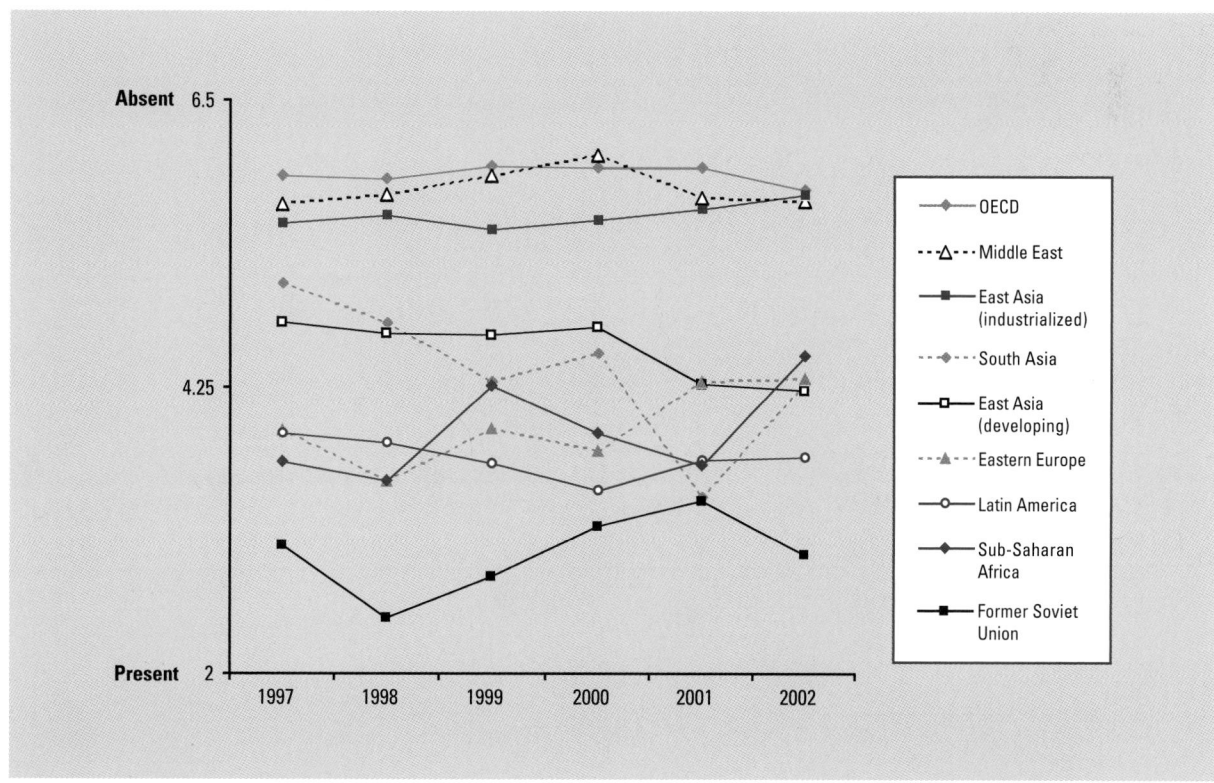

Source: Executive Opinion Survey, 1997–2002

Figure 3e: Quality of infrastructure, regional averages

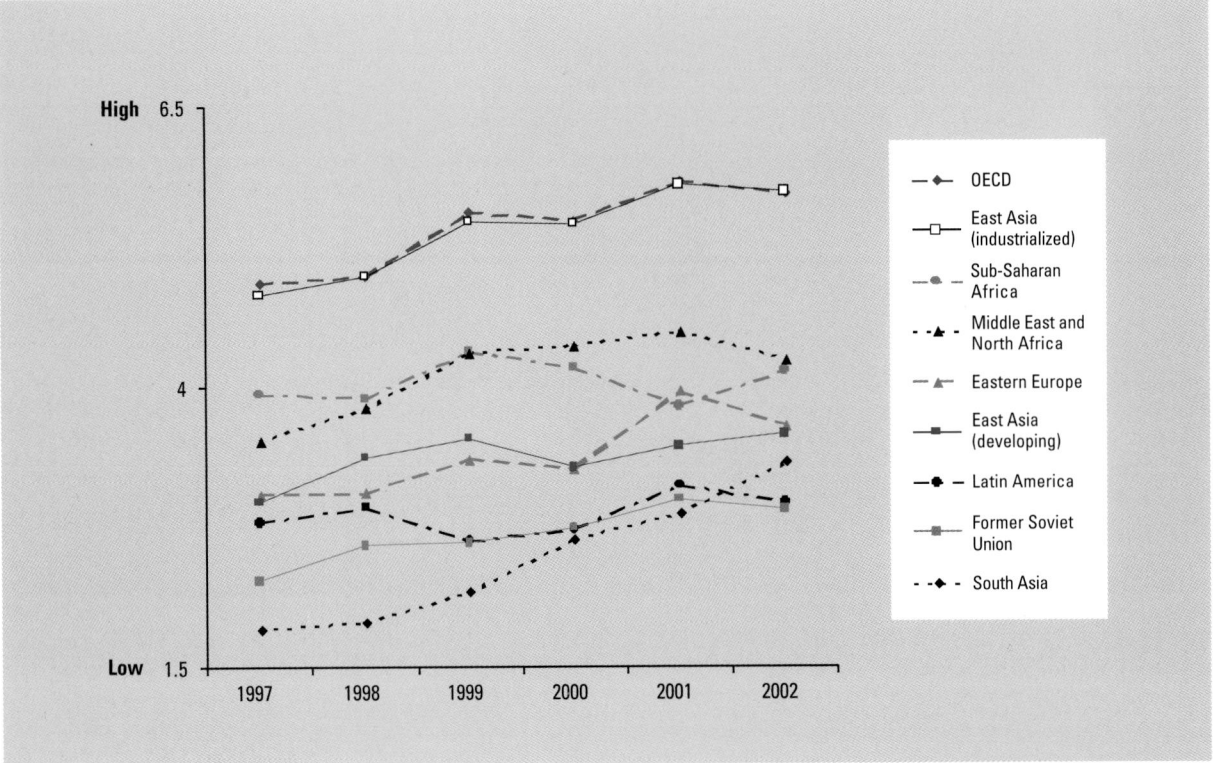

Source: Executive Opinion Survey, 1997–2002

Figure 3f: Effective absorption of new technologies, regional averages

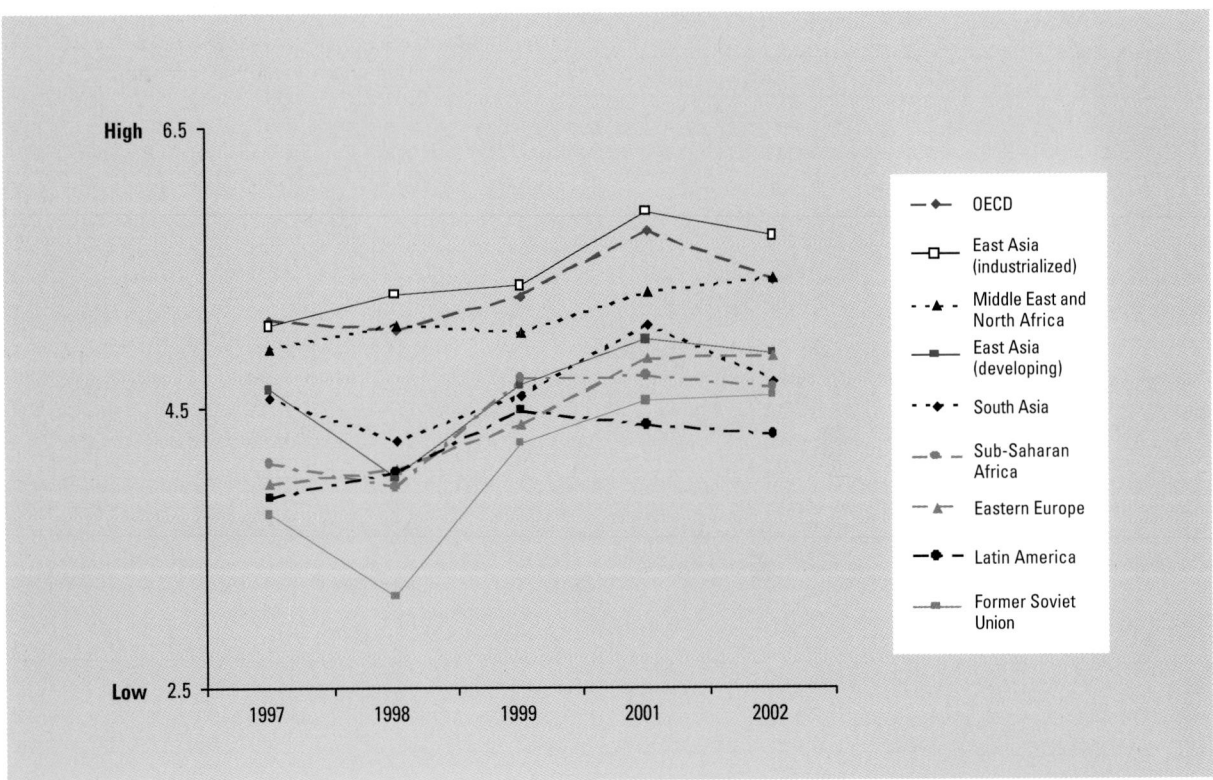

Note: No data exist for 2000.
Source: Executive Opinion Survey, 1997–2002

Box 1: Chile at a crossroads: will the "star" perform brilliantly this decade?

The number of Chile's firms participating in this year's Executive Opinion Survey was significantly above the average country sample for the Survey, at 137 (and particularly relative to its population). On this basis, and by comparing with the rest of the Survey countries, it is of interest to evaluate Chile's reported performance based on the enterprise responses. Given that the Survey is but one input to any comprehensive assessment, no conclusive inferences can be made until they are complemented by other evidence and further in-depth analysis. Rather, the focus on one country is intended to illustrate the early detection of strengths as well as vulnerability "warning flags" that the enterprise may signal through these surveys.

A puzzle emerges through the review of the Survey data for this Chile country case study illustration. Chile was a "star" performer among emerging economies through most of the 1990s. Over the past five years, however, there has been a significant slowdown in growth and productivity. And while the Executive Opinion Survey responses this year still support the view of Chile's institutions being rather strong in many areas, it is also the case that the Survey data point to more complex, and at times mixed, evidence when a broad view is taken. Some core areas of strength in governance, which are well known, are supported by the evidence from this year's Survey. Notable is the relative success in maintaining relatively low levels of corruption, in contrast with much of the rest of the region—and with many other countries as well. For instance, in terms of extent of bribery related to external trade, Chile rates in the top 7 among the sample of 80 countries, implying that the country enjoys nowadays a better rating than most of the OECD countries. Similarly, there is a low reported extent of bribery for access to public utilities and for evading taxes (see Box 1 Figure A), very low illicit diversion of public funds, and far more public trust in the financial honesty of politicians than the vast majority of the rest of the countries. There is also a high regard for some key institutions such as the police, excellent rating for the protection of financial assets and wealth, and there is a rather small estimated unofficial economy—in itself a sign of relatively good governance. And there are also good ratings for the auditing and accounting standards in the corporate sector. Other commendable dimensions of the Chilean success story during the past decade are very well known—such as the quality of macroeconomic management—so these are not detailed further here.

However, not all good things automatically go hand in hand. The unbundling through the Executive Opinion Survey also points to a number of areas of relative vulnerability. This matters, given the significant slowdown in Chile's growth in recent years, and the internal debate about possible areas of improvement and policy intervention needed to restart vigorous productivity growth and attain higher levels of competitiveness. Specifically, in the following areas, Chile appears to be well below the excellent standards attained in other dimensions (discussed above), and also significantly below OECD averages:

- Ease of entry for new firms and removal of remaining administrative barriers to business (including in the labor regulation area).

- Common crime is seen as rather costly to business.

- Competence of public sector personnel, relative to the private sector, and (related) the efficiency of the government bureaucracy, are seen as a constraint to business.

- The quality of parliament, the independence of the judiciary, and also to some extent judiciary-related corruption (relative to the extremely low incidence of some other forms of corruption), are identified as vulnerable areas (see Box 1 Figure A). In general Chile rates relatively well on various corruption dimensions, yet not only are there some (relative) vulnerability dimensions such as in the judiciary, but firms this year also report an apparent recent deterioration in the (admittedly low) incidence of corruption.

- Elite influence is another area of vulnerability: to the question of "when deciding upon policies and contracts, government officials usually favor well-connected firms and individuals," the reported evidence for Chile is very mixed. Similarly, Chile does not rate well in relative terms on the reported extent of illegal donations to political parties, and in the very substantial gap between the rich and the poor in access to quality healthcare (Box 1 Figure A). This suggests the need to probe more deeply into the complex political economy of inequality and influence.

Box 1: Chile at a crossroads: will the "star" perform brilliantly this decade? *(cont'd.)*

Box 1 Figure A: Chile in perspective: Selected governance dimensions

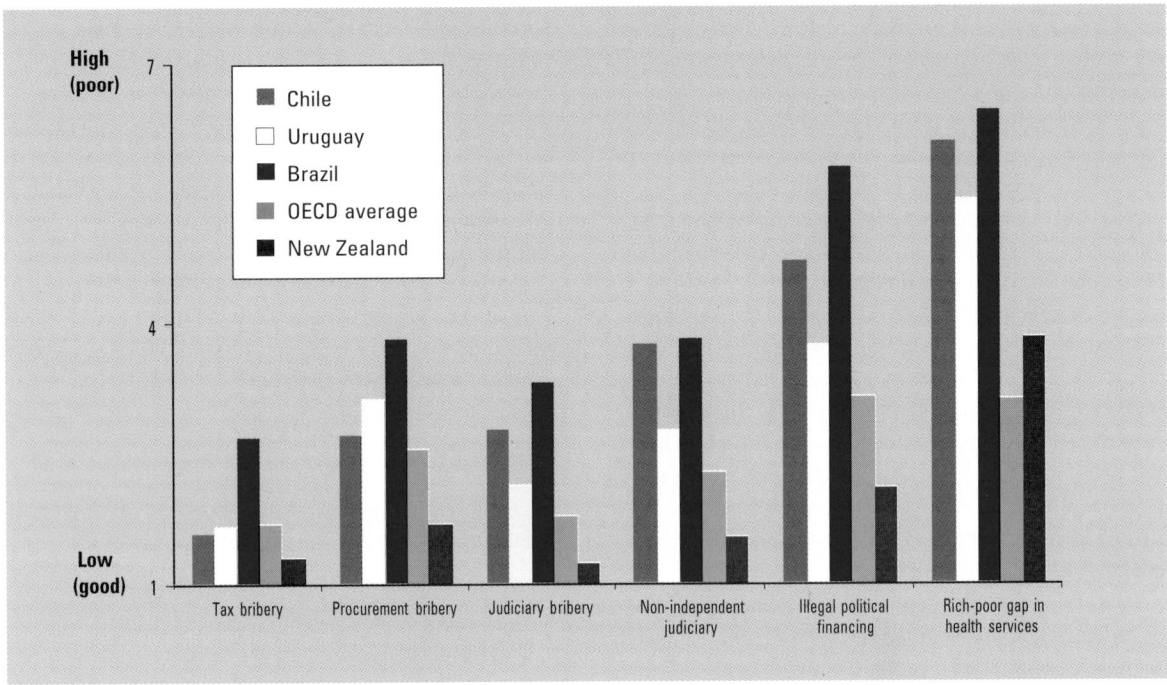

Source: Executive Opinion Survey, 2002

- In tandem with these potential governance vulnerabilities, among areas of weakness outside the conventional realm of governance, the following dimensions are also candidates for further scrutiny: (1) low levels of reported quality of public schools, and, consistent with this, firms consider an inadequately educated labor force to be a major obstacle; (2) low labor market flexibility; (3) the quality of infrastructure; (4) intellectual property protection; and, importantly, (5) the remaining challenges of the "New Economy"/ICT area, where the results are distinctly mixed and the potential for substantial improvement is large.

In sum, by flagging the potential areas of relative strength and vulnerability for a country based on the Survey results, properly qualified and complemented by further analysis (see, for instance, Engel and Velasco [2002] and others), it is possible to suggest focus areas to enhance competitiveness and productivity growth in the future.

Box 2: Variance across countries within a region—and across governance dimensions within a country: results from a survey of 10 Arab world countries

The competitiveness Survey for countries in the Arab World was carried out in late 2001/early 2002, as an input to the *The Arab World Competitiveness Report 2002–2003*, for which additional countries are also analyzed. The cross-country variance within the region, as well as the within-country variation across different governance dimensions, is illustrated in Box 2 Figures A and B for selected dimensions of governance. In some Gulf countries, such as Oman, there is low reported awarding of public contracts according to favoritism and influential contacts, for instance, in contrast with a number of other countries in the Middle East (see Box 2 Figure A). There is also significant variation in tax evasion, which is related to the tax regime burden. With few exceptions, however, in relative terms there appears to be a common challenge across the surveyed countries in enhancing the effective-

ness of antimonopoly policies (Box 2 Figure A). From an analysis of the worldwide governance indicators database discussed early in this chapter, also worthy of note is the extent of intraregional variation across countries in a dimension where, on average, the region rates low—namely "voice and external accountability." This suggests the importance of focusing on the country specifics and not relying unduly on country averages.

There are also significant differences across countries in the frequency of illegal payments, as illustrated in Box 2 Figure B, based on the reports by the firms, respectively, for the cases of bribery to attain public utilities connections, for public procurement contracts, and for obtaining bank loans.

Box 2 Figure A: Governance as reported by firms, selected variables (*Arab World Competitiveness Report 2002–2003*)

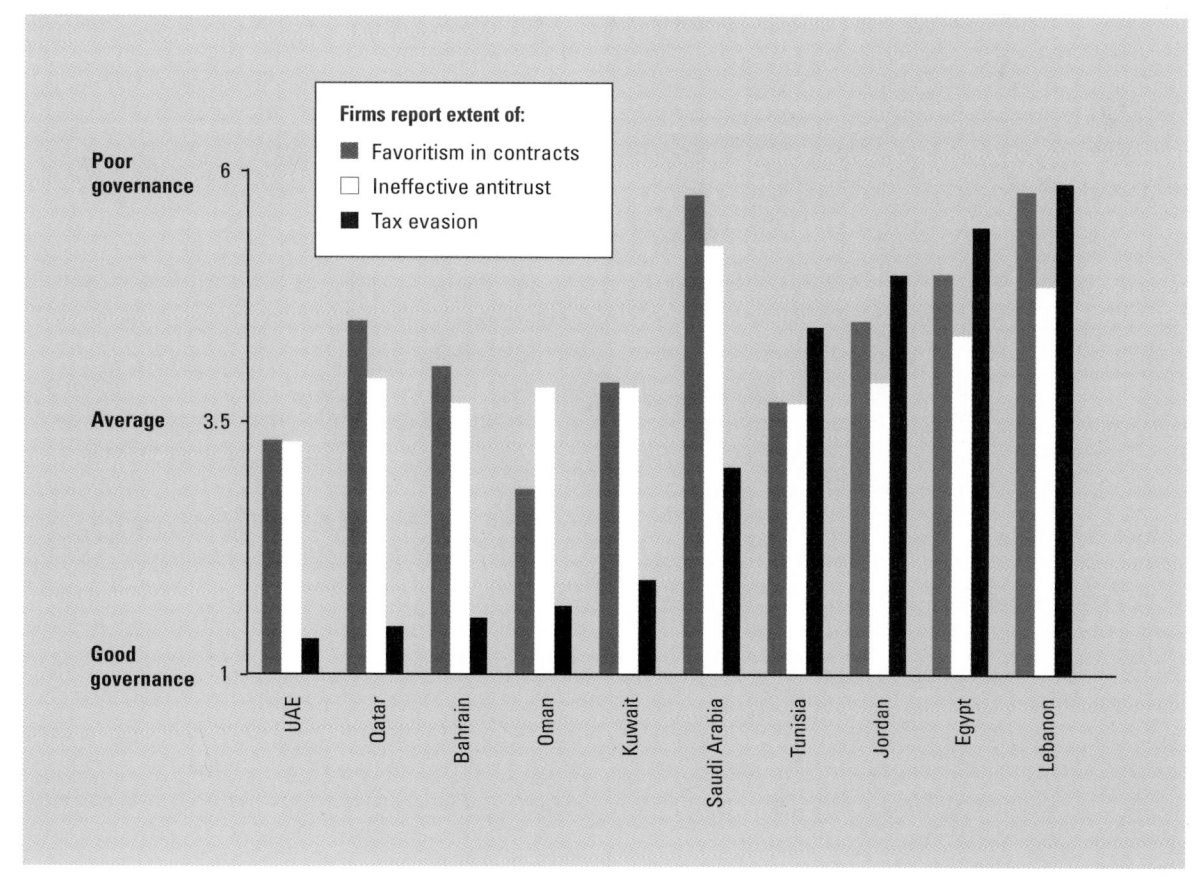

Box 2: Variance across countries within a region—and across governance dimensions within a country: results from a survey of 10 Arab world countries *(cont'd.)*

Box 2 Figure B: Frequency of bribery as reported by firms (*Arab World Competitiveness Report 2002–2003*)

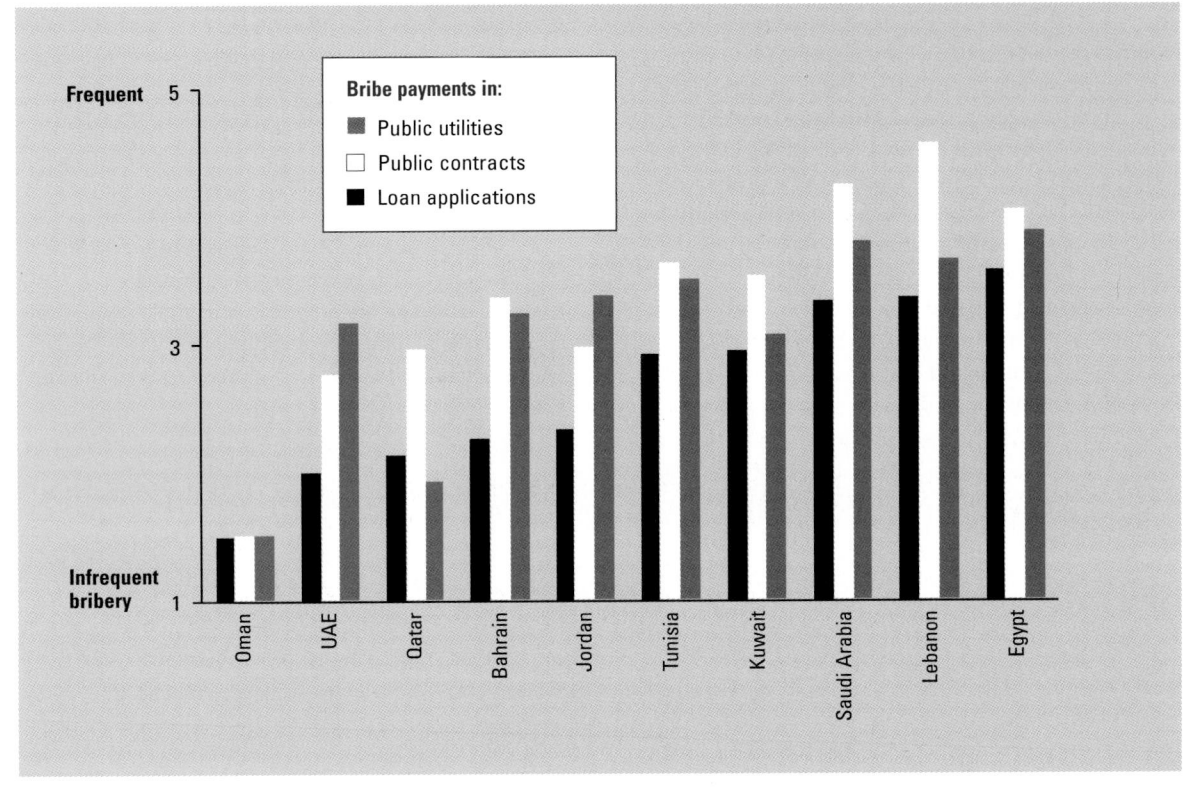

Does governance actually matter?

Through the data emerging from worldwide governance indicators, and from enterprise surveys, systematic assessments of the benefits of good governance worldwide have been performed by a number of researchers. Recent empirical studies confirm the importance of institutions and governance for development outcomes. One study (Knack and Keefer 1997) performed cross-national tests of institutions using various indicators of institutional quality; they found that the institutional environment for economic activity determines, in large part, the ability of emerging economies to catch up to industrialized country standards. Further work has been carried out by La Porta et al. (1999); Acemoglu, Johnson, and Robinson (2001); Engerman and Sokoloff (2002); Mauro (1995) Easterly and Levine (2002); and Rodrik et al. (2002); among others, showing the importance of governance for growth and development.

The set of six worldwide governance research indicators that we have developed over the past few years allows systematic assessment of the benefits of good governance in a large sample of countries. At the most basic level, the data at first reveal a very high correlation between good governance and key development outcomes across countries. Yet this is a "weak" finding in terms of policy application, since such correlations do not shed light on the direction of causality or on whether an omitted ("third") correlated variable is the fundamental cause accounting for the effects on developmental outcomes. In recent research we find, in fact, little evidence of a significant positive effect going from higher incomes to better governance, challenging the notion of governance simply being a luxury good (Kaufmann and Kraay 2002). By contrast, the analysis suggests a *large direct causal effect* from better governance to better development outcomes. Indeed, an improvement in the rule of law (or, say, control of corruption) from relatively poor to merely average performance would result in the long run in an estimated fourfold increase in per capita incomes, a reduction in infant mortality of a similar magnitude, and significant gains in literacy. Since at the same time we find no support for income growth guaranteeing improved governance, we thus challenge the notion that governance is a "luxury good" that automatically accrues with wealth accumulation—an assertion often used as a justification for complacency or to explain away misgovernance in a country. Instead, concerted efforts to improve governance and address corruption are required even during periods of robust growth.

A number of studies at the firm level also point to the paramount importance of governance variables for growth in private-sector development. In-depth research of this type with the new Survey dataset is in the agenda for the future, yet an initial exploration of the evidence suggests support for this link as well. At a very basic level, it is illustrative to perform a simple analysis of the last question of the Executive Opinion Survey instrument, which—instead of asking for a severity rating in the firm response—requested from the firms a list of the top constraints to business development faced by them. Firms were asked to list a maximum of five key constraints in descending order of importance, from a list of fourteen options, thereby prodding the enterprises to choose among the most important obstacles for their development.

As depicted in Figure 4, showing the responses in terms of the most constraining obstacle, in emerging economies after the common concern (in every type of enterprise survey) about finance, the enterprise sector faces on balance its most severe constraint from corruption and an ineffective government bureaucracy. Again, there are important regional differences, however (not depicted): in South Asia, for instance, infrastructure constraints are listed as an even higher priority than control of corruption, while infrastructure is less of a constraint in other regions. Within OECD countries there is less variation, and there is a more dichotomous choice of what constitutes an obstacle (relative to the other obstacles): tax rates, labor and tax regulations, and the government bureaucracy.

Voice, oversight and transparency are key—and not only in the public sector

Transparency matters, and outside of the public sector as well Governance within the public sector matters significantly in many complex ways, not merely in terms of the extent of corruption, but also in terms of broader dimensions of governance such as transparency. Transparency challenges, however, afflict both the public and private sectors. Often the inclination has been to place the full onus of the governance challenge on the public sector, and the approaches to data collection and analysis tended to magnify such bias

341

Figure 4: Most problematic constraint to business in your country

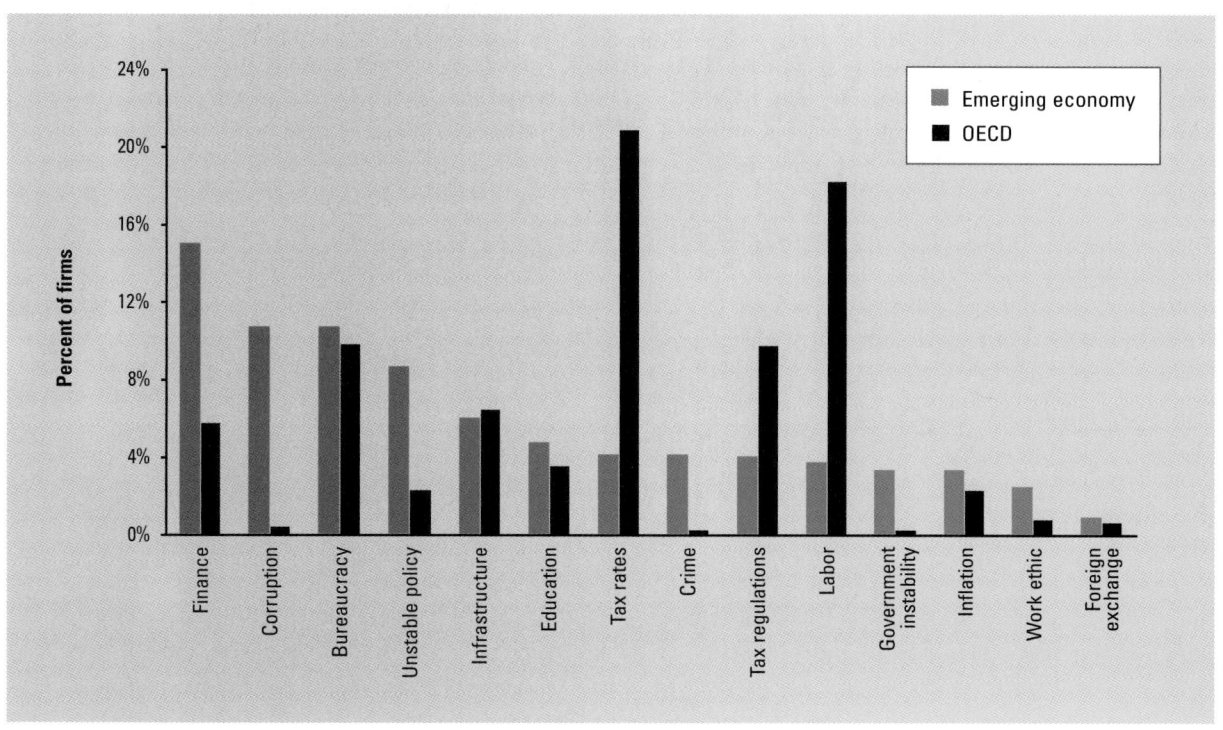

Figure 5: Transparency and GDP growth

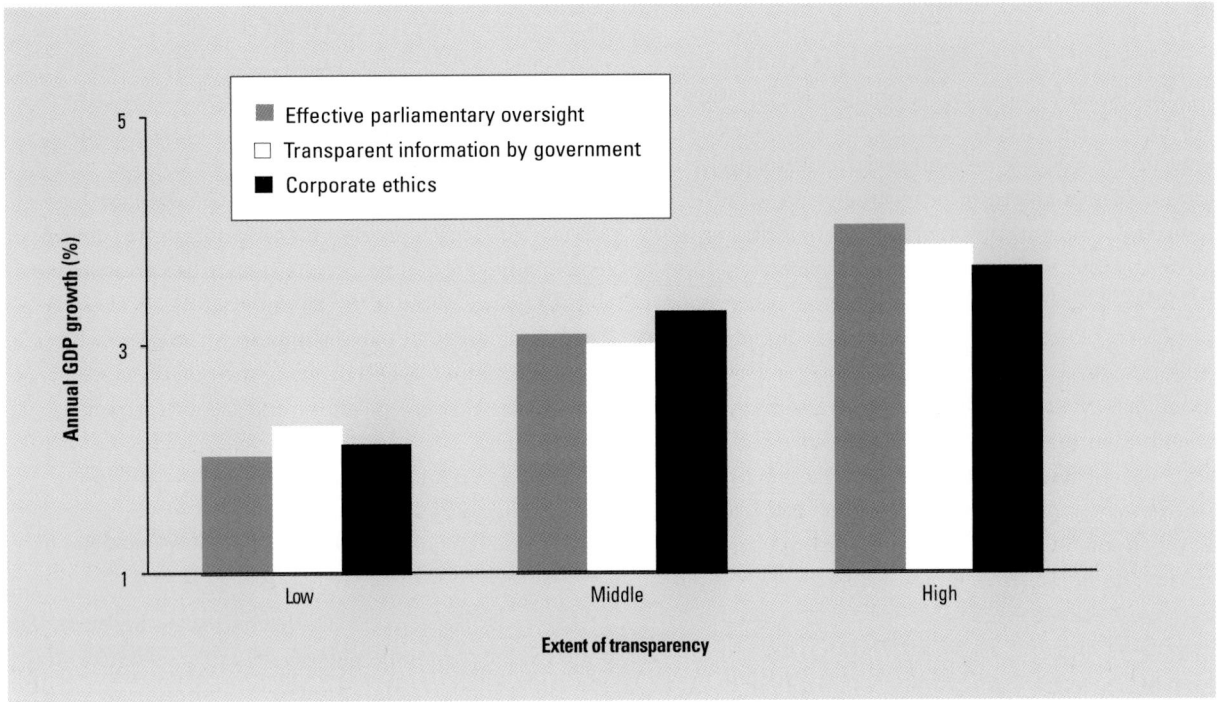

Sources: Annual GDP growth for 1999–2001 is taken from WDI 2002; GDP is computed in PPP terms. The various transparency and governance variables are drawn from the Executive Opinion Survey 2002.

at times. Thus, it is important to recognize explicitly that many measures of misgovernance, such as bribery, tend to involve agents in both the public and private sectors (in some cases, such as bribery for bank loans, it may in fact be a transaction between two private-sector agents). Further, probing the uniqueness of each setting and type of misgovernance is warranted in order to determine whether it is the public-sector official (or politician) who holds most of the power in the transaction (hence the transaction is akin to extortion) or the private-sector agent (in this case, the transaction is closer to "capture," as described in more detail below). And, finally, it is timely to go beyond traditional measures of bribery in the public sector, also measuring the firm's own assessment of the corporate ethics within their industry. This has in fact been done in this year's Survey, via a dedicated question on corporate ethics.

Not surprisingly, the average country ratings based on the enterprise responses to the Survey vary significantly from country to country, and are very highly correlated with measures of public-sector governance and corruption. Clearly, the challenge of corporate ethics cannot be divorced from public-sector governance. The link is either through perverse, and often illicit, forms of influence (such as capture) or, conversely, through legal and competitive

forms of influence on public policy or lawmaking by private interests (such as lobbies).

The importance of institutions outside of government for good national governance is also exemplified by the key legal institution, the parliament, not only because of their lawmaking role but also because of their oversight duties over the executive. In this year's Survey, firms have also provided an assessment of the parliament in their country. Furthermore, they have also given an assessment of the extent of a transparent and effective information flow from government related to the policies affecting them, another important mechanism of accountability. As depicted in Figure 5, in those settings with high levels of transparency, effective parliamentary oversight, and high standards of corporate ethics, there was a higher rate of GDP growth over the previous three years than in countries with lower standards of transparency, parliamentary oversight, and corporate ethics.

Transparency is nonetheless an area where public policy has a key responsibility as well—alongside the role of the private sector. In fact transparency and governance, while distinct concepts, are linked. It is apt in this context to define the often-vague notion of transparency, which refers to the key characteristics of an effective flow of information—namely access, timeliness, and relevance, as well as quality of economic, social, and political information—accessible to all relevant stakeholders. It is thus about private investors' use of loans and the credit-worthiness of borrowers; about properly audited accounts of key governmental, private, and multinational institutions; about the budgetary process and data from the government; about monetary and real economy statistics from the central bank and government service provision; about political and campaign finance disclosure and the voting records of parliamentarians; and about the effective oversight role of parliament, the media, and the citizenry in the public budgetary accounts—as well as about the activities of international institutions and foreign investors. Conversely, a lack of transparency occurs when an agent—whether a government minister, a public institution, a corporation, or a bank—deliberately withholds access to or misrepresents information or fails to ensure that the information provided is timely, relevant, or of adequate quality.

Hence, *access* (including timeliness and nondiscrimination), *comprehensiveness* (ensuring inclusion of key items, such as off-line financial and budgetary items), *relevance* (avoiding superfluous information overload), *quality*, and *reliability* are key attributes, which together help policy-making and provide market confidence to investors. Yet markets on their own rarely induce socially desirable levels of transparency, partly because there can be payoffs from nondisclosure. Further, some key information related to transparency—such as economywide economic and financial statistics—can emanate only from government institutions. Thus, the government has a role in promoting a transparent flow of relevant information from its institutions, and, as suggested by the results illustrated in Figure 5, the transparency and effectiveness of such information flows do matter.

Similarly—and potently illustrated by the recent corporate scandals afflicting a few large conglomerates in the United States—in the context of measures enhancing corporate ethics and transparency, it is important to address in depth the challenges of corporate governance and corporate responsibility in general, and the problems of effective audit and accounting in particular. A new variable measuring the effectiveness of audit and accounting standards was thus also included in this year's Survey, alongside questions on corporate governance, permitting further research on these issues (see discussion below). The data suggest a relatively high correlation between the country's audit standard effectiveness and economic performance as well (not shown in Figure 5). In a broader context of transparency, the evidence also suggests that many countries in the OECD (including the United States) and elsewhere face a challenge in how political financing by enterprises directly affects policy outcomes, a topic deserving separate in-depth analysis in the near future.

Beyond bureaucratic corruption: confronting the challenge of state capture

In the anticorruption arena, the focus on "pettier" forms of administrative bribery is giving way to the need to address explicitly the enormously costly challenges of "grander" forms of corruption, such as the tendency by some elite firms and conglomerates to shape illicitly the formation of the state laws, policies, and regulations, which we refer to as *state capture*.[7] Until recently, however, these more political and "grander" forms of corruption were not regarded as subject to measurement. We have challenged this tenet through recent surveys, which led to empirical research pointing to the extent of state capture by some elite firms (including some with foreign interests) in selected countries in transition and in Latin America, and to their substantial socioeconomic costs and consequences. For the first time, this year's Survey included measures of state capture, which was illustrated in the unbundling of various types of corruption in Figure 2. From the evidence in this Survey, it is clear that there are many countries where the challenge of state capture is present, while in other countries it is less so. Such variance suggests the need to probe further into the determinants and consequences of state capture in the next stage of research, based on this dataset for 80 countries.

The prevalence of state capture by powerful conglomerates (including some transnationals) brings out four corollaries challenging orthodox views about how we have tended to view governance and investment climate. First, the extent of capture by private agents backstops the importance of rethinking the traditional approach to assessing the business environment and investment climate. Such an approach has been predicated on the notion that the government provides such a "climate" to the passive enterprise sector. The public sector has been thought of as the business climate "maker," while the private sector is the climate "taker." The reality turns out to be more complex, with powerful elites and conglomerates (including some multinationals) playing an important role in shaping the rules of the game for the business environment. Second, the existence of state capture constitutes an extreme manifestation (yet a realistic one in many settings) of the importance of understanding the private-public sector governance nexus, and as a result requires rethinking the traditional advice of controlling corruption as if it were solely a problem within the bureaucracy.

Third, in terms of focusing on the causes of misgovernance, state capture implies that corruption is not always merely a symptom of more fundamental factors; instead, the very political and economic forces associated with capture play a pivotal role in shaping policies and political economy outcomes. Fourth, the prevalence of state capture in many settings implies that further emphasis will be needed to understand and empirically assess the key institution of "influence," which exists everywhere and challenges the simplistic interpretation of Adam Smith's invisible hand (in fact, he did understand that influence plays an important role in the market economy).

Implications of the private-public governance nexus

Indeed, where capture is prevalent, we need to rethink the strategies to address misgovernance. Instead of focusing on changes in the internal bureaucratic structures and on organizational rules and regulations, the implication of this work points again to the need to focus on broader external accountability measures, prominently featuring voice and transparency mechanisms—including disclosure of parliamentary votes, asset declaration, publicly available surveys, and higher standards for the media (including investigative journalism and media independence). Furthermore, it is important to have an improved understanding of the institution of "influence": the political and economic incentives shaping the legal, regulatory, and policymaking process. Bureaucracies, senior public officials, and the political leadership do not operate in a vacuum but rather are influenced by diverse forces outside of the public sector. And more focus is required in working with the competitive segments of the private sector (business associations for traders/exporters or medium-sized enterprises, for instance).

The need to focus increasingly on these issues is partly due to the growing evidence that outright transplants of OECD "templates" of *internal* accountability of government to emerging economies have not met with the best results. Similarly, creating new public agencies to address governance challenges (such as new anticorruption agencies or commissions) have often failed. Thus, the challenge is to encourage the pendulum to swing toward *external* accountability mechanisms, with new participatory approaches, providing voice and feedback mechanisms to stakeholders outside the executive—complementing the key priority areas of institutional strengthening within government (see also Box 3).

Evidence from country governance diagnostics points to how important the feedback mechanisms from public-service users are, alongside transparency tools, in contrast with traditional internal rule-making measures (see Box 3). In this context, focusing more on parliamentary, NGO, and citizen oversight is crucial, as is the transparent use of new tools such as citizen scorecards; diagnostics based on survey reports from public officials, public-service users, and firms; and tools to track public expenditures in detail. In a number of settings, such as in Latin America, these have been backstopped by innovative web-based applications—as in procurement, tax collection, and the budget, as well as in disseminating comparative data on governance indicators. A full-fledged embracing of the role of the youth (and leaders of the future) in these collective-action approaches is also needed. Finally, where it has not been captured by the monopolistic state's or elite's vested interests, the media can play a key role in pro-transparency governance reforms.

Box 3: Country governance diagnostics for transparency and action programs

The collection, analysis, and dissemination of multi-country data on governance and corruption—as well as the in-depth, in-country Governance and Anti-Corruption (GAC) diagnostics supported in many countries by the World Bank (in partnership with bilateral agencies and NGOs)—are altering the policy dialogue on governance and corruption and empowering reformists in government and civil society as well as the competitive segments of the private sector through collective action. These in-depth self-diagnostic tools are tailored to the needs of each country that opts to subject itself to such transparent governance review, and are implemented by local institutions. The first set of in-depth governance and corruption diagnostic surveys of public officials, firms, and citizens at the country level were carried out in eastern Europe. More recently such surveys have been conducted in countries in the other emerging regions. The analysis of the links between various institutional variables has significantly expanded the understanding of corruption and its causes, particularly its governance and political roots.

These country surveys ask *citizens* (service-delivery users), *enterprises*, and *public officials* detailed questions about types, manifestations, extent, costs, and private returns of misgovernance and corruption. Survey respondents report on budget transparency and embezzlement of public funds; theft of state property; bribery to shorten processing time; bribery in procurement, banking, and state capture, as well as many other dimensions of governance such as the functioning of merit-based systems in the public sector and the access and quality to public services by the enterprise sector and citizenry. Detailed statistics collected on the access and quality of public services and on the various dimensions of governance and corruption,

discussed here, see Repetto et al. 1989; Bartelmus, Lutz, and Schweinfest 1993; Pearce 1993; and van Tongeren et al. 1993).

The economists' ideas about sustainability at the national level become more intuitive if considered in the light of the work done by the late Raymond Goldsmith (1982, 1985) on national balance sheets. National balance sheets are rarely compiled today, but could be created by consolidating the balance sheets of the firms, households, and government entities within the nation. Domestic financial claims would cancel (for example, a corporate bond is a liability of the issuing firm but an asset of the bondholder), leaving a balance sheet with real assets (buildings, infrastructure, untapped natural resources, and so on) and claims on the rest of the world on the left-hand side, and claims by the rest of the world and national net worth on the right-hand side. The national income accounts and the balance of payments accounts as conventionally constructed show changes to some (although not all) of these asset and liability categories. Solow, Weitzman, and Hartwick advocate the consideration of the excluded measures so that one can tell whether the national net worth is expanding or shrinking. National net worth has value precisely because it enables the nation to generate future income for its citizens. So if national net worth is stable, the country's ability to generate future income is neither increasing nor decreasing; it is (barely) sustainable. If national net worth is increasing, the country's development path is sustainable; if it is decreasing, the path is unsustainable. If, as seems intuitively appealing, we are interested in sustaining per capita consumption rather than aggregate consumption, then sustainability requires that national net worth rise at least as rapidly as population.

Measurement problems are obviously significant. The biggest ones involve human capital and uncertainty. Human capital is excluded from the investment accounts in national income accounting, and is absent from Goldsmith's balance sheets, despite its obvious importance in economic development. These exclusions arise not only because it is difficult to measure human capital but also because, in most modern societies, an individual's human capital cannot legally be owned by a second individual or by a corporation. In effect, then, sustainability accountants are assuming that the possibilities of substituting human capital for conventional and/or natural capital are limited, so that it makes sense to amalgamate natural and human-made capital but to leave human capital out of the picture. Fortunately, human capital is increasing in most societies, so that its exclusion tends to overstate rather than understate any problems of sustainability.

The other significant measurement problem involves uncertainty and shocks. A severe shock to a comfortable country's capital stock (because of earthquake, war, or some other catastrophe) could obviously make the previously prevailing levels of production and consumption unsustainable. Since we can never entirely rule out the possibility of such cataclysms, *sustainable* really has to mean "sustainable with some unspecified but very high probability," and, indeed, this is its meaning in common parlance. The only level of human activity that is sustainable with a probability of 1 is no activity at all. This state of affairs complicates any tests for sustainability that one might devise.

Despite these problems, empirical tests of these ideas have shown relationships between the sustainability of the country's strategy as defined here and its long-term economic performance. Countries that draw down their stocks of natural resources and consume the rents tend to suffer in the long term compared to those that increase aggregate capital stocks over time by replacing the natural capital with other forms of physical capital (Vincent 2001, 2002).

Sustainability at the firm level

Hence at the national level the economists' definition of sustainability is narrow enough to give rise to conceptually plausible measures, but broad enough to be interesting from a policy perspective. The definition has clear firm-level analogs: for a firm, too, a sustainable strategy is one that involves no net decrease in total assets or, equivalently, involves the creation of value. This notion of sustainability is tightly linked to ideas about strategy and competitive advantage that have long been understood in business circles: it is necessary only to integrate these ideas with equally well established notions of social cost.

In other words, we can imagine a test for sustainability in firms analogous to the one proposed by Solow, Weitzman, and Hartwick at the macroeconomic level. If the firm is adding value when inputs and outputs are valued at their social costs, its operations are sustainable; otherwise not.

Sustainability is a somewhat more complicated question for firms than it is for governments, because, in addition to this social-cost test, firms need to pass a similar private-cost test if they are to remain in business. This complication does not, however, invalidate the basic insight: that the economic tests for evaluating sustainability can be applied to firms as well as to national economies. Widely used innovations in the collection and analysis of information, especially those in contingency accounting and life-cycle analysis, facilitate assessments of the sustainability of business operations. Social costs are increasingly built into the private cost structures of firms through regulatory requirements and through the voluntary corporate provision of public goods.

357

Traditional views of the sustainability of a firm

Consider first what microeconomists and students of business strategy mean when they talk about sustainable competitive advantage or sustainable growth at the firm level. Analysts of competitive strategy have long used the notion of a sustainable competitive advantage to describe a firm's ability to generate supernormal returns (ie, to earn rents for its shareholders) over long periods of time (see Ghemawat 2001 for a historical overview of this thinking and a summary of current ideas in the field). In fact, the techniques useful in analyzing private-sector sustainability have roots reaching back at least 80 years. In the early 20th century, Donaldson Brown of E. I. du Pont de Nemours and Company (DuPont) invented a procedure for evaluating the financial performance of diverse businesses that is still used today. Brown expressed a business's return on equity as the product of three ratios:

> ROE = return on equity
> = profits/equity
> = profits/sales × sales/assets × assets/equity.

The first of these three ratios is return on sales; the second is asset returns, a measure of the efficiency with which the business can generate sales from its assets; and the third is a measure of financial leverage, negatively correlated with the debt-to-capital ratio more commonly seen today (Chandler 1962, p 67; Chandler 1977; see also Palepu, Healy, and Bernard 2000). In conventional financial accounting, the profits figure already reflects depreciation and depletion. That is, in the income statement of a firm, depreciation and depletion are subtracted from revenues as operating expenses.

By making a small modification to Brown's procedure, multiplying the ROE by the fraction of earnings retained, an analyst can identify the rate of sustainable growth for a firm (see, for example, Porter 1980, p 66; see also Palepu, Healy, and Bernard 2000):

> Sustainable
> growth rate = asset turnover
> × after-tax return on sales
> × assets/debt
> × debt/equity
> × fraction of earnings retained.

Here the sustainable growth rate is the rate at which the firm can grow from internally generated capital. After-tax return on sales reflects depreciation and depletion. Notice that we are assuming implicitly that earnings retained in the firm can be invested in projects that earn the same rates of return as the company's current projects. The terms in the equation are evaluated at their private, not their social, costs.

This equation gives a private-cost firm-level analog to the macroeconomic test for sustainability. A sustainable firm generates enough revenue to pay its suppliers (including workers, executives, sellers of raw materials, and providers of debt capital) and still have enough to invest so that its capability to generate revenues in the future is unimpaired. If the value of the earnings retained and reinvested in the corporation exactly equals the depreciation and depletion, the sustainable growth rate will be zero: the firm's balance sheet will neither grow nor shrink.

A company's owners have an obvious interest in knowing whether their company's performance is sustainable according to this definition. Hence the rules of the Financial Accounting Standards Board (FASB) and the Securities and Exchange Commission (SEC) require publicly traded companies to disclose the information that equity holders need to evaluate firms' financial sustainability. For example, standard financial reports make it easy for shareholders to determine whether a company delivered dividends by generating profits on sales of goods and services or by selling plant and equipment. The first of these strategies would be sustainable on its face from a private-cost standpoint, but the second would not.

Two tests for firm-level sustainability

In addition to this private-cost firm-level analog to the macroeconomic definition of sustainability, it makes sense to think about a social-cost firm-level analog. That is, we can imagine modifying the DuPont test to accommodate environmental concerns by valuing the relevant flows—income statement quantities and changes in the balance sheet amounts—at their social costs, and then looking to see what the DuPont formulas tell us about sustainability. This leaves us with two complementary tests of firm-level sustainability: a private-cost test and a social-cost test.

Under the first test, a sustainable firm is one that augments its shareholder value when all stocks and flows are measured at the prevailing private costs, as those costs are determined by market forces and by the current government regulations. Companies deliver profits to their shareholders either by creating value (that is, by producing goods and services that are worth more in the marketplace than the aggregate costs of the inputs necessary to produce them) or by diverting value from other entities that do create it (for example, by exploiting monopoly power). A company that fails the private-cost test will not stay in business in a market economy in which it must compete for capital and other resources.

Under the second test, a sustainable firm is one that creates value when all of its costs and revenues are measured at their social costs. This test is exactly analogous to the national-level sustainability requirement discussed above. To be sustainable from a social-cost perspective, a firm must be creating value and reinvesting enough of that value to maintain its capital stock at an undiminished level. As was true for national economies, it is necessary, in assessing the sustainability of a firm's operations, to consider conventional accounting measures (in this case profitability and investment) as well as environmental performance.

Companies must pass two tests instead of one because they face an additional constraint that governments do not. Governments will succeed in the long run only by delivering value to constituents, and this value should be measured using social costs. If a company is to pass the Solow/Hartwick/Weitzman test, it too must deliver value measured using social cost—but its shareholders will not thank it for passing this test unless it also delivers profits that are measured, not according to social costs, but by market prices.

Measurement issues

So far there have been no well-publicized attempts to apply social-cost accounting comprehensively to any firm's operations. Two sorts of measurement activities directly relevant to sustainability are in widespread use, however. The first encompasses a set of accounting techniques designed to provide more robust assessments of environmental assets and liabilities. The second involves the creation of more detailed assessments of the environmental impacts of business activities, typically concentrating on materials and energy flows over the life cycle of a product. These accounting exercises provide some initial hints about the forms that tests for sustainability in the private sector might take.

Attempts to improve the information available to corporate managers and other stakeholders about assets and liabilities that relate to natural resources and the environment have recently become more widespread. Although typically motivated by a need to track private costs accurately, not by a desire to engage in social cost accounting, they reveal some of the opportunities and difficulties that analysts encounter in portraying private-sector environmental information in ways that are useful to executives, shareholders, government officials, and other parties.

For example, companies have long included depletion of natural resource assets both on their income statements and on their balance sheets, in accordance with generally accepted accounting principles. But since the assets are valued at historic acquisition costs, depletion figures may bear little resemblance to the true opportunity costs of the resource extraction, and the asset values net of these depletion charges may have no clear relationship to the market value of the assets. Recently, accounting boards have changed the standards to require more complete treatment of natural resource economics.

In the early 1980s, in the aftermath of the oil shocks, the FASB required "publicly traded enterprises with sig-

nificant oil and gas activities" to prepare supplements to their regular financial statements that provided additional information on their holdings of natural capital. Under Statement of Financial Accounting Standards No. 69 (SFAS No. 69), these companies were required to disclose the amounts of their proved oil and gas reserves, the capitalized costs of production activities, and a "standardized measure of discounted future net cash flows relating to proved oil and gas reserve quantities" using a discount rate of 10 percent (FASB 1982, p 1). For these firms, oil and gas holdings could be a large part of total capital assets, and shareholders were thought to need a more accurate picture of the values of those assets than historical cost data would provide.

Impediments obviously remain. The companies themselves regard this system as highly imperfect. The sections of their annual reports that contain the figures required by SFAS No. 69 typically also include language such as the following: "The information provided does not represent management's estimate of the company's expected future cash flows or of value of proved oil and gas reserves. . . . The arbitrary valuation prescribed under SFAS No. 69 requires assumptions as to the timing and amount of future development and production costs. The calculations . . . should not be relied upon as an indication of the company's future cash flows or value of its oil and gas reserves" (ChevronTexaco Corporation 2002, p 78). So far, procedures such as those spelled out in SFAS No. 69 have not been applied to firms in other industries, such as forest products or minerals, for which natural capital might represent a significant fraction of total asset values.

Given increasing attention to long-term resource trends among governments and nongovernmental organizations, and given the suspicion that such trends may materially affect firms' equity values, shareholders of such firms may come to expect and receive more information on asset values than is currently available. The current tendency in the capital markets toward the vertical disintegration of hitherto integrated natural resource firms will tend to increase this pressure.

Another area in which the FASB has changed accounting standards to ensure the disclosure of information relevant to sustainability is that of environmental cleanup liabilities. FASB Statement No. 5, issued in 1975, requires companies to record contingencies when (1) it is probable that an asset has been impaired or a liability incurred, and (2) the amount of loss can be reasonably estimated (FASB 1975). More recently, the US Securities and Exchange Commission's Staff Accounting Bulletin No. 92 (1993) and the American Institute of Certified Public Accountants Statement of Position 96-1 (1996) spelled out procedures for quantifying contingencies under FASB No. 5.

FASB Statement No. 121 is a more general attempt to bring about accounting changes in the private sector to reflect market values that are lower than historical book values. This statement "requires that long-lived assets and certain identifiable intangibles to be held and used by an entity be reviewed for impairment whenever events or changes in circumstances indicate that the carrying amount of an asset may not be recoverable. In performing the review for recoverability, the entity should estimate the future cash flows expected to result from the use of the asset and its eventual disposition. If the sum of the expected future cash flows (undiscounted and without interest charges) is less than the carrying amount of the asset, an impairment loss is recognized" (FASB 1995, p i). It is worth observing that this requirement has been criticized by former SEC Chairman Arthur Levitt, among others, for offering corporate managers too much discretion in when and to what extent they recognize asset impairments (see Palepu, Healy, and Bernard 2000, p 7-14).

The accounting innovations just discussed pertain to the measurement of assets and liabilities. Similar innovations that relate to the flows or activities portrayed in a company's income statement can be imagined. Many companies have tried to compare the environmental impacts of alternative products or processes as a way of setting managerial priorities, improving their understanding of regulatory risks, and identifying the areas in which further information would be most valuable. Such studies often involve a life-cycle analysis of material and energy flows arising from a product's manufacture, use, and disposal (see, for example, Schaltegger, Müller, and Hindrichsen 1996). Once these flows are quantified, explicit or implicit systems for weighting or pricing the various flows can be used to compare overall effects of alternative production schemes (see, for example, Monsanto 1998, p 4).

Some weighting or pricing system is necessary because, although a few product or process changes may result in superior economic and environmental performance along every relevant dimension, more commonly a new product or process will improve performance along some dimensions while increasing some other costs, environmental impacts, or risks. For example, genetically altered seeds result in "fewer inputs, less labor, less manufacturing of inputs, reduced insecticides, reduced fuel use," and so on (Monsanto 1998, p 5), but are more expensive to produce than conventional seeds and also may increase the risk of pests rapidly developing resistance to the natural toxins on which the biotechnology draws.

In principle, it ought to be possible to use numerical conversion factors to reduce all private and social costs to a single value. Although one might see this practice as reductionist and arbitrary, firms employ similar methods

when measuring assets and liabilities to record on their balance sheets. In practice, most corporate attempts at life-cycle analysis (or at least those that the firms share with the public) do not explicitly quantify social costs, instead leaving quantities entirely unpriced or, perhaps, showing the costs of various activities relative to some nonmonetized benchmark.

All of these accounting procedures involve the disclosure of information not previously divulged by most firms. The firms may have decided not to disclose the information in part because of concerns that by doing so they would increase their vulnerability to lawsuits, and also in part because of difficulties in measurement. As with any accounting issue, tradeoffs exist between relevance and reliability. "The general acceptance of an accounting principle or practice usually depends on how well it meets three criteria: relevance, objectivity, and feasibility" (Anthony and Reece 1983, p 14). As the relevance to shareholders of natural capital assets and environmental liabilities increases, more complete disclosure is appropriate even if problems of objectivity remain unresolved.

At the same time, the increased relevance of the environmental information for investment and management decisions creates incentives to find reliable and replicable methods to generate that information. Information of the sort discussed here is exactly what managers require to assess the impact of environmental concerns on their strategies and operations, to identify risks, and to assess potential opportunities (see Reinhardt 2000a, 2001). This development is exactly analogous to developments at the macroeconomic level, where increasing concern about natural asset values is pushing governments and international organizations to require provision of more information even though it may not be completely objective, and where the increased relevance of the information creates incentives to devise more reliable and replicable ways to capture it.

It is this tension between relevance and reliability that underlies the familiar debate about rules versus discretion. In arenas where measurement systems are imperfect, systems that rely on rigid rules can constrain managers' ability to report what they truly believe to be relevant: this is the criticism of the oil company managers with respect to SFAS No. 69. At the same time, however, systems that provide managers with more discretion create opportunities for potentially misleading accounting, as demonstrated by Arthur Levitt's concerns about SFAS No. 121. In fact, the historical development of accounting standards can be usefully viewed as a search for the optimal balance between rules and discretion, with the optimum shifting as new accounting techniques reduce the costs (in terms of lost accuracy) of standardization, and as new business practices whose effects are not well captured in existing rules increase the benefits of policies that allow more discretion. In this context, the problems of measuring stocks and flows relevant to sustainability are neither new nor dissimilar to ones that we are collectively experienced in solving.

Firm-level environmental sustainability in its economic context

A firm makes money and is sustainable in a private-cost sense if its outputs can be sold for more than the total private opportunity costs of its inputs. It is sustainable in a social-cost sense if its operations pass a social cost–benefit test. Where private costs and social costs are equal, the two definitions are the same. (Private and social costs might be equal because the firm operates in competitive markets where externalities are unimportant, or because government policies have forced them to converge.)

It follows that a particular company's operations are more likely to be unsustainable if the company's margins are low according to conventional accounting, if resource rents represent a significant fraction of the accounting profits that the company produces, if private costs are likely to be substantially lower than social costs because of externalities in production processes, or especially if more than one of these problems is significant. For example, firms harvesting fish in open-access ocean fisheries confront all three of these problems. Because of crowding externalities, accounting profits in the industry are low and resource rents are a significant fraction of whatever accounting profits the firms generate (in fact, resource rents may exceed accounting profits if, as is common in open-access fisheries, excessive entry dissipates the resource rents). In addition to these problems, firms in many fisheries also employ technologies that generate negative externalities (for example, some stun ocean fish with cyanide so that they can be transported live to restaurants), so that the direct social costs of fishing are higher than the private costs.

Note that it is possible, even common, for a profitable firm to pursue a deliberate strategy of nonsustainability. A mining firm, for example, may generate large accounting profits by mining and selling high-quality ores with substantial resource rents, and then pass those rents to its shareholders in the form of dividends. It might deliberately plan to continue to do so until its ore bodies become exhausted. This activity would not necessarily be incompatible with sustainability at the macro level if the shareholders reinvested these resource rents in other productive activities.

By contrast, firms that earn large accounting profits are likely to be sustainable by the definitions developed here unless they operate businesses in which private costs are far lower than social costs or in which resource rents

are a significant fraction of total profits. Put another way, accounting profits can represent value created by the firm for its shareholders and also value that the firm diverts to its shareholders from other parties. Social costing corrects for the second of these (and also for value that the firm creates but does not capture for its shareholders) to determine whether the firm is adding value from a social perspective. If this correction is small and if the firm shows robust accounting profits, then the firm's operations would pass the social-cost sustainability test. For example, in the year ending January 31, 2002, Wal-Mart Stores made over $6.6 billion in after-tax profits on revenues of $218 billion; its book assets at year end were $83.4 billion (Wal-Mart 2002). In calendar year 2001, the Coca-Cola Company earned almost $4 billion on $20.1 billion in revenue, with book assets at year end of $22.4 billion (Coca-Cola 2002). These profit numbers include significant rents, but they are rents to efficient distribution systems and brand names; they are not resource rents. It seems likely that Wal-Mart and Coca-Cola would pass the social-cost sustainability test just outlined.

For other companies whose operations or products rely on large quantities of goods and services for which private and social costs may diverge widely, preliminary calculations paint a murkier picture. Since these calculations illustrate some of the difficulties in operationalizing the accounting ideas discussed in this chapter, it is worth considering them in some detail. Consider, for example, how one might assess the social-cost sustainability of oil and gas giant BP or of the Tokyo Electric Power Company (TEPCO), one of the world's largest electric utilities. One obvious question is how to adjust the published accounts for externalities involving climate change.

In 2001, BP earned after-tax profits (excluding some exceptional items) of $9.88 billion. In the same year, it produced in its operations greenhouse gases equal in warming potential to 80.5 million metric tons of carbon dioxide (BP 2002). That same year, TEPCO generated profits of ¥319.5 billion, or $2.42 billion at the year-end exchange rate of 132 yen to the dollar. Emissions of carbon dioxide from its power plants were 55.4 million metric tons (TEPCO 2002). Thus BP generated about $122 in profit for each ton of carbon dioxide it emitted and TEPCO generated about $44. (The figures as given are not directly comparable because the BP figure aggregates carbon dioxide and methane emissions, with tons of carbon dioxide as the unit of account; the TEPCO figure is for carbon dioxide only. Moreover, the TEPCO figure is for power plant emissions only, while the BP figure is a comprehensive total emissions number for all of the firm's operations. Before making direct comparisons one would want to adjust one firm's numbers.)

To put these numbers in context, note that during Janet Yellen's term on President Clinton's Council of Economic Advisers she estimated that American compliance with the Kyoto Protocol's 7 percent reduction in carbon emissions from 1990 levels by about 2010 would, if done efficiently through a carbon tax, require "an emissions price in the range of $14 to $23 per ton of carbon equivalent" (Yellen 1998), or $51 to $84 per ton of carbon dioxide.[2] In trying to use these numbers to gauge the social-cost sustainability of BP's or TEPCO's operations, one first needs to assume that the $14 to $23 figure has something to do with the social cost of carbon. One also needs to take into account the elasticities of demand and supply in energy markets, since the imposition of a tax such as that imagined by Yellen would result in a decrease in the total sales volumes for BP or for TEPCO. One also needs to know about the other external environmental impacts of the firms' operations besides global climate change. Without a more detailed understanding of these three factors, it is not possible to determine whether BP or TEPCO would pass a social-cost sustainability test.

One obvious difference between the two firms is that much of the carbon associated with BP's value chain is emitted when its customers burn the product in their vehicles. TEPCO, by contrast, does more of the combustion itself and delivers to its customers a product that has fewer externalities in use. The managements of both firms should be interested in the private and social costs of activities throughout their value systems, from extraction of the resource through ultimate consumption. At the same time, however, it makes sense when analyzing the sustainability of a firm's operations to take the firm's boundaries as they are drawn by the scope of the activities in which it has chosen to participate. Managers' choices about the scope of the firm affect sustainability accounting just as they do conventional accounting. But accountants ordinarily have to take as given the scope of the firm as it has been defined by the firm's actual activities and investments.

Forest products companies present another interesting case because they generate both positive and negative externalities in the course of their operations. To focus on the positive externalities, assuming again that the $14 to $23 per ton emissions price for carbon is related to the social cost of the carbon, and noting that growing forests sequester "one to eight tons of carbon per hectare per year" (Intergovernmental Panel on Climate Change 1996, p 247), we can get some idea of the value of the carbon sequestration services provided by timberland holdings and compare that figure with the income of timber-rich firms. In 2000 and 2001, for example, International Paper had on its balance sheet about 6 million acres (ie, roughly 2.4 million hectares) of timberland on which it had planted trees (note that this is a stock number, not an annual

flow), suggesting a value of sequestration services between $34 million and $450 million. To put these numbers in context, in 2000, International Paper earned $142 million on revenues of $28 billion, and year-end book assets were $42 billion; the following year it lost $1,204 million on sales of $26 billion, and year-end book assets were $37 billion.

These simple calculations about BP, TEPCO, and International Paper show both that environmental externalities—positive or negative—can be quite large, and that the externalities are very difficult to measure precisely. It is necessary to complement simple breakeven analyses of the sort discussed here with careful economic analysis of the social cost of various environmental insults (or, to put it differently, with the demand for environmental services and public goods) in order to work toward an improved ability to assess the sustainability of firms' operations. Pricing environmental externalities is especially difficult because of possible nonlinearities in the relationships between human activities such as environmental pollution and environmental effects such as climate change or biodiversity loss. Even simple breakeven analyses can, however, highlight the areas in which additional information would be most valuable to company executives or government policymakers, so that efforts are concentrated where progress is most needed.

As was true at the macroeconomic level, measurement problems involving human capital and uncertainty are significant at the level of the firm. Perhaps the most important omission from the accounting exercises discussed here is human capital. Human capital is difficult to measure, and it seems impossible to incorporate in company balance sheets in a legally and morally defensible way. At the same time, its historic omission from company accounts has not completely undermined the usefulness of those accounts for assessing sustainability in the traditional business sense, and its continued omission should not serve as an excuse to end experimentation with the sustainability tests discussed here.

Now consider uncertainty and shocks. Just as a shock to a country's capital stock can make previously prevalent consumption levels unsustainable, so a shock to a firm can make previous levels of profits and investment inadequate for sustainability, either from the private-cost or from the social-cost perspective (or both). Businesses that made and distributed DDT were first shown to be value-destroying from a social-cost perspective and then, as a consequence, were rendered unsustainable from a private-cost perspective as well. Shocks that threaten the sustainability of firms are familiar outside the environmental arena as well: consider Polaroid, which possessed what looked to be a sustainable competitive position until the advent of digital photography slashed the value of its asset base. A principal job of senior executives in fast-moving businesses is to ensure their assets against the possibility of discontinuous change or, failing that, to hedge the risks by owning other assets with negatively correlated returns. This is true in the environmental arena as well, and the increased likelihood of shocks in this area will itself create incentives for executives to demand improved information about them.

Integrating microeconomic and macroeconomic tests

It seems plausible from the examples just discussed that the operations of a large number of companies would pass the social-cost sustainability test just outlined. At the same time, many well-informed people feel that loss of biodiversity, global climate change, and other environmental problems place the sustainability of the economy as a whole in serious doubt. Is it possible to reconcile these two ideas? In other words, must it be that the tests proposed here are flawed or that concern about the sustainability of the current development path is misplaced?

The two views—that the social-cost test makes sense as a sustainability criterion for firms and that the global society faces some potentially serious environmental problems—can be reconciled by noting that a great deal of the economic activity for which private and social costs seem most likely to diverge takes place in households or in household-sized firms. For example, forest degradation for agriculture or fuel production in developing countries falls largely into this category; so does automobile use in the developed world. So, too, does an operation as simple and apparently innocuous as washing clothes. For example, scientists at Ciba Specialty Chemicals calculated that the total energy consumed when a household washes and dries a polyester shirt 20 times exceeds, by a factor of four, the total energy required to make the polyester, produce the textile, manufacture the shirt, and deliver it to the customer (Büttler 1998). Similarly, researchers at clothing manufacturer Patagonia concluded that consumer care of a typical cotton t-shirt entailed greater environmental (not total) costs than all other stages of the product's life cycle combined (Walsh and Brown 1995; Chouinard and Brown 1997).

Firms may facilitate unsustainable behavior in the household sector. They may also actively encourage it. Further, subsidies to natural resource use, whether implicit or explicit, are enemies of sustainability. For example, recent controversies over global climate change suggest that energy consumption by firms and households may be subsidized quite heavily because energy prices do not reflect the social costs of global warming. This would imply that firms, particularly firms with energy-intensive operations or energy-intensive products, might analyze whether their activities would still be profitable if private fossil fuel prices rose to reflect the social cost of global climate change. More generally, firms whose own operations are sustainable but whose suppliers or customers behave unsustainably need to understand—and manage—the resultant business risk.

Sustainability, substitution of capital for natural resources, and total factor productivity

As Solow, Weitzman, and Hartwick all show, the development trajectory of a national economy can be sustained by ongoing substitution of capital for natural resources, continued improvements in total factor productivity (TFP), or both. The same logic applies at the firm level. Substitution of capital for natural resources counteracts the effects of natural resource depletion and of population growth, both of which work against sustainability. TFP changes enable economies or firms to create more consumption possibilities from a given collection of capital, labor, and natural resource inputs. If TFP increases at a sufficient rate, it can dominate the effects of natural resource depletion and population growth and also those of diminishing returns to manufactured capital.

In the ordinary course of competition, firms will optimally substitute capital for natural resources as long as their relative prices reflect their relative scarcity. For example, the prices of logs from large trees rose in the United States during the 1970s and 1980s in response to shortages of those resources. Lumber and plywood produced from those large trees also rose in price. This created incentives for wood products firms to find ways to create similar products using cheaper natural resource inputs—in this case, wood from smaller trees. Medium-density fiberboard, oriented strandboard, and other engineered board products resemble plywood but can be produced from small, inexpensive, rapidly growing trees. They do require larger investments in factories and skilled labor than plywood mills, which are relatively inexpensive to build and operate. Similar transformations are taking place in other parts of the building materials industry, where glued and laminated timbers made from small trees are increasingly competitive with conventional lumber.

In fact, firms are one of the primary engines through which total factor productivity increases, again because they are interested in finding ways to compete more effectively against other firms. Innovations in biotechnology, for example, involve the substitution of scientific knowledge for materials in the agricultural sector. If plants can be genetically altered so as to be resistant to insects, this can make the manufacture, transportation, and application of broad-scale pesticides unnecessary, avoiding both the private costs of these activities and the negative externalities that they impose on nearby ecosystems and human communities. From the firm's perspective, these innovations are a source of competitive advantage: they increase total factor productivity, enabling the firm to deliver the same value to consumers using fewer capital, natural resource, and labor inputs.

The more closely market prices reflect social cost, the more incentive firms will have to unleash their creativity in figuring out ways to substitute away from natural resources, increase TFP, or both. Simple economic theory predicts, and much historical business practice bears out, that firms tend to exploit differences between private and social cost for short-run advantage. On the other hand, Gary Becker showed theoretically that government interventions that increase efficiency and social welfare are more likely, on average, to persist than those that do not: "Political policies that raise efficiency are more likely to be adopted than policies that lower efficiency" (Becker 1983, p 384). The reason is not that government officials in Becker's model consciously maximize social welfare; on the contrary, they are interested only in maintaining their power by helping the social groups that help them. They are driven toward more efficient policies because these policies enable them to deliver more wealth to their favorites at a lower cost in opposition from the people who are hurt by the policies. "Competition among pressure groups favors efficient methods of taxation" (Becker 1983, p 386) and, by extension, efficient methods of providing environmental public goods.

Given this understanding, business executives need to prepare for convergence of private and social costs even if this development does not appear to be in their own short-term interest. Further, well-run firms should want prices to reflect social costs, both because this reduces overall distortions in the economy, and because the equalization of private and social costs through government policy precludes competitors that are unconcerned with their long-term reputations from deliberately externalizing social costs of operations. In fact, some managers appear to believe, like Becker, that private and social costs will converge over the long term, and that strategies that anticipate this convergence will, if timed properly, yield a competitive advantage. This is the strategy pursued aggressively by agricultural biotechnology firms such as Monsanto and Syngenta, and also by energy firms such as BP and Shell that are investing in solar technology in anticipation of a need for less carbon-intensive forms of energy. As with any strategy that involves anticipating changes in demand, timing is critical: although the penalties if the firm is too late to the market with new offerings are obvious, it is also possible to come to the market too early. Successful strategy formulation in this arena depends on an ability to assess the interrelated market and regulatory risks and to understand the ways in which considerations of social cost may affect the private costs of various economic activities in the future.

Conclusions

The environmental sustainability of a national economy or a firm must be considered in the context of the entity's overall economic activity. Sensible tests of sustainability at the macroeconomic level examine savings and investment as well as environmental degradation and resource depletion. Sensible tests of sustainability at the level of the firm consider profits and investment as well as pollution and resource use. Environmental sustainability at the firm level cannot be viewed in isolation from the business fundamentals of the firm.

Managers concerned about sustainability—from the point of view of social costs or of private costs—should encourage and accelerate the development of public policies that force private and social costs to converge. Over the long term, well-managed firms will benefit if the governmental regulatory regime is stable. Regulatory regimes that do not equate private and social costs are less stable than those that do. The behavior of government is especially important for firms engaged in economic activities for which market price signals may not contain all of the information about social costs: activities, that is, where property rights are nonexistent or poorly enforced. These interrelated conditions (divergence of private and social costs, and incomplete or insecure property rights) are especially prominent in global climate change and the loss of biodiversity; hence they are especially important to the energy, forestry, and agriculture industries.

If business executives are worried about sustainability, they should examine those parts of their operations in which social and private costs may diverge widely, those parts of their operations in which a large fraction of profit is resource rent, and those parts of their operations that are only marginally profitable. Firms whose current operations benefit from unsustainable environmental subsidies in the form of inefficiently lax regulation are no different from those that benefit from more direct government handouts: they should be thinking about how they will make a transition to activities that are sustainable in the traditional business sense of the term.

Today's typical corporate sustainability report resembles the front half of an annual report to shareholders. It relates anecdotes and facts about particular initiatives, indicating that the firm is managerially astute and socially well-meaning. It does not, however, contain much information that is comparable across firms or that can be integrated with the financial reports. Such omissions from the front half of the annual report to shareholders are inconsequential because of the presence, in the back half of the report, of audited data constructed according to accounting principles that are generally understood and thought to be broadly replicable across firms. If firms and governments are serious about sustainable development, their most pressing job is to make progress in designing similar structures for the reporting of data relevant to sustainability. Comprehensive compilations of potential externalities such as those advocated by the Global Reporting Initiative are part of this agenda, but a necessary complement is the development of pricing systems for the externalities, positive and negative, that are most likely to have significant effects on the outcomes of the tests for sustainability discussed in this chapter.[3]

Notes

1 An *economic rent* is a payment to a factor of production larger than what would be necessary to keep that factor in its current employment. Owners of unusually efficient manufacturing or distribution processes earn economic rents. A subcategory of economic rent, called *resource rent*, accrues to owners of highly productive agricultural land or of low-cost deposits of oil or minerals. The distinction between resource rents and other types of rent has important implications for the arguments about sustainability at the firm level developed later in this chapter.

2 Recall that the atomic weight of carbon is almost exactly 12 and that of oxygen almost exactly 16, so a ton of carbon dioxide contains 12/(12 + 16 + 16) = 0.27 tons of carbon.

3 This chapter draws on earlier research, especially Reinhardt (2000b). I am grateful to Peter Cornelius, Richard Johnson, Andrea Larson, Elizabeth Teisberg, and two anonymous referees at *Interfaces*, a journal of the Institute for Operations Research and the Management Sciences. I also benefited from conversations with Bill Bruns, Alexander Dyck, Jim Levitt, David Moss, Julio Rotemberg, Bruce Scott, Dick Vietor, and Lou Wells. Remaining errors are mine.

References

American Institute of Certified Public Accountants. 1996. "Statement of Position 96-1, Environmental Remediation Liabilities." New York: American Institute of Certified Public Accountants.

Anthony, R. N. and J. S. Reece. 1983. *Accounting: Text and Cases.* Homewood, IL: Richard Irwin.

Bartelmus, P., E. Lutz, and S. Schweinfest. 1993. "Integrated Environmental and Economic Accounting: A Case Study for Papua New Guinea." In Lutz, E., ed., *Toward Improved Accounting for the Environment.* Washington, DC: World Bank.

Becker, G. S. 1983. "A Theory of Competition among Pressure Groups for Political Influence," *Quarterly Journal of Economics* 98(1983): 371–400.

BP. 2002. *Annual Report and Annual Accounts 2001.* London: BP.

Büttler, B. 1998. Personal communications (June 23; June 30).

Chandler, A. D., Jr. 1962. *Strategy and Structure: Chapters in the History of the American Industrial Enterprise.* Cambridge, MA: MIT Press.

———. 1985. "Du Pont: The Centralized Structure," Harvard Business School Case # 377-033 (Boston: Harvard Business School, 1977); Reprinted in A. D. Chandler, Jr. and R. S. Tedlow, eds., *The Coming of Managerial Capitalism: A Casebook on the History of American Economic Institutions.* Homewood, IL: Richard Irwin.

ChevronTexaco Corporation. 2002. *ChevronTexaco Corporation 2001 Annual Report.* San Francisco: ChevronTexaco.

Chouinard, Y. and M. S. Brown. 1997. "Going Organic: Converting Patagonia's Cotton Product Line," *Journal of Industrial Ecology* 1(1): 117–129.

Coca-Cola Company. 2002. *2001 Annual Report.* Atlanta: Coca-Cola.

Esty, D. C. 2001. "A Term's Limits," *Foreign Policy* 126 (September–October 2001): 74–75.

Financial Accounting Standards Board of the Financial Accounting Foundation (FASB). 1975. "Statement of Financial Accounting Standards No. 5: Accounting for Contingencies." Stamford, CT: Financial Accounting Standards Board.

———. 1982. "Statement of Financial Accounting Standards No. 69: Disclosures about Oil and Gas Producing Activities." Stamford, CT: Financial Accounting Standards Board.

———. 1995. "Statement of Financial Accounting Standards No. 121: Accounting for the Impairment of Long-Lived Assets and for Long-Lived Assets to Be Disposed Of." Norwalk, CT: Financial Accounting Standards Board.

Ghemawat, P. 2001. *Strategy and the Business Landscape.* Upper Saddle River, NJ: Prentice-Hall.

Global Reporting Initiative. 2002. *Sustainability Reporting Guidelines.* Boston: Global Reporting Initiative.

Goldsmith, R. W. 1982. *The National Balance Sheet of the United States, 1953–1980.* Chicago: University of Chicago Press.

———. 1985. *Comparative National Balance Sheets: A Study of Twenty Countries, 1688–1978.* Chicago: University of Chicago Press.

Hartwick, J. M. 1977. "Intergenerational Equity and the Investing of Rents from Exhaustible Resources," *American Economic Review* 67(5): 972–974.

Intergovernmental Panel on Climate Change. 1996. *Climate Change 1995: Economic and Social Dimensions of Climate Change.* Cambridge, UK: Cambridge University Press.

International Paper Company. 2002. *2001 Annual Report.* Stamford, CT: International Paper Company.

Monsanto Company. 1998. *1997 Report on Sustainable Development Including Environmental, Safety and Health Performance.* St. Louis, MO: Monsanto Company.

Palepu, K. G., P. M. Healy, and V. L. Bernard. 2000. *Business Analysis and Valuation Using Financial Statements.* Second edition; no place of publication given: South-Western College Publishing.

Pearce, D., 1993. *Economic Values and the Natural World.* Cambridge, MA: MIT Press.

Porter, M. 1980. *Competitive Strategy.* New York: Free Press.

PricewaterhouseCoopers LLP. 2002. *2002 Sustainability Survey Report.* No place of publication given: PricewaterhouseCoopers.

Reinhardt, F. 2000a. *Down to Earth: Applying Business Principles to Environmental Management.* Boston: Harvard Business School Press.

———. 2000b. "Sustainability and the Firm," *Interfaces* 30(3): 26–41.

———. 2001. "Bridging the Gap: How Improved Information Can Help Companies Integrate Shareholder Value and Environmental Quality." In Daniel E. Esty and Peter K. Cornelius, eds., *Environmental Performance Measurement: The Global Report 2001–2002.* New York: Oxford University Press for the World Economic Forum.

Repetto, R. et al. 1989. *Wasting Assets: Natural Resources in the National Income Accounts.* Washington, DC: World Resources Institute; reprinted in part in A. Markandya and J. Richardson, eds., *Environmental Economics: A Reader.* New York: St. Martin's Press, 1992.

Schaltegger, S., K. Müller, and H. Hindrichsen. 1996. *Corporate Environmental Accounting.* Chichester, England: John Wiley and Sons.

Solow, R. M. 1974. "Intergenerational Equity and Exhaustible Resources," *Review of Economic Studies* (Symposium 1974): 29–45.

———. 1991. "Sustainability: An Economist's Perspective," J. Seward Johnson Lecture to the Marine Policy Center, Woods Hole Oceanographic Institution, June 14, 1991; reprinted in R. N. Stavins, ed., *Economics of the Environment: Selected Readings,* fourth edition. New York: Norton, 2000.

365

———. 1992. *An Almost Practical Step Toward Sustainability*. Washington, DC: Resources for the Future.

Tokyo Electric Power Company (TEPCO). 2002. *TEPCO Environmental Action Report 2002*. Tokyo: Tokyo Electric Power Company.

United States Securities and Exchange Commission (SEC). 1993. "Staff Accounting Bulletin No. 92." Washington, DC: US Securities and Exchange Commission.

van Tongeren, J. et al. 1993. "Integrated Environmental and Economic Accounting: A Case Study for Mexico." In E. Lutz, ed., *Toward Improved Accounting for the Environment*. Washington, DC: World Bank.

Vincent, J. R. 2001. "Are Greener National Accounts Better?" Harvard University Center for International Development Working Paper No. 63. Cambridge, MA: Center for International Development.

———. 2002. "Genuine Savings and Long-run Competitiveness in Latin America." In J. Vial and P. K. Cornelius, eds., *The Latin American Competitiveness Report 2001–2002*. New York: Oxford University Press for the World Economic Forum.

Wal-Mart Stores. 2002. *2002 Annual Report*. Bentonville, AR: Wal-Mart.

Walsh, J. A.H. and M. S. Brown. 1995. "Pricing Environmental Impacts: A Tale of Two T-shirts," *Ilahee* 11(3&4): 175–182.

Weitzman, M. L. 1976. "On the Welfare Significance of National Product in a Dynamic Economy," *Quarterly Journal of Economics* 90(1): 156–162.

World Commission on Environment and Development. 1987. *Our Common Future*. Oxford and New York: Oxford University Press.

Yellen, J. 1998. Testimony before the House Commerce Committee on the Economics of the Kyoto Protocol, March 4, 1998.

Part 4

Country Profiles and Data Presentation

The Executive Opinion Survey

JENNIFER BLANKE, World Economic Forum

FREDERIC DAVIER, Laboratory of Applied Economics,
University of Geneva[1]

FIONA PAUA, World Economic Forum

The Executive Opinion Survey findings,[2] combined with quantitative data published by major international institutions, underpin the analysis in the *Global Competitiveness Report*. The Survey is indispensable to the *Report* because it captures a broad array of intangible factors that cannot be found in official statistics but that nonetheless affect a country's ability to achieve sustained economic growth. Such factors include many of the most important aspects of an economy, such as the efficiency of government institutions, corruption, and the sophistication of local supply networks. In many cases, such as that of environmental regulation, the Survey provides unique insight into the gaps between economies' *de jure* regulatory frameworks and their *de facto* enforcement.

The Executive Opinion Survey aims to obtain accurate information about the economic environment in which firms operate. Although the operating environments are dynamic and tremendously complex, the underlying premise of the Survey is that one can begin to develop an understanding of an environment only by recording the experiences of those who live and work within that economy. The Survey thus solicits the views of business leaders and entrepreneurs, asking them to compare their respective operating environments with global standards across a range of dimensions. By capturing their responses, we aim to provide textured measures of the competitive environment across many countries.

369

Expanded coverage

Over the years, the *Global Competitiveness Report* has expanded its geographic coverage. The 2002 Executive Opinion Survey, which was executed by the World Economic Forum in coordination with partner institutes, gathered data from a record number of 80 countries with the addition of Botswana, Croatia, Haiti, Morocco, Namibia, and Tunisia.[3] Combined, the country coverage of the GCR accounts for 95.2 percent of the world's economic output.

The new economies in the coverage are all developing and transition economies, and with the exception of Croatia and Haiti, are all in Africa. We are particularly pleased to have added more developing countries to our coverage so we can enhance our knowledge about the varying relative roles played by competitiveness factors at different stages of development. Predicated on the availability of current data, both publicly available information ("hard data") and Survey data, we plan to continue expanding the list of countries covered in the *Report* in the years ahead.

Within the Survey instrument itself, we continue to include well over 100 questions that have allowed us to derive 131 qualitative data variables concerning the quality of government and public institutions, the macroeconomic environment, national technology levels, and domestic competition structures, as well as company operations and strategy. We also continue to include an entire section on the environment, as well as a new section on the effectiveness of international organizations.

Many of the questions are carried over from previous years, and several have been restated and refined in an attempt to distinguish more clearly the results across countries. Many other questions are new, reflecting ongoing updates in our research agenda, frequently as informed by past *Global Competitiveness Report* results.

Methodology

In order to ensure that the Survey data gathered are sufficiently representative of each economy, we work very closely with partner institutes. The target sample of firms is designed to have a distribution across economic sectors of the economy that is proportional to the distribution of the country's labor force sectors, excluding agriculture, as much as possible. The employment distribution was taken from data in the most recent issue of the Yearbook of Labour Statistics of the International Labour Office.

Our partner institutes then prepare a roster of firms from which we ask them to choose firms randomly within these broad sectors. Participation in the Survey is purely voluntary and the respondent is typically a company's CEO or a member of its senior management. The resulting sample usually includes a diversity of executives and managers across many business sectors and firm sizes. We aim, through the use of these various perspectives within each country, to paint as complete a picture as possible of the current economic conditions, particularly those related to growth and productivity. The goal is not to form specific inferences about the population of firms in a country; but rather to construct a sample of firms that is adequately broad and representative to estimate non-firm information about an economy.

The typical Executive Opinion Survey question asks the respondent to assess an issue by choosing a number between 1 and 7 that best reflects their perception of their business environment, with the value 1 representing one end of the spectrum and the value 7 representing the other end. A typical question is presented in Box 1. This question, like most others, is intentionally framed so that 7 represents the top standard in the world and 1 represents a bottom standard. Once completed, the Survey results are compiled and country-level means are calculated to create a country score on each question.

Box 1: Typical Executive Opinion Survey Question

The level of sophistication of financial markets in your country is:

Lower than international norms   **1 2 3 4 5 6 7**   Higher than international norms

Circling 1.....means you agree wholeheartedly with the answer on the left-hand side
Circling 7.....means you agree wholeheartedly with the answer on the right-hand side
Circling 2.....means you largely agree with the left-hand side
Circling 3.....means you agree somewhat with left-hand side
Circling 4.....means your opinion is indifferent between the two answers
Circling 5.....means you agree somewhat with the right-hand side
Circling 6.....means you largely agree with the right-hand side

Key characteristics of the Survey respondents

The Survey was conducted in the early months of 2002, and as Table 1 shows, we received a total of 4,735 surveys, or an average of 59 surveys per country. This ratio is basically in line with last year's Survey, although the response rate fell in a number of countries, presumably due to difficult economic and political situations in some of the countries that have prevented business executives from participating in the Survey.

Table 1 shows some important descriptive statistics concerning this year's Survey respondents. In a third of the countries, more than 70 firms completed the Survey, while in more than half of the countries the figure was greater than 50. Examining the sample in another way, in over 60 of the countries at least one firm completed the Survey per one million inhabitants. The main exceptions are found in countries with huge populations—Brazil, China, India, Japan, Nigeria, the Philippines, and the United States.

Looking at the distribution of respondents by country, one sees that the industrialized economies in the sample tend to have fewer firms in relation to GDP than developing economies. The sample's average firm in an industrialized economy thus "represents" a substantially larger part of national output than its average counterpart firm from a developing economy.

370

Table 1: Distribution of respondents by firm size and type

	Sample size	Surveys per million population	Distribution of respondents by firm size (# employees in country)						Distribution of respondents by firm type				
			<101	101–500	501–5,000	5,001–20,000	>20,000	No response	Dom[1] ≥50%	Gov[2] ≥50%	Fgn[3] ≥50%	D, G, F[4] ≤50%	No response
Argentina	81	2.16	25%	19%	41%	15%	0%	1%	36%	2%	59%	2%	0%
Australia	28	1.45	0%	4%	57%	21%	18%	0%	54%	18%	14%	4%	11%
Austria	35	4.28	11%	23%	51%	11%	0%	3%	43%	11%	34%	3%	9%
Bangladesh	72	0.51	14%	29%	49%	3%	1%	4%	74%	3%	19%	0%	4%
Belgium	18	1.76	11%	17%	11%	50%	11%	0%	17%	11%	44%	11%	17%
Bolivia	55	6.46	64%	24%	9%	0%	0%	4%	76%	5%	11%	2%	5%
Botswana	52	30.95	62%	33%	6%	0%	0%	0%	48%	8%	25%	2%	17%
Brazil	40	0.23	8%	13%	48%	18%	15%	0%	55%	8%	30%	0%	8%
Bulgaria	170	21.44	49%	30%	17%	0%	0%	4%	61%	15%	8%	1%	15%
Canada	33	1.06	24%	12%	21%	21%	21%	0%	76%	6%	9%	3%	6%
Chile	137	8.84	20%	34%	42%	4%	0%	0%	61%	4%	29%	5%	1%
China	80	0.06	10%	23%	49%	10%	3%	6%	36%	30%	11%	0%	23%
Colombia	66	1.53	21%	39%	35%	3%	0%	2%	56%	2%	35%	8%	0%
Costa Rica	71	18.04	38%	38%	23%	0%	0%	1%	61%	7%	31%	0%	1%
Croatia	101	23.06	23%	38%	36%	4%	0%	0%	52%	20%	23%	3%	2%
Czech Republic	46	4.47	46%	22%	26%	2%	2%	2%	46%	11%	28%	2%	13%
Denmark	40	7.49	10%	18%	53%	15%	5%	0%	58%	5%	25%	5%	8%
Dominican Republic	60	6.95	57%	20%	22%	0%	0%	2%	62%	3%	17%	2%	17%
Ecuador	73	6.03	55%	25%	16%	1%	0%	3%	77%	8%	14%	1%	0%
El Salvador	64	9.98	53%	23%	22%	0%	0%	2%	86%	0%	13%	0%	2%
Estonia	78	54.55	59%	27%	9%	3%	0%	3%	49%	23%	18%	0%	10%
Finland	33	6.35	3%	15%	52%	21%	6%	3%	39%	9%	36%	9%	6%
France	36	0.60	19%	17%	42%	11%	11%	0%	47%	6%	36%	6%	6%
Germany	41	0.50	7%	15%	24%	22%	29%	2%	49%	5%	22%	5%	20%
Greece	40	3.78	5%	40%	50%	5%	0%	0%	50%	10%	33%	0%	8%
Guatemala	57	4.88	58%	28%	14%	0%	0%	0%	82%	9%	2%	2%	5%
Haiti	47	5.91	55%	28%	9%	0%	0%	9%	83%	0%	11%	2%	4%
Honduras	62	9.39	48%	27%	23%	2%	0%	0%	68%	0%	21%	6%	5%
Hong Kong SAR	19	2.82	11%	21%	47%	16%	5%	0%	53%	5%	42%	0%	0%
Hungary	31	3.07	10%	32%	48%	6%	0%	3%	29%	16%	45%	0%	10%
Iceland	23	82.14	17%	61%	17%	0%	4%	0%	83%	9%	4%	0%	4%
India	26	0.03	8%	15%	42%	15%	15%	4%	58%	0%	27%	8%	8%
Indonesia	18	0.09	17%	44%	11%	22%	0%	6%	50%	11%	22%	6%	11%
Ireland	27	7.09	30%	19%	44%	0%	4%	4%	19%	26%	37%	4%	15%
Israel	10	1.55	0%	20%	60%	10%	10%	0%	50%	10%	30%	10%	0%
Italy	37	0.64	14%	22%	32%	19%	14%	0%	49%	3%	24%	3%	22%
Jamaica	38	14.50	29%	45%	24%	0%	0%	3%	53%	13%	26%	3%	5%
Japan	71	0.56	3%	14%	34%	27%	20%	3%	77%	0%	18%	0%	4%
Jordan	94	18.11	74%	15%	10%	0%	0%	1%	74%	4%	12%	2%	7%
Korea	103	2.16	3%	25%	62%	7%	3%	0%	71%	5%	11%	5%	9%
Latvia	65	27.43	29%	38%	26%	3%	0%	3%	49%	31%	12%	2%	6%
Lithuania	143	38.75	14%	56%	27%	1%	0%	1%	52%	34%	13%	1%	1%
Malaysia	47	1.98	15%	43%	30%	4%	6%	2%	62%	6%	19%	4%	9%
Mauritius	39	32.77	23%	38%	33%	5%	0%	0%	77%	3%	10%	5%	5%
Mexico	91	0.91	29%	22%	26%	9%	9%	5%	49%	8%	31%	2%	10%
Morocco	82	2.81	66%	17%	10%	2%	0%	5%	67%	6%	10%	2%	15%
Namibia	86	47.07	62%	21%	15%	1%	1%	0%	56%	8%	20%	6%	10%
Netherlands	29	1.81	7%	14%	34%	31%	14%	0%	34%	7%	48%	0%	10%
New Zealand	46	11.95	11%	48%	33%	7%	2%	0%	35%	22%	41%	2%	0%
Nicaragua	60	11.53	57%	18%	8%	0%	0%	17%	62%	0%	10%	13%	15%
Nigeria	15	0.13	20%	47%	13%	13%	0%	7%	87%	0%	13%	0%	0%
Norway	33	7.33	3%	48%	36%	9%	3%	0%	48%	6%	39%	3%	3%
Panama	67	23.26	57%	22%	18%	0%	0%	3%	67%	3%	25%	0%	4%
Paraguay	48	8.52	33%	48%	19%	0%	0%	0%	79%	0%	17%	4%	0%
Peru	61	2.34	21%	44%	33%	0%	0%	2%	69%	5%	20%	0%	7%
Philippines	36	0.43	28%	36%	25%	6%	0%	6%	69%	0%	25%	0%	6%
Poland	71	1.84	27%	13%	34%	7%	3%	17%	20%	8%	44%	1%	27%
Portugal	22	2.19	23%	14%	45%	9%	5%	5%	64%	14%	5%	5%	14%
Romania	96	4.28	74%	15%	7%	0%	0%	4%	80%	1%	15%	0%	4%
Russian Federation	247	1.71	28%	34%	30%	5%	2%	2%	65%	17%	9%	1%	9%
Singapore	90	21.95	31%	39%	24%	4%	1%	0%	6%	9%	81%	3%	1%
Slovak Republic	64	11.83	27%	42%	25%	6%	0%	0%	55%	5%	34%	3%	3%
Slovenia	40	20.08	38%	20%	35%	5%	0%	3%	58%	10%	23%	5%	5%
South Africa	43	0.97	12%	7%	44%	21%	16%	0%	60%	7%	23%	7%	2%
Spain	62	1.54	24%	26%	44%	5%	2%	0%	63%	3%	24%	2%	8%
Sri Lanka	77	3.94	35%	36%	25%	0%	1%	0%	61%	3%	13%	4%	19%
Sweden	14	1.58	14%	29%	29%	21%	7%	0%	36%	14%	29%	14%	7%
Switzerland	74	10.19	35%	27%	22%	8%	5%	3%	73%	7%	16%	0%	4%
Taiwan	50	2.24	0%	10%	72%	16%	2%	0%	62%	12%	10%	8%	8%
Thailand	48	0.76	0%	19%	48%	23%	10%	0%	33%	35%	19%	8%	4%
Trinidad and Tobago	92	70.77	41%	32%	23%	2%	1%	1%	47%	18%	23%	3%	9%
Tunisia	78	8.05	41%	36%	17%	3%	0%	4%	58%	6%	23%	5%	8%
Turkey	17	0.26	29%	24%	35%	12%	0%	0%	35%	6%	47%	0%	12%
Ukraine	89	1.80	51%	30%	18%	1%	0%	0%	67%	21%	3%	0%	8%
United Kingdom	26	0.43	15%	8%	31%	23%	19%	4%	50%	0%	35%	8%	8%
United States	67	0.24	9%	13%	25%	24%	28%	0%	66%	3%	15%	0%	16%
Uruguay	54	16.07	56%	35%	4%	2%	0%	4%	69%	7%	24%	0%	0%
Venezuela	26	1.06	15%	46%	31%	8%	0%	0%	42%	8%	42%	4%	4%
Vietnam	91	1.15	48%	38%	11%	2%	0%	0%	24%	30%	44%	2%	0%
Zimbabwe	36	2.92	0%	14%	75%	11%	0%	0%	61%	3%	28%	0%	8%
Total	**4,735**												

1 Companies majority-owned by the domestic private sector (more than 50%)
2 Companies majority-owned by the government (more than 50%)
3 Companies majority-owned by foreign groups (more than 50%)
4 Mixed companies (not more than 50% owned by any one of the three sectors)

371

Firm size

Firm size varies greatly, with the United States and Germany having nearly a third of the respondents consisting of firms with more than 20,000 employees and about a quarter of the respondents consisting of firms with 5,000 to 20,000 employees. Among the middle-income and developing economies, South Africa, Thailand, and Brazil had country samples where over a third of the companies surveyed had more than 5,000 employees.

At the other end of the spectrum, there is significant participation of smaller businesses in this year's sample. Among these countries are the additions to this year's coverage such as Botswana, Morocco, and Namibia, which, along with 10 other countries, derive over 80 percent of their respondents from firms with fewer than 500 employees. In Latin America, Uruguay, Bolivia, Guatemala, Nicaragua, and Panama have over half of the respondents from companies with fewer than 100 employees.

Firm ownership and market orientation

Table 1 provides further information about the nature of ownership structure and market orientation of firms represented in our Survey. Seventy-one of the eighty countries covered in the *Report* have over half of the companies surveyed with a domestic (private sector or government) majority ownership, led by Iceland, Guatemala, Ukraine, and Nigeria. Countries with a significant proportion of the sample from firms that have majority government ownership include Thailand, Lithuania, Latvia, China, and Vietnam. We note that for certain countries such as Poland and China there are significant no-response rates for this question, at 27 percent and 23 percent, respectively.

Thirty-four of the eighty countries we covered have over a quarter of their sample size represented by firms with majority foreign ownership. Singapore tops this list with 81 percent of the sample comprised of firms with a majority foreign ownership. Other countries that have significant proportion of respondents with majority foreign ownership include Argentina, Netherlands, Turkey, and Hungary.

Robustness of the Survey results

Having analyzed the characteristics of the Survey respondents, in order to determine whether the Survey results are representative and consistent, we examine the standard deviations among responses in each country for Survey questions within different issue areas. Figure 1 shows the responses to an Executive Survey question on the availability of mobile or cellular telephones (question 4.01). The thick bars indicate the average score in each country and the thin lines on the right side of each bar indicate the standard deviations. Countries are listed from top to bottom by the average response, the highest-ranked countries being at the top, and the lowest at the bottom. The graph therefore provides information about the "average" perspective in a given country, as well as the diversity of perspectives within individual countries on a given question. For question 4.01 we see that the standard deviations in Iceland, Israel, and Sweden are in fact 0, demonstrating that every respondent from these countries answered with a value of 7 for this question. We further note that the level of dispersion increases as the average perception of quality gets worse, implying that consensus is less obvious at the bottom end of the spectrum, as we might expect. However, the overall level of dispersion for this, and many other questions, is relatively small, with standard deviations ranging from 1 to 1.5 in many cases (which, of course, must be compared with the value of the mean).

Another way of testing the robustness of the Survey results is to compare the country mean responses to Survey questions of the entire sample to the country mean responses once half of the responses in each country have been randomly dropped from the sample. Figure 2 shows the results of this test for a question asking about the frequency of irregular payments in getting connected to public utilities (question 7.02). We specifically choose to test this question, as it has relatively higher dispersion and would thus be the type most at risk of providing less robust results. To create this figure, we asked the computer to drop one half of its responses randomly from each country. We then recalculated mean country scores for the same question as above on irregular payments and compared them with the results obtained using the full sample. If the results for the full sample and half sample were precisely the same, the collection of dots would form a perfectly straight line along the diagonal. Figure 3 presents the results of the same type of "drop test" for question 4.01 on the availability of mobile telephones, which as we have already established presents little dispersion, and therefore provides a useful benchmark.

Looking at Figure 3, we note that the data points for the drop test on question 4.01, our benchmark, lie very close to the diagonal, as we would have expected, given the relatively lower level of dispersion in this question. Contrasting Figures 2 and 3, we can then assess the robustness of the results for question 7.02 with regards to the benchmark. In fact, what we note is that in Figure 2, each dot representing a country's full-sample versus half-sample country average is also very close to the diagonal, demonstrating that despite greater dispersion, the test also leads to quite robust results. We also see that Finland, the country with the highest mean on this question, has no change in its score when half the sample is dropped. Similarly, the countries with the lowest means, Bangladesh and the Philippines, have almost no change. India, Jordan,

Argentina

Key Economic Indicators

Total population (in millions), 2001 ....37.5
Population rank 25
GDP per capita (PPP), 2001 ....$12,098
GDP per capita rank...31
Real growth in GDP per capita, 2000 to 2001 ....−4.8
Growth rank 78
Unemployment rate, 2001 ....16.40
Unemployment rank 67
Government surplus/deficit, 2001 ....−3.06
Government surplus/deficit rank 49
National savings rate, 2001 ....13.70
National savings rank 73
Investment rate, 2001 ....14.40
Investment rank..76
Inflation, 2001 ....−1.10
Inflation rank 2
Exports of goods (as a percentage of GDP),
     2001 ....9.9
Exports rank...72
Imports of goods (as a percentage of GDP),
     2001 ....7.5
Imports rank...80
Internet users (per 10,000 inhabitants), 2001 ...800.28
Internet users rank 41

Competitiveness Rankings

Growth Competitiveness Rank	**63**

Technology Index Rank **44**
     Innovation Subindex Rank 30
     ICT Subindex Rank 47
     Technology Transfer Subindex Rank
          (out of 56 non-core innovators) 20
Public Institutions Index Rank...**66**
     Contracts and Law Subindex Rank 76
     Corruption Subindex Rank...................................58
Macroeconomic Environment Index Rank **65**
     Macroeconomic Stability Subindex Rank 65
     Country Credit Rating Rank.................................72
     Government Expenditure Rank 20

Microeconomic Competitiveness Rank	**65**

Company Operations and Strategy Rank **57**
Quality of the National Business Environment Rank ...**68**

Trade Performance of Leading Export Sectors

Sector	Share in national exports	Value of exports (US$ millions)	Value of net exports (US$ millions)	Share in world market	TPI current index	TPI change index
Fresh food	23.4%	5,924	5,269	2.49%	9	145
Processed food	23.1%	5,853	5,171	2.71%	11	107
Minerals	17.7%	4,471	3,436	0.64%	24	7
Transport equipment	9.0%	2,265	−676	0.33%	43	8
Chemicals	7.9%	1,995	−2,798	0.33%	49	38

Source: International Trade Centre UNCTAD/WTO

Real GDP (annual percent change)

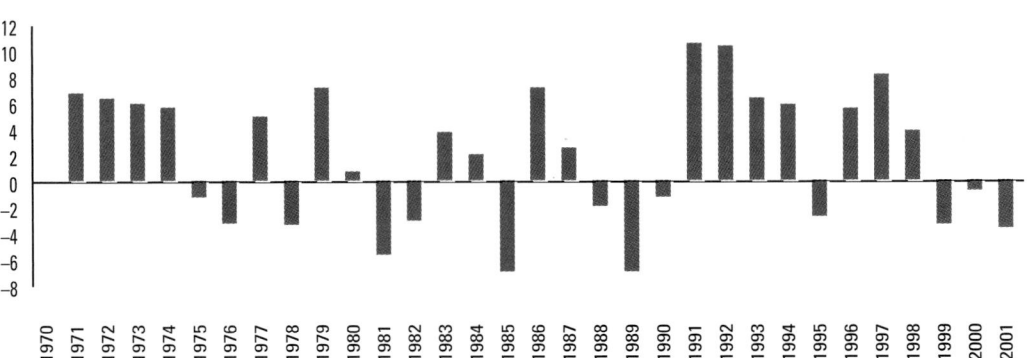

Source: IMF *World Economic Outlook Database,* April 2002

National competitiveness balance sheet

NOTABLE COMPETITIVE ADVANTAGES

Criteria		Rank

Growth Competitiveness

Macroeconomic Environment

2.19	Inflation, 2001	2
2.16	Government expenditure, 2001	20

Technology

3.04	FDI and technology transfer	21
3.18	Tertiary enrollment	23
4.03	Quality of competition in the ISP sector	33
4.09	Internet hosts, 2001	33
3.15	Utility patents, 2001	35
3.05	Prevalence of foreign technology licensing	36
4.08	Internet users, 2001	41

Public Institutions

7.02	Irregular payments in public utilities	38

Microeconomic Competitiveness

Sophistication of Company Operations and Strategy

10.07	Extent of marketing	35
10.10	Extent of regional sales	38
10.06	Production process sophistication	40

Quality of the National Business Environment

3.12	Availability of scientists and engineers	24
10.16	Quality of management schools	30
8.03	Sophistication of local buyers' products and processes	46

Other Indicators

2.20	M2 growth, 2001	1
2.32	Bank liquid reserves	18
8.11	Cost of starting a business relative to GNP per capita	22

NOTABLE COMPETITIVE DISADVANTAGES

Criteria		Rank

Growth Competitiveness

Macroeconomic Environment

2.05	Access to credit	80
2.01	Recession expectations	77
2.17	National savings rate, 2001	73
2.28	Interest rate spread, 2001	69
2.21	Real exchange rate, 2001	58
2.15	Government surplus/deficit, 2001	49

Technology

4.05	Government success in ICT promotion	79
4.04	Government prioritization of ICT	78
3.09	University/industry research collaboration	73
4.06	Laws relating to ICT	73
3.07	Company spending on research and development	72
3.02	Firm-level innovation	70
4.02	Internet access in schools	53
4.07	Cellular telephones, 2001	48
4.10	Telephone lines, 2001	46
4.11	Personal computers, 2001	46
3.01	Technological sophistication	45

Public Institutions

6.03	Property rights	80
6.01	Judicial independence	77
6.09	Favoritism in decisions of government officials	72
7.03	Irregular payments in tax collection	64
7.01	Irregular payments in exports & imports	61
6.15	Organized crime	55

Microeconomic Competitiveness

Sophistication of Company Operations and Strategy

10.02	Value chain presence	75
10.03	Extent of branding	74
3.07	Company spending on research and development	72

Quality of the National Business Environment

2.04	Ease of access to loans	78
8.04	Administrative burden for startups	76
8.05	Effectiveness of antitrust policy	74

Other Indicators

1.04	Real growth in GDP per capita, 2000 to 2001	78
2.03	Soundness of banks	80
2.13	Moody's sovereign debt ratings, 2002	74
2.23	Imports, 2001	80
2.24	Average tariff rate, 2002	70
2.31	Liquid liabilities, 2001	72
6.06	Competence of public officials	80
6.07	Burden of regulation	79
6.11	Effectiveness of law-making bodies	79
6.12	Efficiency of the tax system	79
6.14	Business costs of crime and violence	65
7.10	Diversion of public funds	71
7.13	Prevalence of illegal political donations	77
7.14	Policy consequences of legal political donations	79
7.15	Misuse of legal political donations	79
10.18	Hiring and firing practices	70
11.08	Compliance with international environmental agreements	76

Australia

Key Economic Indicators

Total population (in millions), 2001 ....19.4
Population rank 34
GDP per capita (PPP), 2001 ....$26,552
GDP per capita rank...11
Real growth in GDP per capita, 2000 to 2001.........1.1
Growth rank 41
Unemployment rate, 2001.....................................6.73
Unemployment rank 31
Government surplus/deficit, 2001 ....–0.40
Government surplus/deficit rank 25
National savings rate, 2001 ....18.25
National savings rank 57
Investment rate, 2001 ....21.03
Investment rank..43
Inflation, 2001 ....4.40
Inflation rank 42
Exports of goods (as a percentage of GDP),
    2001 ....17.7
Exports rank..63
Imports of goods (as a percentage of GDP),
    2001 ....18.0
Imports rank..69
Internet users (per 10,000 inhabitants),
    2001 ....3,723.05
Internet users rank 14

Competitiveness Rankings

| **Growth Competitiveness Rank** | **7** |

Technology Index Rank **9**
   Innovation Subindex Rank 9
   ICT Subindex Rank 14
Public Institutions Index Rank............................**5**
   Contracts and Law Subindex Rank 4
   Corruption Subindex Rank......................................8
Macroeconomic Environment Index Rank **4**
   Macroeconomic Stability Subindex Rank.............20
   Country Credit Rating Rank 20
   Government Expenditure Rank 27

| **Microeconomic Competitiveness Rank** | **14** |

Company Operations and Strategy Rank **19**
Quality of the National Business Environment Rank ...**11**

Trade Performance of Leading Export Sectors

Sector	Share in national exports	Value of exports (US$ millions)	Value of net exports (US$ millions)	Share in world market	TPI current index	TPI change index
Minerals	36.7%	21,036	14,667	3.01%	1	60
Fresh food	20.1%	11,511	10,182	4.83%	2	58
Basic manufactures	11.1%	6,327	2,285	1.46%	14	106
Processed food	7.7%	4,397	2,192	2.04%	5	63
Chemicals	4.9%	2,791	–6,091	0.46%	39	42

Source: International Trade Centre UNCTAD/WTO

Real GDP (annual percent change)

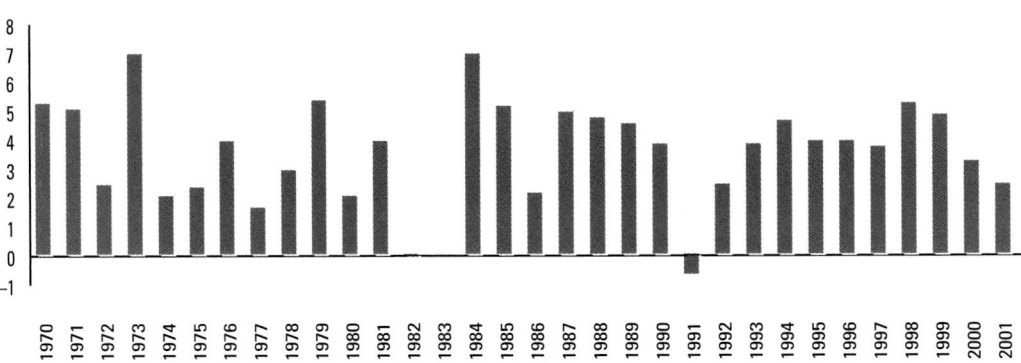

Source: IMF *World Economic Outlook Database,* April 2002

National competitiveness balance sheet

NOTABLE COMPETITIVE ADVANTAGES

Criteria	Rank

Growth Competitiveness

Macroeconomic Environment

2.01	Recession expectations	1

Technology

3.18	Tertiary enrollment	2
4.11	Personal computers, 2001	3
4.06	Laws relating to ICT	5
4.09	Internet hosts, 2001	5
4.08	Internet users, 2001	14
4.02	Internet access in schools	13

Public Institutions

6.01	Judicial independence	1
6.09	Favoritism in decisions of government official	4
7.03	Irregular payments in tax collection	5
6.15	Organized crime	12
7.01	Irregular payments in exports & imports	12
6.03	Property rights	11
7.02	Irregular payments in public utilities	9

Microeconomic Competitiveness

Sophistication of Company Operations and Strategy

10.15	Reliance on professional management	1
10.14	Extent of incentive compensation	3
10.07	Extent of marketing	6

Quality of the National Business Environment

2.07	Local equity market access	2
6.02	Efficiency of legal framework	3
10.17	Efficacy of corporate boards	3

Other Indicators

2.03	Soundness of banks	8
2.32	Bank liquid reserves	5
3.03	Firm-level technology absorption	12
6.05	Freedom of the press	9
6.11	Effectiveness of law-making bodies	4
6.17	Strength of auditing and accounting standards	8
6.18	Pervasiveness of insider trading	4
6.19	Pervasiveness of money laundering through banks	7
6.20	Pervasiveness of money laundering through non-bank channels	4
7.04	Irregular payments in public contracts	7
7.07	Irregular payments in judicial decisions	4
7.15	Misuse of legal political donations	7
8.06	Number of procedures to resolve a dispute	2
8.08	Number of procedures to start a busines	1
11.10	Flexibility of environmental regulations	7
11.04	Chemical waste regulations	9
11.13	Political context of environmental gains	9

NOTABLE COMPETITIVE DISADVANTAGES

Criteria	Rank

Growth Competitiveness

Macroeconomic Environment

2.17	National savings rate, 2001	57
2.19	Inflation, 2001	42
2.28	Interest rate spread, 2001	36
2.16	Government expenditure, 2001	27
2.15	Government surplus/deficit, 2001	25
2.21	Real exchange rate, 2001	17
2.05	Access to credit	16

Technology

4.04	Government prioritization of ICT	44
3.02	Firm-level innovation	43
4.05	Government success in ICT promotion	27
4.07	Cellular telephones, 2001	27
3.07	Company spending on research and development	21
4.03	Quality of competition in the ISP sector	21
3.15	Utility patents, 2001	20
3.01	Technological sophistication	19

Microeconomic Competitiveness

Sophistication of Company Operations and Strategy

10.02	Value chain presence	51
10.01	Nature of competitive advantage	38
10.03	Extent of branding	35

Quality of the National Business Environment

10.20	Cooperation in labor-employer relations	44
3.10	Government procurement of advanced technology products	32

Other Indicators

2.18	Investment rate, 2001	43
2.22	Exports, 2001	63
2.23	Imports, 2001	69
2.25	Corporate income tax rate, 2002	55
2.26	Individual income tax rate, 2002	67
6.12	Efficiency of the tax system	58
8.07	Number of days to resolve a dispute	53
10.18	Hiring and firing practices	42
10.19	Flexibility of wage determination	49
11.08	Compliance with international environmental agreements	47

385

Austria

Key Economic Indicators

Total population (in millions), 2001 ....8.2
Population rank 49
GDP per capita (PPP), 2001 ....$27,518
GDP per capita rank...9
Real growth in GDP per capita, 2000 to 2001.........0.8
Growth rank 46
Unemployment rate, 2001....................................3.86
Unemployment rank 14
Government surplus/deficit, 2001 ....−0.20
Government surplus/deficit rank 21
National savings rate, 2001 ....20.90
National savings rank 42
Investment rate, 2001 ....23.15
Investment rank...30
Inflation, 2001..2.30
Inflation rank 23
Exports of goods (as a percentage of GDP),
    2001 ....34.2
Exports rank..29
Imports of goods (as a percentage of GDP),
    2001 ....36.7
Imports rank..32
Internet users (per 10,000 inhabitants),
    2001 ....3,194.10
Internet users rank 19

Competitiveness Rankings

Growth Competitiveness Rank	**18**

Technology Index Rank **23**
    Innovation Subindex Rank 16
    ICT Subindex Rank 18
Public Institutions Index Rank...........................**11**
    Contracts and Law Subindex Rank 8
    Corruption Subindex Rank...................................19
Macroeconomic Environment Index Rank **23**
    Macroeconomic Stability Subindex Rank 17
    Country Credit Rating Rank...................................8
    Government Expenditure Rank 75

Microeconomic Competitiveness Rank	**12**

Company Operations and Strategy Rank **12**
Quality of the National Business Environment Rank ...**12**

Trade Performance of Leading Export Sectors

Sector	Share in national exports	Value of exports (US$ millions)	Value of net exports (US$ millions)	Share in world market	TPI current index	TPI change index
Nonelectronic machinery	18.7%	10,273	2,551	1.77%	11	55
Basic manufactures	13.7%	7,501	889	1.73%	9	56
Transport equipment	12.4%	6,785	−1,956	0.97%	16	23
Miscellaneous manufacturing	10.9%	5,959	−1,125	1.28%	25	68
Wood products	9.6%	5,275	2,040	2.86%	4	33

Source: International Trade Centre UNCTAD/WTO

Real GDP (annual percent change)

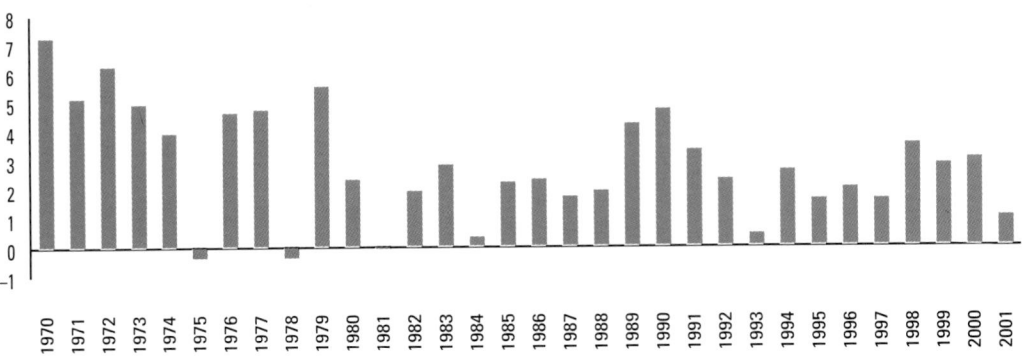

Source: IMF *World Economic Outlook Database,* April 2002

National competitiveness balance sheet

NOTABLE COMPETITIVE ADVANTAGES

Criteria		Rank

Growth Competitiveness

Technology

4.07	Cellular telephones, 2001	7
3.02	Firm-level innovation	11
4.06	Laws relating to ICT	11
3.15	Utility patents, 2001	13
3.01	Technological sophistication	14
3.09	University/industry research collaboration	14
3.07	Company spending on research and development	15
4.09	Internet hosts, 2001	16
3.18	Tertiary enrollment	17
4.03	Quality of competition in the ISP sector	17

Public Institutions

6.03	Property rights	5
6.15	Organized crime	9
6.09	Favoritism in decisions of government officials	11
6.01	Judicial independence	12
7.01	Irregular payments in exports & imports	17

Microeconomic Competitiveness

Sophistication of Company Operations and Strategy

10.10	Extent of regional sales	7
10.01	Nature of competitive advantage	9
10.04	Capacity for innovation	10

Quality of the National Business Environment

5.08	Quality of public schools	1
9.03	Local supplier quality	4
10.20	Cooperation in labor-employer relations	4

Other Indicators

1.09	Employment to population ratio, 2001	8
2.08	Business costs of terrorism	4
5.09	Difference in the quality of healthcare	6
6.05	Freedom of the press	6
6.08	Transparency of government policy-making	9
6.14	Business costs of crime and violence	5
6.17	Strength of auditing and accounting standards	8
6.18	Pervasiveness of insider trading	6
6.21	Military expenditure relative to central government expenditure	3
7.12	Public trust of politicians	9
11.01	Air pollution regulations	2
11.04	Chemical waste regulations	5
11.07	Compliance with environmental regulations	6
11.11	Consistency of environmental regulation enforcement	3

NOTABLE COMPETITIVE DISADVANTAGES

Criteria		Rank

Growth Competitiveness

Macroeconomic Environment

2.16	Government expenditure, 2001	75
2.17	National savings rate, 2001	42
2.05	Access to credit	34
2.28	Interest rate spread, 2001	34
2.19	Inflation, 2001	23
2.15	Government surplus/deficit, 2001	21
2.21	Real exchange rate, 2001	19
2.01	Recession expectations	18

Technology

4.04	Government prioritization of ICT	37
4.10	Telephone lines, 2001	25
4.05	Government success in ICT promotion	24
4.11	Personal computers, 2001	20
4.08	Internet users, 2001	19
4.02	Internet access in schools	18

Public Institutions

7.02	Irregular payments in public utilities	22
7.03	Irregular payments in tax collection	20

Microeconomic Competitiveness

Sophistication of Company Operations and Strategy

10.07	Extent of marketing	23
10.14	Extent of incentive compensation	23

Quality of the National Business Environment

2.02	Financial market sophistication	34
2.07	Local equity market access	42
8.04	Administrative burden for startups	42

Other Indicators

2.09	Regulatory obstacles to business	52
2.18	Investment rate, 2001	30
2.25	Corporate income tax rate, 2002	55
2.26	Individual income tax rate, 2002	70
2.27	Value added tax rate, 2002	60
6.12	Efficiency of the tax system	41
8.07	Number of days to resolve a dispute	64
8.10	Total cost of starting a business	69
10.18	Hiring and firing practices	45
10.19	Flexibility of wage determination	67

Bangladesh

Key Economic Indicators

Total population (in millions), 2001 ....140.3
Population rank 7
GDP per capita (PPP), 2001 ....$1,644
GDP per capita rank...78
Real growth in GDP per capita, 2000 to 2001.........2.4
Growth rank 25
Unemployment rate, 2001.....................................2.50
Unemployment rank 5
Government surplus/deficit, 2001 ....–6.40
Government surplus/deficit rank 71
National savings rate, 2001 ....22.60
National savings rank...34
Investment rate, 2001 ....24.07
Investment rank..27
Inflation, 2001 ....1.80
Inflation rank 15
Exports of goods (as a percentage of GDP),
   2001 ....9.6
Exports rank...74
Imports of goods (as a percentage of GDP),
   2001 ....17.2
Imports rank...71
Internet users (per 10,000 inhabitants), 2001 .....11.43
Internet users rank 80

Competitiveness Rankings

Growth Competitiveness Rank	74

Technology Index Rank **79**
   Innovation Subindex Rank.....................................79
   ICT Subindex Rank 78
   Technology Transfer Subindex Rank
      (out of 56 non-core innovators) 45
Public Institutions Index Rank...........................**79**
   Contracts and Law Subindex Rank 66
   Corruption Subindex Rank....................................80
Macroeconomic Environment Index Rank **39**
   Macroeconomic Stability Subindex Rank............42
   Country Credit Rating Rank.................................71
   Government Expenditure Rank 5

Microeconomic Competitiveness Rank	74

Company Operations and Strategy Rank **76**
Quality of the National Business Environment Rank ...**74**

Trade Performance of Leading Export Sectors

Sector	Share in national exports	Value of exports (US$ millions)	Value of net exports (US$ millions)	Share in world market	TPI current index	TPI change index
Clothing	79.0%	5,003	4,973	2.68%	23	5
Fresh food	7.6%	479	165	0.20%	91	105
Textiles	5.7%	361	–633	0.24%	68	18
Leather products	4.4%	278	262	0.43%	21	28
Chemicals	1.1%	69	–581	0.01%	120	63

Source: International Trade Centre UNCTAD/WTO

Real GDP (annual percent change)

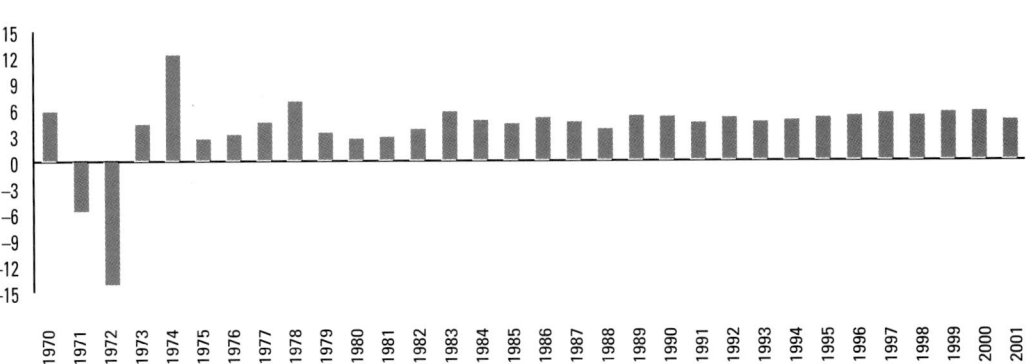

Source: IMF *World Economic Outlook Database*, April 2002

National competitiveness balance sheet

NOTABLE COMPETITIVE ADVANTAGES

Criteria	Rank

Growth Competitiveness

Macroeconomic Environment

2.16	Government expenditure, 2001	5
2.19	Inflation, 2001	15
2.17	National savings rate, 2001	34
2.21	Real exchange rate, 2001	46
2.05	Access to credit	49

Technology

4.03	Quality of competition in the ISP sector	46
4.04	Government prioritization of ICT	46

Microeconomic Competitiveness

Sophistication of Company Operations and Strategy

10.15	Reliance on professional management	56

Quality of the National Business Environment

2.07	Local equity market access	33
8.01	Intensity of local competition	51
9.06	State of cluster development	53

Other Indicators

1.08	Unemployment rate, 2001	5
1.09	Employment to population ratio, 2001	27
2.09	Regulatory obstacles to business	12
2.18	Investment rate, 2001	27
2.26	Individual income tax rate, 2002	6
8.06	Number of procedures to resolve a dispute	15
8.08	Number of procedures to start a business	14
10.18	Hiring and firing practices	27
10.19	Flexibility of wage determination	34

NOTABLE COMPETITIVE DISADVANTAGES

Criteria	Rank

Growth Competitiveness

Macroeconomic Environment

2.15	Government surplus/deficit, 2001	71
2.01	Recession expectations	59
2.28	Interest rate spread, 2001	51

Technology

4.08	Internet users, 2001	80
4.10	Telephone lines, 2001	80
4.06	Laws relating to ICT	79
4.07	Cellular telephones, 2001	79
4.11	Personal computers, 2001	78
3.01	Technological sophistication	77
3.09	University/industry research collaboration	77
3.18	Tertiary enrollment	77
4.02	Internet access in schools	76
3.07	Company spending on research and development	75
3.04	FDI and technology transfer	70
4.05	Government success in ICT promotion	69
3.15	Utility patents, 2001	68
3.05	Prevalence of foreign technology licensing	65
3.02	Firm-level innovation	64

Public Institutions

7.02	Irregular payments in public utilities	80
7.03	Irregular payments in tax collection	80
7.01	Irregular payments in exports & imports	78
6.15	Organized crime	73
6.09	Favoritism in decisions of government officials	66
6.03	Property rights	64
6.01	Judicial independence	56

Microeconomic Competitiveness

Sophistication of Company Operations and Strategy

10.13	Willingness to delegate authority	79
10.01	Nature of competitive advantage	78
10.10	Extent of regional sales	78

Quality of the National Business Environment

6.13	Reliability of police services	80
4.06	Laws relating to ICT	79
7.11	Business costs of corruption	79

Other Indicators

2.22	Exports, 2001	74
2.23	Imports, 2001	71
2.24	Average tariff rate, 2002	74
2.25	Corporate income tax rate	79
2.29	FDI, 2001	77
3.03	Firm-level technology absorption	71
3.13	Brain drain	77
3.17	Secondary enrollment	73
6.07	Burden of regulation	69
6.14	Business costs of crime and violence	71
6.17	Strength of auditing and accounting standards	70
7.08	Frequency of payments or bribes	76
7.13	Prevalence of illegal political donations	78
11.14	Prevalence of environmental management systems	76

389

Belgium

Key Economic Indicators

Total population (in millions), 2001 ....10.3
Population rank 42
GDP per capita (PPP), 2001 ....$27,912
GDP per capita rank...8
Real growth in GDP per capita, 2000 to 2001.........1.0
Growth rank 43
Unemployment rate, 2001....................................6.59
Unemployment rank 30
Government surplus/deficit, 2001 ....0.27
Government surplus/deficit rank 16
National savings rate, 2001 ....25.79
National savings rank...20
Investment rate, 2001 ....20.86
Investment rank..44
Inflation, 2001 ....2.40
Inflation rank 24
Exports of goods (as a percentage of GDP),
    2001 ....82.7
Exports rank..4
Imports of goods (as a percentage of GDP),
    2001 ....77.8
Imports rank..5
Internet users (per 10,000 inhabitants),
    2001 ....2,799.26
Internet users rank 23

Competitiveness Rankings

Growth Competitiveness Rank	25

Technology Index Rank **22**
   Innovation Subindex Rank 15
   ICT Subindex Rank 20
Public Institutions Index Rank..............................**22**
   Contracts and Law Subindex Rank 22
   Corruption Subindex Rank.................................30
Macroeconomic Environment Index Rank **26**
   Macroeconomic Stability Subindex Rank 25
   Country Credit Rating Rank.................................12
   Government Expenditure Rank 72

Microeconomic Competitiveness Rank	13

Company Operations and Strategy Rank **11**
Quality of the National Business Environment Rank ...**15**

Trade Performance of Leading Export Sectors

Sector	Share in national exports	Value of exports (US$ millions)	Value of net exports (US$ millions)	Share in world market	TPI current index	TPI change index
Chemicals	20.3%	36,939	6,104	6.12%	3	13
Transport equipment	14.0%	25,459	3,564	3.65%	5	51
Minerals	11.4%	20,851	−9,726	2.98%	12	16
Basic manufactures	11.1%	20,153	4,971	4.66%	5	76
Nonelectronic machinery	7.6%	13,769	−1,094	2.37%	13	32

Source: International Trade Centre UNCTAD/WTO

Real GDP (annual percent change)

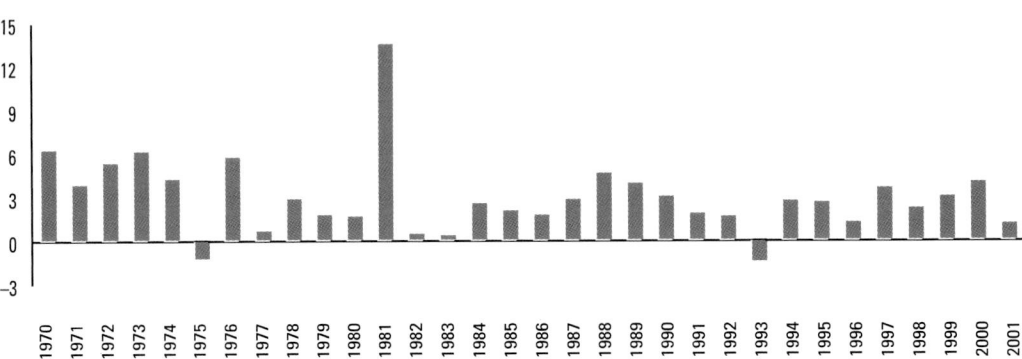

Source: IMF *World Economic Outlook Database,* April 2002

National competitiveness balance sheet

NOTABLE COMPETITIVE ADVANTAGES		
Criteria		Rank

Growth Competitiveness

Macroeconomic Environment

2.21	Real exchange rate, 2001	2
2.01	Recession expectations	12
2.05	Access to credit	25

Technology

3.04	FDI and technology transfer	6
3.05	Prevalence of foreign technology licensing	10
3.02	Firm-level innovation	17
4.05	Government success in ICT promotion	19
4.03	Quality of competition in the ISP sector	24
3.07	Company spending on research and development	25
3.09	University/industry research collaboration	26

Public Institutions

| 6.09 | Favoritism in decisions of government officials | 33 |

Microeconomic Competitiveness

Sophistication of Company Operations and Strategy

3.05	Prevalence of foreign technology licensing	10
10.07	Extent of marketing	19
10.15	Reliance on professional management	25

Quality of the National Business Environment

2.02	Financial market sophistication	11
8.02	Extent of locally based competitors	4
9.08	Local availability of components and parts	1

Other Indicators

2.03	Soundness of banks	28
2.25	Corporate income tax rate, 2002	2
2.26	Individual income tax rate, 2002	19
2.29	FDI, 2001	9
3.03	Firm-level technology absorption	19
6.05	Freedom of the press	24
7.08	Frequency of payments or bribes	17

NOTABLE COMPETITIVE DISADVANTAGES		
Criteria		Rank

Growth Competitiveness

Macroeconomic Environment

2.28	Interest rate spread, 2001	80
2.17	National savings rate, 2001	69
2.19	Inflation, 2001	56
2.15	Government surplus/deficit, 2001	51
2.16	Government expenditure, 2001	48

Technology

3.18	Tertiary enrollment	60
4.07	Cellular telephones, 2001	51
4.08	Internet users, 2001	49
4.10	Telephone lines, 2001	45
4.11	Personal computers, 2001	45
4.04	Government prioritization of ICT	44
3.15	Utility patents, 2001	43
4.06	Laws relating to ICT	43
3.01	Technological sophistication	37
4.02	Internet access in schools	36
4.09	Internet hosts, 2001	36

Public Institutions

6.15	Organized crime	58
7.03	Irregular payments in tax collection	51
7.01	Irregular payments in exports & imports	48
6.01	Judicial independence	45
6.03	Property rights	44
7.02	Irregular payments in public utilities	42

Microeconomic Competitiveness

Sophistication of Company Operations and Strategy

| 10.01 | Nature of competitive advantage | 52 |

Quality of the National Business Environment

2.11	Cost of importing foreign equipment	75
3.11	Quality of math and science education	58
5.08	Quality of public schools	58

Other Indicators

2.18	Investment rate, 2001	68
2.22	Exports, 2001	70
2.23	Imports, 2001	77
2.24	Average tariff rate, 2002	70
3.17	Secondary enrollment	72
5.09	Disparity in healthcare quality	72
6.12	Efficiency of the tax system	77
6.14	Business costs of crime and violence	63
6.16	Informal sector	64
7.13	Prevalence of illegal political donations	66
8.08	Number of procedures to start a business	67

Bulgaria

Key Economic Indicators

Total population (in millions), 2001 ....7.9
Population rank 51
GDP per capita (PPP), 2001 ....$6,182
GDP per capita rank..56
Real growth in GDP per capita, 2000 to 2001.........5.6
Growth rank 7
Unemployment rate, 2001.................................17.52
Unemployment rank 69
Government surplus/deficit, 2001 ....–0.86
Government surplus/deficit rank 28
National savings rate, 2001 ....13.83
National savings rank 71
Investment rate, 2001 ....17.76
Investment rank..66
Inflation, 2001 ....7.50
Inflation rank 59
Exports of goods (as a percentage of GDP),
    2001 ....40.2
Exports rank...20
Imports of goods (as a percentage of GDP),
    2001 ....56.9
Imports rank...10
Internet users (per 10,000 inhabitants), 2001 ...746.27
Internet users rank 42

Competitiveness Rankings

Growth Competitiveness Rank	62

Technology Index Rank **56**
    Innovation Subindex Rank.................................39
    ICT Subindex Rank 44
    Technology Transfer Subindex Rank
        (out of 56 non-core innovators) 50
Public Institutions Index Rank...**47**
    Contracts and Law Subindex Rank 67
    Corruption Subindex Rank.................................27
Macroeconomic Environment Index Rank **75**
    Macroeconomic Stability Subindex Rank 68
    Country Credit Rating Rank................................56
    Government Expenditure Rank 61

Microeconomic Competitiveness Rank	68

Company Operations and Strategy Rank **72**
Quality of the National Business Environment Rank ...**63**

Trade Performance of Leading Export Sectors

Sector	Share in national exports	Value of exports (US$ millions)	Value of net exports (US$ millions)	Share in world market	TPI current index	TPI change index
Basic manufactures	22.3%	1,000	559	0.23%	30	122
Clothing	15.6%	699	523	0.37%	12	13
Minerals	15.5%	697	134	0.10%	55	34
Chemicals	11.6%	521	–120	0.09%	30	117
Nonelectronic machinery	6.1%	275	–326	0.05%	35	95

Source: International Trade Centre UNCTAD/WTO

Real GDP (annual percent change)

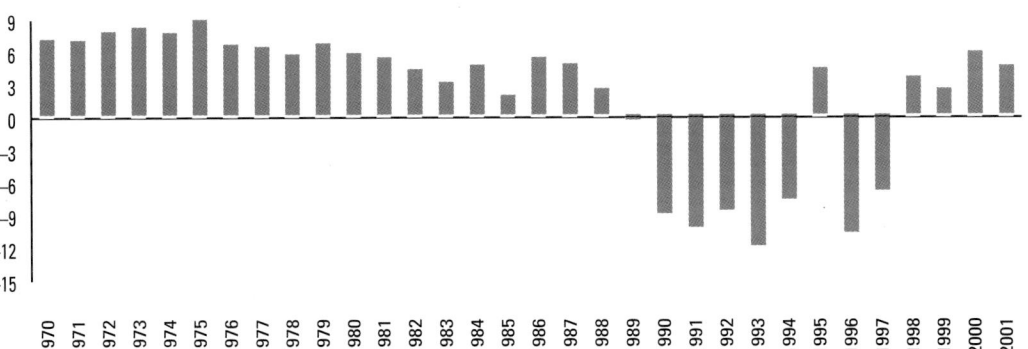

Source: IMF *World Economic Outlook Database,* April 2002

National competitiveness balance sheet

NOTABLE COMPETITIVE ADVANTAGES

Criteria	Rank

Growth Competitiveness

Macroeconomic Environment

2.15	Government surplus/deficit, 2001	28

Technology

3.18	Tertiary enrollment	30
4.10	Telephone lines, 2001	32
4.08	Internet users, 2001	42
4.09	Internet hosts, 2001	45
4.07	Cellular telephones, 2001	47

Public Institutions

7.03	Irregular payments in tax collection	21
7.01	Irregular payments in exports & imports	26
7.02	Irregular payments in public utilities	33

Microeconomic Competitiveness

Sophistication of Company Operations and Strategy

10.04	Capacity for innovation	48
10.08	Degree of customer orientation	48

Quality of the National Business Environment

3.11	Quality of math and science education	23
9.09	Local availability of process machinery	30
9.08	Local availability of components and parts	37

Other Indicators

2.22	Exports, 2001	20
2.23	Imports, 2001	10
2.25	Corporate income tax rate, 2002	8
6.06	Competence of public officials	35
8.09	Number of days to start a business	16
8.10	Total cost of starting a business	6
10.18	Hiring and firing practices	35
10.19	Flexibility of wage determination	17
10.21	Pay and productivity	35

NOTABLE COMPETITIVE DISADVANTAGES

Criteria	Rank

Growth Competitiveness

Macroeconomic Environment

2.17	National savings rate, 2001	71
2.01	Recession expectations	67
2.05	Access to credit	67
2.21	Real exchange rate, 2001	65
2.16	Government expenditure, 2001	61
2.19	Inflation, 2001	59
2.28	Interest rate spread, 2001	59

Technology

3.02	Firm-level innovation	78
3.05	Prevalence of foreign technology licensing	74
3.01	Technological sophistication	70
3.09	University/industry research collaboration	69
4.05	Government success in ICT promotion	68
3.04	FDI and technology transfer	67
3.07	Company spending on research and development	66
4.02	Internet access in schools	64
4.04	Government prioritization of ICT	64
4.03	Quality of competition in the ISP sector	63
4.06	Laws relating to ICT	55
3.15	Utility patents, 2001	51
4.11	Personal computers, 2001	51

Public Institutions

6.15	Organized crime	74
6.03	Property rights	69
6.01	Judicial independence	62
6.09	Favoritism in decisions of government officials	58

Microeconomic Competitiveness

Sophistication of Company Operations and Strategy

3.05	Prevalence of foreign technology licensing	74
10.07	Extent of marketing	74
10.12	Extent of staff training	74

Quality of the National Business Environment

8.04	Administrative burden for startups	79
2.02	Financial market sophistication	78
2.07	Local equity market access	74

Other Indicators

2.04	Ease of access to loans	75
2.09	Regulatory obstacles to business	62
2.18	Investment rate, 2001	66
2.20	M2 growth, 2001	69
2.24	Average tariff rate, 2002	67
3.03	Firm-level technology absorption	72
3.13	Brain drain	76
4.01	Availability of mobile or cellular telephones	70
6.08	Transparency of government policy-making	75
6.12	Efficiency of the tax system	70
6.16	Informal sector	67

Canada

Key Economic Indicators

Total population (in millions), 2001 ....31.1
Population rank 26
GDP per capita (PPP), 2001 ....$28,611
GDP per capita rank...6
Real growth in GDP per capita, 2000 to 2001 ....0.5
Growth rank 49
Unemployment rate, 2001....................................7.21
Unemployment rank 32
Government surplus/deficit, 2001 ....2.30
Government surplus/deficit rank 5
National savings rate, 2001 ....21.98
National savings rank..39
Investment rate, 2001 ....19.82
Investment rank..50
Inflation, 2001 ....2.50
Inflation rank 26
Exports of goods (as a percentage of GDP),
    2001 ....37.1
Exports rank..24
Imports of goods (as a percentage of GDP),
    2001 ....32.6
Imports rank..39
Internet users (per 10,000 inhabitants),
    2001 ....4,352.73
Internet users rank 10

Competitiveness Rankings

Growth Competitiveness Rank	**8**

Technology Index Rank 8
  Innovation Subindex Rank 8
  ICT Subindex Rank 11
Public Institutions Index Rank..............................9
  Contracts and Law Subindex Rank 14
  Corruption Subindex Rank.....................................7
Macroeconomic Environment Index Rank 12
  Macroeconomic Stability Subindex Rank 13
  Country Credit Rating Rank.................................10
  Government Expenditure Rank 52

Microeconomic Competitiveness Rank	**10**

Company Operations and Strategy Rank 13
Quality of the National Business Environment Rank 7

Trade Performance of Leading Export Sectors

Sector	Share in national exports	Value of exports (US$ millions)	Value of net exports (US$ millions)	Share in world market	TPI current index	TPI change index
Transport equipment	26.0%	66,265	19,549	9.51%	13	22
Minerals	14.4%	36,726	22,142	5.26%	9	72
Wood products	12.5%	31,831	25,203	17.23%	10	45
Nonelectronic machinery	7.6%	19,331	−15,258	3.33%	32	52
Basic manufactures	7.1%	18,227	−972	4.21%	38	59

Source: International Trade Centre UNCTAD/WTO

Real GDP (annual percent change)

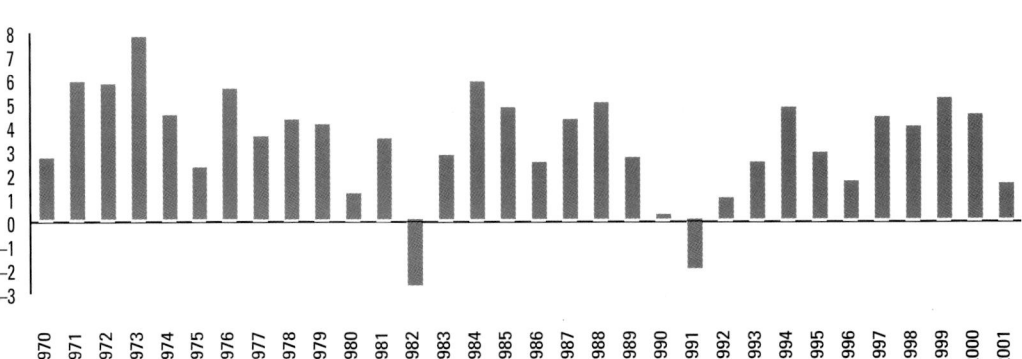

Source: IMF *World Economic Outlook Database*, April 2002

National competitiveness balance sheet

NOTABLE COMPETITIVE ADVANTAGES

Criteria	Rank

Growth Competitiveness

Macroeconomic Environment

2.01	Recession expectations	3
2.15	Government surplus/deficit, 2001	5
2.28	Interest rate spread, 2001	6

Technology

4.03	Quality of competition in the ISP sector	3
4.02	Internet access in schools	5
4.10	Telephone lines, 2001	7
3.02	Firm-level innovation	8
4.06	Laws relating to ICT	8
4.09	Internet hosts, 2001	8
3.09	University/industry research collaboration	12
4.11	Personal computers, 2001	12
4.05	Government success in ICT promotion	11
3.18	Tertiary enrollment	10
4.08	Internet users, 2001	10
3.15	Utility patents, 2001	9

Public Institutions

6.01	Judicial independence	6
7.02	Irregular payments in public utilities	6
7.03	Irregular payments in tax collection	8
6.03	Property rights	14
7.01	Irregular payments in exports & imports	9

Microeconomic Competitiveness

Sophistication of Company Operations and Strategy

10.08	Degree of customer orientation	2
10.10	Extent of regional sales	3
10.14	Extent of incentive compensation	4

Quality of the National Business Environment

10.16	Quality of management schools	3
3.12	Availability of scientists and engineers	6
6.01	Judicial independence	6

Other Indicators

2.03	Soundness of banks	4
2.27	Value added tax rate, 2002	8
2.29	FDI, 2001	10
2.32	Bank liquid reserves	7
3.08	Subsidies and tax credits for firm-level research and development	4
3.17	Secondary enrollment	8
5.09	Disparity in healthcare quality	7
6.06	Competence of public officials	6
6.08	Transparency of government policy-making	10
6.11	Effectiveness of law-making bodies	8
6.17	Strength of auditing and accounting standards	7
6.19	Pervasiveness of money laundering through banks	9
8.11	Cost of starting a business relative to GNP per capita	3
10.05	Ethical behavior of firms	4
10.21	Pay and productivity	9
11.14	Prevalence of environmental management systems	7

NOTABLE COMPETITIVE DISADVANTAGES

Criteria	Rank

Growth Competitiveness

Macroeconomic Environment

2.16	Government expenditure, 2001	52
2.05	Access to credit	45
2.17	National savings rate, 2001	39
2.21	Real exchange rate, 2001	34
2.19	Inflation, 2001	26

Technology

4.07	Cellular telephones, 2001	34
4.04	Government prioritization of ICT	20
3.07	Company spending on research and development	17
3.01	Technological sophistication	15

Public Institutions

6.15	Organized crime	23
6.09	Favoritism in decisions of government officials	17

Microeconomic Competitiveness

Sophistication of Company Operations and Strategy

10.11	Breadth of international markets	35
10.01	Nature of competitive advantage	27
10.02	Value chain presence	26

Quality of the National Business Environment

2.12	Extent of distortive government subsidies	42
6.10	Extent of bureaucratic red tape	34
8.02	Extent of locally based competitors	20

Other Indicators

2.08	Business costs of terrorism	41
2.09	Regulatory obstacles to business	70
2.18	Investment rate, 2001	50
6.12	Efficiency of the tax system	34
8.07	Number of days to resolve a dispute	63

Chile

Key Economic Indicators

Total population (in millions), 2001 ....15.5
Population rank 36
GDP per capita (PPP), 2001 ....$9,753
GDP per capita rank...36
Real growth in GDP per capita, 2000 to 2001.........1.5
Growth rank 34
Unemployment rate, 2001 ....9.20
Unemployment rank 47
Government surplus/deficit, 2001 ....–0.10
Government surplus/deficit rank 18
National savings rate, 2001 ....19.30
National savings rank 51
Investment rate, 2001 ....21.40
Investment rank..41
Inflation, 2001 ....3.60
Inflation rank 36
Exports of goods (as a percentage of GDP),
    2001 ....26.2
Exports rank...42
Imports of goods (as a percentage of GDP),
    2001 ....25.9
Imports rank..58
Internet users (per 10,000 inhabitants),
    2001 ....2,001.99
Internet users rank 29

Competitiveness Rankings

Growth Competitiveness Rank	20

Technology Index Rank **33**
    Innovation Subindex Rank 37
    ICT Subindex Rank 33
    Technology Transfer Subindex Rank
        (out of 56 non-core innovators) 24

Public Institutions Index Rank..........................**19**
    Contracts and Law Subindex Rank 24
    Corruption Subindex Rank...............................10

Macroeconomic Environment Index Rank **13**
    Macroeconomic Stability Subindex Rank 33
    Country Credit Rating Rank.................................28
    Government Expenditure Rank 21

Microeconomic Competitiveness Rank	31

Company Operations and Strategy Rank **35**

Quality of the National Business Environment Rank ...**31**

Trade Performance of Leading Export Sectors

Sector	Share in national exports	Value of exports (US$ millions)	Value of net exports (US$ millions)	Share in world market	TPI current index	TPI change index
Basic manufactures	31.1%	5,402	4,252	1.25%	22	83
Minerals	17.5%	3,044	219	0.44%	34	67
Fresh food	17.1%	2,976	2,302	1.25%	16	26
Wood products	13.1%	2,280	1,772	1.23%	11	22
Processed food	9.6%	1,667	991	0.77%	18	102

Source: International Trade Centre UNCTAD/WTO

Real GDP (annual percent change)

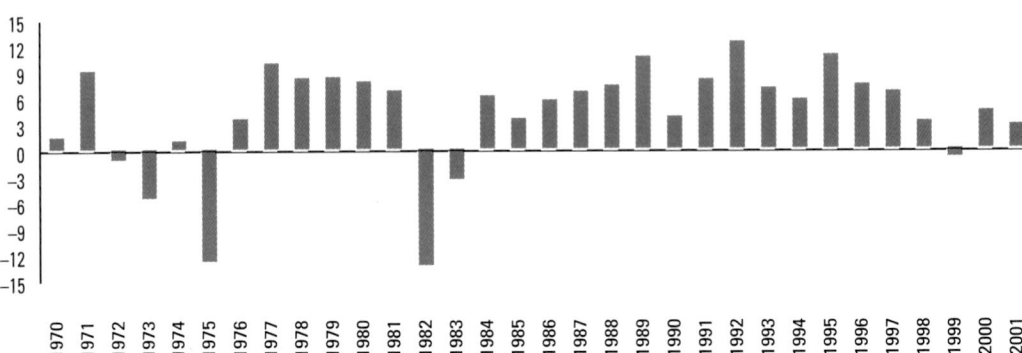

Source: IMF *World Economic Outlook Database,* April 2002

National competitiveness balance sheet

NOTABLE COMPETITIVE ADVANTAGES

Criteria	Rank

Growth Competitiveness

Macroeconomic Environment

2.15	Government surplus/deficit, 2001	18
2.05	Access to credit	19
2.16	Government expenditure, 2001	21

Technology

4.03	Quality of competition in the ISP sector	9
3.04	FDI and technology transfer	26
3.01	Technological sophistication	27
4.08	Internet users, 2001	29

Public Institutions

7.01	Irregular payments in exports & imports	7
7.02	Irregular payments in public utilities	12
7.03	Irregular payments in tax collection	15
6.09	Favoritism in decisions of government officials	18
6.15	Organized crime	20
6.03	Property rights	26

Microeconomic Competitiveness

Sophistication of Company Operations and Strategy

10.11	Breadth of international markets	17
10.07	Extent of marketing	25
10.15	Reliance on professional management	27

Quality of the National Business Environment

2.10	Hidden trade barriers	4
8.01	Intensity of local competition	5
10.17	Efficacy of corporate boards	11

Other Indicators

2.03	Soundness of banks	13
2.25	Corporate income tax rate, 2002	2
3.13	Brain drain	8
5.14	Electric power	9
6.08	Transparency of government policy-making	21
6.12	Efficiency of the tax system	16
6.16	Informal sector	21
6.19	Pervasiveness of money laundering through banks	13
7.05	Irregular payments in loan applications	15
7.12	Public trust of politicians	16
10.19	Flexibility of wage determination	12
10.21	Pay and productivity	21
11.06	Subsidies for energy or materials	11

NOTABLE COMPETITIVE DISADVANTAGES

Criteria	Rank

Growth Competitiveness

Macroeconomic Environment

2.17	National savings rate, 2001	51
2.28	Interest rate spread, 2001	44
2.21	Real exchange rate, 2001	42
2.01	Recession expectations	41
2.19	Inflation, 2001	36

Technology

3.05	Prevalence of foreign technology licensing	49
3.09	University/industry research collaboration	47
3.07	Company spending on research and development	44
4.10	Telephone lines, 2001	43
3.15	Utility patents, 2001	40
4.09	Internet hosts, 2001	40
4.11	Personal computers, 2001	39
3.18	Tertiary enrollment	37
4.06	Laws relating to ICT	35
3.02	Firm-level innovation	33
4.05	Government success in ICT promotion	33
4.07	Cellular telephones, 2001	33
4.02	Internet access in schools	30
4.04	Government prioritization of ICT	30

Public Institutions

6.01	Judicial independence	43

Microeconomic Competitiveness

Sophistication of Company Operations and Strategy

10.02	Value chain presence	63
10.03	Extent of branding	60
10.04	Capacity for innovation	52

Quality of the National Business Environment

5.02	Railroad infrastructure development	63
5.08	Quality of public schools	61
3.11	Quality of math and science education	57

Other Indicators

1.08	Unemployment rate, 2001	47
1.09	Employment to population ratio, 2001	57
2.23	Imports, 2001	58
2.26	Individual income tax rate, 2002	61
2.31	Liquid liabilities, 2001	52
5.09	Disparity in healthcare quality	58
6.05	Freedom of the press	54
6.06	Competence of public officials	55
6.22	Military expenditure relative to GNI	60
7.08	Frequency of payments or bribes	61
10.18	Hiring and firing practices	55
11.10	Flexibility of environmental regulations	63

China

Key Economic Indicators

Total population (in millions), 2001 ....1,271.2
Population rank 1
GDP per capita (PPP), 2001 ....$4,329
GDP per capita rank...62
Real growth in GDP per capita, 2000 to 2001.........6.8
Growth rank 3
Unemployment rate, 2001......................................3.60
Unemployment rank 9
Government surplus/deficit, 2001 ....–2.50
Government surplus/deficit rank 40
National savings rate, 2001 ....38.90
National savings rank...2
Investment rate, 2001 ....37.40
Investment rank..1
Inflation, 2001 ....0.70
Inflation rank 7
Exports of goods (as a percentage of GDP),
    2001 ....23.0
Exports rank...49
Imports of goods (as a percentage of GDP),
    2001 ....21.0
Imports rank...66
Internet users (per 10,000 inhabitants), 2001 ...260.00
Internet users rank 59

Competitiveness Rankings

Growth Competitiveness Rank	**33**

Technology Index Rank **63**
    Innovation Subindex Rank 61
    ICT Subindex Rank 62
    Technology Transfer Subindex Rank
        (out of 56 non-core innovators) 29
Public Institutions Index Rank..**38**
    Contracts and Law Subindex Rank 44
    Corruption Subindex Rank....................................39
Macroeconomic Environment Index Rank **8**
    Macroeconomic Stability Subindex Rank 5
    Country Credit Rating Rank.................................32
    Government Expenditure Rank 16

Microeconomic Competitiveness Rank	**38**

Company Operations and Strategy Rank **38**
Quality of the National Business Environment Rank ...**38**

Trade Performance of Leading Export Sectors

Sector	Share in national exports	Value of exports (US$ millions)	Value of net exports (US$ millions)	Share in world market	TPI current index	TPI change index
IT and consumer electronics	15.5%	38,144	14,873	6.03%	10	51
Miscellaneous manufacturing	14.7%	36,168	25,035	7.76%	10	73
Clothing	14.6%	36,061	34,872	19.31%	2	14
Electronic components	9.7%	24,017	–11,615	4.02%	23	23
Basic manufactures	8.3%	20,493	195	4.73%	16	34

Source: International Trade Centre UNCTAD/WTO

Real GDP (annual percent change)

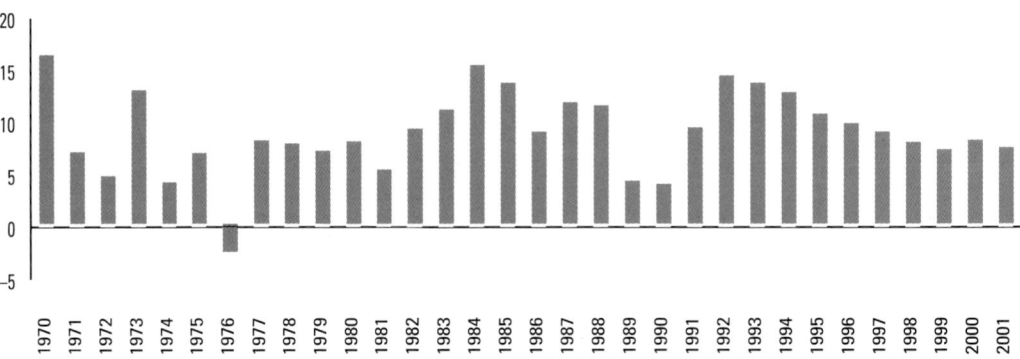

Source: IMF *World Economic Outlook Database,* April 2002

National competitiveness balance sheet

NOTABLE COMPETITIVE ADVANTAGES	
Criteria	Rank

Growth Competitiveness

Macroeconomic Environment

2.17	National savings rate, 2001	2
2.01	Recession expectations	4
2.19	Inflation, 2001	7
2.16	Government expenditure, 2001	16
2.28	Interest rate spread, 2001	16
2.05	Access to credit	30

Technology

4.05	Government success in ICT promotion	13
3.09	University/industry research collaboration	16
4.04	Government prioritization of ICT	18

Public Institutions

6.09	Favoritism in decisions of government officials	29

NOTABLE COMPETITIVE DISADVANTAGES	
Criteria	Rank

Growth Competitiveness

Macroeconomic Environment

2.21	Real exchange rate, 2001	62
2.15	Government surplus/deficit, 2001	40

Technology

3.18	Tertiary enrollment	74
4.09	Internet hosts, 2001	74
4.11	Personal computers, 2001	65
3.15	Utility patents, 2001	62
4.07	Cellular telephones, 2001	60
4.08	Internet users, 2001	59
4.02	Internet access in schools	58
4.03	Quality of competition in the ISP sector	57
3.05	Prevalence of foreign technology licensing	54
4.10	Telephone lines, 2001	53
4.06	Laws relating to ICT	50
3.04	FDI and technology transfer	44
3.01	Technological sophistication	39
3.02	Firm-level innovation	38
3.07	Company spending on research and development	34

Public Institutions

6.03	Property rights	54
6.15	Organized crime	43
7.02	Irregular payments in public utilities	43
6.01	Judicial independence	39
7.01	Irregular payments in exports & imports	38
7.03	Irregular payments in tax collection	36

405

Microeconomic Competitiveness	

Sophistication of Company Operations and Strategy

10.04	Capacity for innovation	22
10.15	Reliance on professional management	29
10.08	Degree of customer orientation	37

Quality of the National Business Environment

9.09	Local availability of process machinery	5
3.10	Government procurement of advanced technology products	10
8.02	Extent of locally based competitors	13

Microeconomic Competitiveness	

Sophistication of Company Operations and Strategy

10.07	Extent of marketing	69
3.05	Prevalence of foreign technology licensing	54
10.10	Extent of regional sales	50

Quality of the National Business Environment

2.07	Local equity market access	67
3.12	Availability of scientists and engineers	64
5.04	Air transport infrastructure quality	65

Other Indicators

1.04	Real growth in GDP per capita, 2000 to 2001	3
1.08	Unemployment rate, 2001	9
1.09	Employment to population ratio, 2001	1
2.18	Investment rate, 2001	1
2.29	FDI, 2001	6
2.30	Domestic credit, 2001	6
2.31	Liquid liabilities, 2001	3
3.08	Subsidies and tax credits for firm-level research and development	21
6.06	Competence of public officials	3
6.07	Burden of regulation	18
6.11	Effectiveness of law-making bodies	10
6.12	Efficiency of the tax system	18
7.08	Frequency of payments or bribes	6
7.12	Public trust of politicians	12
7.15	Misuse of legal political donations	17
10.21	Pay and productivity	7

Other Indicators

2.03	Soundness of banks	65
2.09	Regulatory obstacles to business	77
2.23	Imports, 2001	66
2.24	Average tariff rate, 2002	75
2.26	Individual income tax rate, 2002	61
4.01	Availability of mobile or cellular telephones	73
6.05	Freedom of the press	75
6.17	Strength of auditing and accounting standards	71
6.18	Pervasiveness of insider trading	70
6.21	Military expenditure relative to central government expenditure	71

Colombia

Key Economic Indicators

Total population (in millions), 2001 ....43.0
Population rank 22
GDP per capita (PPP), 2001 ....$6,202
GDP per capita rank...54
Real growth in GDP per capita, 2000 to 2001 ....–0.2
Growth rank 61
Unemployment rate, 2001....................................16.67
Unemployment rank 68
Government surplus/deficit, 2001 ....–5.20
Government surplus/deficit rank 62
National savings rate, 2001 ....13.80
National savings rank..72
Investment rate, 2001 ....13.30
Investment rank..78
Inflation, 2001 ....8.00
Inflation rank 61
Exports of goods (as a percentage of GDP),
   2001 ....15.0
Exports rank...65
Imports of goods (as a percentage of GDP),
   2001 ....15.8
Imports rank...74
Internet users (per 10,000 inhabitants), 2001 ...269.61
Internet users rank 58

Competitiveness Rankings

Growth Competitiveness Rank	**56**

Technology Index Rank **58**
Innovation Subindex Rank.....................................55
ICT Subindex Rank 56
Technology Transfer Subindex Rank
(out of 56 non-core innovators) 40
Public Institutions Index Rank.........................**54**
Contracts and Law Subindex Rank 64
Corruption Subindex Rank....................................41
Macroeconomic Environment Index Rank **51**
Macroeconomic Stability Subindex Rank 66
Country Credit Rating Rank.................................55
Government Expenditure Rank 18

Microeconomic Competitiveness Rank	**56**

Company Operations and Strategy Rank 51
Quality of the National Business Environment Rank ...57

Trade Performance of Leading Export Sectors

Sector	Share in national exports	Value of exports (US$ millions)	Value of net exports (US$ millions)	Share in world market	TPI current index	TPI change index
Minerals	41.7%	5,229	5,063	0.75%	39	100
Fresh food	20.1%	2,519	1,613	1.06%	37	91
Chemicals	11.1%	1,395	–1,568	0.23%	60	67
Basic manufactures	5.6%	706	–272	0.16%	58	4
Processed food	4.8%	606	–103	0.28%	48	11

Source: International Trade Centre UNCTAD/WTO

Real GDP (annual percent change)

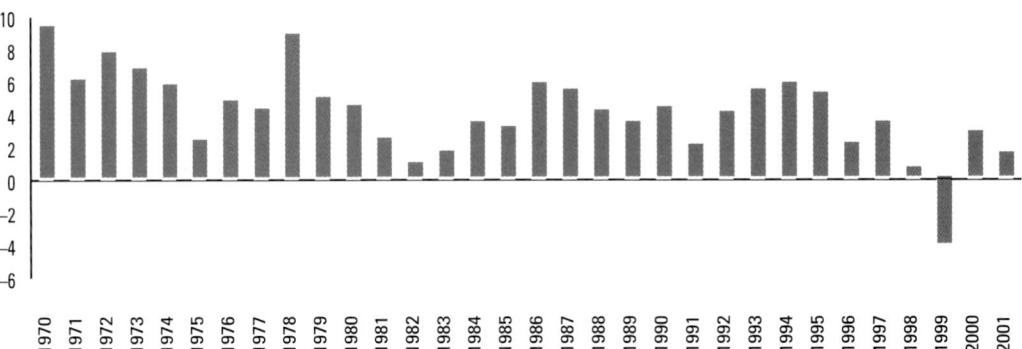

Source: IMF *World Economic Outlook Database,* April 2002

National competitiveness balance sheet

NOTABLE COMPETITIVE ADVANTAGES	
Criteria	Rank

Growth Competitiveness

Macroeconomic Environment

2.16	Government expenditure, 2001	18
2.05	Access to credit	24

Technology

4.06	Laws relating to ICT	28
4.03	Quality of competition in the ISP sector	38
4.05	Government success in ICT promotion	41

Public Institutions

7.01	Irregular payments in exports & imports	35
7.03	Irregular payments in tax collection	41
7.02	Irregular payments in public utilities	44
6.03	Property rights	48

Microeconomic Competitiveness

Sophistication of Company Operations and Strategy

10.08	Degree of customer orientation	35
10.01	Nature of competitive advantage	42
10.02	Value chain presence	46

Quality of the National Business Environment

4.06	Laws relating to ICT	28
8.02	Extent of locally based competitors	28
6.10	Extent of bureaucratic red tape	29

Other Indicators

2.09	Regulatory obstacles to business	31
2.16	Government expenditure, 2001	18
2.26	Individual income tax rate, 2002	34
2.32	Bank liquid reserves	35
8.10	Total cost of starting a business	24

NOTABLE COMPETITIVE DISADVANTAGES	
Criteria	Rank

Growth Competitiveness

Macroeconomic Environment

2.17	National savings rate, 2001	72
2.01	Recession expectations	65
2.15	Government surplus/deficit, 2001	62
2.19	Inflation, 2001	61
2.21	Real exchange rate, 2001	60
2.28	Interest rate spread, 2001	56

Technology

3.02	Firm-level innovation	68
4.07	Cellular telephones, 2001	63
3.05	Prevalence of foreign technology licensing	62
3.01	Technological sophistication	60
4.02	Internet access in schools	59
4.08	Internet users, 2001	58
3.04	FDI and technology transfer	57
3.15	Utility patents, 2001	55
4.04	Government prioritization of ICT	54
4.09	Internet hosts, 2001	54
3.09	University/industry research collaboration	52
3.18	Tertiary enrollment	52
4.11	Personal computers, 2001	52
3.07	Company spending on research and development	51
4.10	Telephone lines, 2001	51

Public Institutions

6.15	Organized crime	80
6.09	Favoritism in decisions of government officials	61
6.01	Judicial independence	52

Microeconomic Competitiveness

Sophistication of Company Operations and Strategy

10.14	Extent of incentive compensation	70
3.05	Prevalence of foreign technology licensing	62
10.06	Production process sophistication	62

Quality of the National Business Environment

9.05	Decentralization of corporate activity	73
7.11	Business costs of corruption	69
5.01	Overall infrastructure quality	65

Other Indicators

2.03	Soundness of banks	64
2.08	Business costs of terrorism	79
2.18	Investment rate	78
2.22	Exports, 2001	65
2.23	Imports, 2001	74
3.03	Firm-level technology absorption	68
3.13	Brain drain	63
5.14	Electric power	71
6.06	Competence of public officials	66
6.11	Effectiveness of law-making bodies	67
6.14	Business costs of crime and violence	73
6.20	Pervasiveness of money laundering through non-bank channels	80
6.21	Military expenditure relative to central government expenditure	65
7.10	Diversion of public funds	69
7.14	Policy consequences of legal political donations	71
10.18	Hiring and firing practices	64
10.21	Pay and productivity	74

Costa Rica

Key Economic Indicators

Total population (in millions), 2001 ....3.9
Population rank 66
GDP per capita (PPP), 2001 ....$8,490
GDP per capita rank...42
Real growth in GDP per capita, 2000 to 2001 ....–1.8
Growth rank 71
Unemployment rate, 2001.......................................6.10
Unemployment rank 27
Government surplus/deficit, 2001 ....–2.72
Government surplus/deficit rank 45
National savings rate, 2001 ....13.50
National savings rank 74
Investment rate, 2001 ....18.01
Investment rank...63
Inflation, 2001 ....11.00
Inflation rank 69
Exports of goods (as a percentage of GDP),
    2001 ....30.0
Exports rank...37
Imports of goods (as a percentage of GDP),
    2001 ....39.3
Imports rank...28
Internet users (per 10,000 inhabitants), 2001 ...933.63
Internet users rank 39

Competitiveness Rankings

Growth Competitiveness Rank	43

Technology Index Rank	**37**
Innovation Subindex Rank	36
ICT Subindex Rank	45
Technology Transfer Subindex Rank (out of 56 non-core innovators)	7
Public Institutions Index Rank	**46**
Contracts and Law Subindex Rank	43
Corruption Subindex Rank	59
Macroeconomic Environment Index Rank	**43**
Macroeconomic Stability Subindex Rank	69
Country Credit Rating Rank	50
Government Expenditure Rank	7

Microeconomic Competitiveness Rank	39

Company Operations and Strategy Rank **32**
Quality of the National Business Environment Rank ...**47**

Trade Performance of Leading Export Sectors

Sector	Share in national exports	Value of exports (US$ millions)	Value of net exports (US$ millions)	Share in world market	TPI current index	TPI change index
IT and consumer electronics	30.1%	1,637	1,350	0.26%	35	21
Fresh food	25.7%	1,399	1,142	0.59%	29	86
Electronic components	7.6%	413	–679	0.07%	54	30
Processed food	7.5%	409	187	0.19%	25	72
Clothing	7.1%	385	79	0.21%	68	16

Source: International Trade Centre UNCTAD/WTO

Real GDP (annual percent change)

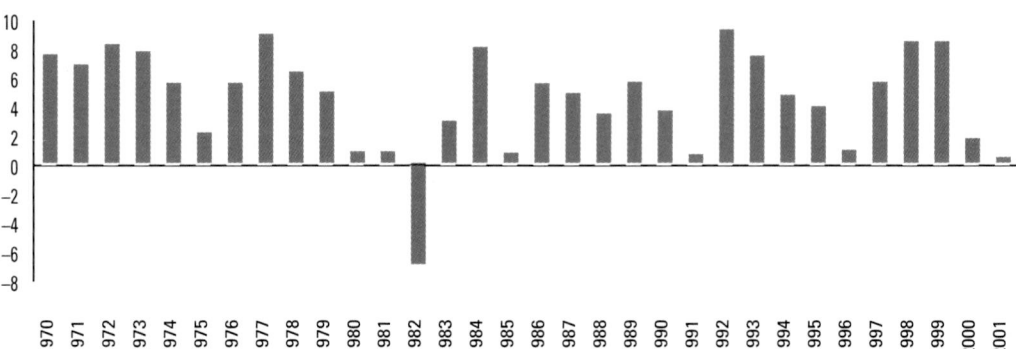

Source: IMF *World Economic Outlook Database,* April 2002

National competitiveness balance sheet

NOTABLE COMPETITIVE ADVANTAGES	
Criteria	Rank

Growth Competitiveness

Macroeconomic Environment

2.16	Government expenditure, 2001	7
2.05	Access to credit	21

Technology

3.04	FDI and technology transfer	3
3.07	Company spending on research and development	22
3.01	Technological sophistication	24
4.11	Personal computers, 2001	27
3.09	University/industry research collaboration	36
4.05	Government success in ICT promotion	36
4.08	Internet users, 2001	39
3.18	Tertiary enrollment	40
3.15	Utility patents, 2001	41

Public Institutions

6.01	Judicial independence	34
6.15	Organized crime	41

Microeconomic Competitiveness

Sophistication of Company Operations and Strategy

3.07	Company spending on research and development	22
10.01	Nature of competitive advantage	23
10.13	Willingness to delegate authority	25

Quality of the National Business Environment

10.20	Cooperation in labor-employer relations	10
3.06	Quality of scientific research institutions	20
10.16	Quality of management schools	27

Other Indicators

1.08	Unemployment rate, 2001	27
2.08	Business costs of terrorism	17
2.09	Regulatory obstacles to business	21
2.26	Individual income tax rate, 2002	6
3.03	Firm-level technology absorption	28
3.13	Brain drain	25
6.22	Military expenditure relative to GNI	3
10.18	Hiring and firing practices	21
11.12	Effects of compliance on business (with environmental regulations)	4

NOTABLE COMPETITIVE DISADVANTAGES	
Criteria	Rank

Growth Competitiveness

Macroeconomic Environment

2.17	National savings rate, 2001	74
2.01	Recession expectations	70
2.28	Interest rate spread, 2001	70
2.19	Inflation, 2001	69
2.21	Real exchange rate, 2001	67
2.15	Government surplus/deficit, 2001	45

Technology

4.03	Quality of competition in the ISP sector	79
4.07	Cellular telephones, 2001	64
4.04	Government prioritization of ICT	55
4.09	Internet hosts, 2001	51
3.02	Firm-level innovation	47
3.05	Prevalence of foreign technology licensing	44
4.02	Internet access in schools	44
4.06	Laws relating to ICT	44
4.10	Telephone lines, 2001	44

Public Institutions

7.02	Irregular payments in public utilities	63
7.01	Irregular payments in exports & imports	58
6.09	Favoritism in decisions of government officials	51
7.03	Irregular payments in tax collection	49
6.03	Property rights	46

Microeconomic Competitiveness

Sophistication of Company Operations and Strategy

10.11	Breadth of international markets	53
10.15	Reliance on professional management	49
3.05	Prevalence of foreign technology licensing	44

Quality of the National Business Environment

5.01	Overall infrastructure quality	70
2.06	Venture capital availability	66
8.04	Administrative burden for startups	60

Other Indicators

2.18	Investment rate, 2001	63
2.31	Liquid liabilities, 2001	64
3.17	Secondary enrollment	62
4.01	Availability of mobile or cellular telephones	80
5.07	Postal efficiency	67
6.06	Competence of public officials	64
6.07	Burden of regulation	62
6.11	Effectiveness of law-making bodies	70
7.14	Policy consequences of legal political donations	67
8.07	Number of days to resolve a dispute	59
10.19	Flexibility of wage determination	62

409

Croatia

Key Economic Indicators

Total population (in millions), 2001 ....4.4
Population rank 64
GDP per capita (PPP), 2001 ....$8,414
GDP per capita rank...44
Real growth in GDP per capita, 2000 to 2001........4.2
Growth rank 14
Unemployment rate, 2001.....................................22.14
Unemployment rank 74
Government surplus/deficit, 2001 ....–5.46
Government surplus/deficit rank 65
National savings rate, 2001 ....20.72
National savings rank 46
Investment rate, 2001 ....21.91
Investment rank..39
Inflation, 2001 ....4.90
Inflation rank 47
Exports of goods (as a percentage of GDP),
     2001 ....22.8
Exports rank..50
Imports of goods (as a percentage of GDP),
     2001 ....44.3
Imports rank..24
Internet users (per 10,000 inhabitants), 2001 ...558.91
Internet users rank 46

Competitiveness Rankings

Growth Competitiveness Rank	**58**

Technology Index Rank **43**
   Innovation Subindex Rank....................................50
   ICT Subindex Rank 37
   Technology Transfer Subindex Rank
     (out of 56 non-core innovators) 35
Public Institutions Index Rank..............................**57**
   Contracts and Law Subindex Rank 60
   Corruption Subindex Rank...................................45
Macroeconomic Environment Index Rank **70**
   Macroeconomic Stability Subindex Rank 41
   Country Credit Rating Rank.................................49
   Government Expenditure Rank 77

Microeconomic Competitiveness Rank	**52**

Company Operations and Strategy Rank **53**
Quality of the National Business Environment Rank ...**54**

Trade Performance of Leading Export Sectors

Sector	Share in national exports	Value of exports (US$ millions)	Value of net exports (US$ millions)	Share in world market	TPI current index	TPI change index
Transport equipment	16.2%	688	–510	0.10%	49	7
Chemicals	13.1%	556	–509	0.09%	48	70
Clothing	11.0%	468	194	0.25%	43	85
Basic manufactures	9.6%	408	–324	0.09%	48	38
Minerals	8.5%	362	–802	0.05%	58	23

Source: International Trade Centre UNCTAD/WTO

Real GDP (annual percent change)

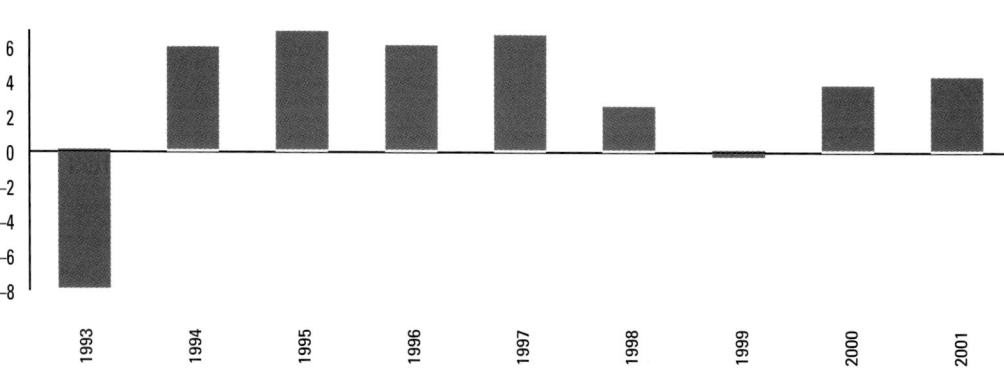

Source: IMF *World Economic Outlook Database,* April 2002

National competitiveness balance sheet

NOTABLE COMPETITIVE ADVANTAGES	
Criteria	Rank

Growth Competitiveness

Macroeconomic Environment

2.16	Government expenditure, 2001	8
2.05	Access to credit	11
2.15	Government surplus/deficit, 2001	13
2.17	National savings rate, 2001	47

Technology

3.04	FDI and technology transfer	11
3.07	Company spending on research and development	31
3.09	University/industry research collaboration	32
4.03	Quality of competition in the ISP sector	36
3.05	Prevalence of foreign technology licensing	39
3.01	Technological sophistication	40
3.02	Firm-level innovation	41
4.06	Laws relating to ICT	42
4.05	Government success in ICT promotion	43
4.09	Internet hosts, 2001	43
4.02	Internet access in schools	49

Microeconomic Competitiveness

Sophistication of Company Operations and Strategy

10.14	Extent of incentive compensation	17
10.08	Degree of customer orientation	18
10.07	Extent of marketing	21

Quality of the National Business Environment

2.04	Ease of access to loans	3
8.01	Intensity of local competition	23
2.06	Venture capital availability	28

Other Indicators

2.25	Corporate income tax rate, 2002	8
2.26	Individual income tax rate, 2002	6
3.03	Firm-level technology absorption	23
6.07	Burden of regulation	25
6.22	Military expenditure relative to GNI	5
11.13	Political context of environmental gains	22

NOTABLE COMPETITIVE DISADVANTAGES	
Criteria	Rank

Growth Competitiveness

Macroeconomic Environment

2.21	Real exchange rate, 2001	72
2.19	Inflation, 2001	65
2.28	Interest rate spread, 2001	60
2.01	Recession expectations	55

Technology

3.15	Utility patents, 2001	56
3.18	Tertiary enrollment	51
4.04	Government prioritization of ICT	60
4.07	Cellular telephones, 2001	55
4.08	Internet users, 2001	63
4.10	Telephone lines, 2001	58

Public Institutions

6.09	Favoritism in decisions of government officials	64
6.03	Property rights	63
7.03	Irregular payments in tax collection	61
6.01	Judicial independence	55
7.01	Irregular payments in exports & imports	54
6.15	Organized crime	51
7.02	Irregular payments in public utilities	51

Microeconomic Competitiveness

Sophistication of Company Operations and Strategy

10.15	Reliance on professional management	69
10.10	Extent of regional sales	48
10.06	Production process sophistication	42

Quality of the National Business Environment

5.05	Quality of electricity supply	77
2.10	Hidden trade barriers	70
3.12	Availability of scientists and engineers	70

Other Indicators

1.08	Unemployment rate, 2001	63
2.09	Regulatory obstacles to business	66
2.22	Exports, 2001	80
5.07	Postal efficiency	73
7.13	Prevalence of illegal political donations	64
7.15	Misuse of legal political donations	70
8.08	Number of procedures to start a business	72
11.02	Water pollution regulations	67
11.06	Subsidies for energy or materials	72

Ecuador

Key Economic Indicators

Total population (in millions), 2001 ....12.1
Population rank 38
GDP per capita (PPP), 2001 ....$3,295
GDP per capita rank..70
Real growth in GDP per capita, 2000 to 2001.........3.3
Growth rank 19
Unemployment rate, 2001.....................................8.10
Unemployment rank 38
Government surplus/deficit, 2001 ....1.22
Government surplus/deficit rank 11
National savings rate, 2001 ....20.84
National savings rank..44
Investment rate, 2001 ....22.84
Investment rank...33
Inflation, 2001 ....37.68
Inflation rank 78
Exports of goods (as a percentage of GDP),
    2001 ....26.3
Exports rank..41
Imports of goods (as a percentage of GDP),
    2001 ....29.7
Imports rank...44
Internet users (per 10,000 inhabitants), 2001 ...254.43
Internet users rank 61

Competitiveness Rankings

Growth Competitiveness Rank	**73**

Technology Index Rank **70**
   Innovation Subindex Rank 60
   ICT Subindex Rank 66
   Technology Transfer Subindex Rank
     (out of 56 non-core innovators) 47

Public Institutions Index Rank...........................**75**
   Contracts and Law Subindex Rank 78
   Corruption Subindex Rank..................................69

Macroeconomic Environment Index Rank **69**
   Macroeconomic Stability Subindex Rank 63
   Country Credit Rating Rank.................................76
   Government Expenditure Rank 30

Microeconomic Competitiveness Rank	**77**

Company Operations and Strategy Rank **74**
Quality of the National Business Environment Rank ...**77**

Trade Performance of Leading Export Sectors

Sector	Share in national exports	Value of exports (US$ millions)	Value of net exports (US$ millions)	Share in world market	TPI current index	TPI change index
Minerals	48.4%	2,216	1,998	0.32%	66	89
Fresh food	33.3%	1,527	1,340	0.64%	31	117
Processed food	8.7%	399	214	0.19%	40	14
Chemicals	2.2%	102	−828	0.02%	90	24
Wood products	1.7%	78	−43	0.04%	66	95

Source: International Trade Centre UNCTAD/WTO

Real GDP (annual percent change)

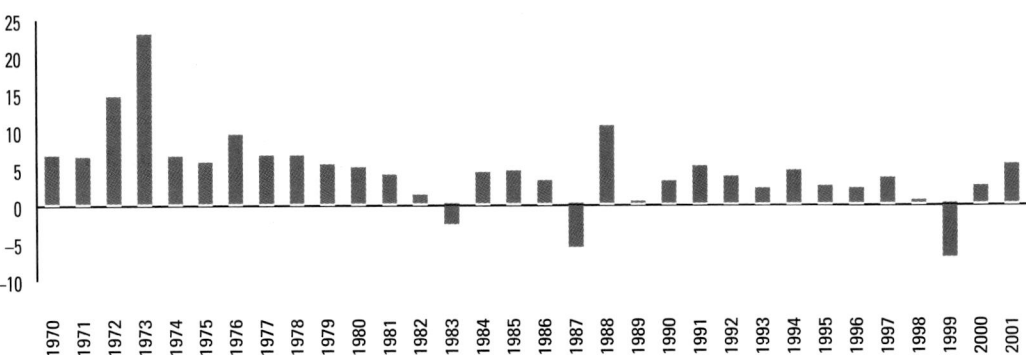

Source: IMF *World Economic Outlook Database,* April 2002

National competitiveness balance sheet

NOTABLE COMPETITIVE ADVANTAGES

Criteria		Rank

Growth Competitiveness

Macroeconomic Environment

2.15	Government surplus/deficit, 2001	11
2.16	Government expenditure, 2001	30
2.01	Recession expectations	38
2.17	National savings rate, 2001	44
2.21	Real exchange rate, 2001	50

Technology

3.02	Firm-level innovation	48
3.15	Utility patents, 2001	54
3.18	Tertiary enrollment	56

Microeconomic Competitiveness

Sophistication of Company Operations and Strategy

10.10	Extent of regional sales	57

Quality of the National Business Environment

6.10	Extent of bureaucratic red tape	46
9.06	State of cluster development	54
9.09	Local availability of process machinery	55

Other Indicators

1.08	Unemployment rate, 2001	38
2.09	Regulatory obstacles to business	23
2.18	Investment rate, 2001	33
2.25	Corporate income tax rate, 2002	8
2.26	Individual income tax rate, 2002	6
2.27	Value added tax rate, 2002	20
2.32	Bank liquid reserves	28
11.12	Effects of compliance on business (with environmental regulations)	35

NOTABLE COMPETITIVE DISADVANTAGES

Criteria		Rank

Growth Competitiveness

Macroeconomic Environment

2.19	Inflation, 2001	78
2.05	Access to credit	76
2.28	Interest rate spread, 2001	61

Technology

3.01	Technological sophistication	74
3.07	Company spending on research and development	73
3.05	Prevalence of foreign technology licensing	71
4.02	Internet access in schools	71
4.05	Government success in ICT promotion	71
3.04	FDI and technology transfer	68
3.09	University/industry research collaboration	67
4.04	Government prioritization of ICT	66
4.09	Internet hosts, 2001	66
4.06	Laws relating to ICT	65
4.07	Cellular telephones, 2001	65
4.08	Internet users, 2001	61
4.11	Personal computers, 2001	61
4.03	Quality of competition in the ISP sector	60
4.10	Telephone lines, 2001	60

Public Institutions

6.01	Judicial independence	78
6.09	Favoritism in decisions of government officials	78
6.03	Property rights	73
7.02	Irregular payments in public utilities	73
6.15	Organized crime	68
7.01	Irregular payments in exports & imports	68
7.03	Irregular payments in tax collection	66

Microeconomic Competitiveness

Sophistication of Company Operations and Strategy

10.15	Reliance on professional management	79
10.12	Extent of staff training	77
10.08	Degree of customer orientation	76

Quality of the National Business Environment

2.06	Venture capital availability	80
9.05	Decentralization of corporate activity	80
2.10	Hidden trade barriers	78

Other Indicators

2.03	Soundness of banks	76
3.03	Firm-level technology absorption	74
3.13	Brain drain	75
4.01	Availability of mobile or cellular telephones	72
5.07	Postal efficiency	76
5.09	Disparity in healthcare quality	79
6.06	Competence of public officials	76
6.07	Burden of regulation	77
6.11	Effectiveness of law-making bodies	77
6.14	Business costs of crime and violence	78
7.07	Irregular payments in judicial decisions	74
7.10	Diversion of public funds	77
7.13	Prevalence of illegal political donations	80
7.15	Misuse of legal political donations	80
10.21	Pay and productivity	80
11.04	Chemical waste regulations	78
11.07	Compliance with environmental regulations	78

419

El Salvador

Key Economic Indicators

Total population (in millions), 2001 ....6.4
Population rank 56
GDP per capita (PPP), 2001 ....$4,603
GDP per capita rank...60
Real growth in GDP per capita, 2000 to 2001.........0.1
Growth rank 57
Unemployment rate, 2001.....................................7.50
Unemployment rank 34
Government surplus/deficit, 2001 ....-3.60
Government surplus/deficit rank 52
National savings rate, 2001 ....14.60
National savings rank...70
Investment rate, 2001 ....16.50
Investment rank..72
Inflation, 2001 ....3.80
Inflation rank 38
Exports of goods (as a percentage of GDP),
    2001 ....20.5
Exports rank..59
Imports of goods (as a percentage of GDP),
    2001 ....36.0
Imports rank..33
Internet users (per 10,000 inhabitants), 2001 .....79.67
Internet users rank 72

Competitiveness Rankings

Growth Competitiveness Rank	57

Technology Index Rank **69**
    Innovation Subindex Rank 59
    ICT Subindex Rank 65
    Technology Transfer Subindex Rank
        (out of 56 non-core innovators) 49
Public Institutions Index Rank...**48**
    Contracts and Law Subindex Rank 58
    Corruption Subindex Rank....................................40
Macroeconomic Environment Index Rank **33**
    Macroeconomic Stability Subindex Rank.............54
    Country Credit Rating Rank...................................52
    Government Expenditure Rank 14

Microeconomic Competitiveness Rank	63

Company Operations and Strategy Rank **61**
Quality of the National Business Environment Rank ...**62**

Trade Performance of Leading Export Sectors

Sector	Share in national exports	Value of exports (US$ millions)	Value of net exports (US$ millions)	Share in world market	TPI current index	TPI change index
Fresh food	27.6%	359	91	0.15%	90	156
Processed food	16.7%	217	−171	0.10%	70	5
Chemicals	13.4%	174	−430	0.03%	76	53
Basic manufactures	8.9%	116	−182	0.03%	75	10
Wood products	6.5%	84	−82	0.05%	70	64

Source: International Trade Centre UNCTAD/WTO

Real GDP (annual percent change)

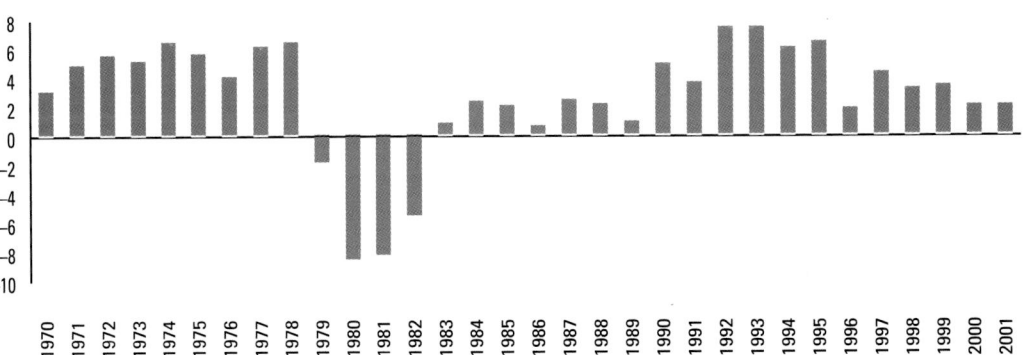

Source: IMF *World Economic Outlook Database,* April 2002

National competitiveness balance sheet

NOTABLE COMPETITIVE ADVANTAGES

Criteria	Rank

Growth Competitiveness

Macroeconomic Environment
2.05	Access to credit	4
2.16	Government expenditure, 2001	14
2.28	Interest rate spread, 2001	25
2.19	Inflation, 2001	38
2.01	Recession expectations	44

Technology
4.03	Quality of competition in the ISP sector	29
3.02	Firm-level innovation	45
3.15	Utility patents, 2001	45

Public Institutions
7.02	Irregular payments in public utilities	32
7.03	Irregular payments in tax collection	38
7.01	Irregular payments in exports & imports	41
6.09	Favoritism in decisions of government officials	45

Microeconomic Competitiveness

Sophistication of Company Operations and Strategy
10.01	Nature of competitive advantage	32
10.13	Willingness to delegate authority	39
10.10	Extent of regional sales	40

Quality of the National Business Environment
6.10	Extent of bureaucratic red tape	14
10.20	Cooperation in labor-employer relations	17
5.04	Air transport infrastructure quality	27

Other Indicators
2.03	Soundness of banks	22
2.26	Individual income tax rate, 2002	6
3.13	Brain drain	43
3.14	Research and development spending	10
6.05	Freedom of the press	32
6.07	Burden of regulation	15
6.12	Efficiency of the tax system	12
7.08	Frequency of payments or bribes	20
10.18	Hiring and firing practices	7
10.19	Flexibility of wage determination	14
10.21	Pay and productivity	16
11.06	Subsidies for energy or materials	13

NOTABLE COMPETITIVE DISADVANTAGES

Criteria	Rank

Growth Competitiveness

Macroeconomic Environment
2.21	Real exchange rate, 2001	78
2.17	National savings rate, 2001	70
2.15	Government surplus/deficit, 2001	52

Technology
3.09	University/industry research collaboration	75
4.09	Internet hosts, 2001	73
4.08	Internet users, 2001	72
3.04	FDI and technology transfer	71
3.05	Prevalence of foreign technology licensing	70
4.04	Government prioritization of ICT	68
3.07	Company spending on research and development	65
4.11	Personal computers, 2001	63
4.10	Telephone lines, 2001	62
4.05	Government success in ICT promotion	60
4.07	Cellular telephones, 2001	58
3.18	Tertiary enrollment	55
4.06	Laws relating to ICT	54
3.01	Technological sophistication	52
4.02	Internet access in schools	51

Public Institutions
6.15	Organized crime	67
6.01	Judicial independence	61
6.03	Property rights	53

Microeconomic Competitiveness

Sophistication of Company Operations and Strategy
3.05	Prevalence of foreign technology licensing	70
10.07	Extent of marketing	70
10.09	Control of international distribution	70

Quality of the National Business Environment
3.06	Quality of scientific research institutions	77
5.02	Railroad infrastructure development	76
9.06	State of cluster development	75

Other Indicators
2.18	Investment rate, 2001	72
2.29	FDI, 2001	68
2.32	Bank liquid reserves	70
5.07	Postal efficiency	75
5.09	Disparity in healthcare quality	73
6.14	Business costs of crime and violence	70
6.16	Informal sector	66
7.07	Irregular payments in judicial decisions	61
11.04	Chemical waste regulations	71

Estonia

Key Economic Indicators

Total population (in millions), 2001 ....1.4
Population rank 77
GDP per capita (PPP), 2001 ....$10,380
GDP per capita rank...34
Real growth in GDP per capita, 2000 to 2001.........6.3
Growth rank 4
Unemployment rate, 2001 ....12.71
Unemployment rank 58
Government surplus/deficit, 2001 ....0.52
Government surplus/deficit rank 12
National savings rate, 2001 ....20.12
National savings rank...48
Investment rate, 2001 ....25.41
Investment rank...18
Inflation, 2001 ....5.80
Inflation rank 52
Exports of goods (as a percentage of GDP),
    2001 ....60.5
Exports rank...8
Imports of goods (as a percentage of GDP),
    2001 ....78.4
Imports rank...4
Internet users (per 10,000 inhabitants),
    2001 ....3,004.59
Internet users rank 21

Competitiveness Rankings

Growth Competitiveness Rank	**26**

Technology Index Rank **14**	
Innovation Subindex Rank.................................28	
ICT Subindex Rank 23	
Technology Transfer Subindex Rank	
(out of 56 non-core innovators) 11	
Public Institutions Index Rank...**28**	
Contracts and Law Subindex Rank 36	
Corruption Subindex Rank.................................25	
Macroeconomic Environment Index Rank **46**	
Macroeconomic Stability Subindex Rank 38	
Country Credit Rating Rank.................................36	
Government Expenditure Rank 50	

Microeconomic Competitiveness Rank	**30**

Company Operations and Strategy Rank **36**	
Quality of the National Business Environment Rank ...**28**	

Trade Performance of Leading Export Sectors

Sector	Share in national exports	Value of exports (US$ millions)	Value of net exports (US$ millions)	Share in world market	TPI current index	TPI change index
IT and consumer electronics	25.0%	953	452	0.15%	34	29
Wood products	13.2%	502	287	0.27%	20	59
Miscellaneous manufacturing	8.7%	332	5	0.07%	27	22
Basic manufactures	8.1%	310	−182	0.07%	47	26
Minerals	7.6%	288	−155	0.04%	32	55

Source: International Trade Centre UNCTAD/WTO

Real GDP (annual percent change)

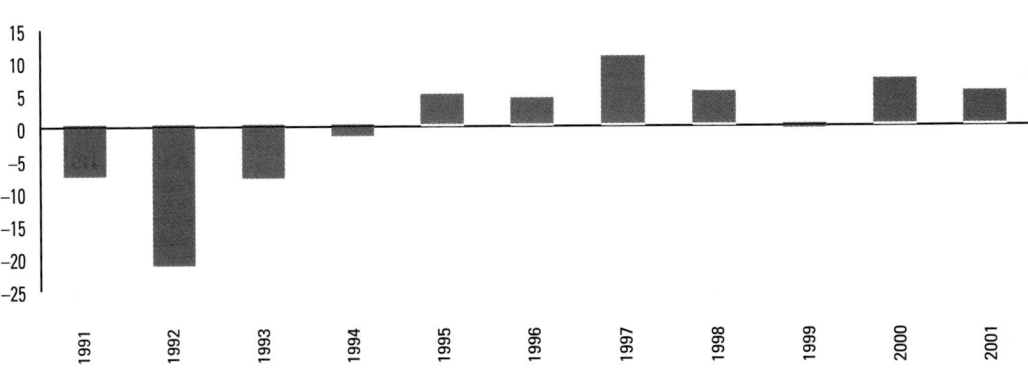

Source: IMF *World Economic Outlook Database,* April 2002

National competitiveness balance sheet

NOTABLE COMPETITIVE ADVANTAGES	
Criteria	Rank

NOTABLE COMPETITIVE DISADVANTAGES	
Criteria	Rank

Growth Competitiveness

Macroeconomic Environment

2.21	Real exchange rate, 2001	11
2.19	Inflation, 2001	15
2.28	Interest rate spread, 2001	22

Technology

3.01	Technological sophistication	8
3.07	Company spending on research and development	8
4.10	Telephone lines, 2001	13
3.15	Utility patents, 2001	16
3.18	Tertiary enrollment	16
4.11	Personal computers, 2001	18
4.06	Laws relating to ICT	20
4.02	Internet access in schools	25
4.07	Cellular telephones, 2001	25
4.08	Internet users, 2001	25
4.03	Quality of competition in the ISP sector	27

Public Institutions

6.09	Favoritism in decisions of government officials	22
7.02	Irregular payments in public utilities	27
7.03	Irregular payments in tax collection	29

Microeconomic Competitiveness

Sophistication of Company Operations and Strategy

10.09	Control of international distribution	2
10.07	Extent of marketing	3
10.04	Capacity for innovation	5

Quality of the National Business Environment

5.02	Railroad infrastructure development	3
3.12	Availability of scientists and engineers	4
10.16	Quality of management schools	5

Other Indicators

2.09	Regulatory obstacles to business	10
2.29	FDI, 2001	7
3.14	Research and development spending	9
3.17	Secondary enrollment	6
6.16	Informal sector	1
7.08	Frequency of payments or bribes	8
8.06	Number of procedures to resolve a dispute	1
8.11	Cost of starting a business relative to GNP per capita	9
11.10	Flexibility of environmental regulations	6

Growth Competitiveness

Macroeconomic Environment

2.16	Government expenditure, 2001	78
2.05	Access to credit	64
2.17	National savings rate, 2001	40
2.01	Recession expectations	36
2.15	Government surplus/deficit, 2001	36

Technology

3.02	Firm-level innovation	53
4.04	Government prioritization of ICT	42
4.05	Government success in ICT promotion	35
3.09	University/industry research collaboration	31
4.09	Internet hosts, 2001	31

Public Institutions

6.01	Judicial independence	40
6.15	Organized crime	36
6.03	Property rights	35
7.01	Irregular payments in exports & imports	31

Microeconomic Competitiveness

Sophistication of Company Operations and Strategy

3.05	Prevalence of foreign technology licensing	50
10.13	Willingness to delegate authority	30

Quality of the National Business Environment

10.20	Cooperation in labor-employer relations	78
8.04	Administrative burden for startups	68
2.12	Extent of distortive government subsidies	43

427

Other Indicators

1.08	Unemployment rate, 2001	44
2.08	Business costs of terrorism	55
2.18	Investment rate, 2001	47
2.25	Corporate income tax rate, 2002	77
2.26	Individual income tax rate, 2002	75
2.27	Value added tax rate, 2002	59
3.13	Brain drain	42
6.07	Burden of regulation	51
6.12	Efficiency of the tax system	67
6.14	Business costs of crime and violence	52
6.22	Military expenditure relative to GNI	57
7.12	Public trust of politicians	40
10.18	Hiring and firing practices	76
10.19	Flexibility of wage determination	56

Germany

Key Economic Indicators

Total population (in millions), 2001 ....82.1
Population rank 12
GDP per capita (PPP), 2001 ....$25,715
GDP per capita rank...13
Real growth in GDP per capita, 2000 to 2001.........0.3
Growth rank 53
Unemployment rate, 2001....................................9.50
Unemployment rank...50
Government surplus/deficit, 2001 ....–2.73
Government surplus/deficit rank 46
National savings rate, 2001 ....22.00
National savings rank...37
Investment rate, 2001 ....22.00
Investment rank...36
Inflation, 2001 ....2.40
Inflation rank 24
Exports of goods (as a percentage of GDP),
    2001 ....30.9
Exports rank...34
Imports of goods (as a percentage of GDP),
    2001 ....26.3
Imports rank...57
Internet users (per 10,000 inhabitants),
    2001 ....3,642.54
Internet users rank 15

Competitiveness Rankings

Growth Competitiveness Rank	**14**

Technology Index Rank **12**
   Innovation Subindex Rank.............................10
   ICT Subindex Rank 16
Public Institutions Index Rank............................**14**
   Contracts and Law Subindex Rank 10
   Corruption Subindex Rank..............................17
Macroeconomic Environment Index Rank **22**
   Macroeconomic Stability Subindex Rank 26
   Country Credit Rating Rank.....................................2
   Government Expenditure Rank 71

Microeconomic Competitiveness Rank	**4**

Company Operations and Strategy Rank 2
Quality of the National Business Environment Rank 4

Trade Performance of Leading Export Sectors

Sector	Share in national exports	Value of exports (US$ millions)	Value of net exports (US$ millions)	Share in world market	TPI current index	TPI change index
Transport equipment	21.0%	106,552	53,901	15.30%	2	48
Nonelectronic machinery	17.3%	87,386	43,518	15.04%	1	94
Chemicals	14.8%	75,125	25,631	12.44%	1	102
Electronic components	9.1%	46,211	6,533	7.73%	1	87
Basic manufactures	9.0%	45,688	7,981	10.55%	1	57

Source: International Trade Centre UNCTAD/WTO

Real GDP (annual percent change)

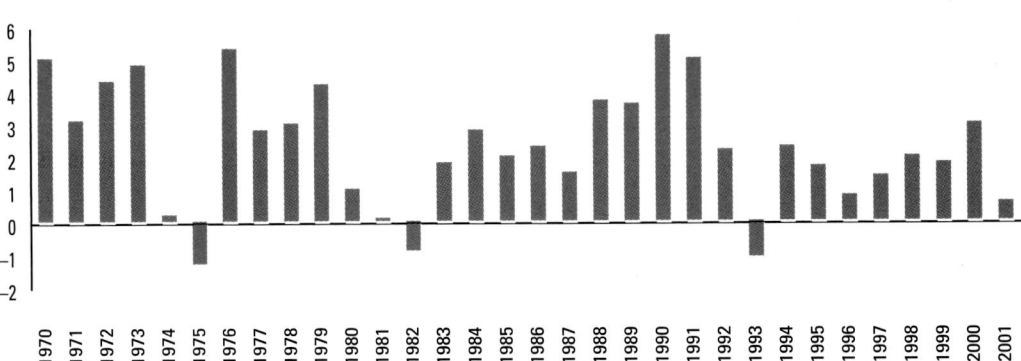

Source: IMF *World Economic Outlook Database,* April 2002

National competitiveness balance sheet

NOTABLE COMPETITIVE ADVANTAGES	
Criteria	Rank

Growth Competitiveness

Global Index
10.02	Value chain presence	1
10.03	Extent of branding	1

Technology Index
3.07	Company spending on research and development	3
3.01	Technological sophistication	7
4.10	Telephone lines, 2001	8

Microeconomic Competitiveness

Sophistication of Company Operations and Strategy
10.01	Nature of competitive advantage	1
10.04	Capacity for innovation	1
10.11	Breadth of international markets	1

Quality of the National Business Environment
9.03	Local supplier quality	1
11.05	Stringency of environmental regulations	1
5.01	Overall infrastructure quality	3

Other Indicators
2.29	FDI, 2001	4
3.08	Subsidies and tax credits for firm-level research and development	7
3.14	Research and development spending	8
5.05	Quality of electricity supply	6
6.05	Freedom of the press	5
6.14	Business costs of crime and violence	7
8.01	Intensity of local competition	4
9.02	Local supplier quantity	2
9.04	Presence of demanding regulatory standards	1
10.06	Production process sophistication	4
10.10	Extent of regional sales	1
11.01	Air pollution regulations	1
11.02	Water pollution regulations	1
11.03	Toxic waste disposal regulations	1
11.07	Compliance with environmental regulations	3

NOTABLE COMPETITIVE DISADVANTAGES	
Criteria	Rank

Growth Competitiveness

Technology Index
3.18	Tertiary enrollment	24

Macroeconomic Index
2.16	Government expenditure, 2001	71
2.15	Government surplus/deficit, 2001	46
2.17	National savings rate, 2001	37

Microeconomic Competitiveness

Quality of the National Business Environment
2.12	Extent of distortive government subsidies	71
3.11	Quality of math and science education	47
8.04	Administrative burden for startups	36

Other Indicators
1.08	Unemployment rate, 2001	50
2.05	Access to credit	40
2.08	Business costs of terrorism	52
2.09	Regulatory obstacles to business	53
2.18	Investment rate, 2001	36
2.26	Individual income tax rate, 2002	73
2.28	Interest rate spread, 2001	47
6.06	Competence of public officials	40
6.07	Burden of regulation	52
6.12	Efficiency of the tax system	75
8.10	Total cost of starting a business	56
10.18	Hiring and firing practices	79
10.19	Flexibility of wage determination	79
10.21	Pay and productivity	44

Greece

Key Economic Indicators

Total population (in millions), 2001 ....10.6
Population rank 40
GDP per capita (PPP), 2001 ....$17,482
GDP per capita rank...28
Real growth in GDP per capita, 2000 to 2001.........3.9
Growth rank 16
Unemployment rate, 2001....................................10.46
Unemployment rank 52
Government surplus/deficit, 2001 ....0.10
Government surplus/deficit rank 17
National savings rate, 2001 ....19.60
National savings rank 50
Investment rate, 2001 ....24.60
Investment rank..24
Inflation, 2001 ....3.70
Inflation rank 37
Exports of goods (as a percentage of GDP),
    2001 ....8.9
Exports rank...76
Imports of goods (as a percentage of GDP),
    2001 ....25.8
Imports rank...59
Internet users (per 10,000 inhabitants),
    2001 ....1,321.25
Internet users rank 33

Competitiveness Rankings

Growth Competitiveness Rank   **38**

Technology Index Rank **30**
  Innovation Subindex Rank 27
  ICT Subindex Rank 31
  Technology Transfer Subindex Rank
    (out of 56 non-core innovators) 31
Public Institutions Index Rank...........................**44**
  Contracts and Law Subindex Rank 40
  Corruption Subindex Rank..............................52
Macroeconomic Environment Index Rank **47**
  Macroeconomic Stability Subindex Rank 27
  Country Credit Rating Rank................................22
  Government Expenditure Rank 76

Microeconomic Competitiveness Rank   **43**

Company Operations and Strategy Rank **47**
Quality of the National Business Environment Rank ...**41**

Trade Performance of Leading Export Sectors

Sector	Share in national exports	Value of exports (US$ millions)	Value of net exports (US$ millions)	Share in world market	TPI current index	TPI change index
Clothing	18.9%	1,718	729	0.92%	26	84
Processed food	18.5%	1,679	−293	0.78%	38	111
Fresh food	17.3%	1,572	−464	0.66%	32	111
Basic manufactures	14.4%	1,305	−866	0.30%	36	116
Chemicals	6.4%	580	−3,127	0.10%	35	105

Source: International Trade Centre UNCTAD/WTO

Real GDP (annual percent change)

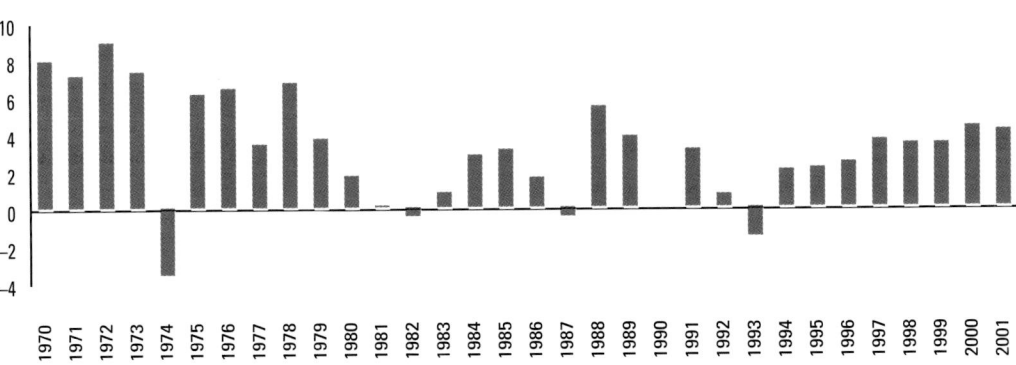

Source: IMF *World Economic Outlook Database,* April 2002

National competitiveness balance sheet

NOTABLE COMPETITIVE ADVANTAGES		NOTABLE COMPETITIVE DISADVANTAGES	
Criteria	Rank	Criteria	Rank

Growth Competitiveness

Macroeconomic Environment

2.05	Access to credit		13
2.15	Government surplus/deficit, 2001		17
2.01	Recession expectations		25
2.21	Real exchange rate, 2001		32
2.19	Inflation, 2001		37

Technology

4.07	Cellular telephones, 2001		13
4.10	Telephone lines, 2001		16
3.18	Tertiary enrollment		18
4.09	Internet hosts, 2001		28
3.15	Utility patents, 2001		30
3.05	Prevalence of foreign technology licensing		32
4.08	Internet users, 2001		33
3.09	University/industry research collaboration		34
3.02	Firm-level innovation		37

Public Institutions

6.15	Organized crime		28
6.01	Judicial independence		36

Microeconomic Competitiveness

Sophistication of Company Operations and Strategy

10.07	Extent of marketing		30
3.05	Prevalence of foreign technology licensing		32
10.09	Control of international distribution		38

Quality of the National Business Environment

2.11	Cost of importing foreign equipment		8
3.12	Availability of scientists and engineers		21
2.04	Ease of access to loans		31

Other Indicators

2.18	Investment rate, 2001		24
2.24	Average tariff rate, 2002		16
3.08	Subsidies and tax credits for firm-level research and development		29
6.05	Freedom of the press		18
6.14	Business costs of crime and violence		22
8.06	Number of procedures to resolve a dispute		15

Growth Competitiveness

Macroeconomic Environment

2.16	Government expenditure, 2001		76
2.17	National savings rate, 2001		50
2.28	Interest rate spread, 2001		41

Technology

4.06	Laws relating to ICT		67
3.04	FDI and technology transfer		58
3.07	Company spending on research and development		56
4.04	Government prioritization of ICT		56
3.01	Technological sophistication		54
4.05	Government success in ICT promotion		52
4.03	Quality of competition in the ISP sector		50
4.02	Internet access in schools		43
4.11	Personal computers, 2001		40

Public Institutions

7.03	Irregular payments in tax collection		70
6.09	Favoritism in decisions of government officials		50
7.02	Irregular payments in public utilities		46
6.03	Property rights		43
7.01	Irregular payments in exports & imports		39

Microeconomic Competitiveness

Sophistication of Company Operations and Strategy

10.15	Reliance on professional management		67
10.13	Willingness to delegate authority		63
10.12	Extent of staff training		57

Quality of the National Business Environment

10.17	Efficacy of corporate boards		76
4.06	Laws relating to ICT		67
9.06	State of cluster development		67

Other Indicators

1.08	Unemployment rate, 2001		52
2.22	Exports, 2001		76
2.23	Imports, 2001		59
2.25	Corporate income tax rate, 2002		79
2.26	Individual income tax rate, 2002		61
3.03	Firm-level technology absorption		67
6.06	Competence of public officials		60
6.08	Transparency of government policy-making		58
6.17	Strength of auditing and accounting standards		59
6.18	Pervasiveness of insider trading		74
8.08	Number of procedures to start a business		67
8.10	Total cost of starting a business		71
10.19	Flexibility of wage determination		68
10.21	Pay and productivity		62

Guatemala

Key Economic Indicators

Total population (in millions), 2001 ....11.7
Population rank 39
GDP per capita (PPP), 2001 ....$3,879
GDP per capita rank..67
Real growth in GDP per capita, 2000 to 2001 ....–0.8
Growth rank 66
Unemployment rate, 2001....................................4.90
Unemployment rank 20
Government surplus/deficit, 2001 ....–1.92
Government surplus/deficit rank 38
National savings rate, 2001 ....10.80
National savings rank..76
Investment rate, 2001 ....15.89
Investment rank...74
Inflation, 2001 ....8.70
Inflation rank 64
Exports of goods (as a percentage of GDP),
   2001 ....12.9
Exports rank...68
Imports of goods (as a percentage of GDP),
   2001 ....30.0
Imports rank...43
Internet users (per 10,000 inhabitants), 2001 ...171.13
Internet users rank 65

Competitiveness Rankings

Growth Competitiveness Rank	70

Technology Index Rank **74**
   Innovation Subindex Rank 75
   ICT Subindex Rank 71
   Technology Transfer Subindex Rank
      (out of 56 non-core innovators) 51
Public Institutions Index Rank............................**74**
   Contracts and Law Subindex Rank 79
   Corruption Subindex Rank....................................66
Macroeconomic Environment Index Rank **56**
   Macroeconomic Stability Subindex Rank 75
   Country Credit Rating Rank 62
   Government Expenditure Rank 2

Microeconomic Competitiveness Rank	73

Company Operations and Strategy Rank **70**
Quality of the National Business Environment Rank ...**73**

Trade Performance of Leading Export Sectors

Sector	Share in national exports	Value of exports (US$ millions)	Value of net exports (US$ millions)	Share in world market	TPI current index	TPI change index
Fresh food	44.3%	1,192	977	0.50%	39	8
Processed food	15.6%	421	–30	0.19%	46	26
Chemicals	12.2%	327	–506	0.05%	68	83
Minerals	7.3%	197	–394	0.03%	118	6
Basic manufactures	6.0%	160	–290	0.04%	74	21

Source: International Trade Centre UNCTAD/WTO

Real GDP (annual percent change)

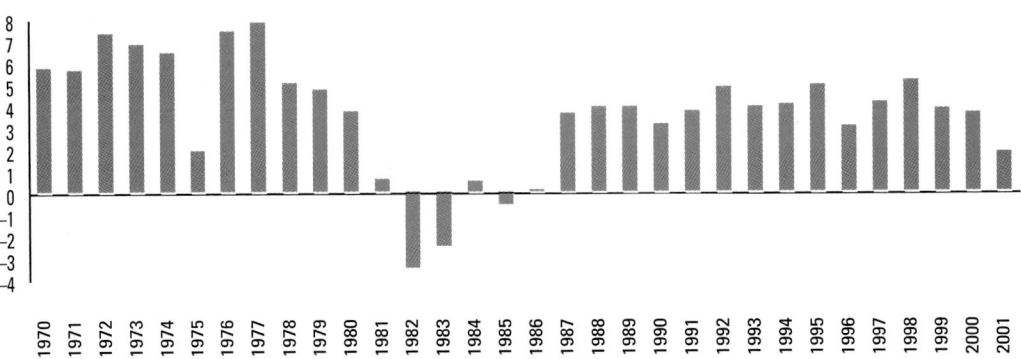

Source: IMF *World Economic Outlook Database,* April 2002

432

National competitiveness balance sheet

NOTABLE COMPETITIVE ADVANTAGES	
Criteria	Rank

Growth Competitiveness

Macroeconomic Environment

2.16	Government expenditure, 2001	2
2.15	Government surplus/deficit, 2001	38

NOTABLE COMPETITIVE DISADVANTAGES	
Criteria	Rank

Growth Competitiveness

Macroeconomic Environment

2.17	National savings rate, 2001	76
2.01	Recession expectations	74
2.05	Access to credit	71
2.21	Real exchange rate, 2001	71
2.19	Inflation, 2001	64
2.28	Interest rate spread, 2001	64

Technology

4.04	Government prioritization of ICT	80
3.05	Prevalence of foreign technology licensing	77
4.05	Government success in ICT promotion	75
4.02	Internet access in schools	74
3.01	Technological sophistication	69
3.18	Tertiary enrollment	69
4.11	Personal computers, 2001	69
3.09	University/industry research collaboration	68
3.15	Utility patents, 2001	68
4.06	Laws relating to ICT	66
4.10	Telephone lines, 2001	66
4.08	Internet users, 2001	65
3.04	FDI and technology transfer	64
4.07	Cellular telephones, 2001	61
3.07	Company spending on research and development	60
4.09	Internet hosts, 2001	59
3.02	Firm-level innovation	58
4.03	Quality of competition in the ISP sector	53

Public Institutions

6.09	Favoritism in decisions of government officials	80
6.15	Organized crime	79
6.01	Judicial independence	71
6.03	Property rights	71
7.03	Irregular payments in tax collection	71
7.01	Irregular payments in exports & imports	66
7.02	Irregular payments in public utilities	65

433

Microeconomic Competitiveness

Sophistication of Company Operations and Strategy

10.10	Extent of regional sales	41
10.14	Extent of incentive compensation	53

Quality of the National Business Environment

2.11	Cost of importing foreign equipment	51
10.17	Efficacy of corporate boards	55

Microeconomic Competitiveness

Sophistication of Company Operations and Strategy

3.05	Prevalence of foreign technology licensing	77
10.06	Production process sophistication	73
10.11	Breadth of international markets	72

Quality of the National Business Environment

3.10	Government procurement of advanced technology products	80
7.11	Business costs of corruption	80
5.08	Quality of public schools	79

Other Indicators

1.08	Unemployment rate, 2001	20
2.09	Regulatory obstacles to business	14
2.24	Average tariff rate, 2002	40
2.27	Value added tax rate, 2002	20
6.22	Military expenditure relative to GNI	5
8.09	Number of days to start a business	25
10.18	Hiring and firing practices	32
10.19	Flexibility of wage determination	39

Other Indicators

2.03	Soundness of banks	72
2.08	Business costs of terrorism	75
2.18	Investment rate, 2001	74
3.03	Firm-level technology absorption	73
5.09	Disparity in healthcare quality	77
6.08	Transparency of government policy-making	77
6.11	Effectiveness of law-making bodies	76
6.12	Efficiency of the tax system	72
6.14	Business costs of crime and violence	80
7.08	Frequency of payments or bribes	80
7.12	Public trust of politicians	76
11.07	Compliance with environmental regulations	79

Haiti

Key Economic Indicators

Total population (in millions), 2001 ....8.0
Population rank 50
GDP per capita (PPP), 2001 ....$1,444
GDP per capita rank...79
Real growth in GDP per capita, 2000 to 2001 ....–3.2
Growth rank 75
Unemployment rate, 2001.................................55.00
Unemployment rank 79
Government surplus/deficit, 2001 ....–2.21
Government surplus/deficit rank 39
National savings rate, 2001 ....18.00
National savings rank..58
Investment rate, 2001 ....22.80
Investment rank..34
Inflation, 2001 ....16.70
Inflation rank 74
Exports of goods (as a percentage of GDP),
     2001 ....8.9
Exports rank...78
Imports of goods (as a percentage of GDP),
     2001 ....26.5
Imports rank...55
Internet users (per 10,000 inhabitants), 2001 .....36.28
Internet users rank 78

Competitiveness Rankings

Growth Competitiveness Rank	80

Technology Index Rank **80**
   Innovation Subindex Rank.................................80
   ICT Subindex Rank 80
   Technology Transfer Subindex Rank
     (out of 56 non-core innovators) 56
Public Institutions Index Rank...............................**80**
   Contracts and Law Subindex Rank 80
   Corruption Subindex Rank....................................79
Macroeconomic Environment Index Rank **68**
   Macroeconomic Stability Subindex Rank 78
   Country Credit Rating Rank...................................79
   Government Expenditure Rank 1

Microeconomic Competitiveness Rank	80

Company Operations and Strategy Rank **80**
Quality of the National Business Environment Rank ...**80**

Trade Performance of Leading Export Sectors

Sector	Share in national exports	Value of exports (US$ millions)	Value of net exports (US$ millions)	Share in world market	TPI current index	TPI change index
Clothing	80.6%	269	111	0.14%	82	29
Fresh food	8.9%	30	–101	0.01%	159	158
Processed food	2.5%	8	–173	0.00%	126	56
Miscellaneous manufacturing	2.1%	7	–28	0.00%	116	115
Textiles	1.9%	6	–20	0.00%	104	24

Source: International Trade Centre UNCTAD/WTO

Real GDP (annual percent change)

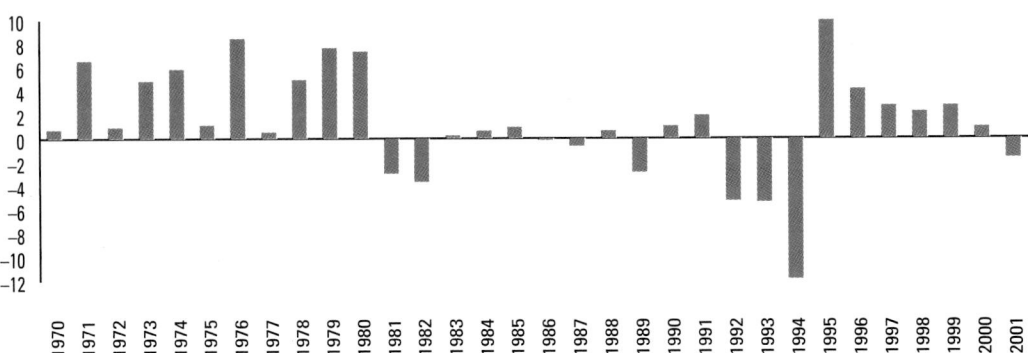

Source: IMF *World Economic Outlook Database,* April 2002

National competitiveness balance sheet

NOTABLE COMPETITIVE ADVANTAGES		NOTABLE COMPETITIVE DISADVANTAGES	
Criteria	Rank	Criteria	Rank

Growth Competitiveness

Macroeconomic Environment

| 2.16 | Government expenditure, 2001 | 1 |
| 2.15 | Government surplus/deficit, 2001 | 39 |

Growth Competitiveness

Macroeconomic Environment

2.21	Real exchange rate, 2001	79
2.01	Recession expectations	76
2.28	Interest rate spread, 2001	75
2.19	Inflation, 2001	74
2.05	Access to credit	70
2.17	National savings rate, 2001	58

Technology

3.01	Technological sophistication	80
3.04	FDI and technology transfer	80
3.05	Prevalence of foreign technology licensing	80
3.07	Company spending on research and development	80
3.09	University/industry research collaboration	80
3.18	Tertiary enrollment	80
4.05	Government success in ICT promotion	80
4.06	Laws relating to ICT	80
4.02	Internet access in schools	79
4.04	Government prioritization of ICT	79
4.08	Internet users, 2001	78
4.10	Telephone lines, 2001	78
3.02	Firm-level innovation	77
4.07	Cellular telephones, 2001	77
4.03	Quality of competition in the ISP sector	75
3.15	Utility patents, 2001	68

Public Institutions

6.01	Judicial independence	80
6.03	Property rights	79
7.02	Irregular payments in public utilities	79
7.03	Irregular payments in tax collection	79
6.15	Organized crime	78
6.09	Favoritism in decisions of government officials	77
7.01	Irregular payments in exports & imports	75

Microeconomic Competitiveness

Quality of the National Business Environment

| 6.10 | Extent of bureaucratic red tape | 7 |
| 10.20 | Cooperation in labor-employer relations | 48 |

Microeconomic Competitiveness

Sophistication of Company Operations and Strategy

3.07	Company spending on research and development	80
10.07	Extent of marketing	80
10.11	Breadth of international markets	80

Quality of the National Business Environment

3.06	Quality of scientific research institutions	80
5.01	Overall infrastructure quality	80
6.04	Intellectual property protection	80

Other Indicators

2.03	Soundness of banks	37
2.09	Regulatory obstacles to business	16
2.18	Investment rate, 2001	34
2.26	Individual income tax rate, 2002	23
2.27	Value added tax rate, 2002	11
6.12	Efficiency of the tax system	38
10.18	Hiring and firing practices	16
10.19	Flexibility of wage determination	2
10.21	Pay and productivity	42
11.13	Political context of environmental gains	39

Other Indicators

1.08	Unemployment rate, 2001	79
2.22	Exports, 2001	78
3.13	Brain drain	80
5.09	Disparity in healthcare quality	80
5.14	Electric power	76
6.11	Effectiveness of law-making bodies	80
6.14	Business costs of crime and violence	79
6.16	Informal sector	80
6.17	Strength of auditing and accounting standards	80
6.20	Pervasiveness of money laundering through non-bank channels	79
7.07	Irregular payments in judicial decisions	79
7.10	Diversion of public funds	80
7.12	Public trust of politicians	79
11.07	Compliance with environmental regulations	80

435

Honduras

Key Economic Indicators

Total population (in millions), 2001 ....6.6
Population rank 54
GDP per capita (PPP), 2001 ....$2,505
GDP per capita rank...73
Real growth in GDP per capita, 2000 to 2001.........0.0
Growth rank 58
Unemployment rate, 2001.................................28.50
Unemployment rank 76
Government surplus/deficit, 2001 ....–6.11
Government surplus/deficit rank 69
National savings rate, 2001 ....24.59
National savings rank..26
Investment rate, 2001 ....24.42
Investment rank...25
Inflation, 2001 ....9.70
Inflation rank 68
Exports of goods (as a percentage of GDP),
    2001 ....21.4
Exports rank...54
Imports of goods (as a percentage of GDP),
    2001 ....49.5
Imports rank...17
Internet users (per 10,000 inhabitants), 2001 .....61.68
Internet users rank 76

Competitiveness Rankings

Growth Competitiveness Rank	**76**

Technology Index Rank **78**	
Innovation Subindex Rank 71	
ICT Subindex Rank 76	
Technology Transfer Subindex Rank	
(out of 56 non-core innovators) 46	
Public Institutions Index Rank...............................**76**	
Contracts and Law Subindex Rank 75	
Corruption Subindex Rank....................................74	
Macroeconomic Environment Index Rank **71**	
Macroeconomic Stability Subindex Rank 70	
Country Credit Rating Rank...................................73	
Government Expenditure Rank 31	

Microeconomic Competitiveness Rank	**78**

Company Operations and Strategy Rank 78
Quality of the National Business Environment Rank ...79

Trade Performance of Leading Export Sectors

Sector	Share in national exports	Value of exports (US$ millions)	Value of net exports (US$ millions)	Share in world market	TPI current index	TPI change index
Fresh food	51.5%	549	387	0.23%	68	126
Miscellaneous manufacturing	15.2%	162	–16	0.03%	89	94
Processed food	8.4%	90	–246	0.04%	87	2
Chemicals	6.1%	65	–399	0.01%	103	22
Wood products	5.9%	63	–80	0.03%	76	36

Source: International Trade Centre UNCTAD/WTO

Real GDP (annual percent change)

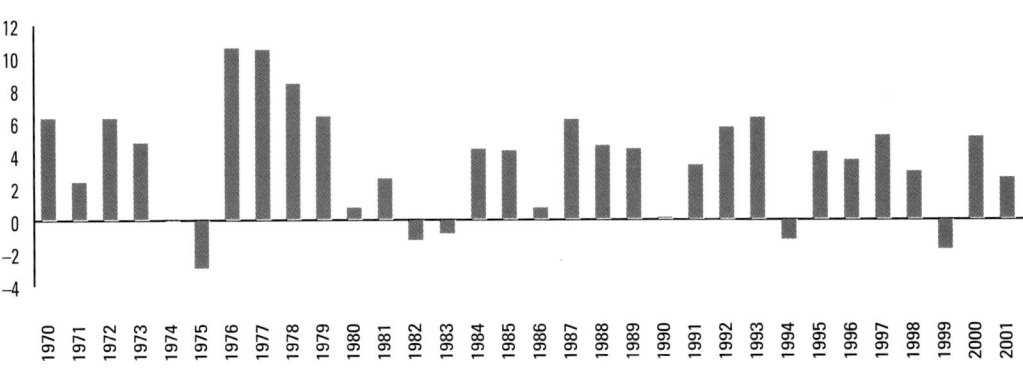

Source: IMF *World Economic Outlook Database,* April 2002

National competitiveness balance sheet

NOTABLE COMPETITIVE ADVANTAGES	
Criteria	Rank

Growth Competitiveness

Macroeconomic Environment

2.17	National savings rate, 2001	26
2.16	Government expenditure, 2001	31

Microeconomic Competitiveness

Quality of the National Business Environment

6.10	Extent of bureaucratic red tape	49
5.03	Port infrastructure quality	52

Other Indicators

2.09	Regulatory obstacles to business	31
2.18	Investment rate, 2001	25
2.25	Corporate income tax rate, 2002	8
2.26	Individual income tax rate, 2002	6
2.27	Value added tax rate, 2002	20
6.22	Military expenditure relative to GNI	5
8.07	Number of days to resolve a dispute	42
8.10	Total cost of starting a business	34

NOTABLE COMPETITIVE DISADVANTAGES	
Criteria	Rank

Growth Competitiveness

Macroeconomic Environment

2.21	Real exchange rate, 2001	75
2.15	Government surplus/deficit, 2001	69
2.19	Inflation, 2001	68
2.05	Access to credit	65
2.01	Recession expectations	64
2.28	Interest rate spread, 2001	63

Technology

3.01	Technological sophistication	78
3.07	Company spending on research and development	78
4.02	Internet access in schools	77
4.05	Government success in ICT promotion	77
3.09	University/industry research collaboration	76
4.08	Internet users, 2001	76
4.04	Government prioritization of ICT	75
4.06	Laws relating to ICT	75
4.09	Internet hosts, 2001	75
4.03	Quality of competition in the ISP sector	74
3.05	Prevalence of foreign technology licensing	73
4.07	Cellular telephones, 2001	72
4.11	Personal computers, 2001	70
4.10	Telephone lines, 2001	69
3.15	Utility patents, 2001	68
3.18	Tertiary enrollment	61
3.02	Firm-level innovation	55
3.04	FDI and technology transfer	55

Public Institutions

7.02	Irregular payments in public utilities	77
6.15	Organized crime	76
6.09	Favoritism in decisions of government officials	73
6.01	Judicial independence	71
7.03	Irregular payments in tax collection	68
6.03	Property rights	67
7.01	Irregular payments in exports & imports	65

Microeconomic Competitiveness

Sophistication of Company Operations and Strategy

10.08	Degree of customer orientation	80
10.11	Breadth of international markets	79
10.12	Extent of staff training	79

Quality of the National Business Environment

2.07	Local equity market access	80
8.04	Administrative burden for startups	80
10.16	Quality of management schools	80

Other Indicators

1.08	Unemployment rate, 2001	76
1.09	Employment to population ratio, 2001	74
2.03	Soundness of banks	71
2.29	FDI, 2001	72
3.03	Firm-level technology absorption	79
3.17	Secondary enrollment	71
4.01	Availability of mobile or cellular telephones	77
5.07	Postal efficiency	78
6.07	Burden of regulation	75
6.14	Business costs of crime and violence	76
6.17	Strength of auditing and accounting standards	75
7.07	Irregular payments in judicial decisions	71
7.14	Policy consequences of legal political donations	78
10.21	Pay and productivity	76
11.04	Chemical waste regulations	79

Hong Kong SAR

Key Economic Indicators

Total population (in millions), 2001 ....6.7
Population rank 53
GDP per capita (PPP), 2001 ....$25,581
GDP per capita rank..15
Real growth in GDP per capita, 2000 to 2001 ....–0.8
Growth rank 67
Unemployment rate, 2001....................................4.93
Unemployment rank 21
Government surplus/deficit, 2001 ....–5.00
Government surplus/deficit rank 60
National savings rate, 2001 ....33.20
National savings rank 7
Investment rate, 2001 ....25.82
Investment rank..13
Inflation, 2001 ....–1.60
Inflation rank 1
Exports of goods (as a percentage of GDP),
    2001 ....117.3
Exports rank..2
Imports of goods (as a percentage of GDP),
    2001 ....124.2
Imports rank..2
Internet users (per 10,000 inhabitants),
    2001 ....4,586.14
Internet users rank 7

Competitiveness Rankings

Growth Competitiveness Rank	**17**

Technology Index Rank **32**
    Innovation Subindex Rank 32
    ICT Subindex Rank 6
Public Institutions Index Rank..**13**
    Contracts and Law Subindex Rank 13
    Corruption Subindex Rank 15
Macroeconomic Environment Index Rank **3**
    Macroeconomic Stability Subindex Rank 9
    Country Credit Rating Rank...................................25
    Government Expenditure Rank 15

Microeconomic Competitiveness Rank	**19**

Company Operations and Strategy Rank **24**
Quality of the National Business Environment Rank ...**16**

Trade Performance of Leading Export Sectors*

Sector	Share in national exports	Value of exports (US$ millions)	Value of net exports (US$ millions)**	Share in world market	TPI current index	TPI change index
Clothing	43.0%	9,932	—	5.32%	25	51
Miscellaneous manufacturing	16.7%	3,863	—	0.83%	36	119
Electronic components	15.8%	3,661	—	0.61%	40	81
IT and consumer electronics	6.4%	1,477	—	0.23%	40	65
Textiles	5.1%	1,174	—	0.79%	40	89

* Hong Kong has a very large percentage of reexports, which are not included in the calculation of these numbers.
** Net exports were not calculated because, although Hong Kong customs data differentiate between exports and reexports, they do not estimate the value of imported goods for reexport.
Source: International Trade Centre UNCTAD/WTO

Real GDP (annual percent change)

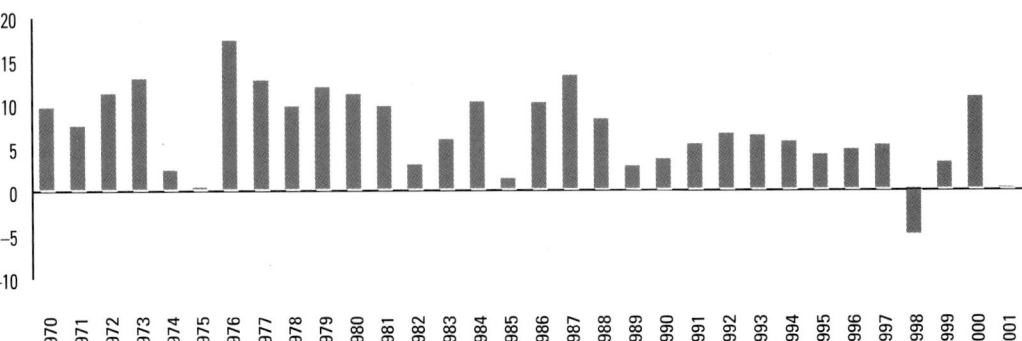

Source: IMF *World Economic Outlook Database,* April 2002

438

National competitiveness balance sheet

NOTABLE COMPETITIVE ADVANTAGES	
Criteria	Rank

Growth Competitiveness

Macroeconomic Environment

2.19	Inflation, 2001	1
2.17	National savings rate, 2001	7
2.28	Interest rate spread, 2001	8
2.05	Access to credit	14
2.16	Government expenditure, 2001	15

Technology

4.03	Quality of competition in the ISP sector	2
4.07	Cellular telephones, 2001	2
4.02	Internet access in schools	7
4.08	Internet users, 2001	7
4.10	Telephone lines, 2001	12
4.09	Internet hosts, 2001	13
4.11	Personal computers, 2001	14

Public Institutions

7.02	Irregular payments in public utilities	8
6.03	Property rights	12
7.03	Irregular payments in tax collection	13
6.01	Judicial independence	14
6.09	Favoritism in decisions of government officials	15
6.15	Organized crime	16

Microeconomic Competitiveness

Sophistication of Company Operations and Strategy

10.07	Extent of marketing	10
10.11	Breadth of international markets	10
10.14	Extent of incentive compensation	10

Quality of the National Business Environment

8.04	Administrative burden for startups	1
5.03	Port infrastructure quality	2
9.01	Buyer sophistication	2

Other Indicators

2.03	Soundness of banks	2
2.22	Exports, 2001	2
2.23	Imports, 2001	2
2.24	Average tariff rate, 2002	1
2.25	Corporate income tax rate, 2002	4
2.26	Individual income tax rate, 2002	5
2.27	Value added tax rate, 2002	1
2.29	FDI, 2001	5
2.31	Liquid liabilities, 2001	1
2.32	Bank liquid reserves	1
6.06	Competence of public officials	9
6.07	Burden of regulation	1
6.12	Efficiency of the tax system	1
6.16	Informal sector	5
7.12	Public trust of politicians	5
8.07	Number of days to resolve a dispute	7
8.08	Number of procedures to start a business	7
10.18	Hiring and firing practices	1
10.19	Flexibility of wage determination	1
10.21	Pay and productivity	1

NOTABLE COMPETITIVE DISADVANTAGES	
Criteria	Rank

Growth Competitiveness

Macroeconomic Environment

2.21	Real exchange rate, 2001	69
2.15	Government surplus/deficit, 2001	60
2.01	Recession expectations	21

Technology

3.18	Tertiary enrollment	46
3.07	Company spending on research and development	37
3.09	University/industry research collaboration	35
4.05	Government success in ICT promotion	29
3.01	Technological sophistication	25
3.02	Firm-level innovation	24
3.15	Utility patents, 2001	22
4.04	Government prioritization of ICT	19
4.06	Laws relating to ICT	19

Public Institutions

7.01	Irregular payments in exports & imports	19

Microeconomic Competitiveness

Sophistication of Company Operations and Strategy

10.15	Reliance on professional management	48
10.04	Capacity for innovation	35
10.13	Willingness to delegate authority	35

Quality of the National Business Environment

10.17	Efficacy of corporate boards	69
3.12	Availability of scientists and engineers	49
8.05	Effectiveness of anti-trust policy	48

Other Indicators

2.09	Regulatory obstacles to business	78
3.03	Firm-level technology absorption	32
3.08	Subsidies and tax credits for firm-level research and development	45
6.18	Pervasiveness of insider trading	35
6.19	Pervasiveness of money laundering through banks	34
8.10	Total cost of starting a business	41
11.01	Air pollution regulations	47
11.07	Compliance with environmental regulations	45

Hungary

Key Economic Indicators

Total population (in millions), 2001 ....10.1
Population rank 43
GDP per capita (PPP), 2001 ....$12,941
GDP per capita rank..30
Real growth in GDP per capita, 2000 to 2001.........4.3
Growth rank 13
Unemployment rate, 2001.....................................5.69
Unemployment rank 26
Government surplus/deficit, 2001 ....–2.85
Government surplus/deficit rank 48
National savings rate, 2001 ....25.10
National savings rank..23
Investment rate, 2001 ....23.42
Investment rank..28
Inflation, 2001 ....9.20
Inflation rank..66
Exports of goods (as a percentage of GDP),
    2001 ....65.8
Exports rank..6
Imports of goods (as a percentage of GDP),
    2001 ....72.7
Imports rank..7
Internet users (per 10,000 inhabitants),
    2001 ....1,484.01
Internet users rank 31

Competitiveness Rankings

Growth Competitiveness Rank	**29**

Technology Index Rank **21**
    Innovation Subindex Rank....................................34
    ICT Subindex Rank 29
    Technology Transfer Subindex Rank
        (out of 56 non-core innovators) 6
Public Institutions Index Rank...........................**30**
    Contracts and Law Subindex Rank 30
    Corruption Subindex Rank...................................29
Macroeconomic Environment Index Rank **49**
    Macroeconomic Stability Subindex Rank 47
    Country Credit Rating Rank.................................27
    Government Expenditure Rank 60

Microeconomic Competitiveness Rank	**28**

Company Operations and Strategy Rank **29**
Quality of the National Business Environment Rank ...**29**

Trade Performance of Leading Export Sectors

Sector	Share in national exports	Value of exports (US$ millions)	Value of net exports (US$ millions)	Share in world market	TPI current index	TPI change index
IT and consumer electronics	25.0%	6,884	2,572	1.09%	17	1
Nonelectronic machinery	14.5%	3,988	–529	0.69%	44	48
Electronic components	12.1%	3,333	–1,766	0.56%	26	32
Transport equipment	9.2%	2,545	116	0.37%	31	59
Chemicals	7.1%	1,960	–1,194	0.32%	25	29

Source: International Trade Centre UNCTAD/WTO

Real GDP (annual percent change)

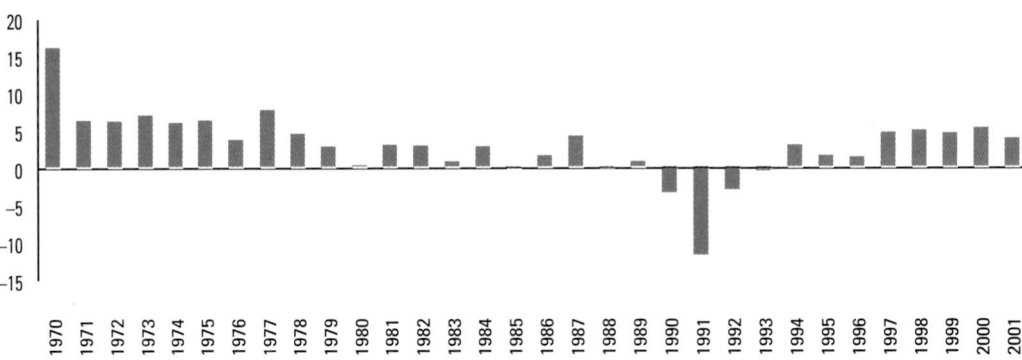

Source: IMF *World Economic Outlook Database,* April 2002

National competitiveness balance sheet

NOTABLE COMPETITIVE ADVANTAGES	
Criteria	Rank

Growth Competitiveness

Macroeconomic Environment

2.28	Interest rate spread, 2001	10
2.01	Recession expectations	14
2.17	National savings rate, 2001	23
2.05	Access to credit	26

Technology

3.04	FDI and technology transfer	2
4.04	Government prioritization of ICT	13
4.06	Laws relating to ICT	13
4.05	Government success in ICT promotion	17
4.02	Internet access in schools	23
4.09	Internet hosts, 2001	26
3.09	University/industry research collaboration	27
3.15	Utility patents, 2001	27
4.07	Cellular telephones, 2001	28

Public Institutions

6.03	Property rights	20
6.15	Organized crime	25
7.01	Irregular payments in exports & imports	27
7.02	Irregular payments in public utilities	29

Microeconomic Competitiveness

Sophistication of Company Operations and Strategy

10.12	Extent of staff training	23
10.15	Reliance on professional management	23
10.11	Breadth of international markets	24

Quality of the National Business Environment

3.11	Quality of math and science education	10
3.12	Availability of scientists and engineers	11
4.06	Laws relating to ICT	13

Other Indicators

2.08	Business costs of terrorism	7
2.22	Exports, 2001	6
2.23	Imports, 2001	7
2.25	Corporate income tax rate, 2002	5
3.08	Subsidies and tax credits for firm-level research and development	20
6.07	Burden of regulation	19
6.12	Efficiency of the tax system	25
6.17	Strength of auditing and accounting standards	25
8.08	Number of procedures to start a business	7
10.18	Hiring and firing practices	12
10.19	Flexibility of wage determination	22
10.21	Pay and productivity	14
11.08	Compliance with international environmental agreements	20

NOTABLE COMPETITIVE DISADVANTAGES	
Criteria	Rank

Growth Competitiveness

Macroeconomic Environment

2.19	Inflation, 2001	66
2.16	Government expenditure, 2001	60
2.15	Government surplus/deficit, 2001	48
2.21	Real exchange rate, 2001	45

Technology

3.02	Firm-level innovation	57
4.03	Quality of competition in the ISP sector	42
3.18	Tertiary enrollment	38
4.11	Personal computers, 2001	36
3.05	Prevalence of foreign technology licensing	35
3.01	Technological sophistication	33
4.08	Internet users, 2001	31
3.07	Company spending on research and development	30
4.10	Telephone lines, 2001	30

Public Institutions

6.09	Favoritism in decisions of government officials	43
6.01	Judicial independence	38
7.03	Irregular payments in tax collection	32

Microeconomic Competitiveness

Sophistication of Company Operations and Strategy

10.09	Control of international distribution	55
10.08	Degree of customer orientation	43

Quality of the National Business Environment

5.03	Port infrastructure quality	57
9.02	Local supplier quantity	57
5.04	Air transport infrastructure quality	55

Other Indicators

2.09	Regulatory obstacles to business	67
2.20	M2 growth, 2001	60
2.27	Value added tax rate	77
2.32	Bank liquid reserves	48
6.05	Freedom of the press	41
6.16	Informal sector	43
7.04	Irregular payments in public contracts	51
8.11	Cost of starting a business relative to GNP per capita	66
11.13	Political context of environmental gains	61

441

Iceland

Key Economic Indicators

Total population (in millions), 2001 ....0.3
Population rank 80
GDP per capita (PPP), 2001 ....$30,725
GDP per capita rank..4
Real growth in GDP per capita, 2000 to 2001.........1.3
Growth rank 38
Unemployment rate, 2001 ....1.40
Unemployment rank 1
Government surplus/deficit, 2001 ....–0.10
Government surplus/deficit rank 18
National savings rate, 2001 ....16.00
National savings rank 66
Investment rate, 2001 ....20.00
Investment rate rank 48
Inflation, 2001 ....6.70
Inflation rank 55
Exports of goods (as a percentage of GDP),
    2001 ....26.7
Exports rank..40
Imports of goods (as a percentage of GDP),
    2001 ....30.0
Imports rank..41
Internet users (per 10,000 inhabitants),
    2001 ....6,794.43
Internet users rank 1

Competitiveness Rankings

Growth Competitiveness Rank   **12**

Technology Index Rank **16**
  Innovation Subindex Rank....................................21
  ICT Subindex Rank 2
Public Institutions Index Rank............................**3**
  Contracts and Law Subindex Rank 3
  Corruption Subindex Rank.....................................2
Macroeconomic Environment Index Rank **24**
  Macroeconomic Stability Subindex Rank 44
  Country Credit Rating Rank..................................24
  Government Expenditure Rank 39

Microeconomic Competitiveness Rank   **17**

Company Operations and Strategy Rank **17**
Quality of the National Business Environment Rank ...**14**

Trade Performance of Leading Export Sectors

Sector	Share in national exports	Value of exports (US$ millions)	Value of net exports (US$ millions)	Share in world market	TPI current index	TPI change index
Fresh food	37.2%	698	597	0.29%	36	99
Processed food	29.7%	558	435	0.26%	28	113
Basic manufactures	22.0%	414	246	0.10%	57	78
Nonelectronic machinery	2.7%	50	–165	0.01%	45	4
Transport equipment	2.3%	43	–329	0.01%	62	54

Source: International Trade Centre UNCTAD/WTO

Real GDP (annual percent change)

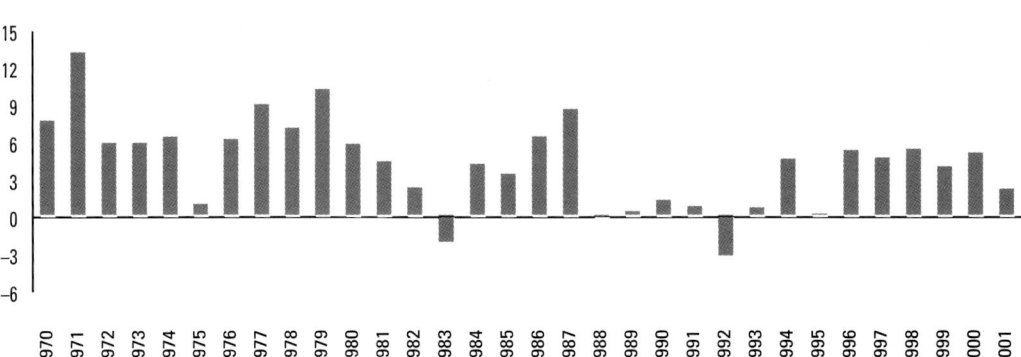

Source: IMF *World Economic Outlook Database,* April 2002

National competitiveness balance sheet

NOTABLE COMPETITIVE ADVANTAGES	
Criteria	Rank

Growth Competitiveness

Macroeconomic Environment
2.21	Real exchange rate, 2001	13

Technology
4.08	Internet users, 2001	1
4.02	Internet access in schools	2
4.09	Internet hosts, 2001	2
3.02	Firm-level innovation	4
4.07	Cellular telephones, 2001	5
4.10	Telephone lines, 2001	6
4.03	Quality of competition in the ISP sector	8
3.01	Technological sophistication	10
4.05	Government success in ICT promotion	10
4.06	Laws relating to ICT	10
4.11	Personal computers, 2001	10

Public Institutions
7.01	Irregular payments in exports & imports	2
7.02	Irregular payments in public utilities	2
6.03	Property rights	3
7.03	Irregular payments in tax collection	3
6.15	Organized crime	4
6.09	Favoritism in decisions of government officials	5
6.01	Judicial independence	8

Microeconomic Competitiveness

Sophistication of Company Operations and Strategy
10.09	Control of international distribution	7
10.13	Willingness to delegate authority	9
10.08	Degree of customer orientation	12

Quality of the National Business Environment
8.03	Sophistication of local buyers' products and processes	1
7.11	Business costs of corruption	2
8.04	Administrative burden for startups	2

Other Indicators
1.08	Unemployment rate, 2001	1
1.09	Employment to population ratio, 2001	9
2.08	Business costs of terrorism	3
2.09	Regulatory obstacles to business	7
3.03	Firm-level technology absorption	4
4.01	Availability of mobile or cellular telephones	1
5.09	Disparity in healthcare quality	1
6.07	Burden of regulation	5
6.08	Transparency of government policy-making	3
6.12	Efficiency of the tax system	6
6.14	Business costs of crime and violence	4
6.17	Strength of auditing and accounting standards	2
6.19	Pervasiveness of money laundering through banks	1
7.12	Public trust of politicians	7
10.18	Hiring and firing practices	5
11.10	Flexibility of environmental regulations	4

NOTABLE COMPETITIVE DISADVANTAGES	
Criteria	Rank

Growth Competitiveness

Macroeconomic Environment
2.28	Interest rate spread, 2001	67
2.17	National savings rate, 2001	66
2.19	Inflation, 2001	55
2.16	Government expenditure, 2001	39
2.01	Recession expectations	31
2.05	Access to credit	18
2.15	Government surplus/deficit, 2001	18

Technology
3.18	Tertiary enrollment	34
4.04	Government prioritization of ICT	21
3.07	Company spending on research and development	20
3.09	University/industry research collaboration	19
3.15	Utility patents, 2001	18

Microeconomic Competitiveness

Sophistication of Company Operations and Strategy
3.05	Prevalence of foreign technology licensing	40
10.02	Value chain presence	33
10.14	Extent of incentive compensation	26

Quality of the National Business Environment
5.02	Railroad infrastructure development	50
2.11	Cost of importing foreign equipment	45
8.02	Extent of locally based competitors	40

Other Indicators
2.18	Investment rate, 2001	48
2.22	Exports, 2001	40
2.23	Imports, 2001	41
2.27	Value added tax rate, 2002	76
2.31	Liquid liabilities, 2001	50
3.08	Subsidies and tax credits for firm-level research and development	37
10.19	Flexibility of wage determination	54
11.14	Prevalence of environmental management systems	47

India

Key Economic Indicators

Total population (in millions), 2001 ....1,030.0
Population rank 2
GDP per capita (PPP), 2001 ....$2,464
GDP per capita rank...74
Real growth in GDP per capita, 2000 to 2001.........2.5
Growth rank 24
Unemployment rate, 2001.....................................9.16
Unemployment rank 46
Government surplus/deficit, 2001 ....–5.70
Government surplus/deficit rank 67
National savings rate, 2001 ....22.40
National savings rank...36
Investment rate, 2001 ....22.70
Investment rank...35
Inflation, 2001 ....3.80
Inflation rank 38
Exports of goods (as a percentage of GDP),
    2001 ....9.1
Exports rank..75
Imports of goods (as a percentage of GDP),
    2001 ....10.4
Imports rank..78
Internet users (per 10,000 inhabitants), 2001 .....68.16
Internet users rank 75

Competitiveness Rankings

Growth Competitiveness Rank	48

Technology Index Rank **57**
  Innovation Subindex Rank 62
  ICT Subindex Rank 69
  Technology Transfer Subindex Rank
    (out of 56 non-core innovators) 2
Public Institutions Index Rank...**59**
  Contracts and Law Subindex Rank 39
  Corruption Subindex Rank....................................73
Macroeconomic Environment Index Rank **18**
  Macroeconomic Stability Subindex Rank 36
  Country Credit Rating Rank...................................46
  Government Expenditure Rank 9

Microeconomic Competitiveness Rank	37

Company Operations and Strategy Rank **40**
Quality of the National Business Environment Rank ...**37**

Trade Performance of Leading Export Sectors

Sector	Share in national exports	Value of exports (US$ millions)	Value of net exports (US$ millions)	Share in world market	TPI current index	TPI change index
Minerals	20.2%	6,560	–9,566	0.94%	84	112
Textiles	15.2%	4,933	4,571	3.34%	16	85
Fresh food	15.0%	4,894	3,744	2.06%	22	121
Clothing	14.9%	4,859	4,855	2.60%	24	38
Chemicals	10.0%	3,262	–1,970	0.54%	43	95

Source: International Trade Centre UNCTAD/WTO

Real GDP (annual percent change)

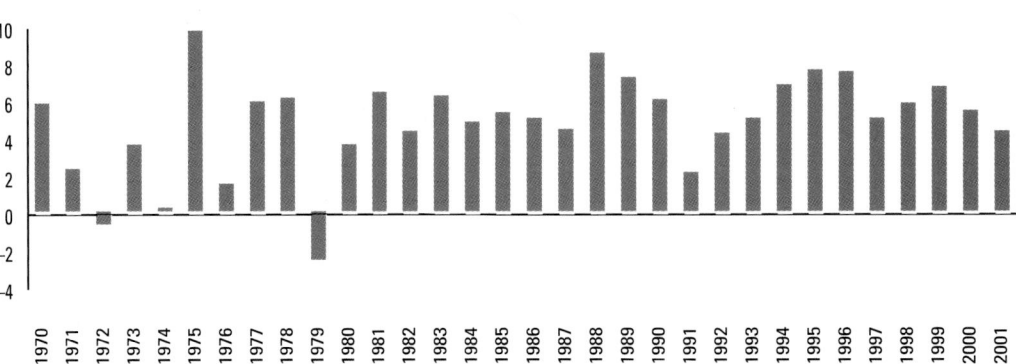

Source: IMF *World Economic Outlook Database,* April 2002

National competitiveness balance sheet

NOTABLE COMPETITIVE ADVANTAGES

Criteria	Rank

Growth Competitiveness

Macroeconomic Environment

2.05	Access to credit	5
2.16	Government expenditure, 2001	9
2.28	Interest rate spread, 2001	11
2.17	National savings rate, 2001	36
2.19	Inflation, 2001	38

Technology

3.05	Prevalence of foreign technology licensing	1
4.04	Government prioritization of ICT	8
4.05	Government success in ICT promotion	8
3.02	Firm-level innovation	12
3.04	FDI and technology transfer	15
4.06	Laws relating to ICT	29
3.07	Company spending on research and development	32
4.03	Quality of competition in the ISP sector	35

Public Institutions

6.01	Judicial independence	24
6.15	Organized crime	40

Microeconomic Competitiveness

Sophistication of Company Operations and Strategy

3.05	Prevalence of foreign technology licensing	1
10.09	Control of international distribution	25
3.07	Company spending on research and development	32

Quality of the National Business Environment

3.12	Availability of scientists and engineers	2
8.01	Intensity of local competition	7
10.16	Quality of management schools	9

Other Indicators

2.18	Investment rate, 2001	35
2.26	Individual income tax rate, 2002	23
3.03	Firm-level technology absorption	16
6.05	Freedom of the press	28
6.11	Effectiveness of law-making bodies	31
6.14	Business costs of crime and violence	27
8.07	Number of days to resolve a dispute	16
8.10	Total cost of starting a business	19

NOTABLE COMPETITIVE DISADVANTAGES

Criteria	Rank

Growth Competitiveness

Macroeconomic Environment

2.15	Government surplus/deficit, 2001	67
2.21	Real exchange rate, 2001	48
2.01	Recession expectations	45

Technology

4.07	Cellular telephones, 2001	78
4.11	Personal computers, 2001	77
4.08	Internet users, 2001	75
4.10	Telephone lines, 2001	75
3.18	Tertiary enrollment	72
4.09	Internet hosts, 2001	71
3.15	Utility patents, 2001	58
4.02	Internet access in schools	55
3.01	Technological sophistication	42
3.09	University/industry research collaboration	42

Public Institutions

7.02	Irregular payments in public utilities	75
7.03	Irregular payments in tax collection	73
7.01	Irregular payments in exports & imports	71
6.09	Favoritism in decisions of government officials	47
6.03	Property rights	42

Microeconomic Competitiveness

Sophistication of Company Operations and Strategy

10.01	Nature of competitive advantage	67
10.14	Extent of incentive compensation	61
10.08	Degree of customer orientation	59

Quality of the National Business Environment

5.05	Quality of electricity supply	75
10.17	Efficacy of corporate boards	74
2.11	Cost of importing foreign equipment	69

Other Indicators

2.08	Business costs of terrorism	71
2.22	Exports, 2001	75
2.23	Imports, 2001	78
2.24	Average tariff rate, 2002	80
5.09	Disparity in healthcare quality	68
6.18	Pervasiveness of insider trading	68
6.20	Pervasiveness of money laundering through non-bank channels	67
7.13	Prevalence of illegal political donations	72
10.18	Hiring and firing practices	78
11.06	Subsidies for energy or materials	66

445

Indonesia

Key Economic Indicators

Total population (in millions), 2001 ....211.2
Population rank 4
GDP per capita (PPP), 2001 ....$3,059
GDP per capita rank...71
Real growth in GDP per capita, 2000 to 2001.........2.0
Growth rank 28
Unemployment rate, 2001....................................10.30
Unemployment rank 51
Government surplus/deficit, 2001 ....–3.70
Government surplus/deficit rank 53
National savings rate, 2001 ....22.90
National savings rank 32
Investment rate, 2001 ....20.85
Investment rank...45
Inflation, 2001 ....11.50
Inflation rank 70
Exports of goods (as a percentage of GDP),
    2001 ....38.7
Exports rank...21
Imports of goods (as a percentage of GDP),
    2001 ....21.3
Imports rank...65
Internet users (per 10,000 inhabitants), 2001 ...186.19
Internet users rank 64

Competitiveness Rankings

Growth Competitiveness Rank	**67**

Technology Index Rank **65**
   Innovation Subindex Rank 63
   ICT Subindex Rank 73
   Technology Transfer Subindex Rank
     (out of 56 non-core innovators) 15
Public Institutions Index Rank...............................**77**
   Contracts and Law Subindex Rank 68
   Corruption Subindex Rank...................................77
Macroeconomic Environment Index Rank **53**
   Macroeconomic Stability Subindex Rank 45
   Country Credit Rating Rank...............................74
   Government Expenditure Rank 19

Microeconomic Competitiveness Rank	**64**

Company Operations and Strategy Rank **55**
Quality of the National Business Environment Rank ...**65**

Trade Performance of Leading Export Sectors

Sector	Share in national exports	Value of exports (US$ millions)	Value of net exports (US$ millions)	Share in world market	TPI current index	TPI change index
Minerals	28.2%	17,280	13,699	2.47%	14	101
Wood products	10.8%	6,611	5,128	3.58%	6	19
IT and consumer electronics	10.7%	6,540	5,923	1.03%	19	22
Clothing	7.7%	4,727	4,690	2.53%	5	73
Fresh food	6.3%	3,828	1,061	1.61%	25	48

Source: International Trade Centre UNCTAD/WTO

Real GDP (annual percent change)

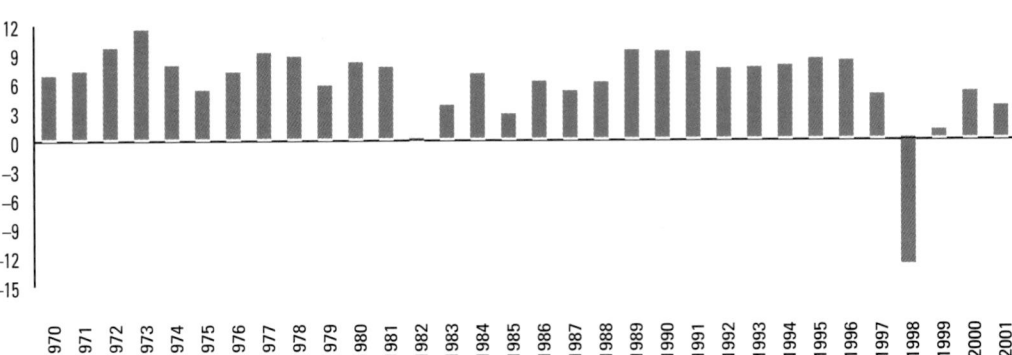

Source: IMF *World Economic Outlook Database,* April 2002

National competitiveness balance sheet

NOTABLE COMPETITIVE ADVANTAGES

Criteria	Rank

Growth Competitiveness

Macroeconomic Environment

2.05	Access to credit	22
2.16	Government expenditure, 2001	46
2.19	Inflation, 2001	48

Technology

4.04	Government prioritization of ICT	10
3.04	FDI and technology transfer	12
3.02	Firm-level innovation	30
4.03	Quality of competition in the ISP sector	32
4.07	Cellular telephones, 2001	38
3.09	University/industry research collaboration	46
4.11	Personal computers, 2001	48
4.10	Telephone lines, 2001	49

Public Institutions

6.01	Judicial independence	37
6.03	Property rights	40
7.03	Irregular payments in tax collection	43
7.01	Irregular payments in exports & imports	49

Microeconomic Competitiveness

Sophistication of Company Operations and Strategy

10.01	Nature of competitive advantage	20
10.15	Reliance on professional management	36
10.07	Extent of marketing	48

Quality of the National Business Environment

5.04	Air transport infrastructure quality	16
5.03	Port infrastructure quality	27
2.07	Local equity market access	31

Other Indicators

2.09	Regulatory obstacles to business	2
2.18	Investment rate, 2001	9
2.26	Individual income tax rate, 2002	6
3.17	Secondary enrollment	34
6.05	Freedom of the press	30
6.12	Efficiency of the tax system	13
6.17	Strength of auditing and accounting standards	33
6.21	Military expenditure relative to central government expenditure	5
7.07	Irregular payments in judicial decisions	28
8.06	Number of procedures to resolve a dispute	2
8.08	Number of procedures to start a business	14
10.19	Flexibility of wage determination	26
11.13	Political context of environmental gains	26

NOTABLE COMPETITIVE DISADVANTAGES

Criteria	Rank

Growth Competitiveness

Macroeconomic Environment

2.21	Real exchange rate, 2001	77
2.15	Government surplus/deficit, 2001	67
2.28	Interest rate spread, 2001	66
2.01	Recession expectations	58
2.17	National savings rate, 2001	54

Technology

3.18	Tertiary enrollment	68
4.02	Internet access in schools	66
4.09	Internet hosts, 2001	60
3.01	Technological sophistication	59
3.07	Company spending on research and development	58
4.05	Government success in ICT promotion	56
4.06	Laws relating to ICT	56
3.05	Prevalence of foreign technology licensing	55
4.08	Internet users, 2001	53
3.15	Utility patents, 2001	52

Public Institutions

6.15	Organized crime	77
6.09	Favoritism in decisions of government officials	54
7.02	Irregular payments in public utilities	52

Microeconomic Competitiveness

Sophistication of Company Operations and Strategy

10.10	Extent of regional sales	75
10.11	Breadth of international markets	74
10.06	Production process sophistication	67

Quality of the National Business Environment

9.09	Local availability of process machinery	80
8.02	Extent of locally based competitors	78
9.02	Local supplier quantity	75

Other Indicators

1.08	Unemployment rate, 2001	64
2.08	Business costs of terrorism	62
2.22	Exports, 2001	69
3.13	Brain drain	67
5.07	Postal efficiency	64
6.14	Business costs of crime and violence	74
6.16	Informal sector	77
6.20	Pervasiveness of money laundering through non-bank channels	70
7.08	Frequency of payments or bribes	69
10.21	Pay and productivity	69
11.01	Air pollution regulations	65

Japan

Key Economic Indicators

Total population (in millions), 2001 ....126.8
Population rank 8
GDP per capita (PPP), 2001 ....$27,101
GDP per capita rank...10
Real growth in GDP per capita, 2000 to 2001 ....–0.6
Growth rank 65
Unemployment rate, 2001.....................................5.03
Unemployment rank 23
Government surplus/deficit, 2001 ....–8.10
Government surplus/deficit rank 77
National savings rate, 2001 ....27.60
National savings rank 16
Investment rate, 2001 ....25.83
Investment rank...12
Inflation, 2001 ....–0.70
Inflation rank 3
Exports of goods (as a percentage of GDP),
    2001 ....9.7
Exports rank...73
Imports of goods (as a percentage of GDP),
    2001 ....8.4
Imports rank...79
Internet users (per 10,000 inhabitants),
    2001 ....4,547.10
Internet users rank 8

Competitiveness Rankings

Growth Competitiveness Rank   **13**

Technology Index Rank **5**
   Innovation Subindex Rank 5
   ICT Subindex Rank 17
Public Institutions Index Rank..........................**25**
   Contracts and Law Subindex Rank 37
   Corruption Subindex Rank....................................21
Macroeconomic Environment Index Rank **29**
   Macroeconomic Stability Subindex Rank 22
   Country Credit Rating Rank................................15
   Government Expenditure Rank 74

Microeconomic Competitiveness Rank   **11**

Company Operations and Strategy Rank **7**
Quality of the National Business Environment Rank ...**17**

Trade Performance of Leading Export Sectors

Sector	Share in national exports	Value of exports (US$ millions)	Value of net exports (US$ millions)	Share in world market	TPI current index	TPI change index
Transport equipment	21.8%	100,426	86,913	14.42%	7	76
Electronic components	18.3%	84,456	49,505	14.12%	2	36
Nonelectronic machinery	17.1%	79,038	62,460	13.60%	10	83
IT and consumer electronics	14.3%	65,724	24,704	10.40%	1	54
Miscellaneous manufacturing	9.3%	42,656	11,532	9.15%	6	90

Source: International Trade Centre UNCTAD/WTO

Real GDP (annual percent change)

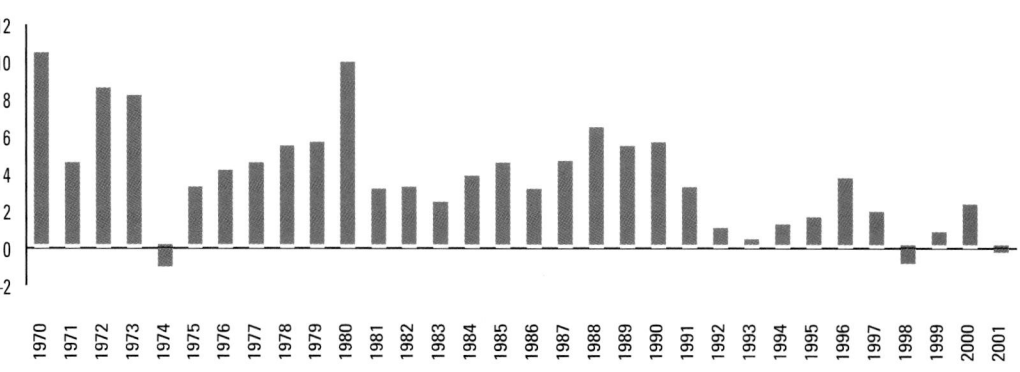

Source: IMF *World Economic Outlook Database,* April 2002

National competitiveness balance sheet

NOTABLE COMPETITIVE ADVANTAGES	
Criteria	Rank

Growth Competitiveness

Macroeconomic Environment

2.28	Interest rate spread, 2001	1
2.19	Inflation, 2001	3
2.17	National savings rate, 2001	16

Technology

3.02	Firm-level innovation	1
3.15	Utility patents, 2001	2
3.01	Technological sophistication	4
3.07	Company spending on research and development	5
4.08	Internet users, 2001	8
4.04	Government prioritization of ICT	9
4.10	Telephone lines, 2001	10
4.09	Internet hosts, 2001	14
4.11	Personal computers, 2001	16

Microeconomic Competitiveness	

Sophistication of Company Operations and Strategy

10.01	Nature of competitive advantage	2
10.06	Production process sophistication	3
10.04	Capacity for innovation	4

Quality of the National Business Environment

5.02	Railroad infrastructure development	1
8.02	Extent of locally based competitors	1
6.10	Extent of bureaucratic red tape	3

Other Indicators

1.09	Employment to population ratio, 2001	6
2.27	Value added tax rate, 2002	4
2.30	Domestic credit, 2001	3
2.31	Liquid liabilities, 2001	2
3.03	Firm-level technology absorption	3
3.13	Brain drain	7
3.14	Research and development spending	4
5.07	Postal efficiency	3
5.09	Disparity in healthcare quality	9
5.14	Electric power	1
6.06	Competence of public officials	5
8.07	Number of days to resolve a dispute	5
10.19	Flexibility of wage determination	8
11.13	Political context of environmental gains	4
11.14	Prevalence of environmental management systems	2

NOTABLE COMPETITIVE DISADVANTAGES	
Criteria	Rank

Growth Competitiveness

Macroeconomic Environment

2.15	Government surplus/deficit, 2001	77
2.16	Government expenditure, 2001	74
2.01	Recession expectations	54
2.05	Access to credit	50
2.21	Real exchange rate, 2001	41

Technology

4.05	Government success in ICT promotion	46
4.03	Quality of competition in the ISP sector	30
4.06	Laws relating to ICT	30
3.18	Tertiary enrollment	28
4.02	Internet access in schools	26
4.07	Cellular telephones, 2001	26
3.09	University/industry research collaboration	24

Public Institutions

6.15	Organized crime	47
6.03	Property rights	33
7.02	Irregular payments in public utilities	31
6.01	Judicial independence	30
6.09	Favoritism in decisions of government officials	27
7.01	Irregular payments in exports & imports	18
7.03	Irregular payments in tax collection	17

Microeconomic Competitiveness	

Sophistication of Company Operations and Strategy

10.14	Extent of incentive compensation	45

Quality of the National Business Environment

10.17	Efficacy of corporate boards	80
2.12	Extent of distortive government subsidies	68
2.04	Ease of access to loans	64

Other Indicators

2.03	Soundness of banks	77
2.08	Business costs of terrorism	58
2.22	Exports, 2001	73
2.23	Imports, 2001	79
2.26	Individual income tax rate, 2002	42
6.07	Burden of regulation	53
6.17	Strength of auditing and accounting standards	54
7.12	Public trust of politicians	50
7.15	Misuse of legal political donations	50
8.08	Number of procedures to start a business	44
8.10	Total cost of starting a business	67
10.18	Hiring and firing practices	59

457

Jordan

Key Economic Indicators

Total population (in millions), 2001 ....5.2
Population rank 62
GDP per capita (PPP), 2001 ....$4,080
GDP per capita rank..65
Real growth in GDP per capita, 2000 to 2001.........1.3
Growth rank 39
Unemployment rate, 2001....................................14.70
Unemployment rank 61
Government surplus/deficit, 2001 ....–7.00
Government surplus/deficit rank 76
National savings rate, 2001 ....27.80
National savings rank 15
Investment rate, 2001 ....25.30
Investment rank..19
Inflation, 2001 ....1.80
Inflation rank 15
Exports of goods (as a percentage of GDP),
    2001 ....26.0
Exports rank..43
Imports of goods (as a percentage of GDP),
    2001 ....54.4
Imports rank..11
Internet users (per 10,000 inhabitants), 2001 ...409.11
Internet users rank 52

Competitiveness Rankings

Growth Competitiveness Rank	**47**
Technology Index Rank **51**	
Innovation Subindex Rank....................................57	
ICT Subindex Rank 50	
Technology Transfer Subindex Rank (out of 56 non-core innovators) 30	
Public Institutions Index Rank..**40**	
Contracts and Law Subindex Rank 27	
Corruption Subindex Rank...................................54	
Macroeconomic Environment Index Rank **57**	
Macroeconomic Stability Subindex Rank 40	
Country Credit Rating Rank...................................58	
Government Expenditure Rank 40	
Microeconomic Competitiveness Rank	**53**
Company Operations and Strategy Rank **59**	
Quality of the National Business Environment Rank ...**48**	

458

Trade Performance of Leading Export Sectors

Sector	Share in national exports	Value of exports (US$ millions)	Value of net exports (US$ millions)	Share in world market	TPI current index	TPI change index
Chemicals	26.2%	242	–279	0.04%	56	20
Minerals	14.0%	130	–101	0.02%	80	44
Clothing	11.3%	105	45	0.06%	80	34
Fresh food	11.3%	104	–381	0.04%	111	43
Basic manufactures	6.8%	63	–275	0.01%	76	36

Source: International Trade Centre UNCTAD/WTO

Real GDP (annual percent change)

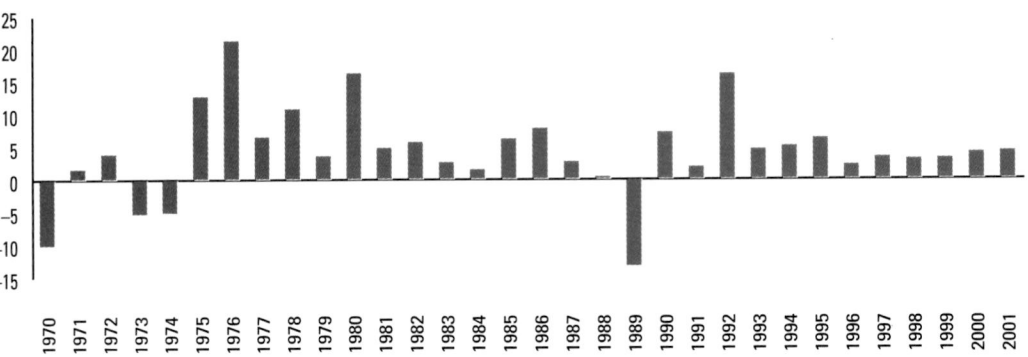

Source: IMF *World Economic Outlook Database,* April 2002

National competitiveness balance sheet

NOTABLE COMPETITIVE ADVANTAGES	
Criteria	**Rank**

Growth Competitiveness

Macroeconomic Environment

2.17	National savings rate, 2001	15
2.19	Inflation, 2001	15
2.28	Interest rate spread, 2001	31

Technology

4.04	Government prioritization of ICT	14
4.05	Government success in ICT promotion	16
4.03	Quality of competition in the ISP sector	20
4.06	Laws relating to ICT	31
4.02	Internet access in schools	33
3.01	Technological sophistication	34

Public Institutions

6.15	Organized crime	10
6.03	Property rights	32

Microeconomic Competitiveness

Sophistication of Company Operations and Strategy

10.01	Nature of competitive advantage	35
10.09	Control of international distribution	43

Quality of the National Business Environment

6.13	Reliability of police services	19
3.12	Availability of scientists and engineers	22
5.01	Overall infrastructure quality	31

Other Indicators

2.18	Investment rate, 2001	19
2.23	Imports, 2001	11
2.26	Individual income tax rate, 2002	23
2.31	Liquid liabilities, 2001	7
6.12	Efficiency of the tax system	26
6.14	Business costs of crime and violence	16
7.13	Prevalence of illegal political donations	20
7.14	Policy consequences of legal political donations	12
10.19	Flexibility of wage determination	24
11.14	Prevalence of environmental management systems	34

NOTABLE COMPETITIVE DISADVANTAGES	
Criteria	**Rank**

Growth Competitiveness

Macroeconomic Environment

2.15	Government surplus/deficit, 2001	76
2.21	Real exchange rate, 2001	66
2.01	Recession expectations	57
2.05	Access to credit	54
2.16	Government expenditure, 2001	40

Technology

3.02	Firm-level innovation	72
3.07	Company spending on research and development	68
4.09	Internet hosts, 2001	63
3.09	University/industry research collaboration	60
3.05	Prevalence of foreign technology licensing	59
4.11	Personal computers, 2001	58
4.07	Cellular telephones, 2001	56
4.10	Telephone lines, 2001	55
3.18	Tertiary enrollment	53
4.08	Internet users, 2001	52
3.15	Utility patents, 2001	44
3.04	FDI and technology transfer	40

Public Institutions

7.02	Irregular payments in public utilities	57
7.03	Irregular payments in tax collection	57
7.01	Irregular payments in exports & imports	44
6.01	Judicial independence	42
6.09	Favoritism in decisions of government officials	40

Microeconomic Competitiveness

Sophistication of Company Operations and Strategy

10.15	Reliance on professional management	74
10.07	Extent of marketing	71
10.14	Extent of incentive compensation	71

Quality of the National Business Environment

6.10	Extent of bureaucratic red tape	73
2.11	Cost of importing foreign equipment	72
10.17	Efficacy of corporate boards	64

Other Indicators

1.08	Unemployment rate, 2001	61
2.08	Business costs of terrorism	67
2.09	Regulatory obstacles to business	64
2.24	Average tariff rate, 2002	60
2.29	FDI, 2001	73
3.13	Brain drain	61
6.05	Freedom of the press	76
6.18	Pervasiveness of insider trading	60
6.22	Military expenditure relative to GNI	77
8.11	Cost of starting a business relative to GNP per capita	61
11.06	Subsidies for energy or materials	52

Korea

Key Economic Indicators

Total population (in millions), 2001 ....47.7
Population rank 20
GDP per capita (PPP), 2001 ....$18,149
GDP per capita rank..26
Real growth in GDP per capita, 2000 to 2001.........2.2
Growth rank 26
Unemployment rate, 2001.................................3.70
Unemployment rank 10
Government surplus/deficit, 2001 ....–1.30
Government surplus/deficit rank 31
National savings rate, 2001 ....28.96
National savings rank 11
Investment rate, 2001 ....26.99
Investment rank..10
Inflation, 2001 ....4.10
Inflation rank 41
Exports of goods (as a percentage of GDP),
  2001 ....35.6
Exports rank...26
Imports of goods (as a percentage of GDP),
  2001 ....33.4
Imports rank..37
Internet users (per 10,000 inhabitants),
  2001 ....5,106.83
Internet users rank 5

Competitiveness Rankings

Growth Competitiveness Rank	21

Technology Index Rank **18**
  Innovation Subindex Rank 11
  ICT Subindex Rank 19
Public Institutions Index Rank..............................**32**
  Contracts and Law Subindex Rank 28
  Corruption Subindex Rank.............................38
Macroeconomic Environment Index Rank **10**
  Macroeconomic Stability Subindex Rank 10
  Country Credit Rating Rank.............................29
  Government Expenditure Rank 23

Microeconomic Competitiveness Rank	23

Company Operations and Strategy Rank **21**
Quality of the National Business Environment Rank ...**23**

Trade Performance of Leading Export Sectors

Sector	Share in national exports	Value of exports (US$ millions)	Value of net exports (US$ millions)	Share in world market	TPI current index	TPI change index
IT and consumer electronics	20.0%	33,993	20,453	5.38%	5	17
Electronic components	18.7%	31,831	3,978	5.32%	7	46
Transport equipment	14.4%	24,379	21,402	3.50%	6	45
Chemicals	9.8%	16,631	2,518	2.75%	10	40
Textiles	7.5%	12,705	9,350	8.60%	3	15

Source: International Trade Centre UNCTAD/WTO

Real GDP (annual percent change)

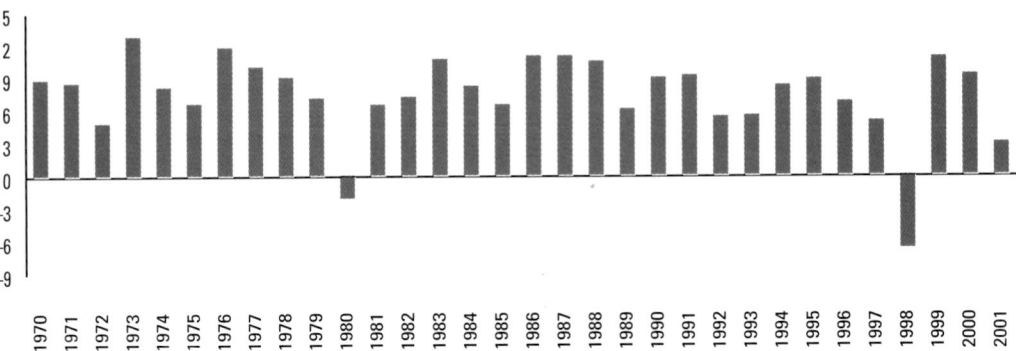

Source: IMF *World Economic Outlook Database,* April 2002

National competitiveness balance sheet

NOTABLE COMPETITIVE ADVANTAGES

Criteria		Rank

Growth Competitiveness

Macroeconomic Environment

2.28	Interest rate spread, 2001	4
2.01	Recession expectations	5
2.05	Access to credit	8
2.17	National savings rate, 2001	11
2.21	Real exchange rate, 2001	16

Technology

4.02	Internet access in schools	3
3.18	Tertiary enrollment	5
4.08	Internet users, 2001	5
4.03	Quality of competition in the ISP sector	6
4.05	Government success in ICT promotion	7
3.07	Company spending on research and development	11
3.15	Utility patents, 2001	12
4.04	Government prioritization of ICT	16
3.01	Technological sophistication	17
4.06	Laws relating to ICT	18
3.09	University/industry research collaboration	20

Microeconomic Competitiveness

Sophistication of Company Operations and Strategy

3.05	Prevalence of foreign technology licensing	8
10.09	Control of international distribution	10
10.11	Breadth of international markets	13

Quality of the National Business Environment

3.10	Government procurement of advanced technology products	6
9.06	State of cluster development	8
8.02	Extent of locally based competitors	11

Other Indicators

1.08	Unemployment rate, 2001	10
2.18	Investment rate, 2001	10
2.27	Value added tax rate, 2002	11
2.31	Liquid liabilities, 2001	14
3.08	Subsidies and tax credits for firm-level research and development	12
3.14	Research and development spending	5
7.08	Frequency of payments or bribes	11
8.07	Number of days to resolve a dispute	8
11.14	Prevalence of environmental management systems	10

NOTABLE COMPETITIVE DISADVANTAGES

Criteria		Rank

Growth Competitiveness

Macroeconomic Environment

2.19	Inflation, 2001	41
2.15	Government surplus/deficit, 2001	31
2.16	Government expenditure, 2001	23

Technology

4.09	Internet hosts, 2001	38
3.02	Firm-level innovation	36
4.07	Cellular telephones, 2001	24
4.11	Personal computers, 2001	22
4.10	Telephone lines, 2001	21

Public Institutions

7.03	Irregular payments in tax collection	50
6.01	Judicial independence	41
7.01	Irregular payments in exports & imports	34
7.02	Irregular payments in public utilities	34
6.09	Favoritism in decisions of government officials	30
6.03	Property rights	27
6.15	Organized crime	26

Microeconomic Competitiveness

Sophistication of Company Operations and Strategy

10.14	Extent of incentive compensation	34
10.15	Reliance on professional management	34
10.07	Extent of marketing	33

Quality of the National Business Environment

10.20	Cooperation in labor-employer relations	55
10.16	Quality of management schools	50
10.17	Efficacy of corporate boards	45

Other Indicators

2.03	Soundness of banks	55
2.08	Business costs of terrorism	47
2.24	Average tariff rate, 2002	51
2.26	Individual income tax rate, 2002	47
6.05	Freedom of the press	53
6.11	Effectiveness of law-making bodies	53
6.17	Strength of auditing and accounting standards	43
6.22	Military expenditure relative to GNI	58
8.08	Number of procedures to start a business	54
8.11	Cost of starting a business relative to GNP per capita	44

Latvia

Key Economic Indicators

Total population (in millions), 2001 ....2.4
Population rank 73
GDP per capita (PPP), 2001 ....$7,750
GDP per capita rank...48
Real growth in GDP per capita, 2000 to 2001.........7.4
Growth rank 2
Unemployment rate, 2001....................................7.70
Unemployment rank 35
Government surplus/deficit, 2001 ....–1.85
Government surplus/deficit rank 37
National savings rate, 2001 ....18.90
National savings rank...56
Investment rate, 2001 ....25.72
Investment rank...14
Inflation, 2001 ....2.50
Inflation rank 26
Exports of goods (as a percentage of GDP),
    2001 ....25.8
Exports rank..45
Imports of goods (as a percentage of GDP),
    2001 ....45.1
Imports rank..23
Internet users (per 10,000 inhabitants), 2001 ...723.10
Internet users rank 43

Competitiveness Rankings

Growth Competitiveness Rank	44

Technology Index Rank **29**
  Innovation Subindex Rank 26
  ICT Subindex Rank 35
  Technology Transfer Subindex Rank
      (out of 56 non-core innovators) 16
Public Institutions Index Rank............................**52**
  Contracts and Law Subindex Rank 50
  Corruption Subindex Rank....................................53
Macroeconomic Environment Index Rank **55**
  Macroeconomic Stability Subindex Rank 32
  Country Credit Rating Rank 44
  Government Expenditure Rank 53

Microeconomic Competitiveness Rank	45

Company Operations and Strategy Rank **48**
Quality of the National Business Environment Rank ...**42**

Trade Performance of Leading Export Sectors

Sector	Share in national exports	Value of exports (US$ millions)	Value of net exports (US$ millions)	Share in world market	TPI current index	TPI change index
Wood products	38.9%	721	573	0.39%	34	30
Basic manufactures	11.0%	204	–104	0.05%	61	68
Clothing	9.4%	174	87	0.09%	48	80
Miscellaneous manufacturing	8.9%	164	–109	0.04%	48	40
Chemicals	6.5%	120	–298	0.02%	75	80

Source: International Trade Centre UNCTAD/WTO

Real GDP (annual percent change)

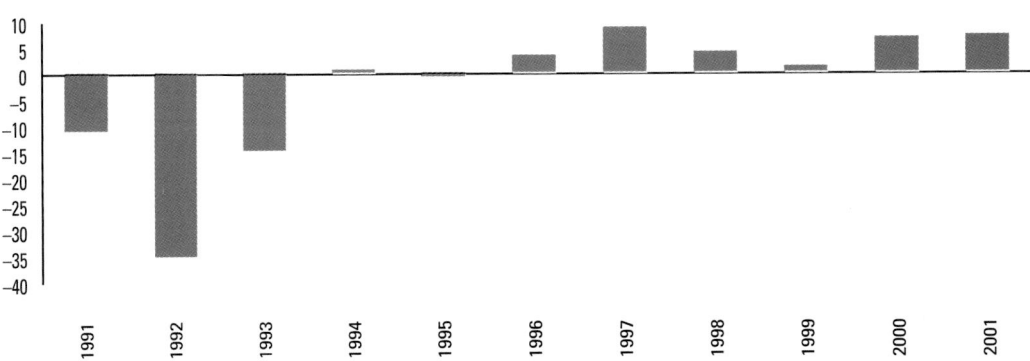

Source: IMF *World Economic Outlook Database,* April 2002

National competitiveness balance sheet

NOTABLE COMPETITIVE ADVANTAGES		NOTABLE COMPETITIVE DISADVANTAGES	
Criteria	Rank	Criteria	Rank

Growth Competitiveness

Macroeconomic Environment

2.01	Recession expectations	9
2.05	Access to credit	9
2.19	Inflation, 2001	26
2.15	Government surplus/deficit, 2001	37

Technology

3.18	Tertiary enrollment	15
3.05	Prevalence of foreign technology licensing	21
3.04	FDI and technology transfer	25
3.02	Firm-level innovation	26
4.11	Personal computers, 2001	29
4.02	Internet access in schools	32
4.04	Government prioritization of ICT	34
4.09	Internet hosts, 2001	35
4.10	Telephone lines, 2001	35
4.07	Cellular telephones, 2001	37

Growth Competitiveness

Macroeconomic Environment

2.21	Real exchange rate, 2001	70
2.17	National savings rate, 2001	56
2.16	Government expenditure, 2001	53
2.28	Interest rate spread, 2001	45

Technology

4.03	Quality of competition in the ISP sector	51
4.06	Laws relating to ICT	49
3.09	University/industry research collaboration	48
3.15	Utility patents, 2001	47
3.01	Technological sophistication	46
4.05	Government success in ICT promotion	45
3.07	Company spending on research and development	43
4.08	Internet users, 2001	43

Public Institutions

7.01	Irregular payments in exports & imports	57
6.03	Property rights	55
7.03	Irregular payments in tax collection	54
6.15	Organized crime	53
6.01	Judicial independence	50
6.09	Favoritism in decisions of government officials	48
7.02	Irregular payments in public utilities	48

Microeconomic Competitiveness

Sophistication of Company Operations and Strategy

3.05	Prevalence of foreign technology licensing	21
10.04	Capacity for innovation	39
10.08	Degree of customer orientation	41

Quality of the National Business Environment

3.11	Quality of math and science education	25
2.12	Extent of distortive government subsidies	29
2.04	Ease of access to loans	30

Other Indicators

1.04	Real growth in GDP per capita, 2000 to 2001	2
2.18	Investment rate, 2001	14
2.24	Average tariff rate, 2002	3
2.25	Corporate income tax rate, 2002	8
2.26	Individual income tax rate, 2002	6
6.06	Competence of public officials	26
6.21	Military expenditure relative to central government expenditure	6
8.09	Number of days to start a business	8
10.19	Flexibility of wage determination	25

Microeconomic Competitiveness

Sophistication of Company Operations and Strategy

10.09	Control of international distribution	67
10.03	Extent of branding	61
10.10	Extent of regional sales	59

Quality of the National Business Environment

8.02	Extent of locally based competitors	73
9.02	Local supplier quantity	61
2.07	Local equity market access	60

Other Indicators

2.20	M2 growth, 2001	65
2.29	FDI, 2001	69
2.30	Domestic credit, 2001	62
2.31	Liquid liabilities, 2001	65
5.14	Electric power	73
6.19	Pervasiveness of money laundering through banks	58
7.06	Irregular payments in government policy-making	57
7.07	Irregular payments in judicial decisions	58
7.14	Policy consequences of legal political donations	64
8.11	Cost of starting a business relative to GNP per capita	57
11.13	Political context of environmental gains	67

463

Lithuania

Key Economic Indicators

Total population (in millions), 2001 ....3.7
Population rank 69
GDP per capita (PPP), 2001 ....$7,764
GDP per capita rank...46
Real growth in GDP per capita, 2000 to 2001.........4.5
Growth rank 11
Unemployment rate, 2001.....................................12.50
Unemployment rank 57
Government surplus/deficit, 2001 ....–1.50
Government surplus/deficit rank 35
National savings rate, 2001 ....16.80
National savings rank..64
Investment rate, 2001 ....19.40
Investment rank...53
Inflation, 2001 ....1.30
Inflation rank 11
Exports of goods (as a percentage of GDP),
    2001 ....38.1
Exports rank..23
Imports of goods (as a percentage of GDP),
    2001 ....52.8
Imports rank..13
Internet users (per 10,000 inhabitants), 2001 ...679.16
Internet users rank 45

Competitiveness Rankings

Growth Competitiveness Rank	**36**

Technology Index Rank **40**
    Innovation Subindex Rank...................................33
    ICT Subindex Rank 40
    Technology Transfer Subindex Rank
        (out of 56 non-core innovators) 32
Public Institutions Index Rank...**36**
    Contracts and Law Subindex Rank 51
    Corruption Subindex Rank...................................16
Macroeconomic Environment Index Rank **45**
    Macroeconomic Stability Subindex Rank 37
    Country Credit Rating Rank..................................47
    Government Expenditure Rank 38

Microeconomic Competitiveness Rank	**40**

Company Operations and Strategy Rank **39**
Quality of the National Business Environment Rank ...**39**

Trade Performance of Leading Export Sectors

Sector	Share in national exports	Value of exports (US$ millions)	Value of net exports (US$ millions)	Share in world market	TPI current index	TPI change index
Clothing	14.9%	481	401	0.26%	20	53
Chemicals	11.5%	370	–362	0.06%	53	98
Processed food	9.8%	317	22	0.15%	34	68
Minerals	9.7%	313	–907	0.04%	69	52
Miscellaneous manufacturing	8.1%	263	–33	0.06%	33	35

Source: International Trade Centre UNCTAD/WTO

Real GDP (annual percent change)

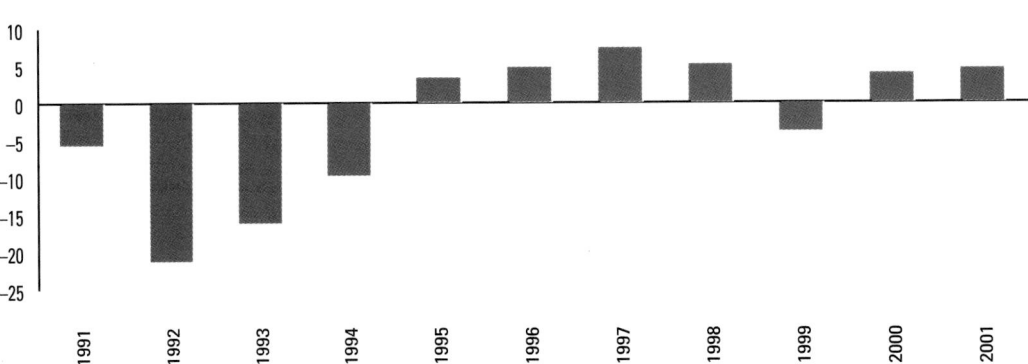

Source: IMF *World Economic Outlook Database,* April 2002

National competitiveness balance sheet

NOTABLE COMPETITIVE ADVANTAGES	
Criteria	Rank

Growth Competitiveness

Macroeconomic Environment

2.19	Inflation, 2001	11
2.05	Access to credit	12
2.01	Recession expectations	27
2.15	Government surplus/deficit, 2001	35
2.16	Government expenditure, 2001	38

Technology

3.18	Tertiary enrollment	32
4.10	Telephone lines, 2001	34
3.15	Utility patents, 2001	37
4.09	Internet hosts, 2001	37
3.07	Company spending on research and development	38
4.04	Government prioritization of ICT	39

Public Institutions

7.03	Irregular payments in tax collection	11
7.02	Irregular payments in public utilities	17
7.01	Irregular payments in exports & imports	22
6.09	Favoritism in decisions of government officials	35

Microeconomic Competitiveness

Sophistication of Company Operations and Strategy

10.02	Value chain presence	25
10.08	Degree of customer orientation	30
10.11	Breadth of international markets	33

Quality of the National Business Environment

2.04	Ease of access to loans	19
3.11	Quality of math and science education	21
8.01	Intensity of local competition	22

Other Indicators

2.22	Exports, 2001	23
2.23	Imports, 2001	13
2.24	Average tariff rate, 2002	7
2.25	Corporate income tax rate, 2002	7
3.17	Secondary enrollment	25
6.16	Informal sector	27
6.21	Military expenditure relative to central government expenditure	13
7.06	Irregular payments in government policy-making	18
8.07	Number of days to resolve a dispute	22
8.10	Total cost of starting a business	11
10.19	Flexibility of wage determination	7
10.21	Pay and productivity	17

NOTABLE COMPETITIVE DISADVANTAGES	
Criteria	Rank

Growth Competitiveness

Macroeconomic Environment

2.21	Real exchange rate, 2001	76
2.17	National savings rate, 2001	64
2.28	Interest rate spread, 2001	49

Technology

3.01	Technological sophistication	62
4.03	Quality of competition in the ISP sector	61
3.02	Firm-level innovation	59
3.05	Prevalence of foreign technology licensing	58
4.05	Government success in ICT promotion	55
3.09	University/industry research collaboration	53
4.06	Laws relating to ICT	53
3.04	FDI and technology transfer	47
4.08	Internet users, 2001	45
4.07	Cellular telephones, 2001	41
4.11	Personal computers, 2001	41
4.02	Internet access in schools	40

Public Institutions

6.15	Organized crime	60
6.01	Judicial independence	58
6.03	Property rights	49

Microeconomic Competitiveness

Sophistication of Company Operations and Strategy

10.14	Extent of incentive compensation	66
3.05	Prevalence of foreign technology licensing	58
10.12	Extent of staff training	58

Quality of the National Business Environment

6.13	Reliability of police services	66
9.01	Buyer sophistication	66
8.04	Administrative burden for startups	64

Other Indicators

2.09	Regulatory obstacles to business	71
2.20	M2 growth, 2001	66
2.29	FDI, 2001	65
2.30	Domestic credit, 2001	72
2.31	Liquid liabilities, 2001	73
3.13	Brain drain	62
6.12	Efficiency of the tax system	62
6.18	Pervasiveness of insider trading	65
7.14	Policy consequences of legal political donations	66
11.10	Flexibility of environmental regulations	64

465

Malaysia

Key Economic Indicators

Total population (in millions), 2001 ....23.8
Population rank 30
GDP per capita (PPP), 2001 ....$8,424
GDP per capita rank..43
Real growth in GDP per capita, 2000 to 2001 ....–1.8
Growth rank...72
Unemployment rate, 2001................................3.80
Unemployment rank 12
Government surplus/deficit, 2001 ....–5.40
Government surplus/deficit rank 64
National savings rate, 2001 ....32.27
National savings rank...8
Investment rate, 2001 ....25.06
Investment rank..22
Inflation, 2001 ....1.40
Inflation rank...12
Exports of goods (as a percentage of GDP),
    2001 ....102.8
Exports rank...3
Imports of goods (as a percentage of GDP),
    2001 ....86.9
Imports rank...3
Internet users (per 10,000 inhabitants),
    2001 ....2,394.96
Internet users rank 26

Competitiveness Rankings

Growth Competitiveness Rank	**27**
Technology Index Rank	**26**
Innovation Subindex Rank	52
ICT Subindex Rank	32
Technology Transfer Subindex Rank (out of 56 non-core innovators)	1
Public Institutions Index Rank	**33**
Contracts and Law Subindex Rank	34
Corruption Subindex Rank	34
Macroeconomic Environment Index Rank	**20**
Macroeconomic Stability Subindex Rank	7
Country Credit Rating Rank	37
Government Expenditure Rank	37
Microeconomic Competitiveness Rank	**26**
Company Operations and Strategy Rank	**27**
Quality of the National Business Environment Rank	**26**

Trade Performance of Leading Export Sectors

Sector	Share in national exports	Value of exports (US$ millions)	Value of net exports (US$ millions)	Share in world market	TPI current index	TPI change index
IT and consumer electronics	34.6%	33,652	25,761	5.32%	7	30
Electronic components	24.8%	24,130	–8,219	4.04%	24	5
Minerals	9.7%	9,414	5,735	1.35%	8	27
Miscellaneous manufacturing	5.7%	5,502	1,144	1.18%	9	19
Processed food	4.8%	4,617	2,967	2.14%	12	66

Source: International Trade Centre UNCTAD/WTO

Real GDP (annual percent change)

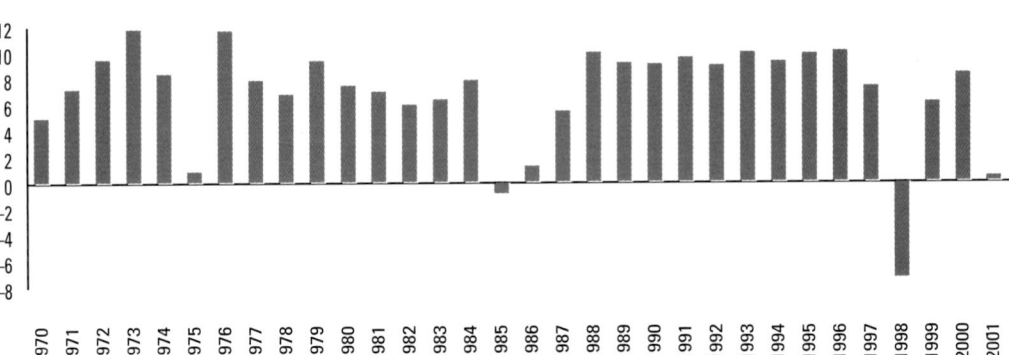

Source: IMF *World Economic Outlook Database,* April 2002

National competitiveness balance sheet

NOTABLE COMPETITIVE ADVANTAGES	
Criteria	Rank

Growth Competitiveness

Macroeconomic Environment

2.01	Recession expectations	2
2.17	National savings rate, 2001	8
2.19	Inflation, 2001	12
2.28	Interest rate spread, 2001	14
2.21	Real exchange rate, 2001	24

Technology

4.04	Government prioritization of ICT	4
3.05	Prevalence of foreign technology licensing	5
4.05	Government success in ICT promotion	6
3.04	FDI and technology transfer	8
3.02	Firm-level innovation	15
4.06	Laws relating to ICT	16
3.01	Technological sophistication	23
3.07	Company spending on research and development	23
4.08	Internet users, 2001	26

Public Institutions

6.03	Property rights	25

Microeconomic Competitiveness

Sophistication of Company Operations and Strategy

3.05	Prevalence of foreign technology licensing	5
10.13	Willingness to delegate authority	22
10.11	Breadth of international markets	23

Quality of the National Business Environment

3.10	Government procurement of advanced technology products	7
8.04	Administrative burden for startups	11
5.01	Overall infrastructure quality	16

Other Indicators

1.08	Unemployment rate, 2001	12
2.20	M2 growth, 2001	6
2.22	Exports, 2001	3
2.23	Imports, 2001	3
2.31	Liquid liabilities, 2001	4
3.17	Secondary enrollment	10
6.07	Burden of regulation	13
6.11	Effectiveness of law-making bodies	9
6.12	Efficiency of the tax system	7
8.07	Number of days to resolve a dispute	13
8.08	Number of procedures to start a business	14
11.10	Flexibility of environmental regulations	15

NOTABLE COMPETITIVE DISADVANTAGES	
Criteria	Rank

Growth Competitiveness

Macroeconomic Environment

2.15	Government surplus/deficit, 2001	64
2.05	Access to credit	41
2.16	Government expenditure, 2001	37

Technology

3.18	Tertiary enrollment	63
4.10	Telephone lines, 2001	48
4.09	Internet hosts, 2001	46
4.03	Quality of competition in the ISP sector	39
4.02	Internet access in schools	37
4.07	Cellular telephones, 2001	36
3.15	Utility patents, 2001	32
4.11	Personal computers, 2001	31
3.09	University/industry research collaboration	28

Public Institutions

6.01	Judicial independence	44
7.01	Irregular payments in exports & imports	42
7.02	Irregular payments in public utilities	40
6.09	Favoritism in decisions of government officials	38
6.15	Organized crime	30
7.03	Irregular payments in tax collection	28

Microeconomic Competitiveness

Sophistication of Company Operations and Strategy

10.01	Nature of competitive advantage	41
10.09	Control of international distribution	37
10.04	Capacity for innovation	36

Quality of the National Business Environment

3.12	Availability of scientists and engineers	52
10.16	Quality of management schools	48
10.17	Efficacy of corporate boards	44

Other Indicators

2.03	Soundness of banks	44
2.09	Regulatory obstacles to business	57
6.05	Freedom of the press	73
7.04	Irregular payments in public contracts	41
8.11	Cost of starting a business relative to GNP per capita	53
10.18	Hiring and firing practices	43
11.06	Subsidies for energy or materials	51

467

Mauritius

Key Economic Indicators

Total population (in millions), 2001 ....1.2
Population rank 79
GDP per capita (PPP), 2001 ....$10,400
GDP per capita rank...33
Real growth in GDP per capita, 2000 to 2001.........5.4
Growth rank 9
Unemployment rate, 2001.................................8.60
Unemployment rank 42
Government surplus/deficit, 2001 ....−6.50
Government surplus/deficit rank 73
National savings rate, 2001 ....28.00
National savings rank 13
Investment rate, 2001 ....23.00
Investment rank...32
Inflation, 2001 ....4.40
Inflation rank 42
Exports of goods (as a percentage of GDP),
    2001 ....34.4
Exports rank..27
Imports of goods (as a percentage of GDP),
    2001 ....47.4
Imports rank..20
Internet users (per 10,000 inhabitants),
    2001 ....1,316.67
Internet users rank 34

Competitiveness Rankings

Growth Competitiveness Rank	35

Technology Index Rank **45**
Innovation Subindex Rank....................................72
ICT Subindex Rank 39
Technology Transfer Subindex Rank
(out of 56 non-core innovators) 36
Public Institutions Index Rank...........................**35**
Contracts and Law Subindex Rank 25
Corruption Subindex Rank...................................42
Macroeconomic Environment Index Rank **36**
Macroeconomic Stability Subindex Rank.............56
Country Credit Rating Rank....................................38
Government Expenditure Rank 24

Microeconomic Competitiveness Rank	49

Company Operations and Strategy Rank **42**
Quality of the National Business Environment Rank ...**50**

468

Trade Performance of Leading Export Sectors

Sector	Share in national exports	Value of exports (US$ millions)	Value of net exports (US$ millions)	Share in world market	TPI current index	TPI change index
Clothing	63.9%	947	929	0.51%	29	87
Processed food	17.7%	262	114	0.12%	63	108
Miscellaneous manufacturing	5.7%	84	−61	0.02%	57	88
Textiles	5.4%	79	−329	0.05%	71	35
Minerals	2.6%	39	−171	0.01%	121	78

Source: International Trade Centre UNCTAD/WTO

Real GDP (annual percent change)

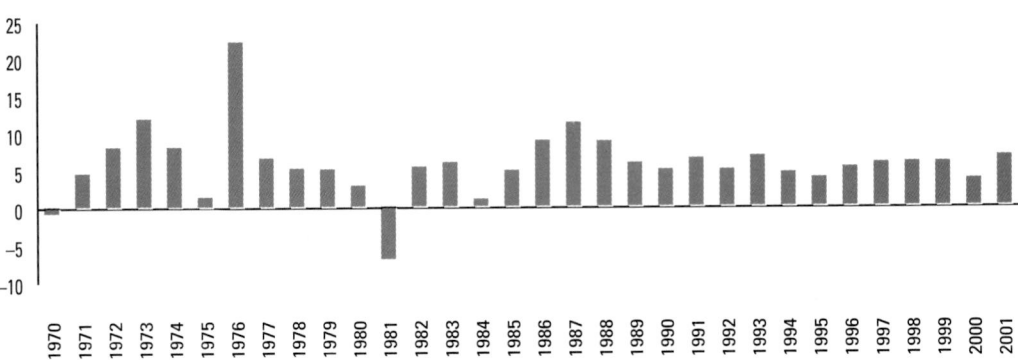

Source: IMF *World Economic Outlook Database,* April 2002

National competitiveness balance sheet

NOTABLE COMPETITIVE ADVANTAGES

Criteria	Rank

Growth Competitiveness

Macroeconomic Environment

2.21	Real exchange rate, 2001	5
2.17	National savings rate, 2001	27
2.05	Access to credit	35

Technology

3.02	Firm-level innovation	14
4.05	Government success in ICT promotion	34
3.04	FDI and technology transfer	35

Public Institutions

6.01	Judicial independence	23
6.03	Property rights	31
6.09	Favoritism in decisions of government officials	37
6.15	Organized crime	44

Microeconomic Competitiveness

Sophistication of Company Operations and Strategy

10.01	Nature of competitive advantage	31
10.15	Reliance on professional management	35
10.12	Extent of staff training	40

Quality of the National Business Environment

6.02	Efficiency of legal framework	20
8.04	Administrative burden for startups	20
5.01	Overall infrastructure quality	22

Other Indicators

2.03	Soundness of banks	26
2.08	Business costs of terrorism	27
2.20	M2 growth, 2001	22
2.22	Exports, 2001	22
2.23	Imports, 2001	18
2.32	Bank liquid reserves	23
6.07	Burden of regulation	12
6.08	Transparency of government policy-making	23
6.12	Efficiency of the tax system	10
6.18	Pervasiveness of insider trading	13
6.19	Pervasiveness of money laundering through banks	18
7.12	Public trust of politicians	28
7.13	Prevalence of illegal political donations	25
11.09	Clarity and stability of environmental regulations	21
11.13	Political context of environmental gains	15

NOTABLE COMPETITIVE DISADVANTAGES

Criteria	Rank

Growth Competitiveness

Macroeconomic Environment

2.15	Government surplus/deficit, 2001	66
2.19	Inflation, 2001	66
2.28	Interest rate spread, 2001	53
2.16	Government expenditure, 2001	51
2.01	Recession expectations	46

Technology

3.18	Tertiary enrollment	70
3.15	Utility patents, 2001	68
4.07	Cellular telephones, 2001	67
4.10	Telephone lines, 2001	65
4.08	Internet users, 2001	62
4.11	Personal computers, 2001	56
3.09	University/industry research collaboration	54
4.03	Quality of competition in the ISP sector	49
4.09	Internet hosts, 2001	49
4.04	Government prioritization of ICT	48
3.01	Technological sophistication	47
3.05	Prevalence of foreign technology licensing	47
4.06	Laws relating to ICT	47
3.07	Company spending on research and development	46
4.02	Internet access in schools	46

Public Institutions

7.02	Irregular payments in public utilities	56
7.03	Irregular payments in tax collection	48
7.01	Irregular payments in exports & imports	47

Microeconomic Competitiveness

Sophistication of Company Operations and Strategy

10.09	Control of international distribution	71
10.08	Degree of customer orientation	68
10.02	Value chain presence	68

Quality of the National Business Environment

3.12	Availability of scientists and engineers	79
10.16	Quality of management schools	77
9.08	Local availability of components and parts	76

Other Indicators

1.08	Unemployment rate, 2001	78
1.09	Employment to population ratio, 2001	71
2.24	Average tariff rate, 2002	61
2.29	FDI, 2001	70
6.05	Freedom of the press	52
6.06	Competence of public officials	56
6.14	Business costs of crime and violence	58
7.04	Irregular payments in public contracts	58

Netherlands

Key Economic Indicators

Total population (in millions), 2001 ....16.0
Population rank 35
GDP per capita (PPP), 2001 ....$26,242
GDP per capita rank..12
Real growth in GDP per capita, 2000 to 2001.........0.4
Growth rank...51
Unemployment rate, 2001....................................2.04
Unemployment rank 3
Government surplus/deficit, 2001 ....0.32
Government surplus/deficit rank 14
National savings rate, 2001 ....25.63
National savings rank 21
Investment rate, 2001 ....21.99
Investment rank...38
Inflation, 2001 ....5.10
Inflation rank...49
Exports of goods (as a percentage of GDP),
    2001 ....56.7
Exports rank..11
Imports of goods (as a percentage of GDP),
    2001 ....51.1
Imports rank..16
Internet users (per 10,000 inhabitants),
    2001 ....3,291.72
Internet users rank 18

Competitiveness Rankings

Growth Competitiveness Rank	15

Technology Index Rank **19**
    Innovation Subindex Rank....................................17
    ICT Subindex Rank..12
Public Institutions Index Rank............................**10**
    Contracts and Law Subindex Rank 11
    Corruption Subindex Rank...................................13
Macroeconomic Environment Index Rank **19**
    Macroeconomic Stability Subindex Rank.............34
    Country Credit Rating Rank...................................3
    Government Expenditure Rank 64

Microeconomic Competitiveness Rank	7

Company Operations and Strategy Rank **8**
Quality of the National Business Environment Rank ...**10**

476

Trade Performance of Leading Export Sectors

Sector	Share in national exports	Value of exports (US$ millions)	Value of net exports (US$ millions)	Share in world market	TPI current index	TPI change index
IT and consumer electronics	17.0%	30,342	–3,244	4.80%	13	36
Chemicals	14.4%	25,733	5,894	4.26%	2	94
Minerals	10.4%	18,498	–3,127	2.65%	18	65
Processed food	9.5%	16,964	7,883	7.86%	2	88
Miscellaneous manufacturing	8.7%	15,513	798	3.33%	2	36

Source: International Trade Centre UNCTAD/WTO

Real GDP (annual percent change)

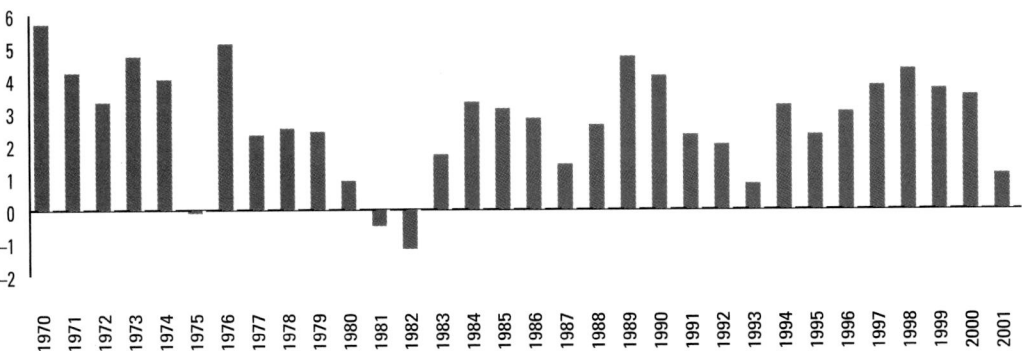

Source: IMF *World Economic Outlook Database*, April 2002

National competitiveness balance sheet

NOTABLE COMPETITIVE ADVANTAGES

Criteria	Rank

Growth Competitiveness

Macroeconomic Environment

| 2.28 | Interest rate spread, 2001 | 5 |
| 2.15 | Government surplus/deficit, 2001 | 14 |

Technology

4.09	Internet hosts, 2001	4
4.11	Personal computers, 2001	8
4.10	Telephone lines, 2001	9
3.15	Utility patents, 2001	11
3.07	Company spending on research and development	12
3.09	University/industry research collaboration	13
4.07	Cellular telephones, 2001	15

Public Institutions

6.01	Judicial independence	4
6.03	Property rights	10
7.02	Irregular payments in public utilities	11
6.09	Favoritism in decisions of government officials	12
7.01	Irregular payments in exports & imports	12
7.03	Irregular payments in tax collection	12

Microeconomic Competitiveness

Sophistication of Company Operations and Strategy

10.13	Willingness to delegate authority	4
10.06	Production process sophistication	5
10.15	Reliance on professional management	6

Quality of the National Business Environment

11.05	Stringency of environmental regulations	3
6.01	Judicial independence	4
6.04	Intellectual property protection	4

Other Indicators

1.08	Unemployment rate, 2001	3
2.03	Soundness of banks	5
2.29	FDI, 2001	8
3.13	Brain drain	3
5.09	Disparity in healthcare quality	5
6.05	Freedom of the press	4
6.17	Strength of auditing and accounting standards	6
6.18	Pervasiveness of insider trading	2
7.12	Public trust of politicians	6
7.13	Prevalence of illegal political donations	4
7.14	Policy consequences of legal political donations	2
7.15	Misuse of legal political donations	6
8.07	Number of days to resolve a disput	2
10.05	Ethical behavior of firms	6
11.02	Water pollution regulations	2
11.08	Compliance with international environmental agreements	2

NOTABLE COMPETITIVE DISADVANTAGES

Criteria	Rank

Growth Competitiveness

Macroeconomic Environment

2.16	Government expenditure, 2001	64
2.05	Access to credit	60
2.19	Inflation, 2001	49
2.01	Recession expectations	47
2.21	Real exchange rate, 2001	26
2.17	National savings rate, 2001	21

Technology

3.02	Firm-level innovation	69
4.05	Government success in ICT promotion	39
4.04	Government prioritization of ICT	36
4.06	Laws relating to ICT	22
3.01	Technological sophistication	21
3.18	Tertiary enrollment	19
4.08	Internet users, 2001	18
4.02	Internet access in schools	16
4.03	Quality of competition in the ISP sector	16

Public Institutions

| 6.15 | Organized crime | 29 |

Microeconomic Competitiveness

Quality of the National Business Environment

6.10	Extent of bureaucratic red tape	50
3.12	Availability of scientists and engineers	39
9.08	Local availability of components and parts	30

Other Indicators

2.09	Regulatory obstacles to business	69
2.18	Investment rate, 2001	38
2.26	Individual income tax rate, 2002	74
3.03	Firm-level technology absorption	44
8.09	Number of days to start a business	51
8.10	Total cost of starting a business	68
10.18	Hiring and firing practices	60
10.19	Flexibility of wage determination	72
10.21	Pay and productivity	60

New Zealand

Key Economic Indicators

Total population (in millions), 2001 ....3.8
Population rank 67
GDP per capita (PPP), 2001 ....$20,725
GDP per capita rank...22
Real growth in GDP per capita, 2000 to 2001.........1.5
Growth rank..35
Unemployment rate, 2001....................................5.30
Unemployment rank 25
Government surplus/deficit, 2001 ....2.00
Government surplus/deficit rank 7
National savings rate, 2001 ....17.10
National savings rank..62
Investment rate, 2001 ....19.18
Investment rank...56
Inflation, 2001 ....2.70
Inflation rank 31
Exports of goods (as a percentage of GDP),
   2001 ....27.7
Exports rank...39
Imports of goods (as a percentage of GDP),
   2001 ....26.9
Imports rank...53
Internet users (per 10,000 inhabitants),
   2001 ....2,806.98
Internet users rank 22

Competitiveness Rankings

Growth Competitiveness Rank	16

Technology Index Rank **27**
   Innovation Subindex Rank 19
   ICT Subindex Rank 21
Public Institutions Index Rank............................**4**
   Contracts and Law Subindex Rank 5
   Corruption Subindex Rank..................................4
Macroeconomic Environment Index Rank **17**
   Macroeconomic Stability Subindex Rank 16
   Country Credit Rating Rank................................21
   Government Expenditure Rank 49

Microeconomic Competitiveness Rank	22

Company Operations and Strategy Rank **25**
Quality of the National Business Environment Rank ...**20**

Trade Performance of Leading Export Sectors

Sector	Share in national exports	Value of exports (US$ millions)	Value of net exports (US$ millions)	Share in world market	TPI current index	TPI change index
Fresh food	31.2%	3,755	3,348	1.58%	6	157
Processed food	23.4%	2,818	2,066	1.31%	8	44
Wood products	12.4%	1,486	1,008	0.80%	17	49
Chemicals	7.7%	931	−908	0.15%	55	85
Basic manufactures	7.5%	902	−39	0.21%	53	98

Source: International Trade Centre UNCTAD/WTO

Real GDP (annual percent change)

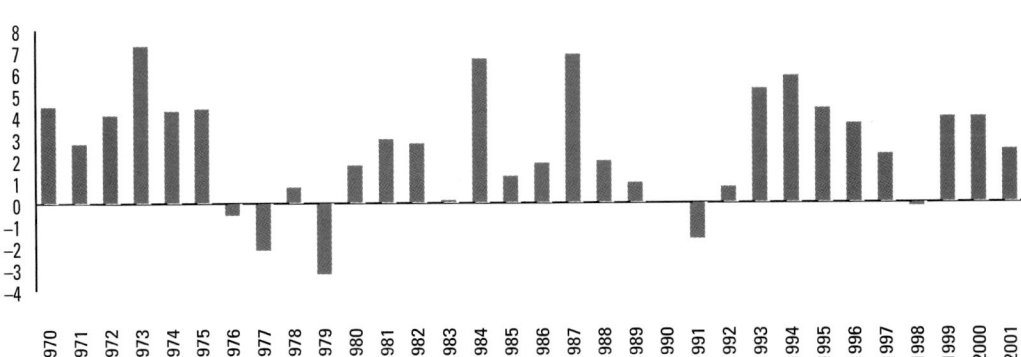

Source: IMF *World Economic Outlook Database,* April 2002

National competitiveness balance sheet

NOTABLE COMPETITIVE ADVANTAGES

Criteria	Rank

Growth Competitiveness

Macroeconomic Environment

2.15	Government surplus/deficit, 2001	7
2.21	Real exchange rate, 2001	12
2.05	Access to credit	15

Technology

4.09	Internet hosts, 2001	6
3.18	Tertiary enrollment	8
4.02	Internet access in schools	12
4.11	Personal computers, 2001	13

Public Institutions

6.01	Judicial independence	3
7.01	Irregular payments in exports & imports	3
7.03	Irregular payments in tax collection	4
7.02	Irregular payments in public utilities	5
6.09	Favoritism in decisions of government officials	6
6.15	Organized crime	7
6.03	Property rights	13

Microeconomic Competitiveness

Sophistication of Company Operations and Strategy

10.15	Reliance on professional management	5
10.13	Willingness to delegate authority	15
10.04	Capacity for innovation	20

Quality of the National Business Environment

6.01	Judicial independence	3
10.17	Efficacy of corporate boards	4
2.11	Cost of importing foreign equipment	5

Other Indicators

2.03	Soundness of banks	10
2.08	Business costs of terrorism	11
2.32	Bank liquid reserves	4
5.07	Postal efficiency	4
6.14	Business costs of crime and violence	10
6.16	Informal sector	2
6.17	Strength of auditing and accounting standards	10
6.18	Pervasiveness of insider trading	5
6.19	Pervasiveness of money laundering through banks	3
7.10	Diversion of public funds	3
7.15	Misuse of legal political donations	2
8.06	Number of procedures to resolve a dispute	5
8.09	Number of days to start a business	1
8.11	Cost of starting a business relative to GNP per capita	2
11.08	Compliance with international environmental agreements	6

NOTABLE COMPETITIVE DISADVANTAGES

Criteria	Rank

Growth Competitiveness

Macroeconomic Environment

2.17	National savings rate, 2001	62
2.16	Government expenditure, 2001	49
2.19	Inflation, 2001	31
2.28	Interest rate spread, 2001	29
2.01	Recession expectations	23

Technology

3.02	Firm-level innovation	63
4.04	Government prioritization of ICT	52
4.05	Government success in ICT promotion	48
4.03	Quality of competition in the ISP sector	31
3.07	Company spending on research and development	28
4.06	Laws relating to ICT	26
3.15	Utility patents, 2001	23
4.07	Cellular telephones, 2001	23
3.01	Technological sophistication	22
4.08	Internet users, 2001	22
4.10	Telephone lines, 2001	22
3.09	University/industry research collaboration	21

Microeconomic Competitiveness

Sophistication of Company Operations and Strategy

10.02	Value chain presence	48
10.01	Nature of competitive advantage	37
10.14	Extent of incentive compensation	28

Quality of the National Business Environment

3.12	Availability of scientists and engineers	50
9.09	Local availability of process machinery	45
9.07	Extent of collaboration among clusters	42

Other Indicators

2.18	Investment rate, 2001	56
2.20	M2 growth, 2001	55
2.25	Corporate income tax rate, 2002	53
3.08	Subsidies and tax credits for firm-level research and development	60
3.13	Brain drain	55
10.18	Hiring and firing practices	44
11.12	Effects of compliance with environmental regulations on business	56

Nicaragua

Key Economic Indicators

Total population (in millions), 2001 ....5.2
Population rank 60
GDP per capita (PPP), 2001 ....$2,514
GDP per capita rank...72
Real growth in GDP per capita, 2000 to 2001.........0.3
Growth rank 54
Unemployment rate, 2001..................................23.08
Unemployment rank 75
Government surplus/deficit, 2001 ....–16.80
Government surplus/deficit rank 80
National savings rate, 2001 ....0.20
National savings rank 80
Investment rate, 2001 ....33.30
Investment rank...2
Inflation, 2001 ....8.30
Inflation rank 62
Exports of goods (as a percentage of GDP),
    2001 ....24.0
Exports rank..47
Imports of goods (as a percentage of GDP),
    2001 ....70.4
Imports rank..8
Internet users (per 10,000 inhabitants), 2001 .....98.54
Internet users rank 71

Competitiveness Rankings

Growth Competitiveness Rank	75

Technology Index Rank 73
   Innovation Subindex Rank 70
   ICT Subindex Rank 75
   Technology Transfer Subindex Rank
     (out of 56 non-core innovators) 42

Public Institutions Index Rank...........................64
   Contracts and Law Subindex Rank 69
   Corruption Subindex Rank................................60

Macroeconomic Environment Index Rank 79
   Macroeconomic Stability Subindex Rank 76
   Country Credit Rating Rank................................77
   Government Expenditure Rank 58

Microeconomic Competitiveness Rank	75

Company Operations and Strategy Rank 75
Quality of the National Business Environment Rank ...76

Trade Performance of Leading Export Sectors

Sector	Share in national exports	Value of exports (US$ millions)	Value of net exports (US$ millions)	Share in world market	TPI current index	TPI change index
Fresh food	75.2%	451	371	0.19%	49	50
Processed food	14.4%	86	–111	0.04%	82	21
Wood products	2.9%	17	–38	0.01%	85	91
Miscellaneous manufacturing	1.4%	9	–103	0.00%	115	76
Leather products	1.2%	7	–9	0.01%	76	41

Source: International Trade Centre UNCTAD/WTO

Real GDP (annual percent change)

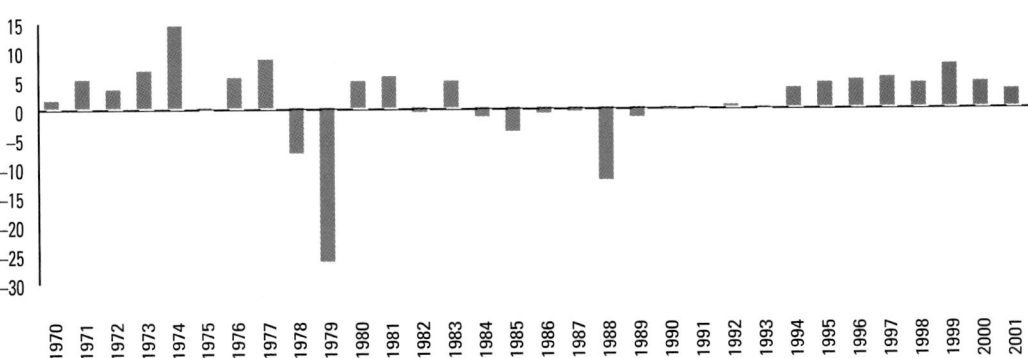

Source: IMF *World Economic Outlook Database,* April 2002

National competitiveness balance sheet

NOTABLE COMPETITIVE ADVANTAGES

Criteria	Rank

Macroeconomic Environment

2.01	Recession expectations	26
2.21	Real exchange rate, 2001	40

Technology

3.04	FDI and technology transfer	28

Public Institutions

6.15	Organized crime	48

Microeconomic Competitiveness

Sophistication of Company Operations and Strategy

10.01	Nature of competitive advantage	36

Quality of the National Business Environment

6.10	Extent of bureaucratic red tape	13
9.09	Local availability of process machinery	43
2.11	Cost of importing foreign equipment	47

Other Indicators

2.18	Investment rate, 2001	2
2.20	M2 growth, 2001	35
2.23	Imports, 2001	8
2.25	Corporate income tax rate, 2002	8
2.26	Individual income tax rate, 2002	6
2.30	Domestic credit, 2001	2
2.31	Liquid liabilities, 2001	16
6.06	Competence of public officials	44
6.21	Military expenditure relative to central government expenditure	9
10.18	Hiring and firing practices	13

NOTABLE COMPETITIVE DISADVANTAGES

Criteria	Rank

Growth Competitiveness

Macroeconomic Environment

2.15	Government surplus/deficit, 2001	80
2.17	National savings rate, 2001	80
2.28	Interest rate spread, 2001	74
2.19	Inflation, 2001	62
2.05	Access to credit	61
2.16	Government expenditure, 2001	58

Technology

4.02	Internet access in schools	78
4.03	Quality of competition in the ISP sector	78
3.07	Company spending on research and development	76
4.10	Telephone lines, 2001	76
4.11	Personal computers, 2001	74
3.01	Technological sophistication	73
4.05	Government success in ICT promotion	73
4.07	Cellular telephones, 2001	73
3.05	Prevalence of foreign technology licensing	72
4.06	Laws relating to ICT	72
4.08	Internet users, 2001	71
4.04	Government prioritization of ICT	70
3.15	Utility patents, 2001	68
3.02	Firm-level innovation	67
3.09	University/industry research collaboration	65
4.09	Internet hosts, 2001	64
3.18	Tertiary enrollment	62

Public Institutions

6.09	Favoritism in decisions of government officials	76
6.01	Judicial independence	74
6.03	Property rights	74
7.03	Irregular payments in tax collection	60
7.02	Irregular payments in public utilities	58
7.01	Irregular payments in exports & imports	56

Microeconomic Competitiveness

Sophistication of Company Operations and Strategy

10.15	Reliance on professional management	80
10.08	Degree of customer orientation	78
10.10	Extent of regional sales	77

Quality of the National Business Environment

2.10	Hidden trade barriers	80
5.08	Quality of public schools	80
8.01	Intensity of local competition	80

Other Indicators

1.08	Unemployment rate, 2001	75
1.09	Employment to population ratio, 2001	70
2.03	Soundness of banks	74
2.29	FDI, 2001	74
3.03	Firm-level technology absorption	78
3.17	Secondary enrollment	67
5.07	Postal efficiency	71
5.09	Disparity in healthcare quality	74
6.08	Transparency of government policy-making	76
7.10	Diversion of public funds	74
7.15	Misuse of legal political donations	76
8.11	Cost of starting a business relative to GNP per capita	72
10.21	Pay and productivity	70
11.03	Toxic waste disposal regulations	79

481

Nigeria

Key Economic Indicators

Total population (in millions), 2001 ....118.3
Population rank 9
GDP per capita (PPP), 2001 ....$898
GDP per capita rank..80
Real growth in GDP per capita, 2000 to 2001........1.9
Growth rank 29
Unemployment rate, 2001....................................3.80
Unemployment rank 13
Government surplus/deficit, 2001 ....–5.30
Government surplus/deficit rank 63
National savings rate, 2001 ....28.60
National savings rank 12
Investment rate, 2001 ....25.50
Investment rank..17
Inflation, 2001 ....18.90
Inflation rank 75
Exports of goods (as a percentage of GDP),
     2001 ....49.3
Exports rank...14
Imports of goods (as a percentage of GDP),
     2001 ....33.4
Imports rank...36
Internet users (per 10,000 inhabitants), 2001 .....17.57
Internet users rank 79

Competitiveness Rankings

Growth Competitiveness Rank	**71**

Technology Index Rank **71**	
Innovation Subindex Rank 78	
ICT Subindex Rank 79	
Technology Transfer Subindex Rank	
(out of 56 non-core innovators) 17	
Public Institutions Index Rank.............................**78**	
Contracts and Law Subindex Rank 61	
Corruption Subindex Rank..................................78	
Macroeconomic Environment Index Rank **61**	
Macroeconomic Stability Subindex Rank 55	
Country Credit Rating Rank................................78	
Government Expenditure Rank 22	

Microeconomic Competitiveness Rank	**71**

Company Operations and Strategy Rank **71**	
Quality of the National Business Environment Rank ...**71**	

Trade Performance of Leading Export Sectors

Sector	Share in national exports	Value of exports (US$ millions)	Value of net exports (US$ millions)	Share in world market	TPI current index	TPI change index
Minerals	99.6%	38,874	38,675	5.56%	29	37

Source: International Trade Centre UNCTAD/WTO

Real GDP (annual percent change)

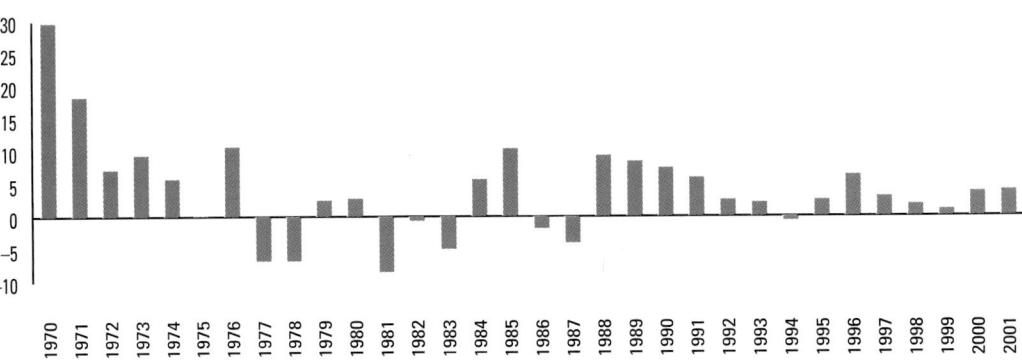

Source: IMF *World Economic Outlook Database,* April 2002

National competitiveness balance sheet

NOTABLE COMPETITIVE ADVANTAGES

Criteria	Rank

Growth Competitiveness

Macroeconomic Environment

2.17	National savings rate, 2001	1
2.15	Government surplus/deficit, 2001	8
2.19	Inflation, 2001	8

Technology

4.04	Government prioritization of ICT	1
4.05	Government success in ICT promotion	1
4.06	Laws relating to ICT	2
4.08	Internet users, 2001	2
3.04	FDI and technology transfer	4
3.02	Firm-level innovation	6
4.02	Internet access in schools	4
4.11	Personal computers, 2001	4

Public Institutions

6.09	Favoritism in decisions of government officials	3
7.02	Irregular payments in public utilities	7
7.03	Irregular payments in tax collection	7
6.15	Organized crime	5
7.01	Irregular payments in exports & imports	5

Microeconomic Competitiveness

Sophistication of Company Operations and Strategy

3.05	Prevalence of foreign technology licensing	4
10.12	Extent of staff training	10
10.06	Production process sophistication	13

Quality of the National Business Environment

2.11	Cost of importing foreign equipment	1
3.11	Quality of math and science education	1
10.20	Cooperation in labor-employer relations	1

Other Indicators

1.09	Employment to population ratio, 2001	3
2.18	Investment rate, 2001	4
2.22	Exports, 2001	1
2.23	Imports, 2001	1
2.24	Average tariff rate, 2002	3
2.27	Value added tax rate, 2002	3
3.04	FDI and technology transfer	4
3.08	Subsidies and tax credits for firm-level research and development	2
6.06	Competence of public officials	1
6.07	Burden of regulation	2
6.08	Transparency of government policy-making	1
6.11	Effectiveness of law-making bodies	1
6.12	Efficiency of the tax system	2
6.14	Business costs of crime and violence	2
7.10	Diversion of public funds	4
7.12	Public trust of politicians	1
7.13	Prevalence of illegal political donations	1
8.07	Number of days to resolve a dispute	3
10.18	Hiring and firing practices	2
10.21	Pay and productivity	4
11.09	Clarity and stability of environmental regulations	1

NOTABLE COMPETITIVE DISADVANTAGES

Criteria	Rank

Growth Competitiveness

Macroeconomic Environment

2.21	Real exchange rate, 2001	43
2.28	Interest rate spread, 2001	27
2.05	Access to credit	17

Technology

3.18	Tertiary enrollment	29
4.10	Telephone lines, 2001	22
4.07	Cellular telephones, 2001	18
3.07	Company spending on research and development	16
4.03	Quality of competition in the ISP sector	15
4.09	Internet hosts, 2001	15

Public Institutions

6.01	Judicial independence	25

Microeconomic Competitiveness

Sophistication of Company Operations and Strategy

10.09	Control of international distribution	40
10.04	Capacity for innovation	25
10.10	Extent of regional sales	22

Quality of the National Business Environment

8.02	Extent of locally based competitors	43
9.08	Local availability of components and parts	43
9.09	Local availability of process machinery	39

Other Indicators

1.04	Real growth in GDP per capita, 2000 to 2001	76
2.08	Business costs of terrorism	38
6.05	Freedom of the press	72
6.22	Military expenditure relative to GNI	72
8.06	Number of procedures to resolve a dispute	37
8.10	Total cost of starting a business	58

Slovak Republic

504

Key Economic Indicators

Total population (in millions), 2001 ....5.4
Population rank 58
GDP per capita (PPP), 2001 ....$11,739
GDP per capita rank...32
Real growth in GDP per capita, 2000 to 2001.........3.2
Growth rank...21
Unemployment rate, 2001.................................18.62
Unemployment rank 71
Government surplus/deficit, 2001 ....–4.60
Government surplus/deficit rank 56
National savings rate, 2001.................................26.60
National savings rank..17
Investment rate, 2001 ....31.86
Investment rank...3
Inflation, 2001 ....7.30
Inflation rank 58
Exports of goods (as a percentage of GDP),
   2001 ....63.3
Exports rank..7
Imports of goods (as a percentage of GDP),
   2001 ....74.0
Imports rank..6
Internet users (per 10,000 inhabitants),
   2001 ....1,203.26
Internet users rank 35

Competitiveness Rankings

Growth Competitiveness Rank	49

Technology Index Rank	**34**
Innovation Subindex Rank 44	
ICT Subindex Rank 34	
Technology Transfer Subindex Rank	
(out of 56 non-core innovators) 22	
Public Institutions Index Rank.............................	**53**
Contracts and Law Subindex Rank 57	
Corruption Subindex Rank....................................44	
Macroeconomic Environment Index Rank	**64**
Macroeconomic Stability Subindex Rank 52	
Country Credit Rating Rank...................................43	
Government Expenditure Rank 59	

Microeconomic Competitiveness Rank	42

Company Operations and Strategy Rank 43

Quality of the National Business Environment Rank ...40

Trade Performance of Leading Export Sectors

Sector	Share in national exports	Value of exports (US$ millions)	Value of net exports (US$ millions)	Share in world market	TPI current index	TPI change index
Transport equipment	22.1%	1,885	377	0.27%	29	53
Basic manufactures	16.0%	1,363	369	0.31%	24	53
Chemicals	11.1%	941	–441	0.16%	44	101
Electronic components	8.9%	760	–28	0.13%	41	44
Nonelectronic machinery	8.9%	756	–601	0.13%	28	60

Source: International Trade Centre UNCTAD/WTO

Real GDP (annual percent change)

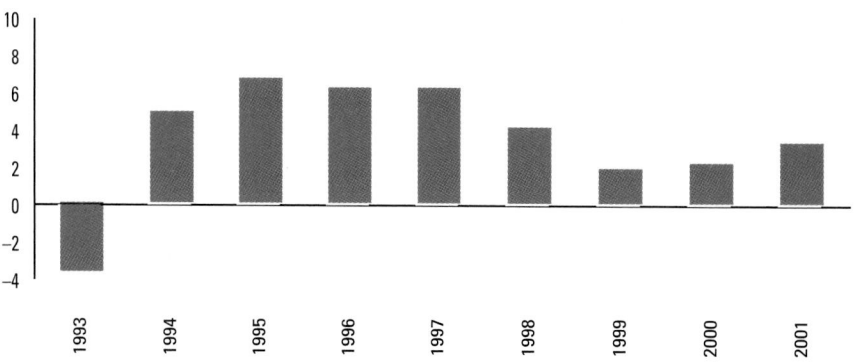

Source: IMF *World Economic Outlook Database*, April 2002

National competitiveness balance sheet

NOTABLE COMPETITIVE ADVANTAGES

Criteria		Rank

Growth Competitiveness

Macroeconomic Environment

2.17	National savings rate, 2001	17
2.05	Access to credit	22
2.28	Interest rate spread, 2001	35

Technology

3.02	Firm-level innovation	28
4.09	Internet hosts, 2001	29
3.05	Prevalence of foreign technology licensing	30
3.09	University/industry research collaboration	30
4.11	Personal computers, 2001	30
4.07	Cellular telephones, 2001	31
3.04	FDI and technology transfer	34
4.02	Internet access in schools	34
4.08	Internet users, 2001	35
4.10	Telephone lines, 2001	37

Microeconomic Competitiveness

Sophistication of Company Operations and Strategy

3.05	Prevalence of foreign technology licensing	30
10.03	Extent of branding	38
10.04	Capacity for innovation	38

Quality of the National Business Environment

3.12	Availability of scientists and engineers	3
3.11	Quality of math and science education	5
6.10	Extent of bureaucratic red tape	10

Other Indicators

2.08	Business costs of terrorism	9
2.18	Investment rate, 2001	3
2.22	Exports, 2001	7
2.23	Imports, 2001	6
2.24	Average tariff rate, 2002	15
3.03	Firm-level technology absorption	26
5.09	Disparity in healthcare quality	22
6.16	Informal sector	8
10.21	Pay and productivity	22
11.03	Toxic waste disposal regulations	19

NOTABLE COMPETITIVE DISADVANTAGES

Criteria		Rank

Growth Competitiveness

Macroeconomic Environment

2.01	Recession expectations	61
2.16	Government expenditure, 2001	59
2.19	Inflation, 2001	58
2.15	Government surplus/deficit, 2001	56
2.21	Real exchange rate, 2001	47

Technology

4.03	Quality of competition in the ISP sector	67
4.05	Government success in ICT promotion	63
4.04	Government prioritization of ICT	59
3.15	Utility patents, 2001	57
4.06	Laws relating to ICT	51
3.07	Company spending on research and development	49
3.18	Tertiary enrollment	47
3.01	Technological sophistication	43

Public Institutions

6.09	Favoritism in decisions of government officials	63
6.15	Organized crime	62
6.01	Judicial independence	57
6.03	Property rights	52
7.01	Irregular payments in exports & imports	51
7.03	Irregular payments in tax collection	47
7.02	Irregular payments in public utilities	41

Microeconomic Competitiveness

Sophistication of Company Operations and Strategy

10.14	Extent of incentive compensation	63
10.09	Control of international distribution	62
10.01	Nature of competitive advantage	60

Quality of the National Business Environment

5.04	Air transport infrastructure quality	80
2.07	Local equity market access	68
8.02	Extent of locally based competitors	67

Other Indicators

1.08	Unemployment rate, 2001	71
2.27	Value added tax rate, 2002	73
6.07	Burden of regulation	64
6.08	Transparency of government policy-making	63
6.11	Effectiveness of law-making bodies	63
7.04	Irregular payments in public contracts	69
8.09	Number of days to start a business	68
11.13	Political context of environmental gains	70

Slovenia

Key Economic Indicators

Total population (in millions), 2001 ....2.0
Population rank 74
GDP per capita (PPP), 2001 ....$18,233
GDP per capita rank...25
Real growth in GDP per capita, 2000 to 2001 ....3.1
Growth rank 22
Unemployment rate, 2001...................................11.60
Unemployment rank 55
Government surplus/deficit, 2001 ....–1.40
Government surplus/deficit rank 33
National savings rate, 2001 ....25.10
National savings rank 23
Investment rate, 2001 ....25.10
Investment rank...20
Inflation, 2001 ....8.40
Inflation rank 63
Exports of goods (as a percentage of GDP),
    2001 ....44.3
Exports rank...18
Imports of goods (as a percentage of GDP),
    2001 ....47.3
Imports rank...21
Internet users (per 10,000 inhabitants),
    2001 ....3,007.52
Internet users rank 20

Competitiveness Rankings

Growth Competitiveness Rank	**28**

Technology Index Rank **25**	
Innovation Subindex Rank 24	
ICT Subindex Rank 26	
Technology Transfer Subindex Rank	
(out of 56 non-core innovators) 38	
Public Institutions Index Rank...............................**23**	
Contracts and Law Subindex Rank 26	
Corruption Subindex Rank.....................................26	
Macroeconomic Environment Index Rank **50**	
Macroeconomic Stability Subindex Rank 35	
Country Credit Rating Rank...................................26	
Government Expenditure Rank 68	

Microeconomic Competitiveness Rank	**27**

Company Operations and Strategy Rank **26**
Quality of the National Business Environment Rank ...**27**

Trade Performance of Leading Export Sectors

Sector	Share in national exports	Value of exports (US$ millions)	Value of net exports (US$ millions)	Share in world market	TPI current index	TPI change index
Basic manufactures	13.9%	1,204	–164	0.28%	26	70
Miscellaneous manufacturing	13.8%	1,196	541	0.26%	19	78
Chemicals	13.4%	1,159	–230	0.19%	22	30
Transport equipment	12.8%	1,114	–108	0.16%	33	42
Electronic components	11.3%	977	345	0.16%	12	40

Source: International Trade Centre UNCTAD/WTO

Real GDP (annual percent change)

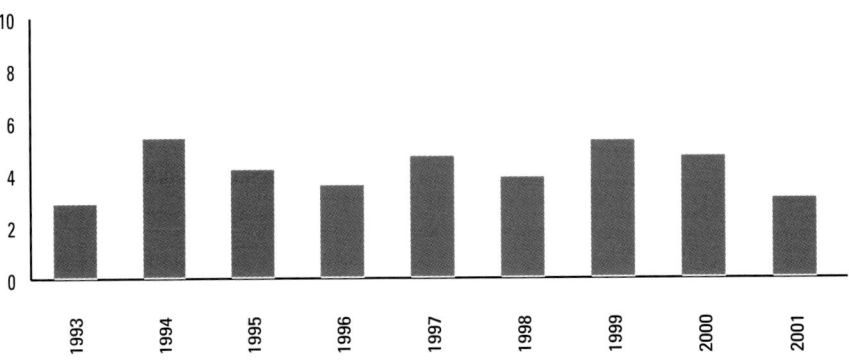

Source: IMF *World Economic Outlook Database,* April 2002

National competitiveness balance sheet

NOTABLE COMPETITIVE ADVANTAGES	
Criteria	Rank

Growth Competitiveness

Macroeconomic Environment
2.05	Access to credit	2
2.21	Real exchange rate, 2001	20
2.17	National savings rate, 2001	23

Technology
4.07	Cellular telephones, 2001	12
3.18	Tertiary enrollment	14
4.02	Internet access in schools	19
4.08	Internet users, 2001	20
4.06	Laws relating to ICT	21
4.11	Personal computers, 2001	21
3.07	Company spending on research and development	24
3.15	Utility patents, 2001	25
3.01	Technological sophistication	26
4.09	Internet hosts, 2001	27
4.10	Telephone lines, 2001	28

Public Institutions
7.03	Irregular payments in tax collection	19
6.15	Organized crime	22
6.01	Judicial independence	26

Microeconomic Competitiveness

Sophistication of Company Operations and Strategy
10.02	Value chain presence	21
10.08	Degree of customer orientation	22
3.07	Company spending on research and development	24

Quality of the National Business Environment
2.11	Cost of importing foreign equipment	18
5.08	Quality of public schools	18
9.10	Local availability of specialized research and training services	20

Other Indicators
2.08	Business costs of terrorism	9
2.18	Investment rate, 2001	20
2.22	Exports, 2001	18
2.23	Imports, 2001	21
2.25	Corporate income tax rate, 2002	8
2.32	Bank liquid reserves	24
3.14	Research and development spending	22
3.17	Secondary enrollment	15
5.07	Postal efficiency	15
5.09	Disparity in healthcare quality	17
6.14	Business costs of crime and violence	15
6.16	Informal sector	22
6.19	Pervasiveness of money laundering through banks	14
6.21	Military expenditure relative to central government expenditure	11
7.08	Frequency of payments or bribes	16
11.10	Flexibility of environmental regulations	10

NOTABLE COMPETITIVE DISADVANTAGES	
Criteria	Rank

Growth Competitiveness

Macroeconomic Environment
2.16	Government expenditure, 2001	68
2.19	Inflation, 2001	63
2.01	Recession expectations	50
2.28	Interest rate spread, 2001	42
2.15	Government surplus/deficit, 2001	33

Technology
3.02	Firm-level innovation	62
3.04	FDI and technology transfer	60
4.03	Quality of competition in the ISP sector	56
4.04	Government prioritization of ICT	47
3.05	Prevalence of foreign technology licensing	46
4.05	Government success in ICT promotion	38
3.09	University/industry research collaboration	33

Public Institutions
6.03	Property rights	38
6.09	Favoritism in decisions of government officials	32
7.01	Irregular payments in exports & imports	30
7.02	Irregular payments in public utilities	30

Microeconomic Competitiveness

Sophistication of Company Operations and Strategy
3.05	Prevalence of foreign technology licensing	46
10.14	Extent of incentive compensation	46
10.07	Extent of marketing	39

Quality of the National Business Environment
9.06	State of cluster development	58
3.12	Availability of scientists and engineers	56
2.07	Local equity market access	51

Other Indicators
1.08	Unemployment rate, 2001	55
2.09	Regulatory obstacles to business	54
2.20	M2 growth, 2001	73
2.24	Average tariff rate, 2002	55
2.26	Individual income tax rate, 2002	70
2.29	FDI, 2001	63
6.18	Pervasiveness of insider trading	64
8.07	Number of days to resolve a dispute	70
10.18	Hiring and firing practices	67
10.19	Flexibility of wage determination	57

South Africa

Key Economic Indicators

Total population (in millions), 2001 ....44.4
Population rank 21
GDP per capita (PPP), 2001 ....$9,565
GDP per capita rank..37
Real growth in GDP per capita, 2000 to 2001.........0.1
Growth rank 56
Unemployment rate, 2001....................................29.50
Unemployment rank 77
Government surplus/deficit, 2001 ....–1.23
Government surplus/deficit rank 30
National savings rate, 2001 ....17.00
National savings rank 63
Investment rate, 2001 ....14.85
Investment rank..75
Inflation, 2001 ....5.70
Inflation rank 51
Exports of goods (as a percentage of GDP),
    2001 ....25.9
Exports rank..44
Imports of goods (as a percentage of GDP),
    2001 ....25.1
Imports rank..60
Internet users (per 10,000 inhabitants), 2001 ...700.58
Internet users rank 44

Competitiveness Rankings

Growth Competitiveness Rank	32

Technology Index Rank **38**
Innovation Subindex Rank 49
ICT Subindex Rank 42
Technology Transfer Subindex Rank
    (out of 56 non-core innovators) 10
Public Institutions Index Rank...**34**
Contracts and Law Subindex Rank 35
Corruption Subindex Rank....................................35
Macroeconomic Environment Index Rank **30**
Macroeconomic Stability Subindex Rank...........30
Country Credit Rating Rank....................................41
Government Expenditure Rank 32

Microeconomic Competitiveness Rank	29

Company Operations and Strategy Rank **31**
Quality of the National Business Environment Rank ...**33**

Trade Performance of Leading Export Sectors

Sector	Share in national exports	Value of exports (US$ millions)	Value of net exports (US$ millions)	Share in world market	TPI current index	TPI change index
Minerals	24.6%	5,425	843	0.78%	3	29
Basic manufactures	20.9%	4,611	3,175	1.06%	7	41
Chemicals	10.2%	2,243	–1,153	0.37%	17	34
Transport equipment	10.0%	2,200	46	0.32%	20	50
Nonelectronic machinery	7.2%	1,581	–1,695	0.27%	34	38

Source: International Trade Centre UNCTAD/WTO
* Data for Southern African Customs Union (includes South Africa, Botswana, Lesotho, Namibia, and Swaziland)

Real GDP (annual percent change)

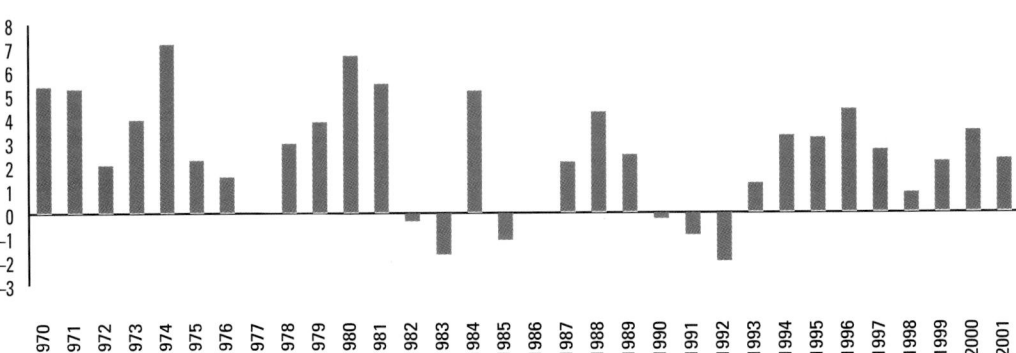

Source: IMF *World Economic Outlook Database,* April 2002

National competitiveness balance sheet

NOTABLE COMPETITIVE ADVANTAGES	
Criteria	Rank

Growth Competitiveness

Macroeconomic Environment

2.21	Real exchange rate, 2001	3
2.28	Interest rate spread, 2001	28
2.15	Government surplus/deficit, 2001	30
2.16	Government expenditure, 2001	32

Technology

3.05	Prevalence of foreign technology licensing	6
3.09	University/industry research collaboration	18
3.07	Company spending on research and development	27
3.15	Utility patents, 2001	29
3.01	Technological sophistication	30
3.02	Firm-level innovation	32

Public Institutions

6.01	Judicial independence	20
6.03	Property rights	21
7.03	Irregular payments in tax collection	30

Microeconomic Competitiveness

Sophistication of Company Operations and Strategy

3.05	Prevalence of foreign technology licensing	6
10.15	Reliance on professional management	13
10.14	Extent of incentive compensation	15

Quality of the National Business Environment

2.12	Extent of distortive government subsidies	9
10.17	Efficacy of corporate boards	12
2.02	Financial market sophistication	13

Other Indicators

2.09	Regulatory obstacles to business	20
2.29	FDI, 2001	24
2.32	Bank liquid reserves	21
6.12	Efficiency of the tax system	19
6.17	Strength of auditing and accounting standards	17
7.07	Irregular payments in judicial decisions	24
7.14	Policy consequences of legal political donations	15
8.06	Number of procedures to resolve a dispute	2
8.10	Total cost of starting a business	16
11.10	Flexibility of environmental regulations	13

NOTABLE COMPETITIVE DISADVANTAGES	
Criteria	Rank

Growth Competitiveness

Macroeconomic Environment

2.17	National savings rate, 2001	63
2.19	Inflation, 2001	51
2.01	Recession expectations	48
2.05	Access to credit	44

Technology

3.18	Tertiary enrollment	58
4.10	Telephone lines, 2001	56
4.07	Cellular telephones, 2001	44
4.08	Internet users, 2001	44
4.11	Personal computers, 2001	44
4.04	Government prioritization of ICT	43
4.05	Government success in ICT promotion	42
4.02	Internet access in schools	41
4.03	Quality of competition in the ISP sector	41
4.09	Internet hosts, 2001	41
4.06	Laws relating to ICT	39
3.04	FDI and technology transfer	33

Public Institutions

6.15	Organized crime	56
7.02	Irregular payments in public utilities	47
6.09	Favoritism in decisions of government officials	39
7.01	Irregular payments in exports & imports	37

Microeconomic Competitiveness

Sophistication of Company Operations and Strategy

10.01	Nature of competitive advantage	68
10.08	Degree of customer orientation	61
10.02	Value chain presence	65

Quality of the National Business Environment

3.11	Quality of math and science education	71
10.20	Cooperation in labor-employer relations	70
3.12	Availability of scientists and engineers	65

Other Indicators

1.08	Unemployment rate, 2001	77
1.09	Employment to population ratio, 2001	75
2.18	Investment rate, 2001	75
2.20	M2 growth, 2001	61
2.24	Average tariff rate, 2002	61
2.26	Individual income tax rate, 2002	61
3.13	Brain drain	60
5.09	Disparity in healthcare quality	65
6.06	Competence of public officials	57
6.14	Business costs of crime and violence	67
10.18	Hiring and firing practices	74
10.19	Flexibility of wage determination	69
10.21	Pay and productivity	66

509

Spain

Key Economic Indicators

Total population (in millions), 2001 ....40.3
Population rank 23
GDP per capita (PPP), 2001 ....$20,374
GDP per capita rank..23
Real growth in GDP per capita, 2000 to 2001.........2.7
Growth rank 23
Unemployment rate, 2001...................................13.05
Unemployment rank 59
Government surplus/deficit, 2001 ....–0.34
Government surplus/deficit rank 24
National savings rate, 2001................................22.88
National savings rank..33
Investment rate, 2001 ....25.06
Investment rank..21
Inflation, 2001 ....3.20
Inflation rank 35
Exports of goods (as a percentage of GDP),
    2001 ....19.8
Exports rank...60
Imports of goods (as a percentage of GDP),
    2001 ....26.4
Imports rank...56
Internet users (per 10,000 inhabitants),
    2001 ....1,827.45
Internet users rank 30

Competitiveness Rankings

Growth Competitiveness Rank	**22**

Technology Index Rank **24**
    Innovation Subindex Rank 23
    ICT Subindex Rank 30
    Technology Transfer Subindex Rank
        (out of 56 non-core innovators) 18
Public Institutions Index Rank...**26**
    Contracts and Law Subindex Rank 41
    Corruption Subindex Rank....................................18
Macroeconomic Environment Index Rank **15**
    Macroeconomic Stability Subindex Rank.............15
    Country Credit Rating Rank....................................16
    Government Expenditure Rank 54

Microeconomic Competitiveness Rank	**25**

Company Operations and Strategy Rank **22**
Quality of the National Business Environment Rank ...25

Trade Performance of Leading Export Sectors

Sector	Share in national exports	Value of exports (US$ millions)	Value of net exports (US$ millions)	Share in world market	TPI current index	TPI change index
Transport equipment	26.7%	29,541	1,242	4.24%	4	43
Chemicals	11.4%	12,578	–5,403	2.08%	19	43
Basic manufactures	10.6%	11,678	501	2.70%	8	105
Fresh food	8.4%	9,343	699	3.92%	7	62
Nonelectronic machinery	7.7%	8,551	–6,516	1.47%	17	73

Source: International Trade Centre UNCTAD/WTO

Real GDP (annual percent change)

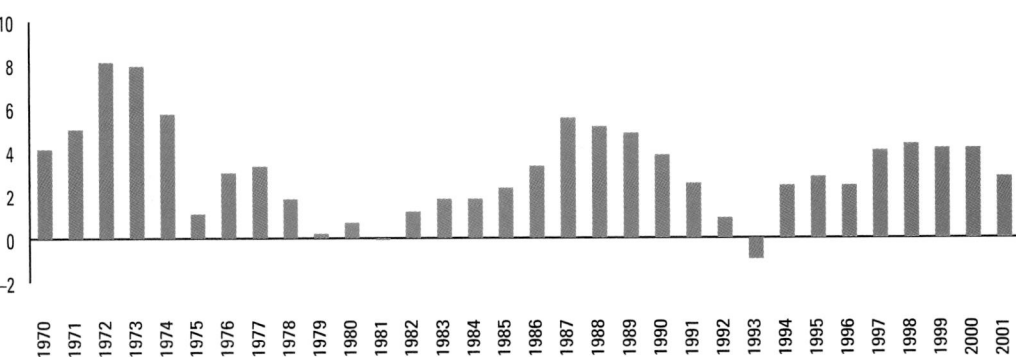

Source: IMF *World Economic Outlook Database,* April 2002

National competitiveness balance sheet

NOTABLE COMPETITIVE ADVANTAGES

Criteria	Rank

Growth Competitiveness

Macroeconomic Environment

2.28	Interest rate spread, 2001	7
2.21	Real exchange rate, 2001	10
2.05	Access to credit	20

Technology

3.18	Tertiary enrollment	12
4.07	Cellular telephones, 2001	22

Public Institutions

7.01	Irregular payments in exports & imports	14
7.02	Irregular payments in public utilities	20

Microeconomic Competitiveness

Sophistication of Company Operations and Strategy

10.03	Extent of branding	17
10.14	Extent of incentive compensation	18
10.02	Value chain presence	19

Quality of the National Business Environment

8.02	Extent of locally based competitors	6
10.16	Quality of management schools	6
9.08	Local availability of components and parts	7

Other Indicators

2.18	Investment rate, 2001	21
2.29	FDI, 2001	11
2.32	Bank liquid reserves	10
3.08	Subsidies and tax credits for firm-level research and development	22
3.13	Brain drain	13
5.09	Disparity in healthcare quality	19
6.11	Effectiveness of law-making bodies	17
6.16	Informal sector	17
7.08	Frequency of payments or bribes	3
11.04	Chemical waste regulations	20

NOTABLE COMPETITIVE DISADVANTAGES

Criteria	Rank

Growth Competitiveness

Macroeconomic Environment

2.16	Government expenditure, 2001	54
2.01	Recession expectations	35
2.19	Inflation, 2001	35
2.17	National savings rate, 2001	33
2.15	Government surplus/deficit, 2001	24

Technology

4.03	Quality of competition in the ISP sector	52
4.05	Government success in ICT promotion	47
4.06	Laws relating to ICT	37
3.01	Technological sophistication	36
3.04	FDI and technology transfer	30
4.08	Internet users, 2001	30
4.09	Internet hosts, 2001	30
3.05	Prevalence of foreign technology licensing	28
4.02	Internet access in schools	28
4.11	Personal computers, 2001	28
3.02	Firm-level innovation	27
3.07	Company spending on research and development	26
3.15	Utility patents, 2001	26
4.04	Government prioritization of ICT	26
4.10	Telephone lines, 2001	26
3.09	University/industry research collaboration	25

Public Institutions

6.01	Judicial independence	46
6.09	Favoritism in decisions of government officials	36
6.03	Property rights	34
6.15	Organized crime	34
7.03	Irregular payments in tax collection	26

Microeconomic Competitiveness

Sophistication of Company Operations and Strategy

10.15	Reliance on professional management	30
3.05	Prevalence of foreign technology licensing	28
10.13	Willingness to delegate authority	26

Quality of the National Business Environment

8.04	Administrative burden for startups	47
10.20	Cooperation in labor-employer relations	43
10.17	Efficacy of corporate boards	41

Other Indicators

1.08	Unemployment rate, 2001	59
2.08	Business costs of terrorism	63
2.09	Regulatory obstacles to business	75
2.22	Exports, 2001	60
2.23	Imports, 2001	56
2.25	Corporate income tax rate, 2002	58
2.26	Individual income tax rate, 2002	69
3.03	Firm-level technology absorption	51
6.18	Pervasiveness of insider trading	50
8.09	Number of days to start a business	64
8.10	Total cost of starting a business	60
10.18	Hiring and firing practices	68
10.19	Flexibility of wage determination	65
11.06	Subsidies for energy or materials	53

Sri Lanka

Key Economic Indicators

Total population (in millions), 2001 ....19.6
Population rank 33
GDP per capita (PPP), 2001 ....$3,634
GDP per capita rank...69
Real growth in GDP per capita, 2000 to 2001 ....–0.5
Growth rank 64
Unemployment rate, 2001.....................................7.80
Unemployment rank 36
Government surplus/deficit, 2001 ....–6.40
Government surplus/deficit rank 70
National savings rate, 2001 ....23.10
National savings rank 30
Investment rate, 2001 ....27.90
Investment rank..7
Inflation, 2001 ....14.00
Inflation rank 73
Exports of goods (as a percentage of GDP),
    2001 ....30.9
Exports rank...35
Imports of goods (as a percentage of GDP),
    2001 ....37.9
Imports rank...31
Internet users (per 10,000 inhabitants), 2001 .....78.52
Internet users rank 73

Competitiveness Rankings

Growth Competitiveness Rank	**59**

Technology Index Rank **67**
    Innovation Subindex Rank....................................74
    ICT Subindex Rank 70
    Technology Transfer Subindex Rank
        (out of 56 non-core innovators) 33
Public Institutions Index Rank.............................**42**
    Contracts and Law Subindex Rank 29
    Corruption Subindex Rank...................................56
Macroeconomic Environment Index Rank **60**
    Macroeconomic Stability Subindex Rank 59
    Country Credit Rating Rank 65
    Government Expenditure Rank 29

Microeconomic Competitiveness Rank	**47**

Company Operations and Strategy Rank **52**
Quality of the National Business Environment Rank ...**43**

Trade Performance of Leading Export Sectors

Sector	Share in national exports	Value of exports (US$ millions)	Value of net exports (US$ millions)	Share in world market	TPI current index	TPI change index
Clothing	55.1%	2,602	2,547	1.39%	10	45
Fresh food	14.2%	669	513	0.28%	26	36
Minerals	5.7%	268	–62	0.04%	91	99
Textiles	5.3%	248	–445	0.17%	64	19
Miscellaneous manufacturing	4.2%	199	–44	0.04%	55	17

Source: International Trade Centre UNCTAD/WTO

Real GDP (annual percent change)

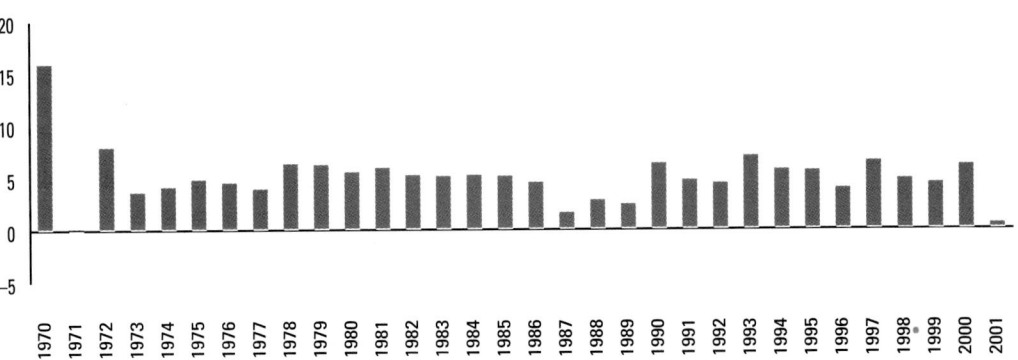

Source: IMF *World Economic Outlook Database*, April 2002

National competitiveness balance sheet

NOTABLE COMPETITIVE ADVANTAGES	
Criteria	Rank

Growth Competitiveness

Macroeconomic Environment
2.01	Recession expectations	13
2.16	Government expenditure, 2001	29
2.17	National savings rate, 2001	30
2.05	Access to credit	37

Technology
4.05	Government success in ICT promotion	22
4.04	Government prioritization of ICT	27
3.04	FDI and technology transfer	32
3.07	Company spending on research and development	39

Public Institutions
6.09	Favoritism in decisions of government officials	10
6.01	Judicial independence	28
6.15	Organized crime	33

Microeconomic Competitiveness

Sophistication of Company Operations and Strategy
10.11	Breadth of international markets	37
10.15	Reliance on professional management	38
3.07	Company spending on research and development	39

Quality of the National Business Environment
3.10	Government procurement of advanced technology products	13
8.04	Administrative burden for startups	22
5.01	Overall infrastructure quality	26

Other Indicators
1.08	Unemployment rate, 2001	36
2.18	Investment rate, 2001	7
2.22	Exports, 2001	35
2.23	Imports, 2001	31
5.09	Disparity in healthcare quality	32
6.06	Competence of public officials	2
6.07	Burden of regulation	3
6.08	Transparency of government policy-making	17
6.11	Effectiveness of law-making bodies	18
6.12	Efficiency of the tax system	15
8.08	Number of procedures to start a business	23
8.10	Total cost of starting a business	8

NOTABLE COMPETITIVE DISADVANTAGES	
Criteria	Rank

Growth Competitiveness

Macroeconomic Environment
2.19	Inflation, 2001	73
2.15	Government surplus/deficit, 2001	70
2.21	Real exchange rate, 2001	55
2.28	Interest rate spread, 2001	55

Technology
3.18	Tertiary enrollment	76
4.11	Personal computers, 2001	75
4.08	Internet users, 2001	73
4.07	Cellular telephones, 2001	71
4.09	Internet hosts, 2001	70
4.10	Telephone lines, 2001	70
3.02	Firm-level innovation	66
3.05	Prevalence of foreign technology licensing	66
3.15	Utility patents, 2001	64
4.02	Internet access in schools	63
3.01	Technological sophistication	58
4.06	Laws relating to ICT	58
3.09	University/industry research collaboration	57
4.03	Quality of competition in the ISP sector	44

Public Institutions
7.02	Irregular payments in public utilities	60
6.03	Property rights	57
7.03	Irregular payments in tax collection	56
7.01	Irregular payments in exports & imports	45

Microeconomic Competitiveness

Sophistication of Company Operations and Strategy
3.05	Prevalence of foreign technology licensing	66
10.09	Control of international distribution	65
10.07	Extent of marketing	62

Quality of the National Business Environment
2.11	Cost of importing foreign equipment	79
5.05	Quality of electricity supply	73
6.10	Extent of bureaucratic red tape	69

Other Indicators
2.08	Business costs of terrorism	78
2.29	FDI, 2001	66
6.05	Freedom of the press	68
6.22	Military expenditure relative to GNI	69
7.13	Prevalence of illegal political donations	63
11.12	Effects of compliance on business (with environmental regulations)	72

Sweden

Key Economic Indicators

Total population (in millions), 2001 ....8.9
Population rank 46
GDP per capita (PPP), 2001 ....$24,978
GDP per capita rank..17
Real growth in GDP per capita, 2000 to 2001.........0.9
Growth rank..44
Unemployment rate, 2001....................................3.98
Unemployment rank 15
Government surplus/deficit, 2001 ....2.92
Government surplus/deficit rank 4
National savings rate, 2001 ....20.80
National savings rank...45
Investment rate, 2001 ....17.49
Investment rank...67
Inflation, 2001 ....2.60
Inflation rank 29
Exports of goods (as a percentage of GDP),
    2001 ....36.0
Exports rank...25
Imports of goods (as a percentage of GDP),
    2001 ....30.0
Imports rank...42
Internet users (per 10,000 inhabitants),
    2001 ....5,162.74
Internet users rank 4

Competitiveness Rankings

Growth Competitiveness Rank	5

Technology Index Rank **4**
    Innovation Subindex Rank 4
    ICT Subindex Rank 1
Public Institutions Index Rank...........................**15**
    Contracts and Law Subindex Rank 18
    Corruption Subindex Rank......................................11
Macroeconomic Environment Index Rank **34**
    Macroeconomic Stability Subindex Rank 14
    Country Credit Rating Rank.................................13
    Government Expenditure Rank 80

Microeconomic Competitiveness Rank	6

Company Operations and Strategy Rank 6
Quality of the National Business Environment Rank 8

Trade Performance of Leading Export Sectors

Sector	Share in national exports	Value of exports (US$ millions)	Value of net exports (US$ millions)	Share in world market	TPI current index	TPI change index
IT and consumer electronics	17.7%	12,756	5,581	2.02%	3	10
Nonelectronic machinery	15.1%	10,840	3,044	1.87%	3	70
Chemicals	11.6%	8,327	1,059	1.38%	12	32
Wood products	11.1%	8,019	6,324	4.34%	1	68
Basic manufactures	10.9%	7,820	1,633	1.81%	2	75

Source: International Trade Centre UNCTAD/WTO

Real GDP (annual percent change)

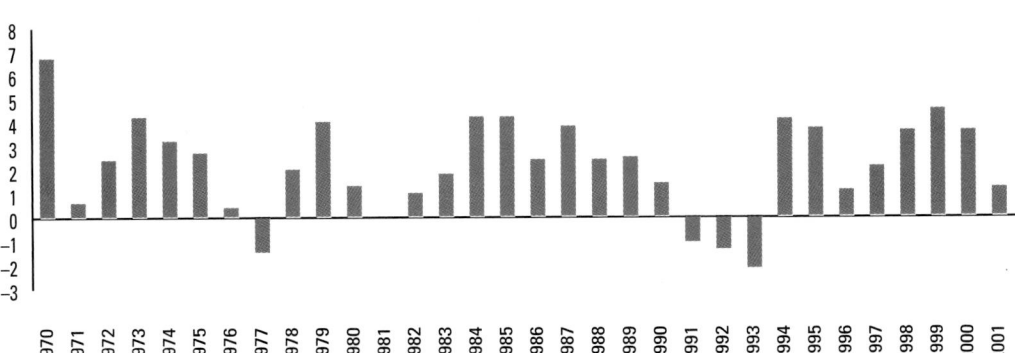

Source: IMF *World Economic Outlook Database,* April 2002

National competitiveness balance sheet

NOTABLE COMPETITIVE ADVANTAGES	
Criteria	Rank

Growth Competitiveness

Macroeconomic Environment

2.15	Government surplus/deficit, 2001	4
2.21	Real exchange rate, 2001	4

Technology

4.10	Telephone lines, 2001	1
3.07	Company spending on research and development	2
4.11	Personal computers, 2001	2
3.09	University/industry research collaboration	4
4.08	Internet users, 2001	4
3.01	Technological sophistication	5
3.15	Utility patents, 2001	5
4.02	Internet access in schools	6
3.18	Tertiary enrollment	7
4.03	Quality of competition in the ISP sector	7
4.06	Laws relating to ICT	7
4.07	Cellular telephones, 2001	8
4.09	Internet hosts, 2001	9
4.05	Government success in ICT promotion	12
4.04	Government prioritization of ICT	11

Public Institutions

7.03	Irregular payments in tax collection	5

Microeconomic Competitiveness

Sophistication of Company Operations and Strategy

10.04	Capacity for innovation	2
10.13	Willingness to delegate authority	2
10.12	Extent of staff training	4

Quality of the National Business Environment

5.05	Quality of electricity supply	3
11.05	Stringency of environmental regulations	4
3.15	Utility patents, 2001	5

Other Indicators

2.32	Bank liquid reserves	3
3.03	Firm-level technology absorption	7
3.14	Research and development spending	1
3.17	Secondary enrollment	1
6.05	Freedom of the press	1
6.17	Strength of auditing and accounting standards	4
7.04	Irregular payments in public contracts	3
7.06	Irregular payments in government policy-making	5
7.10	Diversion of public funds	6
7.13	Prevalence of illegal political donations	3
8.11	Cost of starting a business relative to GNP per capita	5
10.05	Ethical behavior of firms	7
11.04	Chemical waste regulations	4
11.14	Prevalence of environmental management systems	4

NOTABLE COMPETITIVE DISADVANTAGES	
Criteria	Rank

Growth Competitiveness

Macroeconomic Environment

2.16	Government expenditure, 2001	80
2.01	Recession expectations	52
2.05	Access to credit	51
2.17	National savings rate, 2001	45
2.19	Inflation, 2001	29
2.28	Interest rate spread, 2001	18

Technology

3.02	Firm-level innovation	28

Public Institutions

6.09	Favoritism in decisions of government officials	21
6.01	Judicial independence	19
6.03	Property rights	19
6.15	Organized crime	17
7.02	Irregular payments in public utilities	16
7.01	Irregular payments in exports & imports	15

Microeconomic Competitiveness

Sophistication of Company Operations and Strategy

3.05	Prevalence of foreign technology licensing	51

Quality of the National Business Environment

2.12	Extent of distortive government subsidies	49
6.10	Extent of bureaucratic red tape	40
9.08	Local availability of components and parts	35

Other Indicators

2.18	Investment rate, 2001	67
2.26	Individual income tax rate, 2002	77
2.27	Value added tax rate, 2002	77
6.12	Efficiency of the tax system	63
10.18	Hiring and firing practices	77
10.19	Flexibility of wage determination	70
10.21	Pay and productivity	48

515

Switzerland

Key Economic Indicators

Total population (in millions), 2001 ....7.3
Population rank 52
GDP per capita (PPP), 2001 ....$29,587
GDP per capita rank...5
Real growth in GDP per capita, 2000 to 2001.........0.9
Growth rank 45
Unemployment rate, 2001.....................................1.78
Unemployment rank 2
Government surplus/deficit, 2001 ....–0.70
Government surplus/deficit rank 26
National savings rate, 2001 ....31.80
National savings rank 9
Investment rate, 2001 ....20.59
Investment rank...46
Inflation, 2001 ....1.00
Inflation rank 8
Exports of goods (as a percentage of GDP),
    2001 ....31.6
Exports rank...33
Imports of goods (as a percentage of GDP),
    2001 ....31.2
Imports rank...40
Internet users (per 10,000 inhabitants),
    2001 ....4,040.17
Internet users rank 12

Competitiveness Rankings

Growth Competitiveness Rank	**6**

Technology Index Rank **6**
  Innovation Subindex Rank 7
  ICT Subindex Rank 9
Public Institutions Index Rank...........................**8**
  Contracts and Law Subindex Rank 7
  Corruption Subindex Rank......................................9
Macroeconomic Environment Index Rank **5**
  Macroeconomic Stability Subindex Rank 4
  Country Credit Rating Rank 1
  Government Expenditure Rank 55

Microeconomic Competitiveness Rank	**5**

Company Operations and Strategy Rank **5**
Quality of the National Business Environment Rank **6**

Trade Performance of Leading Export Sectors

Sector	Share in national exports	Value of exports (US$ millions)	Value of net exports (US$ millions)	Share in world market	TPI current index	TPI change index
Chemicals	26.8%	21,732	7,562	3.60%	9	57
Miscellaneous manufacturing	20.3%	16,491	4,670	3.54%	3	113
Nonelectronic machinery	19.1%	15,465	8,142	2.66%	4	89
Basic manufactures	10.6%	8,617	–896	1.99%	25	20
Electronic components	6.7%	5,408	971	0.90%	3	56

Source: International Trade Centre UNCTAD/WTO

Real GDP (annual percent change)

Source: IMF *World Economic Outlook Database,* April 2002

National competitiveness balance sheet

NOTABLE COMPETITIVE ADVANTAGES

Criteria	Rank

Growth Competitiveness

Macroeconomic Environment

2.21   Real exchange rate, 2001 35

Technology

4.07   Cellular telephones, 2001 35
3.05   Prevalence of foreign technology licensing 37
4.10   Telephone lines, 2001 38
4.03   Quality of competition in the ISP sector 47

Public Institutions

6.15   Organized crime 37

Microeconomic Competitiveness

Sophistication of Company Operations and Strategy

10.09   Control of international distribution 31
10.02   Value chain presence 32
10.03   Extent of branding 34

Quality of the National Business Environment

9.08   Local availability of components and parts 17
8.02   Extent of locally based competitors 19
6.10   Extent of bureaucratic red tape 21

Other Indicators

2.24   Average tariff rate, 2002 16
4.01   Availability of mobile or cellular telephones 29
6.14   Business costs of crime and violence 17
8.07   Number of days to resolve a dispute 15

NOTABLE COMPETITIVE DISADVANTAGES

Criteria	Rank

Growth Competitiveness

Macroeconomic Environment

2.15   Government surplus/deficit, 2001 79
2.19   Inflation, 2001 79
2.05   Access to credit 74
2.16   Government expenditure, 2001 67
2.17   National savings rate, 2001 59
2.28   Interest rate spread, 2001 58
2.01   Recession expectations 53

Technology

3.04   FDI and technology transfer 73
3.02   Firm-level innovation 71
3.09   University/industry research collaboration 71
3.07   Company spending on research and development 69
3.01   Technological sophistication 66
4.05   Government success in ICT promotion 64
4.06   Laws relating to ICT 63
4.04   Government prioritization of ICT 61
3.15   Utility patents, 2001 59
3.18   Tertiary enrollment 59
4.02   Internet access in schools 54
4.08   Internet users, 2001 54
4.09   Internet hosts, 2001 53
4.11   Personal computers, 2001 53

Public Institutions

7.01   Irregular payments in exports & imports 80
7.02   Irregular payments in public utilities 76
7.03   Irregular payments in tax collection 63
6.01   Judicial independence 60
6.09   Favoritism in decisions of government officials 52
6.03   Property rights 50

Microeconomic Competitiveness

Sophistication of Company Operations and Strategy

10.13   Willingness to delegate authority 76
10.15   Reliance on professional management 70
3.07   Company spending on research and development 69

Quality of the National Business Environment

2.06   Venture capital availability 79
3.10   Government procurement of advanced technology
      products 75
10.17   Efficacy of corporate boards 73

Other Indicators

2.03   Soundness of banks 78
2.20   M2 growth, 2001 79
6.05   Freedom of the press 70
6.06   Competence of public officials 71
6.07   Burden of regulation 69
6.16   Informal sector 76
6.17   Strength of auditing and accounting standards 64
6.22   Military expenditure relative to GNI 74
7.05   Irregular payments in loan applications 76
7.13   Prevalence of illegal political donations 68
11.12   Effects of compliance on business (with
       environmental regulations) 75

Ukraine

Key Economic Indicators

Total population (in millions), 2001 ....49.3
Population rank 19
GDP per capita (PPP), 2001 ....$4,224
GDP per capita rank...63
Real growth in GDP per capita, 2000 to 2001.......10.1
Growth rank 1
Unemployment rate, 2001 ....4.53
Unemployment rank 17
Government surplus/deficit, 2001 ....0.30
Government surplus/deficit rank 15
National savings rate, 2001 ....25.50
National savings rank..22
Investment rate, 2001 ....22.00
Investment rank...37
Inflation, 2001 ....12.00
Inflation rank 71
Exports of goods (as a percentage of GDP),
    2001 ....45.5
Exports rank..16
Imports of goods (as a percentage of GDP),
    2001 ....42.0
Imports rank..27
Internet users (per 10,000 inhabitants), 2001 ...119.29
Internet users rank 69

Competitiveness Rankings

Growth Competitiveness Rank	**77**

Technology Index Rank **72**
    Innovation Subindex Rank....................................38
    ICT Subindex Rank...67
    Technology Transfer Subindex Rank
        (out of 56 non-core innovators) 53
Public Institutions Index Rank...........................**72**
    Contracts and Law Subindex Rank 73
    Corruption Subindex Rank....................................70
Macroeconomic Environment Index Rank **77**
    Macroeconomic Stability Subindex Rank 72
    Country Credit Rating Rank 75
    Government Expenditure Rank 44

Microeconomic Competitiveness Rank	**69**

Company Operations and Strategy Rank **66**
Quality of the National Business Environment Rank ...**69**

Trade Performance of Leading Export Sectors

Sector	Share in national exports	Value of exports (US$ millions)	Value of net exports (US$ millions)	Share in world market	TPI current index	TPI change index
Basic manufactures	39.0%	5,011	4,351	1.16%	17	40
Minerals	18.7%	2,405	−1,799	0.34%	31	21
Chemicals	11.9%	1,527	280	0.25%	29	72
Nonelectronic machinery	5.4%	699	−458	0.12%	43	79
Processed food	5.1%	649	272	0.30%	45	9

Source: International Trade Centre UNCTAD/WTO

Real GDP (annual percent change)

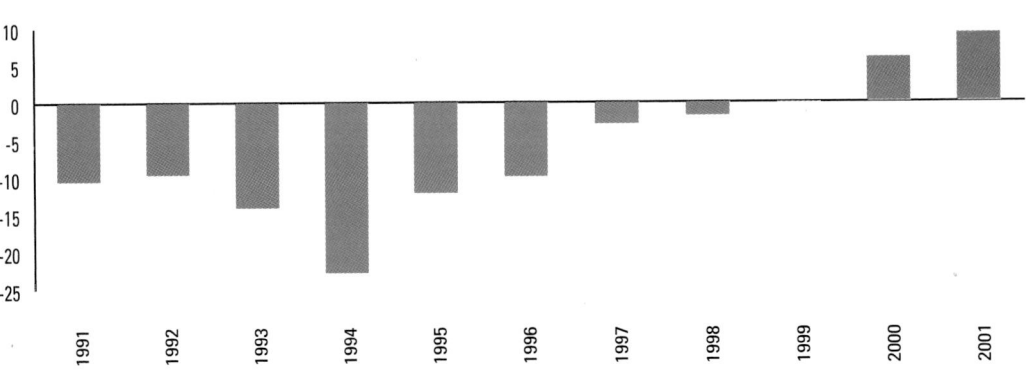

Source: IMF *World Economic Outlook Database,* April 2002

National competitiveness balance sheet

NOTABLE COMPETITIVE ADVANTAGES	
Criteria	Rank

Growth Competitiveness

Macroeconomic Environment
2.15 Government surplus/deficit, 2001 ...15
2.17 National savings rate, 2001 ...22
2.16 Government expenditure, 2001 ...44

Technology
3.18 Tertiary enrollment ...31
4.10 Telephone lines, 2001 ...47
3.15 Utility patents, 2001 ...48

Microeconomic Competitiveness

Sophistication of Company Operations and Strategy
10.04 Capacity for innovation ...28
10.09 Control of international distribution ...20
10.03 Extent of branding ...31

Quality of the National Business Environment
5.02 Railroad infrastructure development ...24
9.08 Local availability of components and parts ...15
9.09 Local availability of process machinery ...11

Other Indicators
1.04 Real growth in GDP per capita, 2000 to 2001 ...1
1.08 Unemployment rate, 2001 ...17
2.22 Exports, 2001 ...16
2.23 Imports, 2001 ...27
3.14 Research and development spending ...30
8.09 Number of days to start a business ...27
8.10 Total cost of starting a business ...14
10.18 Hiring and firing practices ...19

NOTABLE COMPETITIVE DISADVANTAGES	
Criteria	Rank

Growth Competitiveness

Macroeconomic Environment
2.28 Interest rate spread, 2001 ...76
2.21 Real exchange rate, 2001 ...73
2.19 Inflation, 2001 ...71
2.01 Recession expectations ...66
2.05 Access to credit ...66

Technology
3.02 Firm-level innovation ...79
3.04 FDI and technology transfer ...79
3.05 Prevalence of foreign technology licensing ...76
4.06 Laws relating to ICT ...74
4.03 Quality of competition in the ISP sector ...73
4.02 Internet access in schools ...72
4.04 Government prioritization of ICT ...72
4.05 Government success in ICT promotion ...72
3.01 Technological sophistication ...71
4.08 Internet users, 2001 ...69
4.07 Cellular telephones, 2001 ...68
4.11 Personal computers, 2001 ...66
3.07 Company spending on research and development ...61
3.09 University/industry research collaboration ...58
4.09 Internet hosts, 2001 ...55

Public Institutions
6.03 Property rights ...78
6.15 Organized crime ...72
7.02 Irregular payments in public utilities ...72
7.03 Irregular payments in tax collection ...72
6.01 Judicial independence ...70
7.01 Irregular payments in exports & imports ...70
6.09 Favoritism in decisions of government officials ...53

Microeconomic Competitiveness

Sophistication of Company Operations and Strategy
3.05 Prevalence of foreign technology licensing ...76
10.12 Extent of staff training ...76
10.01 Nature of competitive advantage ...70

Quality of the National Business Environment
2.02 Financial market sophistication ...79
2.10 Hidden trade barriers ...79
6.10 Extent of bureaucratic red tape ...77

Other Indicators
2.03 Soundness of banks ...75
2.09 Regulatory obstacles to business ...80
2.20 M2 growth, 2001 ...76
2.31 Liquid liabilities, 2001 ...77
3.13 Brain drain ...72
4.01 Availability of mobile or cellular telephones ...79
6.05 Freedom of the press ...79
6.08 Transparency of government policy-making ...74
6.19 Pervasiveness of money laundering through banks ...80
11.06 Subsidies for energy or materials ...75

529

United Kingdom

Key Economic Indicators

Total population (in millions), 2001 ....60.0
Population rank 16
GDP per capita (PPP), 2001 ....$24,421
GDP per capita rank..19
Real growth in GDP per capita, 2000 to 2001.........1.8
Growth rank 30
Unemployment rate, 2001....................................5.03
Unemployment rank 22
Government surplus/deficit, 2001 ....–0.20
Government surplus/deficit rank 21
National savings rate, 2001 ....15.53
National savings rank..68
Investment rate, 2001 ....16.96
Investment rank..70
Inflation, 2001 ....2.10
Inflation rank 21
Exports of goods (as a percentage of GDP),
    2001 ....18.9
Exports rank...62
Imports of goods (as a percentage of GDP),
    2001 ....22.8
Imports rank...61
Internet users (per 10,000 inhabitants),
    2001 ....3,995.01
Internet users rank 13

Competitiveness Rankings

Growth Competitiveness Rank	11

Technology Index Rank **15**
  Innovation Subindex Rank 14
  ICT Subindex Rank 13
Public Institutions Index Rank..**6**
  Contracts and Law Subindex Rank 6
  Corruption Subindex Rank.....................................6
Macroeconomic Environment Index Rank **16**
  Macroeconomic Stability Subindex Rank 31
  Country Credit Rating Rank....................................4
  Government Expenditure Rank 56

Microeconomic Competitiveness Rank	3

Company Operations and Strategy Rank **3**
Quality of the National Business Environment Rank **3**

Trade Performance of Leading Export Sectors

Sector	Share in national exports	Value of exports (US$ millions)	Value of net exports (US$ millions)	Share in world market	TPI current index	TPI change index
IT and consumer electronics	14.7%	40,006	–8,813	6.33%	11	47
Chemicals	13.4%	36,445	3,837	6.04%	8	86
Nonelectronic machinery	12.9%	35,100	6,724	6.04%	8	81
Transport equipment	12.7%	34,493	–12,110	4.95%	12	58
Minerals	10.8%	29,347	5,123	4.20%	4	43

Source: International Trade Centre UNCTAD/WTO

Real GDP (annual percent change)

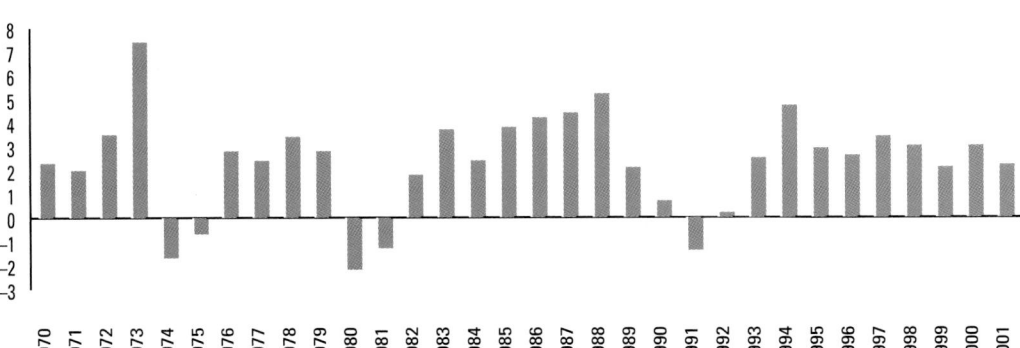

Source: IMF *World Economic Outlook Database,* April 2002

National competitiveness balance sheet

NOTABLE COMPETITIVE ADVANTAGES	
Criteria	Rank

Growth Competitiveness

Macroeconomic Environment
2.28	Interest rate spread, 2001	9

Technology
4.06	Laws relating to ICT	6
3.07	Company spending on research and development	9
4.07	Cellular telephones, 2001	9
3.09	University/industry research collaboration	10
4.03	Quality of competition in the ISP sector	10

Public Institutions
7.02	Irregular payments in public utilities	4
7.01	Irregular payments in exports & imports	6
6.01	Judicial independence	7
6.09	Favoritism in decisions of government officials	8
6.03	Property rights	9
7.03	Irregular payments in tax collection	9

Microeconomic Competitiveness

Sophistication of Company Operations and Strategy
10.09	Control of international distribution	1
10.15	Reliance on professional management	1
10.11	Breadth of international markets	2

Quality of the National Business Environment
2.02	Financial market sophistication	1
9.10	Local availability of specialized research and training services	1
10.17	Efficacy of corporate boards	1

Other Indicators

2.03	Soundness of banks	1
2.29	FDI, 2001	2
2.30	Domestic credit, 2001	5
2.32	Bank liquid reserves	2
3.13	Brain drain	5
3.17	Secondary enrollment	7
6.06	Competence of public officials	4
6.11	Effectiveness of law-making bodies	3
6.17	Strength of auditing and accounting standards	1
6.18	Pervasiveness of insider trading	1
6.20	Pervasiveness of money laundering through non-bank channels	7
7.15	Misuse of legal political donations	8
10.05	Ethical behavior of firms	2
10.19	Flexibility of wage determination	6
10.21	Pay and productivity	6
11.06	Subsidies for energy or materials	2
11.14	Prevalence of environmental management systems	3

NOTABLE COMPETITIVE DISADVANTAGES	
Criteria	Rank

Growth Competitiveness

Macroeconomic Environment
2.17	National savings rate, 2001	68
2.16	Government expenditure, 2001	55
2.21	Real exchange rate, 2001	52
2.05	Access to credit	46
2.01	Recession expectations	29
2.15	Government surplus/deficit, 2001	21
2.19	Inflation, 2001	21

Technology
4.05	Government success in ICT promotion	54
4.04	Government prioritization of ICT	28
3.02	Firm-level innovation	18
3.15	Utility patents, 2001	17
4.09	Internet hosts, 2001	17

Microeconomic Competitiveness

Sophistication of Company Operations and Strategy
3.05	Prevalence of foreign technology licensing	31

Quality of the National Business Environment
5.02	Railroad infrastructure development	30
3.11	Quality of math and science education	28
5.08	Quality of public schools	23

Other Indicators

2.08	Business costs of terrorism	70
2.18	Investment rate, 2001	70
2.22	Exports, 2001	62
2.23	Imports, 2001	61
5.09	Disparity in healthcare quality	33

531

United States

Key Economic Indicators

Total population (in millions), 2001 ....284.4
Population rank 3
GDP per capita (PPP), 2001 ....$34,888
GDP per capita rank...1
Real growth in GDP per capita, 2000 to 2001.........0.2
Growth rank 55
Unemployment rate, 2001.................................4.79
Unemployment rank 19
Government surplus/deficit, 2001 ....1.25
Government surplus/deficit rank 10
National savings rate, 2001 ....11.92
National savings rank..75
Investment rate, 2001 ....16.58
Investment rank...71
Inflation, 2001 ....2.80
Inflation rank 33
Exports of goods (as a percentage of GDP),
     2001 ....7.2
Exports rank...79
Imports of goods (as a percentage of GDP),
     2001 ....11.2
Imports rank...76
Internet users (per 10,000 inhabitants),
     2001 ....4,995.10
Internet users rank 6

Competitiveness Rankings

Growth Competitiveness Rank	1

Technology Index Rank **1**
   Innovation Subindex Rank...1
   ICT Subindex Rank 4
Public Institutions Index Rank..**16**
   Contracts and Law Subindex Rank 15
   Corruption Subindex Rank..................................20
Macroeconomic Environment Index Rank **2**
   Macroeconomic Stability Subindex Rank 46
   Country Credit Rating Rank 6
   Government Expenditure Rank 12

Microeconomic Competitiveness Rank	1

Company Operations and Strategy Rank **1**
Quality of the National Business Environment Rank **1**

Trade Performance of Leading Export Sectors

Sector	Share in national exports	Value of exports (US$ millions)	Value of net exports (US$ millions)	Share in world market	TPI current index	TPI change index
Nonelectronic machinery	15.1%	102,543	1,018	17.64%	9	65
Transport equipment	14.6%	99,111	−86,580	14.23%	19	56
Electronic components	13.2%	89,758	−21,006	15.01%	22	59
Chemicals	12.7%	86,375	1,602	14.31%	6	69
Miscellaneous manufacturing	11.2%	75,865	−47,210	16.27%	17	71

Source: International Trade Centre UNCTAD/WTO

Real GDP (annual percent change)

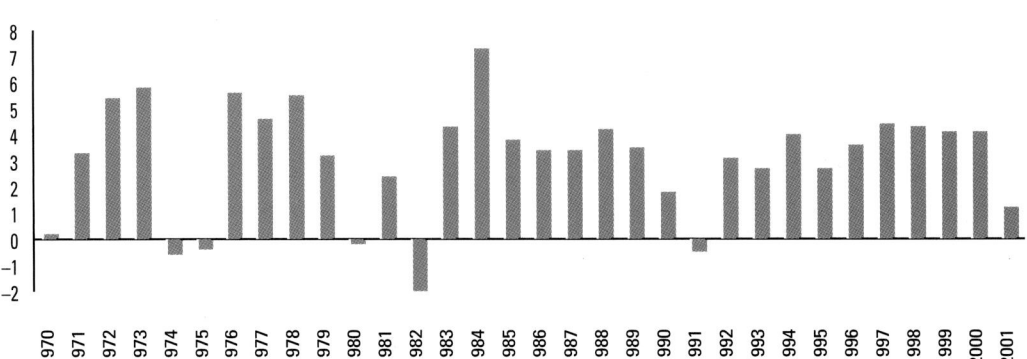

Source: IMF *World Economic Outlook Database,* April 2002

National competitiveness balance sheet

NOTABLE COMPETITIVE ADVANTAGES

Criteria		Rank

Growth Competitiveness

Macroeconomic Environment

| 2.15 | Government surplus/deficit, 2001 | 10 |

Technology

3.01	Technological sophistication	1
3.07	Company spending on research and development	1
3.15	Utility patents, 2001	1
4.09	Internet hosts, 2001	1
4.11	Personal computers, 2001	1
3.02	Firm-level innovation	2
3.09	University/industry research collaboration	2
4.06	Laws relating to ICT	3
3.18	Tertiary enrollment	4
4.03	Quality of competition in the ISP sector	4
4.10	Telephone lines, 2001	5
4.08	Internet users, 2001	6
4.02	Internet access in schools	10

Public Institutions

| 6.03 | Property rights | 7 |

Microeconomic Competitiveness

Sophistication of Company Operations and Strategy

10.07	Extent of marketing	1
10.08	Degree of customer orientation	1
10.14	Extent of incentive compensation	1

Quality of the National Business Environment

2.06	Venture capital availability	1
3.15	Utility patents, 2001	1
8.01	Intensity of local competition	1

Other Indicators

2.03	Soundness of banks	6
2.27	Value added tax rate, 2002	1
2.29	FDI, 2001	1
3.03	Firm-level technology absorption	2
3.13	Brain drain	1
3.14	Research and development spending	6
6.08	Transparency of government policy-making	6
6.11	Effectiveness of law-making bodies	2
8.07	Number of days to resolve a dispute	4
8.09	Number of days to start a business	4
10.18	Hiring and firing practices	3
10.19	Flexibility of wage determination	3
10.21	Pay and productivity	2
11.14	Prevalence of environmental management systems	6

NOTABLE COMPETITIVE DISADVANTAGES

Criteria		Rank

Growth Competitiveness

Macroeconomic Environment

2.17	National savings rate, 2001	75
2.21	Real exchange rate, 2001	68
2.05	Access to credit	48
2.19	Inflation, 2001	33
2.01	Recession expectations	17

Technology

4.07	Cellular telephones, 2001	30
4.04	Government prioritization of ICT	15
4.05	Government success in ICT promotion	15

Public Institutions

7.02	Irregular payments in public utilities	23
7.03	Irregular payments in tax collection	22
6.15	Organized crime	21
6.01	Judicial independence	16
7.01	Irregular payments in exports & imports	16

Microeconomic Competitiveness

Sophistication of Company Operations and Strategy

| 3.05 | Prevalence of foreign technology licensing | 63 |

Quality of the National Business Environment

3.11	Quality of math and science education	38
5.08	Quality of public schools	29
2.12	Extent of distortive government subsidies	28

Other Indicators

2.08	Business costs of terrorism	74
2.18	Investment rate, 2001	71
2.20	M2 growth, 2001	48
2.22	Exports, 2001	79
2.23	Imports, 2001	76
2.25	Corporate income tax rate, 2002	58
6.12	Efficiency of the tax system	32
6.21	Military expenditure relative to central government expenditure	64
7.14	Policy consequences of legal political donations	48
11.06	Subsidies for energy or materials	47
11.08	Compliance with international environmental agreements	58

533

Uruguay

Key Economic Indicators

Total population (in millions), 2001 ....3.4
Population rank 70
GDP per capita (PPP), 2001 ....$8,781
GDP per capita rank..41
Real growth in GDP per capita, 2000 to 2001 ....–3.8
Growth rank 77
Unemployment rate, 2001................................14.90
Unemployment rank 62
Government surplus/deficit, 2001 ....–4.60
Government surplus/deficit rank 56
National savings rate, 2001 ....10.20
National savings rank 77
Investment rate, 2001 ....12.20
Investment rank...79
Inflation, 2001 ....4.40
Inflation rank 42
Exports of goods (as a percentage of GDP),
    2001 ....11.0
Exports rank..71
Imports of goods (as a percentage of GDP),
    2001 ....16.0
Imports rank..73
Internet users (per 10,000 inhabitants),
    2001 ....1,190.12
Internet users rank 36

Competitiveness Rankings

Growth Competitiveness Rank	42

Technology Index Rank 50	
Innovation Subindex Rank.............................43	
ICT Subindex Rank 38	
Technology Transfer Subindex Rank	
(out of 56 non-core innovators) 48	
Public Institutions Index Rank.........................**20**	
Contracts and Law Subindex Rank 21	
Corruption Subindex Rank.................................24	
Macroeconomic Environment Index Rank **73**	
Macroeconomic Stability Subindex Rank 79	
Country Credit Rating Rank..................................42	
Government Expenditure Rank 41	

Microeconomic Competitiveness Rank	62

Company Operations and Strategy Rank **63**
Quality of the National Business Environment Rank ...**61**

Trade Performance of Leading Export Sectors

Sector	Share in national exports	Value of exports (US$ millions)	Value of net exports (US$ millions)	Share in world market	TPI current index	TPI change index
Fresh food	40.5%	912	728	0.38%	17	131
Processed food	13.8%	310	55	0.14%	44	76
Leather products	10.5%	237	139	0.37%	23	38
Chemicals	8.3%	186	–456	0.03%	71	11
Transport equipment	7.2%	161	–138	0.02%	55	14

Source: International Trade Centre UNCTAD/WTO

Real GDP (annual percent change)

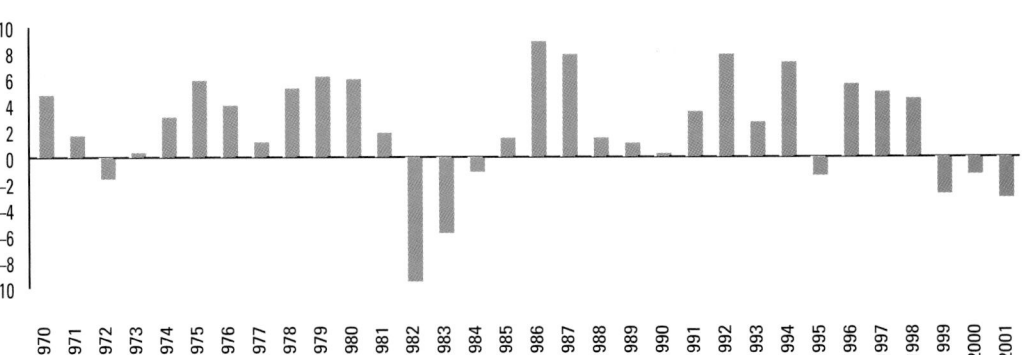

Source: IMF *World Economic Outlook Database,* April 2002

National competitiveness balance sheet

NOTABLE COMPETITIVE ADVANTAGES

Criteria		Rank

Growth Competitiveness

Macroeconomic Environment

2.16	Government expenditure, 2001	40

Technology

4.09	Internet hosts, 2001	24
4.11	Personal computers, 2001	34
3.18	Tertiary enrollment	36
4.08	Internet users, 2001	36
4.02	Internet access in schools	39
4.10	Telephone lines, 2001	39

Public Institutions

6.15	Organized crime	8
7.02	Irregular payments in public utilities	15
6.01	Judicial independence	21
6.03	Property rights	22
7.03	Irregular payments in tax collection	23
6.09	Favoritism in decisions of government officials	31
7.01	Irregular payments in exports & imports	32

Microeconomic Competitiveness

Sophistication of Company Operations and Strategy

10.01	Nature of competitive advantage	39
10.10	Extent of regional sales	39
10.09	Control of international distribution	44

Quality of the National Business Environment

6.01	Judicial independence	21
5.06	Telephone/fax infrastructure quality	22
3.12	Availability of scientists and engineers	23

Other Indicators

2.08	Business costs of terrorism	1
2.09	Regulatory obstacles to business	4
2.20	M2 growth, 2001	19
2.26	Individual income tax rate, 2002	1
6.05	Freedom of the press	17
6.18	Pervasiveness of insider trading	21
7.07	Irregular payments in judicial decisions	22
7.10	Diversion of public funds	22
7.12	Public trust of politicians	22
7.13	Prevalence of illegal political donations	23
7.15	Misuse of legal political donations	16
8.09	Number of days to start a business	15
11.06	Subsidies for energy or materials	25

NOTABLE COMPETITIVE DISADVANTAGES

Criteria		Rank

Growth Competitiveness

Macroeconomic Environment

2.28	Interest rate spread, 2001	79
2.17	National savings rate, 2001	77
2.01	Recession expectations	75
2.05	Access to credit	73
2.15	Government surplus/deficit, 2001	56
2.21	Real exchange rate, 2001	56
2.19	Inflation, 2001	42

Technology

3.04	FDI and technology transfer	77
3.02	Firm-level innovation	73
3.07	Company spending on research and development	71
3.15	Utility patents, 2001	68
4.06	Laws relating to ICT	68
3.05	Prevalence of foreign technology licensing	67
4.03	Quality of competition in the ISP sector	66
3.09	University/industry research collaboration	64
4.05	Government success in ICT promotion	58
4.07	Cellular telephones, 2001	54
4.04	Government prioritization of ICT	53
3.01	Technological sophistication	49

Microeconomic Competitiveness

Sophistication of Company Operations and Strategy

3.07	Company spending on research and development	71
10.04	Capacity for innovation	71
10.11	Breadth of international markets	70

Quality of the National Business Environment

2.07	Local equity market access	78
9.06	State of cluster development	78
8.01	Intensity of local competition	71

Other Indicators

1.08	Unemployment rate, 2001	62
2.18	Investment rate, 2001	79
2.22	Exports, 2001	71
2.23	Imports, 2001	73
2.24	Average tariff rate, 2002	70
2.27	Value added tax rate, 2002	73
2.29	FDI, 2001	67
3.03	Firm-level technology absorption	76
6.06	Competence of public officials	73
6.07	Burden of regulation	67
10.18	Hiring and firing practices	66
11.07	Compliance with environmental regulations	65

Venezuela

Key Economic Indicators

Total population (in millions), 2001 ....24.6
Population rank 29
GDP per capita (PPP), 2001 ....$5,966
GDP per capita rank..58
Real growth in GDP per capita, 2000 to 2001.........1.7
Growth rank 31
Unemployment rate, 2001....................................12.10
Unemployment rank 56
Government surplus/deficit, 2001 ....–6.70
Government surplus/deficit rank 75
National savings rate, 2001 ....21.00
National savings rank 41
Investment rate, 2001 ....16.44
Investment rank 73
Inflation, 2001 ....12.50
Inflation rank 72
Exports of goods (as a percentage of GDP),
    2001 ....20.9
Exports rank..57
Imports of goods (as a percentage of GDP),
    2001 ....14.4
Imports rank...75
Internet users (per 10,000 inhabitants), 2001 ...527.77
Internet users rank 48

Competitiveness Rankings

Growth Competitiveness Rank	68

Technology Index Rank **53**
  Innovation Subindex Rank 47
  ICT Subindex Rank 51
  Technology Transfer Subindex Rank
    (out of 56 non-core innovators) 37
Public Institutions Index Rank...............................**73**
  Contracts and Law Subindex Rank 77
  Corruption Subindex Rank...................................65
Macroeconomic Environment Index Rank **72**
  Macroeconomic Stability Subindex Rank 77
  Country Credit Rating Rank.................................61
  Government Expenditure Rank 25

Microeconomic Competitiveness Rank	72

Company Operations and Strategy Rank **73**
Quality of the National Business Environment Rank ...**72**

Trade Performance of Leading Export Sectors

Sector	Share in national exports	Value of exports (US$ millions)	Value of net exports (US$ millions)	Share in world market	TPI current index	TPI change index
Minerals	82.3%	18,652	18,358	2.67%	26	119
Basic manufactures	8.6%	1,950	593	0.45%	34	102
Chemicals	4.3%	978	–1,259	0.16%	58	61
Fresh food	1.2%	280	–405	0.12%	114	87
Transport equipment	1.0%	225	–1,471	0.03%	68	83

Source: International Trade Centre UNCTAD/WTO

Real GDP (annual percent change)

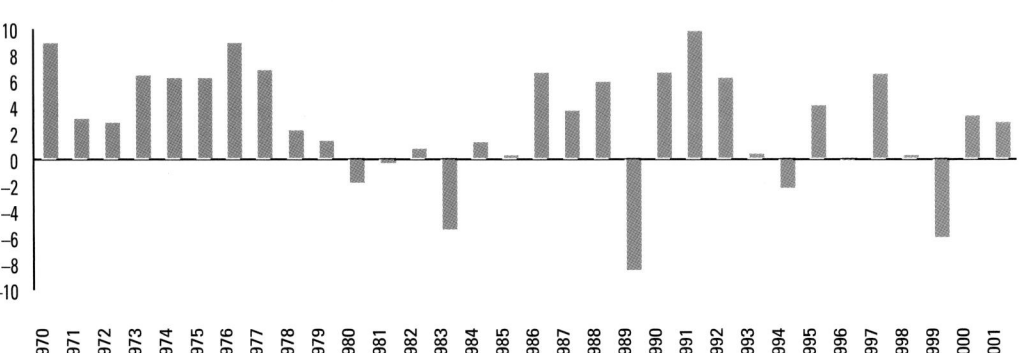

Source: IMF *World Economic Outlook Database,* April 2002

National competitiveness balance sheet

NOTABLE COMPETITIVE ADVANTAGES	
Criteria	Rank

Growth Competitiveness

Macroeconomic Environment

2.16	Government expenditure, 2001	25
2.17	National savings rate, 2001	41

Technology

3.05	Prevalence of foreign technology licensing	29
3.15	Utility patents, 2001	38
4.07	Cellular telephones, 2001	39
4.03	Quality of competition in the ISP sector	40
4.06	Laws relating to ICT	40
3.01	Technological sophistication	44
3.02	Firm-level innovation	44
3.18	Tertiary enrollment	44
4.11	Personal computers, 2001	47
4.08	Internet users, 2001	48

Microeconomic Competitiveness

Sophistication of Company Operations and Strategy

3.05	Prevalence of foreign technology licensing	29
10.07	Extent of marketing	50
10.14	Extent of incentive compensation	54

Quality of the National Business Environment

3.15	Utility patents, 2001	38
4.06	Laws relating to ICT	40
11.05	Stringency of environmental regulations	44

Other Indicators

2.09	Regulatory obstacles to business	8
2.26	Individual income tax rate, 2002	33
2.27	Value added tax rate, 2002	32
2.29	FDI, 2001	32

NOTABLE COMPETITIVE DISADVANTAGES	
Criteria	Rank

Growth Competitiveness

Macroeconomic Environment

2.21	Real exchange rate, 2001	80
2.01	Recession expectations	78
2.15	Government surplus/deficit, 2001	75
2.19	Inflation, 2001	72
2.05	Access to credit	69
2.28	Interest rate spread, 2001	50

Technology

4.04	Government prioritization of ICT	74
3.07	Company spending on research and development	70
4.05	Government success in ICT promotion	70
3.04	FDI and technology transfer	69
4.02	Internet access in schools	69
3.09	University/industry research collaboration	62
4.09	Internet hosts, 2001	57
4.10	Telephone lines, 2001	57

Public Institutions

6.01	Judicial independence	79
6.03	Property rights	76
7.01	Irregular payments in exports & imports	72
6.15	Organized crime	70
7.03	Irregular payments in tax collection	69
6.09	Favoritism in decisions of government officials	67
7.02	Irregular payments in public utilities	59

Microeconomic Competitiveness

Sophistication of Company Operations and Strategy

10.02	Value chain presence	78
10.09	Control of international distribution	78
10.04	Capacity for innovation	77

Quality of the National Business Environment

5.02	Railroad infrastructure development	80
6.02	Efficiency of legal framework	80
2.07	Local equity market access	76

Other Indicators

2.18	Investment rate, 2001	73
2.30	Domestic credit, 2001	73
3.17	Secondary enrollment	70
5.07	Postal efficiency	79
5.09	Disparity in healthcare quality	75
6.05	Freedom of the press	77
6.06	Competence of public officials	79
6.07	Burden of regulation	78
6.08	Transparency of government policy-making	80
6.11	Effectiveness of law-making bodies	78
6.14	Business costs of crime and violence	77
7.08	Frequency of payments or bribes	79
10.21	Pay and productivity	77
11.06	Subsidies for energy or materials	71

Vietnam

Key Economic Indicators

Total population (in millions), 2001 ....78.9
Population rank 13
GDP per capita (PPP), 2001 ....$2,130
GDP per capita rank..77
Real growth in GDP per capita, 2000 to 2001.........3.2
Growth rank 20
Unemployment rate, 2001....................................6.13
Unemployment rank 28
Government surplus/deficit, 2001 ....–5.10
Government surplus/deficit rank 61
National savings rate, 2001 ....33.40
National savings rank..5
Investment rate, 2001 ....28.90
Investment rank..5
Inflation, 2001 ....0.10
Inflation rank 5
Exports of goods (as a percentage of GDP),
    2001 ....48.9
Exports rank...15
Imports of goods (as a percentage of GDP),
    2001 ....51.8
Imports rank..15
Internet users (per 10,000 inhabitants), 2001 .....49.31
Internet users rank 77

Competitiveness Rankings

Growth Competitiveness Rank	**65**

Technology Index Rank **68**
    Innovation Subindex Rank 65
    ICT Subindex Rank 74
    Technology Transfer Subindex Rank
        (out of 56 non-core innovators) 28
Public Institutions Index Rank................................**62**
    Contracts and Law Subindex Rank 55
    Corruption Subindex Rank 68
Macroeconomic Environment Index Rank **38**
    Macroeconomic Stability Subindex Rank 6
    Country Credit Rating Rank...................................67
    Government Expenditure Rank 33

Microeconomic Competitiveness Rank	**60**

Company Operations and Strategy Rank **67**
Quality of the National Business Environment Rank ...**58**

Trade Performance of Leading Export Sectors

Sector	Share in national exports	Value of exports (US$ millions)	Value of net exports (US$ millions)	Share in world market	TPI current index	TPI change index
Minerals	28.2%	3,731	2,725	0.53%	57	39
Leather products	19.0%	2,515	2,293	3.88%	7	4
Fresh food	18.9%	2,507	2,282	1.05%	23	76
Clothing	12.3%	1,632	1,586	0.87%	39	11
Miscellaneous manufacturing	5.8%	763	306	0.16%	32	14

Source: International Trade Centre UNCTAD/WTO

Real GDP (annual percent change)

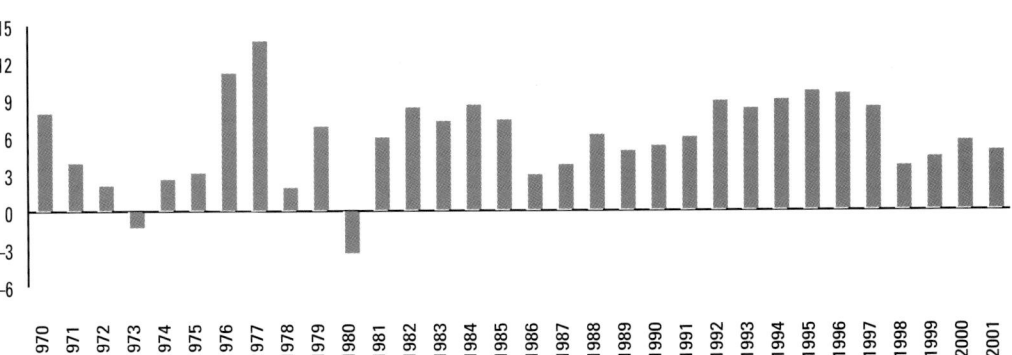

Source: IMF *World Economic Outlook Database,* April 2002

4.3: Data Tables

Index of tables

Section XI. Environmental Policy

Section XII. International Institutions

Section I: Aggregate Country Performance Indicators

1.01 Total GDP, 2001

Gross Domestic Product in billions of US dollars, 2001

RANK	COUNTRY	HARD DATA
1	United States	10,208.13
2	Japan	4,148.65
3	Germany	1,847.35
4	United Kingdom	1,424.49
5	France	1,307.06
6	China	1,158.70
7	Italy	1,089.41
8	Canada	699.99
9	Mexico	617.87
10	Spain	582.23
11	Brazil	504.39
12	India	480.90
13	Korea	422.17
14	Netherlands	380.32
15	Australia	357.43
16	Russian Federation	309.95
17	Taiwan	282.24
18	Argentina	269.48
19	Switzerland	246.95
20	Belgium	227.37
21	Sweden	209.82
22	Austria	188.68
23	Poland	176.27
24	Norway	163.71
25	Hong Kong SAR	161.87
26	Denmark	161.41
27	Turkey	147.95
28	Indonesia	145.50
29	Venezuela	124.91
30	Finland	119.93
31	Greece	116.90
32	Thailand	114.77
33	South Africa	111.70
34	Israel	110.47
35	Portugal	109.48
36	Ireland	101.62
37	Singapore	88.23
38	Malaysia	87.54
39	Colombia	81.48
40	Philippines	71.44
41	Chile	66.45
42	Czech Republic	56.71
43	Peru	52.94
44	New Zealand	49.52
45	Bangladesh	47.07
46	Hungary	46.39
47	Nigeria	41.11
48	Romania	39.64
49	Ukraine	37.59
50	Morocco	33.49
51	Vietnam	30.88
52	Slovenia	21.08
53	Dominican Republic	20.52
54	Croatia	20.43
55	Tunisia	19.99
56	Slovak Republic	19.95
57	Uruguay	19.12
58	Guatemala	18.72
59	Ecuador	17.83
60	Costa Rica	16.70
61	Sri Lanka	15.60
62	El Salvador	13.97
63	Bulgaria	12.71
64	Lithuania	12.02
65	Panama	10.24
66	Jamaica	9.85
67	Zimbabwe	9.20
68	Jordan	8.83
69	Trinidad and Tobago	8.32
70	Bolivia	7.99
71	Latvia	7.77
72	Iceland	7.51
73	Paraguay	7.18
74	Honduras	6.12
75	Estonia	5.42
76	Botswana	4.50
77	Mauritius	4.50
78	Haiti	3.69
79	Namibia	3.17
80	Nicaragua	2.52

SOURCE: IMF World Economic Outlook Database, April 2002

1.02 Total population, 2001

Population in millions, 2001

RANK	COUNTRY	HARD DATA
1	China	1,271.2
2	India	1,030.0
3	United States	284.4
4	Indonesia	211.2
5	Brazil	174.5
6	Russian Federation	144.5
7	Bangladesh	140.3
8	Japan	126.8
9	Nigeria	118.3
10	Mexico	100.4
11	Philippines	82.8
12	Germany	82.1
13	Vietnam	78.9
14	Turkey	66.5
15	Thailand	62.9
16	United Kingdom	60.0
17	France	59.7
18	Italy	57.5
19	Ukraine	49.3
20	Korea	47.7
21	South Africa	44.4
22	Colombia	43.0
23	Spain	40.3
24	Poland	38.6
25	Argentina	37.5
26	Canada	31.1
27	Morocco	29.2
28	Peru	26.1
29	Venezuela	24.6
30	Malaysia	23.8
31	Romania	22.4
32	Taiwan	22.4
33	Sri Lanka	19.6
34	Australia	19.4
35	Netherlands	16.0
36	Chile	15.5
37	Zimbabwe	12.3
38	Ecuador	12.1
39	Guatemala	11.7
40	Greece	10.6
41	Czech Republic	10.3
42	Belgium	10.3
43	Hungary	10.1
44	Portugal	10.1
45	Tunisia	9.7
46	Sweden	8.9
47	Dominican Republic	8.6
48	Bolivia	8.5
49	Austria	8.2
50	Haiti	8.0
51	Bulgaria	7.9
52	Switzerland	7.3
53	Hong Kong SAR	6.7
54	Honduras	6.6
55	Israel	6.4
56	El Salvador	6.4
57	Paraguay	5.6
58	Slovak Republic	5.4
59	Denmark	5.3
60	Nicaragua	5.2
61	Finland	5.2
62	Jordan	5.2
63	Norway	4.5
64	Croatia	4.4
65	Singapore	4.1
66	Costa Rica	3.9
67	New Zealand	3.8
68	Ireland	3.8
69	Lithuania	3.7
70	Uruguay	3.4
71	Panama	2.9
72	Jamaica	2.6
73	Latvia	2.4
74	Slovenia	2.0
75	Namibia	1.8
76	Botswana	1.7
77	Estonia	1.4
78	Trinidad and Tobago	1.3
79	Mauritius	1.2
80	Iceland	0.3

SOURCE: Economist Intelligence Unit

1.03 GDP per capita (PPP), 2001

Gross Domestic Product per capita in US dollars, measured at Purchasing Power Parity, 2001

RANK	COUNTRY	HARD DATA
1	United States	34,888
2	Ireland	32,133
3	Norway	30,727
4	Iceland	30,725
5	Switzerland	29,587
6	Canada	28,611
7	Denmark	28,342
8	Belgium	27,912
9	Austria	27,518
10	Japan	27,101
11	Australia	26,552
12	Netherlands	26,242
13	Germany	25,715
14	Finland	25,611
15	Hong Kong SAR	25,581
16	France	25,074
17	Sweden	24,978
18	Italy	24,510
19	United Kingdom	24,421
20	Singapore	23,250
21	Taiwan	22,559
22	New Zealand	20,725
23	Spain	20,374
24	Israel	19,867
25	Slovenia	18,233
26	Korea	18,149
27	Portugal	17,571
28	Greece	17,482
29	Czech Republic	14,885
30	Hungary	12,941
31	Argentina	12,098
32	Slovak Republic	11,739
33	Mauritius	10,400
34	Estonia	10,380
35	Trinidad and Tobago	10,018
36	Chile	9,753
37	South Africa	9,565
38	Poland	9,327
39	Mexico	8,969
40	Russian Federation	8,948
41	Uruguay	8,781
42	Costa Rica	8,490
43	Malaysia	8,424
44	Croatia	8,414
45	Botswana	8,196
46	Lithuania	7,764
47	Brazil	7,759
48	Latvia	7,750
49	Romania	7,036
50	Tunisia	6,769
51	Turkey	6,716
52	Namibia	6,650
53	Thailand	6,630
54	Colombia	6,202
55	Dominican Republic	6,198
56	Bulgaria	6,182
57	Panama	5,986
58	Venezuela	5,966
59	Peru	4,797
60	El Salvador	4,603
61	Paraguay	4,379
62	China	4,329
63	Ukraine	4,224
64	Philippines	4,113
65	Jordan	4,080
66	Jamaica	3,890
67	Guatemala	3,879
68	Morocco	3,787
69	Sri Lanka	3,634
70	Ecuador	3,295
71	Indonesia	3,059
72	Nicaragua	2,514
73	Honduras	2,505
74	India	2,464
75	Bolivia	2,439
76	Zimbabwe	2,406
77	Vietnam	2,130
78	Bangladesh	1,644
79	Haiti	1,444
80	Nigeria	898

SOURCES: International Comparison Program (ICP) of The World Bank; IMF World Economic Outlook Database, April 2002; Economist Intelligence Unit; and authors' calculations

1.04 Real growth in GDP per capita, 2000 to 2001

Real growth in GDP per capita from 2000 to 2001

RANK	COUNTRY	HARD DATA
1	Ukraine	10.1
2	Latvia	7.4
3	China	6.8
4	Estonia	6.3
5	Botswana	6.3
6	Russian Federation	5.6
7	Bulgaria	5.6
8	Romania	5.5
9	Mauritius	5.4
10	Ireland	4.9
11	Lithuania	4.5
12	Morocco	4.5
13	Hungary	4.3
14	Croatia	4.2
15	Trinidad and Tobago	4.0
16	Greece	3.9
17	Czech Republic	3.7
18	Tunisia	3.7
19	Ecuador	3.3
20	Vietnam	3.2
21	Slovak Republic	3.2
22	Slovenia	3.1
23	Spain	2.7
24	India	2.5
25	Bangladesh	2.4
26	Korea	2.2
27	Jamaica	2.1
28	Indonesia	2.0
29	Nigeria	1.9
30	United Kingdom	1.8
31	Venezuela	1.7
32	France	1.6
33	Italy	1.6
34	Chile	1.5
35	New Zealand	1.5
36	Dominican Republic	1.4
37	Philippines	1.4
38	Iceland	1.3
39	Jordan	1.3
40	Poland	1.2
41	Australia	1.1
42	Norway	1.0
43	Belgium	1.0
44	Sweden	0.9
45	Switzerland	0.9
46	Austria	0.8
47	Denmark	0.7
48	Thailand	0.6
49	Canada	0.5
50	Panama	0.5
51	Netherlands	0.4
52	Finland	0.4
53	Germany	0.3
54	Nicaragua	0.3
55	United States	0.2
56	South Africa	0.1
57	El Salvador	0.1
58	Honduras	0.0
59	Brazil	0.0
60	Peru	0.0
61	Colombia	–0.2
62	Portugal	–0.2
63	Namibia	–0.2
64	Sri Lanka	–0.5
65	Japan	–0.6
66	Guatemala	–0.8
67	Hong Kong SAR	–0.8
68	Bolivia	–1.2
69	Paraguay	–1.7
70	Mexico	–1.8
71	Costa Rica	–1.8
72	Malaysia	–1.8
73	Israel	–2.7
74	Taiwan	–2.8
75	Haiti	–3.2
76	Singapore	–3.8
77	Uruguay	–3.8
78	Argentina	–4.8
79	Turkey	–7.7
80	Zimbabwe	–10.9

SOURCES: IMF World Economic Outlook Database, April 2002, and authors' calculations

1.05 GDP per capita relative to the US, 2001

GDP per capita (PPP) as a proportion of US GDP per capita, 2001

RANK	COUNTRY	HARD DATA
1	United States	1.00
2	Ireland	0.92
3	Norway	0.88
4	Iceland	0.88
5	Switzerland	0.85
6	Canada	0.82
7	Denmark	0.81
8	Belgium	0.80
9	Austria	0.79
10	Japan	0.78
11	Australia	0.76
12	Netherlands	0.75
13	Germany	0.74
14	Finland	0.73
15	Hong Kong SAR	0.73
16	France	0.72
17	Sweden	0.72
18	Italy	0.70
19	United Kingdom	0.70
20	Singapore	0.67
21	Taiwan	0.65
22	New Zealand	0.59
23	Spain	0.58
24	Israel	0.57
25	Slovenia	0.52
26	Korea	0.52
27	Portugal	0.50
28	Greece	0.50
29	Czech Republic	0.43
30	Hungary	0.37
31	Argentina	0.35
32	Slovak Republic	0.34
33	Mauritius	0.30
34	Estonia	0.30
35	Trinidad and Tobago	0.29
36	Chile	0.28
37	South Africa	0.27
38	Poland	0.27
39	Mexico	0.26
40	Russian Federation	0.26
41	Uruguay	0.25
42	Costa Rica	0.24
43	Malaysia	0.24
44	Croatia	0.24
45	Botswana	0.23
46	Lithuania	0.22
47	Brazil	0.22
48	Latvia	0.22
49	Romania	0.20
50	Tunisia	0.19
51	Turkey	0.19
52	Namibia	0.19
53	Thailand	0.19
54	Colombia	0.18
55	Dominican Republic	0.18
56	Bulgaria	0.18
57	Panama	0.17
58	Venezuela	0.17
59	Peru	0.14
60	El Salvador	0.13
61	Paraguay	0.13
62	China	0.12
63	Ukraine	0.12
64	Philippines	0.12
65	Jordan	0.12
66	Jamaica	0.11
67	Guatemala	0.11
68	Morocco	0.11
69	Sri Lanka	0.10
70	Ecuador	0.09
71	Indonesia	0.09
72	Nicaragua	0.07
73	Honduras	0.07
74	India	0.07
75	Bolivia	0.07
76	Zimbabwe	0.07
77	Vietnam	0.06
78	Bangladesh	0.05
79	Haiti	0.04
80	Nigeria	0.03

SOURCES: International Comparison Program (ICP) of The World Bank; IMF World Economic Outlook Database, April 2002; Economist Intelligence Unit; and authors' calculations

1.06 GDP per capita relative to the US, 1995

GDP per capita (PPP) as a proportion of US GDP per capita, 1995

RANK	COUNTRY	HARD DATA
1	United States	1.00
2	Switzerland	0.92
3	Norway	0.90
4	Japan	0.86
5	Denmark	0.84
6	Canada	0.83
7	Iceland	0.83
8	Belgium	0.81
9	Austria	0.80
10	Hong Kong SAR	0.79
11	Germany	0.78
12	Australia	0.77
13	Netherlands	0.75
14	France	0.75
15	Italy	0.74
16	Sweden	0.73
17	United Kingdom	0.71
18	Singapore	0.69
19	Finland	0.68
20	Ireland	0.63
21	New Zealand	0.63
22	Israel	0.62
23	Taiwan	0.61
24	Spain	0.55
25	Korea	0.49
26	Portugal	0.49
27	Greece	0.47
28	Slovenia	0.47
29	Czech Republic	0.44
30	Argentina	0.39
31	Hungary	0.34
32	Slovak Republic	0.31
33	South Africa	0.31
34	Uruguay	0.28
35	Chile	0.28
36	Mauritius	0.27
37	Malaysia	0.27
38	Mexico	0.26
39	Russian Federation	0.26
40	Trinidad and Tobago	0.25
41	Poland	0.24
42	Costa Rica	0.24
43	Brazil	0.24
44	Romania	0.23
45	Estonia	0.23
46	Thailand	0.22
47	Colombia	0.22
48	Venezuela	0.21
49	Croatia	0.21
50	Turkey	0.21
51	Botswana	0.21
52	Bulgaria	0.20
53	Lithuania	0.20
54	Namibia	0.19
55	Panama	0.18
56	Latvia	0.18
57	Tunisia	0.18
58	Paraguay	0.16
59	Peru	0.16
60	Dominican Republic	0.16
61	El Salvador	0.14
62	Jordan	0.14
63	Ukraine	0.14
64	Jamaica	0.13
65	Philippines	0.13
66	Guatemala	0.12
67	Ecuador	0.11
68	Morocco	0.11
69	Indonesia	0.10
70	Sri Lanka	0.10
71	China	0.10
72	Zimbabwe	0.09
73	Honduras	0.09
74	Nicaragua	0.08
75	Bolivia	0.08
76	India	0.07
77	Vietnam	0.05
78	Haiti	0.05
79	Bangladesh	0.05
80	Nigeria	0.03

SOURCES: World Bank *World Development Indicators 2002* and authors' calculations

553

1.07 Change in GDP per capita relative to the US, 1995–2001

Average annual percentage change in ratio of GDP per capita (PPP) to US GDP per capita from 1995 to 2001

RANK	COUNTRY	HARD DATA
1	Ireland	6.43
2	China	4.52
3	Estonia	4.29
4	Latvia	3.68
5	Trinidad and Tobago	2.27
6	Dominican Republic	2.25
7	Vietnam	2.21
8	Croatia	2.12
9	Botswana	2.09
10	Slovenia	1.83
11	Lithuania	1.81
12	Poland	1.72
13	Tunisia	1.68
14	Mauritius	1.61
15	Slovak Republic	1.50
16	Hungary	1.46
17	Finland	1.24
18	India	1.12
19	Spain	1.11
20	Korea	1.06
21	Taiwan	1.04
22	Iceland	0.96
23	Greece	0.92
24	Sri Lanka	0.88
25	Portugal	0.52
26	Bangladesh	0.52
27	Chile	0.26
28	Costa Rica	0.21
29	Netherlands	0.08
30	Mexico	0.04
31	Russian Federation	0.04
32	Namibia	0.00
33	United States	0.00
34	Australia	–0.13
35	United Kingdom	–0.14
36	Belgium	–0.23
37	Sweden	–0.25
38	Canada	–0.28
39	Austria	–0.34
40	Norway	–0.35
41	Morocco	–0.37
42	Denmark	–0.46
43	Singapore	–0.51
44	Czech Republic	–0.63
45	France	–0.66
46	New Zealand	–0.88
47	Italy	–0.90
48	Germany	–0.99
49	Brazil	–1.22
50	Panama	–1.22
51	Hong Kong SAR	–1.30
52	Nicaragua	–1.38
53	Switzerland	–1.38
54	Israel	–1.42
55	Turkey	–1.47
56	Philippines	–1.48
57	El Salvador	–1.48
58	Guatemala	–1.50
59	Malaysia	–1.58
60	Japan	–1.60
61	South Africa	–1.82
62	Ukraine	–1.84
63	Bolivia	–1.85
64	Argentina	–1.87
65	Uruguay	–2.03
66	Bulgaria	–2.13
67	Nigeria	–2.14
68	Peru	–2.18
69	Romania	–2.33
70	Thailand	–2.58
71	Indonesia	–2.73
72	Honduras	–2.95
73	Jordan	–2.96
74	Jamaica	–3.02
75	Ecuador	–3.11
76	Haiti	–3.12
77	Colombia	–3.56
78	Venezuela	–3.65
79	Paraguay	–4.28
80	Zimbabwe	–4.37

SOURCES: International Comparison Program (ICP) of The World Bank; IMF World Economic Outlook Database, April 2002; Economist Intelligence Unit; World Bank *World Development Indicators 2002*; and authors' calculations

1.08 Unemployment rate, 2001

Recorded official unemployment rate as a percentage of total labor force, 2001

RANK	COUNTRY	HARD DATA
1	Iceland	1.40
2	Switzerland	1.78
3	Netherlands	2.04
4	Mexico	2.40
5	Bangladesh	2.50
6	Thailand	3.30
7	Singapore	3.33
8	Norway	3.55
9	China	3.60
10	Korea	3.70
11	Ireland	3.74
12	Malaysia	3.80
13	Nigeria	3.80
14	Austria	3.86
15	Sweden	3.98
16	Portugal	4.05
17	Ukraine	4.53
18	Taiwan	4.58
19	United States	4.79
20	Guatemala	4.90
21	Hong Kong SAR	4.93
22	United Kingdom	5.03
23	Japan	5.03
24	Denmark	5.16
25	New Zealand	5.30
26	Hungary	5.69
27	Costa Rica	6.10
28	Vietnam	6.13
29	Brazil	6.23
30	Belgium	6.59
31	Australia	6.73
32	Canada	7.21
33	Bolivia	7.46
34	El Salvador	7.50
35	Latvia	7.70
36	Sri Lanka	7.80
37	Peru	8.07
38	Ecuador	8.10
39	Turkey	8.53
40	Czech Republic	8.54
41	Romania	8.59
42	Mauritius	8.60
43	Russian Federation	8.66
44	France	9.00
45	Finland	9.10
46	India	9.16
47	Chile	9.20
48	Israel	9.28
49	Italy	9.43
50	Germany	9.50
51	Indonesia	10.30
52	Greece	10.46
53	Trinidad and Tobago	10.90
54	Philippines	11.15
55	Slovenia	11.60
56	Venezuela	12.10
57	Lithuania	12.50
58	Estonia	12.71
59	Spain	13.05
60	Panama	14.40
61	Jordan	14.70
62	Uruguay	14.90
63	Dominican Republic	15.00
64	Jamaica	15.10
65	Tunisia	15.60
66	Poland	16.22
67	Argentina	16.40
68	Colombia	16.67
69	Bulgaria	17.52
70	Paraguay	17.80
71	Slovak Republic	18.62
72	Botswana	19.60
73	Morocco	20.30
74	Croatia	22.14
75	Nicaragua	23.08
76	Honduras	28.50
77	South Africa	29.50
78	Namibia	30.00
79	Haiti	55.00
	Zimbabwe	N/A

SOURCES: Economist Intelligence Unit, US Department of State, 2001 Country Report on Economic Policy and Trade Practices, Bureau of Economic and Business Affairs, and national sources

1.09   Employment to population ratio, 2001

Ratio of recorded employed persons to population, 2001

RANK	COUNTRY	HARD DATA
1	China	56.03
2	Switzerland	54.12
3	Singapore	51.87
4	Thailand	51.84
5	Denmark	50.92
6	Japan	50.58
7	Norway	50.55
8	Austria	50.46
9	Iceland	49.30
10	Portugal	49.04
11	Canada	48.45
12	Hong Kong SAR	48.35
13	Australia	47.73
14	Sweden	47.68
15	United States	47.48
16	New Zealand	47.39
17	Germany	47.10
18	United Kingdom	47.07
19	Netherlands	46.71
20	Latvia	46.34
21	Czech Republic	46.16
22	Ireland	45.55
23	Finland	45.45
24	Russian Federation	45.22
25	Korea	44.64
26	Brazil	43.09
27	Bangladesh	42.74
28	Estonia	42.61
29	Ukraine	42.59
30	Indonesia	42.05
31	Taiwan	41.93
32	Lithuania	41.50
33	Mauritius	41.48
34	France	40.65
35	Slovak Republic	40.01
36	India	39.95
37	Costa Rica	39.44
38	Romania	39.28
39	Belgium	39.24
40	Trinidad and Tobago	39.07
41	Uruguay	39.00
42	Malaysia	38.85
43	Slovenia	38.74
44	Hungary	38.19
45	Poland	37.78
46	Venezuela	37.54
47	Greece	37.32
48	Colombia	37.20
49	Italy	37.12
50	Dominican Republic	36.89
51	Spain	36.70
52	Jamaica	36.29
53	Ecuador	35.94
54	El Salvador	35.93
55	Israel	35.29
56	Philippines	35.19
57	Chile	34.85
58	Tunisia	34.67
59	Bulgaria	34.33
60	Turkey	34.13
61	Mexico	33.19
62	Panama	32.69
63	Argentina	32.31
64	Sri Lanka	31.72
65	Paraguay	29.77
66	Croatia	29.69
67	Guatemala	29.30
68	Morocco	28.84
69	Peru	28.36
70	Nicaragua	28.08
71	Namibia	26.82
72	Botswana	26.70
73	Bolivia	25.27
74	Honduras	24.81
75	South Africa	24.38
	Haiti	N/A
	Jordan	N/A
	Nigeria	N/A
	Vietnam	N/A
	Zimbabwe	N/A

SOURCES: Economist Intelligence Unit and national sources

Section II: Macroeconomic Environment

2.01 Recession expectations

Your country's economy (1 = will likely be in a recession in 2003, 7 = will have strong growth in 2003)

RANK	COUNTRY	SCORE	1 MEAN: 4.2 7
1	Australia	5.8	
2	Malaysia	5.3	
3	Canada	5.3	
4	China	5.2	
5	Korea	5.2	
6	Czech Republic	5.2	
7	Vietnam	5.1	
8	Finland	5.1	
9	Latvia	5.0	
10	Trinidad and Tobago	5.0	
11	Botswana	4.9	
12	Brazil	4.9	
13	Sri Lanka	4.9	
14	Hungary	4.9	
15	Singapore	4.9	
16	Ireland	4.9	
17	United States	4.8	
18	Austria	4.8	
19	Mexico	4.8	
20	Estonia	4.8	
21	Hong Kong SAR	4.8	
22	Norway	4.8	
23	New Zealand	4.8	
24	Italy	4.8	
25	Greece	4.7	
26	Nicaragua	4.7	
27	Lithuania	4.7	
28	Morocco	4.7	
29	United Kingdom	4.7	
30	Denmark	4.7	
31	Iceland	4.6	
32	Belgium	4.6	
33	Germany	4.5	
34	Switzerland	4.5	
35	Spain	4.5	
36	France	4.5	
36	Philippines	4.5	
38	Ecuador	4.5	
39	Thailand	4.5	
40	Tunisia	4.4	
41	Chile	4.4	
42	Taiwan	4.4	
43	Nigeria	4.4	
44	El Salvador	4.4	
45	India	4.4	
46	Namibia	4.3	
47	Netherlands	4.3	
48	South Africa	4.3	
49	Russian Federation	4.2	
50	Slovenia	4.2	
51	Indonesia	4.2	
52	Sweden	4.2	
53	Turkey	4.1	
54	Japan	4.1	
55	Dominican Republic	4.1	
56	Peru	4.0	
57	Jordan	4.0	
58	Jamaica	4.0	
59	Bangladesh	4.0	
60	Croatia	3.9	
61	Slovak Republic	3.9	
62	Romania	3.8	
63	Mauritius	3.8	
64	Honduras	3.7	
65	Colombia	3.7	
66	Ukraine	3.7	
67	Bulgaria	3.7	
68	Poland	3.5	
69	Portugal	3.5	
70	Costa Rica	3.4	
71	Panama	3.1	
72	Israel	2.8	
73	Bolivia	2.6	
74	Guatemala	2.4	
75	Uruguay	2.4	
76	Haiti	2.2	
77	Argentina	2.2	
78	Venezuela	2.0	
79	Paraguay	1.9	
80	Zimbabwe	1.3	

2.02 Financial market sophistication

The level of sophistication of financial markets in your country is (1 = lower than international norms, 7 = higher than international norms)

RANK	COUNTRY	SCORE	1 MEAN: 4.1 7
1	United Kingdom	6.8	
2	United States	6.7	
3	Switzerland	6.4	
4	Hong Kong SAR	6.3	
5	Australia	6.1	
6	Netherlands	6.0	
7	Finland	5.8	
8	Belgium	5.8	
9	Canada	5.8	
10	Germany	5.6	
11	Brazil	5.6	
12	Denmark	5.4	
13	South Africa	5.4	
14	Singapore	5.4	
15	Sweden	5.2	
16	New Zealand	5.2	
17	Ireland	5.1	
18	Israel	5.1	
19	Chile	5.1	
20	France	5.1	
21	Spain	5.0	
22	Panama	4.9	
23	Estonia	4.8	
24	Norway	4.7	
25	Portugal	4.7	
26	Iceland	4.6	
27	Taiwan	4.6	
28	Malaysia	4.6	
29	Hungary	4.5	
30	Italy	4.5	
31	Sri Lanka	4.4	
32	Korea	4.3	
33	Japan	4.2	
34	Austria	4.2	
35	Uruguay	4.1	
36	Thailand	4.1	
37	Zimbabwe	4.0	
38	El Salvador	4.0	
39	Jamaica	4.0	
40	Greece	3.9	
41	Latvia	3.9	
41	Namibia	3.9	
43	Dominican Republic	3.9	
44	India	3.8	
45	Turkey	3.8	
46	Slovenia	3.8	
47	Trinidad and Tobago	3.8	
48	Mexico	3.8	
49	Peru	3.7	
50	Poland	3.7	
51	Colombia	3.6	
52	Costa Rica	3.5	
53	Tunisia	3.5	
54	Philippines	3.5	
55	Nigeria	3.5	
56	Venezuela	3.5	
57	Botswana	3.5	
58	Indonesia	3.4	
59	Jordan	3.4	
60	Mauritius	3.3	
61	Lithuania	3.3	
62	Argentina	3.2	
63	China	3.2	
64	Slovak Republic	3.1	
65	Morocco	3.0	
66	Guatemala	3.0	
67	Paraguay	2.9	
68	Croatia	2.8	
69	Nicaragua	2.7	
70	Czech Republic	2.7	
71	Ecuador	2.7	
72	Romania	2.6	
73	Bolivia	2.6	
74	Russian Federation	2.5	
75	Honduras	2.3	
76	Vietnam	2.3	
77	Bangladesh	2.2	
78	Bulgaria	2.1	
79	Ukraine	2.0	
80	Haiti	1.5	

2.03 Soundness of banks

Banks in your country are (1 = insolvent and may require government bailout, 7 = generally healthy with sound balance sheets)

RANK	COUNTRY	SCORE
1	United Kingdom	6.8
2	Hong Kong SAR	6.7
3	Switzerland	6.7
4	Canada	6.7
5	Netherlands	6.6
6	United States	6.6
7	Denmark	6.6
8	Australia	6.6
9	Belgium	6.6
10	New Zealand	6.5
11	Finland	6.5
12	Ireland	6.5
13	Chile	6.3
14	Sweden	6.3
15	Norway	6.2
16	Botswana	6.2
17	Trinidad and Tobago	6.2
18	Singapore	6.2
19	Estonia	6.1
20	Panama	6.1
21	Austria	6.1
22	El Salvador	6.1
23	Germany	6.1
24	France	6.1
25	Israel	6.0
26	Namibia	6.0
27	Spain	6.0
28	Brazil	5.9
29	Iceland	5.9
30	Portugal	5.8
31	South Africa	5.8
32	Dominican Republic	5.7
33	Italy	5.6
34	Hungary	5.5
35	Mauritius	5.5
36	Morocco	5.5
37	Haiti	5.3
38	Slovenia	5.3
39	Costa Rica	5.2
40	Greece	5.2
41	Jamaica	5.2
42	Tunisia	5.1
43	Latvia	5.1
44	Malaysia	5.1
45	Lithuania	5.0
46	Slovak Republic	5.0
47	Jordan	4.9
48	Sri Lanka	4.9
49	India	4.9
50	Zimbabwe	4.9
51	Poland	4.8
52	Peru	4.7
53	Paraguay	4.7
54	Uruguay	4.6
55	Korea	4.6
56	Croatia	4.6
57	Czech Republic	4.5
58	Philippines	4.4
59	Bulgaria	4.4
60	Nigeria	4.3
61	Taiwan	4.3
62	Bangladesh	4.2
63	Venezuela	4.2
64	Colombia	4.1
65	China	4.0
66	Mexico	4.0
67	Thailand	3.8
68	Bolivia	3.8
69	Romania	3.7
70	Vietnam	3.7
71	Honduras	3.6
72	Guatemala	3.6
73	Russian Federation	3.5
74	Nicaragua	3.4
75	Ukraine	3.1
76	Ecuador	2.6
77	Japan	2.6
78	Indonesia	2.6
78	Turkey	2.6
80	Argentina	2.2

MEAN: 5.1

2.04 Ease of access to loans

How easy is it to obtain a bank loan in your country with only a good business plan and no collateral? (1 = impossible, 7 = easy)

RANK	COUNTRY	SCORE
1	Denmark	4.8
2	United States	4.8
3	Dominican Republic	4.8
3	Finland	4.8
5	United Kingdom	4.6
6	Hong Kong SAR	4.6
7	Norway	4.6
8	Iceland	4.6
9	Sweden	4.5
10	New Zealand	4.5
11	Australia	4.5
11	Ireland	4.5
13	Israel	4.3
14	Switzerland	4.3
15	Belgium	4.3
16	Chile	4.3
17	Singapore	4.2
18	Netherlands	4.1
19	Lithuania	4.1
20	Portugal	4.1
21	Austria	4.1
22	Slovenia	4.0
23	Canada	4.0
24	Sri Lanka	3.9
25	Estonia	3.9
26	Panama	3.9
27	France	3.9
28	Taiwan	3.9
29	Spain	3.8
30	Latvia	3.7
31	Greece	3.6
32	Germany	3.5
33	Korea	3.5
33	South Africa	3.5
35	Botswana	3.5
36	Mauritius	3.4
37	Italy	3.4
38	Poland	3.4
39	Tunisia	3.3
40	Croatia	3.3
41	El Salvador	3.2
42	Trinidad and Tobago	3.2
43	Malaysia	3.1
44	Hungary	3.1
45	Namibia	3.1
46	Thailand	3.1
47	Brazil	3.1
48	Colombia	3.0
49	Slovak Republic	3.0
50	Jordan	3.0
51	Czech Republic	2.9
52	Morocco	2.9
53	Zimbabwe	2.8
54	Costa Rica	2.8
55	India	2.8
56	Uruguay	2.7
57	Romania	2.7
58	Paraguay	2.6
59	Nicaragua	2.6
60	China	2.5
61	Guatemala	2.4
62	Peru	2.4
63	Indonesia	2.4
64	Japan	2.4
65	Turkey	2.4
66	Mexico	2.3
67	Venezuela	2.3
68	Philippines	2.3
69	Bangladesh	2.3
70	Jamaica	2.2
71	Honduras	2.2
72	Vietnam	2.1
73	Russian Federation	2.1
74	Bolivia	2.1
75	Bulgaria	2.1
76	Ukraine	2.1
77	Haiti	2.0
78	Argentina	2.0
79	Ecuador	2.0
80	Nigeria	1.9

MEAN: 3.3

558

2.05 Access to credit

During the past year, obtaining credit for your company has become (1 = more difficult, 7 = easier)

RANK	COUNTRY	SCORE
1	Croatia	5.5
2	Slovenia	5.5
3	Estonia	5.4
4	El Salvador	5.3
5	India	5.2
5	Taiwan	5.2
7	Finland	5.0
8	Korea	5.0
9	Latvia	5.0
10	Trinidad and Tobago	5.0
11	Dominican Republic	4.9
12	Lithuania	4.9
13	Greece	4.9
14	Hong Kong SAR	4.9
15	New Zealand	4.9
16	Australia	4.8
17	Singapore	4.8
18	Iceland	4.8
19	Chile	4.7
20	Spain	4.7
21	Costa Rica	4.7
22	Jamaica	4.6
22	Slovak Republic	4.6
24	Colombia	4.6
25	Brazil	4.5
26	Hungary	4.5
27	Israel	4.4
28	Thailand	4.4
29	Italy	4.4
30	China	4.4
31	Botswana	4.3
31	Vietnam	4.3
33	Denmark	4.3
34	Austria	4.3
35	Namibia	4.3
36	Russian Federation	4.3
37	Sri Lanka	4.2
38	Norway	4.2
38	Zimbabwe	4.2
40	Germany	4.2
41	Malaysia	4.2
42	Tunisia	4.1
43	Switzerland	4.1
44	South Africa	4.1
45	Canada	4.1
46	United Kingdom	4.0
47	Poland	4.0
48	United States	4.0
49	Bangladesh	4.0
50	Japan	4.0
51	Sweden	3.9
52	Paraguay	3.9
53	Ireland	3.9
54	Jordan	3.9
55	Peru	3.8
56	Mauritius	3.8
56	Morocco	3.8
58	Panama	3.7
59	Romania	3.7
60	Netherlands	3.7
61	Nicaragua	3.6
62	Nigeria	3.6
63	Mexico	3.6
64	France	3.6
65	Honduras	3.5
66	Ukraine	3.5
67	Bulgaria	3.5
68	Philippines	3.5
69	Venezuela	3.3
70	Haiti	3.3
71	Guatemala	3.2
72	Bolivia	3.1
73	Uruguay	3.1
74	Turkey	3.1
75	Belgium	3.1
76	Ecuador	3.0
77	Czech Republic	3.0
78	Portugal	3.0
79	Indonesia	2.6
80	Argentina	1.8

MEAN: 4.1

2.06 Venture capital availability

Entrepreneurs with innovative but risky projects can generally find venture capital in your country (1 = not true, 7 = true)

RANK	COUNTRY	SCORE
1	United States	5.7
2	United Kingdom	5.5
3	Finland	5.2
4	Israel	5.1
5	Sweden	4.9
6	Ireland	4.8
7	Netherlands	4.7
8	Hong Kong SAR	4.6
9	Norway	4.6
10	Denmark	4.4
11	Belgium	4.4
12	Canada	4.4
13	Iceland	4.4
14	France	4.3
15	Singapore	4.3
16	Taiwan	4.3
17	Germany	4.2
18	New Zealand	4.2
19	Korea	4.1
20	Spain	4.1
21	Switzerland	4.0
22	Australia	4.0
22	Austria	4.0
24	Estonia	3.8
25	Italy	3.8
26	South Africa	3.7
27	Lithuania	3.7
28	Dominican Republic	3.7
29	Tunisia	3.7
30	India	3.7
31	Trinidad and Tobago	3.5
32	Slovenia	3.5
33	Morocco	3.5
34	Panama	3.5
35	Poland	3.4
36	Portugal	3.4
37	Malaysia	3.4
38	Greece	3.3
39	Latvia	3.3
40	Hungary	3.3
41	Botswana	3.2
42	Thailand	3.2
43	Sri Lanka	3.2
44	Japan	3.1
45	Brazil	3.1
46	Chile	3.1
47	El Salvador	3.0
48	Mauritius	3.0
49	China	3.0
50	Nigeria	2.9
51	Namibia	2.9
52	Zimbabwe	2.9
53	Jordan	2.9
54	Slovak Republic	2.7
55	Croatia	2.7
56	Czech Republic	2.7
57	Ukraine	2.6
58	Russian Federation	2.6
59	Vietnam	2.6
60	Bulgaria	2.5
61	Romania	2.5
62	Bangladesh	2.4
63	Guatemala	2.4
64	Philippines	2.4
65	Indonesia	2.4
66	Costa Rica	2.4
67	Colombia	2.4
68	Jamaica	2.3
69	Nicaragua	2.3
70	Uruguay	2.3
71	Argentina	2.2
72	Mexico	2.2
73	Haiti	2.2
74	Venezuela	2.2
75	Peru	2.1
76	Bolivia	2.1
77	Paraguay	2.0
78	Honduras	1.9
79	Turkey	1.7
80	Ecuador	1.7

MEAN: 3.3

2.07 Local equity market access

Raising money by issuing shares on the local stock market is (1 = nearly impossible, 7 = quite possible for a good company)

RANK	COUNTRY	SCORE		MEAN: 4.8	
			1		7
1	Hong Kong SAR	6.7			
2	Australia	6.4			
3	United Kingdom	6.3			
4	Nigeria	6.2			
5	United States	6.2			
6	Zimbabwe	6.2			
7	France	6.1			
8	Iceland	6.0			
9	Finland	6.0			
10	Japan	6.0			
11	Switzerland	6.0			
12	Taiwan	6.0			
13	New Zealand	5.9			
14	Singapore	5.8			
15	Canada	5.8			
16	South Africa	5.8			
17	Norway	5.8			
18	Italy	5.8			
19	Israel	5.8			
20	Germany	5.8			
21	Thailand	5.8			
22	Denmark	5.7			
23	Malaysia	5.7			
24	Korea	5.7			
25	Netherlands	5.6			
26	Tunisia	5.5			
27	Trinidad and Tobago	5.5			
28	Turkey	5.5			
29	Ireland	5.4			
30	Sweden	5.4			
31	Jamaica	5.3			
32	Estonia	5.3			
33	Bangladesh	5.3			
34	India	5.3			
35	Botswana	5.2			
36	Greece	5.2			
37	Mauritius	5.2			
38	Spain	5.1			
39	Portugal	5.0			
40	Chile	5.0			
41	Namibia	4.9			
42	Austria	4.9			
43	Morocco	4.9			
44	Sri Lanka	4.8			
45	Poland	4.7			
46	El Salvador	4.7			
47	Brazil	4.7			
48	Lithuania	4.6			
49	Indonesia	4.6			
50	Costa Rica	4.6			
51	Slovenia	4.6			
52	Colombia	4.5			
53	Hungary	4.4			
54	Belgium	4.4			
55	Philippines	4.4			
56	Russian Federation	4.4			
57	Panama	4.3			
58	Jordan	4.3			
59	Vietnam	4.3			
60	Latvia	4.2			
61	Romania	4.1			
62	Croatia	4.1			
63	Dominican Republic	4.0			
64	Peru	4.0			
65	Mexico	3.9			
66	Bolivia	3.7			
67	China	3.5			
68	Slovak Republic	3.3			
69	Ukraine	3.3			
70	Guatemala	3.2			
71	Nicaragua	3.1			
72	Ecuador	3.1			
73	Paraguay	3.0			
74	Bulgaria	2.8			
75	Czech Republic	2.8			
76	Venezuela	2.5			
77	Haiti	2.4			
78	Uruguay	2.4			
79	Argentina	2.3			
80	Honduras	2.1			

2.08 Business costs of terrorism

The threat of terrorism in your country (1 = imposes significant costs on business, 7 = does not impose significant costs on business)

RANK	COUNTRY	SCORE		MEAN: 4.9	
			1		7
1	Uruguay	6.6			
2	Finland	6.3			
3	Iceland	6.3			
4	Austria	6.3			
5	Denmark	6.2			
6	Norway	6.1			
7	Hungary	6.1			
8	Estonia	6.1			
9	Slovak Republic	6.0			
9	Slovenia	6.0			
11	New Zealand	6.0			
12	Portugal	5.9			
13	Belgium	5.8			
14	Tunisia	5.8			
15	Panama	5.8			
16	Hong Kong SAR	5.8			
17	Costa Rica	5.8			
18	Latvia	5.7			
19	Czech Republic	5.7			
20	Taiwan	5.7			
21	Romania	5.7			
22	Thailand	5.7			
23	Brazil	5.7			
24	Mauritius	5.6			
25	Chile	5.6			
26	Sweden	5.6			
27	Namibia	5.6			
28	Lithuania	5.5			
29	Australia	5.4			
30	Argentina	5.4			
31	Poland	5.3			
32	Netherlands	5.3			
32	Nigeria	5.3			
34	Botswana	5.3			
35	Croatia	5.2			
36	South Africa	5.2			
37	Greece	5.2			
38	Malaysia	5.2			
38	Singapore	5.2			
40	Dominican Republic	5.1			
41	Canada	5.1			
42	Italy	5.0			
43	Switzerland	5.0			
44	Paraguay	5.0			
45	Ukraine	4.9			
46	Trinidad and Tobago	4.9			
47	Korea	4.9			
48	China	4.9			
49	Mexico	4.9			
50	Ireland	4.9			
51	Bolivia	4.8			
52	Germany	4.8			
53	Vietnam	4.7			
54	Nicaragua	4.7			
55	France	4.7			
56	Turkey	4.6			
57	Russian Federation	4.5			
58	Japan	4.5			
59	Bulgaria	4.4			
60	Morocco	4.4			
61	El Salvador	4.3			
62	Jamaica	4.3			
63	Spain	4.3			
64	Venezuela	4.3			
65	Haiti	4.3			
66	Indonesia	4.2			
67	Jordan	4.2			
68	Honduras	4.1			
69	Ecuador	4.1			
70	United Kingdom	4.1			
71	India	4.1			
72	Peru	4.0			
73	Zimbabwe	3.4			
74	United States	3.2			
75	Guatemala	3.2			
76	Bangladesh	3.1			
77	Philippines	2.8			
78	Sri Lanka	2.6			
79	Colombia	1.8			
80	Israel	1.4			

2.09 Regulatory obstacles to business

Regulatory obstacles to your firm's investment and operations are encountered more often at the (1 = city/regional government authorities, 7 = federal/central government authorities)

RANK	COUNTRY	SCORE
1	Israel	6.0
2	Jamaica	5.5
3	Zimbabwe	5.3
4	Uruguay	5.2
5	Paraguay	5.2
6	Nigeria	5.2
7	Iceland	5.2
8	Venezuela	5.0
9	Trinidad and Tobago	5.0
10	France	5.0
11	Thailand	5.0
12	Bangladesh	4.9
13	United States	4.9
14	Guatemala	4.9
15	Japan	4.9
16	Haiti	4.9
17	Singapore	4.8
18	Denmark	4.8
19	Ireland	4.8
20	South Africa	4.8
21	Costa Rica	4.7
22	Korea	4.7
23	Ecuador	4.7
24	Australia	4.7
25	Chile	4.6
26	Tunisia	4.6
27	Argentina	4.6
28	Panama	4.6
29	Sweden	4.6
30	Slovak Republic	4.6
31	Colombia	4.6
31	Honduras	4.6
33	Namibia	4.5
34	Peru	4.5
35	Norway	4.5
36	Czech Republic	4.5
37	Sri Lanka	4.5
38	El Salvador	4.5
39	United Kingdom	4.5
40	Mauritius	4.5
41	Portugal	4.4
42	Italy	4.4
42	Turkey	4.4
44	Estonia	4.4
44	Poland	4.4
46	Greece	4.3
47	Brazil	4.3
48	Taiwan	4.3
49	Latvia	4.3
50	Mexico	4.3
51	Belgium	4.3
52	Austria	4.2
53	Germany	4.2
54	Slovenia	4.2
55	Botswana	4.2
56	India	4.1
57	Malaysia	4.1
58	Bolivia	4.1
58	Indonesia	4.1
60	Philippines	4.0
61	Russian Federation	4.0
62	Bulgaria	4.0
63	Nicaragua	4.0
64	Jordan	4.0
65	Romania	4.0
66	Dominican Republic	4.0
67	Hungary	3.9
68	New Zealand	3.9
69	Netherlands	3.9
70	Canada	3.8
71	Lithuania	3.8
72	Finland	3.7
73	Switzerland	3.7
74	Vietnam	3.7
75	Spain	3.7
76	Croatia	3.6
77	China	3.5
78	Hong Kong SAR	3.4
79	Morocco	3.3
80	Ukraine	3.2

MEAN: 4.4

2.10 Hidden trade barriers

In your country, hidden import barriers (i.e., barriers other than published tariffs and quotas) are (1 = an important problem, 7 = not an important problem)

RANK	COUNTRY	SCORE
1	Finland	6.5
2	Portugal	6.3
3	Hong Kong SAR	6.3
4	Chile	6.2
5	Singapore	6.2
6	Denmark	6.1
7	New Zealand	6.1
8	Netherlands	6.1
9	Ireland	6.0
9	Sweden	6.0
11	Austria	6.0
12	Belgium	5.9
13	United Kingdom	5.9
14	Australia	5.8
15	Estonia	5.8
16	Germany	5.7
17	Spain	5.7
18	United States	5.6
19	Hungary	5.5
20	Iceland	5.5
21	Israel	5.5
22	Canada	5.5
23	Slovenia	5.4
24	Norway	5.3
25	Switzerland	5.3
26	Botswana	5.3
27	Italy	5.2
28	France	5.2
29	South Africa	5.1
30	Taiwan	5.1
31	Greece	5.0
32	Trinidad and Tobago	5.0
33	Mauritius	4.9
34	China	4.9
35	Tunisia	4.9
36	Namibia	4.9
37	Czech Republic	4.8
38	Korea	4.8
39	Malaysia	4.8
40	Slovak Republic	4.8
41	El Salvador	4.7
42	Peru	4.7
43	Uruguay	4.6
44	Croatia	4.5
45	Thailand	4.5
46	Brazil	4.4
47	Latvia	4.4
48	India	4.3
49	Mexico	4.2
50	Panama	4.2
51	Lithuania	4.2
52	Jordan	4.2
53	Morocco	4.1
54	Poland	4.1
55	Argentina	4.0
56	Japan	4.0
57	Colombia	4.0
57	Costa Rica	4.0
59	Sri Lanka	4.0
59	Zimbabwe	4.0
61	Turkey	3.9
62	Jamaica	3.9
63	Paraguay	3.8
64	Venezuela	3.8
65	Bangladesh	3.7
66	Vietnam	3.7
67	Bulgaria	3.6
68	Haiti	3.5
69	Indonesia	3.5
70	Dominican Republic	3.5
71	Guatemala	3.4
72	Philippines	3.4
73	Russian Federation	3.4
74	Romania	3.3
75	Honduras	3.2
76	Bolivia	3.2
77	Nigeria	3.1
78	Ecuador	3.0
79	Ukraine	2.9
80	Nicaragua	2.9

MEAN: 4.7

561

2.11 Cost of importing foreign equipment

When your firm needs to import foreign equipment, the combined effect of import tariffs, license fees, bank fees, and the time required for administrative red tape raises the cost by (approximately) (1 = less than 10%, 2 = 11–20%, 3 = 21–30%, 9 = greater than 80%)

RANK	COUNTRY	SCORE	1 ——— MEAN: 2.4 ——— 9
1	Singapore	1.2	
2	Denmark	1.2	
3	Finland	1.3	
4	Hong Kong SAR	1.3	
5	New Zealand	1.3	
6	United Kingdom	1.3	
7	Estonia	1.3	
8	Greece	1.3	
9	Belgium	1.3	
10	Spain	1.3	
11	Sweden	1.4	
12	Italy	1.4	
13	Australia	1.5	
14	United States	1.5	
15	France	1.5	
16	Germany	1.5	
17	Switzerland	1.5	
18	Slovenia	1.6	
19	Portugal	1.6	
20	Austria	1.6	
21	Netherlands	1.6	
22	Japan	1.6	
23	Ireland	1.7	
23	Taiwan	1.7	
25	Lithuania	1.8	
26	Czech Republic	1.8	
27	Canada	1.8	
28	Chile	1.8	
29	Hungary	1.9	
30	Slovak Republic	1.9	
31	Thailand	1.9	
32	Korea	2.0	
33	Norway	2.1	
34	Malaysia	2.1	
35	South Africa	2.1	
36	Croatia	2.2	
37	Tunisia	2.2	
38	Botswana	2.2	
39	Latvia	2.2	
40	Panama	2.2	
41	El Salvador	2.3	
42	Bulgaria	2.3	
43	China	2.3	
44	Israel	2.3	
45	Iceland	2.3	
45	Vietnam	2.3	
47	Nicaragua	2.5	
48	Trinidad and Tobago	2.5	
49	Poland	2.5	
50	Indonesia	2.5	
51	Guatemala	2.5	
52	Namibia	2.6	
53	Mexico	2.6	
54	Costa Rica	2.6	
55	Jamaica	2.8	
56	Uruguay	2.9	
57	Philippines	2.9	
58	Dominican Republic	3.0	
59	Venezuela	3.0	
60	Mauritius	3.1	
61	Peru	3.1	
62	Paraguay	3.1	
63	Colombia	3.2	
64	Bangladesh	3.2	
65	Nigeria	3.3	
66	Turkey	3.4	
67	Honduras	3.4	
68	Romania	3.4	
69	India	3.4	
70	Argentina	3.5	
71	Haiti	3.7	
72	Jordan	3.8	
73	Morocco	3.9	
74	Ukraine	3.9	
75	Brazil	4.0	
76	Ecuador	4.0	
77	Russian Federation	4.0	
78	Bolivia	4.1	
79	Sri Lanka	4.5	
80	Zimbabwe	4.5	

2.12 Extent of distortive government subsidies

Government subsidies to business in your country (1 = keep uncompetitive industries alive artificially, 7 = improve productivity of industries)

RANK	COUNTRY	SCORE	1 ——— MEAN: 3.4 ——— 7
1	Singapore	5.5	
2	Tunisia	4.7	
3	Finland	4.6	
4	Ireland	4.6	
5	Hong Kong SAR	4.6	
6	Estonia	4.5	
7	Israel	4.4	
8	Taiwan	4.4	
9	South Africa	4.3	
10	New Zealand	4.2	
11	Austria	4.2	
12	United Kingdom	4.2	
13	Chile	4.2	
14	China	4.1	
15	Hungary	4.1	
16	Netherlands	4.1	
17	Thailand	4.0	
18	Malaysia	3.9	
19	Botswana	3.9	
20	Denmark	3.8	
21	Czech Republic	3.8	
22	Portugal	3.8	
23	Korea	3.7	
24	Brazil	3.7	
25	Australia	3.7	
26	Sri Lanka	3.7	
27	Namibia	3.7	
28	United States	3.7	
29	Latvia	3.7	
30	Morocco	3.6	
31	Slovenia	3.6	
32	Italy	3.5	
33	El Salvador	3.5	
34	Jordan	3.5	
35	Belgium	3.5	
36	Spain	3.5	
37	Colombia	3.5	
38	Iceland	3.4	
39	Peru	3.4	
40	Vietnam	3.4	
41	Mauritius	3.3	
42	Canada	3.3	
43	France	3.3	
44	Norway	3.2	
45	Trinidad and Tobago	3.2	
46	Dominican Republic	3.2	
47	Switzerland	3.1	
48	Nicaragua	3.1	
49	Sweden	3.1	
50	Greece	3.0	
51	Costa Rica	3.0	
52	Panama	3.0	
53	Jamaica	3.0	
54	India	3.0	
55	Lithuania	2.9	
56	Mexico	2.9	
57	Guatemala	2.9	
58	Uruguay	2.9	
59	Paraguay	2.8	
60	Philippines	2.8	
61	Russian Federation	2.8	
62	Honduras	2.7	
63	Slovak Republic	2.7	
64	Poland	2.7	
65	Bolivia	2.7	
66	Argentina	2.7	
67	Haiti	2.6	
68	Japan	2.6	
69	Turkey	2.6	
70	Bulgaria	2.5	
71	Germany	2.5	
72	Indonesia	2.5	
73	Croatia	2.5	
74	Venezuela	2.4	
75	Ukraine	2.4	
76	Bangladesh	2.3	
77	Ecuador	2.1	
78	Zimbabwe	2.1	
79	Nigeria	2.0	
80	Romania	1.7	

2.13 Moody's sovereign debt ratings, 2002

Long-term rating in foreign currency, July 2002

RANK	COUNTRY	RATING
1	Austria	Aaa
1	Canada	Aaa
1	Denmark	Aaa
1	Finland	Aaa
1	France	Aaa
1	Germany	Aaa
1	Ireland	Aaa
1	Norway	Aaa
1	Spain	Aaa
1	Sweden	Aaa
1	United Kingdom	Aaa
12	Netherlands	Aaa***
12	Singapore	Aaa***
12	Switzerland	Aaa***
12	United States	Aaa***
16	Belgium	Aa1
16	Japan	Aa1
18	Australia	Aa2
18	Italy	Aa2
18	New Zealand	Aa2
18	Portugal	Aa2
22	Iceland	Aa3
23	Taiwan	Aa3***
24	Greece	A2
24	Israel	A2
24	Slovenia	A2
27	Botswana	A2***
28	China	A3
28	Hungary	A3
28	Korea	A3
31	Hong Kong SAR	A3***
32	Chile	Baa1
32	Czech Republic	Baa1
32	Poland	Baa1
35	Estonia	Baa1***
36	Malaysia	Baa2*
36	Latvia	Baa2
36	Mexico	Baa2
36	South Africa	Baa2
40	Mauritius	Baa2***
41	Croatia	Baa3
41	Slovak Republic	Baa3
41	Thailand	Baa3
41	Trinidad and Tobago	Baa3
45	El Salvador	Baa3***
45	Tunisia	Baa3***
47	Costa Rica	Ba1
47	Lithuania	Ba1
47	Morocco	Ba1
47	Panama	Ba1
47	Philippines	Ba1
52	Bolivia	Ba2
52	Colombia	Ba2
52	Dominican Republic	Ba2
52	Guatemala	Ba2
56	Uruguay	Ba2**
56	India	Ba2***
58	Jamaica	Ba3
58	Jordan	Ba3
58	Peru	Ba3
58	Russian Federation	Ba3
62	Brazil	B1
62	Bulgaria	B1
62	Turkey	B1
65	Vietnam	B1***
66	Romania	B2
66	Ukraine	B2
66	Venezuela	B2
69	Honduras	B2***
69	Nicaragua	B2***
69	Paraguay	B2***
72	Indonesia	B3***
73	Ecuador	Caa2
74	Argentina	Ca
	Bangladesh	N/A
	Haiti	N/A
	Namibia	N/A
	Nigeria	N/A
	Sri Lanka	N/A
	Zimbabwe	N/A

SOURCE: Moody's, July 2002
*On review for possible upgrade.
**On review for possible downgrade.
***Issuer Rating.

2.14 Standard & Poor's sovereign debt ratings, 2002

Long-term rating in foreign currency, July 2002

RANK	COUNTRY	RATING
1	Austria	AAA
1	Denmark	AAA
1	Finland	AAA
1	France	AAA
1	Germany	AAA
1	Ireland	AAA
1	Netherlands	AAA
1	Norway	AAA
1	Singapore	AAA
1	Switzerland	AAA
1	United Kingdom	AAA
1	United States	AAA
13	Australia	AA+
13	Belgium	AA+
13	Canada	AA+
13	New Zealand	AA+
13	Spain	AA+
13	Sweden	AA+
19	Italy	AA
19	Portugal	AA
19	Taiwan	AA
22	Japan	AA–
23	Hong Kong SAR	A+
23	Iceland	A+
25	Botswana	A
25	Greece	A
25	Slovenia	A
28	Chile	A–
28	Czech Republic	A–
28	Estonia	A–
28	Hungary	A–
28	Israel	A–
33	Korea	BBB+
33	Poland	BBB+
35	China	BBB
35	Latvia	BBB
35	Lithuania	BBB
35	Malaysia	BBB
35	Tunisia	BBB
40	Croatia	BBB–
40	Mexico	BBB–
40	Slovak Republic	BBB–
40	South Africa	BBB–
40	Thailand	BBB–
40	Trinidad and Tobago	BBB–
46	El Salvador	BB+
46	Philippines	BB+
48	Colombia	BB
48	Costa Rica	BB
48	Guatemala	BB
48	India	BB
48	Morocco	BB
48	Panama	BB
54	Brazil	BB–
54	Bulgaria	BB–
54	Dominican Republic	BB–
54	Jordan	BB–
54	Peru	BB–
54	Uruguay	BB–
54	Vietnam	BB–
61	Bolivia	B+
61	Jamaica	B+
61	Romania	B+
61	Russian Federation	B+
65	Paraguay	B
65	Ukraine	B
65	Venezuela	B
68	Turkey	B–
69	Ecuador	CCC+
70	Indonesia	Selective Default
70	Argentina	Selective Default
	Bangladesh	N/A
	Haiti	N/A
	Honduras	N/A
	Mauritius	N/A
	Namibia	N/A
	Nicaragua	N/A
	Nigeria	N/A
	Sri Lanka	N/A
	Zimbabwe	N/A

SOURCE: Standard & Poor's, July 2002

2.15 Government surplus/deficit, 2001

Government fiscal surplus/deficit as a percentage of GDP, 2001

RANK	COUNTRY	HARD DATA	
1	Norway	16.40	
2	Finland	4.45	
3	Russian Federation	2.93	
4	Sweden	2.92	
5	Canada	2.30	
6	Denmark	2.10	
7	New Zealand	2.00	
8	Singapore	1.98	
9	Ireland	1.70	
10	United States	1.25	
11	Ecuador	1.22	
12	Estonia	0.52	
13	Dominican Republic	0.39	
14	Netherlands	0.32	
15	Ukraine	0.30	
16	Belgium	0.27	
17	Greece	0.10	
18	Chile	–0.10	
18	Iceland	–0.10	
18	Trinidad and Tobago	–0.10	
21	Austria	–0.20	
21	United Kingdom	–0.20	
23	Botswana	–0.30	
24	Spain	–0.34	
25	Australia	–0.40	
26	Switzerland	–0.70	
27	Mexico	–0.72	
28	Bulgaria	–0.86	
29	Paraguay	–1.10	
30	South Africa	–1.23	
31	Korea	–1.30	
32	Italy	–1.37	
33	Panama	–1.40	
33	Slovenia	–1.40	
35	Lithuania	–1.50	
36	France	–1.60	
37	Latvia	–1.85	
38	Guatemala	–1.92	
39	Haiti	–2.21	
40	China	–2.50	
40	Morocco	–2.50	
42	Peru	–2.55	
43	Thailand	–2.60	
43	Tunisia	–2.60	
45	Costa Rica	–2.72	
46	Germany	–2.73	
47	Portugal	–2.80	
48	Hungary	–2.85	
49	Argentina	–3.06	
50	Romania	–3.10	
51	Brazil	–3.50	
52	El Salvador	–3.60	
53	Indonesia	–3.70	
54	Philippines	–3.91	
55	Poland	–4.50	
56	Israel	–4.60	
56	Slovak Republic	–4.60	
56	Uruguay	–4.60	
59	Czech Republic	–4.75	
60	Hong Kong SAR	–5.00	
61	Vietnam	–5.10	
62	Colombia	–5.20	
63	Nigeria	–5.30	
64	Malaysia	–5.40	
65	Croatia	–5.46	
66	Namibia	–5.50	
67	India	–5.70	
67	Jamaica	–5.70	
69	Honduras	–6.11	
70	Sri Lanka	–6.40	
71	Bangladesh	–6.40	
71	Taiwan	–6.40	
73	Bolivia	–6.50	
73	Mauritius	–6.50	
75	Venezuela	–6.70	
76	Jordan	–7.00	
77	Japan	–8.10	
78	Zimbabwe	–8.80	
79	Turkey	–15.75	
80	Nicaragua	–16.80	

SOURCES: IMF International Financial Statistics, June 2002, and Economist Intelligence Unit

2.16 Government expenditure, 2001

Government expenditure as a percentage of GDP, 2001

RANK	COUNTRY	HARD DATA	
1	Haiti	10.05	
2	Guatemala	13.21	
3	Russian Federation	14.66	
4	Mexico	15.62	
5	Bangladesh	15.90	
6	Romania	15.94	
7	Costa Rica	15.97	
8	Dominican Republic	16.31	
9	India	17.60	
10	Thailand	17.82	
11	Singapore	18.15	
12	United States	18.37	
13	Paraguay	18.40	
14	El Salvador	18.50	
15	Hong Kong SAR	18.87	
16	China	19.30	
17	Philippines	19.39	
18	Colombia	20.30	
19	Indonesia	20.60	
20	Argentina	22.21	
21	Chile	22.40	
22	Nigeria	23.00	
23	Korea	23.80	
24	Mauritius	24.50	
25	Venezuela	24.70	
26	Taiwan	25.00	
27	Australia	25.20	
28	Trinidad and Tobago	25.50	
29	Sri Lanka	25.62	
30	Ecuador	25.64	
31	Honduras	25.91	
32	South Africa	26.35	
33	Vietnam	26.80	
34	Peru	27.03	
35	Panama	28.60	
36	Ireland	30.20	
37	Malaysia	30.70	
38	Lithuania	31.50	
39	Iceland	31.60	
40	Jordan	32.60	
40	Uruguay	32.60	
42	Tunisia	32.90	
43	Poland	33.50	
44	Ukraine	34.20	
45	Morocco	34.30	
46	Jamaica	34.40	
47	Zimbabwe	35.30	
48	Brazil	35.40	
49	New Zealand	35.80	
50	Estonia	36.21	
51	Namibia	37.60	
52	Canada	37.70	
53	Latvia	38.02	
54	Spain	38.50	
55	Switzerland	38.70	
55	United Kingdom	38.70	
57	Bolivia	39.10	
58	Nicaragua	39.70	
59	Slovak Republic	40.60	
60	Hungary	40.68	
61	Bulgaria	40.83	
62	Portugal	41.00	
63	Norway	41.30	
64	Netherlands	41.97	
65	Botswana	42.20	
66	Czech Republic	43.99	
67	Turkey	44.31	
68	Slovenia	44.70	
69	Finland	45.17	
70	Italy	45.30	
71	Germany	46.30	
72	Belgium	46.56	
73	Israel	46.70	
74	Japan	46.90	
75	Austria	47.20	
76	Greece	49.50	
77	Croatia	49.51	
78	France	50.60	
79	Denmark	51.30	
80	Sweden	53.42	

SOURCES: IMF International Financial Statistics, June 2002, and Economist Intelligence Unit

2.17 National savings rate, 2001

National savings rate as a percentage of GDP, 2001

RANK	COUNTRY	HARD DATA
1	Singapore	51.50
2	China	38.90
3	Botswana	35.70
4	Norway	35.30
5	Vietnam	33.40
6	Russian Federation	33.38
7	Hong Kong SAR	33.20
8	Malaysia	32.27
9	Switzerland	31.80
10	Thailand	29.40
11	Korea	28.96
12	Nigeria	28.60
13	Mauritius	28.00
13	Morocco	28.00
15	Jordan	27.80
16	Japan	27.60
17	Slovak Republic	26.60
18	Finland	26.11
19	Czech Republic	25.98
20	Belgium	25.79
21	Netherlands	25.63
22	Ukraine	25.50
23	Hungary	25.10
23	Slovenia	25.10
25	Taiwan	24.92
26	Honduras	24.59
27	Namibia	24.40
28	Philippines	23.90
29	Denmark	23.69
30	Panama	23.10
30	Sri Lanka	23.10
32	Indonesia	22.90
33	Spain	22.88
34	Bangladesh	22.60
34	Tunisia	22.60
36	India	22.40
37	Germany	22.00
37	Ireland	22.00
39	Canada	21.98
40	France	21.80
41	Venezuela	21.00
42	Austria	20.90
42	Trinidad and Tobago	20.90
44	Ecuador	20.84
45	Sweden	20.80
46	Croatia	20.72
47	Dominican Republic	20.40
48	Estonia	20.12
49	Italy	19.90
50	Greece	19.60
51	Chile	19.30
51	Mexico	19.30
53	Israel	19.29
54	Jamaica	19.00
55	Portugal	18.96
56	Latvia	18.90
57	Australia	18.25
58	Haiti	18.00
59	Turkey	17.83
60	Paraguay	17.80
61	Poland	17.59
62	New Zealand	17.10
63	South Africa	17.00
64	Lithuania	16.80
65	Peru	16.15
66	Iceland	16.00
66	Romania	16.00
68	United Kingdom	15.53
69	Brazil	14.81
70	El Salvador	14.60
71	Bulgaria	13.83
72	Colombia	13.80
73	Argentina	13.70
74	Costa Rica	13.50
75	United States	11.92
76	Guatemala	10.80
77	Uruguay	10.20
78	Bolivia	8.30
79	Zimbabwe	7.20
80	Nicaragua	0.20

SOURCES: Economist Intelligence Unit, IMF Country Reports, and national sources

2.18 Investment rate, 2001

Gross fixed investment as a percentage of GDP, 2001

RANK	COUNTRY	HARD DATA
1	China	37.40
2	Nicaragua	33.30
3	Slovak Republic	31.86
4	Singapore	29.21
5	Vietnam	28.90
6	Czech Republic	28.08
7	Sri Lanka	27.90
8	Portugal	27.49
9	Jamaica	27.20
10	Korea	26.99
11	Tunisia	26.30
12	Japan	25.83
13	Hong Kong SAR	25.82
14	Latvia	25.72
15	Botswana	25.70
16	Panama	25.60
17	Nigeria	25.50
18	Estonia	25.41
19	Jordan	25.30
20	Slovenia	25.10
21	Spain	25.06
22	Malaysia	25.06
23	Morocco	24.90
24	Greece	24.60
25	Honduras	24.42
26	Dominican Republic	24.10
27	Bangladesh	24.07
28	Hungary	23.42
29	Thailand	23.32
30	Austria	23.15
31	Ireland	23.08
32	Mauritius	23.00
33	Ecuador	22.84
34	Haiti	22.80
35	India	22.70
36	Germany	22.00
37	Ukraine	22.00
38	Netherlands	21.99
39	Croatia	21.91
40	Poland	21.57
41	Chile	21.40
42	Denmark	21.12
43	Australia	21.03
44	Belgium	20.86
45	Indonesia	20.85
46	Switzerland	20.59
47	France	20.22
48	Iceland	20.00
48	Paraguay	20.00
50	Canada	19.82
51	Italy	19.81
52	Finland	19.62
53	Lithuania	19.40
53	Mexico	19.40
55	Taiwan	19.20
56	New Zealand	19.18
57	Namibia	19.10
58	Romania	19.00
59	Norway	18.99
60	Trinidad and Tobago	18.80
61	Israel	18.75
62	Peru	18.35
63	Costa Rica	18.01
64	Turkey	17.82
65	Russian Federation	17.80
66	Bulgaria	17.76
67	Sweden	17.49
68	Brazil	17.32
69	Philippines	17.14
70	United Kingdom	16.96
71	United States	16.58
72	El Salvador	16.50
73	Venezuela	16.44
74	Guatemala	15.89
75	South Africa	14.85
76	Argentina	14.40
77	Bolivia	14.11
78	Colombia	13.30
79	Uruguay	12.20
80	Zimbabwe	9.40

SOURCES: Economist Intelligence Unit and national sources

2.19 Inflation, 2001

Percentage change in consumer price index, 2001

RANK	COUNTRY	HARD DATA	
1	Hong Kong SAR	−1.60	
2	Argentina	−1.10	
3	Japan	−0.70	
4	Taiwan	0.00	
5	Vietnam	0.10	
6	Morocco	0.50	
7	China	0.70	
8	Singapore	1.00	
8	Switzerland	1.00	
10	Israel	1.10	
11	Lithuania	1.30	
12	Malaysia	1.40	
13	Bolivia	1.60	
14	Thailand	1.70	
15	Bangladesh	1.80	
15	France	1.80	
15	Jordan	1.80	
15	Panama	1.80	
19	Tunisia	1.90	
20	Peru	2.00	
21	Denmark	2.10	
21	United Kingdom	2.10	
23	Austria	2.30	
24	Belgium	2.40	
24	Germany	2.40	
26	Canada	2.50	
26	Latvia	2.50	
26	Trinidad and Tobago	2.50	
29	Finland	2.60	
29	Sweden	2.60	
31	Italy	2.70	
31	New Zealand	2.70	
33	United States	2.80	
34	Norway	3.00	
35	Spain	3.20	
36	Chile	3.60	
37	Greece	3.70	
38	El Salvador	3.80	
38	India	3.80	
40	Ireland	4.00	
41	Korea	4.10	
42	Australia	4.40	
42	Mauritius	4.40	
42	Portugal	4.40	
42	Uruguay	4.40	
46	Czech Republic	4.70	
47	Croatia	4.90	
48	Jamaica	5.00	
49	Netherlands	5.10	
50	Poland	5.40	
51	South Africa	5.70	
52	Estonia	5.80	
53	Philippines	6.10	
54	Mexico	6.40	
55	Iceland	6.70	
56	Brazil	6.80	
57	Botswana	7.20	
58	Slovak Republic	7.30	
59	Bulgaria	7.50	
60	Paraguay	7.70	
61	Colombia	8.00	
62	Nicaragua	8.30	
63	Slovenia	8.40	
64	Guatemala	8.70	
65	Dominican Republic	8.90	
66	Hungary	9.20	
66	Namibia	9.20	
68	Honduras	9.70	
69	Costa Rica	11.00	
70	Indonesia	11.50	
71	Ukraine	12.00	
72	Venezuela	12.50	
73	Sri Lanka	14.00	
74	Haiti	16.70	
75	Nigeria	18.90	
76	Russian Federation	20.70	
77	Romania	34.50	
78	Ecuador	37.68	
79	Turkey	54.40	
80	Zimbabwe	76.70	

SOURCE: IMF World Economic Outlook Database, April 2002

2.20 M2 growth, 2001

Annual percentage growth in money and quasi money, 2001

RANK	COUNTRY	HARD DATA	
1	Argentina	−19.10	
2	Hong Kong SAR	−0.27	
3	Peru	2.08	
4	Japan	2.18	
5	Bolivia	2.24	
6	Malaysia	2.46	
7	Switzerland	3.90	
8	Austria*	4.15	
8	Belgium*	4.15	
8	Finland*	4.15	
8	France*	4.15	
8	Germany*	4.15	
8	Greece*	4.15	
8	Italy*	4.15	
8	Ireland*	4.15	
8	Netherlands*	4.15	
8	Portugal*	4.15	
8	Spain*	4.15	
19	Uruguay	4.30	
20	Philippines	4.32	
21	Taiwan	4.38	
22	Namibia	4.48	
23	Chile	4.52	
24	Slovak Republic	5.10	
25	Thailand	5.50	
26	Singapore	5.86	
27	Canada	6.56	
28	Sweden	7.43	
29	Jordan	8.10	
30	Jamaica	8.60	
31	Norway	8.74	
32	United Kingdom	8.79	
33	Israel	9.20	
34	Panama	9.60	
35	Nicaragua	9.90	
36	Tunisia	10.10	
37	Costa Rica	10.37	
38	Mauritius	10.93	
39	Denmark	11.00	
40	Brazil	11.91	
41	Iceland	12.00	
42	El Salvador	12.09	
43	Czech Republic	12.10	
44	Indonesia	12.84	
45	Korea	13.20	
46	Australia	13.23	
47	India	13.80	
48	United States	13.86	
49	Morocco	14.08	
50	Mexico	14.10	
51	Haiti	14.12	
52	Sri Lanka	14.14	
53	China	14.40	
54	Bangladesh	14.68	
55	New Zealand	14.75	
56	Poland	15.04	
57	Venezuela	15.27	
58	Colombia	15.96	
59	Paraguay	16.38	
60	Hungary	16.67	
61	South Africa	16.84	
62	Honduras	17.43	
63	Guatemala	18.13	
64	Vietnam	19.50	
65	Latvia	19.81	
66	Lithuania	21.38	
67	Estonia	22.99	
68	Trinidad and Tobago	23.30	
69	Bulgaria	26.05	
70	Ecuador	26.68	
71	Dominican Republic	26.90	
72	Nigeria	30.00	
73	Slovenia	30.44	
74	Botswana	31.22	
75	Russian Federation	36.08	
76	Ukraine	43.25	
77	Croatia	45.70	
78	Romania	46.18	
79	Turkey	90.09	
80	Zimbabwe	128.46	

SOURCES: Economist Intelligence Unit, IMF International Financial Statistics, June 2002, European Central Bank Annual Report, and national sources
*Same M2 growth value used for entire euro area

2.21   Real exchange rate, 2001

2001 period average real exchange rate relative to the United States (1990 to 1995 average = 100, 1995 = 100 for transition economies). Values greater (less) than 100 indicate depreciation (appreciation) relative to the United States.

RANK	COUNTRY	HARD DATA
1	Indonesia	200.7
2	Brazil	196.7
3	South Africa	189.2
4	Sweden	168.3
5	Namibia	167.3
6	Nigeria	161.2
7	Finland	155.9
8	Thailand	155.8
9	Botswana	151.9
10	Spain	151.3
11	France	148.5
12	New Zealand	148.0
13	Iceland	148.0
14	Italy	146.8
15	Belgium	145.6
16	Korea	145.5
17	Australia	145.5
18	Germany	145.5
19	Austria	144.8
20	Slovenia	141.7
21	Croatia	140.5
22	Tunisia	140.2
23	Norway	140.1
24	Malaysia	139.8
25	Denmark	139.7
26	Netherlands	138.6
27	Ireland	138.5
28	Taiwan	138.1
29	Switzerland	137.6
30	Portugal	136.4
31	Paraguay	136.1
32	Greece	135.6
33	Philippines	134.0
34	Canada	131.8
35	Turkey	130.9
36	Mauritius	130.7
37	Vietnam	130.0
38	Morocco	127.4
39	Russian Federation	126.5
40	Nicaragua	124.1
41	Japan	123.8
42	Chile	123.5
43	Singapore	123.1
44	Peru	122.8
45	Hungary	120.5
46	Bangladesh	120.5
47	Slovak Republic	118.7
48	India	118.0
49	Bolivia	117.7
50	Ecuador	115.2
51	Czech Republic	114.7
52	United Kingdom	114.6
53	Panama	114.2
54	Israel	113.4
55	Sri Lanka	111.8
56	Uruguay	109.0
57	Zimbabwe	108.6
58	Argentina	108.6
59	Estonia	106.4
60	Colombia	105.9
61	Trinidad and Tobago	105.8
62	China	104.1
63	Romania	103.3
64	Poland	102.1
65	Bulgaria	102.1
66	Jordan	101.7
67	Costa Rica	101.5
68	United States	100.0
69	Hong Kong SAR	97.5
70	Latvia	96.2
71	Guatemala	92.7
72	Dominican Republic	91.5
73	Ukraine	90.3
74	Mexico	84.8
75	Honduras	83.2
76	Lithuania	79.1
77	Jamaica	78.7
78	El Salvador	77.6
79	Haiti	72.7
80	Venezuela	62.2

SOURCES: IMF World Economic Outlook Database, April 2002; IMF International Financial Statistics, June 2002; and authors' calculations

2.22   Exports, 2001

Exports of goods as a percentage of GDP, 2001

RANK	COUNTRY	HARD DATA
1	Singapore	138.0
2	Hong Kong SAR	117.3
3	Malaysia	102.8
4	Belgium	82.7
5	Ireland	81.7
6	Hungary	65.8
7	Slovak Republic	63.3
8	Estonia	60.5
9	Czech Republic	58.8
10	Thailand	56.7
11	Netherlands	56.7
12	Botswana	54.0
13	Trinidad and Tobago	49.6
14	Nigeria	49.3
15	Vietnam	48.9
16	Ukraine	45.5
17	Philippines	45.0
18	Slovenia	44.3
19	Taiwan	43.5
20	Bulgaria	40.2
21	Indonesia	38.7
22	Namibia	38.3
23	Lithuania	38.1
24	Canada	37.1
25	Sweden	36.0
26	Korea	35.6
27	Mauritius	34.4
28	Norway	34.2
29	Austria	34.2
30	Russian Federation	33.3
31	Tunisia	33.1
32	Finland	32.7
33	Switzerland	31.6
34	Germany	30.9
35	Sri Lanka	30.9
36	Denmark	30.8
37	Costa Rica	30.0
38	Romania	28.7
39	New Zealand	27.7
40	Iceland	26.7
41	Ecuador	26.3
42	Chile	26.2
43	Jordan	26.0
44	South Africa	25.9
45	Latvia	25.8
46	Mexico	25.6
47	Nicaragua	24.0
48	Israel	23.3
49	China	23.0
50	Croatia	22.8
51	France	22.4
52	Italy	22.2
53	Portugal	21.8
54	Honduras	21.4
55	Morocco	21.2
56	Turkey	21.1
57	Venezuela	20.9
58	Poland	20.5
59	El Salvador	20.5
60	Spain	19.8
61	Zimbabwe	19.2
62	United Kingdom	18.9
63	Australia	17.7
64	Bolivia	16.1
65	Colombia	15.0
66	Paraguay	13.8
67	Peru	13.4
68	Guatemala	12.9
69	Jamaica	12.3
70	Brazil	11.5
71	Uruguay	11.0
72	Argentina	9.9
73	Japan	9.7
74	Bangladesh	9.6
75	India	9.1
76	Greece	8.9
77	Panama	8.9
78	Haiti	8.9
79	United States	7.2
80	Dominican Republic	3.9

SOURCE: Economist Intelligence Unit

2.23 Imports, 2001

Imports of goods as a percentage of GDP, 2001

RANK	COUNTRY	HARD DATA
1	Singapore	131.5
2	Hong Kong SAR	124.2
3	Malaysia	86.9
4	Estonia	78.4
5	Belgium	77.8
6	Slovak Republic	74.0
7	Hungary	72.7
8	Nicaragua	70.4
9	Czech Republic	64.3
10	Bulgaria	56.9
11	Jordan	54.4
12	Thailand	54.1
13	Lithuania	52.8
14	Ireland	52.6
15	Vietnam	51.8
16	Netherlands	51.1
17	Honduras	49.5
18	Namibia	48.1
19	Tunisia	47.5
20	Mauritius	47.4
21	Slovenia	47.3
22	Botswana	46.3
23	Latvia	45.1
24	Croatia	44.3
25	Trinidad and Tobago	44.2
26	Philippines	43.9
27	Ukraine	42.0
28	Costa Rica	39.3
29	Romania	39.3
30	Taiwan	38.0
31	Sri Lanka	37.9
32	Austria	36.7
33	El Salvador	36.0
34	Portugal	34.7
35	Jamaica	34.3
36	Nigeria	33.4
37	Korea	33.4
38	Morocco	32.7
39	Canada	32.6
40	Switzerland	31.2
41	Iceland	30.0
42	Sweden	30.0
43	Guatemala	30.0
44	Ecuador	29.7
45	Israel	29.6
46	Panama	29.5
47	Dominican Republic	28.9
48	Poland	28.6
49	Paraguay	27.7
50	Turkey	27.4
51	Mexico	27.3
52	Denmark	27.0
53	New Zealand	26.9
54	Finland	26.5
55	Haiti	26.5
56	Spain	26.4
57	Germany	26.3
58	Chile	25.9
59	Greece	25.8
60	South Africa	25.1
61	United Kingdom	22.8
62	France	22.6
63	Bolivia	21.6
64	Italy	21.4
65	Indonesia	21.3
66	China	21.0
67	Zimbabwe	20.8
68	Norway	19.3
69	Australia	18.0
70	Russian Federation	17.3
71	Bangladesh	17.2
72	Peru	16.3
73	Uruguay	16.0
74	Colombia	15.8
75	Venezuela	14.4
76	United States	11.2
77	Brazil	11.0
78	India	10.4
79	Japan	8.4
80	Argentina	7.5

SOURCE: Economist Intelligence Unit

2.24 Average tariff rate, 2002

Average tariff rate (%), 2002

RANK	COUNTRY	HARD DATA
1	Estonia	0.0
1	Hong Kong SAR	0.0
3	Israel	1.0
3	Latvia	1.0
3	Singapore	1.0
3	Switzerland	1.0
7	Lithuania	1.1
7	Norway	1.1
9	Czech Republic	1.2
10	Iceland	1.4
11	Mexico	1.9
12	Japan	2.3
13	Hungary	2.5
13	Taiwan	2.5
15	Slovak Republic	2.6
16	Austria	2.7
16	Belgium	2.7
16	Denmark	2.7
16	Finland	2.7
16	France	2.7
16	Germany	2.7
16	Greece	2.7
16	Ireland	2.7
16	Italy	2.7
16	Netherlands	2.7
16	Portugal	2.7
16	Spain	2.7
16	Sweden	2.7
16	Turkey	2.7
16	United Kingdom	2.7
31	United States	2.8
32	Poland	3.1
33	Canada	3.2
34	New Zealand	3.3
35	Thailand	3.6
36	Australia	3.8
36	El Salvador	3.8
38	Romania	5.3
39	Bolivia	5.4
40	Guatemala	5.7
41	Indonesia	6.2
42	Sri Lanka	6.5
43	Philippines	6.7
44	Chile	6.8
45	Costa Rica	7.0
45	Ukraine	7.0
47	Honduras	7.6
47	Colombia	7.6
49	Croatia	8.1
49	Haiti	8.1
51	Korea	8.7
52	Jamaica	9.1
52	Trinidad and Tobago	9.1
54	Malaysia	9.2
55	Slovenia	10.4
56	Nicaragua	10.9
57	Mauritius	11.1
58	Ecuador	11.3
58	Russian Federation	11.3
60	Jordan	11.8
61	Botswana	12.0
61	Namibia	12.0
61	Panama	12.0
61	South Africa	12.0
65	Dominican Republic	12.1
66	Peru	12.3
67	Bulgaria	12.4
68	Zimbabwe	12.6
69	Venezuela	13.1
70	Argentina	13.5
70	Brazil	13.5
70	Paraguay	13.5
70	Uruguay	13.5
74	Bangladesh	14.7
75	China	15.7
76	Vietnam	17.5
77	Morocco	19.5
78	Nigeria	20.0
79	Tunisia	28.9
80	India	29.1

SOURCE: G. P. O'Driscoll Jr., K. Holmes, and M. A. O'Grady, 2002 Index of Economic Freedom (Heritage Foundation and *The Wall Street Journal*.)

2.25 Corporate income tax rate, 2002

Top corporate tax rate (%), 2002

RANK	COUNTRY	HARD DATA
1	Estonia	0.0
2	Brazil	15.0
2	Chile	15.0
4	Hong Kong SAR	16.0
5	Hungary	18.0
6	Ireland	20.0
7	Lithuania	24.0
8	Bolivia	25.0
8	Botswana	25.0
8	Bulgaria	25.0
8	Dominican Republic	25.0
8	Ecuador	25.0
8	El Salvador	25.0
8	Honduras	25.0
8	Latvia	25.0
8	Mauritius	25.0
8	Nicaragua	25.0
8	Romania	25.0
8	Slovenia	25.0
8	Taiwan	25.0
21	Singapore	25.5
22	Germany	26.4
23	Canada	27.0
24	Korea	28.0
24	Malaysia	28.0
24	Norway	28.0
24	Poland	28.0
24	Sweden	28.0
29	Finland	29.0
29	Slovak Republic	29.0
31	China	30.0
31	Costa Rica	30.0
31	Denmark	30.0
31	Iceland	30.0
31	Indonesia	30.0
31	Japan	30.0
31	Nigeria	30.0
31	Panama	30.0
31	Paraguay	30.0
31	Peru	30.0
31	South Africa	30.0
31	Thailand	30.0
31	Turkey	30.0
31	Ukraine	30.0
31	United Kingdom	30.0
31	Uruguay	30.0
47	Czech Republic	31.0
47	Guatemala	31.0
49	Philippines	32.0
49	Portugal	32.0
49	Switzerland	32.0
49	Vietnam	32.0
53	New Zealand	33.0
53	Jamaica	33.3
55	Australia	34.0
55	Austria	34.0
55	Venezuela	34.0
58	Argentina	35.0
58	Colombia	35.0
58	Croatia	35.0
58	Haiti	35.0
58	India	35.0
58	Jordan	35.0
58	Mexico	35.0
58	Morocco	35.0
58	Namibia	35.0
58	Netherlands	35.0
58	Russian Federation	35.0
58	Spain	35.0
58	Sri Lanka	35.0
58	Trinidad and Tobago	35.0
58	Tunisia	35.0
58	United States	35.0
58	Zimbabwe	35.0
75	Israel	36.0
75	Italy	36.0
77	France	36.4
78	Belgium	39.0
79	Bangladesh	40.0
79	Greece	40.0

SOURCE: G. P. O'Driscoll Jr., K. Holmes, and M. A. O'Grady, 2002 Index of Economic Freedom (Heritage Foundation and *The Wall Street Journal*.)

2.26 Individual income tax rate, 2002

Top income tax rate (%), 2002

RANK	COUNTRY	HARD DATA
1	Paraguay	0.0
1	Uruguay	0.0
3	Bolivia	13.0
3	Russian Federation	13.0
5	Hong Kong SAR	17.0
6	Bangladesh	25.0
6	Botswana	25.0
6	Costa Rica	25.0
6	Dominican Republic	25.0
6	Ecuador	25.0
6	El Salvador	25.0
6	Honduras	25.0
6	Jamaica	25.0
6	Latvia	25.0
6	Mauritius	25.0
6	Nicaragua	25.0
6	Nigeria	25.0
18	Estonia	26.0
19	Brazil	27.5
20	Singapore	28.0
21	Canada	29.0
21	Malaysia	29.0
23	Haiti	30.0
23	India	30.0
23	Indonesia	30.0
23	Jordan	30.0
23	Panama	30.0
23	Peru	30.0
29	Guatemala	31.0
30	Czech Republic	32.0
30	Philippines	32.0
32	Lithuania	33.0
33	Venezuela	34.0
34	Argentina	35.0
34	Colombia	35.0
34	Croatia	35.0
34	Iceland	35.0
34	Sri Lanka	35.0
34	Trinidad and Tobago	35.0
34	Tunisia	35.0
41	Namibia	36.0
42	Japan	37.0
42	Thailand	37.0
44	Finland	37.5
45	New Zealand	39.0
46	United States	39.6
47	Bulgaria	40.0
47	Hungary	40.0
47	Korea	40.0
47	Mexico	40.0
47	Poland	40.0
47	Portugal	40.0
47	Taiwan	40.0
47	Turkey	40.0
47	Ukraine	40.0
47	United Kingdom	40.0
47	Zimbabwe	40.0
58	Slovak Republic	42.0
59	Ireland	44.0
59	Morocco	44.0
61	Chile	45.0
61	China	45.0
61	Greece	45.0
61	Romania	45.0
61	South Africa	45.0
66	Italy	45.1
67	Australia	47.0
68	Norway	47.5
69	Spain	48.1
70	Austria	50.0
70	Israel	50.0
70	Slovenia	50.0
73	Germany	51.0
74	Netherlands	52.0
75	France	54.0
76	Belgium	55.0
77	Sweden	60.0
77	Vietnam	60.0
79	Denmark	63.3
	Switzerland	N/A

SOURCE: G. P. O'Driscoll Jr., K. Holmes, and M. A. O'Grady, 2002 Index of Economic Freedom (Heritage Foundation and *The Wall Street Journal*.)

569

2.27 Value-added tax rate, 2002

Representative value-added tax (%), 2002

RANK	COUNTRY	HARD DATA
1	Hong Kong SAR	0.0
1	United States	0.0
3	Singapore	3.0
4	Japan	5.0
4	Nigeria	5.0
4	Panama	5.0
4	Taiwan	5.0
8	Canada	7.0
8	Thailand	7.0
10	Switzerland	7.6
11	Australia	10.0
11	Botswana	10.0
11	Haiti	10.0
11	Indonesia	10.0
11	Korea	10.0
11	Malaysia	10.0
11	Paraguay	10.0
11	Philippines	10.0
11	Vietnam	10.0
20	Dominican Republic	12.0
20	Ecuador	12.0
20	Guatemala	12.0
20	Honduras	12.0
20	Mauritius	12.0
25	New Zealand	12.5
25	Sri Lanka	12.5
27	Bolivia	13.0
27	Costa Rica	13.0
27	El Salvador	13.0
27	Jordan	13.0
31	South Africa	14.0
32	Venezuela	14.5
33	Bangladesh	15.0
33	Jamaica	15.0
33	Mexico	15.0
33	Namibia	15.0
33	Nicaragua	15.0
33	Trinidad and Tobago	15.0
39	Colombia	16.0
39	Germany	16.0
39	India	16.0
39	Spain	16.0
43	Brazil	17.0
43	China	17.0
43	Israel	17.0
43	Portugal	17.0
47	United Kingdom	17.5
48	Chile	18.0
48	Estonia	18.0
48	Greece	18.0
48	Latvia	18.0
48	Lithuania	18.0
48	Peru	18.0
48	Tunisia	18.0
48	Turkey	18.0
56	Netherlands	19.0
56	Romania	19.0
56	Slovenia	19.0
59	France	19.6
60	Austria	20.0
60	Bulgaria	20.0
60	Ireland	20.0
60	Italy	20.0
60	Morocco	20.0
60	Russian Federation	20.0
60	Ukraine	20.0
67	Argentina	21.0
67	Belgium	21.0
69	Croatia	22.0
69	Czech Republic	22.0
69	Finland	22.0
69	Poland	22.0
73	Slovak Republic	23.0
73	Uruguay	23.0
75	Norway	24.0
76	Iceland	24.5
77	Denmark	25.0
77	Hungary	25.0
77	Sweden	25.0
77	Zimbabwe	25.0

SOURCES: Ernst & Young, Worldwide Corporate Tax Guide 2002, and national sources

2.28 Interest rate spread, 2001

Average interest rate spread, 2001 (difference between typical lending and deposit rates)

RANK	COUNTRY	HARD DATA
1	Japan	1.34
2	Norway	1.71
3	Switzerland	1.77
4	Korea	1.92
5	Netherlands	1.92
6	Canada	1.96
7	Spain	2.10
8	Hong Kong SAR	2.75
9	United Kingdom	2.84
10	Hungary	2.85
11	India	2.98
12	Indonesia	3.07
13	United States	3.24
14	Malaysia	3.29
15	Panama	3.50
16	China	3.60
17	Philippines	3.66
18	Sweden	3.70
19	Portugal	3.72
20	Estonia	3.75
21	Finland	3.85
22	France	3.98
23	Israel	4.00
24	Czech Republic	4.05
25	El Salvador	4.12
25	Vietnam	4.12
27	Singapore	4.12
28	South Africa	4.40
29	New Zealand	4.53
30	Italy	4.57
31	Jordan	4.60
32	Thailand	4.71
33	Ireland	4.74
34	Austria	4.79
35	Slovak Republic	4.81
36	Australia	4.88
37	Denmark	4.90
38	Tunisia	5.00
39	Belgium	5.06
40	Taiwan	5.25
41	Greece	5.27
42	Slovenia	5.30
43	Botswana	5.60
44	Chile	5.70
45	Latvia	5.93
46	Croatia	6.40
47	Germany	6.45
48	Poland	6.56
49	Lithuania	6.63
50	Venezuela	6.94
51	Bangladesh	7.34
52	Nigeria	7.50
53	Namibia	7.68
54	Trinidad and Tobago	8.00
55	Sri Lanka	8.09
56	Colombia	8.30
56	Morocco	8.30
56	Turkey	8.30
59	Bulgaria	8.35
60	Dominican Republic	8.65
61	Ecuador	8.88
62	Mexico	9.13
63	Honduras	9.30
64	Guatemala	10.20
65	Peru	10.50
66	Jamaica	10.97
67	Iceland	11.00
68	Mauritius	11.32
69	Argentina	11.55
70	Costa Rica	12.06
71	Romania	12.14
72	Russian Federation	13.00
73	Bolivia	13.56
74	Nicaragua	13.80
75	Haiti	14.97
76	Ukraine	21.29
77	Paraguay	23.25
78	Zimbabwe	24.07
79	Uruguay	37.39
80	Brazil	39.76

SOURCES: Economist Intelligence Unit and national sources

2.29　FDI, 2001

Foreign direct investment inward stock (in millions of US dollars), 2001

RANK	COUNTRY	HARD DATA
1	United States	1,321,063
2	United Kingdom	496,776
3	Belgium**	482,107
4	Germany*	480,899
5	Hong Kong SAR*	451,870
6	China*	395,192
7	France*	310,430
8	Netherlands	284,212
9	Brazil*	219,342
10	Canada	201,489
11	Spain	158,405
12	Mexico	115,952
13	Australia	111,127
14	Italy	107,291
15	Singapore*	104,323
16	Switzerland	90,308
17	Sweden	81,275
18	Argentina*	76,269
19	Ireland*	74,831
20	Denmark	64,397
21	Indonesia*	57,361
22	Malaysia*	53,302
23	Japan	50,319
24	South Africa*	50,115
25	Chile*	48,441
26	Korea	47,228
27	Poland*	42,433
28	Austria	34,400
29	Norway*	33,178
30	Portugal	32,671
31	Taiwan*	32,033
32	Venezuela	30,352
33	Thailand*	28,227
34	Czech Republic	26,764
35	Finland	26,267
36	Hungary	23,562
37	Israel	23,089
38	India*	22,319
39	Russian Federation*	21,795
40	Nigeria*	21,289
41	New Zealand	20,408
42	Vietnam*	15,923
43	Colombia	14,777
44	Philippines*	14,232
45	Greece*	14,059
46	Turkey*	12,601
47	Tunisia	11,672
48	Peru*	11,000
49	Morocco*	8,798
50	Ecuador*	8,271
51	Trinidad and Tobago*	7,825
52	Romania	7,636
53	Panama	7,257
54	Croatia*	6,597
55	Dominican Rep.*	6,413
56	Slovak Republic*	6,109
57	Bolivia*	5,699
58	Costa Rica*	5,654
59	Ukraine*	4,615
60	Jamaica*	4,040
61	Guatemala*	3,875
62	Bulgaria*	3,850
63	Slovenia*	3,250
64	Estonia	3,155
65	Lithuania	2,665
66	Sri Lanka*	2,620
67	Uruguay*	2,408
68	El Salvador	2,241
69	Latvia	2,216
70	Namibia*	1,906
71	Botswana	1,734
72	Honduras*	1,684
73	Jordan*	1,679
74	Nicaragua*	1,505
75	Paraguay*	1,389
76	Zimbabwe*	1,090
77	Bangladesh*	1,059
78	Mauritius*	693
79	Iceland	626
80	Haiti*	218

SOURCE: UNCTAD Handbook of Statistics Online, 2002
* estimate
** Includes Luxembourg FDI

2.30　Domestic credit, 2001

Domestic credit as a percentage of GDP, 2001

RANK	COUNTRY	HARD DATA
1	Switzerland	173.6
2	Nicaragua	151.3
3	Japan	145.2
4	Hong Kong SAR	142.5
5	United Kingdom	140.5
6	China	134.2
7	Austria*	122.0
7	Belgium*	122.0
7	Finland*	122.0
7	France*	122.0
7	Germany*	122.0
7	Greece*	122.0
7	Italy*	122.0
7	Ireland*	122.0
7	Netherlands*	122.0
7	Portugal*	122.0
7	Spain*	122.0
18	Malaysia	119.3
19	New Zealand	117.1
20	Panama	114.1
21	Iceland	105.0
22	Thailand	100.9
23	Korea	100.1
24	Australia	97.0
25	Israel	93.4
26	Singapore	91.5
27	Jordan	89.7
28	United States	87.8
29	Morocco	87.8
30	South Africa	81.6
31	Canada	79.4
32	Mauritius	79.2
33	Chile	73.0
34	Turkey	69.9
35	Tunisia	66.1
36	Sweden	63.5
37	Slovak Republic	63.2
38	Indonesia	61.1
39	Philippines	58.6
40	Brazil	57.0
41	Uruguay	56.9
42	India	55.7
43	Hungary	55.3
44	Bolivia	53.2
45	Croatia	51.4
46	Czech Republic	51.3
47	Denmark	51.3
48	Slovenia	49.5
49	Sri Lanka	46.7
50	Estonia	44.5
51	Zimbabwe	43.4
52	Vietnam	41.7
53	Namibia	39.6
54	Poland	37.7
55	Bangladesh	37.4
56	Argentina	36.3
57	Norway	34.7
58	Dominican Republic	31.9
59	Costa Rica	31.6
60	Honduras	31.6
61	Haiti	31.5
62	Latvia	31.3
63	Colombia	30.2
64	Trinidad and Tobago	29.5
65	Paraguay	26.0
66	Peru	25.4
67	Russian Federation	24.3
68	Ukraine	23.8
69	Jamaica	21.2
70	Bulgaria	19.2
71	Mexico	18.9
72	Lithuania	15.8
73	Venezuela	14.9
74	Guatemala	14.9
75	Romania	12.4
76	Nigeria	11.3
77	Botswana	-72.4
	Ecuador	N/A
	El Salvador	N/A
	Taiwan	N/A

SOURCES: IMF International Financial Statistics, June 2002; IMF country data; national sources; and authors' calculations
*Same domestic credit and GDP value used for entire euro area

2.31 Liquid liabilities, 2001

Liquid liabilities as a percentage of GDP, 2001

RANK	COUNTRY	HARD DATA
1	Hong Kong SAR	237.1
2	Japan	198.4
3	China	156.7
4	Malaysia	135.0
5	Switzerland	132.1
6	Thailand	116.9
7	Jordan	116.6
8	Singapore	114.4
9	United Kingdom	104.2
10	Israel	103.4
11	Panama	92.1
12	New Zealand	88.8
13	Morocco	88.2
14	Korea	85.8
15	Mauritius	84.4
16	Nicaragua	81.1
17	Austria*	78.8
17	Belgium*	78.8
17	Finland*	78.8
17	France*	78.8
17	Germany*	78.8
17	Greece*	78.8
17	Italy*	78.8
17	Ireland*	78.8
17	Netherlands*	78.8
17	Portugal*	78.8
17	Spain*	78.8
28	Canada	75.9
29	Czech Republic	74.9
30	Denmark	74.9
31	Australia	73.4
32	Slovak Republic	69.8
33	United States	68.2
34	Croatia	62.0
35	India	59.6
36	Tunisia	59.2
37	Philippines	59.1
38	Turkey	58.4
39	Trinidad and Tobago	58.0
40	Slovenia	57.3
41	Indonesia	56.1
42	Bolivia	56.0
43	Uruguay	55.8
44	Honduras	55.6
45	Vietnam	54.6
46	Norway	53.5
47	Hungary	51.9
48	South Africa	48.8
49	Sweden	47.9
50	Iceland	47.0
51	Poland	46.9
52	Chile	46.9
53	Jamaica	46.6
54	El Salvador	46.1
55	Zimbabwe	43.4
56	Estonia	43.3
57	Namibia	43.2
58	Bulgaria	39.4
59	Paraguay	39.1
60	Dominican Republic	39.0
61	Sri Lanka	38.7
62	Haiti	37.7
63	Bangladesh	36.0
64	Costa Rica	35.6
65	Latvia	33.2
66	Peru	32.3
67	Colombia	32.1
68	Botswana	30.8
69	Guatemala	30.7
70	Brazil	30.0
71	Nigeria	27.5
72	Argentina	27.2
73	Lithuania	26.4
74	Mexico	24.8
75	Russian Federation	23.5
76	Romania	23.4
77	Ukraine	22.2
78	Venezuela	18.6
	Ecuador	N/A
	Taiwan	N/A

SOURCES: IMF International Financial Statistics, June 2002; IMF country data; European Central Bank Monthly Bulletin, July 2002; national sources; and authors' calculations
*Same M3 and GDP value used for entire euro area

2.32 Bank liquid reserves

Ratio of bank liquid reserves to bank assets, 2000

RANK	COUNTRY	HARD DATA
1	Hong Kong SAR	0.25
2	United Kingdom	0.36
3	Sweden	0.37
4	New Zealand	0.54
5	Australia	0.64
6	Italy	0.68
7	Canada	0.73
8	Belgium	0.84
8	Switzerland	0.84
10	Spain	1.01
11	United States	1.13
12	Germany	1.38
13	Japan	1.45
14	Thailand	1.92
15	Korea	1.99
16	Norway	2.22
17	Finland	2.49
18	Argentina	2.52
19	Singapore	2.53
20	Tunisia	2.57
21	South Africa	2.70
22	Chile	3.07
23	Namibia	3.16
24	Slovenia	3.46
25	Botswana	3.60
26	Portugal	3.64
27	Iceland	3.72
28	Ecuador	3.81
29	Poland	4.65
30	Mauritius	5.10
31	Slovak Republic	5.70
32	Bolivia	5.80
33	Latvia	5.81
34	Mexico	5.85
35	Colombia	5.92
36	Morocco	6.29
37	Bulgaria	6.60
38	Turkey	7.07
39	Philippines	7.40
40	Brazil	7.57
41	Sri Lanka	7.63
42	Bangladesh	7.64
43	India	7.95
44	Indonesia	8.15
45	Zimbabwe	8.70
46	Vietnam	9.05
47	Croatia	10.67
48	Hungary	10.80
49	Uruguay	11.14
50	Lithuania	11.98
51	China	12.68
52	Israel	13.56
53	Malaysia	14.04
54	Trinidad and Tobago	14.44
55	Nicaragua	15.36
56	Russian Federation	15.38
57	Nigeria	15.41
58	Guatemala	15.59
59	Ukraine	17.89
60	Honduras	18.03
61	Czech Republic	18.42
62	Costa Rica	18.92
63	Jamaica	18.99
64	Estonia	19.95
65	Peru	21.58
66	Paraguay	22.71
67	Dominican Republic	27.45
68	Jordan	29.03
69	Venezuela	29.47
70	El Salvador	29.77
71	Romania	36.37
72	Haiti	37.28
	Austria	N/A
	Denmark	N/A
	France	N/A
	Greece	N/A
	Ireland	N/A
	Netherlands	N/A
	Panama	N/A
	Taiwan	N/A

SOURCE: World Bank World Development Indicators 2002

2.33 Market capitalization, 2001

Market capitalization in millions of US dollars, end of period levels for 2001

RANK	COUNTRY	HARD DATA
1	United States	13,983,849
2	Japan	3,910,014
3	United Kingdom	2,149,501
4	Belgium*	1,843,529
4	France*	1,843,529
4	Netherlands*	1,843,529
7	Germany	1,071,749
8	Italy	672,097
9	Canada	615,266
10	Spain	597,544
11	China	523,952
12	Switzerland	521,190
13	Hong Kong SAR	506,131
14	Australia	374,269
15	Taiwan	293,486
16	Sweden	232,561
17	Korea	220,046
18	Argentina	192,499
19	Finland	190,456
20	Brazil	186,238
21	South Africa	139,750
22	Mexico	121,403
23	Malaysia	120,007
24	Singapore	117,053
25	India	110,396
26	Greece	86,538
27	Denmark	85,146
28	Ireland	78,696
29	Russian Federation	76,198
30	Norway	69,054
31	Portugal	60,718
32	Chile	56,310
33	Israel	55,964
34	Turkey	47,150
35	Philippines	41,523
36	Thailand	36,340
37	Poland	26,017
38	Austria	25,204
39	Indonesia	23,006
40	New Zealand	17,778
41	Colombia	13,217
42	Peru	11,134
43	Hungary	10,367
44	Czech Republic	9,331
45	Morocco	9,087
46	Zimbabwe	7,972
47	Jordan	6,316
48	Venezuela	6,216
49	Nigeria	5,404
50	Trinidad and Tobago	5,035
51	Jamaica	4,703
52	Iceland	3,552
53	Croatia	3,319
54	Slovenia	2,839
55	El Salvador	2,672
56	Panama	2,602
57	Tunisia	2,303
58	Romania	2,124
59	Bolivia	1,555
60	Estonia	1,483
61	Ecuador	1,417
62	Ukraine	1,365
63	Sri Lanka	1,332
64	Botswana	1,269
65	Lithuania	1,199
66	Bangladesh	1,145
67	Mauritius	1,063
68	Latvia	697
69	Slovak Republic	665
70	Bulgaria	505
71	Guatemala	232
72	Uruguay	153
73	Namibia	151
	Costa Rica	N/A
	Dominican Republic	N/A
	Haiti	N/A
	Honduras	N/A
	Nicaragua	N/A
	Paraguay	N/A
	Vietnam	N/A

SOURCE: World Bank 2002 and World Bank *World Development Indicators 2002*
*Market capitalization of Euronext; Euronext was created in September 2000 by the merger of the exchanges in Amsterdam, Brussels, and Paris.

2.34 Value traded, 2001

Value traded as a percentage of GDP, end of 2001

RANK	COUNTRY	HARD DATA
1	Switzerland	233.62
2	United States	225.61
3	Finland	188.90
4	Taiwan	185.81
5	Belgium*	165.69
5	France*	165.69
5	Netherlands*	165.69
8	Korea	164.43
9	Spain	156.02
10	Sweden	140.53
11	United Kingdom	133.72
12	Hong Kong SAR	121.35
13	Germany	77.65
14	Singapore	71.43
15	Australia	67.15
16	Canada	63.76
17	China	61.99
18	Denmark	56.85
19	India	51.84
20	Italy	50.16
21	Turkey	43.75
22	Japan	40.90
23	Norway	32.00
24	Greece	31.89
25	Portugal	31.75
26	South Africa	31.03
27	Thailand	27.05
28	Malaysia	26.94
29	Ireland	23.17
30	Iceland	17.33
31	New Zealand	16.99
32	Zimbabwe	16.62
33	Indonesia	15.99
34	Israel	13.53
35	Brazil	11.47
36	Hungary	10.66
37	Jordan	10.58
38	Mexico	9.78
39	Russian Federation	7.39
40	Chile	6.23
41	Czech Republic	6.18
42	Poland	6.01
43	Philippines	4.23
44	Austria	4.07
45	Estonia	4.04
46	Slovenia	3.68
47	Morocco	3.48
48	Slovak Republic	2.71
49	Argentina	2.46
50	Mauritius	2.33
51	Trinidad and Tobago	2.09
52	Latvia	2.08
53	Bangladesh	2.04
54	Lithuania	1.75
55	Tunisia	1.58
56	Peru	1.37
57	Botswana	1.29
58	Jamaica	1.25
59	Nigeria	1.05
60	Croatia	0.99
61	Sri Lanka	0.97
62	Venezuela	0.91
63	Bulgaria	0.58
64	Ukraine	0.57
65	Panama	0.44
66	Colombia	0.33
67	Romania	0.27
68	El Salvador	0.17
69	Namibia	0.16
70	Guatemala	0.04
71	Ecuador	0.03
72	Bolivia	0.02
73	Uruguay	0.00
	Costa Rica	N/A
	Dominican Republic	N/A
	Haiti	N/A
	Honduras	N/A
	Nicaragua	N/A
	Paraguay	N/A
	Vietnam	N/A

SOURCES: World Bank 2002 and IMF World Economic Outlook Database, April 2002; national sources; and authors' calculations
*Value traded of Euronext; Euronext was created in September 2000 by the merger of the exchanges in Amsterdam, Brussels, and Paris.

2.35 Number of listed companies, 2001

Number of listed domestic companies as a percentage of market capitalization, end of 2001

RANK	COUNTRY	HARD DATA
1	United States	0.04
2	Italy	0.04
3	Switzerland	0.05
4	Argentina	0.06
5	Belgium*	0.06
5	France*	0.06
5	Netherlands*	0.06
8	Germany	0.07
9	Finland	0.08
10	Ireland	0.09
11	Japan	0.09
12	United Kingdom	0.11
13	Sweden	0.12
14	Mexico	0.13
15	Portugal	0.16
16	Hong Kong SAR	0.17
17	Taiwan	0.20
18	Canada	0.21
19	China	0.22
20	Brazil	0.23
21	Denmark	0.24
22	Norway	0.27
23	Russian Federation	0.31
24	Australia	0.36
25	Singapore	0.36
26	Austria	0.39
27	Greece	0.40
28	Spain	0.41
29	Chile	0.44
30	Hungary	0.55
31	Morocco	0.60
32	Korea	0.61
33	South Africa	0.61
34	Turkey	0.65
35	Malaysia	0.68
36	Trinidad and Tobago	0.80
37	New Zealand	0.82
38	Poland	0.89
39	Zimbabwe	0.90
40	Jamaica	0.90
41	Colombia	0.93
42	Venezuela	1.02
43	Czech Republic	1.03
44	Philippines	1.09
45	Israel	1.10
46	Panama	1.11
47	Estonia	1.15
48	Thailand	1.24
49	Botswana	1.24
50	Slovenia	1.37
51	Indonesia	1.37
52	Iceland	1.72
53	Bolivia	1.86
54	Tunisia	2.00
55	Croatia	2.01
56	Peru	2.11
57	Ecuador	2.19
58	Jordan	2.55
59	El Salvador	2.56
60	Mauritius	4.12
61	Nigeria	4.16
62	Guatemala	4.31
63	Lithuania	4.50
64	India	5.25
65	Romania	5.39
66	Ukraine	8.61
67	Namibia	8.72
68	Latvia	9.17
69	Uruguay	9.80
70	Sri Lanka	17.87
71	Bangladesh	20.09
72	Bulgaria	78.85
73	Slovak Republic	156.88
	Costa Rica	N/A
	Dominican Republic	N/A
	Haiti	N/A
	Honduras	N/A
	Nicaragua	N/A
	Paraguay	N/A
	Vietnam	N/A

SOURCES: World Bank, *World Development Indicators 2002,* and authors' calculations
*Number of companies listed on Euronext; Euronext was created in September 2000 by the merger of the exchanges in Amsterdam, Brussels, and Paris.

Section III: Technological Innovation and Diffusion

3.01 Technological sophistication

Your country's position in technology (1 = generally lags behind most other countries, 7 = is among the world leaders)

RANK	COUNTRY	SCORE
1	United States	6.8
2	Israel	6.7
3	Finland	6.4
4	Japan	6.2
5	Sweden	6.0
6	Switzerland	6.0
7	Germany	6.0
8	France	5.6
9	Singapore	5.6
10	Iceland	5.4
11	United Kingdom	5.4
12	Norway	5.3
13	Taiwan	5.3
14	Austria	5.2
15	Canada	5.2
16	Denmark	5.2
17	Korea	5.2
18	Ireland	5.1
19	Australia	5.0
20	Belgium	4.8
21	Netherlands	4.8
22	New Zealand	4.7
23	Malaysia	4.6
24	Costa Rica	4.5
25	Hong Kong SAR	4.5
26	Slovenia	4.4
27	Chile	4.4
28	Estonia	4.3
29	Czech Republic	4.2
30	South Africa	4.2
31	Trinidad and Tobago	4.2
32	Tunisia	4.1
33	Hungary	4.1
34	Jordan	4.1
35	Italy	4.0
36	Spain	4.0
37	Brazil	4.0
38	Panama	3.9
39	China	3.9
40	Dominican Republic	3.9
41	Thailand	3.8
42	India	3.8
43	Slovak Republic	3.7
44	Venezuela	3.5
45	Argentina	3.5
46	Latvia	3.5
47	Namibia	3.5
48	Poland	3.5
49	Uruguay	3.4
50	Morocco	3.4
51	Mauritius	3.4
52	El Salvador	3.4
53	Botswana	3.3
54	Greece	3.3
55	Portugal	3.2
56	Philippines	3.2
57	Mexico	3.2
58	Sri Lanka	3.2
59	Jamaica	3.1
60	Colombia	3.1
61	Peru	3.0
62	Lithuania	3.0
63	Indonesia	3.0
64	Russian Federation	3.0
65	Zimbabwe	2.8
66	Turkey	2.8
67	Croatia	2.8
68	Vietnam	2.6
69	Guatemala	2.6
70	Bulgaria	2.5
71	Ukraine	2.5
72	Romania	2.4
73	Nicaragua	2.4
74	Ecuador	2.4
75	Nigeria	2.3
75	Paraguay	2.3
77	Bangladesh	2.3
78	Honduras	1.9
79	Bolivia	1.9
80	Haiti	1.5

MEAN: 3.9

3.02 Firm-level innovation

In your business, continuous innovation plays a major role in generating revenue (1 = not true, 7 = true)

RANK	COUNTRY	SCORE
1	Japan	6.5
2	United States	6.3
3	Switzerland	6.2
4	Iceland	6.1
5	Nigeria	6.0
6	Singapore	6.0
7	Paraguay	6.0
8	Canada	5.9
9	Germany	5.9
10	Taiwan	5.9
11	Austria	5.9
12	India	5.9
13	Israel	5.8
14	Namibia	5.8
15	Malaysia	5.8
16	Finland	5.7
17	Brazil	5.6
18	United Kingdom	5.6
19	Denmark	5.5
20	Botswana	5.5
21	Thailand	5.5
22	Norway	5.5
23	Tunisia	5.5
24	Hong Kong SAR	5.5
24	Mauritius	5.5
26	Latvia	5.4
27	Spain	5.4
28	Slovak Republic	5.4
28	Sweden	5.4
30	Jamaica	5.4
31	Morocco	5.4
32	South Africa	5.4
33	Chile	5.4
34	Peru	5.4
35	Mexico	5.4
36	Korea	5.4
37	Greece	5.4
38	China	5.4
39	Czech Republic	5.3
39	Trinidad and Tobago	5.3
41	Dominican Republic	5.3
42	Belgium	5.3
43	Australia	5.3
44	Venezuela	5.3
45	El Salvador	5.3
46	Ireland	5.3
47	Costa Rica	5.3
48	Ecuador	5.3
49	Vietnam	5.3
50	Panama	5.3
51	Philippines	5.3
52	Romania	5.2
53	France	5.2
54	Italy	5.2
55	Honduras	5.2
56	Indonesia	5.1
57	Hungary	5.1
58	Guatemala	5.1
59	Lithuania	5.1
60	Estonia	5.1
61	Zimbabwe	5.1
62	Slovenia	5.0
63	New Zealand	5.0
64	Bangladesh	5.0
65	Poland	5.0
66	Sri Lanka	4.9
67	Nicaragua	4.9
68	Colombia	4.9
69	Netherlands	4.9
70	Argentina	4.8
71	Turkey	4.8
72	Jordan	4.8
73	Uruguay	4.7
74	Bolivia	4.7
75	Portugal	4.5
76	Russian Federation	4.5
77	Haiti	4.2
78	Bulgaria	4.1
79	Ukraine	4.0
80	Croatia	2.9

MEAN: 5.3

3.03 Firm-level technology absorption

Companies in your country are (1 = not interested in absorbing new technology, 7 = aggressive in absorbing new technology)

RANK	COUNTRY	SCORE
1	Israel	6.6
2	United States	6.6
3	Japan	6.3
4	Iceland	6.3
5	Finland	6.2
6	Taiwan	6.0
7	Sweden	5.9
8	Switzerland	5.9
9	Singapore	5.9
10	Korea	5.8
11	Germany	5.8
12	Australia	5.6
13	Estonia	5.6
14	Morocco	5.6
15	France	5.5
16	India	5.5
17	Canada	5.5
18	Ireland	5.4
19	Brazil	5.3
20	Norway	5.3
20	Tunisia	5.3
22	Denmark	5.3
23	Dominican Republic	5.3
24	United Kingdom	5.3
25	Malaysia	5.3
26	Slovak Republic	5.3
27	New Zealand	5.3
28	Costa Rica	5.2
29	South Africa	5.2
30	Austria	5.2
31	Thailand	5.2
32	Hong Kong SAR	5.2
33	Lithuania	5.1
34	Belgium	5.1
35	Czech Republic	5.0
36	Vietnam	5.0
37	Chile	5.0
38	Trinidad and Tobago	5.0
39	Hungary	5.0
39	Latvia	5.0
41	Panama	5.0
42	Turkey	4.9
43	Italy	4.8
44	Netherlands	4.8
45	Croatia	4.8
46	Slovenia	4.8
47	Jordan	4.8
48	China	4.7
49	Indonesia	4.7
50	Jamaica	4.7
51	Spain	4.7
52	Namibia	4.6
53	Ukraine	4.6
54	Mauritius	4.6
55	Nigeria	4.6
56	Russian Federation	4.6
57	Sri Lanka	4.6
58	Poland	4.6
59	Zimbabwe	4.5
60	Peru	4.4
61	El Salvador	4.4
62	Botswana	4.4
63	Philippines	4.4
64	Argentina	4.3
65	Mexico	4.3
66	Romania	4.3
67	Greece	4.3
68	Colombia	4.2
69	Venezuela	4.2
70	Portugal	4.1
71	Bangladesh	4.1
72	Bulgaria	4.0
73	Guatemala	3.9
74	Ecuador	3.9
75	Haiti	3.8
76	Uruguay	3.7
77	Paraguay	3.5
78	Nicaragua	3.5
79	Honduras	3.4
80	Bolivia	3.3

MEAN: 4.9

3.04 FDI and technology transfer

Foreign direct investment in your country (1 = brings little new technology, 7 = is an important source of new technology)

RANK	COUNTRY	SCORE
1	Ireland	6.2
2	Hungary	6.1
3	Costa Rica	6.0
4	Singapore	6.0
5	Czech Republic	5.9
6	Brazil	5.8
7	Israel	5.8
8	Malaysia	5.8
9	Estonia	5.7
10	Trinidad and Tobago	5.6
11	Dominican Republic	5.5
12	Jamaica	5.4
13	Philippines	5.4
14	Thailand	5.4
15	India	5.4
16	Nigeria	5.3
17	Portugal	5.3
18	Canada	5.3
19	Morocco	5.2
20	Panama	5.2
21	Argentina	5.2
21	Indonesia	5.2
23	Mexico	5.1
24	Taiwan	5.1
25	Latvia	5.1
26	Chile	5.1
27	Vietnam	5.1
28	Nicaragua	5.1
29	Poland	5.1
30	Spain	5.1
31	Australia	5.1
32	Sri Lanka	5.1
33	South Africa	5.0
34	Slovak Republic	5.0
35	Namibia	5.0
36	Botswana	5.0
37	Denmark	4.9
38	Italy	4.9
39	France	4.9
40	Jordan	4.9
41	Peru	4.9
42	Sweden	4.9
43	New Zealand	4.8
44	China	4.8
45	Austria	4.8
46	Norway	4.8
47	Lithuania	4.8
48	Romania	4.7
49	Korea	4.7
50	Germany	4.7
51	Belgium	4.7
52	United Kingdom	4.7
53	Netherlands	4.6
54	Hong Kong SAR	4.6
55	Honduras	4.5
56	Zimbabwe	4.5
57	Colombia	4.4
58	Greece	4.4
59	Japan	4.3
60	Mauritius	4.3
60	Slovenia	4.3
60	Tunisia	4.3
63	Switzerland	4.3
64	Guatemala	4.2
65	Croatia	4.2
66	Finland	4.2
67	Bulgaria	4.2
68	Ecuador	4.2
69	Venezuela	4.1
70	Bangladesh	4.1
71	El Salvador	4.0
72	United States	4.0
73	Turkey	4.0
74	Bolivia	4.0
75	Russian Federation	3.8
76	Iceland	3.7
77	Uruguay	3.7
78	Paraguay	3.5
79	Ukraine	3.4
80	Haiti	2.6

MEAN: 4.8

3.05 Prevalence of foreign technology licensing

In your country, licensing of foreign technology is (1 = uncommon, 7 = a common means of acquiring new technology)

RANK	COUNTRY	SCORE
1	India	5.9
2	Israel	5.8
3	Thailand	5.7
4	Singapore	5.6
5	Malaysia	5.6
6	South Africa	5.4
7	Taiwan	5.4
8	Korea	5.4
9	Italy	5.4
10	Brazil	5.3
11	Portugal	5.3
12	Germany	5.2
13	Belgium	5.2
14	Australia	5.2
15	Hong Kong SAR	5.2
16	Czech Republic	5.2
17	Ireland	5.1
18	Philippines	5.1
19	Netherlands	5.1
20	Canada	5.1
21	Latvia	5.0
22	Austria	5.0
23	Morocco	5.0
24	Japan	5.0
25	Indonesia	5.0
25	Switzerland	5.0
27	New Zealand	5.0
28	Spain	4.9
29	Venezuela	4.9
30	Slovak Republic	4.9
31	United Kingdom	4.9
32	Greece	4.9
33	Croatia	4.9
34	Nigeria	4.8
35	Hungary	4.8
36	Argentina	4.8
37	Turkey	4.8
38	Mauritius	4.8
39	Dominican Republic	4.7
40	Iceland	4.7
41	Panama	4.7
42	Poland	4.7
43	Botswana	4.7
44	Costa Rica	4.7
45	Trinidad and Tobago	4.7
46	Slovenia	4.7
47	Namibia	4.7
48	Denmark	4.6
49	Chile	4.6
50	France	4.6
51	Sweden	4.6
52	Estonia	4.6
53	Tunisia	4.6
54	China	4.6
55	Jamaica	4.6
56	Norway	4.5
57	Mexico	4.5
58	Lithuania	4.5
59	Jordan	4.5
60	Finland	4.5
61	Vietnam	4.4
62	Colombia	4.4
63	United States	4.4
64	Romania	4.4
65	Bangladesh	4.2
66	Sri Lanka	4.2
67	Uruguay	4.1
68	Zimbabwe	4.0
69	Peru	3.9
70	El Salvador	3.8
71	Ecuador	3.7
72	Nicaragua	3.7
73	Honduras	3.5
74	Bulgaria	3.5
75	Russian Federation	3.4
76	Ukraine	3.4
77	Guatemala	3.3
78	Paraguay	3.2
79	Bolivia	2.7
80	Haiti	2.5

MEAN: 4.6

3.06 Quality of scientific research institutions

Scientific research institutions in your country (e.g., university laboratories, government laboratories) are (1 = nonexistent, 7 = the best in their fields)

RANK	COUNTRY	SCORE
1	Israel	6.7
2	United States	6.7
3	Finland	5.9
4	Germany	5.7
5	Switzerland	5.7
6	United Kingdom	5.7
7	Netherlands	5.6
8	Sweden	5.6
9	Canada	5.5
10	Singapore	5.3
11	Austria	5.3
12	Japan	5.3
13	France	5.3
14	Australia	5.3
15	Taiwan	5.2
16	Denmark	5.2
17	India	5.1
18	Belgium	5.1
19	Ireland	5.0
20	Costa Rica	5.0
21	South Africa	4.9
22	Korea	4.9
23	New Zealand	4.8
24	Norway	4.7
25	Estonia	4.7
26	Hungary	4.6
27	Iceland	4.6
28	Malaysia	4.5
29	Portugal	4.5
30	Slovenia	4.4
31	China	4.4
32	Russian Federation	4.4
33	Lithuania	4.4
34	Czech Republic	4.4
35	Poland	4.3
36	Spain	4.3
37	Croatia	4.2
38	Brazil	4.2
39	Jamaica	4.2
40	Chile	4.1
41	Tunisia	4.1
42	Slovak Republic	4.1
43	Hong Kong SAR	4.1
44	Sri Lanka	4.0
45	Thailand	4.0
46	Latvia	4.0
47	Vietnam	4.0
48	Italy	3.9
49	Trinidad and Tobago	3.8
50	Morocco	3.8
51	Greece	3.8
52	Mauritius	3.7
53	Dominican Republic	3.7
54	Jordan	3.7
55	Uruguay	3.7
56	Botswana	3.7
57	Colombia	3.6
58	Philippines	3.6
59	Mexico	3.6
60	Indonesia	3.6
61	Bulgaria	3.5
62	Ukraine	3.5
63	Zimbabwe	3.5
64	Argentina	3.4
65	Turkey	3.4
66	Namibia	3.4
67	Panama	3.4
68	Bangladesh	3.3
69	Peru	3.3
70	Nigeria	3.1
71	Guatemala	3.1
72	Venezuela	3.1
73	Romania	3.0
74	Bolivia	3.0
75	Ecuador	2.9
76	Nicaragua	2.7
77	El Salvador	2.7
78	Honduras	2.7
79	Paraguay	2.4
80	Haiti	1.7

MEAN: 4.2

3.07 Company spending on research and development

Companies in your country (1 = do not spend money on research and development, 7 = spend heavily on research and development relative to international peers)

MEAN: 3.6

RANK	COUNTRY	SCORE
1	United States	6.1
2	Sweden	5.9
3	Germany	5.8
4	Switzerland	5.7
5	Japan	5.7
6	Israel	5.7
7	Finland	5.5
8	France	5.2
9	United Kingdom	5.1
10	Taiwan	4.9
11	Korea	4.8
12	Netherlands	4.8
13	Denmark	4.8
14	Belgium	4.7
15	Austria	4.6
16	Singapore	4.6
17	Canada	4.6
18	Norway	4.4
19	Ireland	4.4
20	Iceland	4.3
21	Australia	4.3
22	Costa Rica	4.2
23	Malaysia	4.1
24	Slovenia	4.1
25	Brazil	4.0
26	Spain	3.9
27	South Africa	3.8
28	New Zealand	3.8
29	Czech Republic	3.8
30	Hungary	3.8
31	Dominican Republic	3.6
32	India	3.6
33	Estonia	3.6
34	China	3.6
35	Poland	3.5
36	Tunisia	3.5
37	Hong Kong SAR	3.4
38	Lithuania	3.4
39	Sri Lanka	3.4
40	Morocco	3.4
41	Russian Federation	3.4
42	Italy	3.4
43	Latvia	3.4
44	Chile	3.4
45	Thailand	3.3
46	Namibia	3.3
47	Trinidad and Tobago	3.3
48	Indonesia	3.3
49	Slovak Republic	3.2
50	Vietnam	3.2
51	Colombia	3.1
52	Portugal	3.0
53	Zimbabwe	3.0
54	Botswana	3.0
55	Philippines	3.0
56	Greece	3.0
57	Mexico	2.9
58	Jamaica	2.9
59	Croatia	2.9
60	Guatemala	2.9
61	Ukraine	2.9
62	Panama	2.8
63	Peru	2.8
64	Nigeria	2.8
65	El Salvador	2.7
66	Bulgaria	2.7
67	Mauritius	2.7
68	Jordan	2.7
69	Turkey	2.7
70	Venezuela	2.7
71	Uruguay	2.7
72	Argentina	2.6
73	Ecuador	2.6
74	Romania	2.5
75	Bangladesh	2.4
76	Nicaragua	2.4
77	Paraguay	2.3
78	Honduras	2.3
79	Bolivia	2.2
80	Haiti	1.7

3.08 Subsidies and tax credits for firm-level research and development

For firms conducting research and development (R & D) in your country, direct government subsidies to individual companies or R & D tax credits (1 = never occur, 7 = are widespread and large)

MEAN: 3.3

RANK	COUNTRY	SCORE
1	Israel	6.3
2	Singapore	5.4
3	Taiwan	5.2
4	Canada	5.2
5	Ireland	5.0
6	United States	4.8
7	Germany	4.8
8	Malaysia	4.7
9	Finland	4.7
10	Tunisia	4.6
11	Belgium	4.6
12	France	4.6
12	Korea	4.6
14	Australia	4.6
15	Austria	4.4
16	Netherlands	4.4
17	United Kingdom	4.3
18	India	4.3
19	Japan	4.1
20	Hungary	4.1
21	China	4.0
22	Spain	4.0
23	Portugal	3.9
24	Italy	3.8
25	Norway	3.8
26	Czech Republic	3.7
26	Denmark	3.7
28	Slovenia	3.6
29	Greece	3.6
30	Thailand	3.4
31	Dominican Republic	3.4
32	Switzerland	3.4
33	Morocco	3.4
34	Sweden	3.3
35	Brazil	3.2
36	Mexico	3.2
37	Iceland	3.1
37	Slovak Republic	3.1
39	Sri Lanka	3.1
40	Namibia	3.0
41	Vietnam	3.0
42	Poland	3.0
42	Trinidad and Tobago	3.0
44	South Africa	3.0
45	Hong Kong SAR	2.9
46	Russian Federation	2.9
47	Chile	2.9
48	Botswana	2.8
49	Colombia	2.8
50	Latvia	2.8
51	Lithuania	2.8
52	Jordan	2.7
53	Ukraine	2.7
54	Costa Rica	2.7
55	Estonia	2.7
56	Mauritius	2.7
56	Nigeria	2.7
58	Croatia	2.7
59	Turkey	2.6
60	New Zealand	2.6
61	Philippines	2.6
62	Romania	2.6
63	Nicaragua	2.4
64	Panama	2.3
65	Bulgaria	2.3
66	Jamaica	2.3
67	Indonesia	2.3
68	Guatemala	2.2
69	Bangladesh	2.2
70	Honduras	2.2
71	Venezuela	2.1
72	Uruguay	2.1
73	Ecuador	2.0
74	Bolivia	2.0
75	El Salvador	2.0
76	Zimbabwe	1.9
77	Peru	1.9
78	Haiti	1.8
79	Argentina	1.7
80	Paraguay	1.5

3.09 University/industry research collaboration

In its R & D activity, business collaboration with local universities is (1 = minimal or nonexistent, 7 = intensive and ongoing)

RANK	COUNTRY	SCORE
1	Finland	5.9
2	United States	5.6
3	Israel	5.6
4	Sweden	5.4
5	Belgium	5.2
6	Ireland	5.2
7	Taiwan	5.2
8	Germany	5.1
9	Singapore	5.0
10	United Kingdom	4.9
11	Switzerland	4.9
12	Canada	4.9
13	Netherlands	4.8
14	Austria	4.6
15	Denmark	4.6
16	China	4.5
17	Australia	4.4
18	South Africa	4.3
19	Iceland	4.3
20	Korea	4.3
21	New Zealand	4.1
22	Norway	4.1
23	Czech Republic	4.1
24	Japan	4.1
25	Spain	3.9
26	Brazil	3.9
27	Hungary	3.9
28	Malaysia	3.8
29	Thailand	3.8
30	Slovak Republic	3.8
31	France	3.8
32	Dominican Republic	3.7
33	Slovenia	3.7
34	Greece	3.7
35	Hong Kong SAR	3.6
36	Costa Rica	3.6
37	Poland	3.5
38	Tunisia	3.5
39	Estonia	3.5
40	Indonesia	3.5
41	Vietnam	3.4
42	India	3.4
43	Portugal	3.4
44	Italy	3.4
45	Russian Federation	3.3
46	Jamaica	3.3
47	Chile	3.3
48	Latvia	3.2
49	Philippines	3.2
50	Mexico	3.2
51	Morocco	3.2
52	Colombia	3.2
53	Lithuania	3.1
54	Namibia	3.0
55	Trinidad and Tobago	3.0
56	Croatia	2.9
57	Sri Lanka	2.9
58	Ukraine	2.8
59	Botswana	2.8
60	Jordan	2.7
61	Zimbabwe	2.7
62	Peru	2.7
62	Venezuela	2.7
64	Uruguay	2.6
65	Nicaragua	2.6
66	Panama	2.6
67	Ecuador	2.5
68	Guatemala	2.5
69	Bulgaria	2.5
70	Mauritius	2.5
71	Turkey	2.4
72	Romania	2.4
73	Argentina	2.3
74	Bolivia	2.3
75	El Salvador	2.3
76	Honduras	2.2
77	Bangladesh	2.2
78	Nigeria	1.9
79	Paraguay	1.9
80	Haiti	1.9

MEAN: 3.6

3.10 Government procurement of advanced technology products

Government purchase decisions for the procurement of advanced technology products are (1 = based solely on price, 7 = based on technology and encourage innovation)

RANK	COUNTRY	SCORE
1	Singapore	5.2
2	Israel	5.1
3	Taiwan	5.1
4	Tunisia	5.1
5	United States	4.9
6	Korea	4.8
7	Malaysia	4.7
8	France	4.7
9	Finland	4.7
10	China	4.7
11	Germany	4.7
12	Switzerland	4.6
13	Sri Lanka	4.5
14	Canada	4.3
15	Ireland	4.3
16	Iceland	4.3
17	Japan	4.3
18	United Kingdom	4.3
19	Sweden	4.3
20	Spain	4.2
21	Czech Republic	4.2
22	Morocco	4.1
23	Hungary	4.1
24	Vietnam	4.1
25	Netherlands	4.0
26	Estonia	3.9
27	Denmark	3.9
28	Trinidad and Tobago	3.9
29	Hong Kong SAR	3.9
30	Namibia	3.9
31	Austria	3.9
32	Australia	3.9
33	Italy	3.8
34	Thailand	3.8
35	Brazil	3.8
36	Belgium	3.8
37	Slovenia	3.8
38	New Zealand	3.8
39	Norway	3.7
40	Indonesia	3.7
41	South Africa	3.7
42	Portugal	3.7
43	Slovak Republic	3.7
44	Botswana	3.7
44	Dominican Republic	3.7
46	Jamaica	3.6
47	Lithuania	3.5
47	Nigeria	3.5
49	Chile	3.4
50	Russian Federation	3.4
51	Croatia	3.4
52	Latvia	3.4
53	Bulgaria	3.4
54	Poland	3.4
55	India	3.3
56	Greece	3.3
57	Costa Rica	3.3
58	Mexico	3.2
59	Uruguay	3.2
60	Colombia	3.2
61	Romania	3.1
62	Jordan	3.1
63	Mauritius	3.0
64	Philippines	3.0
65	Ukraine	2.9
66	Zimbabwe	2.9
67	Nicaragua	2.9
68	Venezuela	2.9
69	El Salvador	2.8
70	Peru	2.8
71	Argentina	2.7
72	Panama	2.6
73	Bangladesh	2.5
74	Ecuador	2.5
75	Turkey	2.5
76	Honduras	2.3
77	Haiti	2.3
78	Paraguay	2.3
79	Bolivia	2.3
80	Guatemala	2.2

MEAN: 3.7

3.11 Quality of math and science education

Math and science education in your country's schools (1 = lag far behind most other countries, 7 = are among the best in the world)

RANK	COUNTRY	SCORE
1	Singapore	6.4
2	Czech Republic	6.0
3	Belgium	5.9
4	Austria	5.9
5	Slovak Republic	5.9
6	Tunisia	5.9
7	Taiwan	5.9
8	Switzerland	5.8
9	Romania	5.8
10	Hungary	5.8
10	Israel	5.8
12	Finland	5.8
13	Hong Kong SAR	5.6
14	France	5.6
15	Australia	5.6
16	Estonia	5.6
17	Iceland	5.6
18	Slovenia	5.6
19	Netherlands	5.5
20	Canada	5.5
21	Lithuania	5.2
22	Russian Federation	5.1
23	Bulgaria	5.1
24	Ireland	5.1
25	Latvia	5.1
26	Korea	5.1
27	Japan	5.1
28	United Kingdom	4.9
29	Croatia	4.9
30	Poland	4.9
31	Sweden	4.8
32	Italy	4.8
33	New Zealand	4.8
34	Jordan	4.8
35	Malaysia	4.8
36	India	4.8
37	Denmark	4.7
38	United States	4.7
39	Trinidad and Tobago	4.6
40	Spain	4.6
41	Thailand	4.6
42	Greece	4.6
43	Morocco	4.5
44	Ukraine	4.5
45	Costa Rica	4.4
46	Turkey	4.4
47	Germany	4.3
48	Norway	4.3
49	Sri Lanka	4.3
50	Vietnam	4.1
51	Uruguay	4.1
52	China	4.1
53	Mauritius	4.1
54	Zimbabwe	3.9
55	Botswana	3.8
56	Argentina	3.8
57	Chile	3.7
58	Brazil	3.6
59	Colombia	3.6
60	Portugal	3.5
61	Indonesia	3.5
62	Panama	3.4
63	Jamaica	3.4
64	Nigeria	3.3
65	Namibia	3.3
66	Ecuador	3.2
67	Nicaragua	3.1
68	Bangladesh	3.0
69	Dominican Republic	3.0
70	Bolivia	2.9
71	South Africa	2.9
72	El Salvador	2.9
73	Venezuela	2.9
74	Philippines	2.9
75	Mexico	2.8
76	Peru	2.8
77	Paraguay	2.5
78	Honduras	2.4
79	Guatemala	2.4
80	Haiti	2.2

MEAN: 4.4

3.12 Availability of scientists and engineers

Scientists and engineers in your country are (1 = nonexistent or rare, 7 = widely available)

RANK	COUNTRY	SCORE
1	Israel	6.6
2	India	6.2
3	Slovak Republic	6.2
4	France	6.1
5	Romania	6.1
6	Canada	6.1
7	Japan	6.1
8	Switzerland	6.0
9	Finland	6.0
10	United States	6.0
11	Hungary	5.7
12	Taiwan	5.7
13	Tunisia	5.7
14	Austria	5.6
15	Australia	5.6
16	Sweden	5.6
17	Iceland	5.6
18	United Kingdom	5.5
19	Singapore	5.5
20	Germany	5.5
21	Greece	5.5
22	Jordan	5.4
23	Uruguay	5.4
24	Argentina	5.4
25	Korea	5.4
26	Chile	5.3
27	Norway	5.3
28	Russian Federation	5.3
29	Czech Republic	5.3
30	Belgium	5.3
31	Ireland	5.3
32	Spain	5.2
33	Italy	5.2
34	Poland	5.2
35	Denmark	5.2
36	Lithuania	5.2
37	Morocco	5.2
38	Bulgaria	5.2
39	Netherlands	5.2
40	Estonia	5.1
41	Costa Rica	5.1
42	Vietnam	5.0
43	Brazil	5.0
44	Ukraine	5.0
45	Croatia	5.0
46	Portugal	4.9
47	Trinidad and Tobago	4.9
48	Sri Lanka	4.8
49	Hong Kong SAR	4.7
50	New Zealand	4.7
51	Turkey	4.7
52	Malaysia	4.7
53	Colombia	4.6
54	Latvia	4.6
55	Thailand	4.4
56	Slovenia	4.3
57	Bangladesh	4.3
58	Venezuela	4.2
59	Mauritius	4.2
60	Nigeria	4.2
61	Panama	4.1
62	Peru	4.1
63	El Salvador	4.1
64	China	4.1
65	South Africa	4.1
66	Jamaica	4.0
67	Indonesia	4.0
68	Philippines	4.0
69	Zimbabwe	3.9
70	Dominican Republic	3.7
71	Ecuador	3.5
72	Botswana	3.4
73	Nicaragua	3.4
74	Guatemala	3.3
75	Mexico	3.3
76	Honduras	3.3
77	Paraguay	3.2
78	Bolivia	3.2
79	Namibia	3.2
80	Haiti	2.9

MEAN: 4.9

581

3.13 Brain drain

Your country's talented people (1 = normally leave to pursue opportunities in other countries, 7 = almost always remain in the country)

RANK	COUNTRY	SCORE
1	United States	6.5
2	Finland	5.7
3	Netherlands	5.7
4	Israel	5.6
5	United Kingdom	5.5
6	Norway	5.4
7	Japan	5.4
8	Chile	5.4
9	Switzerland	5.3
10	Iceland	5.2
11	Austria	5.0
12	Belgium	5.0
13	Spain	5.0
14	Taiwan	5.0
15	Czech Republic	4.9
16	Germany	4.9
17	Singapore	4.9
18	Ireland	4.9
19	Denmark	4.8
20	Hong Kong SAR	4.7
21	Brazil	4.7
22	Sweden	4.6
23	Portugal	4.6
24	Panama	4.6
25	Costa Rica	4.6
26	Thailand	4.5
27	Korea	4.3
28	Australia	4.2
29	Malaysia	4.2
30	Canada	4.2
31	Slovenia	4.1
32	Estonia	4.1
33	Tunisia	4.1
34	Botswana	4.0
35	Italy	4.0
36	Poland	4.0
37	Indonesia	3.9
38	Hungary	3.8
39	Greece	3.8
40	China	3.7
41	Trinidad and Tobago	3.6
42	France	3.6
43	El Salvador	3.6
44	Namibia	3.5
45	Mauritius	3.5
46	Vietnam	3.4
47	Turkey	3.3
48	Russian Federation	3.2
49	Mexico	3.2
50	Dominican Republic	3.2
51	Slovak Republic	3.2
52	India	3.1
53	Latvia	3.1
54	Morocco	3.0
55	New Zealand	3.0
56	Uruguay	3.0
57	Paraguay	3.0
58	Honduras	3.0
59	Venezuela	2.9
60	South Africa	2.9
61	Jordan	2.8
62	Lithuania	2.7
63	Colombia	2.7
64	Guatemala	2.7
65	Sri Lanka	2.7
66	Peru	2.7
67	Jamaica	2.6
68	Argentina	2.6
69	Croatia	2.5
70	Nicaragua	2.5
71	Bolivia	2.4
72	Ukraine	2.4
73	Philippines	2.3
74	Nigeria	2.3
75	Ecuador	2.2
76	Bulgaria	2.2
77	Bangladesh	2.1
78	Romania	1.9
79	Zimbabwe	1.8
80	Haiti	1.7

MEAN: 3.8

3.14 Research and development spending

Overall research and development spending as a percentage of gross national income, 2000 or most recent year

RANK	COUNTRY	HARD DATA
1	Sweden	3.76
2	Israel	3.69
3	Finland	3.31
4	Japan	2.80
5	Korea	2.70
6	Switzerland	2.55
6	United States	2.55
8	Germany	2.31
9	France	2.21
10	El Salvador	2.20
11	Iceland	2.08
11	Taiwan	2.08
13	Netherlands	2.01
14	Denmark	1.94
15	United Kingdom	1.81
16	Australia	1.71
17	Canada	1.68
17	Norway	1.68
19	Austria	1.64
20	Belgium	1.55
21	Ireland	1.54
22	Slovenia	1.47
23	Czech Republic	1.27
24	New Zealand	1.21
25	Croatia	1.18
26	Singapore	1.13
27	Russian Federation	1.08
28	Italy	1.04
29	Slovak Republic	0.98
30	Ukraine	0.97
31	Spain	0.84
32	Romania	0.79
33	Estonia	0.78
34	Brazil	0.77
35	Poland	0.73
36	Hungary	0.71
37	Lithuania	0.67
38	Portugal	0.63
39	India	0.62
39	South Africa	0.62
41	Bulgaria	0.61
42	Chile	0.56
43	Bolivia	0.50
44	Argentina	0.48
44	Greece	0.48
44	Turkey	0.48
47	Mauritius	0.45
48	Malaysia	0.42
49	Latvia	0.40
50	Mexico	0.36
51	Venezuela	0.34
52	Tunisia	0.30
53	Philippines	0.21
54	Botswana	0.14
54	Trinidad and Tobago	0.14
56	Thailand	0.10
57	Indonesia	0.07
58	China	0.06
58	Costa Rica	0.06
60	Bangladesh	0.03
61	Ecuador	0.02
	Colombia	N/A
	Dominican Republic	N/A
	Guatemala	N/A
	Haiti	N/A
	Honduras	N/A
	Hong Kong SAR	N/A
	Jamaica	N/A
	Jordan	N/A
	Morocco	N/A
	Namibia	N/A
	Nicaragua	N/A
	Nigeria	N/A
	Panama	N/A
	Paraguay	N/A
	Peru	N/A
	Sri Lanka	N/A
	Uruguay	N/A
	Vietnam	N/A
	Zimbabwe	N/A

SOURCES: World Bank, *World Development Indicators 2002*; OECD Main Science and Technology Indicators, 2002; and national sources

4.11 Personal computers, 2001

Personal computers per 100 inhabitants, 2001

RANK	COUNTRY	HARD DATA
1	United States	62.25
2	Sweden	56.12
3	Australia	51.71
4	Singapore	50.83
5	Norway	50.80
6	Switzerland	49.97
7	Denmark	43.15
8	Netherlands	42.85
9	Finland	42.35
10	Iceland	41.81
11	Ireland	39.07
12	Canada	39.02
13	New Zealand	38.56
14	Hong Kong SAR	38.46
15	United Kingdom	36.62
16	Japan	34.87
17	Belgium	34.45
18	France	33.70
19	Germany	33.60
20	Austria	27.95
21	Slovenia	27.57
22	Korea	25.14
23	Israel	24.59
24	Taiwan	22.32
25	Italy	19.48
26	Estonia	17.48
27	Costa Rica	17.02
28	Spain	16.82
29	Latvia	15.31
30	Slovak Republic	14.81
31	Malaysia	12.61
32	Czech Republic	12.14
33	Portugal	11.74
34	Uruguay	11.01
35	Mauritius	10.83
36	Hungary	10.03
37	Croatia	8.59
38	Poland	8.54
39	Chile	8.39
40	Greece	8.12
41	Lithuania	7.06
42	Trinidad and Tobago	6.92
43	Mexico	6.87
44	South Africa	6.85
45	Brazil	6.29
46	Argentina	5.34
47	Venezuela	5.28
48	Jamaica	5.00
49	Russian Federation	4.97
50	Peru	4.79
51	Bulgaria	4.43
52	Colombia	4.21
53	Turkey	4.07
54	Botswana	3.89
55	Panama	3.79
56	Namibia	3.64
57	Romania	3.57
58	Jordan	3.28
59	Thailand	2.67
60	Tunisia	2.37
61	Ecuador	2.33
62	Philippines	2.20
63	El Salvador	2.19
64	Bolivia	2.05
65	China	1.93
66	Ukraine	1.83
67	Paraguay	1.42
68	Morocco	1.31
69	Guatemala	1.28
70	Honduras	1.22
71	Zimbabwe	1.21
72	Indonesia	1.07
73	Vietnam	0.99
74	Nicaragua	0.96
75	Sri Lanka	0.79
76	Nigeria	0.68
77	India	0.58
78	Bangladesh	0.19
	Dominican Republic	N/A
	Haiti	N/A

SOURCE: International Telecommunication Union, July 2002

Section V: General Infrastructure

5.01 Overall infrastructure quality

General infrastructure in your country (1 = is poorly developed and inefficient, 7 = is among the best in the world)

RANK	COUNTRY	SCORE
1	Switzerland	6.7
2	Finland	6.7
3	Germany	6.6
4	Singapore	6.6
5	United States	6.6
6	Denmark	6.5
7	Iceland	6.4
8	Canada	6.4
9	Sweden	6.4
10	France	6.3
11	Australia	6.3
12	Austria	6.2
13	Belgium	6.1
14	Hong Kong SAR	5.9
15	Netherlands	5.8
16	Malaysia	5.8
17	New Zealand	5.5
18	United Kingdom	5.5
19	Norway	5.4
20	Japan	5.4
21	Korea	5.3
22	Namibia	5.0
23	Taiwan	5.0
24	South Africa	5.0
25	Spain	4.9
26	Sri Lanka	4.9
27	Israel	4.9
28	Czech Republic	4.8
29	Thailand	4.8
30	Tunisia	4.7
31	Jordan	4.7
32	Portugal	4.6
33	Botswana	4.6
34	Mauritius	4.4
35	Italy	4.4
36	Slovenia	4.3
37	Estonia	4.3
38	Trinidad and Tobago	4.3
39	Hungary	4.3
40	Chile	4.2
41	Panama	4.0
42	Zimbabwe	4.0
43	Lithuania	3.8
44	Uruguay	3.8
45	Brazil	3.8
46	Argentina	3.8
46	Slovak Republic	3.8
48	Greece	3.7
49	Turkey	3.7
50	Latvia	3.7
51	Dominican Republic	3.6
52	China	3.4
53	Ireland	3.4
54	Jamaica	3.3
55	Morocco	3.2
56	El Salvador	3.2
57	Russian Federation	3.1
58	Mexico	3.1
59	Bulgaria	3.0
60	Poland	2.9
61	Croatia	2.8
62	India	2.8
63	Guatemala	2.8
64	Indonesia	2.8
65	Colombia	2.7
66	Ukraine	2.7
67	Peru	2.6
68	Venezuela	2.6
69	Honduras	2.6
70	Costa Rica	2.6
71	Vietnam	2.5
72	Romania	2.5
73	Ecuador	2.4
74	Philippines	2.3
75	Bangladesh	2.3
76	Paraguay	2.0
77	Nigeria	1.9
78	Nicaragua	1.8
79	Bolivia	1.8
80	Haiti	1.3

MEAN: 4.2

5.02 Railroad infrastructure development

Railroads in your country are (1 = underdeveloped, 7 = as extensive and efficient as the world's best)

RANK	COUNTRY	SCORE
1	Japan	6.7
2	Switzerland	6.6
3	France	6.5
4	Germany	6.2
5	Belgium	6.1
6	Denmark	6.0
6	Finland	6.0
8	Hong Kong SAR	5.6
9	Singapore	5.6
10	Austria	5.4
11	Sweden	5.4
12	Canada	5.3
13	Korea	5.3
14	Taiwan	5.1
15	Australia	5.0
15	Netherlands	5.0
17	Malaysia	4.9
18	India	4.9
19	Czech Republic	4.8
20	Russian Federation	4.7
21	Slovak Republic	4.7
22	United States	4.6
23	Spain	4.3
24	Ukraine	4.3
25	South Africa	4.3
26	Namibia	4.1
27	Hungary	4.0
27	Norway	4.0
29	Botswana	4.0
30	United Kingdom	4.0
31	New Zealand	3.9
32	Latvia	3.9
33	Slovenia	3.8
34	China	3.7
35	Tunisia	3.7
36	Italy	3.7
37	Portugal	3.7
38	Sri Lanka	3.7
39	Thailand	3.6
40	Estonia	3.6
41	Lithuania	3.6
42	Bulgaria	3.5
43	Zimbabwe	3.4
44	Morocco	3.2
45	Poland	3.2
46	Romania	2.9
47	Israel	2.9
48	Greece	2.8
49	Argentina	2.7
50	Iceland	2.6
51	Panama	2.6
52	Indonesia	2.6
53	Brazil	2.5
54	Ireland	2.5
55	Vietnam	2.5
56	Jordan	2.4
57	Bangladesh	2.3
58	Croatia	2.3
59	Turkey	2.2
60	Mauritius	2.1
61	Mexico	2.0
62	Nicaragua	1.8
63	Chile	1.8
64	Peru	1.7
65	Philippines	1.6
66	Bolivia	1.5
67	Dominican Republic	1.4
68	Trinidad and Tobago	1.4
69	Uruguay	1.4
70	Guatemala	1.3
71	Colombia	1.3
72	Honduras	1.2
73	Jamaica	1.2
74	Nigeria	1.2
75	Haiti	1.1
76	El Salvador	1.1
77	Costa Rica	1.1
78	Ecuador	1.1
79	Paraguay	1.0
80	Venezuela	1.0

MEAN: 3.4

5.03   Port infrastructure quality

Port facilities and inland waterways in your country are (1 = underdeveloped, 7 = as developed as the world's best)

RANK	COUNTRY	SCORE
1	Singapore	6.7
2	Hong Kong SAR	6.6
3	Netherlands	6.5
4	Belgium	6.5
5	Germany	6.4
6	Finland	6.3
6	United States	6.3
8	Canada	6.3
9	Denmark	6.2
10	Iceland	6.1
11	Panama	6.0
12	Sweden	6.0
13	New Zealand	5.8
14	Australia	5.8
15	France	5.7
16	Malaysia	5.7
17	Japan	5.7
18	Norway	5.7
19	United Kingdom	5.4
20	Taiwan	5.3
21	Israel	5.2
22	Korea	5.2
23	Estonia	5.1
24	Switzerland	5.1
25	Namibia	5.0
26	Slovenia	5.0
27	Jamaica	4.9
28	Mauritius	4.9
29	Spain	4.9
30	Sri Lanka	4.9
31	South Africa	4.7
32	Austria	4.6
33	Trinidad and Tobago	4.5
34	Latvia	4.4
35	Thailand	4.4
36	Tunisia	4.4
37	Chile	4.3
38	Portugal	4.2
39	Russian Federation	4.1
40	Jordan	4.0
41	Italy	3.9
42	Lithuania	3.9
43	Slovak Republic	3.8
44	China	3.8
45	Argentina	3.8
46	Uruguay	3.7
47	Morocco	3.7
48	Greece	3.7
49	Ireland	3.6
50	Brazil	3.6
51	Bulgaria	3.6
52	Honduras	3.5
53	Turkey	3.5
54	Ukraine	3.5
55	Poland	3.3
56	Romania	3.3
57	Hungary	3.2
58	Ecuador	3.1
59	Mexico	3.1
60	Nigeria	3.1
61	India	3.0
62	Dominican Republic	3.0
63	Botswana	2.9
64	Indonesia	2.9
65	Vietnam	2.9
66	Czech Republic	2.7
67	Peru	2.7
68	El Salvador	2.7
69	Colombia	2.5
70	Croatia	2.5
71	Guatemala	2.3
72	Venezuela	2.3
73	Paraguay	2.2
74	Bangladesh	2.2
74	Philippines	2.2
76	Nicaragua	2.1
77	Costa Rica	2.0
77	Zimbabwe	2.0
79	Haiti	1.6
80	Bolivia	1.5

MEAN: 4.2

5.04   Air transport infrastructure quality

Air transport in your country is (1 = infrequent and inefficient, 7 = as extensive and efficient as the world's best)

RANK	COUNTRY	SCORE
1	Singapore	6.8
2	United States	6.7
3	Hong Kong SAR	6.6
4	Germany	6.6
5	Netherlands	6.5
6	United Kingdom	6.3
7	Finland	6.3
8	Sweden	6.2
9	Denmark	6.2
10	Canada	6.1
11	Belgium	6.1
12	Australia	6.0
13	Austria	6.0
14	Malaysia	5.9
15	France	5.9
16	Jamaica	5.8
17	Israel	5.8
18	Iceland	5.7
19	Korea	5.7
20	New Zealand	5.7
21	South Africa	5.6
22	Chile	5.5
23	Taiwan	5.5
24	Norway	5.5
25	Panama	5.4
26	Switzerland	5.4
27	El Salvador	5.4
28	Tunisia	5.4
29	Spain	5.4
30	Dominican Republic	5.3
31	Mauritius	5.3
32	Thailand	5.2
33	Portugal	5.2
34	Brazil	5.2
35	Trinidad and Tobago	5.1
36	Japan	5.1
37	Turkey	5.0
38	Sri Lanka	5.0
39	Italy	4.9
40	Jordan	4.9
41	Czech Republic	4.9
42	Estonia	4.9
43	Greece	4.8
44	Morocco	4.8
45	India	4.8
45	Mexico	4.8
47	Slovenia	4.7
48	Namibia	4.7
49	Ireland	4.6
50	Latvia	4.5
51	Colombia	4.5
52	Botswana	4.3
53	Argentina	4.3
54	Lithuania	4.3
55	Hungary	4.2
56	Indonesia	4.2
57	Russian Federation	4.1
58	Nigeria	4.0
59	Venezuela	4.0
60	Croatia	3.9
61	Costa Rica	3.8
61	Poland	3.8
63	Romania	3.7
64	Vietnam	3.6
65	China	3.6
66	Philippines	3.6
67	Peru	3.5
68	Guatemala	3.4
69	Ukraine	3.4
70	Paraguay	3.3
71	Zimbabwe	3.3
72	Nicaragua	3.3
73	Uruguay	3.2
74	Bolivia	3.1
75	Haiti	3.1
76	Honduras	3.0
77	Bulgaria	2.9
78	Bangladesh	2.8
79	Ecuador	2.8
80	Slovak Republic	2.5

MEAN: 4.8

594

5.05 Quality of electricity supply

The quality of electricity supply in your country (in terms of lack of interruptions and lack of voltage fluctuations) is (1 = worse than most other countries, 7 = equal to the highest in the world)

RANK	COUNTRY	SCORE
1	Denmark	7.0
2	Iceland	7.0
3	Sweden	6.9
4	Switzerland	6.9
5	Netherlands	6.9
6	Germany	6.9
7	Austria	6.8
8	Finland	6.8
9	United Kingdom	6.8
10	Canada	6.7
11	Japan	6.7
12	Hong Kong SAR	6.7
13	Belgium	6.7
14	United States	6.6
15	Singapore	6.6
16	Norway	6.6
17	France	6.5
18	Czech Republic	6.5
19	Australia	6.4
20	Israel	6.4
21	New Zealand	6.3
22	Korea	6.2
23	Ireland	6.0
24	Slovenia	5.9
25	Italy	5.9
26	South Africa	5.8
27	Hungary	5.8
28	Slovak Republic	5.8
29	Malaysia	5.7
30	Chile	5.6
31	Namibia	5.6
32	Portugal	5.5
33	Jordan	5.5
34	Uruguay	5.5
35	Tunisia	5.3
36	Taiwan	5.3
37	Thailand	5.3
38	Argentina	5.2
39	Trinidad and Tobago	5.2
40	Estonia	5.2
41	Lithuania	5.1
42	Panama	5.1
43	Latvia	5.0
44	Poland	5.0
45	Croatia	4.9
46	Mauritius	4.9
47	El Salvador	4.9
48	Spain	4.9
49	Greece	4.8
50	Botswana	4.8
51	Costa Rica	4.8
52	Morocco	4.7
53	Peru	4.6
54	China	4.6
55	Colombia	4.5
56	Brazil	4.4
57	Bulgaria	4.1
58	Bolivia	4.1
59	Turkey	3.9
60	Venezuela	3.8
61	Guatemala	3.8
62	Russian Federation	3.7
63	Romania	3.6
64	Zimbabwe	3.6
65	Mexico	3.6
66	Paraguay	3.5
67	Jamaica	3.5
68	Nicaragua	3.5
69	Indonesia	3.4
70	Philippines	3.1
71	Honduras	3.1
72	Vietnam	3.0
73	Sri Lanka	2.9
74	Ecuador	2.9
75	India	2.7
76	Ukraine	2.6
77	Dominican Republic	2.0
78	Bangladesh	2.0
79	Nigeria	1.8
80	Haiti	1.1

MEAN: 5.0

5.06 Telephone/fax infrastructure quality

New telephone lines for your business are (1 = scarce and difficult to obtain, 7 = widely available and highly reliable)

RANK	COUNTRY	SCORE
1	Finland	7.0
2	Iceland	7.0
3	Denmark	6.9
4	Hong Kong SAR	6.9
5	Switzerland	6.9
6	Singapore	6.8
7	Germany	6.8
8	United States	6.8
9	Israel	6.8
10	Canada	6.7
11	New Zealand	6.7
12	Sweden	6.7
13	Japan	6.7
14	Chile	6.7
15	Austria	6.7
16	France	6.7
17	Netherlands	6.7
18	United Kingdom	6.7
19	Norway	6.6
20	Australia	6.6
21	Taiwan	6.4
22	Belgium	6.4
22	Uruguay	6.4
24	Korea	6.4
25	Hungary	6.4
26	Ireland	6.3
27	Czech Republic	6.2
28	Thailand	6.2
29	El Salvador	6.2
30	Croatia	6.2
31	Estonia	6.2
32	Portugal	6.2
33	Slovenia	6.2
34	Morocco	6.1
35	Spain	6.0
36	Brazil	6.0
37	Greece	6.0
37	Slovak Republic	6.0
39	Malaysia	6.0
40	Jordan	5.9
41	Peru	5.9
42	Italy	5.9
43	Argentina	5.8
44	Panama	5.7
45	Latvia	5.7
46	Lithuania	5.7
47	India	5.6
48	Dominican Republic	5.5
49	China	5.5
50	Colombia	5.5
51	Tunisia	5.5
52	Sri Lanka	5.4
53	Venezuela	5.3
54	Mauritius	5.2
55	Turkey	5.2
56	Namibia	5.1
57	Poland	5.1
58	South Africa	5.1
59	Mexico	5.0
60	Vietnam	4.8
61	Trinidad and Tobago	4.8
62	Guatemala	4.7
63	Jamaica	4.7
64	Bolivia	4.7
65	Botswana	4.6
66	Bulgaria	4.5
67	Indonesia	4.5
68	Russian Federation	4.5
69	Romania	4.4
70	Philippines	4.4
71	Ukraine	3.7
72	Paraguay	3.2
73	Nigeria	3.1
74	Zimbabwe	2.9
75	Ecuador	2.8
76	Costa Rica	2.7
77	Nicaragua	2.3
78	Bangladesh	1.8
79	Haiti	1.8
80	Honduras	1.6

MEAN: 5.5

595

5.07 Postal efficiency

Do you trust your country's postal system sufficiently to have a friend mail a small package worth US$ 100 to you? (1 = not at all, 7 = yes, trust the system entirely)

RANK	COUNTRY	SCORE
1	Denmark	6.8
2	Finland	6.8
3	Japan	6.8
4	New Zealand	6.7
5	Iceland	6.7
6	Switzerland	6.7
7	Germany	6.7
8	United States	6.7
9	Sweden	6.6
10	Hong Kong SAR	6.5
11	Singapore	6.5
12	Canada	6.5
13	Israel	6.5
14	Australia	6.5
15	Slovenia	6.4
16	Austria	6.4
17	Taiwan	6.3
18	Norway	6.2
19	Portugal	6.1
20	United Kingdom	6.1
21	France	6.0
22	Korea	6.0
23	Netherlands	6.0
24	Czech Republic	6.0
25	Belgium	5.8
26	Ireland	5.7
27	Estonia	5.6
28	Slovak Republic	5.4
29	Tunisia	5.3
30	Croatia	5.3
31	Brazil	5.3
32	Botswana	5.2
33	Malaysia	5.2
34	Morocco	5.2
35	Spain	5.2
36	Thailand	5.1
37	Hungary	5.1
38	China	4.9
39	Chile	4.7
40	Vietnam	4.7
41	Italy	4.6
42	Greece	4.5
43	Mauritius	4.5
44	Poland	4.4
45	Trinidad and Tobago	4.4
46	Jordan	4.4
47	Latvia	4.3
48	Lithuania	4.2
49	Namibia	4.1
50	Turkey	4.1
51	Uruguay	4.0
52	Colombia	3.9
53	India	3.9
54	Romania	3.8
55	Russian Federation	3.7
56	Argentina	3.5
57	Bulgaria	3.5
58	South Africa	3.3
59	Sri Lanka	3.3
60	Indonesia	3.3
61	Peru	3.2
62	Bolivia	3.1
63	Panama	3.1
64	Jamaica	3.1
65	Ukraine	3.0
66	Guatemala	3.0
67	Costa Rica	3.0
68	Haiti	2.8
69	Bangladesh	2.8
70	Zimbabwe	2.8
71	Nicaragua	2.7
72	Mexico	2.6
73	Dominican Republic	2.6
74	Paraguay	2.3
75	El Salvador	2.3
76	Ecuador	2.2
77	Nigeria	1.9
78	Honduras	1.9
79	Venezuela	1.9
80	Philippines	1.8

MEAN: 4.6

5.08 Quality of public schools

The public (free) schools in your country are (1 = of poor quality, 7 = equal to the best in the world)

RANK	COUNTRY	SCORE
1	Austria	6.4
2	Finland	6.4
3	Belgium	6.3
4	Switzerland	6.3
5	Iceland	6.3
6	Ireland	6.1
7	Netherlands	6.1
8	Canada	5.9
8	Singapore	5.9
10	Israel	5.9
11	Czech Republic	5.9
12	Australia	5.8
12	France	5.8
14	Taiwan	5.7
15	Denmark	5.7
16	New Zealand	5.7
17	Sweden	5.6
18	Slovenia	5.5
19	Tunisia	5.4
20	Slovak Republic	5.4
21	Estonia	5.3
22	Italy	5.2
23	United Kingdom	5.2
24	Malaysia	5.1
25	Hungary	5.1
26	Norway	5.0
27	Japan	5.0
28	Germany	5.0
29	United States	4.9
30	Hong Kong SAR	4.8
31	Sri Lanka	4.8
32	Spain	4.7
33	Croatia	4.6
34	Korea	4.5
35	Romania	4.5
36	Lithuania	4.5
37	Latvia	4.4
38	Portugal	4.3
39	Poland	4.3
40	Trinidad and Tobago	4.2
41	Bulgaria	4.2
42	Costa Rica	4.1
43	Botswana	4.1
44	Uruguay	4.0
45	Russian Federation	4.0
46	Mauritius	3.9
47	Thailand	3.7
48	Namibia	3.5
49	Ukraine	3.4
50	South Africa	3.3
51	Turkey	3.3
52	Greece	3.3
53	Jamaica	3.3
54	China	3.2
55	Jordan	3.2
56	Vietnam	3.2
57	Morocco	3.1
58	Argentina	2.9
58	Brazil	2.9
60	Zimbabwe	2.8
61	Chile	2.8
62	Panama	2.7
63	Mexico	2.6
64	Colombia	2.5
65	Indonesia	2.4
66	Dominican Republic	2.3
67	Philippines	2.3
68	El Salvador	2.2
69	India	2.2
70	Bangladesh	2.1
71	Paraguay	2.0
72	Honduras	1.8
73	Bolivia	1.8
74	Nigeria	1.8
75	Peru	1.8
76	Venezuela	1.6
77	Ecuador	1.6
78	Haiti	1.6
79	Guatemala	1.5
80	Nicaragua	1.4

MEAN: 4.0

5.09 Difference in the quality of healthcare

The difference in the quality of the healthcare available to rich and poor people in your country is (1 = large, 7 = small)

RANK	COUNTRY	SCORE
1	Iceland	6.5
2	Denmark	6.4
3	Belgium	6.1
4	Finland	6.0
5	Netherlands	5.8
6	Austria	5.7
7	Canada	5.7
8	Switzerland	5.7
9	Japan	5.5
10	France	5.4
11	Norway	5.3
12	Hong Kong SAR	5.3
13	Taiwan	5.3
14	Czech Republic	5.2
15	Sweden	5.0
16	Israel	4.9
17	Slovenia	4.8
18	Singapore	4.8
19	Spain	4.7
20	Germany	4.6
21	Australia	4.5
22	Slovak Republic	4.3
23	New Zealand	4.2
24	Tunisia	4.1
25	Estonia	4.1
26	Korea	4.0
27	Italy	4.0
28	Malaysia	3.8
29	United States	3.7
30	Hungary	3.7
31	China	3.7
32	Sri Lanka	3.6
33	United Kingdom	3.5
34	Costa Rica	3.4
35	Croatia	3.4
36	Portugal	3.2
37	Botswana	3.1
38	Lithuania	3.0
39	Thailand	2.9
40	Poland	2.8
41	Vietnam	2.8
42	Mauritius	2.7
43	Greece	2.7
44	Ireland	2.6
45	Romania	2.6
46	Uruguay	2.6
47	Latvia	2.5
48	Bulgaria	2.5
49	Namibia	2.5
50	Jordan	2.4
51	Jamaica	2.3
52	Indonesia	2.2
53	Panama	2.1
54	Morocco	2.1
55	Dominican Republic	2.0
56	Trinidad and Tobago	1.9
57	Colombia	1.9
58	Chile	1.9
59	Russian Federation	1.8
60	Bolivia	1.8
61	Ukraine	1.7
62	Bangladesh	1.7
63	Mexico	1.7
64	Turkey	1.7
65	South Africa	1.7
66	Honduras	1.6
67	Peru	1.6
68	India	1.6
68	Philippines	1.6
70	Argentina	1.6
71	Paraguay	1.6
72	Brazil	1.5
73	El Salvador	1.5
74	Nicaragua	1.4
75	Venezuela	1.4
76	Zimbabwe	1.4
77	Guatemala	1.3
78	Nigeria	1.3
79	Ecuador	1.2
80	Haiti	1.1

MEAN: 3.2

5.10 Paved roads

Paved roads as a percentage of total roads, 1999

RANK	COUNTRY	HARD DATA
1	Austria	100.00
1	Czech Republic	100.00
1	Denmark	100.00
1	France	100.00
1	Hong Kong SAR	100.00
1	Israel	100.00
1	Italy	100.00
1	Jordan	100.00
1	Singapore	100.00
1	Slovenia	100.00
1	United Kingdom	100.00
12	Spain	99.00
13	Thailand	97.50
14	Ukraine	96.60
15	Mauritius	96.00
16	Sri Lanka	95.00
17	Ireland	94.10
18	Bulgaria	92.00
19	Greece	91.80
20	Lithuania	91.30
21	Netherlands	90.00
21	Uruguay	90.00
23	Slovak Republic	86.70
24	Portugal	86.00
25	Croatia	84.60
26	Belgium	78.20
27	Sweden	78.10
28	Malaysia	75.80
29	Norway	75.50
30	Korea	74.50
31	Jamaica	70.10
32	Russian Federation	67.40
33	Poland	65.60
34	Finland	64.50
35	Tunisia	63.80
36	New Zealand	61.90
37	United States	58.80
38	Morocco	56.30
39	Botswana	55.00
40	Romania	53.00
41	Trinidad and Tobago	51.10
42	Dominican Republic	49.40
43	Zimbabwe	47.40
44	Indonesia	46.30
45	Japan	46.00
46	India	45.70
47	Hungary	43.40
48	Latvia	38.60
49	Panama	34.60
50	Guatemala	34.50
51	Turkey	34.00
52	Venezuela	33.60
53	Mexico	32.80
54	Nigeria	30.90
55	Argentina	29.40
56	Iceland	28.10
57	Vietnam	25.10
58	Haiti	24.30
59	China	22.40
60	Costa Rica	22.00
61	Estonia	21.30
62	Honduras	20.40
63	South Africa	20.30
64	Philippines	20.00
65	El Salvador	19.80
66	Chile	18.90
66	Ecuador	18.90
68	Colombia	14.40
69	Namibia	13.60
70	Peru	12.80
71	Nicaragua	9.70
72	Bangladesh	9.53
73	Bolivia	6.40
74	Brazil	5.60
	Australia	N/A
	Canada	N/A
	Germany	N/A
	Paraguay	N/A
	Switzerland	N/A
	Taiwan	N/A

SOURCE: World Bank *World Development Indicators 2002*

5.11 Aircraft departures

Number of domestic and international takeoffs, 2000

RANK	COUNTRY	HARD DATA	
1	United States	8,766,300	
2	United Kingdom	871,700	
3	France	788,900	
4	Germany	743,400	
5	Brazil	723,200	
6	Japan	642,300	
7	Taiwan	586,560	
8	China	572,800	
9	Spain	479,200	
10	Italy	374,600	
11	Norway	363,300	
12	Australia	351,000	
13	Canada	315,500	
14	Russian Federation	314,600	
15	Mexico	291,200	
16	Switzerland	288,300	
17	Sweden	247,700	
18	Korea	226,900	
19	Belgium	225,800	
20	Netherlands	225,400	
21	New Zealand	215,200	
22	India	198,500	
23	Colombia	197,100	
24	Argentina	195,900	
25	Malaysia	169,300	
26	Indonesia	153,100	
27	Denmark	152,200	
28	Austria	148,100	
29	Ireland	145,900	
30	Venezuela	138,500	
31	Finland	125,100	
32	Turkey	114,000	
33	South Africa	110,400	
34	Portugal	110,200	
35	Thailand	101,600	
36	Greece	99,200	
37	Chile	87,900	
38	Hong Kong SAR	78,400	
39	Singapore	71,000	
40	Poland	49,100	
41	Peru	46,000	
42	Israel	45,400	
43	Morocco	44,500	
44	Philippines	44,000	
45	Czech Republic	39,500	
46	El Salvador	37,100	
47	Hungary	32,200	
48	Ukraine	28,100	
49	Vietnam	28,000	
50	Costa Rica	26,800	
51	Trinidad and Tobago	25,700	
52	Panama	25,200	
53	Jamaica	23,600	
54	Bolivia	21,600	
55	Romania	20,700	
56	Tunisia	19,900	
57	Croatia	17,000	
58	Ecuador	16,800	
59	Jordan	16,400	
60	Zimbabwe	14,000	
61	Iceland	12,400	
62	Mauritius	12,200	
63	Slovenia	12,100	
64	Bulgaria	11,600	
65	Lithuania	10,200	
66	Uruguay	9,400	
67	Estonia	9,200	
67	Nigeria	9,200	
69	Latvia	8,600	
70	Paraguay	7,600	
71	Botswana	6,700	
72	Bangladesh	6,300	
73	Namibia	5,800	
74	Sri Lanka	5,200	
75	Slovak Republic	3,100	
76	Nicaragua	500	
77	Dominican Republic	400	
	Guatemala	N/A	
	Haiti	N/A	
	Honduras	N/A	

SOURCES: World Bank *World Development Indicators 2002* and national sources

5.12 Total air transport passengers

Total aircraft passengers of air carriers registered in the country, in millions, 2000

RANK	COUNTRY	HARD DATA	
1	United States	655.65	
2	Japan	108.41	
3	United Kingdom	70.36	
4	China	61.89	
5	Germany	59.36	
6	France	51.93	
7	Taiwan	46.43	
8	Spain	39.56	
9	Korea	34.33	
10	Australia	32.22	
11	Brazil	31.84	
12	Italy	30.59	
13	Canada	25.78	
14	Mexico	21.00	
15	Netherlands	20.79	
16	Russian Federation	17.69	
17	Thailand	17.39	
18	India	17.34	
19	Switzerland	17.22	
20	Singapore	16.70	
21	Malaysia	16.56	
22	Norway	15.16	
23	Hong Kong SAR	14.39	
24	Ireland	14.01	
25	Sweden	13.35	
26	Turkey	11.51	
27	Belgium	10.74	
28	New Zealand	9.89	
29	Indonesia	9.48	
30	Argentina	9.26	
31	Colombia	8.54	
32	South Africa	8.00	
33	Austria	7.26	
34	Greece	7.10	
35	Portugal	6.56	
36	Finland	6.42	
37	Denmark	5.92	
38	Philippines	5.44	
39	Chile	5.17	
40	Venezuela	4.30	
41	Israel	4.07	
42	Morocco	3.67	
43	Vietnam	2.88	
44	Poland	2.37	
45	Czech Republic	2.23	
46	Peru	2.13	
47	Hungary	2.06	
48	El Salvador	1.96	
49	Jamaica	1.92	
50	Tunisia	1.91	
51	Bolivia	1.76	
51	Sri Lanka	1.76	
53	Iceland	1.43	
54	Bangladesh	1.33	
55	Jordan	1.28	
56	Trinidad and Tobago	1.25	
57	Romania	1.19	
58	Ecuador	1.18	
59	Panama	1.12	
60	Ukraine	0.96	
61	Mauritius	0.95	
62	Croatia	0.93	
63	Costa Rica	0.86	
64	Slovenia	0.63	
65	Uruguay	0.62	
66	Zimbabwe	0.61	
67	Bulgaria	0.51	
68	Nigeria	0.42	
69	Estonia	0.28	
69	Lithuania	0.28	
71	Paraguay	0.27	
72	Namibia	0.24	
73	Latvia	0.22	
74	Botswana	0.17	
75	Slovak Republic	0.12	
76	Nicaragua	0.06	
77	Dominican Republic	0.01	
	Guatemala	N/A	
	Haiti	N/A	
	Honduras	N/A	

SOURCES: World Bank *World Development Indicators 2002* and national sources

5.13 Total air transport freight

Total air transport freight in million tons per km, 2000

RANK	COUNTRY	HARD DATA
1	United States	30,130.7
2	Japan	8,549.4
3	Korea	7,773.6
4	Germany	7,128.4
5	Singapore	6,004.9
6	France	5,227.1
7	United Kingdom	5,160.9
8	Hong Kong SAR	4,840.7
9	Netherlands	4,254.1
10	China	3,900.1
11	Switzerland	1,936.6
12	Malaysia	1,863.8
13	Australia	1,860.2
14	Canada	1,806.3
15	Italy	1,748.4
16	Thailand	1,712.9
17	Brazil	1,523.3
18	Chile	1,312.0
19	Russian Federation	1,041.4
20	Belgium	1,016.4
21	Israel	885.7
22	Spain	871.5
23	New Zealand	817.1
24	South Africa	687.5
25	Colombia	595.4
26	India	544.8
27	Austria	444.0
28	Indonesia	422.6
29	Turkey	374.8
30	Mexico	317.9
31	Argentina	295.1
32	Sweden	289.3
33	Finland	265.8
34	Sri Lanka	255.7
35	Philippines	241.0
36	Portugal	224.6
37	Jordan	204.0
38	Norway	201.0
39	Denmark	198.9
40	Bangladesh	193.9
41	Mauritius	183.0
42	Ireland	167.6
43	Zimbabwe	159.4
44	Greece	129.2
45	Vietnam	116.3
46	Iceland	115.3
47	Costa Rica	79.0
48	Poland	75.9
49	Namibia	74.9
50	Morocco	62.5
51	Hungary	50.8
52	Jamaica	48.2
53	Peru	34.6
54	Venezuela	33.1
55	Czech Republic	31.9
56	El Salvador	31.2
57	Trinidad and Tobago	24.2
58	Panama	22.0
59	Tunisia	20.8
60	Bolivia	15.3
61	Ecuador	14.6
62	Uruguay	14.2
63	Romania	12.2
64	Ukraine	11.2
65	Nigeria	9.5
66	Bulgaria	5.8
67	Slovenia	3.9
68	Croatia	2.6
69	Lithuania	1.6
70	Estonia	1.4
71	Nicaragua	0.5
72	Latvia	0.4
73	Botswana	0.3
73	Slovak Republic	0.3
75	Dominican Republic	0.0
75	Paraguay	0.0
	Guatemala	N/A
	Haiti	N/A
	Honduras	N/A
	Taiwan	N/A

SOURCE: World Bank *World Development Indicators 2002*

5.14 Electric power

Electric power transmission and distribution losses as a percentage of output, 1999

RANK	COUNTRY	HARD DATA
1	Israel	3
1	Japan	3
1	Paraguay	3
4	Finland	4
4	Germany	4
4	Korea	4
4	Morocco	4
4	Singapore	4
9	Belgium	5
9	Chile	5
9	Denmark	5
9	Iceland	5
9	Netherlands	5
9	Slovenia	5
15	France	6
15	Switzerland	6
17	Canada	7
17	China	7
17	Greece	7
17	Italy	7
17	Slovak Republic	7
17	Sweden	7
23	Australia	8
23	Austria	8
23	Costa Rica	8
23	Czech Republic	8
23	Ireland	8
23	Malaysia	8
23	Norway	8
23	Portugal	8
23	South Africa	8
23	Thailand	8
23	Trinidad and Tobago	8
23	United Kingdom	8
23	United States	8
36	Jamaica	10
36	Lithuania	10
36	Poland	10
36	Spain	10
36	Tunisia	10
41	Jordan	11
41	Russian Federation	11
43	Indonesia	12
43	New Zealand	12
43	Peru	12
46	El Salvador	13
46	Hong Kong SAR	13
46	Hungary	13
46	Romania	13
50	Mexico	14
51	Argentina	15
51	Philippines	15
51	Vietnam	15
54	Bangladesh	16
55	Brazil	17
55	Bulgaria	17
55	Croatia	17
55	Zimbabwe	17
59	Bolivia	18
59	Estonia	18
59	Ukraine	18
62	Panama	19
62	Turkey	19
62	Uruguay	19
65	Guatemala	20
66	India	21
66	Sri Lanka	21
68	Honduras	22
69	Ecuador	23
69	Venezuela	23
71	Colombia	24
72	Nicaragua	26
73	Dominican Republic	27
73	Latvia	27
75	Nigeria	32
76	Haiti	53
	Botswana	N/A
	Mauritius	N/A
	Namibia	N/A
	Taiwan	N/A

SOURCE: World Bank *World Development Indicators 2002*

General Infrastructure

5.15 Health expenditure per capita

Health expenditure per capita in current US dollars, 1999 or most recent year

RANK	COUNTRY	HARD DATA
1	United States	4,271
2	Switzerland	3,857
3	Norway	3,182
4	Denmark	2,785
5	Iceland	2,701
6	Germany	2,697
7	France	2,288
8	Japan	2,243
9	Netherlands	2,173
10	Sweden	2,145
11	Belgium	2,137
12	Austria	2,121
13	Canada	1,939
14	Australia	1,714
15	Finland	1,704
16	Italy	1,676
17	United Kingdom	1,675
18	Israel	1,607
19	Ireland	1,569
20	New Zealand	1,163
21	Spain	1,043
22	Greece	965
23	Portugal	859
24	Slovenia	746
25	Singapore	678
26	Argentina	654
27	Taiwan	650
28	Uruguay	621
29	Korea	470
30	Czech Republic	380
31	Hungary	318
32	Brazil	308
33	Chile	289
34	Slovak Republic	285
35	Costa Rica	257
36	Poland	248
37	Panama	246
38	Estonia	243
39	Mexico	236
40	South Africa	230
41	Colombia	227
42	Trinidad and Tobago	204
43	Lithuania	183
44	Venezuela	171
45	Latvia	166
46	Jamaica	157
47	Turkey	153
48	El Salvador	143
49	Namibia	142
50	Peru	141
51	Jordan	139
52	Botswana	127
53	Mauritius	120
54	Thailand	112
55	Tunisia	108
56	Dominican Republic	95
57	Paraguay	86
57	Romania	86
59	Malaysia	81
60	Guatemala	78
61	Honduras	74
62	Bolivia	69
63	Bulgaria	62
64	Ecuador	59
65	Nicaragua	54
66	China	40
67	Philippines	37
68	Zimbabwe	36
69	Nigeria	30
70	Sri Lanka	29
71	Ukraine	28
72	Haiti	21
73	Vietnam	17
74	Bangladesh	12
75	Indonesia	8
	Croatia	N/A
	Hong Kong SAR	N/A
	India	N/A
	Morocco	N/A
	Russian Federation	N/A

SOURCES: World Bank *World Development Indicators 2002* and national sources

5.16 Hospital beds

Hospital beds per 1,000 people, 1999 or most recent year

RANK	COUNTRY	HARD DATA
1	Switzerland	18.10
2	Japan	16.40
3	Iceland	14.80
4	Norway	14.40
5	Russian Federation	12.10
6	Netherlands	11.30
7	Latvia	10.30
8	Lithuania	9.40
9	Germany	9.30
10	Austria	8.70
10	Czech Republic	8.70
12	Bulgaria	8.60
13	Australia	8.50
13	France	8.50
15	Hungary	8.30
16	Romania	7.56
17	Finland	7.50
18	Estonia	7.40
19	Belgium	7.30
20	Slovak Republic	7.10
21	New Zealand	6.20
22	Taiwan	5.70
23	Italy	5.50
23	Korea	5.50
25	Trinidad and Tobago	5.11
26	Poland	5.10
27	Greece	5.00
28	Denmark	4.50
29	Uruguay	4.39
30	Canada	4.10
30	United Kingdom	4.10
32	Portugal	4.00
33	Spain	3.90
34	Ireland	3.70
34	Sweden	3.70
36	United States	3.60
37	Argentina	3.29
38	Brazil	3.11
39	Chile	2.67
40	Turkey	2.60
41	China	2.39
42	Panama	2.21
43	Jamaica	2.12
44	Malaysia	2.01
45	Jordan	1.80
46	Tunisia	1.70
47	Costa Rica	1.68
48	Bolivia	1.67
48	Vietnam	1.67
50	El Salvador	1.65
51	Ecuador	1.55
52	Dominican Republic	1.50
53	Nicaragua	1.48
54	Peru	1.47
54	Venezuela	1.47
56	Colombia	1.46
57	Paraguay	1.34
58	Mexico	1.10
59	Honduras	1.06
60	Guatemala	0.98
60	Morocco	0.98
62	Haiti	0.71
	Israel	N/A
	Bangladesh	N/A
	Botswana	N/A
	Croatia	N/A
	Hong Kong SAR	N/A
	India	N/A
	Indonesia	N/A
	Mauritius	N/A
	Namibia	N/A
	Nigeria	N/A
	Philippines	N/A
	Singapore	N/A
	Slovenia	N/A
	South Africa	N/A
	Sri Lanka	N/A
	Thailand	N/A
	Ukraine	N/A
	Zimbabwe	N/A

SOURCES: World Bank *World Development Indicators 2002* and national sources

600

6.01 Judicial independence

The judiciary in your country is independent from political influences of members of government, citizens or firms (1 = no, heavily influenced, 7 = yes, entirely independent)

RANK	COUNTRY	SCORE
1	Australia	6.6
2	Denmark	6.6
3	New Zealand	6.5
4	Netherlands	6.4
5	Finland	6.3
6	Canada	6.3
7	United Kingdom	6.2
8	Iceland	6.2
9	Germany	6.2
10	Ireland	6.0
11	Portugal	6.0
12	Austria	6.0
13	Israel	5.9
14	Hong Kong SAR	5.8
15	Norway	5.8
16	United States	5.7
17	Switzerland	5.7
18	Botswana	5.6
19	Sweden	5.6
20	South Africa	5.6
21	Uruguay	5.2
22	Trinidad and Tobago	5.2
23	Namibia	5.2
24	India	5.2
25	Singapore	5.1
26	Slovenia	5.0
27	Tunisia	5.0
28	Sri Lanka	4.9
29	Mauritius	4.9
30	Japan	4.9
31	Belgium	4.7
32	Estonia	4.7
33	Thailand	4.6
34	Costa Rica	4.5
35	Italy	4.5
36	Greece	4.5
37	Jamaica	4.4
38	Hungary	4.4
39	China	4.4
40	France	4.3
41	Korea	4.3
42	Jordan	4.3
43	Chile	4.2
44	Malaysia	4.2
45	Brazil	4.2
46	Spain	4.1
47	Taiwan	4.0
48	Czech Republic	3.9
49	Poland	3.7
50	Latvia	3.5
51	Philippines	3.4
52	Colombia	3.4
53	Vietnam	3.3
54	Morocco	3.3
55	Dominican Republic	3.3
56	Bangladesh	3.2
57	Slovak Republic	3.2
58	Lithuania	3.1
59	Nigeria	3.1
60	Turkey	3.0
61	El Salvador	3.0
62	Bulgaria	2.9
63	Croatia	2.9
64	Mexico	2.8
65	Romania	2.7
66	Russian Federation	2.5
67	Indonesia	2.5
68	Panama	2.5
69	Peru	2.3
70	Ukraine	2.2
71	Guatemala	2.0
71	Honduras	2.0
71	Paraguay	2.0
74	Nicaragua	1.9
75	Zimbabwe	1.8
76	Bolivia	1.8
77	Argentina	1.6
78	Ecuador	1.6
79	Venezuela	1.3
80	Haiti	1.3

MEAN: 4.2

6.02 Efficiency of legal framework

The legal framework in your country for private businesses to settle disputes and challenge the legality of government actions and/or regulations (1 = is inefficient and subject to manipulation, 7 = is efficient and follows a clear, neutral process)

RANK	COUNTRY	SCORE
1	Finland	6.2
2	Denmark	6.2
3	Australia	6.1
4	Hong Kong SAR	6.1
5	Israel	6.1
6	United Kingdom	6.1
7	Switzerland	6.1
8	Germany	6.0
9	New Zealand	6.0
10	Netherlands	5.9
11	Iceland	5.8
12	United States	5.8
13	Canada	5.8
14	Sweden	5.8
15	Austria	5.8
16	Singapore	5.7
17	South Africa	5.4
18	Ireland	5.3
19	Norway	5.3
20	Namibia	5.1
21	Botswana	5.1
22	Tunisia	5.0
23	Belgium	4.9
24	Malaysia	4.8
25	Sri Lanka	4.6
26	Trinidad and Tobago	4.6
27	Mauritius	4.6
28	India	4.5
29	Estonia	4.5
30	France	4.5
31	China	4.4
32	Costa Rica	4.3
33	Korea	4.3
34	Slovenia	4.3
35	Chile	4.2
36	Portugal	4.2
37	Hungary	4.2
38	Japan	4.2
39	Spain	4.2
40	Uruguay	4.1
41	Taiwan	4.1
42	Jamaica	4.0
43	Greece	4.0
44	Thailand	3.9
45	Morocco	3.9
46	Jordan	3.9
47	Italy	3.8
48	Brazil	3.7
49	Vietnam	3.5
50	Latvia	3.4
51	Colombia	3.4
52	El Salvador	3.4
53	Czech Republic	3.3
54	Poland	3.3
55	Slovak Republic	3.1
56	Mexico	3.1
57	Dominican Republic	3.0
57	Nigeria	3.0
59	Panama	2.9
60	Lithuania	2.9
61	Peru	2.8
62	Philippines	2.8
63	Bulgaria	2.7
64	Turkey	2.7
65	Croatia	2.7
66	Bangladesh	2.6
67	Romania	2.6
68	Russian Federation	2.6
69	Zimbabwe	2.4
70	Indonesia	2.3
71	Nicaragua	2.3
72	Bolivia	2.3
73	Ukraine	2.3
74	Honduras	2.2
75	Paraguay	2.2
76	Guatemala	2.1
77	Argentina	1.8
78	Ecuador	1.8
79	Haiti	1.5
80	Venezuela	1.5

MEAN: 4.0

6.03 Property rights

Financial assets and wealth (1 = are poorly delineated and not protected by law, 7 = are clearly delineated and well protected by law)

RANK	COUNTRY	SCORE
1	Finland	6.7
2	Switzerland	6.5
3	Iceland	6.5
4	Germany	6.5
5	Austria	6.4
6	Denmark	6.3
7	United States	6.3
8	Singapore	6.3
9	United Kingdom	6.3
10	Netherlands	6.2
11	Australia	6.2
12	Hong Kong SAR	6.1
13	New Zealand	6.0
14	Canada	6.0
15	Belgium	5.9
16	Ireland	5.8
17	Israel	5.7
18	Norway	5.7
19	Sweden	5.5
20	Hungary	5.5
21	South Africa	5.5
22	Uruguay	5.5
23	Portugal	5.5
24	Botswana	5.5
25	Malaysia	5.4
26	Chile	5.4
27	Korea	5.4
28	Tunisia	5.4
29	Mauritius	5.4
30	Taiwan	5.3
31	Namibia	5.3
32	Jordan	5.3
33	Japan	5.2
34	Spain	5.2
35	France	5.1
36	Italy	5.0
37	Thailand	5.0
38	Slovenia	5.0
39	Trinidad and Tobago	4.9
40	Jamaica	4.9
41	Panama	4.8
42	India	4.8
43	Greece	4.8
44	Brazil	4.8
45	Estonia	4.8
46	Costa Rica	4.8
47	Morocco	4.3
48	Colombia	4.3
49	Lithuania	4.2
50	Turkey	4.2
51	Poland	4.1
52	Slovak Republic	4.1
53	El Salvador	4.1
54	China	4.1
55	Latvia	4.0
56	Mexico	4.0
57	Sri Lanka	4.0
58	Nigeria	3.9
59	Czech Republic	3.8
60	Vietnam	3.8
61	Peru	3.8
62	Philippines	3.7
63	Dominican Republic	3.7
64	Bangladesh	3.5
65	Paraguay	3.3
66	Indonesia	3.2
67	Honduras	3.2
68	Croatia	3.1
69	Bulgaria	3.1
70	Bolivia	3.1
71	Guatemala	2.9
72	Romania	2.9
73	Ecuador	2.8
74	Nicaragua	2.7
75	Russian Federation	2.6
76	Venezuela	2.6
77	Zimbabwe	2.6
78	Ukraine	2.2
79	Haiti	2.0
80	Argentina	1.9

MEAN: 4.7

6.04 Intellectual property protection

Intellectual property protection in your country (1 = is weak or nonexistent, 7 = is equal to the world's most stringent)

RANK	COUNTRY	SCORE
1	United States	6.4
2	United Kingdom	6.4
3	Finland	6.2
4	Netherlands	6.1
5	Austria	6.1
6	Australia	6.0
7	Switzerland	6.0
8	Sweden	6.0
9	Denmark	6.0
10	Germany	5.9
11	Canada	5.8
12	Singapore	5.7
13	Belgium	5.7
14	Iceland	5.6
15	France	5.6
16	New Zealand	5.3
17	Hong Kong SAR	5.2
18	Israel	5.1
19	South Africa	5.0
20	Norway	5.0
21	Ireland	4.9
22	Tunisia	4.9
23	Italy	4.8
24	Slovenia	4.8
25	Portugal	4.6
26	Hungary	4.6
27	Taiwan	4.6
28	Spain	4.6
29	Korea	4.5
30	Czech Republic	4.4
31	Estonia	4.4
32	Japan	4.4
33	Malaysia	4.4
34	Namibia	4.4
35	Jordan	4.1
36	Chile	4.0
37	Sri Lanka	4.0
38	Thailand	4.0
39	Botswana	3.9
40	Brazil	3.9
41	Greece	3.8
42	El Salvador	3.8
43	Trinidad and Tobago	3.8
44	Costa Rica	3.7
45	China	3.6
46	Slovak Republic	3.6
47	Colombia	3.6
48	Panama	3.6
49	Mauritius	3.5
50	Uruguay	3.4
51	India	3.4
52	Morocco	3.4
53	Poland	3.4
54	Jamaica	3.4
55	Dominican Republic	3.3
56	Latvia	3.2
57	Lithuania	3.2
58	Mexico	3.0
59	Zimbabwe	3.0
60	Croatia	3.0
61	Bulgaria	2.9
62	Guatemala	2.8
63	Turkey	2.7
64	Philippines	2.7
65	Romania	2.6
66	Peru	2.6
67	Argentina	2.5
68	Honduras	2.5
69	Russian Federation	2.4
70	Nicaragua	2.4
71	Nigeria	2.4
72	Indonesia	2.4
73	Vietnam	2.3
74	Venezuela	2.3
75	Paraguay	2.3
76	Ecuador	2.2
77	Bangladesh	2.1
78	Ukraine	2.1
79	Bolivia	1.8
80	Haiti	1.5

MEAN: 4.0

6.05 Freedom of the press

In your country, can newspapers publish stories of their choosing without fear of censorship or retaliation? (1 = no, 7 = yes, whatever they want)

RANK	COUNTRY	SCORE
1	Sweden	7.0
2	Finland	6.9
3	Denmark	6.9
4	Netherlands	6.9
5	Germany	6.8
6	Austria	6.7
7	Norway	6.7
8	United States	6.7
9	Australia	6.6
10	Switzerland	6.6
11	Portugal	6.5
12	Belgium	6.5
12	Canada	6.5
14	United Kingdom	6.5
15	Iceland	6.4
16	New Zealand	6.4
17	Uruguay	6.3
18	Greece	6.3
19	France	6.1
19	Philippines	6.1
21	Hong Kong SAR	6.1
22	Spain	6.1
23	Japan	6.1
24	Brazil	6.1
25	Estonia	6.0
26	Italy	6.0
27	Mauritius	6.0
28	India	6.0
29	Czech Republic	6.0
30	Jamaica	5.9
31	Israel	5.9
32	El Salvador	5.9
33	South Africa	5.8
34	Slovak Republic	5.8
35	Ireland	5.7
36	Paraguay	5.7
37	Indonesia	5.7
38	Argentina	5.6
39	Slovenia	5.6
40	Costa Rica	5.6
41	Hungary	5.6
42	Taiwan	5.5
43	Trinidad and Tobago	5.5
44	Lithuania	5.5
45	Romania	5.5
46	Peru	5.5
47	Mexico	5.4
48	Poland	5.4
49	Bolivia	5.3
50	Honduras	5.3
51	Nicaragua	5.2
52	Namibia	5.2
53	Korea	5.2
54	Chile	5.2
55	Nigeria	5.2
56	Latvia	5.2
57	Dominican Republic	5.1
58	Panama	5.1
59	Botswana	5.0
60	Colombia	4.8
61	Croatia	4.8
62	Ecuador	4.8
63	Bangladesh	4.8
64	Bulgaria	4.7
65	Thailand	4.5
66	Guatemala	4.4
67	Russian Federation	4.4
68	Sri Lanka	4.0
69	Haiti	3.9
70	Turkey	3.9
71	Tunisia	3.9
72	Singapore	3.5
73	Malaysia	3.5
74	Vietnam	3.3
75	China	3.3
76	Jordan	3.3
77	Venezuela	3.2
78	Morocco	3.2
79	Ukraine	2.8
80	Zimbabwe	2.5

MEAN: 5.4

6.06 Competence of public officials

The competence of personnel in the civil service is (1 = lower than the private sector, 7 = higher than the private sector)

RANK	COUNTRY	SCORE
1	Singapore	5.1
2	Sri Lanka	4.5
3	China	4.1
4	United Kingdom	4.0
5	Japan	4.0
6	Canada	3.8
7	Israel	3.8
8	Finland	3.8
9	Hong Kong SAR	3.7
10	Switzerland	3.7
11	Ireland	3.6
12	Denmark	3.5
13	Australia	3.5
14	Vietnam	3.5
15	New Zealand	3.5
16	Netherlands	3.4
17	Tunisia	3.4
18	Taiwan	3.4
19	Austria	3.3
19	Estonia	3.3
21	France	3.2
22	Sweden	3.2
23	Malaysia	3.1
24	Korea	3.1
25	United States	3.1
26	Latvia	3.1
27	Hungary	3.0
28	Norway	3.0
29	Iceland	3.0
29	Slovenia	3.0
31	Morocco	3.0
32	Botswana	2.9
33	Lithuania	2.9
34	Belgium	2.9
35	Bulgaria	2.8
36	India	2.8
37	Thailand	2.8
38	Spain	2.7
39	Czech Republic	2.7
40	Germany	2.7
41	Jamaica	2.6
42	Mexico	2.6
43	Trinidad and Tobago	2.6
44	Nicaragua	2.5
45	El Salvador	2.5
46	Bangladesh	2.4
47	Italy	2.4
48	Mauritius	2.4
49	Brazil	2.4
50	Jordan	2.4
51	Portugal	2.4
52	Croatia	2.3
53	Slovak Republic	2.3
54	Poland	2.3
55	Chile	2.3
56	Namibia	2.3
57	South Africa	2.2
58	Dominican Republic	2.2
59	Ukraine	2.2
60	Greece	2.2
61	Honduras	2.2
62	Russian Federation	2.2
63	Haiti	2.1
64	Costa Rica	2.1
65	Nigeria	2.1
66	Colombia	2.1
67	Indonesia	2.1
68	Philippines	2.0
69	Romania	2.0
70	Peru	2.0
71	Turkey	1.8
72	Bolivia	1.8
73	Uruguay	1.7
74	Zimbabwe	1.7
75	Panama	1.7
76	Ecuador	1.6
77	Paraguay	1.5
78	Guatemala	1.5
79	Venezuela	1.4
80	Argentina	1.4

MEAN: 2.7

6.07 Burden of regulation

Administrative regulations in your country are (1 = burdensome, 7 = not burdensome)

RANK	COUNTRY	SCORE
1	Hong Kong SAR	5.1
2	Singapore	5.0
3	Sri Lanka	4.6
4	Finland	4.4
5	Iceland	4.3
6	Tunisia	4.2
7	Estonia	4.1
8	Ireland	3.7
9	United Kingdom	3.6
10	Switzerland	3.6
11	Canada	3.5
12	Namibia	3.5
13	Malaysia	3.5
14	Taiwan	3.5
15	El Salvador	3.4
16	United States	3.4
17	Botswana	3.4
18	China	3.3
19	Hungary	3.3
20	Spain	3.3
21	Chile	3.2
22	Australia	3.2
23	New Zealand	3.2
24	Denmark	3.1
25	Dominican Republic	3.1
26	Morocco	3.0
27	Korea	3.0
28	Thailand	3.0
29	Austria	3.0
30	Latvia	3.0
31	South Africa	3.0
32	Israel	2.9
33	Sweden	2.9
34	Jordan	2.8
35	Slovenia	2.8
36	Lithuania	2.8
37	Netherlands	2.8
38	Paraguay	2.7
39	Trinidad and Tobago	2.7
40	Portugal	2.7
41	Brazil	2.7
42	Norway	2.7
43	Bulgaria	2.7
44	Czech Republic	2.6
44	Greece	2.6
46	Russian Federation	2.5
47	Panama	2.5
48	Poland	2.5
49	Haiti	2.5
50	Nicaragua	2.4
51	France	2.4
52	Germany	2.3
53	Japan	2.3
54	Jamaica	2.3
55	Belgium	2.3
56	Vietnam	2.3
57	Mexico	2.3
58	Peru	2.3
59	Colombia	2.3
60	Italy	2.2
61	India	2.2
62	Costa Rica	2.2
63	Croatia	2.2
64	Slovak Republic	2.1
65	Mauritius	2.1
66	Guatemala	2.1
67	Uruguay	2.1
68	Bolivia	2.0
69	Bangladesh	2.0
69	Turkey	2.0
69	Zimbabwe	2.0
72	Ukraine	2.0
73	Philippines	2.0
74	Nigeria	1.9
75	Honduras	1.9
76	Indonesia	1.8
77	Ecuador	1.8
78	Venezuela	1.7
79	Argentina	1.7
80	Romania	1.6

MEAN: 2.8

6.08 Transparency of government policymaking

Firms in your country are usually informed clearly and transparently by the government on changes in policies and regulations affecting your industry (1 = never informed, 7 = always fully and clearly informed)

RANK	COUNTRY	SCORE
1	Singapore	5.9
2	Finland	5.5
3	Iceland	5.3
4	Israel	5.3
5	United Kingdom	5.2
6	United States	5.2
7	Tunisia	5.2
8	Hong Kong SAR	5.1
9	Austria	4.9
10	Canada	4.9
11	Netherlands	4.9
12	Denmark	4.8
13	New Zealand	4.8
14	Australia	4.8
15	Switzerland	4.8
16	Taiwan	4.8
17	Sri Lanka	4.7
18	Botswana	4.7
19	Germany	4.7
20	Malaysia	4.6
21	Chile	4.5
22	Ireland	4.5
23	Namibia	4.5
24	Sweden	4.4
25	South Africa	4.4
26	Morocco	4.2
27	Slovenia	4.2
28	Norway	4.2
29	Thailand	4.1
30	Korea	4.1
31	China	4.1
32	Estonia	4.1
33	Hungary	4.0
34	Vietnam	3.9
35	Spain	3.9
36	Trinidad and Tobago	3.8
37	France	3.8
38	Portugal	3.8
39	Mauritius	3.8
40	Czech Republic	3.7
41	El Salvador	3.7
42	Jamaica	3.7
43	Belgium	3.7
44	Lithuania	3.6
45	Japan	3.6
46	India	3.5
47	Nigeria	3.5
48	Colombia	3.5
49	Latvia	3.5
50	Italy	3.5
51	Costa Rica	3.5
52	Indonesia	3.4
53	Brazil	3.4
54	Uruguay	3.4
55	Jordan	3.3
56	Philippines	3.3
57	Dominican Republic	3.3
58	Greece	3.3
59	Croatia	3.1
60	Turkey	3.1
61	Panama	3.1
62	Mexico	3.1
63	Slovak Republic	3.0
64	Bolivia	3.0
65	Peru	3.0
66	Honduras	2.9
67	Bangladesh	2.9
68	Poland	2.8
69	Ecuador	2.6
70	Russian Federation	2.6
71	Haiti	2.5
72	Zimbabwe	2.4
73	Paraguay	2.4
74	Ukraine	2.4
75	Bulgaria	2.4
76	Nicaragua	2.3
77	Guatemala	2.1
78	Romania	2.1
79	Argentina	2.1
80	Venezuela	2.0

MEAN: 3.8

605

6.09 Favoritism in decisions of government officials

When deciding upon policies and contracts, government officials (1 = usually favor well-connected firms and individuals, 7 = are neutral among firms and individuals)

MEAN: 3.3

RANK	COUNTRY	SCORE
1	Denmark	5.6
2	Finland	5.5
3	Singapore	5.2
4	Australia	5.1
5	Iceland	4.9
6	New Zealand	4.8
7	Tunisia	4.8
8	United Kingdom	4.7
9	Switzerland	4.7
10	Sri Lanka	4.5
11	Austria	4.5
12	Netherlands	4.4
13	Belgium	4.4
14	United States	4.3
15	Hong Kong SAR	4.3
16	Norway	4.3
17	Canada	4.2
18	Chile	4.2
19	Germany	4.1
20	Taiwan	4.1
21	Sweden	4.1
22	France	4.0
22	Israel	4.0
24	Morocco	4.0
25	Botswana	3.8
26	Portugal	3.8
27	Japan	3.7
28	Ireland	3.7
29	China	3.7
30	Korea	3.7
31	Uruguay	3.6
32	Slovenia	3.6
33	Brazil	3.6
34	Estonia	3.6
35	Lithuania	3.5
36	Spain	3.4
37	Namibia	3.4
38	Malaysia	3.3
39	South Africa	3.3
40	Jordan	3.3
41	Mauritius	3.3
42	Italy	3.2
43	Hungary	3.1
44	Mexico	3.1
45	El Salvador	3.1
46	Thailand	3.1
47	India	3.1
48	Latvia	3.1
49	Vietnam	3.1
50	Greece	3.0
51	Costa Rica	3.0
52	Turkey	2.9
53	Ukraine	2.9
54	Jamaica	2.8
55	Trinidad and Tobago	2.8
56	Czech Republic	2.8
57	Croatia	2.8
58	Bulgaria	2.7
59	Peru	2.7
60	Poland	2.6
61	Colombia	2.6
62	Russian Federation	2.6
63	Slovak Republic	2.5
64	Dominican Republic	2.5
65	Indonesia	2.4
66	Bangladesh	2.3
67	Nigeria	2.2
67	Venezuela	2.2
69	Panama	2.2
70	Philippines	2.1
71	Romania	2.1
72	Argentina	1.9
73	Honduras	1.9
74	Bolivia	1.9
75	Zimbabwe	1.9
76	Nicaragua	1.8
77	Haiti	1.7
78	Ecuador	1.7
79	Paraguay	1.6
80	Guatemala	1.6

6.10 Extent of bureaucratic red tape

How much time does your firm's senior management spend dealing/negotiating with government officials? (as a percentage of work time) (1 = 0%, 2 = 1–10%, 3 = 11–20%, 8 = 81–100%)

MEAN: 2.8

RANK	COUNTRY	SCORE
1	Romania	1.8
2	Croatia	1.9
3	Japan	2.0
4	Norway	2.1
5	Finland	2.1
6	Denmark	2.1
7	Haiti	2.1
8	Switzerland	2.1
9	Iceland	2.1
10	Slovak Republic	2.2
11	Spain	2.2
11	United Kingdom	2.2
13	Nicaragua	2.2
14	El Salvador	2.2
15	Italy	2.3
16	New Zealand	2.3
17	Tunisia	2.3
18	Hungary	2.4
19	Singapore	2.4
20	United States	2.4
21	Turkey	2.4
22	Australia	2.4
23	Germany	2.4
24	France	2.5
25	Slovenia	2.5
26	Chile	2.5
27	Korea	2.5
28	Brazil	2.5
29	Colombia	2.6
30	Panama	2.6
31	Czech Republic	2.6
32	Poland	2.6
33	Austria	2.6
34	Canada	2.6
35	Paraguay	2.6
36	Hong Kong SAR	2.6
37	Malaysia	2.7
38	Peru	2.7
39	Mauritius	2.7
40	Greece	2.7
40	Sweden	2.7
42	Uruguay	2.7
43	Zimbabwe	2.7
44	Taiwan	2.7
45	Dominican Republic	2.7
46	Ecuador	2.8
47	Lithuania	2.8
48	Morocco	2.8
49	Honduras	2.8
50	Netherlands	2.8
51	Jamaica	2.8
52	Costa Rica	2.9
53	South Africa	2.9
54	Ireland	2.9
55	Venezuela	2.9
56	Namibia	2.9
57	China	3.0
58	Philippines	3.0
59	Argentina	3.0
60	Trinidad and Tobago	3.1
61	Guatemala	3.1
62	Portugal	3.1
63	Estonia	3.1
64	Bolivia	3.3
65	Vietnam	3.3
66	Mexico	3.3
67	India	3.3
68	Bulgaria	3.4
69	Sri Lanka	3.4
70	Latvia	3.4
71	Botswana	3.5
72	Russian Federation	3.5
73	Jordan	3.6
74	Belgium	3.6
75	Israel	3.6
76	Bangladesh	3.7
77	Ukraine	3.7
78	Nigeria	3.8
79	Thailand	3.8
80	Indonesia	4.4

6.11 Effectiveness of law-making bodies

How effective is your national Parliament/Congress as a law-making and oversight institution? (1 = very ineffective, 7 = very effective—the best in the world)

RANK	COUNTRY	SCORE	MEAN: 3.4
1	Singapore	6.0	
2	United States	5.3	
3	United Kingdom	5.3	
4	Australia	5.3	
5	Iceland	5.1	
6	Finland	5.1	
7	Denmark	5.1	
8	Canada	5.0	
9	Malaysia	4.9	
10	China	4.8	
11	Switzerland	4.6	
12	Austria	4.6	
13	New Zealand	4.5	
14	Botswana	4.5	
15	Ireland	4.4	
16	Germany	4.3	
17	Spain	4.3	
18	Sri Lanka	4.3	
19	Sweden	4.3	
20	Israel	4.2	
21	Norway	4.2	
22	Tunisia	4.1	
23	Netherlands	4.1	
24	Mauritius	4.1	
25	Hong Kong SAR	4.1	
26	South Africa	4.0	
27	Namibia	4.0	
28	Estonia	3.9	
29	Hungary	3.9	
30	Italy	3.9	
31	India	3.8	
32	Thailand	3.7	
33	Taiwan	3.7	
34	Portugal	3.6	
35	Belgium	3.6	
36	Jamaica	3.6	
37	Chile	3.6	
38	Turkey	3.5	
39	France	3.5	
40	Slovenia	3.5	
41	Vietnam	3.5	
42	Japan	3.4	
43	Trinidad and Tobago	3.4	
44	Jordan	3.3	
45	Latvia	3.2	
46	Greece	3.2	
47	Morocco	3.2	
48	Brazil	3.2	
49	Czech Republic	3.1	
50	Lithuania	3.0	
51	Russian Federation	2.9	
52	Poland	2.9	
53	Korea	2.9	
54	Indonesia	2.9	
55	Croatia	2.8	
56	Bangladesh	2.8	
57	Uruguay	2.6	
58	Philippines	2.6	
59	Bulgaria	2.5	
60	Dominican Republic	2.5	
61	Honduras	2.5	
62	Nigeria	2.5	
63	Slovak Republic	2.4	
64	Peru	2.3	
65	El Salvador	2.3	
66	Romania	2.2	
67	Colombia	2.2	
68	Mexico	2.2	
69	Ukraine	2.1	
70	Costa Rica	2.0	
71	Bolivia	2.0	
72	Panama	2.0	
73	Nicaragua	1.9	
74	Zimbabwe	1.8	
75	Paraguay	1.7	
76	Guatemala	1.6	
77	Ecuador	1.5	
78	Venezuela	1.5	
79	Argentina	1.4	
80	Haiti	1.2	

6.12 Efficiency of the tax system

Your country's tax system is (1 = highly complex and distortive on business decisions, 7 = simple and transparent)

RANK	COUNTRY	SCORE	MEAN: 3.2
1	Hong Kong SAR	6.6	
2	Singapore	5.8	
3	Botswana	5.6	
4	Estonia	5.5	
5	Tunisia	5.0	
6	Iceland	4.9	
7	Malaysia	4.8	
8	Trinidad and Tobago	4.7	
9	Mauritius	4.7	
10	Namibia	4.7	
11	Ireland	4.7	
12	El Salvador	4.4	
13	Jamaica	4.4	
14	Switzerland	4.4	
15	Sri Lanka	4.2	
16	Chile	4.2	
17	New Zealand	4.1	
18	China	4.1	
19	South Africa	4.1	
20	Finland	4.1	
21	Taiwan	4.1	
22	United Kingdom	4.0	
23	Thailand	4.0	
24	Netherlands	3.8	
25	Hungary	3.5	
26	Jordan	3.5	
27	Slovenia	3.5	
28	Spain	3.5	
29	Paraguay	3.4	
30	Croatia	3.4	
31	Morocco	3.3	
32	United States	3.3	
33	Portugal	3.2	
34	Canada	3.2	
35	India	3.2	
36	Korea	3.2	
37	Panama	3.2	
38	Haiti	3.1	
39	Latvia	3.0	
40	Norway	2.9	
41	Austria	2.9	
42	Zimbabwe	2.9	
43	Costa Rica	2.8	
44	Nigeria	2.8	
45	Bolivia	2.8	
46	Greece	2.7	
47	Japan	2.6	
48	Peru	2.6	
49	Dominican Republic	2.6	
50	Philippines	2.6	
51	Slovak Republic	2.6	
52	Israel	2.6	
53	Honduras	2.6	
54	Bangladesh	2.5	
55	Colombia	2.5	
56	Poland	2.5	
57	Vietnam	2.5	
58	Australia	2.4	
59	Czech Republic	2.4	
59	Nicaragua	2.4	
61	Uruguay	2.3	
62	Lithuania	2.3	
63	Sweden	2.3	
64	Italy	2.3	
65	Russian Federation	2.3	
66	Indonesia	2.3	
67	Belgium	2.2	
67	France	2.2	
69	Denmark	2.2	
70	Bulgaria	2.2	
71	Venezuela	2.2	
72	Guatemala	2.1	
73	Mexico	2.1	
74	Ecuador	2.0	
75	Germany	2.0	
76	Turkey	1.9	
77	Brazil	1.8	
78	Ukraine	1.7	
79	Argentina	1.5	
80	Romania	1.4	

6.13 Reliability of police services

Police services (1 = cannot be relied upon to protect businesses from criminals, 7 = can be relied upon to protect businesses from criminals)

RANK	COUNTRY	SCORE
1	Finland	6.6
2	Iceland	6.5
3	Denmark	6.5
4	Singapore	6.4
5	Austria	6.4
6	United States	6.2
7	Tunisia	6.2
8	Switzerland	5.9
9	Australia	5.9
10	Germany	5.9
11	Hong Kong SAR	5.8
12	Canada	5.8
13	New Zealand	5.8
14	Norway	5.7
15	Sweden	5.7
16	Israel	5.7
17	Chile	5.7
18	United Kingdom	5.7
19	Jordan	5.5
20	Spain	5.4
21	Ireland	5.3
22	Japan	5.3
23	Belgium	5.1
23	Korea	5.1
25	Netherlands	5.1
26	Portugal	5.1
27	Italy	5.1
28	Morocco	5.0
29	Malaysia	5.0
30	France	4.9
31	China	4.8
32	Thailand	4.8
33	Taiwan	4.7
34	Sri Lanka	4.7
35	Uruguay	4.7
36	Panama	4.6
37	Hungary	4.5
38	Slovenia	4.5
39	El Salvador	4.5
40	Czech Republic	4.3
41	Botswana	4.2
42	India	4.2
43	Estonia	4.2
44	Colombia	4.2
45	Vietnam	4.1
46	Costa Rica	4.0
47	Greece	4.0
48	Trinidad and Tobago	3.9
49	Turkey	3.8
50	Latvia	3.7
51	Mauritius	3.7
52	Croatia	3.7
53	Poland	3.5
54	Nicaragua	3.4
55	Peru	3.4
56	Dominican Republic	3.4
57	Brazil	3.4
58	Namibia	3.2
59	South Africa	3.2
60	Romania	3.1
61	Jamaica	3.1
62	Slovak Republic	3.1
63	Honduras	3.0
64	Russian Federation	2.9
65	Bulgaria	2.8
66	Lithuania	2.8
67	Philippines	2.8
68	Ukraine	2.7
69	Paraguay	2.7
70	Nigeria	2.7
71	Mexico	2.6
72	Venezuela	2.6
73	Argentina	2.5
74	Ecuador	2.5
75	Indonesia	2.4
76	Guatemala	2.2
77	Zimbabwe	2.2
78	Bolivia	2.2
79	Haiti	2.0
80	Bangladesh	2.0

MEAN: 4.3

6.14 Business costs of crime and violence

Common crime and violence (eg, street muggings, firms being looted) (1 = impose significant costs on businesses, 7 = do not impose significant costs on businesses)

RANK	COUNTRY	SCORE
1	Finland	6.6
2	Singapore	6.6
3	Israel	6.4
4	Iceland	6.4
5	Austria	6.4
6	Denmark	6.3
7	Germany	6.3
8	Hong Kong SAR	6.3
9	Switzerland	6.2
10	New Zealand	6.0
11	Portugal	6.0
12	Australia	5.9
12	Sweden	5.9
14	Tunisia	5.9
15	Slovenia	5.8
16	Jordan	5.7
17	Turkey	5.7
18	Norway	5.7
19	Canada	5.6
20	United States	5.5
21	Thailand	5.4
22	Greece	5.3
23	Taiwan	5.3
24	Japan	5.3
25	Hungary	5.3
26	Korea	5.3
27	India	5.1
28	Belgium	5.1
29	United Kingdom	5.0
30	Morocco	5.0
31	Malaysia	5.0
32	Ireland	4.9
33	China	4.9
34	Mauritius	4.9
35	Chile	4.9
36	Estonia	4.8
37	Uruguay	4.7
38	Czech Republic	4.7
39	Netherlands	4.7
40	Spain	4.7
41	Sri Lanka	4.6
42	Italy	4.4
43	Croatia	4.4
44	Slovak Republic	4.3
45	Botswana	4.3
46	Romania	4.3
47	Latvia	4.2
48	Panama	3.9
49	Vietnam	3.9
50	Poland	3.8
51	Lithuania	3.7
52	France	3.7
53	Bolivia	3.7
54	Nicaragua	3.6
55	Costa Rica	3.5
56	Dominican Republic	3.5
57	Trinidad and Tobago	3.4
58	Namibia	3.3
59	Russian Federation	3.2
60	Peru	3.2
61	Philippines	3.2
62	Indonesia	3.1
63	Brazil	3.0
64	Zimbabwe	3.0
65	Argentina	2.9
66	Ukraine	2.9
67	South Africa	2.9
68	Bulgaria	2.8
69	Paraguay	2.7
70	El Salvador	2.5
71	Bangladesh	2.5
72	Nigeria	2.4
73	Colombia	2.3
74	Jamaica	2.2
75	Mexico	2.2
76	Honduras	2.0
77	Venezuela	2.0
78	Ecuador	2.0
79	Haiti	1.8
80	Guatemala	1.7

MEAN: 4.4

6.15 Organized crime

Organized crime (mafia-oriented racketeering, extortion) in your country (1 = imposes significant costs on businesses, 7 = does not impose significant costs on businesses)

RANK	COUNTRY	SCORE	Chart (1 / MEAN: 4.7 / 7)
1	Finland	6.8	
2	Denmark	6.7	
3	Israel	6.6	
4	Iceland	6.6	
5	Singapore	6.5	
6	Portugal	6.5	
7	New Zealand	6.4	
8	Uruguay	6.4	
9	Austria	6.4	
10	Jordan	6.3	
11	Switzerland	6.2	
12	Australia	6.2	
13	Norway	6.2	
14	United Kingdom	6.2	
15	Tunisia	6.0	
16	Hong Kong SAR	5.9	
17	Sweden	5.9	
18	Mauritius	5.9	
19	Germany	5.8	
20	Chile	5.7	
21	United States	5.7	
22	Slovenia	5.7	
23	Canada	5.6	
24	Belgium	5.6	
25	Hungary	5.6	
26	Korea	5.5	
27	Ireland	5.5	
28	Greece	5.5	
29	Netherlands	5.4	
30	Malaysia	5.3	
31	Estonia	5.3	
32	Thailand	5.3	
33	Sri Lanka	5.2	
34	Spain	5.1	
35	Botswana	5.1	
36	France	5.1	
37	Taiwan	5.0	
37	Turkey	5.0	
39	Panama	4.9	
40	India	4.8	
41	Costa Rica	4.7	
42	Morocco	4.7	
43	China	4.6	
44	Namibia	4.6	
45	Trinidad and Tobago	4.5	
46	Czech Republic	4.4	
47	Japan	4.4	
48	Nicaragua	4.4	
49	Peru	4.3	
50	Croatia	4.2	
51	Dominican Republic	4.2	
52	Romania	4.2	
53	Latvia	4.0	
54	Bolivia	4.0	
55	Argentina	3.9	
56	South Africa	3.9	
57	Zimbabwe	3.8	
58	Brazil	3.8	
59	Poland	3.8	
60	Lithuania	3.8	
61	Vietnam	3.8	
62	Slovak Republic	3.7	
63	Nigeria	3.5	
64	Paraguay	3.5	
65	Italy	3.4	
66	Philippines	3.3	
67	El Salvador	3.1	
68	Ecuador	3.1	
69	Indonesia	3.1	
70	Venezuela	3.0	
71	Russian Federation	2.9	
72	Ukraine	2.9	
73	Bangladesh	2.8	
74	Bulgaria	2.8	
75	Mexico	2.7	
76	Honduras	2.7	
77	Jamaica	2.4	
78	Haiti	2.2	
79	Guatemala	2.1	
80	Colombia	2.0	

6.16 Informal sector

What percentage of businesses in your country would you guess are unofficial or unregistered? (1 = less than 5% of all businesses, 2 = 6–10%, 3 = 11–20%, 9 = more than 70%)

RANK	COUNTRY	SCORE	Chart (1 / MEAN: 3.4 / 7)
1	France	1.4	
2	New Zealand	1.4	
3	Denmark	1.5	
3	Norway	1.5	
5	Hong Kong SAR	1.5	
6	Finland	1.5	
7	Singapore	1.6	
8	Slovak Republic	1.6	
9	United States	1.7	
10	United Kingdom	1.7	
11	Australia	1.8	
12	Japan	1.8	
13	Netherlands	1.8	
14	Iceland	1.8	
15	Canada	1.9	
16	Tunisia	2.0	
17	Spain	2.0	
18	Taiwan	2.0	
19	Switzerland	2.0	
20	Estonia	2.1	
21	Chile	2.1	
22	Slovenia	2.1	
23	Ireland	2.1	
24	Austria	2.2	
25	Germany	2.2	
26	Korea	2.3	
27	Lithuania	2.4	
28	Israel	2.5	
29	Botswana	2.6	
30	Sweden	2.6	
31	Malaysia	2.6	
32	Vietnam	2.8	
33	Czech Republic	2.8	
34	Belgium	2.9	
35	Jordan	2.9	
36	Portugal	2.9	
37	China	2.9	
38	Morocco	3.0	
39	Panama	3.1	
40	Mauritius	3.1	
41	Nicaragua	3.2	
42	Poland	3.3	
43	Hungary	3.4	
44	Croatia	3.5	
45	Italy	3.6	
46	South Africa	3.6	
47	Costa Rica	3.7	
48	India	3.7	
49	Greece	3.7	
50	Uruguay	3.8	
51	Trinidad and Tobago	3.8	
52	Dominican Republic	4.1	
53	Namibia	4.1	
54	Sri Lanka	4.1	
55	Latvia	4.2	
56	Colombia	4.2	
57	Ecuador	4.4	
58	Thailand	4.4	
59	Argentina	4.4	
60	Indonesia	4.4	
61	Mexico	4.6	
62	Romania	4.6	
63	Venezuela	4.7	
64	Brazil	4.7	
65	Honduras	4.8	
66	El Salvador	4.9	
67	Bulgaria	4.9	
68	Bangladesh	5.1	
69	Guatemala	5.2	
70	Nigeria	5.3	
71	Philippines	5.3	
72	Russian Federation	5.5	
73	Zimbabwe	5.6	
74	Paraguay	5.7	
75	Peru	5.7	
76	Turkey	5.8	
77	Jamaica	5.9	
78	Ukraine	6.0	
79	Bolivia	6.0	
80	Haiti	7.2	

609

6.17 Strength of auditing and accounting standards

Financial auditing and accounting standards in your country are (1 = extremely weak, 7 = extremely strong—the best in the world)

RANK	COUNTRY	SCORE
1	United Kingdom	6.5
2	Iceland	6.2
3	Finland	6.2
4	Sweden	6.1
5	Israel	6.1
6	Netherlands	6.1
7	Canada	6.0
8	Australia	6.0
8	Austria	6.0
10	New Zealand	6.0
11	Belgium	5.9
12	Denmark	5.9
13	France	5.9
14	Hong Kong SAR	5.8
15	Switzerland	5.8
16	Singapore	5.8
17	South Africa	5.8
18	Germany	5.8
19	Ireland	5.7
20	United States	5.7
21	Norway	5.7
22	Zimbabwe	5.6
23	Chile	5.5
24	Malaysia	5.5
25	Hungary	5.5
26	Tunisia	5.4
27	Estonia	5.4
28	Namibia	5.4
29	Italy	5.4
30	Botswana	5.4
31	Brazil	5.2
32	Slovenia	5.2
33	Jamaica	5.2
34	Spain	5.1
35	Taiwan	5.1
36	Trinidad and Tobago	5.1
37	Mauritius	5.1
38	Portugal	5.0
39	Sri Lanka	5.0
40	Costa Rica	5.0
41	India	5.0
42	Uruguay	4.9
43	Korea	4.9
44	Morocco	4.8
45	Panama	4.7
46	Jordan	4.7
47	Thailand	4.7
48	Latvia	4.7
49	Nigeria	4.7
50	Croatia	4.6
51	Colombia	4.6
52	El Salvador	4.5
53	Mexico	4.5
54	Japan	4.5
55	Poland	4.5
56	Peru	4.5
57	Slovak Republic	4.4
58	Lithuania	4.4
59	Greece	4.4
60	Dominican Republic	4.3
61	Philippines	4.3
62	Argentina	4.1
63	Bulgaria	4.1
64	Turkey	4.1
65	Czech Republic	4.1
66	Venezuela	4.0
67	Guatemala	3.8
68	Romania	3.7
69	Ecuador	3.7
70	Bangladesh	3.6
71	China	3.5
72	Nicaragua	3.5
73	Vietnam	3.4
74	Russian Federation	3.4
75	Honduras	3.4
76	Paraguay	3.4
77	Indonesia	3.4
78	Bolivia	3.3
79	Ukraine	3.3
80	Haiti	3.0

MEAN: 4.9

6.18 Pervasiveness of insider trading

Insider trading in your country's stock markets is (1 = pervasive, 7 = extremely rare)

RANK	COUNTRY	SCORE
1	United Kingdom	6.2
2	Netherlands	5.8
3	Romania	5.7
4	Australia	5.7
5	New Zealand	5.6
6	Austria	5.5
6	Finland	5.5
8	Singapore	5.5
9	Denmark	5.5
10	United States	5.5
11	Ireland	5.4
12	Paraguay	5.4
13	Namibia	5.3
14	Switzerland	5.3
15	Canada	5.2
16	Tunisia	5.2
17	Honduras	5.2
18	France	5.1
19	Belgium	5.1
20	Japan	5.1
21	Sweden	5.0
21	Uruguay	5.0
23	Portugal	4.9
24	Germany	4.9
25	Israel	4.9
26	Haiti	4.9
27	Botswana	4.8
28	Croatia	4.7
29	Ukraine	4.7
30	Hungary	4.7
31	Guatemala	4.5
32	Bulgaria	4.5
33	Korea	4.4
34	Russian Federation	4.4
35	Hong Kong SAR	4.4
36	Iceland	4.4
37	Malaysia	4.4
38	Chile	4.3
39	Bolivia	4.3
40	South Africa	4.3
41	Taiwan	4.2
42	Dominican Republic	4.2
43	Vietnam	4.2
44	Morocco	4.2
45	Italy	4.2
46	Sri Lanka	4.2
47	El Salvador	4.2
48	Estonia	4.2
49	Jamaica	4.1
50	Spain	4.1
51	Norway	4.1
52	Latvia	4.1
53	Ecuador	4.1
54	Nigeria	4.1
55	Brazil	4.0
56	Colombia	4.0
57	Slovak Republic	4.0
58	Costa Rica	4.0
59	Mauritius	3.9
60	Jordan	3.8
61	Mexico	3.8
62	Poland	3.8
63	Turkey	3.8
64	Slovenia	3.7
65	Lithuania	3.7
66	Argentina	3.5
67	Peru	3.5
68	India	3.5
69	Nicaragua	3.5
70	China	3.5
71	Trinidad and Tobago	3.4
72	Thailand	3.3
73	Venezuela	3.3
74	Greece	3.2
75	Zimbabwe	3.2
76	Panama	3.2
77	Bangladesh	2.9
78	Philippines	2.9
79	Czech Republic	2.9
80	Indonesia	2.8

MEAN: 4.4

6.19 Pervasiveness of money laundering through banks

Money laundering through the banking system in your country is (1 = pervasive, 7 = extremely rare)

RANK	COUNTRY	SCORE
1	Iceland	6.5
2	Denmark	6.5
3	New Zealand	6.3
4	Tunisia	6.2
5	Finland	6.2
6	Singapore	6.1
7	Australia	6.0
8	United Kingdom	6.0
9	Canada	5.8
10	United States	5.8
11	Sweden	5.8
12	Netherlands	5.6
13	Chile	5.6
14	Slovenia	5.6
15	Botswana	5.5
16	Norway	5.5
17	Austria	5.5
18	Namibia	5.5
19	France	5.5
20	Japan	5.4
21	Germany	5.3
22	Portugal	5.3
23	Belgium	5.3
24	Estonia	5.3
25	China	5.2
26	Taiwan	5.1
27	South Africa	5.1
28	Vietnam	5.1
29	Ireland	5.1
30	Spain	5.1
31	Croatia	5.0
32	Malaysia	5.0
33	Jordan	4.9
34	Hong Kong SAR	4.9
35	Switzerland	4.9
36	Italy	4.8
37	Korea	4.8
38	Hungary	4.7
39	Israel	4.7
40	Greece	4.7
41	El Salvador	4.7
42	Uruguay	4.7
43	Mauritius	4.6
44	Costa Rica	4.6
45	Brazil	4.5
46	Morocco	4.5
47	Slovak Republic	4.4
48	Sri Lanka	4.4
49	Lithuania	4.4
50	Thailand	4.3
51	India	4.3
52	Dominican Republic	4.3
53	Zimbabwe	4.2
54	Turkey	4.2
55	Poland	4.1
56	Czech Republic	4.1
57	Trinidad and Tobago	4.0
58	Latvia	4.0
59	Jamaica	4.0
60	Panama	3.9
61	Peru	3.9
62	Bulgaria	3.9
63	Nigeria	3.9
64	Venezuela	3.8
65	Mexico	3.7
66	Bangladesh	3.7
67	Bolivia	3.5
68	Romania	3.5
69	Ecuador	3.5
70	Guatemala	3.5
71	Honduras	3.5
72	Nicaragua	3.3
73	Philippines	3.3
74	Haiti	3.2
75	Paraguay	3.2
76	Colombia	3.1
77	Indonesia	3.1
78	Russian Federation	3.0
79	Argentina	2.9
80	Ukraine	2.9

MEAN: 4.6

6.20 Pervasiveness of money laundering through non-bank channels

Money laundering through non-bank channels (eg, exchange or retail shops, exports/imports, gems, real estate) is (1 = pervasive, 7 = extremely rare)

RANK	COUNTRY	SCORE
1	Iceland	6.5
2	Finland	5.9
3	Denmark	5.9
4	Australia	5.9
5	Tunisia	5.9
6	New Zealand	5.8
7	United Kingdom	5.5
8	Singapore	5.5
9	Canada	5.4
10	United States	5.4
11	Japan	5.3
12	Austria	5.2
13	China	5.1
14	Germany	5.1
15	Norway	5.0
16	Israel	4.9
17	Chile	4.9
18	Botswana	4.8
19	Switzerland	4.8
20	Sweden	4.8
21	Jordan	4.6
22	Ireland	4.6
23	France	4.6
24	Netherlands	4.6
25	Namibia	4.6
26	Taiwan	4.5
27	Malaysia	4.5
28	Slovenia	4.4
29	Korea	4.4
30	Portugal	4.4
31	Hong Kong SAR	4.3
32	Uruguay	4.1
33	Belgium	4.1
34	Spain	4.1
35	South Africa	4.1
36	Estonia	4.0
37	Vietnam	4.0
38	Mauritius	4.0
39	Greece	3.9
40	El Salvador	3.9
41	Morocco	3.9
42	Hungary	3.8
43	Lithuania	3.8
44	Croatia	3.7
45	Italy	3.7
46	Sri Lanka	3.6
47	Dominican Republic	3.5
48	Latvia	3.5
49	Slovak Republic	3.4
50	Honduras	3.3
51	Panama	3.3
52	Turkey	3.3
53	Costa Rica	3.2
54	Trinidad and Tobago	3.2
55	Philippines	3.2
56	Peru	3.2
57	Nigeria	3.1
58	Venezuela	3.1
59	Brazil	3.1
60	Czech Republic	3.1
61	Poland	3.0
62	Ecuador	3.0
63	Russian Federation	3.0
64	Thailand	3.0
65	Bulgaria	2.9
66	Zimbabwe	2.9
67	India	2.9
68	Indonesia	2.9
69	Bolivia	2.8
70	Jamaica	2.8
71	Mexico	2.8
72	Nicaragua	2.7
73	Bangladesh	2.7
74	Romania	2.7
75	Guatemala	2.7
76	Ukraine	2.6
77	Argentina	2.6
78	Paraguay	2.6
79	Haiti	2.2
80	Colombia	2.1

MEAN: 3.9

611

6.21 Military expenditure relative to central government expenditure

Military expenditure as a percentage of central government expenditure, 1999

RANK	COUNTRY	HARD DATA	
1	Iceland	0.0	
2	Mauritius	0.9	
3	Austria	1.5	
4	Costa Rica	2.0	
5	Jamaica	2.1	
6	Latvia	2.5	
7	Honduras	2.6	
7	Ireland	2.6	
9	Nicaragua	2.9	
10	Belgium	3.1	
11	Slovenia	3.4	
12	New Zealand	3.5	
13	Hungary	3.9	
13	Lithuania	3.9	
13	Paraguay	3.9	
16	Uruguay	4.1	
17	Denmark	4.2	
18	Dominican Republic	4.4	
18	Slovak Republic	4.4	
20	Estonia	4.5	
21	Germany	4.7	
21	Italy	4.7	
21	Romania	4.7	
24	Guatemala	5.0	
24	Norway	5.0	
24	South Africa	5.0	
27	Panama	5.1	
28	Indonesia	5.3	
29	Portugal	5.4	
29	Tunisia	5.4	
31	Sweden	5.5	
31	Trinidad and Tobago	5.5	
33	Canada	5.9	
33	France	5.9	
33	Netherlands	5.9	
36	Japan	6.1	
36	Poland	6.1	
36	Spain	6.1	
36	Thailand	6.1	
40	Czech Republic	6.3	
41	United Kingdom	6.9	
42	Venezuela	7.1	
43	Namibia	7.2	
44	Philippines	7.3	
45	Australia	7.6	
46	Bolivia	8.0	
47	Nigeria	8.1	
48	Ukraine	8.2	
49	Bulgaria	8.7	
50	El Salvador	8.8	
51	Argentina	9.1	
52	Malaysia	9.3	
53	Botswana	9.8	
53	Croatia	9.8	
55	Bangladesh	10.1	
56	Korea	11.0	
57	Taiwan	11.4	
58	Zimbabwe	12.1	
59	Chile	12.3	
59	Peru	12.3	
61	Morocco	13.5	
62	Turkey	13.9	
63	India	14.6	
64	United States	15.7	
65	Colombia	15.9	
66	Ecuador	16.2	
67	Greece	16.4	
68	Sri Lanka	18.4	
69	Israel	18.5	
70	Singapore	20.5	
71	China	22.2	
72	Russian Federation	22.4	
73	Jordan	27.5	
	Brazil	N/A	
	Haiti	N/A	
	Hong Kong SAR	N/A	
	Mexico	N/A	
	Switzerland	N/A	
	Vietnam	N/A	
	Finland	N/A	

SOURCES: World Bank *World Development Indicators 2002* and Economist Intelligence Unit

6.22 Military expenditure relative to GNI

Military expenditure as a percentage of GNI, 1999

RANK	COUNTRY	HARD DATA	
1	Iceland	0.0	
2	Mauritius	0.2	
3	Costa Rica	0.5	
4	Mexico	0.6	
5	Dominican Republic	0.7	
5	Guatemala	0.7	
5	Honduras	0.7	
8	Austria	0.8	
8	Jamaica	0.8	
10	El Salvador	0.9	
10	Latvia	0.9	
12	Ireland	1.0	
12	Japan	1.0	
14	Indonesia	1.1	
14	Paraguay	1.1	
16	New Zealand	1.2	
16	Nicaragua	1.2	
16	Switzerland	1.2	
19	Bangladesh	1.3	
19	Lithuania	1.3	
19	Spain	1.3	
19	Uruguay	1.3	
23	Belgium	1.4	
23	Canada	1.4	
23	Finland	1.4	
23	Panama	1.4	
23	Philippines	1.4	
23	Slovenia	1.4	
23	Trinidad and Tobago	1.4	
23	Venezuela	1.4	
31	Estonia	1.5	
31	South Africa	1.5	
33	Argentina	1.6	
33	Denmark	1.6	
33	Germany	1.6	
33	Nigeria	1.6	
33	Romania	1.6	
38	Hungary	1.7	
38	Thailand	1.7	
40	Australia	1.8	
40	Bolivia	1.8	
40	Netherlands	1.8	
40	Slovak Republic	1.8	
40	Tunisia	1.8	
45	Brazil	1.9	
46	Italy	2.0	
47	Poland	2.1	
47	Portugal	2.1	
49	Norway	2.2	
50	China	2.3	
50	Czech Republic	2.3	
50	Malaysia	2.3	
50	Sweden	2.3	
54	Peru	2.4	
55	India	2.5	
55	United Kingdom	2.5	
57	France	2.7	
58	Korea	2.9	
58	Namibia	2.9	
60	Bulgaria	3.0	
60	Chile	3.0	
60	Ukraine	3.0	
60	United States	3.0	
60	Taiwan	3.0	
65	Colombia	3.2	
66	Croatia	3.3	
67	Ecuador	3.7	
68	Morocco	4.3	
69	Botswana	4.7	
69	Greece	4.7	
69	Sri Lanka	4.7	
72	Singapore	4.8	
73	Zimbabwe	5.0	
74	Turkey	5.3	
75	Russian Federation	5.6	
76	Israel	8.8	
77	Jordan	9.2	
	Haiti	N/A	
	Hong Kong SAR	N/A	
	Vietnam	N/A	

SOURCES: World Bank *World Development Indicators 2002* and Economist Intelligence Unit

7.01 Irregular payments in exports & imports

In your industry, how commonly would you estimate that firms make undocumented extra payments or bribes connected with export and import permits? (1 = common, 7 = never occurs)

RANK	COUNTRY	SCORE
1	Finland	6.9
2	Iceland	6.6
3	New Zealand	6.6
4	Denmark	6.6
5	Singapore	6.4
6	United Kingdom	6.4
7	Chile	6.3
8	Switzerland	6.3
9	Canada	6.3
10	Norway	6.2
11	Ireland	6.2
12	Australia	6.1
12	Netherlands	6.1
14	Spain	6.1
15	Sweden	6.0
16	United States	6.0
17	Austria	5.9
18	Japan	5.9
19	Hong Kong SAR	5.9
20	Germany	5.9
21	Taiwan	5.8
22	Lithuania	5.7
23	Israel	5.7
24	Portugal	5.6
25	Tunisia	5.6
26	Bulgaria	5.6
27	Hungary	5.5
28	Estonia	5.5
29	Belgium	5.5
30	Slovenia	5.5
31	France	5.4
32	Uruguay	5.3
33	Italy	5.3
34	Korea	5.3
35	Colombia	5.2
36	Peru	5.1
37	South Africa	5.1
38	China	5.1
39	Greece	5.0
40	Botswana	5.0
41	El Salvador	4.9
42	Malaysia	4.8
43	Mexico	4.7
44	Jordan	4.7
45	Sri Lanka	4.6
46	Croatia	4.6
47	Namibia	4.5
48	Brazil	4.5
49	Jamaica	4.4
50	Trinidad and Tobago	4.4
51	Slovak Republic	4.4
52	Mauritius	4.4
53	Czech Republic	4.3
54	Dominican Republic	4.3
55	Thailand	4.3
56	Nicaragua	4.2
57	Latvia	4.2
58	Costa Rica	4.2
59	Panama	4.1
60	Zimbabwe	3.9
61	Argentina	3.9
62	Poland	3.9
63	Morocco	3.8
64	Russian Federation	3.8
65	Honduras	3.6
66	Guatemala	3.6
67	Paraguay	3.6
68	Ecuador	3.5
69	Vietnam	3.5
70	Ukraine	3.5
71	India	3.4
72	Venezuela	3.4
73	Bolivia	3.3
74	Romania	3.2
75	Haiti	3.0
76	Nigeria	2.9
77	Philippines	2.7
78	Bangladesh	2.5
79	Indonesia	2.4
80	Turkey	2.4

MEAN: 4.8

7.02 Irregular payments in public utilities

In your industry, how commonly would you estimate that firms make undocumented extra payments or bribes when getting connected to public utilities (eg, telephone or electricity)? (1 = common, 7 = never occurs)

RANK	COUNTRY	SCORE
1	Finland	6.9
2	Iceland	6.8
3	Denmark	6.8
4	United Kingdom	6.7
5	New Zealand	6.7
6	Canada	6.6
7	Singapore	6.6
8	Hong Kong SAR	6.6
9	Australia	6.5
10	Switzerland	6.5
11	Netherlands	6.5
12	Chile	6.4
13	Israel	6.4
14	Ireland	6.4
15	Uruguay	6.4
16	Sweden	6.4
17	Lithuania	6.4
18	Norway	6.3
19	Germany	6.3
20	Spain	6.2
21	Estonia	6.2
22	Austria	6.1
23	United States	6.1
24	Portugal	6.0
25	Taiwan	6.0
26	Belgium	5.9
27	France	5.9
28	Italy	5.9
29	Hungary	5.9
30	Slovenia	5.9
31	Japan	5.9
32	El Salvador	5.6
33	Bulgaria	5.6
34	Korea	5.6
35	Tunisia	5.5
36	Botswana	5.5
37	Thailand	5.5
38	Argentina	5.5
39	Czech Republic	5.5
40	Malaysia	5.4
41	Slovak Republic	5.3
42	Brazil	5.3
43	China	5.3
44	Colombia	5.3
45	Peru	5.2
46	Greece	5.2
47	South Africa	5.1
48	Latvia	5.1
49	Croatia	5.1
50	Trinidad and Tobago	5.0
51	Dominican Republic	4.9
52	Jamaica	4.9
53	Mauritius	4.9
54	Mexico	4.9
55	Panama	4.8
56	Namibia	4.8
57	Jordan	4.7
58	Nicaragua	4.6
59	Venezuela	4.5
60	Sri Lanka	4.4
61	Morocco	4.4
62	Poland	4.4
63	Costa Rica	4.3
64	Russian Federation	4.3
65	Guatemala	4.2
66	Vietnam	4.2
67	Bolivia	4.0
68	Romania	4.0
69	Philippines	3.9
70	Zimbabwe	3.9
71	Paraguay	3.9
72	Ukraine	3.8
73	Ecuador	3.7
74	Indonesia	3.7
75	India	3.4
76	Turkey	3.3
77	Honduras	2.9
78	Nigeria	2.5
79	Haiti	2.0
80	Bangladesh	1.9

MEAN: 5.2

7.03   Irregular payments in tax collection

In your industry, how commonly would you estimate that firms make undocumented extra payments or bribes connected with annual tax payments? (1 = common, 7 = never occurs)

RANK	COUNTRY	SCORE
1	Denmark	6.8
2	Finland	6.8
3	Iceland	6.8
4	New Zealand	6.8
5	Australia	6.6
5	Sweden	6.6
7	Singapore	6.6
8	Canada	6.5
9	United Kingdom	6.5
10	Norway	6.5
11	Lithuania	6.3
12	Netherlands	6.3
13	Hong Kong SAR	6.3
14	Switzerland	6.2
15	Chile	6.2
16	Ireland	6.2
17	Japan	6.1
18	Germany	6.1
19	Slovenia	6.0
20	Austria	6.0
21	Bulgaria	6.0
22	United States	6.0
23	Uruguay	5.9
24	Taiwan	5.9
25	Estonia	5.9
26	Spain	5.8
27	Israel	5.8
28	Malaysia	5.7
29	France	5.7
30	South Africa	5.6
31	Mauritius	5.6
32	Hungary	5.5
33	Botswana	5.3
34	Belgium	5.3
35	Peru	5.3
36	China	5.2
37	Portugal	5.1
38	El Salvador	5.0
39	Trinidad and Tobago	5.0
40	Italy	4.9
41	Colombia	4.9
42	Tunisia	4.9
43	Jamaica	4.9
44	Mexico	4.9
45	Croatia	4.8
46	Thailand	4.8
47	Slovak Republic	4.8
48	Namibia	4.8
49	Costa Rica	4.8
50	Korea	4.7
51	Brazil	4.7
52	Panama	4.6
53	Russian Federation	4.6
54	Latvia	4.5
55	Zimbabwe	4.4
56	Sri Lanka	4.4
57	Jordan	4.4
58	Czech Republic	4.2
59	Romania	4.2
60	Nicaragua	4.1
61	Dominican Republic	4.1
62	Poland	4.1
63	Turkey	4.1
64	Argentina	3.9
65	Morocco	3.8
66	Ecuador	3.8
67	Vietnam	3.7
68	Honduras	3.7
69	Venezuela	3.7
70	Greece	3.6
71	Guatemala	3.6
72	Ukraine	3.5
73	India	3.4
74	Bolivia	3.4
75	Paraguay	3.2
76	Indonesia	2.9
77	Philippines	2.6
78	Nigeria	2.5
79	Haiti	2.3
80	Bangladesh	2.1

MEAN: 5.0

7.04   Irregular payments in public contracts

In your industry, how commonly would you estimate that firms make undocumented extra payments or bribes connected with public contracts (investment projects)? (1 = common, 7 = never occurs)

RANK	COUNTRY	SCORE
1	Finland	6.6
2	Denmark	6.4
3	Sweden	6.4
4	Iceland	6.3
5	New Zealand	6.3
6	Singapore	6.2
7	Australia	6.1
8	United Kingdom	6.0
9	Hong Kong SAR	5.9
10	Norway	5.8
11	United States	5.6
12	Canada	5.6
13	Switzerland	5.5
14	Lithuania	5.4
15	Taiwan	5.4
16	Israel	5.3
17	Netherlands	5.3
18	Chile	5.3
19	Bulgaria	5.2
20	Ireland	5.1
21	Austria	5.1
22	Germany	5.0
23	Belgium	5.0
24	Tunisia	4.9
25	Uruguay	4.9
26	Spain	4.9
27	China	4.8
28	Botswana	4.7
29	France	4.6
30	Slovenia	4.6
31	Japan	4.6
32	Estonia	4.6
33	Italy	4.6
34	Portugal	4.5
35	Korea	4.3
36	South Africa	4.2
37	Sri Lanka	4.2
38	Dominican Republic	4.2
39	Brazil	4.2
40	Colombia	4.1
41	Malaysia	4.1
42	Jordan	4.1
43	Mexico	4.0
44	Costa Rica	3.9
45	Croatia	3.8
46	Thailand	3.8
47	Nicaragua	3.8
48	Russian Federation	3.8
49	El Salvador	3.8
50	Greece	3.8
51	Hungary	3.7
52	Ukraine	3.7
53	Venezuela	3.7
54	Panama	3.7
55	Latvia	3.6
56	Mauritius	3.6
57	Trinidad and Tobago	3.6
58	Namibia	3.5
59	Vietnam	3.5
60	Peru	3.5
61	Jamaica	3.5
62	Morocco	3.3
63	Honduras	3.3
64	Poland	3.2
65	Czech Republic	3.1
66	Ecuador	2.9
67	India	2.9
68	Argentina	2.9
69	Slovak Republic	2.8
70	Romania	2.8
71	Indonesia	2.6
71	Turkey	2.6
73	Bolivia	2.6
74	Guatemala	2.6
75	Paraguay	2.6
76	Zimbabwe	2.5
77	Haiti	2.3
78	Bangladesh	2.2
79	Philippines	2.1
80	Nigeria	2.0

MEAN: 4.2

7.05 Irregular payments in loan applications

In your industry, how commonly would you estimate that firms make undocumented extra payments or bribes connected with loan applications? (1 = common, 7 = never occurs)

RANK	COUNTRY	SCORE		MEAN: 5.0	
1	Finland	6.8			
2	Denmark	6.8			
3	New Zealand	6.6			
4	United Kingdom	6.6			
5	Iceland	6.5			
6	Sweden	6.5			
7	Australia	6.4			
8	Norway	6.4			
9	Singapore	6.4			
10	Canada	6.3			
11	Netherlands	6.3			
12	Lithuania	6.2			
13	Ireland	6.2			
14	Switzerland	6.2			
15	Chile	6.1			
16	Germany	6.0			
17	Austria	6.0			
17	Hong Kong SAR	6.0			
19	Spain	5.9			
20	Uruguay	5.9			
21	France	5.8			
22	United States	5.8			
23	Japan	5.8			
24	Belgium	5.8			
25	Estonia	5.7			
26	Bulgaria	5.6			
27	Taiwan	5.6			
28	Slovenia	5.6			
29	Portugal	5.6			
30	Israel	5.4			
31	South Africa	5.4			
32	Italy	5.3			
33	Colombia	5.2			
34	Trinidad and Tobago	5.2			
35	Mauritius	5.1			
36	Greece	5.1			
37	Jamaica	5.1			
38	Thailand	5.1			
39	Botswana	5.1			
40	Malaysia	5.1			
41	El Salvador	5.1			
42	Brazil	5.0			
43	Tunisia	5.0			
44	Peru	5.0			
45	China	5.0			
46	Hungary	4.9			
47	Korea	4.9			
48	Mexico	4.8			
49	Panama	4.8			
50	Latvia	4.7			
51	Costa Rica	4.7			
52	Jordan	4.6			
53	Namibia	4.5			
54	Nicaragua	4.5			
55	Zimbabwe	4.5			
56	Dominican Republic	4.5			
57	Croatia	4.5			
58	Argentina	4.3			
59	Russian Federation	4.3			
60	Sri Lanka	4.2			
61	Slovak Republic	4.2			
62	India	4.2			
63	Haiti	4.1			
64	Honduras	4.1			
65	Guatemala	4.0			
66	Vietnam	4.0			
67	Poland	3.9			
68	Venezuela	3.9			
69	Ecuador	3.9			
70	Bolivia	3.9			
71	Philippines	3.8			
72	Ukraine	3.8			
73	Nigeria	3.7			
74	Paraguay	3.6			
75	Czech Republic	3.6			
76	Turkey	3.6			
77	Morocco	3.5			
78	Romania	3.3			
79	Bangladesh	2.7			
80	Indonesia	2.6			

7.06 Irregular payments in government policymaking

In your industry, how commonly would you estimate that firms make undocumented extra payments or bribes connected with influencing laws and policies, regulations, or decrees to favor selected business interests? (1 = common, 7 = never occurs)

RANK	COUNTRY	SCORE		MEAN: 4.4	
1	Finland	6.6			
2	Denmark	6.4			
3	Singapore	6.3			
4	New Zealand	6.3			
5	Sweden	6.3			
6	Iceland	6.2			
7	Norway	6.0			
8	Australia	5.9			
9	United Kingdom	5.8			
10	Hong Kong SAR	5.7			
11	Netherlands	5.6			
12	Switzerland	5.6			
13	Austria	5.5			
14	Germany	5.5			
15	Israel	5.5			
16	United States	5.5			
17	Canada	5.4			
18	Lithuania	5.4			
19	Ireland	5.3			
20	Bulgaria	5.2			
21	Taiwan	5.2			
22	Chile	5.2			
23	Tunisia	5.1			
24	Portugal	5.1			
25	France	5.1			
26	Botswana	5.0			
27	Belgium	5.0			
28	Spain	5.0			
29	Malaysia	4.9			
30	China	4.9			
31	Uruguay	4.8			
32	Slovenia	4.8			
33	Japan	4.8			
34	South Africa	4.7			
35	Hungary	4.7			
36	Estonia	4.6			
37	Italy	4.6			
38	Jordan	4.5			
39	Brazil	4.5			
40	Mauritius	4.5			
41	Sri Lanka	4.4			
42	Vietnam	4.4			
43	Jamaica	4.3			
44	Namibia	4.3			
45	Thailand	4.3			
46	Korea	4.2			
47	Trinidad and Tobago	4.1			
48	Greece	4.1			
49	Croatia	4.1			
50	Mexico	4.1			
51	Dominican Republic	4.0			
51	El Salvador	4.0			
53	Colombia	3.9			
54	Nicaragua	3.9			
55	Costa Rica	3.9			
56	Morocco	3.8			
57	Latvia	3.8			
58	Venezuela	3.7			
59	Russian Federation	3.6			
60	Peru	3.5			
61	Panama	3.5			
62	Poland	3.5			
63	Czech Republic	3.4			
64	Slovak Republic	3.4			
65	Ukraine	3.4			
66	Zimbabwe	3.4			
67	India	3.2			
68	Turkey	3.2			
69	Argentina	3.1			
70	Honduras	3.0			
71	Paraguay	3.0			
72	Guatemala	2.9			
73	Ecuador	2.9			
74	Bolivia	2.8			
75	Romania	2.8			
76	Haiti	2.8			
77	Nigeria	2.7			
78	Bangladesh	2.7			
79	Indonesia	2.6			
80	Philippines	2.5			

7.07 Irregular payments in judicial decisions

In your industry, how commonly would you estimate that firms make undocumented extra payments or bribes connected with getting favorable judicial decisions? (1 = common, 7 = never occurs)

RANK	COUNTRY	SCORE
1	Finland	6.9
2	Denmark	6.8
3	New Zealand	6.8
4	Australia	6.7
4	Iceland	6.7
6	United Kingdom	6.7
7	Sweden	6.6
8	Germany	6.5
9	Singapore	6.5
10	Switzerland	6.4
11	Netherlands	6.4
12	Hong Kong SAR	6.4
13	Austria	6.4
14	Ireland	6.3
15	Canada	6.3
16	Norway	6.3
17	Israel	6.1
18	Portugal	6.1
19	United States	6.1
20	Japan	5.9
21	Belgium	5.9
22	Uruguay	5.9
23	Slovenia	5.7
24	South Africa	5.7
25	Spain	5.6
26	France	5.6
27	Botswana	5.5
28	Jamaica	5.4
29	Mauritius	5.3
30	Trinidad and Tobago	5.3
31	Taiwan	5.3
32	Namibia	5.3
33	Estonia	5.3
34	Lithuania	5.3
35	Chile	5.2
36	Tunisia	5.2
37	Jordan	5.1
38	Hungary	5.1
39	Malaysia	5.1
40	Bulgaria	5.0
41	Italy	5.0
42	China	4.9
43	Korea	4.8
44	Costa Rica	4.8
45	Sri Lanka	4.7
46	Thailand	4.7
47	Brazil	4.7
48	Greece	4.7
49	Vietnam	4.5
50	Colombia	4.4
51	India	4.4
52	Czech Republic	4.2
53	Croatia	4.2
54	Zimbabwe	4.1
55	Dominican Republic	4.1
56	Nicaragua	4.0
57	Poland	3.9
58	Latvia	3.9
59	Mexico	3.8
60	Panama	3.7
61	El Salvador	3.6
62	Russian Federation	3.6
63	Bangladesh	3.4
64	Ukraine	3.4
65	Turkey	3.4
66	Morocco	3.4
67	Slovak Republic	3.3
68	Nigeria	3.2
69	Argentina	3.1
70	Guatemala	3.1
71	Honduras	3.0
72	Romania	2.9
73	Venezuela	2.9
74	Ecuador	2.7
75	Peru	2.7
76	Paraguay	2.6
77	Bolivia	2.5
78	Philippines	2.5
79	Haiti	2.5
80	Indonesia	2.0

MEAN: 4.8

7.08 Frequency of payments or bribes

In the past three years, the frequency and extent of additional payments or bribes such as those listed in questions 7.01–7.07 (1 = has increased significantly, 7 = has decreased significantly)

RANK	COUNTRY	SCORE
1	Israel	6.3
2	Taiwan	5.7
3	Spain	5.6
4	Belgium	5.3
5	Singapore	5.3
6	China	5.2
6	Estonia	5.2
8	France	5.1
9	Croatia	5.1
10	Ireland	5.1
11	Korea	5.1
12	Australia	5.0
13	Finland	4.9
14	Canada	4.8
15	Mexico	4.8
16	Slovenia	4.8
17	Brazil	4.8
18	Italy	4.8
19	Lithuania	4.8
20	El Salvador	4.8
21	Japan	4.7
22	Hong Kong SAR	4.7
23	Portugal	4.6
24	Botswana	4.6
24	United States	4.6
26	Latvia	4.6
27	Malaysia	4.6
28	Austria	4.5
29	United Kingdom	4.5
30	Norway	4.4
31	Thailand	4.4
32	India	4.4
33	New Zealand	4.4
34	Turkey	4.4
35	Czech Republic	4.3
36	Uruguay	4.3
37	Slovak Republic	4.3
38	Tunisia	4.3
39	Mauritius	4.3
40	Switzerland	4.3
41	Vietnam	4.3
42	Greece	4.2
43	Sri Lanka	4.2
44	Denmark	4.2
45	Jordan	4.1
46	Namibia	4.0
47	Colombia	4.0
47	Iceland	4.0
47	Sweden	4.0
50	Bulgaria	4.0
51	Dominican Republic	4.0
52	Hungary	4.0
53	South Africa	4.0
54	Morocco	3.9
55	Costa Rica	3.9
56	Poland	3.8
57	Russian Federation	3.8
58	Germany	3.8
59	Netherlands	3.8
60	Peru	3.7
61	Chile	3.6
62	Nigeria	3.5
63	Honduras	3.5
64	Philippines	3.5
65	Ukraine	3.4
66	Indonesia	3.4
67	Ecuador	3.3
68	Argentina	3.3
69	Jamaica	3.3
70	Trinidad and Tobago	3.1
71	Nicaragua	3.0
72	Paraguay	3.0
73	Romania	2.9
74	Haiti	2.8
75	Panama	2.6
76	Bangladesh	2.5
77	Bolivia	2.4
78	Zimbabwe	2.4
79	Venezuela	2.1
80	Guatemala	2.0

MEAN: 4.1

617

7.09　Reliability of payments or bribes

When paying bribes, how confident can business people be that the service is delivered as promised? (1 = not at all confident, 7 = very confident)

RANK	COUNTRY	SCORE
1	Czech Republic	5.0
2	Thailand	4.7
3	Austria	4.7
4	Sri Lanka	4.7
5	Finland	4.7
6	Italy	4.6
6	Slovenia	4.6
8	Jordan	4.6
9	Hungary	4.6
9	Turkey	4.6
11	Estonia	4.6
12	Portugal	4.6
13	Iceland	4.5
13	Korea	4.5
13	Nigeria	4.5
16	Latvia	4.4
17	Jamaica	4.4
18	Hong Kong SAR	4.3
18	Japan	4.3
20	Poland	4.3
21	Greece	4.3
22	India	4.3
22	Taiwan	4.3
24	Bangladesh	4.3
24	Norway	4.3
26	Brazil	4.2
27	Germany	4.2
28	Mexico	4.2
29	Mauritius	4.2
30	Uruguay	4.1
31	Botswana	4.1
31	Dominican Republic	4.1
33	Panama	4.1
34	Lithuania	4.1
35	El Salvador	4.1
36	Romania	4.1
37	Vietnam	4.1
38	Indonesia	4.1
39	Spain	4.0
40	Australia	4.0
40	Malaysia	4.0
40	Netherlands	4.0
40	Sweden	4.0
44	Slovak Republic	4.0
45	Zimbabwe	4.0
46	Trinidad and Tobago	3.9
47	Philippines	3.9
47	Honduras	3.8
47	Chile	3.8
50	Tunisia	3.8
51	Ireland	3.8
52	Russian Federation	3.7
53	Ukraine	3.7
54	Nicaragua	3.7
55	China	3.7
56	Argentina	3.7
57	Bulgaria	3.6
58	Paraguay	3.6
59	Croatia	3.6
60	Denmark	3.6
61	Singapore	3.5
62	Ecuador	3.5
63	Costa Rica	3.4
64	Belgium	3.4
65	South Africa	3.4
66	New Zealand	3.3
67	Switzerland	3.2
68	Peru	3.2
69	Namibia	3.1
70	Bolivia	3.1
71	Morocco	3.1
72	Haiti	3.1
73	Canada	3.0
74	United States	3.0
75	Colombia	3.0
76	Guatemala	2.9
77	France	2.8
78	Venezuela	2.4
79	United Kingdom	2.0
80	Israel	1.0

MEAN: 3.9

7.10　Diversion of public funds

In your country, diversion of public funds to companies, individuals or groups due to corruption (1 = is common, 7 = never occurs)

RANK	COUNTRY	SCORE
1	Finland	6.7
2	Denmark	6.4
3	New Zealand	6.4
4	Singapore	6.3
5	Iceland	6.3
6	Sweden	6.2
7	Switzerland	6.1
8	Australia	6.1
9	Norway	6.0
10	Austria	5.9
11	United Kingdom	5.8
12	Israel	5.8
13	Netherlands	5.8
14	Canada	5.8
15	Hong Kong SAR	5.6
16	United States	5.5
17	Germany	5.4
18	Belgium	5.3
19	Ireland	5.2
20	Botswana	5.2
21	Portugal	5.1
22	Uruguay	5.1
23	Spain	4.9
24	Chile	4.9
25	Slovenia	4.8
26	Tunisia	4.8
27	Taiwan	4.6
28	France	4.4
29	Korea	4.3
30	Malaysia	4.2
31	Greece	4.2
32	Jordan	4.2
33	Estonia	4.1
34	Croatia	4.1
35	Hungary	4.0
36	South Africa	4.0
37	Namibia	3.9
38	Italy	3.7
39	Japan	3.7
40	China	3.6
41	El Salvador	3.6
42	Lithuania	3.5
43	Thailand	3.4
44	Latvia	3.4
45	Mauritius	3.4
46	Sri Lanka	3.3
47	Costa Rica	3.2
48	Czech Republic	3.2
49	Poland	3.1
50	Vietnam	3.1
51	Trinidad and Tobago	3.1
52	Brazil	3.1
53	Slovak Republic	3.0
54	Morocco	3.0
55	Peru	2.9
56	India	2.9
57	Panama	2.8
58	Turkey	2.7
59	Dominican Republic	2.6
60	Jamaica	2.6
61	Ukraine	2.6
62	Bulgaria	2.6
63	Mexico	2.6
64	Russian Federation	2.5
65	Romania	2.5
66	Honduras	2.3
67	Bangladesh	2.3
68	Philippines	2.3
69	Colombia	2.2
70	Zimbabwe	2.1
71	Argentina	2.0
72	Indonesia	1.9
73	Bolivia	1.9
74	Nicaragua	1.9
75	Paraguay	1.7
76	Venezuela	1.7
77	Ecuador	1.7
78	Nigeria	1.5
79	Guatemala	1.5
80	Haiti	1.4

MEAN: 3.8

7.11 Business costs of corruption

Do other firms' illegal payments to influence government policies, laws, or regulations impose costs or otherwise negatively affect your firm? (1 = impose large costs, 7 = impose no costs/not relevant)

RANK	COUNTRY	SCORE
1	Finland	6.9
2	Iceland	6.8
3	Denmark	6.8
4	Australia	6.7
5	United Kingdom	6.7
6	Norway	6.6
7	New Zealand	6.6
8	Singapore	6.4
9	Hong Kong SAR	6.3
10	Ireland	6.3
11	Switzerland	6.2
12	Sweden	6.2
13	Canada	6.1
14	Austria	6.0
15	Israel	6.0
16	Netherlands	6.0
16	United States	6.0
18	Germany	5.9
19	Portugal	5.7
20	Belgium	5.7
21	Spain	5.5
22	Estonia	5.5
23	Japan	5.4
24	Hungary	5.3
25	South Africa	5.3
26	Slovenia	5.3
27	Chile	5.1
28	Italy	5.1
29	France	5.0
30	Taiwan	5.0
31	Greece	4.9
32	Uruguay	4.8
33	Namibia	4.8
34	Korea	4.8
35	Botswana	4.8
36	Mauritius	4.8
37	Tunisia	4.7
38	Lithuania	4.7
39	Malaysia	4.7
40	Latvia	4.7
41	Slovak Republic	4.6
42	Trinidad and Tobago	4.6
43	Jamaica	4.6
44	Turkey	4.6
45	Jordan	4.6
46	Thailand	4.5
47	Costa Rica	4.4
48	Croatia	4.4
49	Brazil	4.4
50	China	4.4
51	India	4.4
52	Russian Federation	4.3
53	Panama	4.2
54	Romania	4.2
55	Peru	4.2
56	Poland	4.2
57	Mexico	4.0
58	Bulgaria	3.9
59	Bolivia	3.9
60	Sri Lanka	3.9
61	Czech Republic	3.9
62	Argentina	3.8
63	Nicaragua	3.7
64	Honduras	3.7
65	Haiti	3.7
66	Vietnam	3.7
67	Dominican Republic	3.7
68	Morocco	3.6
69	Colombia	3.6
70	Ukraine	3.5
71	Zimbabwe	3.5
72	El Salvador	3.5
73	Philippines	3.5
74	Ecuador	3.5
75	Paraguay	3.4
76	Nigeria	3.4
77	Indonesia	2.9
78	Venezuela	2.9
79	Bangladesh	2.8
80	Guatemala	2.8

MEAN: 4.8

7.12 Public trust of politicians

Public trust in the financial honesty of politicians is (1 = very low, 7 = very high)

RANK	COUNTRY	SCORE
1	Singapore	6.4
2	Denmark	6.0
3	Finland	5.8
4	Switzerland	5.4
5	Hong Kong SAR	5.2
6	Netherlands	5.1
7	Iceland	5.0
8	Norway	4.7
9	Austria	4.7
10	New Zealand	4.6
11	Canada	4.5
12	China	4.4
13	Tunisia	4.4
14	Botswana	4.3
15	United States	4.3
16	Chile	4.1
17	Sweden	4.1
18	Australia	4.0
19	Israel	3.9
20	United Kingdom	3.9
21	Vietnam	3.8
22	Uruguay	3.7
23	Belgium	3.7
24	Malaysia	3.6
25	Portugal	3.6
26	Germany	3.6
27	Spain	3.4
28	Namibia	3.3
29	Slovenia	3.2
30	Taiwan	3.2
31	South Africa	2.9
32	Estonia	2.8
33	Jordan	2.8
34	Italy	2.7
35	Greece	2.6
36	Thailand	2.6
37	Morocco	2.6
38	Hungary	2.4
39	Korea	2.3
40	France	2.3
41	Mexico	2.3
42	Latvia	2.2
43	Poland	2.2
44	Mauritius	2.2
45	Czech Republic	2.2
46	Sri Lanka	2.1
47	Ireland	2.1
48	Croatia	2.1
49	Costa Rica	2.0
50	Japan	2.0
51	Brazil	2.0
51	El Salvador	2.0
53	Lithuania	2.0
54	Bulgaria	2.0
55	Trinidad and Tobago	1.9
56	Russian Federation	1.9
57	India	1.9
58	Dominican Republic	1.8
59	Jamaica	1.7
60	Slovak Republic	1.7
61	Indonesia	1.7
62	Honduras	1.7
63	Romania	1.6
64	Turkey	1.6
65	Peru	1.6
66	Ukraine	1.6
67	Colombia	1.6
68	Bangladesh	1.6
69	Philippines	1.5
70	Nicaragua	1.4
71	Venezuela	1.4
72	Panama	1.3
73	Zimbabwe	1.3
74	Nigeria	1.3
75	Ecuador	1.2
76	Guatemala	1.2
77	Bolivia	1.2
78	Paraguay	1.2
79	Haiti	1.1
80	Argentina	1.1

MEAN: 2.8

7.13 Prevalence of illegal political donations

How common are illegal donations to political parties in your country? (1 = common, 7 = never occurs)

MEAN: 3.5

RANK	COUNTRY	SCORE
1	Singapore	6.3
2	Finland	6.2
3	Sweden	6.1
4	Netherlands	6.0
5	Denmark	6.0
6	New Zealand	5.9
7	Norway	5.9
8	Iceland	5.8
9	Australia	5.7
10	Switzerland	5.6
11	Hong Kong SAR	5.5
12	Austria	5.5
13	United Kingdom	5.3
14	China	5.2
15	United States	5.2
16	Belgium	5.1
17	Vietnam	5.0
18	Canada	5.0
19	Tunisia	4.9
20	Jordan	4.9
21	Botswana	4.4
22	Israel	4.4
23	Uruguay	4.3
24	South Africa	4.2
25	Namibia	4.2
26	Slovenia	4.2
27	Malaysia	4.1
28	France	3.9
29	Japan	3.8
30	Taiwan	3.6
31	Portugal	3.5
32	Hungary	3.5
33	El Salvador	3.5
34	Germany	3.5
35	Korea	3.5
36	Ireland	3.4
37	Spain	3.4
38	Chile	3.3
39	Italy	3.3
40	Morocco	3.3
41	Jamaica	3.2
42	Haiti	3.2
43	Croatia	3.2
44	Estonia	3.2
45	Greece	3.1
46	Lithuania	3.0
47	Bulgaria	2.9
48	Thailand	2.9
49	Costa Rica	2.9
50	Latvia	2.8
51	Poland	2.8
51	Slovak Republic	2.8
53	Trinidad and Tobago	2.8
54	Russian Federation	2.7
55	Colombia	2.6
56	Zimbabwe	2.5
57	Mexico	2.5
58	Czech Republic	2.5
59	Peru	2.5
60	Panama	2.5
61	Ukraine	2.5
62	Honduras	2.4
63	Sri Lanka	2.3
64	Dominican Republic	2.3
65	Romania	2.2
66	Brazil	2.2
67	Nigeria	2.1
68	Indonesia	2.1
68	Turkey	2.1
70	Mauritius	2.1
71	Nicaragua	2.0
72	India	2.0
73	Venezuela	1.9
74	Bolivia	1.9
75	Paraguay	1.8
76	Guatemala	1.8
77	Argentina	1.8
78	Bangladesh	1.7
79	Philippines	1.6
80	Ecuador	1.6

7.14 Policy consequences of legal political donations

To what extent do legal contributions to political parties have a direct influence on specific public policy outcomes? (1 = very close link between donations and policy, 7 = little direct influence on policy)

MEAN: 3.9

RANK	COUNTRY	SCORE
1	Finland	6.0
2	Netherlands	5.9
3	Singapore	5.8
4	Sweden	5.8
5	New Zealand	5.7
6	Denmark	5.6
7	Norway	5.6
8	Hong Kong SAR	5.5
9	Iceland	5.3
10	Austria	5.1
11	Australia	5.0
12	Jordan	4.9
13	Switzerland	4.7
14	China	4.7
15	South Africa	4.7
16	Tunisia	4.6
17	Belgium	4.6
18	United Kingdom	4.5
19	Namibia	4.5
20	Botswana	4.5
21	Portugal	4.4
22	France	4.4
23	Chile	4.4
24	Nigeria	4.3
25	Israel	4.3
26	Germany	4.3
27	Canada	4.3
28	Uruguay	4.2
29	Slovenia	4.2
30	Vietnam	4.2
31	Malaysia	4.2
32	India	4.1
33	Morocco	4.1
34	Korea	4.1
35	Japan	4.1
36	Spain	4.0
37	Hungary	4.0
38	Zimbabwe	4.0
39	Jamaica	3.9
40	Italy	3.9
41	Greece	3.9
42	Ireland	3.8
43	Taiwan	3.8
44	Bangladesh	3.8
45	Mauritius	3.8
46	Haiti	3.8
47	Estonia	3.7
48	United States	3.7
49	Mexico	3.6
50	Indonesia	3.5
51	Thailand	3.5
52	Poland	3.5
53	Sri Lanka	3.5
54	El Salvador	3.4
55	Paraguay	3.4
56	Czech Republic	3.4
57	Croatia	3.4
58	Romania	3.3
59	Bulgaria	3.3
60	Dominican Republic	3.3
61	Brazil	3.2
62	Slovak Republic	3.2
63	Peru	3.2
64	Latvia	3.1
65	Nicaragua	3.0
66	Lithuania	3.0
67	Costa Rica	3.0
68	Trinidad and Tobago	3.0
69	Bolivia	2.9
70	Guatemala	2.8
71	Colombia	2.8
72	Turkey	2.8
73	Ukraine	2.7
74	Venezuela	2.7
75	Russian Federation	2.6
76	Philippines	2.5
77	Panama	2.4
78	Honduras	2.4
79	Argentina	2.3
80	Ecuador	2.0

7.15   Misuse of legal political donations

To what extent do legal contributions to political parties end up being misused by politicians or diverted to private individuals or organizations? (1 = commonly, 7 = rarely)

RANK	COUNTRY	SCORE
1	Finland	6.5
2	New Zealand	6.3
3	Sweden	6.3
4	Singapore	6.3
5	Denmark	6.2
6	Netherlands	6.2
7	Australia	6.1
8	United Kingdom	5.9
9	Iceland	5.9
10	Switzerland	5.8
11	Hong Kong SAR	5.8
12	Austria	5.7
13	Norway	5.7
14	Canada	5.5
15	United States	5.4
16	Uruguay	5.2
17	China	5.0
18	Belgium	5.0
18	Israel	5.0
20	Botswana	5.0
21	Germany	4.9
22	Tunisia	4.9
23	Slovenia	4.6
24	Portugal	4.5
25	Chile	4.5
26	South Africa	4.3
27	Estonia	4.2
28	Vietnam	4.2
29	Taiwan	4.2
30	France	4.2
31	Jordan	4.2
32	Malaysia	4.1
33	Namibia	4.0
34	Italy	4.0
35	Morocco	3.9
36	Spain	3.9
37	Ireland	3.8
38	Hungary	3.8
39	Korea	3.8
40	Latvia	3.8
41	Greece	3.6
42	Jamaica	3.6
43	India	3.5
44	Croatia	3.5
45	El Salvador	3.5
46	Poland	3.5
47	Trinidad and Tobago	3.5
48	Slovak Republic	3.4
49	Czech Republic	3.3
50	Japan	3.3
51	Turkey	3.3
52	Mauritius	3.2
53	Thailand	3.2
54	Costa Rica	3.1
55	Brazil	3.1
56	Colombia	3.1
57	Lithuania	3.1
58	Bulgaria	3.1
59	Sri Lanka	2.8
60	Russian Federation	2.8
61	Mexico	2.7
62	Romania	2.7
63	Panama	2.7
64	Bangladesh	2.6
65	Ukraine	2.5
66	Peru	2.4
67	Indonesia	2.4
68	Haiti	2.4
69	Honduras	2.3
70	Dominican Republic	2.2
71	Nigeria	2.1
72	Guatemala	2.0
73	Zimbabwe	2.0
74	Philippines	2.0
75	Bolivia	2.0
76	Nicaragua	2.0
77	Paraguay	1.9
78	Venezuela	1.9
79	Argentina	1.9
80	Ecuador	1.7

MEAN: 3.9

Section VIII: Domestic Competition

8.01 Intensity of local competition

Competition in the local market is (1 = limited in most industries and price-cutting is rare, 7 = intense in most industries as market leadership changes over time)

RANK	COUNTRY	SCORE	1 MEAN: 4.8 7
1	United States	6.1	
2	Taiwan	5.7	
3	Hong Kong SAR	5.7	
4	Germany	5.7	
5	Chile	5.7	
6	United Kingdom	5.7	
7	India	5.6	
8	Belgium	5.6	
9	Japan	5.5	
10	Australia	5.5	
11	Netherlands	5.4	
12	Austria	5.4	
12	Canada	5.4	
14	New Zealand	5.4	
15	Korea	5.4	
16	Sweden	5.4	
17	Spain	5.3	
18	Israel	5.3	
19	Finland	5.3	
20	Singapore	5.3	
21	Hungary	5.2	
22	Lithuania	5.2	
23	Norway	5.2	
23	Dominican Republic	5.2	
25	South Africa	5.1	
26	Italy	5.1	
27	Czech Republic	5.1	
28	Malaysia	5.1	
29	Thailand	5.1	
30	Jordan	5.1	
31	China	5.1	
32	Latvia	5.0	
33	Switzerland	5.0	
34	Brazil	5.0	
35	Sri Lanka	5.0	
36	Iceland	5.0	
37	Vietnam	4.9	
38	Denmark	4.9	
39	Ireland	4.9	
40	Greece	4.8	
40	Slovenia	4.8	
42	Mexico	4.8	
43	El Salvador	4.8	
44	Panama	4.8	
45	Estonia	4.7	
46	Peru	4.7	
47	Turkey	4.7	
48	Poland	4.7	
49	Colombia	4.7	
50	Jamaica	4.7	
51	Bangladesh	4.7	
51	France	4.7	
53	Trinidad and Tobago	4.7	
54	Costa Rica	4.6	
55	Portugal	4.5	
56	Paraguay	4.5	
57	Morocco	4.5	
58	Mauritius	4.4	
59	Argentina	4.4	
60	Croatia	4.4	
61	Philippines	4.4	
62	Botswana	4.4	
63	Namibia	4.4	
64	Bulgaria	4.4	
65	Slovak Republic	4.4	
66	Russian Federation	4.4	
67	Tunisia	4.3	
68	Indonesia	4.2	
69	Nigeria	4.1	
70	Zimbabwe	3.9	
71	Uruguay	3.8	
72	Romania	3.7	
73	Ukraine	3.6	
74	Bolivia	3.6	
75	Guatemala	3.6	
76	Venezuela	3.5	
77	Honduras	3.5	
78	Ecuador	3.5	
79	Haiti	3.3	
80	Nicaragua	3.0	

8.02 Extent of locally based competitors

Competition in the local market (1 = comes primarily from imports, 7 = comes primarily from local firms or local subsidiaries of multinationals)

RANK	COUNTRY	SCORE	1 MEAN: 4.3 7
1	Japan	5.8	
2	United States	5.6	
3	United Kingdom	5.5	
4	Brazil	5.5	
5	Norway	5.5	
6	Spain	5.4	
7	Australia	5.3	
8	Taiwan	5.3	
9	Germany	5.3	
10	Netherlands	5.3	
11	Korea	5.2	
12	Hong Kong SAR	5.2	
13	China	5.1	
14	Thailand	5.1	
15	Switzerland	5.1	
16	Italy	5.1	
17	India	5.0	
18	France	5.0	
19	Turkey	4.9	
20	Canada	4.9	
21	Sweden	4.9	
22	Austria	4.9	
23	South Africa	4.9	
24	Malaysia	4.8	
25	Portugal	4.8	
26	Chile	4.7	
27	Zimbabwe	4.7	
28	Colombia	4.6	
29	Ireland	4.6	
30	Denmark	4.6	
31	New Zealand	4.5	
32	Russian Federation	4.5	
33	Costa Rica	4.5	
34	Ukraine	4.4	
35	Finland	4.4	
36	Lithuania	4.4	
37	Vietnam	4.4	
38	Estonia	4.4	
39	Poland	4.4	
40	Iceland	4.4	
41	Hungary	4.4	
42	Greece	4.4	
43	Singapore	4.3	
44	Israel	4.3	
45	Slovenia	4.3	
46	Belgium	4.2	
47	Argentina	4.2	
48	Dominican Republic	4.1	
49	Venezuela	4.1	
50	Namibia	4.1	
51	Mexico	4.1	
52	Romania	4.1	
53	Panama	4.0	
54	Morocco	4.0	
55	Nicaragua	4.0	
56	Sri Lanka	4.0	
57	Tunisia	4.0	
58	Philippines	4.0	
59	Czech Republic	4.0	
60	Botswana	3.9	
61	El Salvador	3.8	
62	Jordan	3.8	
63	Trinidad and Tobago	3.8	
64	Honduras	3.7	
64	Nigeria	3.7	
66	Bangladesh	3.7	
67	Slovak Republic	3.6	
68	Paraguay	3.6	
69	Bulgaria	3.5	
70	Guatemala	3.5	
70	Indonesia	3.5	
72	Peru	3.5	
73	Latvia	3.3	
74	Croatia	3.3	
75	Mauritius	3.2	
76	Uruguay	3.1	
77	Ecuador	3.1	
78	Jamaica	3.1	
79	Bolivia	3.0	
80	Haiti	2.5	

8.03 Sophistication of local buyers' products and processes

Buyers in your country are (1 = slow to adopt new products and processes, 7 = actively seeking the latest products, technologies, and processes)

RANK	COUNTRY	SCORE
1	Iceland	6.2
2	United States	6.1
3	Finland	6.0
3	United Kingdom	6.0
5	Japan	6.0
6	Australia	5.9
7	Sweden	5.8
8	Hong Kong SAR	5.8
9	Taiwan	5.8
10	New Zealand	5.7
11	Canada	5.6
12	Singapore	5.6
13	Korea	5.5
14	Israel	5.4
15	Denmark	5.4
16	France	5.4
17	Netherlands	5.3
18	Belgium	5.3
19	Ireland	5.3
20	Norway	5.3
21	Thailand	5.2
22	Austria	5.2
23	Germany	5.2
24	Czech Republic	5.2
25	Estonia	5.1
26	Hungary	5.1
27	Switzerland	5.0
28	Brazil	5.0
29	Malaysia	5.0
30	India	5.0
31	Spain	4.9
32	Slovenia	4.9
33	Turkey	4.9
34	Italy	4.8
35	Tunisia	4.7
36	Dominican Republic	4.7
37	Chile	4.7
38	Trinidad and Tobago	4.7
39	Vietnam	4.6
40	Costa Rica	4.6
41	Morocco	4.5
42	Jamaica	4.5
43	Panama	4.5
44	Slovak Republic	4.5
45	Portugal	4.5
46	Argentina	4.4
47	Latvia	4.4
48	South Africa	4.3
49	Poland	4.3
50	Lithuania	4.2
51	Mauritius	4.2
52	Greece	4.2
53	Croatia	4.1
54	Nigeria	4.1
55	Mexico	4.1
56	Philippines	4.1
57	Russian Federation	4.1
58	Indonesia	4.1
59	Sri Lanka	4.0
60	China	4.0
61	Venezuela	4.0
62	Namibia	3.9
63	Botswana	3.9
64	Jordan	3.8
65	El Salvador	3.7
66	Bangladesh	3.6
67	Zimbabwe	3.6
68	Colombia	3.6
69	Bulgaria	3.6
70	Ukraine	3.5
71	Romania	3.5
72	Peru	3.4
73	Paraguay	3.3
74	Uruguay	3.3
75	Ecuador	2.9
76	Haiti	2.9
77	Nicaragua	2.8
78	Guatemala	2.8
79	Honduras	2.8
80	Bolivia	2.6

MEAN: 4.6

8.04 Administrative burden for startups

Starting a new business in your country is generally (1 = extremely difficult and time consuming, 7 = easy)

RANK	COUNTRY	SCORE
1	Hong Kong SAR	6.3
2	Iceland	6.2
3	Singapore	5.9
4	United States	5.8
5	Finland	5.8
6	Estonia	5.6
7	New Zealand	5.5
7	United Kingdom	5.5
9	Canada	5.5
10	Australia	5.5
11	Malaysia	5.4
12	Tunisia	5.3
13	Taiwan	5.3
14	Israel	5.2
15	Vietnam	5.2
16	Thailand	5.1
17	Hungary	5.1
18	Ireland	4.8
19	Norway	4.8
20	Namibia	4.8
21	Switzerland	4.7
22	Sri Lanka	4.7
23	Netherlands	4.7
24	Slovenia	4.6
25	Indonesia	4.5
26	Trinidad and Tobago	4.5
27	Korea	4.5
28	Denmark	4.5
28	South Africa	4.5
28	Sweden	4.5
31	Botswana	4.5
32	Mauritius	4.5
33	Croatia	4.3
34	China	4.3
35	El Salvador	4.1
36	Germany	4.0
37	Portugal	4.0
38	Jordan	4.0
39	India	4.0
40	Panama	4.0
41	Chile	3.9
42	Austria	3.9
43	Turkey	3.9
44	Dominican Republic	3.9
45	Japan	3.8
46	Slovak Republic	3.8
47	Spain	3.8
48	Latvia	3.8
49	Brazil	3.8
50	Philippines	3.7
51	Czech Republic	3.7
52	Poland	3.7
53	Italy	3.6
54	Zimbabwe	3.6
55	Morocco	3.6
56	Nigeria	3.5
57	Paraguay	3.5
58	Belgium	3.5
59	Nicaragua	3.4
60	Costa Rica	3.4
61	Greece	3.4
62	Guatemala	3.3
63	Bangladesh	3.3
64	Lithuania	3.3
65	Russian Federation	3.2
66	Jamaica	3.2
67	Uruguay	3.1
68	France	3.1
69	Colombia	3.0
70	Venezuela	2.8
71	Mexico	2.8
72	Ukraine	2.8
73	Peru	2.8
74	Ecuador	2.7
75	Bolivia	2.7
76	Argentina	2.6
77	Romania	2.6
78	Haiti	2.5
79	Bulgaria	2.3
80	Honduras	2.2

MEAN: 4.1

8.05 Effectiveness of antitrust policy

Antimonopoly policy in your country is (1 = lax and not effective at promoting competition, 7 = effective and promotes competition)

RANK	COUNTRY	SCORE
1	United Kingdom	6.0
2	Finland	5.9
3	Australia	5.9
4	United States	5.8
5	Netherlands	5.6
6	New Zealand	5.6
7	Israel	5.5
8	Denmark	5.5
9	Belgium	5.5
10	Germany	5.4
11	Canada	5.4
12	Norway	5.3
13	France	5.2
14	Taiwan	5.2
15	Korea	5.1
16	Ireland	5.1
17	Iceland	5.0
17	Sweden	5.0
19	Austria	4.9
20	Singapore	4.9
21	Italy	4.9
22	South Africa	4.9
23	Hungary	4.9
24	Brazil	4.9
25	Chile	4.7
26	Switzerland	4.7
27	Japan	4.7
28	Slovenia	4.6
29	India	4.5
30	Tunisia	4.4
31	Spain	4.4
32	Portugal	4.3
33	Malaysia	4.2
34	Mexico	4.1
35	Thailand	4.1
36	Jamaica	4.0
37	Morocco	4.0
38	China	3.9
38	Estonia	3.9
40	Greece	3.9
41	Lithuania	3.9
42	Czech Republic	3.9
43	Panama	3.8
44	Latvia	3.8
45	Sri Lanka	3.7
46	Jordan	3.7
47	Poland	3.6
48	Hong Kong SAR	3.6
49	Namibia	3.6
50	Colombia	3.6
51	Slovak Republic	3.6
52	Croatia	3.5
53	Peru	3.5
54	Dominican Republic	3.5
55	Philippines	3.4
56	Turkey	3.4
56	Zimbabwe	3.4
58	Botswana	3.4
59	Costa Rica	3.4
60	Venezuela	3.4
61	Indonesia	3.4
62	Mauritius	3.2
63	Bulgaria	3.1
64	Nigeria	3.1
65	Russian Federation	3.0
66	Ukraine	3.0
67	Trinidad and Tobago	2.9
68	Bolivia	2.9
69	Paraguay	2.9
70	Bangladesh	2.9
71	Vietnam	2.9
72	Romania	2.8
73	El Salvador	2.8
74	Argentina	2.7
75	Haiti	2.4
76	Guatemala	2.2
77	Uruguay	2.2
78	Nicaragua	2.2
79	Honduras	2.1
80	Ecuador	2.0

MEAN: 4.0

8.06 Number of procedures to resolve a dispute, 2002

Number of procedures required to resolve a contract dispute

RANK	COUNTRY	HARD DATA
1	France	10
2	Australia	11
2	Jamaica	11
2	South Africa	11
5	New Zealand	12
5	Norway	12
5	United Kingdom	12
5	United States	12
9	Hong Kong SAR	13
9	Zimbabwe	13
11	Denmark	14
11	Germany	14
11	Switzerland	14
11	Tunisia	14
15	Bangladesh	15
15	Greece	15
15	Taiwan	15
18	Belgium	16
18	Brazil	16
18	Czech Republic	16
18	Italy	16
18	Japan	16
18	Russian Federation	16
24	Canada	17
24	Hungary	17
24	Morocco	17
24	Sri Lanka	17
28	Poland	18
28	Turkey	18
30	Dominican Republic	19
30	Finland	19
30	Guatemala	19
30	Ireland	19
30	Israel	19
30	Latvia	19
30	Thailand	19
37	Austria	20
37	Botswana	20
37	China	20
37	Croatia	20
37	Singapore	20
37	Spain	20
37	Ukraine	20
44	Chile	21
44	Costa Rica	21
44	Netherlands	21
44	Sweden	21
48	India	22
48	Malaysia	22
48	Portugal	22
48	Slovenia	22
52	Korea	23
53	Nigeria	25
54	Bulgaria	26
55	Philippines	28
55	Romania	28
55	Vietnam	28
58	Indonesia	29
59	Lithuania	30
60	Argentina	32
60	Honduras	32
60	Jordan	32
63	Ecuador	33
64	Peru	35
65	Colombia	37
66	Uruguay	38
67	Venezuela	41
68	Bolivia	44
68	Panama	44
70	Mexico	47
	El Salvador	N/A
	Estonia	N/A
	Haiti	N/A
	Iceland	N/A
	Mauritius	N/A
	Namibia	N/A
	Nicaragua	N/A
	Paraguay	N/A
	Slovak Republic	N/A
	Trinidad and Tobago	N/A

SOURCE: Doing Business, World Bank web site

625

8.07 Number of days to resolve a dispute, 2002

Number of days required to resolve a contract dispute

RANK	COUNTRY	HARD DATA
1	Tunisia	7
2	Netherlands	39
3	Singapore	46
4	United States	54
5	Japan	60
5	New Zealand	60
7	Hong Kong SAR	61
8	Korea	75
9	Botswana	77
10	Denmark	83
11	South Africa	84
12	Norway	87
13	Malaysia	90
14	United Kingdom	101
15	Turkey	105
16	India	106
17	Belgium	120
17	Vietnam	120
19	Ireland	131
20	Jordan	147
20	Spain	147
22	Lithuania	150
23	Germany	154
24	Russian Federation	160
25	Philippines	164
26	Brazil	180
26	China	180
28	France	181
29	Latvia	189
30	Sweden	190
31	Morocco	192
32	Panama	197
32	Zimbabwe	197
34	Chile	200
35	Jamaica	202
36	Taiwan	210
36	Thailand	210
38	Dominican Republic	215
39	Guatemala	220
40	Switzerland	223
41	Ukraine	224
42	Honduras	225
42	Indonesia	225
42	Romania	225
45	Finland	240
46	Nigeria	241
47	Bangladesh	270
47	Czech Republic	270
49	Mexico	283
50	Argentina	300
51	Greece	315
51	Israel	315
53	Australia	319
54	Croatia	330
55	Ecuador	333
56	Uruguay	360
56	Venezuela	360
58	Hungary	365
59	Costa Rica	370
60	Peru	381
61	Bulgaria	410
62	Portugal	420
63	Canada	421
64	Austria	434
65	Sri Lanka	440
66	Bolivia	464
67	Colombia	527
68	Italy	645
69	Poland	1,000
70	Slovenia	1,003
	El Salvador	N/A
	Estonia	N/A
	Haiti	N/A
	Iceland	N/A
	Mauritius	N/A
	Namibia	N/A
	Nicaragua	N/A
	Paraguay	N/A
	Slovak Republic	N/A
	Trinidad and Tobago	N/A

SOURCE: Doing Business, World Bank web site

8.08 Number of procedures to start a business, 2002

Number of administrative procedures required to register a business

RANK	COUNTRY	HARD DATA
1	Australia	2
1	Canada	2
1	New Zealand	2
4	Denmark	3
4	Ireland	3
6	Norway	4
7	Hong Kong SAR	5
7	Hungary	5
7	Israel	5
7	Sweden	5
7	United Kingdom	5
7	United States	5
13	Switzerland	6
14	Bangladesh	7
14	Belgium	7
14	Finland	7
14	Jamaica	7
14	Latvia	7
14	Malaysia	7
14	Mexico	7
14	Panama	7
14	Singapore	7
23	Botswana	8
23	Netherlands	8
23	Peru	8
23	Sri Lanka	8
23	Taiwan	8
23	Thailand	8
29	Austria	9
29	Germany	9
29	Nigeria	9
29	Romania	9
29	Slovenia	9
29	South Africa	9
29	Tunisia	9
36	Bulgaria	10
36	Chile	10
36	Czech Republic	10
36	France	10
36	India	10
36	Uruguay	10
36	Vietnam	10
36	Zimbabwe	10
44	Costa Rica	11
44	Indonesia	11
44	Japan	11
44	Lithuania	11
44	Poland	11
44	Slovak Republic	11
44	Spain	11
51	China	12
51	Nicaragua	12
51	Portugal	12
54	Croatia	13
54	Guatemala	13
54	Italy	13
54	Korea	13
54	Morocco	13
54	Turkey	13
54	Ukraine	13
61	Argentina	14
61	Ecuador	14
61	Jordan	14
61	Philippines	14
61	Venezuela	14
66	Honduras	15
67	Brazil	16
67	Greece	16
69	Colombia	18
70	Bolivia	19
71	Russian Federation	19
72	Dominican Republic	20
	El Salvador	N/A
	Estonia	N/A
	Haiti	N/A
	Iceland	N/A
	Mauritius	N/A
	Namibia	N/A
	Paraguay	N/A
	Trinidad and Tobago	N/A

SOURCE: Doing Business, World Bank web site

8.09 Number of days to start a business, 2002

Number of days required to register a business

RANK	COUNTRY	HARD DATA
1	Canada	2
1	New Zealand	2
3	Denmark	3
4	United Kingdom	5
4	United States	5
6	Australia	6
7	Singapore	8
8	Latvia	11
9	Ireland	16
10	Sweden	18
11	Panama	19
12	Switzerland	20
13	Hong Kong SAR	22
14	Norway	24
15	Uruguay	29
16	Austria	30
16	Bangladesh	30
16	Bulgaria	30
16	Japan	30
20	South Africa	32
21	Chile	34
22	Belgium	35
23	Finland	36
24	Jamaica	37
25	Guatemala	41
25	Korea	41
27	Ukraine	42
28	Taiwan	43
29	Israel	44
30	Germany	45
30	Thailand	45
32	Greece	46
33	Romania	48
34	Nigeria	50
34	Russian Federation	50
36	Croatia	51
36	Mexico	51
38	France	53
38	Turkey	53
40	Malaysia	56
41	Tunisia	57
42	Poland	58
43	Lithuania	62
43	Philippines	62
43	Slovenia	62
46	Argentina	63
47	Italy	64
48	Hungary	66
49	Vietnam	68
50	Botswana	70
51	China	72
51	Netherlands	72
53	Sri Lanka	73
54	Morocco	76
55	Costa Rica	80
56	Colombia	81
57	Czech Republic	89
58	Brazil	90
58	Ecuador	90
58	Jordan	90
61	India	95
62	Bolivia	104
63	Portugal	106
64	Spain	110
65	Peru	114
66	Dominican Republic	117
67	Zimbabwe	123
68	Slovak Republic	125
69	Nicaragua	128
70	Honduras	146
71	Indonesia	158
72	Venezuela	201
	El Salvador	N/A
	Estonia	N/A
	Haiti	N/A
	Iceland	N/A
	Mauritius	N/A
	Namibia	N/A
	Paraguay	N/A
	Trinidad and Tobago	N/A

SOURCE: Doing Business, World Bank web site

8.10 Total cost of starting a business, 2002

Total cost in US dollars to register a business

RANK	COUNTRY	HARD DATA
1	Denmark	0
2	New Zealand	25
3	Zimbabwe	58
4	China	111
5	Russian Federation	114
6	Bulgaria	120
7	Canada	126
8	Sri Lanka	127
9	Thailand	134
10	Vietnam	138
11	Lithuania	143
12	Philippines	150
13	Indonesia	160
14	Ukraine	164
15	Sweden	189
16	South Africa	195
17	United States	210
18	Morocco	217
19	India	221
20	Nigeria	230
21	Finland	254
22	Bangladesh	273
23	Czech Republic	279
24	Colombia	286
25	Australia	368
26	United Kingdom	372
27	Jamaica	420
28	Brazil	430
29	Tunisia	439
30	Peru	465
31	Slovak Republic	488
32	Botswana	505
33	Romania	543
34	Honduras	570
35	Chile	617
36	France	632
37	Venezuela	712
38	Argentina	774
39	Croatia	798
40	Costa Rica	802
41	Hong Kong SAR	804
42	Jordan	806
43	Ecuador	815
44	Taiwan	821
45	Dominican Republic	853
46	Malaysia	921
47	Panama	948
48	Latvia	981
49	Poland	986
50	Nicaragua	1,025
51	Mexico	1,059
52	Guatemala	1,143
53	Turkey	1,189
54	Norway	1,265
55	Slovenia	1,360
56	Germany	1,461
57	Bolivia	1,484
58	Singapore	1,629
59	Korea	1,688
60	Spain	2,338
61	Ireland	2,348
62	Portugal	2,396
63	Uruguay	2,957
64	Hungary	3,143
65	Israel	3,510
66	Belgium	3,622
67	Japan	3,964
68	Netherlands	4,291
69	Austria	4,336
70	Italy	4,535
71	Greece	6,691
72	Switzerland	6,709
	El Salvador	N/A
	Estonia	N/A
	Haiti	N/A
	Iceland	N/A
	Mauritius	N/A
	Namibia	N/A
	Paraguay	N/A
	Trinidad and Tobago	N/A

SOURCE: Doing Business, World Bank web site

8.11 Cost of starting a business relative to GNP per capita, 2002

Cost as a percentage of GNP per capita to register a business

RANK	COUNTRY	HARD DATA
1	Denmark	0.00
2	New Zealand	0.19
3	Canada	0.59
4	United States	0.69
5	Sweden	0.70
6	Finland	1.01
7	United Kingdom	1.52
8	Australia	1.82
9	France	2.59
10	Hong Kong SAR	3.10
11	Norway	3.66
12	Lithuania	4.89
13	Czech Republic	5.30
14	Singapore	5.50
15	Germany	5.82
16	Taiwan	5.92
17	South Africa	6.46
18	Thailand	6.69
19	Russian Federation	6.76
20	Bulgaria	7.92
21	Ireland	10.36
22	Argentina	10.38
23	Japan	11.13
24	Brazil	12.02
25	Zimbabwe	12.68
26	China	13.18
26	Slovak Republic	13.18
28	Chile	13.44
29	Slovenia	13.53
30	Colombia	14.13
31	Philippines	14.45
32	Belgium	14.76
33	Sri Lanka	14.96
34	Botswana	15.29
35	Israel	15.49
36	Spain	15.50
37	Jamaica	16.08
38	Venezuela	16.51
39	Netherlands	17.18
40	Austria	17.19
41	Croatia	17.27
42	Switzerland	17.59
43	Morocco	18.38
44	Korea	18.94
45	Mexico	20.88
46	Tunisia	20.89
47	Costa Rica	21.06
48	Portugal	21.55
49	Peru	22.38
50	Italy	22.50
51	Ukraine	23.45
52	Poland	23.54
53	Malaysia	27.25
54	Indonesia	28.00
55	Panama	29.09
56	Romania	32.54
57	Latvia	33.59
58	Vietnam	35.36
59	Turkey	38.35
60	Dominican Republic	40.05
61	Jordan	47.16
62	India	49.16
63	Uruguay	49.28
64	Greece	55.95
65	Honduras	66.31
66	Hungary	66.72
67	Ecuador	67.34
68	Guatemala	68.01
69	Bangladesh	73.78
70	Nigeria	88.61
71	Bolivia	149.89
72	Nicaragua	256.25
	El Salvador	N/A
	Estonia	N/A
	Haiti	N/A
	Iceland	N/A
	Mauritius	N/A
	Namibia	N/A
	Paraguay	N/A
	Trinidad and Tobago	N/A

SOURCE: Doing Business, World Bank web site

9.01 Buyer sophistication

Buyers in your country are (1 = unsophisticated and make choices based on the lowest price, 7 = knowledgeable and demanding and buy based on superior performance attributes)

RANK	COUNTRY	SCORE	1 MEAN: 4.1 7
1	United Kingdom	6.2	
2	Hong Kong SAR	6.0	
3	Switzerland	6.0	
4	United States	5.9	
5	Finland	5.9	
6	Australia	5.9	
7	Japan	5.8	
8	Belgium	5.7	
9	Germany	5.7	
10	France	5.6	
11	Sweden	5.5	
12	Canada	5.5	
13	Singapore	5.5	
14	Netherlands	5.4	
15	Denmark	5.4	
16	Austria	5.4	
17	Italy	5.3	
18	New Zealand	5.2	
19	Israel	5.1	
20	Iceland	5.1	
21	Taiwan	5.1	
22	Ireland	5.0	
23	Slovenia	5.0	
24	Korea	5.0	
25	Spain	4.8	
26	Norway	4.8	
27	Malaysia	4.8	
28	Tunisia	4.5	
29	India	4.5	
30	Estonia	4.4	
31	Brazil	4.3	
32	Czech Republic	4.3	
33	Thailand	4.3	
34	Vietnam	4.2	
35	Chile	4.2	
36	Trinidad and Tobago	4.2	
37	Greece	4.1	
38	South Africa	4.1	
39	Costa Rica	4.1	
40	Botswana	4.1	
41	China	4.0	
42	Sri Lanka	4.0	
43	Portugal	4.0	
44	Dominican Republic	3.9	
45	Philippines	3.9	
46	Mauritius	3.8	
47	Panama	3.8	
48	Jamaica	3.8	
49	Argentina	3.8	
50	Namibia	3.7	
51	Hungary	3.7	
52	Russian Federation	3.6	
53	Latvia	3.6	
54	Nigeria	3.6	
54	Poland	3.6	
56	Mexico	3.5	
57	Colombia	3.5	
58	Morocco	3.5	
59	Croatia	3.5	
60	Uruguay	3.4	
61	Turkey	3.4	
62	Indonesia	3.4	
63	Jordan	3.4	
64	Slovak Republic	3.3	
65	Zimbabwe	3.3	
66	Lithuania	3.2	
67	Bangladesh	3.0	
68	Venezuela	3.0	
69	Ukraine	2.9	
70	Bulgaria	2.8	
71	El Salvador	2.7	
72	Romania	2.6	
73	Guatemala	2.6	
74	Peru	2.5	
75	Paraguay	2.4	
76	Nicaragua	2.3	
77	Honduras	2.2	
78	Ecuador	2.0	
79	Bolivia	1.9	
80	Haiti	1.9	

9.02 Local supplier quantity

Local suppliers in your country are (1 = largely nonexistent, 7 = numerous and include the most important materials, components, equipment, and services)

RANK	COUNTRY	SCORE	1 MEAN: 4.7 7
1	Japan	6.4	
2	Germany	6.3	
3	United States	6.2	
4	United Kingdom	6.2	
5	France	5.9	
6	Canada	5.8	
7	Australia	5.8	
8	Italy	5.7	
9	Czech Republic	5.7	
10	Austria	5.6	
11	Netherlands	5.6	
12	India	5.6	
13	Belgium	5.6	
14	Spain	5.5	
15	Taiwan	5.5	
16	Brazil	5.5	
17	Switzerland	5.5	
18	Sweden	5.4	
19	Malaysia	5.4	
20	Korea	5.4	
21	Hong Kong SAR	5.4	
22	Chile	5.3	
22	Finland	5.3	
24	Norway	5.2	
25	Singapore	5.1	
26	Lithuania	5.1	
27	Denmark	5.1	
28	South Africa	5.1	
29	Thailand	5.1	
30	Iceland	5.0	
31	Ireland	5.0	
32	Morocco	4.9	
33	Portugal	4.9	
34	New Zealand	4.8	
35	Indonesia	4.8	
35	Turkey	4.8	
37	Slovenia	4.8	
38	Slovak Republic	4.8	
39	Tunisia	4.8	
40	Poland	4.7	
41	Vietnam	4.7	
42	China	4.7	
43	Costa Rica	4.6	
44	Trinidad and Tobago	4.6	
45	Panama	4.6	
46	Mexico	4.6	
47	Greece	4.6	
48	Philippines	4.5	
49	Dominican Republic	4.5	
50	Russian Federation	4.5	
51	Colombia	4.4	
51	Mauritius	4.4	
53	Estonia	4.4	
54	Sri Lanka	4.4	
55	Ukraine	4.3	
56	Nigeria	4.3	
57	Hungary	4.3	
58	Jordan	4.2	
59	Bulgaria	4.1	
60	Peru	4.1	
61	Latvia	4.1	
62	Israel	4.1	
63	Croatia	4.1	
64	Guatemala	4.0	
65	Romania	4.0	
66	Zimbabwe	4.0	
67	Bangladesh	3.9	
68	Uruguay	3.9	
69	Venezuela	3.9	
70	Paraguay	3.8	
71	Argentina	3.8	
72	El Salvador	3.8	
73	Ecuador	3.8	
74	Namibia	3.7	
75	Jamaica	3.6	
76	Honduras	3.5	
77	Botswana	3.3	
77	Nicaragua	3.3	
79	Haiti	3.2	
80	Bolivia	3.1	

9.03 Local supplier quality

The quality of local suppliers in your country is (1 = poor as they are inefficient and have little technological capability, 7 = very good as they are internationally competitive and assist in new product and process development)

RANK	COUNTRY	SCORE
1	Germany	6.3
2	United States	6.2
3	Japan	6.1
4	Austria	6.0
5	Netherlands	5.9
6	United Kingdom	5.9
7	Finland	5.9
8	Sweden	5.9
9	Canada	5.8
10	Belgium	5.8
11	Denmark	5.8
12	Switzerland	5.8
13	Australia	5.7
14	France	5.6
15	Italy	5.6
16	Israel	5.5
17	Taiwan	5.5
18	Spain	5.5
19	Czech Republic	5.4
20	Korea	5.3
21	Hong Kong SAR	5.2
22	Brazil	5.2
23	New Zealand	5.2
24	Iceland	5.2
25	Singapore	5.2
26	Norway	5.2
27	Ireland	5.1
28	Chile	5.0
29	India	5.0
30	South Africa	4.9
31	Malaysia	4.9
32	Turkey	4.7
33	Thailand	4.7
34	Hungary	4.7
35	Slovenia	4.6
36	Portugal	4.6
37	Dominican Republic	4.6
38	Trinidad and Tobago	4.6
39	Estonia	4.5
40	Lithuania	4.5
41	Costa Rica	4.5
42	Tunisia	4.4
43	Morocco	4.4
44	Panama	4.3
45	Mexico	4.3
46	Colombia	4.2
47	Mauritius	4.2
48	Poland	4.2
49	Greece	4.2
50	Slovak Republic	4.2
51	Latvia	4.1
52	Philippines	4.0
53	China	4.0
54	Indonesia	3.9
55	Peru	3.9
56	Croatia	3.8
57	Guatemala	3.8
58	Namibia	3.8
59	Uruguay	3.8
60	Vietnam	3.8
61	Ukraine	3.7
62	Argentina	3.7
63	Jordan	3.7
64	Russian Federation	3.7
65	Sri Lanka	3.7
66	El Salvador	3.7
67	Bulgaria	3.7
68	Zimbabwe	3.6
69	Nigeria	3.5
70	Ecuador	3.5
71	Paraguay	3.5
72	Botswana	3.4
73	Jamaica	3.3
74	Venezuela	3.2
75	Bangladesh	3.2
76	Romania	3.2
77	Honduras	3.0
78	Nicaragua	3.0
79	Haiti	2.7
80	Bolivia	2.5

MEAN: 4.5

9.04 Presence of demanding regulatory standards

Standards on product/service quality, energy, and other regulations (outside environmental regulations) in your country are (1 = lax or nonexistent, 7 = among the world's most stringent)

RANK	COUNTRY	SCORE
1	Germany	6.3
2	United Kingdom	6.3
3	Switzerland	6.2
4	Netherlands	6.1
5	Austria	6.1
6	United States	6.1
7	Denmark	6.1
8	Sweden	6.1
9	Belgium	5.9
10	Finland	5.9
11	France	5.9
12	Canada	5.8
13	Australia	5.8
14	Norway	5.7
15	Iceland	5.7
16	Japan	5.7
17	Singapore	5.6
18	New Zealand	5.5
19	Slovak Republic	5.3
20	Ireland	5.2
21	Israel	5.2
22	Slovenia	5.2
23	Czech Republic	5.1
24	Italy	5.1
25	Korea	5.1
26	Hong Kong SAR	5.1
27	Spain	5.0
28	Taiwan	5.0
29	Brazil	4.9
30	Malaysia	4.8
31	Tunisia	4.8
32	Chile	4.7
33	Hungary	4.7
34	South Africa	4.7
35	Portugal	4.7
36	Thailand	4.6
37	Estonia	4.6
38	Lithuania	4.5
39	Latvia	4.4
40	Poland	4.2
41	Greece	4.2
42	Panama	4.1
43	Costa Rica	4.1
44	India	4.1
45	Mauritius	4.1
46	Croatia	4.0
47	Russian Federation	4.0
48	Colombia	4.0
49	Morocco	3.9
50	Namibia	3.9
51	China	3.9
52	Mexico	3.9
53	Turkey	3.9
54	Trinidad and Tobago	3.9
55	Jordan	3.9
56	Zimbabwe	3.8
57	Jamaica	3.8
58	Ukraine	3.8
59	Argentina	3.7
60	Sri Lanka	3.7
61	Uruguay	3.7
62	Botswana	3.5
63	Peru	3.4
64	Dominican Republic	3.4
65	Bulgaria	3.4
66	Romania	3.4
67	Philippines	3.4
68	Venezuela	3.3
69	Indonesia	3.2
70	Nigeria	3.2
71	El Salvador	3.2
72	Vietnam	3.1
73	Bolivia	3.0
74	Paraguay	3.0
75	Guatemala	3.0
76	Bangladesh	2.8
77	Ecuador	2.6
78	Nicaragua	2.5
79	Honduras	2.2
80	Haiti	1.6

MEAN: 4.4

631

9.05 Decentralization of corporate activity

Corporate activity in your country is (1 = dominated by a few business groups, 7 = spread among many firms)

RANK	COUNTRY	SCORE
1	United States	6.2
2	United Kingdom	6.2
3	Japan	5.8
4	Netherlands	5.8
5	Germany	5.6
6	Denmark	5.5
7	Belgium	5.5
8	Taiwan	5.4
9	Finland	5.3
10	Australia	5.3
11	Switzerland	5.2
12	China	5.1
13	Austria	5.0
14	France	4.9
15	Canada	4.9
16	Singapore	4.9
17	Ireland	4.8
18	Tunisia	4.8
19	Malaysia	4.7
20	Vietnam	4.7
21	Norway	4.7
22	Nigeria	4.6
23	Hungary	4.5
24	India	4.5
25	Brazil	4.4
26	Spain	4.3
27	New Zealand	4.3
28	Thailand	4.2
29	Korea	4.1
30	Morocco	4.1
31	Slovenia	4.1
32	Italy	4.0
33	Sweden	4.0
34	Poland	3.9
35	Iceland	3.9
36	Estonia	3.9
37	Slovak Republic	3.9
38	Portugal	3.9
39	Hong Kong SAR	3.8
40	Czech Republic	3.8
41	Bulgaria	3.8
42	Costa Rica	3.8
43	Greece	3.8
44	Romania	3.7
45	Lithuania	3.7
46	Chile	3.6
47	South Africa	3.6
48	Israel	3.6
49	Latvia	3.5
50	Jordan	3.4
51	Zimbabwe	3.4
52	Trinidad and Tobago	3.3
53	Uruguay	3.3
54	Dominican Republic	3.3
55	Indonesia	3.2
56	Namibia	3.2
57	Jamaica	3.2
58	Botswana	3.2
59	Sri Lanka	3.2
60	Panama	3.2
61	Russian Federation	3.1
62	Croatia	3.1
63	Philippines	2.9
64	Turkey	2.9
65	Paraguay	2.8
66	Venezuela	2.8
67	Mexico	2.8
68	Argentina	2.8
68	Ukraine	2.8
70	Peru	2.7
71	Bangladesh	2.6
72	El Salvador	2.5
73	Colombia	2.5
74	Mauritius	2.5
75	Bolivia	2.3
76	Nicaragua	2.2
77	Honduras	2.1
78	Guatemala	2.1
79	Haiti	2.1
80	Ecuador	1.8

MEAN: 3.9

9.06 State of cluster development

How common are clusters in your country? (1 = limited and shallow, 7 = common and deep)

RANK	COUNTRY	SCORE
1	Italy	5.7
2	Taiwan	5.5
3	United States	5.4
4	Finland	5.3
5	United Kingdom	4.9
6	Singapore	4.8
7	Germany	4.7
8	Korea	4.6
9	Sweden	4.4
10	Ireland	4.3
11	Hong Kong SAR	4.3
12	Canada	4.3
13	Japan	4.2
14	Netherlands	4.1
15	Norway	4.0
16	Austria	3.9
17	Iceland	3.9
18	Brazil	3.9
19	India	3.8
20	Switzerland	3.8
21	France	3.7
22	Denmark	3.7
23	Thailand	3.7
24	Belgium	3.6
24	Indonesia	3.6
26	Australia	3.5
27	China	3.5
27	Malaysia	3.5
27	Turkey	3.5
30	Spain	3.5
31	Mexico	3.4
32	Portugal	3.4
33	Morocco	3.3
34	Lithuania	3.3
35	South Africa	3.2
36	Dominican Republic	3.2
37	New Zealand	3.2
38	Nigeria	3.2
39	Hungary	3.2
40	Russian Federation	3.2
41	Israel	3.1
42	Poland	3.1
43	Philippines	3.0
44	Romania	3.0
45	Chile	3.0
46	Sri Lanka	3.0
47	Botswana	2.9
48	Nicaragua	2.9
49	Mauritius	2.9
50	Costa Rica	2.9
51	Jordan	2.9
52	Trinidad and Tobago	2.9
53	Bangladesh	2.9
54	Ecuador	2.9
55	Colombia	2.8
56	Latvia	2.8
57	Panama	2.8
58	Slovenia	2.7
59	Ukraine	2.7
60	Vietnam	2.7
61	Slovak Republic	2.7
62	Namibia	2.7
63	Croatia	2.7
64	Tunisia	2.7
65	Czech Republic	2.6
66	Peru	2.6
67	Greece	2.6
68	Guatemala	2.6
69	Jamaica	2.6
70	Bulgaria	2.5
71	Bolivia	2.5
72	Zimbabwe	2.5
73	Argentina	2.5
74	Estonia	2.5
75	El Salvador	2.4
76	Venezuela	2.4
77	Honduras	2.3
78	Uruguay	2.2
79	Paraguay	2.0
80	Haiti	1.9

MEAN: 3.3

9.07 Extent of collaboration among clusters

Collaboration in your clusters with suppliers and partners is (1 = almost nonexistent, 7 = extensive and involves suppliers, local customers, and local research institutions)

RANK	COUNTRY	SCORE
1	Finland	5.6
2	Japan	5.5
3	United States	5.4
4	Germany	5.2
5	Italy	5.2
6	Taiwan	5.0
7	Sweden	4.9
8	United Kingdom	4.8
9	Austria	4.8
10	Canada	4.8
11	Belgium	4.8
11	Brazil	4.8
13	France	4.7
14	Korea	4.7
15	Netherlands	4.7
16	China	4.6
17	Thailand	4.6
18	Australia	4.6
19	Switzerland	4.6
20	Singapore	4.5
21	Croatia	4.4
22	India	4.4
23	Spain	4.3
24	Hong Kong SAR	4.3
25	Slovak Republic	4.2
26	Czech Republic	4.2
27	South Africa	4.2
28	Ireland	4.2
29	Israel	4.2
30	Denmark	4.1
31	Malaysia	4.1
32	Romania	4.1
33	Hungary	4.0
34	Morocco	4.0
35	Norway	3.9
36	Latvia	3.9
37	Mexico	3.9
38	Poland	3.8
39	Iceland	3.8
40	Lithuania	3.8
40	Turkey	3.8
42	New Zealand	3.8
43	Russian Federation	3.8
44	Dominican Republic	3.8
45	Vietnam	3.7
46	Indonesia	3.7
47	Slovenia	3.6
48	Sri Lanka	3.6
49	Chile	3.6
50	Portugal	3.6
51	Philippines	3.5
52	Ukraine	3.4
53	Costa Rica	3.4
54	Jordan	3.4
55	Bulgaria	3.4
56	Tunisia	3.3
57	Estonia	3.3
58	Zimbabwe	3.3
59	Peru	3.3
60	Guatemala	3.2
61	Trinidad and Tobago	3.2
62	Jamaica	3.2
63	Argentina	3.2
64	Colombia	3.1
65	Greece	3.1
66	Panama	3.1
67	Nigeria	3.1
68	Botswana	3.0
69	Mauritius	3.0
70	Venezuela	3.0
71	Ecuador	3.0
72	El Salvador	2.9
73	Namibia	2.9
74	Uruguay	2.8
75	Bolivia	2.7
76	Nicaragua	2.7
77	Honduras	2.6
78	Bangladesh	2.6
79	Haiti	2.5
80	Paraguay	2.4

MEAN: 3.8

9.08 Local availability of components and parts

In your industry, how are components and parts obtained? (1 = almost always imported, 7 = almost always sourced locally)

RANK	COUNTRY	SCORE
1	Brazil	5.2
2	Taiwan	5.2
3	Italy	5.0
4	United States	5.0
5	India	5.0
6	China	4.9
7	Spain	4.8
8	Czech Republic	4.8
9	United Kingdom	4.7
10	Japan	4.7
11	Canada	4.6
12	Korea	4.6
13	South Africa	4.6
14	Germany	4.5
15	Ukraine	4.4
16	Russian Federation	4.4
17	Turkey	4.4
18	Thailand	4.3
19	Finland	4.2
20	Malaysia	4.2
21	Austria	4.2
22	France	4.2
23	Portugal	4.1
24	Australia	4.0
25	Norway	4.0
26	Denmark	3.9
27	Switzerland	3.9
28	Lithuania	3.9
29	Poland	3.9
30	Netherlands	3.8
31	New Zealand	3.8
32	Indonesia	3.8
33	Belgium	3.7
34	Mexico	3.7
35	Sweden	3.7
36	Ireland	3.7
37	Bulgaria	3.7
38	Slovenia	3.6
39	Iceland	3.6
40	Hungary	3.6
41	Chile	3.6
42	Romania	3.5
43	Singapore	3.5
44	Morocco	3.5
45	Latvia	3.5
46	Hong Kong SAR	3.4
47	Costa Rica	3.3
48	Slovak Republic	3.3
49	Colombia	3.3
50	Croatia	3.3
51	Dominican Republic	3.3
52	Argentina	3.3
53	Peru	3.2
54	Tunisia	3.1
55	Uruguay	3.1
56	Sri Lanka	3.1
57	Estonia	3.1
58	Philippines	3.1
59	Nicaragua	3.1
60	Greece	3.1
61	Israel	3.0
62	Venezuela	3.0
63	Paraguay	2.9
64	Ecuador	2.9
65	Trinidad and Tobago	2.8
66	Jordan	2.8
67	Vietnam	2.8
68	Panama	2.8
69	Guatemala	2.8
70	Nigeria	2.8
71	El Salvador	2.7
72	Bangladesh	2.6
73	Bolivia	2.6
74	Zimbabwe	2.5
75	Mauritius	2.4
76	Namibia	2.3
77	Jamaica	2.3
78	Honduras	2.1
79	Botswana	2.0
80	Haiti	1.8

MEAN: 3.6

9.09 Local availability of process machinery

In your industry, how is process machinery obtained? (1 = almost always imported, 7 = almost always available locally from world-class suppliers)

RANK	COUNTRY	SCORE
1	Japan	5.7
2	United States	5.3
3	Germany	5.1
4	Italy	5.0
5	China	4.7
6	Czech Republic	4.6
7	Taiwan	4.6
8	Canada	4.5
9	United Kingdom	4.5
10	Korea	4.4
11	Ukraine	4.2
12	Brazil	4.2
13	Finland	4.2
14	Netherlands	4.1
15	Switzerland	4.1
16	Russian Federation	4.1
17	Belgium	4.1
18	Spain	4.0
19	India	4.0
20	Austria	3.8
21	France	3.7
22	Poland	3.6
23	Denmark	3.5
24	Iceland	3.5
24	Malaysia	3.5
26	Hong Kong SAR	3.5
27	Sweden	3.5
28	Australia	3.5
29	Turkey	3.4
30	Bulgaria	3.3
31	Romania	3.3
32	Norway	3.3
33	South Africa	3.2
34	Chile	3.1
35	Ireland	3.1
36	Lithuania	3.1
37	Thailand	3.0
38	Portugal	3.0
39	Singapore	3.0
40	Dominican Republic	2.9
41	Latvia	2.9
42	Morocco	2.9
43	Hungary	2.8
43	Nicaragua	2.8
45	New Zealand	2.8
46	Vietnam	2.7
47	Mexico	2.7
48	Slovenia	2.7
49	Croatia	2.7
50	Indonesia	2.6
51	Slovak Republic	2.6
52	Philippines	2.5
53	Sri Lanka	2.4
54	Greece	2.4
55	Ecuador	2.4
56	Estonia	2.4
57	Colombia	2.4
58	Israel	2.4
59	Costa Rica	2.3
60	Trinidad and Tobago	2.3
61	Argentina	2.2
62	Tunisia	2.2
63	Jordan	2.2
64	Uruguay	2.2
65	Peru	2.1
66	Paraguay	2.1
67	El Salvador	2.1
68	Panama	2.0
69	Bangladesh	2.0
70	Namibia	2.0
71	Bolivia	2.0
72	Venezuela	2.0
73	Nigeria	1.9
74	Guatemala	1.9
75	Honduras	1.9
76	Haiti	1.8
77	Zimbabwe	1.7
78	Botswana	1.7
79	Mauritius	1.6
80	Jamaica	1.5

RANK: 3.1

9.10 Local availability of specialized research and training services

In your industry, specialized research and training services are (1 = not available in the country, 7 = available from world-class local institutions)

RANK	COUNTRY	SCORE
1	United Kingdom	6.3
2	United States	6.2
3	Finland	5.9
4	Japan	5.9
5	Germany	5.8
6	Canada	5.7
7	Israel	5.6
8	Netherlands	5.6
9	Belgium	5.5
10	Switzerland	5.4
11	Austria	5.3
12	France	5.3
13	Sweden	5.3
14	Italy	5.2
15	Denmark	5.1
16	Australia	5.1
17	Taiwan	5.1
18	Brazil	5.0
19	Czech Republic	5.0
20	Slovenia	4.9
21	Spain	4.8
22	New Zealand	4.8
23	Norway	4.8
24	Ireland	4.7
25	India	4.7
26	Singapore	4.6
27	Hungary	4.6
28	Korea	4.6
29	Estonia	4.4
30	Poland	4.4
31	Chile	4.4
32	Iceland	4.4
33	Russian Federation	4.4
34	Malaysia	4.3
35	Costa Rica	4.3
36	Slovak Republic	4.3
37	Hong Kong SAR	4.3
38	Tunisia	4.2
39	Turkey	4.2
40	Thailand	4.2
41	China	4.2
42	Dominican Republic	4.1
43	Croatia	4.1
44	South Africa	4.1
45	Ukraine	4.1
46	Lithuania	4.1
47	Latvia	4.0
48	Mexico	4.0
49	Argentina	3.9
50	Portugal	3.9
51	Bulgaria	3.9
52	Jordan	3.9
53	Venezuela	3.8
54	Morocco	3.8
55	Vietnam	3.7
56	Romania	3.7
57	Greece	3.7
58	Ecuador	3.7
59	Sri Lanka	3.7
60	Colombia	3.7
61	Nigeria	3.7
62	Indonesia	3.6
63	Trinidad and Tobago	3.5
64	Peru	3.5
65	Mauritius	3.3
66	Panama	3.3
67	Jamaica	3.3
68	Uruguay	3.2
69	Guatemala	3.1
70	El Salvador	3.1
71	Philippines	2.9
72	Paraguay	2.9
73	Bolivia	2.8
74	Zimbabwe	2.8
75	Honduras	2.8
76	Namibia	2.7
77	Botswana	2.6
78	Bangladesh	2.6
79	Nicaragua	2.5
80	Haiti	2.2

MEAN: 4.2

Section X: Company Operations and Strategy

10.01 Nature of competitive advantage

Competitiveness of your country's companies in international markets is primarily due to (1 = low cost or local natural resources, 7 = unique products and processes)

RANK	COUNTRY	SCORE
1	Germany	6.2
2	Japan	6.1
3	United States	6.0
4	Switzerland	6.0
5	Israel	5.9
6	United Kingdom	5.8
7	Finland	5.8
8	Denmark	5.8
9	Austria	5.8
10	Sweden	5.8
11	Netherlands	5.4
12	France	5.4
13	Italy	5.3
14	Belgium	5.3
15	Singapore	4.9
16	Hong Kong SAR	4.7
17	Taiwan	4.6
18	Iceland	4.6
19	Korea	4.5
20	Jamaica	4.5
21	Spain	4.5
22	Norway	4.3
23	Costa Rica	4.3
24	Botswana	4.3
25	Ireland	4.3
26	Panama	4.1
27	Canada	4.0
28	Croatia	3.9
29	Slovenia	3.8
30	Dominican Republic	3.7
31	Namibia	3.6
32	El Salvador	3.5
33	Philippines	3.5
34	Hungary	3.5
35	Jordan	3.4
36	Nicaragua	3.4
37	New Zealand	3.4
38	Australia	3.4
39	Uruguay	3.4
40	Tunisia	3.3
41	Malaysia	3.3
42	Colombia	3.3
43	Greece	3.3
44	Chile	3.3
45	Thailand	3.3
46	China	3.2
47	Sri Lanka	3.2
48	Lithuania	3.2
49	Mexico	3.2
50	Portugal	3.1
51	Peru	3.1
52	Brazil	3.1
53	Poland	3.0
54	Mauritius	3.0
55	Morocco	3.0
56	Latvia	2.9
57	Trinidad and Tobago	2.9
58	Venezuela	2.9
59	Argentina	2.9
60	Slovak Republic	2.8
61	Estonia	2.8
62	Bolivia	2.8
63	Guatemala	2.8
63	Turkey	2.8
65	Bulgaria	2.7
66	Ecuador	2.7
67	India	2.7
68	South Africa	2.7
69	Indonesia	2.7
70	Ukraine	2.7
71	Czech Republic	2.7
72	Russian Federation	2.6
73	Haiti	2.6
74	Honduras	2.6
75	Vietnam	2.5
76	Paraguay	2.5
77	Nigeria	2.3
78	Bangladesh	2.3
79	Romania	2.2
80	Zimbabwe	2.1

MEAN: 3.7

10.02 Value chain presence

Exporting companies in your country are (1 = primarily involved in resource extraction or production, 7 = not only produce but also perform product design, marketing, sales, logistics, and after-sales services)

RANK	COUNTRY	SCORE
1	Germany	6.4
2	United Kingdom	6.3
3	Japan	6.3
4	United States	6.2
5	Switzerland	6.1
6	Sweden	6.1
7	Denmark	6.1
8	France	6.0
9	Finland	6.0
10	Italy	5.9
11	Belgium	5.8
12	Hong Kong SAR	5.8
13	Netherlands	5.8
14	Austria	5.7
15	Singapore	5.4
16	Ireland	5.4
17	Israel	5.4
18	Taiwan	5.1
19	Spain	5.1
20	Korea	5.1
21	Slovenia	4.7
22	Czech Republic	4.7
23	Tunisia	4.7
24	Mauritius	4.6
25	Lithuania	4.6
26	Canada	4.6
27	Malaysia	4.3
28	Costa Rica	4.3
29	Hungary	4.3
30	Morocco	4.2
31	Dominican Republic	4.2
32	Turkey	3.9
33	Iceland	3.9
34	Thailand	3.8
35	Portugal	3.8
36	Norway	3.8
37	India	3.8
38	Brazil	3.7
39	Mexico	3.7
40	Greece	3.7
41	China	3.7
42	Jordan	3.7
43	Estonia	3.6
44	Philippines	3.6
45	Croatia	3.6
46	Colombia	3.5
47	Poland	3.5
48	New Zealand	3.5
49	Sri Lanka	3.5
50	Panama	3.4
51	Australia	3.3
52	Romania	3.3
53	Slovak Republic	3.3
54	Vietnam	3.2
55	Latvia	3.2
56	Jamaica	3.2
57	Ukraine	3.1
58	Bulgaria	3.1
59	Trinidad and Tobago	3.1
60	El Salvador	3.0
61	Indonesia	2.9
62	Haiti	2.9
63	Chile	2.9
64	Uruguay	2.8
65	South Africa	2.8
66	Bangladesh	2.8
67	Russian Federation	2.8
68	Namibia	2.7
69	Guatemala	2.6
70	Nicaragua	2.6
71	Botswana	2.5
72	Peru	2.5
73	Bolivia	2.4
74	Honduras	2.4
75	Argentina	2.3
76	Zimbabwe	2.3
77	Ecuador	2.1
78	Venezuela	2.0
79	Paraguay	1.8
80	Nigeria	1.7

MEAN: 4.0

10.03 Extent of branding

Companies in your country that sell internationally (1 = sell into commodity markets or to other companies that handle marketing, 7 = have well-developed international brands and sales organizations)

RANK	COUNTRY	SCORE
1	Germany	6.5
2	United Kingdom	6.3
3	Switzerland	6.1
4	United States	6.1
5	France	6.1
5	Japan	6.1
7	Sweden	6.1
8	Netherlands	6.0
9	Finland	5.9
10	Italy	5.7
11	Denmark	5.3
12	Belgium	5.2
13	Austria	5.0
14	Singapore	4.9
15	Ireland	4.9
16	Israel	4.9
17	Spain	4.8
18	Korea	4.7
19	Iceland	4.6
20	Hong Kong SAR	4.6
21	Taiwan	4.5
22	Canada	4.4
23	Slovenia	4.2
24	China	4.1
25	Hungary	4.0
26	Dominican Republic	3.9
27	New Zealand	3.8
28	Tunisia	3.7
29	Mauritius	3.6
30	Czech Republic	3.6
31	Ukraine	3.6
32	Malaysia	3.6
33	Brazil	3.6
34	Turkey	3.6
35	Australia	3.6
36	Norway	3.6
37	Portugal	3.5
38	Slovak Republic	3.4
39	Costa Rica	3.4
40	Morocco	3.4
41	Thailand	3.4
42	Mexico	3.4
43	Jamaica	3.4
44	Croatia	3.3
45	Russian Federation	3.3
46	Poland	3.3
47	Greece	3.2
48	Vietnam	3.2
49	Jordan	3.2
50	Sri Lanka	3.1
51	South Africa	3.1
52	Indonesia	3.1
53	Colombia	3.0
53	Lithuania	3.0
55	Namibia	3.0
56	Nicaragua	3.0
57	Philippines	3.0
58	India	3.0
59	Panama	3.0
60	Chile	2.9
61	Latvia	2.9
62	Estonia	2.8
63	Trinidad and Tobago	2.8
64	Bulgaria	2.8
65	Romania	2.8
66	Uruguay	2.6
67	Botswana	2.6
68	El Salvador	2.5
69	Guatemala	2.5
70	Bolivia	2.3
71	Peru	2.3
72	Venezuela	2.3
73	Ecuador	2.3
74	Argentina	2.3
75	Bangladesh	2.2
76	Honduras	2.2
77	Zimbabwe	2.1
78	Haiti	2.1
79	Nigeria	2.0
80	Paraguay	1.9

MEAN: 3.7

10.04 Capacity for innovation

Companies obtain technology (1 = exclusively from licensing or imitating foreign companies, 7 = by conducting formal research and pioneering their own new products and processes)

RANK	COUNTRY	SCORE
1	Germany	6.0
2	Sweden	6.0
3	Finland	5.9
4	Japan	5.8
5	France	5.8
6	United States	5.7
7	Switzerland	5.7
8	Israel	5.6
9	United Kingdom	5.6
10	Austria	5.3
11	Netherlands	5.2
12	Belgium	5.2
13	Denmark	5.2
14	Taiwan	4.7
15	Korea	4.7
16	Canada	4.6
17	Norway	4.5
18	Iceland	4.4
19	Italy	4.4
20	New Zealand	4.4
21	Spain	4.4
22	China	4.3
23	Ireland	4.2
24	Slovenia	4.2
25	Singapore	4.1
26	Czech Republic	3.9
27	Australia	3.9
28	Ukraine	3.8
29	Brazil	3.8
30	Russian Federation	3.7
31	Costa Rica	3.7
32	Hungary	3.6
33	Dominican Republic	3.6
34	Estonia	3.5
35	Hong Kong SAR	3.4
36	Malaysia	3.4
37	Lithuania	3.4
38	Slovak Republic	3.4
39	Latvia	3.3
40	Portugal	3.3
41	Croatia	3.3
42	Poland	3.2
43	South Africa	3.2
44	Sri Lanka	3.2
45	India	3.2
46	Vietnam	3.2
47	Tunisia	3.1
48	Bulgaria	3.1
49	Thailand	3.0
50	Colombia	3.0
51	Mexico	3.0
52	Chile	3.0
53	Romania	2.9
54	Morocco	2.9
55	Mauritius	2.9
56	Jordan	2.9
57	Greece	2.9
58	Namibia	2.9
59	Indonesia	2.8
60	Guatemala	2.7
61	El Salvador	2.7
62	Jamaica	2.7
63	Nicaragua	2.7
64	Peru	2.7
65	Botswana	2.7
66	Turkey	2.6
67	Trinidad and Tobago	2.5
68	Panama	2.5
69	Argentina	2.5
70	Philippines	2.4
71	Uruguay	2.4
72	Ecuador	2.3
73	Honduras	2.2
74	Zimbabwe	2.2
75	Bolivia	2.2
76	Bangladesh	2.2
77	Venezuela	2.2
78	Paraguay	2.1
79	Nigeria	1.9
80	Haiti	1.9

MEAN: 3.6

10.05   Ethical behavior of firms

The corporate ethics (ethical behavior in interactions with public officials, politicians, and other enterprises) of your country's firms in your industry are (1 = among the world's worst, 7 = the best in the world)

RANK	COUNTRY	SCORE
1	Finland	6.6
2	United Kingdom	6.5
3	Denmark	6.3
4	Canada	6.1
4	United States	6.1
6	Netherlands	6.0
7	Sweden	5.9
8	New Zealand	5.9
9	Singapore	5.9
10	Norway	5.8
11	Iceland	5.8
12	Switzerland	5.7
13	Australia	5.7
14	Austria	5.7
15	France	5.6
16	Belgium	5.4
17	Germany	5.4
18	Chile	5.1
19	Israel	5.1
20	Ireland	5.1
21	Hong Kong SAR	5.1
22	Tunisia	4.9
23	Spain	4.8
24	Taiwan	4.8
25	Japan	4.8
26	Brazil	4.7
27	Hungary	4.6
28	Slovenia	4.6
29	South Africa	4.6
30	Italy	4.6
31	Estonia	4.5
32	Botswana	4.5
32	Malaysia	4.5
32	Portugal	4.5
35	Thailand	4.5
36	Uruguay	4.5
37	Costa Rica	4.4
38	Korea	4.3
39	Morocco	4.3
40	China	4.3
41	Lithuania	4.2
42	Namibia	4.2
43	Dominican Republic	4.1
43	India	4.1
45	Colombia	4.1
46	Greece	4.1
47	Latvia	4.1
48	Mexico	4.1
49	Trinidad and Tobago	4.0
50	El Salvador	4.0
51	Jordan	3.9
52	Peru	3.9
53	Zimbabwe	3.9
54	Slovak Republic	3.8
55	Philippines	3.8
56	Jamaica	3.8
56	Mauritius	3.8
58	Sri Lanka	3.8
59	Panama	3.8
60	Czech Republic	3.7
61	Turkey	3.6
62	Poland	3.6
63	Croatia	3.6
64	Bulgaria	3.6
65	Vietnam	3.6
66	Guatemala	3.4
67	Argentina	3.3
68	Haiti	3.3
69	Nigeria	3.3
70	Romania	3.3
71	Venezuela	3.3
72	Indonesia	3.2
73	Russian Federation	3.2
74	Ukraine	3.2
75	Bangladesh	3.2
76	Nicaragua	3.2
77	Honduras	3.2
78	Ecuador	3.0
79	Paraguay	3.0
80	Bolivia	2.8

MEAN: 4.4

638

10.06   Production process sophistication

Production processes use (1 = labor-intensive methods or previous generations of process technology, 7 = the world's best and most efficient process technology)

RANK	COUNTRY	SCORE
1	Finland	6.2
2	United States	6.2
3	Japan	6.2
4	Germany	6.1
5	Netherlands	6.0
6	Switzerland	5.9
7	Denmark	5.8
8	Sweden	5.8
9	United Kingdom	5.8
10	Belgium	5.7
11	Israel	5.7
12	France	5.6
13	Singapore	5.6
14	Norway	5.5
15	Iceland	5.5
16	Austria	5.4
17	Australia	5.4
18	Taiwan	5.4
19	Ireland	5.3
20	Canada	5.2
21	Italy	5.2
22	Korea	5.0
23	Spain	4.8
24	New Zealand	4.8
25	Tunisia	4.7
26	Hong Kong SAR	4.6
27	Estonia	4.5
28	Slovenia	4.3
29	Brazil	4.2
30	Malaysia	4.2
31	Hungary	4.1
32	Chile	4.1
33	Czech Republic	4.0
34	Lithuania	4.0
35	Morocco	4.0
36	Costa Rica	4.0
37	Trinidad and Tobago	3.9
38	South Africa	3.9
39	Slovak Republic	3.8
40	Argentina	3.8
41	Greece	3.8
42	Dominican Republic	3.8
43	China	3.8
44	Mauritius	3.8
45	Thailand	3.7
46	Poland	3.7
47	Latvia	3.6
48	Mexico	3.5
49	India	3.5
50	Croatia	3.4
51	Turkey	3.4
52	Portugal	3.4
53	Uruguay	3.3
54	Russian Federation	3.3
55	Panama	3.3
56	Jordan	3.2
57	Sri Lanka	3.1
58	Namibia	3.1
59	Peru	3.0
60	Vietnam	3.0
61	El Salvador	3.0
62	Colombia	3.0
63	Haiti	3.0
64	Venezuela	2.9
65	Ukraine	2.9
66	Romania	2.8
67	Jamaica	2.7
68	Botswana	2.7
69	Bulgaria	2.7
70	Indonesia	2.6
71	Philippines	2.6
72	Nicaragua	2.5
73	Guatemala	2.5
74	Ecuador	2.5
75	Bangladesh	2.4
76	Paraguay	2.3
77	Honduras	2.3
78	Bolivia	2.3
79	Zimbabwe	2.2
80	Nigeria	1.9

MEAN: 4.0

10.07 Extent of marketing

The extent of marketing in your country is (1 = limited and primitive, 7 = extensive and employs the world's most sophisticated tools and techniques)

RANK	COUNTRY	SCORE
1	United States	6.7
2	United Kingdom	6.6
3	France	6.1
4	Germany	6.0
5	Canada	6.0
6	Australia	5.9
7	Switzerland	5.8
8	Netherlands	5.8
9	Japan	5.8
10	Hong Kong SAR	5.7
11	Sweden	5.7
12	Belgium	5.7
13	Italy	5.6
14	Denmark	5.6
15	Finland	5.5
16	Singapore	5.4
17	Ireland	5.3
18	South Africa	5.3
19	Brazil	5.3
20	Spain	5.2
21	Dominican Republic	5.2
22	New Zealand	5.2
23	Austria	5.1
23	Iceland	5.1
25	Chile	5.1
26	Norway	5.0
27	Israel	5.0
28	Taiwan	5.0
29	Hungary	4.9
30	Greece	4.8
31	Panama	4.8
32	Costa Rica	4.8
33	Korea	4.7
34	Thailand	4.6
35	Argentina	4.6
36	Malaysia	4.6
37	India	4.6
38	Czech Republic	4.6
39	Slovenia	4.6
40	Poland	4.5
41	Estonia	4.4
42	Trinidad and Tobago	4.4
43	Tunisia	4.4
44	Mexico	4.3
45	Philippines	4.3
46	Mauritius	4.2
47	Colombia	4.2
48	Jamaica	4.1
49	Latvia	4.1
50	Venezuela	4.1
51	Peru	4.1
52	Indonesia	4.1
53	Slovak Republic	4.1
54	Turkey	4.1
55	Nigeria	4.0
56	Portugal	3.9
57	Lithuania	3.9
58	Morocco	3.9
59	Croatia	3.9
60	Guatemala	3.8
61	Uruguay	3.8
62	Sri Lanka	3.7
63	Ecuador	3.7
64	Paraguay	3.7
65	Namibia	3.5
66	Zimbabwe	3.5
67	Nicaragua	3.5
68	Romania	3.5
69	China	3.4
70	El Salvador	3.4
71	Jordan	3.4
72	Botswana	3.3
73	Bolivia	3.2
74	Bulgaria	3.1
75	Russian Federation	3.1
76	Ukraine	3.1
77	Bangladesh	3.0
78	Honduras	2.9
79	Vietnam	2.9
80	Haiti	2.8

MEAN: 4.5

10.08 Degree of customer orientation

Customer orientation: Firms in your country (1 = generally treat their customers badly, 7 = are highly responsive to customers and customer retention)

RANK	COUNTRY	SCORE
1	United States	6.1
2	Canada	6.0
3	Japan	5.9
4	Switzerland	5.9
5	Finland	5.8
6	Taiwan	5.8
7	Belgium	5.7
8	Denmark	5.7
9	United Kingdom	5.7
10	Netherlands	5.7
11	Sweden	5.6
12	Iceland	5.5
13	Germany	5.5
14	Austria	5.5
15	Singapore	5.5
16	Australia	5.5
17	Korea	5.5
18	Dominican Republic	5.5
19	France	5.4
20	Spain	5.4
21	Hong Kong SAR	5.3
22	Slovenia	5.3
23	Norway	5.3
24	Thailand	5.2
25	Estonia	5.2
26	Ireland	5.2
26	New Zealand	5.2
28	Italy	5.0
29	Malaysia	5.0
30	Lithuania	4.9
31	Israel	4.9
32	Chile	4.9
33	Tunisia	4.8
34	Brazil	4.8
35	Colombia	4.7
36	Morocco	4.7
37	China	4.7
38	Costa Rica	4.6
39	Czech Republic	4.5
40	Philippines	4.5
41	Latvia	4.5
42	Mauritius	4.5
43	Hungary	4.5
44	Greece	4.4
45	Sri Lanka	4.4
46	Mexico	4.4
47	Panama	4.3
48	Bulgaria	4.3
49	Russian Federation	4.3
50	Slovak Republic	4.2
51	Turkey	4.2
52	Trinidad and Tobago	4.2
53	Peru	4.2
54	Vietnam	4.2
55	Poland	4.2
56	Indonesia	4.2
57	Portugal	4.1
58	Bangladesh	4.1
59	India	4.1
60	Uruguay	4.1
61	South Africa	4.0
62	El Salvador	4.0
63	Paraguay	4.0
64	Croatia	4.0
65	Guatemala	3.9
66	Jordan	3.9
67	Ukraine	3.9
68	Namibia	3.9
69	Argentina	3.8
70	Nigeria	3.8
71	Jamaica	3.8
72	Botswana	3.7
73	Zimbabwe	3.6
74	Romania	3.6
75	Venezuela	3.4
76	Ecuador	3.3
77	Haiti	3.1
78	Bolivia	3.0
78	Nicaragua	3.0
80	Honduras	3.0

MEAN: 4.6

639

10.09 Control of international distribution

International distribution and marketing from your country (1 = takes place through foreign companies, 7 = is owned and controlled by local companies)

RANK	COUNTRY	SCORE
1	United Kingdom	5.6
2	France	5.6
3	Japan	5.5
4	Finland	5.3
5	United States	5.3
6	Germany	5.2
7	Iceland	5.2
8	Switzerland	5.0
9	Denmark	4.9
10	Korea	4.9
11	Canada	4.9
12	Italy	4.8
13	Netherlands	4.8
14	Sweden	4.8
15	Taiwan	4.7
16	Belgium	4.7
17	Australia	4.7
18	Austria	4.7
19	Spain	4.7
20	Ukraine	4.5
21	Norway	4.3
22	Ireland	4.3
23	Dominican Republic	4.3
24	Slovenia	4.2
25	India	4.2
26	New Zealand	4.1
27	Croatia	4.1
28	Chile	4.1
29	Brazil	4.1
30	Costa Rica	4.1
31	Turkey	4.1
32	Lithuania	4.1
33	Hong Kong SAR	4.1
34	Russian Federation	4.0
35	Mauritius	4.0
36	South Africa	4.0
37	Malaysia	3.9
38	Greece	3.9
39	Panama	3.9
40	Singapore	3.9
41	China	3.9
42	Tunisia	3.8
43	Jordan	3.8
44	Uruguay	3.8
45	Peru	3.8
45	Thailand	3.8
47	Colombia	3.8
48	Romania	3.8
49	Indonesia	3.7
50	Argentina	3.7
51	Morocco	3.6
52	Portugal	3.6
53	Poland	3.6
54	Bulgaria	3.5
55	Hungary	3.5
56	Philippines	3.5
57	Trinidad and Tobago	3.5
58	Israel	3.5
58	Mexico	3.5
60	Nicaragua	3.5
61	Estonia	3.5
62	Slovak Republic	3.5
63	Bangladesh	3.4
63	Paraguay	3.4
65	Sri Lanka	3.4
66	Nigeria	3.4
67	Latvia	3.3
68	Ecuador	3.3
69	Guatemala	3.2
70	El Salvador	3.2
71	Namibia	3.2
72	Jamaica	3.1
73	Honduras	3.1
74	Czech Republic	3.0
75	Bolivia	2.9
76	Botswana	2.9
77	Haiti	2.9
78	Venezuela	2.9
79	Vietnam	2.8
80	Zimbabwe	2.8

MEAN: 4.0

10.10 Extent of regional sales

Exports from your country to neighboring countries are (1 = limited, 7 = substantial and growing)

RANK	COUNTRY	SCORE
1	Germany	6.6
2	Belgium	6.4
3	Canada	6.4
4	Finland	6.3
5	United Kingdom	6.2
6	Ireland	6.2
7	Austria	6.2
8	Denmark	6.2
9	Netherlands	6.0
10	United States	6.0
11	France	5.9
11	Italy	5.9
13	Czech Republic	5.9
14	Sweden	5.8
15	Iceland	5.8
16	Japan	5.8
17	Switzerland	5.8
18	Hong Kong SAR	5.7
19	Korea	5.7
20	New Zealand	5.6
21	Thailand	5.6
22	Singapore	5.6
23	Australia	5.5
23	Spain	5.5
25	Taiwan	5.5
26	Slovenia	5.5
27	Malaysia	5.4
28	South Africa	5.4
29	Trinidad and Tobago	5.4
30	Colombia	5.3
31	Hungary	5.3
32	Costa Rica	5.2
33	Norway	5.2
34	Estonia	5.1
35	Mexico	5.1
36	Brazil	5.1
37	Portugal	5.0
38	Argentina	5.0
39	Uruguay	4.9
40	El Salvador	4.9
41	Guatemala	4.8
42	Tunisia	4.8
43	Greece	4.8
44	Indonesia	4.7
45	Slovak Republic	4.7
46	Lithuania	4.7
47	Poland	4.6
48	Dominican Republic	4.6
49	Jordan	4.6
50	China	4.5
51	Turkey	4.5
52	Chile	4.4
53	Nigeria	4.4
54	India	4.4
55	Vietnam	4.3
56	Paraguay	4.3
57	Ecuador	4.2
58	Sri Lanka	4.2
59	Latvia	4.2
60	Philippines	4.2
61	Croatia	4.1
62	Russian Federation	3.9
63	Mauritius	3.9
64	Morocco	3.8
65	Zimbabwe	3.8
66	Bulgaria	3.7
67	Namibia	3.7
68	Peru	3.6
69	Panama	3.5
70	Ukraine	3.4
71	Honduras	3.4
72	Romania	3.3
73	Venezuela	3.3
74	Botswana	3.2
75	Jamaica	3.2
76	Bolivia	3.0
77	Nicaragua	2.4
78	Bangladesh	2.3
79	Haiti	2.0
80	Israel	1.6

MEAN: 4.8

10.11 Breadth of international markets

Exporting companies from your country sell (1 = primarily in a small number of foreign markets, 7 = in virtually all international markets)

RANK	COUNTRY	SCORE
1	Germany	6.6
2	United Kingdom	6.4
3	Japan	6.3
4	United States	6.3
5	Sweden	6.2
6	Finland	6.0
7	Switzerland	5.9
8	Italy	5.9
9	Netherlands	5.9
10	Hong Kong SAR	5.8
11	France	5.7
12	Taiwan	5.5
13	Korea	5.5
14	Australia	5.4
15	Ireland	5.3
16	Singapore	5.3
17	Chile	5.2
18	Denmark	5.2
19	Iceland	5.0
20	Austria	5.0
21	Belgium	5.0
22	Thailand	4.9
23	Malaysia	4.8
24	Hungary	4.8
25	Spain	4.8
26	Israel	4.7
27	New Zealand	4.6
28	Brazil	4.6
29	Czech Republic	4.6
30	Slovenia	4.4
31	South Africa	4.3
32	Norway	4.3
33	Lithuania	4.2
34	India	4.1
35	Canada	4.0
36	Turkey	4.0
37	Sri Lanka	3.9
38	Indonesia	3.9
39	China	3.9
40	Slovak Republic	3.7
41	Portugal	3.5
42	Dominican Republic	3.5
43	Estonia	3.4
44	Poland	3.4
45	Tunisia	3.4
46	Mexico	3.3
47	Greece	3.3
48	Mauritius	3.2
49	Philippines	3.2
50	Argentina	3.2
50	Russian Federation	3.2
52	Latvia	3.2
53	Costa Rica	3.2
54	Jordan	3.1
55	Trinidad and Tobago	3.1
56	Romania	3.0
57	Morocco	3.0
58	Bulgaria	3.0
59	Vietnam	3.0
60	Namibia	3.0
61	Colombia	3.0
62	Ecuador	2.9
63	Croatia	2.9
64	Panama	2.8
65	El Salvador	2.8
66	Peru	2.7
67	Zimbabwe	2.7
68	Ukraine	2.6
69	Botswana	2.6
70	Uruguay	2.5
71	Bangladesh	2.5
72	Guatemala	2.4
73	Nicaragua	2.4
74	Jamaica	2.3
75	Nigeria	2.2
76	Venezuela	2.2
77	Bolivia	2.2
78	Paraguay	2.1
79	Honduras	2.1
80	Haiti	1.6

MEAN: 3.9

10.12 Extent of staff training

The general approach of companies in your country to human resources is (1 = to invest little in training and employee development, 7 = to invest heavily to attract, train and retain employees)

RANK	COUNTRY	SCORE
1	Switzerland	5.9
2	Finland	5.8
3	United States	5.8
4	Sweden	5.8
5	Germany	5.8
6	Japan	5.6
7	United Kingdom	5.5
8	Denmark	5.5
9	Netherlands	5.5
10	Singapore	5.4
11	Australia	5.3
12	Austria	5.3
13	Iceland	5.2
14	Ireland	5.2
15	France	5.2
16	Belgium	5.2
17	Canada	5.1
18	Norway	5.0
19	Israel	4.9
20	Taiwan	4.8
21	Korea	4.8
22	New Zealand	4.7
23	Hungary	4.7
24	Spain	4.6
25	Dominican Republic	4.6
26	Tunisia	4.5
27	Malaysia	4.5
28	South Africa	4.4
29	Brazil	4.4
30	Slovenia	4.4
31	Hong Kong SAR	4.4
32	Italy	4.3
33	Czech Republic	4.3
34	Estonia	4.3
35	Mauritius	4.2
36	Thailand	4.1
37	Costa Rica	4.1
38	Chile	4.1
39	Slovak Republic	4.0
40	Namibia	4.0
41	Trinidad and Tobago	3.9
42	Zimbabwe	3.9
43	Botswana	3.7
44	El Salvador	3.7
45	Latvia	3.7
46	India	3.7
47	Portugal	3.6
48	Colombia	3.6
49	China	3.6
50	Sri Lanka	3.6
51	Philippines	3.5
52	Nigeria	3.5
53	Mexico	3.5
54	Morocco	3.5
55	Indonesia	3.5
56	Panama	3.5
57	Greece	3.5
58	Lithuania	3.4
59	Peru	3.4
60	Uruguay	3.3
61	Jamaica	3.3
62	Jordan	3.3
63	Poland	3.3
64	Turkey	3.3
65	Argentina	3.3
66	Venezuela	3.2
67	Croatia	3.2
68	Guatemala	2.8
69	Vietnam	2.8
70	Romania	2.8
71	Russian Federation	2.8
72	Paraguay	2.6
73	Nicaragua	2.6
74	Bulgaria	2.6
75	Bolivia	2.6
76	Ukraine	2.6
77	Ecuador	2.6
78	Bangladesh	2.5
79	Honduras	2.4
80	Haiti	2.3

MEAN: 4.0

641

10.13 Willingness to delegate authority

Willingness to delegate authority to subordinates is (1 = low; top management controls all important decisions, 7 = high; authority is mostly delegated to business unit heads and other lower-level managers)

RANK	COUNTRY	SCORE	1	MEAN: 3.8	7
1	Denmark	6.1			
2	Sweden	5.9			
3	Finland	5.9			
4	Netherlands	5.7			
5	Switzerland	5.7			
6	United States	5.7			
7	United Kingdom	5.6			
8	Norway	5.5			
9	Iceland	5.4			
10	Canada	5.3			
11	Belgium	5.2			
12	Germany	5.2			
13	Austria	5.2			
14	Australia	5.1			
15	New Zealand	4.9			
16	Ireland	4.8			
17	Israel	4.8			
18	Japan	4.5			
19	Singapore	4.5			
20	Taiwan	4.4			
21	Dominican Republic	4.2			
22	Malaysia	4.2			
23	South Africa	4.1			
24	Korea	4.1			
25	Costa Rica	4.1			
26	Spain	4.1			
27	Estonia	4.0			
28	Hungary	4.0			
28	Thailand	4.0			
30	France	4.0			
30	Philippines	4.0			
32	Tunisia	4.0			
33	Brazil	3.9			
34	Slovenia	3.9			
35	Hong Kong SAR	3.8			
36	Italy	3.8			
37	Chile	3.7			
38	Mauritius	3.6			
39	El Salvador	3.6			
40	China	3.6			
41	Slovak Republic	3.6			
42	Colombia	3.6			
43	Peru	3.5			
44	Argentina	3.5			
45	Zimbabwe	3.5			
46	Namibia	3.5			
47	Mexico	3.4			
48	Trinidad and Tobago	3.4			
49	Latvia	3.4			
50	Panama	3.4			
51	Lithuania	3.4			
52	Morocco	3.4			
53	Croatia	3.3			
54	Portugal	3.3			
55	Poland	3.2			
56	Botswana	3.2			
57	Sri Lanka	3.2			
58	Indonesia	3.2			
59	India	3.2			
60	Venezuela	3.1			
61	Jordan	3.0			
62	Nigeria	3.0			
63	Greece	2.9			
64	Jamaica	2.9			
65	Romania	2.9			
66	Uruguay	2.9			
67	Vietnam	2.8			
68	Russian Federation	2.8			
69	Guatemala	2.8			
70	Nicaragua	2.7			
71	Czech Republic	2.7			
72	Bulgaria	2.7			
73	Ukraine	2.7			
74	Ecuador	2.7			
75	Honduras	2.4			
76	Turkey	2.4			
77	Paraguay	2.3			
78	Bolivia	2.3			
79	Bangladesh	2.2			
80	Haiti	1.9			

10.14 Extent of incentive compensation

Cash compensation of management (1 = is based exclusively on salary, 7 = includes bonuses and stock options, representing a significant portion of overall compensation)

RANK	COUNTRY	SCORE	1	MEAN: 4.2	7
1	United States	6.3			
2	United Kingdom	6.0			
3	Australia	5.6			
4	Canada	5.5			
5	Sweden	5.5			
6	Ireland	5.4			
7	Netherlands	5.3			
8	Germany	5.3			
9	Finland	5.2			
10	Hong Kong SAR	5.2			
11	Belgium	5.2			
12	Switzerland	5.2			
13	France	5.1			
14	Singapore	5.1			
15	South Africa	5.0			
16	Israel	5.0			
17	Dominican Republic	4.9			
18	Spain	4.9			
19	Italy	4.9			
20	Taiwan	4.8			
21	Denmark	4.8			
22	Estonia	4.8			
23	Austria	4.8			
24	Norway	4.8			
25	Hungary	4.8			
26	Iceland	4.7			
27	Chile	4.6			
28	New Zealand	4.6			
29	Brazil	4.5			
30	Zimbabwe	4.5			
31	Czech Republic	4.5			
32	Mexico	4.5			
33	Malaysia	4.5			
34	Korea	4.4			
35	Costa Rica	4.3			
36	Trinidad and Tobago	4.3			
37	Panama	4.2			
38	Poland	4.2			
39	Thailand	4.2			
40	Argentina	4.1			
41	Portugal	4.1			
42	El Salvador	4.1			
43	Philippines	4.1			
44	Namibia	4.0			
45	Japan	3.9			
46	Slovenia	3.9			
47	Greece	3.8			
48	Latvia	3.8			
49	China	3.7			
50	Romania	3.7			
51	Indonesia	3.7			
52	Mauritius	3.6			
53	Guatemala	3.6			
54	Venezuela	3.6			
55	Sri Lanka	3.5			
56	Turkey	3.5			
57	Tunisia	3.5			
58	Ukraine	3.5			
59	Botswana	3.5			
60	Jamaica	3.4			
61	India	3.4			
62	Croatia	3.4			
63	Slovak Republic	3.3			
64	Vietnam	3.3			
65	Russian Federation	3.3			
66	Lithuania	3.3			
67	Honduras	3.2			
68	Peru	3.2			
69	Uruguay	3.2			
70	Colombia	3.2			
71	Jordan	3.2			
72	Bulgaria	3.1			
73	Paraguay	3.1			
74	Ecuador	3.0			
74	Morocco	3.0			
76	Nicaragua	3.0			
77	Bangladesh	2.9			
78	Nigeria	2.9			
79	Haiti	2.7			
80	Bolivia	2.5			

10.15 Reliance on professional management

Senior management positions in your country are (1 = usually held by relatives, 7 = held by professional managers chosen based on superior qualification)

RANK	COUNTRY	SCORE
1	Australia	6.5
1	United Kingdom	6.5
3	Finland	6.5
4	United States	6.4
5	New Zealand	6.2
6	Netherlands	6.2
7	Denmark	6.2
8	Germany	6.1
9	Switzerland	6.0
10	Sweden	6.0
11	Canada	5.9
12	Ireland	5.9
13	South Africa	5.8
14	Norway	5.8
15	Japan	5.8
16	Singapore	5.7
17	Austria	5.6
18	Iceland	5.6
19	France	5.5
20	Belgium	5.5
20	Israel	5.5
22	Czech Republic	5.4
23	Hungary	5.4
24	Zimbabwe	5.3
25	Brazil	5.3
26	Estonia	5.2
27	Chile	5.2
28	Taiwan	5.2
29	China	5.2
30	Spain	5.1
31	Nigeria	5.1
32	Botswana	5.0
32	Malaysia	5.0
34	Korea	5.0
35	Namibia	4.9
36	Jamaica	4.9
37	Italy	4.9
38	Sri Lanka	4.9
39	Slovenia	4.8
40	Trinidad and Tobago	4.8
41	Slovak Republic	4.7
42	Philippines	4.6
43	Latvia	4.6
44	Argentina	4.5
45	India	4.5
46	Morocco	4.5
46	Portugal	4.5
48	Hong Kong SAR	4.5
49	Costa Rica	4.4
50	Tunisia	4.4
51	Lithuania	4.3
52	Colombia	4.2
53	Thailand	4.2
54	Poland	4.1
55	Croatia	4.1
56	Bangladesh	4.0
57	Mexico	4.0
58	Vietnam	4.0
59	Russian Federation	4.0
60	Peru	4.0
61	Indonesia	3.9
62	Venezuela	3.9
63	Mauritius	3.8
64	Ukraine	3.8
65	Romania	3.7
66	El Salvador	3.7
67	Greece	3.7
68	Uruguay	3.6
69	Dominican Republic	3.6
70	Turkey	3.5
71	Guatemala	3.5
72	Bulgaria	3.4
73	Panama	3.4
74	Jordan	3.4
75	Haiti	3.0
76	Paraguay	2.8
77	Bolivia	2.7
78	Honduras	2.7
79	Ecuador	2.6
80	Nicaragua	2.5

MEAN: 4.7

10.16 Quality of management schools

Management or business schools in your country are (1 = limited or of poor quality, 7 = the best in the world)

RANK	COUNTRY	SCORE
1	United States	6.8
2	United Kingdom	6.2
3	Canada	6.1
4	Switzerland	6.0
5	France	5.9
6	Spain	5.8
7	Sweden	5.7
8	Netherlands	5.7
9	India	5.6
10	Finland	5.6
11	Israel	5.6
12	Ireland	5.5
13	Chile	5.4
14	Norway	5.4
15	Taiwan	5.3
16	Australia	5.2
17	Singapore	5.2
18	Belgium	5.2
19	Tunisia	5.1
20	South Africa	5.1
21	New Zealand	5.1
22	Iceland	5.0
23	Denmark	5.0
24	Austria	5.0
25	Germany	5.0
26	Philippines	4.9
27	Costa Rica	4.8
28	Estonia	4.8
29	Czech Republic	4.7
30	Argentina	4.7
30	Brazil	4.7
32	Italy	4.7
33	Hungary	4.6
34	Thailand	4.6
35	Slovenia	4.6
36	Peru	4.4
37	Morocco	4.4
38	Jamaica	4.4
39	Uruguay	4.4
40	Portugal	4.3
41	Hong Kong SAR	4.3
42	Latvia	4.3
43	Lithuania	4.2
44	Colombia	4.2
45	Mexico	4.2
46	Poland	4.2
47	Trinidad and Tobago	4.2
48	Malaysia	4.1
49	Slovak Republic	4.1
50	Korea	4.0
51	Japan	4.0
52	Turkey	3.9
53	Nigeria	3.9
54	Russian Federation	3.9
55	Venezuela	3.7
56	Sri Lanka	3.7
57	Indonesia	3.6
58	Dominican Republic	3.6
59	Romania	3.6
60	Ukraine	3.6
61	Jordan	3.5
62	Greece	3.5
63	Mauritius	3.4
64	China	3.4
65	Zimbabwe	3.3
66	El Salvador	3.3
67	Bangladesh	3.3
68	Botswana	3.2
69	Guatemala	3.2
70	Croatia	3.2
71	Paraguay	3.1
72	Bulgaria	3.1
73	Panama	3.1
74	Ecuador	3.1
75	Nicaragua	3.0
76	Vietnam	2.9
77	Namibia	2.7
78	Haiti	2.6
79	Bolivia	2.5
80	Honduras	2.2

MEAN: 4.3

643

10.17 Efficacy of corporate boards

Corporate boards in your country are (1 = controlled by management, 7 = powerful and represent outside shareholders)

RANK	COUNTRY	SCORE
1	United Kingdom	5.8
2	Finland	5.8
3	Australia	5.6
4	New Zealand	5.4
5	United States	5.3
6	Norway	5.3
7	Iceland	5.3
8	Sweden	5.2
9	Denmark	5.2
10	Canada	5.1
11	Chile	4.9
12	South Africa	4.9
13	Germany	4.9
14	Belgium	4.8
15	Taiwan	4.8
16	Austria	4.7
17	Switzerland	4.6
18	Israel	4.6
19	Estonia	4.5
20	Zimbabwe	4.5
21	Peru	4.3
22	Ireland	4.3
23	Slovak Republic	4.3
24	Nigeria	4.3
25	Netherlands	4.2
26	Singapore	4.2
27	Slovenia	4.2
28	Lithuania	4.2
29	Trinidad and Tobago	4.1
30	Namibia	4.1
31	Botswana	4.1
32	Ukraine	4.1
33	Hungary	4.1
34	Costa Rica	4.1
35	Latvia	4.1
36	Russian Federation	4.0
37	Thailand	4.0
38	China	4.0
39	Jamaica	4.0
40	Tunisia	4.0
41	Spain	3.9
42	Italy	3.9
42	Poland	3.9
44	Malaysia	3.9
45	Korea	3.8
46	Colombia	3.8
47	Croatia	3.8
48	France	3.8
49	Brazil	3.8
50	Panama	3.8
51	Portugal	3.7
52	Dominican Republic	3.7
53	Argentina	3.7
54	Mexico	3.6
55	Guatemala	3.6
56	Indonesia	3.5
57	El Salvador	3.5
58	Vietnam	3.5
59	Sri Lanka	3.4
60	Uruguay	3.4
61	Czech Republic	3.4
62	Bulgaria	3.3
63	Bolivia	3.3
64	Jordan	3.3
65	Mauritius	3.3
66	Morocco	3.3
67	Ecuador	3.2
68	Honduras	3.1
69	Hong Kong SAR	3.1
70	Romania	3.1
71	Venezuela	3.1
72	Philippines	3.1
73	Turkey	3.1
74	India	3.0
75	Paraguay	3.0
76	Greece	2.9
77	Haiti	2.7
78	Bangladesh	2.5
79	Nicaragua	2.3
80	Japan	2.2

MEAN: 4.0

10.18 Hiring and firing practices

Hiring and firing of workers is (1 = impeded by regulations, 7 = flexibly determined by employers)

RANK	COUNTRY	SCORE
1	Hong Kong SAR	5.7
2	Singapore	5.6
3	United States	5.2
4	Denmark	5.2
5	Iceland	5.2
6	Nigeria	5.1
7	El Salvador	4.8
8	Czech Republic	4.8
9	Russian Federation	4.7
10	Taiwan	4.7
11	United Kingdom	4.7
12	Hungary	4.6
13	Nicaragua	4.5
14	Estonia	4.5
14	Switzerland	4.5
16	Haiti	4.4
17	Israel	4.4
18	Canada	4.4
19	Ukraine	4.3
20	Brazil	4.3
21	Costa Rica	4.3
22	Thailand	4.2
23	Tunisia	4.1
24	China	4.1
25	Romania	4.1
26	Latvia	4.1
27	Bangladesh	4.0
28	Vietnam	4.0
29	Peru	3.9
30	Turkey	3.9
31	Trinidad and Tobago	3.8
32	Guatemala	3.8
33	Sri Lanka	3.8
34	Dominican Republic	3.8
35	Bulgaria	3.7
36	Morocco	3.7
37	Jordan	3.7
38	Finland	3.6
39	Korea	3.6
40	Slovak Republic	3.6
41	Ireland	3.5
42	Australia	3.5
43	Malaysia	3.4
44	New Zealand	3.4
45	Austria	3.4
46	Bolivia	3.3
47	Jamaica	3.2
48	Poland	3.2
49	Botswana	3.2
50	Lithuania	3.2
51	Croatia	3.0
52	Namibia	3.0
53	Honduras	3.0
54	Greece	3.0
55	Chile	2.9
56	Venezuela	2.9
57	Indonesia	2.9
58	Mexico	2.9
59	Japan	2.8
60	Netherlands	2.8
61	Norway	2.8
62	Belgium	2.8
63	Ecuador	2.7
64	Colombia	2.7
65	Philippines	2.7
66	Uruguay	2.6
67	Slovenia	2.6
68	Spain	2.5
69	Panama	2.5
70	Argentina	2.4
71	Portugal	2.4
72	Mauritius	2.4
73	Italy	2.4
74	South Africa	2.3
75	Paraguay	2.3
76	France	2.2
77	Sweden	2.1
78	India	2.1
79	Germany	1.9
80	Zimbabwe	1.8

MEAN: 3.5

10.19 Flexibility of wage determination

Wages in your country are (1 = set by a centralized bargaining process, 7 = up to each individual company)

RANK	COUNTRY	SCORE
1	Hong Kong SAR	6.7
2	Haiti	6.3
3	United States	6.2
4	Estonia	6.2
5	Taiwan	6.1
6	United Kingdom	5.9
7	Lithuania	5.9
8	Japan	5.9
9	Russian Federation	5.9
10	Singapore	5.8
11	New Zealand	5.8
12	Chile	5.8
13	Canada	5.8
14	El Salvador	5.7
15	Peru	5.6
16	Switzerland	5.6
17	Bulgaria	5.6
18	Vietnam	5.5
19	Malaysia	5.5
20	Czech Republic	5.5
21	Morocco	5.5
22	Hungary	5.4
23	Romania	5.4
24	Jordan	5.4
25	Latvia	5.4
26	Jamaica	5.3
27	Dominican Republic	5.3
28	Slovak Republic	5.2
29	China	5.2
30	Trinidad and Tobago	5.2
31	Thailand	5.1
32	Nigeria	5.1
33	Uruguay	5.1
34	Bangladesh	5.1
35	Korea	5.1
36	Botswana	5.0
37	Namibia	5.0
38	Ukraine	4.9
39	Guatemala	4.9
40	Turkey	4.9
41	Croatia	4.9
42	Poland	4.8
43	Colombia	4.8
44	Bolivia	4.7
45	Israel	4.7
46	Sri Lanka	4.6
47	Mexico	4.6
48	Nicaragua	4.6
49	Australia	4.6
50	Panama	4.6
51	Portugal	4.6
52	Venezuela	4.6
53	Philippines	4.4
54	Iceland	4.4
55	Paraguay	4.3
56	France	4.3
57	Slovenia	4.2
58	Ecuador	4.2
59	Brazil	4.2
60	Indonesia	4.1
61	India	4.1
62	Costa Rica	4.1
63	Argentina	4.1
64	Denmark	3.9
65	Spain	3.8
66	Honduras	3.8
67	Austria	3.7
68	Greece	3.6
69	South Africa	3.5
70	Sweden	3.5
71	Norway	3.5
72	Netherlands	3.4
73	Italy	3.3
74	Belgium	3.3
75	Mauritius	3.2
76	Ireland	3.0
77	Tunisia	2.9
78	Finland	2.7
79	Germany	2.5
80	Zimbabwe	2.3

MEAN: 4.7

10.20 Cooperation in labor-employer relations

Labor-employer relations in your country are (1 = generally confrontational, 7 = generally cooperative)

RANK	COUNTRY	SCORE
1	Singapore	6.2
2	Switzerland	6.1
3	Denmark	6.1
4	Austria	5.9
5	Japan	5.8
6	Sweden	5.7
7	Iceland	5.6
8	Finland	5.6
9	Thailand	5.6
10	Costa Rica	5.5
11	Netherlands	5.5
12	Taiwan	5.5
13	Norway	5.4
14	Hong Kong SAR	5.3
15	Ireland	5.3
16	Czech Republic	5.2
17	El Salvador	5.2
18	United Kingdom	5.2
19	Malaysia	5.2
20	Germany	5.2
21	United States	5.1
22	Canada	5.1
23	Hungary	5.0
24	Estonia	5.0
25	Tunisia	4.9
26	Botswana	4.9
27	Vietnam	4.8
28	Slovak Republic	4.8
29	New Zealand	4.8
30	Chile	4.8
31	Dominican Republic	4.7
32	China	4.7
33	Jordan	4.6
34	Slovenia	4.5
35	Belgium	4.5
35	Israel	4.5
37	Turkey	4.5
38	Sri Lanka	4.4
39	Mexico	4.4
40	Peru	4.4
41	Latvia	4.4
42	Russian Federation	4.3
43	Spain	4.3
44	Australia	4.3
45	Portugal	4.3
46	Romania	4.2
47	Brazil	4.2
48	Haiti	4.2
49	Nicaragua	4.2
50	Mauritius	4.2
51	Colombia	4.1
52	Lithuania	4.1
53	Namibia	4.1
54	Bulgaria	4.0
55	Greece	4.0
55	India	4.0
55	Korea	4.0
58	Bangladesh	4.0
59	Trinidad and Tobago	3.9
60	Morocco	3.9
61	Guatemala	3.8
62	Ukraine	3.8
63	Panama	3.8
64	Paraguay	3.8
65	Uruguay	3.6
66	Argentina	3.6
67	Zimbabwe	3.6
68	Ecuador	3.5
69	Venezuela	3.5
70	South Africa	3.5
71	Jamaica	3.5
72	Italy	3.5
73	Poland	3.5
74	Indonesia	3.5
75	Nigeria	3.5
76	Philippines	3.4
77	Croatia	3.4
78	France	3.3
79	Honduras	3.2
80	Bolivia	2.9

MEAN: 4.5

10.21 Pay and productivity

Pay in your country is (1 = not related to worker productivity, 7 = strongly related to productivity)

RANK	COUNTRY	SCORE
1	Hong Kong SAR	6.0
2	United States	5.9
3	Taiwan	5.7
4	Singapore	5.6
5	Switzerland	5.5
6	United Kingdom	5.2
7	China	5.2
7	Estonia	5.2
9	Canada	5.0
10	Vietnam	4.9
11	Austria	4.9
12	Iceland	4.9
13	Australia	4.8
14	Hungary	4.8
15	New Zealand	4.7
16	El Salvador	4.7
17	Lithuania	4.7
18	Czech Republic	4.7
19	Denmark	4.7
20	Malaysia	4.7
21	Chile	4.7
22	Slovak Republic	4.6
23	Ireland	4.6
24	Russian Federation	4.6
25	Slovenia	4.6
26	Thailand	4.6
27	Dominican Republic	4.6
28	Korea	4.5
29	Latvia	4.4
30	Finland	4.4
31	Israel	4.4
32	Romania	4.3
33	Morocco	4.3
34	Ukraine	4.3
35	Bulgaria	4.2
36	Costa Rica	4.2
37	France	4.1
38	Tunisia	4.1
39	Brazil	4.1
40	Poland	4.0
41	Botswana	4.0
42	Haiti	3.9
43	Japan	3.9
44	Germany	3.8
45	Norway	3.8
46	Jordan	3.8
47	Namibia	3.8
48	Sweden	3.8
49	Nigeria	3.7
50	Belgium	3.7
51	Portugal	3.7
52	Trinidad and Tobago	3.7
53	Uruguay	3.7
54	Peru	3.7
55	Italy	3.6
56	Spain	3.6
57	Argentina	3.6
58	Croatia	3.6
59	Mexico	3.6
60	Netherlands	3.5
61	Turkey	3.5
62	Greece	3.5
63	Indonesia	3.4
64	Philippines	3.3
65	Sri Lanka	3.3
66	South Africa	3.2
67	Bangladesh	3.1
67	India	3.1
69	Jamaica	3.1
70	Nicaragua	3.0
71	Mauritius	3.0
72	Panama	2.9
73	Guatemala	2.9
74	Colombia	2.9
75	Paraguay	2.9
76	Honduras	2.7
77	Venezuela	2.6
78	Bolivia	2.5
79	Zimbabwe	2.2
80	Ecuador	2.2

MEAN: 4.0

11.01 Air pollution regulations

The stringency of air pollution regulations in your country is (1 = lax compared with most other countries, 7 = among the world's most stringent)

RANK	COUNTRY	SCORE
1	Germany	6.7
2	Austria	6.5
3	Netherlands	6.4
4	Denmark	6.4
5	Switzerland	6.3
6	Sweden	6.3
7	Finland	6.3
8	Norway	6.0
9	United Kingdom	6.0
10	Iceland	5.8
11	Belgium	5.7
12	United States	5.7
13	Japan	5.7
14	Canada	5.5
15	Czech Republic	5.5
15	Singapore	5.5
17	Australia	5.5
18	New Zealand	5.4
19	France	5.3
20	Taiwan	5.2
21	Slovenia	5.1
22	Slovak Republic	4.9
23	Hungary	4.8
24	Spain	4.8
25	Italy	4.8
26	Tunisia	4.6
27	Portugal	4.6
28	Chile	4.6
29	Brazil	4.5
30	Israel	4.5
31	Korea	4.5
32	Estonia	4.4
33	Malaysia	4.4
34	Ireland	4.3
35	Latvia	4.2
36	Lithuania	4.0
37	Thailand	3.9
38	Croatia	3.9
39	Greece	3.8
40	Colombia	3.8
41	Namibia	3.7
42	Poland	3.7
43	Mexico	3.6
44	South Africa	3.6
45	India	3.6
46	Costa Rica	3.6
47	Hong Kong SAR	3.5
48	China	3.4
49	Jordan	3.4
50	Venezuela	3.3
51	Botswana	3.1
52	Bulgaria	3.1
53	Mauritius	3.1
54	Russian Federation	3.0
55	Argentina	2.9
56	Panama	2.9
57	Morocco	2.9
58	Turkey	2.8
59	Sri Lanka	2.8
60	Uruguay	2.8
61	Trinidad and Tobago	2.8
62	Dominican Republic	2.8
63	Ukraine	2.7
64	Romania	2.7
65	Jamaica	2.5
66	El Salvador	2.5
67	Indonesia	2.5
68	Philippines	2.5
69	Vietnam	2.4
70	Zimbabwe	2.3
71	Peru	2.3
72	Bolivia	2.3
73	Paraguay	2.2
74	Honduras	2.1
75	Guatemala	2.1
76	Nicaragua	2.0
77	Ecuador	2.0
78	Bangladesh	1.9
79	Nigeria	1.8
80	Haiti	1.1

MEAN: 4.0

11.02 Water pollution regulations

The stringency of water pollution regulations in your country is (1 = lax compared with most other countries, 7 = among the world's most stringent)

RANK	COUNTRY	SCORE
1	Germany	6.7
2	Netherlands	6.6
3	Austria	6.6
4	Finland	6.5
5	Denmark	6.5
6	Switzerland	6.5
7	Sweden	6.5
8	United Kingdom	6.2
9	Norway	6.1
10	Iceland	6.1
11	Belgium	5.9
12	New Zealand	5.9
13	United States	5.8
14	Australia	5.8
15	Singapore	5.8
16	Canada	5.7
17	Japan	5.5
18	France	5.5
19	Tunisia	5.5
20	Czech Republic	5.4
21	Spain	5.2
22	Taiwan	5.1
23	Slovak Republic	5.1
24	Slovenia	5.0
25	Portugal	5.0
26	Italy	4.8
27	Hungary	4.8
28	Israel	4.7
29	Korea	4.6
30	Estonia	4.5
31	Chile	4.5
32	South Africa	4.4
33	Ireland	4.4
34	Latvia	4.4
35	Malaysia	4.4
36	Lithuania	4.2
37	Croatia	4.2
38	Brazil	4.2
39	Namibia	4.1
40	Hong Kong SAR	4.1
41	Greece	4.0
41	Thailand	4.0
43	Colombia	3.9
44	Botswana	3.9
45	Costa Rica	3.9
46	Uruguay	3.8
47	Mauritius	3.6
48	Poland	3.6
49	Venezuela	3.6
50	Jordan	3.4
51	Mexico	3.4
52	China	3.3
53	Morocco	3.3
54	Jamaica	3.2
55	India	3.2
56	Sri Lanka	3.2
57	Bulgaria	3.0
58	Panama	3.0
59	Argentina	2.9
60	Trinidad and Tobago	2.9
61	Zimbabwe	2.9
62	Russian Federation	2.9
63	Romania	2.8
64	El Salvador	2.7
65	Ukraine	2.7
66	Philippines	2.7
67	Dominican Republic	2.6
68	Turkey	2.6
69	Peru	2.6
70	Vietnam	2.5
71	Paraguay	2.5
72	Bolivia	2.5
73	Indonesia	2.5
74	Honduras	2.2
75	Ecuador	2.0
76	Guatemala	2.0
77	Bangladesh	2.0
78	Nicaragua	1.9
79	Nigeria	1.8
80	Haiti	1.2

MEAN: 4.1

11.03 Toxic waste disposal regulations

The stringency of toxic waste disposal regulations in your country is (1 = lax compared with most other countries, 7 = among the world's most stringent)

RANK	COUNTRY	SCORE
1	Germany	6.7
2	Denmark	6.7
3	Netherlands	6.6
4	Finland	6.6
5	Sweden	6.5
6	Switzerland	6.4
7	Austria	6.4
8	Norway	6.3
9	New Zealand	6.1
10	Australia	6.1
11	Iceland	6.0
12	United Kingdom	6.0
13	Belgium	5.9
14	United States	5.9
15	Canada	5.8
16	Singapore	5.8
17	France	5.4
18	Tunisia	5.3
19	Slovak Republic	5.3
20	Japan	5.3
21	Spain	5.2
22	Slovenia	5.2
23	Taiwan	5.1
24	Italy	5.0
25	Korea	4.8
26	Estonia	4.7
27	Israel	4.7
28	Hungary	4.7
29	Portugal	4.5
30	Malaysia	4.5
31	South Africa	4.5
32	Czech Republic	4.3
33	Namibia	4.3
34	Latvia	4.3
35	Hong Kong SAR	4.2
36	Chile	4.2
37	Croatia	4.2
38	Brazil	4.1
39	Greece	4.1
40	Lithuania	3.9
41	Ireland	3.9
42	Mauritius	3.8
43	Thailand	3.8
44	Costa Rica	3.7
45	Poland	3.6
46	Uruguay	3.6
47	Jordan	3.6
48	Botswana	3.5
49	Colombia	3.5
50	China	3.5
51	Mexico	3.3
52	Bulgaria	3.3
53	Venezuela	3.3
54	Morocco	3.1
55	India	3.1
56	Argentina	3.1
57	Sri Lanka	3.0
58	Jamaica	3.0
59	Trinidad and Tobago	3.0
60	Zimbabwe	2.9
61	Russian Federation	2.9
62	Ukraine	2.8
63	Panama	2.8
64	Indonesia	2.8
65	Romania	2.8
66	Dominican Republic	2.6
67	El Salvador	2.6
68	Turkey	2.6
69	Vietnam	2.5
70	Peru	2.5
71	Philippines	2.5
72	Paraguay	2.4
73	Bolivia	2.3
74	Guatemala	2.1
75	Nigeria	2.1
76	Honduras	2.1
77	Ecuador	1.9
78	Bangladesh	1.9
79	Nicaragua	1.8
80	Haiti	1.4

MEAN: 4.1

11.04 Chemical waste regulations

The stringency of regulations concerning chemicals used in manufacturing in your country is (1 = lax compared with most other countries, 7 = among the world's most stringent)

RANK	COUNTRY	SCORE
1	Germany	6.6
2	Denmark	6.5
3	Finland	6.4
4	Sweden	6.4
5	Austria	6.3
6	Switzerland	6.3
7	Netherlands	6.2
8	Norway	6.2
9	Australia	5.9
10	United States	5.9
11	Iceland	5.9
12	United Kingdom	5.9
13	New Zealand	5.8
14	Belgium	5.8
15	Singapore	5.7
16	Canada	5.7
17	Japan	5.6
18	France	5.5
19	Tunisia	5.4
20	Spain	5.1
21	Slovenia	5.1
22	Taiwan	5.1
23	Italy	5.0
24	Hungary	5.0
25	Slovak Republic	4.9
26	Portugal	4.7
27	Estonia	4.6
28	Israel	4.6
29	Korea	4.6
30	Ireland	4.4
31	Malaysia	4.4
32	Brazil	4.4
33	South Africa	4.3
34	Hong Kong SAR	4.3
35	Latvia	4.2
36	Czech Republic	4.2
37	Namibia	4.1
38	Lithuania	4.0
39	Greece	4.0
40	Croatia	4.0
41	Chile	4.0
42	Thailand	3.8
43	Costa Rica	3.8
44	Mauritius	3.7
45	Uruguay	3.6
46	Poland	3.6
47	Mexico	3.5
48	China	3.5
49	Venezuela	3.5
50	Jordan	3.5
51	Colombia	3.4
52	Morocco	3.4
53	Botswana	3.4
54	Sri Lanka	3.2
55	Zimbabwe	3.2
56	Bulgaria	3.1
57	Trinidad and Tobago	3.1
58	Jamaica	3.0
59	Argentina	3.0
60	Romania	3.0
61	India	3.0
62	Russian Federation	2.9
63	Panama	2.9
64	Indonesia	2.9
65	Philippines	2.7
66	Dominican Republic	2.7
67	Turkey	2.7
68	Peru	2.7
69	Vietnam	2.6
70	Ukraine	2.6
71	El Salvador	2.6
72	Paraguay	2.6
73	Bolivia	2.2
74	Guatemala	2.2
75	Bangladesh	2.1
76	Nicaragua	2.1
77	Nigeria	2.1
78	Ecuador	2.1
79	Honduras	2.0
80	Haiti	1.4

MEAN: 4.1

11.05 Stringency of environmental regulations

How stringent is your country's overall environmental regulation? (1 = lax compared with most other countries, 7 = among the world's most stringent)

RANK	COUNTRY	SCORE
1	Germany	6.6
2	Denmark	6.6
3	Netherlands	6.5
4	Sweden	6.4
5	Austria	6.4
6	Finland	6.3
7	Switzerland	6.3
8	Norway	6.2
9	New Zealand	6.0
10	United Kingdom	5.9
11	Belgium	5.9
12	Canada	5.8
13	Australia	5.8
14	United States	5.7
15	Singapore	5.6
16	Iceland	5.5
17	France	5.4
18	Japan	5.4
19	Czech Republic	5.3
20	Tunisia	5.2
21	Taiwan	5.2
22	Portugal	5.0
23	Spain	4.9
24	Slovenia	4.8
25	Slovak Republic	4.8
26	Italy	4.8
27	Korea	4.7
28	Chile	4.6
29	Brazil	4.6
30	Estonia	4.6
31	Malaysia	4.5
32	Costa Rica	4.5
33	Hungary	4.5
34	Ireland	4.4
35	Israel	4.4
36	Croatia	4.3
37	South Africa	4.3
38	Latvia	4.2
39	Thailand	4.2
40	Lithuania	4.1
41	Colombia	4.1
42	Namibia	4.1
43	Hong Kong SAR	4.0
44	Venezuela	3.8
45	Mauritius	3.8
46	Mexico	3.8
47	Poland	3.7
48	Botswana	3.6
49	Sri Lanka	3.5
50	Greece	3.5
51	Jordan	3.5
52	Panama	3.5
53	India	3.5
54	China	3.5
55	Uruguay	3.4
56	Trinidad and Tobago	3.3
57	El Salvador	3.3
58	Zimbabwe	3.2
59	Jamaica	3.2
60	Philippines	3.2
61	Bulgaria	3.2
62	Romania	3.0
63	Argentina	3.0
64	Dominican Republic	2.9
65	Ukraine	2.9
66	Russian Federation	2.9
67	Indonesia	2.9
68	Peru	2.8
69	Morocco	2.8
70	Vietnam	2.8
71	Honduras	2.7
72	Turkey	2.7
73	Bangladesh	2.7
74	Bolivia	2.6
75	Paraguay	2.5
76	Ecuador	2.4
77	Guatemala	2.2
78	Nicaragua	2.2
79	Nigeria	2.0
80	Haiti	1.2

MEAN: 4.2

11.06 Subsidies for energy or materials

Government subsidies in your country (1 = encourage inefficient use of energy or materials, 7 = are not provided for energy or materials usage)

RANK	COUNTRY	SCORE
1	New Zealand	6.2
2	United Kingdom	5.6
3	Finland	5.5
4	Austria	5.5
5	Switzerland	5.5
6	Singapore	5.3
7	Iceland	5.3
8	Belgium	5.3
9	Ireland	5.2
10	Canada	5.1
11	Chile	5.1
12	Hong Kong SAR	5.1
13	El Salvador	5.0
14	Czech Republic	4.9
15	Israel	4.9
16	Denmark	4.9
17	Taiwan	4.9
18	Sweden	4.8
19	Australia	4.8
20	Netherlands	4.8
21	Estonia	4.8
22	Argentina	4.7
22	Japan	4.7
24	Brazil	4.7
25	Uruguay	4.7
26	Peru	4.6
27	Jamaica	4.6
28	Germany	4.6
29	South Africa	4.6
30	Norway	4.5
31	France	4.5
32	Mauritius	4.5
33	Tunisia	4.5
34	Slovenia	4.5
35	Croatia	4.5
36	Colombia	4.5
37	Latvia	4.4
38	Namibia	4.4
39	Korea	4.4
40	Costa Rica	4.4
41	Botswana	4.4
42	Slovak Republic	4.4
43	Lithuania	4.3
44	Zimbabwe	4.3
45	Italy	4.3
46	Paraguay	4.3
47	United States	4.3
48	Portugal	4.3
49	Trinidad and Tobago	4.2
50	Bulgaria	4.2
51	Malaysia	4.2
52	Jordan	4.2
53	Spain	4.2
54	Vietnam	4.2
55	Hungary	4.2
56	China	4.2
57	Bangladesh	4.2
58	Greece	4.1
59	Turkey	4.1
60	Mexico	4.1
61	Thailand	4.1
62	Panama	4.0
63	Honduras	3.9
64	Sri Lanka	3.9
65	Bolivia	3.8
66	India	3.8
67	Philippines	3.8
68	Guatemala	3.7
69	Morocco	3.7
70	Poland	3.7
71	Venezuela	3.7
72	Dominican Republic	3.6
73	Russian Federation	3.5
74	Indonesia	3.4
75	Ukraine	3.2
76	Romania	3.0
77	Ecuador	2.9
78	Haiti	2.9
79	Nicaragua	2.8
80	Nigeria	2.8

MEAN: 4.4

11.07 Compliance with environmental regulations

Your country normally enacts environmental regulations (1 = much later than other countries, 7 = ahead of most other countries)

RANK	COUNTRY	SCORE
1	Denmark	6.6
2	Netherlands	6.4
3	Germany	6.3
4	Finland	6.3
5	Sweden	6.2
6	Austria	6.2
7	Switzerland	6.1
8	Norway	5.9
9	New Zealand	5.9
10	Canada	5.7
11	United Kingdom	5.5
12	Belgium	5.4
13	Japan	5.2
14	United States	5.1
15	Singapore	5.0
16	Iceland	5.0
17	Tunisia	4.9
18	Australia	4.8
19	France	4.7
20	Taiwan	4.6
21	Slovenia	4.6
22	Spain	4.3
23	Israel	4.3
24	Portugal	4.3
25	Hungary	4.3
26	Costa Rica	4.3
27	Korea	4.2
28	Italy	4.2
29	Slovak Republic	4.2
30	Malaysia	4.2
31	Estonia	4.1
32	Czech Republic	4.1
33	Brazil	4.1
34	Thailand	3.8
35	Latvia	3.8
36	Ireland	3.8
37	South Africa	3.8
38	Chile	3.8
39	Namibia	3.7
40	Lithuania	3.7
41	Croatia	3.7
42	Colombia	3.6
43	Mauritius	3.6
44	Jordan	3.6
45	Hong Kong SAR	3.5
46	Poland	3.4
47	Botswana	3.3
48	China	3.3
49	Indonesia	3.2
50	Morocco	3.1
51	Greece	3.1
52	Mexico	3.1
53	Philippines	3.1
54	Venezuela	3.0
55	Jamaica	3.0
56	India	3.0
57	Panama	2.9
58	Bulgaria	2.9
59	Sri Lanka	2.9
60	Zimbabwe	2.9
61	Trinidad and Tobago	2.8
62	Turkey	2.8
63	El Salvador	2.8
64	Dominican Republic	2.8
65	Uruguay	2.7
66	Peru	2.7
67	Argentina	2.7
68	Bolivia	2.6
69	Ukraine	2.6
70	Romania	2.6
71	Russian Federation	2.6
72	Vietnam	2.3
73	Bangladesh	2.2
74	Honduras	2.1
75	Nigeria	2.1
76	Nicaragua	2.1
77	Paraguay	2.0
78	Ecuador	2.0
79	Guatemala	1.7
80	Haiti	1.4

MEAN: 3.8

11.08 Compliance with international agreements

Compliance with international environmental agreements is a high priority in your country's government (1 = strongly disagree, 7 = strongly agree)

RANK	COUNTRY	SCORE
1	Finland	6.4
2	Netherlands	6.3
3	Denmark	6.3
4	Germany	6.2
5	Sweden	6.2
6	New Zealand	6.2
7	Austria	6.1
8	Switzerland	6.1
9	Norway	5.9
10	Japan	5.7
11	Canada	5.7
12	United Kingdom	5.6
13	Tunisia	5.5
14	Czech Republic	5.4
15	Singapore	5.4
16	Taiwan	5.4
17	China	5.2
18	Belgium	5.2
19	Estonia	5.2
20	Hungary	5.2
21	Iceland	5.2
22	Slovenia	5.1
23	Slovak Republic	5.1
24	France	5.1
25	Brazil	4.9
26	Portugal	4.9
27	Spain	4.8
28	Korea	4.8
29	Costa Rica	4.8
30	Israel	4.7
31	Croatia	4.6
32	Malaysia	4.6
33	Vietnam	4.6
34	Namibia	4.6
35	Latvia	4.5
36	Chile	4.5
37	Mauritius	4.4
38	Colombia	4.4
39	Romania	4.4
40	Italy	4.4
41	South Africa	4.4
42	Hong Kong SAR	4.4
43	Thailand	4.3
44	Lithuania	4.3
45	Ireland	4.3
46	Morocco	4.3
47	Australia	4.3
48	Jordan	4.2
49	Mexico	4.0
50	Poland	4.0
51	Bulgaria	3.9
52	Sri Lanka	3.9
53	Dominican Republic	3.8
54	Botswana	3.8
55	Russian Federation	3.8
56	Indonesia	3.8
57	Greece	3.8
58	United States	3.7
59	Uruguay	3.7
60	Ukraine	3.7
61	Bangladesh	3.6
62	Jamaica	3.6
63	Peru	3.6
64	India	3.5
65	Panama	3.5
66	Trinidad and Tobago	3.4
67	Turkey	3.4
68	Honduras	3.3
69	El Salvador	3.3
70	Venezuela	3.2
71	Philippines	3.1
72	Bolivia	3.0
72	Nigeria	3.0
74	Ecuador	2.9
75	Zimbabwe	2.9
76	Argentina	2.8
77	Nicaragua	2.7
78	Paraguay	2.5
79	Guatemala	2.1
80	Haiti	1.5

MEAN: 4.4

11.09 Clarity and stability of regulations

Environmental regulations in your country are (1 = confusing and frequently changing, 7 = transparent and stable)

RANK	COUNTRY	SCORE
1	Singapore	5.8
2	Finland	5.8
3	Switzerland	5.8
4	Sweden	5.7
5	Tunisia	5.5
6	Austria	5.5
7	Iceland	5.5
8	Norway	5.4
9	Germany	5.2
10	Canada	5.2
11	United Kingdom	5.1
12	Taiwan	5.1
13	Netherlands	5.0
14	Slovenia	5.0
15	France	4.9
16	Denmark	4.8
17	Estonia	4.8
18	Hong Kong SAR	4.8
19	Japan	4.8
20	Australia	4.7
21	Namibia	4.6
22	Spain	4.6
23	Hungary	4.6
24	New Zealand	4.6
25	Portugal	4.6
26	Israel	4.6
27	United States	4.5
28	Malaysia	4.5
29	Brazil	4.5
30	South Africa	4.4
31	Botswana	4.4
32	Korea	4.4
33	Czech Republic	4.3
34	Thailand	4.3
35	Latvia	4.3
36	Slovak Republic	4.2
37	Belgium	4.2
38	Costa Rica	4.2
39	Croatia	4.2
40	China	4.1
41	Ireland	4.1
42	Jamaica	4.1
43	Mauritius	4.0
44	Colombia	4.0
45	Italy	3.9
46	Uruguay	3.9
47	Trinidad and Tobago	3.9
48	Lithuania	3.8
49	Jordan	3.8
50	India	3.8
51	Poland	3.8
52	Romania	3.7
53	Morocco	3.7
54	Mexico	3.6
55	Turkey	3.6
56	Bulgaria	3.6
57	Greece	3.6
58	Sri Lanka	3.5
59	Zimbabwe	3.5
60	Panama	3.5
61	Vietnam	3.5
62	Chile	3.5
63	Venezuela	3.4
64	Russian Federation	3.4
65	Peru	3.4
66	Dominican Republic	3.4
67	Nigeria	3.3
68	Bangladesh	3.3
69	Philippines	3.2
70	El Salvador	3.2
71	Ukraine	3.1
72	Argentina	3.1
73	Bolivia	3.1
74	Indonesia	3.1
75	Paraguay	2.9
76	Honduras	2.9
77	Nicaragua	2.9
78	Ecuador	2.8
79	Guatemala	2.2
80	Haiti	1.6

MEAN: 4.1

11.10 Flexibility of regulations

Environmental regulations in your country (1 = offer no options for achieving compliance, 7 = are flexible and offer many options for achieving compliance)

RANK	COUNTRY	SCORE
1	Tunisia	5.2
2	Singapore	5.2
3	Switzerland	5.1
4	Iceland	4.9
5	Finland	4.8
6	France	4.7
7	Australia	4.6
8	United States	4.6
9	Taiwan	4.5
10	Slovenia	4.5
11	Austria	4.5
12	Canada	4.4
13	South Africa	4.4
14	United Kingdom	4.3
15	Hong Kong SAR	4.3
15	Malaysia	4.3
15	Sweden	4.3
18	Netherlands	4.3
19	Brazil	4.3
20	Norway	4.3
21	Namibia	4.3
22	Spain	4.3
23	Ireland	4.3
24	Israel	4.2
25	Denmark	4.2
26	New Zealand	4.2
27	Japan	4.2
28	Thailand	4.1
29	Costa Rica	4.1
30	Botswana	4.1
31	Estonia	4.1
32	Germany	4.1
33	Korea	4.1
34	Colombia	4.1
35	Czech Republic	4.1
36	Russian Federation	4.0
37	Belgium	4.0
37	Jordan	4.0
39	Slovak Republic	4.0
40	Jamaica	4.0
41	China	3.9
42	Hungary	3.9
43	Croatia	3.9
44	Portugal	3.9
45	Trinidad and Tobago	3.9
46	Morocco	3.9
47	Latvia	3.8
48	Mexico	3.8
49	Mauritius	3.8
50	Ukraine	3.8
51	Sri Lanka	3.8
52	Indonesia	3.8
53	Greece	3.8
54	Panama	3.7
55	India	3.6
56	Vietnam	3.6
57	Uruguay	3.6
58	Romania	3.5
59	Poland	3.5
60	Turkey	3.5
61	Italy	3.5
62	Dominican Republic	3.5
63	Chile	3.5
64	Lithuania	3.4
65	Bulgaria	3.4
66	Peru	3.4
67	Venezuela	3.3
68	Bangladesh	3.3
69	Argentina	3.3
70	Zimbabwe	3.3
71	El Salvador	3.2
72	Paraguay	3.1
73	Nigeria	3.0
74	Honduras	3.0
75	Philippines	2.9
76	Ecuador	2.8
77	Nicaragua	2.8
78	Bolivia	2.8
79	Guatemala	2.4
80	Haiti	1.7

MEAN: 3.9

11.11 Consistency of regulation enforcement

Environmental regulations in your country are (1 = not enforced or enforced erratically, 7 = enforced consistently and fairly)

RANK	COUNTRY	SCORE
1	Denmark	5.8
2	Finland	5.8
3	Austria	5.7
4	Switzerland	5.7
5	Singapore	5.7
6	New Zealand	5.5
7	Germany	5.4
8	Tunisia	5.4
9	United Kingdom	5.4
10	Iceland	5.3
11	Canada	5.3
12	Belgium	5.2
13	Australia	5.2
13	Netherlands	5.2
15	Sweden	5.2
16	Norway	5.2
17	United States	5.1
18	Japan	4.9
19	Taiwan	4.7
20	France	4.6
21	Slovenia	4.6
22	Korea	4.5
23	Portugal	4.3
24	Brazil	4.3
25	Hong Kong SAR	4.3
26	Spain	4.2
27	Estonia	4.2
28	Slovak Republic	4.1
29	Hungary	4.1
30	Namibia	4.1
31	China	4.0
32	Israel	4.0
32	Latvia	4.0
32	Malaysia	4.0
35	Chile	4.0
36	Lithuania	3.9
37	South Africa	3.9
38	Ireland	3.9
39	Italy	3.9
40	Thailand	3.8
41	Russian Federation	3.7
42	Jordan	3.6
43	Botswana	3.6
44	Poland	3.6
45	Colombia	3.6
46	Czech Republic	3.5
47	Costa Rica	3.5
48	Mauritius	3.5
49	Mexico	3.5
50	Croatia	3.4
51	Greece	3.3
52	Uruguay	3.3
53	Romania	3.3
54	Ukraine	3.3
55	Dominican Republic	3.2
56	Morocco	3.2
57	Panama	3.1
58	Bulgaria	3.1
59	Sri Lanka	3.0
60	India	3.0
61	Jamaica	2.9
62	Trinidad and Tobago	2.8
63	El Salvador	2.8
64	Turkey	2.8
65	Peru	2.8
66	Vietnam	2.7
67	Zimbabwe	2.7
68	Nicaragua	2.7
69	Venezuela	2.6
70	Bangladesh	2.5
71	Honduras	2.5
72	Indonesia	2.4
73	Philippines	2.4
74	Ecuador	2.4
75	Argentina	2.4
76	Nigeria	2.3
77	Paraguay	2.3
78	Bolivia	2.2
79	Guatemala	1.9
80	Haiti	1.4

MEAN: 3.8

11.12 Effects of compliance on business

Complying with environmental standards in your country (1 = hurts competitiveness, 7 = helps long-term competitiveness by prompting companies to improve products and processes)

RANK	COUNTRY	SCORE
1	Singapore	5.6
2	Japan	5.5
3	Croatia	5.3
4	Costa Rica	5.3
5	Switzerland	5.3
6	Finland	5.3
7	Tunisia	5.3
8	Iceland	5.3
9	Taiwan	5.2
10	United Kingdom	5.1
11	Germany	5.1
12	Canada	5.1
13	Norway	5.0
14	Sweden	5.0
15	Austria	4.9
16	Netherlands	4.9
17	Namibia	4.9
18	Slovenia	4.9
19	Australia	4.9
20	Denmark	4.9
21	Hong Kong SAR	4.9
22	China	4.9
23	United States	4.8
24	Dominican Republic	4.8
25	Malaysia	4.8
26	Korea	4.8
27	Mexico	4.7
28	Spain	4.7
29	Brazil	4.7
30	France	4.7
31	Israel	4.7
32	Colombia	4.7
33	Ireland	4.6
34	Thailand	4.6
35	Ecuador	4.6
36	Slovak Republic	4.6
37	Estonia	4.6
38	South Africa	4.6
39	Hungary	4.5
40	Botswana	4.5
41	India	4.5
42	Jamaica	4.5
43	Jordan	4.4
44	Paraguay	4.4
45	Belgium	4.4
46	Czech Republic	4.4
47	Panama	4.4
48	Chile	4.3
49	Uruguay	4.3
50	Honduras	4.3
51	Peru	4.3
52	Latvia	4.3
53	Portugal	4.2
54	Vietnam	4.2
55	Morocco	4.2
56	New Zealand	4.2
57	Romania	4.2
58	Zimbabwe	4.1
59	Lithuania	4.1
60	Greece	4.1
61	Guatemala	4.1
62	Trinidad and Tobago	4.0
63	Mauritius	4.0
64	Italy	4.0
65	Bangladesh	3.9
66	Bulgaria	3.9
67	Nigeria	3.9
68	Russian Federation	3.9
69	Poland	3.8
70	Argentina	3.8
71	Nicaragua	3.7
72	Sri Lanka	3.7
73	El Salvador	3.7
74	Venezuela	3.7
75	Turkey	3.6
76	Ukraine	3.6
77	Bolivia	3.5
78	Philippines	3.5
79	Indonesia	3.4
80	Haiti	3.4

MEAN: 4.5

653

11.13 Political context of environmental gains

Environmental gains in your country are achieved through (1 = adversarial and legal means, 7 = government-business cooperation and voluntary corporate action)

RANK	COUNTRY	SCORE
1	Switzerland	5.5
2	Tunisia	5.3
3	Singapore	5.3
4	Japan	5.3
5	Finland	5.2
6	Netherlands	5.1
7	Morocco	5.1
8	Canada	5.0
9	Australia	4.9
10	Iceland	4.8
11	United Kingdom	4.7
12	Germany	4.7
13	Israel	4.7
14	New Zealand	4.6
15	Namibia	4.6
16	Malaysia	4.6
17	Botswana	4.6
18	Taiwan	4.6
18	United States	4.6
20	Costa Rica	4.6
21	Croatia	4.5
22	Dominican Republic	4.5
23	Hong Kong SAR	4.4
24	Norway	4.4
25	Denmark	4.4
26	Jamaica	4.4
27	France	4.3
28	South Africa	4.3
29	Spain	4.3
30	Jordan	4.2
31	Austria	4.2
32	Brazil	4.2
33	Ireland	4.2
33	Sweden	4.2
35	Slovenia	4.2
36	Colombia	4.1
37	Thailand	4.1
38	Korea	4.1
39	Haiti	4.1
40	Mexico	4.0
41	Italy	4.0
42	Portugal	4.0
43	Zimbabwe	4.0
44	Trinidad and Tobago	4.0
45	Chile	4.0
46	Estonia	3.9
47	Mauritius	3.9
48	Lithuania	3.9
49	Uruguay	3.9
50	Paraguay	3.9
51	Bangladesh	3.9
52	Nigeria	3.9
53	Nicaragua	3.8
53	Turkey	3.8
55	Guatemala	3.8
56	Sri Lanka	3.8
57	Philippines	3.8
58	Belgium	3.8
59	Panama	3.7
60	India	3.7
61	Hungary	3.6
62	Bulgaria	3.6
63	Ecuador	3.6
64	China	3.6
65	Greece	3.6
66	Vietnam	3.6
67	Latvia	3.5
68	Argentina	3.5
69	Poland	3.5
70	Slovak Republic	3.5
71	Peru	3.5
72	Venezuela	3.5
73	Indonesia	3.5
74	Honduras	3.5
75	Czech Republic	3.4
76	Romania	3.3
77	Ukraine	3.3
78	El Salvador	3.2
79	Bolivia	3.2
80	Russian Federation	3.0

MEAN: 4.1

11.14 Prevalence of environmental management systems

How many companies in your country utilize environmental management systems such as ISO 14000? (1 = almost no companies, 7 = most companies)

RANK	COUNTRY	SCORE
1	Finland	5.5
2	Japan	5.1
3	United Kingdom	5.0
4	Sweden	4.9
5	Germany	4.8
6	United States	4.6
7	Canada	4.6
8	Israel	4.5
9	Singapore	4.5
10	Korea	4.5
11	Austria	4.4
12	Czech Republic	4.4
13	Australia	4.4
14	Denmark	4.4
15	Switzerland	4.4
16	Norway	4.4
17	Netherlands	4.3
18	Italy	4.3
19	Taiwan	4.3
20	South Africa	4.3
21	Belgium	4.2
21	Ireland	4.2
23	Slovenia	4.0
24	New Zealand	3.9
25	Thailand	3.8
26	Spain	3.8
27	France	3.8
28	Brazil	3.8
29	Hungary	3.8
30	Malaysia	3.7
31	Hong Kong SAR	3.5
32	China	3.4
33	India	3.4
34	Jordan	3.3
35	Costa Rica	3.3
36	Slovak Republic	3.3
37	Namibia	3.3
38	Tunisia	3.3
39	Poland	3.2
40	Lithuania	3.2
41	Philippines	3.2
42	Trinidad and Tobago	3.2
43	Morocco	3.1
44	Sri Lanka	3.1
45	Vietnam	3.1
46	Indonesia	3.1
47	Iceland	3.1
48	Argentina	3.0
49	Estonia	3.0
50	Botswana	3.0
51	Colombia	3.0
52	Nigeria	2.9
53	Zimbabwe	2.9
54	Portugal	2.9
55	Mexico	2.9
56	Jamaica	2.9
57	Chile	2.8
58	Greece	2.8
59	Latvia	2.8
60	Turkey	2.8
61	Croatia	2.8
62	Russian Federation	2.7
63	Bulgaria	2.6
64	Romania	2.6
65	Uruguay	2.6
66	Dominican Republic	2.6
67	Ukraine	2.5
68	Mauritius	2.4
69	Ecuador	2.4
70	Bolivia	2.4
71	Venezuela	2.3
72	Peru	2.3
73	Panama	2.3
74	Nicaragua	2.2
75	Honduras	2.0
76	Bangladesh	1.9
77	Paraguay	1.9
78	El Salvador	1.9
79	Haiti	1.7
80	Guatemala	1.7

MEAN: 3.4

Section XII: International Institutions

12.01 World Bank effectiveness in business development/investment

The World Bank performs a very effective role in promoting a pro-private sector development/pro-investment climate (1 = strongly disagree, 7 = strongly agree)

	COUNTRY	SCORE			MEAN: 3.9	
1	Tunisia	4.9				
2	Belgium	4.8				
2	Netherlands	4.8				
4	Dominican Republic	4.7				
5	Canada	4.7				
6	Japan	4.6				
7	Austria	4.6				
8	Denmark	4.5				
8	India	4.5				
10	Finland	4.4				
11	United States	4.4				
12	Estonia	4.4				
13	China	4.4				
14	New Zealand	4.4				
15	Sri Lanka	4.4				
16	Slovak Republic	4.3				
17	Korea	4.3				
18	Norway	4.3				
19	Germany	4.3				
20	Portugal	4.3				
21	Vietnam	4.3				
22	Jordan	4.2				
23	Italy	4.2				
23	Taiwan	4.2				
25	Spain	4.2				
26	Brazil	4.2				
27	Hong Kong SAR	4.2				
28	United Kingdom	4.2				
29	Mauritius	4.1				
30	Ireland	4.1				
31	Morocco	4.1				
32	Trinidad and Tobago	4.1				
33	Singapore	4.1				
34	Romania	4.1				
35	Switzerland	4.0				
36	Nicaragua	4.0				
37	Latvia	4.0				
38	Mexico	4.0				
39	Malaysia	4.0				
39	Nigeria	4.0				
41	Botswana	4.0				
42	Lithuania	3.9				
43	Sweden	3.9				
44	Philippines	3.9				
45	Australia	3.8				
45	Hungary	3.8				
47	Thailand	3.8				
48	Poland	3.8				
49	South Africa	3.8				
50	Bangladesh	3.8				
51	Turkey	3.8				
52	Colombia	3.8				
53	Indonesia	3.8				
54	Peru	3.8				
55	France	3.8				
56	Namibia	3.8				
57	Jamaica	3.7				
58	Iceland	3.7				
59	Costa Rica	3.7				
60	Greece	3.7				
61	Guatemala	3.6				
62	Honduras	3.6				
63	Zimbabwe	3.6				
64	El Salvador	3.6				
65	Chile	3.5				
66	Bulgaria	3.5				
67	Czech Republic	3.5				
68	Ukraine	3.4				
69	Ecuador	3.4				
70	Slovenia	3.4				
71	Uruguay	3.4				
72	Israel	3.3				
73	Croatia	3.3				
74	Bolivia	3.3				
75	Panama	3.3				
76	Paraguay	3.1				
77	Venezuela	3.0				
78	Russian Federation	2.9				
79	Argentina	2.9				
80	Haiti	2.4				

12.02 World Bank effectiveness in socioeconomic development/poverty alleviation

The World Bank performs a very effective role in promoting socioeconomic development and poverty alleviation (1 = strongly disagree, 7 = strongly agree)

	COUNTRY	SCORE			MEAN: 3.8	
1	Tunisia	4.9				
2	Japan	4.9				
3	Belgium	4.9				
4	Vietnam	4.7				
5	Nicaragua	4.7				
6	India	4.7				
7	Finland	4.5				
8	Austria	4.5				
9	New Zealand	4.4				
10	Australia	4.3				
11	China	4.3				
12	Indonesia	4.3				
13	Dominican Republic	4.3				
14	Denmark	4.3				
15	Malaysia	4.3				
16	Italy	4.3				
17	United States	4.2				
18	Hong Kong SAR	4.2				
19	Korea	4.2				
20	Taiwan	4.2				
21	Netherlands	4.2				
21	United Kingdom	4.2				
23	Portugal	4.2				
24	Germany	4.2				
25	Canada	4.2				
26	Latvia	4.2				
27	Jordan	4.1				
28	Bangladesh	4.1				
29	Thailand	4.1				
30	Norway	4.1				
31	Singapore	4.0				
32	Morocco	4.0				
33	Estonia	4.0				
34	Peru	4.0				
35	Brazil	3.9				
36	Switzerland	3.9				
37	Spain	3.9				
38	Sri Lanka	3.9				
39	Iceland	3.9				
40	Namibia	3.8				
41	Botswana	3.8				
42	Mexico	3.8				
42	Trinidad and Tobago	3.8				
44	Greece	3.8				
45	Mauritius	3.8				
46	Honduras	3.8				
47	Turkey	3.8				
48	South Africa	3.7				
49	Jamaica	3.7				
50	Romania	3.7				
51	Poland	3.7				
52	Israel	3.7				
52	Nigeria	3.7				
54	Colombia	3.7				
55	France	3.6				
56	Zimbabwe	3.6				
57	Slovak Republic	3.6				
58	Chile	3.5				
59	Costa Rica	3.5				
60	Lithuania	3.5				
61	Philippines	3.4				
62	Sweden	3.4				
63	Hungary	3.4				
64	El Salvador	3.4				
65	Panama	3.4				
66	Bulgaria	3.4				
67	Paraguay	3.3				
68	Ireland	3.3				
68	Slovenia	3.3				
70	Bolivia	3.3				
71	Guatemala	3.3				
72	Ecuador	3.3				
73	Uruguay	3.2				
74	Venezuela	3.0				
75	Croatia	3.0				
76	Czech Republic	2.8				
77	Ukraine	2.6				
78	Russian Federation	2.6				
79	Argentina	2.5				
80	Haiti	2.2				

12.03 IMF effectiveness in business development

The International Monetary Fund (IMF) performs a very effective role in promoting a pro-private sector development/pro-investment climate (1 = strongly disagree, 7 = strongly agree)

	COUNTRY	SCORE	MEAN: 3.9
1	Canada	5.1	
2	Tunisia	5.0	
3	Austria	4.9	
4	Belgium	4.9	
5	Estonia	4.9	
6	Netherlands	4.9	
7	Denmark	4.8	
8	Nicaragua	4.6	
9	Turkey	4.6	
10	Finland	4.6	
11	New Zealand	4.6	
12	Sri Lanka	4.5	
13	Germany	4.5	
14	Korea	4.4	
15	United States	4.4	
16	Norway	4.4	
17	United Kingdom	4.3	
18	Sweden	4.3	
19	Mauritius	4.3	
20	Australia	4.3	
21	Japan	4.2	
22	Singapore	4.2	
23	Jordan	4.2	
24	India	4.2	
25	Switzerland	4.2	
26	Ireland	4.1	
26	Slovak Republic	4.1	
28	Portugal	4.1	
29	Hungary	4.1	
30	Taiwan	4.1	
31	Botswana	4.1	
32	China	4.1	
33	Italy	4.1	
34	Mexico	4.0	
35	Trinidad and Tobago	4.0	
36	Iceland	4.0	
37	Chile	4.0	
38	Lithuania	4.0	
39	Vietnam	4.0	
40	South Africa	3.9	
41	Costa Rica	3.9	
42	Hong Kong SAR	3.9	
42	Spain	3.9	
44	Namibia	3.9	
45	Dominican Republic	3.9	
46	Poland	3.9	
47	Thailand	3.9	
48	Indonesia	3.8	
49	Peru	3.8	
50	Philippines	3.8	
51	France	3.8	
52	Latvia	3.8	
53	Jamaica	3.8	
54	Greece	3.7	
55	Morocco	3.7	
56	Bangladesh	3.7	
57	Czech Republic	3.6	
58	Honduras	3.6	
59	Bulgaria	3.6	
60	El Salvador	3.6	
61	Brazil	3.6	
62	Zimbabwe	3.5	
63	Colombia	3.5	
64	Malaysia	3.5	
65	Slovenia	3.4	
66	Guatemala	3.4	
67	Nigeria	3.4	
68	Croatia	3.3	
69	Panama	3.2	
70	Ukraine	3.1	
71	Uruguay	3.1	
72	Bolivia	3.1	
73	Israel	3.0	
73	Romania	3.0	
75	Ecuador	2.8	
76	Russian Federation	2.8	
77	Venezuela	2.7	
78	Haiti	2.5	
79	Paraguay	2.5	
80	Argentina	2.3	

12.04 IMF effectiveness in socioeconomic development

The International Monetary Fund (IMF) performs a very effective role in promoting socioeconomic development and poverty alleviation (1 = strongly disagree, 7 = strongly agree)

	COUNTRY	SCORE	MEAN: 3.5
1	Tunisia	4.7	
2	China	4.3	
3	Japan	4.3	
4	New Zealand	4.2	
5	Belgium	4.2	
6	Vietnam	4.2	
7	Denmark	4.2	
8	United States	4.2	
9	India	4.2	
10	Korea	4.1	
11	Iceland	4.1	
11	Netherlands	4.1	
11	Sweden	4.1	
14	Estonia	4.1	
15	Canada	4.1	
16	Taiwan	4.0	
17	Austria	4.0	
17	Norway	4.0	
19	United Kingdom	3.9	
20	Hong Kong SAR	3.9	
20	Indonesia	3.9	
22	Australia	3.9	
23	Finland	3.9	
24	Jordan	3.9	
25	Nicaragua	3.9	
26	Singapore	3.9	
27	Sri Lanka	3.8	
28	Mauritius	3.8	
29	Germany	3.8	
29	Hungary	3.8	
31	Switzerland	3.8	
32	Namibia	3.8	
33	Morocco	3.8	
34	Bangladesh	3.7	
35	Latvia	3.7	
36	South Africa	3.7	
37	Spain	3.7	
38	Botswana	3.7	
39	Poland	3.7	
39	Portugal	3.7	
41	Lithuania	3.6	
42	Turkey	3.6	
43	Dominican Republic	3.6	
44	Italy	3.6	
45	Slovak Republic	3.5	
46	Philippines	3.5	
47	Honduras	3.5	
47	Malaysia	3.5	
49	Greece	3.5	
50	Trinidad and Tobago	3.4	
51	France	3.3	
51	Nigeria	3.3	
53	Chile	3.3	
54	Mexico	3.3	
55	Zimbabwe	3.2	
56	Bulgaria	3.2	
57	Slovenia	3.2	
58	Czech Republic	3.2	
59	Ireland	3.2	
60	Costa Rica	3.2	
61	Peru	3.2	
62	Guatemala	3.1	
63	Thailand	3.1	
64	El Salvador	3.1	
65	Panama	3.1	
66	Bolivia	3.1	
67	Colombia	3.1	
68	Israel	3.0	
68	Romania	3.0	
70	Brazil	2.9	
71	Croatia	2.9	
72	Jamaica	2.8	
73	Venezuela	2.7	
74	Russian Federation	2.7	
75	Ukraine	2.7	
76	Uruguay	2.7	
77	Ecuador	2.6	
78	Paraguay	2.6	
79	Haiti	2.3	
80	Argentina	1.9	

12.05 Regional development bank effectiveness in business development/investment

The Regional Development Bank in your region (AfDB in Africa, EBRD in E. Europe, IADB in Latin America, ADB in Asia) performs a very effective role in promoting a pro-private sector development/pro-investment climate (1 = strongly disagree, 7 = strongly agree)

	COUNTRY	SCORE
1	Austria	5.0
2	Estonia	4.8
3	Belgium	4.8
4	Canada	4.7
5	Finland	4.7
6	Japan	4.6
7	Slovak Republic	4.6
8	Germany	4.5
8	Hungary	4.5
8	Netherlands	4.5
8	United Kingdom	4.5
12	Vietnam	4.5
13	Trinidad and Tobago	4.4
14	Tunisia	4.4
15	Sri Lanka	4.4
16	Romania	4.4
17	United States	4.3
18	Latvia	4.3
19	Slovenia	4.3
20	Czech Republic	4.3
21	Denmark	4.3
21	Uruguay	4.3
23	Malaysia	4.3
24	China	4.3
25	Norway	4.2
26	Philippines	4.2
27	Korea	4.2
28	Peru	4.2
29	Switzerland	4.2
30	India	4.2
30	Italy	4.2
32	Costa Rica	4.2
33	Australia	4.2
34	Lithuania	4.2
35	Singapore	4.1
36	Jamaica	4.0
37	Bangladesh	4.0
37	Hong Kong SAR	4.0
37	Iceland	4.0
37	Mexico	4.0
41	Honduras	4.0
42	Brazil	4.0
43	Poland	4.0
44	Dominican Republic	3.9
45	Namibia	3.9
46	Ecuador	3.9
47	Panama	3.9
48	Jordan	3.9
49	Thailand	3.9
50	Taiwan	3.9
51	Portugal	3.9
52	El Salvador	3.9
53	Spain	3.8
54	Indonesia	3.8
55	New Zealand	3.8
56	Nicaragua	3.8
57	Bulgaria	3.8
58	Croatia	3.8
59	Mauritius	3.7
59	Morocco	3.7
61	Colombia	3.7
62	Bolivia	3.6
63	Greece	3.6
64	Nigeria	3.6
65	Guatemala	3.6
66	Sweden	3.6
67	Paraguay	3.6
68	Ireland	3.5
69	France	3.5
70	Chile	3.5
71	Botswana	3.5
72	Venezuela	3.3
73	Ukraine	3.3
74	Russian Federation	3.3
75	South Africa	3.2
76	Argentina	3.0
77	Israel	2.8
78	Zimbabwe	2.7
79	Turkey	2.6
80	Haiti	2.5

MEAN: 4.0

12.06 Regional development bank effectiveness in socioeconomic development/poverty alleviation

The Regional Development Bank in your region (AfDB in Africa, EBRD in E. Europe, IADB in Latin America, ADB in Asia) performs a very effective role in promoting socioeconomic development and poverty alleviation (1 = strongly disagree, 7 = strongly agree)

	COUNTRY	SCORE
1	Austria	4.9
2	Belgium	4.8
3	Vietnam	4.7
4	Japan	4.6
5	United States	4.5
6	Germany	4.4
7	Tunisia	4.3
8	Indonesia	4.3
9	United Kingdom	4.3
10	China	4.3
11	Estonia	4.2
12	India	4.2
13	Korea	4.2
14	Trinidad and Tobago	4.2
15	Philippines	4.2
16	Denmark	4.2
16	Dominican Republic	4.2
18	Bangladesh	4.2
19	Thailand	4.1
20	Uruguay	4.1
21	Malaysia	4.1
22	Netherlands	4.1
23	Slovak Republic	4.1
24	Finland	4.1
24	Sri Lanka	4.1
26	Peru	4.0
27	Singapore	4.0
28	Latvia	4.0
29	Costa Rica	4.0
30	Australia	4.0
30	Canada	4.0
30	Hong Kong SAR	4.0
30	Iceland	4.0
34	Paraguay	4.0
35	Nicaragua	3.9
36	Poland	3.9
37	Norway	3.9
38	Hungary	3.9
38	Italy	3.9
40	El Salvador	3.9
41	Mauritius	3.9
42	Jamaica	3.8
43	Jordan	3.8
43	Mexico	3.8
45	Switzerland	3.8
46	Ecuador	3.8
47	Romania	3.8
48	Taiwan	3.8
49	Brazil	3.8
50	Portugal	3.8
51	Panama	3.8
52	Honduras	3.8
52	Namibia	3.8
52	New Zealand	3.7
55	Slovenia	3.7
56	Lithuania	3.7
57	Spain	3.7
58	Colombia	3.6
59	Czech Republic	3.6
60	Nigeria	3.6
61	Chile	3.5
62	Morocco	3.5
63	Guatemala	3.5
64	Bolivia	3.5
65	Bulgaria	3.4
66	Botswana	3.4
67	Greece	3.4
68	Sweden	3.4
68	Venezuela	3.4
70	Croatia	3.3
71	France	3.3
72	Ireland	3.3
73	South Africa	3.2
74	Turkey	2.9
75	Argentina	2.8
76	Israel	2.8
77	Russian Federation	2.7
78	Zimbabwe	2.7
79	Ukraine	2.6
80	Haiti	2.4

MEAN: 3.8

Technical Notes and Sources

The data used in this *Report* represent the best available estimates from various national authorities, international agencies, and private sources at the time the *Report* was prepared (July/August 2002). It is possible that some data will have been revised or updated by national sources after publication. Throughout the statistical tables in this publication, "N/A" denotes that the value is not available.

The following outlines some notes on sources for specific variables listed in the Data Tables of this *Report*. Not all of these variables are used in the calculations for the Growth Competitiveness Index or the Microeconomic Competitiveness Index. For specific descriptions of the variables included in those indexes, see Chapters 1.1 and 1.2, respectively.

Section 1. Aggregate country performance indicators

1.01 Total GDP, 2001. Source: Gross domestic product (GDP) in current US dollars was taken from the International Monetary Fund's *World Economic Outlook Database, April 2002*. Available online at http://www.imf.org/external/pubs/ft/weo/2002/01/data/index.htm.

1.02 Total population, 2001. Source: Population data were taken from the Economist Intelligence Unit's Country Data. Available online at http://countrydata.bvdep.com.

1.03 GDP per capita (PPP), 2001. Source: Per capita GDP adjusted for purchasing power across countries was obtained from the International Comparison Program (ICP) of The World Bank. Five missing values (Hong Kong, Israel, Nicaragua, Singapore, and Taiwan) were calculated as follows: 2001 GDP values from the *IMF World Economic Outlook Database, April 2002* "Gross Domestic Product, Current Prices (billions of local currency units)," were divided by 1.02 Total population, 2001, to produce GDP per capita values in national currency. These values were then converted using the World Bank *World Development Indicators 2002* "purchasing power parity conversion factor." For Nicaragua, a high-inflation country, this value was additionally scaled by the *IMF World Economic Outlook Database, April 2002* "Inflation (annual percent change)."

1.04 Real growth in GDP per capita, 2000 to 2001. Source: *IMF World Economic Outlook Database, April 2002*. These values were constructed by calculating the year-on-year change in "Per capita Gross Domestic Product, Constant Prices."

1.05 GDP per capita relative to the United States, 2001. Source: These values present the same underlying data as variable 1.03, but instead show GDP as a proportion of that of the United States rather than at an absolute level.

1.06 GDP per capita relative to the United States, 1995. Source: Data come from the World Bank *World Development Indicators 2002*.

1.07 Change in GDP per capita relative to the United States, 1995 to 2001. Source: Using the data listed in variables 1.05 and 1.06, average annual growth rates from 1995 to 2001 were calculated.

1.08 Unemployment rate, 2001. Source: Economist Intelligence Unit, US Department of State, 2001 Country Report on Economic Policy and Trade Practices, Bureau of Economic and Business Affairs, and various national sources. The data list the recorded unemployment figures for 2001. Readers should note that, regarding this variable, strict comparisons across all countries are particularly difficult due to countries' differing definitions of both *labor force* and *unemployment*. Measurement problems are often most acute in developing economies.

1.09 Employment to population ratio, 2001. Source: Economist Intelligence Unit and various national sources.

Section 2. Macroeconomic Environment

2.13 Moody's sovereign debt ratings, 2002. Source: Moody's, July 2002. The most recent ratings are available online at http://www.moodys.com/moodys/cust/RatingAction/bl_rList.asp?bus LineId=7

2.14 Standard & Poor's sovereign debt ratings, 2002. Source: Standard & Poor's, July 2002. The most recent ratings are available online at http://www.standardandpoors.com/RatingsActions/RatingsLists/Sove reigns/SovereignsRatingsList.html

2.15 Government surplus/deficit, 2001. Source: IMF International Financial Statistics, June 2002, and Economist Intelligence Unit.

2.16 Government expenditure, 2001. Source: IMF International Financial Statistics, June 2002, and Economist Intelligence Unit.

2.17 National savings rate, 2001. Source: Economist Intelligence Unit, IMF Country Reports, and various national sources.

2.18 Investment rate, 2001. Source: Economist Intelligence Unit and various national sources.

2.19 Inflation, 2001. Source: IMF *World Economic Outlook Database, April 2002*.

2.20 M2 growth, 2001. Source: Economist Intelligence Unit, IMF *International Financial Statistics, June 2002*, European Central Bank *Annual Report*, and national sources.

2.21 Real exchange rate, 2001. Using consumer price index data and period average annual (nominal) exchange rate data from the IMF's *International Financial Statistics, June 2002*, this variable was created by setting the average real exchange rate between 1990 to 1995 for most economies and the real exchange rate in 1995 to 100 for transition economies (in some cases missing consumer price values were reconstructed using the IMF's *World Economic Outlook Database, April 2002* inflation data). The results thus show the relative appreciation, for numbers less than 100, or depreciation, for numbers greater than 100, of each currency relative to the US dollar up to 2001. The basis of the real exchange rate calculation was:

$$\left(\begin{array}{c} \text{period average exchange rate} \\ \text{(in national currency per US\$)} \end{array} \right) \times \left(\frac{\text{US Consumer Price Index}}{\text{national Consumer Price Index}} \right)$$

2.22 Exports, 2001. Source: Economist Intelligence Unit. This variable represents exports of goods as a percentage of GDP in 2001.

2.23 Imports, 2001. Source: Economist Intelligence Unit. This variable represents imports of goods as a percentage of GDP in 2001.

2.24 Average tariff rate, 2002. Source: G. P. O'Driscoll Jr., K. Holmes, and M. A. O'Grady, *2002 Index of Economic Freedom* (Heritage Foundation and *The Wall Street Journal*).

2.25 Corporate income tax rate, 2002. Source: G. P. O'Driscoll Jr., K. Holmes, and M. A. O'Grady, *2002 Index of Economic Freedom* (Heritage Foundation and *The Wall Street Journal*).

2.26 Individual income tax rate, 2002. Source: G. P. O'Driscoll Jr., K. Holmes, and M. A. O'Grady, *2002 Index of Economic Freedom* (Heritage Foundation and *The Wall Street Journal*).

2.27 Value added tax rate, 2002. Source: Ernst & Young *Worldwide Corporate Tax Guide 2002* and national sources.

2.28 Interest rate spread, 2001. Source: Economist Intelligence Unit and national sources. This variable is equal to the difference between the typical short-term lending and deposit rates over the 2001 period.

2.29 FDI, 2001. Source: UNCTAD *Handbook of Statistics Online, 2002.* Available online at http://www.unctad.org/en/subsites/dite/FDIstats_files/FDIstats.htm

2.30 Domestic credit, 2001. Domestic credit as a percentage of GDP in 2001 was calculated using domestic credit data in US dollars from the IMF's *International Financial Statistics, June 2002*, IMF country data, and national sources. For the 11 euro area countries covered by the *Report*, a single domestic credit value was used. These domestic credit values were then converted into national currency units and divided by GDP values from the IMF's *World Economic Outlook Database, April 2002* (current prices, national currency).

2.31 Liquid liabilities, 2001. Liquid liabilities as a percentage of GDP in 2001 was calculated using liquid liabilities data from the IMF's *International Financial Statistics, June 2002*, IMF country data, the *European Central Bank Monthly Bulletin, July 2002*, and national sources. For the 11 euro area countries covered by the *Report*, a single M3 value was used. These liquid liabilities values were then converted into national currency units and divided by GDP values from the IMF's *World Economic Outlook Database, April 2002* (current prices, national currency).

2.32 Bank liquid reserves, 2000. Source: World Bank, *World Development Indicators 2002.*

2.33 Market capitalization, 2001. Source: World Bank, *World Development Indicators 2002.*

2.34 Value traded, 2001. Source: Value traded as a percentage of GDP was calculated by taking value traded data obtained from the World Bank and national sources. These values were then divided by GDP (current Prices, billions of US dollars) from the IMF's *World Economic Outlook Database, April 2002.*

2.35 Number of listed companies, 2001. Source: The number of listed domestic companies as a percentage of market capitalization was calculated using data on the number of listed companies obtained from the World Bank, *World Development Indicators 2002.* This value was then divided by variable 2.33.

Section 3: Technological Innovation and Diffusion

3.14 Research and development spending. Source: World Bank, *World Development Indicators 2002*, OECD *Main Science and Technology Indicators, 2002*, and national sources.

3.15 Utility patents, 2001. Source: United States Patent and Trademark Office. *Patent Counts, States and Countries of Origin Calendar Year 2001.* April 2002. Available online at http://www.uspto.gov/web/offices/ac/ido/oeip/taf/st_co_01.htm. Utility patents (ie, patents for invention) are recorded such that the origin of the patent is determined by the first-named inventor at the time of the grant. Patents per million population are calculated by dividing the number of patents granted to a country in 2001 by that country's population in the same year.

3.16 Utility patents, 1980s. Source: United States Patent and Trademark Office. *Patent Counts by Country/State and Year - Utility Patents.* February 2001. Available online at http://www.uspto.gov/web/offices/ac/ido/oeip/taf/cst_utl.pdf. Here the values listed are the average number of patents per million population from 1980 to 1989.

3.17 Secondary enrollment. Source: World Bank, *World Development Indicators 2002* and national sources. This is the net secondary school enrollment for 1998 or the most recent year available. According to the *World Development Indicators*, the net enrollment ratio is the ratio of the number of children of official school age (as defined by the national education system) who are enrolled in school to the population of the corresponding official school age. This is based on the International Standard Classification of Education 1976 (ISCED76) and 1997 (ISCED97).

3.18 Tertiary enrollment. Source: World Bank, *World Development Indicators 2002* and national sources. According to the *World Development Indicators*, the gross tertiary enrollment rate is the ratio of total enrollment, regardless of age, to the population of the age group that officially corresponds to the level of education shown. Tertiary education, whether or not leading to an advanced research qualification, normally requires, as a minimum condition of admission, the successful completion of education at the secondary level. Also according to the *World Development Indicators*, "in 1998, ISCED97 was introduced and UNESCO's data collection program and country reporting of education statistics were adjusted to this new classification. This was to facilitate the international compilation and comparison of educational statistics, as well as to take into account new types of learning opportunities and activities available for both children and adults. Thus the time series up to 1997 are not consistent with the data for 1998 and after." The revision to the classification had an important impact on the tertiary enrollment ratio of some countries covered by the *Report*, the most notable case being Canada, which dropped by 30 percentage points from 1997 to 1998.

661

Section 4. Information and communications technology

4.07 Cellular telephones, 2001. Source: International Telecommunication Union, July 2002. Available online at http://www.itu.int/ITU-D/ict/statistics/

4.08 Internet users, 2001. Source: International Telecommunication Union, July 2002. Available online at http://www.itu.int/ITU-D/ict/statistics/

4.09 Internet hosts, 2001. Source: International Telecommunication Union, July 2002. Available online at http://www.itu.int/ITU-D/ict/statistics/

4.10 Telephone lines, 2001. Source: International Telecommunication Union, July 2002. Available online at http://www.itu.int/ITU-D/ict/statistics/

4.11 Personal computers, 2001. Source: International Telecommunication Union, July 2002. Available online at http://www.itu.int/ITU-D/ict/statistics/

Section 5. General Infrastructure

5.10 Paved roads. Source: World Bank, *World Development Indicators 2002.*

5.11 Aircraft departures. Source: World Bank, *World Development Indicators 2002* and national sources.

5.12 Total air transport passengers. Source: World Bank, *World Development Indicators 2002* and national sources.

5.13 Total air transport freight. Source: World Bank, *World Development Indicators 2002.*

5.14 **Electric power.** Source: World Bank, *World Development Indicators 2002*.

5.15 **Health expenditure per capita.** Source: World Bank, *World Development Indicators 2002* and national sources.

5.16 **Hospital beds.** Source: World Bank, *World Development Indicators 2002* and national sources.

Section 6. Public Institutions: Contracts and Law

6.21 **Military expenditure relative to central government expenditure.** Source: World Bank, *World Development Indicators 2002* and the Economist Intelligence Unit.

6.22 **Military expenditure relative to GNI.** Source: World Bank, *World Development Indicators 2002* and the Economist Intelligence Unit.

Section 8. Domestic Competition

8.06 **Number of procedures to resolve a dispute.** Source: *Doing Business*, The World Bank Group. Available online at http://rru.worldbank.org/DoingBusiness/TopicReports/Default.aspx

8.07 **Number of days to resolve a dispute.** Source: *Doing Business*, The World Bank Group. Available online at http://rru.worldbank.org/DoingBusiness/TopicReports/Default.aspx

8.08 **Number of procedures to start a business.** Source: *Doing Business*, The World Bank Group. Available online at http://rru.worldbank.org/DoingBusiness/TopicReports/Default.aspx

8.09 **Number of days to start a business.** Source: *Doing Business*, The World Bank Group. Available online at http://rru.worldbank.org/DoingBusiness/TopicReports/Default.aspx

8.10 **Total cost of starting a business.** Source: *Doing Business*, The World Bank Group. Available online at http://rru.worldbank.org/DoingBusiness/TopicReports/Default.aspx

8.11 **Total cost of starting a business relative to GNP per capita.** Source: *Doing Business*, The World Bank Group. Available online at http://rru.worldbank.org/DoingBusiness/TopicReports/Default.aspx

The World Economic Forum would like to thank KPMG for their support in making this *Report* possible.

KPMG International

KPMG is the global network of professional services firms whose aim is to turn understanding of information, industries, and business trends into value. With more than 100,000 people worldwide, KPMG member firms provide assurance, tax and legal, and financial advisory services from more than 750 cities in 152 countries.

Fundamental to KPMG's approach is its focus on industry sectors. We believe that we can add value for our clients if we truly understand their business. This is why we invest in continuously improving our knowledge of the industries we serve.

KPMG is best defined by its strong commitment to quality. Accountancy—together with other advisory services—is still a profession of integrity and independence. We embrace a set of core values that emphasizes qualities such as responsive leadership and personal accountability—all aimed at best serving our clients and retaining the public's trust.

On a global basis, KPMG coordinates its national and local resources—people, ideas, skills, technologies, and knowledge—through three operating regions, offering clients flexibility, responsiveness, and critical mass in a host of problem-solving disciplines.